The Threefold Paradise
of Cotton Mather

The Threefold Paradise
of Cotton Mather

AN EDITION OF
"TRIPARADISUS"

EDITED BY
Reiner Smolinski

COMMITTEE ON
SCHOLARLY EDITIONS

AN APPROVED EDITION

MODERN LANGUAGE
ASSOCIATION OF AMERICA

The University of Georgia Press

ATHENS AND LONDON

© 1995 by the University of Georgia Press
Athens, Georgia 30602
All rights reserved
Designed by Betty Palmer McDaniel
Set in 9/12 Trump Mediaeval by Tseng Information Systems, Inc.
Printed and bound by Braun-Brumfield, Inc.
The paper in this book meets the guidelines for permanence and
durability of the Committee on Production Guidelines for Book
Longevity of the Council on Library Resources.

Printed in the United States of America
99 98 97 96 95   C   5 4 3 2 1

Library of Congress Cataloging in Publication Data
Mather, Cotton, 1663–1728.
[Triparadisus]
The threefold paradise of Cotton Mather : an edition of
Triparadisus / edited by Reiner Smolinski.
p.   cm.
Includes bibliographical references and index.
ISBN 0-8203-1519-2 (alk. paper)
1. Eschatology—Early works to 1800. 2. Millennialism—New
England—History—Sources. 3. Theology, Doctrinal—New
England—18th century. I. Smolinski, Reiner. II. Title.
BT820.M34   1995
236—dc20   92-29850

British Library Cataloging in Publication Data available

Frontispiece: Hans Holbein's "The Last Judgment" (*The Dance
of Death*). By permission of Special Collections Department,
Robert W. Woodruff Library, Emory University.

CONTENTS

Meinen Eltern, Horst Smolinski
und Anneliese Emma Dähne Smolinski,
in Liebe und Dankbarkeit gewidmet

Whatever our Elysiums *seem to the rash and injudicious, they are really no other thing than pure Paradises of intellectual pleasures*

Henry More, *The Immortality of the Soul* (London, 1659), "The Preface," p. b4

ACKNOWLEDGMENTS

During the ten years of intermittent effort since I first began to prepare this project, I have received much help from many kind individuals, whose generosity I wish to acknowledge here. I am indebted to John B. Hench, Director of Research and Publication, the American Antiquarian Society, for permission to edit and publish Cotton Mather's "Triparadisus" manuscript; to the Department of English of the Pennsylvania State University for financial support through a grant from the Ben Euwema Memorial Scholarship fund for dissertation research; and to the College of Arts and Sciences of Georgia State University for granting me a graduate research assistant during the final stages of this project.

Editing and annotating "Triparadisus" proved to be a formidable task, and many experts in theology, history, bibliography, language, and literature freely shared their time and knowledge. For his relentless guidance during the dissertation stage of this project, I wish to thank my thesis director, Professor Harrison T. Meserole, who generously shared his expertise in and enthusiasm for the colonial New England experience—even after his Errand took him into Texas. I am indebted to Patrick Barker and Oded Zyssman for translating the Latin, Greek, and Hebrew passages and for making my own translations more felicitous; and to Mita Choudhury and Caffilene Allen for their unrelenting assistance in collating—again and again—"Triparadisus" with my own typescript. The following scholars have read all or parts of the present edition and have generously offered their advice and encouragement in more ways than one: David Levin (University of Virginia); Ronald A. Bosco (University of Albany, SUNY); William J. Scheick (University of Texas, Austin); John Hayes and E. Brooks Holifield (Emory University); John T. Harwood, Robert N. Hudspeth, Joseph J. Kockelmans, and Ernest B. Lowrie (Pennsylvania State University); Gary A. Stringer (University of Southern Mississippi, Chair of the MLA Committee on Scholarly Editions); Robert D. Sattelmeyer and Virginia Spencer Carr (Georgia State University).

I owe special thanks to Charles Mann and the staff of the Pennsylvania State University Libraries; to Pat Graham and his colleagues at the Pitts Theological Library, Emory University; to Jane Hobson of Georgia State University Library; and to Thomas Knoles and the many helpful librarians at the American Antiquarian Society.

Finally—and not least of all—I wish to thank Danutia Piestrzynska, who greatly indulged me during the completion of these magnalia and—when I waltzed with Cotton Mather on the head of a pin—was kind enough to flick me off; Käthe Ristow, who is responsible for my fascination with things Puritan (and not so puritan); Jeffrey Mares and my graduate and undergraduate students, who patiently allowed me to test my ideas in the various seminars on early American literature at Georgia State University and Johannes Gutenberg Universität, Mainz; Linda Smith Rhodes, associate editor of the *New England Quarterly*, for permission to excerpt parts of my article "*Israel Redivivus*: The Eschatological Limits of Puritan Typology in New England," vol. 63, no. 3 (1990): 357–95; Bernard Bailyn, Benjamin Woods Labaree, Edmund Sears Morgan, and the Colonial Society of Massachusetts for awarding that article the 1989 Walter Muir Whitehill Prize in Colonial History; Karen Orchard, associate director and executive editor, the University of Georgia Press, for her enthusiastic support of this project; Madelaine Cooke, managing editor, for seeing the manuscript through the press; Janis Bolster, copyeditor, for her Herculean task of enforcing consistent editorial principles; and most of all Ronald A. Bosco, scholar and editor par excellence, for his wholehearted endorsement of my abilities as a junior editor in his reviews for the University of Georgia Press and for the MLA Committee on Scholarly Editions, for boosting the fortunes of the *Threefold Paradise* (and its editor's) when both seemed on the verge of vanishing in the "Mather bog"; and Virginia Spencer Carr, for her friendship and encouragement during the many winters of despair.

ILLUSTRATIONS

ABBREVIATIONS OF
COTTON MATHER'S WORKS

AB	*The Angel of Bethesda*, ed. Gorden W. Jones (Barre, Mass.: American Antiquarian Society and Barre Publishers, 1972)
AC	*The Armour of Christianity* (Boston, 1704)
ACF	*An Advice, to the Churches of the Faithful* (Boston, 1702)
ATC	*American Tears Upon the Ruines of the Greek Churches* (Boston, 1701)
B	*Bonifacius: Essay Upon the Good* (Boston, 1710)
"BA"	"Biblia Americana," ms., 6 folio vols., Massachusetts Historical Society
BKD	*Batteries upon the Kingdom of the Devil* (London, 1695)
BO	*Boanerges* (Boston, 1727)
BS	*Brontologia Sacra* (London, 1695)
BV	*Balsamum Vulnerarium* (Boston, 1692)
C	*Coelestinus* (Boston, 1723)
CA	*Corderius Americanus* (Boston, 1708)
"CAm"	"Curiosa Americana," ms., American Antiquarian Society
CC	*A Companion for Communicants* (Boston, 1690)
CCC	*A Christian Conversing with the Great Mystery of Christianity* (Boston, 1709)
CH	*Coheleth* (Boston, 1720)
CP	*The Christian Philosopher* (London, 1720/21)
CPI	*Christianus per Ignem* (Boston, 1702)
CTM	*The Case of a Troubled Mind* (Boston, 1717)
D 1–2	*The Diary of Cotton Mather*, ed. Worthington C. Ford, Collections of the Massachusetts Historical Society, 7th series, vols. 7–8 (Boston, 1911–12)
D 3	*The Diary of Cotton Mather . . . for the Year 1712*, ed. William R. Manierre II (Charlottesville: University Press of Virginia, 1964)
DL	*Decennium Luctuosum* (Boston, 1699)
DWD	*The Day, & the Work of the Day* (Boston, 1693)
FD	*Fair Dealing between Debtor and Creditor* (Boston, 1715/16)
FE	*Faith Encouraged* (Boston, 1718)
FF	*The Faith of the Fathers* (Boston, 1699)
FW	*Fair Weather* (Boston, 1692)
FWD	*Frontiers Well-Defended* (Boston, 1707)
GE	*A Glorious Espousal* (Boston, 1719)

GT	*The Glorious Throne* (Boston, 1714)
HC	*The Heavenly Conversation* (Boston, 1710)
HL	*An Heavenly Life* (Boston, 1719)
IC	*India Christiana* (Boston, 1721)
LTS	*A Letter Concerning the Terrible Sufferings of our Protestant Brethren* (Boston, 1701)
M	*Malachi* (Boston, 1717)
MAM	*Manuductio ad Ministerium* (Boston, 1726)
MC	*A Midnight Cry* (Boston, 1692)
MCA	*Magnalia Christi Americana* (London, 1702; facsimile rpt., New York: Arno Press, 1972)
ME	*Menachem* (Boston, 1716)
MP	*Memorable Providences* (Boston, 1689)
NC	*The Negro Christianized* (Boston, 1706)
O	*Observanda* (Boston, 1695)
ODZ	*Ornaments for the Daughters of Zion* (Cambridge, 1691; facsimile rpt. of the third edition, Boston, 1741), ed. Pattie Cowell (Delmar, NY: Scholar's Facsimiles & Reprints, 1978)
PA	*Parentator* (1724), in *Two Mather Biographies*, ed. William J. Scheick (Bethlehem, Pa.: Lehigh University Press, 1989)
PB	*The Palm-bearers* (Boston, 1725)
PMDJ	*Preparatory Meditations upon the Day of Judgment*, prefixed to Samuel Lee, *The Great Day of Judgment* (Boston, 1692)
PN	*Paterna: The Autobiography of Cotton Mather*, ed. Ronald A. Bosco (Delmar, N.Y.: Scholar's Facsimiles & Reprints, 1976)
PS	*Psalterium Americanum* (Boston, 1718)
PSNE	*The Present State of New England* (Boston, 1690)
"PT"	"Problema Theologicum," ms., American Antiquarian Society, 1703
PTL	*Perswasion from the Terror of the Lord* (Boston, 1711)
"Quo"	"Quotidiana," ms., American Antiquarian Society
RDF	*Ratio Disciplinae Fratrum* (Boston, 1726)
SCM	*The Stone Cut out of the Mountain* (Boston, 1716)
SD	*Shaking Dispensations* (Boston, 1715)
SHNE	*A Short History of New-England* (Boston, 1694)
SME	*A Speech made unto His Excellency, Samuel Shute* (Boston, 1720)
SSC	*The Salvation of the Soul Considered* (Boston, 1720)
SSE	*Some Seasonable Enquiries Offered* (Boston, 1723)
SV	*Suspiria Vinctorum* (Boston, 1726)
T	"Triparadisus: A Discourse Concerning the Threefold Paradise," ms., American Antiquarian Society, 1712, 1726/27. All references are to the present edition of this text.
TA	*Theopolis Americana* (Boston, 1710)
TB	*Terra Beata* (Boston, 1726)
TD	*Terribilia Dei* (Boston, 1697)
TDP	*Things for a Distressed People to think upon* (Boston, 1696)

TDR   *Thoughts for the Day of Rain* (Boston, 1712)
TFC   *Tokens for the Children of New-England*, third edition (Boston, 1728)
TL   *The Terror of the Lord* (Boston, 1727)
TLF   *Things to be Look'd for. Discourses on the Glorious Characters, with Conjectures on the Speedy Approaches of that State, which is reserved for the Church of God in the Latter Days* (Cambridge, 1691)
TMT   *Things to be More Thought upon* (Boston, 1713)
TP   *Tela Praevisa* (Boston, 1724)
TRR   *The Triumphs of the Reformed Religion in America* (Boston, 1691)
U   *Utilia* (Boston, 1716)
UGV   *Une Grande Voix Du Ciel A La France* (Boston, 1725)
UN   *Unum Necessarium* (Boston, 1693)
V   *Victorina* (Boston, 1717)
VFH   *A Voice from Heaven* (Boston, 1719)
VGT   *The Voice of God in a Tempest* (Boston, 1723)
WA   *The World Alarm'd* (Boston, 1721)
WIW   *The Wonders of the Invisible World* (Boston, 1693), in *The Witchcraft Delusion in New England*, 3 vols., ed. Samuel G. Drake (1866; rpt., New York: Burt Franklin, 1970), vol. 1
WM   *Winter-Meditations* (Boston, 1693)
WMTU   *What Should be most of all Tho't upon* (Boston, 1713)
WWG   *The Wonderful Works of God Commemorated* (Boston, 1690)

PART I
Introduction

The Authority of the Bible and Cotton Mather's "Triparadisus: A Discourse Concerning the Threefold *Paradise*"

No other American Puritan has fueled both the popular and the academic imagination as has Cotton Mather, whose highly complex character and cornucopia of published and unpublished works have yielded all things to all people. At his worst, he has been dubbed America's national gargoyle—an execrable, neurotic, superstitious hunter of witches and persecutor of the Quakers; at his best, he has been styled the first unmistakably American figure—an individualistic, erudite, urbane shaper of the American self, who fostered New England's transition into the Enlightenment. In short, as one of the most learned Americans of his time, Cotton Mather embodies both the best and worst that American Puritanism has to offer.[1]

The eldest son of New England's leading divine, Increase Mather (1639–1723), grandson of the colony's eminent spiritual founders Richard Mather (1596–1669) and John Cotton (1584–1652), Cotton Mather was born in Boston, Massachusetts, 12 February 1662/63, educated at Harvard (B.A. 1678; M.A. 1681), and awarded an honorary doctor of divinity degree from Glasgow University (1710). As his father's assistant and pastor of Boston's Second Church (Congregational), he stepped into the political limelight during the Glorious Revolution in New England with the ousting of the royal governor, Sir Edmund Andros (April 1689). During the Salem witchcraft debacle (1692–93), Mather not only warned the Salem judges against admitting "spectral evidence" as grounds for indictment, advocating instead prayer, fasting, and consolation as cures for the afflicted, but also wrote New England's official defense of the court's procedures, on which his modern reputation still largely depends: *The Wonders of the Invisible World* (1693). As the Lord's remembrancer and keeper of the Puritan conscience, he wrote the grandest of American jeremiads, his epic church history *Magnalia Christi Americana* (1702). Like his father a staunch defender of Puritan orthodoxy, Cotton Mather persuaded Elihu Yale, a London diamond merchant and practicing Anglican, to endow Yale College as the new nursery of Puritanism, when Harvard seemed to become too liberal in its teaching and independent in its thinking. If such endeavors bespeak Mather's partisan politics on the one hand and his transcendent thinking on the other, it was his chiliastic credo that led him to champion Pietist ecumenism, his effort to unite all Christian denominations in New England—nay, all Christians, Jews, and Moslems in the Orient and Occident alike—under the umbrella of his three maxims of piety to hasten the Second Coming.

Likewise, his interest in the new sciences and in new medical theories distinguishes Cotton Mather from his American contemporaries. He was elected Fellow of the Royal Society of London (1713), defended and popularized the new natural sciences in America even in the face of the Deist menace, and staunchly advocated a new germ theory and inoculation against smallpox—notwithstanding the united opposition of Boston's physicians during the epidemic of 1721. Whereas Increase Mather never quite made the transition into the Enlightenment, Cotton Mather had come full sway; his *Christian Philosopher* (1720/21) represents the best of early Enlightenment thinking in colonial America. His contributions to the New England Errand are as diverse as his publications are prolific and inexhaustible. In all, he published more than four hundred works—although thousands of manuscript pages remain unpublished—on all aspects of the contemporary debate: theological, historical, biographical, political, and scientific. It is therefore unfortunate that Cotton Mather's popular reputation is still overshadowed by the specter of Salem witchcraft. He died in Boston, 13 February 1727/28.

Cotton Mather's lifelong preoccupation with millennialism and its significance to his thought and work have only recently attracted full-scale attention. Although several fine studies have examined his typology within the context of his millenarian rhetoric, the Pietist ecumenism fostered by his eschatological fervor, and his contributions to the Society for the Propagation of the Gospel to the Indians in America, none of these studies have traced Cotton Mather's millenarian ideology throughout the body of his work, his lifelong revisions of his eschatological theories, his hermeneutical break from the tenets of Increase Mather and Joseph Mede.[2] Cotton Mather's modern biographers have done little better. Of the seven nineteenth- and twentieth-century biographers—Barrett Wendell, 1891; Abijah P. Marvin, 1892; Ralph and Louise Boas, 1928; Robert Middlekauff, 1971; David Levin, 1978; Babette M. Levy, 1979; and Kenneth Silverman, 1984—only three touch on Mather's millenarian theories: Middlekauff summarizes them (ch. 18), Levin employs them as a thematic device (ch. 6), and Silverman treats the topic *en passant*. Most recently, John S. Erwin (1990) has provided a historical and theological analysis of Mather's millennialism, but he does not examine how the new philological and hermeneutical challenges of Scripture prophecies in Europe caused Mather to break away from his inherited traditions, or how the emerging preterite-contextual exegesis sponsored by English and Continental Deists shaped Mather's defense of revealed religion in his definitive treatise "Triparadisus." Nor does Erwin investigate how Mather's millenarian theories—old and new—fly in the face of some widely held historiographical paradigms: the Puritan concept of God's *peculium*, New England as the millennial New Jerusalem, and the American hemisphere with its ambiguous role in the Christianography of the millennial New World.[3]

Beginning with *Things to be Look'd for* (1691), Cotton Mather published more than fifty works in which his eschatology played a major role. In fact, it is hard to read any of Mather's writings without finding some reference to the imminence of Christ's Second Coming. Of his unpublished works on that topic, three stand out: "Problema Theologicum" (1703), a 95-page manuscript reflecting the principal issues in Mather's early millennialism; "Triparadisus" (1712, 1726/27), his definitive treatment of his millenarian theories (387 ms. pages) and his response to the contemporary hermeneutical debate in Europe; and his "Biblia Americana," a gargantuan and unfinished critical commentary on the Bible in six folio volumes, fortified with synopses of the best hermeneutical scholarship of the day.

Apocalyptic studies, however numerous, were often plagued by embarrassing inaccuracies and wishful thinking. Mather, too, was given to such conjectures and, as a consequence, had to revise his ideas frequently. "Problema Theologicum"—largely following the theories of Increase Mather and those of Joseph Mede (1586–1638), England's most influential exegete on millennialism in the early seventeenth century—well illustrates the volatile nature of such endeavors. So, too, does "Biblia Americana," from which Mather never got around to expunging those passages and tables of millenarian calculations that the truth of time, or the light of better judgment, had proved vain. Begun in 1712 and finished sometime in 1726/27, "Triparadisus" is Mather's most comprehensive study of apocalypticism (D 3:91). As a hermeneutical defense of revealed religion, Mather's discourse on the threefold paradise seeks to negotiate between orthodox exegesis of the prophecies and the new philological and historical-contextual challenges to the Scriptures by such scholars as Hugo Grotius, Thomas Hobbes, Isaac de La Peyrère, Benedict de Spinoza, Richard Simon, Henry Hammond, Thomas Burnet, William Whiston, and Anthony Collins. "Triparadisus," then, marks a decisive break from the hermeneutical positions he had inherited from his intellectual forebears. While Cotton Mather had originally subscribed to his father's orthodox position on the national conversion of the Jews (Romans 11) as the most significant event to occur before the Second Coming, he abandoned this literalist mainstay of prophetic exegesis a few years before his death and joined the allegorical camp of Henry Hammond, John Lightfoot, and Richard Baxter, who insisted on a preterite reading of Paul's Epistle to the Romans. As Mather understood prophetic Scriptures toward the end of his life, all signs announcing Christ's Coming had long been given in the past and "there is nothing to hinder the immediate Coming of our Saviour" (D 2:733). From 1720 to 1726, Mather's hermeneutics underwent a radical shift from a futurist interpretation of the prophecies to a preterite position—from arguing that several signs of Christ's return were still to be fulfilled to asserting that all signs had already been given several times over. "I purpose quickly to write on these things," he confided to his diary, and he began composing parts II and III of "Triparadisus" approximately eighteen months later (31 January 1725/26), evidently finishing by February 1726/27 (D 2:733, 811; *Selected Letters*, p. 415). "Triparadisus," then, not only marks a decisive break with his

earlier millennialism but also represents the culmination of his lifelong interest in apocalypticism, which lay at the core of his cosmology and which was
the fundamental mainspring of his ministerial and theological office.

Available only in often illegible microfilm copies, the "Triparadisus" manuscript is part of the Mather Family Papers, purchased by Isaiah Thomas and
housed in the American Antiquarian Society, Worcester, Massachusetts. To
make this important document accessible in print and to furnish scholars with
a critical edition seems long overdue, for as an important link between Mather's
premillennialism in the early 1720s and Jonathan Edwards's postmillennial-
ism that came to fruition in the 1740s, "Triparadisus" provides important biographical insight into Mather's last years, when, liberated from the immediate
pressure of his filio-pietistic attachment to his father's exegesis, Cotton finally
came into his own. More significant, "Triparadisus" challenges a number of
deeply cherished paradigms in the scholarship on American Puritanism: the
consensus among modern historians who have traced the Puritan origin of the
American self to the idea of the Errand into the wilderness with its system of
typological adumbration and abrogation as Jehovah's *peculium*, the common-
place argument that New England represented for the Mathers and their colleagues the culmination of prophetic history in an American New Jerusalem,
and the widely held view that the American hemisphere would play a special
role in the Christianography of the coming millennium. Finally, as an exegetical work harmonizing the old with the new biblical criticism, "Triparadisus"
represents the most original contribution by an American theologian before
Jonathan Edwards to the marketplace of hermeneutical ideas.

"Triparadisus" can also be compared with Cotton Mather's magnum opus,
Magnalia Christi Americana, in that the two works converge on a number
of points. The *Magnalia*, as the church history of New England, is generally
regarded as a retrospective jeremiad, bewailing the failure of the younger generation to measure up to the gigantic achievements of the New England fathers,
whom Mather commemorates in his Puritan hagiography. But in chronicling
the declension of New England, Mather also records the *magnalia Christi*, the
providential accomplishments of Christ in America, thus safely lodging New
England within God's eternal time scheme. At the same time, this providence
history prefigures the cosmic revolution, which Mather expected during his
own lifetime. "Triparadisus," too, is retrospective, but only insofar as it links
the history of the Jews and of the Christian church with God's prophetic history of the future—horologicals with chronometricals, to borrow a phrase from
Sacvan Bercovitch's 1970 article.

Moreover, the structure of "Triparadisus," like that of Mather's *Magnalia*,
seems hopelessly unbalanced. Mather's contemporaries, just like some modern
critics, often stumbled over his "undigested" disquisitions and uneven arrange-
ments of material in the various books of his ecclesiastical history. On that
score, "Triparadisus" appears to be similarly flawed. For instance, the tripartite
division of the manuscript (seven fascicles) ranges from 28 manuscript pages
in "The First Paradise," to 68 manuscript pages in "The Second Paradise," to

291 manuscript pages in "The Third Paradise." Part I delineates the history and location of the Garden of Eden as evidenced in the Pentateuch, ancient histories, patristic literature, and contemporary travel literature. Part II is largely a refutation of psychopannychism, that is, a rebuttal of the idea that the soul is dormant and a defense of the doctrine of the soul's immortality. Part III is by far the longest and the most valuable discussion and covers in twelve subsections a variety of topics affected by the hermeneutical debate then taking shape in Europe: from the tradition of the conflagration at the Second Coming to the New Heavens and the New Earth during the millennium. "The Third Paradise" is justifiably the longest section, for it provides Mather's *"Golden Key"* to prophetic literature and covers the events leading up to and following the grand revolution: Christ's millennial reign and the restoration of the earth and mankind to their prelapsarian condition. As Mather's renumbering of his manuscript pages suggests, he chose twelve subdivisions for his "Third Paradise" to tally with the auspicious number twelve—signaling completion and balance in Christian numerology. A similar intent operates in the seven books of his *Magnalia,* the number seven here representing a cycle of completion that can be traced in both Old and New Testaments.

"The First Paradise" is for the generalist a tedious (though not uninviting) philological and linguistic delineation of Old Testament geography. If Mather's explanation can be trusted, the largest part of this section is excerpted from Samuel Lee's now lost manuscript *"Of a Threefold Paradise"* (c. 1689), a discourse on the geography of the Old Testament, which Mather "carefully Epitomized" (*T*, p. 94) and included in his "Biblia Americana" ("Genesis 2 : 25"). How much Mather relied on his father-in-law's lost geography is debatable; much more certain is the influence of Edward Wells (1667–1727), whose *Historical Geography of the Old Testament* (1711–12) supplied Mather with many cribbed passages. Such second- and thirdhand descriptions of the OT geography were standard until the late seventeenth century; in the early eighteenth century, however, a mere recitation of the traditional Mosaic geography proved to be no longer satisfactory. The challenges to the authority of the Bible as the revealed Word of God could no longer be answered in traditional ways.

For instance, the new scientific cosmogonies in Thomas Burnet's *Sacred Theory of the Earth* (1684) and those in William Whiston's Newtonian *New Theory of the Earth* (1696) had seriously challenged the validity of the Mosaic accounts of the Creation, of the location of paradise, and of the Flood itself. Even though Mather substantially retained his excerpt from Samuel Lee's manuscript, the textual and substantive changes (1726/27) in "The First Paradise" not only reflect his sensitivity to the best of early Enlightenment thought but also reveal his nervous reaction to Deist natural science and its threat to the authority of the Bible. It does not come as a surprise that Mather—like most of his contemporaries—mocked his Deist colleague Thomas Burnet (c. 1635–1715), successively Fellow of Christ College, master of the Charterhouse, and chaplain to William III. In his *Sacred Theory* and more so in his later *Archaeologia philosophicae* (1692), Burnet dismissed on scientific grounds the veracity of the Mosaic Creation story—and so did William Whiston, the disciple of Sir Isaac Newton. Moses did not provide a scientifically sound explanation of the Creation, they maintained, but merely furnished "a narration suited to the capacity of the people." Any effort, therefore, to make the natural world and its laws conform to the Bible "in opposition to Reason" was dangerous; time would prove "evidently false [that] which we had made Scripture to assert" (*Sacred Theory*, p. 9). As Whiston put the issue squarely in his *New Theory*, intended to replace Burnet's earlier work, "the *Mosaick* Creation extends no farther than our Earth" and its immediate atmosphere; it excluded all other celestial bodies, which had a separate creation not covered in Genesis. The biblical narrative was therefore limited to the earth only, "because neither the Intentions of the Author require, nor the Capacities of the People could bear either a strictly philosophical, or a truly universal Account of the Origin of Things." Given the didactic intent of the inspired lawgiver, "the *Mosaick* History is not a nice, exact, and philosophick Account of the several Steps and Operations of the whole; but such an historical Relation of each Mutation of the Chaos, each successive Day, as the Journal of a Person on the Face of the Earth all that while would naturally have contained" (pt. I, pp. 81, 88).

If such disputes over biblical authority were not enough, Burnet postulated in his *Sacred Theory* that the surface of the antediluvian earth had been uniformly level and contained neither mountains nor oceans. By this argument the waters that deluged the globe were contained in caverns below the earth's thin crust, which, upon its collapse, caused the inundation described by Moses. Any geographical endeavors to locate the prelapsarian Eden in the ruins of the present earth seemed therefore frivolous, all traces of the original Garden having totally vanished in the chaos and ruins of the collapsing earth (pp. 42–101).

Indubitably, Noah's deluge "caus'd and left very Considerable Alterations on the Face of the Earth," Mather readily conceded, yet the surviving "Reliques and Ruines discovered in *our Days*" more than corroborated the Mosaic geography and could not but "make the *Burnettian* Romance come to nothing" (*T*, p. 94). Mather's triumph, however, was short-lived, for by the time he had reached the end of his "First Paradise," he could not help but confess that the numerous and contradictory OT geographies compiled by such "Ungeographical Gentlemen" as the early church fathers were painfully unreliable and highly damaging to any geographical verification of the prelapsarian Eden. "After all this Labour," Mather whimsically surrendered his argument, "the Issue and Result" may prove to be "little better than . . . a *Fools Paradise*," for the terrestrial Garden "is gone like a great Milstone thrown into the Sea," never to be found any more (*T*, p. 110).

"The Second Paradise" of Cotton Mather's discourse on the threefold paradise must also be set in its proper historical context if we are to appreciate why he elected to fortify the embattled doctrine of the soul's immortality with choice stories of ghosts, poltergeists, and deathbed narratives seemingly more worthy of his *Wonders of the Invisible World* (1693) and of Salem witchcraft than of an enlightened treatise on the new hermeneutics, with its emphasis on philological contextualization and preterite allegorization of the Scriptures. The belief in the soul as a separate incorporeal substance continuing after the death of the body in distinct receptacles, or "Second Paradise," was questioned by few of the dominant Protestant branches in the English Reformation. However, toward the latter part of the seventeenth century, the traditional belief in the *ubi sunt* of departed souls could no longer be taken for granted—not even among the various Protestant denominations. On the one side of the issue, Roman Catholics posited in *Benedictus Deus* (1336) and elsewhere that the disembodied souls of the just, cleansed in a temporary purgatory, would be admitted to the immediate Beatific Vision in paradise even before the Resurrection of the body at Judgment Day.

This position, however, was staunchly opposed by Protestants, especially the Anabaptists in John Calvin's day, who tried to combat the "leaven" of Rome by insisting that the souls of both the just and the unjust were inactive and would sleep insensibly until Judgment Day, when body and soul would rise united. These sectarian "soul-sleepers," dubbed "psychopannychists" in John Calvin's *Psychopannychia* (1542), rendered themselves obnoxious when they went so far in combating purgatory as inadvertently to threaten the whole belief in the immortality of the soul. Trying to contain the damage done to the Protestant Reformation in France, Calvin mediated between the extremes. "For those who admit that the soul lives, and yet deprive it of all sense," he charged in his *Psychopannychia*, "feign a soul which has none of the properties of soul, or dissever the soul from itself, seeing that its nature, without which it cannot possibly exist, is to move, to feel, to be vigorous, to understand" (p. 427). Just souls do not sleep insensibly, he insisted, but are alive and active in separate receptacles until Resurrection, at which time they are admitted to the Beatific Vision (pp. 435–36). If Calvin's mediation temporarily satisfied Protestant sectarians in the sixteenth century, it certainly required buttressing in the seventeenth, when the English philosopher Thomas Hobbes (1588–1679) seemingly revived the old Epicurean materialist position that the *anima* and *animus* (soul and living spirit) have no separate existence from the body but are merely its vitalizing or animating force, vanishing into thin air at the death of the body. Revived in *Leviathan* (1651), this Hobbesian materialism threatened the very superstructure of doctrinal belief in the afterlife, with its attending systems of reward or punishment meted out to immortal souls.

To carry his point, Hobbes tried first to delineate from the biblical texts a consistent definition of the crucial terms *body* and *spirit* (substances "*corporeal*" and "*incorporeal*") and then to show how these terms were misused by exegetes in their assertions of the soul's independent existence from the body (pt. III, ch. 34). In a masterpiece of scholastic *reductio ad absurdum*, Hobbes set out to confound his opponents: "*substance* and *body* signify the same thing; and therefore *substance incorporeal* are words, which when they are joined together, destroy one another, as if a man should say, an *incorporeal body*" (pt. III, ch. 34, p. 286). Such a contradiction in terms rendered illogical the belief in bodies without substance, Hobbes contended as he rose to dismiss the soul or incorporeal body of man. "That the soul of man is in its own nature eternal, and a living creature independent on the body . . . is a doctrine not apparent in Scripture" (pt. III, ch. 38, p. 328), Hobbes lambasted the church, with its armor of control over the people. For "the *soul* in Scripture, signifieth always, either the life, or the living creature; and the body and soul jointly, the *body alive*. . . . If by *soul* were meant a *substance incorporeal*, with an existence separated from the body, it might as well be inferred of any other living creature as of man" (pt. IV, ch. 44, p. 445).

Truth to tell, Hobbes struck at the very core of the issue by hinting that even cats and dogs and other living creatures might thus be endowed with an inalienable right to a living soul. The belief in a distinct soul separate from the body bespoke to Hobbes nothing less than the worst heathenism and "contagion of the demonology of the Greeks," which gave rise to all sorts of dark doctrines of the church: "first, of eternal torments; and afterwards of purgatory, and consequently of the walking abroad, especially in places consecrated, solitary, or dark, of the ghosts of men deceased; and thereby to the pretences of exorcism and conjuration of phantasms; as also of invocation of men dead" (pt. IV, ch. 44, p. 445). Had Hobbes restrained his attack to those dogmas dear to Roman Catholicism, he might have found a receptive audience in Protestant England. Yet given the scope and sweep of his argument, he could not fail to antagonize all of Christendom. Small wonder, then, that in one of the great ironies of the seventeenth century, Hobbes succeeded in uniting against himself such powerful enemies as Roman Catholics, Lutherans, and the Calvinist branches of Protestantism.

Cotton Mather's defense of the soul's immortality in "The Second Paradise" therefore must be appreciated against the contemporary debate lingering on into the eighteenth century. His tall tales of walking ghosts and audible poltergeists intruding on the realm of the living became tangible and extrabiblical evidence to rebut the Hobbesian *Leviathan*. Even the very existence of witchcraft proved Hobbes and the modern *"Sadducees"* liars: "Since there are *Witches* and *Devils*," Mather countered in *Memorable Providences* three years before Satan would descend on New England, "we may conclude that there are also *Immortal Souls. Devils* would never contract with *Witches* for their Souls if there were no such things to become a prey unto them" (pt. III, pp. 14, 16; see also *PN*, pp. 110–13). In this endeavor, Mather was certainly not alone, nor was he the only one among his contemporaries who collected such energumenical specimens to demonstrate the soul's activity in a Second Paradise. Mather's success (or failure), then, must be measured against those of his famous forebears and contemporaries: John Calvin, Hieronymous Zanchius, Moïse Amyraut, Henry More, William Bates, Richard Baxter, Thomas Burnet—all of whom Cotton Mather emulated and mustered in defense of the wonders of the invisible world.[4]

His most significant contribution to the hermeneutical debate then raging in the marketplace of ideas occurs, however, in "The Third Paradise"—his response to the new philological and preterite-allegorist hermeneutics in the early eighteenth century. Here, Mather devises a key to reinterpreting biblical prophecies in light of the new textual and contextual criticism developed by Hugo Grotius, Henry Hammond, Thomas Hobbes, Benedict de Spinoza, Richard Simon, William Whiston, and Anthony Collins, and harmonizes the new hermeneutics with the earlier eschatological theories he had inherited mostly from Joseph Mede and Increase Mather. As noted earlier, "The Third Paradise" covers in twelve subsections a variety of topics affected by the new hermeneutics, from the tradition of the conflagration (secs. i–viii), the New Heavens and the New Earth (secs. ix–x), and the conversion of the Jewish nation (sec. xi) to the prophetic timetables (sec. xii). His "Third Paradise," therefore, is not only the longest subdivision but also the most valuable part of the entire manuscript.

Until the middle of the seventeenth century, few scholars openly questioned the time-honored tradition that the Bible was inspired by God, that his re-vealed Word had been recorded by holy men, that it had been transmitted and preserved intact down through the ages. In Cotton Mather's day, however, the authority of the Bible had been seriously challenged by a number of English and Continental scholars, whose philological and contextual studies of the ancient manuscript versions seemed to reveal serious flaws. One of the most vociferous and outspoken critics in England, Thomas Hobbes, scrutinized the issue of tex-tual transmission and charged in his *Leviathan* that *"The Pentateuch* [was] *not written by Moses"* (pt. III, ch. 33, p. 277), that it was not compiled into a single text until long after the divine lawgiver had died, that the OT textual renditions in their present form must be attributed to the period after King Antiochus Epiphanes (d. 163 B.C.) and the Maccabean revolt, when the temple at Jerusa-lem and its holy books had been destroyed. In fact, if the apocryphal Esdras is admissible evidence, Hobbes conjectured, then "the Scripture was set forth in the form we have it in, by Esdras" (2 Esd. 14:21–22, 45), "who by the direction of God's spirit retrieved [it], when [it was] lost," and therefore dates back no fur-ther than to the second century B.C.[5] Similar problems of textual transmission also encumbered the authority of the New Testament, whose final text was not approved by "the Council of Laodicea" until "the 364th year after Christ," when the early church canonized what its authorities believed were "the writings of those apostles and disciples, under whose names they go" (Hobbes, pt. III, ch. 33, pp. 281–82; Spinoza, *Tractatus*, ch. XI, pp. 157–64).

If that were not enough, Hobbes seemingly cast aspersions on the Scriptures on logical grounds as well, for such egregious problems of textual variants, he argued, would naturally arouse the suspicion of discriminating minds. He raised the inevitable question: *"How* [do] *we know them to be the word of God,* or, *why* [do] *we believe them to be so"*? Naturally, all good Christians *believe* that the Scriptures are authored by God, but by the same token "none can know they are God's word" except for those prophets and apostles to whom he "hath re-vealed it supernaturally." Therefore to *believe* the Bible is God's word is not the same as to *know* that it is so. Hence, the question should not be of "our *belief"* in the Scriptures (for that is personal and individual) but *"by what authority they are made law"* of the land. The Bible therefore attains its legal status not from our belief but from the decree of a ruler of a Christian commonwealth, who demands that the Good Book be observed as the law of God (pt. III, ch. 33, pp. 283–85).

Had Thomas Hobbes been the only critic to challenge the Bible and its authority on philological grounds, his contemporaries might have been able to ignore his startling thesis. Yet Hobbes's research was well received by his colleagues on the Continent and would not disappear so easily. Corroborating the evidence of the French biblical scholar Isaac de La Peyrère, whose *Prae-adamitae* (1655) postulated that the different races populating the various continents had a separate creation from that told in Genesis, Benedict de Spinoza (1632–77), the great Jewish scholar of the Netherlands, spoke for all those who concerned themselves with problems of textual transmission: If one examines how the Pentateuch and much of the Old Testament are put together, he argued in his *Tractatus Theologico-Politicus* (1670), one can easily "discern that all the materials were promiscuously collected and heaped together." The text is "faulty, mutilated, tampered with, and inconsistent" and therefore remains valuable at best for its moral and ethical teachings or merely as the history of the Israelites (ch. IX, p. 135; ch. XII, p. 165). Following in Spinoza's steps, Richard Simon (1638–1712), the renowned French Catholic exegete and professor of philosophy, published his highly controversial *L'Histoire critique du Vieux Testament* (1678), in which he argued that the surviving OT text had been compiled by "Publick Writers" appointed for the task, who had arranged in a single text more or less imperfect synoptical abstracts of no-longer-extant originals. Yet unlike Spinoza, Simon maintained shrewdly that these compilations remained the "inspired" word of God, because "the Authours of these additions and alterations were real Prophets directed by the Spirit of God."[6] If Richard Simon sought to contain the inevitable damage done by his own philological researches, his warrant of God's divine guidance in the endeavors of these "Publick Writers" did little to regulate the intellectual and theological dilemma that his argument posed to his contemporaries. Clearly, the new challenges to biblical authority surpassed even those that had informed the worst sectarian excesses during the English Reformation. Such formidable guns pointed at the very foundation of the Book of Books required every responsible theologian to take his stand. Such "Men are a Sort of *Monsters*, which are the Blemish of Mankind, & ought always to be treated with Terms of Pitty, and of Contempt & of Detestation," Cotton Mather lashed out in exasperation. "An *Argument* is meerly thrown away upon these Detestable Creatures" (*T*, p. 172).

Like his colleagues Benedict de Spinoza and Richard Simon, Sir Isaac Newton was keenly aware of the indelible dilemma surrounding the Bible as a textual document and was greatly concerned about how such problems might affect its authority and traditional claim as the revealed word of God. Newton freely shared his distress in his posthumously published *Observations upon the Prophecies of Daniel, and the Apocalypse of St. John* (1733). The earliest copies of the Bible, he wrote, "are now lost; and such marginal notes, or other corruptions, as by the errors of the transcribers, before this Edition was made, had crept into the text, are now scarce to be corrected" (pt. I, p. 12; Spinoza, *Tractatus*, ch. IX, pp. 133–45). Yet Newton did not dismiss the Bible so readily as Hobbes and Spinoza seemed to do. For if God manifested his will for all times through his prophetic spirit encapsulated in the Scriptures, then the harmony of the prophetic books in the Old Testament when juxtaposed with those in the New might serve as an appropriate barometer. The prophecies of Daniel when compared with those of Revelation, for instance, could reliably measure the extent to which the revealed word of God remained unhampered by problems of textual transmission.

Newton's unswerving loyalty to the prophecies, flying in the face of his own philological challenges to the biblical texts, is particularly revealing: "The authority of the Prophets is divine," Newton avowed, "and comprehends the sum of religion, reckoning *Moses* and the Apostles among the Prophets." Textual problems notwithstanding, the Bible contains God's "instructions for keeping this covenant . . . and predictions of things to come." All true believers could therefore adhere to the revealed will of God by observing the dictums of the prophets, for "the predictions of things to come relate to the state of the Church in all ages," and "to reject his Prophecies, is to reject the Christian religion," which "is founded upon his Prophecy concerning the *Messiah*" (pt. I, pp. 14, 15, 25). Naturally, good men throughout the ages had devoted themselves to the study of the prophecies, but their endeavor was only too often led astray by their zeal for predicting cataclysmic future events. Instead of gratifying "men's curiosities" about things to come, God intended for the prophecies to be validated post facto, *after* the historical event had occurred: "For the event of things predicted many ages before, will then be a convincing argument that the world is governed by providence" (pt. II, pp. 251–52; Spinoza, *Tractatus*, ch. XII, pp. 165–74). Verifying the abrogation of OT and NT prophecies in secular history became a formidable weapon against all those who spurned revealed religion. It is therefore not surprising that predictions about Christ's Second Coming were central to the millenarian exegeses of biblical prophecies, for not only did they establish the prophetic timetables of the church, whose historical development could post facto validate the accuracy of the prophecies, but they also were intrinsic proof that no matter how flawed the surviving versions of the Bible, God had seen to it that his prophetic spirit had not diminished.

If the renewed study of prophetic literature in Newton's day could have lived up to such an important task, then the battle over the prophetic books might yet have been won. Unfortunately, the prophecies had been assailed from yet another battalion in the hermeneutical camp, which posed an even more formidable threat. The Dutch Arminian theologian Hugo Grotius (1583–1645), now best remembered for his acclaimed works on jurisprudence, challenged one of the most valued proofs of the Christian religion when he championed a preterite-contextual interpretation of biblical prophecies. A new departure in the hermeneutical science, Grotius's *Annotationes in Vetus et Novum Testamentum* (1642) insisted that many of the OT prophecies applied by the apostles in the New Testament as literal abrogations in Christ actually violated the

OT prophets' intended primary sense. This primary and literal sense, Grotius claimed, had to be found in the historical and contextual events of the prophets' own time and could not be appropriated in any literalist sense to NT times. Only if a double fulfillment were allowed—a literal and primary abrogation in OT times adumbrating an allegorical and secondary fulfillment in NT times— could the apostles' adaptation of OT sources be admitted as proof of the Christian religion.[7]

One of Grotius's most prominent apologists, the Anglican scholar and member of the Westminster Assembly Henry Hammond (1605–60), came to his defense in the subsequent turmoil engulfing his thesis (1655–57). Hammond insisted that Grotius did not exclude the literal fulfillment in Christ of certain OT prophecies but that in his famous hermeneutical work *Annotationes* he was primarily concerned with "the *first* and *literal interpretation*" of the OT prophets, "where there is one *immediate completion* of each *Prophecy* among the *Jews* of or near *that* time, wherein it was written, another more *remote* and *ultimate* concerning *Christ*, or the times of the *Gospel*." In his *Annotationes*, Grotius therefore established "most *distinctly* the *first*, or *literal* sense, as that is *terminated* in the *immediate completion* . . . because it was most *neglected* by other *interpreters*, who were more *copious* in rendring the *mystical notation*" as it applied to the New Testament (*Second Defence*, p. 81). But Hammond could not stem the avalanche of criticism coming down on Grotius. In thus questioning the exegetical method of none less than Christ's own apostles, his opponents charged, Grotius's contextual preterization of the prophecies watered down the grounds and reasons of Christianity to mere allegories and inadvertently shattered the very foundation of the Christian religion, with its bulwark of typology literally abrogated in Christ. The ever-widening debate, which involved the best of contemporary exegetes in Cotton Mather's time, cannot here be discussed in detail.[8] Suffice it to sketch some of the main responses to Grotius's historical method, which determined much of the hermeneutical debate in the early eighteenth century.

In "Triparadisus," Cotton Mather voiced his discontent with the method of his Dutch colleague, whose missionary handbook *De Veritate Religionis Christianae* (1627) Mather still praised as a major contribution to Christian apologetics. But Grotius's biblical commentary *Annotationes* carried the author's Arminianism too far. Mather was exasperated "that so *Great* a Man among us *Christians*, as *Grotius* . . . should make such *Mad Work* in his *Judaizing* Figments on this wonderful Chapter [Isa. 53]. How poorly would the *Ethiopian Lord-Treasurer*, have been accommodated with a Commentary on this Chapter, if instead of a *Philip*, he had mett with a *Grotius*, for a Commentator? . . . The Bright Coruscations of a CHRIST, in every Line of the Chapter, are enough, even to convert a *Rochester*!" (*T*, pp. 164–65).[9] Subsequent attempts to rescue the OT prophecies and their literal abrogation in Christ from the clutches of the "new" historicists included such scholars as John Greene, Samuel White, John Lightfoot, William Lowth, Arthur Ashley Sykes, Edward Chandler—all of whom tried to harmonize Grotius's preterite contextualization with its tendency to disallow a single and literal abrogation in the New Testament by expanding the "Prophetic Intent" to include a double fulfillment: a smaller one in OT times and the larger one in NT times.

Sir Isaac Newton's disciple William Whiston, the Lucasian Professor of Mathematics at Cambridge, had been wrestling with Hugo Grotius's historical method for some time and vehemently objected to the double and secondary application of the OT prophecies to Christ in his much-acclaimed *Accomplishment of Scripture Prophecies* (1708). Here he countered dogmatically:

> I observe that the Stile and Language of the Prophets . . . is always single and determinate, and not capable of those double Intentions, and typical Interpretations, which most of our late Christian Expositors are so full of upon all Occasions. A single and determinate sense of every Prophecy, is the only natural and obvious one; and no more can be admitted without putting a force upon plain words, and no more assented to by the Minds of inquisitive Men, without a mighty bias upon their rational faculty. (P. 13)

It was absolutely necessary for Whiston that the messianic prophecies in the Old Testament "have been properly and literally without any recourse to Typical, Foreign and Mystical Expositions, fulfill'd in Jesus" if the cause of Christianity were not to relinquish altogether its bedrock of prophetic proof (*Accomplishment*, p. 13). In spurning Grotius's double sense and in categorically ruling out the apostles' supposed allegorical proof of Christ, Whiston had aptly gauged the hermeneutical dilemma surrounding the prophecies. For if Grotius's double sense were allowed to facilitate the NT abrogation, Whiston insisted, then "we can never be satisfy'd but they may have as many [senses] as any Visionary pleases; and . . . will be lyable to the foolish application of fanciful and enthusiastick men." With Grotius's double intention, "we lose all the real advantages as to the proof of our common Christianity" (*Accomplishment*, pp. 15, 16). Unfortunately for Whiston, his own literalism created a problem, for he painted himself into a literalist corner from which he could extricate himself only with difficulty.[10]

In his controversial treatise *An Essay Towards Restoring the True Text of the Old Testament* (1722), Whiston examined the textual difficulties surrounding the apostles' use of OT citations and hypothesized that when compared to the Samaritan Pentateuch used in the times of Jesus, the Hebrew and Septuagint versions of the Old Testament are corrupted precisely in those points where they concern the prophecies of the Messiah's First and Second Coming (pp. 164, 172, 220). In his desperation to uphold the primary and literal abrogation of the OT prophecies in Christ in the face of the apostles' alleged allegorization, Whiston was forced to argue that textual corruptions were introduced in the Old Testament either deliberately to thwart the proof of Christianity or accidentally by scribal error. It is for this reason, he claimed, that many of the apostles' quotations of the OT messianic prophecies deviate in wording and intent from their OT source. The apostles' NT renditions are therefore not allegories but the true and original texts that, if restored to their proper places in the Old Testament, would nullify the need for Grotius's double sense: The OT prophecies would then be singly and literally abrogated in the New Testament. Whiston, however, was quick to discover that his deus-ex-machina device to make the prophecies safe for Christianity aroused the ire of his Deist colleague Anthony Collins (1676–1729), who charged in his famous *Discourse of the Grounds and Reasons of the Christian Religion* (1724) that Whiston's "restoration" of the true text amounted to little more than "a mere WHISTONIAN BIBLE, a BIBLE confounding and not containing *the true Text* of the Old Testament" (pt. II, p. 196). Without doubt, Collins's refutation of Whiston's literalism poured out the baby with the bathwater by repudiating Christianity as little more than Judaism allegorized. As a Socinian who rejected the divinity of Christ, Collins could well afford to look unflinchingly at the "fables" of a Jesus yet still praise the Creator for his "Divine Machine" and the harmony of its universal laws.[11]

A single example must suffice here to illustrate the nature of the contemporary debate and to explain how Cotton Mather's "Triparadisus" was designed as a hermeneutical bulwark against the allegorizing Deists, with their battery of preterite contextualization. Collins's basic argument was that the New Testament proves Christianity out of the Old, that the NT writers delineate Christ and his disciples as abrogating by their works and doctrines the prophecies of the Old Testament, that the apostles reinterpret the Mosaic Laws as prophetic types of Christianity, that Christianity, therefore, is Judaism allegorized (*Grounds and Reasons*, pt. I, ch. 1). In short, the apostles grafted the New Testament on the Old by insisting that the new revelation was to supplant the religion of their fathers, that the new dispensation rescued the Word of God from all manner of corruptions and innovations that had crept into the sacred texts. Yet in presenting the new dispensation as fulfilling the old, Collins maintained, the NT writers seemed to forget that "the old *revelations*, far from intending any change, engraftment, or new dispensation, did for the most part declare they were to last *for ever*, and did forbid all alterations and innovations, they being the *last dispensations* intended" (pt. I, ch. 4, p. 24).

Determined to legitimize their new religion, Collins insisted, the apostles were forced to demonstrate that the Old Testament adumbrated the New, the OT messianic types singly and literally accomplished in Jesus of Nazareth. In their zeal to hail the promised Messiah, however, Christ's disciples took considerable hermeneutical liberties by quoting OT prophecies out of context, by ignoring their literal fulfillment during the time of the prophets' utterance, and, worse yet, by citing messianic predictions that are nowhere to be found in the Hebrew Scriptures:

> These *Proofs* taken out of the *Old*, and urg'd in the *New* Testament, being sometimes, either not to be found in the *Old*, or not urg'd in the *New*, according to the literal and obvious sense, which they seem to bear in their suppos'd places in the *Old*, and therefore not proofs according to Scholastick Rules; almost all Christian *Comentators* on the Bible, and *Advocates* for the Christian Religion, both antient and modern, have judg'd them to be

apply'd in a secondary, or typical, or mystical, or allegorical, or enigmatical sense, that is, in a sense different from the obvious and literal sense, which they bear in the Old Testament. (Pt. I, ch. 8, pp. 39–40)

This misappropriation of the OT prophet Isaiah, Collins argued, echoing Grotius's historical contextualization, is evident in a number of hotly debated messianic prophecies, which the Apostle Matthew had applied to Jesus of Nazareth: "Now all this was done, that it might be fulfilled which was spoken of the Lord by the Prophet, saying, Behold, a Virgin shall be with childe, and shall bring foorth a sonne, and they shall call his name Emmanuel, which being interpreted, is, God with vs" (Matt. 1:22–23; Isa. 7:14). In applying Isaiah's prophecy to Jesus Christ in a literal sense, Matthew had inadvertently violated the historical context of the Scripture. Isaiah's words do not apply to Christ in the New Testament, Collins retorted, but "in their obvious and literal sense, relate to a *young woman* in the days of AHAZ, King of *Judah*," who, besieged by his enemies Rezin and Pekah, was promised a sign that "a Virgine shall conceiue and beare a Sonne" (Isa. 7:14) as a token that Judah's enemies would soon be vanquished (pt. I, p. 41). Since the people of Judah were expecting their speedy delivery from the hands of their approaching enemies, what good would it have done King Ahaz to receive a revelation predicting the Messiah's birth seven hundred years later? "How could a virgin's conception and bearing a son seven hundred years afterwards, be a *sign* to AHAZ" in his present predicament? Such "*absurdity*" would have appeared "a banter instead of a sign" to the people of Judah. Surely, Collins quipped, the historical context of the prophecy clearly establishes that Isaiah's prophecy applied in its primary and literal sense to his own son, born during King Ahaz's reign; Matthew therefore employs Isaiah "in a secondary, or typical, or mystical, or allegorical sense," which is to say in a nonliteral sense (pt. I, pp. 42, 43, 44).

Indeed, with the preterite and contextual commentaries of Hugo Grotius, Henry Hammond, Richard Simon, and Samuel White at his elbow, Collins demonstrated that Matthew's literal application of Isa. 7:14 to Jesus Christ was impossible. The only way out of this dilemma was to embrace Grotius's double fulfillment, a literal one in Ahaz's time and an allegorical, secondary application of this prophecy to Christ in Matthew's time—only then could Isaiah's prophecy be of any use at all in establishing the promised Immanuel. Collins summed up his argument: "The Anti-allegorists" who revile Grotius's method and take the New Testament's "remote-enigmatical sense to be the literal sense, are guilty of the highest absurdity imaginable." In short, Isaiah's prophecies are so misconstrued by the self-styled literalist commentators that "they put a sense upon the words subversive of the true literal sense; whereby properly speaking they are no interpreters at all, or rather worse than none, being mere indulgers of fancy" (pt. II, ch. 21, pp. 244–45). Those who claim to be literalists are really the worst allegorists, for in conveniently ignoring the historical context, they force a secondary sense upon the prophecies.[12]

Such a declaration of war on the Holy Scriptures was too much to bear for the aged Cotton Mather, who entered the hermeneutical debate then raging in the marketplace of ideas by composing his manuscript essay "Triparadisus: A Discourse Concerning the Threefold Paradise." Here he devised a *"Golden Key"* to harmonize his prophetic literalism with the preterite-allegorical hermeneutics of Hugo Grotius as a means to safeguard revealed religion from the onslaught of Deists like Collins. In denying the apostles' supernatural ability "to *know* the Intention of the *Prophecies* in the *Old Testament*" and the events that are to occur in Christ's millennial kingdom (*T*, p. 162), Collins and his ilk "won't own the *Interpretation* which the *New Testament* putts upon the *Old*." Such "Blind *Infidels*" rob all true expositors of "this *Comfort of the Scriptures*," Mather retorted; "And except in a very few Places, we must suppose no more, than here or there *something*, that what we have in the *History* of our SAVIOUR there may be some faint *Allusion* to" (*T*, p. 172). At first glance, Mather's defense of the apostles' literalist hermeneutics seems to beg the question; for in resorting to miraculous causes, Mather knew only too well that he could not dismantle his opponents' exegetical stance. Beginning in 1724 (*D* 2:733), Mather revamped virtually all of the eschatological theories he had inherited from his father and Joseph Mede and adapted his exegesis of the prophecies to the higher criticism, with its emphasis on philological and preterite-contextual scholarship:

> In the *Divine Prophecies* there were THREE *Grand Events*, One or other of which the *Prophetic Spirit* usually had in His View; And tho' His Design were sometimes to foretel some *Lesser Events*, which were more Quickly to be accomplished, yett His *Main Design* was to lead the Minds of His People unto those THREE *Greater Events*. For this Purpose, He often tack'd unto those Prophecies of those *Lesser Events* diverse Expressions which must not be *fully* answered in them; Nor were these *Lesser Events* to be any other than Little *Figures* and *Praeludes* of those *Greater Events*, which GOD would have the Minds of the Faithful to be chiefly fixed upon; wherein those Things have been and will be accomplished. . . . (*T*, pp. 162–63)

Indeed, Mather here acknowledged in the best manner of Hugo Grotius the need to contextualize prophetic proclamation and abrogation in their historical setting. At the same time, he relegated literal fulfillment in OT times to a minor event, to a partial accomplishment, or to a mere prelude of its larger application in NT times. But in elevating the NT accomplishment to the primary event intended by the prophetic spirit governing divine revelation, Mather in essence imposed a double signification and thus expanded prophetic literalism to encompass the realm of typological allegory. Ever the mediator between the old literalism and its expanded application as a kind of "allegorical literalism," Mather inadvertently joined the camp of Grotius and his preterite-contextualist disciples, whose new philological scholarship became a precursor to the higher criticism of a later age.

To be sure, Mather's eschatological views underwent considerable revision during his long, productive life, but especially in his old age. Apart from his sermons, essays, and commentaries on the millennium, his millenarian references to the Second Coming and his exegeses of prophecies lie scattered through-out the body of his work. I have therefore traced the development of Mather's millennialism by drawing on his most significant published and unpublished works, insofar as such an undertaking is possible within the boundaries of an introduction. Moreover, I have attempted to place "Triparadisus" in the context of his earlier works on the subject, always trying to set off the eschatological ideas of his old age against those of his younger years. Without claiming to be comprehensive, I have emphasized a number of important paradigms that are crucial to an understanding of Mather's millennialism. The second part of my introduction therefore focuses on his premillennialist position on the national conversion of the Jews, its importance to Mather's changing views on the role of God's chosen people, and its implication for Puritan self-perception in New England. The third part investigates how the new hermeneutics af-fected Mather's views on the conflagration, on the New Jerusalem, and on the New Earth during the millennium. And the fourth part delineates Mather's changing calculations of the cycles of prophetic adumbration and abrogation in sacred and secular history. Here I have also tried to outline how his calculations settled on specific dates, their importance to Mather's interpretation of the witchcraft phenomenon in his day, his interpretation of natural phenomena as signs of Christ's Coming, and his relentless faith in the imminence of Christ's kingdom—despite repeated disappointments.

In stressing one issue more than another, I have been almost overwhelmed by the myriad of ramifications of Mather's eschatology and his response to the hermeneutical challenge from abroad. I have therefore been compelled to leave untouched many aspects that, perhaps, deserve at least as much attention as those that I have included here. However, such a decision can be justified in light of the many fine studies that have treated Mather's Pietism, his use of typology, and his place within the rhetorical tradition of the jeremiad. To stay within the reasonable limits of an introduction and to avoid overstepping the prerogatives of an editor, I have had to keep my discussion of the issues included here concise. But wherever possible, I have pointed in my notes to other studies to allow the reader to follow those avenues left untraveled.

TRIPARADISUS.

Some ESSAYS to direct such as are willing to Travel
unto a ~~Fair~~ PARADISE, would now Bespeak a
favourable Reception with them. And the Title
of these ESSAYS, which was once the Name of
a City in Syria, will invite their expectation of
a TREBLE PARADISE to be discoursed on.
Accordingly, There are to come under a Cultivation
with us; First, The PARADISE of the old World.
Then; The PARADISE of separated Spirits. Lastly,
The PARADISE of the New Earth under the New
Heavens.

O ~~Father of mercies~~, & our most merciful Father
in our Lord Jesus Christ; Send forth, I may say, thy
Light & thy Truth; & Let us by thereby led & brought
into thy Holy Garden. And Let us anon have a Portion
in the PARADISE, where we shall See the Good of thy
Chosen, & Shine with the Joy of thy Nation, & gloriously
triumph with thine Inheritance. By the Second Adam
Let us obtain a better PARADISE, than what the
First Adam has depriv'd us of.

The
First PARADISE.

The Book of Truth has informed us, That when
the glorious God had finished His Works of Creation, in the Formation of MAN, He placed His
Noble Creature, in a Garden of Delights, of which
we have some Idea under the Denomination of
a PARADISE Served unto us. But, ~~thy~~ poor
mankind. By the Sin of thy First parents, thou
hast Lost thy First Habitation, and art become a
miserable Exile from it, Spending all thy days
in Vanity! Yea, Lost the very Knowledge as
well as the comfort of that wonderful Garden.
This have we got by o[ur] Sacrilegious meddling
with the Tree of Knowledge, that we have left

Cotton Mather's "Triparadisus."
Courtesy, American Antiquarian Society.

The "New" Hermeneutics and the Jewish Nation in Cotton Mather's Eschatology

Until late in his life, Cotton Mather held fast to the premillennialist tenet of the literal restoration of the Jewish nation, whose return to the Holy Land was foretold in Paul's Epistle to the Romans. Virtually all seventeenth- and early eighteenth-century millennialists on both sides of the Atlantic agreed that even though the Jews were still languishing in their Diaspora, Jehovah had not forgotten his chosen people and would, in due time, restore them to their once-elevated position among the nations. Paul, foretelling the restoration of Abraham's natural seed (Romans 11), predicted that God would remove their blinding veil of unbelief in due time and they would then embrace Christianity in everlasting communion with the Ancient of Days. The literal accomplishment of this prophecy just before the Second Coming was affirmed in the *Savoy Declaration of Faith* (1658, 1680) and doubted by few, as Christopher Hill and others have shown. Indeed, this position was shared by such diverse exegetes as Johann Alsted, Thomas Brightman, Joseph Mede, Thomas Goodwin, William Twisse, John Dury, Henry More, John Toland, William Whiston, and even Sir Isaac Newton. Only those who viewed Romans 11 as an allegory of the Christian church would eventually dismiss its inherent typological correspondence with OT precedent and reject altogether the tenet of the literal conversion in the latter days.[1]

In interpreting Paul's prophetic promise in its literal sense, millennialists followed the lead of Joseph Mede (1586–1638), the foremost early seventeenth-century English authority on the Apocalyptic, whose *Clavis Apocalyptica* (1627) had triggered a renaissance of millennialist thinking in both Old and New England. Mede theorized, however, that nothing short of a miracle could effect this promised conversion, whose smaller type was evidenced in Paul's own mystical conversion on the road to Damascus: "That of the *Jews* may be like it; *viz.* That though many were present with S. *Paul* at that time, yet none saw the apparition of Christ, nor heard him speak, but *Paul* alone."[2] In like manner, New England's Peter Bulkeley announced in *The Gospel-Covenant* (1646, 1651), echoing Mede's exegesis of Paul, "There shall be a more full degree of calling home the *Jewes*. And in this the Apostle is cleare and full in *Rom.* 11.12, where speaking of the calling of the *Jewes* he saith, *That if their fall was the riches of the Gentiles, how much more shall their abundance be?* That is, their calling, (which shall be in great abundance) so that, *then* properly is the time, wherein the Nations shall be gathered to *Jerusalem*, namely, when the multitude of the *Jewes* shall be called, and all Nations then added unto them."[3] One of the leading first-generation nonconformists to define Puritan covenant theology in America, Bulkeley was certainly not alone in expounding a literal interpretation of the Jews' spiritual resurrection and return to Palestine. In fact, he was in good company among his colleagues not only of the first generation (John Cotton, John Davenport, William Hooke, William Greenhill, Edward Johnson) but also of the second (Urian Oakes, Nicholas Noyes, Samuel Willard, Increase Mather), the third (Cotton Mather [before 1726], Samuel Sewall), and beyond to Jonathan Edwards.[4]

As Increase Mather explained the doctrine in his *Mystery of Israel's Salvation* (1669), "one of those great and glorious things which the world . . . are in expectation of at this day, is, *The general conversion of the* Israelitish *Nation. . . .* The *Jews* who have been trampled upon by all Nations, shall shortly become the most glorious Nation in the whole world, and all other Nations shall have them in great esteem and honour" (pp. 1, 11). Mather's *Mystery* is the most detailed and most representative publication on this issue by an American Puritan of the period. In it he responded to the frenzied millennial expectations of European divines, which in the 1660s followed in the wake of Shabb'tai Zvi's self-proclaimed messiahship in Turkey, where he inspired European and Ottoman Jews to return to Judea to claim their ancestral seat.[5] Backed by the best of authorities, from the church fathers to his own contemporaries, Mather took his thesis from Rom. 11:26, "*All* Israel *shall be saved*," and opened his Scripture text by conceding that the expression "*all Israel*" admits of "diverse interpretations." Some take it to include only "some Few of *all Israel*," or "all the *elect of God*," or "all and every one of the natural posterity of *Jacob*." Cautioning that "a literal interpretation of Scripture ought never to be rejected for an allegorical one," he asserted that the true meaning of "*all Israel*" was that "very many *Israelites* shall be saved. Yea, *all* here noteth, not only many, but most; it signifieth not only a *Majority*, but a very full and large *Generality*." Likewise, their salvation was not only "*Temporal*" but also "*Spiritual*," for as their temporal salvation signified their restoration to and possession of "the Land promised unto their *Father Abraham*," so their spiritual salvation signified their acceptance of Christianity in the latter days (pp. 1, 5, 9, 53).

When less than thirty years later his aged friend Richard Baxter propounded a strictly allegorical and spiritual reading of Romans 11, in *The Glorious Kingdom of Christ* (1691), Increase Mather defended his earlier *Mystery* in his popular essay *A Dissertation Concerning the Future Conversion of the Jewish Nation* (1709): "But it is clear that the Design of the Apostle is to convince those *Gentiles* of their Error" in assuming that they had irrevocably supplanted the Jewish nation as God's elect. "To say that he intends the Elect, or *Spiritual Israel*, is against the Drift of his whole Discourse," which "speaks of *Israel according to the Flesh*" (p. 10).

How vital their literal conversion was to the Puritans' expectation of the Second Coming and how much New England's eschatologists depended for their own temporal and eternal salvation on the Jews' restoration can be gathered from a variety of sources. Once they were restored to their ancient possession, Joseph Mede conjectured, God would effect their conversion in an instant, just as he had done in Paul's time on the road to Damascus, "by *Vision and Voice from Heaven"* (*Works*, p. 761). William Hooke of New Haven, Connecticut, wrote in his preface to Increase Mather's *Mystery* that the calling of the Jews and their "conversion shall greatly inlighten the world, like the rising Sun which runs his race from East to West." Through the "plentiful effusions of the spirit of God upon the Tribes of *Israel*," Increase Mather warranted, they "shall have most Seraphical gifts bestowed upon them, yea, *they shall be like to the Angel of the Lord"* and their ministers become "burning and shining lights" to the Gentile nations gathering around them (*Mystery*, pp. 98, 99, 113). They will be so enlightened with the knowledge of God, Samuel Sewall corroborated, that the Jews will "be a guide and blessing unto the residue of the Gentiles" and "be entrusted with great Empire, and Rule in the World."[6]

Such promises of power and glory for the Jewish nation could also be employed as a bait to effect their conversion, Increase Mather asserted in his *Mystery*. For to insist on an allegorical rather than literal reading of Israel's restoration to prominence had given "great offence to the *Jews*, when they perceive Christians deny that which their Prophets have so abundantly affirmed." The best way to bring them into the Christian fold was not by allegorizing Paul's Scripture and applying it to the Christian church but by upholding its literal abrogation in the restoration of natural Israel: "It is not . . . the best way to deal with the *Jews*" and their promised glory, Mather admonished his reader, by telling "them that all those things must be understood spiritually, and not literally, which in the Prophets look that way; but it were better [to] yield to them, that they shall have such glory as the like never was, only that this must not be at *Messias* first appearing."[7] An allegorical reading of the prophetic promises to the Jews would thus not only impede their conversion but also postpone the Second Coming; a literal exegesis was therefore infinitely more felicitous.

However eagerly eschatologists were looking for signs of Israel's national conversion, there was one major problem that encumbered their most confident conjectures: the *ubi sunt* of the Ten Lost Tribes, who had not returned from their Shalmanesarian deportation (c. 722 B.C.). While many believed that the descendants of the Ten Tribes could still be found in Medo-Persia on the banks of the upper Euphrates River, as the book of Tobit (14:1–15) seemed to suggest, others were convinced that a remnant of *all* Twelve Tribes had returned from Babylonian Captivity (c. 597–557/27 B.C.). Still others believed with the apocryphal tradition of Esdras (2 Esd. 13:40–49) that the Ten Tribes had removed to a faraway country, "Arsareth," from which they would return at the Second Coming to take possession of their rightful inheritance. The latter theory was, perhaps, the most intriguing and, at once, the most fantastic of them all, for it gave rise to sporadic rumors when eyewitness accounts from the New World sought to deliver proof of the Lost Tribes found in hiding in the Peruvian mountains of Quito. In his *Chronographia in duos Libros Distincta* (1567), Gilbert Genebrard suggested South America as the mysterious country mentioned in 2 Esdras 13 to which the Ten Tribes had moved. Although the Spanish Jesuit José de Acosta rejected this conjecture on ethnological grounds in *The Natural & Moral History of the Indies* (1590), yet his detailed comparison between Indian and Hebrew customs encouraged his Carmelite missionary colleague Fray Antonio Vázquez de Espinosa (d. 1630) to infer from his own ethnological observations, in *Description of the Indies* (c. 1620), that the Peruvian and Mexican Indians were indubitably the offspring of the Lost Israelites. And when the renowned Dutch Hebraist Rabbi Menasseh ben Israel (1604–57), in the second English edition of his *Hope of Israel* (1652), authenticated a similar eyewitness account by Antonius Montezinus, he fueled the millenarian fervor of John Dury, in *Epistolicall Discourse . . . that the Americans are descended from the Israelites* (1650), of Thomas Thorowgood, in *Iewes in America* (1650), and of New England's own missionary to the Algonquian Indians, John Eliot.[8]

While the first generation among New England's settlers was generally convinced that the timely discovery of the Lost Tribes in America was not accidental—in fact, that it confirmed their own place in God's grand scheme—later generations "would be less sure of the origin of the natives," Alden T. Vaughan points out, "but no less certain of their place in the scheme of things" (p. 20). Cotton Mather, too, was committed to "gospellizing" the Indians of America, but while he did not believe that the New World Indians were of "Judaical Origin," he was no less concerned than his predecessors about bringing them into the Christian fold. Smiling graciously at the wishful disposition of the New England patriarchs, whom he immortalized in his *Magnalia Christi Americana*, Mather could look compassionately at the foibles of the first generation, even those of an Eliot:

> I confess, that was one, I cannot call it so much *guess* as *wish*, wherein he [Eliot] was willing a little to indulge himself; and that was, *That our Indians are the Posterity of the dispersed and rejected* Israelites. . . . He saw the *Indians* using many *Parables* in their Discourse; much given to anointing of their *Heads*; much delighted in *Dancing* . . . computing their Times by *Nights* and *Months*; giving *Dowries* for Wives, and causing their Women to *dwell by themselves*, at certain Seasons, for secret Causes; and accustoming themselves to grievous *Mournings* and *Yellings* for the Dead; all which were usual things among the *Israelites*. They have too a great unkindness for our *Swine*; but I suppose that is because our *Hogs* devour the *Clams* which are a Dainty with them. He also saw some learned Men, looking for the lost *Israelites* among the *Indians* in *America*, and counting that they had *Thorow-good* Reasons for doing so. And a few small *Arguments*, or indeed but *Conjectures*, meeting with a favourable Disposition in the Hearer, will carry some Conviction with them; especially, if a Report of a *Menasseh ben Israel* be to back them. (3.3.192–93)

To the modern reader, Mather's level-headed assessment of what the first generation took to be evidence for the Jewish origin of the American Indians is
certainly appealing, and modern ethnology would agree with his conclusions.
So, too, would his knowledge of Hebrew morphology lead him to reject any similarities between the languages of the Israelites and of the Algonquian Indians—
similarities that John Eliot and Roger Williams had tried to establish for New
England's native tribes, just as Vázquez de Espinosa and Menasseh ben Israel
had done for the Lost Tribes of Peru.

But such erudition in light of his colleagues' wishful thinking could be deceiving. Only a paragraph later, Mather revealed that he could be as superstitious
as his intellectual forebears were gullible. Desiring proof that the Algonquian
language was definitely no derivation of ancient Hebrew, as Eliot, Williams, and
Samuel Sewall wished to believe, Mather put it to the test.[9] While trying to cure
a young Charlestown girl from her demonic possessions, he discovered that "the
Daemons . . . understood the *Latin* and *Greek* and *Hebrew* Languages." However, when "this Indian Language" was put to trial, "the *Daemons* did seem as
if they did not understand it" (*MCA* 3.3.193).[10] Certainly, this was proof positive
that the American Indians were not of "Judaical Origin." Mather rejected the
whole thesis. "Be sure," he advised his readers in a 1717 letter to Bartholomew
Ziegenbalg, a German Pietist missionary in the East Indian Malabar, "They
who have Entertained us, with *Dissertations* upon that *Obscure Subject*, have
been sufficiently Luxuriant in their *Fancies*; and have sometimes allow'd a little
Resemblance in *Sound*, (as, for instance, *Massagetae*, and *Massachusetts*,) to be
a Sufficient Bottom for their most Confident Conjectures." And with a flourish of the pen, tongue in cheek, Mather brushed aside the vanity of his British
colleague Thomas Burnet, whose reading of Isaac de La Peyrère's *Men Before
Adam* (1656) had led Burnet to speculate that the American Indians were not
at all descendents of Noah but had had a separate creation and separate providence altogether: "We are sure, that the *Americans* are of the *Noetic Original*"
(*IC*, pp. 22–23). The most Mather would allow was that through the diaspora of
the Jews throughout the Old World, "some of their Blood, passing from *Scythia*
may be found among the *Indians* of *North-America*" (*T*, p. 298).[11]

This is not to say, however, that Mather was any less interested than his New
England fathers in preaching the gospel to the Indians in the remote wilderness
of America. For if the eschatological conjectures of José de Acosta, of Antonio
Vázquez de Espinosa, and of Joseph Mede were correct, then Satan, posing in
former ages as the Aztec god "Vitzlipultzli," had "Seduced numbers of Miserables into *America*" (*IC*, p. 4) to keep them out of reach of the saving gospel of
Christ.[12] It was therefore imperative for Mather almost single-handedly to set
himself "to countermine the whole PLOT of the Devil, against *New-England*, in
every Branch of it" (*WIW*, p. 3). John Eliot's Praying Indian communities of Rox-
bury and Matthew Mayhew's on Martha's Vineyard were certainly proof that
"The *Deceiver of the Nations* has been *Deceived*, if this were his Expectation"
(*IC*, p. 24).

But when was this miraculous conversion of the Jews to be expected? When was the blinding veil of their unbelief to be removed as Paul had predicted (Rom. 11:7–10, 25, 32)? For most of his life, Cotton Mather agreed with Increase that natural Israel would accept Christ just before the millennium commenced, when the prophetic *"Dry Bones"* (*ATC*, p. 38) of ancient Israel would be revived.[13] Cotton Mather's unpublished essay "Problema Theologicum" is perhaps the best of his early treatments of the subject (*D* 1:502, 571). Originally addressed to Nicholas Noyes of Salem, this epistolary treatise attempts to persuade Mather's colleague that the Happy State of the church, which was to usher in the millennium, had indeed not yet come. All signs indicated that Satan was still ruling over the world and that the fall of Antichrist had not yet come to fruition. The Jewish nation, Mather maintained, "is to have no little share in the *Happy State* of the Church; You, are *to Rejoice, O Yee Nations, with that People. But, that Nation* we are sure, is horribly *Deceived* and by *Satan* too, unto this Day" (p. 20).

And in this manner, Mather bolstered his first postulate: "That which will be *Immediately after the Long Tribulation* under which the *Jewish Nation* is now Languishing, will be *at the Beginning of the Happy State, which we Expect for the Church in the Latter Dayes"* ("PT," p. 23; see also *PA*, pp. 117–19). Indeed, Romans 11 explicitly demonstrated, Mather argued, that the return of the Jews to Christ had to be accomplished before the millennium could begin, for the rejection of Christ and the state of the unregenerate church of Israel in the latter days was foreshadowed in Miriam's leprosy, the OT type of Israel's apostasy. Surely, Miriam's condition, like that of its antitype, was divine retribution for challenging the authority of her brother Moses, and her rebellious conduct foreshadowed the Jews' spurning of Christ in NT times. Yet however loathsome her disease and horrible her punishment, Miriam's expulsion from the camp of the Israelites en route to Canaan was not final, for her brethren waited for seven days for her restoration (Num. 12:15). In like manner, "The Church of God must be retarded in its progress, towards its *Happy State*, untill Excluded *Israel* be restored and this restoration will not be, untill the approach of the *Seventh Day*, or the blessed *Sabbatism"* ("PT," p. 26; see also *IC*, pp. 46–47). In the same vein, natural Israel, the modern antitype of Miriam, was to be restored and to resume its ancient position of prominence within the Christian church, whose progress toward the millennium could not be accomplished until Israel embraced the Messiah. In fact, with the miraculous intercession of Christ on the Jews' behalf at his return, then "their Soul will *Escape as a Bird out of the Snare of the Fowler"* ("PT," p. 31).

No matter how convincing Mather's exegesis of the signs of the End might have appeared to Nicholas Noyes or to the unnamed governor to whom Mather finally decided to dedicate his "Problema Theologicum," Mather's argument was filled with much doubt and uncertainty (pp. 84–87). Whereas his calculations of Daniel's prophetic chronology suggested that the time of Antichrist was now near its completion, the Jewish nation was still as unwilling as ever to embrace Christianity. If his calculations about the coming End in 1697 and

1716 did not fail him, then their conversion had to come about any time now. Thus he wondered and eagerly awaited any news from Europe: "The *Israellitish* Nation is a *Numerous* Nation, even at this *Day*; (when to our Surprize we find near Ten Thousand of them, even at *Prague*, and more then [sic] Ten Thousand of them even at *Rome*, in the very midst of their Popish Persecutors!)" ("PT," p. 7). Likewise Mather had wondered in 1702, when he informed his Boston parishioners of the state of the church in the world:

Alas, The ancient *Israel of God*, are now scattered about the World, *Aliens from the Common-wealth of Israel*, without *Hope*, without *Christ*, without *God*, in the World. The *Ten Tribes*, who can tell, where are the *Graves*, wherein they have laid buried for these *many Dayes*? Their State calls for our *Prayers*. . . . The *Two Tribes* are still under the Miseries of their Dispersion among the *Gentiles*, a wondrous *Evidence* to the Truth of the *Christian Religion*, even by their *Denial* of it, and a standing *Monument* of the Divine Vengeance on them, for their *Denial* of the Blessed JESUS. The vast Numbers of them in *Constantinople* and *Salonichi*, and other parts of the *Turkish* Dominions are under Temptations to turn *Turks* (as they often do) rather than *Christians*. The vast Numbers of them in *Poland*, and in other *Popish* Countries, (and by a late List, there are above ten thousand in the City of *Rome* it self,) are infinitely scandalized by the *Idolatries* of the *Christians*, from ever being their Proselytes. (*ACF*, p. 5)

In light of all evidence to the contrary, nothing short of a miracle could effect their conversion—if the Happy State of the church were to commence in Mather's own lifetime.

Naturally, Mather was not the only one who could not reconcile himself to the disparity between the chronology of his prophetic timetable and the state of the contemporary church. Checking his substantial library for evidence of past conversions that might shed light on what was to occur in the very near future, Mather lit on the ever-popular sixth-century legend of the miraculous conversion of Homeric Jews in Tephar (Arabia). Often copied and republished throughout the ages, *Sancti patris nostri Gregentii Tephrensis Archiepiscopi disputatio cum Herbano Judaeo* (1586) reports that during a debate between Gregentius (archbishop of Tephar) and Herban (a Jewish leader) on whether Jesus was indeed the Messiah, Christ appeared visibly in the clouds with scepter and sword and denounced all unbelievers, and "the Jews were all stricken blind, and received not their sight till they were all baptized" (Mede, *Works*, p. 768). In this manner, millions of Jews were converted in a single day. Needing to find a parallel for a latter-day conversion, Mather conjectured that a transient appearance of Christ just before the millennium might effect such a conversion, and he drew on Joseph Mede (*Works*, pp. 767–68) and patristic lore to explain what might occur shortly:

I am sensible, that many Learned Men, do probably Conjecture, a *Transient appearance* of our Lord, for the *Conversion of Israel*, a little before His *Ap-*

pearing [at the Second Coming], for a more *Constant Residence*, to *Rule* and *Judge* the World. This Conjecture finds no little Countenance, from that Wonderfull History, concerning the Conversion of many. Thousands of *Jews*, among the *Homerites* in *Arabia*, (after the Disputation between *Gregentius* & *Herbanus*) a Little after the Dayes of *Julian*. I suppose You may have perused that History, not only as Quoted by *Mede* and *Hornbeck*, & others, but as published by it self; it is well worth Your perusall; and pardon me, if I add (without staying here to give You any Reasons for their Thought,) I Think, tis no *Romance!*" ("PT," p. 33–34)[14]

Nothing short of a transient appearance of the Messiah, as in the days of old, could actually precipitate such a large-scale conversion. Here was good precedent; and had Christ not made such appearances in biblical days more than ten times after his resurrection, and at one time to more than five hundred people all at once? He had done it before and would do it again to save his ancient people (*TMT*, p. 24).

But despite his need to search for evidence in the past to explain the future, Mather could never fully bring himself to accept this legend. Roughly ten years after he had laid aside his "Problema Theologicum," he addressed the issue again, this time registering serious doubts about the veracity of the account: "I confess," he wrote in *Things to be More Thought upon* (1713), "the Relation of great Numbers *Converted* in such an extraordinary Way, in the close of the Disputation which *Gregentius* had with *Herbanus* . . . tho' it arrive to us with many Circumstances that carry some Credibility in them, yet it is encumbred with some other Circumstances which very much Enfeeble, and very near Extinguish the Credit of it" (p. 104). So, too, in 1727, while working on his "Triparadisus" (pt. III, sec. vii), Mather again questioned the accuracy of the account. Here he rejected the visible appearance of Christ during Gregentius's time, because "in little more than Twenty Years after the pretended Conversion of the whole Jewish People . . . [they] are found still as Numerous as ever" (*T*, p. 228). Ironically, Mather changed his mind again as he finished his "Triparadisus," never realizing that a little more than a hundred pages later he negated his previous argument. This time, however, Mather's marginal interpolation pointed out that "the Confession made in the Disputation . . . was verified . . . and no Part of the Earth, had such a Proportion of *Christian Churches*, as the Land of *Judaea*" (*T*, p. 309). Mather's indecisiveness is rather revealing, even as he tried to ground his new position in the preterite hermeneutics of the Pauline prophecy.[15]

Notwithstanding his later indecision, Mather engaged in a lifelong pursuit of bringing the gospel to Jehovah's *peculium*. He therefore went into the field to harvest the natural seed of Abraham, whose conversion as a nation, most literalists believed, was a prerequisite to the Coming of the Lord. In fact, by gospelizing the Jews and by bringing them into the Christian fold, the watchmen of Christ could actively partake in God's providential plan and hasten the return of their Messiah. And so Mather prayed to his God to use his poor servant as an instrument in his divine harvest: "This Day," Mather recorded in his diary for 18 July 1696, "from the Dust, where I lay prostrate, before the Lord, I lifted up my Cries; For the coming of the *Kingdome* of my Lord. . . . For the Conversion of the *Jewish Nation*, and for my own having the Happiness, at some Time or other, to baptise a *Jew*, that should by my Ministry, bee brought home unto the Lord" (*D* 1:200). When his prayer was long in being answered, Mather published the first of a series of works designed to carry the gospel to the "Obstinate Jews."[16]

The Faith of the Fathers (1699) is a brief catechism "To Engage the JEWISH NATION, unto the RELIGION of their *Patriarchs*" (*FF*, title page). For if only the natural seed of Abraham returned to the faith of the fathers, if only the Jews returned to the religion of the Old Testament, which, Mather believed, was nothing but the religion of Christ, then they might recognize their error; then the veil might be lifted from their eyes. For "the *Christian Religion*" is "in reality, but, *The Faith of the Fathers*, and, *The Religion of the Old Testament*, from whence the modern Jews are fallen" (*ATC*, p. 58). Mather's diary entry for 9 April 1699 reveals his design most conspicuously:

> I considered, that when the Evangelical *Elias*, was to prepare the *Jewish Nation*, for the coming of the *Messiah*, hee was to do it, by, *bringing down the Heart of the Fathers upon the Children.* And I considered, that it would not only confirm us *Christians* in our *Faith* exceedingly to see every Article of it, asserted in the express Words of the *Old Testament*, but that it would mightily convince, and confound the *Jewish* Nation. Yea, who knowes, what Use the Lord may make of such an *Essay*? Wherefore, with much Contrivance, I drew up a *Catechism* of the whole *Christian Religion*, and contrived the *Questions* to fitt the *Answers*, whereof I brought every one out of the *Old Testament*. I prefaced the *Catechism*, with an Address unto the Jewish Nation, telling them in some lively Terms, That if they would but Return to the Faith of the *Old Testament*, and beleeve with their own ancient and blessed *Patriarchs*, this was all that wee desired of them or for them. (*D* 1:298)[17]

The specific questions and answers in Mather's "*Irresistible and Irrefragable*" (*FF*, p. 4) catechism need not concern us here, for they reflect the traditional Christology of Protestantism; what is more important is that he received great satisfaction from his "Contrivance" to buttress his argument with those OT prophecies in Isaiah, Psalms, and Daniel that even in Judaism foreshadowed the Messiah. Moreover, by drawing for support on the works of messianic Jews, as, for instance, Rabbi Samuel Marochitanus's *Coming of the Messiah* (1648) (*FF*, p. 2), Mather could cast out his net among the Jewish population.

A few months after his catechism appeared, Mather's efforts were blessed with some surprising success. He recorded in his diary (2 Sept. 1699), "This Day, I understand by Letters from *Carolina*, a thing that exceedingly refreshes mee; a *Jew* there embracing the *Christian Faith*, and my little Book, *The Faith of the*

Fathers, therein a special Instrument of good unto him" (*D* 1:315). Nevertheless, his moderately good fortune is rather astonishing, for Mather's prefatory address to the Jewish nation is anything but flattering. His "lively Terms" of persuasion were nothing less than Christian arrogance through which he sought to provoke to jealousy his Jewish readers (Rom. 11:11): "*Your own Inspired Prophets, who are now more* Ours, *than* Yours, *foretold your being paenally given up to the* Deafness, Blindness, and Hardness *now upon you. But, behold, a Proclamation here sent you from Heaven* [Mather's catechism], *inviting you, to persist no longer in your Damnable* Rebellion *against the* CHRIST *of God! Here is now put into your Hands, an Irresistible and Irrefragable* Demonstration, *That tho' you say, You are* Jews, *you are not so . . .*" (pp. 3–4). Such Christian condescension is certainly not unique in Mather's works or in those of his contemporaries; it is therefore not surprising that his diary remains silent about any further conversions in which his catechism was instrumental. In the same patronizing vein, Mather pressed his Jewish audience in 1713 to refrain from offering any further insults to their promised Messiah and to return to the faith of the fathers: "I know you do it *Ignorantly in Unbelief*: But we are Waiting and Longing for the approaching Time. *Ah! Lord how Long?*" (*TMT*, p. 11).

Several years later, Mather reprinted his catechism in *Faith Encouraged* (1718) to emulate the Jewish conversion successes reported by August Hermann Francke, a German Pietist of Halle, Saxony, whose ecumenism greatly influenced Mather's own eschatological endeavors (*D* 2:494, 503).[18] Through this work, Mather hoped that "the same *Spirit,* who wrought upon the Babes at *Berlin,* will fall upon some of that *Beloved People,* while they have these Words before them" (*FE*, p. 16). The surprising conversion of three Jewish children of Berlin betokened to Mather the nearness of the Second Coming, when God would pour out his grace (Joel 2:28–32) and bring in a mighty harvest (*FE*, p. 14). "These Children, under Twelve Years of Age," Mather reported in his earlier *Menachem* (1716), "make unaccountable Flights unto the Protestant Ministers, to be Initiated in the Christian Religion. They Embrace Christianity, with a mighty Zeal; and they cannot see the Name of our JESUS, in a Book, but they discover a Transport of Affection to it, and fall into a Flood of Tears. They are so firm in their Adherence unto HIM, that all the Endeavours of their Parents to reclaim them, have only this Reply from them, *We never shall Return to you; 'Tis time for you to come over to us*" (pp. 39–40). Such accounts were, of course, ever popular among millenarians, whose eschatological time frame depended on the national conversion of Israel. If nothing else, such conversions—like those of "several Hundreds of *Jews,* (and some *Rabbi's*)" in Hamburg (*ACF*, pp. 4–6)—betokened the Great Sabbatism of Christ, whose signs of the approaching time Mather recorded faithfully wherever he could. "Oh! That you would at last make the happy Experiment!" he beckoned; "*Come and see; see, see,* whether you do not find Him so! Do not go on, under the *Blindness that has happened* unto you, to treat Him as your *Enemy,* who is your only *Saviour*" (*TMT*, p. 27).[19]

Yet despite all efforts, the expected conversion of the Jews remained as slow in coming as ever, and the Happy State of Christ's Church Universal seemed farther off than ever before. Repeated disappointments about the anticipated End in 1697 and again in 1716 led Mather to reevaluate the signs of the times: The authority of the Bible as the revealed word of God was being progressively undermined by the new historicist philological hermeneutics of Hobbes, Spinoza, La Peyrère, and Simon, who spurned the authorized texts as unreliable compilations of lost originals synopsized by "Public Scribes." Worse yet, the divine inspiration of the Mosaic Creation account had been debunked as scientific confusion by Burnet, Whiston, and Newton, who brushed it aside as historical literature of the Jews; and still worse, the time-honored typological literalism of the apostles in quoting OT messianic prophecies as proof of their accomplishment in Jesus Christ (Isa. 7:14; Matt. 1:22–23) had been thrown out as inadmissible evidence for the truth of the Christian religion.

Grotius, Hammond, Lightfoot, and most vociferously Anthony Collins, their Deist brainchild, had irrevocably shown that Matthew's citation of Isa. 7:14 (Matt. 1:23), "Behold, a Virgine shall conceiue and beare a Sonne, and shall call his name Immanuel," could not be applied *in a literal sense* to Jesus Christ as the promised Messiah because Isaiah's prophecy had already been fulfilled *literally* and *historically* in King Ahaz's own time. Any literal application of this prophecy to Jesus Christ in NT times was therefore impossible. In fact, only if one allowed as admissible evidence a double fulfillment—a literal abrogation in Ahaz's time adumbrating an allegorical, secondary application of this prophecy in Christ in Matthew's time—could Isaiah's prophecy be of any use at all in establishing the verity of Christianity. If Collins's exegesis could be trusted, then Matthew's proof of Christ as the Messiah amounted to little more than a weak allegorization of Isaiah's prophecy, which, applied in this secondary or mystical sense to the New Testament, could not serve as the rock of the ages. As Collins put the issue so incisively and, at the same time, so threateningly in his *Grounds and Reasons*:

> In fine, the Prophecies, cited from the Old Testament by the Authors of the New, do so plainly relate, in their obvious and primary sense, to other matters than those which they are produc'd to prove; that to pretend they prove, in that sense, what they are produc'd to prove, is, *to give up the cause* of Christianity to *Jews* and other *Enemies* thereof; who can so easily show, in so many undoubted instances, the Old and New Testament to have no manner of connection in that respect, but to be in an *irreconcilable state*. (Pt. I, ch. 8, p. 48)

With such guns pointing at the grounds and reasons of the Christian religion, it does not come as a surprise that Mather and his contemporaries felt compelled to rise in defense of their religion. Unquestionably, all manner of "heresies" were rampant in Cotton Mather's world, from the machinelike universe of the Deists, who had done away with God's special providence; to the anti-Trinitarian Arians, who revived the Athanasian controversy; to the menace of the Socinians, who regarded Christ as little more than a good man or moral teacher. Such heresies were the order of the day among the most prominent physico-theologians: Thomas Burnet, John Ray, John Toland, and even Mather's much-admired friends Sir Isaac Newton and Newton's disciple William Whiston.[20] "Doubtless," Mather recorded in "Triparadisus," the scoffers of this world will say, *The Days are Prolonged, and Every Vision faileth* (p. 339).

Unwilling to give up so easily, Mather devised "A *Golden Key to open the Sacred Prophecies*" (*T*, pt. III, sec. iii). Here Mather entered the hermeneutical debate then raging in England by embracing the preterite-allegorist interpretation of Romans 11 as championed by Grotius, Hammond, and Lightfoot. No doubt this philological interpretation, though damaging to other prophecies, could be enlisted in the defense of the grounds and reasons of the Christian religion—if Paul's prophecy of Israel's restoration could be shown to apply literally to *spiritual* rather than *carnal* Israel. Henceforth, Mather abandoned the orthodox view on the literal conversion and restoration of the Jewish nation by asserting, with Grotius, Samuel White, Thomas Sherlock, William Lowth, and Edward Chandler at his elbow, a double fulfillment of Paul's prophecy: first, a literal but smaller historical accomplishment of Romans 11 in the first-century church of Jewish Christians, and secondly, a larger literal and spiritual abrogation in the surrogation of the Gentiles in Christ. Mather took this step by combining a preterite interpretation with a quasi-literalist and a quasi-allegorical reading of Paul's Epistle to the Romans (*T*, pp. 172–80). This extraordinary departure from orthodoxy, naturally, required deep meditation before Mather could approve of such drastic measures. And poring again over the prophecies about the End, lying prostrate on the floor of his study, as he had done so often, his head covered in sackcloth and ashes, Mather prayed for illumination. And then on 21 June 1724 he jotted down in his diary:

> The glorious Lord has led me into fuller Views than I have ever yett had, and such as I have exceedingly longed for and asked for, of what shall be the true State of Things in His Kingdome. And I am now satisfied, that there is nothing to hinder the immediate Coming of our Saviour, in these Flames, that shall bring an horrible Destruction on this present and wicked World, and bring on the new Heaven, and the new Earth, wherein shall dwell Righteousness. I purpose quickly to write on these things. In the mean time, I would in all holy Conversation and Godliness, mightily endeavour to maintain such a Disposition of Mind, as the tremendous Descent of my glorious Lord, is to be entertained withal. (*D* 2:733)

One can only surmise the exact nature of Mather's mystical communication, yet this conversation with heaven was the final breakthrough that led him to rework his eschatological views and to recant his belief in the conversion of the Jewish nation before the Second Coming. In 1726/27, while composing part III of "Triparadisus," Mather launched his caveat against the literalist hermeneutics of the day, which still insisted on a futurist fulfillment of Romans 11: "A Strong *Opiate*, which binds on the Chains of the *Dead Sleep*, wherein the Church is to be found, when the *Day of the Lord*, shall break in *like a Thief in the Night* upon the World, is a Strong Opinion, 'That before the Coming of the Lord, there shall be a *National Conversion* of the Circumcised People . . . who are to Return unto their Ancient Seats in *Palaestine*, and make a *Singular Figure* in the Kingdom of God, and be *Distinguished* from, and *Superiour* to, the Rest of the Nations, that shall then also be generally converted unto Christian Piety' " (*T*, p. 296). Such was the conviction of many "zelous Abetters & Asserters" who were of "as great Sagacity and Erudition" as indeed the "*Best of Men*" (*T*, p. 296).[21]

Mather himself had, of course, subscribed to this position for most of his life, and he made haste to step forth and take this shame upon himself: "I was myself a very long While in your Opinion," he moaned. "Alas, I was a very Young Man; . . . I understood not the True *Israel*; I *Recant*; I *Revoke*; and I now make my most public *Retraction*" (*T*, pp. 314–15; see also p. 182). And in a rare moment of disagreement with his deceased father, the aged Cotton Mather begged to differ with his *pater familias*, whom he lovingly addressed with the Hebrew epithet that translates, "My Lord, My Father": "That Excellent Person, *Adoni Avi*," Mather apologized, "who has with the most Erudition of any Man" (*T*, p. 315) written on the subject, held to his dying days that the millennium could not come until the Jewish nation had been restored to Christ. "This was what a Person of his Great Penetration could not but find himself under a Necessity of coming to," Mather lamented. "I insisted upon it unto him, that I was not able to see, how such a *National Conversion* . . . could be consistent" with the Petrine conflagration at the beginning of the millennium, which would rule out any gradual or even sudden conversion of Israel while the *diluvium ignis* was inundating the earth (*T*, p. 315; see also *Selected Letters*, pp. 415–16).[22]

Instrumental in Cotton Mather's disowning of orthodox literalism was an anonymous treatise by "P.G.B.," whose *Good Things to Come* (1675) proved to be of far-reaching consequence to Mather's later eschatology. This homily "explained the *Mystery* of the *Translated* whereof the Apostle writes to the *Corinthians* and the *Thessalonians*" (*T*, p. 316) and held the key to the complex problem of what would happen to the "Saved Nations" whose remaining mortality confined them to the earth and rendered them susceptible to the fire of the global conflagration. "From that Moment," Mather jubilated, "I thought I might say, *I have found it*" (*T*, p. 316). Mather rightfully exclaimed, "Eureka," for this publication reshaped his eschatological views completely. The author of *Good Things to Come* armed Mather with the crucial distinction between the *Raised Saints* and the *Changed Saints*, the former being the martyred witnesses of Christ, who would rise at the First Resurrection (Rev. 20: 4–6) and rule with Christ in the heavenly Jerusalem above, and the latter being the Saints alive on earth at the Coming of the Lord, translated into immortality to escape the grand conflagration then ravaging the earth (1 Cor. 15; 1 Thess. 4:15–17). While Mather had adopted the belief in a global conflagration as early as 1721 (*WA*, pp. 12–16), he was still unable to reconcile this global holocaust with the fate of the Saved Nations that were to survive the flood of fire. His great teacher Joseph

Mede was of little help, for Mede had not yet harmonized the "Rapture" with his own eschatological system (see "Epistle XXI" and "Epistle XXII," in *Works*, pp. 773–76). In discovering *Good Things to Come*, Mather solved this nagging problem of what to do with the Saved Nations during the conflagration. They would be caught up in the clouds, would miraculously change their sin-stained bodies for immortalized ones, and would then return to the purified earth and restore the globe to its prelapsarian condition. To underscore this crucial distinction between the different classes of Saints, Mather's Saved Nations were henceforth renamed Changed Saints.

In harmonizing Paul's Epistle to the Romans with the historicist method of Grotius, Hammond, Lightfoot, and Baxter, whose "feeble Essayes" he had attacked in "Problema Theologicum" (p. 24), Mather drew particularly on the work of Sir John Lightfoot of Ely (1602–75), whose *Harmony, Chronicle, and Order of the New Testament* (1655) had done invaluable spadework: "For, though I am unwilling to recede from that charitable opinion of most Christians, that there shall once be a calling of them [Jews] home," Lightfoot wrote, "yet see I not how that supposal of the universal call of the whole nation . . . can be digested, without some allay and mitigation" (*Works* 3:409, quoted in *T*, p. 297). And more emphatically in *Hebrew and Talmudical Exercitations upon the Romans* (Rom. 11:5), Lightfoot argued that "the Jewish nation, as to the more general mass of it, was cast off before the times of Christ; yet no question, there was in all ages . . . 'A remnant according to the election of grace,'— and in that age more especially, wherein Christ and his gospel began to shine out. And that he [St. Paul] meant the calling of this *remnant* in that age and time wherein the apostle wrote, and not any call of the whole nation to be hereafter" (*Works* 12:445; see also 6:393–94).

Section xi of Mather's "Third Paradise" is largely devoted to justifying his hermeneutical shift from the traditional literalism of the Pauline prophecy and its futurist fulfillment in the days of the Second Coming to a preterite abrogation in an elect remnant of Christianized Jews and a quasi-allegorist application of the prophecy to the Christian church of the nations. This position had gained greater currency in the seventeenth century through the preterite hermeneutics of Jacob Batalerio, Grotius, James Calvert, Hammond, Lightfoot, and Baxter and was also taking its toll on other millenarian literalist interpretations.[23]

Because the Jews rejected their promised Messiah and chose a Vespasian over a Jesus, Mather explained, natural Israel was cast off and the promise once given to Abraham passed on to a "Surrogate Israel" among the Gentiles, to whom the God of Abraham became the God of the nations: "'Tis true," Mather assured his audience, "'Tis *thro' the Fall of the Jews that Salvation is come unto the Gentiles*: and, as our SAVIOUR foretold it would be, on their Murdering the SON of GOD, the *Kingdome of GOD was taken* from the Jewish Nation, and *given to others*, that would *bring forth the Fruits thereof*" (*T*, p. 307). But Mather certainly knew that by merely reciting the allegorist position he could not easily sway his literalist colleagues to abandon hermeneutical orthodoxy. To present a more compelling argument, he resorted to the physiology of Theophrastus, which underlies Paul's typological parable of the olive tree (Rom. 11:13–26):

> The CHURCH, [or say, The CHRIST] of GOD, is to be considered as the *Stock* of an Illustrious *Olive-tree*. Now, it is *Contrary to Nature* to make use of *Cyons* more Ignoble than the *Stock*. . . . Every body knows, the *Oleaster*, or the *Wild Olive-tree*, can by no Managery of Art, be brought unto the Producing of any other, than those *Olives* which for their Ill Qualities were called *Phaulia*. An *Oleaster*, becoming an *Olive-tree* would have been esteem'd a Prodigy; and the Grafting of it on an *Olive-tree*, would be *Unnatural*. But yett, this is what the Sovereign Providence of our GOD has done, in His *Grafting* the *Gentiles* upon the *Church* by the *Faith*, of His CHRIST. (*T*, pp. 307–8)

Thus, God had wrought a miracle and grafted on the fruitful olive tree of the Jews the inferior shoot of the wild oleaster, the Gentile nations, which henceforth were to bring forth the spiritual oil of Christ's olive tree.[24]

The same typological metaphor of inoculation or grafting informed Mather's argument a few pages later when he likened the Christian church to the "Mystical *Body*" of Christ from which unbelieving Israel had been cut off: "The *Falling off* of so many who were *Literally Israelites*, leaves a *Chasm*, in . . . the Mystical *Body*, whereof CHRIST is the *Head*. There must be a *Filling up*, to repair this *Falling off*. . . . Tis a, *Filling up with the Gentiles*, that must accomplish it. There is no other *Israel*, that is to be look'd for" (*T*, p. 309). Indeed, Mather here did not overstep the boundaries of conventional Christology, which he outlined in his "*Key of Prophecy*" (*T*, pp. 172–80). Nor did he pour any new wine into old skins by telling his audience that the Christian church had become Jehovah's Surrogate Israel en route to the City of God. Forever trying to harmonize incongruent points of biblical hermeneutics, he rendered Paul's Romans 11 in preterite fashion by arguing that Natural Israel had *already* been brought in during the apostle's time, when an elect remnant of Christianized Jews were absorbed through intermarriage with their Gentile brethren in Christ. Patristic church histories had given ample proof of such a preterite position. For did they not show that Jews in "Great Numbers" had embraced Christianity after the fall of Jerusalem to the Romans (A.D. 70) when they discovered that the God of Israel had become the God of the nations?[25] In fact, Mather continued, "the most Learned Masters of Computation . . . think, that the Biggest Part of the Jews" who escaped the destruction of Jerusalem under Titus "were *Christians*" and a large part of the Christian churches in Judea "did consist of *Christianized Jews*" who "were soon so united with the *Gentiles*, in *Marriages* and all other Communions, and particularly the dropping of *Circumcision*, that there was no longer any *Israelitish Distinction* left upon them. . . . If [therefore] the *Jews* were all made *Christians* . . . To what Purpose then a Church of the *Jews*!" (*T*, pp. 308, 309, 311).

To continue holding the "Modern Opinion" of those who still believed in a future restoration and conversion of the Jewish nation before the millennium would disenfranchise the Christianized Jews and their offspring, who had long been absorbed into the Christian fold. "This Opinion," Mather countered his literalist colleagues, "excludes the Offspring of that *Holy People*, the *Jews, who First Hoped in CHRIST*, from a share in the Singular Priviledges of the *Restored Nation*, and confines the Priviledges to the Offspring of a *Cursed Remnant*, whom GOD reserves among the Nations, as a Monument and a Spectacle of His Vengeance for the greatest Crime that ever was committed in the World" (*T*, p. 309). And those who were to this day "found in their *Unbeleef*" and who continued to reject their Savior "must perish, among them, who *obey not the Gospel*, & must feel the *Flaming Fire* take *Vengeance* on them" (*T*, p. 311). And invoking the curses of the Mosaic lawgiver (Deut. 28:45, 46) on the "Nation of *Crucifiers*," Mather brushed aside unregenerate Israel and, with it, Christendom's expectation of its future delivery: "*These Curses shall pursue thee, till thou be destroy'd, and they shall be upon thee and upon thy Seed FOREVER. Forever!* What a Word is *That!*" (*T*, pp. 311, 310). Mather's sudden outburst of hostility bespeaks a type of latent anti-Semitism endemic among those whose eschatological ideology is grounded exactly on this kind of reasoning; it illustrates the danger of how the Word of God, no matter how well-intentioned, can sanction all sorts of atrocities when biblical hermeneutics is exploited by demagogues and by the masses.

In his old age, Mather thus completely rejected the views of his father, Increase, whose *Mystery of Israel's Salvation* and *Dissertation Concerning the Future Conversion of the Jewish Nation* had been the basis of Cotton Mather's own eschatological views for most of his life. Cotton Mather's going over to the preterite-allegorist cabal was received with some alarm by New England's literalist millenarians, most notably by his lifelong friend Judge Samuel Sewall, an avid eschatologist. A little more than a year after Cotton Mather's death, Sewall voiced his great concern in a letter to Cotton's son Samuel (6 Mar. 1728/29): "I have one unhappiness befallen me, vizt., Dr. Cotton Mather's vehemently insisting on the Conflagration, so that he seems to think there is no general Calling or convertion of the Jews, Or that it is already past and gone" (*Letter-Book* 2:263). Perhaps it was Mather's abandonment of his literalist orthodoxy that prompted Sewall to update and republish his 1697 work, *Phaenomena quaedam Apocalyptica* (1727), and to append an excerpt of Samuel Willard's orthodox *The Fountain Opened*. Perhaps Sewall intended to stay any further inroads of the preterite-allegorist menace so rampant among English Deists when he included in his 1727 edition a second appendix urging his readers to follow Increase Mather's orthodox *Future Conversion*, an incisive refutation of the allegorist hermeneutics of Lightfoot and Baxter. But Cotton Mather was not easily deterred by such opposition, not even by that of his ancient friend, with whom he had shared his lifelong penchant for millenarian prophecies.[26]

It is perhaps most remarkable that Cotton Mather in his old age had come closer to English Deist exegesis than ever before. The broadening of his hermeneutic horizons also helped him to transcend parochial concerns and myopic visions of Christ's *Heilsgeschichte*. For in "Triparadisus," as indeed in his much earlier work *American Tears Upon the Ruines of the Greek Churches* (1701), Mather's Pietism viewed God's work of redemption as a worldwide scheme that embraced all nations and creeds. "Will our Glorious Lord fetch His People, from one *Circumcised Nation* only!" Mather asked confidently in his *Terra Beata* (1726). "No, No; This Blessed People shall be fetched out of *Many Nations*. Even, the *Indians*, and the *Negro's*" (p. 35). His Pietist ecumenism surcharged with his eschatological fervor transmuted sectarian exclusivity into a type of interdenominationalism that paved the way for Christian world missions of the nineteenth century: "*Now*, One found in the Sultry Regions of *Africa*, or, among the *Tranquebarians* in the Eastern *India*, or the *Massachusettsians* in the Western," is acceptable to God through faith in Christ (*T*, p. 312). Not just the Protestant churches of New England and Europe but "*All Nations* do *Desire* a *Reconciliation* to GOD, or Good Terms with Heaven: 'Tis the Aim of all the *Religions* in the several Forms used among the *Nations* . . . *All Nations do desire*, to come at *Knowledge*, or have *Truth* discovered unto them. They are continually seeking for *Illuminations*" (*TB*, p. 20).[27] Mather's hermeneutical shift from a Pauline to a Johannine interpretation notwithstanding, his allegorical exegesis remained safely within the precepts of the *Savoy Declaration of Faith* (1658, 1680), whose broadly based millennialism was flexible enough to accommodate both views (p. 396).

THREE

The Bang or the Whimper?
The Grand Revolution
and the New World to Come

Still was the night, Serene and Bright,
when all Men sleeping lay;
Calm was the season, and carnal reason
thought so 'twould last for ay.
Soul, take thine ease, let sorrow cease,
much good thou hast in store:
This was their Song, their Cups among,
the Evening before.

Thus Michael Wigglesworth envisioned the sleeping world on the eve of the grand revolution that would rouse drowsy sinners from their downy feather-beds.[1] Cotton Mather could not have agreed more completely with Wigglesworth's depiction of the apocalyptic cataclysm. And in like manner, Mather kept warning his parishioners sixty years after Wigglesworth's *Day of Doom* (1662) had become something of a colonial best-seller. For even the most unregenerate disbelievers, Mather thought, knew deep down that the world could not continue forever in its sinful ways, though they never expected that the day of retribution would call them to justice. "Do not wonder now," the New World Jeremiah admonished his readers, "that *This World*, which has in it so many Millions of Sins unrepented of, do in a *Conflagration* become an *Holocaust*! I say, *Millions of Sins*; For truly, the State of *This World*, even of a, *Whole World lying in Wickedness*, may be Reported in those Terms; *The Earth is full of Bloody Crimes*: Therefore, *Destruction cometh*" (*T*, p. 232).[2]

Most literal-minded millenarians of the day would have agreed on moral grounds with this simple and straightforward justification of the conflagration. The prophecies in both Old and New Testaments certainly foretold the world's destruction on the day of atonement, when the wrath of God's fire would purge the earth of all wickedness. Surely God would not stop short of punishing the world a second time, as he had done before in Noah's days, the smaller type, when a flood of water inundated the entire earth. Nothing less than a second flood would do this time, a *diluvium ignis* that would usher in the New Heavens and the New Earth at the coming of Christ.[3]

Even the most orthodox millenarians of Mather's generation corroborated such biblical predictions with external proof from the Sibylline Oracles to demonstrate "what *Expectation* the Nations had in the *former Ages*, and how, FIRE, was cried among them" (*T*, p. 194; see also pp. 197–201). Yet they did not agree among themselves about either the extent or the time of its occurrence.[4] Nor was there unanimous agreement on whether the conflagration spoken of in the Petrine prophecies, in Isaiah, and in Revelation was indeed literal at all. Most of the ancient Fathers—among them Irenaeus, Eusebius, Origen, Jerome, Augustine, and Gregory the Great—asserted either a partial but not global conflagration on the one hand, or, on the other, a renovation or cleansing of the outward appearance but not substance of the earth (*T*, pp. 269–72). So, too, John Calvin and, a little later, Hugo Grotius, Thomas Hobbes, Henry Hammond, John Lightfoot, and Richard Baxter did not have a consensus on whether the predicted deluge of fire was at all to be taken in a literalist and futurist sense. To the disciples of Origen, the conflagration was but a metaphor; those following Grotius viewed the predicted conflagration as an event already fulfilled in the past: in the double destruction of ancient Jerusalem by the Babylonians in the captivity of Judah and by the Romans in the final diaspora of the Jews (A.D. 70).[5]

Such swings of the hermeneutical compass had been in the making ever since the debate over the spurious authorship of the Second Epistle of Peter had caused Origen and Eusebius to voice their dissatisfaction. In Mather's day, the debate on its authorship had been reopened by Grotius. In examining the most ancient copies of the text available, Grotius established new guidelines for a philological and contextual critique of the Bible and insisted that Peter could not have authored the Second Epistle, because he had died during the reign of the emperor Nero (54–68). The apocalyptic doom pronounced on Jerusalem (2 Peter 3), Grotius argued, must have been written *after* the Roman destruction of Jerusalem; Grotius's candidate for author was Simeon, bishop of Jerusalem, who lived until Trajan's time (*Annotationes* 2:390–94).

Although disagreeing with this conclusion, Hammond, a pioneer of modern biblical criticism, admired the historical method of Grotius and took the argument to its inevitable conclusion. Internal evidence suggested to Hammond that Peter's Epistle was written "*Anno Chr.* 67 about the beginning of *October*" while Peter, imprisoned for preaching the gospel, expected his speedy execution. Peter, therefore, did not foretell the Second Coming of Christ but merely comforted "the persecuted afflicted Christians in their expectation of that deliverance which they should now shortly meet with, by the destruction of their persecuters." He consoled early Christians like himself that their persecution and oppression would soon terminate in the destruction of Jerusalem by the Romans and in the punishment of their zealous persecutors. Internal evidence (2 Pet. 3:7) suggested therefore that Peter's doomsday prophecy "belong[s] all to that judgment of the *Jews*," Hammond insisted, "and not to the day of universal doom or destruction of the whole world" (*Paraphrase*, pp. 719–20; see also pp. 728–30). The Petrine conflagration, he argued, applied in a historical and literal sense only to Peter's own time; any futurist application of the fire dissolving the heavens and the earth violated the historical context of the prophecy and had to be understood in an allegorical and anagogical sense. Preterists like Hammond historicized Peter's prophecies and allegorized his eschatology and thus threatened altogether the very foundation of this prophetic book on which much of the literalists' expectation of the future conflagration depended.[6] Even though Mather had embraced the allegorists' preterite hermeneutics on the restoration of the Jewish nation, he was not at all satisfied with the metaphorists' narrow reading of the *diluvium ignis*, which ridiculed the hyperbolical language of Israel's OT prophets: *"Thus a Storm,"* they were given to objecting, *"is often represented in such Pompous Terms, as if the whole Frame of Nature had been convuls'd & the Universe on the Point of Dissolution"* (T, p. 192). Grotius's allegorist disciples missed the whole point by ignoring the prophetic intent of the Scripture, Mather countered. Nor did they understand the typological design of the "Prophetic Spirit," for which "the lesser *Particular Judgments"* were "an *Earnest* as well as a *Figure*, of the *General One*, wherein the *Frame* of Nature shall be dissolved" (T, p. 184). Those who "play their *Allegorical Engines* to putt out the formidable *Fire"* (T, p. 156) here spoken of positively misjudge the true significance of these prophecies: "The True Reason why in our Sacred Books a *Storm* is represented in such *Pompous Terms*, tis because the *Prophetic Spirit* had an Eye to . . . a *Storm*, wherein the *whole Frame of Nature* shall be indeed *Convuls'd*, & our *Universe* undergo a *Dissolution*: An Event upon which the Old Testament never used one Word that was *Hyperbolical*; and it is impossible to use too *Pompous Terms*. The Figures are all short of the Reality" (T, p. 192). Mather had certainly been sensitized to what John Ray, his confrere in the Royal Society, had discouraged as "tumid Metaphors, and excessive *Hyperbola's"* of "Oriental Rhetorick." Taking Spinoza's *Tractatus* as his matrix, Ray argued that such flights of the "Poetick Style" should not be taken too literally but had to be decoded "as a *Jew* or an *Asiatick* would then have understood them" (pp. 316–17; Spinoza, ch. VI, pp. 94–96). Yet such historical-contextual limitations by the metaphorists, Mather believed, attenuated the prophetic spirit, which, true to God's design, intended a double fulfillment: The smaller event generally accomplished in the historical past of the prophet's own time really signified a second but much larger fulfillment in the latter days. This was certainly the case with the Petrine prophecy, Mather judged, which in predicting the immediate fall of Jerusalem actually intended the passing away of heaven and earth at Christ's Second Coming (2 Peter 3). Ever the mediator between the old literalism and the new philological hermeneutics, Mather employed this double interpretation fostered by his colleagues Samuel White, John Ray, Thomas Sherlock, Edward Chandler, and William Lowth, who were rather resourceful in controlling the damage done by the new hermeneutics.[7]

Had the allegorists been the only critics to contend with, Mather's key to unlocking the prophetic mystery of the conflagration might have been much more concise. Unfortunately, his literalist colleagues were of little help in this hermeneutical battle of the books, for they were equally divided among themselves, their speculations as diverse as their works were voluminous. Such renowned millenarians as Johann Alsted, Thomas Brightman, Thomas Goodwin, Joseph Mede, John Ray, Thomas Burnet, Samuel Sewall, and Increase Mather viewed the conflagration quite differently from Cotton Mather. To them, the flood of fire at the coming of Christ was not at all global but partial and progressive at first, with a general conflagration at the end of the millennium, as Augustine seemed to intimate (*City of God* 20.16, 18). With such mighty opponents even in one's own ranks, it is not surprising that Mather devoted more than half of his "Third Paradise" (*T*, pt. III. secs. i–viii) to his defense of the predicted conflagration.

But Mather was not always so firmly convinced of these occurrences as he was in his old age. Just as he had changed his mind on the national conversion of the Jews as a prerequisite for the Second Coming, he also kept changing his views on the extent of the conflagration and the condition of the New Heavens and New Earth during the seventh chiliad. In fact, for most of his life, Mather in his eschatology was under the sway of his father, who with Joseph Mede believed "that the *Conflagration* will be at first *partial*, and *liesurely* and *progressive*: And that the first Efforts and Effects of it, are like to be felt by *Italy*, whose horrendous *Volcano's*, together with the like Shakings and Breakings of the Earth, in the Bowels of it, would suggest further suspicions of such a *Catastrophe* impending over that *Seat of the Beast*" (*CPI*, p. 69).[8]

Such an interpretation of the last things seemed quite logical at first, and the new theories of the earth with fiery magma in its interior popularized by Burnet, Ray, Whiston, and Newton would certainly bear out this assertion. So, too, logistical problems with the Saved Nations to be sheltered on earth during the conflagration required a spatial limitation of its initial desolation. In "Problema Theologicum" (1703), the younger Mather still confined the Petrine conflagration to the Roman Sodom, "the Seat of *Antichrist*," whose destruction, foretold in Rev. 14:20, would occur "*By the Space of One Thousand & Six Hundred furlongs; or, Two Hundred Miles.*" This desolation by fire was restricted to the "*Roman Territories*," but the ancient terrain "occupied by the *Babylonian*, and *Persian*, and *Graecian* Kingdomes, will yett remain untouched," while the vials of God's wrath were emptied out on the Roman Antichrist (p. 79).[9]

But even here the main proponents disagreed sharply. For while most readily conceded an initial limitation in size and scope to allow the Saved Nations of Christ to escape the wrath of God, Mede had argued in his "*De Gogo et Magogo*" (*Works*, pp. 574–76; see also pp. 809–10) that the American continent, too, would escape the flood of fire—not, however, because it was to shelter some of the Saved Nations, but because America was to be the abyss of Satan and his minions during their future confinement. The Scythian wilderness of America was the habitat of Gog and Magog, whence Satan would rise to attack the Saved Nations during his final stand in the Battle of Armageddon at the end of the millennium (Revelation 20). Mather, however, was never quite satisfied with Mede's legerdemain denigration of the American continent as hell or with his restricting the Christianography of the messianic kingdom to "*Strabo*'s Cloak" in the Old World (*TA*, p. 46; *MCA* 1.1.2, 7). For when Mede wrote his *Clavis Apocalyptica* (1627), he simply did not know about the *magnalia* of Christ, which the Son of God had wrought since then in America and especially in New England. "I that am an *American,*" Mather rebuffed Mede's conjecture, "must needs be Lothe to allow all *America* still unto the *Devils* possession, when our Lord shall possess all the rest of the World" ("PT," p. 68). The churches of New England were far too reformed to be counted among the hay and stubble of the latter days. In fact, "the *American Hemisphere*" had been prepared by the fathers "to anticipate the State of the *New-Jerusalem,* as far as the unavoidable *Vanity* of *Humane Affairs,* and *Influence* of *Satan* upon them would allow of it" (*MCA* 1.1.4–5).[10] Rather than being the hiding place for Gog and Magog, Mather countered in *Theopolis Americana* (1710), "'Tis thought by Some, that *America* might be intended, as a Place where the Worshippers of the Glorious JESUS, may be Sheltered, while fearful Things are doing in the *European World*" (p. 48).[11]

Such counterclaims in Mather's early eschatology seemed only warranted at a time when the Puritan Errand into the howling wilderness appeared to be thwarted by Mede's conjectures, when Christ's millennial kingdom seemed confined to the European world, when the Saved Nations on earth still required a hiding place from the localized fire descending on the Roman territory. In his early millenarian works, Mather was still uncertain about the spiritual condition of these Saved Nations at the time of the conflagration. They would attain immortality only gradually as they ripened to perfection, but their body would still be imbued with the Adamic curse. Though liberated from Satan's luring influence during the millennium, the seed of sin, however, had not yet been extirpated—carnal lust would likely break forth unless curbed by an "Iron Rod" wielded by the Raised Saints of the Celestial City.

Admittedly, Mather entered such paradoxical points in his collection of "Insolubilia" as he searched for answers. His numerous queries in "Problema Theologicum" sufficiently indicate how much his early eschatology was permeated with perplexing inconsistencies: "*Quaere;* How far *Sin* shall be extinguished and Extirpated among the *Righteous,* by whom the *New Earth* is now Inhabited? *Answer;* Tis One of the, *Things hard to be understood*" ("PT," pp. 81–82). Evidently, such troubling questions were the subject of tireless studies and endless debates with his friends as Mather confessed in "Triparadisus" (p. 278; *D* 1:163, 225–26, 243, 2:668, 673, 685–86).

The harmony of Mather's later eschatology, however, was no longer frustrated by geography or by the enigma of the "Rapture" (1 Cor. 15:51–54; 1 Thess. 4:15–17), not yet fully understood even by Mede, the dean of early seventeenth-century millennialism. Even Mede's own harmony required two separate conflagrations to shelter the Saved Nations in various places on the earth (*Works,* pp. 773–76). As noted earlier, Mather evidently discovered the anonymous treatise *Good Things to Come* in 1724 (*D* 2:733), whereafter it became a cornerstone of his eschatology. This treatise harmonized the Rapture with the holocaust attending Christ's return and unraveled the mystery of the double conflagration. It elucidated in the manner of Enoch and Elijah the Saints' translation into the clouds of heaven, their miraculous transformation into immortal bodies, and their restoration as Changed Saints to the earth cleansed by the fire of the conflagration. With these obstacles removed, Mather's harmony no longer needed a hiding place for what he formerly called the Saved Nations. It no longer mattered where the Saints lived at the time of the conflagration nor what hemisphere they would call their home in the millennial New Earth. For then the celestial City would dispense its blessings unhampered by geography, space, and time.

By 1721, Mather had sufficiently harmonized his views on the conflagration to assert a single inundation by fire at the beginning of Christ's Sabbatism. Citing Henry More to corroborate the eyewitness account of Captain John Robertson that Mather published in *The World Alarm'd* (1721), Mather stated his current conviction that the Lord of Hosts would muster at his coming

> such an Universal Thunder and Lightning, that it shall rattle over all the Quarters of the Earth; and discharge such claps of Unextinguishable Fire, that it will do sure Execution wherever it falls; So that the ground being Excessively heated, the Subterraneous Mines of Combustible Matter will also take Fire; which inflaming the Inward Exhalations of the Earth, will cause a terrible Murmur under Ground; So that the Earth will seem to thunder against the Tearing and Rattling of the Heavens, and all will be filled with sad remugient Echo's. Earth-quakes and Eruptions of Fire there will be every where; and whole Cities & Countries Swallowed down, by the vast Gapings and Wide Divulsions of the Ground.—And this fiery Vengeance, shall be so thirsty, that it shall drink deep of the very Sea; nor shall the Water quench her devouring Appetite, but Excite it.—The whole Earth shall be Enveloped, in One Entire Cloud of an Unspeakable Thickness . . . which added to the choaking Heat and Stench, will compleat this *External Hell*. (P. 13)[12]

One last problem that had troubled Mather for many years required elucidation if his argument were to be cogent enough to hold up against ridicule from both allegorists and literalists alike. His studies of the signs of the approaching time (Matthew 24, 25; Mark 13; Luke 21; Joel 2; 2 Peter 3; etc.) indicated that the arrival of Christ was to be attended by wars, earthquakes, persecutions, famines, and pestilences—all signs from which the watchmen of the latter days could infer the imminence of the Second Coming. But if these signs were indeed to be given before the second advent of Christ and the burning of the world, as Matthew 24 seemed to suggest, how could they be consistent with the scriptural warnings "That His *Coming* will be with all possible *Surprize* upon the World; That it shall be like that of a *Thief in the Night*, altogether unlook'd for. . . . In a Word, when all the *deep Sleep* of a *Midnight* is upon the whole World, without so much as a *Dream* of any such Event being so near" (*T*, p. 202)?[13]

For many years, Mather tried to harmonize these contradictory passages and wondered whether these signs might "not be really *Parts*" of the oncoming conflagration, "not *Signs* that will *Prognosticate* it, but *Signs* that will *Concomitate* it . . . and so the Character of His *Coming Suddenly* still be answered" (*T*, p. 202). It seemed reasonable, therefore, to argue that the signs of the approaching day would accompany Christ's return or come upon the earth so shortly before it that the drowsy world would still be caught off its guard—in a word, all dead asleep, as Wigglesworth had suggested vividly in *The Day of Doom*. This conjecture, however, Mather laid aside in 1724, after having received assurances from God that all signs had already been given and nothing was left to inhibit Christ's immediate return (*D* 2:733). "We find in the Bible," Mather wrote two years later in "Triparadisus," "some *Signs* of Things given *Long Before* the Things came to pass. And the *Signs* of the *Conflagration* may be given so *Long Before* it, as to leave room for the Reign of the *Man of Sin* [Antichrist] to intervene between *Them*, and *It*" (p. 203). The signs that were to announce the Second Coming had been given so long ago (and then repeatedly) that the prophecy of the five foolish virgins—their extinguished oil lamps signifying their spiritual sleep at their master's return at midnight—was already fulfilled. Put in another way, Mather enlisted in his battle of the books his enemies' own munition by employing their preterite-contextual hermeneutics to prove his point. The signs of the End so fittingly described by Matthew (24:1–44) yet so unfairly limited by Hammond and his disciples to the historical destruction of Jerusalem (*Paraphrase*, pp. 101–8) served Mather's own point that all prognosticating signs had been given already.

And rummaging through ancient histories, Mather found plentiful evidence to corroborate his preterite thesis (*T*, pt. III, sec. vi): the dreadful eruption of Mt. Vesuvius (A.D. 79), fittingly described by Dion Cassius and Pliny; the horrific earthquakes at Antioch in the reign of Trajan (A.D. 115/16); the repeated eruptions of Aetna, attended by plagues and famines; and the destruction of Jerusalem by the Romans (A.D. 70) (*T*, pp. 204–18).[14] These prodigies of nature given in former ages "were so Abundant," Mather assured his readers, "that if there should never be any more exhibited, Mankind has no Cause to say, *We see not our Signs*; or the Sleeping World must own, *The Signs have appeared, & we have not seen them*" (*T*, p. 208). With such unmistakable portents given in the past, Mather could tremble with awe in expectation of the day when the King would be witnessed in the clouds and "the World . . . Burned for a Witch" (*WA*, p. 15).

But the paradise of the New Earth was not the only elysium that Mather envisioned in "Triparadisus" or in his other millenarian writings. His experience with formidable cases of witchcraft (1692–93) and his pastoral care at the bedsides of dying parishioners had taught him that there was yet another paradise, the paradise of departed spirits. For if the soul of man was indeed immortal, what would happen to the soul once it had left its deceased shell? If the spirit animating matter did not cease with the body or vanish into thin air as that old Epicurean Lucretius had insisted it does in the first century B.C. (*De rerum natura* 3.195–258), would it lie dormant and inactive until resurrection, or would it remain active and enjoy the company of the departed spirits of former ages? Questions of this nature gave rise to heated debates among the principal schools of thought even in the early eighteenth century, and Mather could not ignore such burning issues if he wanted his "Triparadisus" to attract attention in the marketplace of hermeneutical ideas.

In "The Second Paradise" of "Triparadisus," Cotton Mather rose in defense of the soul's embattled immortality, the doctrine that the soul as a separate incorporeal substance survives the body after death. In Mather's time, the traditional belief in this dogma could no longer be taken for granted. In 1331/32, Pope John XXII had inadvertently contested the belief in the immediate Beatific Vision of just souls. Pope Benedict XII's edict *Benedictus Deus* (1336) essentially failed to halt the ensuing debate and fostered roughly four separate schools of thought: (1) *Roman Catholic position*: After purgatory, just souls are admitted to an immediate Beatific Vision in paradise *even before* the Resurrection of the body at Judgment Day; (2) *psychopannychist position*: The souls of the just are inactive and sleep insensibly *until* the Resurrection of the body at Judgment Day; (3) *Calvinist position*: Just souls do not sleep but are alive and active in separate receptacles (the Second Paradise) until the Resurrection, upon which they are admitted to the Beatific Vision; (4) *materialist position*: The soul is *not* an incorporeal substance separate from the body but merely its moving force, which vanishes completely upon the death of the body. At the Resurrection, this force merely revitalizes the beatified body. Awakened from its age-old slumber, this materialist view of body and soul threatened the very superstructure of doctrinal beliefs in the afterlife.

The latter theory had made a surprising comeback in mid-century, when Thomas Hobbes's *Leviathan* seemingly swept off the cobwebs of superstition and with it the belief in ghosts, ghouls, and goblins haunting the visible world (pt. III, chs. 34, 38, pt. IV, chs. 44–46). Hobbes's rationalist-materialist refutation of the soul's continuance after the death of the body was particularly ticklish for the church and its authority, because it seemed to render null and void the crucial dogma of reward or punishment of souls in the hereafter. This revived Epicurean heresy, coupled with the spread of the psychopannychist idea of "soul-sleepers" so formidably countered in John Calvin's *Psychopannychia* (1542), threatened the literalist orthodoxy to the very core. Small wonder that in this dangerous development Mather saw crumbling yet another pillar of the Bible's authority, which rested for the most part on the shaky foundation of the Scriptures as the revealed word of God. And it is against this background that we must appreciate Mather's incessant efforts and seeming superstition as he again defended the wonders of the invisible world in "The Second Paradise."[15]

To corroborate the existence of the immortal soul and its lively continuation after the death of the body, many respected theologians and scientists of the day compiled their own collections of ghost stories, which enjoyed wide popularity. Among the best known are those in Henry More's appendix to his *Treatise Against Atheisme* (1653), which like his *Immortality of the Soul* (1659, bk. 1, ch. xiii; bk. 2, ch. xvi) sought to invalidate Hobbes's contention that incorporeal substances, like apparitions, are contradictions in terms and chimerical fancies of idle brains (*Leviathan*, pt. III, ch. 34, pp. 286–87). "Wee may not Imagine," Mather echoed Calvin's *Psychopannychia* in his own *Midnight Cry* (1692), "that our Souls do fall into the Sleep of a **Senseless Condition**, when we *Dy;* no, the least suspicion of such a thing would make me cry out, and every good man would joyn with me in that Exclamation, *God forbid!* The Opinion of the *Psychopannychist,* or, Soul-sleeper, is too vile a thing for any *man* to swallow" (p. 9).[16] Mather certainly knew what he was talking about. The "incontestable and incontrovertible" evidence found in his day in the learned treatises of Sir George Villiers, Major Thomas Sydenham, Henry More, and William Smythies had revealed "undoubted Histories" of apparitions, which would "compel the Beleef of all but Conceited & Obstinate *Fools"* (*T,* p. 114).[17]

Mather did not have to rely for more tangible proof on such cross-Atlantic accounts by his colleagues. His own Boston neighborhood, time and again, had been visited by such departed spirits from the other world. "My own Vicinity," Mather assured his readers in "Triparadisus," just as he had done more than thirty years before in *Wonders of the Invisible World,* "has been more than once or twice visited, with *Spirits,* who have been *seen* and *heard* asserting themselves to be the *Souls* of Persons departed; and my own most *Critical Enquiries* have putt it out of all Doubt with me, that the Persons more immediately addressed in these Visits, have not been impos'd upon" (p. 115; see pp. 115–18; *D* 2:383). The apparition of Joseph Beacon's brother murdered in London and coming across the Atlantic to Boston to tell Joseph of his murderer; the poltergeist of Mary Johnson of Haverhill, whose voice from the invisible world and whose "Violent and very *Audible Knocks* from an *Invisible Hand"* (*T,* p. 116) kept the whole neighborhood alarmed for several weeks together; the spirit of John Watts's sister of Boston, who had died in childbirth and appeared to her brother in London to exhort him "to a Life of *Serious Piety"* (*T,* p. 117)—all proved that a corporeal soul existed after the death of the body and that the departed enjoyed an active life to boot in the invisible world. If nothing else, these apparitions established that Boston, and New England at large, had its fair share of ghostly visitors:

> Tis no Rare thing among us, for People to have *Apparitions* of their Friends, as *Drown'd* or otherwise *Dead,* who have been at the same time abroad, at Sea, or in other Countreys. At the Time of the *Apparitions,* they have been much talk'd of in the alarum'd Neighbourhood; And I have myself at the Time, enquired into them, and made a Record of them, and concurr'd with the Neighbours in expecting the *Event.* The *Event* has been, that our first News of them has been, that at that very Time, they were *Drown'd,* or otherwise *Dead,* as they had been represented. (*T,* p. 117)

Such tales from the dark side, surely, were no fireside diversions for long wintry nights in Boston. Nor were such accounts to be taken lightly. For they proved beyond doubt, if they proved anything at all, that there was life after death—and an active one at that. Certainly no psychopannychism here! Calvin's treatise was vindicated, and the "soul-killing swine," the Epicureans, were refuted in every letter! Cotton Mather's uncompromising interest in the invisible world should therefore not be interpreted as his singular gullibility at a time when the Enlightenment seemed to sweep away the vestiges of darkest medieval-ism; his fascination with the subject must be seen as his counterattack on the psychopannychism so popular among the Anabaptists of the day and as his war-fare against Hobbesian materialism, which undermined nothing less than the revealed Word of God (Burnet, *Departed Souls*, pp. 61–125).

Without doubt, such ghostly communications from the other world followed a logic all their own and surpassed in tangible evidence the skepticism of the Deists and the scholasticism of contemporary logicians. The case was plain:

> Now, I see no Cause to think any other, but that these were the *Humane Souls*, which they Appeared for. And who can tell, but that the Glorious GOD who enables our *Will*, while we are yett in our *Bodies* . . . may so extend the Sphaere of Activity to *Souls* taken out of their *Bodies*, that they shall be able, when they *Will*, to form such an Human *Voice*, or *Shape*, as they have been us'd unto, and render it *sensible* to the Survivers? . . . The *Spirit* that said, *I am the Soul of your Sister* [the John Watts case]: An *Evil Spirit* would not come upon such an Intention, as to animate *Serious Piety*: A *Good Spirit*, would not *Ly*, and assert himself to be a Person, which he is *not*: Then, it must be the *Soul* of the Deceased. But suppose the *Appearing Spirits* to be *not* the *Souls* they appear for; still they were such *Spirits*, as would plainly induce any one, to beleeve the Existence of such *Humane Souls* in a State of *Separation*. (*T*, p. 117; see also pp. 138–47; *PN*, pp. 111–13, 117)

Mather here relied on the authority of the Cambridge Platonist Henry More, who could not help but feel that demons did not impersonate the souls of the departed and promote Christian piety, "it being below so noble a nature to tell a Lie" (*Immortality*, bk. 2, p. 296). That Mather hedged his argument, how-ever, does not come as a surprise, for his father had explicitly warned against "Those *Apparitions* [who] were *Cacodaemons*, which feigned themselves to be the Spirits of Men departed" (*Illustrious Providences*, p. 211). Hence great care had to be taken if one did not want to be deceived after all.[18]

Whatever their precise nature, the souls of the just continued in a Second Paradise, assuredly not yet enjoying the Beatific Vision until the Resurrection of the body, but certainly living in anticipation of their future happiness. Here the *"unsheathed"* spirits dwelled in a makeshift paradise, or *"Intermediate State"* (the Second Paradise), where they awaited the happy day. Mather's English col-league Thomas Burnet, though agreeing in many details, was less determined to spell out the intermediate condition of the disembodied souls in literal terms. To Burnet, souls would attain a state of anticipated bliss, or "internal heaven," immediately after their departure from the body, "But without their Bodies can-not enjoy the external one" in the Beatific Vision of God. Consequently, this "Intermediate State" must be taken as a metaphor for the future happiness of the resurrected and reembodied souls in the presence of God (*Departed Souls*, pp. 95–105). In contrast to Burnet's quasi-allegorization of the Beatific Vision,

Mather held fast to the Second Paradise as the place to which Enoch and Elijah of old had been translated and of which the dying Redeemer had spoken when he promised his fellow sufferer on the cross: "Verily, I say vnto thee, to day shalt thou be with me in Paradise" (Luke 23:43). Here, in the "Heavenly Mansions" inferior only to those "Distinct Apartments" of the Third Heaven of which the *sanctum sanctorum* of the temple was the smaller type, the good souls were to reap some of the fruits for their faithfulness on earth (*T*, pt. II, sec. iii, esp. pp. 132–34; *C*, pp. 138–40).

The receptacles of the Second Paradise, however, did fall short of the glory to be expected in the mansions of the third, Mather was convinced. "While our *Spirits* are in *Paradise* [Second Heaven], there is an *Essential Part* of us yett remaining under the *Curse*: As long as we are in the *State of the Dead*, the *Curse* is not wholly taken off. Until we are *Embodied Spirits*, we are not in a *Natural State*" (*T*, p. 128). In other words, as long as the souls of the dead had not yet been restored to their former prelapsarian bodies, they still remained under the Adamic curse. Only after the First Resurrection (Rev. 20:4–5), at the beginning of the millennium, could this curse be lifted and the "*Luminous Garment*" that distinguished Adam and Eve before the Fall be restored to the Saints in heaven (*T*, p. 136).[19]

The physical reunion of body and soul, which both just and unjust would undergo at the First and Second Resurrections, was hardly a unique feature of Mather's eschatology. It can be traced to Johann Heinrich Alsted's *Diatribe de mille annis Apocalypticis* (1627). Translated into English by William Burton and published as *The Beloved City* (1643), Alsted's work left a lasting impression on such important chiliasts as Joseph Mede, William Twisse, Henry More, William Sherwin, and Isaac Newton—to mention just a few.[20] Such proponents did not go unnoticed among the New World millenarians. It is therefore not surprising that Cotton Mather's own "Problema Theologicum," as indeed all of his works on the subject, should argue that the souls of the dead would presently rejoin their immortal bodies: "Some, att the *Beginning* of the *Thousand Years*; others, not untill the *Thousand Years* are *Finished*. But the *Latter* then *Live again*, as to their *Bodyes*; and therefore so must the *Former* too" (p. 60). Mather never changed his mind on that issue, even though it took him until the end of his life to resolve the inconsistencies that characterized his earlier millenarian works. Two years before his own death, he was convinced that

Of so fine, & so pure, & so strong a Temper will their *Bodies* be, that they will never be in any danger to *See Corruption*. Their *Bodies* will be so *Salted* by the *Garments of Light*, which GOD will putt upon them, that they will become *Incorruptible* under it. *Luminous Bodies!* We are informed, *They shall shine as the Brightness of the Firmament, & as the Stars forever & ever.* There shall be no *Deformities* on them; nothing Ugly, nothing Lothsome, nothing out of Shape. No; They shall be sett off with a dazzling *Beauty & Brightness. . . . Spiritual Bodies!* Not ceasing to be *Bodies*, or turned into meer *Spirits*; They will be *Material* still; but highly

Spiritualized. . . . Equal to the Angels: Doubtless, Able to Move, and Mount, and Fly, as the *Angels* do. An Heavy Tendency to the *Earth*, doubtless, they will be so disencumbred from it, that *They shall mount up with Wings as Eagles*. (*T*, p. 255; see also 261).[21]

And as the Raised Saints soared with their luminous bodies in the New Jerusalem above, so did Mather's imagination take wing, unshackled by the clay of his Maker but not by the law of gravity.

"The NEW HEAVENS opened" (*T*, pt. III, sec. ix) is Mather's fullest treatment of the subject and surpasses in figural imagination and pictorial description his father's treatise "New Jerusalem."[22] Cotton Mather's description of the New Jerusalem above is far more daring than that of his father, whose typology seldom strayed too far from its biblical source. In fact, the younger Mather's chronometrical delineation of the things to come often came dangerously close to what Charles Chauncey and others would have considered "enthusiasm," for which crime the Quakers in Massachusetts faced persecution and, in some cases, execution—even in Mather's own time (*MCA* 7.4).[23] One case in point may suffice here. Describing in the manner of St. Thomas Aquinas the Hypostatic Union of the beatified soul in the New Heavens, Mather imagined that the Raised Saints would experience such a spiritual and intellectual union with the Deity that the joy of the soul would decant into the body. Their bodies restored to incorruptibility, the Saints would become so holy, so purified, that their conjugation with the Creator would even transcend the bliss that Solomon envisioned with his Shulamite shepherdess:

How *Clean* the *Hands*, How *Pure* the *Hearts*, of all that *ascend* into this *Hill of the Lord*, and *Stand in this Holy Place*! . . . Indeed these *Elect* of GOD, will continue *Distinct Beings*; They will not putt off their *Individuation*; In their becoming *One* with GOD, it must not be blasphemously imagined, that they become the *Same* with GOD. But yett, they shall be brought so *Near* to GOD, that GOD will become *All in All* unto them; and they shall be *Filled with all the Fulness of GOD*; Even so *Filled*, as a Piece of Gold thrown into the Glowing Furnace, is filled with the *Fire*. GOD will Penetrate them: GOD will Replenish them; GOD will wondrously Possess them, and Swallow them up in the Tendencies of a Mind Closing with Him, and Communicate unto them *Fulness of Joy*, and *Pleasures forevermore*. (*T*, pp. 250, 249)[24]

Had "Triparadisus" been published in his own lifetime, as Mather intended, some Oldmixon or Robert Calef would surely have stumbled over such daring speculations. But to imagine that the Raised Saints were to be united with the Trinity did not necessarily imply that they were equal to God. Nor was there total equality among the various stations or mansions to be occupied by the Raised Saints in the celestial City. Naturally, each citizen would here occupy "a Palace bigger than the Biggest in *Great Britain*" (*T*, p. 247), as the Redeemer had promised long ago (John 14:2). However, the Raised Saints' relative stations of glory would correspond to their former trials on earth and to their degrees of serviceableness to God. But the *"Less Glorious"* would not be *"Vex'd* at being overlook'd in those *Distinctions,"* nor the *"More Glorious* . . . be *Proud"* at their preferment in heaven. The Saints of the City would long have been weaned from such carnal vanity—their *"Will* . . . entirely swallowed up in the *Will* of GOD" (*T*, p. 258).[25]

In many respects the celestial society of the City, as Mather envisioned it, was structured like feudal society, its hierarchy relegating stations of relative glory to each of its members. The City of God was to be devoid of any strife intrinsic to such a hierarchy, however, and the perfection of the immortal Saints would preclude envy and malicious joy, the distinguishing characteristics of mortality. The Raised Saints would embrace one another in complete concord, in which even a *"Luther* and *Zuinglius"* would be united in filial love (*T*, p. 261).[26] Imagining what this mystical union with God would be like, Mather drew infinite satisfaction from the marvelous promises that defied human understanding (*C*, p. 145). To be fruitful in the field of the Lord and to be serviceable to his fellowman had always been the core of Mather's pastoral care. His neighbors, however, only too often despised this Bonifacius as a "Public Enemy" and loathed his do-gooding, a matter about which his *Bonifacius: Essay Upon the Good* (1710) bears testimony.[27] With such malevolence all around him, Mather dreamed of the celestial City, where, loosed from the shackles of his ingrate neighbors, he could fulfill his heart's desire: "And our *Heart* had many *Intents* to do this and that *Service*, which to our Grief we were prevented from the doing of." But God, who "saw all the *Thoughts ⅋ Intents of our Heart* . . . will now give us to see, that none of our, GOOD DEVISED, is forgotten with Him" (*T*, p. 259; see also *PN*, p. 197). In fact, all Mather's thwarted intentions of doing good would come to fruition and receive their just rewards, just as the loyalty of old Mordecai to Artaxerxes of Persia had been rewarded with royal favor (Esth. 6:11, 10:1–3): "If the Humble Servant of GOD, be not carried thro' the *Holy City*, with Special Marks of the Divine Favour, & it be not proclamed, *Thus it shall be done to the Man, who made it his Continual Endeavour to do all he could for the Honour of his GOD; and whom the Great KING has Honoured, by giving Him to Do and to Bear for Him!*—Something as Great shall be done for him" (*T*, p. 259).

The guardian angels who had invisibly assisted God's servants in their former duties would, of course, partake in these revelries and would hold "a most intimate *Communion*" with their former wards (*T*, p. 261).[28] Yet such delights of the City would be surpassed by even greater honors for the Raised Saints. They would not only be "made equal" to the angels but would also succeed them as messengers of God, visibly commuting between the New Heavens and the New Earth, and would become princes and rulers over the world below:

As the *Angels* do at this Day, the *Raised Saints* will then come and go, at the Bidding of the Lord. Yea, The Glorious KING will say to them, *You shall be over my House in the Lower World, and according to Your Word shall my People there be Ruled; Only in the Throne I will be greater than You.* He will send them [Raised Saints] to Govern *Cities* and *Nations*, and they will fly down with *Orders* from Him, for the Management of their

Grand Affairs: and *Speak to them of Things pertaining to the Kingdome of GOD*. (*T*, pp. 262–63; see also p. 264; "PT," pp. 82–83; *PN*, pp. 110–13, 119, 121)

Thus, in the world to come, the Raised Saints would become the guardian angels of the new order. Like their ethereal friends in bygone ages, they would then assist and instruct the Changed Saints on the New Earth in the ways of the New Jerusalem and help restore the incinerated planet to an antediluvian paradise, more *"Refined"* than what it was before the Fall (*T*, p. 271). The Changed Saints, who had escaped the cataclysm in the clouds of heaven, would be brought into complete unison with the City in their exercises of theocratic devotion (*T*, p. 273). So, too, would they replenish the earth with millions of their own progeny to carry out God's original commission to Adam and Eve: Be fruitful and multiply. Thus, much work would have to be done, and it would be incumbent upon the Raised Saints above to see it carried out below: the Changed Saints "shall be Visited, & Instructed & Ordered, by the *Citizens* of the *Holy City* coming down as there may be Occasion to them: And while they *Walk with GOD* at an High Rate of *Sanctity* and *Purity*, they shall *Begett Sons and Daughters*: & they shall continue in this Condition, until it shall please the Great KING to have them *Translated*, either *Successively* one after another as they may Ripen for it, or, anon *all at once* in His Time for it, into the Superiour Circumstances of the *Holy City*" (*T*, p. 273).[29]

The Changed Saints would attain, through the ministration of the City, such standards of divine perfection, such heights of learning in matters of divinity, that the least in the earthly kingdom would outshine Solomon in all his wisdom. No doubt there would be colleges in this New Earth (as there were in the Old), with proper curricula, fitting books, and holy teachers, through whom all the nagging questions of hermeneutics would be answered unambiguously. Often enough, Mather's proposal to implement a Pietist curriculum at Harvard had been rebuffed by the overseers, who preferred the philosophy of Greece and Rome to books of practical piety. All this was to change in the New Earth: "The Learning of the World," Mather promised triumphantly, "will not then be the Jargon of a fumivendutous *Aristotle*, and such Trash as the Colledges in our days have sometimes valued themselves upon. But the World will be filled with the most Noble & Useful Knowledge, and all the *Sciences* will terminate in *Living unto GOD*" (*T*, p. 286).[30] In fact, the divine learning under the influence of the Raised Saints would be so universal, "the Messengers of the Lord . . . *forever* conveying of Messages from *Him* down unto them," that even Christ "in *His Times* for it, [would] make His *Visits* to the *Earth*, and show Himself in His Radiant Glory to His *Holy People* here." Such visitations would continue until all the work was finished on earth and the Changed Saints themselves were translated into the City above to "be with a yett nearer Access *forever with the Lord*" (*T*, pp. 287–88). At the end of time, the Changed Saints would leave their earthly habitat as well and join the brethren of the First Resurrection in the New Jerusalem above.[31]

The heavenly Jerusalem, as Mather envisioned it, was not to be mistaken for a metaphor, nor was it a mere representation of God's grace residing in the heart of mankind, as some of the allegorist church fathers had interpreted the visions of Ezekiel and John to be (Ezekiel 40–47; Revelation 4, 21–22).[32] No doubt the description of the City so admirably given in the Scriptures invited allegorization, but it could never be mere metaphor in Mather's hermeneutics: "Tho' we may allow some *Figure* in many Expressions concerning it," Mather conceded, "yett, I entreat You, Syrs, turn it not all into meer *Shadow*, and Lett not your *Metaphysicks* operate & sublimate upon it, until you have made it no better than one of your *Entia Rationis*, & a meer *Non Entity*" (*T*, p. 246). Quite to the contrary: The celestial City described in Ezekiel and Revelation could be nothing less than a "*Material City*" (*T*, p. 244) if it were to accommodate the corporeal bodies of the Raised Saints. "*Spiritualize* the Matter as much as You please," Mather challenged the cabal of English allegorists.[33] "But if you think, a *Visible City*, of a *Cubical* Form is too *Corporeal* a Thing, yett you must allow, That there will be a *Place* of Reception for Bodies" (*T*, p. 245).

Even though Increase Mather had opted for an allegorical and figurative reading of this New Jerusalem, his son never wavered about the literal City of God hovering in the clouds of heaven as Tertullian reported in *Against Marcion* (3.24).[34] To mistake the New Jerusalem for a metaphor would violate the literalism employed throughout; for if the New Jerusalem had accommodated the physical body of the resurrected Messiah and if the City were to provide mansions for the embodied Saints, how then could the City be mere allegory? Neither was its size nor its precious building material far from tangible reality. No, the New Jerusalem above, as Mather saw it described in Revelation 21, was as literal as the restored Jerusalem below:

> A CITY, that has a *Wall Great & High*, having *Twelve Foundations*, with *Twelve Gates*; A CITY, consisting of *Pure Gold*, exceedingly Burnished; and having its *Foundations garnished with all Manner of Precious Stones*; and the *Twelve Gates* entire *Pearles*: A CITY that has no *need of the Sun or the Moon to shine on it*; for the *Glory of GOD Lightens it, and the Lamb is the Light of it*: The *Length* & the *Breadth* and the *Heighth* of the CITY, aequal; each being *Twelve Thousand Furlongs*; or *Fifteen Hundred Miles*, every Way, in each of the Three Dimensions. The *Cubical Arrangement* of the *Mansions*, will not at all obtenebrate any of them, while the *City* is thus filled with the *Glory of the Lord*. No; It will be *the Inheritance of the Saints in Light*. (*T*, p. 244)[35]

Granted, the hyperbolical dimensions outlined in John's Apocalypse seemed unfathomable and naturally would give rise to metaphoric interpretations, especially in light of such Newtonian precepts as "What Ancient Tradition asserts of the Constitution of Nature . . . is to be allow'd for True, where 'tis fully agreeable to Scripture, Reason, and Philosophy" (Whiston, *New Theory*, "Postulata," p. 95; see also Spinoza, *Tractatus*, ch. XV, pp. 190–99). Increase Mather, for one, was much more circumspect than his son, as Increase's "Discourse Concerning the glorious state of the church on earth under the New Jerusalem" (c. 1692–95)

indicates. For instance, the cubic dimensions described in John's vision signified to Increase in the best Augustinian sense "the Fixed and unchangable state
of happiness, that the church of god shall then be in" (p. 405). The perfect cubical shape of the City foreshadowed to Increase the happiness of the millennial
church on the New Earth and its complete harmony with the will of God, "a
restoration and renovation of the earth" in which "a 'new heavens and a new
earth' shall be joined together" (p. 352).[36] Increase's allegorization of the New
Jerusalem does not come as a surprise, however, for the celestial influences
that Cotton Mather ascribed to the literal Jerusalem, visibly hovering in the
clouds of the New Heavens, Increase Mather attributed to the restored City of
David in the New Earth below. Until the end of his life, Increase held fast to
the restoration of the Jewish nation, when the Jews' miraculous conversion to
Christianity, attended by their return to Judea and their rebuilding of ancient
Jerusalem, would usher in a time of unprecedented bliss for all the world. The
center of the messianic kingdom would then be there, the New Jerusalem above
in complete harmony with the administration of the restored Jerusalem below.

Although Cotton Mather rendered the latter doctrine in a preterite and allegorical sense in his old age, yet he always spoke of two separate Jerusalems: the
New above and the Old below. During Christ's Sabbatism "There shall then be
Two Jerusalems," Mather explained the issue in 1703. "Johns New Jerusalem,
in which there is No Temple, and Ezekiels New Jerusalem, in which there shall
be a Temple" ("PT," p. 82). Interestingly enough, in this passage Mather did not
identify Ezekiel's vision of the temple in the Old Jerusalem with John's in the
New, as he would do in "Triparadisus" twenty-three years later (T, pp. 304–6).
For as he saw it in "Problema Theologicum," John's vision applied to the celestial City in the New Heavens, while Ezekiel's applied to the restored Jerusalem
in the New Earth. Assuredly, the two Jerusalems would be in complete concord
with each other, for the City of God in the clouds would send down its winged
messengers, the Raised Saints, with instructions to the rulers below.

Modern readers may smile at such hermeneutical niceties of long-forgotten
lore. However trivial it may appear to us today, though, Mather's distinction between the two Jerusalems has significant ramifications for modern intellectual
historiography concerning the period. While Increase Mather's figural interpretation of the New Jerusalem was closely aligned with Augustine's allegorization
of these visions "as the Church of Christ extending over the whole world" (City
of God 20.11, 17), Cotton Mather's literalism followed Tertullian's Five Books
Against Marcion (3.24) and placed the New Jerusalem in the New Heavens, but
visibly hovering over the Israelitish Jerusalem in the New Earth: "The City of
God in the New Heavens," he postulated in 1703, will extend "Fifteen Hundred
Miles," and "It will be seated over the Land of Israel, which will now again
be possessed by the Israelitish Nation" ("PT," p. 82; see also p. 80). So, too, he
maintained in 1726/27: "The Situation of it [New Jerusalem], will be in a Part
of the Atmosphaere, which will be nearer to the Earth, where the Nations are
to Walk in the Light of it, than as yett it is, and it will be conspicuous to the
Nations" (T, p. 245; see also pp. 268–69, 287–88).

The placement of the New Jerusalem in the clouds above the terrain of ancient Israel has hitherto gone unnoticed and flies in the face of the popular notion among modern intellectual historians that Cotton Mather's myopia limited the New Jerusalem chiefly to Puritan America and proclaimed Boston as the *Theopolis Americana*, the millennial seat of the City of God. According to this received tradition, Cotton Mather was the chief promulgator of the City in America, and his jeremiad *Theopolis Americana* most clearly identifies Boston as the seat of the American New Jerusalem.[37] A cursory glance at Mather's much-quoted sermon seems to suggest that he celebrates the future glory of America by typologically identifying New England as the future site of Christ's millennial throne: "*GLORIOUS Things are Spoken of thee, O thou City of God!* The STREET be in THEE, O NEW-ENGLAND; *The Interpretation of it,* be unto you, O *American* Colonies. . . . There are many Arguments to perswade us, That our Glorious LORD, will have an **Holy City** in AMERICA; a *City*, the **Street** whereof will be *Pure* **Gold**. . . . Yea, the Day is at hand, when this Voice will be heard concerning *thee, Putt on thy beautiful Garments, O* America, *the Holy City!*" (pp. 1, 43, 46). Indeed, on the surface, the apocalyptic overtones of this homily appear to confirm the representative argument of a well-known critic that Mather proclaims "America" as "the seat of the Lord's Kingdom, a New Jerusalem whose streets were paved with gold."[38]

Similar conclusions have been drawn from Increase Mather's jeremiad *A Call from Heaven* (1685), in which the minister of Boston's Second Church bewails New England's declension by contrasting the gargantuan accomplishments of the first generation with the failures of its offspring: "Where was there ever a place so like unto New Jerusalem as New-England hath been? It was once Dr. *Twiss* his Opinion . . . that when New Jerusalem should come down from Heaven *America* would be the seat of it. Truly that such a Type and Embleme of New Jerusalem, should be erected in so dark a corner of the world, is matter of deep Meditation and Admiration" (pp. 77–78). Urian Oakes's well-known election sermon *New-England Pleaded with* (1673) is also frequently cited as evidence for the Puritans' predilection for describing themselves as God's special possession, for when the minister of Cambridge proclaims, "this our Commonwealth seems to exhibit to us a *specimen*, or a *little model of the Kingdome of Christ upon Earth*," in which "You have been *as a City upon an hill*" (p. 21), Oakes apparently reaffirms John Winthrop's vision of God's celestial City in an American wilderness. In like manner, Judge Samuel Sewall's proclivity to herald America as the millennial seat of Christ's theocracy seems obvious in his often misunderstood *Phaenomena quaedam Apocalyptica* (1697, 1727): "*I propound the New-World: as being so far from deserving the Nick-names of* Gog *and* Magog; *that it stands fair for being made the Seat of the Divine Metropolis.*"[39]

Passages like these are legion in the annals of early Americana. And to legions of modern scholars they corroborate that New England's second and third generations not only arrogated the celestial City as their own exclusive domain but also identified themselves as the latter-day antitype of God's ancient Israelites, whose special position had now been assumed by the most reformed people in Christendom. How else are we to read Cotton Mather's arrogant hyperbole, "The *First Age* was the *Golden Age*: To return unto *That*, will make a Man a *Protestant*, and I may add, a *Puritan*" (*MCA*, "General Introduction," 3, sig. Cv)? To understand whether the figurative language employed here is conclusive evidence of the Puritans' myopic vision of Christ's *Heilsgeschichte*, we must tally these claims against Puritan eschatological theories.

The spatial location of the City of God and the nature of its inhabitants were much on the mind of Dr. William Twisse, an English premillennialist, resident of New England in the 1630s, and later member of the Westminster Assembly. In one of his frequent letters to Joseph Mede on eschatological subjects, Twisse hailed the timely discovery of America and the progress of the Puritan gospel in New England and eagerly inquired of his famous colleague: "*Why may not that* [America] *be the Place of* New Jerusalem?"[40] Mede, however, was not at all impressed with Twisse's argument.[41] He ventured that the American hemisphere so lately discovered was not the locus of Christ's millennial throne, as George Herbert's "Church Militant" (1633) might suggest: "Religion stands on tip-toe in our land, / Readie to passe to the *American strand*" (lines 235–36). Rather, to Mede America was the kingdom of Satan and his minions, Gog and Magog, whose armies would once more rise against the City and its inhabitants in the Battle of Armageddon at the end of the millennium. In fact, according to Mede, the geography of Christ's millennial kingdom lay *within* the boundaries of the former Roman Empire as it existed in the apostles' times and therefore excluded all other hemispheres from future bliss: "Concerning our Plantation in the *American* world," Mede responded to Twisse's hopeful inquiry, "I wish them as well as any body; though I differ from them far, both in other things, and in the grounds they go upon." While Christ might be pleased with their efforts to convert "those Natives" and "to *affront* the Devil with the sound of the Gospel and Cross of Christ in those places where he had thought to have reigned securely," yet "I will hope they shall not so far degenerate (not all of them) as to come in that Army of *Gog* and *Magog* against the Kingdom of Christ."[42]

To Joseph Mede, the New Jerusalem as described in the visions of Ezekiel and of John was not a metaphor for the Church Universal in the Augustinian sense but the literal metropolis of Christ's millennial kingdom, with its throne in his restored Judea. Mede explained this mystery to his colleague Dr. Samuel Meddus: "We must distinguish between the State of the *New Jerusalem* and the State of the *Nations which shall walk in the light thereof*; they shall not be both one, but much differing. Therefore what is spoken particularly of the *New Jerusalem*, must not be applied to the whole Church which then shall be: *New Jerusalem* is not the whole Church, but the Metropolis thereof and of the [millennial] New world" (*Works*, p. 772). While the Saved Nations huddling around Christ's future metropolis in "*the land of* Jury [Jewry]" would partake of the City's saving influences, they would again fall prey to Gog and Magog at the end of the Seventh Chiliad. These less fortunate followers of Christ differed from those in the capital city because they still retained their mortality and with it their sinful propensity, while the Saints of the First Resurrection and

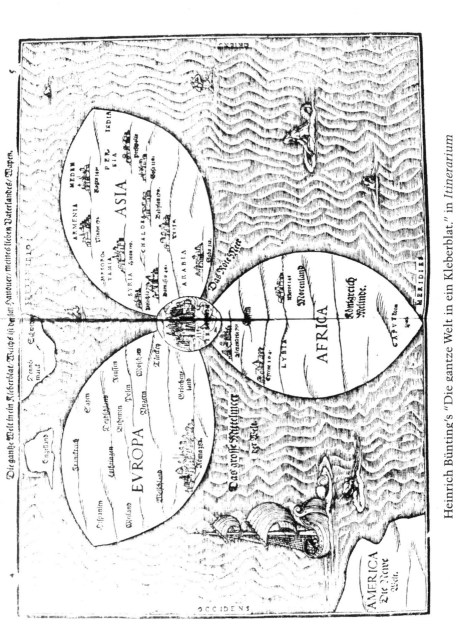

Heinrich Bünting's "Die gantze Welt in ein Kleberblat," in *Itinerarium sacre scripturae* (Helmstedt, 1581), does not pretend to be an accurate depiction of the world but presents the geography of salvation with Jerusalem as its spiritual center.

rulers of the city here below had life everlasting and would thus be immune to the Devil's attack. Against Mede's authority and force of argument, Twisse and most of his contemporaries were unable to stand, and the disciple humbly thanked his master for having *"handsomely and fully clear'd me from such odd conceits"* as that New England rather than the *"land of* Jury" would be the site of the holy City (Twisse's "Epistle," p. 799).

The significance of Mede's restriction of Christ's future kingdom to the territory of the Roman Empire as it existed in the apostles' time and his identification of America as the place from which Christ's adversaries would again rise to destroy his Saints cannot be overemphasized, for in essence he had consigned America to outer darkness. If Mede was right and the American hemisphere was not to share in the sacred geography of Christ's kingdom, then the Puritan Errand in the American wilderness was *nolens volens* an errand in futility, an errand, ironically, not into the future Garden of Eden but to the very gates of hell itself! By transplanting themselves to America, Puritans had in effect foolishly traded Christ's future paradise in the Old World for Satan's abode in the New.

It is in this context that we must appreciate Nicholas Noyes's defense of the New World, written in Salem, Massachusetts, against Mede's singular exclusion: "Now as for *New England*, if the *First Planters* of it had dream'd that the very Situation or Climate of this Land had been crime enough to make men *aliens from the Covenants of promise*; they would not have Sold their *Europaean Birthright*, for a mess of *American Pottage"* (p. 76; see also pp. 68–75). And it is in this context, too, that we must assess Cotton Mather's early eschatological hopes for the fate of his country as he expressed them in *The Present State of New England* (1690): "if the Blessed God intend that the Divel shall keep *America* during the Happy *Chiliad* which His Church is now very *quickly* Entring into . . . then our Lord Jesus will within a few Months break up House among us, and we go for our Lodging either to *Heaven* or to *Europe* in a very little while. But if our God will wrest *America* out of the Hands of its old Land-Lord, *Satan*, and give these *utmost ends of the Earth* to our Lord Jesus," then the Great Sabbatism of Christ would soon be on the horizon (pp. 34–35; see also *SHNE*, pp. 38–39).

Symptomatic of those critics who overlook the context of Mather's oft-cited passage, Charles L. Sanford insists that "When everything looked black even in New England, Cotton Mather questioned whether the next lodging place of the saints would be removal 'to Heaven or to Europe,' that is, to Heaven or Hell." More important, Sanford—like his colleagues—arrives at conclusions diametrically opposed to those intended by the Mathers and their fellow eschatologists precisely because he approaches their millenarian responses with a predetermined notion, just as Cecelia Tichi does when she concludes that, come the millennium, "Boston" would be "a plausible (and perhaps comfortable) locus for the New Jerusalem."[43]

At the center of modern critics' confusion about the Puritans' expectations regarding the Second Coming is the vexed term *New Jerusalem*, which bears a richness of meaning rarely appreciated by twentieth-century commentators. Mede and his American disciples pointed to Judea as the locus of the divine metropolis, but Mede also made an important distinction between the New Jerusalem as the restored *capital* of Christ's throne and the New Jerusalem as the spatial *terrain* of Christ's future kingdom. This important nuance alone, however, does not fully cover the spectrum of the ways *New Jerusalem* was used in the millennialist literature of the period. The majority of the biblical commentators applied the term indiscriminately to signify the restored metropolis in Judea, or the literal and corporeal City of God in the clouds of heaven as described by Tertullian, or the Augustinian Church Universal, whose harmony with the New Heavens was expressed in metaphoric terms, or a combination of those meanings.[44]

Mather never wavered in his literal reading of the New Jerusalem as a city with corporeal inhabitants located in the New Heavens above the terrain of Judea. Especially in his early eschatology, the Raised Saints from the City above and the restored Jerusalem below would govern the Saved Nations of the Gentiles huddling around Judea. In this early eschatology, the Saved Nations did not attain perfection and immortality suddenly and rapturously (as the Changed Saints did in his later theories), but would ripen gradually over a thousand-year period through the nurturing influence of their teachers (the Raised Saints) in the City. Because of their remaining sin, the Saved Nations were prone to relapse and needed special care, as Joseph Mede had conjectured as well (*Works*, pp. 772–75). "The Nations in the Remoter Skirts of the World," Mather echoed Mede in "Problema Theologicum," "will not be under so high a Dispensation of Christianity, as those that ly nearer to ye *City of God*, & under its more Direct and Shining Influences" (p. 81). Indeed, in Mather's early millenarian theories, the spatial distance between the City of God and the City of Man would be a hindrance during the millennium, just as a similar distance would encumber travel in Mather's own lifetime.

In fact, because of their geographic separation from the center of Christ's kingdom in Judea, the Saved Nations would benefit less from the divine dispensations and therefore require more prodding and shoving about than the Changed Saints on earth in Mather's later eschatology: "The *Rulers* of the New World," Mather surmised, "may have more occasion to Employ a *Rod of Iron* among those *Nations*, and *break them to Shivers as the Vessels of a Potter*, and *Execute Punishments upon them*" ("PT," p. 81). During Christ's reign on earth, Mather pleaded in *Theopolis Americana*, "it will be impossible, for the *Holy People*, and the *Teachers* and *Rulers* of the *Reformed World* in the other *Hemisphere*, to leave *America* unvisited. . . . Can you think, that *America*, shall be nothing but *Miery Places and Marishes, given to Salt*? By no means. O wide *Atlantick*, Thou shalt not stand in the way as any Hindrance of those Communications! . . . *They that are of the City*, shall have something to do here for Him. O NEW-ENGLAND, There is Room to hope, That thou also shalt belong to the CITY" (pp. 48, 50).

Clearly, then, Cotton Mather and his confreres did not contest Mede's exclusion of America by claiming the City of God for New England alone. As Mather put it, "It was never intended, that the Church of our Lord, should be confined always within the Dimensions of *Strabo's* Cloak; and that, *All the World*, should always be no more, than it was, when *Augustus* taxed it" (*TA*, p. 46; see also *MCA* 1.1.2). Instead, Mather and others countered Mede by expanding the boundaries of Christ's geography of salvation beyond the Old World into the American hemisphere, thus safeguarding New England's membership in Christ's millennial kingdom. The inevitable problems attending the harmony of Mather's early literalist hermeneutics disappeared, however, when the Changed Saints in his later eschatology attained their immortality and perfection by miraculous intervention from above (the Rapture). Now the Saints were no longer victims of space, time, or geography. It no longer mattered whether they lived in the restored Jerusalem in the old or in Salem in the new hemisphere, for the Raised Saints in the New Jerusalem above dispensed their spiritual munition indiscriminately to the Changed Saints below, no matter what hemisphere they called their home or what lineage they claimed for their ancestry.

To the modern reader, such hermeneutical niceties may reek of the mildew of Puritan antiquarianism. However trivial it may appear to us today, Cotton Mather's placement of the New Jerusalem in the clouds above Judea and his views on the Jewish nation open up vistas that have gone unnoticed. The disciples of Perry Miller and of Sacvan Bercovitch trace the origin of the American sense of mission and manifest destiny to the Puritans' penchant for presenting New England as the typological abrogation of the prophetic New Jerusalem. Unquestionably, Puritan typology, with its figural use of language, played a central role in nurturing a uniquely American identity that came to full flower in the nineteenth century; but in divorcing language from doctrine, critics have fundamentally misunderstood the Puritan position on such crucial issues as the restoration of the Jews, America's millennial role, and the function and location of the New Jerusalem. Perhaps the Mather family provides a good case in point and Cotton Mather's frequently cited *Theopolis Americana* a good testing ground. For when scholars argue that the chiliasm of the Mathers " 'clearly and emphatically expressed the belief that . . . New England was certain to be the site of the New Jerusalem,' " they seem to mistake what Nicholas Noyes calls the *"Analogical sence"* and *"Analogical Accommodation"* of the Old Testament prophetic types for New England's literal abrogation of God's promises to his people.[45] Future studies of Puritan typology must reconcile this discrepancy and assess how the Puritans' vision of Christ's Bride and of his reign in the two Jerusalems affected their sense of purpose and mission in their lone wilderness outpost of America.

FOUR

When Shall These Things Be?
Cotton Mather's Chronometry
of the Prophecies

The question of biblical prophecies and their verity took on new significance in Cotton Mather's day beyond the millenarian penchant for establishing chrono-metrical timetables to foretell the future. As Richard H. Popkin has demon-strated, however, the study of the prophecies could be a double-edged sword in the hands of zealous abettors who chose to ignore the textual and herme-neutical problems of the Bible.[1] For if the philological criticism of Isaac de La Peyrère, Thomas Hobbes, Benedict de Spinoza, and Richard Simon was correct, then the text of the Bible was plagued by hopelessly flawed compilations and inaccurate transcriptions of copies no longer extant.[2] No doubt Spinoza (1632–77), the great Jewish scholar of the Netherlands, spoke in 1670 for all those who concerned themselves with problems of textual transmission: "The history of the Bible is not so much imperfect as untrustworthy: the foundations are not only too scanty for building upon, but are also unsound." Consequently, "If any-one pays attention to the way in which all the histories and precepts in these five books [Pentateuch] are set down promiscuously and without order, with no regard for dates . . . he will easily, I say, discern that all the materials were promiscuously collected and heaped together," as were the remaining books of the Old Testament (*Tractatus*, ch. VIII, p. 120; ch. IX, p. 135).

Like his French colleague Richard Simon, Sir Isaac Newton was keenly aware of the indelible dilemma surrounding the Bible as a textual document and was greatly concerned about how such problems might affect the authority of the Bible and its traditional claim to be the revealed Word of God. Newton freely shared his distress in his posthumously published *Observations*, where he pin-pointed many textual corruptions (pt. I, ch. I). Given such irreparable damage to biblical authority, what could he do? Spinoza and before him Hobbes had been unable to avoid spurning the Bible's claim of exclusivity. At best, they argued, the Book of Books retained its value for its moral teachings, but as an ancient document of prophecies it was little more than the history of the Israelites.

Newton, however, could not dismiss the Bible so readily. For if God's will was made manifest throughout the ages through his prophetic spirit encapsu-lated in the Scriptures, then the harmony of Daniel's prophecies with those of John's Revelation, for instance, could reliably measure the extent to which the revealed Word of God remained unhampered by problems of textual transmission. Newton's unswerving loyalty to the prophecies in the face of his own philological challenge to the biblical texts is particularly revealing: "The authority of the Prophets is divine," he avowed, "and comprehends the sum of religion, reckoning *Moses* and the Apostles among the Prophets." Textual problems notwithstanding, he went on, the Bible contains God's "instructions for keeping this covenant . . . and predictions of things to come." All true believers could therefore adhere to the revealed will of God by observing the dictums of the prophets, for "the predictions of things to come relate to the state of the Church in all ages," and "to reject his Prophecies, is to reject the Christian religion," which "is founded upon his Prophecy concerning the *Messiah*" (pt. I, pp. 14, 15, 25).

Biblical prophecies were therefore of central importance not only to the millenarians of the day but also to those who desperately searched for verifiable means to uphold against the hermeneutical challenge the revealed Word of God—nay, the legitimacy of Christianity itself. Naturally, good men throughout the ages had devoted themselves to the study of the prophecies, but their endeavor was only too often misled by their zeal to predict the End. As Newton put the issue squarely: "The folly of Interpreters has been, to foretel times and things by this Prophecy [Revelation], as if God designed to make them Prophets. By this rashness they have not only exposed themselves, but brought the Prophecy also into contempt." Instead of gratifying "men's curiosities" of things to come, God intended for the prophecies to be validated post facto, after the historical event had occurred: "For the event of things predicted many ages before, will then be a convincing argument that the world is governed by providence" (pt. II, pp. 251–52). Any other use of the prophecies was a dangerous undertaking and could not but court dissension among the various expositors, and even within the church itself.

It is therefore not surprising that predictions about Christ's Second Coming were central to millenarian exegeses of biblical prophecies, for not only did they establish the prophetic timetables of the church, whose historical development could post facto validate the accuracy of the prophecies, but they also were intrinsic proof that no matter how flawed the surviving editions of the Bible, God had seen to it that his prophetic spirit did not diminish. Small wonder that the question of the Messiah's return had engaged myriads of eschatologists in the latter ages, just as it had the apostles in the days of his Crucifixion. When could man expect the risen Savior in glory and when the dissolution of the world? Assuredly, Christ had spoken of ominous portents from which his watchmen could infer the imminence of the Second Coming (Matthew 24; Luke 21), but he had also warned his disciples, "It is not for you to knowe the times or the seasons, which the Father hath put in his owne power" (Acts 1:7). Naturally, such caveats were intended to curb the more zealous millenarians, whose impatience to unveil the mysteries of the Bible could easily lead them astray.[3]

Cotton Mather, too, was highly aware of such warnings, but he knew better than to be discouraged. To him, Christ's stricture applied not to the millennialists of the latter days but to the apostles themselves, whose task was not to inquire into the time of the Second Coming but to preach the gospel among the nations. Mather contextualized this issue for all those who mistook Christ's reprimand of the apostles as evidence that all eschatological studies were to be discouraged: "It was none of their *Present Business* to Ask after the *Times* and *Seasons.*" Rather, the apostles' *"Present Business* was to go, and be *Witnesses unto Him,* and by the *Testimony* Acquaint and Convince the World, *Who He was,* and *What* had been *done* by Him, and *What* He would have them to do; Not, *When* His Coming again was to be look'd for" (*T*, p. 323).[4] Christ did not reveal the time for his return to the early Christians because "It would have broke the *Hearts* of them" to know how long their suffering would have to continue (*TLF*, p. 24; see also 23–25). That sober inquiries into the time were indeed lawful and opportune Mather was more than convinced. In fact, God had given to the postexilic Jews Daniel's prophecy of the Seventy Weeks (9:24–27), which provided his people with clear indications about when the birth of the Messiah was to be expected (*TLF*, p. 24).[5] Furthermore, God had given to man a whole host of Scriptures from which the watchmen of Christ could always infer where in God's chronometry they were.

This did not mean that many expositors had not been thoroughly mistaken in their calculations and incurred, as a consequence, the scoffers' ridicule and censure. But such errors in judgment could hardly deter the faithful, nor were such blunders proof that only God knew the times and the seasons. Rather, the miscalculations of the learned could serve as a beacon for those who were to come hereafter: "The mistakes which they fell into," Mather was quick to point out, "may rather *Advantage* us, than *Discourage* us; and prove so many *Sea-marks* to prevent our *Ship-wreck*" (*TLF*, p. 23).[6] The study of the sacred prophecies was more than a mere theological exercise for gentlemen of leisure, because apocalyptic studies afforded man the greatest of benefits: they not only allowed him to find out where he was in God's eternal plan but could also incite him to action—could even bring about the accomplishment of the prophecies. Even Newton insisted that the prophecies were "not only for predicting but also for effecting a recovery and re-establishment of the long-lost truth, and setting up a kingdom wherein dwells righteousness" (pt. II, p. 252). This millenarian zeal, of course, had informed the Fifth Monarchists in Cromwell's time, when such men as Thomas Venner, William Aspinwall, John Clarke, and a whole host of the misguided fringe almost single-handedly took on the government to bring about the reign of Christ (see *T*, p. 343) as foretold in Daniel's prophecy (2:31–44, 7:1–28). This Protestant militancy, however, did not effect its desired end, nor did Christ appear in the clouds of heaven in mid-century England. If anything, such revolutionary agitation contributed to the collapse of Cromwell's government and the restoration of Charles II to the British throne. Despite the general disdain for such zealotry, the millenarian hope of specific segments of society was never fully extinguished. It was kept alive largely by ministers who reassessed the prophecies and settled on a later date for the Second Coming.[7]

Cotton Mather was no exception. Even though he came to maturity long after the Interregnum, he was not wholly unaffected by the revolutionary zeal of his fellow millenarians in England. On the eve of New England's witchcraft excesses, Mather betrayed his own Fifth-Monarchist hope—hope that had propelled him to action during the Glorious Revolution in New England (1689): "In a Word, An Acquaintance with *Prophecy's* may have more than a little Influence upon the *Accomplishments* of those *Prophecies*. . . . Thus, if at this Day, any Potent Prince, would suffer himself to be Convinced, *That this were the Time for Distresses to be brought upon the state holders of Antichrist;* how much Vigour and Conduct might the Affayrs of such a Prince be thence inspired with?" (*TLF*, pp. 47–48). Mather certainly knew what he was talking about, for his own leadership in the overthrow of Governor Andros (18 Apr. 1689) had catapulted young Cotton into the religious and political limelight in Boston while his father was absent in England to negotiate the Second Charter.[8] But unlike his more radical counterparts in Old England, Mather felt that such political dispensations were fit only for kings and princes. His own impatience to hasten the Coming of the Lord is apparent in his allusion to William and Mary, who had thwarted in the nick of time the Antichristian plot of James II and Louis XIV ("that French Leviathan") to bring the British Isles again under pontifical sway:

> Doubtless, their present MAJESTIES of Great BRITAIN, have seen cause to Consider on the Praediction of the Incomparable JURIEU . . . before the Late Revolutions in *England*, which have so Eminently made good that Praediction; *God has placed you* (says he, speaking of the then Prince and Princess of *Orange*) *for Miracles in Israel, and for Signs, that he ha's intended your Highnesses to be the Principal Instruments of that Grand Deliverance, which He hath prepared for His Church, when the storm shall be over.* (*TLF*, p. 48)[9]

Not every theologian, however versed in the Scriptures, was as eminently qualified as the Huguenot Pierre Jurieu (1637–1713), whose *Balance of the Sanctuary* (1686) had provoked his fellow millenarians to political action. Nor was zeal in and of itself the key to understanding the Word of God. Rather, studies of apocalyptic prophecies "are fittest for those Raised Souls, whose *Heart-strings* are made of a Little Finer *Clay*, than other mens" (*TLF*, p. 46; see also *PN*, pp. 100, 110–11, 249). The very angels themselves, Mather was convinced, assisted such men in an invisible manner and guided them in their studies of the Scriptures. The "*Food* of such Studies is marvellously Scattered all the Bible over; so that you may almost every where, after some *Digging*, throw up some unsuspected Intimations of this kind, whereat you will find impossible to forbear crying out, with some Transport of Soul, *I have found! I have found!*" (*TLF*, p. 46; see also *MC*, pp. 30–32; *TDP*, pp. 32–33).

Naturally, it was easy enough to get carried away in such pursuits, and a long list of almost forgotten fanatics "Like the Honest Old Man upon *Tenderton Steeple*" (*VFH*, p. 13) had done much harm to the study of the prophecies. No doubt Mather knew only too well.[10] Had not young James Franklin derided such misguided prognostications on the front page of Boston's own *New-England*

Courant? *"And inasmuch as such Adventures, which sometimes Captivate whole Herds of the Vulgar, can never be enough expos'd to the publick Scorn* . . . [they] *are enough to check Presumptuous Men in their Aspirations to be wise above that which is written, and (as perpetual Monitors) may serve to remind them, that it is not for them to know the Times and Seasons, which the ETER-NAL has reserv'd in his own Power"* (No. 8, Sept. 18–25, 1721, col. 1–2, p. 1). But if man's "well-Regulated Researches into This Time" were guided by due modesty, Mather countered with all humility, "God may permit us to *Hit Right* in some considerable guesses about the *Time of our Day"* (*MC*, p. 32). Apocalyptic studies were not only lawful, Mather argued, but also required by God, if the watchmen of Christ were to rouse the "Sleepy World" from false security. Thus "for men to hiss at all sober Attempts to Learn, how far we are got on towards the *Rest which Remains for the People of God, in the* **Latter Dayes**, 'tis an affront unto that Holy Spirit of God, who has given us a Prophetical as well as an Historical *Calender* of our Times" (*MC*, p. 31; see also *D* 1:145–47).

The prophetic calendars to which Mather refers were of crucial importance to all millenarians, for they provided the key to calculating God's eternal timescheme. Properly interpreted, they would allow the watchmen of Christ not only to outline the sequence of distinct historical periods but also to determine the end of time from the very beginning. The Reverend Nicholas Noyes of Salem had put it aptly: "If we consider what cognation there is between *History* and *Prophesy*, it will not seem strange. For *Prophesie* is History *antedated*; and History is *Postdated Prophesie*: the same thing is told in both" (*New-Englands Duty and Interest*, p. 43). Much to the chagrin of those millennialists who lived to see their own predictions come to naught, apocalyptic calculations about the exact time of the Second Coming were too often plagued by embarrassing inaccuracies and wishful thinking.

Mather, too, rehearsed such numerological conjectures and, as a result, had to revise his calculations repeatedly. By 1726, however, he had learned to be much more cautious about predicting the exact year of the cosmic event (*T*, pp. 322–23). Previous disappointments about the years 1697 and 1716 and—had Mather lived to see his calculations frustrated a third time—1736 required much more careful reasoning, lest he become the laughingstock of the neighborhood—nay, be dismissed as an enthusiast in the marketplace of hermeneutical ideas. For instance, in his most significant early millenarian sermons and homiletic tracts— *Memorable Providences* (1689), *The Wonderful Works of God Commemorated* (1690), *Things to be Look'd for* (1691), *Preparatory Meditations upon the Day of Judgment* (1692), *A Midnight Cry* (1692), *The Wonders of the Invisible World* (1693), and *Things for a Distressed People to think upon* (1696)—Mather was still arguing that the destruction of Antichrist could be expected in 1697. When 1697 passed and the old world was still lying in corruption, Mather's fervor was curbed, although moderately. While still expecting the End to come daily, he was less given to announcing any specific year in public. Consequently, his sermons between 1698 and 1703 did not project any dates beyond the statement of Christ's sudden return in the clouds of heaven: *Decennium Luctuosum* (1699),

The Faith of the Fathers (1699), *American Tears Upon the Ruines of the Greek Churches* (1701). But while he restrained his tongue in public, his calculations nevertheless continued to flourish in private. Mather's unpublished manuscript treatise "Problema Theologicum" (1703) is perhaps the best exemplum, for it again ventures a new date: 1716. And a whole number of sermons over the next several years blew again the Trumpets of Zion: the preface to *Bonifacius* (1710); *Things to be More Thought upon* (1713); *Menachem* (1716); *The Stone Cut out of the Mountain* (1716), to mention just a few.

With 1716 passing and the Lord still tarrying, Mather again scrutinized his prophetic timetables and reconsidered his evidence. In a letter to a German Pietist missionary in the East Indian Malabar (31 Dec. 1717), Mather shared his characteristic sentiments and asked "whether the Time appointed by GOD for such an Effusion of the Holy Spirit, may quickly come on, & the *Kingdom of GOD be suddenly to appear?* For my part, I do not Know. But that it is not very far off, I do Believe" (*IC*, p. 74).[11] The new date in Mather's premillennialist eschatology was 1736; but this time, Mather was much less given to outright predictions of the year: *Coelestinus* (1723); *Terra Beata* (1726); "Triparadisus," pt. III, sec. xii (1726/27); *The Terror of the Lord* (1727); and *Boanerges* (1727). Mather's "Biblia Americana" perhaps best illustrates the volatile nature of such eschatological endeavors: he never got around to expunging those passages and tables of numerological calculations that had proved wrong. In his old age, while writing his definitive treatise on eschatology, "Triparadisus," Mather had to be much more careful if he wanted to avoid the pitfalls and disappointments that had rendered his earlier calculations suspect: "About the tremendous DAY OF GOD, which will burn up the *Old World* and bring on a *New* One, tis One thing to say, *IT WILL Come Immediately*; Another thing to say, *IT MAY Come Immediately*. The Former I *Dare* not say. The Latter I *Do* say. And Lett the *Sleepy* World be ever so Angry at being disturbed by an *Awakener*, I will do the Part of a *Voice crying in the Wilderness*, and from an *American* Wilderness, and insist upon it; *Repent, For the Kingdome of the Heavens draws very nigh upon us*" (*T*, pp. 322–23). This ambidextrous argument of saying and at once unsaying barely hides Mather's true conviction, one of the most deep-seated impulses behind his ministerial mission, an engine that had propelled him into action during his long, prolific career and a dynamo that had generated numerous sermons fueling countless debates among the members of his Boston "Junto," his private circle of fellow millenarians.[12]

But however circumspect Mather had become in his old age, his chronometry was much bolder and more daring in his younger years. In his early sermons on the subject, he was certain that the Great Sabbatism of Christ could begin in 1697. Following the detailed argument of Thomas Beverley's *Scripture-line of Time* (1684), Mather believed with his English colleague that the binding of the Devil was to be expected "To the End of the Half-time, or to the seventh Trumpet, containing the State of the Reformation, and since to the Expectation of the Witnesses Rising about 1697."[13] Mather's interpretation of Daniel's prophecies of the four empires and the four beasts (2:31–45, 7:1–7), as well as

John's prophecy of the seven-headed hydra (Rev. 11:2–3, 13:1–5), indicated that Antichrist's reign of 1,260 years and the wilderness condition of the church were rapidly drawing to a close. As Mather understood the prophecies, then, Antichrist's last half-time (or 180 years) had begun with the Protestant Reformation of Martin Luther in 1517, when almost half of the pope's Roman Catholic dominions in Europe were wrenched from the influence of the "Beast." His calculations of Antichrist's downfall, furnished in great detail in *Things to be Look'd for*, are indicative of Mather's lifelong penchant: Counting from the fixed date 1517 "makes the Business to be Reasonably and Seasonably Look'd for within a *Score of years*." And "I am verily perswaded," he told his parishioners six years before the expected End in 1697, "A great part of this Assembly may live to see those Blowes given to the *man of Sin*, that shall be more Mortal and more direful Blows, than any that have yet been given him" (*TLF*, pp. 30–31).[14] With such clear evidence of the End at hand, Mather expected the cosmic revolution to occur within his own lifetime.

His calculation largely agreed with that of Joseph Mede, who dated Antichrist's reign from A.D. 456, the year after the dissolution of the old Roman Empire. Genseric the Vandal had just sacked the Eternal City and appointed his vassal rulers of Rome for the next twenty years. Mede therefore dated the beginning of Antichrist's 1260-year rulership over the defunct empire from A.D. 456 and, through a simple addition, arrived at 1716 as the *annus mirabilis*. Mather, of course, did not rule out this later date. Nevertheless, the year 1697 seemed infinitely more desirable in the early 1690s, for it coincided with his speculation about the fall of the Ottoman Empire (the Second Woe Trumpet), which then lay in its last throes. Interestingly enough, even though the world did not come to its end then, Mather's speculations about the fall of the Turks came true in 1698, when Prince Eugene of Savoy and his Holy League crushed the Turkish invaders who besieged Vienna and sealed their fall in the Treaty of Carlowitz (1699).[15]

Yet Mather did not have to turn to Europe for evidence that the Coming of Christ was surely imminent. The astonishing acts of witchcraft in his own Boston neighborhood and New England at large showed all the signs that the reign of Antichrist at Rome and Satan's dominion over the world were hastening toward their inevitable termination. "It is plain," Mather recorded in his *Wonders of the Invisible World*, "that until the second coming of our Lord the Devil must have a time of plagueing the World." Satan's "Reign is to continue until the time when our Lord himself shall *take to himself his great Power and Reign*. Then 'tis that the *Devil* shall hear the Son of God swearing with loud Thunders against him, *Thy time shall now be no more!*" (pp. 72–73; see also pp. 89–90). Since the "wily dragon" himself had only a short while longer until the expiration of the reign of Antichrist, "the Devils *Eldest Son*" (*WIW*, p. 89), Satan, would naturally try his best to afflict God's Saints more than he had ever done before. If, therefore, Satan's descent on New England seemed more frequent and more horrid in the 1690s than in former ages, it did not at all come as a surprise—at least not to those who truly understood the chronometrical signs of the End:

> Toward the *End* of his *Time* the *Descent* of the Devil in *Wrath* upon the World will produce more *woful Effects*, than what have been in *former Ages*. The dying Dragon, will bite more cruelly and sting more bloodily than ever he did before. . . . A little before we [Saints] step into Heaven, the *Devil* thinks with himself, *My time to abuse that Saint is now but short; what Mischief I am to do that Saint, must be done quickly, if at all; he'l shortly be out of my Reach for ever*. And for this cause he will now fly upon us with the Fiercest Efforts and Furies of his *Wrath*. (*WIW*, pp. 72, 83, and passim)

Mather felt certain he was walking on solid ground here; his studies of the invisible world had long occupied his attention and had produced some surprising revelations about the work of the Devil. Besides, Mather's public exorcisms, performed in his own home on Martha Goodwin, Mercy Short, and Margaret Rule a little before that old "Prince of Darkness" began to manifest himself throughout the Bay Colony, had given him firsthand experience and incontrovertible evidence of the power of Satan and his witches.[16] Likewise, his consultations with the Salem judges and his collection of documents to be incorporated in New England's official justification of the witchcraft proceedings, *Wonders of the Invisible World*, all evinced that Satan's attacks on New England were far from being hallucinations.[17] That the Devil would single out New England in his last stand against the Almighty seemed quite logical: The churches of Christ in the New World seemed so free from corruption, their pastors and teachers so holy and devout in their duties, their flocks so regenerate, that those "who mistook Sir *Thomas Moor's* UTOPIA" for a truly existing country might find "a Truth in their Mistake; *New-England* was a true *Utopia*" (*WIW*, pp. 13–14).[18] Even Richard Baxter, the renowned English Presbyterian and patriarchal friend of the Mathers, agreed that Satan was still palpable, notwithstanding Hobbes's disarming ratiocinations against energumenical phenomena: "*If any are Scandalized, that* New-England, *a place of as serious Piety, as any I can hear of, under Heaven, should be troubled so much with Witches; I think, 'tis no wonder: Where will the Devil show most Malice, but where he is hated, and hateth most*" (in *WIW*, p. 10).[19] It therefore appeared logical to believe that Satan, resenting Christ's encroachments on the Devil's formerly unchallenged territory in America, would do his utmost to frustrate such efforts, "Wherefore the Devil is now making one Attempt more upon us," Mather was convinced, "an Attempt more Difficult, more Surprizing, more snarl'd with unintelligible Circumstances than any that we have hitherto Encountred; an Attempt so *Critical*, that if we get well through, we shall soon Enjoy *Halcyon* Days with all the *Vultures* of Hell *Trodden under our Feet*" (*WIW*, p. 16).

The millenarian overtones in Mather's assessment of Satan's war on New England are not at all unique among his sermons of the period. In fact, eschatological speculations among ministers and laymen of the time were quite common. The sermons of Increase Mather, John Eliot, John Davenport, Ephraim Huit, William Hooke, Judge Samuel Sewall, and Nicholas Noyes, to mention only some of the most prominent figures, were all charged with apocalyptic expectations of the End.[20] Even Lieutenant Governor William Stoughton, in charge of the Bay Colony while Increase Mather was negotiating in England for the colony's Second Charter (1692) and for a new governor, gave his official stamp of approval on the proceedings in the witchcraft trials and complimented young Cotton for his acumen: "*such* [is] *your clear discerning of Divine Providences and Periods, now running on apace towards their Glorious Issues in the World; and finally, such your good News of* The Shortness of the Devil's Time, *that all Good Men must needs desire, the making of this your Discourse publick to the World; and will greatly rejoyce, that the* Spirit of the Lord *has thus enabled you to* lift up a Standard *against the Infernal Enemy, that hath been* coming in like a Flood upon us" (in *WIW*, pp. 5–6; see *D* 1:153–54). If nothing else, Stoughton's endorsement indicates that the political leadership of Massachusetts stood firmly behind the ministers' millenarian response to the events of the time.

In light of this evidence, it is probable that such conjectures about the End fostered a climate of opinion that may have kindled the witchcraft hysteria in New England. Of course, it is common knowledge that belief in the power of witches and devils was widespread among New Englanders at the time, for they found it inconceivable to believe in the redemptive power of Christ without also believing in the dark workings of his adversary. Moreover, if indeed the ministers published from their pulpits the conviction that Satan's time was running short, that the Devil was therefore afflicting with might and main God's churches in New England, it is not at all improbable that the parishioners grew more sensitive, their awareness more heightened, to any signs of deviltry in the neighborhood. To be sure, we can only surmise the effects of such sermons on their audience; nor is there time and space here to investigate the various ramifications of such an argument. But if we listen to the din of the arguments and picture the Devil and his demons come alive in haunting images and evocative sermons of the period, we might look afresh at Robert Calef's old sneer that New England's ministry may have had a hand in conjuring up the Devil.[21] We need only read over the pages of Mather's *Memorable Providences* and his *Wonders of the Invisible World* to discover how the Devil was omnipresent in New England. Young Cotton warned his audience in 1689, in 1692, and even in 1704:

> Christian, There are *Devils*: and so many of them too, that sometimes a *Legion* of them are spar'd for the vexation of *one man*. The *Air* in which we breathe is full of them. . . . There are Troops of *Tempters* on every side of thee. *Awake*, O Soul, Awake, Those *Philistines* of Hell *are upon thee*. . . . The *Sovereign* GOD hath . . . confined the *Fallen Spirits* unto this *Atmosphere*; but with their *Confinement*, they have so much *Liberty*, that until the *Second coming* of the *Messiah* into this lower world, they may range

and rove about, and molest the poor Children of men. Our *Air* is fill'd with them, as with *Flies* in *Mid-Summer*. We draw our breath in the *place of Dragons*. . . . O ungodly Sinner, If thy Soul expire in ill Terms with Heaven, tell me, I pray, how tis possible it should get safe to Heaven? It must pass through a Region that swarms with Devils which are waiting to sieze upon it. (*MP*, pt. III, p. 16; *AC*, p. 6; see also *WIW*, pp. 50–85)

If, therefore, the oyers and terminers in the Salem trials were guided by similar millenarian vistas, we need not marvel at the ruthless proceedings of the Salem judges in their effort, as Mather put it, "to countermine the whole PLOT of the Devil, against *New-England*, in every Branch of it" (*WIW*, p. 3).[22]

Despite the upheaval of the witchcraft trials and the damage they did to the reputation of New England's ministry—to the Mathers in particular—Cotton Mather never relinquished his belief in the power of the Devil and his witches, nor did he change his conviction that Satan's afflictions of New England had something to do with the impending millennium. Even if Christ did not set up his Fifth Monarchy in 1697, and even if 1716 did not bring on the revolution of the Saints, Cotton Mather never gave up hope that he would witness the Sabbatism during his own lifetime. Seen on a cosmic plane, the failure of predictions throughout the centuries contributed to the last signs before the End: the general stupor of mankind in the eye of the storm. "There have been *the Devices of Satan* in such things," Mather told his audience in "Triparadisus," "to strengthen the General Security of the World, and furnish & hearten the *Scoffers of the Last Days*, with Matter for even an *Inextinguishable Laughter*" (p. 342). Allegorically considered, the lamps of the Five Foolish Virgins extinguished—like their faith in the sudden return of the master at midnight—typified the whole world caught in a dead sleep at the Messiah's return: "If there should be a Grant of any more *Signs* there would be as little notice taken of them," Mather quipped, "as there has been of those that have already been granted. The foolish, and flouting, & bruitish, & short-winded Way of passing a Sentence upon *Extraordinary Descents from the Invisible World*, which we have seen in our Days, is a sufficient Indication, how much the most Shocking *Signs of the Times* are lost upon us" (*T*, p. 342).

The failure of calculations did not mean that there had been any inaccurate prophecies, Mather was persuaded, nor would such setbacks cast doubt on the divine inspiration of the Book of Books, as some of the more vocal Deists—like Thomas Woolston, Thomas Chubb, Matthew Tindal, and Anthony Collins—argued it did.[23] Rather, such failures were an indication that man did not fully understand how to interpret the epoch of Christ's return (*T*, pp. 324–25). Certainly, many Judeo-Christian traditions could assist the watchmen of Christ in their computations. The Apocalypse of Elias the Prophet, for one, enjoyed a wide popularity among millenarians throughout the ages. According to this talmudic tradition, the horological and chronometrical history of the world corresponds to the six creative days of God, by which precedents "the Continuance of this World, is limited unto *Six Thousand* Years" (*T*, p. 325), the first two thousand years being the period of desolation; the second, the period of the Torah; and the third, the messianic era. Here was a good paradigm, and the same hexameral tradition was accepted by Hippolytus Martyr, Barnabas, Irenaeus, Lactantius, Cyprian, Augustine, and many, many others in the early church.[24]

Mather was rather disappointed with this venerable tradition, for "there are still *Two Hundred and Seventy* Years" left to fulfill the last millennium of the messianic era, which would run out in the year 2000. "Behold, what we have here, to spoil our Praesumption of so *many Years to come*" (T, p. 326). Mather was hardly satisfied with allowing the old world to continue for that many more years. The Samaritan Pentateuch, he pointed out, was much more accurate than any of the much later versions of the Jewish Talmud and projected a much earlier date, according to which "the World will be, in A.C. 1736. just *Six Thousand Years* old" (T, p. 327).[25] Even Increase Mather had held, in his *Dissertation, Wherein the Strange Doctrine*, that the chronology of the ancient Samaritan Pentateuch is infinitely more accurate than the Torah of the Diaspora, whose chronology differs by 311 years.[26] So, too, the "Elegant System" of Pierre Jurieu, in *Accomplishment of the Prophecies* (1686, 1687), pointed to the typological tradition of God's six creative days as an indication that the "Little Stone" in Daniel's prophecy might become the "Great Mountain" of Christ's Church Universal in 1736. The old Separatist minister at Amsterdam, Henry Ainsworth, had furnished a similar key to calculating the six ages of the world in his *Annotations upon the Five Bookes of Moses* (1627):

> We may compare with these *Six Days*, the *Six Ages* of the World, as they are manifestly distinguished in Scripture. The FIRST from *Adam* to *Noahs* Flood; which was of *Ten* Generations; This is called, *The Old World*. The Second, From the *Flood* unto *Abraham*; which also was of *Ten* Generations. At Him the New Testament begins the Genealogy of CHRIST. The Third, From *Abraham* to *David, Fourteen* Generations. The Fourth from *David*, to the Captivity of *Babylon, Fourteen* Generations. The Fifth, from the Captivity of *Babylon* unto CHRIST, *Fourteen* Generations. All which are so reckoned by the Holy Ghost. The Sixth, is the Age after CHRIST, called, *The Last Days*, and, *The Last Time*. After which *remains the Rest* [or, Sabbatism,] *for the People of GOD*; to begin at our Lords Second Coming & to endure forever. (In T, p. 327)[27]

Such a projection appeared infinitely wiser to Mather than that which Muhammad had given in his Alcoran, for in Islamic tradition, the Day of Judgment was yet fifty thousand years off (T, p. 328). Even the Christian world, as Mather perceived the signs of his time, acted as if all the visions had failed and the End were truly as far off as Muhammad had predicted: "I would as far as I can," Mather countered impatiently, "do my Part, by crying, FIRE, awaken a World, whose *Delilahs* had dozed it; and tho' I can't prove that IT SHALL, yett challenge any Living to prove, that it SHALL NOT, be in less than *Ten Years* upon us"—that is, in 1736 (T, p. 328). Postponing the Day of Judgment as far into the future as Muhammad was believed to have done would certainly lull the world into a dead sleep. Mather believed that the prophecies of the Bible, no matter how imperfect its transmitted copies, were infinitely more accurate, its interpreters infinitely more inspired, than any Alcoran could ever claim.

Joseph Mede's *Clavis Apocalyptica* (1627, 1643), William Whiston's *Accomplishment of Scripture Prophecies* (1708), and Governor William Burnet's *Essay on Scripture-Prophecy* (1724) had offered a much more convincing scheme, Mather thought, than any that had yet been developed.[28] In his *Clavis*, Mede had argued that Daniel's prophecy of the four empires—represented by the various metals of Nebuchadnezzar's golden-headed statue (Dan. 2:31–45)—was synchronous with the four beasts mentioned in Dan. 7:1–7. Accordingly, Daniel's prophecies signified the succession of four distinct empires—Babylon, Medo-Persia, Greece, and Rome—at whose destruction Christ would return and set up his millennial kingdom. Moreover, the ten toes of Nebuchadnezzar's statue found their correlative in the ten horns of Daniel's fourth beast.[29] These ten horns, as Mede saw it, were identical with the ten horns of John's seven-headed hydra (Rev. 13:1–5), whose composite body (part leopard, bear, lion, and dragon) related to the same description of the four beasts in Daniel 7. Likewise, the ten horns here spoken of signified ten kingdoms, which would arise out of the ashes of the Roman Empire. These kingdoms, however, would be ruled not by independent monarchs but by a "little horn" (Dan. 7:8), which would exercise dominion over the ten sovereigns for the space of 42 prophetical months or 1,260 years (Rev. 11:2, 3, 13:5).[30] Most Protestant millenarians of the time agreed with Martin Luther that Daniel's little horn and John's hydra were none other than Antichrist and his Papal See at Rome, whose seven hills were here represented by the seven heads of John's dragon (*T*, pp. 328–29 and passim).

For an understanding of Mather's chronometry concerning the reign of Antichrist, a brief summary is here in order (see Figure): According to John's Revelation, Mather and his colleagues argued, Antichrist was given power for "a thousand two hundred and threescore dayes," that is, "fourty and two moneths" (Rev. 11:2–3, 13:5), during which period Antichrist was to sit at Rome. These prophetic days, however, were not literal days but years and were to be counted according to Ezekiel's prophetic time scheme (4:6). Accordingly, Antichrist's rule was to last for 1,260 years. During this period, the Woman (the church) with "two wings of a great Eagle" was to be in a wilderness condition and "nourished for a time, and times, and halfe a time, from the face of the serpent" (Rev. 12:14; see also Dan. 7:25) trying to destroy the Woman. Through a simple equation of these prophetic time periods, that is, of Antichrist's reign on earth and of the Woman's wilderness condition, Mather arrived at the following calculation, which Mede, Huit, Whiston, Burnet, and even Newton were employing as well: 1,260 years = 3½ "times." If the former figure is divided by the latter, we arrive at 360 years per "time" period. Thus, the "time, and times, and halfe a time" for Antichrist's reign on earth and the Woman's wilderness condition respectively equaled 360 years, 720 years, and 180 years, increments of prophetic time that Mather sought to align with specific secular and ecclesiastical events in history.[31]

COTTON MATHER'S CHRONOMETRY OF THE PROPHECIES

1260 + 75 years (Dan. 12: 11, 12)

1260 + 75 years (Dan. 12: 11, 12)

Woman's Wilderness Condition (1260 years)

Antichrist's Reign (1260 years)

Woman's Wilderness Condition (1260 years)

Antichrist's Reign (1260 years)

GRANDEUR 720 years   DECLINE 180 years

| Woman's Labor | Woman's Rest | RISE 360 years | | | GRANDEUR 720 years | | DECLINE 180 years | | | | |

476											1811
456										1791	
476									1736		
								1716			

| AD 33 | 313 | 456 | 476 | 816 | 1517 | 1536 | 1697 | 1716 | 1736 | 1791 | 1811 |

| 280 years | 142 years | | | | | | | | | | |

Christ's Resurrection

Constantine's Baptism

Fall of Last Roman Emperor (W) Romulus Augustulus

Antichrist's Decline 180 years (Mather's early Eschatology)

Pause before Conflagration

CHRONOLOGY OF THE SAMARITAN PENTATEUCH

6,000 years of human history

Fall of Roman Empire (455) Antichrist's Reign begins (456); 10 Kingdoms begin to rise

Charlemagne's Death (814) Antichrist gains full control over secular and ecclesiastical affairs of 10 Kingdoms

Luther's Reformation begins

Protestant Reformation in full sway

Antichrist's Fall expected

| | | | | | | | | 1716 | 1736 | | |
| | | | | | | 1697 | | | | | |

Antichrist loses 1/3 of his Estates

BC 4264

Synchronizing the prophetic time schemes of Daniel and Revelation, Mather could fix the *"Three States"* of Antichrist's *"Rise," "Grandeur,"* and *"Decline"* (*T*, p. 336) and ultimately determine the approximate year of Antichrist's fall at the coming of the conflagration. What now remained to be determined, as Mather saw it, was the fixed date from which the prophetic period of 1,260 years was to be counted: "Now, if we can with Certainty fix the *Epocha*, for these dreadful M.CC.LX. Years, we may certainly know, when they have their Expiration" (*T*, p. 334). For once that crucial date was firmly established, Mather could easily ascertain the beginning of the millennium.

Mather's study of the rise and fall of the Roman Empire led him to the year 455, the year when the Vandal ruler Genseric invaded Italy and sacked the seven-hilled city, and to the celebrated *Definition of Chalcedon* (451), which conferred papal primacy on the See of Rome and established the pontiff as *"Caput Ecclesiarum."* With this Archimedian fulcrum established, Mather was able to apply his lever: Beginning with A.D. 456, which marked the dissolution of the Roman Empire and the rise of ten separate kingdoms in its place, Mather arrived through a simple addition of 360 years (the "time" of Antichrist's *"Rise"*) at the year 816, almost coinciding with Charlemagne's death in 814. At this point the sovereign power of Pope Leo III, Mather believed, was fully established when Charlemagne's son Louis I (the Pious) relinquished to the Roman See the imperial prerogative to veto papal elections. With this final controlling device removed, Mather argued, the pontiff became supreme ruler over the secular and ecclesiastical estates.[32] This second period of Antichrist's reign marked his *"Grandeur"* and was to terminate 720 years ("times") later, in 1536, when the Protestant Reformation was in full sway in England. The final period of Antichrist, his *"Decline,"* could thus be dated from this historic moment, and in 180 years ("half a time")—that is, in c. 1716—the destruction of Antichrist could be expected to occur.

The year A.D. 456 could be ascertained in yet another way, Mather avowed. For if the fall of the Roman Empire ushered in the rise of Antichrist, then the rise of the church and its "wilderness condition," also encompassing 1,260 days/years, could also be linked to that auspicious year:

From the Ascension of our LORD, until the Emperour *Constantine* became a Christian, the Church is represented as a *Travailing Woman*. And there now ran just as many *Years*, as there are *Days*, from the *Conceiving* to the *Travailing* of a Woman with Child; that is to say, *Two hundred & Eighty*. From A.C. 33 to A.C. 313.—It will take some Time for a Woman after her Delivery, to be in a Condition for Transportation into a *Wilderness*. This Time was, while the *Roman Eagle* has *Two* Mighty *Wings*; the *Eastern* and the *Western* Empire: A space of *One hundred & fourty* two Years. The *Left Wing* was then lost; and the *Woman* was dropt unto the Earth; A.C. 456. From this Time she is to continue in the *Wilderness*, for M.CC.LX. *Days*, or Years; which again brings us to M.DCC.XVI. (*T*, pp. 336–37)

As the cabal of Mather and his fellow millenarians unveiled this mystery, then, the prophecies of Daniel and Revelation could be linked with clearly identifiable periods and events in human history. Even Newton had said so in his *Observations* when he employed Daniel's prophecies as the key for unlocking the mystery of John's Apocalypse: "The predictions of things to come relate to the state of the Church in all ages: and amongst the old Prophets, *Daniel* is most distinct in order of time, and easiest to be understood: and therefore in those things which relate to the last times, he must be made the key to the rest" (pt. I, pp. 15; see also pp. 16–23). Millennialists could also employ their timetables in defense of revealed religion (as Sir Isaac had done in private); they could use their tables as potent weapons against the new philological hermeneutics of Grotius, of Hobbes, of Spinoza, of Simon, of Collins, for whom the hopelessly flawed compilations of biblical texts rendered obnoxious any assertions about the prophetic spirit governing political events foretold in the Bible. Chronometrical timetables could also be employed against the coterie of Deist scientists so prominent in the Royal Society in the second decade of the eighteenth century. To them the antiquated argument of God's special, miraculous providence continually intervening in human affairs flatly contradicted the perfection of the "Divine Machine" that, once established on firm laws, ran all on its own. Even as early as the 1680s Thomas Burnet had established rules to distinguish between purely natural and miraculous causes in nature and had helped to pave the way for the spread of Deism: "We must not flie to miracles, where Man and Nature are sufficient," for "it argues a defect of Wisdom in all Oeconomies to employ more and greater means than are sufficient."[33] Reason sufficed to infer the eternal laws of nature; enlightened scholars could no longer pay serious attention to the claptrap of prophetic history in the face of scientific advances.[34]

Such mighty opposition coming from the prestigious confreres of the Royal Society could not be simply ignored. It was therefore imperative that chronometrical conjectures by well-intentioned defenders of the orthodox faith not jeopardize their transcendent mission by rendering frivolous their sacred endeavor. Cotton Mather's own efforts had been thwarted often enough when his speculations did not fully correspond with actual historical dates, or with the dates that Christian tradition had attached to specific occurrences. For example, he argued that the baptism of Constantine the Great, the first Christian emperor of Rome, had occurred in 313. This date correlates neither with modern historiography (which places Constantine's baptism in 336/7) nor with the fifth-century Christian legend that Pope Sylvester I had baptized Constantine in 324.

But Mather could not well afford to prolong the pregnancy of the Woman beyond the 280 prophetic days/years that he had allotted to the gestation of Christ's church. Consequently, his calculations required some juggling and readjusting if he wanted to link prophetic events and their unfolding with significant geopolitical occurrences such as the baptism of Constantine the Great. Counting, then, from Christ's resurrection in 33, Mather added 280 years (allotted to the Woman's pregnancy) and arrived at 313. But he was still a long while from the crucial date of 456, the year that marked the beginning of Antichrist's reign. Mather was attentive to this incongruence, for it would have extended the pregnancy of the *"Travailing Woman"* to a period far exceeding the nine months commonly assigned to such labor. As a result, he developed an explanation to account for the remaining 142 prophetic days, which he called the Woman's rest after giving birth before she could be transported into the wilderness (Rev. 12:1, 6; see also "BA"). At the end of this interlude, the *"Left Wing"* (i.e., the Western Empire) of the *"Roman Eagle"* was permanently lost, "and the *Woman* was dropt unto the Earth; A.C. 456." This year, then, marked the beginning of the church's wilderness condition and the concomitant rise of Antichrist, who was to reign until his 1,260 years were up in 1716.

Unfortunately, this *annus mirabilis* came and went; vice remained triumphant and virtue veiled; the old, sinful world still turned as from the beginning of time. The only remarkable incident near that date was the demise of that "Old French Leviathan" Louis XIV, who died 1 September 1715.[35] Even though Mather must have been chagrined by his second failure to decipher the revealed will of God accurately, he had already, several months in advance, prepared his parishioners for the inevitable. "The World will not presently come to *This*," Mather lamented in 1715, noting the failure of his "Generous MAXIMS" of piety to effect any greater readiness among the nations "to Embrace One another." "*One Year*" won't bring them to it. But it may be infallibly foretold unto you, God will go on to *Shake all Nations* until they come to *This*. GOD will *Overturn, Overturn, Overturn!* And, O Unrighteous *Nations*, O Foolish People & Unwise; You shall never see *Rest* until you come to *This*" (*SD*, pp. 27–28; see also *PN*, pp. 138–39).

Such repeated disappointments notwithstanding, Mather's confidence in the integrity of his chronometrical schemes was never seriously shaken. While working on his "Triparadisus" in 1726/27, Mather could look back on 1716 and taunt his critics without admitting defeat:

> Well; But M.DCC.XVI. is come on; and we see nothing Extraordinary. *The Harvest is Passed, and the Summer is Ended,* and we are still as we were. *All things continue as they were from the Beginning of the Creation.* What are they better, or other than they were, Seven times Ten Years, before the last *Half-Time* of Antichrist, according to our Notion, came unto its Period. The M.CC.LX. Years run out, and the *Man of Sin* Reigning still!— Doubtless, it will now be said, *The Days are Prolonged, and Every Vision faileth.* But I must Reply, *The Days are at hand,* & *the Effect of Every Vision.* (P. 339)

Apparent inconsistencies of this nature never deeply troubled Mather; his resourcefulness in explaining away problems allowed him to bridge the gap between 1716 and 1736, the year on which his millennial hope came to center. For just as he had allowed for a period of prophetic rest between 313 and 456, Mather now argued that a brief interlude could be expected between the fulfillment of one event and the beginning of the next: "When a Period is up, there is not always a Necessity that there should be *No Pause*, between, the *Thing* that has been done, and the *Next Thing* to be done; Especially when the *Next Thing* is not some Great Good for which there has been a Promise of the *Praecise Year* then fixed for it. What I mean, is, That *Some Space* of *Praeparation* for the Following Event, may sometimes be well enough supposed" (*T*, p. 339). This rather revealing circumlocution indicates how Mather could justify, without admitting defeat, why the End had not come in 1716. He now found it opportune to date the beginning of Antichrist's reign not from 456 but from 476, when Genseric's last vassal ruler of Rome, young Emperor Romulus Augustus, was deposed by Odoacer the Hun, marking the end of Rome's 500-year imperial reign.[36] If Antichrist's 1,260-year reign dated from 476, Mather pointed out, "This will bring us to, A.C. 1736." (*T*, p. 339), the year that the Samaritan Pentateuch had also pinpointed as the chronometrical culmination of 6,000 years of human history.[37]

A pause between two chronometrical events seemed to be hinted at in Daniel's prophecies (12:11–12) as well, Mather thought. They suggested that the End might not come immediately after the reign of Antichrist was over. "After the M.CC.LX. Years for the Reign of *Antichrist* are up," Mather cautioned his readers, "we find in the Numbers of *Daniel*, the running on of XXX Years more, making up M.CC.XC. Years; And then the running on, of XLV Years more, making up, M.CCC.XXXV. Years: which *Blessed is he that looks for & comes to.* Now, who can say, what is to be done in the remaining LXXV Years" (*T*, p. 341).[38] Admittedly, he was uncertain how to explain these additional seventy-five years. Did Daniel's prophecy indicate that Antichrist was to reign for 1,335 rather than 1,260 years, as Mather had assumed all along, or did God allow for a seventy-five-year period of rest between the destruction of Antichrist and the Second Coming itself? Such an additional period would certainly postpone the New Heavens and the New Earth far beyond Mather's own lifetime—far beyond the risk of living long enough to see his own computations confuted again. The Seventh Chiliad might therefore not be expected until sometime between 1791 and 1811, depending on whether one chose 456 or 476 as the starting point. Nevertheless, since no one could tell "whether all these Years have to a Minute just the same *Epocha*" (*T*, p. 341), the Second Coming might still occur sooner than anyone had expected. If nothing else, this interlude allowed the modern-day Jeremiahs to awaken the sleepy world for the day when the King would be witnessed in the clouds (*D* 2:737–38; *Selected Letters*, pp. 405–6).

When on the eve of the Sabbath, 29/30 October 1727, a series of earthquakes began to rock the Bay Colony and sounded a "horrid rumbling like a Noise of many Coaches together, driving on the paved Stones with the utmost Rapidity" (*TL*, p. 1), many frightened Bostonians fled their houses and tumbled onto the dark streets, not knowing where to turn for shelter. The earthquake, as Mather reported in *The Terror of the Lord* and in *Boanerges*, was not confined to Boston alone but was also felt in other parts of New England, so terrifying the good people of Methuen that they wondered whether this "was the Great Day of the Son of man's appearing in the clouds of heaven."[39] Even the ships off the New England shore felt the quiver of the sea and reported "terrible Flames and Lights, in the Atmosphere" (*TL*, p. 2). Cotton Mather and his fellow watchmen of the Lord certainly knew what this prodigy of nature signified. And so did the frightened Bostonians who thronged into their churches throughout the night. The next morning, when Mather rang the bells of his Old North Church on Clarke's Square, he addressed one of the largest crowds he had ever witnessed in his church. As frightful reports trickled in, eyewitnesses described the event in words echoing Michael Wigglesworth's all-time favorite, *The Day of Doom* (1662): "The *Air* [was] never more *Calm*, the *Sky* never more *Fair*; every thing in all imaginable Tranquility," when the finger of God struck and "Rocque[d] the Houses, and cause[d] . . . the falling of some smaller Things, both within Doors and without" (*TL*, p. 1). In all of its ninety-seven years of existence, Boston had never seen "such a *Night*, as what we saw a few Hours ago." In the sermon hurriedly put together for his waiting congregation, Mather coached his parishioners: "A MIDNIGHT CRY was heard; The Consternation whereof is not this Morning over with us; An *Anguish* like that of a *Travailing Woman*, siezed upon *Men* as well as *Women*. What *Fear*, from the Apprehension of going to the *Pit*, by a stroke like a *snare* upon us!" (*TL*, pp. 6–7).[40]

The morning after the earthquake was one of Mather's few remaining opportunities to improve the occasion with timely words of warning to those parishioners who were not easily shaken out of their apathy. His cries of "FIRE! FIRE!" had gone unheeded often enough. But with such unmistakable portents of the End at hand, and with such trembling crowds of people applying for spiritual munition, Mather could not resist the call to offer his interpretation:

I do not speak these things, as a *Melancholy Visionary*, or because of any *Delight* I can take in keeping my Neighbours under a *Fear* which has *Torment* in it. . . . But I am certain, a Greater *Earthquake* than all of those, is what we have cause to live in *Expectation* of: Even that *Earthquake*, whereof we are warned, Rev. XVI.18. A *Great Earthquake, such as had not been since Men were on the Earth, so Mighty an Earthquake, and so Great an one.* I again, and again, declare it unto you; *The Coming of the Son of Man in the Clouds of Heaven,* 'tis what we know of Nothing to Retard it or Protract it. . . . It may, *for any thing I know*, be the *Next Thing* that is to be look'd for. All that the *Oracles* of GOD have mentioned, as Things to be done before it, are Accomplished: I say, *All Accomplished!* Certainly, The *Kingdom of GOD is at hand*. (*BO*, pp. 41, 43, 44)

With such words of warning, which would also well serve Jonathan Edwards some fourteen years later, when he preached *Sinners in the Hands of an Angry God* to awaken his Enfield, Connecticut, congregation (8 July 1741), Mather's call for reform could not go unheeded, nor his caveats be easily mocked. In fact, the tremors continued to rumble well into November, as young Ebenezer Parkman recorded in his *Diary* (pp. 27–28), guaranteeing a quivering audience for Mather and his colleagues. When reports arrived in December 1727 that earthquakes had ravaged Barbados, the West Indies, England, and even Sicily, in the Mediterranean, where no fewer than fifteen thousand people had perished in the rubble of its cities, Mather impatiently rebuffed his doubting critics:

> I confess, I cannot but admire, how any Men of Thought can content them-selves, with the commonly Received Opinions, about the *Coming* of our SAVIOUR in His *Kingdom*, which are indeed calculated, as if on purpose, to lay and keep the *World* in that profound SLEEP, wherein the *Day of GOD* is to find it. . . . If I should own, That this Word, is, *like a Fire in my Bones, and I am not easy in forbearing;* If I should make the Cry, FIRE, FIRE! *The Fire of GOD will sooner than is generally thought for, fall upon a wretched World, which dreams little of it!*—I should be as much *mocked,* and as little *minded,* as *Lot* was in the *Morning* of the Day when he went out of *Sodom.* The *Sleepy* People of GOD, will not bear to be Awakened: Our SAVIOUR has foretold, *That it must be so!* (*TL*, pp. 28–29)

Assuredly, his parishioners could not forbear reading the "MENE, TEKEL" on the wall, as Mather spelled it out for them vividly in his *Terror of the Lord.* In fact, this sermon was so popular that it saw three editions in no less than four weeks, with *Boanerges* following in late December of the same year. Nor was his congregation insensitive to Mather's speculation that the conflagration was about to begin and swallow up the globe in one cosmic *diluvium ignis.*[41] How effective Mather's sermons of hellfire and brimstone were at that time can be seen in the number of new communicants joining the Old North Church. By the end of 1727, a few months away from his grave in Copp's Hill cemetery, Mather had admitted seventy-one new members, the largest ever in a single year, more even than his old record of 1691, when fifty-five new members pleaded the benefit of the Half-Way Covenant and sought protection from the turmoil with which the witchcraft hysteria was disrupting New England society.

On 24 December 1727, Mather addressed his congregation for the last time, drawing on Isa. 26:20, "Come my People, Enter thou into thy Chambers" (*The Comfortable Chambers,* 1728). Unlike his sermons of terror and warnings, this one serenely assured his listeners that the soul and body of man reunited in the New Jerusalem above would be filled with the joy of the Beatific Vision. Shortly thereafter, his son Samuel and Mather's assistant, Joshua Gee, filled the vacated post in the pulpit of the Old North Church.[42]

FIVE

Note on the Text

Sometime in 1726/27, Cotton Mather evidently sent a clean manuscript copy of "Triparadisus" for publication to John Wyatt, a nonconformist bookseller and printer, Rose and Crown, St. Paul's Churchyard, London. Unfortunately, "Triparadisus" was never printed. Wyatt having died meanwhile (c. 1720), the clean copy was never recovered, as Mather's son Samuel reported in 1729 in his biography of his father: "Since which I am informed the *Bookseller* is dead, and know not what is become of the *Manuscript*" (p. 72). Cotton Mather's bibliographer, Thomas J. Holmes, conjectured that a transcript of "Triparadisus" was sent to Wyatt "some time before 1720" (3:1124). Apparently, Holmes grounded his argument on the estimated dates available for John Wyatt, who flourished in London c. 1690–1720 (see Plomer). Holmes's date, however, appears to be inaccurate for several reasons: Cotton Mather's post-factum annotation in his diary for 1712 reveals that he "Resumed and Finished, in the Winter of the year, 1726," his "Discourse concerning the Threefold *Paradise*," which he had planned (but "Laid aside") as early as the beginning of November 1712 (D 3:91). So, too, Mather's hermeneutics shifted in 1724 from a literalist to a preterite-allegorist interpretation of Romans 11, on the conversion of the Jewish nation; he recorded in his diary on 21 June 1724 that God had given him to understand that all signs of Christ's Second Coming were already fulfilled, and Mather therefore promised, "I purpose quickly to write on these things" (D 2:733). This hermeneutical shift informs much of his argument in part III ("The Third Paradise") of "Triparadisus," which therefore could not have been completed before 1720. A much later date may also be inferred from a letter to Thomas Prince of 31 January 1725/26, where Mather commented, "I am hastening unto the Work of my *Triparadisus*" (D 2:811). However, Mather may not have begun part III, the most significant and longest division of his manuscript, until later in the spring, for he recorded and then erased the date "May 28" on its first page (upper left-hand corner [ms. III, 1]).[1] In fact, he may not have completed his treatise until early 1727, because his chronometrical calculations in the final section of part III imply that he was still working on it as late as that year (p. 326). And finally, a still later missive to Prince (11 February 1726/27) indicates that Mather's holograph was ready for transcription by a copyist (*Selected Letters*, pp. 415–16). This internal and external evidence, then, suggests that Mather did not send a clean copy of "Triparadisus" to London before 1726/27. At any rate, the only extant version is the holograph now in the possession of the American Antiquarian Society, Worcester, Massachusetts, which is the text of the present edition.

"Triparadisus" consists of 387 pages in seven fascicles, ranging in length from 28 to 143 manuscript pages. As is evident from the different watermarks and qualities of paper, Mather used sheets from different quires. The size of the leaves varies from approximately 190/195 millimeters in length to about 150/ 155 millimeters in width. Apparently, all seven fascicles were at one time bound as one book. Unfortunately, the binding has disintegrated, and the manuscript now consists of several parts poorly sewn and loosely held together with coarse twine. As far as I have been able to determine, parts I and II each consist of conjugate leaves still connected. Part III, however, shows that Mather detached several leaves from the manuscript: Two stubs left in the binding indicate that he removed two leaves preceding ms. III, 1; and three stubs following III, v71, and preceding III, ix, 72, indicate that he removed three additional leaves. So, too, one leaf is torn off following III, x, {34v}, as is evident from the stub left in the binding. To III, x, {34v}, Mather attached two leaves (four pages) with four wax wafers (now loose). Likewise, one leaf appears to have been removed preceding III, xi, 107, and another leaf between III, xi, 36v, and III, xii, 136v. One oversized leaf (III, 4, and III, v4), roughly 15 millimeters longer than most other manuscript pages, has been inserted. This leaf is folded at the bottom to line up with the other pages. In addition, Mather added one half-sheet, merely marking its intended location at the bottom of III, xii, 28v, with three number signs (# # #). This half-sheet is loosely placed between III, xii, 28v, and III, xii, 133.

Generally, the manuscript is in fair condition, excepting the final leaf (III, xii, r40v, and III, xii, {42v}), which is heavily torn along the edges. Fortunately, I have been able to reconstruct from the context or from parallel passages most words that were completely obliterated or partially obscured by the careless binding of the manuscript or by wear and tear along the edges.

The text of "Triparadisus" is further plagued by innumerable marginal and interlinear interpolations and excisions. However problematic, these editorial revisions provide much information about the evolution of the work. They furnish invaluable insight into Mather's thoughts during the early stages of composition and reveal his hermeneutical shifts as he finished the manuscript. During these fourteen years, his eschatological views underwent drastic changes. To record these innumerable textual intrusions as completely as possible without sacrificing readability, I have opted for a literal transcription that preserves the text as Mather intended it for the press and have relegated his excised passages to appendix A. And to preserve the integrity of the text, I have abstained as much as possible from "improving" the manuscript with editorial intrusions. The following guidelines explain my editorial decisions, which are informed by G. Thomas Tanselle's "Editing of Historical Documents."

I have relied on Microsoft Word 5.0 to maintain a faithful and accurate transcription of "Triparadisus." The typescript has been subjected to twelve complete verification processes: eight collations of typescript and copyflo made from microfilm; two comparisons between typescript and copyflo by Mita Choudhury, formerly of Pennsylvania State University; and three careful on-site collations of typescript and holograph manuscript during three extended stays at the American Antiquarian Society. Finally, to maintain utmost fidelity of my electronic files following the typesetting, Jeffrey Mares and Caffilene Allen graciously served as co-readers in harmonizing page and line references in the appendixes, in double-checking Greek and Hebrew letters, accent marks, and hyphenations, and in collating the master copy with the galley and page proofs.

1. I have placed all of Mather's marginal and interlinear interpolations, which he designated by single, double, triple, or quadruple carets, in the text. To identify these interpolations, I have used various symbols explained at the beginning of appendix A. However, to provide a clean text unencumbered by countless editorial symbols, I have recorded these markers only in that appendix. Those who wish to see Mather's very many interpolations recorded in the genetic text itself may consult my dissertation.

2. Mather canceled punctuation marks, letters, words, sentences, paragraphs, and pages for a number of reasons: to search for a more precise word during his rapid composing process; to replace one quotation with another; to excise names, titles, places, dates, and figures about whose accuracy he was in doubt or whose anonymity he decided to preserve; to correct spelling and capitalization; to cancel false starts; to revise punctuation and upper- and lowercasing of letters or words as necessitated by insertions and cancellations; to emphasize or deemphasize specific words; to restore matter obliterated or otherwise obscured by ink spots or smudges. All of these excisions have been recorded in appendix A.

Generally, Mather canceled matter by drawing a thick wavy line through the passage. Deciphering and reconstructing these excisions proved fairly easy. But when he wanted to be sure that the passage could not be deciphered, he obliterated it by repeatedly drawing a wavy line through the excision, by smudging it, or both.

I have used the following symbols wherever letters or words have been permanently lost through defacement, illegibility, or mutilation:

[.], [. .], [*], [* *] to indicate the loss of, respectively, one or more letters or one or more words by Mather's *defacement;*
[. *illeg.*], [. . *illeg.*], [* *illeg.*], [* * *illeg.*] to indicate the loss of, respectively, one or more letters or one or more words through *illegibility* of Mather's paleography;
[. *torn*], [. . *torn*], [* *torn*], [* * *torn*] to indicate the loss of, respectively, one or more letters or one or more words by mutilation.

If a lost letter or word can be inferred with reasonable certainty, the inferred reconstruction is rendered in braces { }. If subject to conjecture, however, the reconstruction is followed by a question mark and rendered in braces { ?}.

3. Mather's use of abbreviations and contractions provides no hardship for scholars of the period. Even general readers unfamiliar with the conventions of the late seventeenth century and early eighteenth century should experience few problems in this respect. But since Mather intended "Triparadisus" for the press, I have silently expanded all those contractions and abbreviations that an early eighteenth-century typesetter would generally have spelled out:

y^t = that y^e = the y^m = them
y^r = their o^r = our   wth = with
w^{ch} = which   wherewth = wherewith aforesd. = aforesaid

However, all of Mather's abbreviations that follow modern conventions, such as *Capt* (*Captain*) or *M^r* (*Master/Mister*) or *D^r* (*Doctor*), have been retained, though they are rendered as *Capt.* or *Mr.* or *Dr.* In his "First Paradise," written in a clear hand in 1712, Mather placed a period below the raised letters of such abbreviations as wch and y^e, but he discontinued use of this mark in the remainder of the manuscript. I have elected to regularize his practice and to omit this abbreviation mark altogether. Virtually all of Mather's other textual abbreviations follow the patterns here listed and have been expanded or modernized accordingly. Those that do not clearly fit these patterns have been retained as they occur in the original manuscript.

4. While Mather distinguished between the minuscules *i* and *j* in his quotations from Latin sources, he generally did not do so for the majuscules *I* and *J*. Since no misreading is possible here, I have retained Mather's archaic convention wherever applicable. His long-tailed minuscule ſ, commonly represented by the lowercase *s*, is somewhat more problematic, for Mather used ſ and *s* interchangeably. Thus both *ſhould* and *should* or *poſſession* and *possession* can be found. Since little appears to be gained by retaining such niceties of archaic calligraphy, I have silently adopted modern conventions throughout.

5. Following homiletic traditions for oral delivery, Mather underscored an unusually large number of words or phrases with single or double underlining to emphasize key words and concepts and to signal quotations. The present edition has adopted the printer's convention of Mather's day (and of the present), which would generally have rendered a passage underscored by a single line in *italics* and that by a double line in SMALL CAPITALS.

6. Mather's pagination, given in arabic numerals, is somewhat more problematic, for his cancellations and insertions necessitated repeated repagination. In his first major subdivision, "The First Paradise," Mather used a continuous recto and verso pagination starting with (1 recto and ending with 28) verso. The recto page numeral appears in the upper right-hand corner with an opening parenthesis, for example, (1. Verso pagination, on the other hand, appears in the upper left-hand corner, for example, 2). He followed the same procedure in "The Second Paradise," which begins with (1 recto and ends with 62) verso.

Mather's longest subdivision, "The Third Paradise," is also the most problematic part of the entire manuscript, for it contains the largest number of excisions and cancellations and therefore many instances of repagination. Whereas parts I and II have only minor divisions, part III contains twelve major sections headed with roman numerals, and these sections, by and large, have separate pagination. Thus the first eight sections bear a continuous recto pagination from 1) recto to 71) recto, the closing parenthesis indicating the position of the page numeral in the upper left-hand corner. Whereas recto pagination continues in section ix, recto 72) to recto 88), Mather introduced a separate verso pagination for this and each of the following sections. However, while his recto pagination continues in numerical order, hence 72), 73), 74) and so on, his verso pagination runs sequentially 2), 4), 6), 8), and so forth, beginning with 2) on the verso of 72) recto and ending with 34) verso.

Section x begins with 89) recto and ends with 106) recto. Verso pagination of this section is problematic, for Mather mispaginated verso 8) as 6) verso, while the verso of 105) recto, which should be verso 34), lacks pagination altogether. Instead Mather paginated the verso of 106) recto as 34) verso, which should properly be 36) verso. To this verso he attached—with sealing wax—two conjugate leaves (four pages, unpaginated).

Section xi begins with 107) recto and ends with 121) recto, with versos numbered from 2) verso to 36) verso. Following verso 14), Mather inserted two conjugate leaves. While verso pagination continues on these leaves in proper sequential order, hence 16) and 18), no recto pagination is given; the recto numbering resumes with 114) recto after the insertion. Between verso 34) and recto 122), Mather inserted four conjugate leaves (eight pages) bearing verso 36) but no recto pagination. This insertion occurs at the end of section xi and at the beginning of section xii.

In section xii, the first three rectos are unpaginated. Recto pagination resumes with 122) recto and ends with 137) recto, even though two more (but unpaginated) rectos follow. Verso pagination on the other hand is continuous from 2) verso to {42?} verso. The corners of the final two leaves are torn; thus pagination of versos 40) and 42) is subject to inference. That the final two verso paginations must have existed can be inferred from the still visible closing parenthesis of verso {40?}).

To facilitate identification of manuscript pages and to establish a permanent source of pagination for "Triparadisus," I have enclosed Mather's pagination in brackets and have placed it in the text at the beginning of each new manuscript page. Where pagination is obliterated by torn corners of the manuscript, it can generally be inferred from the partially remaining numeral or from the sequence of the preceding and succeeding page numbers. I have indicated such an inference by a question mark after the numeral.

But since Mather began each of the three major sections of "Triparadisus" with page numeral 1, further means of identification are required. Consequently, I have used the roman capital numerals I, II, and III to identify, respectively, "The First Paradise," "The Second Paradise," and "The Third Paradise." Further means of identification are necessary in the third division. As described above, Mather used a continuous recto pagination throughout part III but no verso pagination in the first eight sections. I have thus placed *v before* the arabic numeral to distinguish the verso following a recto pagination from the recto itself. Thus v46 designates the verso following 46 recto, while 46 without prefix or suffix signifies 46 recto.

Beginning with section ix, as noted, Mather introduced separate verso pagination. I have indicated these sections with lowercase roman numerals, followed by Mather's arabic page numbers. The abbreviation *v after* an arabic numeral here indicates Mather's separate verso pagination. With these principles in mind, the reader can easily decipher the following representations:

[ms. I, 25]   =   part I, "The First Paradise," p. 25
[ms. II, 14]   =   part II, "The Second Paradise," p. 14
[ms. III, vii, v55] =   part III, "The Third Paradise," section vii,
                       verso following 55 recto
[ms. III, ix, 4v] =   part III, section ix, 4 verso
[ms. III, ix, 73] =   part III, section ix, 73 recto
[ms. III, xii, r2v] =   part III, section xii, recto following 2 verso

7. Even though Mather's spelling was remarkably consistent and, by our own standards, remarkably modern, occasional slips of the pen did occur. If Mather's misspelling does not give rise to any confusion, I have retained his variant. For instance, he rendered *foretell* as either *foretel* or *fortell* and consistently spelled *carcass* as *carcase*. Since no misreading seems possible even in the second example, I have retained Mather's exact spelling throughout. So, too, his archaic Latin spelling of the suffix -*qe* for -*que* has been retained—for example, *utrumqe* rather than *utrumque*. If, on the other hand, Mather misspelled such names as *Peutinger* or *White*, rendering them as *Pentinger* or *Wite*, serious misreading is possible. In such cases, I have corrected the erroneous spelling in the text and recorded my editorial intrusions in appendix B. Such obvious slips as "ye the heavens," often a result of Mather's inaccurate cancellations of earlier passages or of his interpolations of words and phrases, have been emended and the deleted words recorded in appendix B. His inconsistent use and archaic mixes of arabic and roman numerals, such as *i2* for *12* or *3i* for *31*, have been silently normalized.

8. Capitalization in "Triparadisus" is rather problematic as well. Whereas the younger Mather carefully distinguished upper- from lowercase letters in "The First Paradise," the older Mather no longer observed such niceties of penmanship. Anybody who has ever seen a sample of Mather's old-age handwriting will be aware of the difficulty. His indiscriminate use of upper and lower cases of *c, e, g, l, m, o, p, s, u, v, w, x, y,* and *z* is confusing to modern expectations, especially when the first letter of a name or the initial letter of a word following a period is lowercased. Generally, a lowercased word at the beginning of a sentence is not problematic. But since there is no evidence to suggest that Mather intentionally used minuscules after sentence-terminal marks, the initial letters of words at the beginning of new sentences, as well as proper names, have been silently capitalized.

A final capitalization usage deserves brief attention. Mather commonly capitalized word-initial letters of nouns or a sequence of nouns, of adjectives modifying nouns, of a sequence of predicate adjectives, or even of sequential adverbs and verbs to emphasize particular words or ideas or to signal to the orator a change of intonation to effect a different meaning. Hence we find "their Thoughts and their Pens," "Beloved City," "Considerable Alterations," "more Copiously or more Accurately." Such conventions are typical of the contem-

porary homiletic tradition intended for oral delivery, and Mather's practice re-
quires no elucidating. It is more problematic, however, when his capitalization
lacks any apparent rationale. His use of upper and lower cases in such a passage
as "GoD the Father, The son, the Holy ghost" follows no recognizable logic.
Since problems of this nature are a distinctive feature of Mather's writing, it
seemed necessary to regularize his use of minuscules or majuscules in those
cases where he does not seem to follow his pattern evident in the text. The
following principles have been applied throughout: All initial letters of nouns
have been capitalized unless Mather used a distinct minuscule not listed in the
above series. Or, if a sequence of parallel nouns, adjectives, verbs, adverbs, and
prepositions obviously demonstrates upper or lower cases, I have regularized
the sequence according to the pattern Mather was following in that instance.
Unfortunately, this system is not completely foolproof; in some cases arbitrary
decisions were necessary when no precedent or patterns were available. At any
rate, I took pains to rule out any unintentional shift in meaning.

    9. Punctuation marks in "Triparadisus" are a constant source of problems.
Mather's innumerable excisions and interpolations necessitated frequent re-
punctuation. Unfortunately, he did not always excise the existing punctuation
mark when he inserted a new one, and as a result, two different marks often
exist side by side. But deciphering Mather's final choice proved to be relatively
easy when I consulted the holograph manuscript at the American Antiquarian
Society, for Mather used two different types of ink, a brown ink for his original
and a blackish ink for his revisions.

    Generally, I have retained Mather's final choices just as they occur in "Tri-
paradisus." Only when his punctuation was likely to obscure the meaning of his
sentence did I intrude into the text. Such intrusions, however rare, are recorded
in appendix B.

    10. I have retained blank spaces between paragraphs where they appear in the
manuscript. Most of the time, Mather signals the beginning of new paragraphs
with indentations of varying lengths. Here I have used standard indentation for
all of his paragraphs. Any extra spaces between words or sentences, possibly
serving Mather as reminders for later insertions, have been silently omitted.
When Mather skipped one or more lines between paragraphs to signal a new
subdivision or to break up long passages into visually recognizable units, I have
regularized his practice and dropped one line. Similarly, when he used one or
more slashes to indicate that a subsequent passage was to be centered, I have
carried out his intent, but recorded the silently omitted slash or slashes in
appendix B.

    11. Mather frequently used dashes of varying lengths. Such a dash often sig-
nifies the end of a quotation, an omission of words (especially in conflated
quotations), or some other unspecified alteration to a quotation. This is not to
say that such dashes occur only within quotations, for they can frequently be
found at the ends of lines, here generally indicating pauses. In all cases, I have
retained Mather's practice in the text of the present edition.

    12. Single and, infrequently, double quotation marks served Mather to high-

light specific passages in "Triparadisus." These markers appear at the opening (but not at the closing) of each citation and in front of each word (along the left-hand margin) beginning a new line. Little seems to be gained, however, by retaining this archaic practice: (1) Mather's line breaks (except for those in his poetry) are different from the line breaks in the present edition. (2) If these lines were run to the same measure as the surrounding copy, Mather's quotation marks would appear midline. (3) And to move the quotation marks back to the left-hand margin would be to impose an archaic convention on this modern setting. For these reasons, modern conventions have been adopted here, and double quotation marks are placed only at the opening and closing of Mather's citations.

13. I have retained Mather's hyphenations of compound names, verbs, nouns, adjectives, and adverbs as they appear in the manuscript. Distinguishing compound hyphenations from end-of-the-line divisions proved easy enough. In "The First Paradise" (1712), Mather clearly identified a word division with a colon placed at the end of the line and at the beginning of the next line, but in 1726/ 27 used hyphens instead for his revisions and for his additions in "The Second Paradise" and "The Third Paradise." Thus no separate record of Mather's divisions of hyphenated compounds is necessary.

PART II

The Text

Tri-Paradisus &c.

Samuel Mather's Book. _1727_[1]

This work is in the Handwriting of
Cotton Mather.[2]

There is likewise his _Triparadisus_, which was sent to Mr. Wyat[3] Bookseller in
London in order to be published: Since which I am informed the Bookseller is
dead, and know not what is become of the _Manuscript_. It is pity it should be
lost; It showed great acquaintance with _divine and human learning_.

Samuel Mather's Life of Cotton
Mather, 1729. pp; 72, 146.

TRIPARADISUS.

ESSAYS on

I.   The PARADISE of the OLD WORLD.
Enriched with Some Instructive *Illustrations* on the SACRED
GEOGRAPHY.

II.   The PARADISE of DEPARTED SPIRITS.
Fortify'd with well-attested RELATIONS to *Demonstrate* as well as
Illustrate, the State of *Such.*

III.   The PARADISE of the NEW EARTH under the Influences of the NEW
HEAVENS.

A Description of the tremendous CONFLAGRATION to be First (and
Soon) look'd for; And of the Things wherein our SAVIOUR has
Already most punctually and marvellously fulfill'd *All* that He fore-
told, for the SIGNS of *it*, & of His *Coming.*

Then, The NEW HEAVENS Opened: And, The NEW EARTH Surveyed.
With a Modest Enquiry after, The TIME of the END; And, Whether a
National Conversion of the JEWS be first of all to be expected.

POINTS, which call for the deepest Consideration of THIS AGE; and are
here prosecuted with a great Variety of Entertainment.

TRIPARADISUS.

Some ESSAYS to direct such as are Willing to Travel unto a PARADISE, would now bespeak a favourable Reception with them. And the *Title* of these ESSAYS, which was once the Name of a City in *Syria*,[4] will invite their Expectation of a TREBLE PARADISE to be discoursed on.

Accordingly, There are to come under a Cultivation with us; First, *The PARADISE of the* Old World. Then; *The PARADISE of* Departed Spirits. Lastly; The PARADISE of *the* New Earth under the New Heavens.

O Father of Mercies, & our most merciful Father in our Lord Jesus Christ; Send forth, I pray thee, thy Light & thy Truth; Lett us be thereby led & brought into thy Holy Garden; And Lett us anon have our Portion in the PARADISE, where we shall see the Good of thy Chosen, & shine with the Joy of thy Nations & gloriously triumph with thine Inheritance. By the Second Adam *Lett us obtain a Better PARADISE, than what the First* Adam *has depriv'd us of.*

The
First PARADISE.

The *Book of Truth* has instructed us, That when the Glorious GOD had *finished His Works* of Creation, in the Formation of MAN, He placed His Noble Creature, in a *Garden of Delights*, of which we have Some Idaea under the Denomination of a PARADISE derived unto us. But, *Poor Mankind*, By the Sin of thy *First Parents*, thou hast Lost thy *First Habitation*, and art become a miserable *Exile* from it, *Spending all thy Days in Vanity!* Yea, Lost the very *Knowledge* as well as the *Comfort* of that *Wonderful Garden*. This have we gott by our Sacrilegious Meddling with the *Tree of Knowledge*, that we have Lost [ms. I, 2] even the *Knowledge* of the Place where it stood. However we *Naturally*, and, I hope, not *Criminally*, have some Appetite for as much *Knowledge* of it, as we can by our best Searches attain to. And tho' our *Main Study* now must be, to make sure of an Entrance in to the *Better Paradise* which our Great REDEEMER has praepared for those whom He takes under His Conduct, yett we may *Look back* on the *Paradise*, from which we have been Banished. And as the *Jews*, when they might no more sett foot on the Spott where once their *Beloved City* stood, had an Allowance to draw so near as to Look and Mourn and Weep, at the rueful Spectacle, so We may with Tears in our Eyes behold the Spott, where we had in our First Parents the *Delectable Seat*, from which the Indignation of our Incensed Maker for our Crime has chased us.

The FLOOD, no doubt, caus'd and left very Considerable Alterations on the Face of the Earth, when *The World which then was, being overflowed with Water, perished.*[1] Nevertheless the inspired Historian, who has written an History of the *Flood,* which is *daily* confirmed by the Reliques and Ruines discovered in *our Days,* has given such an Account of the *Ancient Rivers* yett remaining, which run still much as they did in the *Antediluvian World,* as not only to make the *Burnettian* Romance come to nothing,[2] but also putt us in a Way, that Steering by the Course of these *Rivers,* we may now very much find out *how the Land lay,* and where the *Place* of the *Terrestrial Paradise* we have now lost, is to be look'd for.

Great Literators have employ'd their Thoughts and their Pens, on this Article of the *Sacred Geography.* But none more Copiously or more Accurately, than those two Prodigies of Literature, *Bochart,* and, *Huet,* the Illustrious Ornaments, of their Two Communions, or, give me Leave to say, of those Two Grand Parties, the *Sethites* and the *Cainites.*[3] The Lucubrations of these Two very Great Men, are so much in all hands, that I shall not propose to [ms. I, 3] Transcribe, or to Abridge, either of their most Elaborate Composures. But instead thereof, I will produce what has hitherto been, *An Hidden Treasure:* and bring to Light the *Stones of Darkness.*

The Learned SAMUEL LEE, whose Noble Treatise, Of *Solomons Temple,* which he entituled, *Orbis Miraculum,* is not unworthy of the Title which he putt upon the *Temple;* began to prepare for the Public, another Treatise, *Of a Threefold Paradise:* In which he never did proceed, that I can learn, any further than the *Terrestrial,* nor indeed had he finished what he purposed upon *That;* but was called away to *taste* of the *Coelestial,* before he had gone so far as to *write* upon it.[4] This Manuscript is lost, I fear, beyond the hopes of any recovery. But it happened, that in the Few Hours, while I had a Copy of it in my hands, I carefully Epitomized it, and Siezed upon all that appeared unto me, Material and Serviceable for the Design of Enriching our, BIBLIA AMERICANA, with a very Entertaining *Illustration* upon, *The Situation of the Terrestrial Paradise;* Intending to have our Collections enjoy the Honour of his Name on that Occasion.[5]

Indeed, one would at first have little Courage to Search after the Seat of *Paradise,* on Reading the *Disagreements* which there have been upon the Problem; and which a *Man of Renown in the Congregation* of the Learned has briefly Summ'd up, in such discouraging Terms as these.[6] "*Paradise* has been placed in the *Third Heaven;* in the *Fourth;* [*where's That?*] in the *Heaven* of the *Moon;* in the *Moon* itself; in the Middle Region of the *Air; Above* the Earth; *Under* the *Earth;* in a Place *Hidden* and *Remote* from the Knowledge of Men. It has been fixed under the *Arctic Pole;* in *Tartary;* in the Place filled at present by the [ms. I, 4] *Caspian* Sea. Others have sent it away to the Extreme Parts of the *South,* in the *Terra del Fuego.* Several have placed it in the *Levant;* or upon the Banks of the *Ganges;* or in the Island of *Ceylon;* even deriving the Name of the *Indies* from that of *Eden.* It has been placed in *China;* or, even beyond the *Levant,* in some Uninhabited Countrey. Some will have it be in *Armenia;*

Others, in *Africa*, under the Equator: Others, at the Equinoctial Orient; Others, under the *Mountains of the Moon*, from whence it was beleeved, the *Nile* proceeded. But most, in *Asia*; Some in *Armenia Major*; Others, in *Mesopotamia*; Others, in *Assyria*; or, in *Persia*; or, in *Babylonia*; or, in *Arabia*; or, in *Syria*; or, in *Palaestine*. There have even some such been found, that have honoured *Europe* with its Situation."[7]

The very learned Author of this List [HUET Bishop of Avranches] yett ventures to determine the Situation.[8] *Calmet* Comes after him, & Praises him, & yett Refutes him; with a Determination of its being in *Armenia*, near the Springs of the *Tigris*, the *Euphrates*, the *Phasis*, & the *Araxis*.[9] And then *Reland* comes with further Speculations.[10]

Notwithstanding these *Variations of the Compass*, in the Successive Attempts to find out the *Seat* of *Paradise*, I will not be disheartened; but that my *Talent* may not ly *buried*, I will bring forth what I have *Contracted* from the *Rich Oar* of that Manuscript, which I have so happily litt upon; and give it in the Terms wherein I have calcined & improv'd & strengthened it.[11] And if it should be so, that we have after all miss'd of the *Place*, we are seeking for, yett, as it has been observed, that the Vain Men who forever miscarry in their Quaest of that which they call, *The Philosophers Stone*,[12] do nevertheless light upon very notable *Experiments*; which make them some Recompence for their Pains; thus, if we miscarry in our Quaest of *Paradise*, we shall nevertheless have our Pains a little recompensed in some notable *Illustrations* upon the *Sacred Geography*. [ms. I, 5 *canceled*][13]

¶ I. Of PARADISE, we find a notable Remembrance and Resemblance, in a City of *Syria*, scituate, on the River *Orontes*, which for the many Delights of it, is call'd *Paradisus*, by *Strabo, Ptolomy*, & *Pliny*, and by *Diodorus* call'd also *Triparadisus*; a City, not far from the *Goodly Mountains* of *Lebanon*; where the Scripture doth report the *House of Eden* [Amos. I. 5.] to have Sway'd the Scepter of Government.[14] In this *Valley of Eden* (which the Ancient Gentiles, do celebrate in their *Adonis* and *Adonius*)[15] there stood the beautifull City of *Damascus*, a City six miles in compass, and the rarest prospect in the World. Here, besides a thousand other Delicacies, there grew, the *Pomegranat*, and the *Pistacho*, (*Jacobs* present unto *Joseph*, Gen. XLIII. 11.) and the rare Figs of the Emperour *Julian*.[16] Here also were the choice Quarries of *Alabaster*, and the Golden Sands of the River *Chrysorrhoas*, the supposed *Pharphar* mentioned in the Bible, not far from the River *Adonis*.[17] In this Valley, some will have *Cain* to have kill'd his Brother; & so they derive the Name, of [ms. I, 7] *Damascus*, from, *Dam-Shach*, the *Blood* of the *Boy*. However, In this Valley, is that *Eden*, wherein the Prophet *Ezekiel* [Ezek. XXVIII. 13, 14,] finds the Prince of *Tyrus*[18] walking; & upon the *Holy Mountain of God*, that is upon *Lebanon*. Moreover, when the Lord foretels [Amos I. 5.] that Hee will send the Syrians of *Damascus* Captives to *Kir*, that is, a Countrey in *Media*, upon the River *Cyrus*, now called *Kur*, Hee also fore-dooms the cutting off the Inhabitant from *Aven*, that is, *Heliopolis* [*Balbek*, or, *Baal-beth*] the House of *Baal*, or, the Sun; which stood in this very Valley; as also, to take the Scepter from the *House of Eden,* which was here scituated. In after-times, wee find these *Damascen* People, in a Captive-State [Isa. XXXVII. 12.] by the Name of, *The Children of Eden,* at *Telassar,* or, the *Tal-atha* of *Ptolomy,* near the River *Tigris* in *Assyria.*[19]

But after all, wee shall seek, and find, the True *Paradise* of our Father *Adam,* somewhere about the Rivers of *Mesopotamia;* where fell Serpents & fierce Dragons are now hissing among the *Thorns,* which the primitive *Curse* has brought upon it.[20]

Yea, perhaps, 'Ere we have done, wee shall have so described it, that an Ingenious Traveller may go directly to it; and carry from the farthest *America* some Informations to the *Armenian* and *Nestorian* Bishops, thereabouts Inhabiting, which they never had before.[21]

Lett us first begin with the Text,

Gen. II. 8, 10.

The Lord God planted a Garden Eastward in Eden,—And a River went out of Eden, to water the Garden; and from thence it was parted, & became into four Heads.

The Hebrew Original more Exactly tells us, It was, *a Garden in Eden from Kedem*: that is, on the East-side of *Kedemah;* or, in the Countrey of *Eden,* towards the East of it. Wee'l thus paraphrase it; This garden lay in the Countrey of *Eden,* East from *Kedemah,* a Territory in & near *Aram-naharaim,* or, *Syria* of the Rivers; that is, *Mesopotamia,* or, *Armenia;* nigh to the River *Uphrates,* where the *Children of the East,* or, *Kedemah,* so often mentioned by *Moses,* & other Sacred Writers, had their Ancient Residence. The Region of *Kedemah,* in a fair Map, would Illustrate Scriptures not a few. Hence it was that the *Wise Men* [ms. I, 8] came to worship our Lord;[22] the King that [Num. XXIV. 7.] is to bee *Higher than Agag* (or, *Gog,* as the Samaritan has it; that is, the *Turk.*)[23] 'Tis the Countrey, which I suppose is called, *Anatole,* or, *Oriens,* in the *Themata* of *Constantine;* & so tis mentioned in the *Notices of the Empire,* exhibited by *Pancirollus;* and here t'was that *Zenobia,* the Queen fam'd in History, Ruled.[24]

Here then, Lett us first Look out for the Land of *Kedemah,* which lay *West* unto the Countrey & Garden of *Eden.*

It had its Denomination from *Kedem,* [Gen. XXV. 15.] one of the Sons of *Ishmael;* whose Children gave Names unto their Cities & Castles, whereof wee find Remnants in the Writings of the Ancient Pagans, & so may from thence deduce their true Scituation.

It is recorded of *Ishmael,* [Gen. XVI. 12.] *Hee was to Dwell in the Presence of His Brethren*: על פני / or, before their Face;[25] that is, on the East-side, of the Habitations of the Sons of *Sarah* & of *Keturah*: the usage of Adoration towards the *East,* made *This* a phrase for *That.*[26] Accordingly, wee find *Abraham* disposing his Children by *Keturah* [Gen. XXV. 6.] into the Land of *Kedem,* a Land, it seems, known by that Name, when this Book was written: That so they might bee seated near to the Posterity of *Ishmael*: For which cause, *Ishmaelites* and *Midianites,* are so Joined, as they sometimes are in the Sacred Story: [see Gen. XXXVII. 25, and Judg. VIII. 1, 24.].

You may now meet with the Children of *Keturah*, on the East-side of Mount *Gilead*, & *Hermon*, towards *Uphrates*; and more Southwardly towards *Edom*: which may bee part of the Reason, why *Laban* went with *Jacob*, no farther than that Mountain; for it was the Limits between those Eastern People, and the *Amorites* in the Land of *Canaan*.

Zimran was the first of these. [Gen. XXV. 2.] of him, the petty Kingdomes of *Zimri* [Jer. XXV. 25.] had their Appellation: called the *Zamareni* by *Pliny*, Lying near the *Cennessari* (now *Quennessari*) in the Nubian Geographer: Twenty Miles West of *Haleb*, or *Aleppo*, by *Ptolomy*, called *Chalybon*.[27]

Jokshan was the next; whose Offspring & Countrey, seems to bee *Casama*, in *Ptolomy*.[28]

[ms. I, 9] As *Medan*, the Third, seems to be the adjacent *Odmana*, in that Author.[29]

Midian Lay near Mount *Gilead* of old; but in their migrations marched further towards the Red-Sea; where *Ptolomy* gives us *Modiana*, and *Madiana*. And in the *Peutinger* Tables, wee have *Medeia*, or *Midian*, a City, about Forty Miles from *Elush*, or, *Alush*, & Eighty Miles from *Paran* near the Red-Sea.[30]

Ishbak, affords us the *Scabiosa Laodicea*, upon the River *Orontes*; near *Emesa*, or *Emissa*; in *Ptolomy*, styled, *Cabiosa*.[31]

Shuach, (whereof was *Bildad* the *Shuhite*, by *Procopius* on the Kings, called, *Sauchaeorum Tyrannus*;) gives us the City *Sucta*, in *Ptolomy*, and in the *Peutinger* Tables, about Sixteen Miles from *Gadara*.[32]

Of *Sheba*, the Grandson of *Abraham*, by *Jokshan*, we have *Sabe* in *Ptolomy*; South west of *Palmyra*, and North of *Aurana*, or *Hauran*: and hence are denominated, the *Arabes Scenitae*, *Sabaei*, of *Pliny*; These were the *Sabaeans* that infested *Job*; & here seems to have been the *Aram-zobah*, in Scripture; and *Asabajah*, in the *Notices* of the Eastern Empire.[33]

Dedan, the brother of *Shebah*, dwelt not far off;—about four miles—from *Punon*; & hence do seem to bee [Isa. XXI. 13.] the *Travelling companies of Dedanim*. This *Punon* was the Place, where the *brazen Serpent* was made, of the *Phennesia Metalla*, often mention'd by the Ancients, & called, *Metallofenum*, by *Jerom*; and *Phenustus*, by *Gul. Tyrius*; and, *Pinon* a Dukedome of *Edom*, [Gen. XXXVI. 41.] and *Diafenis* in the *Notices*.[34]

As for *Ashur*, the Son of *Dedan*, as *Assyria* is by *Strabo* called *Atyria*, So hee may well afford us, the *Atera* of *Ptolomy*, near *Casama*; Lying somewhat North of Mount *Alsadamus*, or Mount *Hermon*, or *Syrion*, the South-Eastern part of *Lebanon*.[35]

Letush may be imprinted on the *Latavi*, of the *Notices*, in parts adjacent unto *Palmyra*.

Leum hath affinitie with *Luma*, in *Ptolomy*, South East of *Aurana*, or *Hauran*, of *Ezekiel* [chap. XLVII. 16.] in the same Wilderness. *Hauran* was a famous Place, built on a Mountain of Three Ridges, mentioned by *Niger*. And may not the *Emims* remember this Name with a / ל / praefixed?[36]

Ephah [whereof see Isa. LX. 6.] is *Papha* with *Ptolomy*; and perhaps *Aphaca* in *Lebanon*, where stood the Temple of *Venus Aphacitis*, between *Heliopolis*, & *Byblus*.[37]

Epher; or, *Geber*; *Gabara*, Lying N.E. of *Aurana*, in *Ptolomy*. *Hanoch*; *Anitha*; or, *Canacha*, in *Arabia Petraea*; Lying East [ms. I, 10] of *Cletharro*, which is a Name Corrupted for *Beth-ar*, in *Moab*.[38]

Abidah; In *Ptolomy*, *Eboda*, near *Maliattha*, or, *Amalek*. This may well bee the "οβοδα, of *Stephanus*, by him call'd, Χωριον Ναβαταιων, a Region of *Neba-joth*.[39]

Eldaàh; possibly, the *Allata*, of *Ptolomy*; among the *Rhaabeni*, in the South of *Arabia Deserta*.[40]

Behold, how much of *Scripture-Geography*, is already Illustrated! You may see, how long the Ancient Names of Places remained upon them, & Laying of *Ptolomy* with *Moses* you see where to find them: especially mountainous Countreys, which were not so Liable to bee subdued, by Strangers.

Thus the Sons of *Abrahams* concubines, were together placed in *Kedemah*, or the East Countrey; East ward from *Canaan*, which was intended for *Isaac*.

But were not the *Ishmaelites*[41] also seated hereabouts? They took their General Name of *Hagarens*, for their Mother *Hagar*: or from a Name of that Sound, signifying a *Rock*. Their First Bounds were in the wilderness of *Paran*, from *Havilah* to *Shur*, [Gen. XXV. 18.] that is, from *Eloth*, or *Elana*, by the Red-Sea, to *El-Toro*, on the same Strand. By some they are styled *Agareni*, and *Agrei*; & their chiefe City is by *Stephanus*, called "Εγρα: And, *Hagiar*, or, *El-hagiar*, by the *Arabians*. *Jerom* (*de Locis*) tells us, That *Hagiar*, or, *Petra*, was Ten miles North of *Eloth* by the Red-Sea.[42]

Lett us now take an orderly View of their Castles and Cities.

Nebajoth, the Eldest Son of *Ishmael*: His countrey is called, *Regio Naba-thaea*, & his Dominions are in *Ovid*, *Regna Nabathaea*; & the chiefe City thereof, *Pliny* calls, *Petra*. Hence came the *Fat Ra*{ms} of *Nebajoth*, [Isa. LX. 7.] whose Tails were so broad & large, that they Laid them upon Sleds to bee drawn after them, & were forty pound in weight.[43] This is the City, from whence tis thought, *Arabia Petraea*, derives its Name: compassed, as Pliny saies, *Montibus Inaccessis*.[44] *Malchus* was King of this *Arabia*, in *Caesars* Time; and *Aretas* [II Cor. XI. 32.] in the Apostle *Pauls*. In this Countrey, with *Stephanus*, wee find *Saraka*, [possibly the same with *Masrekah*, Gen. XXXVI. 36.] whence the *Saracens* had their Name: And several other Places & Peoples, which it will not much serve our present purpose, to mention.[45]

[ms. I, 11] *Kedar*; from / קדר / *obscurus fuit*;[46] because Living in a Dark Wilderness. [Compare Psa. CXX. 5. *Mesech* was *Kedars* Brother.] The Name of their City Lies buried in *Ptolomies* "Αδρα, in the South part of *Arabia Petraea*, not far from *Petra*.[47] They are called, *Cedraei*, by *Pliny*; and, they are those Men of *Kedemah*, joined with *Hazor*, [Jer. XLIX. 28.].

Abdeel; or, the *Adubeni*, or, *Augubeni*, in *Junius*.[48]

Chisbam; the *Muasaemones*, near Mount *Zamatha*, in *Arabia faelix*.[49]

Mishmah; where *Zagmais*, and the *Rhaabeni*, in *Ptolomy*, near to *Rabba*.[50]

Dumah; *Dumaetha*, among the *Rhaabeni*; and *Dumatha*, in *Stephanus*.

Massah; Μεσυνη in *Stephanus*; the *Masani*, between *Euphrates* and *Tigris*, in *Ptolomy*; and the *Mesech* of the Psalmist. [Psal. CXX. 5.][51]

Hadar, or *Chadar*: the *Atharitae* or *Athritae*, in *Junius*. I take this to be the *Hazor* of *Jeremiah*, [Jer. XLIX. 28.] where the petty Kingdomes of *Hazor*, are those of the *Nabathaeans*; *Napata*, and *Adara*.

Tema, or, *Thema*; near the Mountains of *Arabia Faelix*. The *Temanite* was here.

Jetur: The *Ituraei* in *Trachonitis*, [Luc. III. 1.] a part of *Hermon*, in *Coelo-Syria*. Here were the Συρμαῖοι, or the *Hermonites*, in a plain between the *Nomaides* and the *Nabathaeans*: and near them, the Σαλάμιοι, or such as Quartered about *Salmon*, [Psal. LXVIII. 14.] in *Stephanus*.[52]

Naphish, or, *Nabis*: the *Nubei Arabes*, of *Junius*; in or near *Lebanon*, possibly *Noba* was here [I Chron. XV. 19.].[53]

Kedemah: in the Land of the *Kadmonites*, giving denomination to the whole countrey.

Here were the posterity of *Hagar* mostly randevouzed.

Wee are still on the West-side of *Paradise*, in the Land of *Kedemah*: and I know not how to Leave that Illustrious Land, until wee have entertained ourselves, with further Observations upon some of its Inhabitants, and Illustrations of the Texts that mention them. That Land, hitherto undescribed by any, Lay, South of *Aram*, or, *Syria*; East, of *Canaan*; North, of *Edom*, & *Arabia* the Happy: And West, of the Region of the Ancient *Eden*.

In this Countrey, wee find *Job*, with his Friends inhabiting. And in the *Notices* of the Eastern Empire, and in the *Themata*, wee find [ms. I, 12] here a peculiar province, termed, *Oriens*, κατ᾽ ἐξοχιαν,[54] whereof *Zenobia*, so often mentioned, was Queen: as has been already told you. *Job*, was the *chiefe* [Job XXIX. 25.] in this Region. His Head-City was / עוץ / *Gutz*; by the Arabian Geographers called, *Algutze*, or, *Algauta*. The people are called, *Autaei*, by *Pliny*, and *Æsitae*, by *Ptolomy*, and by *Niger*, his Explanator:[55] The City itself, *Ciasa*, or *Caeasa*, and *Caesa*, South-East of *Palmyra*. The Countrey, Αυσιτις, by the LXX, and the City, *Auza*, somewhat North of *Teman*. This *Caesa*, or, *Uz*, is by *Ptolomy* placed in the Latitude of 32. gr. 50. min.[56] The *Æsitae*, which are by some thought so called, from / אש / *Ignis*;[57] because they were Worshippers of the *Fire*, the *Sun*, & the *Stars*; and judg'd the same with the *Zabis*, celebrated in many Authors, who may be so styled from Worshipping, *Zabaoth*, or the Hosts of Heaven: people of the same Complexion, with the Chaldaeans of *Ur*,[58] who worshipped *Ur*, the great *Light* of the *Sun*, and were great Students in *Astronomy*. These Extended their vain Superstitions thro' all the adjacent Regions; the *Superstitions* infinitely detested & condemned [Jer. X. 2.] in the Word of God. They dwelt all along the Banks of *Uphrates*, up as far as *Haran*, where dwelt *Laban*, one of those poor *Star-gazers*, who composed (as is judged) his *Talismanical* Gods of certain Metals, imprinted with a *Lion*, or *Scorpion*, or the Like, when the Sun & Moon faced one another with benign Aspects; from the same Triplicitie, & inproper Houses & Mansions of the Heavens; for the Designe of Divinations: and therefore, by *Rachel*, his Daughter, stolen from him.[59]

Teman, the City of *Eliphaz*, was well known to the Romans; having long been a *Praesidium*, or Garrison of theirs, among the *Arabians*. *Jerom*, in his Book of

Hebrew places, putts it a five miles distance off *Petra*; but it is fifteen, in the Greek Copy of *Eusebius*, which was *Jeroms* Original.[60] The *Peutinger* Tables have it, one & Twenty Miles from the Temple, *Ad Dianam*; which I suppose, was the Idolatrous *Fanum* of the Romans, on, or, near Mount *Horeb*.[61]

Sue, the City of *Bildad*, had its Name from a Rock. It is called, *Socho, Sueth,* and *Sueta*, by the Romans *Capitolias*; & it is described at large by *Gulielmus Tyrius*. Its exact position is in the *Peutinger* Tables: and the Prince of it is called, *Sauchaeorum Tyrannus*, who are the *Saccaei* of *Ptolomy*, near the *Agrei*, or *Agarens*, in the same Vicinage of *Arabia Petraea*.

[ms. I, 13] *Capitolias*, is by *Peutinger* fixed Ten miles from *Edrei*, and this, Twenty four, from *Dozzats*; the same it may bee, is, whats called, *Saveh*, or, *Kings-dale*, in *Genesis*. [Gen. XIV. 17.][62]

Naguamathi, was the Seat of *Zophar*. It is corrupted into *Nazama*, in *Ptolomy*, and the Imperial *Notitiae*.[63] It signifies an *Ostrich*, which was a Creature frequent in those Wildernesses. It was near *Palmyra*: but if you would know the Position, with a more Critical Exactness, I refer you to the Tables. All I am doing, at this Instant, is, to show you, with some General Hints, whereabouts you are, when you read the Scriptures.

In this Countrey of *Kedemah*, you'l find *Balaam* also. His Town, *Pethor*, was by the River *Uphrates*, and the Mountains of *Kedem*, on the East, by *Aram*; that is, *Aram Naharaim*, or, *Mesopotamia*. It seems to bee the *Betthara*, of *Ptolomy*, near the Mountains of *Aramenia*.[64]

And in this Countrey you'l find *Jacob*, fled unto his Uncle, at *Haran*, & *Padan-aram*; for *Laban* probably had a great Interest in both of those places. *Padan* I take to bee the *Aphadana*, of *Ptolomy*; and *Haran* to bee the ancient *Carrae*, famous for the overthrow of *Crassus*; & called *Charran*, by Holy *Stephen*. Tis not the same with *Hauran* mentioned by *Ezekiel* [Ezek. XLVII. 16.] which is the *Aurana*, of *Ptolomy*; standing in the *Peutinger*-Maps, Eighteen miles East of *Adrianople*, or *Palmyra* of *Stephanus*, famous for Palm-trees, & answering the Name *Tamar*, or *Tadmor*, i.e. the *Palm-City*, a Stronghold built by King *Solomon*, in this Wilderness.[65]

Moreover, To pass by what wee read about this Land of *Kedemah*, in the Book of *Judges*: [Judg. VI. 3. & VIII. 10. & XXIV. 8. 11.][66] Wee find it mentioned in the Story of mens planting the World soon after the *Flood*. [Gen. XI. 2.]. The Ark resting on Mount *Ararat*, in the Northern parts of *Armenia*, they travelled thence first unto this *Kedemah*; the Countrey called, *East*, not in respect of *Ararat*, but of *Canaan*. As *Abraham* has it said of him, in another place [Gen. XIII. 1.] *Hee went out of Ægypt into the South*; altho' indeed it was *North* from *Ægypt*: and the Original Word should still be kept here untranslated, *Negob*;[67] *Hee went into Negob*; that is, a Countrey in the South of *Canaan*, so called. But the *Plain of Shinar*, whereto those first Companies came, is that which is called *Senagjar*, in *Golius*,[68] and *Sinigarus*, in *Ptolomy*, which gave Name, as well to a *City*, as a *Plain*, on the South of the *Gordiaean*, or *Ararat* Mountains.

[ms. I, 14] In this *Kedemah* wee likewise find [Gen. X. 30.] Mount *Sephar*, or, *Saphir*,—that is, the Shining Mountain; where the posteritie of *Shem* dwelt

in the parts adjacent unto *Mesha*, that is, Mount *Masius*.[69] A Mount of this
Name, *Shapher*, wee have in the Journeyes of *Israel*, thro' the Wilderness:
[Numb. XXXIII. 23.] it was in *Arabia Petraea*. And this might Lead us to Illustrate the Scituation of other Stages taken by *Israel* in those Journeyes, from
the Tables of *Peutinger*, & *Ptolomy*: But I suspect you begin to grow weary of
tarrying thus Long at *Kedemah*: and perhaps you wonder, where I design to
carry you.

To content you, I'l so far anticipate the Entertainment, which I have anon for
you, as to tell you, That I hope, I shall anon determine the Countrey of *Paradise* to have been, the *Inter omnia*,[70] or the principal part, if not the whole, of
Mesopotamia, between the two famous Rivers, of *Tigris*, & *Uphrates*: the same
Countrey which the *Arabians* call *Algerive*. But wee are not yett got so far;
Wee have hitherto been only Surveying the *West*-side of *Eden*; the *Countrey*
of *Eden*, is to be sought in the East of *Kedemah*, and the *Garden* of *Eden*, in a
particular part of that Countrey, to bee e're Long discovered. Before wee come
thither, Lett us a Little View the *North*-side of *Eden*. Famous Rivers ran down
the Mountainous Crags, in the *North* of *Assyria* and *Mesopotamia*, and im-
parted Innumerable Excellencies, to the Transcendent & Illustrious Countrey,
which was of old called, / עֵדֶן / *Voluptas*,[71] the Countrey of *Eden*, or, Delight:
and by the Greeks, Ἡδονὴ and *Adonis*.[72] But, if you ask, which of those two
Rivers, *Tigris*, or, *Euphrates*, did strike thro' the *Garden* of this *Eden*, before its
Departure, into its four Branches, or *Divortia*, mention'd in the Second Chapter of *Genesis*; I must shortly show you, that it was *Tigris*: *Tigris*, that sprang
from the Mountains of *Elwend*,[73] or *Ararat*, a Long Ledge of *Taurus* and *Caucasus*, on the North of *Media* and *Armenia*. Near here unto Rose the River
Phasis of *Iberia*; and the City *Cholcis* was near the Head of *Tigris*, where the
Golden-Fleece, as the Poets remarkably tell us, was kept by a *Dragon*.[74]

You shall now Travel with mee, to the *East*-side of *Eden*. *Moses* acquaints us,
[Gen. III. 24.] There were *Cherubims* placed with *Flaming Swords*, to keep the
way of the Tree of Life; and [ms. I, 15] these were on the *East-side of the Garden*. Some Learned Men Judge these to bee the Sulphureous *Lakes* thereabouts
continually Flaming Day & Night; which were beheld Long after, by *Alexander*
the Great, with Great Admiration: a Notable *Emblem*, & a Probable *Effect*, of
Angels, who are called *Flames of Fire*.[75]

These Fiery, Bituminous, and Stupendous *Lakes*, are found in *Plutarchs* Life
of *Alexander*, near *Ecbatana*, the Head-City of *Media*, call'd *Acbatana*, by
Ptolomy, and in Sacred Writ, [Ezr. VI. 2.] *Achmetha*: His Words are, χασμα πυρὸς
'εν Εκβατανοις. Wee read also in *Pliny*, of a *Burning Mountain* among the *Bac-
trians*, and *Medians*: And wee read of a Field of *Babylon*, that Burns, as it were
in a Fish-pond of an Acre in Quantity; and the same is by *Tibullus* glanced at;
Ardet Aractaeis aut unda per hospita campis: The strange Lake that Burns in
the Fields of *Aracta*; that is, of *Erech*, [Gen. X. 10.] not far from *Babylon*. These
Conflagrations worse than *Sodoms*, continued for many Ages; and I suppose,
do still continue, or are apt on the Least occasions, to Enkindle.[76]

Moreover, when *Cain* went out from the Worship of God, in his Fathers

Samuel Bochart's "Map of Eden." By permission of Special Collections Department, Robert W. Woodruff Library, Emory University.

Family, tis said, Hee *dwelt in the Land of Nod, on the East of Eden*: [Gen. IV.
16.] which is called *Naid*, by *Jerom*. And it is added, *Hee built a City, & call'd
it by the Name of his Son, Enoch*. Here probably is the Land, which the *Nubian*
Geographer, calls, *Nodha*; where is the City *Kir*, which is the same with the
City *Cyrus*, or, *Cyropolis*, of *Ptolomy*; upon the River *Kur*, in *Media*; mentioned by the Ingenious *Olearius*: whither the people of *Syria* and *Damascus*
were as I have told you, carried captive. [Amos. I. 5.][77]

And as for the City, *Enoch*, tis Embalmed by *Mela*, by *Solinus*, by *Pliny*, and
by *Ptolomy*, among the *Eniochi*, or *Heniochi*, in the Land of *Enochia*. And in
the *Nubian*, wee read of the Clime called, *Kir-cajan*, and another called *Abil*,
near *Nodha*, and *Candaul*. Hee speaks also of other places, called, *Tel-becain*,
that is, *Tel-beth-cain*, or, The Mount of the House of *Cain*. So, the first Man,
that built a *City*, was the first *Wicked Man* in the World.[78]

But Lett us now take our course to the *South* side of *Eden*. And, Remembring
our former distinction between the Countrey of *Eden*, and the Garden of *Eden*,
wee may here observe, That the Land of *Eden*, is the same, that the *Arabians*
now call, [ms. I, 16] *Gesire*, or, *Diarbeck*; that is, the Province Lying between
the Two Rivers *Uphrates* and *Tigris*; & reaching to the South Sea, into which
those Rivers are Disembogued. Unto this purpose, *Ethicus*, in his Cosmography,[79] notes, that the River *Armodius*, illustrates the Region of *Adonis*—(i.e.
Eden, or *Gezre*) and *Mesopotamia*; and is Received into the *Persian* Gulf. This
Armodius, I suppose to bee *Armodus*, or the River of *Ormuz*, that is, *Tigris*.
This was the *Countrey*. But now the *Garden*, of *Eden* Lies on the East side of
this Land of *Adonis*; It is an Island of *Tigris*; on the South side whereof, the
River *Tigris* issuing out of that pleasant Spott, is by several Cutts Lett into
Euphrates; which, with its branches, disciphers the *Four Rivers*, or Heads of
Water, mentioned in the Second of *Genesis*, to bee divided, on the South-side
of the Garden.

I. The River *Pison*, or, the *Fish-ful* River.

Omitting what *Pliny* writes, of *Eels* Thirty foot Long, to bee caught in this
River: I shall only tell you, That this River is called *Pasitigris*. *It compasses
the Land of Havilah*; [Gen. II. 11.] the Land, by *Strabo* called, *Chalonites*; and
by some, *Chaulan*; but by *Benjamen* of *Tudela*, *Haoula*.[80] Its *compassing* that
Land, means not an *Encircling* of it, but a winding in and out, upon its bor-
ders. Tis true, there was an Ancient *Havilah*, upon the Strand of the Red Sea:
[Gen. XXV. 18. and I. Sam. XV. 7.] the same with *Alah*, or, *Eloth*, or, *Elanoh*, or
Hailah, in *Magirus* upon *Ptolomy*.[81] Here dwelt *Havilah*, the Son of *Cush*; the
Ethiopian of *Arabia*. But near this place, there is no notable River to detain us.
There is another *Havilah*, which Lay, in or near the East-*Indies*, in the Golden
Chersonese; where is the Island of *Ceilan*, or *Chaulan*, that is, *Havilah*: and the
Plantation of *Ophir*, couched in *Hiphouros*, or, *Hippurus*, is in the same Island,
of *Zeilan*. But there was a Third *Havilah*, from *Havilah*, the Son of *Joktan*,
who dwelt near his Brother *Ophir*, and the rest of *Shems* Issue, in the Golden

Countrey of *Arabia*, and afterwards Colonised into more Eastern Countreyes of *Asia*, where wee find, a New *Havilah*, and a New *Ophir*. This is the *Havilah* of the Text now before us.[82]

In the very Mouth of the *Persian* Sea, wee Light upon the *Diving-places*, or Oister-banks, for *Pearl*; and anon, sais *Arrian*, in his *Periplus*, of the *Red-Sea*, you have the χωρα πασινη,—[ms. I, 17] *Regio Pasini*, or, Countrey of *Pison*; called also, *Vallum Pasini*, near the United Falls of *Tigris* & *Uphrates* into the *Persian* Gulf.[83] The People of *Chelfa* there, affirm themselves to have their Habitation in *Eden*. The *Bedolach*, *Bdellium*, or true Oriental *Pearl*, is here found, abundantly, near the Isle of *Baharem*.[84] As for the *Gold* of *Havilah*, Wee know the best *Gold* is in that part of *Arabia*; ['υαιλα of *Ptolomy*,[85] is near the *Homerites* of *Arabia*:] & in such plenty, that they Exchange it for aequal Quantities of *Coper* and *Iron*. Here, *Ophir* was at first planted, near *Chesens*, or, the *Cassanitae*; & the place called *Auphar*, in *Arrian* & *Ptolomy*; but by Removes carried further into *Asia*. *Solomons Ophir*, Lay in the Second Plantation of the Sons of *Joktan*; & not far from the Bay of *Persia*, where *Strabo* affirms, that *Gold*, & transparent Stones were to bee mett withal.[86] There is one Raritie more, by *Moses* assigned unto *Havilah*; and that is, the *Onyx*, which some take for the *Sardonyx*: as indeed Metalls & Jewels, use to Ly together; for our precious Stones are but the Flowers, Ebullitions or Exudations, of *Minerals*. The *Onyx* is here called, *Soham*; and the *Nubian* Geographer, saies, *Du-Sohaim* was in the Land of *Chaulan*, or, *Havilah*. The Upshott is, This Land Lay in the Easterly part of *Arabia*, Environed by the River *Pison*, which was a Fish-ful Branch of *Tigris*, after the Conjunction of *Uphrates*, & its Running down towards the *Persian* Sea, at *Teredon*, now *Belsara*, where all these Waters Tumble into the *Erythraean* Ocean.[87] The Prophet *Ezekiel*, you know, fetches *Pearl* & *Coral*, out of *Eden*; in the South part of the aforesaid Countrey.

II. *Gihon.*

This River is the same that is called, *Gyndes*, by *Herodotus*, *Tibullus*, *Ammianus Marcellinus*, and *Orosius*. The Poet speaks of,

Rapidus Cyri Dementia Gyndes.[88]

A Channel cutt out of *Tigris* by *Cyrus*, was called so.[89] But the Ancient *Gihon*, gave Title, in the Dayes of *Moses* to another Branch of Waters, issuing out from *Tigris*. *It compassed the whole Land of Ethiopia*: [Gen. II. 13.] which wee must understand of the *Arabian Ethiopia*; or, the Eastern, mentioned by *Homer*, of old:[90] From whence came *Zerah*, with his vast Army, against *Judah*: [II Chron. XIV. 9.] The Land of *Midian*, was a part of that *Ethiopia*; where *Moses* [ms. I, 18] married his Wife. The Word הַטֹּבֵב / *Circuiens*, may bee rendred, *Alluens*, *Allambens*.[91] This River, in its pleasant *Maeanders*, ran down, on the Eastern side, of the *Arabian* Deserts; at last, it spreads itself in Great Circuits, into the Lakes of *Chaldaea*; & joining with *Tigris* & *Uphrates* united, they fall together, with a Joyfull Roar, from a vast Mouth, into the Persian Gulf. Tis the

Flood, which *Ptolomy* calls *Maarsares*, or, *Naarsares*; or the *Regius Fluvius*, issuing out of *Uphrates*, at *Sipphara*, near *Naarda*, the University of the Jewish Rabbins;[92] it rowls up & down in many Voluminous Windings, West of *Babylon*, & thence to *Volgesia, Borsita, Bibla Beana, Didigna*; and falls into *Tigris* at *Apamia*.

III. Hiddekel.

The Name of this River, is from, *Dekel*, a *Dart*, for the Swiftness of it; & therefore called also, *Tigris*. The Springs of this Rapid River, tis true, are in the Northern Mountains of *Armenia*; & *Media*, about *Caucasus*. But our present concern Lies in that part of it, where the main Single Stream, rowles out of *Paradise*, on the South-side of the Garden, & runs nimbly towards the East of *Assyria*. Of old, *Assyria* contained itself within the Bounds of these two Rivers; called since, *Mesopotamia*: hence *Lucan* calls, *Haran*, or *Carrae*, where *Crassus* came to his End, *An Assyrian City*.

Assyrias Latio maculavit Sanguine Carras.[93]

Nimrod (afterwards constellated into *Orion*) at first passed into that Land of *Ashur*, [Gen. X. 4.] and there he built *Ninive*, or, *Nini-nave*, i.e. the Habitation of *Nimrod*;[94] and *Rehoboth, Calah* and *Resen*; that is, *Oroba, Calicala*, and *Rhesnea*, near *Ptolomies Ingine*, or *Engannim*, the Fountain of Gardens, or *Edens*, East ward of *Chebar*, or, *Aboras*.

IV. Euphrates.

That is, *Huperath*, or *Phrat*, in English, The *Fruitful River*. This Goodly Stream, ran thro' the midst of *Babylon*; and it is afterward spent, partly in the Chaldaean Lakes, near *Urchoa*, and the *Orcheni*, or the *Ur* of *Abraham*; and partly recollects itself into *Tigris*, & then Envelops itself, in the Bosom of the *Persian* Sea, and so is Lost in what *Solinus* & others call, the *Ethiopian Ocean*.[95]

[ms. I, 19] So Famous is this River, that it needs no Description; or, if you would have it, go to *Pliny* for it; But beware you do not so affront the Scripture, as to take the present *Bagdat*, upon *Tigris*, for *Babylon*; for the old *Babylon*, is, as the Scripture foretold, now in desolate *Heaps*; nothing of Building is in it, or near it, but *Felugea* of Late, a Little Warehouse, for Merchants.[96]

Tis Remarkable to see how the Four *Monarchies*, have been accomodated unto these Rivers; The *Assyrian* to *Tigris*, the *Persian* to *Pison*, the *Graecian* to *Gihon*, and the *Roman* to *Euphrates*, the Old & New *Babylon*.[97]

But passing That Curiositie, *tanquam Canis ad Nilum*;[98] The River that Runs thro' the Garden of *Eden*, must needs be *Tigris*. Accordingly, wee shall find a very beautiful *Island*, in the midst of the River *Tigris*, called, *Gesire*, or, The *Garden*, from / גְזַר / *secuit*.[99] It were Easy, but it would be Tedious, now to produce, the proofs of undoubted *Geography*, that such an *Island* there is, not far from the place, where *Noahs* Ark rested, abundantly answering all

the Scriptural Circumstances of *Paradise*. Wee might Especially, insist on the
Testimony of Sir *Walter Rawleigh*, taken out of *Masius*, reciting the Epistle
of the *Nestorian* Bishops, who Live at & near the place.[100] Whereto wee may
add, the Accounts of Travellers, in *Purchas*,[101] who assert, that the true Ancient Garden of *Eden*, was in the Island *Gozoria*, Ten miles in Circuit; a matter
of Twelve Miles North of *Mosul*, a City now on the West side of *Tigris*, over
against *Niniveh*. This *Mosul*, in Lat. 36. gr. 50. min. is a famous place, at this
Day, tho' *Ninive*, over the Water, on the East side, bee, as was prophesied, a
Desolate Heap.

This *Island*, is called, *Zegira*, by *Ptolomy*; *Gizirra*, by *Ferrarius*; *Zizira*, by
Jansonius; *Jasirey*, by *Olearius*; and Mr. *Tavernier* mentions, *Gezire*, a Little
City, in an Island of *Tigris*.[102]

[The doubled ם *clausum*, in Gen. II. 8. may intimate, that *Paradise* was a,
Locus Circumseptus,[103] walled with Water.]

Thevet, in his *Cosmography*, sais, *Gesire*, in the middle of *Tigris*, is, the most
fertile Soyl, of all *Asia*.[104] [Compare Gen. II. 9]. And all *Mesopotamia*, is, by the
Arabians hence called *Algezire*.

[ms. I, 20] This is the Island whereto *Eliphaz* the *Temanite* alludes, who lived
not far from it: [Job. XXII. 30.] *Hee shall deliver the Island of the Innocent*;
and perhaps hee prophecies, that God will deliver this *Island* of the Innocent
Adam, in the Latter Dayes, into some wonderful Circumstances of Glory, not
yett comprehended.

Every Quarter of the World, has had its Memorials, of this glorious Island.
Asia had sundry *Tempe's*; *Africa* its *Fortunate Islands* & *Hesperides*; *America*,
its *Atlantis* of *Plato*; And *Europe* the Island of Great *Brittain*, by *Hesiod* called,
The Happy: the *Elysian* Fields, & the Gardens of *Alcinous*.[105]

Here was the *Garden Enclosed* [Cant. IV. 12.] the Pinacle of Terrestrial Delight & Glory, and the Palace, where *Adam* and *Eve* were together a Type of our
Lord Jesus Christ, with His Church, in the Latter Dayes. This was the Place,
Watered, & by God Himself Defended & *watched, Night & Day*. Here all Creatures waited on the Harp of the True *Orpheus*, & presented themselves before
the *High-priest of the Creation*.[106]

> *Magna Viri merces, parat ultima Terra Triumphos,*
> *Tigris et Euphrates, sub Tua Jura fluunt.*
>   Propert. L. 3. p. 206.[107]

¶ 2. In these Remarks, which have so far determined the Scituation of the
Primitive PARADISE, and at the same time illustrated the *Geography* of the Bible
in very many other Instances; I have chiefly subsisted on the Manuscript, I have
boasted of.[108] Yett because I have mentioned the great Names of *Bochart* and
Huet; I will offer a Taste or two from them; with observing that one whose
Name is *Wells*, who has published some things on the *Geography of the Old
Testament*, and he does out of *Bochart* and *Huet* further insist on this mat-
ter, with a Discourse, from which I shall not think it amiss to offer a few
Delibations.[109]

The Scituation of *Havilah*, in the Eastern Tract of *Arabia*, near and on the Bottom of the *Persian* Gulf, is no longer to be doubted of. Here we find a *River*, which *Encompasses*, that is, with a winding Stream washes, *all one side* of such a Land, & hath a Communication with the Three other Rivers mentioned in the History, by one Common Channel.

[ms. I, 21] This must needs be our *Pison*. To confirm this, *Huet* observes, it must be remembred, that *Moses* wrote his History in *Arabia Petraea*, or somewhere thereabouts. This River was therefore the nearest unto him; and so it was very Natural and proper for him, to Name it first. The Etymology of the Word, *Pison*, is also to be considered. Most of the Hebrew Grammarians agree, that it comes Either, of / פוש / To *be Full*, or, / פשה / To *spread*. Because the Tides are so high, so violent, so Boisterous, at the End of the *Persian* Gulf, that no Trenches can defend the Neighbouring Grounds from their Incursions. It is therefore observed by *Strabo*, that all the Coast is full of Lakes & Marishes. The Author of the Apocryphal *Ecclesiasticus*, makes an Allusion to this Etymology, where he saies of God, [c. XXIV. 25.] *He fills all with Wisdome, Like the Pison*.[110]

The Province washed by the *Gihon*, was formerly called, *Cush*. Now, the Countrey adjoining to the Easterly Mouth of *Euphrates*, and which by the *Greeks*, and *Latins*, was called, *Susiana*, had formerly that Name of *Cush*; yea, tis at present called so. The Journals of all Travellers inform us, That *Susiana* is now called, *Chuzestan*; which carries plain Footsteps of *Chus*, or *Chuz*, as the Name of *Chush* uses to be written. *Benjamin* of *Navarre*, saies, the great Province of *Elam*, whereof *Susa* is the Metropolis, is called so.[111] That Province is *Elymais*, which Extends itself as far as the *Persian* Gulf, at the East of the Mouth of the *Euphrates*. When the Nubian Geographer calls it, *Churestan*, it is doubtless a Mistake of the Copiers, not well distinguishing the Letter R from Z of the Arabians. The Inhabitants of the Land call it absolutely, *Chus*, if you will beleeve *Marius Niger*.[112] The same Region is called, *Cushah*, [2 Kings. XVII. 24.] And it was partly from thence, that *Salmanassar*,[113] transported a Colony into *Samaria*. This New Colony, afterwards known under the Name of, *Samaritans*, kept also the Name of its Origin, & was called, the *Cuthaeans*. *Dion* has observed, That the Letter, S, is often changed into T, or, TH, by the *Chaldaeans*. We find here also, the *Cossaeans*, Neighbours to the *Uxians*, according to *Pliny*, *Ptolomy*, and *Arrian*, whose Name is doubtless from *Chus*. From hence Likewise the Name of *Cissia*, and of the *Cissians*; a Little Province of *Susiana*, and used some times to denote all the *Susians*.[114]

[ms. I, 22] The Poet *Æschylus*, takes Notice of a City of that Name, seated in the same Land, & remarkable for its Antiquity.[115]

The Third River is Hiddekel. You must not be surprised, if you are now told, That the Name of *Hiddekel* here given by *Moses*; and that of *Diglath*, which they give it in the East; and that of *Tigris*, which the *Europaeans* give it; are but one & the same, Varied by diverse Nations. Take away the Aspiration from the word, *Hiddekel*, and the word, *Dekel*, remains; which the Syrians disguised into *Diklat*. *Josephus*, and the *Chaldaean* Paraphrasts, the *Arabians* and the *Per*-

sians, turned it into *Diglath;* [116] Other Modern Orientals into *Degil,* and *Degola; Pliny,* or those who informed him, into *Diglito;* [117] And the Greeks, who gave to all strange Words, the Turn of their own Tongue, turned the *Diglis,* into *Tigris;* to which they might be the rather induced, because they were inform'd of an Extreme *Swiftness* in the River. From the place where *Moses* was writing, this is the *Third River* that in our Travelling along, we must meet withal.[118] It is here added, (for so it may rather be rendred,) *That is it, which goes before Assyria.* There was as yett no *Assyria,* but only the Province that was first so called, whereof *Niniveh* was the Capital City. Now from the parts where *Moses* was writing, there was no going into that *Assyria,* without crossing the *Tigris,* as running along *before* it.[119]

   The River *Euphrates* is by this time, so well known, as to need no particular Marks for the distinguishing of it. The *Greeks* turned *Perath* into *Euphrates;* partly to suit the Genius of their own Language; and perhaps partly to allude unto the *Pleasantness* or *Fruitfulness* of the Countrey, washed with it. The Greek word, ευφραινειν, signifies, both, To *Rejoice,* and, To *make Fruitfull;* agreable to the Latin Expression, *Loetum facere;* whence *Vergil, Quid Loetas faciat Segetes.*[120] Compare, Psal. LXV. 12, 13. The Words of *Moses,* imply, That in *Eden,* the River was but one; that is, it had but one single Channel; but *from thence,* or, out of *Eden,* it was parted, & became *Four Heads,* or Four principal Channels. The Place he assigns for *Paradise,* is the *Eastern* part of *Eden.* And as Dr. *Wells* expresses it, It must be scituated on one of the Turnings of this River, that goes from West to East, & probably at the Easterly End of the Southernly Branch of the Lowest great Turning, which *Ptolomy* takes Notice of.[121]

   [ms. I, 23] It is probable, That this *Garden of Eden,* was the Original of those curious Gardens, with which the Princes of the East, were so curious to accomodate themselves, and by which they would represent the *Garden of Eden.* Such an one was that *Golden Garden,* valued at Five-hundred Talents, which *Aristobulus* King of the Jews, presented unto *Pompey;* and which *Pompey* afterwards carried in Triumph, & consecrated unto *Jupiter* in the Capitol. The Garden was called, τερπωλη, and, τερπνον, which in strictness of speech, is, *Eden,* or, *Pleasure.* And the Conformity between the very words, *Garden of Eden,* and, Garden of *Adon,* seems to shew, that unto the *Garden of Eden,* was owing the Rise of those Gardens, consecrated unto *Adonis,* which the *Greeks, Egyptians* and *Assyrians,* planted in Earthen Vessels, and Silver Baskets, to adorn their Houses withal, & carried about in their Processions. And there is no doubt, that out of this pattern, the Poets formed, their *Fortunate Islands,* the *Elysian Fields,* the *Meadows of Pluto,* the Gardens of the *Hesperides,* of *Pluto,* & of *Alcinous.*[122]

   We may add this one Curiosity. The *Land of Nod,* whereto *Cain* was banished, it is here said, *It lay before Eden.* This is to be understood, with respect unto the place where *Moses* was now writing. Consequently it was on the *West* of *Eden.* One would therefore incline unto the Opinion of *Grotius;* who supposes *Cain* doom'd of God, unto a withdraw into the Desarts of *Arabia,* which does join unto the *West* of *Eden.*[123] Such a place, (rather than a Pleasant & Fruitfull

Susiana) is most proper for a Banishment. And unto the Barrenness of this part of *Arabia*, may pertain the Curse, Gen. IV. 12. *When thou tillest the Ground, it shall not henceforth yeeld her strength unto thee.*[124]
   Thus our Collector.[125] [ms. I, 24 canceled]

[ms. I, 25]
¶ 3. Tho' I have thus offered, what may be sufficient for our Present Entertainment, yett I must present the Reader with a *Dessert*, of a short Passage, which I fetch from the Travels of M. *Tournefort*.[126] His Words are these:
   "If we follow the Letter of that Passage, wherein *Moses* describes the Situation of the *Terrestrial Paradise*, nothing seems more Natural, than the Opinion of M. *Huetius*, the ancient Bishop of *Avranches*, one of the most Learned Men of his Time.[127] *Moses* assures us, That a River went out of that Delightful Place, and divided itself into Four Channels, the *Euphrates*, the *Tigris*, *Pison*, and *Gihon*. But no such River can be found in any Part of *Asia*, except this of *Arabia*; That is to say, the *Euphrates* and *Tigris* joined together, and divided into Four great Channels, which empty themselves into the Bay of *Persia*. *Huetius* therefore seems indeed to have fully answered the Letter of the Text, in fixing *Paradise* in this Place. But notwithstanding this, his Notion cannot be maintained; it being so very manifest from the *Greek* and *Latin* Geographers & Historians, [Plin. l. 6. c. 26. Polyb. Hist. l. 5. Strabo. l. 16. Appian de Civ. Bel. l. 2. Arrian. de Exped. Alex. l. 7. Ptolom. Geogr. l. 5. c. 17. Ammian. Marcel. l. 24. c. 21. Zosim. l. 3. c. 24.][128] That the *Euphrates* and *Tigris* formerly ran in Separate Beds; and likewise, that there was a Design to make a Canal of Communication between the Two Rivers, and that afterwards Several Canals were actually made by Commands of the King of *Babylon*, and *Alexander* the Great, and even of *Trajan*, and *Severus*, for the facility of Commerce, and to render the Countrey more Fruitful.[129] There is no Reason therefore to doubt, but these Branches of this River of *Arabia*, were made by the Art of Man, and Consequently were not in the *Terrestrial Paradise*.
   "The Commentators upon *Genesis*; even those who are most confined unto the *Letter*, don't think it necessary, in order to assign the Place of *Paradise*, to find a River, which divides itself into Four Branches; because of the very Great Alterations which [ms. I, 26] the *Flood* may have introduced:[130] But think it enough to shew the *Heads* of the Rivers mention'd by *Moses*; namely, the *Euphrates*, *Tigris*, *Pison*, and *Gihon*. And thus, it cannot be doubted, but that *Paradise* must have been in the Way, between *Erzeron* and *Teflis*;[131] if it be allow'd to take the *Phasis* for *Pison*, and *Araxes* for *Gihon*. And then, not to remove *Paradise* too far from the *Heads* of these *Rivers*, it must of necessity be placed in the beautiful Vales of *Georgia*, which furnish *Erzeron* with all sorts of Fruits. And, if we may suppose *Paradise* to have been a Place of Considerable Extent, and to have retained some of its Beauties, notwithstanding the Alterations made in the Earth at the *Flood*, and since that time, I don't know a finer Spott, to which to assign this *Wonderful Place*, than the *Countrey of the Three Churches*, about twenty French Leagues[132] from the Heads of *Euphrates* and *Araxes*; and near as many from the *Phasis*. The Extent of *Paradise* must

at least reach to the Heads of these Rivers; and so it will comprehend the ancient *Media,* and Part of *Armenia,* and *Iberia.* Or, if this be thought too large a Compass, it may be confined only to Part of *Iberia,* and *Armenia,* that is, from *Erzeron* to *Teflis.* For it can't be doubted, that the Plain of *Erzeron,* which is at the Head of *Euphrates* and *Araxis,* must be taken in." Thus our French Traveller and Botanist.

§ 4. After such Views as we have thus had, of the *Roads* leading to the *Terrestrial Paradise,* and of the *Ancient Landmarks* by which we may find it, how Surprizing must it be, to find a very Learned *Heidegger* maintain, That the True Seat of *Paradise,* was in that Part of the *Holy Land,* which was called *Genesar,* [or, *Hortus Principis,*[133] that is, of *Adam,*] and which comprehends the Sea of *Galilee,* the illustrious Field and Vale of *Jericho,* and the Countrey which the *Dead Sea* has [ms. I, 27] now buried under Water. The *River of Paradise* he takes to be the *River of Jordan,* [its Name originally being / נהר עדן / *The River of Eden.*] The Four famous Rivers of *Pison* and *Gihon* and *Hiddekel* and *Euphrates,* he takes to hold such a Subterraneous Communication with *Jordan,* which we know has no Outlett above ground, that *Jordan* may justly be esteemed the Source of them all. He imagines, an Inspection of the Maps, would invite one to such Apprehensions. And indeed both *Brocardus* and *Villamontius* do mutter something of such a matter. Tis with an *Uncommon* (tho' with HIM *Usual*) Erudition, that my rare *Helvetian* endeavours to support his *Paradox.*[134] But if the *Geography* of this Gentleman look ever so *Improbable,* it is yett more Defensible, than that of old *Epiphanius,*[135] who [to show us, no doubt, that the Fathers were as accurate in their *Geography* as they were in their *Astronomy,*] tells us, That *Pison,* one of the Rivers that watered *Paradise,* was the Same that the Indians and the Ethiopians called, *Ganges,* and that the Greeks called, *Indus;* which River at length passing thro' *Ethiopia,* discharged itself at length into the Ocean at *Cales.* The Mention of which putts one in Mind, That all the Fathers do by *Gihon,* another of the Rivers wherewith *Paradise* was watered, understand the River *Nilus.* And even so late a Modern as Cardinal *Perron* was herein so deceived, that he delivered it, as an *Express Text* of the Scriptures: which both *Scaliger* and *Petavius* do chastise him for.[136] But when we pardon *Tertullians* unphilosophical fancy of the *Plants,* and *Ambrose's* of the *Sun;* and the Scorn wherewith *Justin* derides the *Sphaerical Figure* of the Heavens, and the Resolution of *Lactantius* never to hear the *Circular Figure* of the *Earth,* and the Antipathy of *Austin* to *Antipodes,* we must have the like Pardon ready for these Ungeographical Gentlemen.[137]

[ms. I, 28] After all this Labour, it may be, the Issue and Result will be; *Probè fecistis; Multò incertior sum quàm dudum.*—[138] And some will complain, that they are left little better than in *a Fools Paradise,* as to the Points they were most in Expectation of.

We will say then; That a *Terrestrial Paradise* cannot be found: It is no more to be look'd for; It is gone like a great Milstone thrown down into the Sea; A

Flood has wash'd it out of the World; Neither *It,* nor the *Ruined Place* of it, is ever to be seen any more. *Quis talia fundo—*[139]

But, O! Blessed be our Glorious REDEEMER! There is by Him a *Better Thing provided* for His People. There is a PARADISE infinitely more Desireable, which, with His Help, Lett us now proceed unto.

The
Second PARADISE.

We are inform'd, and it is allow'd, That until the Age of *Ezra*,[1] the People whom GOD had *known above all the Families of the Earth*, applied, and perhaps appropriated, the Term of PARADISE, unto the Delicious Garden of EDEN, the amiable, the admirable, the richly accommodated Spott of *Earth*, where our First Parents were placed by our most Gracious Creator. But the Condition of the *Church upon Earth* was now growing more and more so full of *Thorns*, and a *Land flowing with Milk & Honey* here, was become so Uncertain, & so Troublesome, as to drive the People that were under the *Covenant* and *Instruction* of GOD, unto more Stedy Thoughts of a more *Heavenly World*; And the nearer they were to the Dawn of the Time when the *Sun of Righteousness* would more fully appear from thence unto them, the more *Distinct Views* of that World were granted them. From this Time, *The GOD of Israel*, is called, *The GOD of Heaven*; And from this Time, there was more Cause than ever, to consider *Heaven* as the Place where the Blessed GOD is to do, what He has to do, for His *Israel*. We are certain, That Good Men long before those Days, *Hop'd* and *Sought* for an *Heavenly Countrey*; And a *Blessedness* to be received at & by a *Resurrection from the Dead*, was their Grand Expectation. From the *Scriptures*, whereof they enjoy'd a Portion, they were advis'd of an *Eternal Life*, whereof the paenitent *Children of Death* were to be made Partakers by a SAVIOUR who would *Redeem them from the Power of the Grave*: And in the *Shechinah*[2] of GOD sometimes visibly exhibited among them, they had a very Plain, Indisputable, Unquaestionable *Demonstration* of *Another World*. But from the Age of *Ezra* downward, when they spoke of that *Intermedial State*, wherein the *Immortal Souls* of the Righteous are to subsist, between their *Expiration* and the *Resurrection*, the Wise among them now distinguished *This*, by the peculiar Name of PARADISE.[3] Their Form of Comprecation and Benediction for a Dying [ms. II, 2] *Israelite* was, *May his Soul be in the Garden of Eden*! They placed *Abraham* and *Moses* in *Paradise*: And it was a celebrated Saying among them; *That none have a Right for to enter* Paradise, *but the Just, the Souls of whom are carried thither by Angels.* They pray'd for the *Comforter to come & open the Gates of* Paradise unto the Souls, of the deceased: And from the *Jewish* it became also a *Chaldaean* Oracle, *Seek* Paradise *the glorious Countrey of Souls*!

It is not at all to be wondred at, That the Name of *Paradise*, by Custome came to signify any Place of uncommon *Delight* and *Beauty*; and that the Greek Version so renders the Words of *Solomon*, [Eccl. II. 5.] I *made me* ΠΑΡΑΔΕΙΣΟΥΣ *Paradises*. When *Cicero* found the Term in *Xenophon*, he rendred it, *Agrum conseptum ac diligenter consitum*: A Field well *hedg'd* and *sow'd*.[4] The Term is affirm'd by *Pollux*, to be of a *Persian* Original: But the *Jewish* Language having adopted it, we may from the *Jewish* Nation best learn the Meaning of it. *Philo* alone will be a Sufficient Interpreter, to satisfy us, That the Term of *Paradise* was used by the *Jews*, to signify, *The Happiness of Souls in a State of Separation from their Bodies.*[5] This *Happiness* was by the *Hellenist Jews* more particularly called, ΑΝΑΠΑΥΣΙΣ, the *Repose*, and, ΠΑΡΑΚΛΗΣΙΣ, the *Comfort*, of *Paradise*; because of the Desireable Enjoyments vouchsafed unto the *Separate Souls* of the Righteous there. A *Gellius* translates the Word, *Paradise*, by, *Vivarium*: A Place wherein Beloved Creatures (and especially *Birds*,) are *Kept alive for Pleasure.*[6] And his Translation seems most agreeably to *Enliven* our Idaea of the *Paradise*, wherein the *Winged Souls* of the Righteous are to be *kept Alive*, until they are fetched from thence into the Faelicities of the *Resurrection*:

This is the PARADISE unto which we must now call off our Thoughts, from that which was *overflown with a Flood*; and from a [ms. II, 3] World which is not a *Paradise* (nor is like to afford one) but is an horrid & howling Wilderness; A *Land of Pitts & of Droughts, & fiery flying Serpents.*[7]

Sect. I. The Faith of a PARADISE praepared by our most Powerful & Merciful REDEEMER, for the *Departed Souls* of Good Men, must suppose, *The Immortatility of the Soul*; must suppose its Existing and Surviving after the *Death* of the *Mortal Body.*[8] The *Dream* of the *Soul Sleeping* after Death, or Ceasing to *Think* or Losing all Faculty to *Think*, which to a *Rational Soul* would at least be little short of Ceasing to *Be*, one would think to have been Sufficiently Disturbed by the Thunderbolts of a *Calvin*, [in his Book, of the, *Psychopannychia*, whereof *Zanchy* very justly says, *Dignissimus est, qui legatur*,] and abundantly Confuted by a mighty Host of acute Writers, wherein if we allow an *Origen* for a *Leader*, an *Amyraut*, a *Baxter*, & a *Bates*, may be esteemed no Contemptible *Bringers* up.[9] Of the *Departing Soul*, they who had buried Theirs in *Sense* and in *Sin*, said in Days as long ago as the Son of *Sirach*, *It vanishes into Soft Air*: which Terms *Lucretius*, a great Apostle of Theirs, made his own, in his, *Tenues evanescit in Auras.*[10] But the *Host of GOD* have made such a *Brick-kiln*, that these *Ammonites* cannot but fall by the Swords which reach them in their *Garloup* of passing thorough it. A Dying *Pope*, has been celebrated, for his declaring, that he was *then* going to be satisfied, *whether he had an Immortal Soul or no!*[11] A fine Qualification for one pretending to be, *The Infallible Head of* [ms. II, 4] *the Church!* Another *Vile Person*, who was of his Countrey, by ordering for himself, that Epitaph, *Totus* Cremoninus *hic jacet*, only erected a Monument of his own *Vileness*;[12] but could not by his *Beastly Order* procure for himself the *Fate* of the *Beast*, of which, tis likely, his having led the *Life* of one, might render him so ambitious. But, *Awake, O my Soul, and assert thy own Immortality; And from fair Probabilities, & strong Praesumptions of it, go on, and rise higher & higher, till thou art come to the most Ungainsayable Demonstrations.*

We are sure, *The Spirit of a Man is the Candle of the Lord.* And such a *Lamp* of GOD, being once enkindled in any *Individual*, tho' it may *go away*, will it ever *go out*? Indeed, The Story of the *Lamp* found burning in the Tomb of

Tulliola, after many Ages, is found a *Fable*:[13] and so is all that we read of that Sort. But certainly, here is a *Lamp* that will hold its Flame to *Endless Ages*. Other Things may *Perish*, but *thou*, O *Lamp* of GOD, *shalt Endure*; *thy Garment may wax old*, *thy Vesture shall be changed*; but *thy Years will have no End*; Such an *Image* thou hast of thy *Eternal Maker* upon thee!

In the whole *Creation* of GOD, there is no one Instance, of any *Inclination* made by Him in any Creature, so Superfluous & so Impertinent, that He has provided no Gratification for it. Now, There is a *Natural Desire* of *Immortality*, which we find very deeply rooted in the *Soul* of Man. Tis not a *Vice* of *Depraved Nature*; tis no *Vicious Inclination*: It is formed in us, by an All-Wise GOD, who does *Nothing in Vain*. Doubtless, Tis to be *Gratified*.

The *General Praesage* of *Immortality*, which operates in the *Soul*, and is discovered, even by the rudest *Pagans*, and the very *Indians* themselves, in the *Scythian Deserts*[14] of *America*: THIS *also* [ms. II, 5] *cometh forth from the Lord of Hosts*: HE has wrought it, who is *Excellent in Working*. It can be no *Delusion*; inasmuch as it is Engraven here, by the GOD that *forms the Spirit of Man within him*. Tis not a meer *Tradition received from their Fathers*; nor a Fancy with which they have been frighted by their *Nurses*: But *Something within them*, dictates it. Indeed, *Cebes* confesses, there was ΤΟΙΣ ΠΟΛΛΟΙΣ ΑΠΙΣΤΙΑ, *A Disbeleef of it in Many*. And *Cicero* confesses, there were *Catervae contradicentium*, & others besides the *Epicureans* that opposed it. Nevertheless, the *Lusts* of these People could not wholly suppress the *Suspicion* of it in them; there still remained in them, Something that *Suspected* it: It was a *Perswasion* kept under, by their Impiety; but it was not wholly extirpated. Our *Zanchy* among others, has made a *Victorious Collection*, of *Testimonies* and *Confessions*, from all Sorts of People, for, *The Immortality of the Soul*. So that here is Room for *Cicero's* Axiom, *In omni re, omnium Gentium consensio Lex Naturae putanda est*. And what can the *Law* & *Light of Nature* be, but the *Voice* of the GOD of *Nature*?[15]

What Judgment shall be passed upon the *Apparitions* of *Spirits*, professing themselves to be *Humane Souls*, after they had by *Death* been forced out of their *Bodies*? The *Witlings* of an *Epicurean* Age and Herd may laugh at all such things; because there have been a few *Impostures* detected.[16] But the Relations of such *Apparitions*, have been many of them as unquaestionable as the *Matters of Fact* which have been delivered unto us in the most undoubted Histories, and such as *no body* can make any Quaestion of. Those of Sir *George Villiers*, and of Major *Sydenham*, and those related by *Webster*, will compel the Beleef of all but Conceited & Obstinate *Fools*. The whole City of *London* had Occasion to take notice of such an one, in the Year, 1695. when the appearing of one *Stockdon*, procured the Apprehension and the Execution of Three Men who had murdered him; whereof Mr. *Smithyes*, a Considerable and Unreproachable Divine, has given us an ample Narrative. In the Year, 1706. we had it as an undisputed Article among the *Memorable Occurrences* of it: That one Mr. *Nailor*, after he had been Two Years among the Dead, came and satt a good while with his Friend Mr. *Shaw*, in *Oxford*; And one Passage in the Conversation was, that the Latter enquired, *How do they do in that World which you are gone to?* the former answered, *Very well, But not as you do here!*[17]

My own Vicinity has been more than once or twice visited, with *Spirits,* who have been *seen* and *heard* asserting themselves to be the *Souls* of Persons departed; and my own most *Critical Enquiries* have putt it out of all Doubt with me, that the Persons more immediately addressed in these Visits, have [ms. II, 6] not been impos'd upon. Out of my Collection, I will single out only Two or Three Instances, that in *the Mouth of Two or Three Witnesses the thing may be established.* And I will praesume to say so much of them; That the Story which the Publishers & Praefacers of M. *Drelincourts* often reprinted Book about, *The Fear of Death,* have thought worth telling to the World, & laying some Stress upon, will not be found more worthy of Consideration, than these, which we shall now proceed unto.[18]

The First is This. On the Second of *May,* in the Year, 1687. an Ingenious, Accomplished, well-disposed Young Gentleman, Mr. *Joseph Beacon,*[19] about five a clock in the Morning, as he lay, whether Sleeping or Waking, he could not certainly say, but judged the Latter, had a View of his Brother then at *London,* tho' he were now at our *Boston,* distanced from him a thousand Leagues. This his Brother appeared now unto him, as having on him a *Bengal* Gown, (which he usually wore) with a Napkin tied about his Head. His Countenance was very pale, ghastly, deadly; and he had a Bloody Wound on one side of his Forehead. *Brother!* sayd the affrighted *Joseph. Brother!* answered the Apparition. *Joseph* said, *What's the Matter, Brother! How came you here!* The Apparition reply'd, *Brother, I have been most barbarously & inhumanely murdered, by a debauched fellow, to whom I never did any wrong in my Life.* Whereupon he gave a Particular Description of the Murderer; Adding; *Brother, This fellow, changing his Name, is attempting to come over unto* New-England, *Either in* Foy *or in* Wild. *I would pray you, on the first Arrival of either of these, to gett an Order from the Governour, to sieze the Person whom I have now described; and then do you gett him indicted for the Murder of me Your Brother: I'l stand by you and prove the Indictment.* And so he vanished. Mr. *Beacon* was extremely astonished at what he had seen and heard; and the People of the Family where he sojourned, not only observed an Extraordinary Alteration upon him, for a Week following, but also gave me under their hands a full Testimony ready to be deposed upon Oath, that he *then* gave them an Account of this Apparition. All this while, Mr. *Beacon* had no Advice of any thing amiss, attending his [ms. II, 7] Brother then in *England.* But about the Latter End of *June* following, he understood by the Common Ways of Communication, that in the preceding *April,* his Brother going in Haste by night for to call a Coach for a Lady, mett a fellow then on Drink, with a Doxy[20] in his hand. Some way or other, the fellow thought himself affronted in the Hasty Passage of this *Beacon;* and immediately ran in to the Fire-side of a neighbouring Tavern; from whence he fetch'd out a Fire-fork, wherewith he grievously wounded *Beacon* on the Skull, in that very Part where the Apparition shew'd his Wound. Of this Wound he Languished, until he Died, on the Second of *May* aforesaid, about five a clock in the Morning, at *London*. The Murderer, it seems, was endeavouring an Escape, as the Apparition affirm'd; but the Friends of the Deceased *Beacon* siez'd him; and prosecuted him. However, he found the Help of such Friends as brought him off, without the Loss of his Life: Since which there was no more heard of the Business.

A Second is this. In the Latter End of the Year, 1695. a Young Woman in *Boston*, whose Name was, *Mehetabel Warner*, was visited by another Young Woman, whose Name was, *Mary Johnson*.[21] The latter of these, being Somewhat Sickly, fell into Discourse with the former, about, *The State of our Spirits after Death*. The Discourse proceeded unto so much of Curiosity, that *Mary* pressed upon *Mehetabel*, an Agreement between them, That which soever of them should have it appointed for them to *Dy first*, would come to the Survivour, and lett her know, whether there be a Real *State of Separate Spirits*, and whether they have any *knowledge of what is done in This World?* *Mehetabel* express'd her Fear of coming into this Agreement; but *Mary* still demanded it; and at her Leaving of her, her Last Words were, *Well, If I dy first, you shall* [ms. II, 8] *hear of me*: And *Mehetabel* afterwards confessed, *That she had gone too far in the Agreement. Mary Johnson* quickly goes to *Haverhil*, a Town thirty Miles off *Boston*; and there she Dies. It was not long before *Mehetabel Warner* heard a Voice diverse times calling to her; *Hitty, Come here!* and with such Circumstances, that it could be concluded, this *Voice* came from none but the *Invisible World*. There ensued Violent and very *Audible Knocks* from an *Invisible Hand*, upon her Mothers House, where she now resided; which continued for *Diverse Weeks*, and sometimes for the best Part of *Whole Nights* together; and the *Knocks* were heard as far off as in other Families of the Neighbourhood; and they shook the *Doors* and *Sides* of the Habitation where they were given. Upon an Experiment made, by *Mehetabels* altering the Place of her Lodging, and the Noise more closely following of her, it was taken for granted, *That it came upon her account*. She had now heard of *Mary's* Death; and she then told her Friends, of the *Agreement* which *Mary Johnson* had propos'd unto her; and she verily beleeved, That it was the *Departed Spirit* of that Young Woman, which was now so Troublesome. She resolved therefore, That the Next Night that there should be any more such *Knocking*, she would speak unto the *Knocker*, and ask, what should be their Meaning? The *Knocking* return'd; and *Mehetabels* Lodging was in a Chamber of the House, where her Mother with another of her Children lay below. The Whole House was made sensible enough of the *Knocking*, and pretty well affrighted with it, tho' they had heard so much of it, and so long a Time. At last, *Mehetabel* took the *Courage*, tho' not without a Sweating *Terror* upon her, to Speak, and Say, *In the Name of the Lord, what is it that you come for?* Immediately, a Shril Voice very audibly answered; *Hitty, Come hither! Hitty, Come hither! Hitty, Come hither!* [ms. II, 9] Not only did *Mehetabel* hear this, but also her Mother, who is a virtuous and credible Woman, and the other Person that was with her. They heard no more after this. But in a few Days *Mehetabel Warner* fell sick; She lay sick but about *Four Days*, and it could hardly be told, what her Distemper was. Then she died, in a very Comfortable Frame of Mind; in the Month of *April*, 1696. when she was a little above twenty Years of Age.

For these Two Instances, I did by the Strictest Enquiries obtain all Possible Confirmation.

I will offer a Third, for which the Credit will rest wholly on the Single Testimony of the Gentleman more immediately concerned: But for my own Part, I have not the Least Haesitation about it. A Worthy Friend of mine, *John Watts* Esqr,[22] assured me; That One Morning about break of Day, he Lodging in or near *London*, he had a Sight of his Beloved Sister, who was then as far from him, as the *American Boston*. He express'd an Astonishment, how she came there; and the more for the bright Circumstances that she appeared in. She told him, That she was *Expir'd*, but *Happy*; and expressing a very tender Concern for him, she mightily encouraged him to a Life of *Serious Piety*: with diverse Particular Directions about it. He afterwards understood, that she died, not many Hours before his being thus entertained with her Apparition. But, as if this his godly, & lovely, & affectionate Sister, had been another *Potamiana*, it had a very holy & lasting Impression upon him, and contributed more than a little to the *Serious Piety*, which he afterwards maintained, unto the End of his Days.[23]

I am furnished with more such well-attested Narratives; and some of them Sworn before the Magistrate. But I am lothe to grow tedious upon the Argument. I will only add [ms. II, 10] this: Tis no Rare thing among us, for People to have *Apparitions* of their Friends, as *Drown'd* or otherwise *Dead*, who have been at the same time abroad, at Sea, or in other Countreys. At the Time of the *Apparitions*, they have been much talk'd of in the alarum'd Neighbourhood; And I have myself at the Time, enquired into them, and made a Record of them, and concurr'd with the Neighbours in expecting the *Event*. The *Event* has been, that our first News of them has been, that at that very Time, they were *Drown'd*, or otherwise *Dead*, as they had been represented.

Now, I see no Cause to think any other, but that these were the *Humane Souls*, which they Appeared for. And who can tell, but that the Glorious GOD who enables our *Will*, while we are yett in our *Bodies*, under certain Limitations to Command and Perform such Motions as we *Will*, may so extend the Sphaere of Activity to *Souls* taken out of their *Bodies*, that they shall be able, when they *Will*, to form such an Human *Voice*, or *Shape*, as they have been us'd unto, and render it *sensible* to the Survivers? On the Third of my Instances, one would argue so. The *Spirit* that said, *I am the Soul of your Sister*: An *Evil Spirit* would not come upon such an Intention, as to animate *Serious Piety*: A *Good Spirit*, would not *Ly*, and assert himself to be a Person, which he is *not*: Then, it must be the *Soul* of the Deceased. But suppose the *Appearing Spirits* to be *not* the *Souls* they appear for; still they were such *Spirits*, as would plainly induce any one, to beleeve the Existence of such *Humane Souls* in a State of *Separation*.[24]

Lett us go on. If we Reasonably Consider the *Constitution* of our *Soul*;—Here we find, it is no *Perishable Substance*; nor does it consist [ms. II, 11] of *Corruptible Principles*. Tis a *Spiritual Substance*; and it has no *Separable Parts*;

nor any *Seeds of Corruption* in it. Our *Soul* has a Conception of Things purely *Spiritual;* a GOD, and *Spirits* that are *Pure Intelligences*, and the *Analogies* and *Relations* of things to one another: And it Rectifies the *False Reports*, which the *Senses* may happen to make unto it. Now, the *Faculty* and the *Object* must be agreeable to one another: If the *Soul* were not itself an *Intellectual Being*, it could not apprehend such a Being. And what can there be, to render such a Being liable to a *Dissolution?* The Roman Orator made this, as a very just Conclusion; *Quum simplex Animi Natura esset, neqe haberet in se quicquam admixtum dispar sui atqe dissimile.*[25]—The *Soul* can, and often does, mortify the most vehement Appetites of the *Body;* yea, against the greatest Reluctances that can be found in *Flesh & Blood*, it wittingly and willingly exposes the *Body* to *Death* itself. Its most grateful *Pleasures*, and its most grievous *Troubles*, are such as *Moral Causes* give unto it. From this, tis very *Certain*, that the *Soul* is a thing very different from the *Body;* and from hence tis very *Likely*, that it will survive the *Body*. And, as one well says, "To imagine, that because the Soul in the Present State, can't understand clearly without the Convenient Disposition of the *Body*, therefore it cannot act at all without it, is as absurd as to fancy, because a Man confined unto a Chamber cannot see the Objects without, but thro' the Windows, therefore he cannot see at all but thro' such a Medium, and that when he is out of the Chamber he has totally lost his Sight."

Or, that I may illustrate it with another Comparison. While the *Spring* of my *Watch* is in it, it moves the Curious Machin, it setts and keeps all the *Wheels* in Motion; and the *Hands* do their Office faithfully. If it be taken out of the *Barrel*, & cease to be employ'd as it was, while it was there, tis a [ms. II, 12] *Spring* still; it loses not its *Elasticity;* nor is it made incapable of being putt into another *Machin* that shall be like the former.

But I will insist no longer on the greatest *Likelihoods*: For tho' they be never so praeponderating, yett *They* alone, will not give to a *Reasonable Soul* all its desired Satisfaction. When the Dying *Socrates* uttered some Thoughts of Something to be enjoy'd *after Death*, he did it, with an, *If, Perhaps;* and broke off with a Mean Passage, *But this I would not speak too confidently, nor does it become any Wise Man to be positive, that it will be so.* As *Tertullian* remarks upon it, All he said was, *Non de Fiducia compertae Veritatis.* We cannot wonder if a *Caesar*, when he comes to speak of *Death*, should say, *Ultrà neqe Curae neqe Gaudio locum esse.* But even a *Cicero* beginning to speak of a Surviving Soul, says, *Expone, si potes*, or, *I wish you could make it out.* And having reckoned up the Different Opinions of the Philosophers about it, he concludes, *which of these Opinions is True* [DEUS aliquis viderit] *Some GOD must inform us, which is most like to Truth, is a Great Quaestion.* Yea, *Plutarch* prates about, ΜΥΘΩΔΗΣ ΕΛΠΙΣ, *The Fabulous Hope of Immortality. Lipsius* owns, That it was a Controverted Point among the *Stoicks;* They were still at their, *Ifs*, or, *Ands*, and fluctuating between their *Disjunctives* upon it. Accordingly, *Seneca* brings it in with a, *Fortasse, Si modò Sapientum vera Fama est*, or, *It may be so, if what wise Men have said about it, be True.*[26] But, Thanks be to our GOD; We can speak it very *Confidently*, and be very *Positive* in it. We can *make it out;* We have a GOD who has *informed* us. We have a *well-bottom'd Hope* of it; We [ms. II, 13] are gott beyond an, *It may be so.* One who neither can *Deceive,* nor be *Deceived,* has infallibly told us, *It will be so.* Shall we not Beleeve, If *One come unto us from the Dead?* There has come One who is not an Ordinary One; but One who by *Rising from the Dead* [whereof we have *many Infallible Proofs!*] has demonstrated Himself to be the *Son of GOD,* and a *Teacher come from GOD,* whose *Revelation* is in all things forever to be relied upon. He that *Made* our *Soul,* and *Bought* our *Soul,* and that instructs us, to *Committ unto Him* our Departing *Soul,* has Expressly told us, concerning the most *Killing* Things in the World, Matth. X. 28. *They kill the Body, but are not able to kill the Soul.* A venemous Insinuation, as if this Gospel had not so fairly recited the Words of our SAVIOUR, that we may depend upon it, would be so foolish & so profane, that it ought forever to be hissed out from the Church of GOD with indignation. *Rash Man!*—Our SAVIOUR also says, [Matth. XVI. 26.] *what is a Man profited, if he gain the whole World, & lose his own Soul.* It is true, that if a Man were presently to lose his *Life* upon such a Purchase, he would be no *Gainer* by it; because there would be no *Time* for the Enjoyment. And such a *Rash Man,* would, no doubt, look on the Parallel Text in the other Gospel, as encouraging him to offer *This,* as *All* that is contained in the Words of our SAVIOUR. But you will soon see *Something further* intended, when you consider, That our SAVIOUR is here shewing the Reasonableness of, *Parting with Life itself,* in Service & Suffering for Him. This could never be made out, if the *Soul* differed not from the *Body,* or were extinguished with it. But this Passage,—*Kill the Body, & not able to kill the Soul;*—Tis *Decisive;* It has Determined the Matter; T'wil be a most Criminal Impiety, to doubt, *The Immortality of the Soul,* after such an Illustrious Determination.

Our *Dying* SAVIOUR Himself, had an *Humane Soul,* (as tis own'd by all who have not lick'd up the *Apollinarian* Haeresy,)[27] which He did *Then* [ms. II, 14] committ into the Hands of His Eternal FATHER; and which after He was Dead, immediately entred into the *Paradise* of GOD.

Instructed by Him, a *Crowned Leader* in His *Army of Martyrs,*[28] did at His Death call upon HIM, as He had before call'd upon His Eternal FATHER, and therein own'd HIM to be GOD, Equal with His Eternal FATHER, [For unto none less than such a GOD, would one dare to committ a *Departing Spirit!*] Saying, *Lord JESUS, Receive my Spirit.* And, like *Stephen,* all the rest of His People, herein *Followers of the GOOD ONE,* have under a Divine Direction and Afflation, expired committing their *Souls* into the Hands of, *The GOOD ONE;* and with a *Lively Hope* in a *Dying Hour* have said, *I know whom I have Beleeved, and I am perswaded that He is Able to keep what I have committed unto Him.* And, as the Psalmist expresses it, Their *Souls* have *gone to lodge with the GOOD ONE,* at the Time when their *Offspring* are dividing the *Earthly Inheritance* which they leave unto them.

Our Apostle PAUL is one, whose *Inspirations* arrive to the Church of GOD, with such Evident Signatures of a *Divine Original* upon them, that our *Satisfied Reason* upon fair & full Evidence receives the *Divine Testimony* in them.

Now this Inspired Servant of GOD, when upon the Occasion of a Great Vouch-safement unto him; [I suppose, when he had his *Trance* in the *Temple*, which is mentioned in the Book of, *The Acts*, wherein He *Saw the Just One*, & was Qualified for his *Apostle-ship* unto the *Idolatrous Gentiles*!] he says, [2. Cor. XII. 3.] *whether I was in the Body or out of the Body, I cannot tell*; He plainly tells us, That a *Soul* may be *Out of the Body*, and THEN *See* and *Hear* Things that are *Unspeakable*. According to his plain Concession and Assertion, the *Soul* when *Separated* from the [ms. II, 15] *Body*, yett has an *Ear* to hear, and an *Eye* to see, what no *Body* in This World has a *Tongue* to utter.

   And, what shall we think of the *Desire* working in the *Soul* of this admi-rable Man? [Phil. I. 23.] *I desire to Depart, & to be with CHRIST, which is far better*. There has been much debate *Pro* and *Con* among the *Romanists*, about their Grand Apostle *Aristotle*, whether he held, *The Immortality of the Soul*, or no. There are Words of this Importance to be found in *Aristotle*; *Tis absurd to say, That any Man can be Happy after Death; Since Happiness does con-sist in Operation*. Upon this, *Atticus* long ago reckon'd him among those, who held that *Souls* could not remain after their *Bodies*. And *Origen* says, He did *Condemn the Doctrine of the Souls Immortality*: However, he has not wanted Vindicators: an *Oregins* among the rest. Be sure, Our Apostle, would not have imagined, that he could have a *Soul Happy* without being *in Operation*.[29] So Fervent, So Active, so well-principled a Servant of GOD; could *he* have desired a *Departure*, into a Condition of all *Operation* ceasing! He could not have har-boured & cherished a *Desire* of a *Dissolution*, if his Holy *Soul* must have come to *nothing*, or have been laid in a *Sleeping Inactivity*, at his *Departure* from the *Body*. I am sure, To, *Be With CHRIST*, and in a *far better State*, than that of one *at Work* for CHRIST, & one fill'd with *Precious Thoughts* of Him, among the *Living on the Earth*; Tis very contrary to the having of *no Being* at all, or being altogether *No where*; or not being *in any State* at all, and vanishing into Nothing.

   It has been said *Quicquid Sufficientiae additur, Superfluitati adscribetur*.[30] But, tho' what has been offered may be *Sufficient* for the Proof of the *Souls Im-mortality*, yett it will not be altogether *Superfluous*, if I go on to prove it, with a Glorious *Argument*, which, Oh! That the Reader may in his *own Soul*, feel the Presence & the Power of! [ms. II, 16] Here and There [Alas, that it is yett but *Here* and *There*!] a Soul Rectified and Replenished with, *The Love of GOD*, is to be mett withal. This *Love of GOD*, which our Bible calls, *A Good Work*, on the *Soul*, is a *Living Principle* in it; A *Principle*, whereof the Sacred Oracles have told us, That it shall *never Dy*, but be a *Seed* of Life *always remaining* in the Man that has it; and be, *A Well of Water springing up to Everlasting Life*. Now, if the *Soul* be Extinguished, this *Divine Principle* in the Soul must suffer an Extinction with it. The Promises of a Perpetual Vigour and Verdure to the *Principle* of PIETY in the *Soul*, do promise as perpetual a Continuation of the *Soul*. No Wonder then, that we read, [Rom. VIII. 10.] *The Body is Dead because of Sin, but the Spirit is Life because of Righteousness*. A Never-dying Principle of *Righteousness* in the *Spirit*, assures us, of its *Living*, and of its having a Good

Life, when the *Body dies.* It is in regard of This, that our SAVIOUR says of the Beleever, not only that he SHALL HAVE, but also that he HATH, *Everlasting Life;* He HATH in him what shall *never Dy.* Indeed, we know not, whether many of the Things, which the *Soul* has laid in as its *Treasures,* will not be lost in the *shipwreck* of *Death.* Doubtless many of them will be lost, as to any Use of them in the *Future State.* But, if a Principle of PIETY be wrought in the *Soul, This* will certainly swim away with it; and if, *Caetera mortis erunt,*[31]—*This* will be still Safe; *This* will Stick by the *Soul,* and be of Everlasting Benefit unto it. *We brought nothing into this World, and it is certain we can carry nothing out.* But if our Soul be Renewed with a Principle of *Sanctity,* which it *brought not into this World,* it is very *Certain* it will carry THAT Out, and find the Everlasting Advantage of it. We have a Little Hint of This, in that the PIETY of Good Men will continue, when thro' *Old Age* all their other Faculties appear to be impaired. Good Men sometimes comfort themselves, as our *Baxter* did, upon reading the Like in the Life of our *Eliot,* in a Letter of his, written a few Weeks before he died, which I have lying by me: *My Understanding fails me, my Memory fails me, my Utterance fails me,* [ms. II, 17] *But I thank GOD, my Charity does not fail; That holds out still.*[32] But now, the *Inference!* Tis This. Neither does the *Soul fail,* that is the *Subject* of it.

It may be yett further argued; If the *Soul* were meerly the Result of the *Bodily Constitution,* the *Prosperity* of the *Soul* would then depend on the *Health* of the *Body.* But it may often be said of a very *Sickly* Man, *Thy Soul Prospers.* And when the *Body* is worn out with *Labours* & *Sorrows,* yett the *Soul* that inhabits it, has a *Consolation* that carries *Immortality* with it: *Tho' the Outer Man Perishes, the Inner Man is Renew'd Day by Day.* Even *Then,* when the *Soul* feels a *Decay,* or I will rather say, a *Restraint,* upon its other Operations, by some Difficulties come upon certain Particular Organs that were of Use unto it, even THEN, the *Love of GOD* will continue *flourishing like a Green Olive-tree.* A *Love,* that will *never Fail;* Nor, by Consequence, the *Soul* that has it!

What now remains, but that we Lash the *Soul-killing Swine* of our Days, with a Line of a very Ancient, and even Pagan Poet; whose Name was *Phocilides.*

ΨΥΧΗ ΔΕ ΑΘΑΝΑΤΟΣ, ΚΑΙ ΑΓΗΡΩΣ ΖΗ ΔΙΑ ΠΑΝΤΟΣ·[33]
The Soul Immortal, never old will grow;
Nor its Existence any Period know.

One might suppose, that after these Things, a Considerate Christian cannot without the utmost Wonder and Contempt reflect on the Strange Attempt of One, who among other *Paradoxes,* has treated the Word with, *An Epistolary Discourse proving from the Scriptures* & *the First Fathers, that the Soul is a Principle Naturally Mortal.*[34] And would have us beleeve, That our *Souls* are to be *Immortalized* only by a *Baptismal Spirit* convey'd thro' the hands of an *Episcopally Ordained* Minister. What *Exalted Folly!* As for the *Scriptures,* we have seen how *they* serve him. Take only that one *Sharp-pointed Stone* from thence, & throw it at him;—*Cannot kill the Soul.* What? And any *Distemper,* any *Murderer,* do it, if a Parson don't see Cause to keep the *Soul* alive! As for the *Fathers*, They will as little serve him. Take only *Justin Martyr*, who (notwithstanding the Pains taken to muddy & obscure the Meaning of what he says in his *Dialogue*,) in his *Apology*, expressly asserts *Departed Souls* to be in a *State of Sensibility*, and the *Wicked* particularly to be [ms. II, 18] in Torments; Yea, over and over again maintains, *All Departed Souls to continue in a State of Sensation*.[35] But Here's enough.

Sect. II. There is a Matter, which I would humbly lay before *The Wise Men of Enquiry*, to be more thoroughly enquired into.

The Glorious GOD, in whom *we live & move & have our Being*, & who is every where continually at Work, as the *Universal Cause* of all things; does by His Almighty *Will* give a Being to *Spirits*, that are in greater or lesser Degrees of Distance from *Grosser Matter*, as it pleases Him. And unto such *Spirits* He has by His *Laws* assigned such *Powers*, that upon their *Tendencies* He does produce what *Effects* He has by His *Laws* assigned unto such *Tendencies*. The more Progress we make in *Experimental Philosophy*, the oftener we shall find ourselves driven to something so much beyond *Mechanical Principles*, as to show us the Insufficiency of a meer *Corpuscularian Hypothesis*.[36]

There is in Man a Wonderful *Spirit*, which from very good Authority, & for the Abbreviation of our Expression, we may call, NISHMATH-CHAJIM, or, *The Breath of Life*: And which may be of a *Middle Nature*, between the *Rational Soul* and the *Corporeal Mass*: But may be the *Medium of Communication*, by which they work upon one another.[37] It wonderfully receives Impressions from Each of them; And perhaps it is the *Vital Ty* between them. The Scriptural *Anatomy* of *Man*, into *Spirit* and *Soul* and *Body*, seems to favour and invite such Apprehensions as [ms. II, 19] we are now therefore proceeding to.[38]

The Great GOD, who *forms the Spirit of Man within him*, has endued this *Nishmath-Chajim* with marvellous *Faculties*; which yett are all of them short of those *Powers*, that enable the *Rational Soul*, to penetrate into the *Causes of Things*; To do Curious and Exquisite Things in the *Mathematical Sciences*; And above all, To act upon a Principle of *Love to GOD*, and with the *Views* of *Another World*.

Some *Rays of Light* concerning this *Nishmath-Chajim*, have been darted into the Minds of many Learned Men, who have yett after all remained very much in the *Dark* about it: Famous have been the Sentiments of *Helmont*, (and some other *Masters of Obscurities*) about it;[39] who would exhibit it under the Name of the *Archaeus*; and with much of Reason press, that in the *Cure of Diseases* there may be more of Regard paid unto it. According to *Grembs* (writing, *De ortu rerum*) it is, *Medium quid inter Vitam et Corpus, et veluti Aura nitens splendensqe*; A sort of a *Luminous Air*, of a *Middle Nature*, between *Spirituous* and *Corporeous*.[40] It has the Name of, *The Astral Spirit*, with some Philosophers, who trouble the *Stars*, more than there is any Need for. Even the *Galenists* themselves, have not been without some *Suspicions*, yea, some *Acknowledgments* of our *Nishmath-Chajim*, and given very *Broad Hints* concerning it. And no doubt, they may thank the Old *Platonists* for instructing of them. The Great *Fernelius*, one of the most Illustrious Men that ever shone among them, [writing, *De Abditis rerum causis.*] gives a very Lively Description of it. Yea, He finds it in the TO ENOPMON of *Hippocrates* and having a great *Power of Incursion* like the *Wind*, he allows it some affinity with the Nature of *Body*:[41] But inasmuch as it is *Invisible* it must also have some Affinity with what is *Incorporeal*: So, he will have it of a *Middle Nature* between *Both*. But he supposes it, the *Vehicle*, and proper Seat of the *Soul*, & all its Fa-[ms. II, 20]culties; and if we call it their *Body*, we shall have his Permission for it. *Heurnius*, whom some reckon & value next unto *Fernelius*, describes it [in his *Institutions*,] as, A Kind of *Ethereal Spirit, elaborated out of the Purest Part of the Blood, and changed into the Substance of a very Subtil Air; and the Prime Instrument of the Soul, for the Performance of its Functions.*[42]

Our *Nishmath-Chajim* seems to be commensurate unto our *Bodies*; and our *Bodies* are conformable to the Shape which GOD our Maker gives to that *Plastic Spirit*, (if we may call it so;) But by what *Principle* the Particles of it, which may be finer than those of the *Light* itself, are kept in their *Cohaesion* to one another; tis a thing yett unknown to us. And, how it fares in the Case of *Amputations* on our *Bodies*:—whether what remains, may not have the Power to produce a *Recruit*, when there shall be a Lodging again provided for it?—

The *Nishmath-Chajim* is the *Spirit* of the Several Parts where it has a Residence; and it is the *Life* by which the Several Parts have their *Faculties* maintained in Exercise. *This* tis, that *Sees*, that *Hears*, that *Feels*; and Performs the Several *Digestions* in the *Body*. And the *Animal World*, having *Animam pro sale*,[43] if it were not for *This*, would quickly *Putrify*.

The *Nishmath-Chajim* is indeed *Generationis Faber ac Rector*;[44] and as it leads to the Acts requisite in *Generation* without any further *Instructor*, so it is the *Spirit*, whose *Way we know not for shaping the Bones*, and other Parts, *in the Womb of her that is with Child.*

There are indeed many things in the *Humane Body*, that cannot be solved by the Rules of *Mechanism*. Our *Nishmath-Chajim* will go very far to help us in the Solution of them. Indeed we can scarce well subsist without it.

There is an astonishing Operation, and indeed some Illustration and Explanation of the *Nishmath-Chajim*, in *Praegnant Women*; whose [ms. II, 21] *Imagination* frequently makes Impressions on the *Unborn Infants*, that would exceed all Beleef, if we had them not continually in View before our Eyes. The Instances are so Numerous and so Various, that one might compile a Large Volumn of them, and the *Formative Power* therein display'd so astonishing, that one would almost ask a *Palaephatus* to afford a Title to it.[45] But in what other Way to be accounted for?

For the *Nishmath-Chajim* we may safely be *Traducians*. It is a *Flame* Enkindled in, and so Derived from, the *Parent*. And this *Traduction* [which is *Luminis È Lumine*,] may help us considerably, in our Enquiries, *How the Dispositions of Original Sin are convey'd & infus'd into us?*[46]

It was of old, Yea, it is at this Day, a prevailing Opinion, among the Strangers to the *Glorious Gospel of the Blessed GOD*; That the *Manes* which remain after *Death*, have still an *Humane Shape*, and all the *Parts* which there were in the *Body* that is now deserted; Yea, that there is a *Food*, which this *Departed Spirit* craves for & lives on. They speak of Punishments on the Wicked, after *Death*, which there must be a sort of *Bodies* to be the Subjects of. And *Plato* speaks of those that are punished in *Hell*, as having such *Members* and *Faces* as they had once upon the *Earth*. Indeed *Justin Martyr* argues from it, that these old Gentlemen must needs have some Knowledge of what we hold, about, *The Resurrection of the Dead*. In reading of *Homer*, we find his Notion to be the same with what was in the *Egyptian* Philosophy;[47] which supposed, that *Man* is composed of Three Parts; An Intelligent *Mind*, called ΦΡΗΝ or ΨΥΧΗ· A *Vehicle*, called ΕΙΛΩΛΟΝ, The *Image*, or the *Soul*: And a Gross *Body*, called ΣΩΜΑ· The *Soul*, in which they looked on the Mind as lodged, they supposed exactly to resemble the *Body*; the Shape, & Bulk, & Features; being in the *Body*, as the *Statue* in the *Mould*, & so after its Departure keeping the *Image* of the *Body*. *Plutarch* very distinctly delivers this Doctrine; and says, when the *Soul* is compounded with the *Understanding*, it makes *Reason*; & when compounded with the *Body*, it makes *Passion*. The one Composition, is the Principle of *Pleasure* & *Pain*, the other of *Virtue* & *Vice*. He adds, Man dies *Two Deaths*. The *First Death* makes him *Two* of *Three*: The *Second* makes him *One* of *Two*.[48] But what shall we say, when our Glorious LORD-REDEEMER in His *Parable* of the *Rich Man* supposes his *Body* in the *Grave*, and yett being in *Hell*, he cries out of a *Body*, and particularly of a *Tongue*, [the Member which the *Wealthy* much abuse in their *Table-Talk*] that is Tormented there? Many of the Ancients thought, there was much of a Real *History* in the *Parable*; [yea, the *Talmuds* have such an *History*, and make the Name of the *Rich Man* to be, *Nimensis*:] And their Opinion was, That there is ΔΙΑΦΟΡΑ ΚΑΤΑ ΤΑΣ ΜΟΡΦΑΣ A [ms. II, 22] *Distinction* (and so, a Resemblance) *of Men, as to their Shapes after Death*.[49] We find, This was the Opinion of *Irenaeus*; who proves, from what our SAVIOUR speaks of the *Dead Man*, that the *Souls*, which have putt off their *Bodies*, do yett *Characterem Corporum Custodire*, preserve the *Shapes* of the Bodies, to which they were united. And from the Same Speech of our SAVIOUR does *Tertullian* infer, *Effigiem Animae et Corporales Lineas*, the *Shape* and the *Corporal Lineaments* of the *Soul*. Of *Thespesius's* Visions, we'l say nothing.[50] The *Nishmath-Chajim* is much like the *Soul*, which animates the *Brutal World*; Even that *Spirit of the Beast which goeth downward unto the Earth*: But is by the Hand of the Glorious Creator impraegnated, with a *Capacity* and *Inclination*, for those Actions, which are necessary for the *Praeservation* of themselves, and the *Propagation* of their *Species*. The *Nidification* of *Birds*, the *Mellification* of *Bees*, the *Architecture* of *Bevers*, and a thousand such Things, how Surprising Works done in the Brutal World, without any *Rational Projection* for them![51] And hence also, there are many Actions done by us, that have a Tendency to our Safety and Welfare, which are not the Effects of any *Rational Projection*; but such as we do, by what we call, *A meer Instinct of Nature*, fall into; The *Sucking Infant*, yea, and the *Nursing Mother* too, do very Needful and Proper Things, without consulting of *Reason* for the doing of them.[52] It is a thing, which who can observe without Astonishment? In every other *Machin*, if any thing be out of Order, it will remain so, till some Hand from abroad, shall rectify it. But the *Humane Body* is a *Machin*, wherein if any thing be out of Order, presently the whole Engine, as under an Alarm, is awakened for the helping of what is amiss, and other Parts of the Engine, strangely putt themselves out of their Way, that they may send in Help unto it, whence can this proceed, but from a *Nishmath-Chajim* in us, with such Regards for the *Law of Self-Preservation*, by GOD imprinted upon it.

Having at some time or other felt a Considerable *Smart*, or been Considerably *Sick*, from Something that we have mett withal, we have an *Abiding Horror* for the Thing perhaps all our Days. Tho' we certainly Know, that the Thing will do us *No Hurt*, but rather do us *Much Good*, yett no Conviction of *Reason* will overcome our *Abiding Horror*. We cannot swallow the *Pill*, or take the *Meat* or the *Drink*, or do an hundred Things, which we have heretofore been horribly frighted at. Our *Nishmath-Chajim* has an Incurable Aversion for them. [ms. II, 23] Tis the *Nishmath-Chajim*, that is the *Strength* of Every Part in our *Body*, and that gives *Motion* to it. Here perhaps the Origin of *Muscular Motion* may be a little accounted for. This is that *Aura Motiva*, which in the Proportion of its *Force* to the *Pondera Elevanda*, so admirably observed and adjusted by the Rare *Borelli*, (and others after him,) carries in it what will *force* the Greatest Astonishment.[53] And This is the *Spirit*, and the *Balsame*, and one might almost say, the *Keeper*, of each Part, which is occupied and befriended with it. Yea, what Construction shall we make of it, when People have lived, without *Brains* in their *Heads*, and after the Destruction of almost all the *Bowels* in their *Bodies*? We are Supplied and Surprized with many most Credible Relations of such Things. And, I quaestion, whether any thing will do so well, or go so far, as our *Nishmath-Chajim*, to account for them.

A Principal Wheel in the *Animal Oeconomy*, is the *Stomach*. And we shall now find That which above all things the *Digestion* there is to be ascribed unto. Dispute, O *Philosophers*, How *Digestion* is performed in the *Stomach*! Tis the *Nishmath-Chajim* after all, that is the *Main Digester*. Else, how could a *Stomach*, that is actually *Cold*, and has in it no very *Tastable* or *Notable* Humour for this Purpose, *Digest* the very *Stones* that are taken down into it? The taking of some *Repast*, is in our Sacred Scripture sometimes called, *The Establishing of the Heart*; And, the *Heart* is not seldom a Term for our *Nishmath-Chajim*.— *Quaere*.[54]

It is the *Nishmath-Chajim*, that is more eminently the *Seat* of our *Diseases*, or the *Source* of them. To pass by what they quote of *Herophilus*, we find *Plato* elegantly demonstrating, That all *Diseases* have their Origin in the *Soul*. Yea, as long ago as the Days of *Hippocrates*, the *Essentials* of *Diseases* began to be discovered, and the Pacifying & Rectifying of the *Enforcing Spirit*, was proposed as the most [ms. II, 24] Ready Way to cure them. Is not this the *Microcosmic Air*, whereto *Tachenius* ascribes the Cure of the *Gout*, by a Strong Perturbation of the Mind; upon which he concludes it animated?[55] Most certainly, The *Physi-*

cian that can find out Remedies, that shall have a more immediate Efficacy to Brighten, and Strengthen, and Comfort, the *Nishmath-Chajim;* Especially, if he can irradiate the Spirit in the *Stomach,* and also fortify the *Blood,* and restore a *Volatil Ferment* in *That,* when it grows Vapid & Languid; and in a Word, if he can *Confirm the System,* which our *Sydenham* supposes, of our *Spirits,* wherein proper *Anodynes,* and *Chalybeates,* are often very potent: Such an one will be the most successful *Physician* in the World. He will be yett more so, if as *Baglivi* advises, he can Skilfully Quiet the *Passions of the Mind,* the *Griefs* and *Cares,* by which his Patient is disordered. Wonders have been done, in the, *Art of Curing by Expectation;* & there would be yett greater Wonders done in the, *Art of Curing by Consolation.*[56]

In the Indisputable and Indubitable Occurrences of *Witchcrafts* and *Possessions,* there are many things, which because they are *Hard to be understood,* the *Epicurean Sadducees* content themselves in their *Bekkerian* Manner, only to laugh at. But the *Nishmath-Chajim* well understood would give to more Sober Men a Key to lett us very far into the Meaning of them.[57]

To have done; It is probable, That when we *Dy* the *Nishmath-Chajim* goes away, as a Vehicle to the *Rational Soul;* and continues unto it an Instrument of many Operations. Here we have some Solution for the Difficulties, about the *Place,* and the *Change* of it, for such an *Immaterial Spirit* as the *Rational Soul;* And some Account for *Apparitions* of the *Dead,* which are called both, *Spirits,* and, *Phantasms,* in our Gospel. Yea, we are certain of it, That Persons before they have *Died,* upon Strong Desires to Visit and Behold Some Objects at a Distance from the *Place* to which they were now confined, have been thrown into a *Trance,* wherein they have lain some Considerable [ms. II, 25] While, without *Sense* or *Breath,* and then Returning have reported what they have seen. But incontestible Witnesses have deposed, that in *This Time,* they were actually *seen* at the Place which they affirm'd they had gone unto.

To annex this *Breath of Life,* unto the *Rational Soul,* appear'd a thing of some Service to the Cause we have in hand: But if it has been too long a *Digression,* tis hoped, the Reader will see Cause to pardon it.

Sect. III. But now, *Man gives up the Ghost; and where is he:* A *Place* for the *Immortal Soul,* ceasing to animate a *Mortal Body,* is to be sought for.

That the *Souls* of the Faithful *unsheathed* from their *Bodies,* are transplanted into a *Place* proper for them, is a thing that cannot be doubted. The *Locality* of *Souls* is indeed an Obscure Matter to us. But, if they have it while *in the Body,* they must as well have it when *out of the Body.* The *ubi* of *Spirits!*—Lett it be ever so dark, yett, Mr. *Nullibist,* I hope, you will allow a *Place* for *Enoch,* and for *Elias,* and for the *Many Saints* whom our Lord caused, as *His Dead Men,* to *Rise together with His Dead Body.*[58] That *Place* will soon lead us to a *Place* designed for the *Departed Souls* of the *Saints.*

But the Oracles of our GOD, have expressly told us, That there is a PARA-

DISE, which is the *Place* intended for them. This PARADISE is now to be a little treated of.

Now, first, the *Sacred Scriptures* do seem to intimate, as if there were some *Difference* between the PARADISE into which the *Departed Spirits* of the Faithful are admitted; and the THIRD HEAVEN in which our SAVIOUR is Enthroned; that *Holy of Holies* wherein the Most *Immediate & Beatific Vision* of GOD is attain'd unto.[59]

When our Apostle in his Rapture was *Caught up to the Third Heaven*, and, *Caught up into Paradise*, other Learned Men, besides Dr. *Bull*, have apprehended, that there are *Two Several Visions* referr'd unto. The Exposition is as old as *Methodius*;[60] Yea, it was the General Apprehension of the Ancients. The Apostle being one called unto more than ordinary Sufferings in the *Faith and Patience of the Kingdom*, that he might be fortified under them and against them, His Gracious LORD, gave him first a *View* of the *Perfect Blessedness* wherewith he was to be Recompensed at the [ms. II, 26] *Resurrection of the Dead*. But because it would be a Long While before he could arrive to *That*, His Lord then gave him a *View* of *Unutterable Comforts*, which he should receive immediately upon his *Dissolution*, and which tho' they would be *Short* of the *Perfect Blessedness* that he should at last be brought unto, yett they were worth longing for. The *Holy of Holies*, which was the *Third House* in the *Temple*, whereof *David* had a *Platform*, from a Vision which GOD gave him of the *Heavenly World*, was a Small Type of the *Third Heaven*; which is by *Moses* and *Solomon* and the *Levites* in the Book of *Nehemiah* called, *The Heaven of Heavens*, because of Peculiar Excellencies, wherein it outshines the rest of that *Habitation* of GOD.[61] But then, it seems as if *Paradise* were an *Apartment* of the *Heavenly World*, not only *Different* from the *Third Heaven*, but also on some Accounts, and in some Glories, *Inferiour* to it; as the *Courts* of the *Temple* were to the *Holy of Holies*. Both of them are *Heaven*; but the one more *Heavenly* than the other: In what Regard—*Such Knowledge is too wonderful for me; it is High; I cannot attain unto it!*

What passed between our SAVIOUR and the *Paenitent*, on the *Cross*, may carry Some Intimation of This. The Paenitent pray'd, *Lord, Remember me, when thou comest in thy Kingdome*. He expected a *Coming* of the *Messiah*, to sett up His *Kingdome* in the World; and it was his Expectation, that the *Messiah* would *Raise the Dead* at His Coming. This was the *Faith of the Fathers*; and it shows, that they beleeved Him to be GOD as well as *Man*. Our SAVIOUR in answer to this Prayer of the Paenitent, says, *Verily, I say unto thee, This Day thou shalt be with me in Paradise*. I cannot accept of *Austins* Exposition of, *Thou shall be with me*. But I think, Dr. *Tailor* has given us a very probable Paraphrase upon it. q.d. Tho' "thou only ask to be *Remembred when I come in my Kingdome*, not only shall *That* be performed in the Due Time of it, but even *To Day* thou shalt have that Great *Refreshment*, which the *Paradise* of GOD affords unto them that are lodged there."[62]

That which would yett further incline one to [ms. II, 27] this Opinion, is;

That the Divine Oracles do not speak of our SAVIOURs Entring into the *Most Holy Place,* [or, the *Third Heaven,*] until as our *High-Priest* He *carried His own Blood* with Him thither, and had Finished all that was to be done towards the *Obtaining of Eternal Redemption* for us. Now, this cannot well be supposed before the *Resurrection* of our SAVIOUR. And therefore the *Paradise* to which He carried the *Soul* of the Expiring *Paenitent,* some Days before His *Resurrection,* seems to be a *Receptacle of Spirits,* different from that Apartment of the *Heavenly World,* where our Glorious *High-Priest, after He had offered one Sacrifice for our Sins, did forever sitt down on the Right Hand of GOD.* Accordingly, It is well-known, That the *Manichees* maintained, that *Good Souls had their whole Reward immediately after Death:* And for the Proof of their Opinion, they brought the Promise of our SAVIOUR to the *Paenitent* on the Cross: *This Day thou shalt be with me in Paradise.* But we also know *Chrysostom's* Way of answering the Objection: He does it with a Concession, that the *Paenitent* was indeed admitted into *Paradise:* But then he adds, That *Paradise* was not the *Heaven* which they supposed it, *For it contains not all the Good Things that GOD has promis'd us.*[63]

When our SAVIOUR has told us, *In my FATHERs House, there are many Mansions;* by the *FATHERs House* we understand, *The Heavenly World.* And Persons less Fanciful than a Conceited *Nestorian* in our Days, have gathered from hence, That there are *Distinct Apartments* in the *Heavenly World.* Rejecting the Whimsyes of the *Jews,* which determine a Vast Extent for those which they call, *The Mansions of Paradise,* they judge that they may justly and safely suppose, that the *Paradise* where our SAVIOUR has *praepared a Place* for the *Departed Spirits* of the Faithful, may be in *Mansions* different from those which they shall have, when He does *COME AGAIN,* to *Receive them unto Himself, that where He is, there they may be also.*

Many things look, as if the Conviction of the *Spirits* in *Paradise,* tho' inconceivably *Happy,* may be supposed, *short* of that Faelicity which is intended for the Righteous, when our Lord-Redeemer shall by the *Resurrection of the Dead* fetch them out from thence, to receive *All the Spiritual Blessings of the Heavenly Places.* The *Intermedial State* seems to be an *Inferiour State;* and tho' it be full of *Blessed Circumstances,* yett it is not the *Perfection of our Blessedness.* While our *Spirits* are in *Paradise,* there is an *Essential Part* of us yett remaining under the *Curse:* As long as we are in the *State of the Dead,* the *Curse* is not wholly taken off. Until we are *Embodied Spirits,* we are not in a *Natural* [ms. II, 28] *State;* neither what we *should* be, nor what we *would* be.

It is intimated, That the *Saints* which are *Dead* before us, [Heb. XI. 40.] *will not be made perfect without us.* It is made an Argument, That the *Patriarchs* have not yett received what GOD Promised and They Expected, because *We* who are to receive the Same with them, are yett where we are. They are, as it should seem, to stay for our Company; & they must not receive the *Perfection of their Blessedness,* until we shall receive it *All together,* at the *Resurrection of the Dead,* when that *Better Thing,* which the Old *Patriarchs* apprehended as laid up for them in the *Covenant* of GOD, shall be dispensed unto us.

Yea, tis a Point of *Deep Meditation*; why the *Salvation* that is to be received at the *Appearing of Jesus Christ*, even that *Salvation* of which the *Prophets* made so *Diligent Enquiry & Scrutiny*, as having in it the *Grace* that should then come to the Chosen People of GOD, is called [1. Pet. I. 9.] *The Salvation of the Soul*. It should seem, as if the *Salvation of the Soul*, were somewhat unfinished, until the *Praise, & Honour, & Glory* to be granted at the *Appearing* of the Lord.

We will not insist on That; [1. Cor. XV. 19.] *We have Hope in CHRIST, not in this Life only*: As meaning, that after *this Life* is ended, we continue still in a Joyful *Hope*, of what our SAVIOUR will do for us, at the *Resurrection of the Dead*. Nor will we insist on That; [Act. II. 34.] *David is not ascended into the Heavens*; As if it meant, that the *Soul* of *David* was yett remaining in that *Hades*, which was not what the *Resurrection of the Dead* will bring him to. But this we may insist upon; That the Sacred Scriptures do seem continually to adjourn our *Main Blessedness* to the Time, when the *Resurrection* shall fetch out our *Souls* from the *State of the Dead*.

When is it that our GOD gives the *Reward* unto them that *Fear His Name*? It is, [Rev. XI. 18.] when the *Last Trumpett* shall bring on *the Time of the Dead, that they shall be Judged*. So our SAVIOUR says, [Luk. XIV. 14.] *Thou shalt be Recompensed at the Resurrection of the Just.*

When is it, that *GOD the Righteous Judge*, will *give the Crown of Righteousness*? It is, [2. Tim. IV. 8.] [ms. II, 29] *At That Day.* [Compare, 2. Tim. I. 12, 18.]

What is our *Blessed Hope*? It is, [Tit. II. 13.] *The Glorious Appearing of our Great GOD & SAVIOUR Jesus Christ.*

We read, [Rom. VIII. 18.] *The Sufferings of the Present Time* weigh'd against the *Glory to be Reveled in us*. But this *Glory* is to be *reveled & received at the Redemption of the Body*. And until That arrive, *we hope for what we see not, but with Patience wait for it.*

When *we are Dead*, [Col. III. 3.] our *Life remains Hid with CHRIST in GOD*, and it won't be fully understood, & therefore not fully possessed, until *CHRIST who is our Life, shall appear; Then shall we also appear with Him in Glory.*

Our *Glory* lies in our *Likeness* to our SAVIOUR. But we read, [1. Joh. III. 2.] *we know, that when He shall appear, we shall be like Him; for we shall see Him as He is.* Does not that look, that until Then, we shall not see *Him as He is*?

Are the faithful Stewards of the *Talents*, rewarded before the *Return* of their Lord? The *Blessed* in the *Beatitudes* of our SAVIOUR, come to *See GOD*, at the Time when they shall also in the *Kingdom of Heaven* come to *Inherit the Earth*. And this will be after the *Resurrection of the Dead*.

And in our *Creed*, the *Resurrection of the Dead*, goes before *Life Everlasting*.

Such Things as these have procured from the Pen of a Judicious *Calvin*, such Limitations to our Expectations of *Glory* for the *Departed Spirits* of the Faithful;—*Contenti fimus his Finibus divinitus nobis praescriptis; Animas piorum militiae labore perfunctas, in beatum Quietem concedere, ubi cum faelici*

Laetitia Fructionem promissae Gloriae exspectant, atqe ita omnia tenere sus-pensa, donec Christus appareat Redemptor.[64] In short, Their *Warfare* being accomplished, they do with an *Happy Joy* keep waiting for the *Promised Glory,* which will not be fully dispensed, until the *Appearing* of the Glorious Re-deemer.

Shall we say with the Psalmist; [Psal. CXIX. 100.] *I gett Understanding from the Ancients?*

It seems to have been the General Opinion of the *Ancients.* Tis true, *Ephrem Syrus,* in his Treatise, *De mansionibus aeternis,* runs pretty much into our Modern Language.[65] He asserts only a *Twofold State,* either of *Happiness* or *Misery,* for Men in the *Future State,* and rebukes the Fancy of a *Third State.* But Some Reconcile his Expressions to the *General Opinion* of his Brethren. Souls may Ly in a State of *Happiness,* while they yett see not the *Perfection* of their *Happiness. Paradise* may be *Heaven,* tho' it be not all that Advancement In *Heaven* which they that are there do look for. *Justin Martyr* in his Dialogue with *Trypho,* complains of the Mistake in those Christians, who held, *That assoon as they died their Souls were taken into Heaven.* And yett, the *Quaes-tions* and *Answers,* which go under the Name of *Justin,* (and are by *Photius* himself, tho' probably by a Mistake, ascribed unto him) tell us, [ms. II, 30] *That the Souls of the Just go to Paradise, and there converse with Christ by Vision.*[66] But *Irenaeus* makes yett a larger Complaint of it; and for the Confutation of it, he urges the Exemple of our SAVIOUR, who (says he) *Observed in Himself the Law of Dead Persons, and did not presently on His Death go to Heaven, but staid three Days in the Place of the Dead.* He took *Paradise* to be not prop-erly *Heaven,* but a Station of *Hades;* and called it, *The Midst of the Shadow of Death. Tertullian* is full this Way, only that (perhaps misunderstanding the Word, *Hades,* as of a Subterraneous repast) he sinks *Paradise* too low, and seems to have the *Elysian Fields* of the Heathen too much in his Eye. So we'l quote nothing from him. Nor shall the Loss of his Book, *On Paradise,* throw us into much Impatience:[67] *Caius* at the same time will tell us, That *Just Souls* are led by *Angels,* ΕΙΣ ΧΩΡΙΟΝ ΦΩΤΕΙΝΟΝ, *Into a Region of Light,* where they are delighted with the Vision of the Just Fathers, *expecting after they have been in this Place their Habitation in Heaven.* Tho' we do not come into all the *Para-doxes* which are fathered (and many of them, I suppose, very Injuriously) upon *Origen,* yett we may think, whether this be one, that may not be allowed of: *The Saints departed, receive not the Reward of their Good Actions, but wait for it.* The Primitive Church had not a Greater Interpreter than *Theodoret;* who says; *The Saints departed have not yett obtained their Crowns; GOD expecting, that those also who were yett to combate, should arrive at the Place, where they are;—it being His Purpose to proclaim them all Victors together. Theophylact* says the Same. *Chrysostom* on the XI to the *Hebrews,* does enlarge upon the Purpose of GOD, that none of the Faithful which are *Dead* shall receive the *Crowns* of their *Combates,* untill *We* shall *All come to receive them together;* ΟΜΟΥ ΔΟΞΑΣΘΗΝΑΙ.[68]

Citations from *Ambrose* and *Austin* might be thrown into our Heap. And it is well known how some of the Reformers expressed themselves in this Matter: who nevertheless with a proper & pious Modesty avoided Peremptory Decisions upon it. *Frith* said, *I dare be bold to say, They* [the Departed Spirits of the Faithful] *are in the* [ms. II, 31] *Hand of GOD; and that GOD would that we should be ignorant where they be, & not take upon us to determine it!* It is added by *Tyndal; I beleeve they are in no worse Case, than the Soul of CHRIST was before His Resurrection.* *Luther* had at first express'd himself too inadvertently in terms too much of a *Psychopannychist* Aspect; of which *Perron* & his other Popish Adversaries made an Handle to reproach him as denying the *Immortality of the Soul.* But he afterwards rectified his Expressions, and made not the *Rest* for the *Souls* of the Praedestinate, such a *Profound Sleep* as to deprive them of the *Vision of GOD & Angels.* Yett he joined with them, who took not that *Rest* for the *Perfection of Blessedness.*[69]

The Ancient Opinion, of a *Distinct Paradise,* wherein the Departed *Spirits* of the Faithful enjoy but a *Lower State of Blessedness* until the Coming of the LORD, is in these Later Ages indeed most generally abandoned, both by the *Romanists* & by the *Protestants.* And which is a little odd; while the *former* have deserted the Opinion, that so they may Support a great Point of *Popery,* the *latter* have done it, that so they may Avoid another great Point of *Popery.* On the one Hand, As we are sensible, this is the Doctrine of the whole *Greek Church* at this Day, so it continued very much the Doctrine of the *Latin Church,* till it was rejected in the Council at *Florence* about three hundred Years ago.[70] The Design of that Council was, to establish, *The Invocation of Saints;* which Idolatrous Practice is destroy'd if it appear that the *Souls* of the *Saints,* are, tho' in a State of *Comfort,* yett not in a State of *Power,* until the *Day of Judgment.* How shall we *Invocate* them, to procure Good Things for us, who are not yett *Perfect,* nor *as they would be,* themselves? On the other hand, They that carried on the *Reformation* were justly desirous to extinguish the *Fires* of *Purgatory;* And how could they do this more Thoroughly, than by lodging the *Souls* of the *Saints* immediately in the *full Fruition* of GOD, & by transporting them to the *Top* of that State which is to be look'd for, & not supposing it a State that has any *Imperfection* in it?

But then, L. *Cappellus,* in his Treatise, *De Statu Animorum Post Mortem,* while he is a declared Enemy to the *Popish Figment,* and allows unto the Departed *Spirits* of the Faithful, a Deliverance from all their Troubles, and especially from *Sin,* the Chief of all their Troubles, and the wondrous *Joy of Hope,* upon what they have in View, [*Inenarrabile quoddam* [ms. II, 32] *atqe Gloriosum ex illa Spe, certissimaqe expectatione, Gaudium:*] yett he makes the State considerably *short* of that *Possession* and *Enjoyment* of *Glory,* whereof they are here detained in the *Joyful Expectation.*[71]

It may be, some Good Men will think that *Cappellus* may sett the State of *Paradise* as much *too Low,* as he has thought it has been sett by others *too High.*

May the *SPIRIT of Truth* keep us from *Errors* on both Hands. *Ponder the Path of thy Feet, that thou mayst neither Turn to the Right nor to the Left!*

This I am sure of; Since the Things which we treat of, are those which the

Ancients called, *ABDITA animarum Receptacula*,[72] it becomes us to be very modest, in our Searches into, & our Judgments upon, Things that are so *Hidden* from us.

Sect. IV. My *Pen* shall be Burnt a thousand times, yea, my very *Hand* shall go with the Martyr *Cranmers*, before it shall make the Least Motion, to blow up any thing like the *Fire* of the *Popish Purgatory*. *Popery*, which is revived *Paganism*, has nothing in the *Sacred Scriptures* to countenance the Least *Spark* of the Opinion which *Antichrist* has invented, about a *Purgatory* for the *Departed Souls*: of which we read in the *Sacred Scriptures*, That *there is no Condemnation to them*; and, That *the Blood of the SON of GOD cleanses them from all Sin*. The *Purgatory* of the *Papists*, is but a *Relique* of a Fancy very rife among the *Pagans*; kept up for an Engine, by which the *Priests* may Exercise their Tyranny over the Souls of the *People*, and Enrich the Treasures of the Church, by their *Indulgences*, for which *Rivet* well assign'd the Term of *Emulgences*, as a fitter Appellation. Tis not from the *Gospel*, but from a *Virgil*, that they have the best Authority for the Tradition [ms. II, 33] of their *Purgatory*: Not the *Third* Chapter in the First Epistle to the *Corinthians*, but the *Sixth* Book of the *Æneids*, is to be quoted for it.[73]

Most certainly, A *Paradise* is the Perfect Reverse of a *Purgatory*. According to *Austin* indeed, *Paradise* is a *General Name*, for, *Ubicunqe benè Vivitur*. Be sure, They that are in a *Paradise* of GOD must be *very well* of it. And the *Upright Ones*, who when they are *taken away* from hence, [Isa. LVII. 2.] *Enter into Peace, and Rest in their Beds*, are not in those Miseries, which the *Purgatorian Flames*, were there any such, must bring upon those that suffer them.[74]

Tho' the *Intermedial* State of *Paradise* be *Inferiour* to what we shall see, when our LORD *shall come, and His Reward is with Him*; Yett it must be unspeakably *praeferrible* to our *Terrestrial* State, which is that of a Pilgrimage through a forlorn & wretched *Wilderness*. They, who, with Dr. *Bull*, somewhat Abate the *Glory* of this *Paradise*, do so express the Sentiments of the Ancients upon it, & their own Concurrence with them. *The Place & State of Good Souls separated from their Bodies, & waiting for the Resurrection, they beleeve to be in an Happiness far exceeding all the Faelicities of this Life: Tho' Inferiour to that Consummate Bliss which follows the Resurrection.* Tho' the Faithful Waiting for the *Resurrection of the Dead*, have not yett all their *Crown of Righteousness*, yett they have glorious *Coronetts* bestow'd upon them. GOD *shows Wonders to the Dead*, even while they are yett in the *State of the Dead*: He *wondrously* gratifies them with Tokens and Effects of His Everlasting *Love* unto them: Their Condition is Exalted and Refined unto a *Wonderment*. Such things are done for them, that we need not scruple to subscribe that Article of our Catechism; *The Souls of Beleevers at their Death do immediately pass into Glory.*

Our Apostle asserting the State of *Absence from the Body*, to have so much *Glory* in it, that we may well be willing to pass into it, argues thus: [2. Cor.

V. 5.] *He that hath wrought us for this very thing is* GOD. The *Work* of *Grace*, which a *Wise* and *Just* GOD has wrought on the *Regenerate Soul*, is an Argument of the *Good State* it shall be in, when it becomes an *Unbodied Soul*. The Word used here ΚΑΤΕΡΓΑΣΑΜΕΝΟΣ, is the Same that is used in the Greek Version of the Old Testament, where the Curious *Work* of *Bezaleel* about the *Tabernacle* is mentioned. When *Bezaleel* [ms. II, 34] with excellent and exquisite *Workmanship* had praepared a *Board* for a Standing in the Silver *Sockets* of the *Tabernacle*, we may be sure, he would not throw it away among the Rubbish. And, when GOD has been at *Work* upon a *Soul*, and the *Soul* is by an admirable *Workmanship of* GOD upon it, *created for Good Works*, the Divine *Wisdom* will not throw it away, but assign it a Place and an Use about His *Tabernacle*. It was also the *Law* that GOD gave unto His *Israel; The Wages of a Labourer shall not abide with thee all night, until the Morning*. And according to that *Law*, our GOD will deal with His *Israel*. Such is the Divine *Justice*, that the *Wages* of their *Work & Labour of Love*, shall not at the *Night* of *Death* be altogether deferr'd, *until the Morning* which they that have a *Soul Waiting for the Lord* are *Watching* for: They shall Immediately have some Convenient *Portion* and *Hansel* of it. Beleevers have here *sown in Tears*, and undergone many Fatigues & many Sorrows. But they have *ploughed in Hope*, that at the End of their Difficulties they shall presently see some Glorious Recompence. They shall not be *Ashamed of their Hope*. Such is the Divine *Goodness*, that even while their *Flesh* is yett lying under the Clods of the Valley, they shall *Reap with Joy* some *First-fruits* of that *Fuller Harvest*, which, when *what had been sown in Corruption* does no longer ly under the Clods; is, intended for them; and when they shall *come again Rejoicing, bringing their Sheaves with them*, even a *Tertullian* will allow; *Decerpitur Gloria dum Sustinent Diem Judicii:* [75]

I have not forgotten our Quotation from *Chrysostom*, referring the *Happiness* of the Saints unto the *Day of Judgment*: And yett I must now take notice, that the Same Father [ms. II, 35] in his *Panegyricks* on the *Saints*, does place them in *Heaven*, and rank them with the *Angels*, and ascribe to them there a Marvellous *Faelicity*. And this is no more than what is done in the *Book of Truth*; which assures us of a Marvellous *Faelicity* for the *Paradised Beleevers*.[76]

Indeed, when we read, [Rev. XIV. 13.] *I heard a Voice from Heaven, Saying unto me, write, Blessed are the Dead which Dy in the Lord, from henceforth:* ΑΠΑΡΤΙ, is as much as to say, *Now very Quickly*: The Time is now very near. And inasmuch as it is uttered, when our SAVIOUR is going to be exhibited, as coming to that Great *Harvest* and *Vintage*, in which the Kingdom of *Antichrist* is to terminate, and our Lord is thereupon to *Appear in His Kingdom*; Some Acute Writers expound this *Blessedness*, not of what is enjoy'd by the *Dead*, before they *Rise from the Dead*; but they look on the Passage as a Prophecy of the *First Resurrection*, which would be *Now very Quickly*, when the *Harvest* & *Vintage* here foretold, was coming on. It seems to be taken from that; [Dan. XII. 12.] *Blessed is he that comes to the One Thousand three hundred & thirty five Days*. For this Cause I will not insist upon it; tho' as our Venerable *Goodwin* has observed, The Faithful have in *that Sense* most generally look'd upon it, as *one of the Strongest and most Spiritful Cordials, that ever was compounded for Men that are a dying, or that live in a continual Expectation of Death.*[77]

If it should be so, that we lose the Countenance of this Text, yett we shall not therewith lose the *Blessedness*, which is to be enjoy'd before we Reassume our *Bodies*: We have enough elsewhere, to assure us, of a wonderful *Blessedness* enjoy'd by the *Souls* of the Faithful departed into the *Paradisian World*.

It is expressly said of such an one; [Luk. XVI. 25.] *He is Comforted.* Inexpressible the *Consolations* of [ms. II, 36] the *Table*, where they ly down with *Abraham*; and where their *Souls* are *satisfied as with Marrow & with Fatness!*—Great GOD, *Thy Consolations cannot be small!* That Invitation; [Isa. XXVI. 20.] *Come, my People, Enter thou into thy Chambers:* is not only by *Clemens*,[78] & others of our Ancients, understood of the Lodgings intended for the *Departed Souls* of the Faithful, but the *Jews* as well as the *Christians*, have expounded these *Chambers*, of the *Receptacles where the Souls of the Righteous are lodged until the Resurrection.* We are sure, these *Chambers* are not *Prisons*; We are sure, they can be no other than Glorious *Mansions!*

The *first* and the *least* thing to be affirmed concerning our *Paradise*, is, *That there the Weary are at Rest.* When we drop our *Bodies*, we drop all our *Burdens* with them; It was by *them* that they were *tied* upon us. Most agreeable will those *Notes* be to these *Birds of Paradise*; [Psal. CXXIV. 7.] *Our Soul is escaped as a Bird out of the Snare of the Fowlers.* Our *Souls* will now be *Escaped* from the *Diseases*, and *Escaped* from the *Enemies*, which have annoy'd us, and *Escaped* from all the Uneasy Things of this *Wearisom Life.* But more than all this, and what is infinitely more considerable; The *Seeds of Sin* which were in our *Flesh*, & the *Snares of Sin* which our *Bodies* laid for us, we have now also made a *Glad Escape* from these most grievous Things. Even the Poor *Jews* themselves have learnt so much *Christianity* as this comes to. In their *Bereschith Rabba*, tis a Saying of theirs, *Quamdiu Justi vivunt, pugnant cum innatâ sua concupiscentiâ; cum mortui sunt, tum quiescunt.*[79] An Excellent Person, from whose Discourse on, *The Blessed State of the Saints in Glory*,[80] I shall anon make an advantageous Quotation, when he lay a dying, said, *I am going to the Three Persons with whom I have had Communion. I shall be Changed in the twinkling of an Eye. All my Lusts & Corruptions, I shall be rid of, which I could not be here: these Croaking Toads will fall off in a Moment!* Or, shall we be beholden to a Scriptural Similitude? The *Leprosy* which infected us, from the tainted Walls of our *Clay-Tabernacle*, will no more infest us, after the Walls of the *Tabernacle* are taken down. It is an *Holy World* which we are now gott into; A World wherein our *Holiness* will be raised unto a Transcendent Elevation: The Thing which we *Long'd* for, which we *Groan'd* for, which has been more valuable to us than all this World, or a thousand such Worlds! The *Ordinances* we enjoy, and the *Afflictions* we endure, in this *Present Time*, are a *Furnace* whereof we may say, *our Iniquity is purged* [ms. II, 37] *here, and the Fruit is to take away our Sin.* But these are a dull & a slow *Furnace.* The near Approach to GOD, which our *Souls* make when our *Blood* ceases to be any longer an Element for them, will be a Quick, Strong, Fiery *Forge*, (as a True Divine well expresses it) that will soon dissolve our *Dross*, and separate our *Souls* from all that was Irregular in them. In short; The Acclamation, which the Jews report that *Mordecai* made upon his Advancement, will now be ours; *Thou hast putt off my Sackclothe, and girded me with Gladness; I will praise thee, O Lord, my Redeemer*. And now there are *Three Satisfactions*, which *Bernard* of old *Saw* rejoicing the *Souls* in *Paradise*: The First, The Remembrance of their former *Virtue*. The Second, The Fruition of their Present *Quiet*. The Third, The *Joyful Expectation* of a *future Consummation* to all their Blessedness.[81]

Can there be any thing more plain than the Promise of our SAVIOUR, unto them who are faithful Stewards of their Possessions: [Luk. XVI. 9.] That *when they fail* they shall find *Friends*, who will *Receive them into Everlasting Habitations*? At our *Death* it is that we *fail*: We are then turned out of House & Home, for the *Debt* we contracted by our Sin. At the *Resurrection from the Dead* we are *Sett up* again. But before That, even when we *Dy*, we are immediately *Received into Everlasting Habitations*. We may be sure, they are *Comfortable Habitations*, and *Houses full of Good Things*, inasmuch as we find in them some *Recompense* of the *Good* we have been doing here.

A Dying *Stephen* cries out; *Lord JESUS, Receive my Spirit*. But unto what? One who was present at the *Death* of *Stephen* and shortly after converted unto the *Faith*, of the Master, shall under the Inspirations of GOD explain the *Faith* of *Stephen*: [Rom. XV. 7.] *CHRIST Receives us unto the Glory of GOD*.

We read concerning *Separate Souls*, waiting and wishing for the *Resurrection of the Dead*; [Rev. VI. 11.] That *White Robes are given to them*; which implies, the Exercises of an *Holy Priesthood*, appointed for them. Certainly, *Priests* must be *Worshippers*. It seems by this, that there is a *Worship of GOD*, carried on among the *Separate Souls* in the *Heavenly World*. But how *Sinless*, how *Sublime*, how *Gladsome* a *Worship*, is it!

[ms. II, 38] On this Occasion I will ask Leave to mention a few *Jewish Curiosities*, which my Reader will be at his Liberty to Judge of, as he pleases. The *Ancients* (as well as the *Scriptures*, which are *Older* and *Wiser* than they!) speak of, a *Cloathing* with which the Faithful are hereafter to be accommodated. Relating to it, there is a Strange Passage, in the Commentaries of *Psellus*, on the *Chaldaic Oracles*. He says; *The Chaldees give the Soul Two Cloathings; The One, of the Spiritual Body, weaved out of that which is Subject to Sense; The Other, a Thinner, but Shining, & not subject unto the Touch, which they call, The Superficies*. The Conjecture of the *Jews*, is; That this *Cloathing* will be of *Light*, or *Fire*; which the Term of, *Glory*, does peculiarly belong unto. So the Old Book *Zohar*, says, *The Bodies of the Just shall be cloathed with the Light of GOD*. It is a Saying of R. *Phineas*, The Blessed GOD will give to the *Bodies* of the Just, An *Ornament*; According to that, [Isa. LVIII. 11.] *He shall satisfy thy Soul with splendid things*. By then R. *Levi* goes on, yett further to the Purpose we are now upon, with saying, *That the Soul in the State of its Glory is accommodated with this Superiour Light*, and when it returns to the *Body* it shall *come with this Light, and then the Body shall shine with the Brightness of the Heavens*. May not this agree somewhat, with the fulgent *Glory*, which came upon the

Body of our Lord, at His *Transfiguration?*—And with what we read in the *Old* Testament, of the Just *Rising* from their Graves, and then *Shining as the Brightness of the Firmament, & the Stars forever & ever;* And in the *New,* That *they shall Shine as the Sun in the Kingdom of the Father?* We have shrowd Reasons to think, That our *First Parents* while they continued in their Sinless Integrity, had something of this *Luminous Garment* upon them, and had, in it, both their *Shelter* and their *Beauty.* Tis called, *Vestis Onychina* in [ms.II, 39] the Jewish Tradition of it; from its Resemblance to an *Onyx* in the Colour of it; and unto the *Nails* on our Fingers, in some other Circumstances. Tis thought, that on the Sin of our First Parents, this *Luminous Garment* vanished from them; and this was the *Nakedness,* wherein they were *Asham'd* and *Afraid* of appearing before the Glorious GOD: and Justly might they be so, when they found, that they had *Sinn'd away* such a Mark of the Divine Favour to them.—To Some, these Communications will appear not contemptible. But I am far from urging of them; Nor will I so much as enquire, whether the *Separate Souls* of the Faithful are lodged in such a *Luminous Garment:* or how far, what was lost in & with the *First Paradise,* may be Regain'd in and by the *Second.* Whether this may be thought a *Proper Indument* for them, or no, the *Love of GOD,* & the *Perfection of Holiness* to which they are arrived, will be a Sufficient *Glory* to render *Paradise* a *Blissful Seat* unto them: that it shall be, even as *Tertullian* himself confesses it, *Locus Divinae Amoenitatis.*[82]

But now what shall be thought concerning that, *Sweetest Fruit of Paradise?* We read of such a Thing as This; [Phil. I. 23.] *To Depart and be with CHRIST;* which is *far Better* than to *Live in the Flesh.* And; [2. Cor. V. 8.] *To be Present with the Lord,* when *Absent from the Body.* The *Views* of a Glorious CHRIST, were the Enjoyments, which the Beleever while he was on Earth, had of all the greatest Relish for. They were the *Salt* & *Soul* of his Life: He *Liv'd* upon them. It was by *Acquainting* himself with a Glorious CHRIST that he saw *Peace* under whatever Storms assaulted him, & thereby *Good* came unto him. This *Acquaintance* was that which brought unto him the *Excellent Knowledge* in Comparison whereof he *counted all Things but Loss,* and it was that which *fill'd him with all Goodness:* And the *Precious Thoughts* of a CHRIST made up unto him, the Want of whatever else might be denied him. [ms. II, 40] He is now in the *Paradise* of GOD admitted unto such a *Vision* of his Glorious LORD, as he never had before. And now, to assail the Difficulty!—

—We have hitherto supposed the *Paradise* of *Separate Souls,* to be distinguished from the *Third Heaven,* which is the more *Constant Residence* of our SAVIOUR: And we have seen Plain Intimations, That it will be *His Appearing* that will bring us to *See Him as He is;* And, That it will be after *the Coming of the Lord* that we shall *be forever with the Lord.* How does this agree with our being *with Him,* while *That Day* is not yett arrived?

Will this be any Solution of the Difficulty? It seems, as if the *Souls* of the Faithful had no sooner left their *Bodies,* but they are by the *Angels* of GOD brought before the Lord, even into His *Glorious Presence,* for Him to take that *Notice,* and give that *Order,* which He Judges proper for them.

Will it be any Solution, to suppose; That our LORD makes His *Transient,* and perhaps, *Frequent, Visitations,* to those Apartments, where the *Souls* of the Faithful, have their *Paradise;* And grants New, and Fresh, and Wonderful *Discoveries* of Himself unto them, in these *Visitations?*

Will it be any Solution, to suppose; That *Souls* can by Raised and Fixed *Contemplations* alone come near to the Objects which they converse withal; and *Local Approaches* are not always necessary: But the Faithful in *Paradise* are fetch'd up to *Contemplations,* whereof they were not capable here below?

Some thus assay to solve the Matter, "The *Paradisial Hades* is a Place wherein CHRIST manifests Himself in a more Glorious Manner than here below. And therefore it may justly be [ms. II, 41] said, That *Comparatively* with the Discoveries given *here,* to be *There,* is to be *more Directly with CHRIST,* than our being *here* can admitt of. Thus, tho' He was Resident on Earth in the *Temple* of old among the *Jews,* so as He was in no Countrey on Earth, yett this did not hinder Men from supposing Him to have been more gloriously present with the *Angels* above, and more directly and conspicuously Resident in the Highest Heavens." And the Truth is; It was no Improper Thing for Men in other Countreys to wish, That they were in the *Holy Land,* that they might *there be with* the GOD of *Israel;* and yett at the same time, there was more of GOD in the *Heavenly World* than there was in that *Holy Land:* for the Sake whereof one might have wish'd, *when shall I come and appear before GOD, in the Better Countrey!* So Dr. *Bull* also expresses it. *Present in the Body, they do not so nearly enjoy CHRIST, as they do, when Absent from the Body.* And again; *They Behold the Glory of CHRIST, tho' not in that full Brightness, wherein it shall be Seen at the Day of His Glorious Appearance.*

Briefly, Tis well observed by our *Goodwin;* That altho' the *Blessedness* of the *Soul* in Both Conditions, (that under the *Separation,* and that after the *Resurrection*) be described by some of the Same Expressions, yett these Expressions are to be understood with a Vast Variety, Difference, Disproportion; So Vast, that we may say, *That which is made glorious now,* while in the State of the Dead, *has no Glory in respect of that which excelleth it;* as that will, which we shall have when Raised from the Dead. It is Remarkable, That some of the Same Expressions are used, for such Special Manifestations of GOD and CHRIST unto the *Soul,* thro' *Faith,* while here on *Earth,* which are used for both the *Successive Conditions* of *Glory* in the *Heavenly World;* Such as, *Beholding the Glory of GOD in the Face of JESUS CHRIST,* and *Being with Him,* and, *Dwelling in Him:* And yett very vast is the *Disproportion* between the Dispensations on *Earth,* and those in the Heavenly *World.* So, says the Doctor, why may not such a *Disproportion* be understood, between the *Two States of Glory,* under the same [ms. II, 42] Expressions? He thinks, the Fruition we shall have of GOD and CHRIST, which we shall have in the *Day of the Lord,* will be so far elevated above all that our Souls enjoy'd before, as it will in *Comparison* be, as if we had never seen them. How much—*None but GOD and CHRIST Himself, do know, or can!* [83]

Finally; Some of the Fathers, when they speak of the Receptacles for the *Sepa-*

rate Souls of the Faithful, call them, *Atrià a longè*: The *Courts* of Heaven. As he of *Caraval* expresses it; The *Souls* of the Faithful do, *Adhuc in Atriis Dei Stare*.[84] From those *Courts* they are not without Glorious *Views*, of what is done in the more *Inner Parts* of the *Coelestial Temple*. *Christian*, Think on those *Courts*, when thou findest a devout *Soul*, so often *Thirsting* for them in the Songs of *Zion*: But then, be of that Perswasion, O *Blessed is the Man of whom Thou mak'st a gracious Choice, and whom thou shalt make to approach near to thy Majesty! Such an one does dwell in thy Courts; We shall be satisfied with the Good of thy House, and with thy Temples Holy Place.*

However *Paradise* may fall short, of *what we shall be*, yett Lett us dy in the *Faith* of those *Dying Beleevers*, whereof so many have had those for their Last Words, *I am going to be with CHRIST*. Such was the Faith of that famous Martyr *Wishart* in *Scotland*; who coming to seal the Truth with his Blood, said, *Some have reported, as if I beleeved, that the Souls of Men sleep till the Day of Judgment; whereas I certainly know, That I shall be this very Night, with CHRIST in Heaven*.[85]

Pious Mr. *Shermerdine* of *Darby-shire*, dying said, *I am going to my Praeferment*. Beleever, Thy *Paradise*, at the Lowest, will be an High *Preferment* for thee![86]

[ms. II, 43]
Sect. V. It may Reasonably be considered, as an Intimation of the Glorious *Blessedness* for the *Souls* of Good Men in the *Paradise* of GOD; That many *Souls* just arrived unto the *Gate* of the *Garden*, have been favoured with some astonishing *Anticipations* of what is there more fully allow'd unto the Faithful; and which doubtless have been intended by Heaven, for the Instruction & Encouragement of the Survivers, that with a *Patient Continuance in well-doing*, they may *Rejoice in the Hope of the Glory of GOD*.

I do most readily grant, that some Relations, which we have had of *Dying Extasies*, may impose upon us, no other than the Delirious and Extravagant *Fancies*, of Whimsical *Visionaries*. They must be read with *Discretion*. But yett some of these *Dying Extasies* have been attended with such Circumstances, that it would be a Rash & a Weak & a very *Indiscreet* thing to make meer *Fancies* of them, and nothing but the *Vapours* of Imagination. Some *Holy Souls* just arrived unto the *Streight Gate*, have had an *Open Entrance* into the *Paradise* of GOD *administred* unto them, in most Regular, but Ravishing, Exhibitions of the *Glory* there waiting for them. The *Views* and the *Joys* to which these *Holy Souls* have been raised, before they have quite left their *Bodies*, have been such as to make them utterly Insensible of their *Bodily Ails*, & strangely take away the *Sting of Death*, and give them a Surprizing Triumph over the *King of Terrors*; and enable them to expostulate, *How cold is thy Kindness, O Death, in being so slow to come & loose a poor tired Prisoner! O Time, How dost thou torment a Soul that would be swallowed up* [ms. II, 44] *in the Love of CHRIST!*

When! What Hand will shovel Time out of the Way, and hasten my Soul away to her Glorious Bridegroom!

Judicious Writers have not thought it any Betraying or Exposing of their Judgment, for them to relate Passages of this Importance: And, *Lett me, I pray thee, also run after them!*

The Last Hours of Dr. *Ames,* and of Dr. *Holland,* have been celebrated, for the Praelibations of *Paradise,* and of an Heavenly *Glory* in them.[87]

That Pious Physician, *Joachimus Curaeus,* on his Death-bed, after a thousand Expressions of a Blessed Soul, inhabited by a JESUS Leading & Ruling in all its Motions, and able to say, *I see the Heavens now open for me,* summ'd up all in This; *Pectus meum iam ardet conspectu vitae aeternae, cujus verè sentio in me Initia.*[88]

That Excellent Lady, *Olympia Fulvia Morata,* celebrated, as by *Melchior Adam,* so by the great *Voetius;* dying in the *Twenty ninth* Year of her Age, said; *For Seven Years, & ever since my Engaging of myself unto the Lord, I have seldome had any Cessation from some Assault or other of the Devil, to shake my Faith. But now, he has lost all his Darts. Now I feel in my Soul nothing but inexpressible Tranquillity, & Peace with GOD thro' Jesus Christ.* She told her incomparable Husband, for whom she had the tenderest Love in the World, *That she had now gott a Sight of a most Excellent & most Delightful Place, ever shining with an astonishing Light & Brightness, whereto she was now hastening.* And said she, TOTA SUM LÆTA—*I am full of Joy; But now, Syr, I know you no more.*[89]

Dr. *Winter,* as he drew near his End, on a certain Morning said unto his Consort; *I have been this night conversing with Spirits. Oh! The Glories that are praepared for the Saints of GOD! The Lord has been pleased to shew me this night, the Exceeding Weight of Glory, which is in Heaven laid up for His Chosen ones. I have studied; and I have thought, that I knew Something of what is the Glory there. But I now see, that all the Divines on Earth are but Children, in the Knowledge of the Great Mystery of the Heavenly Glory: A Mystery which cannot be comprehended by the Will of Man. Oh! If you had but a Thorough Sight thereof, it would make you all to love the Lord JESUS CHRIST and Holiness, which is the only Way to attain this Happiness.*[90]

Thus, *Ibat ovans Anima, et sic Spe sua damna levabat.*[91]

A Late Writer on, *The Glory of Heaven,* recites diverse Exemples of these *Dying Extasies.* One Person [ms. II, 45] on his Death-bed, particularly, being told, that it was hoped GOD would Restore him to his Health again, replied; *You are much mistaken, if you apprehend, that the Thoughts of Life & Health are pleasing to me. All this World has quite lost its Excellency. In my Judgment, it is but a poor contemptible thing in all its Glory, compared with the Glory of the Invisible World, which I now live in the Sight of. It would be a far more delightful thing to me, if you could tell me for certain, that I am no more for this World, and that before to Morrow I should be in Eternity: For I do so long to be with CHRIST, that I could be content to be cutt in Pieces, & putt to*

*the most Exquisite Torments, might I but Dy, & be with CHRIST; Death is,
thro' Grace, nothing to me. It hath lost its Terribleness; It may do its worst; I
fear it not; I can as easily Dy as shutt my Eyes, or turn my head & fall asleep.
Yea, I long to Dy, that I may be with CHRIST. Come therefore, O Lord JESUS,
Come Quickly. Why is thy Chariot so long a coming! Why tarry the Wheels of
thy Chariots!*[92]

I will not Swell my *Treatise,* & Load my *Reader,* with Stories fetched from
former Ages, or other Places. More particularly what *Austin* writes of one
Curma, whom he knew; and who after it was thought that he had been Dead,
came to Life again, & related Strange Things upon it: Shall not be now repeated. But those that would see more such things, I will refer to a *Wanly* for
them.[93] And yett I know not how to forbear the Mention of Two, which are so
well-attested, that I am not ashamed of them.

The one from a former *Age,* is related, not only by *Fulgosus,*[94] but by other
very approved Historians. A Godly Young Man who was a Servant unto a Person
of Quality in *Rome,* at a time when the Plague raged there, was look'd upon as
actually Dead of it. But he Revived, and Lived for Two Days after it. In this time,
he told his Masters, that he had been *in a Most Glorious World;* and added, That
such & such in the Family were to Dy of the Pestilence, but that his Master
himself should Survive them all: Which came to pass accordingly.

The other from another *Place,* is related by Mr. *Tho. Wadsworth,* in his Book
of, *The Immortality of the Soul.* Mr. *Mather* a Minister at *Nantwich* in *Chesh-
ire,* lay at the [ms. II, 46] Point of Death; with no Strength, & scarce any Breath
left unto him. His Friends apprehended him to be in Slumber; but were surprised at their hearing him fall to *Singing,* with the Strength & Voice of one that
had nothing ailing him. After some time, they asked him the Meaning of it. He
told them, that he had been where he had seen what appeared unto him as a
Glorious Palace; and having Liberty to look in at the Door, he saw it filled with
a *Glorious People,* all of them *Singing* at a rate that ravished him. He would
fain have entred; but one at the Door denied him Entrance; with informing
him, That his Friends having been very Importunate in their *Prayers* for his
Life, GOD would gratify their Importunity with letting him live *Three Days*
longer: But at the End of *Three Days* he should have Admission. He lett his
Friends know, that he could not forbear *Singing* at the Door, because of what he
had heard within; But he call'd for his Flock to visit him; which they did with
much Resort. He spent those *Three Days* as one that had no Weakness upon
him, in such Instructions and Admonitions and Exhortations, as left greater
Impressions than his *Ordinary Ministry* might perhaps in so many *Years* have
made upon them. And just at the End of the *Three Days* he expired.[95]

The Narrative which Dr. *Atherton,* a Physician of *Caermarthen,* has given the
World, concerning a Godly Sister of his, Mrs. *Ann Atherton,* who after having
lain Six Days without any Signs of Life, returned unto her Friends, and gave an
Account of a *Glorious Place* that she had seen, confirming it with what she had
seen of Persons Dying in the Time of her Long *Extasy;* tis worth perusing. And
what both *Manlius* and *Borellus* have given us, of the like Instances, deserves

to be considered. But I shall here offer to the Public only a few Relations, of, *Occurrences on the Borders of Paradise*, with which *my own* Observation has furnished me, and which have upon my Enquiries into them not wanted the Proofs that have entirely satisfied me.[96]

[ms. II, 47]

I. There died at our *Salem-Village*, a Man called *Wilkins*, who for fifty Years had led a very Wicked Life, but for some Weeks before he died, he was become a most Remarkable Paenitent. After the Impressions of the Divine Grace had begun to be conspicuous on him, he fell into a Distemper that proved Mortal to him; And in the Sick & Last Weeks of his Life, there occurr'd a great Variety of *Extraordinary Passages.* I shall relate only the Conclusion of them. After he had sometimes cried out, O *the Riches of Free Grace! There are thousands of thousands, & ten thousand times ten thousand, in Heaven, rejoicing over a great & an old Sinner coming to Glory!*—At last he grew Speechless & Senseless, and his Friends apprehended him come to the Last Gasp. He lay for diverse Hours thus drawing on; But at Length, to their Amazement, he revived so far, that he Sprang up in his Bed, and Spred his Arms abroad as going to leap into Arms ready to receive him; and gave a Shout, saying, O my Friends, *Heaven rings all over at This; A great & an old Sinner coming to Heaven! Behold, In my Fathers House there are many Mansions. If it had not been so, my SAVIOUR would not have said it. But He is gone to praepare a Place for me. Oh! The Riches of Free Grace! Oh! Glorify Free Grace forevermore!*—And so he immediately lay down & expired.[97]

II. A Shipmaster whose Name was Mr. *Thomas Parker*, in a Long Sickness made that Progress in a Serious Conversion to GOD, which enabled him to say, *He had found one Minutes Communion with a Lovely JESUS, better & sweeter, than all the Enjoyments of this World.* Seven Days before he died, he fell into a *Trance*, in which he lay for some considerable while. Coming out of it, he said unto me; He had been admitted into a *Most Glorious Place*, where every thing was extremely *Regular.* The Persons there all in the greatest *Rest* imaginable; and yett always at *Work*; very much of which *Work* was, the *Worship* of GOD. He saw Great *Praeparations* making there, that he understood were for the *Resurrection of the Dead*; which is now shortly [ms. II, 48] coming on. He said; *If whole Mountains of Gold were offered me,—all the Glory of this World, were it a thousand times more than it is, would not hire me to stay one Minute out of that Heavenly Glory. Oh! If People did but know that Glory, they would think much of no Pains to make sure of an Interest in it. Syrs You told me some time ago,* "That if a Man gott safer to Heaven, the odds is little between going thither just now, or going thither Twenty Years hence; and they who came thither, would not complain, if it were Twenty Years before Sixty were up." *I did not then so well apprehend the Glorious Truth of what you spoke; But now I apprehend it!—Twenty Years! NO! Tis impossible to come too Soon or too Young to the Glory of Heaven! Oh! Tis nothing to Dy; I would freely Dy Ten Deaths to come at the Glory, to which I am agoing!* Some time after this,

he had a sharp Conflict with an *Invisible Adversary*. But he overcame it; &
recovered his *Views*, and *Joys*, to which on the *Seventh* Day after his *Extasy*,
he departed.[98]

III. *John Goodwin*, a Young Man of Exemplary Piety and Honesty, and Industry,
and one in Comfortable Circumstances, lay indisposed for something above a
Week before he died. *Before this*, when the Least Illness arrested him, a discern-
ible *Fear of Death* siezed upon him. *Now*, the perfect Reverse; *Now*, he longed
for *Death*, and said unto his Consort; he would not have her take it unkindly,
that he did so: For if she knew so much as *he* now did, of a Glorious CHRIST,
and of His *Heavenly World*, she would not wonder at his Disposition. He express'd a most flaming and eager Desire to leave *This World*: and he declared
himself afraid of returning back into it, as being lothe to have the Satisfactions
of the *Heavenly World* which now fill'd him, suffer any Interruption. When he
first began to droop, he lay down in his Cloathes; And his Friends coming to
him, he told them, That he had newly heard a *Voice*, a sweet, pleasant, charming & melodious *Voice*, which had audibly declared unto him, *That he should
Dy that Day Se'n night*. He had a Soul now as full of Comfort, as he could [ms.
II, 49] bear; It seem'd long to him e'er the Week roll'd about. There appeared
nothing Singular, or indeed Threatening, in his Distemper. It was only a gentle
Fever on taking a Cold. But he did accordingly *Dy that Day Se'n night*.[99]

IV. There died in our *Salem*, a Gentlewoman whose Name was Mrs. *Rix*; One
of real *Piety*, and of aequal *Patience*; a Disciple of the Cross, who had endured
much Affliction, especially by Sickness, with much Submission to the Will of
GOD. Unto her Pastor, my Intimate Learned, & Worthy Friend, who visited her
before she died, she related and affirmed, That there had newly appeared unto
her, Several *Shining Persons*, who told her, *That they were not now come for
her, but on that Day Six Weeks hence, they would come for her, & fetch her
away with a Glorious Equipage*. And then she immediately asked her Pastor,
*I pray, Syr, what is the Meaning of the Word, EQUIPAGE? I don't remember,
that I have ever heard that word, EQUIPAGE*. Her Pastor wisely advised her,
by no means to build her Hopes on any *Visionary Matters*, but have them forever built on the *Sure Foundation*, which the *Covenant of Grace* as declared in
the Gospel, afforded for them. She gave him abundant Satisfaction, that she did
so; Yett she kept in an Heavenly Manner Praying and Waiting, & full of agreeable anhelations, to see the *Six Weeks* expired; and praecisely at the Expiration
thereof, *she died*.[100]

V. Mrs. *Katharin Mather*, after a short Life of Early & Substantial and Retired
Piety, enjoy'd a *Death*, whereof they that stood by and saw it, said, *Such a
Death were well worth all the Pains and all the Prayers of the Longest Life
upon Earth!* Lingring and Painful Sickness wasted her, yett she could keep say-
ing; *I am even broken to Peeces, but I Love, I Love the Hand that breaks me!*
She could say, *I am in great Misery, but while GOD is Glorified, I cannot be*

miserable. She could say; *I am going to a Glorious World, but I have been times without number already there.* Death came upon her at an Age that is most fond of *Life;* And yett her [ms. II, 50] *Death* was beyond all Expression welcome to her, with some Holy *Impatience,* and yett profound *Submission,* longed for. When she was told of any Symptoms, that her *Death* was drawing on, she replied, *Oh! I could even Sing for Joy, at what you tell me!* She could say, *I have now left no Will of my own; But, Oh! the Peace & Joy, which I find in this Extinction of my Will! I know, that GOD will be Glorified in all that He will have to be done concerning me; and therein I shall be forever satis-fied.* She could say, *I find an astonishing Fulfilment of that Word,* If GOD give Quiet, who can cause Trouble? *I am not able to Trouble myself, tho' I should even Try to do it. Nothing on Earth, Nothing in Hell, can cause Trouble to me, while I feel Heaven in me.* She said, *I have nothing to do, but Resign & Rejoice!* As the Hour drew near, she said, *Strong as Death is my Love to thee, O my SAVIOUR; I am willing to go thro' any Death unto thee!* On her Last *Satureday,* she long'd, that she might have her *Sabbath* in the *Paradise* of GOD. In the Evening, when it was told her, it was thought she might live another Day, she replied; *No, I have received other Advice; It has been said unto me,* THIS DAY THOU SHALT BE WITH ME IN PARADISE. A little after Midnight, she said, *My Soul is in perfect Ease;*—And with those Words expired.[101]

VI. Mrs. *Jerusha Oliver,* had been of a very Timerous Constitution, and *all her Life kept in Bondage by the Fear of Death.* She was one of uncommon *Piety:* Among the written Memorials whereof, I found after her Death, she had often made this an Article of her most fervent Supplications; *That she might Dy Be-leevingly, Willingly, Joyfully;* And, *That she might thro' CHRIST obtain the Victory over Death, & the Fear of Death;* And, That *she might have such Fore-tastes of the Joys of Heaven, as might cause her to long to be there.* About a Week after a Travail, she felt a Change come upon her. Whereupon she told us, [ms. II, 51] That she was very sure, the *Time of her Death* was now arrived. But, said she, *Here is a Strange Thing! When I was in Health, Death was a Terror to me. But now I know I shall Dy, I am not at all afraid of it. This is a Wonderful Work of GOD! I know, that I am going to CHRIST: That I shall shortly be with an Innumerable Company of Angels, and among the Spirits of the Righteous. I see things that are unutterable! O the Glory of Heaven! O the Glory of Heaven! O the Glory of Heaven! I see a Glory which cannot be expressed: Persons and Matters, which I want a Language to declare what they are!* She continued her Ovations over the *Last Enemy;* and at last she expired with these Words, *I am in Distress to be gone!* [102]

VII. A Virtuous Young Woman, called *Sarah Frothingam,* died of a Consump-tion. Having lain speechless for several Days together, she fell into an Agony, that appeared somewhat convulsive; and that Fitt ceasing, she lay stretched out, with her *Eyes* fixed, without *Breath,* without *Pulse,* without any Observable Sign of Life; but only some Little Working perceived in her Breast. After she had been thus the best Part of an Hour, she Return'd, she Reviv'd; she address'd a Room full of Spectators, with as plain & free & audible a *Speech* as ever she had in her Life, and such as threw them all into an Astonishment. She told them, that she had been in *Heaven*, and that a Glorious One had assured her, she should by 'nd by go thither again, & come back no more: And she blessed the Lord, who had permitted her to come back a few Minutes, and say what she had now to say unto them. She said, *The Glory of the Place is inexpressible!* She kept magnifying to the best of her Capacity the *Glory* of it; and she Pittied those who were to stay here; which for her Part she would not be willing to do, for all the Poor *Glory* of *This World*. Her Exclamations were; *Oh! Heaven! Tis a Glorious Place! I cannot express the Glory of it! My Joy, my Joy, my Joy, tis inexpressible!* She gave them Lively Exhortations to praepare for Heaven, and gett an Interest in the CHRIST, who alone can bring them thither. [ms. II, 52] She dispensed Pungent Admonitions, to some whom she thought Wandring from the Way of Life; And she begg'd them, that they would not imagine her to be Delirious in these Discourses. When she had finished, she call'd for a Cup of *Cold Water*, and having *Drunk* it, she said, *I will now go to the Fountain of Living Water.* And so she died.[103]

VIII. Mrs. *Sarah Brown* of *Salem*, was a Gentlewoman of Conspicuous Piety, as well as other Accomplishments. But she was one who thro' *Fear of Death* had been always kept in Degrees of Consternation, beyond most of the Children of GOD. And she was of a very *Tearful* as well as of a very *Fearful* Temper: *Tears in a Great Measure*, and almost beyond Measure, had been given her. When she was within a few Days of her Travail, Sitting alone, in a *Dark Room*, Weeping and full of Thought, she saw a *Light* break into the Room, and heard a *Voice* therewith speak to her; *Be of Good Comfort; Thou art going to have all Tears wiped from thine Eyes; From this Time, thou shalt never weep any more!* She now foretold her dying in Childbed; and her excellent Mother-in-Law, who was more than a Mother to her, (to whom she related what had passed,) could by no means bring her out of that Perswasion. But she never shed One *Tear*, after the *Light* & *Voice*, that had so comforted her; and her Triumph over the *Fear* of the *Disarmed Snake*, was wonderful. Her Travail was Easy & Happy, beyond what is ordinary: But she died in her Childbed.[104]

IX. Mrs. *Lydia Baily*, when she lay a dying, made much Complaint, that her Friends did her a Diskindness, by keeping her back, & not Sufficiently Resigning her up to GOD in CHRIST, whom she did love above all, & long to be withal. She said, That HE had appeared unto her, and that the *Peace* and *Joy* of His Holy SPIRIT now filled her; and that she had whole Floods of the *Love* of [ms. II, 53] GOD in her Soul, and more than she was well able to bear. She would not be pacified, until her affectionate Husband, would promise before all the Witnesses present, and before the *Holy Angels*, who, she said, should Seal it with their *Golden Seals*, That he would lett her go, & give up his *All*, and *her* with the rest, unto the Lord. After a Thousand Praises to the SAVIOUR, who had filled her with His Marvellous *Love,* she could say, *Death has now no Terror in it; I can as freely Dy, as ever I fell asleep; I deserve none of this Love: But if my SAVIOUR will give it, who shall hinder Him? O Go to Him; He is no Niggard; He has Love & Grace enough for you all. I cannot bear it; it is too heavy.* As well as *I Love my invaluable Husband here, and I now Love that Servant of GOD better than ever I did, & I shall bless GOD thro' all Eternity for him, yett I would not be hired by Millions of Worlds, to Live a Day or an Hour with him, & Stay from my dear SAVIOUR. And yett, if GOD would have me to Live, I would Live. This Hour is the Happiest Hour that ever I had since my Mother bound my Head. I am going to the Lord, and if thousands of Devils tell me otherwise, I will not beleeve them. GOD has now made me amends for all the Troubles I ever mett withal in the World!* And in this Frame she expired. Her Husband, a Worthy Minister, well-known in *Ireland* as well as *New-England,* concludes his Narrative with a Surprising Passage. "She desired, that we would Sing some *Psalm* of Praise to the Riches of Free-Grace. But our *Harps* were hang'd in the Willows; We did it not. Yett there was a most Melodious *Singing* at that very time. *I heard it myself;* but intended never to speak of it; until *Two More* spoke of it. They went unto the Fire, thinking it was there; But they heard it best within the Curtains. GOD, by His *Holy Angels,* putt an Honour upon my dear Consort; and by it reproved us, that Seeing we could not Sing, (being bad at it,) *They* would." *Some of the Witnesses have since asserted this, unto the Author.*[105]

X. It is not easy to apprehend, what may be the Meaning of that Strange *Music* which has been plainly heard, by many, who have stood by the Bedsides of several Godly Persons on their Deathbeds among us, & who were sure that their Imaginations were not imposed upon. Who can ap-[ms. II, 54]prehend, how *Materially* the *Invisible World* may be circumstanced, and what *Senses* may be enjoy'd and employ'd in the *Heavenly Paradise;* and on what accounts a *Paul,* when *Caught up* thither, might *hear Words* uttered there? In this Place, there have been several Instances of it; wherein, they who have agreed in hearing of the *Music,* before they have invited each other to take notice of it, have nicely at the Moment of it, examined, whence it might proceed, & found that it could come from none but the *Invisible World.*

Among the rest, we had one in the Month of *September.* A.C. 1721. A Gentleman who abounded in the Works of Piety and Charity, and who had been also a Justice of Peace in the City of *Boston,* died about the Middle of the Month. His Domesticks took notice, that in the Last Prayer which he made with his Family, before his Retirement unto the Chamber of his Decumbiture, he did with an Extraordinary Fervency, insist on a Petition, *For a Conduct & a Convoy of Good ANGELS in a Dying Hour.*[106] About four or five Hours before he died, having lost the Sight of every thing in this World, he gave a mighty Spring towards the Heavens, crying out, *Sweet JESUS, I come unto thee!*—and so fell down upon his Face, as if he had expired. At this time, there was heard about his Bed, by no less than Four Persons, which attended upon him, a Soft *Music,*

which was beyond all Expression Delectable & Admirable to them. He continued still Four or Five Hours, under the Approaches of *Death*: But the *Music*
was in this while heard Five or Six times, Four or Five Minutes at a Time. They
did every thing they could think of, to inform themselves, whether the *Music*
might not come from some Quarter or other in the Neighbourhood: But it was
to be heard no where but about the Sick Man: and they were fully convinced,
That it must come from the *Invisible World*. It was heard somewhat after his
Death, and even when the Corpse was just laid out: But unspeakably charming,
& with a Melody that could not be described. [ms. II, 55] Don't these things
appear a little of a Peece, with the *Singing of Psalms* in the *Invisible World*,
often heard in the Air, by Hundreds of Witnesses, in the time when the *Scotch*,
and afterwards the *French*, Persecutions, were in the Heat & the Heighth of
them? [107] *GOD knows what they are!*

But, *what shall we say to these things?*—Lett not any One censure all these
Communications, as *Enthusiasms* unworthy of all Regard from *Judicious Readers*. No, Master *Epicurus*; The most *Judicious Writers* in the World have not
thought such things unworthy to be communicated, and contemplated. In the
German Ephemerides for A.C. 1682. there are diverse Instances of such *Extasies*, wherein the *Extatics* returning from the Degrees of *Death*, in which they
had lain Insensible of This World for a considerable while, not only complained
of their being fetch'd back from the *Wondrously Delicious Place* where they
had newly been entertained, but also told *Secret & Remote & Future* Things,
which they learnt in their *Extasies*, and which were found afterwards to be
punctually *True*.[108] A Noble Young Lady particularly, mentioned in the French,
Lodiacus Medicus, An. 2.—*Restitua, non Gratias egit officiorum sibi praesti-
torum, sed Querelas fudit, quod ereptu sibi fuerit incomprehensa et ineffabilis
animi Tranquillitas, et voluptas gratissima ac talis, quâ mortales frui, nisi ad
statum illum deducti fuerint, nequeant, Faelicitas: Quicquid Gaudii nomine
venit, levissimam tantum idaeam exhibere ejus, quo gavisa fuerat.*[109] Most Expressive Terms; and how Pertinent unto our Present Occasion! For the Sake of
some who do not ken the Latin, wee'l bestow a Translation on them. "She Being
Recovered, conn'd very Little Thanks [110] to them who had been the Instruments
of it. But she made heavy Complaints, that she had been robb'd of an incomprehensible & unutterable *Tranquillity of Soul*, and most grateful Satisfaction,
& such a Faelicity as no Mortals can have any Taste of, without being brought
into the State, that she was now reduced from. Whatsoever is called, *Joy*, in
this World [*she said*] could give but a very mean & low Idaea, of what she had
rejoiced in." The ingenious Professor *Hanneman* says upon them; That these
Things must by no means be despised as *Meer Fancies*. But we have Cause to
think, that the *Souls* of People, withdrawing so far from a Conversation with
This World, as they do in these *Extasies*, they fall into a Conversation with
the *Spirits* in the *Invisible World*: Either *Good* ones, or *Bad* ones, according to
Quality of the *Extatics*; and from these they learn what they do. And whereas
the [ms. II, 56] Vulgar Philosophy knows not how to *Explain* these Things, and

therefore [very *Humbly*, and *Wisely!*] chuses to *Deride* them, he quotes the very just Remark of the Excellent *Spener* upon it; *Vera fortasse caremus philosophia.* Dear Syr, There's no room for a, *Fortasse*, upon it! It is most *certainly* so.[111]

There are Several Circumstances in my *Narratives*, and especially that of *Death* arriving just at the *Time* foretold for it, that cannot but recommend them to some attentive Consideration. But if they may serve to no other Purpose, they will yett serve to that which I mainly produced them for; That is, To illustrate the *Consolations* of *Paradise*, and the *Dispositions* of *Souls* well-praepared for it. And the *Triumphant Way of Dying* exemplified in them, cannot but make the Worst of *Mortals* to wish.—*Sic mihi contingat!*—[112]

Sect. VI. A Departed Servant of GOD, appearing to a Brother of his, [*whom I know!*—] and it being enquired of him, *Is it well?* He replied, *Infinitely well! Infinitely well! Infinitely well! The Glory is Infinitely beyond all that I ever imagined.* His Brother answering, *Well, I shall be with you Anon; It won't be long!* He proceeded; *In the mean time, keep up a Good Intercourse with our World; It may be done!*—And so he disappeared.

There is an *Intercourse* with *Paradise*, and Communion with the *Departed Spirits* of the Faithful there, which is indeed so far from *Unlawful* to be ask'd for, and sought for, that our *Sanctity*, & our *Conversation with Heaven* lies very much, in the Study of it. It is indeed said, They have *no more a Portion forever in any thing that is done under the Sun*. But if they have *Nothing* to do with [ms. II, 57] *Us*, we have *Something* to Do with *Them*; and we should as far as we can affect ourselves, & inflame our *Zeal*, and confirm our *Peace*, and strengthen our *Hope*, from what we know concerning *them*. This will be no Criminal *Necromancy!*[113] The *Saints*, whose *Bodies* are *Laid in the Earth*, are the *Excellent Ones* in whom we are to have a Singular *Delight*, and are the Nobler Members of the *Family*, which we in a *Lower State* belong unto. And they may be thus convers'd withal. To bring some *Warmth* into us, & make our *Hearts burn within* us, Lett us thus bring down the Rays of *Paradise* upon our Souls. Are we too ready like *Fools*, to make Light of *Sin*, and *Sport* with *Firebrands* & *Arrows* & *Death?* Lett us *lift up our Eyes to Heaven*, and a Right *Understanding will return unto us*. Think, How odious is all *Sin*, to the Purified *Souls* in *Paradise*. Doubtless, It would be a *Second Death* unto them, to *Sin* any more.[114] Do we Dote upon the Things of *This World*, with *Dreams* that have *Diverse Vanities* in them? Lett the Glories of *This World*, appear to us, as they do to them that are gott into the more glorious Regions of *Paradise*. Think, *How contemptible does this World appear, & how does all the Pomp of it vanish, and what are all the Deceitful Riches of it, unto the Souls, which have taken to themselves Wings, & are flown away into Heaven?* Are we here in a *Frozen Zone*, where the *Love of many waxes cold?* Lett a *Seraph* bring a *Red-hot Stone* from the *Altar in Paradise* to render us, *Fervent in Spirit serving the Lord*.[115] Think, *Do they love GOD so poorly in Heaven? Do they love one another no better in Heaven?* When we fail in our *Compliance* with the Will of GOD, with what a Pungency may we thus reprove ourselves; *Is this to do the Will of GOD on Earth, as it is done in Heaven?* This *Reproof GOD* may sound like a Peal of Thunder in *Heaven* over us. Are we engaging in the *Worship* of our GOD? Lett us call to Mind, how the *Host of Heaven do worship Him!* In what an Holy Manner, do our *Brethren in Paradise* prostrate themselves before the *Glorious High Throne* of our GOD. If we grow *Dull* in our Approaches unto GOD, call down the *Spirits* that are Above, to be *Swift Witnesses* against our *Lukewarmness* [ms. II, 58] in what we have before us. Think; *Do our Brethren in Heaven worship the Great GOD, so unconcernedly, so unattentively?* Have not those who are *Living to GOD* in His *Paradise,* an *Earnest Expectation of the Resurrection from the Dead?* As their *Flesh,* in the *Dry & Thirsty Land* of the *Grave,* is *Longing for the Lord,* and for the falling of the *Dew* from Heaven, by the Virtue whereof they shall be *Born again*; So, their *Soul* is *Thirsting* for Him, & for His bringing their *Body* from the *Land of the Enemy.* Lett us Join with them in the *Lively Hope of the Inheritance reserved in Heaven for us, & the Salvation to be Reveled in the Last Time*; Join with them, in their Cry, *How Long, Lord, Holy & True!* Are not the Manifestations of a Glorious CHRIST, the Delicious *Manna,* which the *Souls* in *Paradise* do feed upon? They therein eat the *Food of Angels!* We may do *This,* even while we are yett in our *Terrible Wilderness.* Every thing of a Glorious CHRIST should now be precious to us. We may *determine to know nothing so much* as Him; and may *live by the Faith* of Him. Thus to *Harmonize* with the Saints in *Paradise!*—We are *caught up to Paradise* in these *Harmonies.* They will be the *Evident Tokens of Salvation* upon us; *Tokens* that e're long we shall be *There.* We may go on, and fetch admirable *Cordials* from the *Spicy Countrey,* to encourage us under the Difficulties of the Way that leads unto it. *We Faint not, while we look to the Things which are not seen!* Are we in danger of growing *Weary* of being *always upon Duty?* Always *Watching & Warding,* and in a continual *Warfair?* Look up to *Paradise,* and see what an *Harvest* the Saints there have already begun to *Reap* of all their *Well-doing* here. Can we think, that they *Repent* of their *Prayers,* of [ms. II, 59] their *Alms,* of all their Laborious and Assiduous Essays to *Do Good?* No, surely; They will tell us, *Hold on, and Hold out, Ye diligent Servants of GOD; Be not wearied, nor faint in your Minds; Our Heaven is already worth all the Pains that can be taken to obtain it.* Is it suggested unto us, by *Satan,* and his *Party,* that they who espouse the Ways of *Holiness,* are but a *Small Party*; As a *Flock or two of Kids,* when the *Enemy fill the Countrey*; Yea, the most of the more *Learned* & more *Splendid* People in the World, not of *This Party?* O *Little, Little Flock,* Look up to *Paradise.* There you will see the Holy Ones make a Party far from *Inconsiderable: They are an Exceeding Great Multitude, which no Man can number.* More *Learned* & more *Splendid* Ones there, approve your Ways, than those which decline them here. *Chuse Holiness*; and Abide by your *Choice*; There are on your Side enow to weigh against all the Foolish & Brutish People of a thousand such Worlds, as you are now so deserted in. The Calamities of *This Life* may tire you. But look into *Paradise*. There the *Wicked cease from Troubling*, and the *Weary are at Rest*. No *Distempers*, no *Reproaches*, no *Discords* disturb them that are there. *Follow* them, and you shall be shortly *with* them. Your *Corruptions*, are, what *Pricking Briars*, what *Vexing Thorns* unto you! Look up to *Paradise*, and see the *Dead free from Sin*: The Sinless Ones, that once complained of the very same *Corruptions*. Their Complaints of a Blind *Mind*, a Vain, Proud, Impure, Slothful, Envious & Earthly *Heart*, were once the very same with Yours. A Busy *Devil* once haunted & frighted *Them*, just as he now does to *You*. *They* once feared a *Shipwreck* as much as *You* can do; and said, *I shall one Day perish by an Heart that is Deceitful above all things & desperately Wicked*. But they are gott safe into the *Harbour* after all. Now think upon it, O *my SAVIOUR, wilt thou not save* [ms. II, 60] *me, as thou hast saved my Brethren before me! Their Experience invites me to hope for thy Salvation!* Finally; Have we *the Desire of our Eyes taken away with a Stroke?* And are we in *Lamentations* on the *Departure* of those, concerning whom, we have not Cause *to Sorrow as those that have no Hope!* Lett us Behold them in the *Paradise* of GOD, and, Hear them from thence *Comforting of us, by the Comfort with which they are themselves Comforted of GOD*: Hear them from their Comfortable Circumstances there calling to us; *As well as we love you, we would not for all this World return unto you!* Thus, Lett our *Thoughts* often go into *Paradise*, before the going up of our *Souls* into it: Lett us often send up our *Thoughts* thither, as *Harbingers* and *Fore-runners* of our *Souls*. Our doing so, will be a *Sign*, that our *Souls* have their *Treasures* there. Now, we need not be afraid of *Dying*: To *Dy*, will be only to be *Caught up to Paradise*!

Sect. VII. And now, If the Readers will *shew themselves Men*, there will be nothing upon Earth a Point of so much Sollicitude unto them, as This; *That their Souls may be sure of an Admission into the Heavenly Paradise, when they leave their Bodies.* Most certainly, there is no Man *Living*, but who, since he knows himself *Dying*, but knows not how soon he is to *Dy*, has Cause to be sollicitous for nothing so much in this World, as This; *That he may not find the Paradise of GOD shutt upon him, at the Time of his Departure out of this World.* Reader, Instead of such an Effect, as they say, what *Plato* wrote about, *The Immortality of the Soul*, had upon some that Readd it, Lett what thou hast now Readd, quicken thee to spend thy *Life* in assiduous Endeavours, to obtain a Part in a *Paradise*, for thy *Immortal Soul*, when it shall in GODs Way be remov'd from hence, and be dislodged from the *Nest*, from whence it must soon *fly away*. [ms. II, 61] None of all the Problems discussed in any of the Schools, where Sciences are pretended to, are of so much Importance as This; *What Course is a Man to take, that upon his Expiration, he may be sure to find the Gates of Paradise open for him?*

Now, in answer to the most Important Quaestion that ever was handled among the Children of Men, what can be more Expressive, or more Directive, than those Words, wherein we may apprehend our SAVIOUR giving His *Orders* to His *Angels* about the *Gates* of *Paradise*! Isa. XXVI. 2. *Open Ye the Gates, that the Righteous Nation, which keeps the Truth, may enter in.* Lett this Passage, *cutt short the Work in Righteousness*, and be taken by Every Christian, into his Most Expanded Meditations.

All that I will add, shall be This. One, who was desirous to have this most weighty Matter well settled with him, formed this Process upon it.

PARADISE made sure of.

Most certainly I am in a *State of Safety* for Eternity, and my approaching *Death* will but call me away to the *Paradise* of GOD; and the *Good Work*, which the *Golden Gates* will stand open to, is upon me, if I can so Declare before Him.

"O my Glorious GOD, my *Love* unto thee, such as it is, disposes me, to a *Choosing* of it, and a *Closing* with it, as my highest *End*, and *Wish*, and *Satisfaction*, *To be & to do that which thou mayst with Delight look down upon.* If I may be made a *Grateful Spectacle* unto Thee, and an *Object* wherein thou mayst be *Gratified* with the Beholding of what thou hast, thro' thy CHRIST, brought me to, I ask for no more: *This is All my Salvation, & all my Desire.* The Thoughts of this *Faelicity*, fill me with *a Joy unspeakable & full of Glory*; Even, laying aside the Views of *Gains to myself* in the Contemplation.

"For this Cause I would forever Abhor and Avoid the *Sin*, which I know to be Displeasing [ms. II, 62] unto thee. And in a Perpetual *Respect unto all thy Commandments*, I would seek the Things that please thee. Yea, I am in a Continual *Struggle*, to be pleased with whatever shall be pleasing unto Thee, and have my *Will* swallowed up in Thine.

"In order to *This*, and that the Blessed GOD may take Delight in me, I do by *Faith* make my Flight unto a Glorious CHRIST, and Beg and Hope to be *Found in Him*. O my GOD, I present before thee, the *Sacrifice* of thy JESUS, that so *Expiation* being thereby made for my Offences, thou mayst for the sake of *That* be Reconciled unto me. I present before thee, the *Righteousness* of thy JESUS, as my Only Plea, that He to whom I would be *united*, having fulfilled thy Law, I may for the sake of *That*, be Justified. And I consent and entreat and with a Comfortable Perswasion of it I expect, That my SAVIOUR should with His Good SPIRIT so take Possession of me, as to Live and Act and Work in me, and be in me a *Principle for Living to GOD*, and bring me to be all that an *Holy Redeemer* would have me to be.

"And now, with a Serious *Repentance*, I Confess and Bewayl my Many *Miscarriages*, wherein I have *denied the GOD that is Above*; and especially the *Fountain of Sin* with me, in an *Heart that is desperately wicked*. And I heartily give Thanks unto Thee, for all the *Bitter Dispensations* of Providence, which *Embitter* my Sin unto me. Yea, That my *Repentance* may be carried on unto its *Perfect Work*, I heartily submitt unto all the Methods, tho' *for the Present* they should be, *not Joyous but Grievous* ones, that thy *Wisdome* and *Goodness* may take for to accomplish it."

Canst thou Declare these Things? Then, *Go thy Way*, Beleever; Go into the PARADISE of thy GOD, *until the End be: For thou shalt Rest, and thou shalt Stand in thy Lott at the End of the Days.*

That END we are now proceeding to.

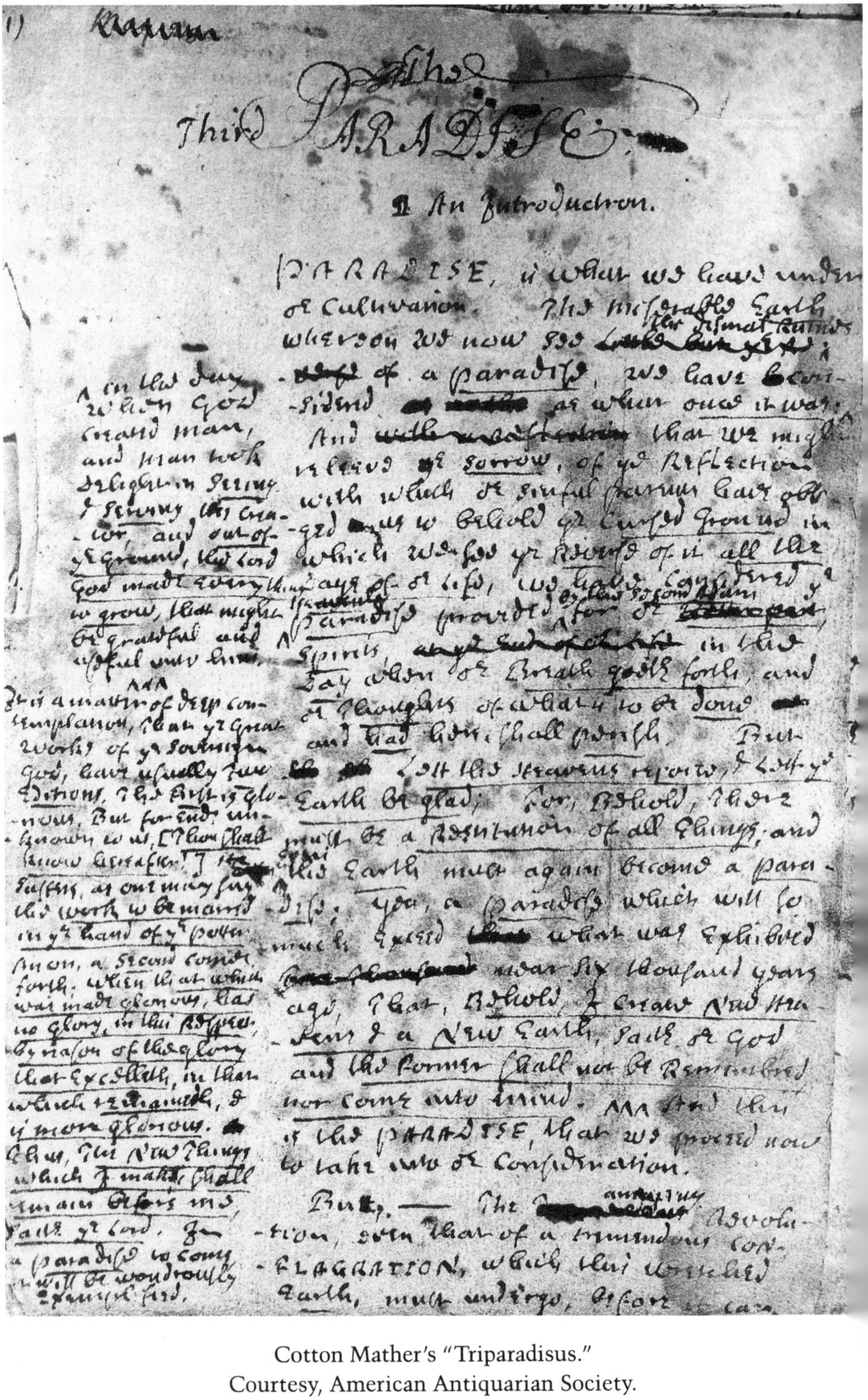
The Third PARADISE.

An Introduction.

Cotton Mather's "Triparadisus."
Courtesy, American Antiquarian Society.

The
Third P A R A D I S E.

An Introduction.

PARADISE, is what we have under our Cultivation. The Miserable *Earth* whereon we now see the dismal Ruines of a *Paradise*, we have considered as what *once it was*: in the day when GOD created Man, and Man took Delight in, *Seeing & Serving* His Creator, and *out of the Ground, the Lord GOD made every thing to grow*, that might be grateful and useful unto him.

And that we might releeve the *Sorrow*, of the Reflection with which our Sinful Parents have obliged us to behold the *Cursed Ground* in which we see the *Reverse* of it *all the Days of our Life*, we have considered the *Heavenly Paradise* provided by the *Second Adam* for our *Spirits*, in the *Day* when our *Breath goeth forth;* and our *Thoughts* of what is to be *done* and *had* here, shall *perish*. But *Lett the Heavens rejoice, & Lett the Earth be glad;* For, Behold, There must be a *Restitution of all Things;* and even the *Earth* must again become a *Paradise;* Yea, a *Paradise* which will so much exceed what was exhibited near Six thousand Years ago, That, *Behold, I create New Heavens & a New Earth,* saith our GOD, and *the Former shall not be Remembred, nor Come into Mind.* It is a Matter of deep Contemplation, That the Great Works of the Sovereign GOD, have usually *Two Editions.* The *First* is glorious. But for Ends unknown to us, [*Thou shalt know hereafter!*] He suffers, as one may say, the *Work to be marred in the hand of the Potter.* Anon, a *Second* comes forth; when *that which was made glorious, has no Glory, in this Respect, by reason of the Glory that excelleth*, in that which *remaineth, & is more glorious.* Thus, *The New Things which I make, shall remain before me, saith the Lord.* In a *Paradise* to come, it will be wondrously exemplified. And this is the PARADISE, that we proceed now to take into our Consideration.

But,—The amazing Revolution, even that of a tremendous CONFLAGRATION, which this Wretched *Earth*, must undergo, before it can [ms. III, v1] have Restored and Augmented unto it, the *Paradisian* Circumstances intended for it! The astonishing *Flames*, that are to take Vengeance for the infinite *Crimes*, that have been perpetrated on it; and that are to *Purify* it, in order to its being made a Seat of these, *Glorious Things which are spoken of thee, O Thou City of GOD!*

These *Flames* will make such a Formidable Desolation upon the *Earth*, in the Enjoyments whereof the Children of Men generally place all their Cares & Hopes & Joys; and the *Flames* are so Ready now to break forth upon a World by black & long Wickedness horribly ripened for them, and every Thing has been so fulfill'd that has been foretold as what must go before them; That, it is impossible to treat Mankind, with a Matter that calls for more universal, or more affectuous Meditation. *O Earth, Earth, Earth, Hear the Word of the Lord!* *Yea, Hear this, All Ye People, Give Ear, All Ye Inhabitants of the World.* A more Certain and a more Awful Matter you never were address'd withal.

I. The Present Earth, perishing in a CONFLAGRATION.

The *Second Epistle* of *Peter* is now to be produced.[1] It is true, Others besides *Grotius* and *Huet*, have observed, that some of the Ancients did suspect whether that *Epistle* might be genuine. But from *Eusebius* who mentions the Suspicion (after *Origen*, who was the First that mention'd it) it appears, That the *Generality* of *Christians* made no quaestion of it, nor were there any *Churches* that rejected it.[2] The whole Doubt was founded [ms. III, 2] on a Peece of Criticism upon, A *Difference* of *Style*: which yett extends no further than the *Second* of the *Three* Chapters that compose the Epistle. We will grant (and have the Help of a *Sherlock*[3] in it) that the *Second* Chapter is a Description of the *False Teachers* infesting of *Primitive Christianity*, that seems an *Extract* from some Ancient *Jewish Writer*, who so described the *False Prophets* of his own, or of perhaps more Early Times. It is likely that *Jude* had the Work of the same *Jewish Writer*, before him, when he is upon his Epistle. And this may be the Reason, of *Jude's* agreeing so much with *Peter*, and of *Peter's* having his own Style a little altered, in transcribing so many Passages, from the *Old Book* which he had his Eye upon.[4]

But what is this to the *Third Chapter*, which is plainly *Peter* in every Line? Lett an Inspired *Peter* be now attended to! An Apostle of our Ascended SAVIOUR, (one of the *First Three*) who before the Ascension of his Lord, had as much Instruction from Him as any Man in things pertaining to the Kingdome of GOD, and after it, was instructed with an Uncommon Degree of *Illumination* from above; This Pen in the hand of GOD, & under the Inspiration, of the Holy SPIRIT, *which it writes* of, has in Plain Terms declared; 2. Pet. III. 5, 6, 7, 10, 11. *By the Word of GOD, the Heavens were of old, & the Earth, standing out of the Water & in the Water: whereby the World which then was, being overflowed with Water, perished. But the Heavens & the Earth which are now, by the Same Word are kept in Store, reserved unto FIRE, against the Day of Judgment, and Perdition of Ungodly Men.—The Day of the Lord will come as a Thief in the Night, in the which the Heavens shall pass away with a Great Noise, & the Elements shall melt with Fervent Heat, the Earth also, & the Works that are therein, shall be burnt up; and, All these Things shall be dissolved.* O Thou Old & Vile *Witch*;[5] This is the Sentence passed by the Judge of the World upon thee. By One whom thy *Judge* has made His *Recorder*, tis in these Terms Readd unto thee.

Can any thing be more *Literal* than these Expressions? But, Many here complain, *The Letter kills them.* Or, It *kills* them to think, that their *dear World* must be so parted with.—To extinguish the Sense of a *Fire*, so Praedicted, & so Terrible, there have been many attempts to make but a *Painted Fire* of it; and expound the whole Praediction, as being only of some *unknown Events*, and Things which are, the Expositors know not *what* [ms. III, v2] themselves, nor *When* to be look'd for, whereof a *Conflagration* serves but as an *Allegory*.[6] But, Syrs, what sort of an *Inundation*, was That, in which *the World being over-*

flowed with Water, perished? The *Fire* for which the Present *Earth* is *kept in Store against* another *Day for the Perdition of ungodly Men*, must certainly be as *Literal* as that *Water*. If the *Inundation* were not, there can be no Manner of Reason why the *Conflagration* should be, meerly *Allegorical*. Had the *Disobedient People* in whose impious Carcases, the *Spirit* which GOD breathes into Man, was but *imprisoned*, come to our Patriarch *Noah*, with such Complements, that they so far beleeved his *Preaching*, as to expect, that at some time or other many *Violent Things* would be done in the World, and many People here & there would be *overwhelmed* in Ruines, and there would be a *Flood of Calamities*, as well as of *Iniquities* which diverse Countreys would be considerably *overflow'd* withal;—What would the Venerable Patriarch, the *Proclaimer of Judgment*, have answer'd unto them? His Answer doubtless would have been of this Importance: *Miserables, Deceive not yourselves. A Flood without a Metaphor will quickly be upon you. There is a Day very near at hand, when you shall be wholly immers'd in the Hurries & Pleasures of an Earth which you will not expect any Changes to be near unto: But, while you are in a Dream of a Dry Summer, the Wrath of GOD will pour in more than Figurative Waters upon you. Wretched Men, There will be more than Figurative Waters, that will shortly have you groaning under them!* And unto them, who in our Times; play their *Allegorical Engines* to putt out the formidable *Fire*, which the Word of our GOD has plainly devoted this *Earth* unto, [ms. III, 3] and are for complementing it with a Concession that many *Consuming Dispensations* of Divine Providence may perhaps be look'd for; and there may perhaps be a *Change of affairs*, which may introduce more of *Religion* into many Parts of the World, than there is at this Day; Shall it not be Replied? *O Ye Sleepers of the Last Times. There is a Day hastening upon you, and in an Hour when you look not for it, it will come upon you, wherein first you shall with an horrible Consternation see the Heavens fill'd with the Flames of that Fire, in which the Son of GOD, attended with His mighty Angels will make His Descent, unto the Place from which He ascended Seventeen Centuries ago. And, You shall then feel this Fire of GOD falling on the Earth, & meeting with the hideous Flames that shall break forth at the Same time from the Bowels of it. Nor shall any of the Figures which you hoped, were Covers under which the Faithful Sayings of God were to be restrained, serve as Rocks & Mountains to cover you from the Wrath of Him that sitteth on the Throne, then to be Reveled.* We have lost the Book, which the pious & skilful *Nepos* long ago wrote under the Title, of ΕΛΕΓΚΟΣ ΑΛΛΗΓΟΡΙΣΤΩΝ, or, *A Confutation of Allegorical Expositors*. But there needs not a *Nepos* to Return unto us, for Confuting of such *Liberties* taken to make the Sacred Scriptures anon, and whenever we please, to signify just *nothing* at all. Indeed, it is a Just Observation of the Incomparable *Hottinger*: *Pessimè christianismo consuluerunt illi, qui justa et gravi sine causa, literales scripturae expositiones repudiarunt*: And perhaps, what he observed, is no where more confirmed, than in the Case, we have now before us. But if no *Reason* will confute our *Allegorizers*, we can tell what will do it; The *Event* will do it.[7]

[ms. III, v3 *blank*]

[ms. III, 4] Among those who have attempted many Ways to *expound away*, the *Conflagration* foretold by the Holy SPIRIT of GOD in our Apostle, from the proper Meaning of it, none appear with more Ostentation, than some that would by the *Fire*, in which the *Heavens shall pass away* and the *Earth shall be burnt up*, understand only the *Fiery Destruction* then coming on the *Church* and *State* and *City* of the *Jews*, and by the *New Heavens* and the *New Earth* succeeding thereupon, understand the *New Administration* of Things under the Gospel. But certainly, this *Exposition* will prove some of the *Stubble* that is to be *Burnt* in the *Fire* now to be enkindled. I could not but wonder, to find *One* very Learned Man once and again quote *This* as a Notable Invention of *Another*, if such *Hallucinations* were not so common among Learned Men, that they are no longer to be wondred at.[8]

That the *Day of GOD* which is to Dissolve This World, cannot be the meer Burning of *Jerusalem*, & some other Towns in *Judaea*, one would think, should be a little evident from This; The People of GOD are directed, not only to *Look*, but also to *Long*, for the Day. Our Lord Himself *Wept* at the forethought of the Lamentable and Formidable *Day*; and what? must it now be a Direction of Importance in Christianity, to *Long* for it? I pray, what was there in the *Day* to be *Longed* for? Our Anhelations for the *Coming* of the Lord, which will bring the *Burning* of the World, have in View a Marvellous *Faelicity* to succeed unto His People upon it. But the Condition of the *Christians* after the Burning of *Jerusalem*, had no *Faelicity* at all in it, which it had not before. The Infidel *Jews* did employ more horrid Cruelties & Massacres upon the *Christians* after the Burning of *Jerusalem*, than they did before. And when *Adrian* finally suppressed them, and finished the Enervation of the Infidel *Jews*, the [ms. III, v4] *Christians* were still as far from *Faelicity* as they were before: They continued still the *Prey* of *Other* Infidels![9] This is plain; The *Scoffers* whom the *Embassador* of GOD rebukes & refutes, made this their Cavil against the Faith, of the Lords *Coming*, to bring a wonderful *Fire* and *Change* upon the World; There is no *Probability* of any such thing; for *All things continue as they were, from the Beginning of the Creation*. If the *Coming* of the Lord here intended, were only for the *Burning* of *Jerusalem*, what Shadow had there been for such a Cavil as this? The *Burning* of a City in a War, was as *Probable* a thing as any in the World; It is a Spectacle very commonly seen in the World. Them that make the *Conflagration* here, to mean only what occurr'd in & on the Destruction of *Jerusalem*, one might almost charge them with *Outscoffing* the very *Scoffers*, that incur the Censures of GOD upon them. And Besides; If this had been the *Day*, about the *Delay* whereof the Apostle was not a little sollicitous to satisfy the Minds of the Faithful, what Need had he to offer Considerations, upon the Supposal of its being a *Thousand Years* off? This *Day* was no more than *Three or Four Years* off, at the Time of his writing this Epistle. Moreover; The *New Earth* of *Peter*, is doubtless the Same with the *New Earth* of *John*. But the *New Earth* of *John*, takes not place, till after the Destruction of *Antichrist*; nor till the *New Jerusalem* comes down *from GOD out of Heaven*, and there is to be seen a *Great City*, whereinto there *enters nothing that defileth;* and there is no *Night* there, nor any *Death*, or *Pain*, or *Sorrow!* Was any such Thing to be seen after the *Burning* of *Jerusalem*, any more than there was before? Add this; In the *New Earth* of *Peter*, there *dwells Righteousness*. The *Mean Attainments* of the Christian Church in *Righteousness*, even at its *Best Estate* hitherto under the Gospel; and its *Quick Apostasies* to what is infinitely the *Reverse* of it, will by no means agree to that Character. Good Syrs, How long was it after the Burning of *Jerusalem*, that honest *Salvian* gave the horrible Pourtraiture of the Christian Church, which we now have in our hands; and in short, so summ'd up the Matter, *Praeter paucissimos quosdam qui mala fugiunt, quid est aliud penè omnis caetus christianorum quam sentina vitiorum?*[10] This is your *New Earth*, wherein *dwells Righteousness*: is it? In fine; Our SAVIOUR did not COME (in the sense His *Coming*, is to be look'd for) at and for the Destruction of *Jerusalem*. No; [Matth. XXII. 7.] *He SENT FORTH His Armies*. This tremendous Dispensation was indeed a *Type* of His *Coming*; But it was not the *Thing* itself: [ms. III, 5] Tis a Perillous *Unsignificating*[11] of the Sacred *Oracles*, to say it was. To argue, That it must intend *Only* what was just going to be executed on the *Jewish* Nation, Because it was a Thing to have *its Peculiar Influence on the Men of that Generation*, seems as if one had forgotten the Last Verses in the *Thirteenth* Chapter of *Mark*.[12] As for what is affirmed by Some, That the Prophecy in the *Sixty fifth* Chapter of *Isaiah*, concerning the *New Earth*, of which our Apostle here propounds & expects the Accomplishment, is only a Prophecy of Such Times, *as We NOW See* under the Gospel: Tis an utter Mistake. An Excellent Person may say, That *Peter* calls the Time of the *Destruction* of the *Judaical* Church and State, expressly, *The Day of Judgment and Perdition of Ungodly Men*. But it is most *Unadvisedly* said! And it is from GOD *Raining Snares* on the World, that such Valuable Authors write, not only so *Fancifully*, but so very *Dangerously*. This we are sure of; The *Primitive Christians*, even *All the Orthodox*, who lived soonest after the Destruction of *Jerusalem*, renounced this Exposition. And, I beleeve, there are few Learned Men in the World at this Day, but what will confess themselves under a Necessity of Exploding it.

[ms. III, v5 *blank*]

II. Plain Praedictions of the CONFLAGRATION, in other Passages of the SACRED SCRIPTURES, besides the *Petrine* Prophecy.

Thro' the tender Mercy of our GOD, who has had Compassion on a World *sitting in Darkness & in the Shadow of Death*, we have had a *Day-spring from on high*, visiting of us, in the Grant of a Book, which is a *Volumn of Truth*, that are of the Greatest Importance unto us. Tis a Book which particularly contains not only *Histories*, of what has befallen the *Peculiar People* of GOD that are called His *Church*, in the World for more than Four thousand Years, from the Beginning of it, but also *Prophecies* of *Great Events* that must occur *till* and *at* the *End* of the World. There is all possible *Evidence*, that this *Book* was written by Men under an *Inspiration* from GOD; and that in the *Prophecies* thereof *Holy Men of GOD wrote as they were moved by His Holy Spirit* instructing of them. There are evident *Signatures* of GOD upon the Book, and it is impossible to derive it from any other than a *Divine Original*. The *Mysteries* Reveled in the Book are so sublime, and so worthy of a GOD that the most High GOD must be the Author of the Revelation. The *Miracles* that have confirmed the Assertions of this Book, are so Illustrious, as undeniably to demonstrate that what is Asserted is to be received as coming from the GOD, who has the Laws of Nature at His Ordering. The *Rules of Life* directed in this Book, and the *Intentions* & the *Tendencies* of it, are so *Holy*, as to render it Necessary, that the Holy Lord GOD should be the Giver of such Directions. The Effects of it on such as *receive it* in *the Love of* it, are such as leave no room to doubt, that it comes from GOD. It is infinitely *Reasonable* to Beleeve, That the Great GOD has in *Some* Instrument or other, made known His Will unto the Children of Men, and acquainted them with Truths [ms. III, v6] the Knowledge whereof is needful in order to their Glorifying of Him, & attaining unto Blessedness. *This Book* must be that Instrument, or there can be *none Such*. It has no Competitors, that can in the *Balance* of *Reason* with it, weigh so much as the *Light Dust of the Balance*. All things conspire, to render it as Indisputable as a *First Principle*, That this Matchless Book is of a *Divine Original*. All that we are sure our Bible has declared unto us, is to be unquaestionably relied upon. They will be none but *Unreasonable Men*, who have so Little *Faith*, as to call in quaestion a Thing which our Bible has with the greatest Perspecuity and Inculcation assured us of. If such a Book hath over and over again most plainly warned us; That the *Earth* on which we are now Sojourners, must ere long be Destroy'd by an horrendous *Fire*, and thereupon Restor'd unto the Condition of a *Paradise* that shall have no *Death*, or *Pain*, or *Sin*, annoying of it; We may depend upon it. These are *Faithful Sayings of GOD, and shall surely be accomplished*.

But besides, what we have in the *Petrine* Prophecy, which comes upon all the Suspicions & Objections of *Infidelity* that would make the Tremendous

Conflagration an Uncertainty, as upon impotent *Briars* and *Thorns*, and *goes thro' them, & burns them together*: No Man, who has read the Bible, can be insensible, that these *Faithful Sayings*, every where ly scattered up & down in it; We walk in the Midst of these Warnings, which ly glittering like the *Stones of Fire*, in this Mount of GOD. We will keep to *Algazels* Maxim, That whatever is brought more than a *Sufficiency*, is to be reckoned a *Superfluity*; And keeping in Resenis an *Host of GOD*, and a Vast Army of Passages to be at proper times introduced from the Sacred Scriptures, to our Purpose, with *Two or Three Witnesses* from the *Old Testament*, and as Many from the *New*, we will count the Matter at Present, *Sufficiently Established*.[1] In the *Old Testament*, it is foretold, [Dan. VII. 9, 10, 11.] that our Lord shall come at the End of the *Fourth Monarchy*,[2] and a *Fiery Stream* shall *issue, & come forth from before Him*, and [ms. III, 7] the World occupied by it shall be *given to the Burning Flame*; and not survive, as that which was occupied by the Three Foregoing Monarchies did *after their Dominion was taken away, for a Season & a Time*. It is foretold [Psal. XI. 6.] *upon the Wicked He shall* [as upon *Sodom*] *rain Snares, Fire & Brimstone, & an horrible Tempest: This shall be the Portion of their Cup*. It is foretold; Psal. L. 3, 4. *Our GOD shall come, and shall not keep Silence; A Fire shall devour before Him, and it shall be very Tempestuous round about Him; He shall call to the Heavens from Above, and to the Earth, that He may judge His People*. That such Oracles as these, may not be *allegorized* away into some *Unintelligible Smoke*, We shall have the Thing delivered in the Plain Terms of the *New Testament*, for which there can be no Pretence of any *Figurative Involutions* to darken them. If it may be thought possible that the Apostle *John*, should speak *metaphorically*, in what he says, about *The Lake of Fire*, or, the World perishing like *Sodom*; and, [Rev. XXI. 1.] *A New Heaven and a New Earth; for the First Heaven & the First Earth were passed away*: It cannot be meer *Metaphor*, that the Apostle *Paul* has foretold, with *Daniels* Vision in his Eye; [2. Thess. I. 7, 8, 9.] *The Lord JESUS shall be reveled from Heaven, with His mighty Angels, in Flaming Fire, taking Vengeance on them that know not GOD & that obey not the Gospel of our Lord JESUS CHRIST; who shall be punished with Everlasting Destruction from the Presence of the Lord, & from the Glory of His Power*. But that the Thing may be putt beyond all Contestation; I will only demand, Is our Blessed JESUS *Risen from the Dead* or, no? I affirm, That since the World began, there never was any *Matter of Fact* in the World, more fully proved, and confirmed with greater Demonstration, than the *Resurrection of our Blessed JESUS from the Dead*. Now, it is most justly argued, That in this Thing, the Great GOD has *given Assurance unto all Men*, that He has [ms. III, v7] *appointed a Day, in which He will Judge the World in Righteousness by that Man*; and that This Man, is more than a Man, even the very SON of GOD, who can be no *Deceiver*, in the *Gospel* which He has brought unto us. Yea, This *True Witness* has in His *Gospel* over & over again most expressly instructed us; [Matth. XXV. 31, 41.] That *He shall come in His Glory, & all the Holy Angels with Him, & He shall sit on the Throne of His Glory*; and, The *Wicked shall then be thrown accursed into an Everlasting Fire praepared for the Devil and His Angels.* And, [Matth. XIII. 40, 41, 42.] *That there shall be an End of this World; and He shall then send forth His Angels, & they shall gather out of His Kingdome all things that offend; and cast them into a Furnace of Fire.* Yea, This was the *Testimony to the Truth*, and the *Good Confession* which He died for; [Matth. XXVI. 64.] *I say unto You, Hereafter shall Ye see the Son of Man, sitting on the Right Hand of Power, & coming in the Clouds of Heaven.* He has assured us, [Joh. V. 27, 28.] *The FATHER has given Him Authority to execute Judgment, because He is the SON OF MAN,* (exhibited in the Visions & Prophecies of *Daniel:*) *The Hour is coming in the which all that are in the Graves shall hear His Voice, and shall come forth.* And [Luk. XIV. 14.] They that follow and obey Him, shall *be Recompensed at the Resurrection of the Just.* After this *Gospel*, I hope, there needs no further *Disquisition!* The *Gospel* of a JESUS *Risen from the Dead*, and Retir'd into the Heavens, having expressly informed us, That He will Return to us, and that at His Return, there will be an astonishing *Fire* in which the Wicked are to perish, and that with a *Resurrection of the Dead*, there shall ensue a *New State* of Things in the World; After such a *Gospel*, how absurd must it be to demand any further Satisfaction?

III. What may be called, A *Digression*, [*But is none*] offering, A *Golden Key* to open the Sacred Prophecies.

Tho' the *Plain Declarations* of the *Gospel*, concerning the *Coming* of the Lord, and the *Burning* of the World, and *the Glory that is to follow*, which have been offered; are enough to satisfy any *Christian* [that is to say, any *Reasonable Man*] in the *Truth of the Matter*, yett there are so many *more Declarations* in our Bible concerning it, and the Sacred Scriptures are so *Full of the Matter*, that it is fitt we should make a further and a deeper Scrutiny and *Search diligently* into the *Book of the Covenant*, concerning the *Salvation* after which the *Prophets have enquired, who prophecied of the Grace that is to come unto us*, when the *Spirit of Christ in them signified such Things*, as even the *Angels* also *desire to look into.*

I know not how to proceed, until I have laid in, and a little prosecuted & cultivated an Observation, which will be a *Golden Key*, to lett us into the Meaning of the *Divine Prophecies*, and enrich us with *Treasures* more valuable *than Gold, yea, than much fine Gold*: And enable us more particularly to see, what will be for our Satisfaction, concerning the *Dissolution* and *Renovation* of the World, in which, Lord, *we are Strangers before thee, and Sojourners, as were all our Fathers; Our Days are as a Shadow, & there is no Abiding for us.*

Know then; One of the most *Illustrious Gifts*, which the Holy SPIRIT of our Ascended SAVIOUR, conferred on His Apostles, was that which is called, *The Word of Knowledge*. Those [ms. III, v8] *Embassadors for CHRIST* unto the World, were in this *Word of Knowledge* gloriously & wonderfully Illuminated by Him, to *know* the Intention of the *Prophecies* in the *Old Testament*, and the *Mysteries* that were *kept from Ages, were then made manifest*; And they had also Reveled unto them the *Grand Events*, which were to occurr in the *Kingdome of GOD* for *Future Ages*. A *Gift*, superiour to all the other *Miraculous Powers* granted unto those Favourites of Heaven, and aequalled by none but that *Word of Wisdome*, that acquainted them, with the *Gospel* which they were to publish unto the Nations, and made them at once to understand the *Sublime System* of the *Christian Religion*, in all the Vast Aims and Parts & Connections of it. This *Heavenly Gift* we don't pretend unto; but yett we reap the *Benefit* of it, from that *Exercise* of it which we find in the Writings of the *Apostles*; and We shall anon have our *Eyes Opened* so far as to *behold Wondrous Things*, in the *Prophecies* of the *Old Testament*, relating to some *Grand Events* more plainly praedicted in the *New*.

Taught of GOD we are now able to say; In the *Divine Prophecies* there were THREE *Grand Events*, One or other of which the *Prophetic Spirit* usually had in His View; And tho' His Design were sometimes to foretel some *Lesser Events*, which were more Quickly to be accomplished, yett His *Main Design* was to lead the Minds of His People unto those THREE *Greater Events*. For this Purpose, He often tack'd unto those Prophecies of those *Lesser Events* diverse Expressions which must not be *fully* answered in them; Nor were these *Lesser Events* to be any other than Little *Figures* and *Praeludes* of those *Greater* [ms. III, 9] *Events*, which GOD would have the Minds of the Faithful to be chiefly fixed upon; wherein those Things have been and will be accomplished, which will at last oblige the Faithful to bring in a full Attestation to the Truth of the Prophecies, and acknowledge, *There has nothing failed of any Good Thing, which the Lord had spoken to the House of Israel; It is all come to pass.*

The *First* of those GRAND EVENTS is, The SON of GOD, His being *Born of a Virgin*, and first *Suffering*, but then *Entring into Glory*.

The *Second* is, The Abdication of the *Natural Israel*, which Carnally and Lineally descended from the *Fountain of Israel*; and the Surrogation of a more *Spiritual Israel*, with the Church of GOD sett up among the *Gentiles*.

The *Third* is, The *Raising* of the Dead, and the *Changing* of the Living, and the *Burning* of the World, at the *Second Coming* of the Lord, and the Holy and Happy State of Things in the *New Heavens* and the *New Earth*, which is to follow thereupon.

Tis the more fairly to introduce the Last of these *Three Events*, that we shall take a little Notice of the Two First: But Far, Far, from Exhibiting *All* the Texts, wherein they who take their Observation of the *Light* in the Firmament of the Sacred Scriptures, may *Consyder* these Events: I will only single out a few, from the Consideration whereof, a Mind that is Master of any Penetration may be led into an Exposition of the rest; and see how they were not of such *Private Interpretation*, as to mean only some *Small Events*, that were to arrive within a few Years after the Writing of them. These *Few* also, shall be *Mostly* taken but from *One Prophet*, and him that in the Volumn is the *First* that appears unto us.

[ms. III, v9]

[1.] The *Key of Prophecy*, applied
unto that GRAND EVENT,
The Incarnation of the REDEEMER.

The *Greatest Event* that ever occurr'd among the Sons of Men, was *GOD manifest in the Flesh* of our Blessed JESUS: the Infinite & Eternal SON of GOD becoming *Incarnate*; and the Arrival of the long Promised REDEEMER, whom the *Protevangelium*[1] in the *Third of Genesis* & *the Fifteenth* had raised in Mankind an Expectation of: Together with what befell Him, in His *Humiliation* and His Following *Exaltation*. Had we been with the Disciples travelling to *Emmaus*, under the Instructions of our SAVIOUR, we should have been Partakers with them, in an uncommon *Light* and *Warmth*, from His *Expounding to them in all the Scriptures, the Things concerning Himself.* But His Church is now so enlightened, and the *Second Temple*[2] so *filled with His Glory*, that we grow more & more sensible of Him shining upon us, in the *Prophecies*, that some would fain muddy, or divert unto other Purposes. Be sure, The *Types* of our

SAVIOUR, ly scattered all over the Old Testament, and are a Noble Study, for the Beleever, who *Seeking of Goodly Pearls*, does in meeting with His Glorious CHRIST find the *Pearl of Great Price*, which yields him an inexpressible Consolation. But a *German Divine*[3] once undertook to Demonstrate, That there is not *One Chapter* in all the *Old Testament*, in which a Glorious CHRIST may not be mett withal; and there is not something wherein *He* is referr'd unto. The Undertaking would not be attended with much of Difficulty! Indeed many of the *Lutheran Writers*, have been very happy in their Discoveries of our Blessed JESUS, where the *Common Readers* are little aware of Him. And, I wish, my admirable *Calvin* had given them less [ms. III, 10] Reason to insult him, for his Overlooking our Great SAVIOUR, in some of his Expositions, where there is Occasion for *Him* to be more thought upon. Tho' they are sometimes unreasonable in their Vociferations, yett there may be some Occasion to make this Apology for that Excellent *Interpreter*, and *Man of a Thousand*; That *no One Man can See and Say every thing*; and the *Grace* given unto that Rare Man in other Points *must be sufficient for him*. The Good Men whom we call, *The Fathers*, were on the other hand sometimes *Excessive*, and even *Whimsical*, in applying of certain *Prophecies* unto our SAVIOUR: what Strange Work does the famous *Austin* sometimes make of it! And more, particularly, among the Notable Things in the Disputation between *Gregentius* and *Herbanus*, how it palls one to read, the Comment on, in that Passage *Thy Life shall hang in Suspense before thee!*[4] But certainly, We may with much *Sobriety*, and in the *Light of GOD*, apprehend a Glorious CHRIST intended in the *Prophecies*, which some would make to look another Way.

The *Prophecies* of ISAIAH, are such, that we commonly quote a Passage from them, as found in such a *Chapter* and *Verse* of, *The Gospel according to* Isaiah. We commonly say as *Jerom* did long ago; *Quod non tam propheta dicendus sit, quam evangelista.*[5] And our Blessed JESUS is in his *Prophecies*, with so much Evidence refer'd unto, that *The Gospel according to* John, says, *These Things said Esaius, when he saw His Glory, & spake of Him.*

Our Glorious CHRIST appears after so evident a Manner, in the *Fifty Third* Chapter of *Isaiah*, that it is an astonishing Thing, how the *Modern* Jews can expound it of any other than the *Messiah*; When, besides the *Chaldee Paraphrase* which expressly assigns it unto *Him*, *Abarbanel* and *Moses Alshec*, Obstinate & Infidel Jews (as well as *Lyranus*, a Converted One) confess, That *their Ancient Wise Men did so expound it.*[6] But as *Hulsius* notes, This Chapter is *Carnificina Rabbinorum*; and reports that some Jews confess'd unto him, The Rabbins could extricate [ms. III, v10] themselves from all the *Prophecies* that favour Christianity, if *Isaiah* were out the Way.[7] It is much more astonishing, that so *Great* a Man among us *Christians*, as *Grotius*, who has written so well, *De Veritate Religionis Christianae*, [a Work worthy to be translated into the *Seven Languages*, which it has appeared in!] should make such *Mad Work* in his *Judaizing* Figments on this wonderful Chapter.[8] How poorly would the *Ethiopian Lord-Treasurer*, have been accommodated with a Commentary on this Chapter, if instead of a *Philip*, he had mett with a *Grotius*, for a Commentator? Even

a Wretched *White* is forced here to desert his *Master!*⁹ The Bright Coruscations of a CHRIST, in every Line of the Chapter, are enough, even to convert a
*Rochester!*¹⁰

Abundance has been written upon that famous *Prophecy*; [Isa. VII. 14.] *Behold,
A Virgin shall conceive, and bear a Son, and shall call His Name, IMMANUEL.*
The Learned have indisputably proved, That the Word, *Alma,* which we translate, *A Virgin,* constantly signifies, *A Virgin untainted by Man*; one whom no
Man has had, what we call, *Carnal Knowledge,* of. The *Greek* Translators, before the Birth of our SAVIOUR, who knew the Signification of *Hebrew* Words,
better than any of the *Jews* in our days, do in this Place render it so. Tis impossible to suppose, That the Prophet, after so pompous an Introduction as he
uses here, should mean only, that a *Young Married Woman* should prove with
Child. Now, what a Struggle has there been, to make this Prophecy understood,
at least, of the Prophets, *own Son* as a *Type,* and then, of the *Messiah,* as the
Antitype? Whereas we don't want the *Typical Explication* at all! One who can
afford *Light* in the Matter, yea, more than one, has now fully clear'd it up.¹¹ The
Two Kings of *Syria* and *Israel,* were now Invading of *Judaea,* and had carried
Great Multitudes into Captivity. At this Dark Time, *Isaiah* called a Son, by the
Name of *Shearjashub,* or, *The Remnant shall return*; in token that the Captives would speedily be sent home again: and they were so! [ms. III, 11] But
the next Year, the *Two* Kings resolved upon razing the Walls of *Jerusalem,* and
setting up a New King, a Stranger to the House of *David* & the Tribe of *Judah,*
a Son of *Tabeal,* as their Deputy. This Wicked Conspiracy, could not be later
than the Fourth Year of King *Ahaz.* It was then, in the Second, or Third Year of
Ahaz, that *Isaiah* now appears, with *Shearjashub,* in his Arms, or newly on his
Feet; which he took with him, for a *Pledge* of *Things to come,* as having been a
Sign of *Things already performed.* Thus accompanied, he found *Ahaz,* and his
Nobles, viewing the Walls of the City, and in much Dejection & Confusion.
Ahaz profanely refuses the Offer of a *Miracle,* either in the *Heav'n,* or on the
Grave. The *Hypocrite* pretended, a Fear of transgressing the Divine Command,
Ye shall not Tempt the Lord Your GOD; But in Reality, he paid more of Re-
spect unto *Baalim* than unto the True GOD, and instead of Waiting upon the
GOD of *Israel,* He was resolved on flying unto the King of *Assyria,* to deliver
him. The Holy One had now, no further Design to comfort *Ahaz,* or force a
Sign upon him after the Sleight he had putt upon the Offer of one. There follow
Threatnings of dreadful Judgments upon *Ahaz,* and a fearful Depopulation of
the Countrey, by the King of *Assyria,* and the Exclusion of the Jews from their
Traffic into the *Southern Sea,* which they had ow'd most of their Wealth unto.
The Prophet now therefore turns to the Nobles of the Blood Royal, and assures
them, that tho' the Line of *Ahaz* which they were in Pain about, should utterly
fail; yea, tho' all the Male-Line of *David* should be extinct; yett, by a Female of
that House, and even by a *Pure Virgin,* He could and would raise up the *Promised Seed* unto *David*: A SAVIOUR, who would be the IMMANUEL, would be
from a *Pure Virgin* produced unto them. Upon this Promise, they were to rest
satisfied, That neither *Syria,* nor *Israel,* nor any other Stranger, should be able

totally to destroy the Kingdome of *Judah*, and the Family of *David*, until He
came to *assume the Kingdome, whose Right it was*, and unto whom the *Land*
belonged. The *Birth* of a *Son*, from [ms. III, v11] a *Young Woman*, foretold as a
Sign, that the Enemies now feared should be defeated, would have signified very
Little. For the very Numerous & hitherto Victorious Enemies had now taken
the Field; yea, probably were on their full March to *Jerusalem*; which t'was
expected would within a very few Months be swallowed up. They wanted some
Consolation under their present Anxiety & Perplexity! And how useless a *Sign*,
would such a *Remote Matter* have been to them, under their *Present Anguish*!
The Prophecy cannot in any sense at all, relate unto a Young Woman in the Days
of *Ahaz*. But *Matthews* Interpretation of it, is *Literal*, and Obvious and Genuine,
and indeed the only one that can be given of it.[12] This makes the Prophecy serve
to a Considerable *End*! It conspicuously distinguishes the *Messiah* from all
other Persons: It gives a Distinction that had never till now, been so clearly and
fully reveled; It makes a Provision against every Imposter that might hereafter
sett up for the Redeemer. An *End*, worthy of the Solemn Introduction, *Behold*!
None but our Blessed JESUS was ever *born of a Virgin*! And None but *He*, could
be called, *Immanuel*. And of none but Him could it be said, *His Name shall
be called, The Mighty GOD*! Here are, as our *Green* remarks, evidently *Two
Praedictions*.[13] The First, That a *Virgin* should *conceive and bear a Son*: The
Second, That the Land of the Enemies to *Judah*, should be *forsaken of its Kings*,
before *Shear-jashub* should *know to chuse the Good & refuse the Evil*. The one
of these Praedictions is made a *Sign* of the other, and was to be fulfilled, in
token that the other should come to pass in the Season of it. GOD here assures
the House of *David*, That a *Virgin* should *bring forth a Son*, who should be
an *Immanuel*. And since many were *staggering at the Promise thro' Unbeleef*,
He kindly tells them, He would give this as a *Sign* for the Accomplishment of
that Glorious Prophecy, The *Land of their Enemies* would be *forsaken of their
Kings*, before *Shearjashub*, (whom we may suppose the Prophet then pointing
at) *should know to refuse the Evil & chuse the Good*; tho' he should *eat Butter
& Honey* and have a Plenty of the Food suitable for his Age, that he might be
in a Capacity of Doing it *as soon* as possible. Thus we have a *Sign*, very *soon*
coming to pass, of a thing to be performed after several *Centuries*. [ms. III, 12]
Christian, I am sure, thou canst now after more than *Seventeen hundred* Years
which have rolled along, since it was fulfill'd, not be in any Doubt, who was
The Son of the Virgin, that was foretold more than *Seven hundred* Years before
His being Born into the World.

   The XXXV and the XL Chapters of *Isaiah*, are to be joined: (the *History* between them, is a *Parenthesis*;) And here, when you read, of, *A Voice crying in
the Wilderness, All Flesh is Grass* will You think of nothing but a Promise,
That the Strongest Empire, being but *as Grass*, would not be able to Resist the
GOD that had espoused the Cause of His People, any more than a *Flower* can
stand before the Blast of an Irresistible Whirlwind? Or, that tho' Men & Means
were weak and frail things, and Instruments would *Vanish*, yett the Return of
the *Jewish Nation* should be brought about, not by Humane Force, but by the

Power and Wisdome and Goodness of GOD? No; The *Holy Spirit of the New Testament* bids you look further than so, and see *John Baptist*, the Harbinger of our SAVIOUR in the Prophecy. And when you Read of; *The Wilderness made Glad*, will you think of nothing but *Judaea*, which had been reduced into the Condition of a *Wilderness*, rejoicing upon the Destruction of such Enemies as the *Assyrians*, and the *Idumaeans*, that had made it so? When you read of, *The High-Way*, and, *The Way of Holiness*, will You think of nothing but their *High-Way* restored, so that it might be safely travelled in; and a Way *sett apart* for the *Jewish Nation*, who were an *Holy People*, so that none other should walk there, without their Leave? And shall, *The Ransomed of the Lord*, be no other, than they who had fled unto *Jerusalem* for Shelter, but after the Defeat of the Besiegers repairing to their own Possessions, when *Jerusalem* was again sett in order did return again unto the Temple, to give Thanks unto their Almighty Deliverer? A *Jew*, or [ms. III, v12] a *White*, may be content with such Commentaries. But a *Lowthe* has *Learned CHRIST* better than so. And so, has a Learned & an Acute *Chandler*; whose Accurate Sentiments on the Answer given by our SAVIOUR to the Disciples of *John* highly deserve to be considered.[14] The *Kingdome* of the *Messiah* is here described. The *Joy of the Wilderness* foretold here, means, that the People & Places least Instructed, should be in as good a Condition for the Knowledge, of Divine Things, as the most Cultivated. *The Glory of Lebanon, the Excellency of Carmel and Sharon;*—the Advantages of *Jerusalem*, & of other Cities, best situated for Fruitfulness in Instruction and Religion, should be offered unto the People that had been disadvantaged with all the rough Circumstances of a *Wilderness*. The *Gifts* of the Holy SPIRIT are promised, under the Figure of *Waters*, to *break forth in Parched Grounds*, because of their having ceased for many Years in the Nation. In this *Wilderness*, the *Way* of the Glorious KING, was to be praepared, by the Preaching of *John Baptist*; A *Way of Holiness*, and *no Lion there, nor any Ravenous Beast*. He should preach up *Repentance*, and *Purity*: Men of *Bruitish* Appetites, & *Unclean* Creatures, would then despise his Preaching, and not come into his *Way*. The *Godly* alone should receive the Doctrine of, *The Kingdome*. There would be no mighty Difficulty in the Learning of it: The *Poor*, Simple, Honest, & Sincere Ones, would not mistake the *Way*. Even the Ancient Jews understood these *Poetical* Expressions, as *Prophetical* of a SAVIOUR to come; and reckoned that the *Leaping of the Lame* here prophesied, carried in it, the *Healing of the Leprosy*, in the Age of the *Messiah*. Four Kinds of Diseases, are here proposed for a *Miraculous Cure* by the Mighty Hand of the Redeemer; [ms. III, 13] as a *Specimen* for all the rest, and such as were to Humane Skill *Incureable*. Tis very plain, how the *Jews*, in the Time of our SAVIOURs Tabernacling among us, understood & applied this Prophecy, from their Forwardness to own Him then for the *Messiah*, after He had wrought some or all of *Isaiahs* Cures before them. Upon the Report of such *Cures* to *John Baptist* he sends Two of His Disciples unto our SAVIOUR, that they might have Opportunities to satisfy themselves, by what they should see & hear of the Glorious Lord, unto whom he had born his Testimony; Their Quaestion was in the very Words of

Isaiah; Art thou He that shall come? Our SAVIOUR answers them in the very Words of *Isaiah*: Adding moreover, *The Dead are raised up.* What He concludes withal, *The Poor have the Gospel preached unto them,* is in other Words, but what *Isaiah* had said; about the *Uncultivated Wilderness.* The Whole is, "You look for *Isaiahs* CHRIST: You see, I do the *Works* which *Isaiahs* CHRIST was to do." The Doctor has by the Way a Curious Observation; It was from what *Isaiah* foretold of the *Desarts,* that all the *Imposters* and *Magicians* and *False Christs,* first of all drew People into *Deserts,* before they would show them their pretended *Miracles.*[15]

After these Essays, it may be hoped, There will need no more, to awaken our Enquiries after a Glorious CHRIST in the Prophecies of *Isaiah*; or to sett us upon *Watching,* for the Rays of the Great REDEEMER appearing therein, *more than they that watch for the Morning, I say, more than they that watch for the Morning.*

In what we read, [Isa. XXII. 20–24.] of an *Eliakim*: we shall not wonder, that our SAVIOUR, after His Ascension, in His Letter to the Church at *Philadelphia,* declares *Himself* to be referr'd unto. [ms. III, v13] Shall we hearken to them, who tell us, That [Isa. XXVIII. 16.] *The Stone laid in Zion for a Foundation,* means only, that *Jerusalem* was to be the only Place, where the People of GOD should find Safety, and a *Foundation* of Security, under the Invasion of *Sennacherib?* from whence they should have no Occasion to *hurry away* into other Countreys? Our Apostle *Peter,* who indeed had in his very *Name* something to mind him of it, has taught us better, and led us to the *Stone,* that such *Builders have refused.*

It may be some will have none but a *Cyrus* meant, when we read, [Isa. XLI. 25.] of, *One Raised up from the North.*—But others will see a JESUS, whose Conception, Habitation, Education, was at *Nazareth,* which was to the *Northward* of *Jerusalem.* He *came from the Rising of the Sun,* and entred the City, by the Way of Mount *Olivet,* which was to the *Eastward* of it. He *called on the Name of GOD,* when He *made known* the *Name* of GOD, and Reformed His Worship. He *came upon the Princes as Mortar,* when He Thunderstruck the Rulers of the Nation with His Terrible Admonitions; and He *trampled* on them as *Clay,* when He exposed their Hypocrisy. And in what follows, which we render, *The First shall say to Zion, Behold, Behold them, and I will give to Jerusalem one that bringeth Good Tidings:* that Christianized & Memorable *Jew,* whose Last Words were, *Not Barabbas but JESUS,* was apprehensive of his Beloved JESUS, when he rendred it; *I will give to Zion that Principal One, in whom behold these things, and to Jerusalem, One that bringeth Good Tidings.*[16]

In those Words [Isa. XLII. 1.–] *Behold, my Servant,*—and what follows; the *Grotian* Impiety may pretend, that the Prophet speaks of himself;[17] and the *Rabbis,* with them which lick up their Spittle, that he speaks of *Cyrus.* But the *Chaldee* [ms. III, 14] does discern and a *Kimchi* himself does confess, the *Messiah* there. Yett, *Abarbanel* does laboriously prove it, against his Friend *Aben Ezra.*[18] And our incomparable *Witsius* makes this just Reflection upon it; *Caeci caeterequin Judaei in Ruborem eos ex nostris dare oportet, quibus tam*

Insigne vaticinium aliovorsum torquere Religio non est.[19] But our Evangelist *Matthew* has determined it for our Blessed JESUS. And a Penetrating and Judicious Expositor,[20] suspects, that with an Eye to what is here, our Apostle says of our SAVIOUR, *He took on Him the form of a Servant.*

What we read, [Isa. L. 8.] *He is near that Justifies me;* Our Dr. *Goodwin* has an Hint upon it, that may lead into the Sense of many other Passages. "They are the Words of CHRIST, and spoken of GODs *Justifying* Him. CHRIST is brought in there, uttering them as standing at the High-Priests Tribunal, when they *Spatt* upon Him: [Ver. 5, 6.] When He was condemned by *Pilate,* then He exercised His Faith on GOD His Father; for His Deliverance & *Justification* from our Sins that were laid on Him, to be given Him at His Resurrection."[21] And *Jerom* thinks, That our Glorious CHRIST is meant, anon in that Chapter, by the *Servant of GOD, who walked in Darkness and saw no Light.*[22] He was unknown and conceal'd; He came in much Obscurity; He appeared *in the Form of a Servant:* He saw nothing but the *Darkness* of sad & sore Affliction & Ignominy. They that *obey'd the Voice* of this *Eclipsed* and *Abased* Servant of GOD, might *Safely Trust in their GOD.*

If we should go to the other Prophets, what we find in *Isaiah,* may intimate unto us, what may be expected from all the rest: *The Holy Child JESUS,* as it were, in *Swaddling-Cloathes!*

If we consult the Prophet *Jeremiah,* to whom some have Profanely & Foolishly [ms. III, v14] & Sacrilegiously applied the most Illustrious Prophecies of his Predecessor concerning the *Messiah;* This *Prophet* will also point us to our JESUS, and say, *Behold, the Lamb of GOD!* I am not Resolved, That I will see no Praediction of our SAVIOURs Conception, at *Nazareth,* a City of the *Ten Tribes,* when I read [Jer. XXXI. 22.] of, *The Lord creating a New Thing in the Earth; A Woman compassing* [or conceiving,] *a Mighty Man:* [A, *Geber,* of whom *Sampson* a Figure,] in one of their Cities, which GOD invites them therefore to Return unto.[23]

However, Whom else, but a Glorious CHRIST could I think upon, when a *Jew* of my Acquaintance becoming a *Christian,*[24] recommended unto me such a Reading [of Jer. XIV. 8, 9.] as This. *The Expectation of Israel is the SAVIOUR thereof in time of trouble. Why; Thou shalt be as a Stranger in the Land, and as a Wayfaring Man, who turneth aside to tarry for a Night. Why; Thou shalt be as a Man astonied, as a Mighty Man that cannot save. Yett thou, O Lord, art in the Midst of us, and we are called by thy Name, Leave us not.*

When we read of our Blessed JESUS *Taken* by them that came to destroy Him, the Evangelist says, *All this was done, that the Scriptures of the Prophets may be fulfilled.* Our Translators of the Bible, have to it very wisely & justly affixed in the Margin, the Text, in the *Lamentations,* [Lam. IV. 20.] concerning, *The Breath of our Nostrils, the Anointed of the Lord, Taken in their Pitts.*[25] While I was Meditating on this; and Remembring that elsewhere the Mourning for the *Messiah* is compared unto the Mourning for *Josiah:* and that what we read, *He was taken in their Pitts,* may be read, *He was taken in their Sins:* [The LXX agrees to it:] I litt upon the [ms. III, 15] *Veri Messiae Parastasis,* written many hundreds of Years ago, by *Samuel Marochianus*, a Converted Jew of *Morocco*; and I found that in this Treatise, he declares his Fears, That our JESUS is that *CHRIST of the Lord*, whom the *Spirit of Prophecy* in this Chapter of the *Lamentations*, has His Eye upon.[26]

If I should now carry the Readers, to those whom we call, *The Smaller Prophets*, and carry my *Samuel* with us, we should hear him, expressing his Fears, That our JESUS is the *Just One Sold*, in the Prophecies of *Amos*; That our JESUS may be He, who has *Horns coming out of His Hand, & there the Hiding of His Power*, in the Prophecies of *Habakkuk*: And that our JESUS, may be the *Shepherd*, the *Man*, who is the *Fellow to the Lord of Hosts, against whom the Sword awakes*, in the Prophecies of *Zechariah*.[27]

But I shall not give any more than a Touch or two more, on what of a CHRIST, those Prophecies are enamell'd withal.

That Passage, [Hos. VI. 1.] *He hath torn*; Pious Mr. *Beart* glosses, *HE hath torn* [the Flesh of His Son.] *and He will heal*, [us Sinners;] *He hath smitten* [Him;] *and He will bind us up*.[28] This he takes for the Meaning of the Text. And, I pray, why not? And, the Clause that follows, *On the Third Day He will raise us up*: Instead of Interpreting it, as the *Modern Jews* do, of a Deliverance from their present Captivity, which will be a *Third Redemption*, if ever it come, I will rather Quote the Words of *Munster, Christiani verius hoc intelligunt, de Tertia Die, qua Christus e mortuis surrexit.*[29]

But that *Grotius* may make some [ms. III, v15] *Honourable Amends*, for the Abuses he has offered unto some other Prophecies, I cannot but Quote a Curiositie of his, upon that; [Hos. IX. 15.] *All their Wickedness is in Gilgal*.[30] The Word *Golgoltha*, is but the *Syriac* Pronunciation of *Gilgal*; and *Syriac* was the Language used among the *Jews* in the Days of our SAVIOUR; *All their Wickedness is in Golgotha!* A Marvellous Praediction, that the Consummation of the Long *Wickedness* found among the *Jews*, would be, what they did in *Golgotha*, where they crucified the Son of GOD. For this *Wickedness* it is, that GOD *hath driven them out of His House*, & now *loves them no more*.

What we read in the Prophecies of *Micha*, about, *The Ruler of Israel*, we are not at a Loss whom to make the Application to. But then, how can I do any other than see the Blessed JESUS *Rising from the Dead*, when I read; [Mic. II. 13.] *The Breaker is come up before them.—Haphoretz; The Breaker;* Tis a Name of the *Messiah*. He was in the Midst of those Infernal Enemies, who had made us their Captives: But He gloriously triumphed over them, when He delivered us from our Captivity. The *Breaker came up*, when our Lord Rose from the Dead, and *Broke* the Bonds of Death which were upon us, and *Broke* the Force of all our Adversaries. He was the *Head* of His People in this Matter. Whereupon it follows; His People, *They also have Broke up, & Passed thro' the Gate, & are gone out by it*. They are delivered from the *Gates* of Hell, upon the Sufficient Price paid for them. And *Their King*, [our Lord] *passes before them, & the Lord on the Head of them*.

All Attempts to make, *The Desire of all Nations*, in *Haggai*, mean any other than our Blessed JESUS, are fruitless ones. [ms. III, 16] And who, I pray, but He is, *The Branch,* and, *The Corner-Stone,* and, *The Pierced JEHOVAH,* and, *The Opened Fountain,* of *Zechariah?* None but *He,* can be, *The Lord whom they sought,* of *Malachi.* Who but He, can be, *The Sun of Righteousness arising,* in him? And what he foretells, of a People that would say, *It is in vain to serve the Lord,* was undoubtedly & eminently fulfilled in the *Sadducees,* whom our SAVIOUR at His Coming found very considerable in the Nation.

But of all the *Prophecies* in the Old Testament, there are none that exhibit a Glorious CHRIST so Conspicuously & so Advantageously unto us, as our Book of PSALMS; of which *Folengius* has made this very True and Just Remark; *Totius Voluminis Psalmorum Argumentum CHRISTUS est.*[31] Christian, come to this matchless *Book of David,* with a Will and Skill to discover a Glorious CHRIST here to be mett withal, and thou dost come with the *Key of David* in thy hand. There is the Word, *Mictam,* found in the Titles of Several *Psalms;* and as Monsr. *Gousset* will have it, the Word signifies, *A Thing that is covered with Gold:*[32] But another Word of the Same Letters, does also signify, *A Sanctified Thing.* We have our Great SAVIOUR and His Works, in these inspired Songs of *Zion.* The Sense which concerns the *Type,* is a Peece of *Canvas,* on which the Holy SPIRIT has inlaid the *Mystical Sense,* which concerns our SAVIOUR, as a *Golden Embroidery.* If *David* sometimes be the *Canvas* in any of the *Mictams,* the Holy SPIRIT has inwrought a *Golden Idaea* of our SAVIOUR into it, and curiously embroidered it, with some of His Incomparable *Glories.*[33] But, verily, there are more *Mictams* in our *Psalter,* than those which have this Term in the *Titles* of them. *David,* whom a Sovereign GOD has made a greater Instrument of Good in His Church, by His Pen, than any one Man that ever was in the World, was indeed such a *Type* of the [ms. III, v16] Promised REDEEMER, that when *Solomon* was gaining & giving a View of the *Messiah,* he represents Him, as having a Countenance very like his admirable Fathers, *White and Ruddy.* Passing by the LXXII Psalm, & the CXVIII Psalm, and several others, wherein the *Blindness that has happened unto the Jews,* has not kept them from See-ing the *King Messiah;* and their Concession, that all the *Psalms* which have in them, *The Lord Reigns,* do refer to Him, I must carry the Observation fur-ther than so. I must observe, That tho' the Troubles, & other Assayes of *David,* occurring in the Psalms, may *sometimes* be Typical of our SAVIOUR, yett ever now & then, we are accosted with Passages, wherein *David* must wholly Dis-appear: There was nothing in *David,* that would give so much as a *Shadow* to them. The XXII Psalm, and the LXVIII Psalm, are not without several such Passages; our Apostle *Peter* also proved that the XVI Psalm could not be meant of *David.* And when a Gentleman lately made an Essay, for an *Historical Sense* of the CX Psalm, even without excluding the Figurative, a Synod of the *French* Churches at *Breda,* severely condemned the Exposition as very Impious, and pass'd a Severe Sentence on, *Une hardiesse si criminelle.* A Synod of the *Dutch* Churches concurr'd unto the Censure; and Learned Monsr. *Martyn* wrote a whole Book, to confute that *Criminal Hardiness.*[34]

I cannot but here enter my Complaint upon an *Evil,* that *I have seen under the Sun.* I thankfully accept much that I see done in many *Modern Refutations*

of Infidelity. But I don't well understand, why such Wretched & Wicked Miscreants, as the *Infidels* which they engage, ever should be thought worthy, to
have not only so much *Argument,* but also *Complement* bestow'd upon them,
with the Air which we use when treating the Best of Gentlemen. The Men are
a Sort of *Monsters,* which are the Blemish of Mankind, & ought always to be
treated with Terms of Pitty, and of Contempt & of Detestation. An *Argument*
is meerly thrown away upon these Detestable Creatures: For it is not a Want
of *Conviction* that carries them away into their Infidelity, but a cursed Hatred
of that *Piety,* which [ms. III, 17] the *Faith* of a Glorious CHRIST leads unto. It
is a vain Imagination in us, if we dream, that the addressing of these *Impious
Creatures* in a Genteel Manner, and with an Air of *Deference,* as if we apprehended they had some Shadow of *Reason* on their Side, or would be gain'd by
Reason; were the Way to win upon them. It may be quaestion'd whether any
of them have been by *Argument* brought over to the *Beleef of the Truth;* But,
if they had been in the *Garden,* and had seen with their own Eyes, the shining
Ministers of Heaven roll away the Stone that covered the Sepulchre, and had
felt the most undoubted Coruscations from the Eyes of the *Risen* JESUS upon
them, they would yett have gone away no better affected than their Brethren,
the *Souldiers,* who turned all into a *Devised Fable.* A *Commiseration* is due
to such *Miserables;* But we think too well of them, if ever we speak of them,
without a Proper *Indignation. Indignities* offered unto our Good King on the
British Throne, would not be beheld with so Small *Emotion,* or so much *Indolence,* by any of his Loyal Subjects, as we can hear the Infinite SON of GOD,
and the Great KING, who has *all Power in Heaven & Earth* belonging to Him,
exploded & blasphemed as, *An Impostor.* But, what gives me a more particular
Dissatisfaction in the Conduct of some that *handle the Pen of the Writer,* when
they come to the *Help of the Lord against the* Infidels, & give Battel to the
Armies of the *Aliens,* is; That altho' an Ability to see a Glorious CHRIST in
the Prophecies of the *Old Testament,* were a most precious & peerless *Gift of
Heaven* to the First *Witnesses* of Christianity, this Invaluable *Gift* must now be
of no Use unto us *Christians,* because these Blind *Infidels* are Strangers to it,
and can't see thro' it. In Complaisance to these *Infidels,* it seems, because they
won't own the *Interpretation* which the *New Testament* putts upon the *Old,*
always to have plain *Demonstration* in it, we must now give up this *Comfort of
the Scriptures;* And except in a very few Places, we must suppose no more, than
here or there *something,* that what we have in the *History* of our SAVIOUR
there may be some faint [ms. III, v17] *Allusion* to; and be sure, the *Psalms* as
Testifying of Him, are generally to be denied unto us. How can we be patient in
being Robbed of such Inaestimable Treasures? *My Brethren, These things ought
not so to be!* [35]

[2.] The *Key of Prophecy* applied unto a Second GRAND EVENT; The
Surrogation of the GENTILES, in the *Peculium* of GOD.

Until this First *Grand Event* was accomplished, and with Regard unto it, it
seemed *Good in the Sight of the Father who is the Lord of Heaven & Earth,* from

the Days of *Moses*, to make the *Israelitish Nation* for many Ages His *Peculiar People*. And when a *Select Part* thereof was enough to answer the Divine Intentions, it pleased Him eternally to throw off a *Greater Part* of the *Ten Tribes*; and none but *Judah* retaining a *Sceptre* of Government, until the promised *Shiloh* came, That which went under the Name of the *Jewish Nation*, and consisted of it, & of such other *Israelites* as were come into a Coalition with it, now became the *Peculium*, in which there was maintained the *Religion* that praepares them that feel the Power of it on their Minds, for the Blessedness of the *World to Come*; and here was the *Israel* of GOD. But in the Accomplishment of what had been foretold concerning the Coming of the *Messiah*, the Glorious REDEEMER was horribly Rejected and Murdered by the *Jewish Nation*; and hereupon, as the Words of *Gabriel* to *Daniel* are to be read, [ch. IX. 26.] they now, *Are not His People*; And the *Gentiles*, who were employ'd as Instruments for the Destruction [ms. III, 18] of their *City* & their *Temple*, are called, *The People that are to become the People of the Prince*, that is, of the *Messiah*. Among the *Gentiles* we are now to look for, *The Israel of GOD*. The *Christian Gentiles* now under the Oppression of *Antichrist*, are in the Prophecies of *Daniel* expressly called, *The Holy People*: which was the Name of *Israel*.[36] As the *Covenant* of GOD with our Father *Abraham*, was for the Blessings of the *Heavenly Countrey* which is to be here, after the *Resurrection of the Dead*, so the true *Israel of GOD* is of a more *Spiritual Sort*, than what has only a *Name* in the Book of *Jewish Genealogies*, and a Lineal Descent from the *Flesh* of our Father *Jacob*, to plead for such an Appellation. The very *Spirit of the Gospel* now is, That all who *walk according to the Rules* of the Gospel are *The Israel of GOD*. Every Sincere Servant of GOD, and Lover of CHRIST, is, *An Israelite indeed*. All (and only) they that Beleeve in the REDEEMER, on whom *Abraham* relied, as the *Seed* in whom *all the Nations of the Earth are to be Blessed*, and rescued from the *Curse* in being *Raised from the Dead*, are the Genuine *Children of Abraham*: [The *Stones* among the *Gentiles*, turned into such, & made *Living Stones*!] And, *He is not a Jew, which is one outwardly*; but *he is a Jew who is one inwardly*; and has a *Circumcision, in the Spirit, & not in the Letter*; and by having his *Praise of GOD*, lays Claim to the Name of *Judah*, in the true Signification of it. They are the truly *Circumcised* ones, who *worship GOD in the Spirit, & rejoice in CHRIST JESUS, & have no Confidence in the Flesh*. An *Ethiopian*, and any one in *Every Nation*, who *fears GOD & works Righteousness*, is as much an *Israelite*, as ever *Simeon* and *Levi* were, or as any one that can prove himself the *Natural Issue* of any that *Moses*, led out of *Egypt*. Now the Amputation of the *Circumcised People* [ms. III, v18] from the *Covenant* of GOD, and the *Religion* of Life; the Sentence of a, *Lo-Ammi*,[37] upon them: And the *Inoculation* of another People, who were *not a People*, but a *Foolish Nation* thereupon; T'was a most *astonishing* Dispensation! The Apostle, who was the most Illustrious of all the Instruments employ'd for the *Israelitizing* of the *Gentiles*, ever speaks of it as a most *Hidden Mystery*! ever falls into Raptures & Wonders & Praises upon it! Almost sinks & faints under the Load of the Speculation! In *astonishment* cries out, *How unsearchable are the Judgments of GOD! And His Ways past finding out*! That the *Temple* of GOD should be erected on the Ground

belonging to the *Jebusites*, and the Church of the Most High, yea, thousands &
myriads of *Living Temples*, every one worth more than that built by *Solomon*,
or that built by *Justinian*, who boasted of having out-done *Solomon*, be found
among the *Gentiles*! That the *Kingdome of GOD* should be *taken* from them,
who *Kill'd the Heir* of it, and be given to other *Nations*, among whom there
have been found the *Fruits* of it! And the *Little Stone*, that will *grind unto
Powder* what it *falls upon*, and anon must become a *Great Mountain*, be found
among those who least look'd for it![38] That the *Faith of the Fathers* now should
be lost among the *Jews*, but found among the *Gentiles*; and the *Bible* be better
understood & embraced & obeyed among the *Gentiles*, than among them unto
whom there were *committed the Oracles of GOD*![39] That the *Heavenly Gifts*,
& the *Powers of the World to come*, which were only tasted now and then
& Little Sprinklings of them granted in the *Holy Land* should come down in
Mighty Showers upon the *Gentiles*, & *refresh* it, as now become the *Heritage of
GOD*! That there should be Hundreds of Thousands among the *Gentiles* found
living unto GOD, and attaining to Degrees of Sanctity, & Purity, & an Heavenly
Life, Triumphing over the *Sting* and Fear of *Death*, and Glorifying of GOD with
Sufferings, and amazing *Martyrdomes*, at a rate beyond what was commonly
found before the Coming [ms. III, 19] of Him who brought in *Everlasting Righteousness*! In fine, That a *Church-State* should be sett up among the *Gentiles*,
more Noble, more Manly, more Sublime, and having more of *Substance* & of
Heaven in it, than what was under the *Mosaic Paedagogy*![40] I say again, Tis a
marvellous, an amazing *Revolution*.

It may now well be allow'd, that the *Prophetic Spirit* should foresee and foretell this Wonderful Dispensation; and lett fall many Passages, which tho' at first
they seem to look *another Way*, yett they that are under this Dispensation, may
in their own Condition see how to apply them, with Edification & inexpressible
Satisfaction. Tis true, He often uses, *Levitical Terms*; but as the sharp-sighted
Calvin observes, *Loquitur Propheta Figuris quae suae aetati conveniunt*.[41] The
Prophets, when they speak of the *Gentiles* coming into the Church, express
their Seeking of the True GOD, with such *Acts of Devotion* as were most used
in their own Time. The *Offering of Sacrifices*, and, *Keeping the Solemn Feasts
at* Jerusalem, intends only in general, the Service & Worship of GOD. There is a
notable Instance of this, in the Prophecy; [Isa. XIX. 19.] *There shall be an Altar
to the Lord, in the Midst of the Land of Egypt*. When *Onias* in after-times built
a *Temple* and an *Altar* in the *Land of Egypt*, for the *Jews*, proposing *Literally* to
fulfill this Prophecy, the *Jews* in the *Land of Canaan* vehemently decried this
Action; and asserted, that no *Temple* could lawfully be built any where but at
Jerusalem.[42] It is plain therefore, that the *Jews* themselves thought that this
Prophecy was to have a *Mystical*, and not a *Literal*, Completion. An *Altar for
the Lord* intends no more than the true Service and Worship of GOD, wherein
we have a glorious *Altar*. The *Pillar* here, alludes to what *Jacob* sett up at *Bethel*:
And the *Altar* alludes to what the Two Tribes & an Half, sett up on the Bor-
ders of Jordan, to keep up their Claim to the true Altar at the Tabernacle. If the
Saviour & the Great One, may mean the Angel that cutt off the Army of *Sen-*

nacherib, we will fly from him, to a *Greater than he*, who delivers the *Gentiles*, that are *led captive by the Wicked One*.[43] *Egypt* and *Assyria*, means those who have been Enemies to the People of GOD, of whom tis here foretold, That they should become *Fellow Heirs, of the Same Body, & Partakers of the Promises*, which was made unto the *Jews*, by the Gospel.

We have a Surprizing Direction, how to expound many *Prophecies* of the *Old Testament*, in the Use which the Apostle *James* made of a Quotation from the Prophet *Amos*: which a late Work entituled, *Miscellanea Sacra*,[44] has most acutely & curiously illustrated.

Of old, there were *Gentiles* called *Proselytes* [ms. III, v19] *of the Gate*, who on the Score of their quitting the *Idolatry* then prevailing among the *Gentiles*, were permitted a *Dwelling* in the *Holy Land*, and had Several *Civic Priviledges* allow'd them, with Liberty to join with the *Jews* in all Acts of Worship which were of the *Patriarchal* Usage, or practised before the Giving of the *Levitic* Institutions. These *Proselytes of the Gate* were obliged only to observe the *Laws of Society*, and such Laws of *Moses* as related particularly unto *Them*; which were *Four*; To *abstain from Things offered unto Idols*; And, from *Blood* separated from the *Flesh*; And, from Creatures that were *Strangled* with Design to keep the *Blood* in them; And from *Fornication*, or, Unchastity of every Sort; which was what belonged unto the very Worship of the Heathens. These *Four Prohibitions* were together imposed on these *Proselytes*, by *Moses*, in the XVII and XVIII Chapters of *Leviticus*: and the Reason thereof was, because these Things in these Times, were *Enticements* to Idolatry, or *Concomitants* and *Evidences* of it. Now some *Zelots* urged, That these *Proselytes* converted unto Christianity, yett should not be admitted unto full Communion with the Church at *Jerusalem*, & the rest of Christian *Jews*, without submitting to *Circumcision*, & other *Mosaic Ceremonies*. The *Quaestion* being brought unto *Jerusalem*, there the Apostle *James* maintains, That the Christianized *Proselytes of the Gate*, should have no *other Burthen* than the *Four Prohibitions* of *Moses* continued upon them; [which also could continue no longer, than their Claim to the Rights of the *Holy Land*, which the *Jews* were yett in the Possession of, was made upon it:] And for the Justifying of his Judgment, he quotes the Words of the Prophet *Amos*: [chap. IX. 11, 12.] *After this I will return, & will build again the Tabernacle of David, which is fallen down, and I will build again the ruins thereof, & I will sett it up: That the Residue of Men might seek after the Lord, and all the Gentiles, upon whom my Name is called, saith the Lord, who doth all these things.* It is here [ms. III, 20] foretold, That after the Sitting of the *Messiah* on the Throne of *David*, not only a *Remnant* of the most abandoned *Idolaters* would become His Faithful Subjects; but *All the Gentiles on whom the Name of GOD was called*, or who were *called by His Name*, or, who *called on His Name*, should be so. By these are meant, *The Proselytes of the Gate*, who generally became *Christians*, when they had *Christianity* preached unto them; and indeed, were the Best *Praepared* of any to receive it, as being already a sort of *Demi-Christians*. GOD, who *knew this from the Beginning*, pointed it out unto the *Jews*, by ordering such Persons to be received among them, on their *Worshipping* of Him, and *Abstaining* from the *Four Prohibited Things*; and yett more fully in His Pouring out His Holy SPIRIT upon them at His Visit by *Peter* to them: wherein it *Seemed Good unto the Holy SPIRIT*, that no further Qualification should be demanded of them. And now, What Pretence could there be for demanding any more?

But the Prophet *Isaiah* again, must be he, whose Prophecies, we shall chiefly touch upon; & no more than *Touch* upon.

His *Ninth Chapter*, I hope, we are all agreed about. In the *Small Remnant*, [mentioned, Isa. I. 9. IV. 2, 3. X. 20, 22. XVII. 6. and several other Places,] the *Prophetic Spirit*, no doubt, saw the *Few Converts* among the *Jews*, who embracing the *Gospel*, should escape the Temporal and Eternal Judgments, that came upon the rest of the Nation for their Vile Rejecting of their SAVIOUR and His Messengers. This *Remnant*, are called, The ΣΩΖΟΜΕΝΟΙ in the *New Testament*; which is the Term the LXX also uses for them. They that were praeserved in *Jerusalem*, from *Sennacheribs* Invasion may pass indeed for a Type of these.[45]

When we read, [Isa. VIII. 14.] of, *The Lord of Hosts being for a Stone of Stumbling, and for a Rock of Offence to both the Houses of Israel*: Tis a Demonstration that the Prophetic Spirit enlarges His Views, beyond the Subject of *Rezins & Pekahs* Association, which was the Immediate Occasion of the Prophecy.[46] For then *Israel* and *Judah* were in very Different Interests: [ms. III, v20] and the Prophet exhorts the King & People of *Judah*, to trust in GOD, who would be their Defence against the Designs of their Brethren, the *Ten Tribes*; whereas the Prophecy here involves them in the Same Sin & Punishment. And the Apostles expressly assert, that CHRIST, is, *The Lord of Hosts*, here spoken of.

When we read, [Isa. XIV. 1, 2.] of *Strangers joining with Israel, & cleaving to the House of Judah*; why should we not think on the *Times of the Gospel*? About the Time of our SAVIOURs Coming, there were Vast Numbers of *Proselytes*; and there soon came on a Time, when these Powers that had been Great Enemies to the Truth, were converted, & conquered, & paid a profound Submission to the Laws of Christianity.

By the Light of the *Morning-Star*, [Isa. XIV. 12.] where Mr. *Despaign* justly complains, that our Translation don't keep to that Word, instead of clapping in the Latin Term of *Lucifer*, (and so producing a very Improper Name for the *Devil*,) it is much if we can't read, the Bishop of *Rome*, his Character & his Destiny.[47]

By [Isa. XVI. 5.] *The Tabernacle of David*; which alludes to *Davids* having been a *Shepherd*, & his Dwelling in *Tents*, before he was advanced unto a Kingdome; why may we not understand, *The Church*; which is also called, *The Tabernacle of GOD*?

By, [Isa. XVIII. 7.] *Presents brought unto the Lord of Hosts from the Nations*; why may we not understand, the Calling of the Nations to & by the Gospel; *Piety* being expressed in making *Presents to the Lord of Hosts*: Tis the very proper Notion of it?

When we read, [Isa. XIX. 18.] of, *Kirheres*, coming to *Speak the Language of Canaan, and Swear to the Lord of Hosts*; is here not an Intimation that many Cities in *Egypt* shall enjoy & embrace the Gospel, which teaches the *Language of Canaan;* and consecrate themselves unto the Glorious JEHOVAH; Yea, that *Heliopolis* itself, though wickeder than any of the rest, [Answer, [ms. III, 21] thou, *Strabo,* for *That!*] shall be one of them? Our Eagle-Eyed *Jameson,* (a miraculous Literator, Stark Blind from his Nativity!) discovers how this Prophecy was fulfilled in the Preaching & Spreading of the Gospel.[48]

Certainly, a More Evangelical View must be taken, of [Isa. XXV. 6.] *The Feast in the Mountain made by the Lord of Hosts unto all People,* than as if it meant only the Joy of the Jews, & of some other Nations, for the Defeat of *Sennacherib.*

Upon Isa. XXIX. 11. *The Sealed Book,* a *Christianized Jew* wrote like one, some hundreds of Years ago; *Quae clausura libri major est, quam clausura qua clausit Deus corda nostra!*[49] And, [ibid. v. 14.] *The Perishing of their Wisdome;* How Remarkably verified, when their Murder of our SAVIOUR for Fear of the *Romans,* was the Thing that brought the *Romans* upon them! And their most Learned Rabbi's have ever since minded almost nothing but *Fables* & *Follies,* and given us *Trifles* for the profoundest *Mysteries!* Tis well noted by an Ingenious Man, [on Isa. XXX. 19.] That an Hint being taken from the prosperous Times that succeeded the Deliverance from *Sennacherib,* the Prophet is carried on to a Contemplation & Exhibition of Things to be under the *Gospel* mett withal.[50]

The Glories [Isa. XXXII. 1–8.] of, *The King that shall Reign in Righteousness,* and, *The Man,*—so maginified; They can belong to none but that *King,* who is more than a *Man.*

When we read; [Isa. XXXIII. 18.] *Where is the Scribe? Where is the Receiver? Where is he that counted the Towres?* Was it only to foretell, That the Delivered People should with *Pleasure* think on the *Terror,* they were in, when they saw the *Assyrian* at their Gates; and now insulting over their Conquered Enemies, ask, where is the *Secretary of War?* And, the *Tribute-gatherer?* And, the *Master of the Artillery?* No; our Apostle has taught us another Application. And the account which Dr. *Templar* gives us, of the Studies followed in the Colledges at *Jerusalem,* helps us in Pursuing the Apostolical Accommodation.[51]

When we find; [Isa. XLI. 5, 6.] *The Isles fearing, & the Ends of the Earth afraid;* we can scarce avoid thinking on the Combination of the Heathen-Powers, to support their [ms. III, v21] Idolatry, & suppress the Christian Religion in the Primitive Times.

That Promise, [Isa. XLV. 14.] *The Labour of Egypt, and the Merchandise of Ethiopia shall come over unto Thee, & they shall be Thine.* It can't be understood of *Cyrus's* Conquests, as the *Men of Letter* would have it.[52] For the Words, *Thee,* and, *Thine,* are of the Faeminine Gender; and so must be understood of *Jerusalem,* the City mentioned just before. It was to be fulfilled, unto the Church under the *Gospel,* [which is often described under the Figure of a City,] when the Gentile World were to Come into it, and Enrich it, and Adorn it, and Submitt unto it as the Temple of Truth.

What we read, [Isa. XLIX. 8.] about, *The Acceptable Time, & the Day of Salvation;* if it had any Aspect on the *Time of Grace* at the Expiration of the *Seventy*

Years for the *Chaldaean* Captivity, our Apostle has carried it unto the *Time*, when GOD first published the *Gospel* unto the World.

That, [ibid. v. 23.] of, *Kings Nursing Fathers*, and, *Queens Nursing Mothers*, was fulfilled in *Constantine*, and *Helen*, as well as in *Artaxerxes* and *Esther*.[53]

What we read, [Isa. LII. 7.] of, *The Beautiful Feet of him who bringeth Good Tidings;* is it a meer Poetical Description, of the Messenger who first brought the *Good Tidings* of *Cyrus's* Decree for the Peoples Return? Our Apostle has taught us to read the First Preachers of the Gospel in it.

That, [Isa. LIV. 1.] *Sing, O Barren;* can't be literally true of the *Jewish Nation*. But our Apostle, in his Epistle to the *Galatians*, gives the True Exposition of it. The Church, after her Spouse, the Blessed JESUS had been taken from her, did from very mean & contemptible Beginnings, come to spread over the World.

There are very many more Prophecies of *Isaiah*, which had their Accomplishment in the Conversion of the *Gentiles;* [ms. III, 22] which rendred them indeed, the *Israel*, that was *accounted unto the Lord for a Generation*. And this Little *Specimen*, may sufficiently show an Attentive & Sagacious Reader, how to operate upon them.

The other Prophets, play the same Tune. Be sure, The Prophet *Jeremiah* is full of it. Yea, some, who do very justly so read the Prophecy, [Jer. XXX. 21.] *Their Excellent One shall be of themselves, & their Governour shall proceed from the Midst of them;* carry the Matter so far, as to argue for *Infant-Baptism* in our Days, from that Clause in the Verse praeceding; *Their Children also shall be as of old*. They are to be Solemnly Dedicated, & given up to GOD, & putt under His Protection, and *Baptised*, as *of old*, in *aforetime* they were circumcised.[54]

We have Evidence enough of This; That *Jeremiah* prophesies about a *Babylon* that is *now* extant, & about a King of *Babylon* that is *now* living. But, Since we are upon the Prophet *Jeremiah*, I will only add, It is extremely probable, That the six last (misplaced) Chapters in the Book of *Zechariah*, might be written by *Jeremiah*, and belong really to his Book: For they contain Things which might well be *Foretold* in *Jeremiahs* Days, but were *Fulfill'd* before *Zechariahs*: And so the Difficulty in *Matthews* Quotation is at once removed.[55]

Now, when we read there; [Zech. X. 4.] *out of him came forth the Corner;*— Our *Munster* carries it so; *From the Flock of the House of Judah*, there shall go forth a Number of *Goodly Horsemen*, who shall wage a *War* with the World: But the *Warfare* will be *Spiritual*, against the *Lusts* of it. Among these there will be *Corners*, that is to say, *Captains*: The *Apostles* were such. And there will be *Nails*; This is a Term for Faithful and Constant Men. It may mean such as the Apostles made their *Successors* in the Ministry.—

For the rest of the Prophets; to pass by the Broad Hints, which there are in the Prophecies of *Malachi*, [Mal. I. 11.] *That from the Rising of the Sun even unto the going down of the Same, the Name of GOD {Almighty?} should be great among the Gentiles, & in every Place Incense offered* [ms. III, v22] *unto His Name, & a Pure Offering*: [A Plain Direction, how to understand the *Levitical Terms*, in the *Prophecies*!] If what the Prophet *Hosaea* speaks, [Hos. XIV. 3.] *In Thee the Fatherless finds Mercy;* be not a Praediction of *Mercy* to the *Gentiles*, who have no *Fathers*, (no *Abraham*, and *Isaac* and *Jacob*, like the *Jews*) to value themselves upon; Yett, we are sure, that the Words of the Prophet *Habakkuk*, [ch. I. 5.] *Behold Ye among the Gentiles, and regard, & wonder marvellously; for I will work a Work in your Days, which Ye will not Beleeve, tho' it be told you;* [A *Marvellous Work,* That the *Chaldaeans* with whom the *Jews* were now in Covenant, should bring the *Babylonian* Captivity upon them!] These Words, are by our Apostle *Paul* applied unto a *Marvellous Work* to be done under the New Testament. How could This be, when the *Babylonian Monarchy* had been for many Ages vanished? Why; The *Roman Empire* was to fill up & compleat that *Babylonish Image,* whereof the *Golden Head* was the *Chaldaean Empire* of the *Literal Babylon.* That old *Literal Babylon,* was a Type of the *Mystical Babylon,* & the whole *Roman* Potentacy. As one well expresses it; *The Spirit of Prophecy furnished the Prophet, with Language which extended, even to this also!*[56]

And that Prophecy, [Zeph. II. 11.] *The Lord will famish all the Gods of the Earth, and Men shall worship Him, every one from his own Place; even all the Isles of the Gentiles.* [All were called, *Isles,* that they went by Water to.] Can any thing more livelily describe the Extinction of *Idolatry,* among the *Gentiles;* wherein the *Idols* did *Eat the Fat of their Sacrifices, & Drink the Wine of their Drink-Offerings?* or the Days wherein *One Place* for Worship, is not better than another? *Plutarchs* Treatise, *Concerning the Ceasing Oracles,* is as fair a Commentary on it, as if it had been written on Purpose to verify this Prophecy.[57]

[ms. III, 23] But scarce can I pass over the Prophecies in the III Chapter of *Zephaniah;* which wondrously describe the Condition of *Jerusalem,* about and after, the Time of our Lords *Coming in our Flesh.* An horrid Corruption was then prevailing: albeit the *Just* Lord was then in the *Midst of the City,* doing of nothing but *Righteousness* Himself, and Preaching of *Righteousness* daily to the People. The Judgments of GOD which had newly been executed upon the Nations in the Neighbourhood, are herewithal commemorated. The *Egyptians* had been destroyed by the *Persians;* The *Philistines* had been destroyed by the *Graecians;* The *Idumaeans* had been subdued by the *Jews* themselves; And the *Romans* had subdued all, just before the Coming of our Lord. Hereupon, says the Lord, *I said, Surely thou wilt fear me.* But the Son of GOD now addresses Himself unto His own People; *Wait Ye upon me, Saith the Lord, until I Rise to Perpetuity.*[58] So it should be rendred: So *Abarbanel* renders it; And not, *unto the Prey.* It is a Praediction of our Lords *Resurrection* from the Grave. The Events that were to follow upon that *Resurrection* are then declared: The *Gathering of all Nations* into the One Roman Empire, that so the *Wrath* of GOD might be the more effectually poured out upon them; and the Conversion of the *Gentiles;* to *call upon the Name of the Lord.*

The Prophecy of the *Locusts* in *Joel;* Even *Bochart* himself quaestions whether it were ever *Literally* accomplished; and so averse is *Abarbanel* to a *Literal Interpretation,* that he cries out, *Absit à me ut hoc credam.* Wherefore, I will not with *Cyril,* and *Jerom,* find the *Four Monarchies,* in the Four several

Sorts of *Locusts* here; but beleeve them to be the Same with the *Locusts* in the *Apocalypse*: from which the *Christians* of the *New Testament* have suffered unutterable *Torments*.[59]

[ms. III, v23] The Book of PSALMS is all over a Book of *Prophecies*: And more particularly, the Condition of the Church under the *New Testament*, is in these *Prophecies*, how often, how plainly referr'd unto! I confess, when the Sufferings of the Faithful are lamented with such a *Poetical Flame* in this *Prophetical Book*, I cannot *now* think (tho' once *unawares*, and when I wrote a *Psalterium Americanum*, I did so,) the Learned Man is in the right, who fancies that it exhibits the Condition of the *Synagogue*, or the Jews dispersed & oppressed under the *Roman* Captivity:[60] No, tis the Condition of that *Holy People*, who are now the Real and Only *Israel* of GOD, that suffers horrid Things under the Tyranny of *Antichrist*. The *Moans* and *Prayers* were never praepared for the Use of the Wretches, that will never use them; Nor is the XLIV Psalm calculated for the State of such abandoned Infidels.

Jerom long ago found *Antichrist* in the *Psalms*; and the Devout Singer thereof, *may be carried away into the Wilderness*, & *be shown the Judgment of the Great Whore that sitteth upon many Waters*. Yea, Tis no Mistake of *Austin*, That not only a Glorious CHRIST, but the State of the *Church*, after both His *Comings*, is very charmingly exhibited unto us in them.[61]

To reckon up the Passages of the *Psalms*, that are Prophecies of the *Church* in our Days, would be to *look towards Heaven*, & *tell the Stars*. I shall only single out a very *Unsuspected Psalm*; even the XXIII: and report, That an ingenious Man whose Name is, *Gurtler*, in his, *Dissertationes de CHRISTO ad Gloriam evecto*, finds here, a *Prophecy* of the Church under the *Shepherdly Care* of our SAVIOUR, in *Four Periods*.[62] After the *Sufferings* of our SAVIOUR, in His *Humiliation*, which are celebrated in the XXII Psalm, we have now the *Benefits* to be expected from our SAVIOUR, in His *Exaltation*. First, In the three first Verses, we have what our SAVIOUR did for His People, by Himself and His Apostles, while the Church at its Beginning, *had Rest* & *was Edified*, & *Walked in the Fear of GOD*, & *the Comfort of the Holy SPIRIT*. Next, In the Fourth Verse, we have the Condition of the Faithful under *Antichrist*, that *Foolish* & *Cruel Shepherd*. Hereupon, in the Fifth Verse, we have the Condition of the Faithful, after the *Reformation*; *Feasted* with the Good Things of the Gospel, but yett surrounded with *Enemies*. Lastly, we have what our SAVIOUR will anon do for us, at His *Coming*, & in His *Kingdome*, when we shall have no Enemies to conflict withal.

[ms. III, 24]

[3.] The *Golden Key* applied unto the Third GRAND EVENT; The CONFLAGRATION, and its Consequences.

But there is yett another GRAND EVENT, which we are still waiting for, And THAT is, *The Blessed Hope, Even the Glorious Appearing of our Great GOD, and Saviour JESUS CHRIST*: The *Raising* of the Dead Saints, and the *Changing* of the Living Ones, to a State of *Sinless Immortality*; and the Purifying of this Polluted World with a tremendous CONFLAGRATION; and thereupon the Succession of *New Heavens* and a *New Earth*, wherein *shall dwell Righteousness*; and there shall be a *Restitution of all things* to *Paradisaic* Circumstances; and a Glorious Kingdome of GOD maintained by the *New Heavens* reigning over the *New Earth*, and the *Raised*, made *Equal to the Angels*, continually descending from the *Holy City* in the *New Heavens*, to teach & rule the *Changed* who on the *New Earth* shall *build Houses and Inhabit them*, & *Plant Vineyards* & *Eat the Fruit of them, and have an Offspring that shall be the Blessed of the Lord.*

This may well be called a GRAND EVENT. Now our Apostle having assured us concerning it; [Act. III. 21.] *It is what GOD hath spoken by the Mouth, of all His Holy Prophets,* [All as with *One Mouth!*] *since the World began:* Tis a Plain Instruction unto us, how to interpret *All the Prophets!* This GRAND EVENT must be look'd for in, *All the Prophets!*

To praepare us, that we may *understand a Prophecy,* & *the Interpretation, the Words of the Wise,* [ms. III, v24] *and their dark Sayings,* Lett it be first of all considered, That the Blessedness of a *Deathless* & *Sinless* World, which is to come after the *Burning* of *This World,* is that COVENANT, in which the Glorious GOD has promised all along to be *the GOD of His People.* Yea, the Godly *Patriarchs* understood it so! When the *Covenant* of GOD, engaged unto *Abraham,* That He would give him the *Land of Canaan for an Everlasting Possession,* and be a *GOD unto him,* did he think, that there was no more intended for him, than that he should enjoy the *Temporal Blessings* of; A Countrey, where he was followed with *Temptations* and *Calamities* all his days; A Countrey, which tho' it were a *Land flowing with Milk* & *Honey,* yett the *First Thing* he saw in it, was a *Grievous Famine!* A Countrey where he was never Owner of so much as *one foot,* except one Little Field for a *Burying-Place*;[63] the First bitt of *Land,* that ever we read purchased in the World! Sufficient Intimations, that the *Covenant* of GOD with him referr'd *unto,* & would not be fulfill'd *until,* the Time of his being brought out from the *Cave of the Treasury* there, by a *Resurrection from the Dead?* This *Friend of GOD,* and *Favourite* of Heaven, what was *he* the better for it, that his Posterity should enter into it, five hundred Years after he was *Dead;* and then have it but a *Little While,* and for the most *Part* see such *Confusions,* & such *Miseries,* & such uneasy Circumstances in it, as often and alone respected this Proclamation unto the Faith of them that had the Fear of GOD in them; *Arise Ye,* & *Depart, for this is not your Rest; because it is polluted.* In the Covenant of GOD, this Word, *I will be thy GOD,* carried this forever in it, *I will Bless thee.* This was the plain Sense of it; Every One took it so; All that understood any thing, sang upon it; *GOD, our own GOD, shall Bless us.* [ms. III, 25] Now if the Glorious GOD shall *Bless* us, it will imply, that He will remove the *Curse* from us; take off the *Curse* which our Sin has brought upon us. But, what is the *Curse?* The *Curse* is, *unto Dust shalt thou Return.* Wherefore, in the Day when we shall be *Blessed* of our *GOD,* we shall be fetched from the *Dead,* and be brought into a World, which *Death* will be a Stranger to. And *in that Day,* the *Ground,* which is *cursed for thy Sake,*

O Man, shall be Delivered and be Disencumbred from all the Things that now Embitter it. There was in the *Covenant* of GOD promised unto our *Patriarch* an *Offspring*: And that *Offspring* is not meerly to be found in such as were Literally & Lineally the issue of his *Loins*; no, nor is it *Meerly*, (tho' more *Truly*) to be found in such as tread in the Steps of *his Faith*, who all are the Children of *Abraham*, and shall, to a Man be and share with him in the *Land of Promise*: But the SPIRIT of GOD has expressly taught us, *That the Seed is CHRIST*; the *Offspring* is the Promised REDEEMER, in whom *all the Nations of the Earth*, [and, *They that go down to the Dust!*] are to be *Blessed*; And *Blessed* they cannot be, I again say, without a *Resurrection from the Dead*. THIS is that which the Blessed GOD has been pleased in a very Distinguishing Manner to call, My *Covenant*. For this Cause, our Blessed REDEEMER going to prove the *Resurrection of the Dead*, with infinite Wisdome He brings His *Argument*, from, *The Covenant of GOD*; Says He, When GOD promised unto the Patriarchs, That He would be *Their GOD*, He most certainly meant, That He would *Bless* them: Now, how could He *Bless* them, if He left them under the *Curse*? *Death* is the *Curse*; and the Patriarchs *Abraham* & *Isaac* & *Jacob*, were actually under it, at the Time when He told *Moses*, That He was *Their GOD*. It must unavoidably follow from hence, That these Patriarchs must see *a Resurrection from the Dead*. Most [ms. III, v25] powerfully and admirably argued! And the Argument is the more Notable, for its Proceeding from the Mouth of that Mighty REDEEMER, who is to accomplish the *Resurrection from the Dead*, wherein the *People of the GOD of Abraham*, are to be the *Blessed of the Lord*. They who are big with an Expectation, that the *Jews*, who are now a Crue of Circumcised and Abandoned *Infidels*, dispersed in many Countreys, will under better Sentiments of *Christianity*, be repossessed of their *Old Countrey*, and be there Distinguished from the rest of the *Christians* in the World, in Circumstances of *Prosperity* & *Fertility* like or above & beyond those of their Fathers in the Days of *Solomon*; but still have *Death* and *Sin*, doing its Part among them; these will do well to examine, how far their *Faith*, is the same with the *Faith of the Patriarchs*. Of *Them* we are assured in the XI Chapter to the *Hebrews*, That they *confessing themselves to be Strangers & Pilgrims on the Earth*, did *seek an Heavenly Countrey*, as That wherein the *Promises* which they had *Embraced* were to be accomplished. Yea, it is affirmed, That *NOW they desire that Heavenly Countrey*; so that they are *not yett* arrived unto it; but it is one which they will *not Without us*, and so *not Before us*, arrive unto. Now this *Heavenly Countrey*, must needs be That, into which we shall be introduced by a *Resurrection from the Dead*; A *Countrey*, where the *New Heavens* will have such an *Influence* on the *New Earth*, as to imprint an *Heavenly Character* on all the People, & Actions, & Enjoyments of it: and the *Will of GOD shall be done on Earth, as it is done in Heaven*. In short, A World that shall have *Death* and *Sin* left in it, cannot be the World, wherein what is promised in the *Covenant* of our GOD shall be fulfill'd unto us. The continual Prayer & Hope of the Faithful, *O that thou wouldest Bless me indeed, & keep me from Evil, that it will not grieve me!*—will not be answered in *this present Evil World*: or where *Death* and *Sin* have any thing to do. The Principle of [ms. III, 26] PIETY in them, Naturally disposes them to look for it in *Another World!* Yea, I would have Learned & Thoughtful Men to enquire, whether there may not be some Dark Hint of this, in what our *Psalterium Americanum* renders, [Psal. CV. 8.] *He hath been very mindful of His Covenant forever: The Word He for the Age mark't by a Thousand did appoint.*⁶⁴ We have readd it, *A Thousand Genera-tions.* But certainly *This World* will not endure a *Thousand Generations!* If we take a *Generation*, in the Signification of the *Law*, for *Seven Years*, then indeed, it leads us into the *Seventh Millennium*, which will be the *Sabbatism* that is to be expected. But the Word is not in the Plural Number. It rather seems to point at one Special *Generation*, or we may rather say, *Revolution.* And if we keep to the Translation of, *A Thousand*, and not read it, as one does, *The First Age*, (which *Bildad* sends *Job* to enquire of,) namely that of the Patriarchs to whom GOD gave the *Covenant*, [So *Kimchi* reads it, *Ad Ducem in Generatione*,⁶⁵ and expounds it of *Abraham*,] why may it not lead us to the *Age*, that shall have the *Millennial* & *Sabbatical* Stamp upon it? It is only an *Hint*, which I do not insist upon. But on *This* I do; That after the *Second Coming* of our Lord, His *Raised* and *Changed* People, shall in an *Heavenly Countrey* here below, in a *Deathless* & a *Sinless* Condition, enjoy the Consolation of an *Heavenly Kingdome* with Him: And that what is promised in the *Covenant* of GOD, is to be expected in that *Countrey* & that *Kingdome*: And that the Expectation of the *Promise*, & of Happy Times for the Church of GOD upon Earth before that *Revolution*, is *Unscriptural*, and *Unreasonable*; I had almost said, somewhat *Irreligious.* [Ponder, Rev. XXI. 3, 4. XXII. 3, 4, 5.]

What remains to be considered, and calls for our Next Contemplation, is This. To introduce that State of a *Deathless* and *Sinless* World [ms. III, v26] wherein the Glorious GOD will *perform the Good Thing which He has promised unto His People*, THIS WORLD must undergo a tremendous CONFLAGRATION, which will make a most amazing Devastation upon it: And a Vengeance once executed by a *Flood* of another Element, will be now repeted in a, *Diluvium Ignis*,⁶⁶ which the *Ancients* did, tho' *We* upon whom it is just going to fall, do very Little, tremble at the Approaches of.

But Lett us now address ourselves unto our *Oracles*, and hear what Plain & Strong Intimations, the *Sacred Prophecies* have given us, of that FIRE, which will fill *This World* with horrid and hideous Desolations, and of the *New World*, that shall succeed it, and be *satisfied with Favour, & be fill'd with the Blessing of the Lord.*

And here, still to begin with the Prophet which has hitherto most enter-tained us;

Lett it be remembred, That when the Prophet uses that Expression, *In That Day*, the Phrase often denotes not the same time that was last mentioned; but some *Extraordinary Season*, Remarkable for some *Signal Event* of Providence, called elsewhere, The *Day of the Lord.* Our Apostle *Paul*, more than once uses that very Phrase, for the Day, wherein GOD shall *Come* and *Burn* and *Judge* the World. [see 1. Thess. I. 10. 2. Tim. I. 18. IV. 8.] Now, *The Spirit of Burning*, [Isa.

IV. 4.] which is to *Purge* the World, *In that Day*, probably refers to what shall be done at the *Conflagration.* And, *The Escaped of Israel,* and, *They that are left in Zion,* may ultimately intend those who shall *Escape* the *Conflagration,* and be *caught up to meet the Lord.*

[ms. III, 27] When we read of such Things occurring, *In that Day,* as [Isa. V. 24, 25.] *The Fire devouring the Stubble, & the Flame consuming the Chaff,* and *the Hills trembling;* a Sensible Interpreter observes, Tis because the lesser *Particular Judgments* foretold in such Phrases, are an *Earnest* as well as a *Figure,* of the *General One,* wherein the *Frame* of Nature shall be dissolved.[67]

That Prophecy, [Isa. XI. 4.] *He shall smite the Earth with the Rod of His Mouth, and with the Breath of His Lips He shall slay the Wicked;* Lett Interpreters Rack their Witts for other Accommodations of it, our *One* Apostle *Paul* is worth Ten *Thousand* of them. And he has determined it, for the Destruction of *Antichrist,* by the *Coming of the Lord in Flaming Fire, to take Vengeance* on a World which *obeys not the Gospel of GOD.* Yea, our SAVIOUR Himself, declares, That the Prophecy here given, of, *An Ensign for the People,* and, *An Ensign for the Nations,* intends what He foretells in saying, *There shall appear the Sign of the Son of Man in Heaven; and then shall the Tribes of the Earth mourn; and they shall see the Son of Man coming in the Clouds of Heaven, with Power & Great Glory. And He shall send His Angels with a Great Sound of a Trumpett, and they shall gather together His Elect from the four Winds, from one End of Heaven to the other.*

We may allow, That the Prophecies describe, sometimes the Desolations brought on *Judaea,* by the *Assyrians,* & sometimes the Desolations brought on the *Jews* by the *Babylonians;* and sometimes the *Desolations* brought on the *Babylonians,* & on the *Idumaeans,* and on other Wicked Peoples & Places. But the Way used by the SPIRIT of GOD in the *Apostles* of the New Testament, enables me & empowers me, to demand, That we [ms. III, v27] apprehend the *Prophetic Spirit* as having in *His* View, and showing to *Ours,* the Stupendous Desolations, which the *Conflagration* will after all bring upon the *Whole World;* wherein there will be done more than all these Pompous Expressions in the Prophecies do come up to. The very Reason why the *Prophetic Spirit* has employ'd these Expressions on those lesser Occasions, was because all these Dreadful Things are to be more Effectually and more Formidably, and unto the uttermost Extremity done, in that *Final Destruction of the World,* whereof He would kindly give Mankind the most frequent Insinuations, & the most awful Admonitions.

Of the mighty *Conflagration,* whereof all the foregoing Desolations, are but little *Emblems,* and *Shadows,* and yett very dismal *Assurances,* we are to think, when we read, [Isa. XIII. 3–] I *have commanded my Sanctified Ones, I have also called my Mighty Ones for mine Anger.—The Lord of Hosts musters the Host of the Battel.—They come from a far Countrey, from the End of Heaven, even the Lord & the Weapons of His Indignation, to destroy the whole Earth. Howl Ye, for the Day of the Lord is at hand; it shall come as a Destruction from the Almighty. Therefore shall all hands be faint, & every Mans heart shall melt;*

And they shall be afraid; Pangs ⅋ Sorrows shall take hold of them, they shall be in Pain as a Woman which Travaileth: [Compare, 1. Thess. V. 3.] *They shall be amazed one at another, at the faces of the Flames. Behold, The Day of the Lord cometh, cruel both with Wrath ⅋ fierce Anger, to lay the Earth desolate; and He shall destroy the Sinners thereof out of it. For the Stars of Heaven, ⅋ the Constellations thereof shall not give their Light; the Sun shall be darkened in his going forth, ⅋ the Moon shall not cause her Light to shine. And I will punish the World for their Evil, ⅋ the Wicked for their Iniquity.*—The whole World shall 'ere long see, that this Prophecy was designed as a Description of a Matter, that was not all accomplished above Two Thousand Years ago.[68]

Of *That* we are to think, when we read, [Isa. XXVI. 11.] *The Fire of thine Enemies shall devour them.* And when we read: [Isa. XXVII. 4.] *Briars ⅋ Thorns* [ms. III, 28] *against me in Battel; I will go thro' them; I will burn them together.* And when we read, [Isa. XXIX. 6.] *Thou shalt be visited of the Lord of Hosts, with Thunder, ⅋ with Earthquake, and great Noise, with Storm ⅋ Tempest, ⅋ the Flame of devouring Fire.* And when we read, [Isa. XXX. 27–] *Behold, the Name of the Lord cometh from far, burning with His Anger,—His Lips are full of Indignation, ⅋ His Tongue as a Devouring Fire.—And the Lord shall cause His Glorious Voice to be heard, and shall show the Lighting down of His Arm, with the Indignation of His Anger, and with the Flame of a Devouring Fire.* What follows, *Tophet is praepared of old;* [if we don't read, *By the King;* but] *Yea, for the King it is praepared, He hath made it Deep and Large; the Pile thereof is Fire ⅋ much Wood; the Breath of the Lord, like a Stream of Brimstone doth kindle it:* I can quote so good an Interpreter for it as to demonstrate that I am not alone; When I interpret, *the King,* to be meant of *Satan,* the *Prince of this World,* with whom *Wicked Men,* as well as *his Angels,* are to be associated, in the *Punishment* of the *Everlasting Fire.* His well-known *Vicar* at *Rome* too, may have a share in the Interpretation.[69]

Of *That* we are to think, when we read; [Isa. XXXI. 9.] *The Lords Fire is in Zion, ⅋ His Furnace in Jerusalem.* And when we read; [Isa. XXXIII. 14.] *The Sinners in Zion are afraid; Fearfulness hath surprized the Hypocrites: Who among us shall dwell with the devouring Fire? Who among us shall dwell with Everlasting Burnings?* And when we read; [Isa. XXXIV. 8–] *It is the Day of the Lords Vengeance, and the Year of Recompenses for the Controversy of Zion. And the Streams thereof shall be turned into Pitch, ⅋ the Dust thereof into Brimstone, and the Land thereof shall become Burning Pitch. It shall not be* [ms. III, v28] *quenched night nor day; the Smoke thereof shall go up forever.* Lett the Gentlemen that are best skilled in History tell us, if they can, when it was that the Countrey of *Edom* was thus in the Letter made a *Sodom!* No; Here is foreseen a more General & a more Terrible Judgment, whereof the Destruction of *Edom* was but a faint Representation. The Term *Edom,* which carries the Colour of *Blood* in it; and *Bozrah,* that signifies a *Vintage,* are how Prophetically and Poetically and Agreeably employ'd, by Way of *Hint,* on this Occasion! The Jewish Writers are altogether in the Right on't, when they give us this Key to the *Prophecies* concerning *Edom; Of Rome are they spoken.* But an Expositor infinitely more to be relied upon, has in our *Apocalypse* determined the Matter.[70] And most certainly, we cannot now be at a Loss, what we have to think of, when we read; [Isa. LXIV. 1–] *Oh! That thou wouldest rend the Heavens! That thou wouldest come down! That the Mountains might flow down at thy Presence! As, when the melting Fire burneth, the Fire causes the Waters to boil, to make thy Name known to thine Adversaries, that the Nations may tremble at thy Presence! When thou* shalt do *terrible Things which we looked not for;* when *thou hast come down, the Mountains* shall flow *down, at thy Presence:* even as Metals heated in the *Fire.* What follows, of, *Meeting him that rejoiceth to work Righteousness,* will be understood by them who will then be *caught up to meet the Lord.* And the unknown *Things* here which *GOD has praepared for him that waiteth for Him,* the Holy Spirit of GOD elsewhere explains of Things which our Gospel refers unto; And when we read, [Isa. LXVI. 15–] *Behold, The Lord will come with Fire, & with His Chariots like a Whirlwind, to render His Anger with Fury, & His Rebuke with Flames of Fire. For by Fire, & by His Sword, will the Lord plead with all Flesh, & the Slain of the Lord shall be many.* This is to be done, when *your Bones shall flourish as an Herb;* which will be understood by them, who in being *Raised from the Dead,* shall have their *Bones* restored unto them. Then, *The Hand of the Lord shall be known,* and what the *Holy Spirit* of GOD can do, will be demonstrated. Compare the L and LI Chapters of *Jeremiah,* with what we have had from *Isaiah,* and with what we have in the Book of *Revelation,* and how sensibly shall we feel the Grand *Fire,* blazing there: And the Territories of Antichrist, *overthrown like Sodom & Gomorrah & the neighbour Cities!* How often is there in the Prophecies of *Ezekiel,* a *Fire* kindled, of which one cannot read, without seeing by the Light of it, *such Things* as we are now to *look for!* So when we read, [Ez. XXIV. 9.] I *will make the Pile for FIRE Great;* Old *Jerom* will tell us, of those who find in it, *Consummationem Saeculi.*[71]

Can we forgett the Grand FIRE, when we read, what *Obadiah* writes, [Ob. 18.] of the *Fire,* & the *Flame,* in which the *House of Esau shall be for Stubble, & they shall kindle in them, and shall devour them, and there shall not be any remaining of the House of Esau;* [Not a *Romanist* left in the World!]

How dreadfully that *Fire* blazes, in the Vibrations of the Prophet *Micah!* [Mic. I. 2–] *Hear, all Ye People; Hearken, O Earth, and all that therein is; and Lett the Lord GOD be Witness against you, the* [ms. III, 29] *Lord from His Holy Table.*[72] *For, Behold, the Lord cometh forth out of His Place, and will come down, and will tread upon the High Places of the Earth; And the Mountains shall be molten under Him, and the Valleys shall be cleft; as Wax before the Fire, and as the Waters that are poured down a steep Place.*

The Flashes of that *Fire* are very visible, when the Prophet *Nahum,* comes thus to brandish them: [Nah. I. 3–] *The Lord hath His Way in the Whirlwind, & in the Storm, and the Clouds are the Dust of His Feet. He rebukes the Sea and makes it dry; & He drieth up all the Rivers. The Mountains quake at Him, and the Hills melt, and the Earth is burnt up at His Presence, Yea, the World, and all that dwell therein, who can stand before His Indignation? And who can abide in the fierceness of His Anger! His Fury is poured out like Fire, and the Rocks are thrown down by Him.*

One would suspect something of this *Fire*, in that *Smoke*: [Hab. II. 13, 14.] *The People shall labour in the very Fire, and the People shall weary themselves for very Vanity.* And then it follows, *The Earth shall be filled with the Knowledge of the Glory of the Lord.* Be sure, The Song of *Habakkuk*, is full of it!

There are very Sensible Glowings of this *Fire*, in what the Prophet *Zephaniah* writes; [Zeph. I. 14–] *The Great Day of the Lord is near, it is near, and hasteth greatly; even the Voice of the Day of the Lord; The Mighty Man shall cry there bitterly,* [O Tripple-Crown'd Monarch, Thou art that *Mighty Man!*][73] *That Day is a Day of Wrath; a Day of Trouble & Distress; a Day of Wastness & Desolation; a Day of Darkness, & Gloominess; a Day of Clouds & thick Darkness. A Day of the Trumpett.—I will bring Distress upon Men, because they have sinned against the Lord; Neither their Silver nor their Gold shall be able to deliver them in the Day of the Lords Wrath; but the whole Earth shall be* [ms. III, v29] *devoured by the Fire of His Jealousy; for He shall make even a Speedy Riddance of all them that dwell in the Earth.* And [Zeph. III. 8.] *All the Earth shall be devoured with the Fire of my Jealousy.*

We will conclude, the *Praedictions* of the *Conflagration*, as the Old Testament concludes. [Mal. IV. 1.] *Behold, The Day comes, that shall burn as an Oven, and all the Proud, yea, and all that do wickedly shall be Stubble, and the Day that cometh shall burn them up, saith the Lord of Hosts.*

But now, for the Concomitants & Consequences of the *Conflagration*, so evidently sett forth, before our Eyes, in a Language, that nothing Humane can Parallel or Imitate; the Divine Oracles have not been altogether silent.

What we read, [Joel. III. 2.] concerning, *The Valley of Jehoshaphat;* borrows a Proper *Name*, to express a Special *Thing;* and points to, *The Judgment of the Lord.*

In the Prophecies of *Hosaea*, we read once and again concerning, A *Jezreel*: And, [Hos. I. 11.] *Great shall be the Day of Jezreel. Jezreel* signifies, *The Offspring of GOD.* And be sure, Their *Blood* will be Revenged upon *Antichrist*, who like *Jehu*, pretends a *Zeal for the Lord of Hosts*, in Shedding of it. But it is here foretold, That the Tribes of Saved *Israel*, shall be called, *The Sons of the Living GOD.* It must be the *Raising* and *Changing* of them into a *Deathless Blessedness*, that makes them so; And indeed, *Great will be the Day*, [The New Testament calls it, The GREAT DAY] when the *Offspring of GOD* shall be brought forth, with a *New Birth*, for the *World to Come.* This will be the True *Return* of *Israel*. When tis foretold, [Hos. II. 21.] That all the *Elements* will then conspire for their Service, honest *Allein* of *Bristol* [ms. III, 30] is in the Right; That the People of the *New World* are the *Jezreel*, whom this Promise will be fulfill'd unto. All the *Creatures* will with one Consent serve that *Jezreel*; They *Groan* for the Time, when they shall do so.[74]

I said but now, *Return of Israel!*—We often read of it, and particularly in the last Chapter of *Hosaea's* Prophecies. Now, Give me Leave humbly to offer a *Key* unto the Sense of the Term. There is a *Return* to GOD, (and so, a *Regeneration*) which must be found in the Experience of all that shall be Partakers of the *Glories* in the *Kingdome* of our SAVIOUR. The *Beginning* of this *Return*, is now in our *Spirits*, by a Work of *Sanctification* upon them, *without which no Man shall see the Lord*. But in the *Perfection* of this *Return*, our *Bodies* are to have a Share, by a Recovery from the *State of the Dead*; the *Deplorable State* in which our Fall from GOD has buried us. That this Phrase, RETURN, is not rarely to be understood of the *Resurrection*, we have a notable Intimation in the Prayer of *Moses*; where, a Prophecy of the *Resurrection* is thus expressed; [Psal. XC. 3.] *Thou sayst, RETURN, Ye Children of Men*. And this leads us, to the fullest & final Sense, (not excluding the praevious and needful Changes of *Repentance*, the Neglect whereof is Damnable,) of that Passage; [Matth. XVIII. 3.] *Except Ye be RETURNED, Ye shall not Enter into the Kingdome of Heaven*. Even in this last Chapter of *Hosaea*, we read, *They shall RETURN, they shall Revive as the Corn, they shall Grow as the Vine*. The Jewish *Rabbi's* themselves, as *Grotius* confesses, apply it unto the Time of the *Resurrection* from the Dead.[75] And coming to that Sacrament of the New Testament, wherein we partake of the *Corn* & of the *Vine*, we consider the *Resurrection* of the *Bodies*, which partake thereof, as therein *Sealed* unto us.

[ms. III, v30] Agreeably to this; When we read in the Prophecies of *Jeremiah*, [ch. XXIII. 20.] *In the Latter Days, YE shall consider it*: The *Chaldee* Paraphrast is Testimony enough, that the Ancient Beleevers among the *Jews*, from hence, as well as from other Places, look'd for the *Resurrection of the Dead*, as the *Thing* & the *Time*, wherein the Promises of Good unto *Israel* were to be accomplished. As his Gloss on the Text last quoted, from *Hosaea*, is; *They shall be gathered out of their Captivity; they shall sitt under the Shadow of their Messias; and the Dead shall Revive, and Good shall be multiplied on the Earth*; So, his Gloss on this Text in *Jeremiah*, is; *In that He saith, YE shall consider it, and not, THEY shall consider it, it intimateth the RESURRECTION of the Dead, in the Days of the Messias*. Yea, *Aben Ezra* [on, Dan. XII. 2.] says, *The Righteous who died in the Captivity, shall REVIVE, when the Redeemer cometh*.

In the Prophecies of *Ezekiel*, we have notable Things foretold about a *Restored Israel*. But there is a *Key* to them, in what we read; [Ezek. XXXVII. 12.] *Behold, O my People, I will open your Graves, and cause you to come up out of your Graves, & bring you into the Land of Israel*. A Thing to be literally accomplished: I say, *Literally accomplished*. In being at the Time, when the Holy One says, *My Tabernacle shall be with them; Yea, I will be their GOD, and they shall be my People*; the Apostle *John* allows me, and invites me, with Assurance to say: That the *Resurrection* here foretold, as the Restoration of *Israel*, is a Thing to be *Literally accomplished*!

Who would *at first* have imagined, That the *Song*, & what follows it, in the XXV Chapter of *Isaiah*, look'd any further, than the Deliverance of the *Jews*, from their *Assyrian*, or their *Chaldaean* Adversaries? But, if honest *Munster* have this brief, but Sharp, and High, Note upon it; *Gratiarum Actio de Gloria Piorum in Die Judicii*; he will have the Apostle *Paul* and *John* to bear him out.[76] The *Day*, when *GOD will swallow up Death in Victory*, and, *The Lord*

GOD will wipe away Tears from all Faces, is by these Two Apostles found in the World, of the *Raised* and *Changed* Ones. This One Exemple, is enough to show us, how we may *handle* the *Matter wisely*, in our Operations upon all the rest. [ms. III, 31] But concerning the *Burning* of *This World*, and what shall follow thereupon, what can be more astonishing, than what we have in the XXIV Chapter of those Prophecies. Read a little of them, and be astonished!—*Behold, The Lord maketh the Earth empty, and maketh it waste.—The Earth shall be utterly emptied, & utterly spoiled.—The Earth is defiled under the Inhabitants thereof; Therefore the CURSE has devoured the Earth, and they that dwell therein are desolated: Therefore the Inhabitants of the Earth are BURNED, and few Men left.* But shall there not Some Escape this Desolation! Yes; *When thus it shall be in the Midst of the Earth, among the People, there shall be, as the Shaking of an Olive-tree, and as the Gleaning Grapes when the Vintage is done!* How shall these Holy Ones, be disposed, when they see the *Heavens* all on a Light *Fire* over their Heads, and behold their Glorious Lord, making His Descent in *flaming Fire*, with His *Angels* about Him, and His *Raised* Ones fetch'd up to come down with Him, and expect every Moment when the *Earth* shall be all in *Flames* about their Ears? *They shall then lift up their Voice; they shall sing for the Majesty of the Lord*, [The Ninth Verse of the Next Chapter, gives their Song:] *they shall cry aloud from the Sea.* Why, *From the Sea*? I'l tell you presently,—Lett us Read on. *Wherefore glorify Ye the Lord in the FIRES, even the Name of the Lord GOD of Israel, from the Isles of the Sea.*—Now I'l tell you. The *Europaean* Parts of the World, were in the Hebrew Style called, *The Isles of the Sea*; because it was by *Water*, that the *Hebrews* went unto them, and because they bordered on the vast *Atlantic* Sea. Now, there will be scarce any where upon the face of the Earth, except in the [ms. III, v31] *Europaean* Parts of the World, [my poor *American* Countrey, Lett me pray and hope, for thy adding some unto the Number!] any considerable Number of those *Humble Walkers with GOD*, who will then be able to *sing for the Majesty of the Lord, and glorify the Lord in the Fires*, and may look to be transported by the *Angels* of GOD, after their Brethren, the *Raised* Ones, who are to have the Start of the *Changed*, in this wonderful Revolution.[77] Well; And what will ensue upon this? The *Prisoners of the Earth*, being *shutt up for many Days*, yea, no less than a Thousand Years, the *Moon shall be confounded & the Sun ashamed, when the Lord of Hosts shall Reign in Mount Zion & in Jerusalem, and there shall be the Glory before His Ancient People.* O Heavenly *Mount Zion, and thou City of the Living GOD, the Heavenly Jerusalem*, Thou shalt see this most gloriously accomplished: when thou shalt have no *Need of the Sun, or of the Moon, to shine in thee, but the Glory of GOD enlightens thee!*

What we read, [Isa. II. 2.] about, *The Mountain of the House of the Lord*, is doubtless to be fulfilled, when the *Stone* in the Visions of *Daniel*, shall become a *Great Mountain*. And the *Peece* that shall arrive unto it, is doubtless, the *Rest*, whereof the Apostle writes to the *Thessalonians*, which will be the *Recompence* of the *Troubled* Saints, when the Lord *JESUS shall be Reveled from Heaven.*

The Promise to the Faithful, [Isa. XL. 31.] *That they shall mount up with Wings as Eagles;* will be fulfilled, when they shall *Renew their Strength;* or, shall be *Raised from the Dead.* Even the *Jews* themselves, take the *Wings of Eagles,* to mean, The *Bodies* of the *Resurrection.* O Beleever, One who lived Three hundred Years before the Writing of this Prophecy has taught thee, that when GOD *Redeems thy Life from Destruction,* at thy *Resurrection* from the *Dead,* Then thou shalt *Renew thy Youth,* and be as the *Eagles.*[78] [ms. III, 32] It is evident from our Apostles applying, the Twenty fourth Verse in XLV Chapter of *Isaiahs* Prophecies, to the *Day of Judgment,* that our *Mede* has done well, to explain the Context; for the *New Heavens* and the *New Earth.*[79] To these there belongs the Prophecy; *Thus saith the Lord, that created the Heavens, GOD Himself that formed the Earth, ⅋ made it, He hath established it; He created it not in Vain; He formed it to be inhabited.* It may be read; *He formed it for the Sabbath;* Even for that Great *Sabbatism,* when the Illustrious Matters here foretold, are to have their full Accomplishment.

It is foretold, [Isa. LI. 6.] *The Heavens shall vanish away like Smoke, and the Earth, shall wax old like a Garment; but my Salvation shall be forever;* And the Gloss of a Judicious Writer upon it, is; "When *Heaven* and *Earth* shall be *Dissolved,* Then is the Time for that *Salvation,* which I promise to my Servants."[80]

There is foretold; [Isa. LIV. 12.] The *Laying of Precious ⅋ Pleasant Stones,* in the *Foundation* of the Church. Our Apostle *John* makes this to be a Description of the *New Jerusalem.* Tis designed here, to exhibit the State of *Paradise* at the First Creation; which is now to see a *Restitution.* By a Plenty of *Gems,* the Glory of *Eden* is represented by the Prophet *Ezekiel;* And when in the Book of *Job,* we read, *As for the Earth, the Stones of it are the Place of Sapphires,* the Targum explains it of *Eden.* From *Ezekiel,* I suppose it was, that *Plato* seems to have borrowed his Picture of the *Paradisaical Earth,* the Beauty whereof he setts forth, from the bright *Stones* of Several Colours, which it abounded with.

Some think, that the Prophecy, [Isa. LV. 13.] *Instead of the Thorn shall come up the Fir-tree;* may import a Renovation of the World, and the Restoration of it unto a *Paradisaical State.* And the Prophecy, [Isa. LX. 21.] *They shall inherit the Land forever;* must be meant of the *Millennium;* in which the *Meek shall inherit the Earth.*[81]

But then, the Apostle *Peter* has putt it beyond all Dispute, That the *New Heavens* and the *New Earth,* in the LXV Chapter of *Isaiah,* are those which are to take place after the *Conflagration.*

[ms. III. v32] If the Book of PSALMS be the *Man of our Counsel,* how frequently, shall we have the Things of the *World to Come,* there pointed at! Among *the Last Words of David,* who wrote *the Melodious Psalms of Israel,* we read concerning the *Sons of Belial,* [2. Sam. XXIII. 7.] *They shall be utterly burnt with FIRE in the Place where they stand.* Or, it may be read, *In the Sabbath,* when the Great *Sabbatism,* (the Kingdome here foretold) arrives, it will come on with a Stupendous *Conflagration,* (which is the Same with the *Third Wo,* even that of the *Seventh Trumpet* in the *Apocalypse,*) & the *Sons of Belial,* which are called, *Those that corrupt the Earth*, shall then be *utterly Burnt with Fire*. Tis what his *Former Words* in the *Melodious Psalms of Israel*, often advise us & assure us of. The Citations made in the *New Testament* from very many of the *Psalms*, have instructed us, *What*, and *How*, we are with *Opened Understanding*, to seek in all the rest. Yea, Our SAVIOUR, in His most memorable Sermon, *at the Mount*, giving the *Characters* of a *Godly Man*, which always are to be all united in *One Man*, and the *Faelicities* rendring him a *Blessed Man*, which are to be all enjoyed at the *Same Time*, and so at the *Same Time* that these Holy Ones, are to have the *Kingdome of Heaven for Theirs*, and are to be *Comforted* in the *Obtaining of Mercy*, and are to *See GOD*, they shall also *Inhabit the Earth*: It is remarkable that in these *Beatitudes* He had the XXXVII *Psalm* in His Eye. The XXXVII *Psalm* then is to have its Fulfilment, in the World of *Blessedness*, which is the World, that will have no *Curse* or *Death* or *Sin*, to damnify it. In that *Psalm*, we see

> *Ill Men shall perish, and the Foes*
> *of the ETERNAL GOD*
> *shall be consum'd like Fat of Lambs;*
> *they shall consume in SMOKE.*

But, *when*

> *All they who are His Blessed Ones*
> *as Heirs shall have the Earth;*
> *then they that are cursed from Him*
> *shall be cutt-off from thence.*[82]

It is here foretold, [Psal. CIV. 35.] That there will a Time come, *Sinners will be from Earth consumed, and the Impious be no more.* It will be at the Time, when the Lord, *He does look down upon the Earth; It falls a Trembling then; He to the Mountains gives a Touch and presently {they smoke.}* This [ms. III, 33] is the first time, that, an, HALLELUIAH occurs in the Bible. HALLELUIAHs won't be heard, as it is to be, until this *New Face* upon the World here foretold, and thus produced, shall bring it on: Lord, *Thou wilt send forth thy Spirit; They created are anew: And thou to the Face of the Earth wilt a Renewal give. The Glory of th' ETERNAL GOD, it shall endure forever; The Joy of the ETERNAL GOD will be in all His Works.*

The Great HALLELUIAH comes on, with a *Conflagration*, so foretold; [Psal. XXI. 8.] *Thy Hand shall apprehend all those that are thine Enemies: Thy Right Hand shall such apprehend as Haters are of thee. Thou'lt make them as a FIERY OVEN, in the Times of thy Wrath: Th' ETERNAL in His Great Wrath will swallow them wholly up: And the FIRE irresistibly shall quite devour them all.*

But of the *Conflagration*, what a Wonderful Description have we, in the *Psalm*, from whence *Homer* borrow'd the Beauties of his *Twentieth Iliad*.[83] *Reader*, Don't think much, to have here a Transcription of it. Thou shalt have it in a Translation keeping strictly to the Original, Word for Word; But yett in

Metre.—*Then the Earth shook, and trembled sore; and of the Mountains then were the Foundations mov'd & shock'd; because He was displeas'd. Out of His Nostrils went a SMOKE; and FIRE out of His Mouth; This did devour; Coals were by Him kindled into a Flame. The Heavens also He bow'd down,* [ms. III, v33] *and He made His Descent: A Cloudy Darkness then there was display'd under His Feet. Upon a Cherub then He Rode, and flew with Spreading Wings; Yea, He flew swiftly on the Wings of the Spirituous Wind. Darkness He made His Secret Place; Surrounding Darkness was His Tent; Darkness of Waters with Clouds which do cloath the Skies. Thro' the Illustrious Brightness which there was before Him then, His thick Clouds pass'd away; there were Hailstones & Coals of FIRE. And the ETERNAL GOD, did in the Heavens thunder forth; and the Most High utter'd His Voice; Hailstones and Coals of FIRE. Yea, He did send His Arrows forth; and so He scatter'd them; His Lightnings too He darted forth, and did discomfit them.—Longinus,* why didst thou not fetch an Exemple of, *The Sublime,* from the XVIII Psalm, as well as from the First Chapter of *Genesis,* to entertain thy brave *Jewess,* the Great *Zenobia?*[84] *Christians,* Do *You* Take these Notes, and *Now* begin to *sing for the Majesty of the* Lord!

A *Mischievous Person* who is infamous for His Employing the little *Smattering of Learning* he had attain'd, in undermining the *Faith* of *Christianity;* values himself upon an Observation: *That the Style of the Old Testament is extremely Hyperbolical.—Thus a Storm is often represented in such Pompous Terms, as if the whole Frame of Nature had been convuls'd, & the Universe on the Point of Dissolution.*[85] Vain Man! The True Reason why in our Sacred Books a *Storm* is represented in such *Pompous Terms,* tis because the *Prophetic Spirit* had an Eye to, & would lead the Faithful to the View of, a *Storm,* wherein the *whole Frame of Nature* shall be indeed *Convuls'd,* & our *Universe* undergo a *Dissolution*: An Event upon which the Old Testament never used one Word that was *Hyperbolical;* and it is impossible to use too *Pompous Terms.* The Figures are all short of the Reality: Nor can the Pen of any *Blackmore* describe a *Storm* in such *Pompous Terms* as would in any Measure aequal it.[86]

The Great *Scaliger* upon the Complements which an Irish Man address'd him in Latin, the *Teaque* had pronounced his Latin so awkwardly that he answered him, *Domine, Non intelligo Irlandicè. Hodequs* explains the Bible so awkwardly, so profanely, & so foolishly, that every Man of Sense must say, *Domine, Non intelligo Irlandica.*[87]

The *Hallelujatic Psalms,* in the End of our *Psalter,* tell us of the Glorious Things that shall be at the *End of the World.*[88]

Then shall the XLVI *Psalm* have a full Explanation. *O Come, Consider well, the Works of the ETERNAL GOD; who does make Desolations be upon the Wasted Earth. Unto the Borders of the Earth He does make Wars to cease; He breaks the Bows & cutts the Spear; Chariots He Burns in FIRE. Be still* [or, Sabbatize] *and Know that I am GOD; Among the Nations I will be exalted; Yea, will be exalted in the Earth.*

What can we see, but the *Conflagration,* and the *Kingdome* of our SAVIOUR that follows upon it? When we sing, [Psal. XCVII. 1–] [ms. III, 34] *Now the ETER-*

NAL GOD does reign, O Lett the Earth rejoice; O Lett the many Isles thereof shine with a cheerful Joy. A Cloud & a dense Darkness does encompass Him about; Justice and Judgment are the firm Foundation of His Throne. FIRE goes before His Face, and burns all round His Enemies; His Lightnings fill the World with Light; the Earth sees it, and shakes. Like Melting Wax the Mountains are dissolv'd before the Face of the ETERNAL GOD; before the Lord of all the Earth. O Lett the Heavens now declare abroad His Righteousness; and of His radiant Glory Lett all People have a View.

I will conclude with a Line or two from the CII Psalm; which is no more than what our Apostle writing to the Hebrews has led us to. And if Daniel were, (as there is Cause to think) the Writer of it, His Visions will help us to understand the Meaning of it. When the ETERNAL GOD shall please to build His Zion up; He shall most visibly appear in His bright Glory there.—In the Beginning thou hast laid Foundations for the Earth; The Heavens also of thy Hands are the rare Workmanship. They'l perish, but Thou shalt endure; Yea, like a Garment they shall all wax old; Thou'lt change them as a Robe; and they'l be chang'd. But as for thee, Thou ever dost continue what thou art; And thy Years, they are such as will not ever be consum'd. But, may Dust & Ashes humbly enquire: Lord; What Place will there be for thy Poor Children, if the present Heavens and Earth must so pass away? Lo, He points us to the New Heavens & the New Earth, and allows us to sing, The Children of thy Servants shall have a fix'd Dwelling-Place; and their Offspring before thy Face shall be established. [ms. III, v34] Tho' I propos'd this for the Conclusion of all, yett I cannot but annex to it a Passage of the Sublimest Song that ever was in the World; A Song that was composed in the Heavens, but copied from the Heavenly Dictates, by the Illustrious Moses, above One & thirty Hundred Years ago; which foretells This, as the Issue of what should follow upon the Impiety and Apostasy of Israel, & the Succession of the Gentiles into their Covenant: A FIRE is kindled in my Anger, and it shall burn unto the Lowest Hell, and it shall consume the Earth with its Increase, & it shall sett on Fire the Foundations of the Mountains. After This;—GOD will be merciful unto HIS LAND, & unto His People.

Such Things as these do we find in the Scripture of Truth. CHRISTIANS, Employ your Best Thoughts upon them!

IV. The *Sibylline* Oracles,
concerning the CONFLAGRATION.

Having seen something of what the *more sure Word of Prophecy* has informed us, concerning the Fate of the *Dark Place*, which does *Enjoy*, but, alas, how much *Despise*, the *Light* communicated in it; what if we should now, *Consult the SIBYLS!*[1]

But tho' in saying so, I seem to speak like one of the Old *Romans*, among whom This was done on far less Occasions, yett I will do it, with no Higher a Value for them, than *Austin* had, when he said, *Sibyllae si vera praedixisse perhibentur, valet quidem aliquid ad paganorum vanitatem revicendam, non tamen ad istarum Auctoritatem amplectendam.* They may be of some Use to show us, what *Expectation* the Nations had in the *former Ages*, and how, FIRE, was cried among them.[2]

I confess, I pay little Regard unto the Tradition, of the *Ten Women*, possessed with a *Prophetic Spirit*, which from the *First* of the Ten, were called, *Sibyls*; or, of the most noted among them, called, the *Cumaean*, from her Settling at *Cumae* in *Italy*,[3] where *Justin Martyr*, who had been There, tells us, that in his Time, there was to be seen the Chappel hewn out of a great Rock, from the innermost Cell whereof she uttered her Enthusiasms;[4] which *Onuphrius* tells us, was to be seen less than Two Hundred Years ago, when an Earthquake overwhelmed it:[5] However, a Vault thereabouts, which they call, *The Grotto of the Sibyl*, is at this Day also shown to Travellers.[6] I pay as little Regard, unto the Odd Story, of the Bargain, which the Strange Woman sold unto *Tarquin*;[7] when the *Augurs* advised him to pay the Price demanded by her, for certain *Fatidical Books* of the *Sibyls*; which were then putt up in a Stone-Coffer, and lodged in a Subterraneous Vault of the *Capitol*; under the Custody of Chosen Keepers, who assisted the Commonwealth to make them Significant *Engines of State* upon Occasion: But they perished in the *Flames*, which consumed the *Capitol*, about Fourscore Years before the Birth of our SAVIOUR.[8] We know, the Pains taken by the *Senate* afterwards, to collect the Vast Numbers of Prophecies, pretending [ms. III, v35] to be the *Sibylline Oracles*, that were scattered every where in the Hands of the People; who were forbidden upon Pain of Death, to retain any of them. *Augustus*, upon an Examination of these, destroy'd no less than Two Thousand Volumns of them, as being Spurious. *Tiberius* upon a further Examination of them, destroy'd a great many more.[9] They that were judged fitt for Public Service, were preserved; and they were now more consulted than ever, because the Pagan Oracles very much *Ceased*, on the Coming of our SAVIOUR.[10] They continued, until the Christian Emperour *Honorius*, about the Period of our Fourth Century, brought as far as he could, a Total Destruction upon them all. We cannot recover them; only this we know, That they were *Devillish Things*; when the *Romans* consulted them, they directed such *Idolatrous* and *Abominable* Rites, as abundantly discover their Diabolical Original.[11]

We have yett Eight Books in Greek Verse, which go under the Name of *Sibylline*; A Collection that could not be made before the Year, of our Lord, CXXXVIII; Because it mentions the next Successor to *Adrian*: And could not be made after the Year CLXVII; Because it is often quoted by *Justin Martyr*.[12] Tis a Just Remark, that *Casaubon* has upon these Books; *Oracula illa, quo Apertiora sunt, eo videri suspectiora*.[13] We find in them such an Abstract of the Bible, as could be writt by none but a *Christian*; Yea, the Writer in one Place expressly confesses himself to be a *Christian*. And yett the *Sibyl* declares, that she was wife to one of *Noahs* Three Sons, & with him in the *Ark*, during the whole Time of the Deluge.[14]

It is a little strange, that *Justin Martyr*, & others of the Fathers, could appeal so much to the *Sibylline* Books; and *Josephus* quote them, for the Tower of *Babel*:[15] yea, *Clemens Alexandrinus* affirm, that *Paul* frequently referr'd unto them, in his Preaching to the *Gentiles*.[16] And yett; There is in *Vopisculus* a Letter of *Aurelian* to the Roman Senate, which signifies, That the *Christian* Churches made no great account of them. The Shrewd Plea for them, from the Report of *Cicero*, that there were *Acrosticks* found in *them*, & there are *Acrosticks* in the *Sibylline* Books that are *now* extant; has nothing in it; For the *Acrosticks* of *Cicero*, were of quite another Sort, than the IXΘΥΣ of our pretended *Sibyls*.[17]

After the many & learned [ms. III, 36] Volumns that have been written upon this Intricate Subject, we have Dr. *Prideaux* aquiescing in this Determination;[18] That the *Jews* dispersed among the Nations, had an Earnest Expectation of the MESSIAH quickly to appear unto the World, and had the Praedictions of *Daniel* to raise it in them. From hence the *Gentiles* gott their Notion, of a Great King to come out of *Judaea*, & reign over the whole World; which we have often heard of. Tis possible also, that the Glorious GOD might make some of the *Pagan Oracles*, to bear some Testimony unto the Approach of the REDEEMER, as He did *Balaam* of old;[19] yea, and He compelled the very *Devils* themselves, in the Days of His Flesh, to own Him. An *Heathen* having digested these things into a Book of *Greek Verses*, about the Time of our SAVIOUR, this operated something to the advantage of *Christianity*; and therefore the Professors of it, make such frequent Citations from them, that (as *Origen* tells us)[20] they gott the Denomination of *Sibyllists*, from their pinched & vexed Adversaries. This Book was afterwards interpolated with many Additions, by a *Christian*, whose *Discretion* and *Honesty* were much of a Piece; and the noble Cause of *Christianity* suffered no little Damage, from the Authority of the *Whole* being brought into quaestion by these *Adulterations*. All that we now have, is this *Wretched Mixture*.

But then Dr. *Chandler* has bestow'd a further Cultivation upon this Important Subject; According to whom, The Tradition of the expected *Messiah* and *Redeemer*, was what the *Graecians* and *Romans* came to be acquainted with, by means of the *Jews*, in *Asia Minor*, and the *Islands* of the Ægean Sea; who turned into *Greek Verses*, the better to be Remembred, what they had learnt from the *Prophets* concerning Him.[21] These Verses were called, *Sibylline*; from an Hebrew or [ms. III, v36] Chaldee Word of the same Sound, that signifies, *To Prophecy*. *Hesychius* calls it, *A Word that signifies, A Prophetess*.[22] It appears not, that there was any Person, which had for her proper Name, that of *Sibyl*: But because these Verses were collected in Different Countreys, a *Sibyl* fancied, & so was Named, from that Countrey where the Verses were collected. The Old *Sibylline* Books of *Tarquin*, seem to have been mainly *Ritual* Books: whereas the Greek *Sibylline* Books were of another Nature, and exhibited the Things foretold in the *Jewish* Prophecies, or grounded on them; and therefore some very Learned Men, such as *Usher*, and *Grotius*, and *Vossius*, take them, to be a *Jewish Composition*, designed for to propagate the Beleef of the *Messiah*, and praepare the Way for His Reception among the *Gentiles*.[23] From the *Graecians* they passed unto the *Romans*; among whom for some time there were Praedictions concerning, *A Glorious King to Come*. They were in every bodies hands; many of them under the Title of *Sibylline*; and they were variously applied, as Men were disposed. *Julius Caesar* contrived a Motion to make him a *King*, from something in these Books, intimating that a *King* must be their Saviour. *Cicero* offered Reasons to doubt whether this could be found in the *Tarquinian Sibyls*; But the Reasons were of no force against the *Jewish* Ones. Upon the Conception of *Augustus*, it was commonly said, *That Nature was then in Labour, to bring forth a King that should rule the Romans*; which *Virgil*, in the Sixth *Æneid*, explains more largely, Of Prophecies concerning One, who should be of the *Race of the Gods*, that should sett up the *Golden Age* again, and subdue the hitherto unconquered Nations, & reduce them all into one *Universal Empire*. All this he ominates of *Augustus*; But as their Hopes from *Augustus* dwindled, *Virgil* would needs revive them, for the Son [ms. III, 37] that *Scribonia*, the Wife of *Augustus*, was then big withal. In his *Fourth Eclog*, he applies to this Child, the Glorious Things which the *Sibylline* Books had foretold of, *The Great King to Come*. To the Disgrace of the Poet, and of his pretended Skill at the Interpretation of Prophecies, the Lady was delivered of a *Daughter*.[24] However, *Virgil* did not quite lose *his* End; which was to ingratiate himself *Augustus*. And *We* also have the Benefit, of knowing, what the *Grand Expectation* of People in his Days turn'd upon: Even in *Substance*, yea, in the very *Language*, much the same, with what we read in the *Jewish Prophecies* concerning the *Messiah*. If the Whole of what *Virgil* writes had not been in the *Sibylline* Books, yett he might have added unto his Knowledge, from great Numbers of *Jews*, which then lived in one Quarter of *Rome*; and from *Herod* & his Followers, who in his Time were *there*, and were probably (as his Two Sons were afterwards) Guests unto that very *Pollio*, unto whom his *Eclogue* is inscribed. However, he plainly teaches us, what the *Sibylline* Books treated of: and it is very affecting to see, how pattly his Expressions hitt with the Prophecies of the *Old Testament*.[25]

Upon the Destruction of the *Sibylline* Books by the Emperour *Honorius*, I would humbly ask Leave to *shew my Opinion*. The Cause pretended for it, was a very poor one! There was a Tradition rife among the Pagans, That our Apostle *Peter* had foretold, That the *Christian Religion* should continue but Three hundred & Sixty five Years in the World; And it was pretended, That

Something in the *Sibylline* Books, intimated and countenanced this Praediction. This Term of Years, had just now run Out, in the Year CCCXCVIII, which was just a CCCLXV Years from the Ascension of our SAVIOUR; and the *Pagans* here upon flattered themselves with mighty hopes of a *Revolution* in their Favour to come on immediately. The Sensible [ms. III, v37] Confutation of the Praediction, in *Christianity* still continuing & even flourishing, afforded unto *Honorius* an Advantage to convict the Books of Imposturs, and order a *General Conflagration* of them; which Order was executed by *Stilico* in the Year ensuing.[26] But, if the *Sibylline* Books had no greater Mistakes in them than This![27]—Alass, The *Christian Religion* in the *Purity* of it, outlived not the Year assigned. The growing Depravations of *Antichrist*, had made fearful Alterations upon it. Lett it be considered, how far the Proportion of the *Inner Court*, unto the *Outer Court*, in the *Temple*, was like that of CCCLXV, to M.CC.LX. and then Lett us consider, the *Christianity* of the Worshippers in the *Inner Court*, as *leaving the Earth* at this Time, and the *Outer Court*, left unto the *Gentiles*, for the Revived *Gentilism* of *Popery* to take Place instead of it: I doubt, we shall find more Truth in the *Petrine Praediction* [If it were so!] than thou, *Honorius*, hadst any Suspicion of.[28]

By this time, we are prepared a little, to spend some Thoughts, on what we find, concerning the *Conflagration* of the World, in the *Sibylline* Books, that have survived the *Conflagration*, which they were by *Honorius* doom'd unto. And, *valeat quantum valere potest.*[29] It will at least *avail* to a Demonstration, That the Destruction of the World by FIRE, was an Ancient & a Received Opinion in the World.

Here, I shall wave what *Lactantius* has quoted from them; representing the Wrath of GOD, as, *Destroying Mankind*, and ΑΠΑΣΑΝ ΥΠ᾽ ΕΜΠΡΗΣΜΟΥ ΜΕΡΘΟΝΤΑ᾽ *Dispeopling the World with a Conflagration.* I shall also wave a Distich that *Prosper* has quoted from them; which tells us—*Tellus confracta peribit.*

> All things shall cease; By FIRE the *Earth*, and all
> Its *Water*, shall into Perdition fall.

These *Quotations* are but *Second-hand* Things. Tis enough that I make Two or three, more directly from them.[30]

These are Two Lines, of more to the like Purpose, in the Second Book of the, *Oracula Sibyllina.*

[ms. III, 38]

ΚΑΙ ΤΟΤΕ ΔΗ ΠΟΤΑΜΟΣ ΤΕ ΜΕΓΑΣ ΠΥΡΟΣ ΑΙΠΗΘΕΝΟΙΟ
ΡΕΥΡΕΙ ΑΠΟΥΡΑΝΟΘΕΝ, ΚΑΙ ΠΑΝΤΑ ΤΟΠΟΝ ΔΑΠΑΝΗΣΕΙ. κ.λ.[31]

> Down a Vast *Flood* of FIRE from *Heav'n* shall flow,
> And lay all waste upon the *Earth* below.

But what can be more expressive than those Lines!

ΠΥΡ ΕΣΤΑΙ ΚΑΤΑ ΚΟΣΜΟΝ ΕΝ Ω ΤΟΔΕ ΣΗΜΑ ΤΕΤΥΚΤΑΙ
ΡΟΜΦΑΙΑΙ. ΣΑΛΠΙΓΓΕΣ ΑΜ᾽ ΗΕΛΙΩ ΑΝΙΟΝΤΙ.κ.λ.[32]

Perhaps the Reader, may be tired, if the Whole should be transcribed. Wherefore instead of a *Transcription* I will give him a *Translation*, of it, which my *Son* happening to stand by me, at the Time of my Writing, entertains me with.[33]

> Behold; The World so Beautiful and Fine,
> Envelop'd in tremendous *Fires* shall shine.
> When this Sad Fate draws near, then *Peace* no more
> Shall spread its Silver Wings from Shore to shore.
> But all shall hear of *War* the dire Alarms;
> They sound the *Trumpetts*, and they shine in *Arms*.
> Then from the *East* a dreadful Noise shall fly;
> And the whole World shall hear the hideous Cry.
> When now a raging *Fire* comes thundring down,
> And all the Globe becomes a *Torrid Zone*.
> The Race of Men unto *Flames* a Prey become;
> Floods, Seas, & Cities feel the *Fiery Doom*.
> The *Fiery Doom* all to Destruction brings;
> The *Men* to Ashes turn'd, to Soot the *Things*.
> When the Great GOD the World so ruin'd sees
> In *Flames*, He then will bid the *Flames* to cease.
> All-powerful then He *Man* again will form;
> His Bones will reunite, his Blood will warm.
> Now when He shall to Man again say, *Live*,
> The *Future Judgment* surely shall arrive.
> And then the Most High GOD His Truth shall prove.
> And show the *Heights* of Justice & of Love.
> [ms. III, v38]
> For those in Sin delighting shall again
> Buried in *Earth* be left among the *Slain*;
> But those who constant in Religion are
> Shall live on *Earth*; Free from all anxious Care.
> To Them their GOD will grant Superiour Joys;
> Their Life maintain with Food which never Cloys.
> They'l know their Friends, and Joyful them Caress;
> Themselves They'l happy know; and see, and Bless.

But we will now leave the Books of the *Sibyls* to a *Third*, and more effectual *Conflagration*.[34]

V. Traditions of the CONFLAGRATION,
with All Nations, in All Ages.

We have done with *Sibyls*; But for the same Cause, that gave us the Patience to hear *Them*, we will use a little more, and see the Tradition little short of *Universal Extent*, which even from Time Immemorial, the Expectation of a *Conflagration* to come upon this World, has had among the Nations of it.[1]

Josephus has told us a Story of *Two Pillars* erected by our Father *Seth*, on one of which there was inscribed a Prophecy of a Double *Destruction* to come on the World, one by *Water*, & then another by *Fire*, which he received from his Father *Adam*: Adding, *That one of those Pillars was at that very time standing in Syria.* Tis, I confess, a very unlikely Story: But, *Josephus* being an Historian who impiously & scandalously complemented his *Pagan Readers*, with forbearing to insert any thing in his Histories, but what might appear credible to *Them*, We may from this Passage argue the Article, of the *Conflagration* to be what *They* had some Notion of.[2]

Among the Sons of *Noah*, we find it an *Early Perswasion*. The *Philosophers* whom it has pleased the self-conceited *Westerlings* to call *Barbarians*, we know, were full of it; And their Offspring in the *East*, as *Maffeus* tells us, to this Day continue so. T'was in the *North* as well as the *East*; and the *Scythians* in their Disputes with the *Egyptians* had it.[3] *Berosus*, in *Seneca*, finds it among the *Chaldaeans*; who not only beleev'd the *Thing*, but also foretold the *Time* of it. It was rife among the *Phaenicians*, as tis evident from their Mystical Books mentioned by *Suidas*.[4] Tis probable, that *Zeno*, the Founder of the *Stoicks*, derived from *Them* his Doctrine of the *Conflagration*. And the *Stoicks* made it so considerable a Part of their Philosophy, that it was almost the Character which distinguished them. But *Zeno* was not the *First*, who published this Doctrine in *Greece*; he only *Revived* it. *Minutius Faelix* reports it, even of the *Epicureans* themselves, That they held the same with the *Stoicks*, about the *Elementorum conflagratio, et mundi Ruina.*[5] I suppose, I shall by 'nd by produce one of that Hand. But *Plato*, who lived several Years in *Egypt*, informs [ms. III, v39] us, that the Doctrine was taught among the *Egyptians*: [Two fatal Catastrophe's for the World, by *Water* & by *Fire*.] *Strabo* traces it, among the *Druids*, who preached it unto the old *Celtae*; the People that have praeserved their *Tongue Alive*, the longest of any that ever were in the Word. So that well might *Jerom* in his Comment on *Isaiah*, assert: *Etiam philosophorum mundi haec est opinio, omnia quae cernimus Igne peritura.*[6] And *Theophilus* of *Antioch*, writing to *Autolycus*, observe; *That the Philosophers whether they would or no, agreed with our Prophets, in the Doctrine of the Conflagration; which indeed* (he says) *they stole from them.* Or, as the other *Theophilus* of *Alexandria* expresses it; Απο πηγης αρυσαμενοι τα δογματα˙ *They Drew their Opinions from the True Fountain.*[7]

Among the *Romans*, how notably do we find *Cicero* in the *Dream* of *Scipio*, representing it, as a more than a Vain *Dream*, That there is no room for any *Lasting Glory* in This World; for the World itself is *Transient*, and a *Conflagration* will sweep away all Records of Humane Actions![8]

Without looking back, on what *Justin Martyr* quotes from *Sophocles*; concerning a FIRE that shall one Day bring a Destruction on the World;

Η ΔΕ ΒΥΣΚΗΘΕΙΣΑ ΦΛΟΞ
ΑΠΑΝΤΑ ΤΑ ΠΙΓΕΙΑ ΚΑΙ ΜΕΤΑΡΣΙΑ
ΦΛΕΞΕΙ ˙ κλ.[9]

Of Things *below* & Things *above*, the Frame
Shall all be burnt in a Devouring *Flame*.

Or, on what *Clemens* of *Alexandria* quotes from *Diphilus*; of the Same Intention, & in very near the Same Expression: We will quote a few Lines from some of the *Roman* Poets.[10]

Ovid complements *Lucretius*, that his Verses would continue in Esteem, and only be lost, *Exitio terras, cum dabit una Dies*. Now this *Lucretius* has *that* very Expression; and the *Bruit*, before he is aware, discovers his Fright of a *Fire* blazing before his Eyes; wherein,

Una dies dabit exitium, multosqe per Annos
Sustentata ruet moles, et machina mundi.
Nec me animus fallit, quàm res nova mirage menti
Accidit, exitium Coeli Terraeqe futurum.[11]

Which an Ingenious & Infamous Pen has thus translated

—First cast an Eye,
And look on all Below, on all on High;
The solid Earth, the Seas, and arched Sky;
One fatal Hour (dear Youth) must ruin all;
This glorious Frame that stood so long, must fall.
I know that this seems strange, & hard to prove;
My word harden'd Prejudice will scarce remove.

[ms. III, 40] His Admirer *Ovid* has a Claim to stand the Next unto him; whose Verses are known to every Schole-boy.

Esse quoque in Fatis reminiscitur; adfore Tempus
Quo Mare, quo Tellus, correptaqe Regia Coeli
Ardeat, et Mundi moles operosa laboret.[12]

Upon which another has bestow'd this Translation.

A Time decreed by Fate, at Length will come,
When Heav'n, and Earth, and Seas shall have their Doom,
A Fiery Doom: And Natures mighty Frame
Shall break, and be dissolv'd into a Flame.

If it were worth our while, we might call in *Lucan*, to join in setting *Fire* to the *Funeral-Pile* of the World; as the Monster that murdered him, they say, did unto the City of *Rome*, (which another *Fire* from a juster Hand is now ready to fall upon.) and cry out,

—*Communis superest mundo Rogus.*[13]

Speaking of the *Dead Bodies*, that *Caesar* would not suffer to be *Burnt*, after the Battel, he Sings,—

> *If now these Bodies want their Fire, & Urn,*
> *At last, with the whole Globe, they'l surely burn.*
> *This World expects One General Fire.—*

So he who sang the *Burning* of *Rome*, now sings the *Burning* of the World.[14] But here's enough.

Only, while we are thus discovering the Footsteps of, *A Conflagration Expected*, among the *Ancient Gentiles*, why should not the Book of *Job*, on this Occasion be look'd into? This Book, to some very Judicious Men appears to be, *the Oldest Book in the World*; and it shows us the *State of Religion* in the World, before the Days of *Moses*. There is not a Syllable of the *Mosaic* Law in it, nor an Allusion to any one Rite thereof; nor any one Peece of History later than the Days of *Moses*, nor any Touch on any Form of the *Idolatry* that was then generally practised. But the Book appears written, as a Late Author observes,[15] in Opposition to the very *Ancient Haeresy*, of, *Two Independent Principles*, the one of *Good*, the other of *Evil*: The most *Ancient Haeresy*, as far as we know, on the Face of the Earth; and one that has not had the Fewest Followers; Now, if in those *Early Days*, and even among the First Sons of *Noah*, we find the *Burning* of the World, in the *Faith* of Good Men, certainly it will be thought a Matter that will call for the *Deepest Meditation*. Wherefore, as we find, the *Flood* expressly mention'd in this Book, so, when we read there, [Job. XV. 34.] *The Congregation of Hypocrites shall be desolate, and FIRE shall consume the Tabernacles of Bribery*; And when we read; [Job. XX. 26, 27.] *A FIRE not* [ms. III, v40] *Blown, shall consume the Wicked; The Heaven shall reveal his Iniquity, & the Earth shall rise up against him*: [see also, Job. IX. 5, 6.] I humbly offer it unto Consideration, whether the *Conflagration* may not be referr'd unto. However, we see, *All Ages*, and *All Nations*, have beleeved it.

VI. SIGNS of the
CONFLAGRATION coming on.

The Men, whom our Lord chose first for His *Disciples*, & then for His *Apostles*, enquired of Him, *What shall be the Sign of thy Coming, & of the End of the World?* And in answer to this Enquiry, our Glorious REDEEMER, has given such *Signs* of His *Coming*, & of the *Burning* which the World is to undergo at & by His *Coming*, as ought greatly to be considered.[1]

Hereupon I have thought, and who would not think?—How can the Appearance of such *Signs*, be consistent with what our Lord has warned us of? His *Warnings* to us are, That His *Coming* will be with all possible *Surprize* upon the World; That it shall be like that of a *Thief in the Night*, altogether unlook'd for; That it shall be as *in the Days that were before the Flood, when they carried on their Saecular Affairs, and Sensual Delights* with utmost Security, *until the very Day that* Noah *entred into the Ark, and knew not until the Flood came & took them all away;* That *the Day shall come as a Snare on all them who dwell on the Face of the whole Earth;* And, That *when they shall say, Peace and Safety, then Sudden Destruction will come, as Travail upon a Praegnant Woman.* In a Word, when all the *deep Sleep* of a *Midnight* is upon the whole World, without so much as a *Dream* of any such Event being so near, and there shall scarce be any *Faith in the Earth* of such a Matter; THEN, shall the *Son of Man* at once break in upon the World. The *First Blaze* of the *Flames* in the Heavens going to be fired, shall be but as an unregarded *Aurora Borealis*, in a *Midnight*. How can such solemn & awful & awakening *Signs* of its Approach, consist with such a *Subitaneous Revolution?* Be sure, the Conjectures of some, That a *Long Drought*, & other Dispositions of Inflammability, [ms. III, v41] and what may carry Plain Indications or Intimations of a *Conflagration* coming on, will praecede it; are what the Sacred Scriptures are far from Countenancing.[2]

In the Multitude of my Thoughts within me, upon this Matter, I have examined, whether some things mention'd for *Signs* of the *Conflagration* coming on, may not be really *Parts* of it; not *Signs* that will *Prognosticate* it, but *Signs* that will *Concomitate* it; and such as will not be seen, until after the *Descent* of our Lord has proceeded so far that the *Day of Grace* for the World will be over, and the Ejulations[3] of the People condemned unto the *Flames* be all *too late*; and so the Character of His *Coming Suddenly* still be answered.

But upon a more Thorough Disquisition, I will now venture to propose; What if the *Signs* which our Lord has given of His *Coming & of the End of the World*, should not meerly mean such as are to be JUST BEFORE His *Coming & the End of the World;* or be the *Immediate Fore-runners* of it: But mean, such as may serve both for a *Demonstration, That* He can and will *Come & Burn* the World; and an *Explanation, How* it shall be done: or, serve to *Signify,* what shall be *Hereafter,* and *in His Time* accomplished: And be so long before the *Grand Event,* that the World shall have Time to fall asleep again before it arrives; and utterly forgett all the *Praemonitions* of it. Yea, *Quaere;* whether the

Signs are not all *giv'n*, and *past*; so that there is *no more to be look'd for*. We find in the Bible some *Signs* of Things given *Long Before* the Things came to pass. And the *Signs* of the *Conflagration* may be given so *Long Before* it, as to leave room for the Reign of the *Man of Sin* to intervene between *Them*, and *It*. When our Apostle had so foretold the *Day of the Lord coming as a Thief in the Night*, that the *Thessalonians* fell into an Immediate Expectation of the Day, he afterwards told them, *The Day of CHRIST would not come* until the *Man of Sin* was *Reveled*, and *Antichrist* had passed thro' the Period intended for him. [ms. III, 42] The *Signs* which our Lord has more particularly assign'd for our Satisfaction, *That* and *How* He will *Come*, and *Burn* the World at His Coming, are thus expressed; [Luk. XXI. 25, 11.] *There shall be Signs in the Sun & in the Moon & in the Stars; and upon the Earth Distress of Nations with Perplexity, the Sea and the Waves thereof roring; Mens Hearts failing them for fear, & for looking after those things that are coming on the Earth; for the Powers of Heaven shall be shaken.—And Great Earthquakes shall be in diverse Places, and Famines, and Pestilences, & fearful Sights & great Signs shall there be from Heaven.* In another Gospel, they are thus expressed; [Matth. XXIV. 29.] *Immediately after the Tribulation of those Days, The Sun shall be darkened, & the Moon shall not give her Light, & the Stars shall fall from Heaven, & the Powers of the Heavens shall be shaken.* To these Lett us add the Words of *Joels* Prophecy; [chap. II. 28.–31.] *I will pour out my Spirit upon all Flesh, & your Sons & your Daughters shall prophesy,—And I will show Wonders in the Heavens, and in the Earth, Blood & Fire & Pillars of Smoke. The Sun shall be turned into Darkness, & the Moon into Blood; before the Great & the Terrible Day of the Lord come.*

Now, I would hereupon humbly propose these Three Remarks;

The first Remark is; That if *Immediately after* the Destruction brought on the Jewish *Temple & City & Countrey & Nation*, which our SAVIOUR calls, *The Tribulation of those Days*, there were such *Prodigious Occurrences*, as those that are foretold by Him, and by the *Prophetic Spirit*, in *Luke* and *Matthew* and *Joel*, We cannot but own that the World has actually seen sufficient *Signs*, to assure us, That His being *Reveled from Heaven in flaming Fire*, is to be look'd for.[4]

The Second Remark is; That if in the Succeeding Ages the World has been alarmed, with many astonishing *Repetitions* of such [ms. III, v42] Prodigies, the *Signs* of that Grand Event are still the more Speaking, the more Potent, and should have the more Notice taken of them.

The Third Remark is This; That if the *Signs* which are *Already Past*, should not be those which our Lord intended in the Prophecies wherewith He has instructed us, yett they will admirably serve to *describe* the *Conflagration* to us; and help us to understand *in what Manner* it will be accomplished.

These Remarks will Qualify us, to Read the History of some Occurrences, which it may be have not yett been Commonly Readd with such Apprehensions as there should be in those that are *wise, & will observe these things*:

(1.) Signs from *Vesuvio*.

And in the First Place, Lett it be now observed, That not long after the *Spirit poured out upon all Flesh*, yea, while it was doing, in the *Gifts* of our Ascended SAVIOUR unto His Primitive Church, and *Immediately after the Tribulation of those Dayes*, in the Destruction & the Dispersion of the *Jewish Nation*, yea, in the very Days of *Titus*, the Emperour, who was the Grand Instrument of it; there was an *Eruption* of the famous Mount *Vesuvius*, which as Dr. *Burnet* says very truly, *was accompanied with such Prodigies & Commotions in the Heavens & the Earth, as made it look like the Beginning of the Last Conflagration.*[5] Without running the Hazards of Admiral *Pliny*, who with the Price of his Life paid for his Curiosity, in approaching too near the Sulphureous Ebullitions of the Mountain, [I suppose, to obtain more Matter for his *Natural History*:] We will take a Short Account of it, from a *Pagan Historian*, of whom we can have no Manner of Apprehension, that he had in his View, the Coming of our SAVIOUR, and the *Signs* of it, whereto he was an utter Stranger; and therefore his Account may be the more Surprizing to us.[6] Tis *Dion Cassius*, who is look'd upon, as one [ms. III, 43] of the *Best Writers*, about the *Roman Affairs*; and who tells us, [Lib. 66.] "That there were first *Fearful Sights and Great Signs* in the Air: Yea, *Viri multi et magni omnem Naturam Humanam excedentes, quales exprimuntur Gigantes, partim in ipso monte, partim in Agro circumjacente, ac in oppidis interdiu noctuqe terram obire, atqe aera permeare videbantur.* And *Then* the *Earth* began to *Tremble* and *Quake*, and the *Concussions* were so Great, that the Ground seem'd in Sundry Places to rise and boil up, and in others the tops of the Mountains either sunk in or tumbled down. At the same time, there were Great *Noises* and *Sounds* heard; whereof some were subterraneous, like Thunder within the Earth; others were above-ground, like hideous Groans and Bellowings. The SEA ROARED; The *Heavens* rattled with a Fearful Noise; And then came a Sudden & a *Mighty Crash*, as if the Frame of Nature had broke, or all the Mountains of the Earth had fallen down at once. At Length *Vesuvius* burst, and threw out of its Womb, first, huge Stones; Then a Vast Quantity of *Fire* and *Smoke*, so as the AIR was all DARKENED, and the SUN was hid, as if he had been under a Great Eclipse. The DAY was turned into NIGHT, and Light into Darkness; and the frighted People fancied they saw the Shapes and Images of GIANTS, in the Smoke, and heard the SOUND of TRUMPETS. Others thought, the WORLD was returning to its first *Chaos*, or going to be ALL consumed with FIRE. In this general Confusion and CONSTERNATION, they knew not where to be safe: Some run out of the Fields into the Houses; others, out of the Houses into the Fields: Those that were at *Sea*, hastened to Land, and those that were at *Land* assay'd for *Sea*: Still thinking every Place to be safer, than *That* where they were. Besides grosser Lumps of Matter, there was thrown out of the Mountain such a Prodigious Quantity of Ashes, as covered the Land and Sea, and fill'd the Air; so as, besides other Damages, the Birds, Beasts, & Fishes, with Men, Women, & Children, were destroy'd before it; Yea, Two Entire Cities, *Herculaneum* and *Pompeios*, were overwhelmed with a showre of

Ashes, as the People were sitting in the Theatre. Nay, [ms. III, v43] these Ashes were carried by the Winds, over the Mediterranean, into *Africa*, and as far as into *Egypt* and *Syria*. And at *Rome*, they so choak'd the Air on a sudden, as to hide the Face of the Sun. Whereupon, the People, not knowing the Cause, as not having yett gott the News from *Campania*, of the Eruption of *Vesuvius*, could not imagine what the Reason should be; but thought the HEAVENS and the EARTH were coming together; the SUN coming down, and the EARTH going to take its Place above." Thus *Dio* does Entertain us; thus Astonish us![7]

Here was a *Becon* fired, with which the *Whole World* was then alarumed, and the Ashes flew from *Europe* as far as into *Africa*, and *Asia*. *Tantus inexhaustis erupit faucibus ardor Ac Vastor.*—So sang *Hieronymus Borgius*[8]—It is a Marvellous Thing, that the *Christian* Writers have left us no large Records of it; and of the awful & joyful Frames, with which they thought of a *Redemption drawing nigh*, & look'd for the Coming of their Glorious REDEEMER in it: and, the more than Humane Figures appearing in the *Fires*, to be the *Angels*, which He had promised them for their Deliverers: Nor have we any Monuments, how they might at this Terrible time *Intercede for Sodom*! If they did leave any, they are lost. But the Providence of our GOD having ordered it, that it must be handed so fully down unto Posterity by *Pagan* Writers, who were *Aliens* from the Faith of our New Testament, the Matter is rendred not only the most *Unquaestionable*, but also the more *Admirable* & *Serviceable* for our Purposes. Wherefore to confirm the Report of *Dio*, Lett us call in another Evidence. It shall be That of Governour *Pliny*; an Eye-Witness of the Matter; who in Two Epistles to the famous *Tacitus*, that had enquired after it, and the Fate of his *Uncle* in it, [Lib. 6. Ep. 16. & 20.] has described that Eruption of Mount *Vesuvius*, just as *Dio* has done it.[9] It is impossible for *us* to Read, what he writes, about the Amazing *Flames*, & *Smokes*, and mighty Showres of *Cinders* which then filled the World; The Swelling & Roaring of the *Sea*; The Shaking and Heaving of the *Earth*; and the unutterable Consternation of the People, *their Hearts failing them for fear, & for looking after those things that were coming*: their Cries to Heaven for Mercy; the Methods they took [ms. III, 44] to cover themselves from the *Puntice-Stones* falling about their Ears;[10] the anxious Cries of Relatives losing one another, in a Darkness like that of a Dungeon which was come upon them; and the dreadful Devastations wherein vast Multitudes of People perished; But we must therein apprehend a Lively Picture, of the *Conflagration* which we are now to look for.—

Among the Remarkables, which this *Pliny* the Younger mentions of this Event, there is one very *Minute Circumstance*, that seems to be mention'd not without a Special Indigitation[11] of the Divine Providence, to point out the Intention of it. The Prophecy of *Joel*, had foretold, That when the *Spirit of GOD* should be *poured out upon all Flesh*, [by means whereof the *Gospel* was to be *preached throughout the whole World*, before the Destruction of *Jerusalem*,] there should be—*Pillars of Smoke*: To intimate, that GOD would be as Terrible a *Judge* unto all those who did not embrace the *Gospel*, as by the like Terrors on Mount *Sinai*, He declared He would be to them who did not obey the

Law. Tis a Criticism of Dr. *Jackson*[12] upon it; That the Word in the *Original*, which we render, *Pillars*, properly signifies, *Palm-trees*. Now, *Pliny* expressing the First Apparition of what broke out on the Top of the Burning Mountain, uses this very Similitude: *Cujus formam non alia magna arbor, quam pinus expresserit*;[13] with a Long *Trunk*, and Spreading *Boughs* above. Had a *Palm-tree*, been as well known in *Italy*, as a *Pine-tree*, no doubt, *that* had been the Term for it.

The *Darkening* of the *Sun* and *Moon*, among the *Signs* given by our SAVIOUR, needs no further Interpretation, than what the Story has already given us. But, that of *Stars falling from Heaven*, has wondrously puzzled Interpreters. They who expound it of *Blazing Stars*, pretend that *Comets* may be called, *Stars falling from Heaven*, in their Elliptic Motions.—*Non placet.*[14] I find *Eugubinus* writing, *De Mundi Exitio*, takes much notice [ms. III, v44] of it; That the Greek Expositors, being utterly averse to the Thoughts of the *Conflagration* reaching the Proper *Stars*, will have this Passage to be understood of the *Devils*, who may be also called, *The Powers of Heaven*, and shall be Driven down from the *High Places* which are now occupied by the *Wicked Spirits*: and *fall from Heaven like the Lightening.*[15] And verily, This will be one *Great Thing*, and almost the *First Thing*, done, at the Coming of the Lord, when the *Heavens will be on Fire*. But what need of Straining so! It may justly be said, *The Stars are fallen from Heaven*, when we can see them no more; when we have lost the Sight of them there. Tis, because on the *Fourth Day* of the *Creation*, in the *Mosaic* History, (which after the first Verse extends no further than our Globe) the *Sun, Moon,* and *Stars*, first became visible, to our *Earth*, and the *Earth* was made capable of receiving Illuminations & other Influences from them, that they are spoken of as being *Then* first placed in the Firmament for us. Thus, when the *Stars of Heaven* are witheld from us, it may be aptly said, They are *fallen from Heaven* to us. And now, who sees not *This* also, most fearfully accomplished, in the *Vesuvian* Desolations![16]

Tis true; *Rome* the Inhabitants whereof were then prodigiously terrified, was not then overwhelmed: No; Thy Time is to come, O Daughter of *Babylon*. But in the Year following, when the Emperour *Titus* was gone to view the Calamities of *Campania*, the Countrey of the Burning Mountain; a Considerable Part of *Rome*, was consumed by *Fire* some say, Descending down from *Above*; others, issuing out of the *Ground*; which burnt for Three Days together. In this Fire many *Temples*, as well as other Dwellings were destroy'd; and among the rest, the Temple of *Jupiter Capitolinus*, unto which the Jews were enjoined a little before, to pay the Tribute, which they had formerly paid unto the Temple of GOD.

And that no *Signs* may be wanting; from the *Vesuvian* Eruption; there spred an Infection, which quickly produced a most grievous & wasting *Pestilence*: Added unto that which went a little before it, wherein the Bill of Mortality for [ms. III, 45] the City alone, was Ten Thousand a Day, for a considerable while together. Yea, there came on such a *Pestilence*, that it look'd as if the World were going to be dispeopled; and the Reliques of it remained, even to the time of our Martyr *Cyprian*.[17]

(2) Signs at *Antioch*.

Well, It might be said; *If they will not hearken to the Voice of the First Sign, they will beleeve the Voice of the Latter Sign*. Great EARTHQUAKES, must afford it. Accordingly, within a very little while after this, and before our Apostle *John* could well be cold in his Grave, one of the most horrendous *Earthquakes* that ever shook the World was produced, with Circumstances that obliged all the World unto some Cognisance of it.[18] The Emperour *Trajan* was now Wintering at the City of *Antioch*; which was the *Second City* of the Empire; and at this time (as Dr. *Jackson* expresses it,) *The Whole Worlds Representative.* Here a Stupendous *Earthquake*, now sett the *Whole World* a trembling.[19] Amazing *Lightenings*, and *Thunders* join'd with it, in doing horrible Execution. The *Sea* wrought and rose and roar'd. The *Earth* heav'd; The *Trees* were thrown up by the roots; The *Winds* rattled so, as to drown the Cries of the Perishing People; The *Air* was fill'd with Dust, & so darkened, that People could not see one another; and the *Heats* become so violent, that many hid themselves naked under ground, where they were famished, the Continual Shaking of the Earth so frighting of them, that they durst not come forth to releeve themselves.[20] *Multitudes, Multitudes*, were buried in the Ruines of the Tumbling Houses. The Emperour himself narrowly escaped with his Life, being drawn out at a Window, [*Dion* says, *By no mortal Creature!*] but so terrified, that he durst not venture to come under a Roof any where, for many Days after the *Earthquake* was over.[21] [ms. III, v45] *He that was on the House-top durst not come down, to take any thing out of his House; and he that was in the field returned not back to take his Clothes;* What had been foretold unto others, now took the Poor *Antiochians*, a Learned Writer says, *At the Rebound.*[22] And as for them, who *gave Suck in those Days*, the Roman Writer tells us, An infinite Company of all Sorts, were starved by their close Imprisonment in Houses, the Foundations whereof were sunk, & only the Roof appearing: Only *One Woman* was found Alive, which had sustained herself & her Child by her *Milk*; and another Child in such a Cavity was found alive, *Sucking* at the Breast of the Expired Mother.[23] Yea, There was hardly any Sort of Disaster which did not now befall the miserable Children of Men. The Mischiefs were not confined unto *Antioch*, and the Cities of the adjacent Regions; which had a dreadful Destruction brought upon them. A Vast Number, not only of Souldiers, but also of other People, were now repaired thither, from *all Parts* of the World, on the account of the *Emperours* residing there. *Embassadors*, with their Attendants; *others* with *Petitions*; *others* with *Merchandises*; and Vast Throngs, to see the *Plays* now celebrated there. In the Midst of the *Plays*, this *Destruction from GOD* came upon them; and, as *Dion* remarks, the Damage did redound unto all the Subjects of the *Whole Roman Empire.* Thus did the Glorious Judge of the World, give to the *Whole*

World, another *Sign*, of what He would bring upon it, at His Coming, in His *Kingdome*; after some Further Trial should be made of the Disposition in Men, to praefer the Kingdome of *Antichrist* before it.

But as our SAVIOUR foretels, *Great Earth-quakes in DIVERSE PLACES*, none that [ms. III, 46] know any thing of the Roman Story, can be ignorant, how prodigiously *Earthquakes* were multiplied in *Diverse Places*, a little before & a little after, that Memorable One at *Antioch*.

And whereas *Famines* also make an Article of our SAVIOURs Praedictions, tis well-known, how much the World in *those Days* languished under them. In particular, the *Drought* that follow'd these *Earth-quakes*, and the Extreme Heat of the Earth, caused the Fruits of the Earth, to fail at such a rate, that the *Non-plus'd World* was at an horrid Loss for a Subsistence; Incredible Myriads *had their skin black like an Oven, because of the terrible Famine*; they *pined away, stricken through, for Want of the Fruits of the Field*. Yea, as *Jerom* expresses it; *Ad nefandos cibos erupit esurientium rabies*; And as *Lipsius* declares upon it; *De Fame, nihil profecto nos, aut nostra aetas, videmus, si videmus Antiqua.*[24]

Now, in the Instances already given, the *Signs*, that might awaken & enlighten the Minds of Men, to expect what is to come, when the *Lord our GOD shall come*, and the *Perdition of Ungodly Men* shall be accomplished, were so Abundant, that if there should never be any more exhibited, Mankind has no Cause to say, *We see not our Signs*; or the Sleeping World must own, *The Signs have appeared, & we have not seen them*. I am sure, no less a Person than our Penetrating *Jackson* sees Cause hereupon to labour for the *Perswading* of his Reader, *That for ought any Man knows, or for any Praecedent Sign that can be expected, it may this Night sound to Judgment*. He justly adds, *Watch we therefore; and pray continually!*

[ms. III, v46]

(3) Repeted Signs; especially *Sicilian* ones.

But our Compassionate SAVIOUR, *Not willing that any should perish, but that all should come to Repentance*, has follow'd the World, with *Incessant Warnings* of His Coming, & of the *Destruction* which is now ready to overtake it. There has been a *Repetition*; a frequent *Repetition*, a wondrous *Repetition*, of the *Signs*, in several Successive Ages, and even in *Our Days*.

First, For *Burnings*. How many times have there been fresh & fierce Eruptions of Mount *Vesuvio*, since that in the Days of *Titus*! There was One, wherein as *Ammianus Marcellinus* tells it the Ashes of the Burning Mountain, covered and obscured all *Europe*; and threw the People as far off as *Constantinople*, into such Consternation, that the Emperour *Leo* had not Courage enough to stay in the City; and on the Twelfth of *November* they kept an Anniversary Commemoration of it.[25] What our *Sandys* relates of this amazing Mountain, is well worth a serious Perusal.[26] But the mention of all the rest, shall be superseded, with the Words of *Kirker*, who notably expresses the *Use*, which the glorious GOD calls Mankind, & which we are now endeavouring to make of the *Shocking Spectacle*. This Gentleman visiting the Mountain, in the Year 1638. was cast into an horrible Amazement at the View of what he there mett withal; & breaks forth into these Words upon it. "I saw it all over of a Light Fire, with a dreadful Combustion, and a Stench of *Sulphur* and burning *Bitumen*: at which being astonished, methoughte I beheld the Habitation of Hell; wherein there seemed nothing to be wanting, but the Apparitions of Devils & of damned Spirits. I then observed horrible Bellowings & Roarings in the Mountain, and inexpressible Stench, Smokes mixt with Darkish Globes of Fire, which both the Bottom & Sides of the Mountain continually belched forth from Eleven Several Places;—*O the Depth of the Riches of the Wisdome & Knowledge of GOD! How Incompre-*[ms. III, 47]*hensible are thy Ways! If thou shewest thy Power against the Wickedness of Mankind, in such formidable and PORTENTOUS Prodigies and OMENS of Nature: What shall it in that LAST DAY, wherein the Earth shall be destroy'd by thy Wrath, and the Elements shall melt with fervent Heat!"* Thus our *Cicero.*[27]

But is *Vesuvio* the only Monitor of a World *buried in Sleep and Vice?* The World has yett *Pyrites* enough in Stock, diffused every where, to keep us at that Note; *Lord, my Flesh trembles for fear of thee, and I am afraid of thy Judgments.* Allow me to *repeat* a little.[28]

What Commotions, what Convulsions has this Planet, in many Parts of it suffered from Subterraneous *Combustions*, and such Amassments of those *Igneous Particles*, which are an *Eternal Fire*, breaking forth at those formidable *Spiracles*, which if they had not been afforded, the Globe would, no doubt, have been torn to Peeces![29] If we range over the *Globe*, a little Geography soon informs us, of many Regions that are signalized and affrighted with them. Yea, such are the Numbers of them, that there needs another *Varenius* to perfect the Reckoning left unfinished by the former.[30] The Empires of *Japan*, (in which alone, as unknown a Countrey as it is, we know of Eight *Volcano's*) of *China*, of *Indoustan*, have their share of Ignivomous Mountains; which give the *Terrors of the Shadow of Death* unto the Beholders of them. The *Islands* that are *East* of those Countreys, and those that are *South*, in many Places undergo a direful *Fever* and *Ague* from them. They are in both of the *Java's*; where Ten thousand People have been killed at a time with 'em: And *Banda* has the Smoke & the Noise thereof sensible at a Mighty Distance.[31] The Relations which our *Philosophical Transactions* give us of the Modern *Volcano's* in the *Molucco Islands*, can't be read, without a *Fear* that shall carry *Amazement* with it.[32] At the *Northward*, we find the Outbreakings of the *Infernal Fires*, on the Shores of *Tartary*;[33] To the *Southward* we find them at New *Guinea*, and the *Lands afar off. Africa* has at least Eight of these *Fiery Furnaces* far surpassing that which *Nebuchadnezzar* kindled on the Plane of [ms. III, v47] *Dura.*[34] And those Islands, which are made such in the Midst of the *Atlantic*, by the Sinking of the Vast Countreys to the *Westward*, between the Continent & them, in the Matchless *Earthquake*, whereof we have such Probable Traditions in Monuments of remote Antiquity. These are not without them. *Fayal* is well-known to Travellers.[35] In the Year, 1638. At St. *Michael*, after Earthquakes for Eight Days together, in the Midst of the Sea, Six Miles from the *Pic*, at the Depth of an hundred & twenty foot under Water, there broke out a *Fire*, which *many Waters could not quench*, nor the Ocean drown it.[36] It reach'd thro' the Water up to the very Clouds, carrying up with it, Water, Earth, Sand & Stones, whereof some were of Enormous Dimension, & falling back again into the Water, added considerably to the Noise of what was doing. The *Fish*, mighty shoals of them, were boiled unto Death, in this dreadful Caldron of the *Deep* thus *boiling as a Pott*. From a Collection of what was thus thrown up, there began a New Island, which grew anon to the Length of no less than Five Miles, and the Heighth of about Sixty Fathoms. As late as the Year 1720. the Inhabitants of *Tercera*, after praevious *Earthquakes*, were astonished at a *Fire*, that broke out in the Sea, near twenty Leagues to the South-East of them;[37] where they perceived anon a New Island risen, both in Length & in Breadth, of two Leagues Extent; which had still two Hummocks hideously flaming in it, with a Noise, as if there had been Fifty Canon at once continually firing: and throwing up Dust & Stones in incomputable and inconceivable Quantities. I am informed, it is again sunk into the Ocean. The Flammivomous *Volcano's* in *America*, are so many, that some, who might have thought of a better Name for it, have called it, *Vulcans Kingdome*: [ms. III, 48] amazed at the *Æstuaries*, that have so many & such bulky, Chimneys to them. There are no less than Fifteen of them, in the *Andian* Mountains of *Chili*; And if out of *Chili* we pass into *Peru*, they tell us, we shall there find as many more. And surely, The *Terra del Fuogo* must have something of them. The *North America* has them, as well as the *South*; Diverse besides that at *Nicaragua*. Some of our Islands have them. And, besides what is to be seen at St. *Christophers*, our *Monserat* has a Mountain sometimes uttering its Cautions, to the People there.[38] Those in *Europe*, every body is apprised of. Besides what is related by *Tacitus*, of one in *Germany* many ages ago, Mount *Carbo* in *Misnia* obliges People sometimes in our Days to think a little.[39] The Frozen Regions of *Lapland*, and *Iseland*, and *Groenland*, are not so cold, as to admitt of no *Burning Mountains* there. Even within the Polar Circle, *Hecla* that has the Shoulders of it covered with *Snow*, has its Belly fill'd with *Fire*; and in its rages, it vomits out, not only Dust & Stones & Ashes with its Flames, but also a Sort of a *Flaming Water*.[40] Visit *Greece*, and there you have particularly, the Island *Santorin*, in the *Archipelago*: formed in the Year, 726. much after the Manner of the Islands I just now showed you, by St. *Michael*, & by *Tercera*.[41] In the Year, 1670. another Island was after the like Manner formed in the neighbourhood of *Santorin*. But, *Italy, Italy*, is to be *Saluted* with a doleful *Clamour*, as a Countrey, singularly devoted for the Fate of *Sodom*, from the *Fires* in a dreadful Conservatory waiting for it. Here, we have already seen *Vesuvio*; And, with what a Shudd'ring Horror must one read *Kirkers* Description of his *Phlegraean* Plains. We shall hasten from them to *Sicily*; and without stopping at the *Vulcanello's* on the *Liparitan* Islands, and particularly, Mount *Strombola*, in its Vicinage, We can by no means be excused from a Visit unto the celebrated *Ætna*.[42]

ÆTNA! One of the *Ancient Mountains*! Famous for its *Flames* in very Early Antiquity! Long before *Virgil*, even more than Three Thousand Years ago, we find [ms. III, v48] it flaming: and, as an *Everlasting Fire*, it flames, and foams, and roars to This Day. The *Ætnaean* Eruptions that are upon Record, are more than we have here Occasion to enumerate. No body will wonder, that a *Caligula* was frighted at them.[43] The wide *Crater* on the Top of that Mountain, has been to whole *Nations* a *Cup of Trembling*. I will only *Single out*, that One Paroxysm, which the Mountain suffered, so lately as in the Year, 1669. whereof the Earl of *Winchelsea* was an Ey-Witness.[44] From the *Instructive* as well as *Affecting* Relation thereof, with which he and some others that were so, have entertained the World, I will also but *Single out* a few Passages, which may a little serve the Design we are upon, and show the *Significancy* of the Prodigy.

The *Sun* first appearing of a Pale and a Dead Colour, so unusual as to fright the People, there ensued a dreadful *Earthquake*, which was accompanied with such horrible Roarings of this *Monte Gibello*,[45] as added yett more to their Affrightment, and caused them to fly out of their Tumbling Houses: And yett the Reeling and Staggering People in the Fields, discerning the Earth in its Violent Concussions begin to open in diverse Places, the Dread of *going down alive into the Pitt*, brought them to such a Distraction, that their Behaviour was entirely that of People bereaved of their Senses. This was quickly followed by *Three terrible Eruptions*, at once, at a little distance from one another. The *Flames* mounted with an unparallel'd Noise, & Force, above an hundred Yards high; and the Roarings in the Bowels of the Mountain, were accompanied with the Thunders, that outsounded the Peals of Ten Thousand Ordinances. [ms. III, 49] Great Stones, whereof some were Three Hundred Pound Weight, were shott thro' the Air, and fell many Miles off; and the whole Air was at the same time filled with Smoke, and Cinders & Ashes, which fell as a Fiery Rain upon the Countrey. Yea, there was a Stone Fifteen foot long, slung out from the Mouth of the Furious Mountain, to a Miles distance; and then fell with such a Weight as to bury itself Eight foot under ground. What are our Silly *Bombs* to this! The *Sea* at this time, Ran much higher than was usual, and Roar'd with the *Mighty Voice of many Waters*. But that which was yett more amazing, was, *A Lake burning with Fire & Brimstone*: Or, a Mighty River of Melted and Burning Matter, which like an Inundation drown'd in a *Fiery Flood*, all the Countrey that it came unto. A *River of Fire*, which was mostly two Miles Broad, yea, there were Places where the Fiery Torrent was no less than Six or Seven Miles Broad, & sometimes Ten or Fifteen Fathoms deep, came down the Side of the Mountain, and marched slowly along, devouring & absorbing all that came in its Way, and forced its Way into the Sea for near a Mile, and there kept burning in the Midst of the Waters: with Red hott Stones, and Cinders & Ashes floating on the Surface of it: The River of a Fiery Red, the Stones of a Paler; All smoaking like a *Furnace of melted Iron*. Thus was the *Mountain carried into the Midst of the Sea; The Waters whereof roared & were troubled*. The Acute *Alphonsus Borelli*, the peerless Mathematician of *Pisa*, upon an accurate Survey, declared the Quantity of Matter thrown out of the Mountain at this time, to amount unto Ninety three Millions, Eight hundred thirty Eight-thousand, Seven hundred & fifty, Cubical Paces: and if it had been extended in Length upon the

Surface of the Earth, at the Breadth & the Depth of Three foot, it would have
reached above Ninety three Millions of Paces; which is more than four times
the Circuit of the Earth.⁴⁶ Almost Incredible! One says upon it, The greatest
Fictions of the Poets, about their *Acheron*, [ms. III, v49] and *Phlogeton*, & the
rest, are nothing to the Reality of these Occurrences.⁴⁷ At the same Time, it was
Remarkable, That the *Fowls of Heaven* lay dead in all Places, thro' the Poisonous Influence with which these Burnings reached them. The Lord *Winchelsea*
tells the *King* to whom he described this *Tophet; I assure Your Majesty, no Pen
can express how terrible it is: Nor can all the Art and Industry of the World,
quench or divert that which is burning in the Countrey. In forty days time, it
has destroyed the Habitations of twenty seven thousand Persons.*

Thus has *the Lord roared out of Zion*, and *uttered His Voice* unto a *World
lying in Wickedness.* From the Mouths of all those *Burning Mountains, Lo,
GOD sends forth His Voice, and that a mighty Voice.* The *Voice* of the Glorious
Lord, unto the World, from the Wide & Loud Mouths of these *Burning Mountains*, is; *Behold, O Sinful World, going on still in thy Trespasses: If thou wilt
go on, Behold, How thou shalt be dealt withal in the Day of my Pleading with
thee. Behold, How thy Earth shall be fitted with Burning Mountains, when I
shall descend in flaming Fire to take Vengeance on thee. Such things as were
done to the People, that were overwhelmed in the Ruines produced by these
Flaming Mountains, will be more universally done unto thee, in the Day of the
Lord, that shall burn like an Oven.* Such as This, is the *Voice* of our GOD; the
Man of Wisdome will hear it, and will conform unto it.⁴⁸

But now, Secondly; For *Earthquakes;* How many times has *Antioch* had
fearful Shocks given to it, since That in the Days of *Trajan?* In one of them
there perished more than Three Score Thousand People. The [ms. III, 50] *History of Earthquakes* would make almost an *Elephantine Volumn;* and cause an
Heart-quake in us, and almost a Swoon with Fear, to think, what an uncertain
Ground we Stand & Build upon, and how liable the Thin *Arched Roof,* over
the dark, hollow, & horrid Recesses of the *Subterraneous World* may be, to
break & sink, upon the Colluctation of Minerals there, or upon other unknown
Occasions.⁴⁹

Particular Countreys must make *Earthquakes* a Memorable Article, & almost
an *Epocha,* in their *History. England* has registred, how many of these, in
her *Chronicles!* One of which produced those *fearful Pitts,* which go by the
Name of *Hell-kettles.*⁵⁰ But none has had more than *Italy. Italy;* How often
hast thou seen, the *Earthquakes,* in which the Sea has overrun many Leagues
of the *Land,* and many Leagues of Land have been laid bare in the bottom of the
Sea; Ships have been convey'd unto the Tops of *Hills;* and Stately *Edifices* have
been demolished, yea, whole Cities destroyed! *Thirty thousand* Souls, yea *Forty
thousand* at a Time, have gone at once down into the *Hell-kettles.* Of What
Earthquakes there were before the Incarnation of our Lord, we have tis true,
tho' *Some,* yett not *Much,* Account! Not only in *Strabo* and others, but even
in Writings as early as *Herodotus,* yea, before him, in our *Sacred Scriptures,*
we find *Earthquakes* written of; *Austin* affirms, There had been one in *Libya,*

wherein an *hundred Cities* perished.[51] Be sure, *Tyre* and *Sidon* felt amazing *Earthquakes*, & vast Numbers of People were buried in the Ruines. In the Time of our Lords being on the *Earth*, we have an Account of One in which *Thirteen Cities* were destroy'd. And that which attended the Crucifixion of our Lord, not only splitt those Great Rocks, on which Travellers that are Judicious and Incredulous *Protestants*, behold at this day the incontestible *Remembrances*, but also, was felt all over the World.[52]

Whether *Sicily* were joined unto *Italy*, whether *Spain* unto *Africa*, whether *France* unto *Britain*, yea, [ms. III, v50] whether *North-America* to *Ireland*, until *Earthquakes* made the *Separation*, is *Uncertain*, tho' Great Literators have judged it *Probable*.[53] But since the Gospel of our Lord has been preached unto the World, we find *Earthquakes* much oftener *Occurring*, or at least oftener *Mentioned.* Some have thought that *Earthquakes* are not mentioned among the *Plagues* in the *Twenty Eighth* Chapter of *Deuteronomy*, because of a Transcendency in This beyond all other *Plagues*, which renders it a more Proper Vengeance for Sins under and against the *Glorious Gospel of the Blessed GOD.* Against all other Strokes, there may some Defence or other be thought upon: There can be none against This. It says, *Tho' they hide in the Top of Carmel, I will find them there.* And now, besides the *Earthquakes* more confined unto a few *Particular Countreys*, there have been some, of a much greater Extent, and a *Great Part of the World* has been in a Tremulous Posture & Horror from them. Thus *Ammianus Marcellinus* tells us; In the Year 365. *Horrendi Tremores per omnem orbis ambitum quassati sunt.*[54] Of that which did such Execution on the World, in the Year, 430. Authors assert, *That almost the whole World was affected with it.* And it continued shaking the World for Six Months together. The *Seventh* and *Eighth* Centuries had many such; in which the *Hell-kettles* had many Towns thrown into them. Thus it has been, when as our *Bulkley* wrote on an *Earthquake* in the Countrey where I am now Writing. *Nutant fulcra orbis, mundi compago soluta est, ex vultu irati contremit ille Dei:* [ms. III, 51] But tho' I wave the rest, it is hardly possible to pass over the *Earthquake* which tore the Island of *Sicily* to Peeces, in the Month of *January:* 1692.[55]

Come, *Behold the Works of the Lord, what Desolations He has made in the Earth.* On the Seventh Day of the Month, Mount *Etna* began to Roar; and it held on, to do so for Two Days together. It was an *Alarm!* On the *Ninth* Day, the Roaring abated, and an *Earthquake* began to Jog many Cities & Villages, which terrified many People, to begin the doing of what their Distraction would allow them to do for their Safety. But on the *Eleventh* came on a Shake, felt by the whole Island; Which tho' it continued but about Six Minutes, the *Desolations made in the Earth*, by it surpass all Imagination. The Ancient and Opulent City of *Catania*, which was most pleasantly situated, & had an University, and very many Persons of Quality, & Illustrious Families, and about Four & Twenty Thousand Inhabitants, in a Minute sunk down forever out of Sight, with a Noise as loud as if Ten Thousand Canons had been at once discharged. A New Little Mountain advanced & appeared near it; which yett presently again became Invisible. Under the same dismal Calamity fell the Ancient and Renowned City of

Syracuse; whereto there belonged Sixteen Thousand Inhabitants.[56] Tho' some of these fled from the Storm, on the *Ninth* day, & so were saved; yett on the *Eleventh,* Two Thirds of the Buildings were thrown down, & in the *Earthquake* were slain *Seven thousand Men,* who were buried in the Rubbish. The City of,—But it would fill Pages to particularize them all. In short, *Whole Cities,* that had *Thousands* of Inhabitants in them, were in a Minute swallow'd [ms. III, v51] up, and not one Person left alive to tell what had happened. Nothing to be seen, but a *Pitt* or a *Pond,* where once Flourishing Cities, and very Populous. O Earthquake, *Thou hast destroyed Cities, their Memorial is perished with them.* In some of the *Cities,* the Poor *Idolaters* fled into their *Churches,* and cried unto their Idols; *They cried, but there was none to save them!* They, and their *Churches* & their *Idols* went all down together. In one Place, the frighted People *ran to a Strong Tower;* but not one where they could be *Safe.* The Heavens blazed with *Lightnings;* one Flash whereof struck the Powder, which blew up Eleven hundred of them. In the whole, the biggest Part of Two Hundred Thousand Souls, were thus *brought into Desolation as in a Moment; They were utterly consumed in Terrible Ways.* And the Damages done, were beyond all Calculation; whole Ages cannot repair them. *Come, and see the Works of GOD! He is terrible in His doing toward the Children of Men.*

    It was in the Same Year, that the Island of *Jamaica,* drank of the Same Cup.[57] That *Principal Mart* of the English West *Indies,* on Jun. 7. 1692. underwent an *Earthquake,* which after a *calm,* & clear & fair Morning, about half an hour after Eleven, in a few Minutes threw down almost all the *Houses,* & *Bridges,* and *Mills,* & *Sugar-Works,* in the whole Countrey; rent the *Rocks* to Peeces, & threw the *Mountains into the Sea.* The *Earth* sunk, & the *Sea* came rolling in, & the Harbour was covered with the *Dead Bodies* of the Inhabitants. In Places without Number, the *Earth Opened,* & out of the dire *Chasms* there spouted up vast Quantities of Water. And tho' some that were swallowed up in these *Chasms,* were thrown up again alive, and are now living in [ms. III, 52] my Neighbourhood, yett others were squeezed & crushed unto Death, by the Ground closing on them, or they were wholly *interred* with an Absorption there. The Town of *Port-royal* alone lost fifteen hundred Persons: And at the same time, while the People had the *Earth* trembling under their Feet, & hideously gaping for its Prey, they had the *Heavens,* rumbling over their Heads with mighty Thunderclaps & hott flashes and firebals flying there, and the *Sea* rolling in, with its Billows passing over them: So that the Reporter says, *Tis impossible for Tongue to speak or Pen to write the Terrors of the Day.*[58] I may add; If we can read them unterrified, *Ambrose's* Exclamation will be called for; *O Hominum pectora, saxis duriora.*[59] Truly, the *Desolations* made by all those *Earthquakes,* have been but the *Decimations* of Rebellious *Legions;* And Intimations, of what the People of the *Earth* going on in Rebellions, and saying to the Almighty, *Depart from us,* must expect, in the Day when *the Lord our GOD shall come, & all His Holy Ones with Him,* and they shall *Flee,* as People *fled from before the Earthquake in the Days of Uzziah the King of Judah.*

    And what? Is there nothing *Signal* in these Things? We are told by *Josephus,* that about the Time of the Battel at *Actium*, so much talk'd of, [when GOD *shook the Earth & the Sea & the Dry Land*, and He that is *what all Nations desire*, immediately *Came!*] there was a sad *Earthquake*, wherein *Judaea* was particularly & astonishingly *Shaken*, and near Ten Thousand People were slain by the Fall of Houses upon them there.[60] Tis likely, that in that *Earthquake*, a *Tower* built over the *Portico's* at the Pool of *Bethesda*, fell, and slew *Eighteen* that were there waiting for a Cure. Now upon this, our SAVIOUR said unto all the People; *Those Eighteen, upon whom the Tower of Siloam fell, and slew them, think Ye that they were Sinners above all the Men who dwelt in Jerusalem? I tell you, Nay; But except Ye Repent, Ye shall all likewise perish.* And the many Thousands, who [ms. III, v52] were miserably overwhelmed in the Ruines of the *Temple* & of the *City*, when the *Towers fell upon them*, found it so.[61] Verily, with a Voice much louder than the Murmurs of the most rugient *Earthquakes*,[62] we have our Glorious Lord in these Dispensations calling unto us; *O Inhabitants of the Earth, and the Earthly-minded Ones, who have Your Souls already buried there; The Thousands, and Hundreds of Thousands, that have perished in the Earthquakes, which convinced them that in all their Hopes of Satisfaction from what the Earth could afford them, they built on a rotten Foundation; Think Ye, that these were Sinners above the rest of the World, who are going on in the Ways of their Folly & approve their Sayings? Nay, If the World will not Repent, it shall all Perish. And because the World will go on in Abominations unrepented of, it shall perish in the Desolation; wherein more extensive Earthquakes, will join with the Fire of my Jealousy, to make the Harvest of the whole Earth an Heap in the Day of Grief & of desperate Sorrow.*

But, alass, as there was a great *Earthquake* in the Hours of a *Battel* between those two great High-Way Men who were disputing the Empire of the World; But the *Business* of the *Battel* so engaged the Combatants, that they took not the least notice of it: thus, People will be generally so engaged in the *Business* of *This World*, that the *Voice* of GOD unto them in all these *Earthquakes*, is what they will take as little notice of.[63]

But, the *Impiety* of our *Stupidity*! We may wonder at what a Bishop of *Sicily* writes; That at the very Time of the *Burning*, wherewith Ætna drove the People to their Devotions, there were Considerable Troops of Robbers, which took the Opportunity of the General [ms. III, 53] Confusion, to steal, & pillage, & murder; and committ most infandous Robberies: Whole Cities were so apprehensive of their Depraedations, that nothing but a Quick Dispatch of them on the Gallows could putt a Stop to them. We may wonder at what the Minister of *Jamaica* writes; That at the very Time of the *Earthquake* there, a Vile Crue took the Opportunity of the General Confusion, to sieze on whatever they pleased, without any regard unto the Owners; to break open Houses, & rush into Shops, and carry away all they could, before the very faces of the Owners; to Rob them in the open Street, of the Things which they were carrying away for their Security; while others were doing the like Mischiefs on the Waters, and stripping the Carcases of the Dead with the utmost Inhumanity; And all this while, belching out against Heaven continual Volleys of Cursed Oathes & Blasphemies: And the Body of the People remain'd so unreformed, that he says; *We have Cause to fear, the Judgment of* Sodom *may be our Next Punishment.* But after all; What is the *Impiety* of a Stupid, & Sottish, & Senseless World, sleighting the *Warnings* it has had, in its *Burnings* and its *Earthquakes,* but all of a Peece with what is our Wonder, in *Sicily* and in *Jamaica!*[64]

(4) The Becon fired at *Jerusalem.*

And now; Are these all the *Signs,* with which the World has been admonished, of a Day, wherein *Destruction upon Destruction shall be cried, & the whole Earth shall be spoiled;* and Men shall *behold the Earth, & Lo, it shall be without form & void; & the Heavens, & they shall yeeld no Light;* They shall *behold the Mountains, & they shall tremble, & the Hills, & they shall be moved?*[65] No; There has been One *Sign* more, and a *Repeted* One. And certainly, it might have been enough to have left us inexcusable, if our Glorious Lord had said; *This Generation seeketh after a Sign, and there shall be no Sign given it, but the Sign given in the* Destruction *of Judaea* & *of Jerusalem.* It [ms. III, v53] pleased the Glorious One, to sett up the *Jewish Nation* even in *the Midst of the Earth,* for the Instruction of the *Whole World;* that from His Dispensations towards that Nation, all the World might learn what would be the Consequences of *Obedience* unto Him, or of *Rebellion* against Him, and what is to be expected in the *Kingdome* of GOD. And more particularly in the *Destruction* brought upon that *Sinful Nation, a People that were laden with Iniquity, a Seed of Evil Doers,* GOD would exhibit unto all the World, a little, but a lively, Representation of what the *Whole World* of the like *Evil-doers* are to look for. Accordingly, Behold, A *Progressive* Proceedure in the *Days of Vengeance!* The *Destruction* brought by the King of the *Chaldaean Babylon* upon the *Jewish Nation,* was but an *Earnest,* or *Foretaste,* of what was brought upon it, by the King of the *Roman Babylon:* The Lamentations of *Jeremiah,* were not only an *History* of what they suffered from *Nebuchadnezzar,* but also a *Prophecy* of what they suffered from *Vespasian.* In the *Double Destruction,* the *former* was as much exeeded by the *latter,* as the *Type* is by the *Antitype.*[66] Yea, In the Praedictions referring to the *former,* there are Passages which are not known to have been entirely fulfilled before the *latter.* Now, that the *Progression* may go on; in the *Final Destruction* of *Jerusalem,* what an astonishing *Figure* was there of what shall be done, in the *End of all things,* which now *is at hand!* I will not here insist upon the Remark, That as the Crime of the Jews lay not so much in the Denying of GOD the FATHER, as in the Denying of GOD the SON, so, it must be not the Emperour who was the *Father,* but he who was the *Son,* that executed the *Vengeance* of Heaven upon them; And thus, *The FATHER has committed all Judgment unto the SON,* for the Executing of His *Vengeance* on a World that He is infinitely offended at. But what I Remark is, That the *Resemblance* which there was in the *Judaeical Desolations,* to those which the World shall undergo at the *Coming* of the Lord, was as expressive as can be imagined. For first, with what *Fire* were they carried on? The [ms. III, 54] *Children of Wrath* saw their *Towns* laid in Ashes; the *City of their Solemnities* in *Flames* that reached up to Heaven; And of their *Temple* they might renew their doleful Ejulations. *Our Holy & our beautiful House, where our Fathers praised thee, is burnt up with Fire; and all our pleasant things are laid waste.* Yea, The Harbinger of our Lord, a *Prophet and more than a Prophet,* warning them of the *Wrath to come,* with an Eye to what yett remains & hastens to be done, told them of an *Unquenchable Fire* for the *Chaff.* And how emphatically was this in Part fulfilled, when *Titus* would fain have preserved the *Temple,* but Souldiers agitated by a Superiour Spirit, in spite of his Orders *fired* it; and when he exerted himself unto his uttermost for the *Quenching* of it, his Orders all signified nothing, but it proved an *Unquenchable Fire.*[67] But, Oh! the hideous *Cries* of them who perished with it! And, then, for the *Number* of the *Slain.* According to the Divine Comminations, *Their Table was made their Snare.* And the Vast Confluence of People from all Parts, to celebrate the *Feast* of their *Passover* which was the very time the *Enemy* now took to *Desire their Land,* [which Circumstance, by the way, argued, that the *Passover* was what GOD now *required not,*] shutt them up for the *Slaughter* which they were now *fatted* for. *Tacitus* makes them Six hundred Thousand, *Josephus* makes them Eleven hundred Thousand, who perished in that Siege; besides what were cutt off in all the rest of *Palaestine,* & some other Countreys; Thus it was in the *Battel of the Day of the Lord.*[68] But with how Resembling Strokes, was the *Day of the Lord* pourtray'd in these Occurrences! Here was not only the *Battel of the Warriour with confused Noise, & Garments rolled in Blood;* but also one that was *with Burning & fuel of Fire.* One cannot from the Pen of their own Historian, form an *Idaea,* of the Superb & Stately *Edifices* horribly blazing & falling; the Anguish of the Desperate People beyond that of a *Travailing Woman,* looking & howling at one another; [ms. III, v54] the Shrieks of *Prayers* for Deliverance, in vain made unto inexorable Justice; the horrendous Noises & Clamours, and universal Confusion, that accompanied the whole Transaction; but at the same time he has an *Idaea* of the Condition which the *Whole World* shall by the *General Conflagration* be thrown into.

Now, as it was of old a thing that the *Jewish Nation* could be reminded of, *The Lord spake unto you from out of the Midst of the Fire;* This Nation, with all its *precious & pleasant Things,* was now on *Fire;* And *Our GOD,* becoming thus a *Consuming Fire* unto them, He *speaks from out of the Midst of that Fire,* unto the rest of the Nations. His Thundring Voice *from out of the Midst of that Fire,* is That; [Jer. XXV. 29.] *Lo, I begin to bring Evil on the City which is called by my Name, and should you be utterly unpunished? You shall not be unpunished; For I will call for a Sword upon all the Inhabitants of the Earth, saith the Lord of Hosts.* What the Glorious GOD speaks unto the *Whole World,* in what He did, when *Jerusalem Remembred not her Last End, but came down wonderfully, and there was no Sorrow like unto her Sorrow, & what was done to her, when GOD afflicted her, in the Day of His fierce Anger, and from Above He sent a Fire into her Bones;* it was of this Importance; *Behold, O all Ye Nations,*

who refuse to pay your Homage to the SON of GOD, Behold, Something of
what you shall undergo in the Day When He shall speak to you in His Wrath;
and you shall perish in and for the Way that you take. Yea, His Wrath will
quickly burn; and then, Blessed will they only be found, that have Beleev'd &
Obey'd that Glorious One.[69]

[ms. III, 55] After all these Things, what need we ask for any further Description of the *Conflagration*, which we have before us? In the *Signs* we have seen given of it, we have it plainly & fully enough described unto us; and it is *evidently sett forth as flaming before our Eyes*. But, perhaps, it may add a little to the Impression of it on our Minds, if we employ a few Lines of Dr. *More*, on this Occasion. Our Glorious Lord,—[*he so expresses it*,] "will cause such an Universal Thunder and Lightning, that it shall rattle over all the Quarters of the Earth, & discharge such Claps of *Unextinguishable Fire*, that it will do sure Execution wherever it falls. The Ground being excessively heated, the *Subterraneous Mines* of Combustible Matter will also take *Fire*; which inflaming the inward Exhalations of the *Earth*, will cause a terrible Murmer under ground: so that the *Earth* will seem to *Thunder* against the Tearing and Rattling of the Heavens, and all will be filled with sad remugient *Echo's*. *Earthquakes*, and Eruptions of *Fire*, there will be every where; and whole *Cities* and *Countreys* swallowed down, by the Vast Gapings and Wide Divulsions of the Ground.— And this *fiery Vengeance* shall be so Thirsty, that it shall drink deep of the very *Sea*; nor shall the *Water* quench her devouring Appetite, but excite it.— The whole *Earth* shall be enveloped in one entire Cloud, of an unspeakable Thickness; which will cause more than *Egyptian* Darkness; which added to the Choaking *Heat* and *Stench*, will compleat this *External Hell*."[70]

Most livelily *painted*! But permitt me over again to say it; As I have my Friends agreeing with me, when we have had our View of a Caged *Lion*; *That the Lion really is more fierce, than he is or can be painted*: We may most certainly say so, of that *Ariel*, by which this *Earth* is one day to be *devoured*, and made a *Sacrifice* to the *Vengeance* of an Incensed & an Infinite GOD.

VII. The CONFLAGRATION described.

The World will have no Expectation of any other, but that, *All things will continue as they were from the Beginning of the Creation*: They will be besotted and buried in a most profound Security; pleased with the *Dreams* that proceed from its *Opiates & Amusements*. Mankind will have no more Apprehension of any Mighty & Sudden *Change* to come upon the World, than the *Chaldaean* Court was of a *Cyrus* being in the Palace before the Morning, when the Unknown Hand was beginning to write the, *Mene Tekel*, on the Wall, and *the Night of their Pleasure was turned into Fear* unto them. *Old* as well as *Young*, will *walk in the Ways of their Heart*, such *Ways* as an *Evil Heart of Unbeleef* inclines unto, & *in the Sight of their Eyes*, and so as to do whatever is *Right in their own distorted Eyes*; Altogether unmindful of any *Judgment* that they shall be brought into.—All Sorts of People, will promise themselves, *Goods laid up for many Years*. Men of *Business*, will be very *Busy*, and violently pursue the *Scent* of Methods to build & fill *Houses*, of which their *Inward Thoughts* will be, *That they will continue forever*. *Wicked* Men will be engaged in the Prosecution of their *Voluptuous* and their *Malicious* and their *Unrighteous* Purposes, as if they were never to be called unto any Account for their Wickedness. And, *they that walk after the Flesh in the Lust of Uncleanness*, will be wallowing in their Unclean & Unchast and Brutal Practices, without the least regard unto a *Day of Judgment*, wherein the *Unjust*, and these *chiefly, shall be punished*: and as *far from Fear*, will they be as the *Blinded* Wretches of *Sodom* were, the Night before the *Vengeance of Eternal Fire* came down, & *Hell* was rained from *Heaven* upon them. How many Millions will have their *Hearts overcharged with Surfeiting & with Drunkenness*! Controversies about *Religion* will be managed in a very *Irreligious* Manner, by Men *smiting their Fellow-Servants*, and perswaded *That the Lord will delay His Coming*. The *Roman Legions* of *Antichrist* will be carrying on the wonted *Persecutions* of the Faithful; *Edicts* will roar, *Dragoons* will rage, *Protestants* will be treated like *Sheep for the Slaughter*; and *Rome* will Flatter itself, with its old Epithet, *Eternal*, vainly putt upon it. They that have Real PIETY distinguishing of them, will be generally *Slumbring*: And a Misinterpretation of *Prophecies*, deluding them [ms. III, 56] into an Imagination, of *Happy Times* to arrive, & be long enjoy'd by the Church of GOD upon Earth, before the Coming of the Lord. In a Word, *All fast Asleep!*[1]—

—Lo, All on the sudden, there appears an astonishing *Light* in the *Heavens*; perhaps first most over the *Italian* Territories: where the *Priests Daughter*, that is to be *burnt* for her *Whoredomes*, has her Paramour, and where is the *Seat* for that Son of Perdition whom our Lord will *Destroy by the Brightness of His Coming*.[2] But it will soon spread thro' all the Welkin. Yea, *As the Lightening issueth out of the East & shineth even unto the West; so shall also the Coming of the Son of Man be*. Both Haemisphaeres will soon be sensible of it. In *both* will be found the *Carcase* which *Eagles* and *Angels* of the Heavens, will see

devoured in the *Flames* which they descend withal. The *Heavens* will soon be
filled with such Blazes, and Flashes, and fiery Coruscations, as will oblige them,
who until now had *so much to do upon Earth, that they had no Liesure to look
up unto the Heavens,* Now to look up, and see what will cause their *Hearts to
fail them for fear, & for looking after those things that are coming on the Earth.*
Our GOD will astonish the World at the *Brightness of His Coming! Heaven on
Fire,* some take to be that *Sign of the Son of Man in Heaven,* with which His
Coming will be ushered in.

One Great Thing intended in, *The Heavens being on Fire,* will be to Dislodge
and Afflict the *Daemons,* which now very much occupy that Part of the Atmosphaere, that is above us, but not very far from us; and which our Bible calls,
Wicked Spirits in High Places.[3] *Men* may talk very confidently, and as their
Praesumpteous *Philosophy* may please to dictate, about the *Nature* of those
Wicked Spirits, and with the *Subtilties* of the *Schoolmen,* who are at best no
better than meer *Dunces,* with all their Metaphysical Jargon about the Matter,
they may entirely *Subtilize* them into a Sort of *Impassibility;*[4] But it is after all
most certain, That the *Wicked Spirits,* notwithstanding their being *Invisible* to
Us, and more *Spiritual* in their *Vehicles* than *We,* yett are of such a Constitution, as that the *Fire* which is to attend the Coming of the Lord, will grievously
torture them. To say nothing of the *Terrors* which *our Obsessed Ones* have often
seen discovered in them, when they have been in danger of *Wounds* from the
Swords of the Standers-by; We will be determined by a *more Sure Word.*[5] Of that
Fire, our SAVIOUR has expressly told us, *It is praepared for the Devil, and his
Angels.* Then it must be for their *Torment.* The *Fire* cannot be on any other account *Praepared* for the *Wicked Spirits,* but this, that they are to be *Tor-*[ms. III,
v56]*mented* in it; It necessarily implies, that they are capable of being, and actually shall be, *Tormented* in it. Accordingly, by the *Fire of GOD* now flying thro'
the *Heavens,* those *Armies,* [which is the Proper Translation of the Greek Term,
which we render, *Elements,*] of *Wicked Spirits,* will find their Quarters become
Too Hott for them: Not only, the *Fowls of Heaven,* but also the *Devils* who are
called, *The Birds of the Air,* those *Unclean & Hateful Birds,* will have a Share
in the *Desolation that shall come from far;* whither, whither will they *fly for
Help,* in this *Day of Visitation?* Those *Fiery Serpents,* will now feel a *Fire,* that
will Exceed, & Revenge all that the Poor Children of Men have suffered from
them. This *Fire* will be that *Sword,* the *Fiery Sword,* even that *Sore & Great &
Strong Sword,* with which the Eternal GOD, will *Punish,* the *Leviathan,* that
Piercing & Crooked & Apostate Serpent. Thus it will be, that the Eternal GOD,
Thundring in the Heavens, will *Send out His Arrows, & Scatter* the Apostate
Legions; He will *Shoot out Lightenings,* and wondrously *discomfit them!* We
scorn to be beholden unto Pagan, or any Humane Poetry, for a—*crebris micat
Ignibus Æther,*—and the like low Flights, to describe this all-devouring *Fire of
GOD.*[6] What the Executioners of the Divine Vengeance, then appearing in our
Heavens, will do, shall be told in higher Terms; *A Fire devours before them,
& behind them a Flame burneth; & nothing shall escape them. They shall be
like the Noise of a Flame of Fire which devoureth the Stubble. Before their face*

the People shall be much pained, all Faces shall gather Blackness. The Earth shall quake before them, the Heavens shall tremble: the Sun & Moon shall be dark, & the Stars shall withdraw their Shining; The Day of the Lord is great, and very terrible; and who can abide it?

While Appearances infallibly & infinitely more praesagious, than the flaming Boards of ten thousand *Comets* would be, of an approaching Destruction upon the Earth, and while our Lord is not yett come down so nigh to the Earth, as now Quickly He will be; There will be accomplished, the *Grand Promise*, which the Faith of all that have lived unto GOD, in Expectation of a REDEEMER to deliver them from the *Curse*, has in all Ages lived upon: [1. Thess. IV. 14.–] *Them who sleep in JESUS, will GOD bring with Him;—For the Lord Himself shall descend from Heaven with a Shout, with the Voice of the Archangel, & with the Trumpett of GOD, and the Dead in CHRIST shall Rise first.* The Divine Oracles do celebrate the GREAT NOISE, which there will be, at the *Passing away of the Heavens;* And, no doubt, the Prodigious Thunderclaps of that awful Time, will bear their Part in [ms. III, 57] *Great Noise.* The *Hearts* of Men *will tremble,* and be *moved out of their Place,* when they *Hear* the *Noise* of that *Voice* of GOD, and the *Sound* that will so *go out of His Mouth:* which He will *direct under the whole Heaven,* with His *Lightning to the Ends of the Earth.* A *Voice will Roar;* GOD will *Thunder* with the *Voice of His Excellency;* GOD will *Thunder marvellously with His Voice;* and *Great Things will He do, which we cannot comprehend!* But then also, *It shall come to pass in that Day, that the Great Trumpett shall be Blown:* A GREAT NOISE Æqualling and Resembling that of a *Trumpet* at the Mouth of an *Archangel,* transcending what was at the giving of the *Mosaic* Law, will reach to the deep Caverns of the Earth. And in the Midst of this GREAT NOISE, we are expressly told, by the SON of GOD Himself; *The Dead shall hear the Voice of the SON of GOD, and they that hear shall live! They that are in the Graves will hear His Voice, and shall come forth.* He that after He had *wept* no doubt, with Tears of transporting & heartmelting Joy, at the Forethought of what He was ere long to do for Millions, *cried with a Loud Voice,* over the *Grave* of Lazarus, COME FORTH;—*and he that was Dead came forth!*—will now *cause His Mighty Voice to be heard.* He will *cry with a Loud Voice* of that Importance; *COME FORTH, my People, out of the Chambers, where I have hid you. Lett my Dead Ones, live again; As my Dead Body, Lett them Arise; Awake, and Sing, Ye who dwell in the Dust. COME FORTH, at the Voice of the REDEEMER now calling for you!—* So shall it be, when, *Behold, The Lord cometh out of His Place, to punish the Inhabitants of the Earth for their Iniquity.* Our Almighty SAVIOUR, the Lord JESUS CHRIST, will now bestow *Changed Bodies* on the *Spirits,* of His *Chosen & Called & Faithful* Ones.[7] He will as with an inexplicable *Magnetism* find as much of their *former Bodies* as may serve the Present Occasion, and *change their Vile Bodies, according to the Working, whereby He is able even to subdue all things unto Himself:* and their *Spirits* will by the *Working of that Power,* find themselves *Cloathed* with *Bodies,* which this *Father of the World to come,* shall give unto them; *Luminous, Vigorous, Incorruptible Bodies,* wherein they shall *mount up as with the Wings of Eagles*, at a more significant rate, than the *Eagles* of old lett fly from the *Funeral Piles* of the Roman Tyrants: [ms. III, v57] And being *made Equal to the Angels*, these *Redeemed* Ones, filled with the High Praises of their Glorious REDEEMER, and amazed at the *Great Things which their Lord has done for them*, wherein they *will be glad*, when GOD shall *Return the Returning of Zion*, transported with Shouts of, *Grace! Grace!* upon thus laying the *Topstone* of what the *Grace* of their Glorious REDEEMER has to do for them; they will be joined with the Vast Squadrons of *Mighty Angels*, and help to make up the Illustrious Retinue, which the *Great GOD our SAVIOUR* will *Bring with Him*. The *Mighty Angels*, as well as these whom GOD has now *Raised out of the Dust, & Lifted up from the Dunghil, & Sett with Princes, even with the Princes of His People*, will doubtless then [what they Now can do when they please,] render themselves *Visible* to the Inhabitants of the Earth; and it will be no Mistake in the Sinful Mortals, generally now upon these Apparitions to conclude; *We shall surely Dy, because we have seen the* Elohim. How awful the Shapes of the now appearing *Seraphim!*[8]

The *Son of Man*, being thus attended with no less than *Thousands of Thousands ministring unto Him, & Myriads of Myriads waiting before Him;* and *sitting on a Throne, which will be like a fiery flame, and have Wheels like burning Fire;* and *a Fiery Stream issuing & coming forth from before Him*: Soon will Mankind be convinced of what is a Coming! Soon will they See, [Yea, *Behold, He cometh with Clouds; and Every Eye shall See Him, and they also which pierced Him; and all the Kindreds of the Earth shall wail because of Him!*] Soon See, that the SON of GOD is come down *in flaming Fire, to take Vengeance*, on a World from which there is gone up a long & a loud *Cry* to Heaven for it; and they will be every Minute now looking to see *all on Fire* about them. When, *Fire! Fire!* is cried in a City at Midnight, it affrightens the Inhabitants. But what will the Cry of, *A World on Fire!* The inexpressible Anguish, and Horror, and Consternation; that a *Woful World* will be thrown into! The *Devils* and their [ms. III, 58] Clergy & Vassals, were in a Sad Uproar, at the *Constantinean Revolution*, when a New Face of Things, with a Demolition of their *Temples* and their *Idols* was coming on, To describe the Distress of the Wicked at that mighty Turn, there are Colours only borrowed from what shall be in the Day, whereof that was no more than a Little Figure and Earnest.[9] What occurr'd in *That*, was but a *Metaphor*, (and in a Vision where *Metaphor* is to be look'd for, tis accordingly represented so,) to what shall Really and Literally, and with Transcendently more of Convulsion on the World be done at *this Day*. The *Frame of Nature* shall now feel, what was then more *Morally* felt in the *Roman Empire*. At *this Day*, there will be *a Great Earthquake*; the *Sun* will appear as *black as a Sackcloth of Hair*, by reason of the Outshining Lustre in the *Chariots* of GOD; and the *Moon become as Blood*, by reason of the Vapour wherewith our Air will be thickened; the *Stars of Heaven* will appear as if they were *falling to the Earth*, by reason of the Vibrations in the Atmosphaere: The *Heaven will depart as a Scrowl when it is rolled together*, not look at all as it use to do. And then, *the Kings of the Earth, & the Great Men, & the Rich*

Men, *&* the Chief Captains, *&* the Mighty Men, *&* every bond-man, *&* every free-man, will hide themselves in the Dens, *&* in the Rocks of the Mountains, and say unto the Mountains *&* Rocks, Fall on us, *&* hide us from the Face of Him that sitteth on the Throne, *&* from the Wrath of the Lamb; For the Great Day of His Wrath shall come and who shall be able to stand? What Wringing of Hands, what Wildness of Looks, what Running to & fro will there be, *for Fear of the Eternal GOD & for the Glory of His Majesty, when He ariseth to shake terribly the Earth!* What *Weeping* and *Howling,* for the *Miseries coming* upon the World, in the *Fire* that will sieze the *Treasure heaped up together for the Last Days!* What Cries, what Shrieks, that will even pierce the flaming Heavens, for, *Mercy! Mercy! Mercy! The Sorrows of Dea{th}* compassing the Miserable People, and *the Pains of Hell getting hold* on them, with what Agony will they *call on the Name of the Lord, O Lord, I Beseech thee, Deliver my Soul!* The Spectacles in every Corner, will be those rueful Ones; *A Voice of Trembling;— Wherefore do I see every Man with his hands on his Loins, & all Faces are turned into Paleness; Alas, For that Day is great, so that none is like it.*—Step in, O *Imagination* of my Reader, and Lend thy Assistences. Use the best of thy Skill, to limn out the *Terrible Day of the Lord,* in Views beyond what any Language can give of it. And [ms. III, v58] after thy *Meditating of Terror* unto the utmost, and calling in all the frightful *Idaeas* which any thing thou hast *Seen,* or any thing thou hast *Read,* can help thee to, confess, *All falls infinitely short of what will be the Truth of the Matter! T'wil surpass all Imagination!*—

At this Time of such *Trouble as has never been from the Beginning of the World unto this Time,* there will be found here and there scattered about the World, *An Holy People,* who will be distinguished from the rest of Mankind, by their not *walking according to the Course of This World.* As they *know the Truth* of the Gospel, so they *Do the Truth,* and are found such as do not *hold the Truth in Unrighteousness* now the *Wrath of GOD is revealed from Heaven* against them who do so. They are such as Repair to & Rely on a Glorious CHRIST for all His *Great Salvation;* and have *Him Living in them.* They are such as by having the *Image* of a JESUS deeply enstamped on them, and a Lively Study to *Resemble & Imitate* Him, are *Sealed for the Day of Redemption.* They *Live* unto GOD and *Acknowledge Him in all their Ways;* and they have a fervent *Love unto their Neighbour* which perpetually disposes them to *do as they would be done unto. Devotions* towards GOD and *Benignities* towards Men, will fill their Lives. And passing thro' this World as meer *Travellers* and *Sojourners,* they will have their Grand *Aims* and *Hopes,* in the *Inheritance reserved in Heaven for them,* & the *Salvation ready to be revealed in the Last Time.* A very great Number of these, will be at this time suffering Hard Things, under the Tyranny of *Antichrist,* shamefully deserted & neglected by their Brethren to whom *Joseph in the Pitt,* in vain cried for Pitty.[10] Such *Characters* will be a *Mark* of GOD upon them; and by such *Characters* they shall be *Marked* for Praeservation, when the SON of GOD now gives Order to the Destroyers, *Go, and Smite. Lett not your* [ms. III, 59] *Eye Spare, neither have Ye Pitty; Slay utterly Old & Young; but come not near any Man that has the Mark upon him.*

No doubt, these *Humble Walkers* with GOD, and genuine Children of *Noah*, will not be altogether without some Share in the *General Agony*. When the *Lord came with His Holy Myriads*, and upon their Descent unto the Mountain in the *Arabian* Wilderness, the *Mountain burned with Fire*, and there was a *Blackness* and a *Darkness* and a *Tempest*, and there was *the Sound of a Trumpett;* we read, *So terrible was the Sight*, that even a *Moses* himself cried out, *I exceedingly fear & quake!* Much more will the Best among the *Saints*, who will be the *Excellent Ones*, now on the *Earth* which they see going to be devoured, apprehend Cause *exceedingly to fear and quake* at the Appearances they now have above them and about them. Will not those Wishes then be enkindled in their Souls; *O! That I had Wings like a Dove; I would hasten my Escape from the Tempest!* These now in their *Distress will call upon the Lord, & cry unto their GOD.* Their Glorious REDEEMER will *hear their Voice*, and their *Cry shall come before Him.* Yea, when the *Earth shakes, & Fire out of His Mouth devours it,* Then will He *send from above,* and will *draw them out of the many Fires.* It will not be long, before He enables them to sing, *Lo, This is our GOD; We have waited for Him and He will save us; This is JEHOVAH; we have waited for Him, we will be glad, & rejoice in His Salvation!*

And now comes on the Transaction, which our SAVIOUR has in the *Twenty-fifth* Chapter of *Matthew*, described unto us. To understand *The Nations gathered before the Son of Man coming in His Glory,* as if it referred unto a *Process of Judgment* upon those that have passed thro' a *Resurrection of the Dead,* is a Mistake, that has filled Thousands of Godly Sermons, but led the People of GOD into some *Wrong Thoughts* [ms. III, v59] about the *Day of the Lord;* Especially in Supposing the *Righteous* and the *Wicked* as *Rising together,* and then *Standing together,* for a *Trial* before the Tribunal of GOD. There is not so much as One of the *Raised,* among them, whom our Glorious LORD here passes a *Doom* upon.[11] A Nameless Dutch Writer, *De Regno Ecclesiae Glorioso,* very truly observes, *Nihil hic refertur de Mortuorum Resurrectione. All Nations,* here means, as *Erasmus* expresses it, *All Ranks & Sorts of Men in all Nations:* And *Gregory Nazianzen* long ago observed, *The Goats here, are wicked Beleevers,—not Foreigners, but offending Citizens.*[12] A Great Part of the Ungodly among those who after the Decursion of the Decreed Ages will be *Raised from the Dead,* will scarce be capable of lying under the Charge, which the *Goats* here have brought in against them. To make a Short Work of this Matter, I will transcribe the Words of our, BIBLIA AMERICANA, upon it. "In this Transaction, the *Nations* that are to be *Judged,* seem to be only such as have *Professed* the Name of the Lord JESUS CHRIST, separate from the Infidel World; Or the Visible People of the Lord JESUS CHRIST; His Professed Souldiers and Servants; His *Flock,* that has been gathered out of the World; And thus the whole Discourse will admirably agree with the Two former Parables. It seems, as if at the Next Coming of GOD our SAVIOUR one of the *First Things,* will be a Glorious Transaction, wherein the Members of *Christian Churches,* will have a Determination of their State, in the *Kingdome of GOD,* on the *New Earth* which is to follow; Either to take their Part in the *Glories* of that *King-*

dome, or to perish among them that are to be *Without*. In short: There is not one of the *Raised*, concerned in this Transaction. But our Glorious Lord making His Descent in *Flaming Fire*, and the *Conflagration* going to begin, among the *Christians* that cry unto Him to be *delivered from the Wrath to come*, under the General and Horrible Consternation the World shall then be filled withal, our Lord will distinguish the *Righteous*, and those *Humble Walkers* with GOD, which will be found [ms. III, 60] with his *Marks* upon them; and by the Assistence of His *Angels*, they shall be *caught up to meet the Lord*, & the *Raised*, whom He will first fetch up, to bring with Him, in His Retinue. The *Wicked* shall be Consigned over to the *Flames*, and Perish as *Bundles of Tares*, in the tremendous *Conflagration*, which will then bring about the *Perdition of Ungodly Men*. These will remain *Prisoners for many Days*, and not be *Raised* unto the *Condemnation* intended for them, until after a Revolution of many Ages."[13]

With our Glorious GOD, *Saying* is *Doing*. And our Lord now being on the Strain of *Parables*, it is but the more agreeable, to express in the *Form*, of a *Dialogue*, the *Works* and the *Frames* of the *Righteous*, with the *Crimes* and the *Frames* of the *Wicked*. It is enough, That the *Things*, which would afford *Matter* for such a *Dialogue*; will then be found in the World: and the Lord, whose *Throne is in Heaven*, will with His *Eyes behold*, and with His *Eylids try*, the *Children of Men*, so as evidently to Distinguish the *Righteous* from the *Wicked*, when He is going to *Rain Snares, Fire & Brimstone, & an horrible Tempest*, on them who are to have *That* for the *Portion of their Cup*. However, it may be proper enough, to suppose, That the *Sentence* here passed, may be most Articulately Pronounced by the *Voice* that will then *Shake not Earth only but also Heaven*, in the *Orders* given unto the mighty *Angels*; Even those *Reapers*, of whom our SAVIOUR has told us; [Matth. XXIV. 31.] *He shall send His Angels, with a Great Sound of a Trumpett; and they shall gather together His Elect from the Four Winds, from one End of Heaven, to the other.* And has again told us; [Matth. XIII. 41.–] *The Son of Man shall send forth His Angels, & they shall gather out of His Kingdome, all things which offend, & them who do Iniquity; and cast them into a Furnace of Fire; There shall be wailing & gnashing of Teeth.* And whereas *Works of Mercy* done to the Suffering Children of GOD, have a Singular Notice taken of them in this Transaction, and are Singularly Considered in Determining what *Christians* they are that shall now *obtain the Mercy of the Blessed*, I pray, that he *who Reads may understand*, what I am going to offer upon it. One of the *Last Things* that shall happen just before the *Coming of the Lord*, will be an horrid *Persecution* employ'd by *Antichrist*, upon the Pure Worshippers of GOD. [ms. III, v60] Yea, the *Furnace* may be heated Seven times hotter by the King of *Babylon*. *French* Confessors; *Hungarians*, & with *Vaudois, Palatines*, & *Polanders*, and many others, will have such Things done upon them, as will *Try* the *Mercy* of their Bretheren, that are not under the same Oppressions.[14] There will be Charitable Christians, that from a Principle of *Love* to our SAVIOUR suffering in these Members of His Body, will abound in *Works of Mercy* to them; and in all possible Methods of *Charity*, make the Condition of These *Their own*. While many, and especially the *Great Ones of* the Earth, who have it *in the Power of their Hands* to help them, will not have it in their *Hearts*, but look upon their Sufferings with an unpardonable Indolence, and not afford so much as *a Little Help* unto the *Holy People*. They may make a *Flourish* of some Zeal for the *Protestant Religion*; But they will Do *nothing*; All will come to *nothing*. An Infamous *Peace* will be once & again concluded, and the *Suffering Protestants* be left rather worse than they were before.[15] Men shall now be dealt withal accordingly; they shall *Eat the Fruit of their Doings*; the *Reward of their Hands will be given them*.

At that time, O Daniel, Thy People shall be delivered. Indeed the Difficulties to be now encountred on their Part may be such, that it may be said, The *Righteous will Scarcely be Saved*. But, yett they shall *Surely be Saved*. Our Glorious REDEEMER, who *knows who are His*, will make Effectual Provision for the Deliverance of His People. But, How shall they be Delivered? It appears Impossible to contrive an *Ark*, that could subsist & shelter, in such a *Flood* as now carries all before it. *What shall we do?* It might satisfy our *Faith*, if we had no more than that Word; *The Lord knows how to deliver the Godly, and reserve the Wicked to be punished*: But our Gracious Lord has condescended so far, as to tell us, which Way it shall be accomplished. *Supernatural Occurrences* which we find Recorded in the Book of our GOD, are left upon Record, partly to give Hints unto us, of what shall be done, in the Kingdome of GOD, and in *the Days of the Voice of the Seventh Angel, when the Mystery of GOD shall be finished*. Here I will not propose the Three Jewish *Hero's*, in the *Midst of the Burning Furnace* on the Plain of *Dura*, upon whose *Bodies the Fire had no Power, nor was an Hair of their head Sinjed, neither were their Coats changed, nor had the Smell of Fire passed on them*, as giving any Intimation to us, that any of the *Righteous* may be kept [ms. III, 61] any time *Untouch't* and *Unhurt* upon the Earth, after it is become a *Fiery Furnace*; or that he who *walketh Righteously, & speaketh Uprightly*, shall be able to *dwell* any where in the *Devouring Fire & the Everlasting Burnings*. No; They shall be rescued out the *Fiery Furnace*; and on every one of them there shall be Cause to make that Acclamation, *Is not this a Brand pluck't out of the Fire!* And as when *Lot* was to be saved from the Flames of the *Wrath to come* on the *Cities which GOD* inexorably *overthrew in His Anger*, the *Angels* of GOD *laid hold on his hand, the Lord being merciful unto him, & brought him forth; & sett him without the City*, thus, the *Good Angels* will be employ'd on this great Occasion. In short, The Oracles of Truth have plainly told us; [1. Thess. IV. 16, 17.] *The Dead in CHRIST shall Rise first: THEN we which are alive, and shall remain, shall be caught up together with them in the Clouds, to meet the Lord in the Air*. And, [1. Cor. XV. 51.] *Behold, I shew you a Mystery; We shall not all sleep, but we shall all be changed, in a Moment, in the twinkling of an Eye, at the Last Trumpett, (for the Trumpett shall sound,) and the Dead shall be Raised Incorruptible, and we shall be changed*. It was a *Mystery*, How the *Righteous* could survive the *Fire* which is to Destroy the Earth, and all that is upon it. They shall be *caught up*, into the Regions where their SAVIOUR will say to them, *With me thou shalt be in Safety*. It is a *Mystery*, how the *Righteous* having the Remainders of *Original Sin* in them, and such terrible Circumstances as now do fetter them, should be admitted into an *Undefiled Inheritance*, and that *Kingdome of GOD*, which *Flesh & Blood cannot inherit.* They shall be *Changed*, and made *New Creatures.* In this Affair, our Lord has told us, The *Angels* will be *Ministring Spirits*; the *Heirs of Salvation* will have their *Ministry* to befriend them. To render this *Translation*, and this *Transmutation*, the more credible to our Faith, tis no more than what we have already seen exemplified. There was a *Man of GOD*, singled out long ago, to exemplify it; of whom we read; [2. King. II. 11.] That having his *Elisha* with him, *It came to pass as they still went on, and talked, that, Behold, there ap-*[ms. III, v61]*peared a Chariot of Fire, and Horses of Fire, and parted them both asunder, and Elijah went up with a Whirlwind into Heaven.*[16] Doubtless, *Elijah* was made *Sinless*, before he had ascended a furlong; and that he became *Deathless* no one can quaestion, upon the Testimony of his being seen Alive Nine hundred Years after his Departure. The Thing is no longer so much a *Mystery*: Tis enough explained unto us; *How these things can be!* And how it *will be*, when, as our Lord has told us, *Two shall be together in one Field, yea, in one Bed; whereof the one shall be taken & the other shall be left.*

Our GOD having thus *made up His Jewels*, and snatched away all that He had any Value for, the *Earth* is now left with none but the *Wicked* upon it; None to intercede for any *Mercy* to it; *Judgment without Mercy*, is now to be its Portion. *Wickedness* which *burns like Fire*, now calls for *Fire* to be sett upon it. Nothing but *Briars* and *Thorns* now appear on the Face of it; It is now *nigh* unto the *Curse* that belongs unto it; The *End* of the Things which it has born, is to be *burned.* It is now come; Those *Briars & Thorns, I will now go thro' them,* says an Incensed GOD, *and I will burn them together!* It is praepared for a *Burnt-Offering* to the Justice of an Infinite GOD: who will now no longer bear with its Incorrigible Impieties. The *Earth* is by *Sulphur* every where filling & fatning of it, ready for Inflammation. And, not one *Vesuvio*, not one *Ætna*, but a Thousand Vast *Volcano's* are now ready to break forth upon the giving of the *Signal.* The Children of Men, with the *Bitterness of Death* upon them, stand all Trembling & Fainting, and their *Countenances changed*, with their *Thoughts troubling* of them, the *joints of their Thighs loosed*, & their *Knees knocking against one another*, and they *crying with a Loud Voice*, for Mercy to be shown unto them. With feeble Hands they smite upon their *Breasts*, in which there are *Hearts moved as the Trees of the Wood are moved with the Wind*, and quivering like an *Aspine-Leaf.* In a most Unutterable Consternation, they see nothing *remaining*, but a *certain fearful Expectation of Judgment, & of a fiery Indignation*, from an Almighty GOD, going to *ease Himself of His Adversaries, & avenge Himself on His Enemies.*

Ah, Wretched Earth, Doom'd unto *Flames*; *An End is come, the End is come upon all Corners of the Earth.* Yea, The Lord GOD will now in formidable Assurances [ms. III, 62] of what He is going to do, declare it unto the *Children of Belial*, who are now to be as *Thorns thrust away, & utterly consumed with Fire*, and cause them with an utter Despair of Mercy, to hear it; *An End is come,*

the End is come; The Time is come, the Day of Trouble is near; Now will I accomplish mine Anger upon thee; and I will Judge thee according to thy Ways,
and I will Recompense thee for all thine Abominations; and my Eye shall not
Spare, neither will I have Pitty; But, O Sinful Ones, You shall know, that I
am JEHOVAH, who am now smiting of You.—But the Manner of its Coming
on!—The History of the famous Disputation with the Jews among the Homerites, written, it seems, by Palladius, has appeared with so Little Character of
Papal Superstitions upon it, that many Learned Men look on it as a Credible
Relation. But that which very much weakens the Credit of the History, is that
in little more than Twenty Years after the pretended Conversion of the whole
Jewish People there, by a Miraculous Appearance of our Lord, in the Kingdome
of the Homerites, the Jewish People are found still as Numerous as ever.[17] However, if the Reader will give himself the Pleasure of Reading it, he will there
find a very Lively Description, of the Manner, wherein the Glorious Appearance of our Great GOD & SAVIOUR, is to be looked for.—JEHOVAH-JESUS,
upon a Throne High & Lifted up, now darts out His Refulgent Rays, thro' the
Dense Clouds, wherein He has had His Dark Pavilion. He now shows Himself
to a World, which had Hid their Faces from Him; He was despised, and they
esteemed Him not! When one of His Persecutors once had only a Sight of the
Glory that covered Him & arrayed Him, [the Chosen Vessel saw not His Face,
till His Trance afterwards in the Temple!] there was a Light from Heaven, above
the Brightness of the Sun, shining round about him, that struck him down to
the Earth: He could not stand before it.[18] How will the Reprobate World now
stand, under the View of that Face, which inconceivably outshines the Sun in
its Meridian Lustre! When, the Disciple whom He loved, came to see that Lamb
of GOD, the Son of Man, in the glittering Habit of His Royal Priesthood, His
Eyes as a flame of Fire, His Feet like Fine Brass, as if they Burned in a Furnace,
His Voice as the Sound of many Waters, and His Face as the Sun shining in
His Strength; He that had once lain in His Bosom, now fell down as Dead at
His Feet. What will a World of those that are the Abhorred of the Lord, now do
when they shall see that wonderful Face of [ms. III, v62] the Great King, who
now comes Glorious in His Apparrel, travelling in the greatness of Strength, to
tread upon them in His Anger, to trample them in His Fury. The Lord GOD
Omnipotent, so seated on His most magnificent Mercavah,[19] now looks down
from Heaven upon the Children of Men, to see if there be any Understanding
Seekers of Him left among them; He sees, They are Corrupt, they do Abominable Things, they are all together become filthy, there is none that doth Good,
no, not One. He sees, No, not One, but of whom He may not say, I know that
you have not the Love of GOD in you. He sees, No, not One but what lives entirely to himself, & setts up Creatures for his Idols. He sees, No, Not One, but
what continually does Things, which by Conscience, if hearkened to, would
condemn him for. He sees the nefandous Impieties that Cry to Heaven for Vengeance, every where abounding in every Part of the World: Lo, The Cry is great,
and their Sin is very grievous! Among the rest, He sees an Horrid Conspiracy,
carried on, among those who are called after His Worthy Name, [They say, they

are CHRISTIANS, *but they are not!*] impiously to Dethrone Him, to Degrade Him, to *Ungod* Him, and make Him no more than a *Subordinate GOD*, and One, that had a *Beginning*; What *High Treason* against Infinite MAJESTY! [20] Upon the Provoking Sight, the Holy One cannot but say, *Shall I not visit for these things; and shall not my Soul be avenged on such a Nation as this!*— At the same time, the Mighty *Angels* of the glorious Lord, [the *Ministers of His, which do His Pleasure!*] will *Visibilize* themselves unto the Children of Men; Their *Eyes* will be *opened* now to see Those, whose *Countenance will be the Countenance of Angels of GOD, very Terrible.* [ms. III, 63] They shall see, upon GOD *Opening* of their *Eyes*; And, Behold, The Sky will *be full* of those who once managed the *Horses & Chariots of Fire* in the *Mountain*, for the Comfort of the Prophet. These *Valiant* Ones, before the Least of whom the biggest Conqueror & Emperour that ever was in the World, is no greater than a *Worm*; These about the Throne of One infinitely *greater than Solomon*, will *all hold Swords, Expert for the War* now going on. These Holy *Seraphim*, full of detestation for the *Detestable Idolatries* and *Iniquities* in which the Children of Death have indulged themselves, as the Prince of Old said unto the Man of GOD, about the *Syrians* that were now his Prisoners, *My Father, Shall I Smite them? Shall I Smite them?* So these now humbly propose it unto the SON of GOD about the *Sinners* which are an *Abomination* to them; O *our Holy Lord, who art of Purer Eyes than to behold Evil; Shall we Smite them? Shall we Smite them?*—Nothing but the WORD is waited for!—

—And now, as in the ancient Visions of GOD, He that had *Power over the Fire*, seeing him that had the *Sickle* ready, *Cried with a Loud Cry to him, Thrust in thy Sickle; The Grapes are fully Ripe*: And it was done; The *Vine of the Earth was gathered, and cast into the Great Winepress of the Wrath of GOD*: Thus, our Almighty Lord, now ready to *Tread the Winepress*, will immediately *cause Judgment to be heard from Heaven, at which the Earth will be afraid*; A Voice infinitely more tremendous than the United Peal of a Million Thunderclaps, will proceed from the Mouth, which now indeed will *Speak so as never Man Spake*; A Voice of this Importance; *Lett the People that would not have me to Reign over them, receive what they deserve!*—STRIKE!— The Blow is given. *Hott Thunderbolts* fall every where as thick as *Hail-Stones!* With what Stupendous Fulminations, will GOD now *thunder out of Heaven upon His Adversaries*, when He shall *Judge the Ends of the Earth!* Ten Million *Canon* playing at once would be nothing to it! All-Scorching [ms. III, v63] Sheets of Liquid *Fire* are showred every where down upon them whom GOD will have to be *devoured* by the *Fire of His Enemies*. Upon the Lords *causing His Glorious Voice to be heard*, He will *presently show the Lighting down of His Arm, with the Indignation of His Anger, & with the Flame of a devouring Fire*. The Veins of *Sulphur*, with which the *Earth* is every where saturated, will take *Fire immediately*; Ten Thousand *Volcano's* will burst out, & throw up Flames, and Vapors & Cinders, with a Rage and a Roar, that will reach unto the Heavens. [21] At the same time, the *Earth* will quake & splitt & open in Thousands of Places; massy *Mountains* will be *overturned in the Anger* of GOD, and mighty *Cities* will be swallow'd up. Yea, the very *First Essay* of these Concussions, as it seems, will be *Fire* from Above, and Below, upon the *Accursed City*, that has long *Reigned over the Kings of the Earth*, & intoxicated them with *the Wine of the Wrath of her Fornication.* That City shall *Sink like a Milstone;* The *Smoke of Her Burning* shall carry astonishments with it; and the Countrey where that City stood, shall be turned into an entire *Lake, burning with Fire & Brimstone,* for [*a thousand and Six hundred furlongs,*] the Space of Two Hundred Miles together.[22] But other Parts of the *Earth* will have their Share in the *Desolation.* In One Word, All the *Combustibles* on the Surface of the Earth, will be destroyed, and it will be an *Universal Desolation.—O Great GOD; At thy Rebuke, what is there done? Thou, even Thou art to be feared; and who or what can stand in thy Sight, when once Thou art angry!—*

If the Satellit of this Earth *walking in her Brightness,* have any Reasonable Inhabitants, we know not what Reflections they will have, at the Beholding of what is done to this Globe, when they see GOD *hath enkindled a Fire, & it hath devoured the Foundations thereof.* Nor know we, how dire, how dismal, how doleful a Spectacle *This* may be to any of the other Planetts, if there be in them any *Rational Spectators,* of what Appearances may now be discovered here.[23] But this we do know.

The Holy *Angels* of GOD, and the Children of the *Resurrection,* together with the *Transported* and *Escaped* Ones, will hereupon all join their Acclamations. *Righteous art thou, O Lord, for that thou hast Judged thus:* Repeated Acclamations, *Lord GOD Almighty, True and Righteous are thy Judgments!—* —For the rest— —No Pen can express it, no Heart can conceive it!

[ms. III, 64]—And now, *Adieu, Vain World! Adieu, Vile World! Thou that hast forever deceived the Expectation of all that ever proposed a Satisfaction in thee & from thee! Thou that hast been to the Children of GOD, a terrible Wilderness, a Land of Pitts & of Droughts & fiery flying Serpents. We never look'd for our Portion in thee. We are now in View of the Portion we have waited for. Come on, O New Heavens, & O New Earth, wherein is all our Salvation & all our Desire: and the Harvest of all that we have been sowing in the Tears of our Pilgrimage!*

VIII. The CONFLAGRATION,
How Reasonably to be look'd for.

But, *what means the Heat of this Anger!*—It seems hardly possible for such a Desolation, ever to come upon a World, that has in it such Vast Numbers of Ingenious & Ingenuous & Well-accomplished *People;* Such Stately *Cities,* Noble *Palaces,* Wondrous *Libraries,* admirable Effects of Humane Industry & Workmanship; Such rich *Clusters of Grapes,* whereof one cannot but say, *Oh! Destroy them not; Is there not a Blessing in them!* To condemn all these unto the *Flames!*—The *Men of This World, who are for a Portion in this Life,* be sure, can't bear the Thoughts of such a Desolation coming upon what they have so sett their Hearts upon. The Mountain in *Lycia,* which had a *Volcano* at the Top,

> *Whose pitchy Nostrils flaky Flames expire*
> *Her gaping Throat emitts infernal Fire;*

went by the Name of *Chimaera;* And every body now knows how to expound the *Fable of the Poets,* describing it.[1] But the World is full of those Unbeleevers, who would make the *Burning World* no more than what we now call a meer *Chimaera,* & no better than a *Fable of the Poets.* Yea, some of a Better Character, may be ready to think, *what a Pitty it is!* And, *How unmercifully it looks!* And with a, *God forbid,* they will try to shake off all Apprehensions of it.—But, The *Purpose* of the Great GOD *shall stand,* and *He will do all His Pleasure.* Tis Peremptorily declared in that Word; *The Earth and the Works of it, shall be burnt up;* And, *All these things shall be dissolved.* There is no Standing before a Word, so brought unto us.

To procure for this Beleef a more Easy Passage unto our Minds, Lett these Things be duely considered with us.

First: SIN; the Evil *Nature* of *Sin,* the Evil *Desire* of *Sin;* Are we well Aware of *That?* Sin, which *Denies the GOD that is Above,* & Setts other Things, nay the Worst of Things, *Above Him;* Disowns the Authority of our Creator to be our Governour; [ms. III, v64] Disturbs the *Good Order,* wherein the *Great GOD that formed all things,* has placed them! *Sin,* which does Reproach Infinite *Wisdom,* Defy Infinite *Power,* Despise Infinite *Goodness,* and Blaspheme the *GOD of Truth,* with giving the *Lye* unto Him. *O Fools that make a Mock of Sin;* As Light a Matter as you make of it, it heaps those Indignities on an Infinite GOD, for which, according to the Demands of His Indisputable *Justice,* No *Punishment* can be enough; *Tis impossible to be too severely punished.* We do not know that it was any more than *One Sin,* that procured the Damnation of more *Angels,* doubtless, more by far, than there will be found *Men* Alive on the Earth, at the *Conflagration.* That ONE SIN brought those *Angels,* to be *reserved in Everlasting Chains under Darkness unto the Judgment of the Great Day.* Now, can it be wondred at, that in the *Conflagration,* which will be the *Judgment of the Great Day,* the *Men* that have such Thousands of *Sins,* even *Innumerable Evils,* chargeable upon them, should be sent into the same

Fire, with the Devil & his Angels? Yea, there is a Contemplation that carries infinitely more of Conviction with it. The *Sin* that you make so Light a Matter of; Have you thought what the Glorious GOD has made of it? Judge of That, by the *Sacrifice* which He has demanded for it. The *Death* of no less a Person than the SON of GOD, was the *Sacrifice* that must be offered, that so the Repenting Sinner may be Released from his Obligations to Suffer the *Penalty* which the Violated Law of GOD is arm'd withal. The *Lamb* of the *Passover*, was Roasted at the *Fire*. Yea, The *Lamb* of the *Daily Offering* was consumed in the *Fire*. This was but a Figure of what the *Lamb of GOD* underwent from the Wrath of GOD at our Sin, the *Fire* whereof threw Him into a *Bloody Sweat*, and fetch'd the Cry, *I Thirst*, from Him, & His *Heart was like Wax melted in the Midst of His Bowels*. O Sinful World, Renouncing the Benefit of that *Sacrifice*, there *does not remain any more Sacrifice for thy Sin*: But thou must now thyself be made a *Sacrifice*. Yea, The tremendous *Wrath of the Lamb will make thee* so! A Glorious CHRIST made a *Sacrifice* for the Sin of His People! Here was a *Sacrifice*, of more Importance, than if Ten such *Worlds* as ours, were made an entire *Burnt-Offering*. Do not wonder now, that *This World*, which has in it so many Millions of Sins unrepented of, do in a *Conflagration* become an *Holocaust*! I say, *Millions of Sins*; For truly, the State of *This World*, even of a, *Whole World lying in Wickedness*, [ms. III, 65] may be Reported in those Terms; *The Earth is full of Bloody Crimes*: Therefore, *Destruction cometh*.[2]

But,—what a dark Scene is now to be opened! What hideous, & shocking Spectacles, are we now to be entertain'd withal! If in the *Visions of GOD*, we were now to be carried, as once one of His Prophets was, to *See what they do* every where, and See the *Great Abominations that are committed* every where in the *Earth*, a Mind that had any Fear of GOD working in it, could not but be amazed at the *Ungodliness* and *Unrighteousness*, reigning in the World.[3] There would be no Part of the *Earth*, where we should not see Incredible Occasions to cry out with another of the Prophets; *Wonderful & Horrible Things are committed in the Land*!

Indeed, all they who do not live unto GOD, spend all their Days in *Continual Rebellions* against Him; and the Best Things they do are but *Splendid Abominations*. Now, how Few of Mankind are they who truly *Live unto GOD*! Ah, Degenerate Mankind; The Genuine Children of GOD found in thee, are but *as the shaking of an Olive-tree, two or three Berries in the top of the uppermost Bough, four or five in the outmost fruitful Branches thereof*. Alas, Those *two Evils*; whereat the SPIRIT of GOD, exclamed, *Be astonished O Ye Heavens, at this, & be horribly afraid, be Ye very desolate, saith the Lord*, are what the whole Unregenerate & Unsanctified Part of Mankind committ continually. Wherefore, *Be astonished, O Thou Earth, & be horribly afraid; for thou shalt for this be very desolate*; And Room shall be made for a Generation that shall render thee truly, *The Land of the Living*! If nothing will do, but all means prove ineffectual, and People will remain *a People of no Understanding*, it must not be murmured at, if *He that made them have no Mercy on them, & He that formed them shew no Favour to them*.

We won't Refine upon the Matter of Real and Vital PIETY, which is almost banished, out of the *Earth*, and where it should be most look'd for, tis by the Men who *mind Earthly things*, decried & exploded as, nothing but *Enthusiasm.* *Son of Man, Turn thee yett again, and thou shalt see Greater Abominations!*

Idolatry may still be called, as it was long ago; *Praecipuum crimen humani generis.*[4] What a Prodigious Proportion of Mankind, are to this Day, the *Heathen that know not* [ms. III, v65] *GOD,* and the Families that *call not on His Name!* [*Lord, what wilt thou pour out upon them!*] Yea, the Plain Worshippers of *Devils!* Among the rest, O thou Extended Empire of *China,* which hast by Computation Fifty Eight Millions of People in thee; what an Homage has the *Dragon* from thee! And how many Millions more, does the Pope of *Barantola,*[5] hold in a Vassalage to the *Powers of Darkness,* adoring of *Idols* that have *Devils* in them! The *Mahometans* indeed, after so *Iconoclastic* a Character has been upon them, would be lothe to be thought *Idolaters*: and it was ridiculous enough in our Old Papists, to call *Idolatry* by the Term of *Mammetry*; But certainly, their *Faith* in the *Imposters* to whom they pay more than *Humane Regards,* carries an *Idolatry* in the Bowels of it: and be sure, their Prayers unto *Fatima,* (whom they call a *Virgin,* tho' they own her a *Mother,*) to Intercede for them, is most notoriously so.[6] The *Romanists,* whereof tis affirmed there are no less than Fourscore Millions at this day in the World, are all of them *Idolaters.* The Religion practised among them, is the *Idolatry* of a *Revived Gentilism.* Every Sort of *Idolatry* is to be found in the *Mystical Babylon,* and that of their *Artolatry* the most Nonsensical, the least Accountable.[7] Now, the glorious GOD ordered the Executioners of His Vengeance on the ancient *Idolaters, Ye shall utterly destroy all the Places, wherein they Served their Gods; and you shall Burn their Groves with Fire.* And if a City of *Israel,* did Apostatize to *Idolatry,* it was ordered, *Thou shalt Burn that City with Fire, and all the Spoil thereof every Whit, for the Lord thy GOD.* What was this *Order,* but a Sort of Sermon & Warning of the Grand *Conflagration* to be inflicted on a World full of *Idols?* Be sure, The Infliction is no longer to be wondred at!

But, Oh! The Cry of *Blood!*—When the *Vials* of the Divine Wrath are poured out upon the World, the *Angels* of GOD express their Satisfaction so; *Thou art Righteous, O Lord; For they have shed the Blood of Saints & Prophets.* When our GOD *comes out of His Place, to punish the Inhabitants of the Earth for their Iniquity,* t'wil be when the *Earth shall disclose the Blood* of the Faithful that have been *Slain* upon it. The Blood of MARTYRS: What Rivers of it shed! And with what cruel, & hideous & horrid *Excarnifications!*[8] The CXXVIII Chapter of *De La Cerda,* in his *Adversaria,* that one Chapter, one can scarce do any other than swoon away at the Reading of it![9] The Spirit of *Persecution* in all Ages, and all Places has gone too far *Abetting* these *Cruelties,* where it has not gone to the Extremity in the Repeting of them. This *Blood* all *Cries* to GOD from the *Earth,* which it has been spilt upon; & will bring down *Fire* from *Heaven* upon it. The *Martyrs,* I say; What an *Army* of them! The Paradoxical Gentleman, who has written, *De Paucitate Martyrum,* has doubtless *Fallen Short* of the Truth, as much as others may have *Gone beyond it.*[10] But if the

Former Centuries did not shed *Blood* enough, the *Latter* have made it up. What nefandous[11] Things have been done, by the *Spirit of Persecution,* and how have the *Followers of the Lamb* all along been treated [ms. III, 66] *like Sheep for the Slaughter?* Pagan *Rome* did such Things to the People of the Blessed JESUS, as made many Thousands of *Souls under the Altar,* whose *Memorials,* go up, to *cry, with a Loud Voice; How Long, O Lord, Holy & True, dost thou not Judge, & avenge our Blood on them who dwell on the Earth.* An Approach of a *New State* upon the Advancement of a *Constantine* unto the *Imperial Throne,* some Way discovered among them, seems to have rowsed that *Cry* among the *Sacrificed Souls.* But they must wait, until Papal *Rome* have done her Part, in *Worrying & Murdering & Sacrificing* the *Flocks* of our GOD. And she has done it unto Astonishment! Our *Martyrologies,* how many *Bulky Folio's* would they make, if they should exhibit a Thousandth Part, of the Barbarities, which the *Scarlett Whore, Drunk with the Blood of the Saints,* has perpetrated on them. An History of the cruel Things occurring in the Sufferings of but *One Church,* in but *One Little Part* of a Countrey, & but for *four Sevens* of Years, & but exhibited with very much *Abridgment,* in the Relation; it has made a Couple of *Heavy Folio's.*

I make no Doubt, That when our Blessed JESUS was in the *Bloody Agony,* which left His *Blood* on the *Earth,* no Little Part of the *Cup* which he deprecated, was, the Hott & Long *Persecution* wherein He foresaw the *Wine of Astonishment* that was to be given unto His *Followers.* But, how deeply & how dreadfully has *He* drunk of the *Cup,* in *Their* Suffering *what was Behind* of His *Afflictions!* And the *Earth* which has *Drunk* in this *Blood,—O GOD unto whom Vengeance belongeth; what wilt thou do unto it?* Indeed, When the *Reformation* came on, the *Holy People* were *Holpen with a Little Help,* in some Nations beginning to *come out of Babylon.* But even since that Revolution, the *Protestant Religion,* has lost near half that Extent of People and of Regions, which it had acquired in the First *Sixty Years* after the Beginning of the *Reformation.* And by what Methods, have such Desolations been brought upon the *Protestant Interest?* The most Barbarous Methods of Bruitish *Injustice,* of Shameless *Treachery,* of *Prisons,* of *Inquisitions,* of *Massacres,* of Executions at the *Stake,* & on the *Wheel,* & by the *Gibbet,* with Tortures, the very Relation whereof were a sort of *Inhumanity.* With what Actions of Matchless *Violence,* and what Inhumane Butcheries, has the Successful *Persecution* been carried on! Even in OUR DAYS, what *Enormous Things* have been done by the Two Houses of *Austria* & of *Bourbon,* for the Extirpation of what they please to call by the Name of, *Haeresy?* O *Dioclesian,* Thy Bloody Doings have been out-done, by a *Leopold,* and a *Louis.* Thou *Nero,* Thou *Domitian,* Ye have been but *Pygmies* to these Two *Giants* in *Perfidy* and *Cruelty!*[12] And, what is at THIS DAY doing, wherever the *Roman Beast* is not muzzled by those, who nevertheless have not the *Wisdom* to *Unite* for their own Safety, not the *Goodness* to *Appear* for the Rescue of [ms. III, v66] their Suffering Brethren? What *Expiation* can be made for these Things, but by a *Desolation* upon an *Earth* so fearfully defiled! Thousands of *Martyrdomes* have been made in the Unutterable Torments of

Burning at the Stake. *Fire and Faggot*, the Word! The *Holy Ones* that have *not loved their Lives unto the Death*, but been willing to lay down their *Lives*, for Testimonies to the *Truths* and *Ways* of their SAVIOUR, before the *Course of Nature* should bring their *Death* upon them, have been *Sacrificed* in the *Flames* of *Antichrist*. How can these things be expiated, but by the *Destroying of the Beast, and giving his Body to the Burning Flames*! O Ye *British Isles*; Are you altogether free from the Guilt of a most *Unreasonable Persecution*; wherein the *Witnesses* of GOD have been, many Hundreds of them, Afflicted, Ruined, Murdered! The *Fires* of your *Smithfield*, are not all the *Cries* that have gone up to Heaven against you; But All still, *How unrepented of*![13]

If we pass from this *Mother of Abominations*, and see the other *Channels of Wickedness*, which the Vices of Mankind run into, where shall we find that Countrey on the Face of the *Earth*, whereof the GOD of Heaven may not utter that grievous Complaint; *It is a Land that sinneth against me by trespassing grievously*! What? Not, if it be a Countrey of professed *Christians*, I hope! Alas, *Christians*, that should be the *Salt of the Earth*, & preserve it from a Dissolution, These have generally *lost their Savour*. *Christians* cannot but confess themselves under the strongest Bonds to be a *Peculiar People*, & *Zealous of Good Works*. But what are the most of them any better than *Infidels*? A *Grotius* complains, *Eo ventum est, ut inter christianos, crucis candidatos, quotidie palam publice fiat, quod profanarum gentium leges severè puniissent.*[14] A *Kidder* complains, *Were a wise Man to choose his Religion by the Lives of them that profess it, perhaps Christianity would be the Last Religion he would choose*.[15] Yea, The Behaviours of *Christians* have been such as infinitely to scandalize the *Infidels*. And in the *East-Indies* at this day, even where we have *Protestant Factories*; the Pagans look on us, as a *Vile Crue*; and if one of Theirs come over to *Us*, they look on him as lost unto all that is *Good*.[16] We may throw all into One Mass of Putrifaction.—*O my GOD, I am ashamed, and I blush to lift up my Face unto thee, my GOD!* What is the Common, one might almost say, the *Vulgar*, Language of People, but that of Tongues that are *Sett on Fire of Hell*? If the *Fire* come, it can't be wondred at! What *Cheats*, what *Frauds*, what *Villianies*, are abounding every where beyond all *Imagination*! *Officers* of almost all Sorts are so frequent in them, & so expert at them, and they are so connived at, and [ms. III, 67] with such Combination carried on, that if any Honest Man go to oblige the Public by detecting of them, he only *makes himself a Prey*. Men are every where & every Day, carrying of *Burning Coals* into *their Nests*. And shall not GOD anon *Burn* the *Nests*! Men of *Integrity*, I find often making their Moans upon it, That as the *Business of the World*, is now carried on, it is become next unto Impossible to steer clear of much *Dishonesty* in doing any thing to Purpose in it.

How commonly is *Government*, that *Ordinance of GOD* for the Good of Mankind, basely prostituted unto quite other Purposes; and made a meer Engine for Avaricious & Rapacious Wretches, [*The wild beasts of the Earth*, our Bible calls 'em!] to fleece their Subjects, and *Extort Riches* to *Consume upon their Lusts*! What *Bribery*, what *Corruption*, what wrong *Sentences*, are found in the

Judges of the Earth! I *saw the Place of Judgment, that Wickedness was there;* And shall it not now be said, *GOD will Judge the Righteous & the Wicked!* The *Church-State* of some Countreys, what is it but an House built upon the *Sand*, which the *Storm* wherein our GOD *shall come, & it shall be very Tempestuous round about Him*, is gathering for? The *Pure Institutions* of our SAVIOUR, either Neglected, & Vacated, or by *Additions* and *Pollutions* rendred Ineffectual in it! And a Combination to *Serve Carnal Interests*, carried on, under the fallacious Cry of, *The Temple of the Lord! The Temple of the Lord!* They that should be the *Prophets of GOD*, and Continually *Speak for GOD*;—Not only the *Magicians* that perform the Superstitious & Unprofitable Rites of the *False Religions*, but they that profess themselves the *Ministers of the Gospel*, what Multitudes of them are *Blind Watchmen*, and *Ignorant* of the Points wherein they pretend themselves to be the *Guides of the Blind*, & the *Instructors of the Foolish?* What, but poor, mean, *Dumb Dogs, that cannot bark; Talking in their Sleep, Lying down, Loving to Slumber; Yea, They are greedy Dogs, which never can have enough; and they are Shepherds that cannot understand; They all look to their own Way, every one for his Gain from his Quarter.* The *Love of Souls* is what they are Strangers to. Their *Ministry* is nothing but the *Trade* they live by. Their main Concern is, *Modò hic sit benè.*[17] They encourage a *Lifeless Religion*, and an *Irreligious Life*: and even build their *Church-State* upon it. If honest Old *Bernard* were living, I know what his Complaint would be; *Ipsa quoque ecclesiasticae Dignitatis officia, in turpem quaestum, et Tenebrarum negotium transiere: nec in iis salus Animarum, sed luxus quaeritur divitiarum.*[18] Hence The least contempt or neglect of the *Little Things* which maintain their Saecular Grandeur, is unpardonable; The most Immoral and Scandalous Miscreants in the World, that will favour *That*, shall be their Favourites. Their *Conduct & Priestcraft*, is the Great Breeder of *Atheism* in the World. As for the Enchanted People, *They love to have it so!*

Turn yett again! Among the Instances, wherein *Iniquity does abound* [ms. III, v67] among the Nations of the *Earth*, most certainly the *Slave-trade*, and the Usage of *Slaves*, almost every where, but very conspicuously in You, O *Caribbee-Islands*, it calls for a *Judgment without Mercy*, on *Men* becoming worse than *Wolves* to one another.[19] But indeed, the *Cry of the Oppressed* is from every Countrey under Heaven, Perpetually & Importunately going up to Heaven. The *Cry* reaches and *enters the Ears* of the *Lord of Sabaoth;*[20] And the Answer to it, is, *Be patient; For the Coming of the Lord draweth nigh. Behold, The Judge standeth before the Door!*

Yea, Thou shalt see yett greater Abominations.

The *Unchastities* and *Impurities* of People *given up to Vile Affections*, and the Irregular Ways taken by them, to quench the *Fires* that render their Souls like an *Heated Oven;* These are so *Epidemical*, and so little short of *Universal*, that they strongly call for, *The Day of the Lord that shall burn like Oven.* There is a black Description of some *Courts*, in the First Chapter to the *Romans;* and *Suetonius* in describing that of *Nero's*, gives a bright Commentary on it. But how many more of them, have been the *Seraglio's* of Debaucheries![21] And the

People, who *Deify* their *Princes,* will according to their Capacity *Imitate* them. Whole Nations wallow in all the Filth of *Polygamy* and *Concubinage.* Yea, Among those that call themselves *Christians,* how are *Adulteries* multiplied!— Insomuch, that a famous Preacher in *Switzerland,* said in a Sermon, That if the Old Punishment of *Adulterers,* even that of *Stoning to Death,* were now to be executed, he quaestioned whether all the *Stones* in the adjacent Mountain would be enough to serve the Executions.[22] But, what if, *Burning to Death,* should now prove the Punishment? There was a *Foul Disease* known & felt in our Nation, some hundreds of Years before *America* was discovered; which was called, *Brenning,* or *Burning.* Tis hardly to be imagined, how many Millions in the World, are *marked* by that *Foul Disease,* for the *Brenning,* or *Burning,* which in the Day when *Flames are to be punished with Flames,* they will be *consigned* unto.[23] Yea, That *Unnatural Crime,* which brought *Fire & Brimstone & an horrible Tempest* upon Sodom & its Neighbourhood, is now, they say, become so rampant, even among them that call themselves *Christians,* as well as *Mahometans,* that the *Horrible Tempest* [ms. III, 68] must needs quickly make a more extensive Desolation.[24]

In short; If we were to single out that *Island,* that is now thought, *The Glory of all Lands,* and were to take a Prospect of the *Abominable Things,* that are a *Reproach to any People,* but are grassant and usual there, what shall be judged concerning the rest of the World?[25] The Proclamed Hatred of *Serious Piety* there, we will say nothing of. But the *Perjury,* which the *Fools* make a *Mock of!* And very particularly, but how *Disagreeably,* in the *Universities!* Must not the *Earth Mourn,* & even *Burn,* which such *Swearing* does invoke the Vengeance of Heaven upon! The *Selling of Places,* and the consequent Rogueries of them that have bought them, would make all *Just Thinkers* to cry out, *Lord, what wilt thou do to a Nation so depraved!* Among One hundred Thousand Gentlemen of the *Law,* in the *Nation,* I have seen a Challenge made, which I am lothe to Repeat—Those *Academies of Hell,* the *Theatres,* how loud Invocations go up from them, for the Cataracts of Heaven to pour down a Vengeance on the *Nation!*[26] The Thousands of *Murders* committed in & by the *Prisons,* on *Debtors* most unrighteously perishing there, are what the *Nation* has to pay for. Besides others that often purchase a too *Easy Pardon.*[27] An Honest Writer of, *An Essay on a Public Spirit,* has enumerated only a Few of our Abominations; But concludes, That the Nation is ripe for the *Conflagration;* wonders that the *Conflagration* does not immediately commence upon it: An Honest Roman could not see such Things as these, without crying out upon them, *Finis ad est rerum.* It's a coming![28]

—But, O Wretched World, There yett remains One Article of thy *Indictment,* and the very Consummation of Wickedness, which, who that has the Heart of a *Christian* in him, can mention without that Exclamation of *Piety* upon it; *Horror hath taken hold on me!* What must be done with the *Earthen Vessel,* in which the *Sin-Offering* underwent what was to be done unto it! Of the *City,* [which is a *World* also!] damned unto the *Flames* of the *Grand Conflagration,* it was a *Small thing* to say, All the Crimes of *Sodom* and of *Egypt* are found in it;

but it is added, WHERE ALSO OUR LORD WAS CRUCIFIED.—This, This is that incomprehensible and unparallelled *Wickedness*, which has rendered *This World* obnoxious unto the *Devouring Flames*, and rendered them unavoidable. When the Plagues of GOD all come upon the Empire of *Antichrist*, and it shall be *utterly burnt with Fire, for strong is the Lord GOD that Judges it*, there is this Account given of it; *In it was found the Blood of Prophets, & of Saints, and of all that were slain upon the Earth.* But, O Wretched [ms. III, v68] World, the *Smoke of whose Burning* will be *seen afar off; In Thee is found the Blood of the SON of GOD!* When the SON of GOD, became a *Man*, how was the *Son of Man* treated among the Children of Men, whom He so loved, as to become Incarnate that He might bring them unto GOD? They *Rejected* Him; They *Reviled* Him; They heaped all possible *Outrages* upon Him. They took Him & Bound Him & arraigned Him as a *Malefactor*; They praeferr'd a Despicable and Execrable *Highway-Man* before Him; They falsely *Accused* Him, and passed a Sentence of *Death* upon Him; They *Mock'd* at Him, they *Spitt* on Him, they *Buffeted* Him. With horrible *Scourging* they tortured Him. They Hang'd Him on a *Tree*, Nail'd Him to a *Cross*, and this between a Couple of Robbers, as being the *Chief of Sinners*. They kept Him in Bitter Torments, in the Midst of which they offered Him *Vinegar dash'd with Gall*, to prolong them & augment them, till He expired in them. This was done to the SON of GOD: and Him whom all the *Angels* in the Heavens adore with Eternal Praises and Wonders! A Fact which the *Sun* could not bear to look upon! And a World, where the Children of Men daily *crucify the Son of GOD afresh*. O Sun, How canst thou *now* look upon! That *Blood* which is the *Blood of GOD*,—We cannot say (with some Devout and Learned Writers,) That the *Angels* received that *Precious Blood* into *Golden Vials*. No, It was in the *Shedding* of it, spilt upon the *Earth*; We expressly read of, *His Blood falling on the Ground*. And, O *Earth, Canst thou cover that Blood, that the Cry of it shall have no Place?* Tho' it *Cries* for a *Pardon*, to them, who *Mourn* for what has *Pierced* Him, and with a *Repenting Faith* do plead it, that they may be *Pardon'd*, and so it *Speaks better things than the Blood of Abel*; yett it *Cries* for a *Vengeance* on them, who *tread under Foot the Son of GOD, & count His Blood an Unholy Thing*; on them, who *crucify to themselves the Son of GOD afresh, & putt Him to an Open Shame*. Thou, O Forlorn *Earth*, art the Polluted Seat of this *Wickedness*. And, The Infinite GOD, full of Resentments for what has been done, to the SON of His Infinite *Love*, says hereupon, *In the Day when I visit the* [ms. III, 69] *Earth, I will visit THAT Sin upon it!* The *Lamb* of GOD now on the *Throne* of GOD, appeared unto His *Beloved* Servant, *As He had been slain*. It seems by This, that He carries to This Day the Scars of the *Wounds* which were given Him on the Day that He was *Crucified*. "Lord, If Thou appear *As thou wast Slain*, the *Earth* from which thou didst carry the Scars of thy *Wounds* to *Heaven* with thee, will see what may stop the Mouth of all Complaint at the Vengeance, that shall render the *Rebukes* of *GOD in Flames of Fire* upon it." What a Detestable *Earth* is it, in which the SON of GOD was murdered! And now, *what shall be given unto thee! Or, what shall be done unto thee, Thou Detestable Earth.*

Sharp Arrows of the Mighty, with Coals more ardent & lasting than those *of Juniper. Thy Reprieve* is every day to be wondred at! Finally, There yett remains One Word more, which will finish the Matter, and which will determine the Load of *Guilt* lying upon Mankind in *Our Days,* upon which the *End of the World is come,* to be heavier than what has lain upon any former Generation. Tis that Word of our SAVIOUR; *Fill ye up the Measure of your Fathers: That upon you there may come, all the Righteous Blood shed upon the Earth, from the Blood of Righteous Abel.—Verily, I say unto You, All these things shall come upon this Generation.* The People of *This Generation,* by *walking in the Way of Cain,* and of others, their Predecessors in Impiety, have entailed upon them the *Guilt* of their Predecessors. *This Generation* going on in the same *Way* that was the *Folly* of their Predecessors, have *Approved their Sayings,* and had a *Fellowship* with all their *Unfruitful Works of Darkness.* It has *heaped up Wrath;* and its *Trespass is grown up unto the Heavens!* How can it be any other than come to That; *The Harvest is Ripe; Gett Ye down,* Ye Executioners of the *Judgment written,* to do what you have to do: *For the Press is full; the Fatts overflow; their Wickedness is Great:* Verily, *The Day of the Lord is near in the Valley of Decision!* When the *Generation* came on, wherein the *Iniquity* of the *Amorites* and the Nations devoted unto Destruction *was full,* and come to the *Fulness of the Measure* allowed for, then they were *Destroy'd,* and the *First* of their *Cities* particularly, was made a Type of the *Last Conflagration.* Such is the Sad Case of *This Generation;* It has the *Guilt* of all the *Wickedness* that ever was committed in the World, lying upon it.

And is not here *Guilt* enough, to procure a *Conflagration?* What can there be pleaded in an *Arrest of Judgment?* Or, what hast thou to say, O *Guilty World,* why the *Holy, Holy, Holy Lord GOD* Almighty, should bear any longer with thee! Every Day now may this Issue be looked for: *The Lord could no longer bear, because of the Evil of your Doings, and because of the Abominations which Ye have committed; Therefore is your Land a Desolation, & an Aston-ishment, & a Curse, without any Inhabitant upon it.* Certainly The *Earth* has *Guilt* enough, to render it *Combustible!* A *Fuel* for the burning Indignation of GOD!

On that Head, there is no more to be said. But, Secondly, Lett us call in some other Considerations, which [ms. III, v69] may abate the *Incredibility* of such a *Catastrophe,* as we have now before us. People would fain have their *Beloved Earth* consist of none but *Asbestine* Clothe, & such as they weave into the *Incombustible Sheets,* in which they sometimes wrapped up the Bodies of the *Dead,* for the Preservation of their *Ashes,* in the Midst of the *Funeral Fire.*[29] But as our Apostle, speaking of *One Great Thing,* which the *Conflagration* is to be attended withal, used those Terms upon it, *Why should it be thought a Thing Incredible with you?* These are Terms which may be agreeably used on this Occasion.

I will not insist on the *Dispatch,* which a *Few Years* makes of All Mankind in Every Generation. We see One *Whole Generation,* in a *Few Years* passing away to make Room for *Another Generation;* and in the Moment of their *Passing away,* their own Dissolution is little other *to them,* than if the *Whole World* underwent a Dissolution. And, *Why should it be thought a thing Incredible with you,* that in GODs Time for it, a *whole Generation* should *at once* pass away; and such a *Generation,* as may on very many of the Greatest Accounts imaginable, be called, *An other Generation,* come on; and *this Earth,* see the End of that, *Forever,* which Vain Man assigns to it, & be no longer what it is, but *Abide forever* in the *Paradisaic Restitution* intended for it!

But I will rather say, Have we not known mighty *Cities,* full of *Wealthy* and *Polite* Inhabitants, many People of Quality; full of admirable *Curiosities,* full of memorable *Antiquities,* and *Seats* whereof the *Charms* were marvellous: All swallowed up at once in astonishing *Earthquakes?* And now, *Why should it be thought a thing Incredible with you,* that vast *Numbers* of such *Cities,* may together perish in their *Sins?* For, O *Cities* yett standing on the *Earth,* what are your *Sins* less than those of the *Cities* that have perished before you? The *Cities* which GOD has *overthrown in His Anger, & Repented not.*

More *Cities,* Yea, More Considerable *Cities,* have been laid waste by *Fire* and *Sword,* when the Sons of *Chain* have been lett loose to spend the *Heat* of their Fury upon them? *Ninive,* for Exemple; *Ninive,* whereof in the Book of *Jonah* we read, *It was, GOD knows, a Great City!* It had in it, Six score thousand Infants under Two Years of Age; which usually making the *Fifth* Part of a People, here must be Six hundred thousand Inhabitants;[30] [Almost as many as the City of *London,* which exceeds *Paris* and *Roan* and *Rome,* if you putt them all together, for the Numbers of the Inhabitants, pretends unto:—But thou, O *London,* hadst once a *Second* of *September* in thee!][31] But, what is become of this Populous *Ninive,* and all her Stately Edifices! This Renowned City is now so lost, that *Lucian* affirm'd in his Days, *There was no Footstep left of it, nor could any Man Living tell where it was.* It is with a very Desultory Levity, that very Ancient Writers direct us where to find it; *Herodotus* and *Diodorus* do with a Strange Inconstancy contradict [ms. III, 70] themselves, as well as one another upon it. Even the Incomparable *Bochart,* whose Exquisite Researches must have discovered some Rubbish of this Eminent City, if any Mans could have done it, after he has consulted a whole University of Authors about it, concludes, *Proindè puto Doctos se fatigare frustrà in loco Ninives praecisè definiendo.*[32] What an Amazing Fulfilment of the Prophecy! [Nah. I. 8.] *He will make an Utter End of the Place thereof!* And, [Nah. III. 17.] *Their Place is not known, where they were!* Yea, besides, what they tell us, of *Sybaris,* tis related by *Strabo,* as well as *Diodorus,* (none of the Vainest Writers,) That there were Cities in *Libya,* which had Seven hundred Thousand Men in them. An Old Inscription remembred by *Tacitus,* asserts, that in *Thebes,* there were Seven hundred Thousand Inhabitants able to bear Arms.[33] But, what is become of these *Wicked Cities?* How many of them, have like the Bright Star of *Cassiopaea,* totally disappeared; Entirely Vanished?[34] And, *Why should it be thought a Thing Incredible with you,* that the rest of the *Wicked Cities,* become at once *Extinct,* in the Day, when *by Fire and by His Sword,* (*Fire* being the *Sword*) *the Lord shall plead with all Flesh, & the Slain of the Lord shall be many?* Thy *Talisman,* O *Paris,*

will be unto thee but a *Lying Vanity!*[35] When the Flourishing City of *Corinth*
had offered Some Indignities to the *Roman Ambassadors*, it was Revenged with
Fire and *Sword*, and *Flames* that laid the whole City in Ashes, & Ruines. I
make no doubt, that our Apostle had Some Eye to This Event, and hoped the
Corinthians would have so too, when he wrote those Words in his Epistle to
them; [2. Cor. V. 20.] *As Ambassadors for CHRIST, as tho' GOD did beseech
You by us; We pray You in CHRISTs stead, Be Ye Reconciled unto GOD.*[36]
The *Ambassadors* of that Glorious LORD, have every where mett with as Vile
Indignities, from a World, refusing an offered *Reconciliation* with GOD. And,
Is it *a thing Incredible with you*, that Such a World, should be by *Flames* reduced unto Ashes & Ruines? [ms. III, v70] When those, which they called, *The
Barbarous Nations*, upon their Call from the *Trumpetts* of GOD, made their Descent upon the *Roman Empire*, tis impossible to comprehend the *Desolations*
which the World was filled withal.[37] The Invasions upon the Peace of Mankind
when the two following *Wo-Trumpetts*, called in first the *Saracen Locusts*, and
then the *Ottoman Horsemen*, upon the World, made Incomprehensible Additions to the Prodigious *Desolations*.[38] In these *Desolations*, whole *Cities* have
been overwhelmed; and such Vast Amassments of *Wealth* have been buried
with them, that All the *American Mines*, have not been able unto this Day to
repair the Damages. And, *Why should it be thought a thing Incredible with
you*, that the Last of the *Trumpetts*, the Sounding of which is now every day
to be looked for, & which is to bring in the Consummation of *Woes* upon a
Wicked & a *Woful* World, should make the *Desolations* no less than *Universal*:
Our GOD sees, That we do *not fear Him*, & *receive Instruction*, to prevent the
Cutting off of our *Dwellings*, but We have *corrupted all our Doings*. What can
be now looked for, but this; *Therefore saith the Lord, All the Earth shall be
devoured by the Fire of my Jealousy!* In these *Desolations*, what *Memorable*
Things have been Irrecoverably Lost, and their *Memorials perished with them!*
The *Epitaphs* of Numinized Emperours, as well as their *Monuments*, all *Buried
in Oblivion*; while at the same time, to exemplify the *Vanity of the World*, the
Epitaphs of those *Lesser Bruits*, the *Horses* that carried some of them, are still
praeserved. Yea, what rare Arts are forgotten; and how many Occasions have the
Pancirollus's of these Later Ages, to weep over the, *Res deperditae!*[39] But why
should not the Things of *Ours*, go after those of the *former Ages*? In the Midst
of the *Desolations*, there has been scarce any thing, that some whom I know,
would more beg to be spared, than the *Libraries*.[40] Their most Pathetical Cry
would be, *Oh! Spare the Libraries!* But, it is reported, That there were Seven
hundred Thousand Volumns in the *Library* at *Alexandria*. And how great a Part
of these perished in the *Flames*, that were kindled by an *Execrable Troubler of
the World*, and Butcher of Mankind, happening to lodge in the City?[41] What is
become of the Library at *Pergamus*, which was a Rival unto this? A *Fire* at *Constantinople*, destroy'd a *Library* that had an Hundred & Twenty Thousand [ms.
III, 71] Volumns in it.[42] A *Protestant* Scholar can't but (with *Salmuth*) weep;—
when he sees the brave & rich Library of *Heidelbergh* which was by *Scaliger*
praeferr'd unto the *Vaticans*, transferred unto the *Vatican*: Tis as bad as *burnt*.[43]

But the *Vatican* too was once *burnt* by the *German* & *Spanish* Souldiers; and
whatever *Collection of Books* be now there, *That* also is quickly to be *Burnt*
in a *Fire* more desolating than that which laid waste the Tower of *Shechem*.[44]
Then, *Why should it be thought a Thing Incredible with you*, that there should
be a *General Bonfire* of Libraries? Especially, when so many *Books* are such
Trash, that the *Burning* of them would be no Loss, if the World could survive it;
but have that Complement upon it, *Nunquam vidi clariorem Ignem*[45]; And so
many are such Stuff, that a Sentence of *Burning* were most justly to be pass'd
upon them; consisting very much of that *Hay & Stubble*, which the *Fire* is to
sieze upon! Be sure, the Inhabitants of the *New Earth*, will have Little Occasion for them; Indeed, there is One BOOK which we cannot bear to see the *Fire*
sieze upon; That BOOK, which one a few Minutes before he died, Reading of it,
said, *If there were any thing that would make one lothe to Dy, it would be the
Reading of it*; Our BIBLE; the Precious & Peerless BOOK, One Leaf of which,
is worth a Thousand Libraries. Must this BOOK of GOD be lost? GOD forbid.
The *Martyr* that had the Book of, *The Revelation*, burnt with him, comforted
himself, upon it; *O Beata Apocalypsis; Quàm benè mecum agitur, qui tecum
comburar!*[46] But, O Wretched World; Thou shalt not be *Burnt* for a *Martyr*;
Thou shalt be *Burnt* for a *Traitor*. This BOOK shall not be *Burn't* in the same
Fire with thee. How our Glorious LORD will deal with this *Wonderful Book*,
and *Gift* of His, we know not. The Story of *John Arndts* Holy Book in the *Oven*,
is famous.[47] But this we know, when *Heaven & Earth shall pass away*, the
Words of this BOOK shall not *pass away*. After the Day when *the Earth shall
become Burning Pitch*, there shall be that Order given, *Seek Ye out of the Book
of the Lord, and Read.*

There is yett one thing more, which *at once* utterly takes away all the *Incredible* of the Matter. It is extremely *Probable*, that the *Antediluvian World*
was extremely *Populous*. The *Longevity* of the *Antediluvians* must necessarily
contribute unto it. Lett us make a *Computation*, with as much Disadvantage to
the Problem as can be asked for. Wee'l abate the Two or Three *First Centuries*,
in which the World might be pretty notably supplied with *Sons* & with *Daughters*: & wee'l suppose a Man to have Children at *Sixty*, and in the next *Forty*
Years to have *Twenty* Children. Single out now, the *Shortest Liver* of any that
you find mentioned as *Dying* before the Flood; and from that one Stock of *Seven
Hundred* Years multiplying still by *Twenty*, we shall find the Produce to be
more than *One Thousand, three Hundred, & forty Seven Millions*.[48] Thus, that
One Family would long before the *Flood*, have afforded People, more *than twice
as many*, as are thought now to be living on the *Earth*. When [ms. III, v71] *the
World being overflow'd with Water*, perished in the *Flood*, there were far more
People *at Once* destroy'd, than there are now in the World: And with the People,
what *Cities*, what *Sciences*, what *Inventions*, and what *Monuments*! What may
have been praeserved, by being stowed in the upper Cockloft of the *Ark*, by
our *Patriarch*, in whom *GOD has comforted us*, we know not. We have indeed
One Peece of *Antediluvian Prophecy*, and we have One Peece of *Antediluvian
Poetry*, rescued out of the dreadful *Inundation*. We can show some Unquaes-

tionable, Subterraneous, & Even *American* Remembrances of the Desolation.[49] The astonishing *Tower* erected not long after the Flood, unto which there is nothing to be parallel'd in our Days, inclines Learned Men to think, That some Tradition and Remembrance of the *Antediluvian Architecture* enabled them to make the Model for such a Building.[50] There were *Cities* before the *Flood*; and GOD knows, how Populous; how Illustrious. But, *All went at once!* Now, *Why should it be thought a Thing Incredible with you*, That GOD should bring upon the *Earth* a *Conflagration* which will *at once* carry all before it! Since, the *World* is as *Wicked* now, as it was before the *Flood*. And there will be a far greater Number *Saved* out of the *Conflagration*, than there were out of the *Inundation*. The *Saved* will be far more than *Eight Persons*; Tis to be hoped, there will be no fewer than *One hundred & forty four Thousand* of them; From whom the NEW EARTH, will be *Replenished*; and, no doubt, Mightily & Speedily Replenished: The NEW EARTH which we are now proceeding to. As for the *Earth which now is*, we have left nothing to be spoken for it.

I have all along supposed it Needless to intimate, That we cannot imagine the *Conflagration* foretold in the *Scripture of Truth*, should extend any further than this *Terraqueous Globe* with its *Atmosphaere*.[51] But lest any Reader should be so unphilosophical, as to dream of a further Extent for it, and bring the inconceivably Distant *Stars* within the Reach of it; I will here entreat him to be content with the Limits that *Salonius* of old assigned for this *Destruction from GOD*, which is a *Terror* to us; *Tantum ardebit quantum malitia Hominum, simul ac Daemonum, Coinquinari potuit*. That's enough![52]

IX. The NEW HEAVENS opened.

We are now to see a *New Heaven* and a *New Earth;* For *the First Heaven and the First Earth are passed away.* What may be the *Intention* of that Clause, *No more Sea,* or, what the *Occasion,* if I do not pretend here to *fathom,* or, if I Defer my Compliance with the Thought of *Minutius Faelix,* upon the Nourishment of it, and of its Fountains, *In Vim Ignis abiturum,*[1] I do no more than what is proper for one Sailing as I yett am on the *Black Sea* of *Ignorance.*

The *Fires* of the tremendous *Conflagration* by which the Globe is to be expiated & purified & marvellously Altered, having done their Work, & being so far extinguished as to make Room for what is to follow, there will now follow, the Fulfilment of that Word; Isa. LXV. 17. *Behold, I create New Heavens, and a New Earth; and the Former shall not be remembred, nor come into Mind.* These are to be now considered. But, as the *Heavens that now are,* will have a little Praecedency in *Burning,* before the *Earth* which the *Fire of GOD* is *then* to fall upon; so, they that are to people the *New Heavens,* are to be *First Raised,* a little before they that are to people the *New Earth* shall be *Changed.* Accordingly, The NEW HEAVENS do in the *First Place* call for our Consideration; and the *Place* as well as the *State* of it, is to be Enquired and Assigned.

Now, the Divine Oracles have informed us, in the XXI Chapter of the *Apocalypse;* Concerning an *Holy CITY, coming down from GOD out of Heaven:* A CITY, that has a *Wall Great & High,* having *Twelve Foundations,* with *Twelve Gates;* A CITY, consisting of *Pure Gold,* exceedingly Burnished; and having its *Foundations garnished with all Manner of Precious Stones;* and the *Twelve Gates* entire *Pearles:* A CITY that has no *need of the Sun or the Moon to shine on it;* for the *Glory of GOD* [ms. III, ix, 2v] *Lightens it, and the Lamb is the Light of it:* The *Length* & the *Breadth* and the *Heighth* of the CITY, aequal; each being *Twelve Thousand Furlongs;* or *Fifteen Hundred Miles,* every Way, in each of the Three Dimensions. The *Cubical Arrangement* of the *Mansions,* will not at all obtenebrate any of them, while the *City* is thus filled with the *Glory of the Lord.* No; It will be *the Inheritance of the Saints in Light;* and while,—O Lord, *In thy Light we see Light,* it cannot be otherwise.—Or, while the Inhabitants themselves, are those who shall *shine as the Brightness of the Firmament, and as the Stars forever and ever.*

This is that CITY, whereof another Apostle of GOD, has told us, with relation to them, who in the Condition of *Strangers & Pilgrims on the Earth, seek an Heavenly Countrey,* [Heb. XI. 16.] *GOD is not ashamed to be called, Their GOD, for He hath praepared for them a CITY:* And, [ver. 18.] *The Patriarchs, dwelling in Tabernacles, looked for a CITY which hath Foundations, whereof the Builder and Maker is GOD.*[2]

It is a *Material City.* For, besides what is observed by our *Peganius, Creatures* as they cannot live out of the World, which is replenished with *Matter,* so, neither can they live out of *Matter.* The *Place* for the Communication of GOD unto us, must be where the most Noble and Sublime Creatures find the Noblest

& Purest *Matter.* This Place is in the *Heavens,* and no doubt in that Part of the *Heavens,* where the best Part of that rare *Matter* is to be mett withal: We have this to Demonstrate its being so. Tis a *City* to be inhabited by *Bodies;* The Inhabitants will be *Embodied Spirits;* The Glorious KING of the *City* Himself, will be so. But insist upon it if you please, that it be an *Ethereal City.* And Lett the *Matter* be so rich, & so fine, & so splendid, that our *Gold* and *Gems* are little better than *Shadows* of it. I object nothing to *That. Spiritualize* the Matter as much as You please; But if you think, a *Visible City,* of a *Cubical* Form is too *Corporeal* a Thing, yett you must allow, That there will be a *Place* of Reception for Bodies; and in this *Place* these *Bodies* must be so much *Together,* that they may *Converse* with one another, and maintain an admirable *Order* among them. Now since there must be such a *Place,* and our GOD has told us, *Tis a City,* and shown us the *Shape* of it, I know not, why we should be fond of having the *Place* to which He leads His *Redeemed,* any other than *A City of Habitation.*[3]

But then, The Situation of it, will be in a Part of the *Atmosphaere,* which will be nearer to the *Earth,* where the *Nations* are to *Walk* in the *Light of it,* than as yett it is, and it will be conspicuous to the Nations. We are expressly told, [1. Thess. IV. 17.] That the *Place* of our *Meeting with the Lord,* and where we *shall ever be with the Lord,* will be *in the Air.* Now, it will be in this *Holy City,* that the LORD will admitt us [ms III, ix, 73] to our *Meeting* with Him. The *Strong* One, will be *in the Clouds. O GOD, How venerable wilt thou be in those Holy Places!* What *Strength* and *Power* will He give to His *Holy People,* whom He will *Strengthen* for the *Flights* and *Works* of those *Holy Places,* and *Empower* to Reign over the *Earth* which will be then putt under them! This do I take to be that *Holy City,* whereof we read, *That the Many Bodies of the Sleeping Saints, which Rose & Came out of the Graves* after the *Resurrection* of our SAVIOUR *went into it,* after they had *Appeared unto many* here.

The *Primitive Christians* had such an *Idaea,* of this *Holy City.* Yea, Tis an astonishing Passage, which *Tertullian* has, towards the End of his Third Book against *Marcion.* While some, with *Tan. Faber,* quaestion the Truth of the Matter, & reckon it a Lye invented by the Heathens to abuse the Christians, & with our *Moyle* deride the good old Man for his *Castles in the Air,* others have had their more Credulous & Serious Enquiries about the Intention of the Divine Providence in Ordring such an Appearance.[4] Lett it be supposed one Way or t'other, the Passage will answer my Design in producing it; which is, To declare what Conception the Faithful then had, of what is *Praepared* for them. After those memorable Words of this venerable *African, Confitemur et in Terra nobis Regnum repromissum, sed alio statu, utpote post Resurrectionem,*[5] he goes on to declare the Expectations which the *Primitive Christians* had, of an *Holy City,* even a *New Jerusalem,* to *come down from Heaven:* The *City,* which, he says, the Apostle calls, *Our Mother which is Above;* and where, the same Apostle assigns, our *Citizenship,* in those Words which we render, *Our Conversation is in Heaven.*[6] He says, *Ezekiel* and *John,* had a Sight of that *Holy City.* And then he adds a Consolation granted unto the *Christians,* even in *his days,* by a Sight of the *City* granted not unto *Them* only, but unto the *Roman* Army. He affirms, that about the Year CXCVIII, there was a Wonderful Appearance of a Walled and a Mighty *City* in the *Air*, over *Judaea*, beheld with Astonishment for Fourty Mornings together. It appeared still in the *Mornings*, he says, but as the *Forenoons* come on it became Invisible: And he appeals to the *Pagans* as well as *Christians*, who had been Spectators of it, for the Truth of his Relation. Then he concludes; *Hanc* [civitatem] *dicimus, excipiendis Resurrectione sanctis, et refovendis omnium Bonorum utique spiritualium copiâ, in compensationem eorum quae in saeculo vel despeximus vel amisimus, a Deo prospectum.*[7] Now tho' I don't know what well to make of the [ms. III, ix, 4v] Relation; Yett I am fully with *Tertullian* [He shall be my *Master!*] in the Faith of such a *City praepared*, as he propounds in the Conclusion.

   Christian Reader, Be not shy of taking the Blessedness of the *New Heavens* into thy Contemplation, under the *Idaea* of a CITY. Tis the *Idaea*, under which the Oracles of our GOD most commonly exhibit it. Call not *That*, an *Idle Notion*, or a *Groundless Fancy*, which the Oracles of our GOD, have so often commended unto us. Our *Faith* will not have the Less of *Wisdome* in it, for *taking* Things as our GOD has *given* them. A perverse *Romanist*, on a very Impertinent & Ridiculous Occasion, that he may do, as they that write *Catalogues* of *Haeresies* use to do, and multiply the *Divisions* of *Protestants*, pretends to find a *Sect* which he exposes under the Title of, METAPHORISTS. Tho' what he prates of be no more than *Chimaerical*, yett we have indeed a Sect of *Metaphorists*, of whom I would entreat, that they would not so *Metaphorize* the *Holy City*, as utterly to *Evaporate* it.[8] Tho' we may allow some *Figure* in many Expressions concerning it, wherein *Wisdome will be profitable to direct*, yett, I entreat You, Syrs, turn it not all into meer *Shadow*, and Lett not your *Metaphysicks* operate & sublimate upon it, until you have made it no better than one of Your *Entia Rationis*,[9] & a meer *Non Entity*. Lett us have some *Substance* for a *City that has Foundations*. I do *affirm constantly*, that the *New Heavens* will have an *Holy City* in them. And the *finest City* that you can show, yea, even your *Seven-hilled City*, shall rather be a *Metaphor*, than our *City* of our GOD, where we have a *Better & a Lasting Substance* laid up, for them who have *taken joyfully, the Spoiling of the Goods*, that have less of *Substance* in them.[10]

   And now, *What Glorious Things are to be spoken of Thee, O Thou CITY of GOD!*[11]

   The *City* of Old *Babylon* was once, *The Wonder of the World.* It was Exactly Square, Fifteen Miles Each Way from Side to side. Its Wall was, as *Herodotus* tells, *Eighty Seven foot* thick, and *Three hundred & fifty foot* high; or, Lett us according to the more probable Account of others, make the Heighth to be but *Fifty Cubits*:[12] That's enough! It was built with Large *Bricks*, but cemented with a *Bitumen*, which soon grows harder than *Bricks*. On every Side of this Vast *Square*, were *twenty five Gates* in the Wall, of Solid *Brass*; and between every *Two Gates*, there were mostly *Three Towers*, which were Ten foot higher than the Wall. From the *Twenty five Gates* on each side of the Square, there went as many *Streets* to the opposite Side in a direct Line; so that there were *Fifty*

Streets, each of them *Fifteen Miles* long; but these were about an *hundred &* *fifty foot* broad. Besides these, there were also *Four Great Streets*, with Houses but on one side, facing the Wall; which were *Two Hundred foot* Broad: By the Streets thus crossing each other, the whole *City* formed Six hundred & Seventy Six *Squares*, each of them Four Furlongs & an half on every side.[13] On that Part of the Square that lay next the Street, there stood the *Houses*; and behind them was room for *Yards, Gardens, Orchards,* all Manner of Conveniences. Neither [ms. III, ix, 74] were the *Houses Contiguous*, but there were Proper *Spaces* between each of them, to render the Abodes more Secure & Healthy & Pleasant: and there were three or four Stories in them. The *Curiosities* that replenished & embellished this *Unparallel'd City*, surpass Imagination! To people this his *Beloved City* did *Nebuchadnezzar* conquer *Judaea*, and many other Countreys, & hither he translated the People over whom he triumphed; So that the City was a Mixture of *Many Nations*, who at first as little understood one another, as People did, at the first *Confusion of Tongues* in *Babel*: It was inhabited by such as were chosen out of *Many Nations.*—But this *Accursed City*, what is now become of it? It was never finished; It is become an *Eternal Desolation!*

Lett us now *Turn away our Eyes from the Beholding of* this *Vanity!* Behold, A *New Jerusalem* that is the Reverse of the *Old Babylon;* and is the *Perfection of Beauty!* Behold, *The City of our GOD, the Mountain of His Holiness; Beautiful for Situation; The Joy of the Whole Earth,* rejoicing in Continual Irradiations and Communications from it! *The City of the Great King; in the Palaces* whereof GOD will be *known.* Come, *Walk about the City,* O *Faith* having a *Confidence of Things hoped for,* & the *Evidence of Things not yett seen:* Go round about it; Count, if thou canst, the *Towers* thereof!—

Here will be a CITY built by the SON of GOD, even *by the Might of His Power, for the House of His Kingdome, &* for *the Honour of His Majesty.* Tis a *City* an *Hundred Times* as Big, as that *Golden City,* which has now *Ceased,* wherein there once lived and grazed the Tyrant, who *smote the People in Wrath with a Continual Stroke:*[14] An *Hundred Times* as *Long* and an *Hundred Times* as *Broad;* But then, add the *Depth* of its *Cubical Figure,* and what a vast Addition, to Superiority in Bulk, above that Idolatrous Rendezvouz of the Nations! I hope, I shall not be detected in a Mistake like that for which the Learned have taxed a *Scaliger* in his Calculating the Weight of his *Colossus,* if I ask the Reader to Try, whether he don't find the *New Jerusalem* to be at least One Thousand & fifty Six Million times, as big as the *Old Babylon.*[15] And then allowing to Every One of the Citizens, a Palace bigger than the Biggest in *Great Britain;* Lett him calculate, how many Thousands of Millions, may be here accommodated, with *Mansions,* which nothing on Earth may be compar'd unto. One that knew the *City,* has told us, *In it there are Many Mansions!* Well may it be called; [Rev. XXI. 10.] That GREAT CITY, the *Holy Jerusalem.* After many Millions have been *Received into the Everlasting Habitations* there, it will be still said, *Yett there is Room.* To people this *Holy City,* our Glorious LORD is continually making the *Conquests of His Grace,* among the Nations of the World. The [ms. III, ix, 6v] Grand Work of the Gospel, is, To subdue the Minds of them, whom

His Purpose according to Election has distinguished; and cull them & call them out from the World, that they may be *translated into His Kingdome,* & become the Inhabitants of His *Holy City.* Tis, to be the *Vehicle* of that *Verticordious Grace,* which in the Way of a *Victorious Delectation,* does Perswade and Incline and Quicken His Chosen, to *yield themselves* up unto Him, consenting to be all that He would have them to be, & come unto all that He would bring them to: And so, to *make Ready a People praepared for the Lord.*[16] These *Captives,* whom GOD *leads in Triumph by CHRIST,* [Lord, *Lett me be found among thy Blessed Captives!*] assembled in His *Holy City,* will now sing that *New Song:* [Rev. V. 9.] *Thou hast Redeemed us to GOD by thy Blood, out of Every Kindred & Language & People & Nation.*

In this HOLY CITY, we shall be made Partakers of those Wonderful Things, which the Word of our GOD has called, [Eph. I. 3.] *All Spiritual Blessings in HEAVENLY PLACES.* This is that STRONG CITY, wherein our GOD will *shew His marvellous Kindness.* And, *O our GOD, our GOD, How Great is thy Goodness which thou hast there laid up for them that fear thee!* This is that STRONG CITY, the *Gates* whereof will be *Open,* for the *Righteous Nation,* which keeps the Truths to Enter in. Tis the CITY, where, *Behold, The Tabernacle of GOD is with Men,* & *He shall dwell with them,* & *they shall be His People,* & *GOD Himself shall be with them,* & *shall be their GOD. And GOD shall wipe away all Tears from their Eyes,* & *there shall be no more Death, neither Sorrow, nor Crying, neither shall there be any more Pain; for the former things are passed away.*

Will it be expected of me, that I should now attempt a Description of the HOLY CITY, and of the *Blessedness,* which the *Raised Saints* who are to Inhabit it, shall Rise unto? Alas, My Reader, It should rather be a *Moses* or an *Elias* on the *Holy Mountain,* that such a Thing were to be expected from![17] One who had been admitted unto as full a View of it, as could be had in the Present State of Mortality, brought us this Report of it: [1. Cor. II. 9.] *Eye hath not seen, nor Ear heard, neither have gone up in the Heart of Man* [or has there been any *Ascent* high enough to conceive] *the things which* [ms. III, ix, 75] *GOD has praepared for them that love Him.* They are, as One well expresses it; *Far more above the Highest Ascent of our Thoughts, than the Marriage Feast of a King, exceeds in Magnificence the Imagination of One that has always lived in an obscure Village, that never saw any Ornaments of State, nor tasted Wine in his Life.*[18] Indeed, the most Effectual and Compendious Way, to come at the Knowledge of what will be found in the *Holy City,* will be, by the Methods of PIETY, to walk in what we *know,* is the *Way to the City. Scies cum fies.*[19]

But if we must aforehand have some View of the CITY, take it, as it is given in those Words: [Rev. XXII. 3–] *There shall be no more Curse; But the Throne of GOD & of the Lamb shall be in it; and His Servants shall serve Him. And they shall see His Face; and His Name shall be in their Foreheads. And there shall be no Night there, and they need no Candle, neither Light of the Sun; for the Lord GOD giveth them Light; and they shall reign forever & ever.* These Words, what Blessings, what Comforts, what Wonders are contained in them!

Words, which, tho! we don't fully understand all that is promised in them, yett
so much is to be understood from them, that we cannot but say, *Lord, It will
be Good for us to be here!* Or, if we must make a little further Use of our Low,
Dark, Scanty Language, to *tell of Heavenly Things*, the *First Thing* that offers
itself unto our Contemplation in the *Holy City*, is that UNION with GOD,
into which it is the Eternal Purpose of His *Love*, to bring His Chosen People.
The *Delights* of the *Union* between the THREE ever to be adored Persons in the
Glorious GOD, are Incomprehensible! But such is His Inconceivable and Unfathomable *Grace*, as to bring some from among the *Sons of Men*, to partake in
those Divine *Delights* as far as it is possible for *Creatures* to be made Partakers
of them. This astonishing Purpose of our GOD, is discovered unto us, in the
Words of our Dying Redeemer: [Joh. XVII. 20–] *I pray for all them who Beleeve
on me, that they all may be One, as thou, Father, art in me, and I in Thee; that
they also may be ONE IN US.* Indeed these *Elect* of GOD, will continue *Distinct Beings*; They will not putt off their *Individuation*; In their becoming *One*
with GOD, it must not be blasphemously imagined, that they become the *Same*
with GOD. [ms. III, ix, 8v] But yett, they shall be brought so *Near* to GOD, that
GOD will become *All in All* unto them; and they shall be *Filled with all the
Fulness of GOD*; Even so *Filled*, as a Piece of Gold thrown into the Glowing
Furnace, is filled with the *Fire*. GOD will Penetrate them: GOD will Replenish them; GOD will wondrously Possess them, and Swallow them up in the
Tendencies of a Mind Closing with Him, and Communicate unto them *Fulness
of Joy*, and *Pleasures forevermore*.[20] We are making our Approaches towards
this *Union* with our GOD, while we are yett here in our *Pilgrimage*, travelling
towards the *Holy City*; and the higher Advances we make in our Approaches
towards it, the more *Holy* we are, and the more do we answer the End of all
the Divine Dispensations towards us. But when we are brought into the *New
Heavens*, the *Union* will have its Glorious Consummation there. In this *One
Thing*, the Inhabitants of the *Holy City*, shall have Things done for them, *Far
above all that they can Ask or Think!*—The Faithful are now in their *Center*.
In an Infinite GOD *Embraced* by them, and *Solacing* of them, they have now,
All their Salvation and all their Desire!

    In the Memorials of One Bound for the *Holy City*, *enquiring the Way to it,
with a Face thitherward*, I have read such Passages as these.

    "There is an Illustration of the Glorious TRINITY in the Eternal GODHEAD,
which apprehends the Great GOD propounding to Himself an Infinite *Satisfaction*; And here is GOD the FATHER. Then, GOD *Reflected* on Himself, that
so He may have that *Satisfaction*; And here is GOD the SON. Lastly, upon this
Contemplation, wherein GOD Beholds and Enjoys Himself, arising a *Love*, a
Joy, an *Acquiescence* and a *Satisfaction* of GOD within Himself; And here is
GOD the HOLY SPIRIT. Now, I sett before me my Admirable SAVIOUR, that
I may *See GOD in Him*, and *Live*. From this *View* of GOD in my SAVIOUR,
my Soul is filled with *Love* to Him, with *Joy* in Him, with an Incomparable
Satisfaction from Him. What a *Communion* with the Glorious GOD, and the
Three Subsistences in Him, is *Dust & Ashes* herein rais'd unto! What a Dem-

onstration will this *Exercise of Piety*, give of ones having the Holy SPIRIT of GOD filling and acting of him! Yea, what a *Praelibation* here have I, of that *Final Blessedness*, wherein all the Gracious Designs of my SAVIOUR for me terminate."[21]

[ms. III, ix, 76] In the *Holy City*, the Servant of GOD will see the *Consummation* of the Blessedness, whereof he has here no more than a *Small*, tho' a *Sure, Inchoation:* [22] The Blessedness, which his *Divinely-touched Soul*, is Perpetually, Importunately, Insatiably aspiring, & ascending to! But, who, who can declare the *Satisfaction*? who can comprehend the *Glory*!

Tis an *HOLY City*. None but *Real Saints*, and indeed *Perfect* Ones, will inhabit it. They will be *Blessed* and *Holy* Ones, and indeed they could not be *Blessed* if they were not *Holy* Ones, who by a Part in the *First Resurrection*, are Qualified for & Introduced into the *New Jerusalem*.[23] In *Rising* from the *Dead*, the *Children* of Men have a *New Birth*, and are *Born of GOD*, and are become none but *His Children*. Of those that are thus *Born of GOD*, we read; *They do not committ Sin; They cannot Sin, because they are Born of GOD*. How *Clean* the *Hands*, How *Pure* the *Hearts*, of all that *ascend* into this *Hill of the Lord*, and *Stand in this Holy Place*! A Total *Freedom from Sin*, is One, and every Good Man will esteem it no Little One, among the inaestimable *Priviledges* of it. It is the *Inheritance undefiled, reserved in the Heavens for us*; and it will be the Reverse of what the *Old Jerusalem* was, when our *Isaiah* made his Complaints of what he observed there; No, *It shall be called, The City of Righteousness, the Faithful City*. T'wil be, indeed, what the Book of GOD has called it, *The Land of Rectitude*. All the Inhabitants of it, will have all their *Faculties* and all their *Appetites*, entirely *Rectified*. Not One *Wrong Step* will ever be taken there; Not One *Vain Word* ever be spoken there; Not One *Irregular Frame* ever gott into any Mind; not any but the *Right Thoughts of the Righteous* ever be formed there. All will be *Just as it should be*. All *Sinful Dispositions* will be wholly extirpated out of Every Soul; Every One will have all the Tempers and Virtues and Blessings of, *An Healed Soul. Self* will be entirely dethroned; The *Love* of GOD will govern every Motion. There will nothing be done, but what shall have an *Homage* to GOD intended & rendered in it. The *Relish* of every thing will be taken from its Use for the *Seeing* & *Serving* of GOD. *The Love of the Saints* to one another, will be *without Dissimulation*; most Cordial; most Generous; and from a Regard unto GOD in one another. All Possible *Obedience* to GOD, will be the *Glory* of the *City*. [ms. III, ix, 10v] The Remainders of *Indwelling Sin*, which in the Days of their Pilgrimage, were the Continual *Grief*, of all whom CHRIST has made *Alive unto GOD*, and fetch'd that Continual *Groan* from them; *O Wretched One that I am! Who shall deliver me from this Body of Death*! will now be entirely abolished in them. The Walls of the *Clay House*, having been beaten down by the Blows of *Death*, all the *Verminous Leprosy* of animated Mischiefs lodged & fastned there, will be forever done away; The *New House*, into which they have now entred, will have nothing of it.— *Be gone, O our Lusts, Be gone! There now no more be done by you, or for you, in us, till the very Heavens be no more.*

In short; We have the *Sum* of the Matter, and the *Source* of it also, in those Words; 1. Joh. III. 2. *Now are we the Sons of GOD, and it doth not yett appear what we shall be; But we know, that when He shall appear, we shall be like Him, for we shall See Him as He is.* They who are the *Children* of GOD, by an *Adoption*, become at the same time the *Children* of His CHRIST by a *Regeneration*. Having lost the *Image* of GOD in and with the *First Adam*, his *Children* have derived from him, an *Evil Heart of Unbeleef, departing from the Living GOD*. But our Blessed JESUS, as a *Second Adam*, is, *The Father of the World to come*; And all the People of the *Holy City*, will be made His *Children*, by a *Transforming* Influence of His Holy SPIRIT upon them: *Forming a People for Himself, to shew forth His Praise*. Every Cell, Every Soul, there will be *Enlivened*, & brought into its Figure & Action, by the Glorious KING Himself, infusing the *Spirit of Life* into it. Our Great REDEEMER, began the Operations of His Grace, upon the *Elect Vessels*, to recover the Lost *Image* of GOD upon them, while they were yett in *This World*; Even in the *Lower Parts of the Earth*, and those things which were many times *not Joyous but Grievous* to them, were but like the Strokes of a Statuary upon the yett unpolished *Stone*, proper Means to carry on the *Image* and finish the *Erudition*. Tis now done unto [ms. III, ix, 77] a *Perfection of Holiness*: and, they who longed for nothing so much as in all things to *Resemble* and *Imitate* that *Good One*, will have their desired *Conformity* to Him gloriously perfected; the *Top-Stone* laid, with a Shout of, *Grace! Grace!* upon it. The REDEEMER has done that on them, which constitutes them His *Children*, and *looking on the Travail of His Soul*, how gloriously is He *Satisfied!* With what a *Satisfaction of Soul*, does He say, *Behold, I, and the Children which GOD has given me!* A Balsamic Virtue, in the Spotless *Righteousness* of our JESUS and Surety, imputed unto the Beleever, while he was yett under the Infirmities of that *Hospital*, which the *Compassionate* One, allows His Church to be in the present *State* & *Seat* of it, inclined him, assiduously to press after a *Conformity* to that *Righteousness*, in the most consummate *Holiness*. Here the Wish of the Faithful is, yea, tis the Firstborn of their Wishes, *Oh! That I may be Holy, as He that has called me, & made me Righteous, is Holy!* They will in the *Heavenly Places*, be brought unto a full *Conformity* to the Holy One: and, *Beholding the Glory of the Lord, they will be changed into the same Image from Glory*. They that were the *Followers of GOD as obedient Children*, will now be all that their Father & Saviour would have them to be. But, what a Wonderful *City* this! A *City*, in which all the *Citizens*, are the *Children* of the KING, whose *Throne is Established* there, & whose *Kingdome ruleth over all!* What an *Holy Nation*, & what a *Peculiar People* will be the *Citizens*, and how will they *shew forth the Praises of Him, who has called them out of Darkness into His Marvellous Light!* O *Citizens* of *Zion!*—*What Manner of Men*, will they be! *Lord, As Thou art, so will they be, Each One resembling the Children of a King!*

The very *Heaven of Heavens*, and the *Life* of these *Heavenly Places*, will be our *Sight* of the Glorious REDEEMER, and of GOD in Him. To *See Him as He is!*—Our *Dying* SAVIOUR, left this as His *Best Legacy* to us, and is Risen

from the *Dead*, that He may be the *Executor* of His own *Will & Testament*:
[Joh. XVII. 24.] *Father, I will, that they whom thou hast given me, be with me,
where I am; that they may behold my Glory, which thou hast given me.* It will
be now executed. In the *Holy City*, They shall have the *Sight* of that Man, who
is GOD as well as *Man*, and in whom there *Dwells the Fulness of the Godhead
Bodily*: The *Sight* of that *Man*, who once *appeared in the Form of a Servant*,
but now is *Highly Exalted with a Name above Every Name*; The *Sight* of that
Man, who sitts on the *Throne of GOD*, and has *All Power given* to Him. They
will See the *Face*, [ms. III, ix, 12v] which has the *Glory of GOD* shining in it:
A Countenance, which is *as the Sun shining in his Meridian*. They will also
hear the *Voice*, as which no Thunder so Big, no Music so Sweet; The *Voice
of the Lord GOD Almighty*. When that *Voice* is uttered, all the *Holy City* is
moved with glad Astonishments! It carries *Life* with it, wherever it reaches.
The Name of the City, will be, JEHOVAH SHAMMAH.[24] And we may be sure,
All that is *Good* is There, if, *The Lord is there*. He is, *The Face of GOD*. In
Conversing with Him, they will See *GOD*; have the *Beatific Vision*. He is the
Sun of Righteousness that has Healing in His Wings. The whole *City* of GOD
is Irradiated from that *Sun of Righteousness*: and *Bless'd* and *Fill'd* with *Righteousness*, which they have been *hungry & thirsty* for. The *Rays* of that *Sun*
will be darted all over the *City*, into every *Corner* of it, and all the Saints there
will greedily take in the *Rays*, with a *Joy unspeakable & full of Glory*. All that
has been *Amiss* in them, will now be fully *Cured*: and they will be *Filled with
all the Fulness of GOD*.

The *Holy Ones* now receiving their *Inheritance*. What a LIGHT, will they be
brought into! In what a *True Light*, will Every Thing be sett before them! And
what will be the *Understanding of the Holy Ones*! We are here very much in the
Dark: Tis a *Dark Place* in which we sojourn. We are here how much deceived
with *Shadows*, and buried in them.[25] We see very few Things as they *are*. But
unto them that are in the *Holy City*, the *Day will break, & the Shadows flee
away*; The *True Light will shine*. The *Treasures of Knowledge*, Precious *Treasures*, Immense *Treasures*, which they will be enriched withal! How *Accurate*
the *Knowledge*! O Seekers of *Truth*; *Now we see thro' a Glass, darkly; but then
Face to Face: Now I know in Part; but then shall I know, even as also I am
known* by the Spirits whom we call *Intelligences*. Alass, To what *Mistakes*, to
what *Errors*, are we liable in this *Land of Darkness*! But in the *Holy City*, they
will be all corrected. Here, the Acutest Men have their very *Different Apprehensions*, of many things; And [ms. III, ix, 78] they often treat one another very ill
upon the Various Apprehensions they have of many things, and the Venemous
Apprehensions they have of one another. In the *Holy City*, there will be no such
Differences; no Dissensions, no Divisions. All *Discords* will be over there. The
Meek Ones how *beautified with Salvation*, will have no *Jars* among them. They
will all see with the *Same Eyes*; and in *the Light of GOD*: Yea, How *Extensive*
the *Knowledge*! In the Works of *Creation*, how *many Things* are there, which
we do *not Know*! Yea, are there *any Things* that we *do*? Even the *Smallest Parts
of Matter*, are too Big for our Comprehension. The *Wise Men of Enquiry* are to

this day puzzled about an *Atom*. In the *Holy City* they will doubtless have all the Difficulties & Phaenomena of our *Philosophy* solved. In the Works of *Providence*, how many *Mysteries* are there! *Mysterious Things*, whereof our Lord says unto us, *What I do, thou knowest not now, but thou shalt know hereafter*. In the *Holy City* all will be unriddled. Those Inscrutable Dispensations, which *to know, tis too painful* for us; they who come into the *Holy Places of GOD*, shall *Understand* them there. In the Book of GOD, there are *Things hard to be understood*. But in the *Holy City*, the *Book will be opened*. What *Illustrations* on the *Bible*, will they that are there be Masters of! Most certainly, The *Light* of the *Holy City*, will be a *Zaphnath-Paaneah*, a *Revealer of Secrets*, beyond any thing, that can here be mett withal.[26] *Truly, the Light will be sweet, and it will be a pleasant thing for the Eyes to behold* what the *Sun of Righteousness*, will show to them, whom He will there have under His Illuminations.

Among some Writings, that were entituled, *Vitalia;*[27] I have read such a Passage as This. "A Candidate of the *Heavenly World*, once insisted upon Two Things, that made his being there, *The One thing that he desired*. The first was, *To behold the Beauty of the Lord;* The next was, *To enquire* [ms. III, ix, 14v] *in His Temple*. Oh! May my Anhelations after a Translation thither, be mightily animated from this Expectation: *I shall be with my JESUS, and behold His Glory there; Yea, JESUS in all His Glory!* The *Sight* of HIM alone, will answer, how many of my *Enquiries!* While I am here, I am full of *Enquiries*: But this is not a Place to have them answered. The *Temple* is the Place for *That!* Even that *Holy City*, which is also the *Temple* of GOD. The Studies of my *Inquisitive Mind* will not bring me an Answer to a Multitude of *Enquiries*. I despair of having the *Enquiries* answered here. What would I give, to have a full Resolution unto Some of my *Enquiries!* But I will be patient; I will be content; In the *Heavenly World*, whither I am going, they will all be resolved. The *Holy Temple* Above, is the Place for the resolving of all my *Enquiries. There* is the *Oracle!* I will *Enquire in the Temple*. I will cease *Enquiring*, till I come to the *Temple*. I will count it a Culpable *Curiosity*, to prosecute *Enquiries* upon which I cannot hope to be satisfied, until I am in the *Holy Temple*. But, how should this endear the *Heavenly World* unto me! There I shall *Enquire* about abundance of Great Things, which I am here at a Loss about, and I shall receive the fullest Satisfaction."

In One Word; An *Eternally Progressive Knowledge*, will undoubtedly be a most glorious Ingredient in the Blessedness of the *Holy City;* But in the Day, when the REDEEMER shall *come down like Rain upon the mown Grass*, to revive what the Sythe of *Death* has done its Part upon, we read, *They that are of the City shall flourish like the Grass of the Earth*. In the *Reviviscence* of the *Blessed* Ones, who become the Burgesses of the *New Jerusalem*, a very Considerable Part of their Faelicity, will be from the *New Bodies*, wherein they shall *glorify GOD*:

To accommodate the *Holy Ones* for and in the *Blessedness*, which the REDEEMER will now bring them to, a *Resurrection from the Dead* now unites their *Spirits* to such *Bodies*, as will be admirably fitt for the Business of the

Heavenly Places. Of these *Bodies,* what an astonishing Account is there given unto us, in those Words! [Phil. III. 20.] *From Heaven we look for the Saviour, our Lord JESUS CHRIST; who shall change our Vile Bodies, that it may be fashioned like unto His Glorious Body, according to the* [ms. III, ix, 79] *Working, whereby He is able even to subdue all things unto Himself.* A *Resurrection from the Dead,* or, a *Living again* in *Bodies* that shall have some Conformity to the *Old Humane Figure,* but a Wonderful Accession of *New Qualities,* agreeable to an *Heavenly World,* was the Expectation, which all the People of GOD, who are now to inhabit the *Holy City,* dropt their Old, and *Vile Bodies* withal. It has all along been an Article of their *Creed;* and their constant Acclamation, *Resurrectio Mortuorum Fiducia Christianorum!*[28] The Eminent Person, who ordered only that Word for his Epitaph, RESURGAM,[29] therein express'd the *Faith* in which all the *Christians* that ever were in the World, expired. This *Faith of Christianity* inspired all the ancient *Patriarchs;* Who of the *Promise,* that the Glorious GOD, would be their GOD, and BLESS them, forever understood This, to be the Intention; That He would rescue them from the *Curse* of *Death,* & *Raise* them from the *Dead.* They all held their *Flesh fast* in the *Teeth* of their *Faith,* and tho' the Lord *Slew them,* yett they *Trusted in Him,* that after their *waiting the Days of their Appointed Time,* a *Change* would *come,* wherein GOD will have a *Desire to the Work of His Hands,* and their *Bodies* reviving shall answer to His Call, *Here am I!* When they sang, [Psal. XXXV. 10.] *Yea, of my Body all the Bones, Lett them declare abroad, O Thou Eternal GOD, who is to be compar'd to Thee;* They had in their View, what would be done for their *Bones,* in that Incomparable Work of the Glorious GOD, *The Resurrection of the Dead.* What a *Melody!* Their Song was, [Psal. XC. 3.] *Thou to Destruction dost reduce poor Miserable Man; And then thou sayst, O Children of Adam, Return again.* Their Song was; [II. Sam. II. 6.] *The ETERNAL GOD brings Men to Death, and then makes them to Live; He brings them down unto the Grave, & brings them up again.* Tis what they *Knew,* when they sang, *The Living One is my Redeemer:* And, *GOD will Redeem my Soul from the Power of the Grave.* What they look'd for, was That *the many who sleep in the Dust shall awake.* To assure us of Such a *Resurrection,* our JESUS has over and over again, bidden us to *Hope* for it; affirming, that none could quaestion it, but Such as did not know the *Power,* and *Scripture* of GOD, whereof the former assures us that He *Can,* and the latter assures us that He *Will* one day *Raise the Dead.* And then He has confirmed us in the *Lively Hope* of it, by His first *Raising One* from the *Dead,* in *every Year* of His Public Ministry, for *Four Years* together, and then *Rising Himself* on the Third Day after His *Death;* at which time He *Raised Many* [ms. III, ix, 16v] more, who were *His Dead Men,* and who anon ascended with Him. He that proposed unto His Followers, His own *Resurrection from the Dead,* as a *Sign* of *Theirs,* is Himself *Risen from the Dead;* and after this *Gospel,* there needs no further *Disquisition:* There can be now no Doubt, but that *He who Raised up the Lord JESUS, will Raise up us also by JESUS.* But that nothing might be wanting to satisfy us in the Matter, as *Calvin* remarks, *The Resurrection of our Bodies, is to be proved from the*

Use of the Sacraments;[30] Our SAVIOUR has instituted *Sacraments* to be observed by us, wherein the *Washing* and the *Feeding* of our *Bodies,* is to Testify from Him unto us, That He will one day give us the *Cleansed Bodies,* wherein we shall *Feast* with Him on the *Good Things of His Holy Temple.* Yea, As the *Resurrection of our Bodies* is Ascribed to, so it may be Inferred from, the *Possession* which the Holy SPIRIT of GOD, has in our *Sanctification* here taken of them. We read, [Rom. VIII. 11.] *If the SPIRIT of Him who Raised up JESUS from the Dead, dwell in you, He that Raised up CHRIST from the Dead, shall also quicken your Mortal Bodies, by His SPIRIT who dwelleth in you.* Now, if these *Bodies* do not *Rise again,* then the SPIRIT of GOD utterly loses His *Possession* of them; He misses the Purpose for which He took *Possession* of them. A thing by no means to be imagined! *Irenaeus* of old prosecuting this Argument, cried out, *It is a Blasphemy to imagine it!*[31]

This was the *Faith,* which the *Holy Ones,* Lived upon, and which they Died withal. And now, in the *Holy City,* they receive that which had been unto them, *The Consolation:* They find it, *An Hope which they have no Cause to be ashamed of.* But in the Day, when GOD will *Ransome them from the Power of the Grave, and Redeem them from Death,* and a *Plastic Spirit* renews the Work, the *first Essay* whereof had been by our Sin, *marred in the hand of the Potter,* what *Bodies* do they find themselves furnished [ms. III, ix, 80] withal:[32] As Easily can our Almighty REDEEMER do this Work, as change *Worms* into *Flies,* which is done Every Year before our Eyes: As Easily, as bring the *Seed* out of the *Ground;* Which Comparison we will rather use, because our Apostle *Paul* used it: Tho' perhaps it was for This, that the foolish & flouting *Athenians* called him, *A Seedmonger,* for it: For that is the Etymology of the Term, which we render, *A Babbler.*—But then, The Glorious *Endowments,* of the *Bodies,* with which the Inhabitants of the *Holy City* will be glorified! *Immortal Bodies!* About the *Children of the Resurrection,* we are instructed, *Neither can they Dy any more.* The Influences from the *Tree of Life,* on their *Bodies* will be such, that no *Death* will prey upon them. Of so fine, & so pure, & so strong a Temper will their *Bodies* be, that they will never be in any danger to *See Corruption.* Their *Bodies* will be so *Salted* by the *Garments of Light,* which GOD will putt upon them, that they will become *Incorruptible* under it. *Luminous Bodies!* We are informed, *They shall shine as the Brightness of the Firmament, & as the Stars forever & ever.* There shall be no *Deformities* on them; nothing Ugly, nothing Lothsome, nothing out of Shape. No; They shall be sett off with a dazzling *Beauty* & *Brightness.* The Splendor on the Face of the *Israelitish* Lawgiver, a little shew'd, how splendid the *Bodies* of the *Just* will be, when they *shall shine like the Sun, in the Kingdome of their Father.*[33] *Powerful Bodies!* When they are *brought forth* from the *Land of Darkness,* that Word shall be fulfilled, *He brought them forth, & there was not one feeble Person among* them. The *Bodies* will be liable to no Diseases; The *Inhabitants* of that Balsamic Air, shall not say, *I am sick.* No *Timothy* will have any *Infirmities* there.[34] Their *Strength* will be beyond that of any *Lions,* that of any *Samsons.* As *Joshua* said, *Behold; The Lord* [ms. III, ix, 18v] *hath kept me alive; And now Lo, I am this Day four-*

score *&* *five Years old; As yett I am as strong this Day, as I was five and fourty Years ago; As my Strength was then, even so my Strength is now*: Thus, after these *Bodies* have been a Thousand Years at Work for GOD, they will have lost nothing of their Vigour, but be able to say, *Behold, The Lord keeps me alive, and my Strength is now the same that it was a thousand Years ago.* Finally; *Spiritual Bodies!* Not ceasing to be *Bodies,* or turned into meer *Spirits;* They will be *Material* still; but highly *Spiritualized.* Their Way of Living will be very *Angelical;* And they that are in them, will be *Equal to the Angels:* Doubtless, Able to Move, and Mount, and Fly, as the *Angels* do. An Heavy Tendency to the *Earth,* doubtless, they will be so disencumbred from it, that *They shall mount up with Wings as Eagles.* They have done well, who have taken the *Wings of Eagles,* to intend the *Bodies* of the *Raised from the Dead.* Our SAVIOUR has expressly called them, *Eagles.* Behold, The Bodies which the Faithful do now *Grone Earnestly,* to be brought into. Take them, O Ye Sons of GOD, and tho' Ye have once *lien among the Potts,* yett now fly about the *City of GOD,* with the *Wings of a Dove, covered with Silver,* & your *Feathers with yellow Gold;* Yea, as with the *Wings of the Morning,* whither soever your Glorious Lord shall please to order you! All the Painful Things which once they suffered in their *Bodies,* bearing Testimonies to *Pure *&* Undefiled Religion,* yea, tho' they had been Burnt at the *Stake,* or Broke on the *Wheel,* or undergone whatever is written, *De Cruciatibus Martyrum,* will now have an Abundant Compensation. Even a *Tharacus* and a *Blandina* will own themselves well paid for all their Sufferings.[35] Thus we read, [2. Cor. V. 10.] *That every one shall receive in his Body, the Things that will be according to what he hath done.*

—It is impossible for us to apprehend, the *Ways* wherein the Glorious LORD will now multiply the *Testimonies* of His *Everlasting* and even Overwhelming *Love,* to those for whom He has been willing to stand engaged unto His Eternal FATHER, and whom He has *Loved* at such a rate as to *wash away their Sins in His own Blood;*—Now He has them together in His *Holy City* with Him. T'wil be the *Love* of a GOD! Infinite! Infinite! Breaking forth in astonishing Demonstrations.

Be sure, *Now* will be the *Time* when, and *Here* will be the *Place* where, [Rev. [ms. III, ix, 81] XI. 18.] *O Lord GOD Almighty, Thou wilt give a Reward unto thy Servants the Prophets, and unto the Saints, and them that Fear thy Name, Small *&* Great.* Now and *Here* will be fulfilled that Promise to them, whose Bounties pass without any *Recompences* from the Present World; *Thou shalt be Recompensed at the Resurrection of the Just.* Now and *Here,* will be the Compleat Fulfilment of that Promise; *Whatsoever Good any Man does, the Same shall he receive of the Lord.* All the *Rewards* promised unto the *Overcomers,* in the Epistles to the *Seven Churches* [36] will be now dispensed in the *Variegated Blessedness* of the Faithful. None but the *Raised from the Dead* are to be esteemed *Overcomers. Beleever,* Distinctly Employ thy Meditations on the *Promises* to the *Overcomers.* In them thou wilt see Something of what is to be look'd for! This is the *Day,* and this the *Field,* where, *The Lord, the Righteous Judge, will give a Crown of Righteousness, unto all them that love His*

Appearing. And when He who says, *Behold I come, and my Reward is with me*, has brought all His Faithful Ones before Him, in His *Holy City*, the *Rewards* of PIETY will be such, as will abundantly assure them that have practiced it, *Verily, There is a Reward for the Righteous!* Yea, A *Full Reward from the GOD of Israel!* When their *Life* is thus *Redeemed from Destruction*, the Glorious GOD will *Satisfy* their *Mouth with Good*. All the *Good* which their *Mouth* opened in *Prayer* unto Him, *according to His Will* has asked for, shall be to their *Satisfaction* granted them. All the *Prayer* which they have made under the Influences of the Holy SPIRIT, tho' they have, it may be, forgotten Thousands of the Petitions which they have uttered in it, the Holy SPIRIT is the Infinite & Eternal GOD, and has not forgotten any one of them all, but will make them feel that He is Perfectly & Forever *answering* of them; Yea, Doing far more than ever they asked for.

Among the *Rewards* of them, that have been *Faithful to the Death*; One will now be a Public *Declaration* of the *Services* and *Sufferings*, wherein the Faithful *Followers of the Lamb* have Glorified God, and an Equal *Assignation* of such *Glories* to them as *GOD the Righteous Judge* will thereon *Distribute in His Love* unto them. This is what we are expressly told: [1. Cor. IV. 5.] *When the Lord comes, He will bring to Light the Hidden Things of Darkness, and THEN shall Every Man have PRAISE of GOD.*

We are by no means to Imagine, That *after* the *Coming* of the LORD, the Faithful will undergo an *Examination*, in order to the *Determining* of their *Title* to Eternal Blessedness: or, that their *Claim* to the Blessedness of the Heavenly World, will be held in *Suspense*, till a *Judicial Process* have passed upon them, that it may be then *Determined*, whether it belong to them, or no. When our Glorious REDEEMER has long before, *United* them to Himself, and pronounced them *Absolved* and *Righteous*, by allowing to them the Benefits [ms. III, ix, 20v] of His Blood, in the Notice which *Heaven with Joy* took of their *Conversion* unto GOD; and has by His Good SPIRIT Inhabited them as His *Temples*; Yea, by Virtue of His *Union* with them has *Raised* them from the Dead that He might *bring them with Him*; can it be imagined that *After all this*, they must pass thro' a *Trial*, to *Decide* whether the *Mansions* of the *Holy City* shall be granted them? Away with such *Inconsistencies!* No, This Matter has abundantly had its *Determination*, when their *Spirits*, at their Departure from their *Bodies*, were taken into that *Paradise*, where the Lord, who has the *Keys* of *Hades* in His Hands, kept them *Rejoicing in the Hope of the Glory of GOD*. At their first Passing into the *Invisible World*, if they could not THEN have shown and proved their *Genealogy*, they would have been forever chased from all *Hope* of any Part in the *Royal Priesthood* of the Blessed.

But now, our Glorious LORD, will have a *Judgment-Seat* in the *Holy City*. And whereas we read, [Mal. III. 16.] concerning, A *Book of Remembrance written before Him, for them that feared the Lord, & that thought upon His Name*; They who have their *Names in the Book of Life*, will have their *Names* by which they stand entred there, successively called upon; and making their Humble Appearance before their Almighty JUDGE, and *in the Congregation of* the *Righteous*, what is found written in that *Book of Remembrance* concerning them, will be publickly recited in the *Great Congregation*. In that Book, there is entred, all that *Work & Labour of Love*, which the Faithful have *shewed unto the Name* of their GOD. Yea, In that *Book*, as in a Golden *Lacrymatory* they will find reserved Every Single *Tear*, which they have shed in the *Sorrows* of a *Repenting*, or the *Ardours* of a *Beleeving* Soul: and in *Suffering according to the Will of GOD*. The Glorious ONE, from whom they long ago received that Encouragement, *I know thy Works, & thy Labour, & thy Service, & thy Patience*, and lived upon it, and in the Faith of it bravely trampled on the *Praise of Men*, and made nothing of being made Nothing among them; will now have it very publickly Reported; How they *Lived unto GOD*, and *Lived by the Faith of the Son of GOD*; How their *Lives* were filled with *Acknowledgments* of GOD, & with *Benefactions* to Men; How *Diligent* they were in the *Business*, to be considered when they come to *Stand before the King of Kings*; and what Husbands they were of the *Time* once indulged unto them! What *Pains* they took to praepare for a Reception where no *Undefiled Thing* may *enter*; and by being [ms. III, ix, 82] *Rich in Good Works, lay up a Good Foundation for the Time to come, and lay hold on Eternal Life*; What *Fruits* they brought forth, by which their *Heavenly Father has been glorified*: With what *Zeal* they paid Regards to the *House* of their GOD: With what *Self-denial*, they went thro' the Duties incumbent on them; What *Stewards* they were of their Various *Talents*; What *Projections* they had, that they might be *Blessings* to all about them, & promote the *Kingdome* of GOD in the World: With what *Resignation* to the Will of GOD, and with what *Perfect Work of Patience* they took every *Cup* that He ordered for them; and, with what *Meekness of Wisdome*, they underwent *Injuries & Oppressions* from those who *troubled* them. That such a *Report* will be made of these Things, is not meer *Conjecture*, or Figurative & Poetical Flourish; Tis in Plain Terms most positively asserted: [1. Pet. I. 7.] *The Trial of your Faith, being much more precious than of Gold that perisheth, tho' it be tried with Fire, will be found unto PRAISE and HONOUR and GLORY, at the APPEARING of JESUS CHRIST*. Their *Tried Faith*, and their Behaviour under their *Trials*, it shall *Then* be *Praised*, and *Crowned*. What the Faithful have been found upon the *Trial*, which their *Faith* had, in their Encounters here, it will *Then* be *found*, that GOD, shall have His *Praise & Honour* and *Glory* from it; and in *His*, they shall have *Their Own*. It unavoidably follows, That there will be *Degrees of Glory* for the Faithful, Proportioned unto what there is found in the *Book of Remembrance* for them. However, there will be no *Discontent* in the *Less Glorious*, nor any *Elation* in the *More Glorious*, where every *Will* is entirely swallowed up in the *Will* of GOD: The *Disciple* whom JESUS has *Loved* with some *Distinguishing* Signs of His Acceptance, will not be *Proud* of what is done for him; and the Rest will not be *Vex'd* at being overlook'd in those *Distinctions*. When these Things are thus in their Exhibition, before our Great REDEEMER, who will take an inconceivable Delight, in seeing the *Effects* of His Purchase, & SPIRIT; and before a Great *Assembly*, who will magnify the

Grace of our GOD in *giving such Gifts unto Men*; We have been informed from Above, that the Holy ANGELS will appear as *Witnesses* to the *Actions* of the Beleever now receiving of his *Recompences*. In our Sacred Oracles, we find *Charges* given us, *Before the Elect of Angels*; and *Comforts* brought us from our being, *A Spectacle to Angels*: which are Plain Intimations, that the *Angels* take much Cognisance of what we do, in [ms. III, ix, 22v] order to their Appearing as *Witnesses* on this bright Occasion. What an Addition to the *Solemnity!* to the *Satisfaction!*—Yea, we read concerning our Glorious LORD, *He is a Judge of the Thoughts & Intents of the Heart.* Accordingly, when we stand before His *Judgment Seat*, He will make all to know, that He saw all the *Thoughts & Intents of our Heart*, and will now pass a favourable *Judgment* upon them. And whereas, we had an *Heart* full of *Thoughts* on that Noble Quaestion; *What Service may I do for the Kingdome of GOD my SAVIOUR?* And our *Heart* had many *Intents* to do this and that *Service*, which to our Grief we were prevented from the doing of; the Glorious One, who said unto a Servant of His about a Real *Purpose*, which Heaven would not allow Him to accomplish, *Thou didst well in that it was in thine Heart for to do it*: will now give us to see, that none of our, GOOD DEVISED, is forgotten with Him.[37] And now, As the Emperour of *Persia*, finding in a *Book of Remembrance*, what had been done by a *Mordecai* for the Good of His Family, ordered him to be carried in great Pomp & State, with Singular Marks of the Royal Favour, thro' the Capital City, and Proclamation to be made, *Thus it shall be done to the Man whom the King delights to honour*: This is probably entred in these Pages, with a *Deep* Design to intimate & illustrate, *What shall be done for the Man*, whose *Attainments* and *Atchievements*, are found Registred in the *Book of Remembrance* to be now opened before a LORD infinitely Greater than any *Persian Emperour*, and before His *Holy Ones*, the Least of whom will be greater than ever an *Artaxerxes Longimanus* in all his Grandeur.[38] If the Humble Servant of GOD, be not carried thro' the *Holy City*, with Special Marks of the Divine Favour, & it be not proclamed, *Thus it shall be done to the Man, who made it his Continual Endeavour to do all he could for the Honour of his GOD; and whom the Great KING has Honoured, by giving Him to Do and to Bear for Him!*—Something as Great shall be done for him.—Some few of the Faithful, have in *This World* had their *Lives* published after their *Deaths*, and had, *A Good Name with Good Men for Good Things*; which is as right a Definition of *Honour*, as ever was offered; and from One whose *Life* has been printed, & who had a share of the *Honour* so rightly defined. But the Most of them, and some of those not Inferiour to any of them that have by our little *Monuments*, been made *Persons of Renown in the Congregation of the Lord*, have been buried in Obscurity and Oblivion. Their *Life* has been *Hid* [ms. III, ix, 83] *with CHRIST in GOD*; They have passed along very unobserved among the Children of Men, and been *His Hidden Ones*. Their GOD has been *Theatre* enough unto them; It has been enough unto them, to be *Visible* unto the *Invisible*; They never affected, but even Avoided, all Public Appearances on any other *Theatre*; or any Discoveries of their *Prayers* and their *Alms*, which went *up as a Memorial before GOD.* Their *Lives* will *now* be published; and all that they have been or done, shall be told in the whole *City* of GOD, for a *Memorial of them.*

At the same time, these Children of GOD, astonished at what the *Sovereign Grace* of their GOD has done for them, and in them, and by them, and full of *Self-Annihilation*, will be transported with an Inexpressible Joy, that they have been made *Vessels of Honour* to their Glorious LORD; *His Glory* they will esteem *Theirs*, and they will reckon they have *No Glory*, but what is entirely *His.* GOD will be *the Joy of their Joy*; And as, while they were yett among the *Potsherds of the Earth* here below, being aware that the most of People who might admire them & applaud them, would foolishly Terminate in *Them*, and look no further than the *Worm*, defrauding the Great GOD of His Praises, they deprecated it as an *Infaelicity* to be made the Objects of that *Sacrilegious Idolatry*; and had no fondness for the *Praise of Men*, but said, *Lord, Lett those that Fear thee, & will See Thee thro' me, be those that shall turn unto me!* So, all that now gratifies them, is, *That GOD their SAVIOUR will be glorified in them.* Their *Echo* upon all that is told of them, will be; *Not I, but the Grace of GOD that was with me!* And, *Not unto me, O Lord, Not unto me, but unto thy Name give the Glory!* And hence, if the Mention of their *Old Miscarriages*, and of the Points wherein *they have sinned & have done very foolishly*, and for which they have *Wept Bitterly*, like *Davids* and *Peters* in the Bible, be necessary to be also published, that the *Grace* of GOD may have its *Glory* in what is done for [ms. III, ix, 24v] them, the *Love of GOD* reigning in them, & filling of them, will *Constrain* them to a marvellous Acquiescence in it: Yea, like the Blessed *Paul*, Themselves to make a frequent Mention of them, with Wonders at the *Grace* that has Forgiven them.[39] GOD has His *Praise* on their Account; and in This their *Joy* is *Full*: Tis *Wonderful*! Tis *Wonderful*! Indeed, after so much as has been spoken, concerning the *Covering* of our *Sins*, and the *Blotting* of them out, and the *Remembring of them no more*, one would not have suspected, that the *Old Miscarriages* of the Faithful could ever have been mentioned any more, if so many *Faults* of the *Ancients that have obtained a Good Report*, in our Bible, had not been mentioned there. This leaves it a *Dubious Matter.*—

But it is no *Dubious Matter*, no, tis very *Certain*, That in the Midst of the *Rewards*, given to the Faithful in the *Holy City*, they will partake of a Marvellous Pleasure in their *Conversations* and *Conferences* with their *Fellow-Citizens.* If any Quaestion, whether the Saints in the *Holy City* shall *know one another*? I would putt that Quaestion to them; Whether *Moses* and *Elias* in the *Holy Mountain* did *know one another*?[40] When our Apostle recommends the *Love*, that shall *Abide*, after we have in the World to come received the Things, that we have here *Beleeved* and *Expected*, it is plain, that he intends the *Love to all the Saints.* But can We *Love*, any further than we *Know*? A Minister of GOD, whose Ministry had brought certain People home unto Him, writes unto that People; [I. Thess. II. 19.] *What is our Hope, or Joy, or Crown of Rejoicing! Are not even Ye, in the Presence of our Lord JESUS CHRIST at His Coming! Ye are our Glory & Joy.*[41] It is very sure, They that have been the Happy Instruments of bringing any into the *Holy City*, and Instructing & Assisting them in the Way leading to it, will there *know* the Persons, whom GOD has made them the Instruments of so much Good unto. O the *Joy* at the Interview! How will they *Rejoice* in one another! But how moving a Call to *Archippus*, in this Contemplation![42] So then, in the *Heavenly World*, the Saints [ms. III, ix, 84] will *know* one another. But how can we that *Sojourn, Wo is me!*—where we do, any otherwise than with Sighs to be there, think as Eminent Persons, when expiring, have sometimes done, *O Beatum illum Diem—O Happy Day, Happy Day!*[43]—When we shall come into that *General Assembly*, where we shall see the *Patriarchs*, & the *Prophets*, and the *Martyrs*, and all the *Just Ones made perfect*; Who will then be wholly free from all the *Imperfections* that might render them at all undesireable, & who will embrace one another [*Luther* and *Zuinglius!*] in the Arms of the dearest Love![44] What entertaining *Relations* may they give to one another, of what occurr'd unto them in their Travels thro' the Wilderness! Especially, of the *Ways devised* by Heaven, to *bring back the Banished Ones*, and the Methods of the *Divine Conduct* in carrying on the *Good Work* of GOD upon their Souls, and in answering of their *Prayers* and in fortifying them against their *Temptations*, & in delivering them out of their *Distresses!* In short, They will be *Associated* in *Acts of Adoration*; They will *together*, and in the sweetest *Consort*, carry on the *Worship* of their GOD. It will be *Strange* indeed, if they *know not one another!*

But the *Communion of Saints* will most certainly take the ANGELS into it. They whom we called, *Just Ones made perfect*, which they are not, until a *Resurrection from the Dead* makes them so, are also called, *Spirits*. Tis true, they are *Embodied Spirits*: But yett their *Bodies* will be so near to *Spirits*, that they will be capable of holding a most intimate *Communion* with the *Angels*, of whom there will be *Myriads* in the *Holy City*. Yea, When we read, That at and by the *Resurrection of their Bodies* the *Just* shall be *Equal to the Angels*, it carries a Shrowd Praesumption with it, that the *Angels* also have a Sort of *Bodies*: Otherwise, in our *Separate Spirits*, before the *Resurrection* of our *Bodies*, we should have more of a *Parity* with them. This we find, when they that have been *Redeemed unto GOD, by the Blood of the* [ms. III, ix, 26v] *Lamb, out of Every Kindred, & Language, & People, and Nation*, do *fall down before the Lamb of GOD*, and *Sing their New Song*; Then *Myriads of Myriads, & thousands of thousands*, of ANGELS, join their *Loud Voice* with them, *Worthy is the Lamb!* They that so compose *One Society* in paying their Homage unto GOD, cannot be *Strangers* to one another. The *Heirs of Salvation*, saw not the *Angels*, when they were *sent forth to minister* unto them, in the Days of their *Minority*, and when even the *Little Ones* had *Their Angels* to be their *Guardians*.[45] Their *Eyes* were not then of a *Texture*, to *Discern such Spirits*. But they shall now *See* these their once *Unknown Friends*, and *Know* them as they were once *known* of them. From These, what Surprising Relations may they have, of the *Good Offices*, which they once did for them; when *like tender Nurses they did in both Hands carry them*! And what Vast Improvements in *Knowledge*, may they gain, by what they may learn from them that have had so long & so far an Insight in the *Works* of GOD, which are *Sought out by all of them who take Delight therein!* Behold, Another Channel of the *River*, that will *make glad the City of GOD.*

But, *Employments* for the *Glorified! Employments*, in the *Rest which remains for the People of GOD!*—What shall we make of those *Expectations?* [Rev. V. 10.] *We shall Reign over the Earth.* And, [Rev. II. 26.] *He that overcometh, unto him will I give Power over the Nations; and he shall Rule them with a Rod of Iron;* that is to say, A Scepter: when *as a Potters Vessel they shall be broken to Peeces*, and wholly divested of the Shape which was formerly upon them.—And, [Luk. XIX. 17.] An *Authority over Cities* given unto them that have been faithful *Stewards* of their various *Talents.* And, [1. Cor. VI. 2.] *Do Ye not know, that the Saints shall Judge the World*: That is to say, *Teach* and *Rule* the World? The *Explanations* commonly given of these *Promises*, [ms. III, ix, 85] are so *Vain*, that it is impossible to keep in Good Terms with the *Third Commandment* upon them. To say, They shall be fulfilled unto the *Faithful*, in what shall be done for their *Successors*, & for People rising up in remote Generations, of the same Religion with them, tis to *Speak Profanely*, and it makes the *Promises* to *Speak just nothing at all.* They are the *Faithful* Themselves, who in their own *Persons*, and after the *Resurrection of the Dead*, are to *Inherit these Promises* of *Power over Nations*: and of *Reigning* with our SAVIOUR. Be sure, The *Nations* to be *Taught* and *Rul'd* are not in the *Holy City.* The Citizens of *That*, are to be the *Teachers* and *Rulers* of the *Nations*.[46] It remains then, that the *Nations* of the *New Earth* are they whom the *Glorified* in the *New Heavens*, will be sent forth to *Lead* in the *Paths of Righteousness*, and *Help* in the Work they have to do for GOD, as there may be Occasion. There is a Notable Passage; [Heb. II. 5.] *Unto the Angels hath He not putt in Subjection the World to Come.* And the Sentiments of some Students in this *Mystery of GOD*, have been express'd in this Manner upon it. The Church of GOD is now greatly befriended, by the Ministration of the *Angels*; which is indeed *Invisibly* carried on. But the *Raised Saints* will be the *Angels* of the *World to Come*, and the Church on the *Earth*, will receive inexpressible Benefits by the Ministration of these *Holy Ones.* The Ministration of the *Angels*, will now either be *Ended*, and they will enjoy unknown *Recompences* of their *Performances* in it, or perhaps the *Object* of it will be *Changed*.[47] The *Evil Angels* now being *Bound*, the *Good Angels* will not have many of those things to do, which once they had. But now, to come into a Sort of *Succession* unto them, *This Honour have all the Saints.* As by the Ministration of *Angels*, our GOD has heretofore made known His Mind unto His People, the *Raised Saints* will now be the *Messengers* to carry the Mind of GOD unto them. The *Law* was of old given on *Sinai* by the *Ministration* of *Angels*; But now the *Law* shall *go forth from Sion*, and the *Raised Saints* will be the Promulgators. The *Raised Saints* will be the *Angels flying thro' the Midst of Heaven*, [ms. III, ix, 28v] having the *Everlasting Gospel to preach unto them who dwell on the Earth.* As the *Angels* do at this Day, the *Raised Saints* will then come and go, at the Bidding of the Lord. Yea, The Glorious KING will say to them, *You shall be over my House in the Lower World, and according to*

Your Word shall my People there be Ruled; Only in the Throne I will be greater than You. He will send them to Govern *Cities* and *Nations,* and they will fly down with *Orders* from Him, for the Management of their Grand Affairs: and *Speak to them of Things pertaining to the Kingdome of GOD.* There will be a *Kingdome of the Heavens* thus administred: And, as the Faithful when they Dy, have their *Spirits* transported by *Angels,* into the *Rest,* wherein they are to wait for the Coming of the *Kingdome,* so when the Time comes for any to be Translated from the *New Earth* into the *New Heavens,* the *Raised Saints* may have something to do, about the Transportation. The *Glorified* Ones will then lose no more *Glory,* by this Ministration, than the *Angels* do, that in *Heaven always behold the Face of our Father,* and yett with Alacrity fly down unto the *Earth,* to execute Commissions there. Certainly, The Sinless Inhabitants of the *New Earth,* will be as Able to bear an *Access* of & a *Discourse* with, their Illustrious and Superiour *Brethren,* as the *Patriarchs* of Old, were able to bear the Approaches of the *Angels* unto them. If their Form should be too *Amazing,* we read in the Visions of *Ezekiel,* of such a thing as that; *When they go to the People, they shall lay aside their Garments, in which they ministred, & putt on other Garments.* But there will be none of this *Amazement,* in a People of such *Holiness* as they will then have to deal withal. While these *Glorified* Ones, were yett in their *Nonage* and under *Tutors,* as they were most Religiously and Exceedingly *Thankful,* for the *Angels,* who were the *Cherubim* [ms. III, ix, 86] that GOD had placed about His Church, and very *Great Wheels* for very many Motions in the Machin of the World; So, it was their Endeavour to be *Angelical Men,* and as far as their *Vermicular State* would allow of it, Resemble the *Angels,* in having their *Eyes continually unto the Lord,* and in their *Burning Zeal* against the Things offensive unto GOD, and in the Pleasure they took, *as they had Opportunity, to do Good unto all Men,* and in the *Quick Dispatch* with which, as with Souls upon the *Wing,* they yeelded Obedience unto the Commands of their Lord.[48] And now, the Glorious Requital! They shall be made *Equal to the Angels,* even in their *Employments,* as well as in their *Qualities;* and be the *Angels,* of that *World to Come, whereof we are speaking.* While these *Angels in Flesh* were as yett in the *State of Probation* it could in some Degree be said, *Projections to Do Good* fill'd their Lives; It was their *Meat* and their *Drink* to *Do Good* continually; Advantages to *Do Good* were inaestimable *Riches* with them; They knew no *Pleasures* comparable to Those of GODs using them to *Do Good* in the World. O Indefatigable *Doer of Good; The Doing of Good,* is with thee Now, what carries its *own Reward.*[49] Arriving to the *State of Retribution,* thy Opportunities to *Do Good* will be Inconceivably Multiplied, unto thee. Thy Glorious Lord, will still employ thee, in Ways that now cannot be conceived of, to do what His *Good Spirit* has made thee so much Love to do. The Faithful at this Day are generally shutt out of all *Places,* wherein *Humane Society* might be, as if their Hands were not unhappily tied, it would be, the Better for them. Among the *Officers* of the Nations, it may be said, *A Faithful Man who can find?* It may be, *Laws* aim'd at the *Establishment of Iniquity,* have enacted those *Tests* for *Employments* in profitable *Places,* that exclude those that would be the most *Faithful Officers*, and would most of all study to be *Blessings* in their *Places*. *Bretheren*, Bear with Patience the *Indignities* that are now cast upon you; *Be Patient, for the Coming of the Lord draws nigh;* At which you shall have more Honourable *Offices*, than any of those that are now denied unto you. Thus, the *Meek Ones*, at the same time, when the *Kingdome of Heaven* will be *Theirs*, and they shall be the *Children of GOD*, & they shall *See GOD*, THEN shall they *Inherit the Earth*. So, The *Patriarchs*, and they who had the Promises of a *Land flowing with Milk & Honey*, will THEN See all in the very *Letter* accomplished. They shall be the *Lords* of such a *Soyl*. The *Holy Ones* who suffered such *Slander* and such *Torture* on [ms. III, ix, 30v] the *Earth*, for their Faithfulness unto their GOD, will on the very *Earth*, and in their *Entertainment & Reception* among the *Nations* there, See a marvellous Compensaton; and be *made Princes in all the Earth*. It is not unlikely that something of this may be hinted, in that Appearance of our Almighty REDEEMER, to *Rule the Nations;* [Rev. XIX. 16.] *Having on His Thigh a Name written, KING OF KINGS, and, LORD OF LORDS*. In the Scriptural Style, the Term of, *The Thigh*, refers usually to the *Offspring*. They who were *from the Thigh* of such or such an one, meant, *His Offspring*. The *Raised Saints* are in a most inexpressible Manner, the *Offspring* of the REDEEMER. And now, On His *Thigh*, that is to say, on His *Offspring*, there will be the Character of, LORDS, Yea, and of KINGS. And THEN, Oh! what a Transcendent Fulfilment will there be of that Word! [Zeph. III. 19.] *I will gett them Praise & Fame in every Land where they have been putt to Shame*. The very *Seat* of their *Sufferings*, will be a *Seat* of their *Triumphs*! *Tertullian* is not the only Christian that has made that Remark: *Justum est et Deo dignum, illic quoqe exultare famulos ejus; ubi sunt et afflicti in nomine ipsius*.[50]

—But, The *Different Sexes*!—No; There will be no *Different Sexes*, in the *Holy City*;[51] And yett the *New Jerusalem* will be far from doing, as that *Anti-Chamber of Hell*, the *Old Babylon* did by their *Women*, when they had the apprehensions of a *Starving Siege* upon them. There will be *Huldahs* in the *New Jerusalem*! The Spirits, that once were in *Bodies*, kept under a *Covert-femme*, and could not move in any Higher Sphaere, than to *Marry, & bear Children, & guide the House*: having been exemplary for their PIETY, & been of *Old time, the Holy Women, who trusted in GOD, and adorned themselves with such things as are of great Price in the Sight of GOD;* These will doubtless now have their Part in the Employments of the *Holy City*: beyond what *Miriam* the Prophetess, & *all the Women that went out after her*, had of old, in the *Songs of the Redeemed*.[52] Even [ms. III, ix, 87] while the *Curse* upon the *Sex* in the Third Chapter of *Genesis* is yett unremoved, we have seen other Ladies, besides the brave Jewess of *Palmyra*, at the Head of mighty Empires.[53] But, in the World, where will be *no more Curse*, who can tell, what the *Daughters*, as well as the *Sons, of the Almighty*, may be advanced unto! Certainly, They will be *Equal to the Males*, who are made *Equal to the Angels*. It will be a Difficult thing to find the *Reality* or the *Original* of that which they call, *The Salique Law*, in a Kingdom that pretends to it. But this we are sure of; There is no *Salique*

Law that will affect the *Holy City*. *Different Sexes*! No; I say again; There will be *none*.[54] Our Lord saying, *That the Raised Marry not, nor are given in Marriage*, takes away the *Difference of Sexes* in the *Holy City*. They will so *Putt on CHRIST*, that there will be *neither Male nor Female*, nor any more Difference, between them, than between *Jew* and *Greek*, in the *Heavenly Places*. Lett it only be considered, *who is their Father*? The Problem is capable of being a little Elucidated, by some Reflection on the *Nativity* [I will take leave to call it *so*!] of the *First Woman* that ever was in the World. For the Formation of that *First Woman*, some Sagacious Men, [particularly, the Ingenious Author of the *Bibliotheca Biblica*,][55] have upon the *Mosaic* Account, formed this *Idaea* of it. The Hebrew Word, *Zelah*, which we translate, *A Rib*, is not in the Signification of it restrained unto any One *Bone* in the whole Humane Fabric. But the *Bone* which has the Best Claim unto it, is the *Back-bone*; in which also is found the famous *Luz*, which the Hebrews talk of.[56] The *Spina Dorsi*, is the first thing Visible in an *Embryo*; and the *Carina* of the *Foetus*: Anon the *Cerebrum* and the *Cerebellum* appear, which are as Appendices to it: Then the *Salient Point* of the *Heart*: And so the *Thirty Pair* of *Nerves* that come out between the *Vertebres*, proceed with their Influences; and with them there goes forth from the *Medullary Matter* in the *Spina Dorsi*, that which is the Foundation of the whole *Corporeal Substance*, from whence the Muscular and Carneous Parts are propagated & have their Nutriment.[57] Now, to produce a Consort for *Adam*, or *First Father* [Who was *Father* to our *First Mother* too!] was by the *Great GOD who formeth all things*, thrown into a *Deep Sleep*, or *Deliquium* and [ms. III, ix, 32v] *Extasy*; wherein his whole Animal *Oeconomy* was thrown into a Sort of *Digestion*, and had a Degree of *Resolution* brought upon it.[58] From *Adam*, even from every Part of his Body, and so originally from that *Bone*, and probably not without an *Image* of the *whole Shape* formed at the same time in his Mind, there was *Extracted* the Matter, [How discharged, *GOD knows*!] that was by a Divine *Energy*, quickly wrought up, into the *Body* of an *Help Meet* for Him. The Proceeding of this Operation, might well be called, an *Opening* of a *Side*; and the Finishing of it called, a *Closing* of it. And thus the *First Adam* had One that was *Bone of his Bone*, and *Flesh of his Flesh*, brought unto him. Here was,— and I have good Authority to say so, *A Great Mystery concerning CHRIST and His Church*. Now all the Remark here to be made upon it, is This: All the *Children of the Resurrection* will be *Born of GOD*; And the *Second Adam*, who is also GOD, will be their *Father*. Yea, they will be so His *Children*, as to be also, *Members of His Body, of His Flesh & of His Bones*. We are expressly told, It is an *Energy* of His, that will *fashion* the *Bodies* of the Glorified, into the *Likeness of His Glorious Body*. And He will doubtless give such a *Configuration* to them, as will best Answer His Designs in forming the People, of whom He has declared, *They are the Work of my Hands, that I may be glorified*. When *Abraham* with regard unto his *Dead Lady*, said, [Gen. XXIII. 4.] *That I may bury my Dead out of my Sight*; it has been observed, that, *My Dead*, is in the *Masculine Gender*. And Interpreters run into such a Variety of Opinions upon it, that an acute *Saurin* smiles at their Disputations.[59] But what if there should be this Intimation in it; That when the *Dead* are brought forth from the Cave of *Macpelah*, and their other *Caemeteries*, there will be no more *Difference of Sexes*; but both Sexes will be again united in *One Body*, as they were before the *Deep Sleep* upon the *Protoplast*, and all shall be *Perfect Men*, and the *Spirits of Just Men made perfect*, according to the Services which they will be *New Creatures* for?[60]

The *Female Sex* may think they have some Cause to complain of us, that we stint them so much in their *Education*, and abridge them of many Points wherein they might be serviceable; But, *the Handmaids of the Lord*, A RE-DEEMER who was once *Born of a Woman*, intends unknown *Dignities* for you, and will make an Use of you beyond what we yett know, to serve His *Kingdome*, when it shall *cease to be with* [ms. III, ix, 88] you as now it is, and your *Subjection* to *Men*, shall with your *Distinction* from them, no longer be considered. *Women* have sometimes had their uncouth Part in the *Priesthood* of some Countreys here. But your most Gracious Lord will most agreeably make you *Priests* unto GOD, among those that attend upon Him in the Regions that are *Above*: & bear a Lovely Part in the Sacrifices there. Yea, tho' the Apostolical Injunctions do *not suffer Women to take* any Part of *Teaching* in the *Christian Assemblies* of these Days, yett your Lord may one day send you to do a Part among the *Teachers* of His Flocks here below. Of old, about the *Temple* of GOD, there were *Women*, (usually the Daughters of the *Levites*) who were employ'd in the *Songs* of His Praise, and with all possible Decency & Modesty & Reserve, bore a Separate Part, in the *Instrumental* as well as *Vocal Music*, which kept up the Religion of the *Holy Nation*. Tis for this Cause, that we find the *Daughters*, as well as the *Sons*, of *Heman*, who was one of the Three Praesidents over the *Temple-Music*, mentioned in, The *Chronicles*. We find *Choirs* of *Damsels* led by the Praesidents of the *Music*; which *Praesidents* the Title of *Muatseach* belong'd unto. And it is at Length demonstrated, That the *Neginoth*, and the *Nehiloth*, and the *Alamoth*, in the *Titles* of Several Psalms, are no other than Various *Bands* of these *Female-Musicians*.[61] But shall not *Women* also have their Work to do about the Coelestial *Temple?* —I forgett myself. The Name, *Women*, is to be heard no more. O *Blessed Ones*, you have lost your *Name*, in your *Marriage* to the SON of GOD. Who were they, that were sent by the *Angel* to carry the *Tidings* of a *Risen* REDEEMER unto His Disciples? And why may not the REDEEMER, having *Raised* these into a very *New Condition*, employ these, to carry His Messages unto the *Earth*, which will have His *Hephsibah* and His *Beulah* dwelling in it?[62]—[ms. III, ix, 34v] In fine, To bring unto a *Period* our Discourse on the *Blessedness* that knows no *Period*; We find, That the Glorious GOD in His Promise to our Patriarch, said, *Look toward HEAVEN; Tell the Stars, if thou canst Number them; SO shall thy Seed be.* An Ingenious *Jew* informed me, the Hebrew Word / כה / is a Note of *Place*: and that the Lord not only said, *Number the Stars if thou canst; SO shall thy Seed be*: but also, *Look toward Heaven, THERE shall thy Seed be*. And I afterwards found, *Petrus Alfonsi*, in his, *Collatio adversus Judaeos*, making the same Observation.[63] Agreeably to This; We are now pointed unto the NEW

HEAVENS, which are in the *Place,* where the *Stars* appear to us. *Abraham* will be THERE; His *Offspring* will be THERE; The *Covenant* of GOD will be fulfill'd unto them THERE. *He* has none that will be own'd as his *Offspring,* but they that *Beleeve* as *he* did. All such *Beleevers,* in *all Nations,* tho' *Stones* fetch'd in from the *Streets* of the *Gentiles,* are His *Offspring.* THERE they are with Him; and THERE they receive *the Good Thing which GOD has promised unto the House of Israel, & unto the House of Judah.* To look for it, among a *Carnal Posterity,* flourishing in an *Earthly Prosperity,* before the *Coming* of the Lord, & the *Raising* of the Dead, & the *Burning* of the World, is, to *Look for the Living among the Dead.*

Thus we have taken a short View, of the *Blissful Seats,* wherein we shall be *forever with the Lord.*

It will not impair our *Portion* there, if we now step down for a while, [*Tis no more than what the Citizens themselves will do!*] to the *New Earth,* which will be the Lower Part of the *Heavenly Countrey* to be *Look'd for.*

X. The NEW EARTH survey'd.

Be Joyful, O Earth; and break forth into Singing, O Mountains! Our GOD is going to *Renew the Face of the Earth;* And we are going to see an *Earth full of His Mercy:* An *Earth,* No longer a Nest of *Serpents,* no longer a Den of *Dragons,* no longer a *Land that Eats up the Inhabitants thereof,* and that affords not unto the Children of GOD, a *Quiet Habitation:* But a *Mountain of Holiness,* & a *Dwelling of Righteousness:* The *Blessed* of the Lord!

We left the *Earth* all on *Fire:* Every where covered and perishing in the *Flames,* whereto a GOD, who *Judges in the Earth,* and is of *Purer Eyes than to behold the Evil, & look on the Iniquity,* which the *Earth* is every where filled withal, has condemned it. How long the *Fire* will persist, and how far it will proceed in its all-devouring Rage, we know not.[1] But in a little while, there will be seen an *Earth,* in all the Beauties of a PARADISE; praepared for an *Holy People,* that shall have no *Satan* to annoy them there. In this *Paradise* they shall continue At Least a *Thousand Years.* If I say, *At Least,* it is because the Repetition of the Term, *A Thousand Years,* no less than *Six times* over in the Prophecy that has informed us & assured us of it, has invited some to think, It may be *Six Thousand* Years, and as long as the Duration of this World has been before the Arrival of it. So *we shall be made Glad according to the Years wherein we have seen Evil.* Yea, from the constant Usage of the Book, in which This Prophecy occurs, & indeed of all Sacred Prophecy, which putts a *Day* for a *Year,* some very considerable Writers, urge that the Space may be prolonged unto Three *Hundred & Sixty Five Thousand Years:* if not *Cubically* to a *Thousand Thousand.*

Can any one tell, how much the *Shape* of the *Earth* shall be changed from what it was, by the *Conflagration* doing the *Strange Work* of GOD upon it? Shall we imagine, that the *Fire* which is to take Vengeance on the *Wickedness* of the World, will have a Commission to make no Impression any where, but on the *Wicked Part* of it: and like the *Fire* which once did not consume the Innocent *Bush* from which the ancient Lawgiver, heard GOD speaking to him, it shall not prey upon Objects that have not been rendred *Combustible,* by *Sin* defiling of them? Or, shall we imagine, that the World will undergo little more than a *Singeing* from the *Fire,* that is to fall upon it; and the *Fire* prove not much more Destructive, than the *Water* that once *Washed* it, when the *Foundation of the Ungodly was overflown with a Flood:* Some have imagined, that the *Old Seats* of the *Earth,* will not be so much altered by the *Conflagration,* but that there may in the Ruines be left some *Remembrances* of them.[2] [ms. III, x, 2v] Some have particularly apprehended, that the Spott of the *Earth,* which was the *Land of Promise,* whereof the Blessed GOD promised unto *Abraham, The Land which thou seest, unto Thee will I give it, and unto thy Seed forever:* will be the Distinguished *Midst of the Earth,* when the *New Earth* is to be brought on. And when the Apostle proves, That the *Patriarchs desired an Heavenly Countrey,* Because they might have had *Opportunity to return unto the Countrey from which they came out, and made no Use of it;* Such Writers as honest *Maton*, think, it looks as if the *Heavenly Countrey* which they desired, were the Land of *Canaan*, to be possess'd by them, when it should be Restored unto an *Heavenly* Condition.[3] And others, improving on that Notion, consider the *Holy City* of the *Raised*, in the *Clouds* of the *New Heavens*, as being more peculiarly over *That Land*, at the Time of the *Restitution*, and *That Land* as having a peculiar share above other *Countreys*, in the Visits which the *Raised Saints* from time to time shall give unto the Lower World.[4] Had *Heaven* in general been the *Heavenly Countrey* here spoken of, it might be argued, that they might as well have obtained *That*, or have expressed their Affection to it, *in their own Countrey from which they came*; They might have returned unto *That*, and have *Lived as Pilgrims* There. But they would *this Way* express their *Faith*, of what GOD had promised One Day to do for them & theirs in *This Land*, when He should *Raise the Dead*, and be *Their GOD*. Indeed, *This Land*, as it should seem, shall then after a Singular Manner be an *Heavenly Countrey*; And it seems to be foretold in *Ezekiel*, That it shall become *Like the Garden of Eden*; in which *Garden*, the SON of GOD in the *Shechinah*, with His *Angels*, was visibly & familiarly conversant. This also, they suppose, may be to the Intention of *Joseph*, in ordering his *Bones*, without any regard unto the Whimsey of, *The rolling of the Caverns*, to be transported into the *Land of Canaan*.[5]

But, We are at a Loss, how this Imagination will stand before the *Fire* of those Oracles, [ms. III, x, 90] which express the Matter to us, in those overwhelming Terms; *The EARTH, and the Works that are therein, shall be BURNT UP*; And, *ALL these things shall be DISSOLVED*. And, *The First Heaven, and the First Earth is PASSED AWAY, and there is NO MORE SEA*: And, *Heaven and Earth shall PASS AWAY*; And, *The former Heavens & Earth shall NOT BE REMEMBRED, nor come into Mind* any more. That Word also looks very suspiciously. They that *inherit the New Earth*, shall *diligently consider the Place of the Wicked, and IT SHALL NOT BE*. One cannot but consider hereupon, whether the *Deed* for the *Promised Land*, will not be more than made Good, by Investing the *Father of the Faithful*, and his Offspring, in the Enjoyments of a *Better Countrey*, which was then uncapable of being described in more intelligible *Idaea's*, than those of such a *Countrey* as the Land of *Canaan* here carried an *Image* of? And, whether the whole or the most, of the *New Earth*, may not be, *The Land of Israel*, in many of the Ancient Prophecies referr'd unto?

Indeed, One may empannel a *Jury* of the *Fathers*, who lett fall Passages, which if *Arnobius* the Younger might be allow'd, as their *Foreman*, to speak for them, would carry the Verdict for an, *Ad Nihilum redigendus mundus in Fine Saeculi*.[6] But, tho' a, *Gerhard* appear as an Atturney, with Several *Scriptures* having such a Sense, as by *Fire* extorted from them, strongly moving for such a *Judgment*, and all the *Lutherans* unite in a Cry for a *Substantial*, Total, Final *Destruction* of the World, in the *Conflagration*, [a ΚΑΤ' ΟΥΣΙΑΝ *Abolition*!] yett there appears enough to be brought in, for an *Arrest of Judgment*.[7] If the VOICE of the *Fathers* were to be taken for it, we should more generally find the *Substance* of the World saved from a *Total Dissipation*. I will mention but a few of many. *Irenaeus* will by no Means consent, that the *Substance* of it be

Exterminated. Cyril of *Jerusalem* expects but such an *Alteration* for it, as may be called a *Renovation* and a *Resurrection. Cyril* of *Alexandria* expects it as an *Innovation* and a *Reparation.* To pass by the ΚΑΘΑΡΣΙΟΝ ΠΥΡ of *Origen,* we find *Basil* will by no Means part with a *Redintegration.*[8] *Theophylact,* is not satisfied, That the *Fate* of the World, should be any other than what the *Creatures* may have an Earnest, & Hopeful, & Longing *Expectation* of. And *Oecumenius* will have it, not a *Perdition,* but a *Purgation* of the World, like that of Metals in the *Fire,* that is to be expected. *Epiphanius* might be call'd for, if he were worth calling for.[9] According to *Proclus; Exardescet quidem ad Purgationem et Renovationem, descensione factâ totus mundus Igne dilutus; non tamen ad perfectum Interitum et corruptionem deveniet.* As *Jerom* understands it, it is very plain, he says, *Perspicuum est Coelum ac Terram non perire, sed in melius commutari.* And quoting the Apostles Words, The [ms. III, x, 4v] *Fashion of this World passes away,* he so glosses it; *Figura praeterit, non substantia.*[10] *Austin* concurs; *Mutatione rerum, non omnimodo Interitu transibit hic mundus;* And so *Salonius; Igne Judicii purgata Meliorabuntur, quoniam Renovabuntur, sed non penitus destruentur.* And so, *Gennadius, Elementa non credamus Abolenda per Ignem, sed in melius commutanda.*[11] And so, *Gregory* whom they complement with the Title of, *The Great; Coelum et Terra per eam quam nunc habent Imaginem Transeunt; Sed tamen per essentiam sine Fine subsistunt.* And so,—But here are enow, to show, that we shall not want for good Company, if we go into the Opinion of the *Cononites,* mentioned by *Nicephorus,* who maintained, That the *Destruction* of the World, would be; *Juxta Formam solummodò, non autem secundum Materiam.*[12]

Tis true, a *Wendelin* will find enough in the *Eighth* Chapter to the *Romans,* to secure the World from such an *Evaporation* and *Evanition* for the *Substance* of it, as a *Valesius* has demanded.[13] But yett Things look as if the *Desolation* of the World must proceed so far, that there will be requisite Something that may be called, A New CREATION, to bring it into the Condition which is to succeed the *Conflagration.* I say nothing, of what has been offered among the *Cosmical Suspicions* of Learned Men, which even such Divines as our *Baxter* subscribe to; "Tis uncertain, whether the *Chaos,* which the *Creation* of our Present World, went upon, might not be the Reliques of a *Former World.*" I neither Offer, nor Humour the Conjecture. But we are sure, that from the *Chaos* of the *Present World* there will be a *New World* CREATED by the Almighty Power of GOD. He that sitts on the Throne says, *Behold, I make all things New.* Yea, *Behold, I CREATE New Heavens & a New Earth.* And we are advised, That *if any Man be in CHRIST,* and look to partake of such things as a CHRIST has to bestow upon the People, who *no more know* Him nor any thing else, *after the Flesh,* and in a Carnal View, he must look for a *New Creation,* wherein *Old things will be pass'd away, and, behold, All things, will become New. Theodoret* understands the NEW CREATURE, whereof the Apostle speaks unto the *Galatians,* to be that *Change* of Things, that shall be after the Coming of the Lord: And *Theophylact,* who understands it of, a *Life according to CHRIST,* adds this Reason, because in the *Age to come,* it will be attended with a *Reno-*

vation that will bring us into a State of *Glorious Incorruptibility*. What *Philo*, a Gentleman who knew the Sacred Scriptures, wrote about the ΑΥΤΑΡΣΙΑ, or, *Incorruptibility* of the Present World, can by no Means be defended, or excused, but by interpreting it, with regard unto *Annihilation*, or being thrown into a *Worse Condition*.[14]

The Thing whereof We are assured, is, [Act. III. 21.] That when our Blessed JESUS does Return from the *Heavens*, which have *received Him*, there will be *a RESTITUTION OF ALL THINGS*. Now, we will not go to any *Pagans* or *Gnosticks* for the Meaning of this, ΑΠΟΚΑΤΑΣΤΑΣΙΣ:[15] but according to the Scriptures, understand it, for [ms. III, x, 91] the *Restauration* of the *Earth*, to the State of a PARADISE, or the Putting of the World into the Condition, in which it was, before the *Apostasy* of Man from the GOD that formed Him; which is the Thing to be understood, by what GOD hath under Various Ways of expressing it, *Spoken by the Mouth of all His holy Prophets that have been since the Beginning of the World*. *Calovius* well notes, [and proves it from what we call, The LXX,] That the Term is to be taken, *De Restitutione in pristinum statum, vel meliorem*.[16] To take it for the Destruction of the *Jews*, & the Vocation of the *Gentiles*;—Away with such Excessive and Exalted *Folly*! Unworthy of a Refutation!—This, *Restitution of all things*, is in the Gospel, [Matth. XIX. 28.] called, ΠΑΛΙΓΓΕΝΕΣΙΑ, The *Regeneration*: which indeed carries, *The First Chapter of GENESIS over again*, in the Signification of it. The Term used for it by the Ancients, & particularly by *Justin Martyr*, [A Man, one who quotes him says, *of profounder Learning than any of our Modern & Modish Infidels*.] was that of an ΑΝΑΚΤΙΣΙΣ, or, *The Creation done over again*.[17] They explained it, by, *The Creature purged from the Irregularity and Imperfection, which the Sin of Man has brought upon it*. Briefly, The *Earth* is to be CREATED over again, into an entire PARADISE; and, no doubt, the *Second Edition* will be, *Auctior et Emendatior*,[18] and the World will be *Recovered* into a Better Condition, than it had before, *Sin did by one Man enter into the World, & Death by Sin, and so Death has passed upon all Men, for that all have sinned*. The Earth will be *Refined* into a Noble, Holy, Heavenly Seat; in which GOD *will govern the Nations upon the Earth; All the People shall Praise Him; and GOD, even their own GOD, will Bless them* wonderfully.

Some have thought, that the *Antediluvian World*, was punished with more *Irregular Seasons*, and a more difficult, ungrateful, unfruitful *Soyl*, than what we *now* enjoy; and more like what the Disobedient *Israelites*, are in the XXVI of *Leviticus* awfully *Cursed* withal: And that by Virtue of the *Covenant* with *Noah*, there has been some Degree of *Releef* sent unto Mankind, and of Comfort [as the Father of *Noah* foretold] relating to, and abating of, the *Work and the Toil of our Hands*, and the *Curse* upon the *Ground*; as a Small *Pledge* of a more perfect Salvation from the whole of the *Curse*, to be one Day brought unto Mankind by the Promised REDEEMER; and that by the Blessings convey'd unto the Earth from the *Clouds*, we see the *Faithfulness of our GOD in the Clouds*, fulfilling the *Covenant* He made with the *Patriarch*; whose *Godliness* had for us the *Promise of the Life that now is*, as our JESUS has for *that which is to come.* I leave a *Burnet* and a *Sherlock,* to dispute this between them: I offer no Sentiments upon it.[19] But This I am sure of; The *Earth* has not *Yett Seen* the Deliverance it *Shall See,* from the *Curse* of GOD upon it. [ms. III, x, 6v] I say again; It shall be a PARADISE. Yea, The *Lord will comfort all her Waste Places, and He will make her Wilderness like Eden, and her Sandy Ground like the Garden of the Lord; Joy and Gladness shall be found therein, Thanksgiving & the Voice of Melody.* And again; THEN *they shall say, This Land that was Desolate, is become like the Garden of Eden.*

THEY shall *Say* so!—*Who* shall *Say* it? They that will then *Inhabit* it, shall *Say* This. Yea, they shall say, *The Waste & the Desolate & the Ruined Cities, are Inhabited.* But, I pray, By whom *Inhabited?*

We see a NEW EARTH CREATED. But shall it remain empty of *Inhabitants?* GOD forbid! Some have apprehended Ground enough, to replenish all the *Planets* with *Inhabitants,* from that Word, [Isa. XLV. 18.] *GOD that formed the Earth, He created it not in Vain, He formed it to be Inhabited.* Be sure, This word may be *Applied* to the *New Earth,* and was indeed *Intended* for it. We find those Things done in the *New Earth,* which cannot be done without *Inhabitants.* Yea, Tis expressly called, OIKOYMENH˙ *An Inhabited World.*[20]

But I again enquire, By whom *Inhabited?* Most certainly, The *Wicked* shall not *Inhabit* it. The *Conflagration* has dispatch'd all of them. *The Day shall burn them up, & leave them neither Root nor Branch.* We are assured, That GOD will then *Destroy them who Corrupt the Earth.* In the Prospect of it, *That Sinners will be consumed out of the Earth, & the Wicked be no more,* we have the first *Hallelujah* that occurs in the Bible: and it calls for one! The *Raised* shall not *Inhabit* it. They are *Elsewhere* provided for. And, of them that are found here after the *Conflagration,* it is expressly said, They shall not only *Build Houses,* and *Plant Vineyards,* but also have an *Offspring.* Whereas, for them that obtain *the Resurrection from the Dead,* our Lord has, as one may say, *Forbidden their Bannes,* and has [ms. III, x, 92] declared, *They neither Marry, nor are given in Marriage.* From whence then, I beseech you, shall the *New Earth* be stocked with Suitable *Inhabitants?*[21]—

The *New Earth* must be mightily, filled with *Inhabitants;* yea, and speedily too: There must be mighty *Nations* of them. And inasmuch as there must be *no Curse* in the *New Earth,* and in what the REDEEMER will do for the Rescue of it, *His Work is perfect;* Hence the *New Earth,* must have no *Dying,* and by Consequence, no *Sinning,* in it: The Inhabitants of it must be a *Deathless,* and by Consequence, a *Sinless* People. I beseech you again, Tell me, From whence will you supply the *New Earth,* with a People proper for it? Or, If I now tell you, O *Ye Sober Enquirers,* Will you receive it? Or, Shall it be hastily rejected, with an, *Ah, Lord, He speaketh Parables!*— —

I say then, It will be Impossible for you to find any where, a People for these Lovely Regions, but the *Saved Nations,* that shall not be *utterly consumed in the Terrors* of the *Conflagration;* Even those that are *Caught up to meet the Lord* at His Coming, to Judge the World.

When the *New Earth* is by the Almighty *Will & Word* of our GOD, [And,

Job upon his *Restoration*, must say, O *Lord, I know that thou canst do every thing!*] brought into the Condition of a PARADISE, the Faithful, who were by the *Angelical* Ministry, *Caught up* to the Place, where the LORD will have His *Holy Ones* with Him, at such a Distance from the *Earth* as to *Deliver* them *from the Wrath to Come*, and from the Flames of a World on Fire; They will be then again Returned unto the *Field* praepared for them, and be on the *New Earth*, as ADAM and EVE was in the *Terrestrial Paradise*, before they Rebelled against their *Maker*, and before they Sinned away those *Garments of Light*, the Loss of which *Defence & Beauty* made them *Ashamed* of Appearing before their *Judge*; and before their *Sin* opened the *Floodgates* for all *Miseries* to break in upon the World: And they shall [ms. III, x, 6, (8v)] here *long enjoy the Work of their Hands.* They shall be Persons of *Heavenly* Tempers tuned unto *Unison* with what is Above: They shall Abound in *Heavenly* Exercises of Devotion: They shall have a Variety of most Suitable *Employments*: They shall serve and please the Holy GOD with a perpetual Homage paid unto Him in all they do; and be *Holy in all Manner of Conversation*: They shall *Taste* the Goodness of GOD in the Fruits of His Bounty plentifully allow'd unto them: They shall in a most Virtuous, and Rational and Regular Manner make Use of those *Oblectations*, with which their *Senses* will be gratified: They shall perfectly & practically understand how, *Frui Deo*, and, *Uti Creaturis*;[22] They shall be Visited, & Instructed & Ordered, by the *Citizens* of the *Holy City* coming down as there may be Occasion to them: And while they *Walk with GOD* at an High Rate of *Sanctity* and *Purity*, they shall *Begett Sons and Daughters*: & they shall continue in this Condition, until it shall please the Great KING to have them *Translated*, either *Successively* one after another as they may Ripen for it, or, anon, *all at once* in His Time for it, into the Superiour Circumstances of the *Holy City*.[23]

These CHANGED Ones will in many Points be Sharers with the RAISED Ones, in their Faelicity. While the Flames of a perishing World are doing their Execution, and the Formation of the *New Earth* is going on, they be *Both* of Them together with the LORD in the *Aerial* Place of Safety. They shall be *Both* of them rid of all Sinful *Pollution*; of *Corruption* and of *Mortality*. They shall *Both* of them have *all Tears wiped from their Eyes*, and see *Rest from Adversity*. Yett, in Sundry Points there will be a *Difference* between them: And if when we read, *He tells the Number of the Stars, He calls them all by Names*, not only *Kimchi* but also *Arnobius* expound it right concerning, *The Just of the World to come*, we may here apply that Passage, *One Star differeth from another Star in Glory.* The *Changed* Ones have not had their *Bodies* passing thro' the Rotting Alterations of *Death feeding on them* in the Grave. But the *Raised* [ms. III, x, 93] Ones may from thence have their *Bodies* on some Accounts in more *Ethereal Aptitudes* for the *Holy City*. And it is most particularly declared in the Divine Oracles, That the *Changed* Ones will on the *New Earth* have some Circumstances of the *Animal Oeconomy*, which the *Raised* Ones will forever have done withal.

Upon the Mention of an *Earth*, inhabited by a People who shall have no *Death*

nor *Sin* among them, and who shall maintain a most Intimate Fellowship with
such as will be *Equal to the Angels*; and yett shall *Build Houses and Inhabit
them*, and shall *Plant Vineyards & Eat the Fruit of them*, and be *the Seed of the
Blessed of the Lord, and their OFFSPRING with them*; we must not wonder if
some angry and froward *Jerom* come in and *Push* with his Invectives, and cry
out, *Carnal*! *Carnal*!—it may be, *Cerinthian*! It may be, *Mahometan*! And rail
against such *Sensuality*, as hee'l call it, with Vociferations as Impertinent and
Ridiculous as those with which that *Furious Man* entertained his Lady *Hedibia*.[24] Or, if we should express the Matter as *Lactantius* has done it; "That those
who shall be at that time alive in their Bodies, will never Die, but shall *begett
an Infinite Multitude*, & have an *Offspring*, during that Space of a *Thousand
Years*, and their Offspring shall be Holy and Beloved of GOD: But, they who
shall be *Raised* from the Graves, will praeside as Judges or Princes over the
rest:"[25] We must not be surprised at it, if they who are *Swifter* to *Speak* than
to *Hear*, tell us at once, *Our Milk boils over*; and refuse to give us a Patient
Hearing. But, O *Vain Man, Born like the Wild Asses Colt*; Wilt thou be Wiser
than the Glorious GOD, who has in His *Promise* expressly bidden us to *Look
for such things*? Or, if we don't *Look for such things*, what *Signification* can
we putt upon His *Promise*, but what will render it utterly *Insignificant*? Will
the *Changed Bodies* of them that are saved out of the *Fire* which will purify
the World, have their *Senses* left unto them; and must their *Senses* be used no
more in Conversing with the Proper *Objects* of them? Or shall the World that
Survives & Succeeds the *Fire* be filled with such Things as are made for the
Use of Man, & are Proper *Objects* for the *Senses* of the *Changed Bodies*; and
shall they have nothing more to do with them? Shall Man be restored unto the
Condition, wherein our *Protoplast* shone before he was chased out of *Paradise*,
and must there be a *Turpitude* in his doing those things which were to be done
in *Paradise*, and which his Creator had in [ms. III, x, 10v] the Tendencies of
His *Plasmation* an Eye unto! The Vile *Marcionites*, who ΑΓΑΜΙΑΝ ΕΚΗΡΥΞΑΝ,
were not such a Sect as we should be ambitious to *Herd* withal![26]

I beseech you, Syrs; Must this *Cursed Baseness* be forever entail'd on all the
Creatures made for the *Taste* and *Use* of *Man*, that *Sin* must be a Necessary
Qualification for the *Tasting* and *Using* of them, and that without *Sin* in the
Partaker, there can be no *Tasting* or *Using* of them; or, except an Homage be
paid unto the *Devil*, as there is in all *Sin*, we can't be fitt for them? GOD forbid!
It is a Vile Affront unto the *Works* of GOD, for us to think so; A Vile Reflection
on His *Wisdom* & on His *Goodness*. Our Glorious LORD condescending to
Eat & to *Drink* after His *Resurrection* from the Dead; and the *Angels* at the
Table of *Abraham*; have confuted such a Froward & Absurd Imagination. Men
may *See GOD*, and yett *Eat & Drink*; I again say, *See GOD*, and yett *Inherit
the Earth*.[27]

Tho' *Tertullians* Book entituled, *Spes Fidelium* is unhappily lost, an Anony-
mous & Ingenious Gentleman has lately entertained and edified us, with an
Epistolary Dissertation, which he has given *Tertullians* Title to. Now, tho' this
Gentleman did not apprehend the Difference between the *Raised Saints*, and

the *Changed Saints*, and therefore, asserts for the *Former*, what the XX Chapter of *Luke* permitts me to propose only for the *Latter*, I will on the behalf of These borrow some Terms and Thoughts, which *he* supplies me withal.[28] "Why may they not be praesumed to act as *Adam* should have done in *Paradise* had he remained there: to have done all things Regularly according to the Designation and Purpose of his Creator, *Eating, Drinking, Procreating*? Since none of these Acts are against, but highly & exactly conformable to, the Pure and Uncorrupt *Law* of *Nature*, the *Laws* of *Reason*, the Will and Pleasure of the Almighty *Creator*, the *Constitution* of *Humane Nature*, consisting of *Body* and *Soul*; and in all Manner of Respects proceeding Regularly, consistent with the highest *Excellencies*, & *Perfection* of Man in this Sublunary State, *Holiness, Purity, Innocence, Obedience*; In a Word, with the Exactest Duty & Obligations, to do all things acceptable & agreeable unto GOD, that he was capable of, and that GOD requir'd of him. Hence then, tis clear, that what was not *Incongruous* or *Inconsistent*, with those *Duties*, that *Perfection*, that *Innocence, Purity*, and *Holiness*, that GOD requir'd from Man in his *Original State*, cannot be *Incongruous* and *Inconsistent*, with his *Repaired State*, when he shall be in all Particulars Restored unto his *Original Innocence*, & *Perfection* of Mind & *Body*." But here's enough. The *Cavillers* at this Dispensation, Lett us leave them, with the *Saturninian* Hereticks in the Hands of an *Irenaeus*, to bestow due Castigations upon them.[29]

This *Holy People*, shall for their Vast Multitude, soon be, *as the Flock of Holy Things, as the Flock of* Jerusalem *in her Solemn Festivals*: The *Waste* World shall be *filled with the Flocks of Men*. Our Glorious [ms. III, x, 94] GOD, will fulfill that Word among them, *They shall be my People, and I will be their GOD; They shall walk in my Judgments, and they shall dwell in the Land that I have given unto my Servant; Even THEY and their CHILDREN, and their CHILDRENS CHILDREN forever*. Thus it will be, when that Word shall be fulfill'd, *My Tabernacle shall be with them*: which is the Character of the *New Earth*, and of the Time, when *GOD shall dwell with Men, and they shall be His People, and GOD Himself shall be with them, & be their GOD; and there shall be no more Death, neither shall there be any more Pain; for the former Things are passed away*. Yea, Now, O *Ye Mountains of Israel*, says our GOD, *Behold, I am for you, and I will turn to you, and Ye shall be till'd and sown, and I will MULTIPLY MEN upon you*. Doubtless, the Inhabitants of the *New Earth* will be greatly & quickly *Multiplied*; and within a very little while, almost as if a *Nation were born at once*, here will soon be mighty *Nations*, and People enough to afford *Subjects* for the *Raised Saints* to find Work among.

To accelerate this Blessing of, *Increase & Multiply*, for this *Holy People*, we need not have Recourse to the Jewish Tradition upon the *Six Words* used by the Sacred Historian, to express the *Fish-like Multiplication* of the *Israelites* in *Egypt*, [which I perceive *Theodoric Hacspan* approves of,] nor to what *Aristotle* reports of the *Egyptians* also, nor to the Exemples of *Polytokie*, of which *Caspar Schottus* has given us a Collection:[30] Unto them, who have admired that in a little above *Two Hundred* Years, there should be a Multiplication of

Seventy Souls, into such a Number, that there should be *Six hundred thou-sand* Fighting Men, besides *Women & Children*;[31] and in the whole by a Just Computation, *Three millions & three hundred & forty odd Thousand* People: What Mathematical Demonstrations have been offered by *Capellus*, [ms. III, x, 12v] and by *Torniellus*, and others, that even in making Allowances of noth-ing *Extraordinary*, there would arise by the *Rule of Progression*, a much larger *Multiplication?*[32] Yea, *Johannes Temporarius* Demonstrates, that even with such Allowances, [of *One* Man to have *Ten* Children, beginning the Generation at the Age of *Twenty*,] ere *Two Hundred & Ten* Years are expired, the Number arises to so many, that if the whole Family of *Jacob* were to perish, the Branch of *Joseph* would yeeld not only *Six hundred Thousand* Armed Men, but also *Ten Millions* of them, *Sine ullo Naturae Prodigio.*[33] But there needs not much *Arithmetick*, to make the Calculation. It is enough to say, Considering, the *un-declared Number* of them, that shall be rescued from the *Second Flood*; and the *Blessing* of GOD on the *New Earth*, and the Release from the *Curse* of *Death* upon the *Holy People* of it, what an astonishing *Multitude* will soon be seen here living unto GOD![34] It is expressly said, [Isa. LX. 22.] *A Little One shall be-come a Thousand, & a Small One a great Nation.* And, [Hos. I. 10.] *The Number shall be as the Sand of the Sea, which cannot be measured nor numbered.* If we are Tempted unto any *Blasphemies* against the *Divine Goodness*, upon the *Few that shall be Saved* among the People of *This Present Evil World*, We need not repair to *Curio's* Method in his Treatise, *De Amplitudine beati Regni DEI*;[35] No, Lett us come and *See the Goodness of GOD in the Land of the Living*, and look into that World, which will be incomparably better peopled than *This*, and the People ALL *Righteous*, ALL *Saved*, ALL *Happy*; and say, *Behold, An Earth full of the Goodness of the Lord! Lord, How Great thy Goodness & thy Beauty!* *Beleever, See them from the Rocks, & behold them from the Hills; Lo, The People will not be reckoned among such Nations as now cover & encumber the Earth; Who can count them, that appear Numerous as the Dust? Who can count the Number of a Quarter of them!*

Of THIS MATTER, there appears to be an Admirable Representation in the VII Chapter [ms. III, x, 95] of the *Apocalypse*: and when I have told *how* I apply what I Read there, I will tell *why* I do so.

We find a Provision made for the *Sealing* of *One Hundred & fourty four Thousand*, from the *Tribes of Israel*, that by the *Mark* of GOD & His CHRIST upon them, they may be praeserved from the *Hurt* which is to be done by the *Angels* of GOD unto the *Earth* and the *Sea*. If we take this *Hurt* ultimately to intend the *Conflagration*, we shall not be alone in the Exposition. And if we look for the *Tribes of Israel*, in the *Surrogate Israel*, and among the *Gentiles*, among whom the Children of GOD are the Genuine *Israel*, we shall do but as it becomes *Christians* to do. We have here then at Least *One Hundred & fourty four Thousand* that are saved out of the *Conflagration*. They are else-where called, *The Redeemed from the Earth*, on the Score of their being so. Well; *After this*, and it won't be long first, we shall *Behold*, and, *Lo, There will be a great Multitude which no Man can number*, that will have the *White Robes* of a *Priesthood* upon them, obtained by *the Blood of the Lamb,* which is applied unto them, & is the *Sacrifice* which they plead before GOD continually. And why may not these be the *Offspring* of the *One Hundred & fourty four Thousand,* Saved Ones? It is Evidently the *Blessedness* of the *World to Come,* which is here assigned unto them. We read, *He that sitts on the Throne shall dwell among them; They shall hunger no more, neither thirst any more; neither shall the Sun light on them, nor any Heat.* For the *Lamb who is in the Midst of the Throne, shall feed them, and shall lead them unto Living Fountains of Waters; and GOD shall wipe away all Tears from their Eyes.* Every Word calculated for the *Blessedness* of the *World to Come!* And yett it seems as if they were the *Holy People,* of the *New Earth,* which this *Blessedness* is intended for.—I am now to answer my Engagement, plainly to confess, wherefore I suspect THIS MATTER to be represented here; Why, we read of these *Marked,* and *Saved* Ones, and of the *Great Multitude* following, *They* [ms. III, x, 14v] *are before the Throne of GOD, and they serve Him DAY and NIGHT in His TEMPLE.* Now, in the *Holy City* the *New Heavens* we read, It is all DAY, there is no NIGHT there; and one who saw it, says, *I saw no TEMPLE therein.* So then, it looks as if the Condition of the *New Earth,* may be what this Prophecy may at least ultimately, refer unto. However *This* I will not insist upon.—*Valeat quantum valere potest.*[36]

What I must and shall insist upon, is; That they who have been *Redeemed from the Earth,* and whom the LORD sends down to the *Earth,* which *He gives to the Children of Men,* whom He will *Bless, and Increase more & more, them & their Children,* shall then be entirely *delivered* from the Worst of all their *Enemies,* even from SIN, and *Serve Him without* any of the *Fear* that SIN forever brings with it, in a Sinless *Holiness and Righteousness before Him all the Days of their Life:* They shall be a *Sinless People.* Whatever *Sin* they had before their being fetch'd up from the *Conflagration,* in which GOD will fulfill that Word unto them; *When thou walkest thro' the Fire, thou shalt not be Burnt, neither shall the Flame kindle upon thee,* they shall be cleared of it, and they shall have nothing of it left in them, to disqualify them for the Favours of the LORD: No *Leven* left in them, to disqualify them for the *Feast* of GOD in the *Holy Mountain.* Certainly, This *Old Leven* was thoroughly *Purged* out of *Enoch,* while the GOD who *Took him* up, was *Translating* of him! When the Lord, in the *Day of His Coming,* shall *Appear,* as *a Refiners Fire,* He will *Sitt as a Purifier of Silver,* and *Purify* them whom He setts apart for Himself, and *Purge them as Gold and Silver, that they may offer to the Lord an Offering of Righteousness.* What shall be done for them, in their Deliverance from the *Terrors* of that formidable *Fire,* will be the True *Purgatory,* of which the *Seducing Spirits* of the *Latter Times,* have made an Handle to trump up the *Fiction,* which the *Priestcraft* of *Rome* lives upon. The Holy SPIRIT of the REDEEMER, will with a marvellous Efficacy fall upon them, & come into them; and so, tho' the *Brands pluckt out of the Fire,* have been *clothed with Filthy Garments,* GOD will say of them, *Take away the Filthy Garments from them;* and say to [ms. III, x, 96] them, *Lo, I have caused thy Iniquity to pass from thee, and I will clothe thee with Change of Raiment.* This is the People to whom that Word will be accomplished; [Jer. L. 20.] *In those Days & at that Time, saith the Lord, the Iniquity of Israel shall be sought for, and there shall be none; and the Sins of Judah, and they shall not be found; for I will pardon them whom I reserve.* I remember, Many Years ago, sitting in a Company of Serious Christians, who were [like the *Primitive*] discoursing on, *The Kingdom,* I moved the Quaestion, *What shall we think about the State of the New Earth, with relation to* SIN? *Shall the Holy People have any* SIN *cleaving to them?* A Grave Old Man, whom at the Schole I had been in my Childhood a Scholar to, turned somewhat short & sharp upon me; *What! The Spouse of CHRIST have the Foul Disease! Never tell me That!* That Word struck deep into my Mind; and has contributed more than a little to produce the Sentiments I am now compell'd unto.[37] The *Holy People,* before the Rapture that saved them from the *Perdition of Ungodly Men,* felt the *Remainders of Indwelling Sin* in them, as the heaviest of all their Calamities, and with *the Groans of a Deadly Wounded Man,* they cried out under the Burden, *O Wretched One that I am!* If our Great REDEEMER should now leave any *Remainders of Indwelling Sin* in them, He would leave them under insupportable Annoyances from the worst Adversary they ever had in the World, and their *Hallelujahs* would be intermixed & interrupted with most grievous Lamentations; yea, their Moans would be, *My Wounds Stink & are Corrupt, because of my Foolishness; I am troubled, I am bowed down greatly, I go mourning all the Day long: For my Loins are filled with a Lothesome Disease!* The true *Israel* of GOD, will not reckon that they see a *Plenteous Redemption,* except they be *Redeemed from all their Iniquities.* How can the *New Earth* have it said concerning it; *There shall be no more Curse;* if SIN, which is the Cause of the *Curse,* and the most *Cursed* thing in the World, continue in it? Has the REDEEMER taught us to pray, *Thy Kingdome come; Thy Will be done on Earth, as it is in Heaven?* And have we no *Faith* of having this *Prayer* answered, with an *Earth* which will be [ms. III, x, 16v] a Place, where SIN will be so abolished; that the *Will of GOD* shall be perfectly complied withal? Was not *the Son of GOD manifested for this Purpose, to destroy the Works of the Devil?* But is not SIN the *Chief of the Works of the Devil,* and that by which the *Wicked One* does effect all the rest? How then shall SIN be left in the World, when the SON of GOD, has made a full Conquest of the *Devil,* and chased him out of it? If SIN be there, the *Devil* is there! When the *New Earth* is brought on, the *Old Serpent* is *bound,* in a *Great Chain; & cast into the Bottomless Pitt, and shutt up,* so that he has nothing to do upon the *Earth,* for a *Thousand Years* together. The *Strong REDEEMER,* having overcome the *Strong Armed* one, will *take away the Armour wherein he trusted.* SIN was that *Armour,* and This will now be all *taken away!* The *Evil Spirit* being chained up from tempting of them, the Holy SPIRIT of GOD, & His CHRIST, will now take an entire *Possession* of the *Holy People,* and they shall be more *Free from Sin,* than the *Inspired Prophets* of old, and the *Holy Men of GOD* who *Spake as they were moved by the Holy SPIRIT,* were even in the very Moments of their *Inspirations* and *Agitations.* The Leader of them that should have been an *Holy People,* said unto them, while they were yett in the *Wilderness,* and were not yett *come to the Rest ఴ the Inheritance which the Lord their GOD gave them;* After you are so *Ye shall not do after the Things that we do here this Day.* Most certainly, the *Holy People,* when they *come to the Rest ఴ the Inheritance, which the Lord their GOD* will give them, will not then *Do after the Things which they do here this Day,* while they were yett in the *Wilderness;* No, nor as the *Israelites* did in the *Rest and the Inheritance which the Lord their GOD gave* to them; wherein they generally did Criminal and Scandalous Things; their Conformity to the *Law* of their GOD was very Defective; and if PIETY now & then gott some Ascendent, it was quickly sunk and lost again; *Their Heart was not Right with GOD; nor were they stedfast in His Covenant.* What was but *Attempted* in the Land of *Canaan,* and the *Theocracy* whereof there was no more than some little *Essay,* some feeble *Display,* in that Land, shall in the *New Earth,* be fully accomplished.

[ms. III, x, 97] A Concomitant of the Deliverance from SIN, wherein the *Holy People* will be *cleansed according to the Purification of the Sanctuary,* and what will inexpressibly contribute unto the *Tranquillity* of the *New Earth,* will be the, *Legatio Satanae,*[38] or, the Confinement of SATAN, with his *Apostate Legions,* unto the *Prison,* which will be a *Place of Torment* unto them; and which will forbid their being such *Prisoners at large* as now they are. *Satan* will no longer be able to pretend unto, *Going to ఴ fro in the Earth, ఴ Walking up ఴ down in it.* The *New Earth* will not be, A *Whole World lying in the Wicked One;* There shall be *no Part* of it left in his Bloody Hands. Who of us can say, how far may extend the Sense of that awful Word; *He that has had the Power of Death, that is, the Devil!* This we can say, *The Wicked Spirits are the Rulers of the Darkness of this World;* a *World,* which they *Rule* very much by keeping it in *Darkness.* And this we can say very much of the *Wickedness* done in the World by the Men who have *not the Fear of GOD,* is done by *Men moved by the Instigation of the Devil.* Of Ungodly Persons, we are told, They *walk after the Prince of the Power of the Air, the Spirit which works in the Children of Disobedience;* and, They are *led captive by Satan to do His Will.* What hideous & horrid Things are implied in it, when *Satan,* the *Head,* and as one may say, the *Sultan,* of the *Devils,* is called, *The Prince of this World!* Yea, *The God of this World!* What *Impieties,* what *Impurities,* what *Iniquities,* and what *Idolatries,* does the *Devil* fill this forlorn World withal! What cruel *Persecutions* has the *Dragon* raised, by inspiring the abominable *Pharaohs,* from the Egyptian *Busiris* to the French *Louis,* and the Tyrants first of the *Pagan,* and then of the *Papal* Empire, to afflict & oppress the People of GOD![39] Indeed, we *know not the Way of the Serpent on the Rock,* and how tis the *Wicked Spirits* apply to the *Heart* of Man, and poison, and excite, *our Spirits,* by their Influences. [ms. III, x, 18v] But the *Matter of Fact* is notorious; and the *Wicked Spirits* do strangely Enchant & Enslave, all but a Few who are *Turned from the Power of Satan unto GOD:* but most notoriously after they have by *Repeted Acts of Sin,* wickedly resign'd themselves up unto the Diabolical *Energy.* And then, when these *Wicked Spirits* have seduc'd the Children of Men into those Miscarriages and

Rebellions which expose them to the *Wrath* of GOD, they thereupon *Desire to have* them in their Hands, & pay them their *Wages* in horrible Plagues, and obtain a Commission to be the *Executioners* of the Divine *Wrath* upon them. On the other Side; If any Man will *Abound* in *Services* to the *Kingdom* of GOD, he shall find such *Dark things* befall him, & such grievous Humiliations and Mortifications, as he cannot but judge to be *Revenges of the Devil* upon him. If any Man will *bring forth much Fruit*, he must be with a *Spirit of Martyrdom* armed for *Sad things*, and be willing to undergo bitter *Colaphisations*[40] from *Satan*, & his *Messengers*. These are the *Idaea's* of the Matter, which the Gospel of our GOD has given us. The applauded & inflated *Venetian* Preacher, when he made a *Crack-brain'd Motion* unto his Vast Auditory, to say Masses for that *Conversion of the Devil*, which, he said, *Origen* expected, was not altogether in the Wrong, when he said, *We should have a much better World than we have, if the Devil had once done molesting us.*[41] But One can scarce imagine, what has ail'd the *Brains*, of those who maintain, that the Time of the Promised *Binding of Satan*, was begun a Great While ago; Some, from *Luthers* Time; Some from *Constantines* Time; [In Spite of *Julian*!] Some from an earlier Date. *What Folly!* No, Syrs, In *your* Time of *Satan bound*, we have seen *Satan loose*, as much as ever since the World began.[42] The *Earth* could not from the *Pandaemonium* of *Hell*, be more supplied with *Devil*, than it has [ms. III, x, 98] in the *Time*, that you so unaccountably torture the Scriptures for. When *Satan* is *Bound*, and *Seal'd up in the Abyss*, it will be another Sort of a *Time*, than any *History* can yett show unto us. The NEW EARTH shall see the *Time*. THEN will the *Oppressor cease*; THEN will the *Whole Earth be at Rest, and be quiet, & break forth into Singing*; and say, *Since thou art laid down, there is no Fetter come up against us. How art thou cutt down, to the Ground, which didst weaken the Nations! Thou hast said in thine Heart, I will exalt my Throne above the Stars of GOD: I will ascend above the Heights of the Clouds; I will be like the Most High; Yett thou shalt be brought down to Hell, to the sides of the Pitt!* Yea; So far will the *Holy People* of the *New Earth* be, from the Infestations of the *Wicked Spirits*, that they may rather have some share in what their Brethren, the *Holy People* of the *New Heavens*, will then be concerned in doing upon these their ancient Adversaries. This will be one admirable *Recompence* of the *Resistence*, with which their *Stedfast Faith* in the Days of their *Trial*, they stood against the *Wiles of the Devil*; and *withstood the Wicked Spirits in the Evil Day*. Of old, even while the *Old Heavens* and the *Old Earth* were yett in Being, there have been *Saints* that have had *Power* over the *Wicked Spirits*, to *cast them out* of their Strong Holds. Much more, the Saints of the *New Heavens*, having those of the *New Earth* in some Degree associated with them, will exert a *Power* over these *Fiends of Darkness*. As they have been once *Cast into Prison* by these *Wicked Spirits*, they shall now *Cast* these into *Prison*; *They shall take them Captives, whose Captives they have been, and rule over their Oppressors*: and, *Bind* those which are at this day, *By the Wrath of GOD, the Kings* of this World, *in Chains, and these Nobles of Babylon, in fetters of Iron. This Honour have all the Saints!* Thus, they *shall Judge the Angels*: They shall do it, in the Acclamations, with which they shall accompany the Act of our Descending REDEEMER, that will in the *Judgment of the Great Day*, lay *Everlasting Chains of Darkness* upon them.

There is yett Another Enemy from which the *Holy People* shall be then *Delivered*; Even that which is called, *The Last Enemy*. DEATH is that *Enemy*; And so we read; [1. Cor. XV. 26.] *The Last Enemy that shall be destroy'd is Death.* None of the *Holy People* on the *New Earth* shall be liable [ms. III, x, 20v] to the Stroke of *Death*. *Immortality* shall be one of their Priviledges: And there shall be granted unto *them* an Admission to the *Tree of Life*; which if it were granted unto *Us* in our present Sinful Circumstances, tis thought, it would but *Immortalize* us in our Miseries. *If the Lord were pleased ever to kill them, would He have shewed them such things* as He did for them, when He snatch'd them out of the *Flames*, which *Destroy'd all the Wicked of the Earth*; and when He wrought such a *Change* upon them! The *Delivered* Ones at *That Time*, are [Dan. XII. 1.] *Every One found written in the Book*: The Same, that in another Prophecy are called, *The Written among* (or, for) *the Living*. The *Curse* is wholly removed from the *New Earth*; and so there will no more be any *Returning into the Earth*. Our LORD-REDEEMER has given a very Plain Declaration of this Matter, which our Preachers not minding, do often gloss with Weak Strains upon it. His Words are; [Joh. XI. 25, 26.] *He that beleeveth in me, tho' he were dead, yett shall he Live. And whosoever liveth and beleeveth in me, shall never Dy.* Here is a Distribution of the Condition, wherein *Beleevers* will be at the Coming of the Lord. First, there will be many *Dead* Beleevers, and such as by *Death* have been laid in their Graves. Of these our Lord says, Tho' they be *Dead*, yett shall they *Live*: They shall be *Raised* from the *Dead*. Secondly, there will be some *Living* Beleevers; Those that will be *found Alive*. Of these our Lord says, *They shall never die*; they shall be so *Changed*, that they shall *never see Death*. Truly, The *Holy People* of the *New Earth*, shall not be *all their Life time, thro' Fear of Death Subject unto Bondage*. With regard unto *Them*, has their LORD-REDEEMER said, *O Death, I will be thy Plagues!* Of *These* there will be that Account given; GOD *will be Gracious to them, and say, Deliver them from going down to the Pitt, I have found a Ransom.* Their *Flesh* will then be *fresher than a Childs*; GOD will *Deliver their Soul from going into the Pitt, and their Life shall see the Light*. When they, whom the Glorious One has *Covered with His Feathers*, and made Safe under the Protection of His Winged Messengers, are so rescued from the *Terror* of the *Wasting Destruction*, that when a *Thousand fall at their Left Side, & ten Thousand at their Right Hand*, it shall not *come nigh them*: they shall only *with their Eyes behold & see, the Reward of the Wicked*, because the *Angels* to whom He has given the *Charge of them shall BEAR THEM UP*, and the Lord will *deliver* them, and Sett them ON HIGH: THEN with *LONG LIFE will* He *Satisfy* them. There is indeed One Text, which in our Translation seems to militate against all Hope of such a *Deathless & Sinless Earth*, as we [ms. III, x, 99] have been Striving for. We read concerning the *New Earth*; [Isa. LXV. 20.] *There shall be no more thence an Infant of Days, nor an Old Man that hath not filled his*

Days; for the Child shall Die an hundred Years old, but the Sinner being an hundred Years old shall be cursed. But we must Read over again. Being fully perswaded, that the *Holy People* on the *New Earth*, being the Subjects of the *Second Adam*, would like *Enoch* the *Seventh from Adam*, in that *Seventh* Age, or Great *Sabbatism* of the World, be *released* from the *Statute* of *Death*, but be in GODs Time *Translated* into the *Holy City*: This Text was to me among the *Difficiliora Loca*; Yea, at first one of the *Insolubilia S. Scripturae*.[43] But upon an Hint from our *Holmes*, I soon perceived, That the Hebrew Particle, which we render, *For*, may & should be rendred, *That*.[44] Now Lett us Read right; *There shall be no more thence an Infant of Days, or an Old Man that hath not filled his Days*: [It shall not be so] *That the Young Man should dy at an hundred Years old*. He that is an *Hundred Years* old, will be but a *Young Man*; and has lived but a *Tenth Part* of the *Thousand Years* whereto Life will be then extended. And as the *Young Man* must not have his *Days cutt off*, so the *Old Man* shall *fill his Days*. It is added, *or that the Sinner an hundred Years old should be cursed*. Neither *Young* nor *Old* shall Die a *Natural Death*; nor shall there be a *Sinner*, who shall bring upon himself the *Curse* of a *Violent Death*, (or, be putt to *Death* in his *Youth*) for his Crimes. Thus the Text Asserts & Confirms, the very Thing, which we thought it at first appear'd against. And Thus it is added, *As the Days of a Tree are the Days of my People*: which both the *Chaldee*, and the *Greek*, Version render, *As the Days of the Tree of Life*; which *Tree*, we know, was to *Immortalize* those that were Partakers of it.[45] Nor were the Pagan Poets altogether Strangers to this Expectation; But in their *Golden Age*, what {*Aforcaeus?*} particularly [ms. III, x, 22v] writes of an, ΕΚΑΤΟΝ ΠΑΙΣ ΕΤΕΩΝ, is well known to them who think it worth the while to dip into them.[46]

Such an *Holy People* will be Able to *bear*, such Easy and Wealthy and Plentiful Circumstances, as the *Church upon Earth* could never yett see any Thing so much as *Tending* to them, without *Swift Apostasies*, and without Occasions for that Cry; *Venenum effusum in Ecclesiam!*[47] To imagine, that without and before such a *Change* upon the Children of Men, as can be produced by nothing but the *Coming of the Lord*, the *Church upon Earth* can enjoy an *Undisturbed Condition*, or a Freedom from the Discipline of the *Cross*, for a *Thousand Years* together, or one *Twentieth* Part of the Time, without falling into a fearful *Decay of Piety*; tis to imagine something much more *Improbable*, and *Miraculous*, than any thing that has been offered in our *Scheme*, whereof a *Nicodemus* cries out, *How can these things be!*[48] And it is infinitely *Unscriptural*: The *Scriptures* having every where taught us, *That thro' much Tribulation we must enter into the Kingdome of GOD*. But a People so *Changed*, and under the Influences of the *New Heavens*, as the *Holy People* of the *New Earth* will be, will find a *Well-accommodated World*, no Praejudice unto their *Holiness*. Accordingly, we every where find the, *New Earth* described as, *A Good Land*; and much more worthy than that which the Five *Danites* brought such a Report of, to be so esteemed, *Behold, It is a very Good Land, and a Place where there is no Want of any thing that is in the Earth*.[49] I say again; and again, *There shall be no more Curse*: And our Father *Isaac* seems to have had some *Scent* of the *New Earth*, when in Pronouncing the *Blessing*, on him whose *Genuine Offspring* are to possess it, he had *the Smell of a Field which the Lord has Blessed*. It was added, *GOD shall give thee of the Dew of Heaven & the Fatness of the Earth, and plenty of Corn & Wine*. And yett, the *Famine* on the *Land* where he sojourned, constrained him to fly into *Egypt*, for a Subsistence. But in the *New Earth*, all the promised *Plenty of Corn and Wine*, will be dispensed, unto the *Israelites indeed*, by whom it will be occupied. After the World has *pass'd thro' the Fire*, as well as *thro' the Water*, the People of GOD shall be *brought into a Fructifying Place*. Yea, we are expressly told; [Psal. LXVII. 6, 7.] *Then shall the Earth yield her Increase, and GOD, even our own GOD shall Bless us: GOD shall Bless us:* [Each of the SACRED THREE concur to it!] *And all the Ends of the Earth shall fear Him*. There is a Memorable Passage, of a Complaint made unto the Prophet, *The Water is Naught, & the Ground is Barren;* whereupon he [ms. III, x, 100] called for a *New Cruse of Salt:* Casting of which into them, [2. King. II, 21.] *He said, Thus saith the Lord, I have healed these Waters; there shall not be from thence any more Death or Barren Land:* And it came to pass. Lett it be Remembred; The *Extraordinary Occurrences* ever now & then mentioned in the Bible, are doubtless designed for Praelibations and Exhibitions, of Things that shall more Notably and more Commonly occur in the *New Heavens* & the *New Earth*, and the *Kingdom of GOD*, the Appearing whereof we are waiting for. This Memorandum, will be of more than Ordinary Use to us, in Reading our *Bible*, which is a *Rich Cabinet of Mysteries*. I take this for one of the Instances. The *Soyl* of the *New Earth*, after the *Fire of GOD*, like the *Salt* of the Prophet here, has done its Part, is what we have here a Praefiguration of. Lett us now read what *Josephus* writes of the *Soyl*, which had these *Healing Waters* to enrich it. He says; "This Fountain which before was the Cause of *Famine* and *Sterility*, was now the Cause of *Plenty* and *Fertility*. It so waters the Ground, that where a little of it comes, it does more Good than all other Waters that may ly long upon it. There are Goodly *Orchards*, and many sorts of *Palm-trees*, growing by the Sides of the Brook; the Fatter whereof being press'd, yield a Juice like Honey." He says afterward; "That we may call *that Part* of the Earth, *Divine;* where indeed whatsoever Fruit is most *Precious*, is in most *Abundance*. In other Fruits, it surpasses all Countreys in the World. It multiplies all things, and increases them sooner than other Places. The Cause whereof I judge to be, the *Pleasant Waters*, and the *Warm nourishing Air* thereabouts."[50] I dismiss this Curiosity; As I also do the Circumstances of the *Sabbatic Year* among the Ancient *Israelites;* wherein there was an Emblem, & Earnest, & Foretaste, & even a *Prophecy*, of what a Soyl the *New Earth* will be to the *Holy People* that shall occupy it: And instead of it, call to Mind, That whereas we read, Of the *Earth* admirably accommodated with Fructifying *Rivers & Streams of Water*, after the *Day of the Great Slaughter;* and of the *Sun* and *Moon* shedding more Benign Influences than ever, [Isa. XXX. 26.] *In the Day that the Lord binds up the Breach of His People, & heals the Stroke of their Wound;* the Gloss of Good old *Irenaeus* upon it, is; "The *Pain of the Stroke*, or, the *Stroke of the Wound* is, that by which Man in *Adam*, in the Beginning, was smitten; that is, *Death:*

which GOD will *Heal*, by Restoring us to the *Inheritance of the Fathers*."[51] And unto this Time, the Excellent Martyr applies That; [Isa. LVIII. 14.] *Thou shalt delight thyself in the Lord, and I will cause thee to ride upon* [ms. III, x, 24v] *the High Places of the Earth, and feed thee with the Heritage of* Jacob *thy Father*. To express the Incomparable *Fruitfulness* of the *New Earth*, we reject with a Proper Contempt, the *Hyperbolical*, and *Parabolical* Fancies of the more *Dreaming Ancients*; concerning Every *Vine* having Ten Thousand *Branches*; in Every *Branch*, ten thousand *Twigs*; on Every *Twig* ten thousand *Clusters*; in Every *Cluster* ten thousand *Grapes*; and Every *Grape*, when pressed, yielding twenty five Measures, containing Ten Gallons of Wine; or, two hundred & fifty Gallons. [Two Trillions, and five hundred Thousand Billions, of Gallons![52]— A fine Quantity truly! Could any Flight of *Persian Poetry* have out-done the *Talmudism!*] We had much better hear our more *Sober* Friend *Lactantius* upon the Matter. *Terra aperiet faecunditatem suam, et uberrimas furges sua sponte generabit. Rupes montium melle sudabunt; per Rivos vina decurrent; et Flumina Lacte inundabunt. Mundus deniqe ipse gaudebit, et omnis rerum Natura Laetabitur, erepta et liberata dominio mali, impietatis et erroris.*[53]—Or, Give me Leave to carry you, unto a more Surprising Expositor upon the *Prophecies*. Be n't surprized, when I tell you; *Virgil* is the Man. Read *Virgil*, I pray. And what says he? "He speaks of an *Age to Come*, which he calls, *The Last Age*: [And so, as Dr. *Chandler* observes, it must be, the *Fifth*,—succeeding to the *Iron Age*, which the Poets counted the *Fourth*;] when the *Grand Revolution* of the Former Times, and a *New Birth* of the *Old World* shall begin, and *Nature* shall resume its Pristine Vigour. When the Simplicity, and Probity and Equity of the *Paradisical State* shall be restored; which was called *Golden*, in respect unto the following Times; And *Manners* would be so Reformed, as if a *New Race* of Men were drop'd down from Heaven. In this *New Kingdom*, the Poet promises an End of all *War*; an *Universal Peace* throughout the World; a benign *Concord* between the most fierce & voracious Animals, and the weakest, & such as are least able to defend themselves: And no Poisonous *Reptile* or *Vegetable* remain in the World. For the *Plenty* and *Security* of that Age, the Poet says, The *Flocks* will need no *Shepherds* to look after them: They shall of their own Accord bring home their *Milk*, unto their Owners: The *Earth* shall not want the Rake, nor the *Corn* the Plow, nor the *Vine* the Knife: nor shall the Merchants bring in *foreign Commodities*, but [ms. III, x, 101] *Every Countrey* shall produce every thing that is Desireable: Ripe *Grapes* hang on the *Bramble*: *Honey* drop from the *Oaks*; and *Spiknard* be as common as *Ivy*." All this appears to be fetch'd out of our *Bible*. And I affirm *Virgil* to be in his *Fourth Eclog*, a better Commentator on the *Prophecies* there, than some that have written professed Commentaries.[54]

NOW, and never until NOW, will that Word be fulfilled, [2. Sam. VII. 10.] *I will appoint a Place for my People Israel, and will plant them, that they may dwell in a Place of their own, and move no more; neither shall the Children of Wickedness afflict them any more as in former times.* Here will be a True *Eutopia!*

A very Natural Consequence will be, *The Inhabitant shall not say, I am sick.* For to taste such Blessings,—*Valeat possessor oportet.*[55] There will be no *Physicians* on the *New Earth: The Whole need them not!* Tho', doubtless, notwithstanding the Hard *Jewish Sentence* upon them, there will in the *New Heavens* be many, besides our *Evangelist,* that have been of their Profession; and will in their *Own Bodies* receive the Reward of what they once did upon a Pious Intention for the *Bodies* of others.[56] The *New Earth* will have in it the *Tree,* the *Leaves* whereof will be *for the Health of the Nations.*

But that which will be of the Last Importance, to the Welfare of the *Nations,* will be their *Walking in the Light of the Holy City.* The *Raised Saints* of the *Holy City,* I again insist upon it, will do the Part of *Angels* to the *Holy People* on the *New Earth:* and be continually doing them all the Good that can be imagined; *Good surpassing all Imagination!* It is expressly said, *They shall REIGN:* and, [Dan. VII. 27.] *The Kingdom, & the Dominion, and the Greatness of the Kingdom UNDER THE WHOLE HEAVEN, shall be given to the People of the Saints of the Most High.* Happy Revolution! The World is at this day most miserably of it, by reason of *Rulers* that are *Unreasonable Men,* and such *Unhappy Wretches* as when they hear of a *Judgment to Come,* wherein *Unrighteousness & Intemperance* will be punished, have Cause to fall a *Trembling* at it. How often do Great Princes, deserve the Character which one of [ms. III, x, 26v] the Greatest that ever sway'd a Sceptre, did confess to belong unto them;—*The Basest of Men!*[57] Those that have swollen with more than *Fourty Titles,* have had *This* omitted in their Instruments, of which they have been more worthy than of all the rest. After all the Honours paid unto an *Alexander,* what was he but an Overgrown *Robber* and *Murderer* and *Madman?* A Deified *Lunatick!* He and his Brethren, that on their Statues have had such Execrable Elogies as there were on *Pompey's;*[58] what have they done, but made the World a *Wilderness,* and then been complemented for giving *Peace* unto it! What Numberless Lives of Poor *Slaves,* have been sacrificed by Thousands, to the *Glory* of their *Grand Monarch,* when the *Idol* was but another *Viltzlipultzli!* On how Trivial Occasions, and Idle Capricio's, have the *Cyclopean* Monsters, butchered their *Subjects* as well as their *Neighbours,* by *Hundreds* of *Thousands!*[59] Perhaps, a Quarrel about a *White Elephant!* Yea, all the Kingdomes of the World were engaged, and their Armies brought unto a Bloody Carnage near *Actium,* and *One Female* the Sole Cause of all!ise[60] How rarely has a *Throne* been filled with one, that might be justly called, *A Protector!* How often have the *Governours* of Provinces merited that Name, *The Wild beasts of the Earth;* which Name our Bible gives to the *Thirty Tyrants,* of whom *Trebellius Pollio* relates the Desolations, which they together made upon the *Roman* Empire? How often have such *Governours* been placed in their Capacities to do Mischief, & on the *Top of the House,* for which if Providence be expostulated withal, why *These* are there, the Answer must be, *Quia non inveni pejorem!* or, How little better have *Governours* often been, than what *Gunnar* sett over the *Norwegians,* and what *Oisten* sett over the *Nidrosians,* to humble them?[61] The Indisposition of the World, unto the Easy & Golden *Yoke* of a merciful SAVIOUR, and the Malignity wherewith Men reject His *Good Laws*, and say, *We will not have this Man to reign over us*: is thus Revenged by a Righteous GOD; and that *Curse* is executed; *Sett thou a Wicked Man over them*! The *New Earth* will have no such *Wild Beasts* in it; No *Roring Lions*, no *Ranging Bears*, no *Wicked Rulers*. *Plato* of old had a Notion, That as in the *Animal World*, they don't sett one of the *Herd* or of the *Flock*, to govern the rest of the Kind, but putt them under the Conduct of a *Man*: So, the [ms. III, x, 102] Love of GOD unto *Mankind*, inclined Him to sett *Angels* over *Men*. But, behold, the Love of GOD unto His *Holy People* in the *New Earth*, setting *Men Equal to Angels* over them: and fulfilling that Word unto them; *I will make thy Officers Peace; Violence shall no more be heard in thy Land; Thy People also shall be all Righteous; They shall Inherit the Earth forever*. The *Officers*, whether Greater or Smaller, coming down from the *New Heavens* to discharge Various Offices among them, will be the fulfilling of that Word unto them: [Psal. LXXII. 3.] *The Mountains to thy People shall bring forth a Prosp'rous Peace; and so the Little Hills shall do, because of Righteousness*. What a *Blessed People* will they be, that shall have *Shepherds* of such *Upright Hearts* and *Skilful Hands*, to *Teach* them and *Lead* them; and be under the Conduct of such *Angelical* Ones, who will be *wise like Angels of GOD*, and like the *Good Angels* forever *full of Goodness*! Under Conductors who will be True *Benefactors*, and whom they will most heartily, & with Cause enough, pay the Salutation of an, *Abrek*, to![62] Under *Commissioners* coming down unto them, with Directions, from a Glorious REDEEMER, who has *loved them, & washed away their Sins in His own Blood*, and will make them sensible in astonishing Ways, that He *Delights* in shewing *Mercy* to them! And as, no doubt, the *Dwellers* on the *New Earth*, will be very much employ'd in Studying the *Works* of GOD, with what marvellous *Illuminations* may their Studies be assisted from such Coelestial *Tutors*! Perhaps, no *Solomon* ever so Illuminated, as *the Least in the Kingdome of GOD*! A very Ordinary Scholar *there*, will much more truly have it allow'd for him, than it was to that *Voluminous* Writer here, of whom it was pretended,—*Scibile discunt omne*:[63]— much more truly be celebrated, as a well-known *Literator* once was by another, in those Terms; *There was nothing that any Man could desire to Learn, but what He was able to Teach*. The Learning of the World will not then be the Jargon of a fumivendutous *Aristotle*, and such Trash as the Colledges in our days have sometimes valued themselves upon.[64] But the World will be filled with the most Noble & Useful Knowledge, and all the *Sciences* will terminate in *Living unto GOD*: Every Part of the World, superiour even to a *Frederician* University.[65] Tho' Dr. *More* had not risen to such Sentiments of a *New Earth* So *Deathless* and *Sinless* as ours, yett he could not but say: "In the *Seventh Thousand* Yeare, I do verily Beleeve, that there will be so great *Union* between GOD and Man, that [ms. III, x, 28v] they shall not only partake of His *Spirit*, but that the Inhabitants of the *Æthereal Regions*, will openly converse with those of the *Terrestrial*: And such frequent Conversation and ordinary Visits of our *Cordial Friends* in that *Other World*, will take away all the Toil of *Life* and Fear of *Death*, among Men.—*Heaven* and *Earth* shall then Shake Hands together, or become as *One House*; and to *Die* shall be accounted, but to ascend into an Higher Room:—tho' this Dispensation for the Present, be but very sparingly sett on foot."[66]—And tho' Dr. *Willet* had not so distinct *Idaeas* of this affair, as there are in our Scheme, yett his *Expressions* are such, That we may clothe *Ours* in them; "There shall be an *Intercourse* between *Heaven* and *Earth*, as the *Angels* sometimes came from *Heaven*, & appeared in Humane Bodies; and *Moses* and *Elias* talked with CHRIST in the Mount: And our SAVIOUR Himself, after He was *Risen again*, was conversant forty Days with the Apostles on *Earth*. All which are Good Probabilities that the Saints shall pass to & fro, from *Heaven* to *Earth*, & shall *follow the Lamb whithersoever He goeth*."[67] But, I hope, we have settled the Matter more to Satisfaction.

There will be no *Carcases of Kings* in the *New Earth*: nor Princes, who, tho' basely flattered with *Blessed Memory*, deserve that their *Memory* should *Rott*. The *Raised Saints* of the *New Heavens*, will be the *Kings* of that *Earth*. And these *Kings of the Earth*, Returning from the Execution of their *Commission*, and with the *Glory* and *Honour* of the *Services*, which the LORD has given them to do in it, they shall *bring their Glory and Honour* into the *Holy City*, [In a much more Illustrious Manner, than the Old Conquerors did *Theirs* into the *Capitol*!][68] and render it all unto their Great REDEEMER on the Throne; And *they shall bring the Glory and Honour of the Nations* thither, in the Reports of what has been done among the Obedient *Nations*.

—Yea, what raises the Faelicity of the *Holy People* on the *New Earth*, to the highest Pitch of Astonishment!—It appears, that not only the *Raised Saints* of the *New Heavens*, will do so, but even the Glorious LORD of the *Holy City* Himself, will in *His Times* for it, make His *Visits* to the *Earth*, and show Himself in His Radiant Glory to His *Holy People* here, and receive their most affectuous Adorations.[69] But, O! the *Times of Refreshment*, that shall *come from the Presence of the LORD*! An Apostle of His, has intimated, that such *Times of Refreshment* would be granted unto others besides the *Raised* from the *Dead*. They that *Behold* & *Possess* the Land that was *very* [ms. III, x, 103] *far off*, Twenty four Hundred Years ago, [but now *the Salvation is near to come*, & the *Righteousness to be reveled*!] shall have their Opportunities, for their *Eyes to see the King in His Beauty*. Who can comprehend the Consequences of these Wonderful *Appearances*! What *Glad Shouts* as of a *Jubilee*, will be made *unto the Lord in all the Earth*! With what a *Shining Joy* will they *Serve the Lord*, and with what *Joyful Acclamations* will they *come into His Presence*! What Confirmations in *Holiness*, will His Reviving and Comforting Rays give unto them; and what *Gifts* will He with a Munificence & Magnificence infinitely more than Royal scatter among them!

They that were *caught up to meet the Lord*, may notwithstanding their having that Part of the *Kingdome* which is to be transacted on the *New Earth* allotted for a while unto them, still very well be comprehended in that Word, *So we shall be forever with the Lord*. For the *New Heavens*, wherein the Lord will be enthroned, will now be *forever* nigh unto them: His *Pavilion* will be *forever* in their View. The Messengers of the Lord will be *forever* conveying of Messages from *Him* down unto them. Yea, the LORD Himself will *Visibly* exhibit Himself unto them, in the proper Seasons for it. And by being SO *caught up again*, with a Translation to the *Holy City*, when their Work on the *Earth* is all finished, SO shall they be with a yett nearer Access *forever with the Lord*.

Finally; That the Faelicity of the *New Earth* may in a more *Summary Way* be declared unto us, We will in One Word say, Tis the State which the WHOLE CREATION is GROANING for. There is a famous Passage of our Apostle *Paul* concerning this Matter; [Rom. VIII. 19–23.] *The Earnest Expectation of the Creature, waiteth for the Manifestation of the Sons of GOD; For the Creature was made Subject unto Vanity, not willingly, but by reason of him who hath subjected the Same, in Hope; Because the Creature itself also shall be delivered from the Bondage of Corruption, into the Glorious Liberty of the Children of GOD; For we know that the whole Creation groneth and Travaileth in Pain together until Now: And* [ms. III, x, 30v] *not only they, but we ourselves also, who have the First-fruits of the Spirit, even we ourselves grone within ourselves, waiting for the Adoption, The Redemption of our Body.* There are those who will have the Apostle *Peter* to refer particularly unto this Passage, when he says, *Our Beloved Brother* Paul, *In all his Epistles speaks of these things* [which we have been speaking of;] *in which there are some Things hard to be understood.* That they may justify this Fanciful Application, of those Words, to what thus occurs in *One Epistle*, they go as far as *Nonsense* can carry them, to make this Passage *understood* so as to mean *just nothing at all*. The *Ancients* who would make the *Angels* to be the *Creature* here spoken of; [What? that are *made Subject unto Vanity?*] The *Moderns* who would make the *Heathens* to be the *Creature* here spoken of; [What? that are *not willingly made Subject unto Idolatry?*] are a Specimen tho' not the only one, of Interpreters not sticking at any *Nonsense*, rather than admitt of a Plain, Clear, Incontestible Interpretation, which may clash with some of their first imbibed Prejudices.—Whether the Passage to the *Romans*, were intended in the cited Words of *Peter*, certainly these Expositors go too far into the reach of his Next Words, which tell us, *There are some who wrest the Scriptures.* I beseech You, Syrs, Do but Read the Text over again; Yea, if You have no more Sense than *Little Children*, yett if You come to it, as free from all *Praepossession* as *Little Children*, there will need no Elaborate Commentary. I say Again, *Do but Read the Text over again*. I durst Appeal to *You*. Is it not here Evident, That there will a *Time* come, when the *Adoption* of the *Faithful*, will have a *Manifestation*, in the *Redemption of their Bodies*, and by a *Resurrection from the Dead*, it shall be made *Manifest* that they are the *Children of GOD?* Is it not Evident, That until the Arrival of this *Time*, the *Creatures* of GOD are abused, & *made Subject unto Vanity*, so that they don't answer the *Purposes* to which their *Creation* first adapted them; [ms. III, x, 104] No; they are perverted, unto the *Dishonour* of their *Creator*, and made the *Instruments* of *Rebellion* against Him? Is it not Evident, That this *Perversion* of the *Creatures* is an *Oppression* upon them; there is a *Violence* done to them in it; they may justly *Complain* of the *Indignity* they suffer from it; Yea, it often exposes them to a *Blast* of Heaven, which breaks the Orderly, the *Natural*, the Regular Course of their Proceedings? Alas, *For the Sake of Man* how are they *Cursed!* Is it not Evident, That the *Nature* which their Maker has given them and their *Constitution*, tends to a Recovery from this *Prostitution*, and calls for a Rescue from such Depravation? And, Lastly, Is it not Evident, That when the *Raised* and *Changed* Saints, are made the *Lords* of the *Creatures*, and have a *Dominion over the Works of* GOD, and *have all things putt under their Feet*, the *Creatures* will then be so applied, as admirably to answer the *Purposes* which they were originally intended for, and have the *Liberty of that Glory* (so the Text is to be rendred) *which the Children of GOD shall have;* they will be sett at *Liberty*, by being entirely applied by the *Glorious Children of GOD* unto the *Service* of Him that made them; GOD will be glorified in them; and, O *Lord, Our Lord, How excellent will be thy Name in all the Earth!* Behold, *The Restitution of all things*, which GOD has declared *by the Mouth of all the Prophets!*

I am sensible, that many *Quaestions* may be ask'd me, concerning the *New Earth*, which I am not capable of Replying to. Unto some of them, I will offer a Short *Reply*, in the Express Words of that Chapter, which has in it, the *Promise of the New Earth*, which the Apostle expressly renders as the Bottom of our Expectation.

Q. Will there be *Minerals* in the *New Earth?*
Reply. [Isa. LXV. 21.] *They shall Build Houses.*
Q. Will there be *Vegetables* in the *New Earth?*
Reply. [Isa. LXV. 21.] *They shall Plant Vineyards.*
Q. Will there be *Animals* in the *New Earth?*
Reply. [Isa. LXV. 25.] *The Wolf & the Lamb shall feed together; and the Lion shall eat Straw like the Bullock; & the Dust shall be the Serpents Meat.*
Q. How do such Things come to appear after such a *Destruction* as the *Old Earth* will undergo in the *Conflagration?* [ms. III, x, 32v]
Reply. [Isa. LXV. 17.] *Behold, I CREATE a New Earth.*

But there yett remains One Quaestion more, which must be a little more largely spoken to.

It is with much Disdain, that upon the least Proposal of any thing relating to the *Coming of the Lord, at the Beginning of the Happy Time to be expected for the Church of GOD upon Earth*, I hear that Quaestion presently thrown at me, as a *Bomb* that will at once destroy all that can be said;[70] *Where will you find* Gog and Magog? The *Deceived Nations* in the *Four Quarters of the Earth*, which besiege the *Beloved City*, after the *New Earth* has been under the *Reign of the Saints* for a Thousand Years together: *What are they; Whence come they;* They that are, till they are better acquainted with the *First Elements* of the True *Chiliasm*, altogether unqualified for passing any *Judgment* on a Right *Answer* to that *Quaestion*; and they that are perhaps determined, they will hearken to no *Answer* of the *Quaestion*, that can claim to be laid in any *Balances*, think they have at once confounded all Essays to search into these things, with only asking, *Where will you find, Gog and Magog?* How Impertinent, this! How Ridiculous! To see a *Lump of Ignorance,* vapouring as if he had at once destroy'd all *Consistent Interpretations* of the *Sacred Prophecies,* and brought a great Part of the Bible to signify *next to nothing,* by a Supercilious Demand, *Where will you find Gog and Magog?*[71]

Now, suppose I can't answer the Quaestion!—What then? As our Blessed JESUS once, to retund & silence the Petulance of some *Litigious Enquirers,* chose to say, *I will also ask you one thing, which if you tell me, I likewise will tell you,* what you ask after: Unto some *Indocible Enquirers,* I have sometimes thought it enough to say; I can *Ask* you more than Twice Seven things about the *Bodies* of the *Raised Saints,* which you cannot *Answer:* And yett you would not have me reckon that Your *Ignorance,* will excuse me from the Beleef of the *Resurrection. I will tell You one thing, which if You will tell me, I likewise will tell You,* where to find *Gog* and *Magog. The Bodies of the Raised, will they have TEETH, or no!*—To speak yett more—*ad Hominem;* Tis promised unto the Overcomers, or the *Raised* from the Dead, *They shall have Power over Nations.* Now, Do you tell me, who am willing to learn of you, where you will find the *Nations,* that the *Raised from the Dead* have *Power* over; Then I will try to tell you, *Where to find* Gog *and* Magog.[72]

Or, what if I should say; That it will be Time enough more than *Five Hundred Years* hence, to *Ask* a *Quaestion,* about an Event, which we are sure is yett above a *Thousand Years* off? If any Gentleman had come to our Father *Abraham, Four hundred* Years before the *Redemption* of his *Offspring* from their *Egyptian Darkness,* he would have expressed [ms. III, x, 105] a *Strong Faith* of the *Promised Redemption.* But, *Syr,* can you satisfy me, which *Way a feeble Handful of People shall be able to make head against a mighty Kingdom?* Or, what shall be the facilitating *Circumstances of their March out of* Egypt? *What their Number; what their Order; who their Leader; which Way they shall be led; and what Miracles will be wrought for them; and how a Theocracy shall be established among them?* Here the Patriarch must have answered: *Indeed, Syr, Here I am in as much Darkness, as I was in my Deep Sleep, when the Horror of Great Darkness fell upon me!* NOW, Why may not one allow me to make the like Answer? I *Strongly Beleeve,* That after the Coming of the Lord, there will be *New Heavens* inhabited by *Raised* Saints, and a *New Earth* inhabited by *Changed* Ones; and these holding a most Suitable *Fellowship* with one another for a *Thousand Years* together. But then, there shall be an Unaccountable Attempt from *Hell* against the *New Jerusalem* in *That World:* The Enemies of GOD shall *Return at Evening* and *make a Noise like a Dog,* & go round about the City. [Which Words of the *Psalm,* some Jewish Rabbi's apply to *Gog* and *Magog:*] But the Attempt shall be blasted with *Fire from Heaven* upon the Fool-hardy Undertakers. I am asked, *Who and Whence will be the Authors of this Enterprize; and what will be the Methods wherein it will be carried on?* To this, I will First of all Answer; *More than Four Hundred Years before the Matter comes to pass, tis possible I may be able to tell more about it.* At present, if the Matter were to have been putt, even among the *Quaeries* of the famous Father *Cotton* the Jesuite,[73] it is Quaestionable, whether the Leader himself of *Gog* and *Magog*, would be able to answer all that might be ask'd concerning it.

One thing which does a little *Encumber* us, [But may it not also a little *Enlighten* us!] about *Gog* and *Magog*, is, That the *Gog* and *Magog* of *Ezekiel*, & the *Gog* and *Magog* of *John*, do not appear to be the same *Gog* and *Magog*, but there is the Distance of a *Thousand Years* between them. In *Ezekiels* Action there seems to be a Terrible *Battel*; In *Johns* there seems not a Stroke to be struck on either Side, but *Fire* from Heaven decides the Controversy. The *Tzemaon David*, composed by R. *David de Pomis*, takes the former *Gog* and *Magog* to be *Armillus*, who is the Same with our *Antichrist*.[74] This Interpretation admirably agrees with what we read, *Thou art he of whom I have spoken in old Time, by my Servants the Prophets*. And *Antichrist* persecuting the true *Israel* of GOD, & at last perishing in the *Conflagration*, will be an admirable Fulfilment of *Ezekiels* Prophecy.

But then, for the *Gog* and *Magog* of *John*:

If the *Curious Enquiries* of some, will not yett be satisfied, without some *Further Accounts*, [ms. III, x, {34v}] One that is an *American*, as I am, will hardly give that of Mr. *Mede*; That the *American* Haemisphaere will escape the *Conflagration*; and that the People there shall not be Partakers in the Blessedness of the *Thousand Years*, but that the Suggestions of the *Devil* shall dispose them, to make an Invasion on them that are.[75] I will rather humbly offer *Two Conjectures*, of which the Enquirers may take their *Choice*, or else use their own Liberty to substitute what may appear Better to them.

First; I will offer what I least praefer to insist upon. I call to Mind the Advice that *Cyrus* in *Xenophon* gave to his Children, ΕΚ ΤΩΝ ΠΡΟΓΕΓΕΝΝΗΜΕΝΩΝ ΜΑΝΘΑΝΕΤΕ, *Learn from the Things that have been done already; This is the Best Way of Learning*.[76] I say then; *What has been done Already?* Did not the *Old Serpent* [I say, *The Old Serpent*, for the Reasons of the Excellent *Langius* have convinced me, that there was no Literal and Corporeal *Serpent* used in the Case,] Did he not by the Divine Permission make his Effectual *Insinuations* into our *First Parents* in *Paradise*?[77] What ensued upon it we *know*, and in the *Increasing* of *Knowledge* we have *Increased Sorrow*. Now, suppose that the *New Earth* may among its *Holy People* have those whom our Lord-Redeemer may leave to stand on the Terms of such a *Covenant* as may admitt of an *Apostasy*. Tis true, The *Covenant of Grace* admitts not of *Apostasy*. And we know, of no other *Covenant* for the *Faithful*. But can we sett Limits, to the Unknown Dispensations of GOD in the *World to Come*? If the *Old Serpent* be *Lett Loose* to try the Force of his Enchantments on the Minds of such as These, and the Influences of Heaven be at all withdrawn from them, why should it seem any more strange to us, that the *Lying Spirit* should go forth, and *perswade them, and prevail also*, upon a Vast Multitude of these, than that he should *Prevail* on our *Sinless* First Parents in the *Paradise* of GOD? The Behaviour of the *Israelites*, in the Business of the *Golden Calf*, at Mount *Sinai*, where they had newly *Seen the very GOD of Israel*, and heard the *Voice* at which the *Pillars of Heaven do tremble*, and their Terrors, & Cries, & Vows, had been what they were; And the Account which *Ezekiel*, and *Amos*, and *Stephen*, [ms. III, x, 106] give of their Be-

haviour in the Wilderness, for *Fourty Years* together, notwithstanding a mighty
Regiment of *Angels* conspicuously hovering over them, sheltering of them as
a *Cloud* by Day, & enlightning of them as a *Fire* by Night, and Pouring down
above Two Hundred and fifty Thousand Bushels of *Manna* for *Daily Bread* upon
them! is an amazing Exemple, of what horrible Things a People will do, when
the *Old Serpent* is *Lett Loose* upon them.[78] Alas, *What won't Men do when
the Devil is in them!* Yea, we know of mighty *Legions*, that were *Sinless* Ones,
which the People at *Sinai* were not, and that had enjoy'd the Visions of GOD,
and made near Approaches,—*He knows, how long!*—unto Him. And yett into
what a Rebellion against their Almighty Maker, and Father, did One *Belzebub*
seduce them?[79]

Secondly; I offer This. Monsr. *Poiret*, in his, *L'Oeconomie Divine*, is not the
only Person, who has look'd for *Gog* and *Magog*, among the *Damned*, or the
Wicked, Rising from the Dead. The Search after them *There*, is ingeniously
prosecuted by Mr. *John Smith*, in his Treatise entituled, *Christian Religions
Appeal*.[80] And Mr. *Thomas Staynoe* by his further Prosecution of it, in his
Treatise entituled, *Salvation by JESUS CHRIST alone*, has placed it in a Light,
which well deserves to be considered. A Learned, but a Nameless, Writer of,
Annotations on the Revelation, has notably cultivated the Notion, and very
near established it.[81] Some Shrewd Intimations of their being Those who had
gone down to Hell, with their Weapons of War, & with the Same Enmity to
GOD with which they had lived, and *laid their Swords under their Heads*,
in a Readiness to act the Same over again; these do seem unto him, a little
to countenance it. And the Truth is, The World, which is to be the Field of
this Action, will be so *Spiritualized*, that it will not be at all Incongruous to
such from *Hades* the Great Actors in it. But I forbear to give the full Detail
of the Sentiments; and more particularly of our *Staynoes*, [*Tho' what I most
incline to!*] for diverse Causes; and for this especially; I think, the *Answer* to
the *Enquiry*, is *Unnecessary*, and the *Demand* of it, *Unreasonable*. Nor was it
any Want of Learning in *Scaliger* to say, *Humanae sapientiae pars est quaedam
aeque animo nescire velle*.[82]

THESE are Some of the Things that will be found in the *Heavenly Countrey*,
which we are looking and waiting for. But, *How little a Portion is heard of it.*

Appendix.

And yett, that I may not leave the Enquiry after *Gog* and *Magog* wholly un-
answered, I have so far conquered my Resolution of Silence, as to add a brief
Disquisition upon it.[83] [ms. III, x, 34, (36v) *blank*]

[ms. III, x, (1)]

Where to find *Gog* and *Magog*.

That Excellent Servant of GOD, and Writer of our Martyrology, our *John Fox*,
being in much Distress & Anguish of Mind, about the Period of such dreadful
Things as he was writing of, he relates, [vol. I. p. 129. Edit. 1632.] *"That on a
Lords-day Morning, lying in his Bed*, and musing about the Numbers in the

Book of the *Revelation*; the Fourty-two Months, the Time, Times & half Time; the Twelve-hundred & Sixty days, it was answered unto his Mind Suddenly, as with a Majesty, thus inwardly Saying within him; *Thou Fool, Count these Months by Weeks, as the Weeks of Daniel are counted by Sabbaths.* Complying as he thought, with this Direction, all that he could make of it, was, That the Persecutions of the Church were to continue *Two Hundred ninety & four Years;* which was the Space that ran out from the Death of *John Baptist,* unto the End of *Maxentius* and *Licinius,* the Two Last Pagan Persecutors, conquered by *Constantine.*"[84] And yett after all, how happy soever the *Hitt* may appear, it is very certain, that altho' the *Pagan Persecutions* might last for such a Term of Years; as is found in this Way of Calculating, yett the Fourty two Months, the Time Times & Half-time, & the Twelve Hundred and Sixty Days, in the Prophecy, are intended for the Period of the *Papal Persecutions,* and must be expounded by the Rule for Calculation given to the Prophet *Ezekiel.*[85]—

I do not pretend unto any *Enthusiasm,* or to such Impulses as that Good Old Man was led withal. But yett I may say, On a certain *Lords-day,* when I was with some Anxiety Wishing & Begging to be more fully instructed, for an answer to that Enquiry, with which the *Scoffers,* or the *Sleepers* of the *Last Time,* hope to cavil away what the Oracles of GOD have in Plain and Strong Terms asserted, concerning the [ms. III, x, (2v)] *Coming* and *Kingdom* of the Lord; *Where will you find* Gog and Magog? It was darted into my Mind, with a Force, almost aequal to that of being spoken to me; *Look into the Chapter over again, & You shall presently find what You are seeking for!*

I look'd into the Chapter, and behold, what I saw immediately!

First; I See it mentioned with a sort of Anticipation, *The rest of the Dead lived not again until the Thousand Years were finished.* An Evident Intimation of something to occur, for the doing of something that is to be done when the *Thousand Years are finished.*

Secondly; I See the *First Resurrection* then reassumed; and the Character of them that have a *Part* in it exhibited. They are *Blessed* and *Holy;* which is as much as to say, They are *Deathless* and *Sinless.* This Character I take to extend not only to the *Raised Saints* in the *New Heavens,* but also the *Changed Saints* in the *New Earth:* All of which have a *Part* in the Benefits of the *First Resurrection.* And this Character secures all of these, from a Capacity of Suffering Seductive Impressions from *Satan deceiving of the Nations.*[86]

Thirdly. I See such as have been *Damned* for Seven Thousand Years, and have even lain in the Torments of Hell for One Thousand Years together, yett released, and putt into a Power to play the *Devil,* as they have used formerly to do among the Nations of the Earth, and accordingly doing of it.[87]

Fourthly; I See a Vast Number,[88] whom GOD permitts the *Devil,* to seduce into an Enterprize full of Malice and Madness, against the People of GOD, by whom the Earth will then be occupied: And it is altogether as easy to conceive, that the Glorious GOD should permitt Some of the *Humane Race,* that have been kept *Prisoners for many Days* [ms. III, x, (3)] in *Hades,* for a Damnation that is not yett fully executed on them, to be concerned in an Enterprize against the *Camp of the Saints,* as it is to conceive, that the *Devil,* after he has been in the *Fiery Oven* for a Thousand Years, yett should be again lett out, and again play his Old Game after his being so.

Fifthly. Some Learned Men, are of the Opinion, that the *Second Resurrection*, will be of all and only those, who in their first Life-time, never had the Offer of a REDEEMER made unto them; & who shall then enjoy the Offer; which Some (as it is *Now*) shall Accept, & be admitted into the *Camp of the Saints*; but the Most (as it is *Now*) shall, thro' the venemous & bewitching Influences of Satan upon them, Refuse, and be drawn into a Plott, which will bring Fire from Heaven upon them. And so, they shall be brought forth again, in that *Resurrection*, which will, after This Transaction, be of all & only those who have Rejected the Offered REDEEMER, whereof Not One is found in the *Book of Life*; but, *All shall be Damned*. If the Conjecture of these Gentlemen may be received, we need *Seek no further*. Be sure, the *Vast Number* of the Assailants here, will be very Agreeable to *The Number of them, as the Sand of the Sea.*[89]

Sixthly. To countenance our Apprehension, That the *Nations* here called *Gog* and *Magog*, are fetched from the Dismal *Receptacles of Wicked Spirits*, there can be nothing more expressive, than the Expression here used for them: *They went up on the Breath of the Earth.* It seems they were such as had been *under the Earth.* Yea, of the Nations upon whom Satan operates, we read, *They are in the Quarters of the Earth.* But every Greek *Lexicon* will inform us, That the Word which we render, *Quarters*, is a Word that signifies, *Hidden Places.* Those of *Hades* are so.

Seventhly. But, finally, I see no Necessity, why the Armies of *Gog* and *Magog* must be at all such as by a *Resurrection* have their *Bodies* restored unto them. It is no unreasonable thing, to suppose, that even *at This Day*, the *Ghosts* of [ms. III, x, (4v)] the Dead which have *died in their Sins*, may be employed in some *Diabolical Services.* They become a Sort of *Devils* before they *Dy*; Even *Devils Incarnate* and very Active & Cunning & Potent *Instruments* for the *Devils*, and *Co-Workers* with them. Why may they not, after they are *Dead*, be associated with the *Devils*, in Essays to give Annoyances unto the Kingdome of GOD? Yea, when *Evil Spirits* have grievously molested Persons and Houses among us, we have sometimes had very Cogent Reasons to Beleeve, That some *Departed Spirits* of the Humane Race, have been Considerable Agents under the *Devils*, in the Molestations. In the affair of *Gog* and *Magog*, it appears very likely, that Satan designing a *Violent Shock of Temptations*, (which may suitably enough be called, *A Battel*) upon the *Camp of the Saints*, may reckon his own Apostate *Legions* not enough to carry on the Design which he has to manage. And therefore, by the Permission of GOD, he calls in a Vast Number of *Humane Ghosts*, to act with him & for him. In order to which, he *Deceives* them with an Expectation of what they shall *do*, & of what shall be *done* for them if they succeed in what they do. He may promise them, and they may beleeve the *Deceiver*, that he is upon Methods, to bring them, with himself, into as Happy Circumstances, as any that are enjoy'd, by the *Camp of the Saints*, or by the *Beloved City.* But such a *Fire* from GOD as once drove the *Wicked Spirits* from their *High Places*, will now putt an End unto this Mysterious Undertaking.[90]

XI. A National Conversion of the *Jews;*
Whether to be look'd for.

But, *O my Lord, what will be the End of these things?* Or, How long will it be, before *This World* will come to an *End?* And the *New World* shall be introduced?

When the *Chosen Witnesses* of our LORD's being *Received up into Glory,* at His going from them enquired of Him, *Whether Now were the Time for Him to bring on the Restitution of all things, wherein His Israel should enjoy the Promised KINGDOM?* His Answer was, *It is not for you to know the Time or the Seasons, which the Father has putt in His own Power.* The SON of GOD, acting in the Man JESUS, this *God-Man* sustained the Quality of a *Servant* unto His Eternal FATHER, and must *know nothing,* so as to communicate the *Knowledge* of it unto His People, any further than He should have the Commission of His Eternal FATHER for it. It is evident, that the Blessed JESUS, was well-acquainted with the illustrious Prophecies of *Daniel,* the *Man greatly Beloved,* & the Elder-Brother (we may call him,) of the *Disciple whom He loved.*[1] He knew Himself to be, *The Son of Man,* celebrated in those Prophecies: and several times told His Attendents, of His being so. He knew, when the *Last Day* of the *Sixty Nine Weeks,* which according to those Prophecies, was to bring on His *Death,* was arrived; and Then plainly told His Followers that it *was so,* and with an astonishing Fortitude, went up to be crucified. He knew, the *Periods* in those Prophecies: and what should come on, when *One Thousand & three hundred & thirty five* Years were expired. But, the *Praecise Time,* for the Epocha & Beginning of those *Periods,* had not been so declared, that the *Hour,* or the *Praecise Time,* for the Expiration could be determined.[2] And, tho' at the Time, when it was asked, *Wilt thou at THIS* [ms. III, xi, 2v] TIME?—the Blessed JESUS, had not yett received a Commission, enabling Him to Instruct the Faithful in the *Times and Seasons,* yett within a very little while after this, He *took the Book & opened the Seals,* and His FATHER gave Him a *Revelation,* wherein He was to *shew unto His Servants the Things that must shortly come to pass.* Whereupon, as He had Illuminated His Apostle *Paul,* in the *Mystery* of the *Man of Sin* to have a Long Reign before His Coming, so He now more particularly Illuminated His Apostle *John,* with the Term for which that *Man of Sin* was to Reign: and the *Number of the Years for the Oppressor* is not altogether so much *Hid,* as once it was.

Nevertheless, Tho' we may *understand by Books,* that the Coming of the LORD, and so the Burning of the World, cannot be *very far off,* and the Allowance of *Gerhard* is very Reasonable, *Non improbem pium eorum studium, qui vaticinia in scriptis propheticis et Apostolicis proposita, cum ipso eventu, optimo vaticiniorum Interprete, prudenter conferant, ac Diem Ultimum IN PROPINQUO esse colligunt:*[3] Yett We ought *Still,* with all humble Modesty to be awed by the Admonition; *It is not for You to know the Times or the Seasons.*

They who seem Resolved upon it, that the GRAND EVENT must be *very far off*, and who are for *putting far away, the Evil Day*, are very confident of a Very Considerable Matter, to be first Accomplished. A Strong *Opiate*, which binds on the Chains of the *Dead Sleep*, wherein the Church is to be found, when the *Day of the Lord*, shall break in *like a Thief in the Night* upon the World, is a Strong Opinion, "That before the Coming of the Lord, there shall be a *National Conversion* of the Circumcised People, descended from the *Twelve Tribes* of *Israel*; who are to Return unto their Ancient Seats in *Palaestine*, and make a *Singular Figure* in the Kingdom of God, and be *Distinguished* from, and *Superiour* to, the Rest of the Nations, that shall then also be generally converted unto Christian Piety."[4] I will express the Prevailing Opinion of the *Time* [I say not, of the *Day*!] in the Terms of the Illustrious *Voetius, Negativè concludi potest; Nondum conversi sunt Judaei; Ergò non adest Mundi Finis*.[5]

Now, it must be confessed, That there are so many Passages in the Sacred Scriptures, which at first seem to have such an Aspect, as to render it not at all [ms. III, xi, 108] Marvellous; that this Opinion has been so much imbibed. And it is to be confessed, That many of those who have been zelous Abetters & Asserters of this Opinion, have been the *Best of Men*, and Persons of as great Sagacity and Erudition, as any that can be found among the Children of Men. But what if after all it should be found, That the Opinion is a *Mistake*, an Opinion, really *Unscriptural* as well as *Irrational*; and not very Agreeable to the whole Tenour & Spirit of the *Gospel*? Or, as the Author of the *Colluctationes* upon it, expresses it, *Opinio et praesumptio, licet epidemica et à toto mundo avidè recepta, proculdubio tamen vana*?[6] And that the Sovereign GOD has permitted so many of His Faithful Servants to be by Plausible Appearances led into it, because it would contribute not a little to the accomplishing of His Glorious Purposes? *How unsearchable are His Judgments, and His Ways past finding out*! As Learned a Pen as ever appeared in the Defence of this Opinion, yett found it necessary to acknowledge; *Illorum sententia, qui Adventum Domini non fore, nisi post nescio quot Annorum, saecula, tradunt, valdè soporem in corda hominum ingerit, ideoqe non statim est recipienda*.[7] As on the One Side, it is not easy to be conceived, how such a Plentiful *Effusion of the Holy Spirit* on Mankind, and such a Wonderful Improvement in *Holiness*, and *Prayerfulness & Watchfulness*, throughout the whole World, as the Followers of this Opinion must look for, can be consistent with such a *Dead Sleep*, and such a Conformity to the Security & Impiety that was *in the Days of Noah*, as the *Day of the Lord* must find the World overwhelm'd withal: So on the other side, we actually feel it, that this Opinion has a Plain Tendency to produce the *Dead Sleep*, which must be upon the World *in our Days*.[8] This tis that obliges me to spend some Thoughts upon it: and enquire, whether we are to look upon ourselves, as excused from all Apprehension, *That the Day of CHRIST is at hand*, until We See the *Israelitish Nation* Miraculously *Converted* unto the *Faith* of CHRIST, and *Restored* unto the Countrey once possessed by their [ms. III, xi, 4v] Fathers? It is with a most Humble, and even Trembling, Heart and Hand, that I think of Disputing against an Opinion, that has had so many & so mighty Patrons. But the *Authorities*, which may be brought as *Demonstrations*, of an Opinion, while they oblige my *Modesty*, they will not oblige my *Compliance*. I can owe them no more of Regard, than *Austin*, writing against *Crescentius*, paid unto *Cyprian*.[9] Hear now my *REASONING*! Our *Lightfoot*, with his usual *Modesty*, said upon this Problem; *Tho' I am unwilling to recede from the Charitable Opinion of Most Christians, yett I see not how the Supposal can be digested without some Alloy & Mitigation*.[10] And I would freely say, *Tho' I am unwilling to recede from the Charitable* and almost Universal, *Opinion*, of the *Christian World*, about a future Conversion of the *Jewish World*, *Yett I see not how to digest* the *Difficulties*, which it is encumbred with. I Beg to be better informed! If I knew the R. *Isaac* that would favour & answer my Addresses, I would humbly address him in those Terms, *Desidero, Domine mi, certificari per te, et Testimoniis legis, et prophetarum, et aliarum scripturarum*.[11]—

I. I desire to be instructed, whether the Sacred Prophecies, which are now frequently interpreted, as importing a *General Conversion* of the *Israelitish Nation* to Christianity, still to be expected, be not really accomplished *Already*; or, whether those that are not so, must not have their Accomplishment in the *World to Come*, and after the Conflagration. After we have had such a *Key* to the Intent and Language of the *Prophetic Spirit* in the ancient Oracles, as we are now furnished withal, we shall soon see ourselves disencumbred from all Necessity to Interpret them of such a Future *Conversion*, & following *Dominion* and *Prosperity*, of the *Israelitish Nation*, as the Persons who sometimes read [ms. III, xi, 109] them with as much Praepossession as what sometimes looks upon the *Clouds*, do imagine in them.

Lett it be considered, That at the Return of the *Two Tribes* from the *Chaldaean* Captivity, there were so many of the *Ten Tribes* returned, as with such of the *Ten Tribes* as were left after the *Salmanasserian* Deportation, and such as had been incorporated with the *Two Tribes* in Religion, before the *Chaldaean* Captivity, and were their Fellow-sufferers in it, were enough to keep up the Appearance of *Twelve Tribes* in the Land of *Israel*. Here was a, DODEKA-PHYLON, enough, to answer the Purposes & Promises of GOD.[12] The *Peculiar* Ones who were to be the Blessed of the Lord, & reckon'd *His People*, were always a *Select*, and often a *Little*, Number, taken out of a *Multitude*. The *Seven Thousand* among the *Ten Tribes*, whom GOD had *Reserved* unto Himself, & Preserved from the Epidemical Idolatry, *These were the Ten Tribes*, in *His* Account. There was an *Holy Offspring*, that were the *Substance* of *Israel*, and the Trunk of the Tree, when the rest were fall'n & lost & blown away, like the Leaves in Autumn. Besides what Refugees the *Two Tribes* had, after the Defection of *Jeroboam*, we find, before the *Chaldaean* Captivity, yea, before the Final Stroke of the *Assyrian*, the People of *Asher*, & of *Menasseh*, & of *Zebulon*, upon the Motion of *Hezekiah*, coming up to the Worship of GOD at *Jerusalem*.[13] And, *when that was finished, they went & utterly destroy'd* the Monuments of *Idolatry, in their Several Cities; Then all the Cities of Israel returned Every Man to his Possession, into their own Cities*. The Cities reached by this Action were not, as *Grotius* thinks, only such as were in the Possession of *Hezekiah*; but the Reformers took advantage from the *Anarchy* and *Confusion* in *Israel* under *Hoshaea*, to do what they did.[14] When the *Salmanasserian* Deportation came on, the People were not ALL carried away; but as *Isaiah* had foretold, *Gleanings were left*; and as *Amos* foretold, *There were some taken by the Shepherd out of the Mouth of the Lion*. We find after this, the *Simeonites*, in the Days of *Hezekiah* doing Exploits; Particularly against the *Amalekites*, of whose Countrey they were the Inhabitants, when the First Book of the *Chronicles* was written. And long after this, we find *Josiah*, the Great Grandson of *Hezekiah*, purging the Cities of *Menasseh*, and *Simeon*, and *Ephraim*, and *Naphthali*, from Idolatry.[15] Indeed many of these, did in Process of Time so intermingle with *Barbarians*, that the *Jews* conceived an *Antipathy* to such a Mungril Generation: But there were [ms. III, xi, 6v] not a few, that better kept their *Israelitism*. The *Israelites*, that were carried unto *Chalachena*, and *Chaboras*, which are the Names in *Ptolomy* for *Halah*, and *Habor*, and unto the City of *Ganzana*, between the two Chanels of the River *Cyrus*, and the other Cities of the *Medians* (who, as *Herodotus* tells us, were also called *Arians*;) tho' their Captivity was not profitable to themselves, as we may gather from the Complaint of *Tobit*, yett the Captivity of the *Jews* was profitable to them, and brought them into Communion with the People & Prophets of GOD.[16] *Jeremiah* Invited, and *Ezekiel* Praedicted, their Coming to *Repentance*; and, the *Jews*, no doubt, communicated the *Prophecies* to them; *Daniel* also in his great Post, could not be unacquainted with them, or unconcerned for them. The Story of the Apocryphal *Esdras*, concerning their Long Travel, and even a Year & half's Ramble, into a far distant Countrey called *Harsaret*, is a meer Fable.[17] Indeed it is not unlikely, that in a Long Tract of Time, their Offspring may be translated into all Corners of the World; yea, albeit the *Best Reasons* which any Fanciful Men may bring to prove, *that it is so*, can't be allow'd for *Thorow-good*, yett the thing is possible, that some of their Blood, passing from *Scythia* may be found among the *Indians* of *North-America*.[18] But, These, and the rest that chose forever to remain where the King of *Assyria* settled them, were but the *Chaff* of the Nation. Part of the *Good Grain* appeared, When the Return from the *Chaldaean* Captivity gave an Opportunity for it. Then, Lett a *Menasseh-ben Israel* say what he please unto the Contrary, there were Numbers of the *Ten Tribes* that accompanied the *Two Tribes*, in returning to the Land of their *Fore-fathers Sepulchres*; and were not worse than the *Moabites*, and *Ammonites* and *Idumaeans*, who laid hold on the Liberty given unto the *Jews*, to repossess their own Countreys also.[19] The *Edicts* of the *Persian* Emperours extended unto *All the Tribes*; And we find, *Men of the People of Israel*, actually taking the Benefit of the *Persian* Proclamations and Indulgences. *Lightfoot*, & long before him, *Seder Olam*, observe, That the *Twelve Thousand* in the *Sum Total* [ms. III, xi, 110] of the Families Returned, and yett not found in all the *Particular Articles* of the Families, were of the *Ten Tribes*, whose Genealogy had not been so exactly praeserved.[20] We find also, *The People coming again, Every One unto his City*. Now, Tis plain, that the Cities of the *Ten Tribes*, as well as the *Two Tribes*, were after this inhabited. And accordingly, in the New Testament, we find most Part of the Land of *Israel* possessed by *Israelites*. In fine, what is reported in the Book of *Ezra*, concerning the *Children of the Captivity keeping the Dedication of the House of GOD with Joy, & offering Twelve Sacrifices according to the Number of the Tribes of Israel;* tis a Decisive Passage, and it has in it a Demonstration, That Each of the *Twelve Tribes* had their *Quota* in the Land, as well as out of it, by and for whom the Worship at the *Temple,* was to be carried on. Their Condition thro' the whole *Persian* Empire, may be a little apprehended from the Book of *Esther*. And the Tribe of *Judah*, being the only one that praeserved a *Sceptre*, or *Government*, after the Losing of the rest, & until the Coming of *Shiloh*, all the *Israelites* of the *Twelve Tribes*, came now to wear the Name of JEWS; which was indeed now become a Name not meerly of a *People*, but of a *Religion*. As the Chaldee Paraphrase brings in *Jonah* saying, I *am a Jew*; so *Elias* in his *Tisbi*, remarks, That after the *Ten Tribes* were carried into Captivity, all *Israelites* were called *Jews*.[21] Yea, the Circumcision of the *Idumaeans* under *Hyrcanus*, procures them the Denomination of *Jews*, with *Josephus*; and with *Dio Cassius*, all *that observed the Institutions of the Jews*, TA NOMIMA AYTΩN, were so denominated.[22] Unto all the *Twelve Tribes* there doubtless belonged many of those whom *Luke* finds come from all Nations to *Jerusalem* at the Feast of *Pentecost*; and therefore they are by *Peter* anon called, *The whole House of Israel.* [ms. III, xi, 8v] *Paul* also testified, *That the Twelve Tribes instantly Served GOD*: and, *Unto the Twelve Tribes*, both *James* and *Peter* direct their Epistles.

We need not a *Josephus* to tell us, That *Ezra* sent Copies of the *Persian* Edicts into *Media*, unto *all his Nation* there, and that many repaired from thence unto him, at *Babylon*, to return with him unto *Jerusalem*.[23] Unto these there was fulfill'd, what was foretold by *Isaiah*; [Ch. XIV. 1.] *The Lord will have Mercy upon Jacob, and will yett choose Israel,* [This denotes more than *Judah* & *Benjamin*:] *and sett them in their own Land, and the Stranger shall be joined with them:* [which was done, in the *Edomites* and *Moabites* & *Ammonites* coming to submitt unto the Rites of the Conquering *Israelites*: and appears a thing intimated in *Obadiahs* Prophecies;] And unto these there was fulfill'd what was foretold by *Micah*; [Ch. II. 12.] *I will surely assemble, O Jacob, all of thee; I will surely gather the Remnant of Israel.* The Meaning of which was, That no *Tribe* should be wanting, tho' many *Persons* in every *Tribe* should be so. *Jeremiah* has yett more distinctly expressed it; [Ch. III. 14.] *I will take you, One of a City, & Two of a Family, & I will bring you unto Zion.* [Compare; Jer. XXX. 3, 4, 10, 18. XXXIII. 7, 13, 14.] Their *Families* indeed, & their *Possessions*, were not now altogether so exactly distinguished, as they had been at the Beginning. Tho', as *Anna* knew she was of *Asher*, so there were many others that knew, to which of the *Tribes*, they ow'd their Original, yett there were many, who could not produce an *uninterrupted Line of Succession*, with the Name of each Successive Ancestor for many Generations.[24] [Consider, 1 Chron. IX. 1. and Neh. VII. 6.] From this time, as tis expressed [Zech. IX. 9, 10.] *Ephraim* and *Jerusalem* were so united under one Government, that *Ephraim* afforded the *Chariot*; and *Jerusalem* afforded the *Horse*, for the same Expedition; and it was actually so in the *Asmonaean* Wars.[25]

The *Twelve Tribes*, according to the Prophecies, quickly grew so numerous, that they not only stock'd [ms. III, xi, 111] their own Countrey with Cities, but sent forth Colonies all over *Asia*, and into *Egypt*, & other Parts of *Africa*, and into *Greece* and *Italy*; and even *Spain* itself scarce made a, *Ne plus ultrà*, for them: And at the same time, they conquered the Nations in the Neighbourhood. Lett *Joppe* a Town of the *Ten Tribes*, be an Instance of their Numbers; where *Strabo* tells us, The *Place did so abound with Men*, that from *Iamnia* the adjoining Village, & the Habitations in the Vicinity, they armed *Forty Thousand Men*.[26] The Gospel was first preached, unto the Towns of the *Ten Tribes*. And what GOD had engaged unto the Returning *Israelites*, [Jer. III. 15.] of, *Pastors after His own Heart*, was eminently fulfilled, in the *Apostles* chosen & called by our Blessed JESUS here, Who are likewise called, [Jer. XXXI. 6.] *Watchmen*, (Hebr. *Notzerim*) upon *Mount Ephraim*, crying, *Arise Ye, & Lett us go up unto Zion, unto the Lord our GOD*. The Princes, as we may call them, of the *Nazarenes*, [tis the note of the Excellent *Witsius*] may very suitably be called, *Notzerim*! Here are all the *Twelve Tribes* that are to be sought for; *These* were they, whom the Glorious GOD kept *for a Seed to serve Him, & who were accounted unto the Lord for a Generation*; The *rest* were lost like a few Drops in the *Ocean* of Mankind. And it is well remarked by the Great *Voetius*, That when our SAVIOUR mentions, *The Lost Sheep of the House of Israel*, He intends no more than the Scattered Ones, which paid their Devotions to and at the *Temple*.[27]

The Remarkable Repentance of the *Twelve Tribes* after the Reduction of them from the Land of their Punishment, and their conspicuous and perpetual Recovery from the *Idolatry*, that had been *Their own Iniquity*, was a notable Fulfilment of the Prophecies, which foretold, [Jer. XXXI. 18–] the *Bemoanings* of Paenitent *Ephraim*. And, [Jer. L. 20.] The *Iniquity of Israel*, not found, if *Sought for*. And, [Ezek. XVI. 53, 61.] That when the *Captivity of Sodom & of her* [ms. III, xi, 10v] *Daughters* (by which, when, A *Lapide* understands the *Moabites* & *Ammonites*, whose Original may well be referr'd unto the Countrey of *Sodom*, he seems to hitt the Mark.) *shall return to their Former State* (which, we know, they did at the same time with the *Jews*;) *Then they should remember their Ways & be ashamed*.[28] And, [Ezek. XXXVI. 26.] *From all Your Idols I will cleanse You; and a New Heart will I give You*. Of these, & many the like Prophecies, there appears no Cause, why a further Fulfilment should in THIS WORLD be look'd for. Here was enough, to stay our Appetites, till ANOTHER WORLD, shall bring on the *Full* & the *Whole* of the *Good Thing*, that has been *promised for the House of Israel*. The unparallel'd *Union* of the *Twelve Tribes*, in this Long Period, is enough to fulfil, the Prophecies, which foretold; [Isa. XI. 13–] That *Ephraim* should *not Envy Judah, and Judah* should *not Vex Ephraim*; and that they should *fly upon the Sea-Coast of the Philistines towards the West*, & should *also spoil them of the East together; and* should *lay their Hand upon*

Edom & Moab, & the Children of Ammon should *obey them.* All done in the very Letter of it! And, [Ezek. XXXVII. 19–] That the *Stick of Joseph,* and the *Stick of Judah,* should be *One Stick*; And, *Thus saith the Lord GOD, I will make them One Nation in the Land upon the Mountains of Israel; & they shall be no more Two Nations, neither shall they be divided into two Kingdomes any more at all; Neither shall they defile themselves any more with their Idols.* Not, but that the BETTER WORLD, will bring on a yett more Illustrious Fulfilment of all.

The Incredible Multitude of those among the Nations, from the Days of *Esther* (whose Book seems to have been written by a *Gentile,* and is a most Congruous Transition from the *Old* to the *New* Testament,) who then and all along became the *Proselytes of the Gate,* and were *Gathered under the Wings of the Divine Majesty,* and [ms. III, xi, 112] of *Gentiles* became a Degree of *Jews,* and made their Oblations to the *Temple* of GOD, might very much help to fulfil the Prophecies, [Isa. II. 2.] of, *All Nations flowing to the Mountain of the House of the Lord*; And [Isa. LVI. 7.] of The *House of GOD* becoming an *House of Prayer for all People.*

From some Things *foretold* as future, in the Last Chapters, of the Book, that we enjoy under the Name of *Zechariah,* which had *Occurr'd,* and been *Fulfill'd,* before the Days of that Prophet, it is evident, that the *Six Last Chapters* of that Book must be written by a Prophet that lived before him; and our Evangelist *Matthew* has particularly determined, that the Prophet *Jeremiah* was the Writer.[29] What we read there; [Ch. X. 6–] *I will strengthen the House of Judah, and I will save the House of Joseph,—and I will bring them again to place them,*—tis what we have seen accomplished in the Return of the *Twelve Tribes*; And whereas it follows, *He shall smite the Waves of the Sea, and all the Deeps of the River shall dry up,* a *Calvin,* a *Vatablus,* a *Gataker,* will find it accomplished in that Exiccation of *Euphrates,* which proved the Taking of *Babylon*:[30] Fl. *Illyricus* wonders, why Expositors torture themselves to find any other Exposition: And *Theodoret* long before any of these was an Author for *this.*[31] The Next Chapter, was evidently and wonderfully fulfilled, in the Destruction, brought by the *Romans* on *Jerusalem,* and the Crimes that introduced it: when they were delivered *into* the Hand of *Their King,* even of *That King* of whom, in Opposition to our SAVIOUR, they said, *We have no King but Him*: Their King *Vespasian.* Then the *Three Factions* into which the *Jews* were divided were *Cutt off*; The *Two Staves,* of their *Political* and *Ecclesiastical* State were utterly broken; and the *Covenant* of their *Peculiarity* was dissolved.[32] The *Foolish Shepherd* that succeeded, if we can find him no where else, Thou, *Rome,* shalt afford him to us! Yea, I would humbly enquire, (being yett no more than a *Seburaean*[33] in it!) whether the *Families,* that are found, [Chap. XII. 12.] *Mourning* in the Lamentations of *Repentance,* for the *Crucifixion* of Him who is JEHOVAH, do not point us to the *Repentance,* which *Pierced* the Beleeving *Jews* [ms. III, xi, 12v] to the *Heart,* upon the Proofs which they saw of His *Resurrection* from the Dead. The Families of *David, Nathan, Levi, & Shimei,* are such as we find *Progenitors* of our SAVIOUR, all recorded in the *Genealogy* which *Luke* has given us, of His Blessed *Mother*; where *Shimei*, who is the Fifth Generation after the *Zorobabel* of *Luke*, was but contemporary with the other *Zorobabel*, mention'd by *Matthew* in the Line of *Joseph*. Then, he that was *Fallen*, was *as David*, for such a Signal *Repentance* as *David* express'd after his *Fall*; And the House of *David*, coming into the Christian Faith, were *like the House of GOD*: the *House* of the Posterity of *David*, were as full of Piety, as if it were the *Temple* itself; yea, so *Angelically* Pious, and Holy, and Watchful, *as if the Angel of the Lord* were always visibly *before their Eyes*. As for the Circumstances of the *Siege* and *Fight*, in the *Last* Chapter of these Prophecies, I refer you, first, unto a *Grotius*, or, if he will not satisfy, unto a *Jackson*, to declare how literally all has been accomplished.[34] Whereas also we read, [Hos. III. 4.] That *Israel* should *abide many Dayes* in abandoned Circumstances, (far above one hundred & fourscore Years, & by Consequence more than Three Times as many, as *Judah*) but, *Afterward* they *should Return and Seek the Lord their GOD,—and Fear the Lord & His Good One in the Latter Days*: not only a *Calvert*, but also a *Calvin*, finds it accomplished, between the *Days* of *Cyrus*, & of our SAVIOUR.[35]

But then, if still we cannot see some of the Prophecies about a *Returning Israel*, to our Satisfaction accomplished, in what we have yett seen done for the *Twelve Tribes* aforesaid, it is now Time to Remember That, *Mens legis est lex*, and there is a *Surrogate Israel*, which putts in a Claim to them; and, *We are the Circumcision*.[36] The *Style* of the Prophecies is indeed such as best suited the *Dispensation* under which they were uttered: Nevertheless, *We* who are the *Heirs of the Promises*, have been taught of GOD; how to interpret them agreeably to our *Dispensation*. We have them Intelligibly and Sufficiently accomplished in our *Evangelical Blessings*; and the *Ordinary* [ms. III, xi, 113] *Gloss* of Interpreters, *Per Cyrum Temporaliter, Per CHRISTUM Spiritualiter*,[37] tis what it becomes *Christians* to pay a Continual Regard unto. They are very Remarkable Passages of our Apostle; *Christian*, I know thou canst not but sett a *Nota Bene*, upon them. [Rom. IV. 14, 16.] *If they which are of the Law be Heirs* [of the Promise] *Faith is made void, & the Promise is made of none Effect.— The Promise to be sure to all the Seed, not only to that which is of the Law, but to that also which is of the Faith of Abraham, who is the Father of us all.* And again, [Rom. III. 3, 29.] *Shall their* [the Jews] *Unbeleef make the Faith of GOD without Effect? GOD Forbid! Is He the GOD of the Jews only? Is He not also of the Gentiles? Yes, of the Gentiles also.* The Sum of it is; Tho' the Carnal *Israel* do by their Unbeleef lose their Claim to the *Promises* of GOD, yett the *Faith* of the *Promises* will not be defeated: A Faithful GOD will find an *Israel*, to whom He will fulfill all His *Promises*. But it is among the *Gentiles* that He will find this *Israel*: The Beleeving *Gentiles*, whom He will become a GOD unto. WE now actually *See* this *Israel*, yea, *Are* this *Israel*; With Pleasure and Wonder We can read a L. *Cappellus*, reckoning up a Score of Praerogatives and Excellencies, in which the *Christian Church* of the *New Testament* has been dignified above the *Israel* of the *Old Testament*. We can with an astonishing

Satisfaction Interpret the *Promises* unto *Israel*, as fulfilled in what is done for *us*; and say, *O our GOD; we are thine Israel, and thy Faithfulness faileth not.*

Finally; If still we want a further Satisfaction, Roll about, O *Yolam Hava!*[38]— There is a *World to Come*, in which *All* will be accomplished; and there shall *not fail aught of any Good Thing which the Lord hath spoken unto the House of Israel: It shall ALL come to pass.* Yea, It shall be said, *The one Half was never told us!* *Eusebius* has informed us, That such as were known to be of the *Davidic* Family, and have some *Kindred* unto the Blessed JESUS, were interrogated concerning *His Kingdom*, so much then talk'd of, They answered, *That His Kingdom was not a Kingdom of a Worldly and an Earthly Character, but Coelestial and Angelical; and it would not come on till the End of the World, when He will come in Glory, to Judge the Quick & the Dead, and give to all Men according to their Works.*[39] These Good Men were entirely in the right of it. THEN truly, will the *Son of the Most High sitt on the Throne of His Father David, and He shall reign over the House of Jacob forever & ever.* THEN the *Mystery of GOD will be finished;* and the Prophecies which now appear so full of *Mystery*, will all have the Best Expositor than can be, to *Unfold* them all unto us. To *Fulfil* them will effectually *Unfold* them!

I cannot but Entreat, That the *Prophecies* of the *Great Good* reserved for the *Israel of GOD* in the *Latter Days*, may be so interpreted, as to leave [ms. III, xi, 14v] room for our Father *Abraham*, & the other Patriarchs, to be Partakers in the Accomplishment of them. And This, the Notion of the *Jews*, in a National Recollection *Christianized*, and *Riding on the High Places of the Earth which now is*, with all other Christians depending on them, does not make a due Provision for.

But I must acknowledge, there lies one thing in my Way, that obliges me a little to *Stand Still*. I am stopt at the *Nine last Chapters of* EZEKIEL, and when the *Book is delivered unto me*, by one *saying, Read this, I pray thee*, I must say, *I am not learned.* Yea, if the *Book be delivered unto one of the Learned*, by one *saying, Read this, I pray thee*, even he must say, *I cannot, for it is sealed.* I am as much at a Loss, about the Deep Sense of these Chapters, as *Cunaeus* was, when he said, The Utmost that we can reach about it is but, *Opinion;* and, *Hominis est haec opinare, Dei scire.* Some are in Pain to see a *Naphthali* with the Aids of a *Villalpandus* & others, *wrestling* to show, that as the Distribution of the *Tribes* in the Land whereof we have the Topography here, was attended by the *Jews* in the Return from the *Babylonian* Captivity, so, that the *Temple* then built, in the Measures of it answered what is here described; And they censure the Time of these Reconcilers as all spent *at the Labour in Vain.*[40] But then, if we bring these *Hard Chapters* to prove a Return of the *Twelve Tribes* to possess their Land, & erect a *Temple*, as to be yett expected in *This World*, they prove *too much.* A *Whiston*, and Company, will here pretend Proofs, That the *Mosaic Paedagogy* is also to be Restored, and a *Worship* like that of the Old Judaic *Temple* revived.[41] But, can a *Christian*, admit such a Vain Imagination? and bring in *Moses* again, and a *Carnal Tabernacle*, which will cutt off a *Right*

unto the *Altar* we now live upon? *Theodoret* long ago, did not amiss to laugh
at *Apollinarius* for it, nor we now, at a *Toland*. What shall we then do?[42]—

[ms. III, xi, (1r)]—And yett, Lett us not ly down like *a Stag in a Nett*, utterly
despairing to gett out of the *Toils*. The *Wise Men of Enquiry*, have at Length
been so Inquisitive, as to be not altogether unsuccessful in their Essays to form
Thoughts upon these Visions of *Ezekiel*, which may a little satisfy us. And
among them, those which our *Lowth* has offered us, in his commentary, would
contribute not a little to our Satisfaction.[43]

This is the Summ of what such Masters have led me to. First, for the TEMPLE,
in the Visions. The *Temple* at *Jerusalem*, having been for the Idolatries, & the
other Impieties of the People, forsaken of GOD, and given up unto Destruction,
our Prophet *Ezekiel* gives unto the *Israelites* that were to Return from their Captivity in *Babylon*, a Direction and Encouragement for their Building of another
Temple.[44] Their *Temple* had been, *The Excellency of their Strength*, and, *The
Desire of their Eyes*: And they would have been very dull about a Return unto
their *Old Seats*, if they had not been animated with a *Prospect* & a *Promise*,
of their having their *Temple* restored. Nor would the Law of *Moses* have been
long observed in their Dispersion, but been lost in *Detestable Idolatries*, if the
Restoration of their *Temple*, to which it was adapted, had not made Provision
for the Praeservation of it. Now to Excite and Assist the People of GOD unto
this Necessary Enterprize, as before the building of the former *Temple*, GOD
shewed unto *David*, the Model of it in the Heavenly World: in like Manner
another *Temple* now being to be built, GOD shewed unto *Ezekiel*, the Model
for this also in the Heavenly World. And whatever Difference there may be, as
to the *Measure* of the *Two Temples*, namely, *Solomons* and *Ezekiels*, which
we leave to the Disputes of the Learned, it is evident, their *Figure* is, for the
Main, the Same. The People of GOD seeing this *Invitation* to, and *Preparation*
for, their Work, in the Visions of the Holy Prophet, fell to work, upon their Arrival at *Jerusalem*, and endeavoured a Conformity to the Model with which the
Prophet had instructed them. For indeed, we cannot suppose an Exact Model
of the Former *Temple*, to have been transmitted unto those, who [ms. III, xi,
16v] returned from the Captivity. *Seventy* Sad Years had rolled along, between
the *Destroying* of the *Former Temple*, and the *Finishing* of the *Latter*: In which
Long Interval, the *Ancient Priests* must all be Dead; and the *Younger* could have
but very Imperfect & Confused *Idaea's* of the Edifice. Doubtless, the *Temple*
of *Zorobabel*, was formed with an Eye to what the Prophet had praescribed.
But their feeble Circumstances made it fall short of the *Magnificence* that was
proposed. The *Tabernacle* of *Moses* was made according to the *Pattern* which
he saw *in the Mount*. And yett the *Pattern* which he saw, was the same that also
David saw, when a *Temple* much more *Magnificent* was but still conformed
unto it. However, the *Zorobabelian Temple* falling so short, This was a Sensible
Mortification unto the People; and it has drawn the *Jews* in succeeding Ages, to
expect, that in the Days of the *Messiah*, they should have a *Temple*, more fully
answering *That* in the Visions of *Ezekiel*.

But here the *Christians* come in, and plead for a *Mystical Temple* to answer the Prophecy: And they urge, That for the more *Circumstantial Embellishments* of the *Prophecy*, the Fulfilment of them, is no more to be insisted on, than in the Explication of a *Parable*.[45] We urge, that *Solomon* was a Type of our SAVIOUR, chiefly in regard of his being, *The Builder of the Temple*; And therefore, Several Passages of *Nathans* Prophecy concerning *Solomon*, [2. Sam. VII. 13, 14.] are in the *New Testament* applied unto our SAVIOUR. [Heb. I. 5. Luk. I. 32.] And other Prophets foretel the Same Thing about our Blessed JESUS. Thus tis foretold; Zech. VI. 12. *The Man whose Name is, The BRANCH, shall build the Temple of the Lord.* Now the *New Testament* comes, and plainly tells us, That the *Christian Church* is the *Temple of GOD*. [1. Cor. III. 16. 2. Cor. VI. 16. Eph. II. 20. 1. Tim. III. 15. Heb. III. 6.] And thus particularly, we there find *Antichrist* sitting in *the Temple of GOD*. Thus our *Ezekiel*, by giving the *Israelites* a View of having a *Temple*, not unlike to that of *Solomon* re-[ms. III, xi, (2r)]stored among them, did something to prevent their defiling themselves with *Babylonian Idolatries* during their Captivity; and Quicken them, when the Time for it should come, to go home, and Rebuild their Temple, and observe the Ordinances of *Moses*; until the *Messiah* should come, whose *Church* would resemble the *Temple* of *Solomon*, yea, exceed it, in Strength, in Grandeur, in Symmetry, & in Duration.

But then, for the CITY and COUNTREY in the Visions: The *Dimensions* of the One; and the *Divisions* of the Other. Here seems to be *Advice* unto the Returned *Israelites*, how to proceed as they were able. But they never came to it!—This is to be ascribed unto their own *Deficiencies* and *Miscarriages*. The *Holy One of Israel* does not therefore *suffer His Faithfulness to fail*. When the *Israelites* made their First *Entrance* into the *Promised Land*, they could not complain, that *there failed ought of any Good Thing which the Lord had spoken to the House of Israel*. And yett we know, how meerly thro' their own Fault, there was a dreadful *Abridgment* on their Enjoyment of the *Promised Land*; and how many *Nations* were left still, to be *Snares* & be *Traps* unto them, *Thorns in their Eyes*, & *Scourges in their Sides*, and they saw not the *Rest*, which the *Promise* told them of! Thus now, had the Redeemed *Israelites*, gone on with a *Strong Faith*, and an Inflexible & Unwearied Resolution, in the Resettlement of their Affairs, the Almighty GOD, who told them, *The Silver is Mine & the Gold is Mine*, would have carried them along. They might anon have had a Countrey Six hundred & Eighty two Miles, [or, adding the *Princes Portion*, Seven hundred & Eight Miles,] in *Length*, and at [ms. III, xi, 18v] Least One hundred & Sixty Miles in Breadth, besides future Enlargements: A *City* fourty two Miles in Compass; with a *Temple*, the *Ground-Plott* whereof would have contained in Compass, four Miles & above a Quarter. But an *Evil Heart of Unbeleef*, and the Sins which it led them to, *kept such Good Things from them*![46]

However, we must retire again to *Yolam Havah*!—If it be true, what is asserted by *David Kimchi*, as *L'Empereur* quotes him, That the *Returned Israelites*, had the Model of *Ezekiel* in their View, when they erected their *Temple*; but as *Cunaeus* notes, no further than they were capable; and as *Lightfoot* adds, they could not come up to the Bulk and Cost of *That*; Yett we must consent unto our *Greenhil* and others, that there was much of the *Mystical* in the Visions.[47] More particularly; There is a *Weight* in what falls from one of the *Romish* Rabbi's: *Omnia quae in Ezekiele de Jerusalem scribuntur, de Sancta Civitate, Superna Jerusalem absqe dubio sunt intelligenda.*[48] Yea, Tis a Saying of the *Jewish* Rabbi's themselves; *The City described in the Last Chapters of Ezekiel, is to be interpreted concerning the Jerusalem that is Above.* And for this Cause, I look on the Essay of that Gracious Man, *William Allein* of *Bristol,* to explain this Dark Prophecy, as the Best of any that I have yett mett withal.[49]

In short; When the *New Heavens* & the *New Earth* arrive, these *Nine Chapters* will be better understood, than they are ever like to be before. That which would yett more incline one to such Sentiments, is; That when *Moses,* and afterwards, the other Favourites of Heaven, were by the *Hand of GOD* upon them, transported into the *Heavenly World,* they all had exhibited unto them, a *Temple,* after the *Pattern* of which, first the *Tabernacle* of *Moses,* & then the *Temple* of *Solomon* were formed: And these *Holy Places* were, as our Apostle tells us, but Small *FIGURES of the TRUE,* even of *Heaven* itself. And in the Heavenly World, *John,* saw such a *Temple;* Even such an one as Ezekiel saw, & such an one as was built by *Solomon,* and such an one as had things in it, which were not in that which was built by *Zorobabel.* But that which yett more confirms the Sentiments, is; That our *Ezekiels* Visions are ushered in, with *The Resurrection of the Dead,* and the State wherein, *The Tabernacle of GOD shall be with Men, & He will be their GOD.*[50]

I may now fairly dismiss the Subject.

But in doing of it, we must briefly gett rid of one Encumbrance more. [ms. III, xi, 114 *canceled*]

[ms. III, xi, 20v] One of the main Props which has been brought for the Hopes of Great Things yett remaining to be done for the *Jews,* and what my rare *Witsius* lays much Stress upon, is, in that Promise; Deut. XXX. 5. *The Lord thy GOD will do thee Good, and multiply thee ABOVE THY FATHERS.* And since we can't find in all the Years after the Return from the *Chaldaean,* and before the Coming of the *Roman* Captivity, any Term of Time, wherein the *Jews* were prospered *Above their Fathers* in the Days of *Solomon,* they say, it remains to be in *This World* accomplished. But are these Excellent Men aware that the Promise expressly runs upon that Condition; *When thou shalt Return unto the Lord thy GOD, and shalt Obey His Voice.* However, I will satisfy myself, That in the *World to Come,* the true ISRAEL of GOD,[51] shall have it most literally & abundantly accomplished.

Thus do we begin to gett clear of our Obligations, to Embrace the Opinion, of an *Exalted Condition* for the *Israelitish Nation* upon *Earth,* before the *Coming* of the Lord, & the *Burning* of the World. We have left the Patrons of the Opinion, very *Little* if any thing at all, to say for it.—

II. Very *Little!*—Yes; Our ELEVENTH CHAPTER to the ROMANS! Tis a *Chapter* which affords a *Triumph* to our Friends, and assures them, That *the Blindness in Part is happened unto Israel, until the Fulness of the Gentiles be come in*, yett they shall be *Graffed in again upon the Olive-tree*; they shall be *Received again*, and in their *National Conversion*, there will be a *Salvation of all Israel*, and a *Life from the Dead unto the Gentiles*. How many admirable Men, besides the Younger *Alting*, & the Later *Junius*, have by their *Comments*, [pardon me, that I use the Word, *Comments!*] on this *Chapter*, thought that they have putt this Matter beyond Contestation![52]

—But not so fast, Syrs. Lett us have a *Review of the Case*; and without much help from a *Bartelerius*, Lett us employ some *Second Thoughts* upon the *Chapter*. It may be, upon *Second Thoughts*, all Things will appear in another Light immediately. I must acknowledge as *Paraeus* did, when he came to the *Twentieth* Chapter of the *Revelation*, *Haec explicare fateor me trepide aggredi*. But I will venture to tender some Thoughts on the *Eleventh* Chapter to the *Romans*.[53]

It is well known, That for the *First Eight Years* after the Ascension of our SAVIOUR, the *Gospel* [ms. III, xi, 115] was preached by the *Twelve Apostles*, unto none but the *Circumcised Israelites*. The Great Conversion among those being over, the Gospel was then preached unto the *Proselyted Gentiles*, who were the most *Prepared*, & prov'd the most *Perswaded*, of any to receive it. For *Four Years* more the Gospel went no further. But then, the *Jews* continuing to Refuse the Gospel, our Lord sent it unto the *Idolatrous Gentiles*, by *Two New Apostles*, namely, *Paul* and *Barnabas*, whom He commission'd for that Purpose.[54] The Most of the *Jews* that for the Present were to be converted, had now been brought in; the Work was much at a Stand among them; and *the Rest*, were growing Ripe for the Destruction which was hastening upon them. This View of Things brought an inexpressible Anguish on the Mind of our Apostle; And now, Behold his Releef upon it. Come and See, whether our Apostle has not his Eye, upon Events that were to occur in or near his *own Time*, and not such as would not arrive till perhaps *Two Thousand* Years after, and be sure, in the *End of the World*.[55]

There were now some among the *Gentiles*, who began to surmise and give out, That the *Jews* would now be so wholly *Rejected of GOD*, as that not only the *Gifts of the Holy Spirit* would no more be granted unto any of that Nation, but also the *Door of Grace* would be entirely & eternally shutt upon them: In short, *Quod Deus alienior esset ab Israele, quam a Gentibus*.[56] Our Apostle would by no Means have the *Gentiles* to *Talk so exceeding proudly*, & *Lett such Arrogancy come out of their Mouth*. Tis true, Tis thro' the *Fall of the Jews that Salvation is come unto the Gentiles*: and, as our SAVIOUR foretold it would be, on their Murdering the SON of GOD, the *Kingdome of GOD was taken* from the Jewish Nation, and *given to others*, that would *bring forth the Fruits thereof*. But then Lett the *Gentiles* consider their Circumstances in this awful Transaction, and, *Be not high-minded but Fear*, lest they also by *Unbeleef* come to be *broken off*. The CHURCH, [or say, The CHRIST] of GOD, is to be considered as the *Stock* of an Illustrious *Olive-tree*. Now, it is *Contrary to Nature* to make use of *Cyons* more Ignoble than the *Stock*: There [ms. III, xi, 22v] is no need of quoting *Theophrastus* for This; who particularly directs the Insition of the *Olive-tree*. Every body knows, the *Oleaster*, or the *Wild Olive-tree*, can by no Managery of Art, be brought unto the Producing of any other, than those *Olives* which for their Ill Qualities were called *Phaulia*.[57] An *Oleaster*, becoming an *Olive-tree* would have been esteem'd a Prodigy; and the *Grafting* of it on an *Olive-tree*, would be *Unnatural*. But yett, this is what the Sovereign Providence of our GOD has done, in His *Grafting* the *Gentiles* upon the *Church* by the *Faith*, of His CHRIST. *How much more shall* the Jews which are *the Natural Branches, be grafted into their own Olive-tree?* Which is agreeable, not only to the Rule of *Theophrastus*, but also to our own *Experience*, That the nearer Consanguinity there is between the *Cyons* and the *Stock*, the nobler is the Fructification. The Metaphor of *Inoculation* is the more emphatically applied unto the *Olive-tree*, inasmuch as this Tree, is best propagated *That Way*; not very well by *Semination*, & not at all by *Surculation*.[58] Says our Apostle; "If you *Gentiles* are by the Extraordinary Favour of GOD, *Grafted* on the *Stock* of *Israel*, and there be good Effects of it; much more the *Jews*, that are on great accounts nearer akin to the *Stock*, will be welcome to their *Mother-Tree*, and if they are *Grafted on* again, (for so they must be, if they Return to GOD,) there will Excellent Fruits be found upon them."[59] However, our Apostle expressly putts it upon this Condition; *If they abide not still in Unbeleef*. And here also, He comforts himself, *GOD is able to Graft them on again*. Yea, He seems not without a glimmering Hope, That the *Emulation* of what they should anon see among the *Gentiles*, would *Provoke* them, to *Think on their Ways, & to turn their feet unto the Testimonies of the Lord*. He hopes, That Great Numbers of the *Jews*, when they saw, how the Glorious GOD own'd the *Gentiles* for *His People*, by the *Gifts of His Holy Spirit* plentifully poured out upon them, and astonishing Tokens of His Gracious Presence among them, would come over into the Tents of *Christianity*.

The Thing accordingly came to pass! Indeed, our *Church-History* for those *First Ages* of Christianity, is miserably Defective and Imperfect. But yett, we find Plain Footsteps, of GOD *Reviving His Work in the Midst of the Years*, and Great Numbers of *Jews* [ms. III, xi, 116] appearing to embrace the Faith of the Risen JESUS. We find a R. *Eliezer* making a Sad Outcry of so many *Jews* turned *Christians*, in the Days of *Trajan*. We find *Justin Martyr* making a Glad Outcry, of *Jews* ΚΑΘ᾽ ΗΜΕΡΑΝ *Every Day* turned *Christians* in his Days. The *Fast*, which the Infidel *Jews* then kept for the Translation of the Bible into *Greek*, is by the most Acute Writers of our Days, assign'd unto their Grief on the account of so many *Jews* made *Christians* by it.[60] When *Adrian*, to finish what the *Vengeance* of Heaven had begun by *Vespasian*, carried on the Destruction of the *Jews*, to so many horrible *Millions*, the most Learned Masters of Computation [without going into the *Talmudic Hyperbole's* upon the Sacking of *Bitter*] think, that the Biggest Part of the *Jews* then left alive in the World were *Christians*;[61] We are informed by *Sulpicius Severus*, that *Adrian* look'd on the *Christians* generally to have been *Jews* originally: And he intimates, as *Drusius* understands him, that *Adrians* chasing the *Jews* from the Sight of *Jerusalem*, contributed unto the *Perfection* of their *Christianity*.[62] Anon, Beholding the desperate Condition of their Nation, and the *Light* of GOD *shining* on the *Tabernacles* of the *Gentiles*, there appears to have been a yett Greater *Ingathering* from among the *Jews*, into the Christian *Floor* of GOD our SAVIOUR. Under the Reign of *Constantine*, the *Christianized Jews* had all possible Encouragements; the Confession made in the Disputation of *Gregentius* with *Herbanus* was verified, That *Christianized Hebrews* were look'd upon as, TIMIΩTEPOI, more to be accounted of than *Christianized Gentiles*: and no Part of the Earth, had such a Proportion of *Christian Churches*, as the Land of *Judaea*, which on the Score of our SAVIOURs former Appearing & Sojourning there had a Vast Respect paid unto it above any Spott of Ground upon the Face of the Earth.[63] A Great Part of these *Christian Churches*, did consist of *Christianized Jews*; and some of them had none but such as were known to be so, for their *Pastors*, in many Long Successions. And what became of these? Why, They were soon so united with the *Gentiles*, in *Marriages* and all other Communions, and particularly the dropping of *Circumcision*, that there was no longer any *Israelitish Distinction* left upon them. The Modern Opinion, That the *Israelitish Nation*, which remains dispersed with the usual Marks of *Judaism* upon them in the Several Parts of the World, shall be converted from their Infidelity, and restored unto the Possession of their old *Little* [ms. III, xi, 24v] *Countrey*, and have a Glorious Kingdom of GOD erected among them, and thorough them extended unto the *Gentiles*; This Opinion excludes the Offspring of that *Holy People*, the *Jews, who First Hoped in CHRIST*, from a share in the Singular Priviledges of the *Restored Nation*, and confines the Priviledges to the Offspring of a *Cursed Remnant*, whom GOD reserves among the Nations, as a Monument and a Spectacle of His Vengeance for the greatest Crime that ever was committed in the World!—*Credat Judaeus Apella!*[64]

But then, Lett us hear our Apostles Conclusion upon the Whole. As the very *Spirit* of the Whole Epistle to the *Romans*, does discountenance this Opinion of Great Things intended for the *Circumcised Jews* in the Latter Days, by still making the *Genuine Offspring* of *Abraham* to be a *Spiritual Offspring*; and showing that *All* were not *Israel* that were *of Israel*, nor were *All Israel* those that were *of Israel*; So the *Conclusion of the Matter* in this Chapter, does utterly confound it. The Words are,—*Until the Fulness of the Gentiles be come in; And SO all Israel shall be saved.* The Sound of that Word, *The FULNESS of the Gentiles!*—I pray, How do you understand it?—It is, ΠΛΗΡΩΜΑ, *The Filling up of the Gentiles*; Even as, *Gemma implet cavitatem Annuli*.[65] There is a *Salvation* from *Death* and *Sin*, and a *Blessedness*, whereof *ALL Israel* shall be made Partakers. The *Falling off* of so many who were *Literally Israelites*, leaves a *Chasm*, in that which is to be the Mystical *Body*, whereof CHRIST is the *Head*. There must be a *Filling up*, to repair this *Falling off*; And that the *Whole Body fitly joined together* may be supplied with all that the Eternal *Praedestination* of GOD has made requisite unto it, what Course will be taken by His amazing *Providence*? Tis a, *Filling up with the Gentiles*, that must accomplish it. There is no other *Israel*, that is to be look'd for [And if we should add, That what is to be done for the full *Restoration* of *Israel*, is to be done at & by the *Resurrection* of the *Dead*, there is a very Broad Hint in this very Chapter for it.] But—SO tis, that ALL *Israel*, comes to be *Saved*. And SO, the Faithful People of GOD, you see yourselves delivered from a *Mistake*, which Your *Hopes* and *Prayers* have gone upon.

I don't see, That the Opinion has now any one Support left unto it.

III. Now, I beseech You, Syrs, Have the Patience to see and weigh what I have to offer against Your Opinion, and hath compelled me to abandon it.

[ms. III, xi, 117] An honest Man called, *Seager*, near Fourscore Years ago, when this Opinion was pretty culminant, bestow'd some Rebukes upon it, in a Treatise entituled, *A Discovery of the World to Come*; and made that Remark on the Maintainers of it.[66] *You balk the New Testament, and hide Yourselves under the dark Prophecies of the Old: Whereas You should consider, that CHRIST and His Apostles have so clearly interpreted the Prophets, as touching the Latter Times, that we need not appeal from them to the Prophets on this Argument.*

Indeed, there are in the *Old Testament* some terrible Intimations, That the *Israelitish Nation* as to the Literal and Lineal Appearance of it, would be so *Cast Off*, as never to be Restored, *Until*, or otherwise than *By*, the *Resurrection of the Dead*. I will not insist on that Word, Mal. IV. 1. *The Day that cometh shall burn them up, & leave them neither Root nor Branch*. But, we will go back, as far as the Prophecy of their Illustrious Lawgiver, in the XXVIII Chapter of *Deuteronomy*. *There*, the *Man of GOD*, having foretold a Variety of Calamities to come upon that People, for their *Idolatries*; when they have gone thro' what we may call, *The First Sett of Plagues*, and were pretty well cured of their *Idolatries*, he, with a MOREOVER, brings on a *Second Sett of Plagues* much longer than the Former. This lays a *Yoke of Iron* on their Neck; being under that Monarchy which is called, the *Iron* One, in the Sacred Oracles: and it comes by a *Nation that came from far, from the End of the Earth*, even from *Europe*, with a *Flying Eagle*; in which, who sees not the *Roman* Banners?[67] A Crime greater than any of their former *Idolatries* must call for this; Especially since they were not Relaps'd into *Them*; And such a Crime it was, To Reject and Murder the only REDEEMER of the World. Now concerning the *Sett of Plagues*, which is thus brought on, we read, *These Curses shall pursue thee, till thou be destroy'd, and they shall be upon thee and upon thy Seed FOREVER*. Forever! What a Word is *That*!

But Lett us repair to the *New Testament*.

There we read; [1. Thess. II. 16.] *The Jews,—Wrath is come upon them to the uttermost*. I pray my [ms. III, xi, 26v] Readers that understand *Greek*, to tell the *English* of, ΕΙΣ ΤΕΛΟΣ.[68] Most certainly, tis, To the END. Say, To the End of *What*?

When our Glorious LORD makes His Descent, [Rev. I. 7.] *Behold, He cometh with Clouds, and Every Eye shall see Him, and they also which pierced Him*; The *Jews*! And these will be some of *the Kindreds of Earth, which are to wail because of Him*. Certainly, They are then found in their *Unbeleef*. The *Faithful* will not *wail because of Him*, when they see Him *come with Clouds*. No,

They will *Sing* upon what they See; and *make a Joyful Noise unto the Lord;* and *lift up their Heads,* to meet a *Redemption which draws nigh.* But if the Nation of *Crucifiers,* be then found in their *Unbeleef,* they must perish, among them, who *obey not the Gospel,* & must feel the *Flaming Fire* take *Vengeance* on them.

It is commonly supposed, That the *Jews,* upon their *National Conversion,* will be still *Distinguished* from the *Gentiles,* [else, what avails *their Conver-sion* more than that of any *other Nation?*] and that they will enjoy their *Peculiar Dignities.* But, what can there be to *Distinguish* them? For the *Language* of a *Distinct Nation,* they have *None;* And their *Circumcision* must cease, with the other *Mosaic* Ordinances. Our *Baxter* very justly says, To propose the Continu-ance of them in a *Jewish Peculiarity* is a downright *Wickedness,* and contrary to the very Nature of *Christianity.*[69] And the Truth is; I would have no more hand in Rebuilding the *Partition-Wall,* between *Jews* and *Gentiles,* which the Blessed JESUS has thrown down so long ago, than I would in Rebuilding the Sunk Walls of *Jericho.*[70] In short; If the *Jews* were all made *Christians,* there would in a few Years be no *Jews* left in the World; No, not so much as One Man, on whom we can imagine any thing to be seen, upon which it might be said, *This Man is a Jew.* To what Purpose then a Church of the *Jews!*—Except you suppose a Church that will admitt none but such as could prove their Descent from *Circumcised Parents* into it? But, *Christian,* can't thou suppose it?

The *Offspring* of the *Jews,* that according to this Opinion, are to be the Par-takers of the *Jewish Monarchy,* that so many Good Men do look for; I would ask, whether they shall be the *Offspring* of All the *Jews,* that have become *Christians* in all the Past Ages? Or, only the *Offspring* of the *Jews* that have continued *Obstinate Infidels* until this *Revolution?* For the Former, tis utterly Impossible: They are *Unknown:* They are *Extinct;* [ms. III, xi, 118] They are *Gentiles.* For the Latter, tis, as we have already hinted, so *Incredible,* that!—*It seems to me unreasonable.*

Many there are, who not only will have the more particular *Distinction* of even the *Twelve Tribes* recovered, [And how *Miraculously!*] for this National Re-establishment of the *Jews;* but also Dream of the *Ten Tribes* existing some-where or other, separate from those who now go under the Name of *Jews,* to be anon found out, & brought in, and come to a Coalition, with such as are now more visibly of the *Jewish Extract.* In this, more charitable to the *Ten Tribes,* than the *Jews* themselves, who in the *Talmuds* consign them over to Eternal Perdition, & exclude them forever from *all Part in the World to Come.* Yea, Some Learned Men have written some Curious Things, to prove, That the *Tartars* are *They.*[71] Amazing Futilities! That ever Men of so much Learn-ing, should throw away their Time and Skill in such Impertinencies! It seems, Father *Jerom* had something of the Fable, about the *Ten Tribes* yett existing in some Northern Parts of *Asia.*[72] But I bestow even too much Pains in answer-ing them, if I only repeat the Words of a *Voetius; Nullas Tribus Israeliticas, aut Reliquias earum, extra Gentem Judaicam hodie superesse.* Or the Words of a *Vorstius: Hodie aliquas genuinas Reliquias istarum Tribuum reperiri in*

orbe, est vanissimum somnium.[73] Tis enough to say, The Idle Stories told by
Benjamin Tudelensis, and by *Abraham Peritsol*, with the ridiculous Romance
more lately palm'd upon the World by *Menasseh Ben Israel;* Away with 'em!
They are all of a Peece with *Aristaeus's* Legend. And they that find any *Ten
Tribes* in the Places, these Gentlemen tell of, I durst say, will also find the *Cave*
built by *Solomon*, where *Jeremiah* hid the Utinsels of the Temple.[74]

In offering these *Objections*, as we go along, what are we doing, but still quoting the *New Testament?* For, what lies at the Bottom of the Opinion, is a Thing
that is every where condemned all over the *New Testament*. The very *Spirit*
of the *New Testament*, is to retund all *Confidence in the Flesh*, and introduce
a more *Spiritual Dispensation*, wherein they that *worship GOD in the Spirit,
& rejoice in CHRIST JESUS*, become the Only True *Israel of GOD*. These are
the True *House of Jacob*, and *are called by the Name of Israel*: while the *Circumcised Infidels*, are no better than so many *Dogs*. According to [ms. III, xi,
28v] the Design, and the Doctrine, and the *Spirit*, of the *New Testament*, in
the *Gentile* World, where it had once been said by the Most High GOD, *Ye are
not my People*, there they that are brought into the Knowledge & Service of
His CHRIST, come to be called, *The Children of the Living GOD*. The *Spirit!*
Yea, how often the very *Letter* of it! The *Four* Last Verses in the *Third* Chapter
to the *Galatians*, are enough to determine who are now the True *Offspring of
Abraham*. Tis very *Unevangelical* now to look for them among an *Abdicated
Generation*. When of old the *Holy One of Israel*, told His People of His being
their *Husband*, he said, *The GOD of the Whole Earth shall He be called*. And
the *New Testament* finds gathered from the *Whole Earth* unto the *Holy One of
Israel*, the People that are to be His *Espoused Israel*. Tis true, there was a Time
when the People descended from *Jacob, & born of the Will of the Flesh*, were a
Peculiar People of GOD. But it was with Relation to the Promised REDEEMER,
and that the World might know *Where* to look for Him, who was to be Born of
that Nation. This Relation was that which procured and secured a *Distinction*
for the more Peculiar Tribe of *Shiloh*, when the Body of the rest became Eternal *Castaways*. And yett, even while this *Distinction* was kept up, how many
Gentiles were brought in, & sett upon the Level with the People on which they
were *Inoculated*, by a *Full Reward from the GOD of Israel, under whose Wings
they were come to shelter themselves!* Thus did the *Wisdome* of GOD, even
Then, Initiate His People to the Principles of our *Gospel*, and begin to make
them learn, That *the Righteousness of GOD, which is by the Faith of JESUS
CHRIST, is unto all & upon all them that Beleeve*, in Every Nation; *for there
is no Difference*. But *Shiloh* is come; and now all Occasion for the *Distinction*
is forever taken away. The Carnal *Children of Israelites*, are to our *Holy One
of Israel*, no better than *Children of Ethiopians*. *Now*, One found in the Sultry
Regions of *Africa*, or, among the *Tranquebarians* in the Eastern *India*, or the
Massachusettsians in the Western, that shall thro' the *Faith* [ms. III, xi, 119]
of the Gospel, be by the SON of GOD made one of His *Members*, and by the
SPIRIT of GOD made one of His *Temples*, is as much valued by GOD, as ever

any *Simeon* or *Levi*, that could show their Descent from the Good Man, who struggled with an *Angel*, & gott a *Blessing* from Him.[75] To imagine, That the Glorious GOD *of the Spirits of all Flesh*, has a *Distinguishing* Regard for the Offspring of the *Flesh*, of One Ancestor more than another; tis an Imagination very Derogatory to the *Glory* of our GOD; very Contradictory to the *Language* of our *Gospel*.

We will not insist on the Vast Confluence of *Miracles*, which our Bretheren find it necessary to expect, for the Accomplishment of what they are so fond of; Among which they are driven particularly to expect a *Transient Appearance* of our SAVIOUR from Heaven to the *Jews*, like what He granted unto the Chosen Vessel in the Way to *Damascus*. I will only say, They had need have a better Warrant for such Expectations, than any that I am yett apprised of![76]

But more *Direct Proofs* from the *New Testament* for the Confutation of their Opinion, are what we must proceed unto. And they shall See, how as we *hold on our Way*, we *grow stronger & stronger*.

I would be informed, whence it comes to pass, that when our LORD had foretold, [Luk. XXI. 24.] *This People shall fall by the Edge of the Sword, and shall be led away Captive into all Nations; and Jerusalem shall be troden down of the Gentiles, until the Times of the Gentiles be fulfilled;* or, until the Expiration of the Fourth Monarchy: He says not One Word, about any Long Time of Prosperity for the *Jewish Nation* to intervene before His Coming to Judge the World? But the Prophecy of *Jerusalem trodden under foot of the Gentiles* does also & chiefly intend the *Christian Church* of *Pure Worshippers*, under the Oppression of the *Papists*. All the *Pious* are now *Israelites*; they that persecute them are now the *Gentiles*. But what? Any thing of the old *Jerusalem* a revived *Phoenix*? No; The very Next Thing is; *THEN shall they see the Son of Man coming in a Cloud with Power & great Glory.* So then, *Jerusalem* is to be *troden down of the Gentiles*, until the *Day of the Lord that shall burn like an Oven*: For such will be the Day, when *the Son of Man comes in Clouds with Power & great Glory.* And then, Syrs, Rebuild Your *Jerusalem* in Your Way, as well as You can!—This Text obliged *Chrysostom* long ago, to *Beleeve* it, That the Present Condition of the [ms. III, xi, 30v] *Jews*, ΕΩΣ ΣΥΝΤΕΛΕΙΑΣ ΚΑΘΕΞΕΙ, *will continue to the End of this World.* And it obliged *Origen* long before him to *Speak* it; ΘΑΡΡΟΥΝΤΕΣ ΕΡΟΥΜΕΝ ΟΤΙ ΟΥΔΕ ΑΠΟΚΑΤΑΣΤΗΣΟΝΤΑΙ, *We confidently declare it, that they shall never be restored.*[77] Once more, Has not our SAVIOUR said, *When the Son of Man cometh, shall He find Faith on the Earth?* But, if the *Jews* be all brought in to the *Faith* of our SAVIOUR, and the *Gentiles* be generally drawn with them & by them into the Same *Faith*, certainly He will then *find Faith in the Earth*, yea, He will *find the Earth* fill'd with *Faith*. Expound it & Limit it, for the *Faith of His Coming*, yett such a Senseless & Secure Frame as *That*, will be incompatible to so Glorious a State as our Good Bretheren look for. Nor can such a State be consistent, with the Groans of the *Elect, crying Day & Night unto GOD*, that He would *avenge them on the Adversaries* oppressing of them, which will be the State in which the *Elect* will be found at the Coming of the Lord. It would grieve one to see, what Poor Work our Friends, and no less Men than a Great *Zanchy* himself, do make to extricate themselves from the *Toils* of this Objection.[78]

But if the Opinion against which we are thus Arguing, be able with desperate shifts, to live under all the Arguments which have hitherto been used for our *Awakening*, there is One yett behind, which will fall with all the Force of an huge *Mountain* upon it, and come indeed like that which appears upon the Sounding of the Second Angel in the Apocalyptical Vision of the *Trumpetts*; *A Great Mountain burning with FIRE*: There will be no Standing before it. In short, It is an Opinion that appears utterly Inconsistent with the *Conflagration* which is to *Destroy all the Wicked of the Earth*, both such as *Know not GOD*, and *such as Obey not the Gospel of our Lord JESUS CHRIST*, at the *Second Coming* of the LORD; And it is utterly Impossible to be Reconciled unto the State of the *New Heavens* and the *New Earth*, before the Arrival whereof there will not come on the *Salvation*, of which the *Prophets have enquired, who prophesied of the Grace that should come to the Israel of GOD*.

If our Bretheren will be satisfied in This; That the *Israel* which is to have the *Kingdom*, and enjoy the *Holy Land* which was in the *Covenant* of GOD promised unto the *Patriarchs*, are to be the *Raised Saints* of the *New Heavens*, who shall have the *Nations* of the *New Earth* under their *Instruction* and *Government*; and a Great Part of whom will be Really such as *according to the Flesh*, were once of the *Israelitish Nation*, which were for *Seventeen Hundred Years* together the *Peculiar People* of GOD, & under His Institutions, from whence He was all along fetching and forming a *People for Himself*, to replenish His *Holy City*: Or, more briefly, If the *Resurrection of the* [ms. III, xi, 120] *Dead*, be the *Return of Israel*, which they will take up withal;—I have no more to say; I am Silent; I am Content; There is no more to be Said.—And I wish, that every Pious Reader, would here make a Pause, and See whether upon a due Reflection, he don't find something within him, disposing him to praefer a *Deathless* and *Sinless* World, for the Seat of the *Good Things* which our GOD has *promised for the House of Israel*.[79]

Bretheren, *Etiam Nos hoc opinati fuimus aliquando*.[80]—I was myself a very long while in your Opinion; Very near Fourty Years ago, I published a Treatise, entituled, EXPECTANDA; wherein this was the *Basis* which I built upon. "There is a *Davidical Kingdom* (if I may call it so) which belongs to our Lord. The Special Property of this *Kingdom* lies in This; As the *Humane Nature* is exalted above other Natures, thus the *Jewish Nation* is exalted above other Nations, upon this Account, That *of Them as concerning the Flesh, CHRIST came, who is over all, GOD blessed forever*. For *That*, and some other Causes, a Distinct Body of the *Jewish Nation* shall be exalted unto a most Particular Acquaintance with our Lord JESUS CHRIST; and be so advanced by Him, in the World, as that by their Means the *Earth* shall be filled with *Heavenly Influences* transcending any that the By-Past Ages have had Experience of."[81]—Alas, I was a very Young Man; [between Twenty and Thirty.][82] I understood not the True

Israel; I *Recant*; I *Revoke*; and I now make my most Public *Retraction.—Then* indeed, and all along, I had no other View, than that the Promised *Kingdom*, could not come on, before the *New Earth*, wherein is to *Dwell Righteousness*. But I must confess I *Then*, and for more than Fourty Years together, felt Myself puzzled about the State of the *New Earth* in regard of the *Conflagration* that is to praecede it and produce it, and as much puzzled in regard of the *Poison of the Old Serpent* remaining in the People of GOD. And I declare it, That I never could gett over the Difficulties. That Excellent Person, *Adoni Avi*, who has with the most Erudition of any Man that ever has written upon it, maintained; *A National Conversion of Israel, still to be look'd for*, did both in that Book, and in another that followed it, maintain, and evince, That *the Second Coming of our* SAVIOUR *will be at the Beginning of the Happy State*, which is to be expected for the Church upon Earth in the Latter Days.[83] And [ms. III, xi, 32v] in the History of his Life, the *Parentator* has told the World, that he died with a Perswasion, *That there will be no settled Good Times, till the Second Coming of the Lord; His Coming will be at the Beginning of the Good Times promised by the Mouth of all the Prophets. His Kingdom takes not place, nor is the Israelitish Nation restored, until His Appearing.*[84] This was what a Person of his Great Penetration could not but find himself under a Necessity of coming to. But now, I insisted upon it unto him, that I was not able to see, how such a *National Conversion* of the *Jews*, with such Consequences as are commonly assign'd unto it, could be consistent with such a *Terrible Conflagration*, as the Second Epistle of *Peter* brings upon the World, *At the Beginning of the Good Times promised by the Mouth of all the Prophets*.[85] His only Return and Retreat was, That the *Scripture* speaks of *Two Conflagrations*; First a *Partial* One, at the Beginning of the *Millennium*: out of which whole Nations would escape; and particularly those which *Lactantius* tells of, *Quaedam relinquentur ut a Justis triumphentur*; and then, a more *General* One, at the Conclusion of the *Millennium*: which was what the *Chiliasts* of the primitive Times, many of them went upon.[86] The *Partial* One he thought might chiefly fall on the *Italian* Territories; and tho' he did not see how *Cresseners* Method of proving, That after the *Burning of the Body of the Beast*, a considerable Part of the Earth would remain unreach't & untouch't by it; & inhabited as formerly, was liable to no Exceptions, yett he inclined unto some such Sentiments; and commended him as a *Judicious Writer*.[87] I laboured, all I could for my Life, to acquiesce in the Opinion. But after all I cannot. I find, It will never do. Tis *Unscriptural*. I do not, I cannot find the *Earth* coming under any *Conflagration* at all, a Thousand Years *after* the Coming of the Lord; tho' I find *Fire Coming down from GOD out of Heaven* upon a Vile Crue then mustering on the *Earth*. But for the *Conflagration*, which the *Earth* undergoes *at the Coming of the Lord*, I find it expressly said, *The Earth & the Works that are therein shall be burnt up* in it, and, *All these things shall be dissolved*. While I was in my anxious Enquiry after the *Truth*, and [ms. III, xi, 121] *I sett my Heart to understand*, a Good Providence brought into my View, a Little Treatise of a Nameless Writer, entituled, *Good Things to Come*: [printed in the Year, 1675.] which explained the *Mystery* of the *Translated* whereof the Apostle writes to the *Corinthians* and the *Thessalonians*; and from that Moment, I thought I might say, *I have found it.*[88]

This is now with me the Plain *State of the Case*; and what, I hope, without coming under the Guilt of the, *Mutatio Dictaminis*, by *Caramuel* & Company infamously pleaded for, I find myself compell'd unto.[89] The *Second Coming* of the Lord is most certainly to be at and for the Destruction of the *Man of Sin*. If my Reader, won't yett own *That*, I hope, that before we part, he will find himself compell'd unto it. But the *Second Coming* of the Lord, will be accompanied with the *Conflagration* which will *Burn up the Earth*, & *the Works that are in it*, and will *Dissolve all these things*. Our Apostle expressly makes, His *Coming*, and that *Burning* and the *Day of the Lord*, all to be One and the Same. Now, Surely no body expects the *National Conversion of Israel*, before the Destruction of the *Man of Sin*, and the Removal of *Antichrist*. Nor can any expect, what is to be done for the *Converted Nation* of the *Jews*, before the *New Earth*: And the *New Earth* takes not place, till after the *Conflagration*. To place the *New Earth* before the *Conflagration*, is a Strain of *Nonsense*, that if I had not been so unhappy as to hear it often uttered, I could not have thought that any *Man* could be guilty of it.[90] But then, Lett any Living show, if he can, how and where an *Infidel Nation* can be converted unto GOD & His CHRIST, in the Midst of the *Flames*, which are to *Scatter Brimstone* on them, and their *Habitations*! Or if the Conviction which the Approaching *Flames* give them could qualify them for the Rapture of the *Saved*, what would the Converting of One *Infidel Nation* signify more than another, for what is then to follow? The only Way that appears, for the Gentleman to evade the Force of this Text, will be, To *Metaphorize* the *Conflagration*, and make it mean,—I know not what. But when their hand is in, at this *Legerdemain*, they had e'en as Good *Metaphorize* the *Apostle* too; and Lett the Name of *Peter* mean, what?—A Gentleman wearing a Triple Crown as a Successor to *Peter*, in a City where it may be proved that *Peter* never once appeared in all his Travels![91]—

These Meditations have at Length forced me [ms. III, xi, 34v] to Resign the Opinion, as Part of the *Hay and Stubble*, which will not *Abide the Fire*, of the *Day which will declare*, what is the *Truth*, and what is not so. Indeed, it appeared unto me a *Paradox*, That an Opinion should prevail so far, & so long, & be embraced by such Good Men, & by an *Host of GOD*, and yett after all, be found an *Error*, calculated for, and contributing to, the *Faulty Sleep* of the *Latter Times*.—But I must say upon it, as our *Mede* said of his *Chiliasm*,—when at last he came into it. *Postquam alia omnia frustrà tentassem, tandem Rei ipsius claritudine perstrictus paradoxo succubus!*[92]

It is to me no less a *Paradox*, [and one that was born before me, says upon it, *Saepe et valde mecum miratus fui*] how it has been possible for *Christians* to give into that Maxim of the *Jews*, which the Talmuds ascribe to a Blade called R. *Samuel: There will be no Difference between our Days*, & *the Days of the Messiah, but This; That in those Days,* [Subjuganda sunt Regna,] *the King-doms of the World will be brought under.*[93] Or what mighty Benefit *Christians* can propose to themselves, by having *Jews* made their *Lords*, and exercising a Dominion over them.

In fine; when we find an Eternal Downfal foretold unto *Israel:* [Hos. I. 6.] *I will NO MORE have Mercy on the House of Israel, but I will UTTERLY take them away:* And, [Amos. V. 2.] *The Virgin of Israel is fallen; She shall Rise NO MORE:* But in other Places a *Restoration* is foretold; It leads one to think, that, *NO MORE,* extends as far as the Duration of *This World;* and that the *Resto-ration* is to be at and for the *Resurrection of the Dead.* According to *Hosaea,* it will be at the *Day of Jezreel,* which is the Time for the *Manifestation of the* [ms. III, xi, r34v] *Sons of GOD;* and that Word is fulfilled, *I will ransom them from the Power of the Grave, I will Redeem them from Death.* According to *Amos,* it will be at, *The Day of the Lord,* and when that Word shall be fulfilled, *Seek Ye me, and Ye shall Live.* And it is with a *Resurrection from the Dead,* that *Ezekiel* introduces it. *Miriam* for her Affronts unto her LORD, is to be excluded from the Camp of GOD, and for the whole *Seven Days,* the Exclusion must continue upon her. Nay, We don't find, that the repudiated *Vashti,* has any more Notice, ever taken of her.[94]

The Learned *Fuller,* in his, *History of the Holy War,* speaking of the Stately *Christian Church,* built on the Floor which was once the Place of *Solomons Temple,* has a Remark.[95] That Heaven seem'd not well pleased, in the Christians not leaving that Floor to its *Perpetual Desolations;* inasmuch as the Christians were often beat out of it, and at this day, whoever enters it, tho' ever so casually, must Renounce his Religion, or Dy for it. On that Remark I pass no Censure. But so much I would say; I am not for Building too much on *Solomons Temple!* I don't See, that *Heaven* will be well pleased with it, or that our *Gospel* will much allow of it, That we should propose any other, than to leave, even the *Nation* as well as the *Temple* of *Solomon,* as to any Revival thereof in Saecular Appearances, under *Perpetual Desolations.*

What has befallen the *Golden Vessels* of the *Temple,* I doubt, carries a Sad Emblem & Symptom of what must be the Fate of the *Nation* which they once be-long'd unto. Those *Golden Vessels* were once transported into *Babylon. Cyrus* returned them. Anon *Vespasian* transported them to *Rome.* When *Gensericus* the *Vandal* sack'd the City, he transported them into *Africa: Justinian* recover-ing them, they were transported unto *Constantinople.* [ms. III, xi, 36v] A Jew told him, that no Potentate that had them could prosper; they must be returned unto *Jerusalem.* So *Justinian* return'd them thither, that they might be laid up in the *Christian Temple* there. By 'nd by, (if they were not lost by Sea, in their Transportation, as tis by some affirm'd they were) the *Mahometans* conquering *Jerusalem,* siez'd upon them;—And so—they are *Irrecoverably gone!*—They have never since been heard of; They will never be seen any more. *Lost, Lost* forever! All that will ever be seen of them, is the Image of them, on *Vespasians* Triumphal Arch, which is it seems, yett surviving. And, surely, the *Carnal,* Rebellious, Abdicated *Israel*, the *Wicked* which GOD has *putt away like Dross*, will not be any other than what they are, till the Time that the *Lost Vessels* of the *Temple* be found again.[96]

If I go to Restore that *Nation* in Circumstances, that shall give them a *Distinction* from, and a *Superiority* to, the rest of the *Christian World*, I am stop'd, as the *Jews* were, when the Impious *Julian* encouraged them to rebuild their *Temple*:—(A Thing, which the Report of *Pagan* Writers will compel us to Beleeve while the Silence of some *Christian* Writers about it, is justly wondred at!)[97]—A FIRE breaks out, and consumes all my Materials.[98]

XII. WHEN shall these Things be!
WHEN the Grand REVOLUTION to be look'd for?

That we may yett more Exactly know, *whereabouts we are*, the First Thing we will do, shall be to look back upon the astonishing Exhibition of, *The Four Grand Monarchies*, which were to Contain and Afflict the Church of GOD, from the Time of that mighty *Chaldaean* unto whom *it* was given to the *Time of the End*, when the SON of GOD shall bring *Them* to a final Period, and shall *take to Himself His Great Power, & shall Reign* over the World.[1] The Discovery and Explanation which our Gracious GOD gave unto His *Beloved Servant*, of what He had exhibited unto the *Chaldaean* Emperour concerning the *Fate* of the World unto the *End* of it, had the Fame thereof so soon & far spred thro' the Empire, that the Renown of *Daniel* for his *Wisdom*, was every where become a *Proverb*, while he was yett but a Young Man, & could not be much above Thirty Years of Age. The *Image* in this Illustrious Vision, doubtless gave Occasion to that *Image*, which the ungrateful *Nebuchadnezzar* sett up to be worshipped in the Plain of *Dura*. And this was doubtless the same *Image* of Massy Gold, that *Xerxes* found in the Temple of *Babylon*; whereof *Diodorus* tells us, it was *Fourty foot* high; to which, if we add the Pedestal, it will make the *Ninety foot* assign'd unto it, in the Sacred Story. According to *Diodorus*, the *Image* contain'd a Thousand *Babylonish Talents* of Gold; And this, according to *Pollux*, will amount unto Three Millions & an half of our Sterling.[2] As the *Fiery Furnace*, in which the Three Children of GOD were praeserved Alive, was a notable Emblem of the Grievous Things, which the Church of GOD should suffer & survive under the *Four Monarchies*, thus the *Worship* of this *Image*, notably represented the whole Scaene of *Tyranny*, which was to follow. *This*, as a very accomplished Governour of a Province, writing on [ms. III, xii, 2v] the *Scriptural Prophecies*, has justly observed, has forever been an *Image* or an *Idol*: And the Superstitious Conceits and Follies of Mankind paying *Divine Honours* to their *Tyrants*, have been the Chief Instruments of their Miseries. We will not here pursue the admirable *Succession* of the *Four Monarchies*, and show how the Figure of the *Body* and the Nature of the *Metal* in the Vision has been accommodated in them, or how the *Poetical Division of Time* was fetch'd from this Vision. We are not now writing a Treatise, *De Quatuor Summis Imperiis*.[3]

What is most for our Present Purpose, is, That there is foretold, *An Heavenly Kingdom of GOD*, which was to arise before the Extinction of these *Four Monarchies*, and appear first in the form of a *Little Stone*, and then in the form of a *Great Mountain*. [Compare, Matth. XXI. 44.] It must be a *Stone* fetch'd from the *Mountain* of the *Heavenly World*; but it must not be *in Hands*, nor carried on by any Humane Force, or Strength, or Means: but be very *Spiritual*; a Quality which the Term of *Made without Hands*, is [Col. II. 11.] used for. Upon the Destruction of the *Last Monarchy*, the *Iron* and *Earthen* One, in this memorable *Image*, the *Stone* becomes a *Great Mountain*, and *fills the Whole Earth*:

Heaven from whence it has its Original, comes down, and the *Whole Earth is filled* with it; which imports the *New Heavens* and the *New Earth*, which we look for.[4]

While this *Kingdom of Heaven* continues in the State of a *Little Stone*, our Glorious LORD is by His *Gospel*, (the *Strong Rod*, with which He *Rules in the Midst of His Enemies*,) Conquering and Gathering and Preparing Subjects, to partake in the Glories of His *Kingdom*, when it shall appear in the State of a *Great Mountain*. This *Holy People*, the Subjects of this *Kingdom*, are to be for [ms. III, xii, r2v] the most Part, not only in a very *Scattered* Condition, [*A certain People, scattered abroad, & dispersed among the People, in all the Provinces of the Monarchy, and their Laws divers from all People!*] but also in a Very *Oppressed* Condition, grievously Maligned, and Abused and Injured, by *the Rulers of the Darkness of this World*: and *thro' much Tribulation* qualified for the *Kingdom of GOD*. The *Kingdom* comes not into the State of a *Great Mountain*, until the *Roman Empire*, under the *Papal* Figure of it, governed by *Ten Sovereigns*, be *broken to Peeces*, and become like *the Chaff of the Summer threshing-floors, & the Wind so carries them away, that no Place will be found for them*.[5] Compare, Psal. I. 4. *The Ungodly like the Chaff*. And upon, *The Ungodly*, mentioned *Four Times* in the Psalm, with surprize feel the Touch of a Jewish Rabbi, *Et Similiter Sunt Quatuor Monarchiae*.[6] Wherefore, it will not be, until the Revolution, which another Vision of these *Four Monarchies* has told us of; not, until the SON OF MAN *comes with the Clouds of Heaven*, to make the *Fourth Beast*, which is the Same with the *Iron & Earthen*, Legs and Feet of the *Nebuchadnezzarian Image*, perish in the CONFLAGRATION; whereupon *the Greatness of the Kingdom under the Whole Heaven shall be given to the People of the Saints of the Most High*.

When the Faithful among the *Jews*, became sensible, that there was come on the *Last* of those *Monarchies*, in the Days whereof the *Heavenly Kingdom of GOD* was to be *sett up*; and their Computation also assured them, that the LXX *Weeks* within which the *Messiah* was to appear, must be near their Expiration; they had, and might well have, a Strong Expectation for this *Kingdom* to begin, about the Time that our Blessed JESUS came into the World. Accordingly, they were not altogether unacquainted with the Meaning of the Expression, when *John* the Baptist, came with his, *Repent, for the Kingdom* [ms. III, xii, 4v] *of Heaven is at hand*; and the Glorious KING Himself *Incognito* among them, told them, *The Time is fulfilled, & the Kingdom of GOD is at hand*. They understood it, as *These* intended it, for the *Kingdom* foretold in the Prophecies of *Daniel*. And as it is well observed by a Learned *Sykes*, whose Thoughts do as much *Please* me as *Help* me, on this Occasion, These *Prophecies* are constantly in View, whenever we find, *The Kingdom of Heaven*, and, *The Kingdom of GOD*, and, *The Kingdom of CHRIST*, mentioned in the Gospel.[7]

In the *Progress* of this *Kingdom*, from Small Beginnings, thro' the State of the *Little Stone*, to the State of the *Great Mountain*, it sees very Different Circumstances; and yett all belonging to the *Same Kingdom*. Very commonly, tis the *Kingdom* in the State of the *Little Stone*, that is in the Gospel referr'd unto;

and particularly in many of the *Parables*; But sometimes tis the *Kingdom* in the State of the *Great Mountain*:

And the Consideration of This, has furnished others, as well as our *Sykes*, with a Golden key, to many Passages in the Sacred Scriptures, which have sometimes puzzled our Expositors. For instance; When we read, *The Least in the Kingdom* of our SAVIOUR, would be *Greater than John*; as it implies, that the Dispensation of the *New Testament*, which took place upon the Ascension of our SAVIOUR to take Possession of the *Promised Kingdom* had many advantages above the *Old*, so *John* did *no Miracle*; whereas the *Least Prophet* of the *New Testament*, was vested with *Miraculous Powers*. When our SAVIOUR said, [Mar. IX. 1.] *There be some that stand here, who shall not taste of Death, till they have seen the Kingdom of GOD come with Power*; it referr'd unto the Commencement of this *Kingdom*, at the *Resurrection*, & following *Ascension* of our SAVIOUR, when *He was declared* [ms. III, xii, 14v] *the Son of GOD with Power*. They that *made themselves Eunuchs for the Kingdom of Heaven*, were those who resolutely mastered their most Natural Inclinations, that they might be more capable to taste the *Comforts* or serve the *Interests*, of this *Kingdom*: Such were they who kept themselves *Pure*, & gave *themselves up to Prayers & Fastings night & day*, so *waiting for the Consolation of Israel*. Our SAVIOURs *Drinking the Fruit of the Vine in the Kingdom of GOD*, was fulfilled after His *Resurrection from the Dead*, when He was entring into *All Power in Heaven & Earth*, which then belong'd unto Him; and when He did yett *Eat & Drink with His Disciples*. This was the *Kingdom*, whereof the Angel *Gabriel* told the Mother of our LORD; And our LORD *Confessed* unto *Pilate*, That He was the KING, whom these Prophecies had spoken of. Accordingly, Tho' this *Kingdom* in the State of the *Little Stone*, *cometh not with Observation*, & is not regarded, as those of *This World* are, with Splendid, Pompous, Magnificent *Appearances*, yett we actually See a *Kingdom* sett up, wherein our Blessed JESUS is Ador'd & Obey'd, as a LORD Superiour to the Greatest *Kings* upon Earth, and *His Laws* are esteemed Paramount unto *Theirs*: If in any Nation (as our *Sykes* remarks) there are published Commands & Edicts contrary to those of our Blessed JESUS, the Subjects of His *Kingdom* look upon them, as of no Obligation. And I may add, the Spirit of true PIETY, wherever it operates, lies in *Kissing the Feet of the SON of GOD*, and Placing our SAVIOUR on the *Throne* in our Souls, and Paying the *Homage*, which our *Thomas* upon a full Conviction pay'd unto this Glorious REDEEMER, *My Lord and my GOD!*[8]—

We may, as we go along, take some Notice of it; That the Glorious KING, whose Perpetual and Universal *Kingdom* we find celebrated in the Prophecies of *Daniel*, is called, *The SON of MAN*. And now, I perfectly concur with our *Sykes* in this also, [ms. III, xii, 6v] That wherever that Phrase, *The Son of Man*, occurs in the New Testament, the Prophecy of *Daniel* is in View; and wherever our JESUS is called, *The Son of Man*, it means, that He is the Person, who in the Prophecy of *Daniel*, has the *Kingdom* assign'd unto Him. Here, more particularly, is the Emphasis of what our SAVIOUR says, *Authority is given Him to execute Judgment, BECAUSE He is the Son of Man*; Even that *Son of*

Man of whom the Prophecy of *Daniel*, about a *Kingdom over all Nations to be given Him*, is to be understood. And when our LORD said, *The Son of Man has not where to lay his Head*, the Emphasis of it, is, That the *Son of Man*, who according to the Prophecy of *Daniel*, was to have a *Kingdom over all*, was now destitute of every thing. When He speaks of the *Son of Man* having *Power on Earth to forgive Sins*; what can these Words, *On Earth*, intend, if there were not in them, an Eye to the *Son of Man* coming with full Power in *the Clouds of Heaven*, as *Daniel* had prophesied? On that Passage, [Matth. X. 23.] *Ye shall not have gone over the Cities of Israel, till the Son of Man be come*, our *Sykes* would have it noted, That wherever the ΠΑΡΟΥΣΙΑ,[9] *Coming* or *Presence* of the Lord, is mentioned in the New Testament, it forever has respect unto the Time, when He shall appear, as *Daniel* describes it, in the *Clouds of Heaven*. His Meaning therefore seems to be, That the Obstinacy of the *Jews* would be such, that before His Disciples could convert them, & bring them to the Beleef of His being the *Messiah*, He should come in the Glory foretold by *Daniel*. The *Twenty Seventh* & *Twenty Eighth* Verses in the *Sixteenth Chapter* of *Matthew*, represent the *Kingdom* under both Exhibitions; That of the *Little Stone*, and that of the *Great Mountain*. Our SAVIOUR, who declares Himself to be, *The Son of Man*, intended in the Prophecy, Comes *Twice*. The *First Coming*, is to *Open* the *Kingdom*, and lay the *Foundations* of it. The *Second Coming* is to be in *Glory*; whereat He will *Reward Men according to their Works*. The Connecting of this *Latter Coming*, with the *Former Coming*, which Some *Then Alive* were to see, is what has brought an Obscurity on this Discourse, that is now taken away. *Stephen* and *John*; in their Extasies, Beheld the SON of MAN, Possessed of *All Power*, as *Daniel* had beheld Him.[10] Yea, The Day is now at hand, when, *Behold, Every Eye shall see Him so!* [ms. III, xii, 122] Well; We have seen the whole *Prophecy* of the *Golden-Headed Image* all accomplished; unto the Existence of the *Ten Toes* belonging to it; which have also been visible for as many Years as they have any Reason from the *Prophecy*, to depend upon. All that remains is, The *Breaking* of them to Peeces, by the SON of MAN, coming in the *Clouds of Heaven*, and Changing the Face of His *Kingdom*, from that of the *Little Stone* to that of the *Great Mountain*; which is to be brought about, by His *Burning* of This World, and bringing on the *New Heavens* and the *New Earth*, which *according to His Promise we look for*.

What we are now proceeding to, is, *WHEN are we to look for these things?* Unto Some, who Seventeen hundred Years ago, thought, *That the Kingdome of GOD should Immediately appear*, our LORD, the KING of it, signified that He must first *go into a Far Countrey*, and *Receiving the Kingdom* there, He would then *Return* from thence, and have the People that had been the *Enemies* of his *Reign*, and that should be Reserved unto His Return, *brought & slain before Him*. The glorious LORD has accordingly *gone into the far Countrey*, and stay'd such a Term of Time, that we may *Now* look on it, as high Time to enquire, *Whether the Kingdome of GOD may not now APPEAR IMMEDIATELY.*

About the tremendous DAY OF GOD, which will burn up the *Old World* and bring on a *New* One, tis One thing to say, *IT WILL Come Immediately*; Another thing to say, *IT MAY Come Immediately*. The Former I *Dare* not say. The Latter I *Do* say. And Lett the *Sleepy* World be ever so Angry at being disturbed by an *Awakener*, I will do the Part of a *Voice crying in the Wilderness*, and from an *American* Wilderness, and insist upon it; *Repent, For the Kingdome of the Heavens draws very nigh upon us.*[11]

While it was yett kept conceal'd, Whether the *Days* assign'd for the Reign of the *Antichrist*, were to be understood of *Natural Days*, as the Primitive Christians generally took them, and Prayed and Acted accordingly; Or to be understood of *Prophetic Days*, even so many *Years*, as it would have broke the Hearts of the Faithful to have been assured of; it might very well be said, That the *Day* and *Hour* for *Heaven and Earth to pass away*, could not as yett be declared. But this Point having been Reveled, since the *Ascending* of our LORD and the *Opening* of the *Book* [ms. III, xii, 8v] that had the Secret in it, the *Day* and the *Hour*, tho' it may still remain so much in the Dark that it cannot be *praecisely determined*, yett we may now be Capable of more Satisfactory Sentiments about the *Age*, wherein it may justly be made a Matter of awful and Earnest Expectation. When our SAVIOUR said unto His Apostles, *It is not for You to know the Times & Seasons*, His Meaning was, That it was none of their *Present Business* to Ask after the *Times* and *Seasons*; Their *Present Business* was to go, and be *Witnesses unto Him*, and by the *Testimony* Acquaint and Convince the World, *Who* He *was*, and *What* had been *done* by Him, and *What* He would have them to do; Not, *When* His Coming again was to be look'd for.[12] Nevertheless the FATHER did anon allow of it, that He should inform them, of what it was convenient for them to *know* of *the Times and Seasons*. He did give them to *Know*, That the *Time* and *Season* for His *Coming in His Kingdom* would be delay'd until an *Apostasy* in the Christian Church would give Opportunity for a *Son of Perdition* to erect his *Throne* in what should have been the *Temple of GOD*. He did give them to *Know*, That the *Time* and *Season* for that *Son of Perdition* to take his *Throne* would be delay'd, until *Ten Sovereign Kings* rose up in the Broken *Roman Empire*. He did give them to *Know*, That the *Time* and *Season* for that *Son of Perdition* to perish in the *Burning Flame* would be delay'd, until after *Twelve hundred & Sixty Years* were expired.[13]

It is very impertinently that such Passages of the Sacred Scriptures have been alledged, as an Inhibition upon all Sober Essays of the Faithful, to *understand by Books*, and learn, *whereabouts we are*, in *Running the Race*, which the Church of GOD has had sett before it. The Common Saying, and Satire, *That all Good Men have been mistaken in their Guesses*, is a Great Mistake, and most notoriously Untrue. When the Better Sort of People among the *Jews*, perceived the *Fourth Monarchy* come on, They concluded, That the Coelestial *Kingdom*, which had been foretold in [ms. III, xii, 123] the Prophecies of *Daniel*, was now to be look'd for; *And they were in the Right on't!* When also they perceived between Four and Five Hundred Years run out, since the *going forth* of the Edict for the Rebuilding of *Jerusalem*, they concluded, That according to the *Weeks* in the Prophecies of *Daniel*, the Birth of the *Messiah* was now to be look'd for; *And they were in the Right on't!* There were those watchful Observers of the

Time, who then *waited for the Consolation of Israel*. And our Lord rebuked the more Carnal & Stupid People, at that *Critical Time*, for their no better *Discerning the Time*. When the more Sagacious Christians beheld the City of *Rome* sack'd by those that were called, *The Barbarous Nations*, and that which *hindred* the Rising of the *Man of Sin*, evidently *removed out of the Way*, they cried out, *We shall see Antichrist immediately. And they were in the Right on't!*[14] Tho', alass, when they saw him, their *Eyes were held* with such Praepossessions, that they did not see him. There are *Computations of the Times*, which will well *become*, and as well *befriend*, the Christians that would not *Sleep as do others*. The *Jews* do *Curse* them indeed; but We know *Why* they do so. The wiser *Christians*, by having *Understanding in the Times*, propose to *know, what they ought to do*; and how the *Kingdome* of their Glorious *David* may be best served by them. *The République des Lettres*, tells of a Pretender to Learning, who seriously enquired, whether *Constantine* the Great lived not before *Julius Caesar*; and when his Enquiry was derided, he seriously justified it from this Text, *It is not for you to know the Times and Seasons.*[15] There is a Prophecy about the *Times* and *Seasons* now obtained for us, whereof the Holy Spirit has told us, *Blessed is he that readeth, & they that hear the Words of this Prophecy*. To discourage all Modest Researches into this *Prophecy*, with alledging the Text, *It is not for you to know the Times and Seasons*, is to abuse it as much as that notable Chronologer.

It is true, In every Generation there have been those, who have made very precarious and precipitous *Computations*, and been seduced by them into vain Conclusions and Confidences about the *Day* and the *Hour* for *The End of the World*, and by their *Temerity* have exposed themselves unto the *Derision* which the World has bestow'd upon their *Disappointed Expectations*. There were those in the Days of the Apostles, who said, *The Day of CHRIST is at hand*: But the Apostles were enabled quickly to teach them otherwise. In the Time of *Lactantius*, the Cry was, *Omnis expectatio non amplius quam Ducentorum videtur Annorum.*[16] [ms. III, xii, 10v] A Whisper among the Primitive Christians, That *Christianity* would come to an End in CCCLXV Years after the First Appearing of it, made it suspected, that the *End of the World* would be no further off. Honest *Hesychius* took it for granted, That *Four hundred & Ninety* Years would be all that should pass between the *First* and *Second* Coming of the Lord.[17] *Gregory* of *Rome*, went upon a Moral Prognostication, and from the *horrid Manners* of his Age, pronounced, *Saeculum suum non longe abfuisse a Fine Mundi*: No, *Gregory*; A *Successor* of thine, of whom thou didst so plainly point out the *Praecursor*, must first have M.CC.LX. Years, allow'd unto him.[18] The Delusions went on. *Trithemius* tells of a *Suevian* Woman, about A.C. 848. who filled *Europe* with the *Noise* of a Revelation from an *Angel* appearing unto her, that the *End of the World* would be in *That Year*. In *Bernards* Epistles we find a Gentleman called *Nortbert* as much Deceived in his *Praedictions* about the *End of the World* then just arriving, as he himself was in his blowing the *Trumpett* for the *Holy War*.[19] *Aventinus* tells us, that about A.C. 1062. all the World was frighted with a Rumour, that the *End of the World* was then presently coming upon it. *Arnoldus de Villa nova* assign'd the Year 1335, as the Last

Year for *Antichrist*, and the *World*.[20] It is not worth our while to mention all the
Freaks of Imagination this Way, in Succeeding Ages, which do stand *Pilloried*
in History, nor the Wild *Enthusiasms* of those, who have even run furiously
roaring about the Streets, *The Day of the Lord! The Day of the Lord!* Yett Lett
us allow a mention, to what *Camerarius* Reports, That a very Learned Man,
& a Good Mathematician, who from the Numeral Letters in, *Videbunt quem
pupugerunt*, sett A.C. 1532. for the Coming of the Lord: *Bucholtzer* does of
another, whose Discoveries ran upon his finding the Like, in; *Jesus Nazarenus
Rex Judaeorum*.[21] Others discovered the Time, in, a Chronogram, of *Adventus Domini*, abbreviating the Period from, *Dies abbreviabuntur*. But all such
Cabalistical Fooleries [ms. III, xii, 124] I leave to the Mercy of *Remaclus*, and
the Contempt of all Judicious Men.[22] *Poyselius* would go another Way to Work,
and finding Forty Years after a Remarkable *Passeover* several times bring on a
great Event, he foretold the *End of the World* about *Fourty Years* after the New
Settling of *Easter* by the *Gregorian Kalender*; Some, from that Word, *It shall be
as it was in the Days of Noah*, inferr'd, that the *End of the World*, would arrive
in as many Years from the Incarnation of our SAVIOUR, as the *Flood of Noah*
did from the *Creation*: And so A.C. 1656. was a Year of mighty Expectation.
But the Terrors of that Year, as well as of some other Periods thereabouts, and
that particularly of the Gentleman who gott the Nickname of *Doomsday* by his
Praedictions, all went over.[23] Then, from the *Number of the Beast*, given in the
Apocalypse, what a Tip-toe Expectation was there of A.C. 1666.[24] I have seen
among the Grammatical *Theses* for a Commencement that Year, one run in that
Punning Style, *VÆ, PAPÆ, Sunt Communes Interiectiones.* But *Rome* was
not Burnt that Year.—How many Determinations besides *Napiers*, were long
ago, for Years that fell between A.C. 1670. and A.C. 1700.[25] But especially the,
Octuagesimus Octavus Mirabilis Annus. [*Cardan* extending his as far as A.C.
1800. keeps yett out of our Catalogue.] All these Computations have had the
same Confutations, with our Honest *Beverly* in his *Ninety Seven*.[26] And if they
go no better to work, than the famous Gentleman of *Mirandola*, who writes,
*Investigare possumus per secretissimam viam Cabalae, futuram esse consum-
mationem saeculi hinc ad Annos* DXIV *et Dies* XXV. the same Confusion will
be their Portion.[27]

   If One could pay any Regard unto *Humane Computations*, it would be to the
Venerable Tradition, which goes under the Name of, ELIAS'S *Prophecy*: That
the Continuance of this World, is limited unto *Six Thousand* Years, answerable
to the *Six Days* of its *Creation*.[28] *Lauterbachius* has versified it; and the First of
his *Distichs*, is;

> *Annorum stabit tantum sex millia mundus;*
> *Post totus misso victus ab Igne ruet.*
> Six Thousand Years!—Vain World, Expect no more:
> *Fire* then to sieze thee must be looked for.[29]

[ms. III, xii, 12v] Tis true the *Elias*, to whom this Tradition is ascribed, was
not the Immortal *Tishbite*, but a *Jew* living about a Couple of Centuries before the Birth of our SAVIOUR; Yett, I find some Learned Men will not be

perswaded, but that it came originally from the *Tishbite*.[30] A Rabbi would not pretend unto *Prophecy* in his *Age*. Tis also very strange, the ancient *Pagans*, before the Age of that *Jew*, had some Inkling of it; Witness the EKTH EN ΓENEH of *Orpheus*, quoted by *Plato*![31] Be sure, the *Christian Fathers*, mightily fell in with it: *Justin*, and *Hippolytus* and *Irenaeus*, and *Cyprian* and *Lactantius*, are full in it; Yea, *Jerom* and *Austin*, lay some Stress upon it: and at least Half a Score more that might be quoted for it.[32] And, the Chronology of their *Greek Bible*, which made the World *Six Thousand Years* old, not long after their Time, was that which led so many of them into that which was then, *Omnis Expectatio*.[33] I suppose, the Tradition will not pass for the more *Infallible* at all with us, because there were *Popes* in the following Ages declaring for it. But it will pass with us for the More *Valuable* because it has made an Impression on the Minds of so many Good Men in Several Ages. That which recommended this Tradition to them, was not, that the Hebrew Letter *Aleph*, which numerically stands for a *Thousand*, occurs just *Six Times*, in the *first* Verse of *Genesis*, and again, in the *Last* Verse of the *Chronicles*; the first & the last Verses of the Old Testament. Few of them knew any thing of *That* Nicety: But it was This, That the Apostle seems to countenance it, when he says, not only, *That a Thousand Years is with the Lord as One Day*, but also, *That One Day is as a Thousand Years*. They considered, the Stamp of *Seven*, which the Glorious GOD, had sett upon the Things that carried in them the Signatures of the *Happy State*, that shall be enjoy'd by the *Faithful* at *the End of the World*.[34] *Enoch* the *Seventh* from *Adam*, is released from the *Law of Death*. Every Week had a *Seventh Day*, which was a *Sabbath*, and a *Type* of the *Rest that remains for the People of GOD*. He himself calls it, *A Sign*; It was a *Sacrament* of our Grand *Sabbatism*. Every *Seventh* Year, was to be spent in *Devotions*, while the *Earth* yielded its Fruits without much of Labour. When the *Seventh* of those Years rolled about, the *Saecular Times* terminated in a *Jubilee*; The *Great Trumpett* was blown, and a *Restitution of all things* came on. Our SAVIOUR having foretold, *The Coming of the Son of Man in His Kingdom*, then, AFTER SIX DAYS, He took some up *into an High Mountain*, and gave them an actual Exhibition of it. It was a Flourish, of Antiquity, (and if you please, Lett it pass for no more than so) That the *Six Water Potts*, wherein was the *Water* which our SAVIOUR turned into *Wine*, were to Answer the *Six Ages*, wherein the *Covenant* of GOD is to remain unaccomplished, in which Periods tis on some accounts like *Water*. But then comes on that when the full Accomplishment shall putt the Character of the richest *Wine* upon it. From these, and *Seven times Seven* more such things, they Reasoned and Reckoned, that the SEVENTH *Millennium* [ms. III, xii, 125] would bring on what these *Types* pointed at, and by Consequence the *End of the World*.[35]

According to This, there are still *Two Hundred and Seventy* Years, [Taking it for granted, that the Vulgar, 1727. is really 1730.] to run before *the Time of the End*.[36] But, since what I am arguing for, is, not our CERTAINTY, but our, UNCERTAINTY in the Matter, and not our KNOWING when the *Day* and *Hour* WILL BE, but our NOT KNOWING When it MAY BE, Behold, what we have here, to spoil our Praesumption of so *many Years to come*.

First, The *Tradition*; What *Foundation* for it? And, if we must have, Six Eminently and Conspicuously distinguished *Periods*, before the *Great Sabbatism*, we can find them, without the Exact Measure of a *Thousand Years* for them. Tho' the *Literal Transaction* of the *Hexaemeron*, be forever unquaestionable; yett there is a *Mystery* in the *History*.[37] And how the *Prophecy* contained in the Successive Works of the *Six Days*, has been all most punctually & elegantly accomplished in the Succeeding Ages of the Church, is a Matter which well deserves to be cultivated. It has been admirably done by a *Jurieu*, in his, *Accomplishment of the Prophecies*.[38] T'wil be too much here to transcribe *his* Elegant System. It will not be so to transcribe a few Lines of an Author, whom the Party Men, that can rarely bear to quote an Author of his Character without some Expression of Indignity, are forced always to quote with Honour. Tis our *Ainsworth*, who [on *Gen. I. 31.*] says, "We may compare with these *Six Days*, the *Six Ages* of the World, as they are manifestly distinguished in Scripture. The FIRST from *Adam* to *Noahs* Flood; which was of *Ten* Generations; This is called, *The Old World*. The Second, From the *Flood* unto *Abraham*; which also was of *Ten* Generations. At Him the New Testament begins the Genealogy of CHRIST. The Third, From *Abraham* to *David*, *Fourteen* Generations. The Fourth from *David*, to the Captivity of *Babylon*, *Fourteen* Generations. The Fifth, from the Captivity of *Babylon* unto CHRIST, *Fourteen* Generations. All which are so reckoned by the Holy Ghost. The Sixth, is the Age after CHRIST, called, *The Last Days*, and, *The Last Time*. After which *remains the Rest* [or, Sabbatism,] *for the People of GOD*; to begin at our Lords Second Coming & to endure forever." [1. Thess. IV. 16, 17.][39]

Again; If I were as well satisfied, that the *Samaritan Pentateuch* may be in such a Thing righter than *Ours*, [which yett it would not enfeeble the Proofs of our *Heaven-born Religion*, to allow of,] as I am, (from the indisputable *Numismatic* Evidence) that the *Samaritan Character*, is what it was always written in before the *Chaldaean* Captivity, I should think it a thing worthy of more than a little Notice, That according to *That*, the World will be, in A.C. 1736. just *Six Thousand Years* old.[40]

Lastly; Who can say, what may be the Whole of what our SAVIOUR means, when He said; *For the Sake of the Elect those Days shall be shortened?*

[ms. III, xii, 14v] Upon the Whole; No Man took more Pains, than the renowned Glory of *Hippo*, to discourage all attempts at Guessing the *Praecise Time* for the Coming of the Lord: Nor is what *Vives* writes hereupon in his Notes on that Great Mans Book, *De Civitate Dei*, unworthy to be thought upon.[41] But the Good Man distinguishes Three Ranks of *Watchful Christians*. The First is, Of them who say, *Vigilemus, et Oremus, quia Citius Veniet Dominus*. The Second is, Of them who say, *Vigilemus et Oremus, quia tardè quidem veniet Dominus, sed Vita nostra est brevis*. The Last is, Of them, *Vigilemus et Oremus, quia Nescimus Quandò Venturus sit Dominus*. The Last of them, is what *Austin* declares for. And I am content, if the *Nescimus Quandò*, be fairly stated.[42] I am content, if the PIETY which the Excellent *Zanchy*, pleaded for, after his going so far, [perhaps *Too far*!] as to assert, *Quo Anno, et quo SECULO Dominus rediturus sit nos Ignorare, et nullo modo POSSE SCIRE*, be complied withal, in these Two Articles; The former, *Perpetuò cuiqe cogitandum, fieri posse ut citius veniat Dominus, quam mundus putet;* The latter, *Vigilandum et orandum est perpetuò, et lampades oleo Fidei et Bonorum operum instructae ita retinendae, perindè ac si cras venturus sit.*[43] Indeed The General Disposition of the World seems to be, as if the *Gospel of the Day,* were what *Mahomet* has in his *Alcoran,* [tho' the Imposter elsewhere contradicts himself,] That the *Day of Judgment* was, when he scribbled on the Spade-bones, *Fifty Thousand Years off.*[44] I would as far as I can, do my Part, by crying, FIRE, awaken a World, whose *Delilahs* have dozed it; and tho' I can't prove that IT SHALL, yett challenge any Living to prove, that it SHALL NOT, be in less than *Ten Years* upon us.[45]

What I would move, is; That, without any Positive Determinations of what WILL BE, or Peremptory Pronunciations on the *Day* and the *Hour,* We NOW come to This; We *know nothing* that must necessarily *praecede* and *putt off* the DAY of GOD, or hinder, but that it MAY Come Immediately; And, For *aught we know,* the *Day that shall burn like an Oven* MAY come on before to Morrow Morning; and before the Reader of this Book has laid it out of his hand, the Flames MAY begin, that will carry all before them.

Sentiments of this Importance have this NOW to give a Vigour to them, which there was not in the Foregoing Ages; *That which did obstruct is now taken out of the Way.*

[ms. III, xii, 126] What I am now coming to demonstrate, is, That the *Second Coming* of the LORD, and so the tremendous *Conflagration* which is to make Way for the *New Heavens* and the *New Earth* wherein shall *dwell Righteousness,* will be at and for the Destruction of the *Romish Antichrist,* which appears to be Now the *Next Thing,* and *Quickly,* to be look'd for.

Lett us consult the Oracle. [2. Thess. II. 8.] *That Wicked One shall be Reveled, whom the Lord shall Consume with the Spirit of His Mouth, & shall Destroy with the Brightness of His Coming.*

There is at this time of Day, no Quaestion to be made among Sound *Protestants,* who should be, *The Wicked One,* whose coming into the World is here foretold unto us. There are Irrefragable and Innumerable Demonstrations, That the *Man of Sin,* or the Supereminently *Sinful* One, foretold here to rise upon the Fall of the *Roman Empire,* and make a powerful & wonderful Figure in the Church, but One that is destined for as great a Figure in the *Perdition of Ungodly Men* which is to come on with the Day when GOD shall come to the *Judging* of the World; This can be no other than the Bishop of *Rome.* Even a good while before the *Revelation* of this *Antichrist,* and as long ago as the Age of *Irenaeus,* the Faithful were sensible of an Invitation to look for him in the *Latin Church,* from the *Number of his Name* in the Word ΛΑΤΕΙΝΟΣ. All the Attempts of *Grotius* and *Hammond* and their Ill-designing Followers, to sett up another *Monster,* with a Claim to these Characters, are such *Monstrous Absurdities,* that it may astonish one to think, how tis possible for any Man of Letters to be guilty of them. The Men of *Sodom* were not under a greater Occaecation![46]

Who can be meant by him, That *shows himself that he is a God:* but the *Pope* of whom *Sylvester de Petra Sancta* published a Book to prove, That he is deservedly called *God*: and of whom the Wretched Idolaters do not stick to speak in that Style, *Dominus Deus noster Papa*?[47] Who can be meant by him, *That opposeth & exalteth himself above all that is called God, or that is worshipped*; but the *Pope*, who not only tramples on the *Kings* of the Earth, but [ms. III, xii, 16v] challenges the Right of *Dispensing with the Laws of GOD*; and the rest of the bigotted Papists, as well as *Perron*, and *Vasquez*, and *Andradius*, affirm it no Error, to think that he can do so;[48] Yea, *Bellarmine* proceeds to such a Degree of Sottish Impiety, as to invest him with a, *Potestas faciendi de peccato non peccatum, et de non peccato peccatum!*[49]—Where is this *Wicked One* to be look'd for? He *sitts in the Temple of GOD*; It is in the *Christian Church*, and verily, in the *See of Rome*, or no where, that he has his Operations. But—What am I doing? Tis not only *Du Moulin*, in his Excellent, *Vates*, but there are a Thousand Judicious and Accurate Writers besides him, that have made it beyond all Contestation evident, that, *The Wicked One*, in the Prophecy before us, must be the *Bishop of Rome*. And among them all, a Treatise of One whose Name is *Walter Garret*, entituled, *A Discourse concerning Antichrist*, has *handled* this *Matter* so *Wisely*, that *he* alone may supersede the Reading of a Thousand more: *He* may be, *Instar Omninum*.[50] Yea, give me leave to say, we need no *Protestant* Writers; *Baronius* and *Bellarmine*, have written mighty Volumns, to magnify the *Greatness* of their *Bishop*, so as unawares to prove *Him* to be *Antichrist*: Such a *Bishop* as that Brace of Writers describe, sitting at *Rome*, can be no other than *Antichrist*.[51]

All the Quaestion before us, is, What should be that, *Coming of the Lord*, the *Brightness* whereof is to *Destroy this Wicked One*? Most certainly, It can be no other than the SECOND COMING of our SAVIOUR; what we call, His *Personal Coming*. There can be nothing more plain than this; That the *Thessalonician* Beleevers, had been in hazard of being *Shaken & Troubled* in their Minds, & putt into the *Uncertain Motions* of a tempestuated Vessel, by an Apprehension that the SECOND COMING of our LORD, or His Promised COMING in *Glory*, to the *Judgment* of the World, was immediately to be look'd for. That which might lead them into this Apprehension, might be either *Spirit*, that is to say, *Revelations* of that Importance, the Pretence of some that it had been *Reveled* unto them; or, *Word*; that is to say, Rational Conjectures, Probable Ratiocinations; or, *Letter*; that is to say, not only the Former Epistle of *Paul* himself to them, which had been misinterpreted, but also it may be some *Forged* Ones. To prevent the Inconveniencies that might follow on such a Misapprehension, his Discourse begins, *Now we beseech you, Bretheren, by the Coming of our Lord Jesus Christ, & our Gathering together unto Him*. The Translation should be changed & mended; and *Fl. Illyricus* notes very truly, that the Praeposition, YПEP which we translate, BY, should be translated, UPON, or, ABOUT; it points to [ms. III, xii, 127] the *Matter* here treated of; *We beseech you, concerning the Coming of our Lord Jesus Christ*. And so, it seems, *Luther* in his Vulgar Version has carried it.[52] Now the Thing about which he besought his Godly *Thessalonicians* to be satisfied, is, That the *Second Coming of our Lord Jesus Christ*, was not so near as was by some thought for, or, not the NEXT THING to be look'd for; Inasmuch as there must be FIRST Reveled, *That Wicked One*, who is to *Sitt For the Temple of GOD*, [so both *Austin* and *Jerom* carry it, q.d. as being himself the *Temple*, or calling himself, *The Church*:] Whom the *Lord will destroy with the Brightness of His Coming*.[53] The *Coming of the Lord* here can be no other than His *Personal Coming*. For it was only the *Personal Coming* of the Lord, about which the *Thessalonicians* were sollicitous. To make, *The Coming of the Lord*, which is to be *after*, the *Reveling of the Wicked One*, quite another Sort of *Coming*, than that which the Apostle had undertaken to show, that it would not be *before* it,—meerly because we will have it so!—To make a meer *Mystical Coming* of it, or, the *Coming* of a *Preached Gospel*,—Men may think what they will, but plainly, tis, *Foolish*; Yea, tis *Profane*; it makes the *Sacred Scripture* a *Waxen* sort of a Thing; It gives us up to *Quakerism*: It leaves us without *all Proof* that our SAVIOUR will *ever come* at all.—One would almost assoon take up with such forlorn Stuff as an Old Bishop of *Ossory* has uttered in his Commentaries on the *Revelation*, as admitt of such Affronts to the Holy Oracles.[54] At best, they are of a Piece with the Egregious Nonsense of making the *First Resurrection* in the *Revelation* to mean a *Resurrection from a State of Sin*, in a Work of Conversion to *Piety* wrought upon the Soul: As if such a *Work* were to be wrought on Men, after they have been *Beheaded for the Witness of JESUS, & for the Word of GOD!* Away with such Impertinencies! At the same time, Lett it be considered, That our Apostle here has a plain Reference, to the *Slaying of the Wicked*, in the *Eleventh* Chapter of *Isaiah*; which was by the Jews themselves as long ago as the *Chaldee* Paraphrast, interpreted concerning *Armillus*, which is their Term for our *Antichrist*; But there tis foretold, That in *That Day, the Lord shall stand as an Ensign for the People*: Upon which our Lord Himself putt this Interpretation; [Matth. XXIV. 30.] *Then shall appear the Sign of the Son of Man in Heaven, and they shall see the Son of Man coming in the Clouds of Heaven with Power & great Glory*. It [ms. III, xii, 18v] may be, one thing, that has misled our Leaders, has been, their Construing of that Expression, *The Lord shall consume him with the Spirit of His Mouth*, as necessarily meaning, The *Preaching of the Gospel*. But of them who make this Construction, the more Sagacious, carry it so; That *Antichrist* must first undergo a *Consumption* by the *Preaching of the Gospel*, as he did at the *Reformation*, and then undergo his *Destruction* by the *Brightness of our Lords Coming* as He shall do at His Return from Heaven. And yett there is no Necessity, that the *Breath of His Mouth*, should signify so. The Prophecy was, *He shall smite the Earth with the Rod of His Mouth, and with the Breath of His Mouth He shall slay the Wicked*. This is a Plain Prophecy of the *Conflagration* wherein the *Son of Perdition* is to *Perish Wonderfully*. Now for the *Conflagration*, we shall find the *Breath of the Lord* used in a much other sense than that of a *Preached Gospel*. We find, [Isa. XXX. 33.] *A Tophet praepared for the King, even for thee, O Thou Wicked One*, and thou *King over the Children of Heighth!*—It is *deep and large, the Pile thereof is Fire & much Wood; the BREATH OF THE LORD, like a Stream of Brimstone, doth kindle it*. Thus, the Time, when our Lord comes to *Fill the*

Dead Bodies, that is to say, To *Raise the Dead;* This will be the Time when He *will wound the Head over many Countreys;* Antichrist, as well as he whose *Vicar* he is, will then be found, *The Head over many Countreys.*

To render it yett more evident, That the *Destruction* of *Antichrist* must be by the *Burning* of the World at the *Coming* of the Lord, the Exhibition of the [ms. III, xii, 128] *Four Monarchies* in the Visions of *Daniel*, will soon give us the fullest Satisfaction. The *Four Monarchies*, when they were to be exhibited unto One who was to be the *Head* unto the First of them, were shown under the more Inoffensive Shape of so many *Metals*. But now they are to be exhibited, where they might with less Provocation be shown as they *are*, the true Shape of *Wild-Beasts* is putt upon them. The First Empire, that appears as a *Lion*, was the *Babylonian*. The Second, like a *Bear*, having *Three Ribs in his Mouth*, was the *Persian*, consisting of the *Persian*, and the *Median*, and the *Chaldaean*. The Third, like a *Leopard*, with the *Wings of a Fowl*, and *Four Heads*, was the *Graecian;* which with incredible Celerity siezed upon the World, and was then divided into *Four Kingdoms*. The *Fourth*, [which Nameless One, if I should say, it was a *Boar* or *Swine*, I should have the General Approbation of the *Jews*, and their Application of the *Eightieth* Psalm unto it, on my Side; But I rather say, it was a Composition of all the other *Three:*] t'was the *Roman*. Of this, if *Austin* in his, *De Civitate Dei*, do not convince us, I hope, the *Thirteenth* Chapter of the *Revelation* will.[55] I will not here detain you with R. *Solomons* nice Observation, That the, *How Long?* repeted *Four times* in the *Thirteenth* Psalm (as, *The Ungodly*, repeted *Four times* in the *First* Psalm) had an Eye to these *Four Monarchies*.[56] The *Fourth* of them is all that we are now concerned withal. All the *Jewish* Doctors both before and after the Birth of our SAVIOUR, for Nine hundred Years after the giving of the Prophecy, understood this to be the *Roman Empire;* Until at last, the Fear lest *Christianity* should bring in the *Kingdome of the Son of Man*, which is to destroy the *Fourth Beast*, made them desirous to have it understood of [ms. III, xii, 20v] the *Graecian Empire*. And herein some *Unhappy Christians*, who frequently are as Pernicious Enemies to the Cause of CHRIST as the Worst of *Jews*, and serve the Worst Intentions of the *Jews*, do sordidly & shamefully lick up their *Spittle*. This is well-known, that all the *Primitive Christians*, at least until *Jeroms* time, did concur to the True Opinion; *Ergò dicamus* (quoth he) *quod omnes scriptores ecclesiastici tradiderunt,*—"Lett us therefore say, what all the *Ecclesiastical Writers* have delivered; That in the End of the World, when the Kingdom of the *Romans* is to be destroyed, there shall be *Ten Kings*, who shall divide the World among themselves, and there shall be an *Eleventh Little King* that shall arise, and overcome *Three* of those *Ten Kings.*"[57] Yea, the most Eminent Writers in the Church of *Rome* itself are forced for to allow, That the *Fourth Kingdom* in the Prophecies is the *Roman*. Tis the irresistible Evidence of the Thing, which compels them to confess, with *Maldonat*, *The Fourth Kingdom is the Kingdom of the Romans, and so* (says he) *all take it to be:* And with *Malvenda*, *That the Fourth Beast is the Roman Empire, tis certain and agreed upon by all that profess the Name of Christ*.[58] The *Roman Empire*, the very *Temper* and *Period* whereof, is by the Spirit of Prophecy admirably painted out unto us, in the *Fourteenth Psalm*, [How agreeably by the Apostle quoted unto the *Romans*!] tis a *Beast* that has *Ten Horns* assign'd unto it.[59] And it is marvellous to see, that not only the *Roman Empire* while *Pagan*, was divided into *Ten Provinces*, but also when the *Northern Invasions* broke the *Roman Empire* in Peeces after it became *Christian*, there were *Ten Kingdoms* that arose out of its Ruins.[60] These *Horns*, the *Midrasch Tillin* understands by, *The Horns of the Wicked*, that sometimes our *Psalms* [ms. III, xii, 129] have spoken of: And perhaps the *Ten Sons of Haman* might be Types of them.[61] Tis astonishing to see, How this Division of the *Ten Horns*, answerable to the *Ten Toes* of the *Golden-Headed Image*, has been preserved all along, by an Overruling Providence of GOD; and if any One has happened by the *Fate of Kingdoms* to drop off, another as in a Moment rose up to supply the Place. Behold, It is at *This very Time* remarkably existing! Yea, in *This our Time* the disappearing of a Distinct *Crown* in *Scotland*, has a remarkable Reparation by another *Crown'd Head* starting up in another Part of *Europe*![62] Tis astonishing to see, How the Attempts of any *One* among the *Ten* to swallow up the Nine, in an, *Universal Monarchy of the West*, have proved Abortive. Both *Spain* and *France* have been upon the very Point of gaining it, & had gain'd their Point if GOD had not *Infatuated* them: How entertaining would be the Story of their *Infatuations*![63] Among the *Seven Forms* of Government which had been exercised in the *Seven-Hill'd City*, One was that of the *Decemvirate*.[64] This *Decemvirate* is after some Sort revived in these *Ten Kings*. And the more properly for This; The first Old Roman *Decemvirs*, were sett up first of all, on Purpose to fetch *New Laws* from *Greece* & establish them in *Rome*. In like Manner, the Barbarous Nations under these *Ten Kings*, brought their own Laws into the Roman Empire. But still This Appearance differed so much from that of the *Decemvirs*, as to make really an *Eighth Head*, while it might be called *One of the Seven*: And it must *go into Perdition*; Tis the *Son of Perdition* that gives *Life* and *Form* unto it. Well; There *comes up among them*, [what we read, *After them*, should be readd, *Behind them*,] a *Little Horn, before which Three of the First Horns were plucked up by the roots*. Lo, The Bishop of *Rome*, and his Kingdom, in most Lively Colours: There can be nothing more to the Life! He was at first, a *Little Thing*: Yea, as late as the Days of *Marcellus*, the Bishop of *Rome*, he was not very Big, when the Emperour honoured him with the Office of *Cleansing his Stables*.[65] By diverse Accidents and Stratagems this *Little Priest*, at Length became the *Grand Monarch* of the *West*; and assumed the Style of, *The Vicar of Christ*, which is indeed but the very English of the Word, ANTICHRIST. Shall we now observe, That he takes away a *Third Part* of the *Estates*, and *Powers*, and *Jurisdictions*, belonging to each of the *Ten Kings* under his Influences? This is not near punctual enough. Lett it be then observed, That he particularly overthrew, & extinguished, and siez'd upon, *Three* of their *Kingdoms*. The Bishop of *Rome* caused a Ruin to be brought, first on the Kingdom of the *Herules*; Then, on the Kingdom of *Ostrogoths*; Lastly, on the Kingdom of the *Lombards*; GOD has employ'd such Pens as that of a *Sigonius*, without the least Eye of [ms. III, xii, 22v] the Authors unto the *Prophecy*, to relate the Events which most notably expound it unto us.[66] The *Eyes of a Man* in this *Little Horn*, and a *Mouth speaking very great things*, and a *Look more stout than his Fellows* and his *Blasphemies against the Most High*, and his *Wearing out the Saints of the Most High*, and his *Thinking to change Times & Laws*; are so plainly fulfilled in the *Papacy* [which indeed is but the *Roman Empire* in the Second and more Spiritual Edition of it,] that if Old *Porphyrro* were now Living, he would Blaspheme the *Seventh* Chapter of *Daniel*, as once he did the *Eleventh*, and say, That it must needs be no *Prophecy*, but an *History*, written after the Things were accomplished.[67]

What I have now to Demand, and I insist upon it, is, That the *Reign* of this *Wicked One* do continue, until the *Thrones* be *Settled* (not, *Cast down*, but, *Pitch'd down*,) for the *Overcomers* unto whom our SAVIOUR has promised, *That He will grant them to sitt with Him in His Throne*: [And we know, *The Compact City*, where *are sett the Thrones for Judgment, the Thrones of the House of David*:] There the *Ancient of Days* will *Sitt*, whose *Throne* will be *the Fiery Flames; & the Wheels thereof a Burning Fire*. A *Fiery Stream* will *issue & come forth from before Him*. THEN, the *Beast* will be *Slain*, and his *Body destroy'd, and given to the Burning Flame*. This will be, when *the Son of Man comes in the Clouds of Heaven*. The *Ancient of Days*, [A Title that had much better be rendred, *The Appointer of Times*,] is the same with the *Son of Man coming in the Clouds of Heaven with Power and Great Glory*. If upon, *One LIKE the Son of Man*, so brought at this Time, any incline to the Conjecture of the Learned *Bisterfield*, Lett them do, as they please.[68] But here we have *evidently sett forth as* enthroned *before our Eyes*, the SON of MAN, who is the *Appointer of Times*, attended [ms. III, xii, 130] with His *Mighty Angels*. From His *Throne*, there issues the *Burning Flame*, in which the *Fourth Beast*, or the *Roman Empire* in the Possession of *Antichrist*, has his *Body destroy'd*. In this the Destruction of this *Beast* is to differ from the Destruction of the *Three* preceding *Monarchies*. They, after their Destruction had a *Prolonging of Life given* unto them; Their Territories were still continued in the World. But this undergoes all the *Perdition* that a *Fire* without a *Metaphor* can bring upon it. The *Fiery Stream coming forth from before* the Glorious Judge, with *the Thousands of Thousands ministring unto Him, and Myriads of Myriads standing before Him*, on this awful Occasion, is but the very same that our Apostle *Paul*, citing the very Words, took to be, [2. Thess. I. 7.] *The Reveling of our Lord JESUS from Heaven, with His Mighty Angels, in Flaming Fire, to take Vengeance*. And surely, no Man will be so *Vain*, or so *take the Name of the Lord our GOD in Vain*, as to deny, that This is the *Second Coming* of the Lord. What Vile Design had *Grotius* in his Head, when he would fain make, *The Son of Man*, in this Prophecy of *Daniel*, to mean, *The Roman People*? But for this we will call in *Grotius* to confute him! This very Man, in his Commentary on the Gospel, owns, that our SAVIOUR does refer to this Prophecy of *Daniel*, when He says, [Matth. XXVI. 64.] *Hereafter shall Ye See the Son of Man Coming in the Clouds of Heaven*.[69] That this must mean His *Personal Coming*, is plain from what the Blessed *Son of Man* has Himself told us, That it will be at the

End of the World. That the *Coming of the Son of Man in the Clouds of Heaven,* means His Literal, Visible, *Personal Coming,* or His Appearing to *Burn* and *Judge* the World, I am so very positive, that I must say, I do not see, how this Interpretation can be laid aside, without an Impious Rejection of all the Proof in the Bible, that ever the *First-begotten* of GOD shall be *brought again into the World.* But that the *Coming of the Son of Man in the Clouds of Heaven,* will be at & for the Extinction of the *Roman Monarchy,* is as plain as any Words can render it. I again and again insist upon it; There can be nothing more clear, than that the *Second Coming of our Lord,* will be at & for, the Destruction of the *Papal Empire!*

But, O *Lord, How long shall our Enemy be Exalted over us?*—The Term assigned for the *Papal Empire,* has been over & over & over again declared, and with a very notable Inculcation. Tis to be, a TIME, TIMES, and, HALF A TIME. It has been also sett for, *Twelve hundred and Sixty Days;* Which are as many as make [ms. III, xii, 24v] up *Three Years and an Half:* whereof doubtless the *Three Years & Six Months by the Space whereof it rained not on the Earth,* in the Days of *Elias,* were Typical.[70] And it is *now* fully understood, that these are *Prophetical Days;* According to the Rule first given to *Ezekiel; I have appointed thee Each Day for a Year.* To express it yett another Way, tis denominated, *Fourty two Months*: No doubt, in allusion to the *Forty two Stations* of *Israel* detained in the *Wilderness.* Thus, *The Days of* ANTICHRIST, *are determined with GOD, and the Number of his Months is with GOD;* GOD has appointed his Bounds that he cannot pass.

Now, if we can with Certainty fix the *Epocha,* for these dreadful M.CC.LX. Years, we may certainly know, when they have their Expiration. But, can any thing be more plain, than those Words; [Rev. XVII. 12.] *The Ten Horns which thou sawest are Ten Kings, which have received no Kingdom as yett; but receive Power as Kings one Hour with the Beast:* As in the Vision of *Daniel,* the *Little Horn* is Contemporary with the *Ten.* When we see *Ten Sovereign Kings* rising in the broken *Roman Empire,* we may take it for granted, That *Antichrist* is now upon his Throne. But then, it is astonishing to see, how in the Fourth and Fifth Century, the Barbarous Nations, made their Violent Assaults and Inroads upon the *Roman Empire,* and made Fearful Devastations upon a People many Ways ripened for the Vengeance of GOD. These *Heathens* themselves had a Strange Impression on their Minds, that they were doing, *The Work of GOD,* in what they did:—*Non Suum esse quod facerent, aqi enim se, et perurgeri divino Jussu,* as the godly Presbyter of *Marseilles* has informed us: *Jornandes* tells us, That some of them affirmed themselves, to have been by some *Heavenly Visions* putt upon their Expeditions.[71] And we know the Name of One mighty Leader among them, who would be called, *Flagellum Dei.*[72] In less Compass than Fourscore Years, *Italy,* which had been the Heart and Strength of the *Roman Empire,* was no less than *Seven times* brought unto what was little short of Desolation, [ms. III, xii, 131] by the Fire and Sword of the *Barbarians.* The City of *Rome* itself was more than once, horribly sack'd, in these Invasions. But what is yett more astonishing, the Invaders, were strangely captivated into the Religion of the People whom they conquered; these *Heathens* quickly declared themselves *Christians,* and most unaccountably the Bishop of *Rome,* soon became an Oracle unto them. The Consummation of the Matter was, That Several *Kingdomes* took advantage from the Confusions come upon the *Roman Empire,* to sett up for themselves; And by the Year, *Four hundred & fifty Six,* there were no less than TEN *Crowned Sovereigns,* appearing, whereof TO ΔΕΚΑΤΟΝ, the TENTH & Last was *France,* which yett for Merits, may be called, *The First-born of Antichrist.*[73] Many Learned Men, have with much Accuracy of Calculation, settled the *Hour,* for the Nativity of these *Ten Kings;* among whom, it may be none has done it with more Learning, than our *Lee,* in his Treatise, *De Excidio Antichristi.*[74] Now, that *Antichrist* was gott into his *Power* at this *Hour,* Lett it be considered, that the Emperour *Honorius* having removed unto *Ravenna,* left *Rome* the ancient Seat of Empire to the Government of the *Roman Bishops.*[75] Behold, the Surprizing Accomplishment of that Prophecy; [2. Thess. II. 7.] *He who now hinders, will hinder, until he be taken out of the Way, and THEN shall that Wicked One be reveled.* The *Imperial Power,* not only in the *Pagan* but also in the *Christian* Appearance of it, flourishing at *Rome,* was now *taken out of the Way;* And what a *Revelation* of *Antichrist* upon it! The Bishop of *Rome* still rose as the *Roman Empire* went down the Wind; Insomuch that *Leo,* who praesided in the *Roman See,* A.C. 456. [And methinks it is agreeably enough, that we find a *Leo,* at the Commencement of the New *Babylonian* Empire!] boasted in a Sermon, *De Apostolis,* that the Government of the *Roman* Emperour was changed into the Power of the [ms. III, xii, 26v] *See of Rome.*[76] It is Exceedingly Remarkable, that at *This very Time,* a General Council held at *Chalcedon,* where the Greek Emperour himself, in Person, and Six hundred & thirty Bishops from all Parts of the World, were present, acknowledged the Bishop of *Rome,* to be, *Caput Ecclesiarum:* And from *This Very Time* does the Cardinal, whom we call, *The Goliath of the Romish Philistines,* derive the Title.[77] The Emperour *Valentinian* III. had newly given Orders unto his General *Ætius,* to provide, that for the future none should ordain Bishops, without Leave of the Pope at *Rome.*[78] Thus does the *Roman Eagle* acknowledge him! He also published an Edict in Conjunction with the Emperour of the East, "That it should not be lawful for any Bishops to undertake any thing, without the Authority of the Venerable *Pope* of the Eternal Town; but that whatever the Authority of the Apostolical See shall ordain, shall be a Law to all other Bishops." On the Death of this *Valentinian,* who was murdered by *Maximus,* there came *Gensericus,* and killed the Usurper and sack'd the City of *Rome:* and after having spent fifteen Days in Sacking & Spoiling of it, left it A.C. 455. The Mock-Emperours, who were changed by the *Gothic General* at Pleasure, for one & twenty Years after this, never had the Power, nor any more than the *Name,* of Emperours.[79] At *This very Time,* they who would see the *Superstition* as well as the *Supremacy,* of ANTICHRIST, sufficiently introduced, may, when they please, call in an Army of Protestant Writers to the Service.[80]

The TIME, and the TIMES, and the HALF-TIME of *Antichrist,* are most admirably suited, unto his *Three States*, his *Rise*, and his *Grandeur*, and his *Decline*.[81] His *Rise*: He kept Thriving, & Prospered in his Encroachments, until not only *Charlemaign* gave him the Temporal Sovereignty in *Italy*, reserving to himself a Negative upon the Election of *Popes*, but his weaker Son had the *Debonnaireté* to resign that also.[82] Here expired the TIME, or the first CCCLX Years of the *Papacy*. A.C. 815. His *Grandeur*: The Second Period; or, the Two TIMES, which contain DCCXX Years, reached unto A.C. 1535. when the *Reformation* was at [ms. III, xii, 132] its Heighth in *Germany*; and fixed in *England*, and first preached in *France* and *Switzerland*. His *Decline*: The Third Period; or the HALF TIME, which contains CLXXX Years, is to be reckoned from the *Reformation*, to the Death of *Lewis* XIV. who was the Last Great Power, that attempted the Extirpation of it; And if *Others have done* Perfidiously and Inhumanely, *Thou*, LOUIS, *hast excelled them all*. It is Remarkable, That *Antichrist* now lost *Half* his Dominion, by Countreys of *Europe* withdrawing their Allegiance from him. It were to be wished, that some of the Countreys who shook off his Corruptions, had not so *done it to Halves* as it may be fear'd they have.

There is an Ingenious & Surprising Remark of our *Mede*, on this Occasion. In the *Eleventh* Chapter of the *Apocalypse*, we find only the *Inner Court* of the *Temple* measured; and the *Outer Court* left unmeasured, and *given to the Gentiles*. By the *Inner Court* may be well intended, the *Primitive Church* in its Evangelical *Purity* of Doctrine and Worship and Manners. By the *Outer Court* may be intended the *Corrupted Church* under the Antichristian Apostasy. The *Inner Court* was much Smaller than the *Outer Court*; it bore to it, the Proportion of *One to Three & an half*. And may we not beleeve, that we have here an *Image* of the *Duration*, which must be extended unto the *Great Revolution*? The Duration of the *Pure Church*, must be *One Time*; or CCCLX Years; And then the Duration of the *Base Church*, must be, *One Time, Two Times, & an Half-time*; or, M.CC.LX. Years. We may well reckon the CCCLX Years of the *Pure Church*, from the Date of the Visions here granted unto the *Beloved Apostle* of the Lord. So they End about A.C. 455. Then follows the *Base Church*; And at *This very Time*, we have seen the Arising of *Antichrist*.[83]

Upon this Last HALF TIME for the *Man of Sin*, there is yett another Thing that is very Notable. There are Two Steps taken for the Abolishing of *Antichrist*: [ms. III, xii, 28v] [Rev. XIV. 15, 18.] There is first, an *Harvest*; and then, a *Vintage*. Accordingly, our Lord had a Mighty *Harvest* of Churches, gathered out of the *Papal Empire*, at the Reformation; and at the Beginning of the Last *Half-Time*. Still the Earth is not cleared: The *Harvest* leaves Work for the *Vintage*; which always comes about a *Seventh Part of the Year after* it. The *Seventh Part* of the *Twelve hundred & Sixty Years*, which constitute the *Grand Year of Antichrist*, is just *One Hundred & fourscore Years*. There we have the Expiring of the Last *Half-Time*; And *Then* it is, that the *Vine of the Earth*, whereof the *Grapes* are the *Grapes of Sodom*, is to be *cast into the Great Winepress of the Wrath of GOD*.

It is also a Matter of the deepest Contemplation. From the Ascension of our LORD, until the Emperour *Constantine* became a Christian, the Church is represented as a *Travailing Woman*. And there now ran just as many *Years*, as there are *Days*, from the *Conceiving* to the *Travailing* of a Woman with Child; that is to say, *Two hundred & Eighty*. From A.C. 33. to A.C. 313.—It will take some Time for a Woman after her Delivery, to be in a Condition for Transportation into a *Wilderness*. This Time was, while the *Roman Eagle* has *Two Mighty Wings*; the *Eastern* and the *Western* Empire: A Space of *One hundred & fourty two* Years. The *Left Wing* was then lost; and the *Woman* was dropt unto the Earth; A.C. 456. From this Time she is to continue in the *Wilderness*, for M.CC.LX. *Days*, or Years; which again brings us to M.DCC.XVI.[84]

But there is a Marvellous Coincidence of many other Computations, as well as a Concurrence of these, to invite us into a Perswasion, That we are come to the *Time of the End*, and that the *Twelve hundred and Sixty Years* wherein the *Man of Sin* is to wear his *Tripple Crown*, are come unto their Period.

[Attachment recto] I will not expatiate into any Long Exinanitions upon the Subject. But I cannot forbear to mention one Computation, which the acute *Walter Cross*, in Prosecution of his *Taghmical Art*, finds an Occasion to fall upon.[85]

Abraham the Father of the Faithful, very notably represented the *Church*, whereof *Lot* was as a Backsliding Part, who falling in Love with the *Fatt Valleys* of the Earth, brought a *Leanness* into his better Part, & a Ruine on his Family. *Melchizedek* as notably represented our glorious JESUS, Meeting & Blessing the Church, with His *Visible Presence*, as their King, after He has by His *Invisible Power* assisted them to triumph over their Enemies.[86] This will be at the *Time of the End*, when One of the Chief Enemies, will be the King of *Shinar*, which was the Countrey of *Babylon*. The *Ten Years* of *Abrahams* Pilgrimage, from *Charran*, thro' *Canaan*, to *Egypt*, & so back to *Mamre*, the Place of his Abode, & from thence to the Victory, did, by putting a *Year* for a *Day*, signify the Pilgrimage of the Church in & thro' this World, until the Coming of *Melchizedek*. Ten times CCCLXV Years, make MMM.DC.L. Years. He then paid his *Tenth* to *Melchizedek*; by which he acknowledged not only this *Victory*, but all his *Riches*, to be from the *Blessing* of the *Lord of Hosts*; and particularly, all his *Protections* during his *Ten Years* Difficulties. It may be [says our *Cross*] this [Attachment verso] *High-Priest* might read a Lecture of this Kind unto him, when He *Blessed* him; and this might more particularly lead him to the Payment of his *Tenth* on this Occasion. However this Gentleman desires us to Reckon *Three Thousand Six hundred & fifty Years*, from the Date when *Abraham's* famous *Four hundred and Thirty Years* began: And Then,—Expect the Appearance of *Melchizedek*, as a Thing to be Quickly look'd for! I look upon This to be as *Conjectural* as many other *Computations*. However, It may not be amiss, *Reader*, to be at the Pains of *Computing* it; and say,—According to This,—*whereabouts are we?*

[ms. III, xii, 133] I shall supersede all Recital of any more with the Marvellous Words of Cardinal *Cusanus*, written the best Part of Three hundred Years ago;—And *such* Words from *such* a Man in *such* an Age, truly must be beyond all Expression *Marvellous!*—He sais, "In the Things done to and by our

SAVIOUR, to the *Twenty Ninth* Year of His Life and to the Day of His *Resurrection from the Dead*, extend every Year, into a *Jubilee*;—and you may be likely to foresee, what will fall out in the Church of GOD. According to this, In the *Thirty Fourth Jubilee* from the *Resurrection* of CHRIST, you may hope to see, by the Mercy of GOD, a *Resurrection* of the CHURCH, and a Pulling down of ANTICHRIST, with her gloriously Victorious over him. And this will be, after the Year *One Thousand Seven hundred* from the Nativity of our Lord, and before the Year One *Thousand Seven hundred & thirty four.*" *Post illud autem Tempus, Ascensio Ecclesiae futura est, CHRISTO Sponso adveniente ad Judicium.* What? A *Cardinal* write thus! O *Cajaphas*, Who inspired thee! *Reader*, canst thou beleeve thy own Eyes! Turn to the 934 Page of his *Works*, and thou shalt Read it there.[87]

I will sum up all, with saying at once. ALL that has been *Foretold* in the *Scripture of Truth*, as what must come to pass before *the Coming of the Day of GOD*, is, as far as we understand, *Fulfill'd*: I say, ALL FULFILL'D! We do not know of any *One Thing* that remains to be accomplished.

For the fullest Satisfaction, of those who are so *Blessed* as to *Read and Hear the Words of the Prophecies, and Observe the Things in them*, I would only entreat, that they would bestow a just Perusal on Two Treatises; The One, is, *An Essay on the Revelation*, written by an Acute *Whiston*, whose unhappy going over to the Tents of *Arius*, needs not make us lose the Benefit of his more profitable & valuable Studies. The other is, *An Essay upon the Scripture-Prophecies*, written by Colonel *Burnet*, the Governour of *New York*, who upon the Encouragement, & not without the Direction, of the Great Sir *Isaac Newton*, has applied his [ms. III, xii, 30v] Thoughts this Way, & obliged the World with some Rare Effects of his doing so.[88] These two, are truly admirable Performances, & full of *Decisive Strokes*; and it is impossible to Read them without being exceedingly charmed with them; It is impossible to see in them, how Exactly, & how Punctually the *Prophecies* have been accomplished, without Adoring the Lord GOD of the Holy Prophets; or indeed, without crying out, Lord *JESUS, Thou wilt come Quickly!* Having seen what has been *Foretol'd*, so surprisingly *Fulfill'd*, in so many Instances, what a well-bottomed Assurance have we for the Fulfilment of *All the rest!* Yea, in the *Spirit of Prophecy*, what a *Testimony of JESUS* have we, and what a Demonstration of the Religion, which beleeves a JESUS *enthroned in the Heavens!*

As for the *Seven Vials*, which the *Arbitrary Interpreters*, make such Wild Work withal, I cannot but recommend the Explications of *Jurieu*, as the best that have yett been offered; According to which, the Thing that is now Daily to be look'd for, is, *That Great Babylon will come in Remembrance before GOD, and He will give unto her, the Cup of the Wine of the Fierceness of His Wrath.*

One thing that somewhat sways me This Way, is, that I am informed, the Incomparable Sir *Isaac Newton*, who has applied himself to the Study of the *Sacred Prophecies*, finds Demonstrations, That the whole Vision of the *Vials* must be Synchronous and Similar to the Vision of the *Trumpetts*.[89]

As for the *Last Slaughter*, & following *Resurrection*, or, at least for the *As-*

cension, of the *Witnesses*, I am very much *in the Dark*: Yea, *An Horror of Great Darkness falls* upon me,—I am Afraid! I am Afraid!—*I tremble in myself, that I may Find Rest in the Day of Trouble.* Well; But M.DCC.XVI. is come on; and we see nothing Extraordinary. *The Harvest is Passed, and the Summer is Ended*, and we are still as we were. *All things continue as they were from the Beginning of the Creation.* What are they better, or other than they were, Seven times Ten Years, before the Last *Half-Time* of *Antichrist*, according to our Notion, came unto its Period. The M.CC.LX. Years run out, and the *Man of Sin* Reigning still!—Doubtless, it will now be said, *The Days are Prolonged, and Every Vision faileth.* But I must Reply, *The Days are at hand, & the Effect of Every Vision.* And I have these Things to say upon it.

I say, First; Even for the M.CC.LX. Years, one may very Reasonably allow a *Latitude*. For the Commencement of them, it may be Reasonable to allow, from A.C. 456. when the [ms. III, xii, 134] Last of the *Ten Kings* is up, to A.C. 476. when upon the Fall of the Last Emperour *Augustulus*, [A little *Name-sake* of the First; a Curiosity sometimes occurring in History,] it utterly gave up the Ghost; until which none of the *Ten Kings* were in the free & safe Possession of their *Crowns*. This will bring us to, A.C. 1736.—Remember now, what has been said of the *Samaritan* Chronology![90]

I say, Secondly; When a Period is up, there is not always a Necessity that there should be *No Pause*, between, the *Thing* that has been done, and the *Next Thing* to be done; Especially when the *Next Thing* is not some Great Good for which there has been a Promise of the *Praecise Year* then fixed for it. What I mean, is, That *Some Space* of *Praeparation* for the Following Event, may sometimes be well enough supposed. Thus, tho' the Period of a little more than *Three hundred and Ninety Six* Years, for the *Ottoman Empire* to do the Part of a *Wo* upon *Europe*, were up in A.C. 1697.[91] Yett, the Sounding of the *Seventh Trumpett* may be a little waited for. [The SEVENTY WEEKS in the famous Prophecy of *Daniel*, will afford us a wondrous Exemple, of a *Parenthesis*, in the Transition from One Great Affair to another in a Prophecy. A Gentleman whose Name is *Marshal*, has cleared up this Matter, beyond all that ever went before him, & so that there now remains no more to be said upon it.[92] From the Time of the *Commandment* and Commission, from *Artaxerxes Longimanus*, in the Twentieth Year of his Reign, unto *Nehemiah*, to rebuild *Jerusalem* & replenish the Waste-Places of it, there were to be *Seven Weeks*, or *Fourty nine* Years; which were spent in that Work accordingly.[93] But a Thing of infinitely greater Consequence was then to come on: Even the Redemption of the World by the Sacrifice of the MESSIAH; the Time of which had hitherto been kept a *Secret*. The Angel *Gabriel* himself seems to be surprised at the Discovery of it, and uses the same *Salutation* to the *Prophet* upon it, that he afterwards used unto the *Mother* of the Redeemer.[94] This was to be upon the Dispatch of *Sixty two Weeks*, or Four [ms. III, xii, 32v] *Hundred and Thirty four* Years more. So that when *Four Hundred and Eighty three* Years, from the *going forth of the Commandment* aforesaid, should be run through, the *Crucifixion* of our SAVIOUR could not be deferred for One Year longer. It must be at the *Passeover;* and accordingly it fell out at the very *Next Passeover* after the Sixty *Nine Weeks* were finished: as from that *Golden Rule* of *Astronomers,* the *Canon* of *Ptolomy,* has now been demonstrated.[95] There yett remains *One Week* more to make up the *Seventy.* Now this was not in a Close Cohaesion, to the *Sixty two,* as the *Sixty two* were to the *Seven.* This did not run on in a Reckoning with the rest. No; It was a *Separate Week;* This *Distinguished Week,* has a Beginning different from those which preceded it. It contains the *Seven Years,* which were employ'd in the Final Destruction of *Jerusalem, the City & the Sanctuary.* The *Continued Reckoning* of all the *Seventy Weeks,* when the Angel plainly leads us, to begin only the *Seven Weeks* and the *Sixty two Weeks* from the same *Epocha,* has been the Rock which all the Expositors of this Illustrious Prophecy have splitt upon. And on this account, it might be said concerning the *Day* and *Hour* for the Final Destruction of *Jerusalem;* It was *known to no Man.* It might be quaestion'd whether the *Angel Gabriel* himself, had been lett into the Secret. But after this miserable People had *with Wicked Hands crucified* the Son of GOD, and were now no more *His People,* the Glorious GOD waited a while; There was a *Little Interval* before He brought on the *Single Week,* which was to be spent in the Destruction which was now waiting for them. *Anon,* the *Seven Years* for the carrying on of the *Desolation* came on; and then as with a raging *Inundation,* it swept all before it. *Then, the People that were to become the People of* Messiah *the Prince,* did *make a Covenant with Many.* The *Week* began, on the Seventeenth of *September* A.C. (V.Æ.) 63. About this very Time, *Tacitus* tells us, how the *Romans* by their General *Corbulo,* made a *Peace* with the Nations, which was, *Haud alias quam immota pax.*[96] GOD ordered it, that they might be entirely at Liesure for the Work now before them! On the Last of *February* [ms. III, xii, 135] A.C. 67. began the *Last-Half* of the *Week.* At the Beginning of This, *Vespasian* entred into the *War,* with the *Jews,* which was praecisely of *Three Years and an Halfs* Continuance. *Jerusalem* was attacked the Year before, by *Cestius;* who had entred the Lower City, and laid Siege to the Upper. One Assault, as *Josephus* tells us, would have carried it; but he most unaccountably desisted from the Enterprize. Yett about Six Days after, he made an Assault upon the *Temple,* so successfully, that he was going to sett it on Fire. But he most unaccountably gave over that Enterprize also. A Secret Operation of GOD, is all the Account that can be given of it! It was before that *February* in which the Last *Half-Week* was to commence for the *Desolation* that was determined.[97] Nor was the *Universal Publication of the Gospel* accomplished, until the Year, *Sixty two;* which was the Year before the *Last Fatal Week* began. In *that Year,* the Apostle *Paul* was able to say; [Col. I. 6, 23.] *The Gospel is now come in ALL THE WORLD.* And, *It has been preached unto EVERY CREATURE which is under Heaven.* How the *Desolation* went on, till the *Sacrifice & Oblation ceased,* with a People thrown into such hideous Hurries that it was no longer possible for them to attend the Customary Devotions, and the *Roman Idolatrous & Abominated* Standards were sett up on the *Holy Place* of the *Temple* then in Flames, on the Tenth of *August;*—Every body knows the

Story. The Reader will pardon this *Parenthesis*. Tis not *unsuitable* to what I am in Prosecution of:]

I say, Thirdly; After the M.CC.LX. Years for the Reign of *Antichrist* are up, we find in the Numbers of *Daniel*, the running on of XXX Years more, making up M.CC.XC. Years; And then the running on, of XLV Years more, making up, M.CCC.XXXV. Years: which *Blessed is he that looks for & comes to*. Now, who can say, what is to be done in the remaining LXXV Years: Or, on the other hand, can any Man say, whether all these Years have to a Minute just the same *Epocha*? So that still, *Of the Day and Hour knoweth no Man!*[98]

[ms. III, xii, 34v] Lastly; I have one thing more to say; Tis That: [2. Pet. III. 9.] *The Lord is not slack concerning His Promise, as some Men count Slackness; but HE is Long-suffering to usward; not willing that any should perish, but that all should come to Repentance.—Account that the Long-suffering of our Lord, is for our Salvation.*

—The *Longsuffering* of the Glorious LORD, gives an Opportunity for the *Midnight Cry* to be rais'd; and for the *Voice* of *Elias* to be heard; and for the Favourites of Heaven to *Make Ready*, and be awakened unto such a *Conduct* as may render them Fitt for the Blessedness of them that shall be *Caught up to meet the Lord*.

Far, Far would I be from rash Determinations about the *Day* and the *Hour*, for the Coming of what is to *Come as a Snare on all them who dwell on the face of the whole Earth*. Church-History has abundantly informed us, how the Determining such and such a *Praecise Time* for the Appearing of the Lord, has carried Men into Pernicious & Ridiculous Extravagancies. At the *Reformation*, there were People pretending to *Revelations*, that the Coming of the Lord, and the *Saeculum Spiritus Sancti*,[99] was *Then* at the Door. But those *Fanaticks*, as *Balduin* justly calls them, did the Reformed Religion very Little Service. *Bullinger* tells us, That there were about A.C. 1530. Some odd People so violently hurried away with the Notion, *That the Day of the Lord was at hand*, as to throw up all *Business*, and imagining, *Tam brevi Temporis spatio se satis opum habere*, spend upon the Stock, & plunge themselves into Impoverishments that were laughed at.[100] Yea, others tell us, That about A.C. 1533. a Pastor in *Saxony*, (called *Stifelius*) had the Vanity to boast himself the *Angel* of the *Seventh Trumpet*, and sett the very *Day* and *Hour*, for the Appearing of the Lord unto the Judgment of the World; whereupon the Countrey-Men ran so mad as to neglect their *Business*, & lay by their Husbandry, and indulge themselves in Sensualities [ms. III, xii, 136] very Disagreeable to such an Expectation.[101] More lately, A.C. 1693. *Switzerland* was troubled with a Sect, which would have brought all into Confusion, with an Assurance, that the *Day of Judgment* would begin at the End of *August* in that Year. And A.C. 1694. One whose Name was *Mason*, a Well-meaning but Melancholy Minister of our Established Church, fancied that our Lord had appeared unto him, and a Couple of his Followers gave out, that they had seen *Angels*; and according to these, the Glorious Reign of the Lord was immediately to begin in *England*, and more particularly at *Water-Stratford*; and they had their Disciples that laid aside all *Business*, and having all things in common, associated in the Devotions that such an Expectation called for.[102] There have been *the Devices of Satan* in such things, to strengthen the General Security of the World, and furnish & hearten the *Scoffers of the Last Days*, with Matter for even an *Inextinguishable Laughter*. *Et quidem sic fieri oportet*.[103]

All that I would propose, is, To animate that PIETY, which would not be unseasonable and unreasonable, if *This World* might have more than a *Thousand Years* yett allow'd for its Continuance. This is most certain, That Every Mortal Man ought so to *Live*, as *Knowing* THAT he is to *Dy*, and as *Not Knowing* WHEN he is to *Dy*; and leave nothing *Undone*, that he shall *wish it had* been *done*, when he comes to *Dy*. And tho' it would be an *Indiscrete* Speech, That a Man ought so to *Live Every Day*, as if he *Knew* it it WILL BE the *Last Day of his Life*; Yett it is the highest Piece of *Discretion*, for a Man to *Live Every Day*, as *not knowing* but that it MAY BE the *Last Day of his Life*. Yea, he is a Madman, who does not make the *Provision* that should be made by one that MAY DY *before To Morrow*. Now, it will add a Considerable Animation to this PIETY if this Consideration may be called in; The COMING of the LORD unto the *Judgment of the World* now CANNOT be very FAR OFF, but MAY BE in OUR TIME, and *before this Generation pass away*: Yea, THOU KNOWEST NOT WHAT A [ms. III, xii, 36v] YEAR MAY BRING FORTH. Our *Zanchy* as earnest a Pleader as any Man, against rash Determinations, *De fine Seculi*, yett will permitt us to conclude upon a, NON PROCUL, and a, CITO, for it; if we forbear praecisely defining the, *Non Procul*, and the, *Cito*; but leave it unto GOD: NEAR, but not say, HOW *Near*.[104]

Andreas Musculus published a Book of this Title; *An ille Puer, qui Diem Supremum Supervicturus sit, calceos modò induent?* [105] For my own Part, I am willing to own, that one Intention of THIS BOOK, is to maintain, *That such as are now born, may, for aught any Man alive can say, be found Alive at the Coming of the Lord*. Yea, As the Thing is now SHORTLY to be look'd for, so, I maintain, *That no further Signs of it than what have been already given us, yett remain to be look'd for*: No, not so much as the *fifteen Signs* of the last *fifteen Days* before the *Last Day*, in the Annals of the *Hebrews*.

Flinsbachius, in his, *Conjecturae Extremorum Temporum*, near an hundred and Seventy Years ago, did in the *Signs of the Times* find no less than *Ten* Grounds for *Conjectures*, & the Most of them very Good Ones, That the *Day of GOD* is now hastening on the World.[106] And *Luther* Thirty Years before That, saw such *Signs of the Times*, as perswaded him, that the *Last Day*, even the *Great Day of the Lord*, then could not be more than *Two Hundred Years* off.[107] If there should be a Grant of any more *Signs* there would be as little notice taken of them, as there has been of those that have been already granted. The foolish, and flouting, & bruitish, & short-winded Way of passing a Sentence upon *Extraordinary Descents from the Invisible World*, which we have seen in our Days, is a sufficient Indication, how much the most Shocking *Signs of the Times* are lost upon us. The fearful Decay of Real and Vital PIETY every where, [ms. III, xii, {1}37] and the *Insignificancy* of all the ancient and usual Means to praeserve it and revive it, is among the most awful *Signs of the Times*; But who is there that makes a due Construction upon it? I make no doubt, That the Reception of THIS BOOK will also be among the *Signs of the Times:* For it must be, *As it was in the Days of* Noah: and *Lot* must *seem as one that mocked,* unto them that have the *Fire of GOD* just going to fall upon them![108]

It is indeed proposed, That we may forbear the *Inconvenient Steps,* into which any may be led, by an *Ungrounded Faith,* of the Church having a Promise and Prospect of seeing a *Long Prosperity* upon Earth, under *Godly Rulers,* before the Coming of the Lord, and of Seeing *Happy Times* in a World, that will have the *Curse* of *Death* and *Sin,* yett remaining on it. And as the Doings of such Mazeheaded and Hare-brained *Fifth-Monarchy Men,* as *Venner* and Company, have their Frenzy now sufficiently & effectually exposed, so some things more usual with even the Best of People, are now to be examined, *How far they should be continued in.*[109] But what is then to be done? Briefly, It is proposed, That all the Honest and Proper *Business* of *This World,* should go on still, as the *Occasions* of the Day call for it. Lett the *Business* be carried on with as much Alacrity and Variety of Application, as if *This World* might yett stand for *Many Years.* But yett, Lett the Prosecution of the *Business* be Moderated and Regulated, with due Suspicions, *That the Day of CHRIST is NOW at hand;* or, *what if it should be so?*

This I insist upon.

Tho' the PIETY to which the *Meditation* of our own LAST DAY, *Nigh* to us but *Hid* from us, be truly *for the Main,* but the Same that the *Meditation* of the LAST DAY now coming on a *Cadaverous* World, even with the *Wings of an Eagle hasting to the Prey,* would oblige unto; Yett, that the Designs of the *Former* Meditation will be sensibly advantageous by annexing the *Latter* Meditation unto it, is evident from our SAVIOURs insisting so much upon it. And if *He* Insist upon it, what Pretence can there be to Deride it or Decry it as a *Folly,* in them [ms. III, xii, 38v] that *handle the Pen of the Writer* for Him to do so too? This we know; They who have enquired into the Causes and Reasons of that astonishing *Fortitude,* with which the *Martyrs* of Primitive Christianity went thro' their Sufferings, make this Return upon it; That it was very much owing to the *Strong Faith,* which they had, of their being surely and fully & speedily Rewarded, in the *Kingdom* of GOD, at the Approaching *Resurrection* of them that were *Beheaded for the Witness of JESUS.* Most certainly, A *Life* influenced by & agreeable to, the *Faith,* of our Glorious LORD *Quickly Coming* to sett *Fire* unto *This World,* & bring on a *Better,* would make Amiable & Admirable *Christians.*

It is an Appeal made unto the *Conscience* of a Reasonable Christian; *Seeing all these things shall be dissolved* [And, How soon, O *my GOD, I know not!*] *What Manner of Persons ought Ye to be in all Holy Conversation and Godliness?* Do Thou say, O CONSCIENCE, Thou *Light of GOD* in the Soul of MAN; Do Thou say: What should be the Conduct of a Christian, who is Assured, that there will a *Day* QUICKLY arrive, wherein the SON of GOD will make His Descent into these Regions, and *Raise from the Dead* all the *Holy People* whose *Bodies* are sleeping in their Graves, and consume This World in those Formidable and All-devouring *Flames*, from which none shall be *Delivered*, but those that by the Ministry of His *Angels*, will be *caught up to meet their SAVIOUR:*—But he has no Assurance that this *Day* shall not arrive before the next Rising of the Sun, or *before our Potts can feel the Thorns!* What is the PIETY that should shine in the whole *Conversation* of such a Christian? And with what Eye should such a Christian look on a *World*, obnoxious to such a Speedy & such a Sudden *Evanition*?

I am supplied with an *Answer of a Good Conscience* to This, in, An Instrument of PIETY, that shall be offered as, *The Conclusion of the Matter.*

[ms. III, xii, r38v]

Vigilantius.[110]
Or, The Dispositions of One
Looking for, and Hasting to,
the Coming of
THE DAY OF GOD.

Seeing, that all the Things of this World shall undergo a DISSOLUTION, and the DAY now draws very Near, but no Man knows how Near, wherein the *Fire of GOD* shall bring a Stupendous Desolation on *the Heavens and Earth which are now,* but our GOD, who is a Consuming Fire, will *create New Heavens & a New Earth* wherein He will give His Children to *Inherit all things, What Manner of Person ought I to be in all Holy Conversation & Godliness!*

I desire in the First Place, that *Seeing I look for Such Things,* I may IMMEDI-ATELY, Yea, IMMEDIATELY, come into a State of *Reconciliation* to GOD; and be in such Terms with Him, that if the Glorious LORD were Immediately to *descend in Flaming Fire to take Vengeance* on His Wicked Enemies, I may not be found One of the Wicked: and a Stranger to the *Life of GOD.* Since *GOD* has *appointed a Day, in which He will Judge the World, by that Man whom He has ordained* for it, He commands me to *Repent,* and with a *Change of Mind* from the Sentiments which I have had, while I have *walked in the Vanity of my Mind,* become Qualified for a Part in His *Kingdom.* IMMEDIATELY, would I now go thro' a Process of REPENTANCE. I would Retire, and own myself *Unable* to Turn unto GOD, and *Unworthy* that He should Enable me; but implore the Help of *Sovereign Grace* on this Grand Occasion. Then, I would Call over, Confess, Bewayl, my Transgressions of what is *Forbidden* and what is *Required,* in the Commandments of GOD: But above all, Mourn over that *Original Sin,* which is the Fountain of all my Transgressions; and an *Evil Heart* sett upon *Departing from the Living GOD.* Hereupon, I would shew and plead the *Blood* of my SAVIOUR, that I may be *cleansed from all Sin;* Pray, Beg, Weep, for the *Pardon* of all my Sin. This would I do, till I have obtained Some Impression from Above, with a Grounded Perswasion of my being *Pardoned.* Now, I would give myself up to GOD, with hearty Wishes that having done with *Iniquity,* I may *not offend any more;* and [ms. III, xii, {40?}v] hearty Resolves, That with His

Help, I will *walk in Holiness & Righteousness before Him*, all the remaining Time of my Pilgrimage.

I Desire, That since the Day which I look for, is the Day when GOD will *make up His Jewels*, I may be sure of my having my own *Soul bound up in the Bundle of Life with the Lord my GOD*; This I would make sure of, by *Coming* to a Glorious CHRIST, and getting into *His Covenant*. He has engaged unto His Eternal FATHER on the behalf of all that are in His *Bundle*, That He will *Satisfy* for their Sins; and, That He will also *Sanctify* them for Himself. I consent unto these Engagements of my SAVIOUR; O *Glorious GOD, I consent, I consent unto it, that the Oblation which thy CHRIST has made unto Divine Justice be my Atonement; and that thy CHRIST should work in me what shall be well pleasing in thy Sight.* I most thankfully accept the Gracious & Marvellous Offers of my SAVIOUR to me. Conquered by a Sense of a *Victorious Delectation* in what is offer'd me, I cry out; O *my SAVIOUR, I am Willing, Thou hast made me Willing, That thou shouldest make me Righteous & make me Holy, & fulfil for me & in me all the Good Pleasure of thy Goodness.* This brings me into the *Covenant*, wherein I am *in the Bundle of Life, with the Lord my GOD.* I hope, I shall not be *gathered* with the *Tares* and I shall not be *bound* with them in the *Bundles* that are to be *Burned in the Fire at the End of This World.* Lord, *Gather not my Soul with Sinners!* My *Groans* unto my SAVIOUR, *Groans* full of *Agony*, are; O *my SAVIOUR, Do Thou take me under the Shadow of thy Wings; and lett me find myself Comprehended in thy Engagements to thy FATHER for thy People.* Herein I am Translated from the *First Adam*, to the *Second Adam*. The *Second Adam* will now own me for one of *His Children*. The *Father of the World to Come*, will bring me to an *Inheritance* among His *Children* in the *World to Come.* I shall be one of those, of whom He will say, *Behold me, and the Children which GOD has given me!*

I Desire, That since a Glorious CHRIST (who *is Our Life,*) is He, at whose *Appearing*, Oh! that *I may appear in Glory!*—my *Life* may be fill'd with all Possible Regards unto that *Lord of Glory*.

I would have Him *Living in me*; and sensible that I can *Do* nothing, *Bear* nothing, any further than I have Him *Strengthening* of me, I would keep continually Resigning myself up to Him, that He may Possess me, & Incline me, & Quicken me, for Living unto GOD. This will assure His having taken a *Vital* & a *Lasting Hold* on me, and my Coming to *Live* with Him.

[ms. III, xii, r40v] I would Study all imaginable *Conformity* to Him; Labour to *Resemble* Him; Labour to *Imitate* Him; As a *Follower of the Good One*, often consider the Lovely Pattern of *Goodness*, which He has given me, till *beholding the Glory* of the Lord, I am *changed into the same Image from Glory to Glory.* Yea, the very *Afflictions* and *Abasements* that carry on my *Conformity* unto Him, I would Rejoice in them, as, *Tokens for Good*; Willing to *Suffer with Him*, in Hopes of *Reigning with Him.* Certainly, He will not now say unto me, *I know thee not!*

I would sett such a Value on Him, that if I may have HIM *Concerned* for me, and HIM Conversing with me, *That* shall be *Enough*: I will easily part with all

Creatures: Easily submitt unto the most *Bereaving Dispensations*, be *Poor*, be *Sick*, be *Friendless*, if I have but a CHRIST left unto me!

I would be always *at Work* for Him; and continually *Devising of GOOD*; Contriving how to promote His *Kingdom* & *Interest*. Oh! That for His *Book of Remembrance* my Numberless Projections, *To Do Good*, may be some Articles!

I Desire, That I may be *Holy in all Manner of Conversation*: Make it the Main End of my Life, to *Serve* and *Please* the Glorious GOD; My Highest Ambition, To be a *Grateful Spectacle* to GOD: With most Explicit & oft Repeted *Intentions*, aim at the *Gratifying* of Him, with an *Obedience*, to Him, which will be *Accepted in His Beloved* SON: Take my Measures of my *Delights* in my *Comforts*, from the *Help* they give me, in *Seeing* of Him, & in *Doing* for Him; And with very frequent & awful *Reflections*; call to Mi{nd} His *All-seeing Eye* upon me. And Hence Whatever I ta{ke} to be a *Sin*, I would forever *Abhor* it, forever *Avoid* it; *Abstain from all Appearance of Evil*.

I would *spend my Time*, with the Wise {Men?} of a *Circumspect Walk*, as one that can at most have but [** torn] and as one tha{t is} on the Wing to a *World of Recompences*.

I would find out what are the *Talents* wherewith GOD has endew'd me, & seek out the most *Exquisite Methods* of Employ{ing} them all as becomes a *Good*, *Steward* of the *Manifold Favours* which GOD showes unto me.

I would by a Serious, Prayerful, & [ms. III, xii, {42?}v] Watchful *Walk with GOD*, and a care to shun the Epidemical Vices of the Age, be distinguished from the *World of the Ungodly*, which are to perish in the *Flood* that is approaching. {I} would forever *Take Heed lest at any Time* I have my *Heart overcharged with Surfeiting or Drunkenness*, any Sensual Excesses, or with the *Cares of this Life*, or Distempered with *Controversies* and *Contentions*, and so *That Day come upon me unawares*. I would not *at any Time* fall into those *Discomposures*, which may unfitt me to *meet the Lord*, if He should presently *Rend the Heavens, & Come down, & Melt the Mountains, & Cause the Nations to tremble at His Presence*. I would often {t}hink, *what if the {G}lorious Judge of the World should Immediately come down upon us*! O my GOD; *Lett not the Day come as a Snare upon me*!

And, as a *Sign*, of my having a Share in the Great *Sabbatism*, which I am waiting for, Oh! That I may very Particularly, very Industriously, maintain the Exercises of, *An Holy Sabbatizer*!

I Desire, That since the *Angels* of the *Lord*, are in many & unknown Ways to befreind His Chosen at His Coming, I may now in all the Ways of *Piety* obtain it of my SAVIOUR, that His *Angels* may be my *Guar{di}ans*, I would much employ {many?} *Praises* as well as {many?} {P}rayers, for the {Servants?} of the Angelical {Min}istry: And I would {in San}ctity, in *Activities*, [** torn], & in *Benignities* [** torn] be as like to {the Holy?} ANGELS as {our Sin}ful Condition {would} allow of.

I Desire, That since the Lord JESUS is going to be *Reveled from Heaven in flaming Fire*, to *Recompense Tribulation unto them who Trouble* His Faithful People, under the Oppressions of *Antichrist*, I may associate myself with His

People, and have a very Tender *Sympathy*, a most Brotherly & Anxious *Condolence* with them in their *Troubles*; Bear them on my Heart; Plead their Cause; Move Heaven & Earth on their behalf. *Lord, Thy People* shall be *My People*. And I will *Remember them that are in Bonds, as bound with them*!

I Desire, That, since *This World* is condemned unto *Flames*, which are Now Quickly, [*I know not, How Quickly!*] to sieze upon it, & make a dismal Havock of it, I may look upon *This World*, with the *Contempt* which is due to such a Wretched Object: That I may not be lothe to comply with *Mean Circumstances* in *This World*, if such must be allotted for me; That I may be very *Moderate* in my Pursuit of *This World*, & since *the Time is short, Purchase* as one that is not to *Possess* any thing of it; That for what of *This World* may in the Way of my *Business* flow in upon me, I may *Devise Liberal Things*, & abound in such Disbursements to *Pious Uses*, as will not be forgotten when a well-bestowed *Cup of Cold Water* shall have its *Reward*: And that my *Hope*, and my *Joy*, and my *Portion*, & all my *Treasure*, may be in the *Future World*.

NOTES

INTRODUCTION

Chapter 1. The Authority of the Bible and Cotton Mather's "Triparadisus"

1. See Levin, "Trying to Make a Monster Human."

2. Brumm, chs. 3, 4; Bercovitch, *Puritan Origins* and *American Jeremiad*, ch. 3; Tichi, *New World*, ch. 1; Lowance, *Language of Canaan*, ch. 7; Lovelace, ch. 2; De Jong, ch. 3.

3. Erwin's *Millennialism* is a slightly revised 1987 Indiana University dissertation in history. My dissertation, also from 1987, includes an analysis of Mather's millenarian theories.

4. Zanchius, *Opera Omnia Theologica*; More, *Immortality*; Bates, *Considerations*; Baxter, *Immortality* and *Certainty*; Burnet, *Departed Souls*. See also K. Thomas, ch. 19.

5. Pt. III, ch. 33, pp. 281, 282. See also Spinoza, *Tractatus*, chs. VIII–X, pp. 120–56. 1 Macc. 1:54–57; Josephus, *Antiquities* 12.5, 6. Newton, pt. I, ch. 1, pp. 11–12.

6. Simon, *Critical History* 3: sig. (a) 1r-1v, 2r-2v. For an excellent discussion of the rise of philological criticism of the Bible, see Popkin, "Newton."

7. 1:258, 2:5–6. For John Lightfoot's opposition to Grotius's interpretation of Matt. 1:23, see Lightfoot's *Works* 11:20.

8. For background see Reventlow, esp. pts. II ("The Crisis over the Authority of the Bible in England") and III ("The Climax of Biblical Criticism in English Deism"); Reedy, chs. 1–2.

9. For Increase Mather's caveat against the poison of Grotius and Hammond, see *Future Conversion*, pp. 7–8.

10. For information on William Whiston, I am greatly indebted to Force's excellent study, *Whiston*, chs. 3–4.

11. For the most thorough study of Anthony Collins, see O'Higgins. Korshin mentions Collins in passing, pp. 115–17. See also Reventlow, pp. 362–69.

12. See esp. Hammond, *Paraphrase*, pp. 1–4; Simon, ch. 21; White; Whiston, *Essay Towards Restoring*, p. 229. Similar hermeneutical problems surround the messianic readings of Matt. 2:15, 23, etc.

Chapter 2. The "New" Hermeneutics and the Jewish Nation in Cotton Mather's Eschatology

1. For historical backgrounding, see Hill, "Till the Conversion"; Toon, "Jewish Immigration"; Culver; Ehle; Scult; Froom, vol. 3, pt. I.

2. *Works*, p. 767. See also Mede, "*The Mystery of St. Paul's Conversion, or, The Type of the calling of the Jewes*," in *Paraleipomena*, pp. 37–40; I. Mather, *Mystery*, p. 90. For a discussion of Mede's influence, see Gilsdorf, pp. 64–70; Clouse, "Rebirth."

3. Pp. 7–8; see also pp. 9, 16–17, 19–24; Whitby, *True Millennium*, pp. 1–24; and "Appendix to [Romans] Chap. XI," pp. 95–107.

4. Cotton, pp. 185–86; the prefaces by Davenport, Greenhill, and Hooke, in I. Mather's *Mystery*, n. p; Johnson, pp, 24, 30, 34–35, 60–61, 138, 250, 255; Oakes, p. 3; Noyes, pp. 4–9, 26–32; Willard, app. 1, pp. 2–16; I. Mather, *Mystery*, pp. 1, 17, 49, 63–64, 77, 127–28, *Diatriba*, pp. 54, 70, *Future Conversion*, pp. 1–34, and "New Jerusalem," pp. 395–97; Sewall, *Phaenomena*, pp. 29–31 and app. 2, pp. 16–24; Edwards, *Work of Redemption*, pp. 487–88, *Revival of Religion*, pp. 313–16, and "Apocalypse," pp. 133–35, 196–97, 333–34, 337.

5. Scholem, "Shabbetai Zevi and the Shabbatean Movement," in *Kabbalah*, pp. 244–86; Bercovitch, *American Jeremiad*, pp. 74–75; Michael G. Hall, pp. 76–78.

6. Quoting William Owen, in *Letter-Book* 2:199.

7. Pp. 127–28; See also Mede, *Works*, pp. 758, 761.

8. Acosta 1:66–69; Vázquez de Espinosa, pp. 18–32. For Menasseh ben Israel's speculation on the fate of the Lost Tribes, see *Hope of Israel*, esp. pp. 20–44, 53–56. The best study of the whole issue is Huddleston, pp. 33–47, 128–37. See also Bercovitch, "Horologicals," pp. 52–74, 115; Sanders, ch. 30; Maclear, pp. 244–48; Mede, *Works*, pp. 74–77, 799–800. For John Eliot's belief in the "Judaical Indians," see De Jong, pp. 34–78; and Holstun, pp. 102–65.

9. Williams; Vázquez de Espinosa, chs. 11–13, pp. 24–32; Sewall, *Phaenomena*, pp. 29–47; Noyes, pp. 68–99; Canup, pp. 55–148. David E. Smith is obviously mistaken in his assertion (p. 540) that Mather believed the American Indians were the Lost Tribes. And so is William R. Hutchison, p. 38.

10. For similar tests, see *MP*, pt. I, pp. 24, 34, and I. Mather, *Illustrious Providences*, pp. 170–71, 201.

11. For Thomas Burnet's debate of La Peyrère's Pre-Adamite theory, see *Sacred Theory*, pp. 193–95; Noyes, pp. 69–75; Hornius (1652); *MCA* 1.1.6; Huddleston, pp. 138–43.

12. Vázquez de Espinosa, pp. 34–35; Acosta 2:326–31; Mede, *Works*, pp. 575–76, 799–801; see also *MCA* 1.1.7.4–5; *WIW*, pp. 201–2; *T*, p. 298; Clendinnen, pp. 23–24.

13. See also I. Mather's *Mystery*, pp. 77–78.

14. See Mede, *Works*, pp. 761, 766–68; Whitby, *True Millennium*, p. 5. For opposition to the idea of Christ's transient appearance, see Cotton, pp. 219, 232; I. Mather, *Future Conversion*, p. 4; Baxter, *Glorious Kingdom*; and Cotton Mather in his later eschatology, *T*, p. 313.

15. See also *TB*, pp. 16–17, 33–34; *BO*, pp. 43–45.

16. See also *D* 1:300, 315, 370, 2:41, 62, 218–19, 233, 500, 741n. For early discussion of this issue, see Huhner; De Sola Pool; Friedman, "Jewish Residents" and "Mather and the Jews."

17. Hugo Grotius wrote one of the earliest Protestant missionary handbooks for the conversion of Jews and Muslims, *De Veritate*. This work may contain the germ for Twisse's "Epistles"; see also I. Mather's *Mystery*, p. 93, and *Future Conversion*, pp. 4–6.

18. Francke's Pietist influence has been established by Kuno Francke and by Benz, "Ecumenical Relations" and "Sources." Mather's millenarian Pietism has been carefully examined by Lovelace, pp. 32–72. For Mather's deliberations on the subject, see *D* 2:23, 196–97, 200, 202, 213, 247–48, 277, 411, 524, 544.

19. See also *ATC*, pp. 58–59; *D* 2:378, 492, 494, 524. Similar reasons guided Mather in translating the Psalms into blank verse without the "*little Jingle at the end of the Line.*" His *PS* was to be "a powerful and perswasive Engine in the *Army of the LORD*" for use in the conversion of the Jewish nation. In fact, "were One to single out a present for a JEW," Mather advised, "it should be a *Psalter* with a *Commentary!* Which no doubt he will consider the more Attentively because he will find his own *Rabbi's* continually brought in as Vouchers for it" (*PS*, pp. xxxiv, xxx).

20. Mather felt deeply threatened by Whiston's revival of the Athanasian controversy and responded to the attack on Trinitarianism through mystical and intellectual measures (*D* 2:12, 15, 106–7, 186, 205, 225, 230, 817; *CCC*). For helpful background on Whiston, see Reventlow, pt. III; Reedy, pp. 20–45; Force, *Whiston*, chs. 3–4, and "Newtonians"; Popkin, "Newton."

21. Since his fellow millenarians believed the restoration of the Jewish nation to be the most reliable sign of Christ's imminence, Mather argued, their deference to this sign would easily lull them asleep "as the *Day of the Lord* must find the World overwhelm'd withal" (*T*, p. 296). See also *D* 2:816–17; I. Mather, *Mystery*, p. 171; Lovelace, pp. 44–47.

22. For *Adoni Avi*, see *D* 2:313, 430. On the debate about a partial vs. a global conflagration, see Mede, *Works*, pp. 766, 773–75, 809; I. Mather, *Future Conversion*, pp. 30–32; Ray, pt. III, pp. 393–96; Burnet, *Sacred Theory*, pp. 289–91; *DL*, p. 193; and my next chapter.

23. See ch. 3 of this Introduction. For the development of the preterite-allegorist exegesis, see Grotius, *Annotationes* 2:270–73, 392–94; Hammond, *Paraphrase*, pp. 433–37, 719–20, 727–30; Lightfoot, *Works* 6:393–94, 7:112–27, 9:328, 354, 11:303–5, 12:445–46; Batalerio; Calvert; Baxter, *Glorious Kingdom*. It was the latter work that caused Increase Mather to write his refutation of this allegorist position in *Future Conversion*. See C. Mather, *Selected Letters*, pp. 415–16.

24. For contrary views, see Whitby's *True Millennium*, pp. 9–10, and "Appendix to [Romans] Chap. XI"; and John Toland's *Nazarenus*, which argues that Christianity as allegorized Judaism is still obligated to observe the Mosaic Laws and Jewish ceremonial rites (pp. iv–xxv).

25. For Mather's careful observations on the diaspora of the Jews after the fall of Jerusalem, see his "Appendix to the Book of *Lamentations*," pp. 1–26, "Addendum to the Book of *Malachi*," and "The Parenthesis, or, some Hutchesonian Hints on the Jewish Nation between the Old and New Testaments," all in "BA."

26. See also De Jong, pp. 93–99. One of the best, though unpublished, discussions of Sewall's millennialism appears in Delmer Davis, pp. ix-c.

27. Mather's interest in Pietist ecumenism was grounded in his millenarian hope for the Second Coming. Like his Frederician colleague of Halle, Saxony, he campaigned to unite all Judeo-Christian churches under his Maxims of Piety, the "Everlasting Gospel" reduced to three simple dogmas. This system of principles, Mather hoped, would not only conquer all sectarian dogmas that divided the various denominations, but also effect the prophetic accomplishment of Joel 2:28: God's spirit poured out on all flesh. Mather's Maxims would thus spread the mantle of brotherly love over all religious contentiousness—mankind, at last, united in Christ's Everlasting Gospel. His *Stone Cut out of the Mountain* (1716) describes how the Church Universal might be brought about:

> Among the diverse Colonies of *Bees*, fierce Wars are sometimes carried on, in which they neither give, nor take any Quarter, but make a very great Slaughter of one another. Of these Opposing Armies, the *Voice* is the same; the *Aspect* is the same; the *Armour* is the same; 'Tis only by their *Scent*, that they distinguish themselves from one another. Wherefore if any one throw among them a *Sweet-scented Liquour*, which may impart the *same Scent* to all the Contenders, presently the *Fight* is over; the *Strife* is at an end; there is a Cessation of all *Hostilities*. Most certainly, the *Maxims of the Everlasting Gospel* exhibit such a *Sweet-scented Liquour*, which being poured, and cast upon the *Church-Militant* [Alas! too *Militant*!] All the Faithful Servants of God, of whose *Union* the *Blood* of their Saviour is the Eternal *Cement*, will presently be sensible, that they all have the *same Scent* upon them; and they will without any more ado, give over wounding one another. *God put an End unto their doing so!* (p. 6)

Chapter 3. The Bang or the Whimper?

1. *The Day of Doom*, p. 55. See also Mather Byles's poem "The Conflagration."

2. See also *T*, pt. III, sec. viii. In contrast to Cotton Mather, John Ray rejects the idea of nature's progressive degeneration and argues for a cyclical increase and decrease of wickedness periodically punished by God (pt. II, pp. 269–71, Pt. III, 338–44, 393–97).

3. See also *CPI*, pp. 67–68; *T*, pp. 154–55, 201, 270.

4. As extrabiblical proof, the Sibylline Oracles greatly gained in significance when the authority of the Bible as the revealed Word of God was threatened by the new sciences. For this reason, Mather devoted a whole section to the Sibyls and their validation of biblical prophecies (*T*, pt. III, sec. iv). Increase Mather's low opinion of the Sibyls is evident in *Future Conversion* (p. 23), but in Cotton Mather's time the issue was much more pressing. The Sibylline Oracles were hotly debated by Whiston (*Vindication*) and by Chandler (ch. 1, sec. 1, pp. 10–35). See also Augustine's *Sibyllinorum Verborum Interpretatio* (*PL* 90.1181–86) and *City of God* 18.23.

5. For an excellent summary of the contemporary debate, see Burnet, *Sacred Theory*, pp. 241–70, 339–46; Ray, pp. 320–39, 406–15; Hobbes, pt. IV, ch. 44, pp. 455–56. Quistorp; Lamont.

6. Hammond applied the same historical-contextual method to Matthew 24 and limited this prophecy to the destruction of Jerusalem in A.D. 70 (*Paraphrase*, pp. 101–8). How volatile the issue was can be seen in Lightfoot's adoption of Hammond's method in *Works* 7:78–79, 112–127, 9:328, 354, 11:303–7; in Burnet, *Departed Souls*, pp. 128–44, and *Sacred Theory*, pp. 295–96, 306–21, 334; in Ray, pp. 300–325, 388–93; and Sherlock, *Use and Intent*.

7. White, of Trinity College, Cambridge (fl. 1700), wrote *Commentary on the Prophet Isaiah*. See also Ray, pp. 311–12; Sherlock, *Use and Intent*; Lowth, *Isaiah*.

8. For the various positions on a partial or global conflagration, see *PSNE*, pp. 34–37; *MCA* 1.1.2, 1.1.7; "PT," pp. 78–79; *D* 2:740, 748; *T*, pp. 315, 316; I. Mather's *Future Conversion*, pp. 30, 31. For their sources, see Mede, *Paraleipomena*, p. 36, and *Works*, pp. 773–76, 809–10; Burnet, *Sacred Theory*, pp. 262, 289–91; Ray, pp. 303–5; Whiston, *New Theory*, pt. II, pp. 285–91, 442–47.

9. See also "PT," pp. 48–52. For the scientific theories on the fluid interior of the earth, see Burnet, *Sacred Theory*, bk. I, chs. 5, 9–10, bk. III, ch. 7; Ray, pp. 373–81, 411–12.

10. See also *PSNE*, pp. 35–37; *MCA* 1.1.7; *BKD*, p. 20; *WIW*, pp. 96–97, 201–2; *TA*, 48; *IC*, pp. 24–27; *T*, p. 291; Mede, *Works*, pp. 776, 798.

11. See Mede, *Works*, pp. 798–802, 808–10; *T*, p. 189; *RDF*, pp. 195–96; Sewall, *Phaenomena*, pp. 27–29, 52–55; Bercovitch, *American Jeremiad*, pp. 72–73.

12. See also *T*, pp. 209–11, 315–16; Ray, pp. 373–81, 384, 411–12; Burnet, *Sacred Theory*, pp. 270–79; Whiston, *New Theory*, pt. II, p. 287.

13. 1. Thess. 5:2; 2 Pet. 3:10; Rev. 3:3, 16:15. For his sentiments on the church caught in her spiritual sleep, see *D* 1:384–85, 2:737–38. Hammond employed a preterite reading (*Paraphrase*, pp. 101–8). See also Burnet, *Sacred Theory*, pp. 293–99. Ray offers the three main theories and commits himself to none (pp. 395–97).

14. For Mather's source, see Burnet, *Sacred Theory*, pp. 95–97, 270–78.

15. The Greek philosopher Epicurus (324–270 B.C.) denied the immortality of the soul (*On Nature*) because, he argued, the soul like the body is only a temporary combination of ever-changing atoms dissolved at death. Consequently, the concept of reward and punishment after death is null and void. The Roman poet-philosopher Carus T. Lucretius adopted the same argument in *On the Nature of the Universe* (c. 58 B.C.), arguing that

the *anima* and *animus* (soul or living spirit) are the same as the body and thus have no independent existence, vanishing with the death of the body. The state of the soul was subsequently debated by the Greek theologian and early church father Origen (c. 185–254), in *De Principiis* 2.3.1–4, 3.4.1–5, and by Lactantius, in *Against Heresies* 2.33. In Mather's day the issue remained relevant, even after Calvin's *Psychopannychia*, written against the Anabaptists in 1534, had appeared in an English translation in 1581. See also Mede, *Works*, p. 801. For Spinoza's refutation of ghosts and their existence, see his correspondence with Hugo Boxel (Letters LIV–LX), in *Works* 2:375–88. Henry More launched his attack on Hobbes in *Immortality*, bk. 1, chs. 3, 9. Thomas Burnet joined More's position in *Departed Souls*, chs. 3–4. And so did the French theologian Moïse Amyraut (1596–1664); Baxter (*Immortality*); Isaac Bates (fl. 1700); and the Presbyterian William Bates (1615–91).

16. See also *PMDJ*, pp. 11–12; *T*, pp. 113–14; I. Mather, "New Jerusalem," pp. 391–94, *Souls of Men*, and *Meditations*; Burnet, *Departed Souls*, pp. 95–125.

17. See *MP*, pt. I, pp. 3–17; *WIW*, pp. 1, 55–57; *MCA* 6.7.66–83; I. Mather, *Illustrious Providences*, pp. 168–247. For background see K. Thomas, chs. 19–20.

18. See *PN*, pp. 131, 133, 162, and Cotton Mather's nightmarish encounter in *D* 1:129–30.

19. See *T*, pp. 122–26; *AB*, pp. 28–38; Erwin, pp. 116–52.

20. See Augustine, *City of God* 20.7, 10; Sherwin, *Glorious Kingdom, Saints Rising*, and *Restitution*; Whitby, *True Millennium*, pp. 5–7; Davidson, pp. 22–23; Tuveson, *Millennium*; Clouse, "Alsted"; Capp, "Political Dimension."

21. See also *C*, pp. 144–50; "PT," pp. 82–84; *WMTU*, pp. 14–15; *SSC*, pp. 8–9; *WA*, p. 15; *SV*, pp. 6–7; *TB*, pp. 13–18; *T*, pp. 250–52, 273–75; Mede, *Works*, pp. 773–76; Augustine, *City of God* 20.18; Baxter, *Glorious Kingdom*, pp. 71, 72; I. Mather, *Future Conversion*, pp. 34–35; Whitby, *True Millennium*, p. 22.

22. On Increase Mather's treatise, see Lowance and Watters.

23. See also *MCA* 7.96–101, app., art. xxix. For the treatment of the Quakers in New England, see Worrall, pp. 3–42.

24. See *C*, pp. 147, 149; *PN*, pp. 119, 121–26. See also Augustine, *City of God* 22.21, 29–30.

25. See William Twisse's "Postscript," in Mede, *Works*, p. 799.

26. The same argument occurs in "PT," pp. 10–11; and in I. Mather's "New Jerusalem," pp. 400–402. On his hopes to unite Lutherans and Calvinists through his *Maxims of Piety*, see *D* 2:663.

27. Mather warned his emulators that the envy of their detractors "will render it a *Dangerous Thing*, to be very *Charitable* and *Beneficent*," for "Men will sooner Forgive Great *Injuries*, than Great *Services*." To such ingrates, "a man *of Good Merit*, is a Kind of *Publick Enemy*. And that by *Engrossing* a great many Applauses, which would serve to gratify a great many others, he cannot but be *Envied*; And that men do naturally *hate*, what they *Esteem* very much, but cannot *Love*" (*B*, pp. viii, x, xi). See also *D* 2:670–71; *PN*, pp. 14–15, 188, 197–201, 217–18; Phyllis Franklin, ch. 2; Levin's introduction to his edition of *Bonifacius*, pp. vii–xxxiii; Silverman, *Life and Times*, pp. 232–38; Breitwieser, pp. 54–56.

28. While still in their mortal bodies, Mather believed, the Saints would be unable to see their angelic helpmates, for the Saints' "*Eyes* were not then of a *Texture*, to *Discern such Spirits*" (*T*, p. 261). See also *C*, pp. 89–108; *D* 1:263–64, 2:190, 520–22, 577, 579, 590; *PN*, pp. 107, 110–13, 119, 121–26, 133, 148, 162, 173; I. Mather, *Angelographia*; and Levin, "Angel."

29. See "PT," p. 84. During one of his mystical experiences, Mather received assurances that he would be among the Raised Saints and rule with Christ (*D* 1:379). For Mather's

sources, see Tertullian, *Against Marcion* 3.24; Mede, *Works*, pp. 775–76. See also Whitby, *True Millennium*, p. 5; I. Mather, *Future Conversion*, p. 30.

30. In *MAM*, Mather left a guideline for those who would follow in his steps. See "A CATALOGUE of BOOKS For a Young Student's Library" (pp. 148–49), chs. 5–11 for his recommendations for the gentleman pastor, and *PN*, p. 42. For a helpful assessment of *MAM*, see Woody, "Cotton Mather's *MAM*" and "Bibliographical Notes."

31. Increase Mather rejected the idea of Christ's corporeal visitation on earth during the millennium, in *Future Conversion*, pp. 34, 35. And so did his predecessor Edward Johnson, pp. 34–35.

32. According to Augustine, *City of God* 20.11, the New Jerusalem was the worldwide church of God. For a review of the debate in the early church, see Mede, *Works*, pp. 815–16; Whitby, *True Millennium*, pp. 4–5.

33. Hugo Grotius, Henry Hammond, John Lightfoot. To Thomas Burnet, the New Jerusalem *was* the millennium (*Sacred Theory*, pp. 358, 362). To Thomas Hobbes, the kingdom of heaven would be on earth with Jerusalem as its capital in Judea (pt. III, ch. 38, pp. 335–37; see also his exegesis of the phrase "Kingdom of God," in pt. III, ch. 55, pp. 297–303).

34. Lowance and Watters, pp. 343–59. Cotton Mather's comment on Tertullian's mirage is revealing: "Now tho' I don't know what well to make of the Relation; Yett I am fully with *Tertullian* [He shall be my *Master*!] in the Faith of such a *City praepared*" (*T*, p. 246).

35. See also *T*, pp. 304–6; "PT," p. 82; Mede, *Works*, p. 593; Whitby, *True Millennium*, pp. 4–5; I. Mather, "New Jerusalem," p. 396, and *Future Conversion*, pp. 27, 33, 34; Edwards, "Notes on the Apocalypse," pp. 149–50, 166–67, 197–98.

36. See also "New Jerusalem," pp. 364, 380–81, 395–96; Lowance, *Language of Canaan*, pp. 145–49.

37. See my "*Israel Redivivus*."

38. Heimert, p. 96. See also *D* 2:19. Others before and after Heimert have reached substantially the same conclusion: Parrington 1:107–11; Niebuhr, p. 171; Miller, *Seventeenth Century*, pp. 463–91, *Jonathan Edwards*, pp. 326–27, and *Colony to Province*, pp. 188–90; Brumm, chs. 3–4; Bercovitch, "Horologicals," pp. 4, 6, 15–17, 20, 37, 43–45, 55–75, 201, and *American Jeremiad*, esp. pp. 8–10, 49–61, 69–80; Tuveson, *Redeemer Nation*, chs. 4–5; Elliott, pp. 186–90; Lowance, *Language of Canaan*, pp. 127–35, 141–42, 154–59, 160–65; Gura, pp. 13, 127; Stout, pp. 8–9, 45, 102–3.

39. Sig. Bv. See also Edward Taylor's letter to Sewall (29 Sept. 1696), in Isani, "Pouring," and Noyes, pp. 44–63. Oakes, Sewall, and Noyes all seem to echo John Winthrop's famous lay sermon *A Model of Christian Charity* (1630), in which he exhorts his fellow colonists on the *Arbella*, "wee must Consider that wee shall be as a Citty upon a Hill, the eies of all people are uppon us" (p. 93). In significant revisionist studies, Theodore D. Bozeman has called this passage the most misquoted and misunderstood expression in American history ("The Puritans' 'Errand'" and his excellent study *Ancient Lives*, ch. 3). This revisionism has been continued by Andrew Delbanco, who also recognizes the conflicting strands of ideological justifications of the Errand (pp. 81–97).

40. Twisse's "Fourth Letter" (2 Mar. 1634) to and debate with Mede are published in Mede's *Works*, pp. 798–99.

41. Mede's position is set forth in *De Gogo & Magogo* and his "*Answer to Dr. Twisse his Fourth Letter*," in *Works*, pp. 574–76, 799–802.

42. *Works*, pp. 799–800. Mede's geography of salvation represents Jerusalem as the spiritual center of the earth and arranges the continents of Europe, Asia, and Africa (but excluding America), like the three leaves of a shamrock, around the Holy Land. For a geographical representation, see Bünting, "Die gantze Welt in ein Kleberblat [Kleeblatt],"

in *Itinerarium*, pp. 4–5. For a select listing of Puritan reactions against Joseph Mede's rejection of America, see app. 3 in my *"Israel Redivivus,"* p. 395.

43. Sanford, p. 95 (see also pp. 82–89); Tichi, *New World*, p. 31 (see also pp. 32–36). See also Baritz, p. 31; Berens, pp. 14–31.

44. The New Jerusalem as a metaphor for the millennial Church Universal can be found in Augustine, *City of God* 20.11, 17, 18, 22.30; and in Brightman, p. 101. Increase Mather's double Jerusalem was at once an allegorization of the New Jerusalem in the clouds of heaven (Revelation 21) and the literal, restored city Jerusalem in Judea; see "New Jerusalem," pp. 364, 380–81.

45. Lowance, *Language of Canaan*, p. 135, quoting Elliott, p. 190; Noyes, pp. 10, 42.

Chapter 4. When Shall These Things Be?

1. "Newton." See also Force, *Whiston*, pp. 63–89.

2. La Peyrère, *Men Before Adam*, bk. 4, p. 208; Hobbes, pt. III, ch. 33, pp. 276–85; Spinoza, *Tractatus*, ch. IX, p. 135 (see also ch. XII, pp. 165–66); Simon, bk. 1, chs. 1–8.

3. Even John Ray mentioned such erstwhile millenarians who set out to know the future (pp. 296–99).

4. Similar justifications are found in William Twisse's "Epistle XIII" to Joseph Mede (Mede, *Works*, p. 758), and in I. Mather's *Mystery*, pp. 130–31.

5. Cotton Mather came to the same conclusions also in *MC*, p. 30; *TDP*, p. 33; *T*, pp. 339–41. Cf. Newton, ch. 10, pp. 128–43. For the similarities between Mather's exegesis of Daniel's Seventy Weeks prophecy and that of Joseph Mede, see Mede's *Works*, p. 105. Yet Mather was most impressed with Arthur Ashley Sykes's *Difference*, which informs Mather's own calculations in *T*, pp. 320–24, 339.

6. See also *MC*, pp. 31–33; Mede, *Works*, p. 603.

7. Thomas Goodwin, *Exposition*, pt. II, chs. 6–7, pp. 157–61, 195–205; Samuel Hutchinson, p. 3; Banks; Maclear. Capp, *Fifth Monarchy Men*; P. G. Rogers; Hill, "Religion and Politics"; Holstun, ch. 3.

8. For discussions of Cotton Mather's involvement in the ousting of Andros, see *D* 1:138–39n; Marvin, pp. 83–88; Wendell, pp. 71–77; Levin, *Cotton Mather*, pp. 162–73; Silverman, *Life and Times*, pp. 55–82; Lovejoy, pp. 235–50.

9. Mather seemed awed by the ideas of the Fifth Monarchists. He pointed out to the members of the Artillery Company of the Massachusetts Bay (1 June 1691) that in Christ's kingdom their swords would be changed into "Plough-shares" and "Pruning-hooks," but he exhorted them meanwhile to *"make as Good use of your Swords and Spears as you can,"* though not *"to do like those mad Fifth-Monarchy men,* who have thought their Turbulent Insurrections would be Acceptable" to Christ (*TLF*, p. 71). See also *WWG; O,* pp. 20, 31–36; *B*, pp. 179–80.

10. See *T*, pp. 324–27, 341–42. Mather and his fellow millenarians often invoked as a perpetual warning to the radical fringe the Anabaptists of Münster, Germany, whose religious excesses had led them to infamy and destruction in the 1530s. See Cohn, pp. 256–80.

11. In letters to Robert Woodrow, Anthony William Boehm, and August Hermann Francke (but most conspicuously in his Reserved Memorials), Mather records his most visceral hopes on how his Maxims of Piety might promote God's providential timetable for 1716, when the Almighty would pour out his prophetic spirit on all nations (Joel 2:28) and bring on the millennium (*D* 2:329, 333, 365–66, 368, 371, 376, 380–81, 387, 396, 397, 406–7, 449, 453–54, 456–57, 462–63, 520–23, 544, 577; *SCM*). See also De Jong, pp. 99–107.

12. See *T*, pp. 277–79; *D* 1:225–26, 243, 2:551, 667–68, 685, 763, 804–6; *PN*, pp. 100, 249; Silverman, *Selected Letters*, p. 343.

13. Beverley, "A Calender of the Whole Time," following the preface of *Scripture-line*. An English millenarian of Hertfordshire, Thomas Beverley seems to have influenced the Mathers to expect the End in 1697, as can be seen in *D* 1:188, 199–200, 207–8, 222–26, 234, 241, 261–63; *WIW*, pp. 51–52; "PT," pp. 87–89; *PN*, pp. 128–29, 138–39, 148–53; *T*, pp. 324–25, 327–28; and in I. Mather's *Future Conversion*, pp. 12–13, *Strange Doctrine*, pp. 92–94. Indeed, Beverley had corresponded with Increase on the issue and made him a gift of a copy of his *Thousand Years Kingdom*. This copy (at the American Antiquarian Society) contains Beverley's letter to Increase while the latter was in London to negotiate the Second Charter. The Mathers owned at least five of Beverley's many millenarian works (Tuttle, "Libraries," p. 317; *National Union Catalogue: Pre-1956* 12:610–13. See also Murdock, p. 269.

14. For the same argument, see *MC*, pp. 63–65; *WIW*, pp. 51–52, 85–90; *DWD*, pp. 56–58, 69; *BS*; *DL*, pp. 186–98; *MCA* 7.101, art. xxx; *TDP*, pp. 34–37; and I. Mather's *Future Conversion*, pp. 12, 13, 25.

15. Middlekauff, pp. 339–40. For Mather's interpretations of the seals, trumpets, and vials and the destruction of the "Turkish Woe" (Revelation 6–18), see "Revelation," in "BA"; *TLF*, pp. 31–44; *WIW*, pp. 90–97; *PSNE*, p. 35; *DWD*; *TDP*; *ATC*, pp. 41–42; "PT," pp. 52–59; *TA*, pp. 3–4, 47–53; *ME*, pp. 40–41; *SV*, pp. 1–22; Goodwin, *Exposition*, pp. 157–61, 195–205.

16. For his treatment of the afflicted Goodwin children, see *MP*, pt. I, secs. xvii-xxxii; Drake, 1:lxxxviii, 2:xxi. For his views on Mercy Short and Margaret Rule, see *D* 1:160–61, 174–75; Drake 2:49–54; Levin, *Cotton Mather*, pp. 223–32; Silverman, *Life and Times*, pp. 120–32; Michael G. Hall, p. 273; Middlekauff, ch. 8.

17. Mather's typological explication of the biblical past to interpret the future states the issue point-blank: "You are not Ignorant, That just before our Lords *First Coming*, there were most observable Outrages committed by the Devil upon the Children of Men: And I am suspicious, That there will again be an unusual Range of the Devil among us, a little before the *Second Coming* of our Lord, which will be, to give the last stroke, in *Destroying the works of the Devil*. The *Evening Wolves* will be much abroad, when we are near the *Evening* of the World" (*WIW*, p. 79).

18. See also Mather's address to William Phips, the future governor of the Bay Colony, whom he had baptized, in *CC*, pp. A2r-vA2r.

19. See *SHNE*, p. 37; Hobbes, pt. III, ch. 34, pt. IV, ch. 45. See also Mede, *Works*, pp. 799–802.

20. Froom 3:19–185; Gilsdorf, esp. pp. 71–158.

21. Calef's attack on Cotton Mather and his colleagues for having incited the witchcraft delusion appeared as *More Wonders of the Invisible World*, this title recalling Mather's own *WIW*. Responding to the ministry's defense of the Salem trials and of Governor William Phips (*Return of Several Ministers* [1692]), Calef lashed out against this mutual whitewashing (158–59). See also Trefz; Owen; Middlekauff, p. 327; Levin, *Cotton Mather*, pp. 240–48, 287–88; Silverman, *Life and Times*, p. 88.

22. See also Mede, *Works*, p. 800. Of the ever-lengthening list of publications on Salem witchcraft, several reliable studies deserve to be mentioned: Kittredge; Starkey; Hansen; Boyer and Nissenbaum; Demos; Weisman; Graubard; Karlsen; David D. Hall.

23. Reventlow, pp. 289–334; Reedy, chs. 2–3; Popkin, "Newton"; Force, *Whiston*, pp. 63–89.

24. St. Barnabas, ch. 15; Irenaeus 5.28, 30; Hippolytus Martyr, ch. 202; Lactantius,

Divine Institutes 7.14; St. Cyprian, *Exhortation to Martyrdom*, ch. 11; Augustine, *City of God*, bk. 20; Mede, *Works*, pp. 776, 813–16; Burnet, *Sacred Theory*, pp. 258–59; Ray, pp. 321–25, 397–402.

25. See also *TLF*, pp. 34–44; "PT," pp. 88–89. Lovelace does not consider all the evidence in suggesting that Mather believed the Second Coming "might occur as late as A.D. 2000" (p. 68). And Erwin (p. 210) suggests the year 1745 by relying on Mather's discussion of Daniel 12 in "BA." In this discussion, however, Mather summarizes the theories of Governor William Burnet's *Scripture-Prophecy*, pp. 146–67. But even Burnet himself suggested that according to his reading of Daniel 12, the first of the *"Three Periods"* would expire "in the Year 1715. The *Second* to be expected to expire in 1745, and the *Last* in 1790" (p. 166). Mather's own chronometrical calculations in "Triparadisus," though echoing Burnet's, arrive at somewhat different conclusions (see Figure) from those that Mather paraphrases in "BA." For Middlekauff's discussion of Mather's millennialism, see ch. 18.

26. Pp. 92–109. See also his *Future Conversion*, p. 26.

27. See also *TLF*, pp. 59–61; Edwards, *Work of Redemption*, p. 306; Gay, ch. 4.

28. For Mather's praise of Governor Burnet, see *D* 2:805–6. In W. Burnet, see esp. pp. 26–27, 40–98.

29. Mede, *Works*, pp. 104–6. Mather followed Mede and synchronized the two dream visions. The Babylonian Empire began with Nebuchadnezzar, son of Nabopolassar, the founder of the Neo-Babylonian Empire (seventh century B.C.). In the Persian Empire, Cyrus the Great, who became king of Persia (c. 559 B.C.), rose against the Median overlords and conquered Media (c. 553 B.C.) and Babylonia (c. 547/537 B.C.), thus becoming the ruler of Medo-Persia and Chaldea. In the Greek Empire, Alexander the Great defeated the last Persian ruler, Darius III (Codomannus) (c. 331/330 B.C.). At Alexander's death (c. 323 B.C.), his empire was divided among his four generals: Seleucus Nicator (who took Syria and Mesopotamia), Lysimachus (Asia Minor and Thrace), Cassander (Macedonia and Greece), and Ptolemy Lagus (Egypt and Palestine). The rise of the Roman Empire began with the subjugation of lower Italy (c. 266 B.C.). After Carthagena had lost Spain to Rome during the Second Punic War (218–201 B.C.), Rome sought to expand its realm of influence in the East and annexed Macedonia (168 B.C.), Greece and Corinth (146 B.C.), and Asia Minor and Syria (after 64 B.C.). See *T*, pp. 331–35; see also Huit, pp. 43–61, 173–195; Fletcher and Lee, pp. 118–25; W. Burnet, pp. 40–51, 63–87.

30. *T*, p. 338; W. Burnet, pp. 103–9, 146–47, 150–67; Whiston, *Revelation of St. John* and *Accomplishment*; Newton, pt. I, pp. 24–127; Manuel, pp. 361–80.

31. Mede, *Works*, pp. 105–6, 586–89; W. Burnet, pp. 98–109.

32. Charlemagne (c. 742–814), king of the Franks, whom Pope Leo III (795–816) crowned first Holy Roman Emperor, consolidated his power over the Western Empire, thus diminishing the influence of his rival in the East, Empress Irene (797–802). But Charlemagne did not want the pontiff to become too powerful and reserved for himself the right to veto papal elections, which traditionally were in the hands of the Roman bishops. In 813, Charlemagne crowned as his successor and heir Louis I (778–840), who relinquished to the Roman See the imperial right to veto papal elections, though he continued to demand the pope's oath of allegiance to the Holy Roman Emperor. Even this last controlling element was relinquished when Louis's son Lothair, ruler of Italy, recognized the pope's institutional independence from the empire in the famous *Constitutio Romana* (824). While this document continued to guarantee the allegiance of the Romans to their emperor, it exempted the pope from any such oath.

33. *Sacred Theory*, p. 281. See also Whiston, *New Theory*, pt. I, pp. 58–66; Spinoza, *Tractatus*, ch. VI, pp. 81–97.

34. Force, *Whiston*, chs. 4–5.

35. Louis XIV's persecution of the Huguenots before and after the Revocation of the Edict of Nantes (1685) and his wars of attrition, especially the War of the Spanish Succession (1701–13), reserved for the Roi du Soleil a special place in Mather's eschatology. Mather devoted particular attention to him in his mock-funeral sermon *SD*. See also *UGV*; Rice.

36. Romulus Augustus (also Augustulus, i.e., little Augustus), last of the Roman emperors of the West (475–76), succeeded to the throne when his father, Orestes, of Gothic descent, deposed Julius Nepos, emperor of the West. Augustulus's reign, however, did not last much longer than that of his predecessor, for Odoacer the Hun killed Orestes in 476 and deposed young Augustulus. With Odoacer becoming king of Italy, 507 years of Roman imperial rule (beginning with the Battle of Actium, 31 B.C.) came to an end.

37. I. Mather, *Future Conversion*, p. 26, and *Strange Doctrine*, p. 109 (app.).

38. See also Mede, *Works*, p. 590. Mather speculated in *BO* that during this pause the slaughter of the witnesses (the Saints of the First Resurrection) might be carried out (Rev. 20:4–5): "There is abundance of cause to think, the Expiration of that *Black Period* may have been above Ten Years ago [1716]. What *Pause* our Glorious LORD may now make, before the *Next Thing* which we have to look for, and what He may please to Do in this *Pause*, and whether in this Pause a more General, and a more Terrible *Slaughter of the Witnesses*, may not be carried on, we can not say" (pp. 43–44).

39. Quoted in Silverman, *Life and Times*, p. 417. Peter Lockwood Rumsey also discusses the 1727 earthquake and its effects on church admissions (*Acts of God*, pp. 140–42).

40. See *BO*, p. 44; Wigglesworth, stanzas 1 and 5, p. 55. Young Ebenezer Parkman described the stillness before the earthquake in surprisingly similar terms (p. 27). See also Sewall, *Diary* 2:1055, and *Letter-Book* 2:229–30. On the providential significance of earthquakes see I. Mather, *Illustrious Providences*, ch. 10.

41. See also *TL*, pp. 10–11, 14–15, for Mather's qualms about Thomas Burnet's Deist explanation of the end of the world in *Sacred Theory*.

42. Silverman, *Life and Times*, pp. 418–19; Pope, pp. 99–101.

Chapter 5. Note on the Text

1. For Mather's manuscript page numbering, see the discussion of pagination later in this chapter (point 6).

THE TEXT

Preliminary Pages

1. Samuel Mather (1706–85), Cotton Mather's only son to follow him into the ministry. The "Triparadisus" ms. and a large part of his father's prized library passed into Samuel's hands at his father's death in 1727/28.

2. While the first line bears Samuel's own signature, the remaining passage on this ms. page is in a different hand, most likely that of a librarian who copied the text from Samuel Mather's biography of his father (*Life*, p. 72). The page citations to Samuel's biography are in yet another hand and are penciled on the ms. For Samuel's summary of his father's eschatological views, see pp. 141–46 of the *Life*.

3. John Wyatt or Wiat (fl. 1690–1720), nonconformist bookseller and publisher in London, Rose and Crown, St. Paul's Churchyard.

4. Paradeisus, an ancient city northwest of Damascus (Strabo 16.2.19).

The First Paradise

1. 2 Pet. 3:6. Syntax, spelling, and word usage suggest that Mather's biblical citation, like most others in "Triparadisus," is from the King James Version (1611). However, Mather frequently adapts biblical passages to suit his own syntax. Unless otherwise noted, all biblical references are to the KJV (first edition).

2. See also *TDR*, pp. 9–14. Mather alludes to the discovery of the bones of a mammoth at Claverack, New York (1705), and he took them as evidence of the giant nephilims living before the flood (Gen. 6:1–4; see Stanford. Mather pokes fun at Thomas Burnet (c. 1635–1715), whose *Sacred Theory* postulated that the surface of the antediluvian earth was uniformly level, with neither mountains nor oceans. By this theory, the waters that deluged the globe were contained in caverns below the earth's thin crust, which, upon its collapse, caused the inundation described by Moses (pp. 42–89). Burnet's theories were frequently attacked by his physico-theological colleagues John Ray, William Derham, and William Whiston, whose *New Theory* replaced Burnet's work.

3. The much-acclaimed *Geographia Sacra* (1646) of Samuel Bochart (1599–1667), Huguenot pastor, biblical scholar, and orientalist, went through several expansions and editions. Bochart's discussion of the terrestrial paradise appears in his *Paradiso terrestri*, pt. II, bk. 5, ch. 6, pp. 9–36. The renowned Pierre Daniel Huet (1630–1721) was a member of the French Academy and bishop of Avranches and Soissons. His *Tractatus* was excerpted in many biblical commentaries of the day.

4. The Puritan divine Samuel Lee (1625–91) settled in Bristol, Rhode Island (1686), but returned to England in 1689. His widowed daughter Lydia Lee George became Cotton Mather's third wife (1715). Mather refers to Lee's *Orbis Miraculum*, a copy of which was in Lee's choice library when it was purchased by the Mathers. See Silverman, *Life and Times*, pp. 281–93, 308–13. For the surviving Mather libraries, see Tuttle, "Libraries."

5. Lee's lost manuscript is excerpted in Mather's discussion of Gen. 2:25 in "BA," his commentary on all books of the Bible. Encyclopedic in design and scope, "BA" gathers from all fields of inquiry the most useful knowledge of the day. Mather translates the title of Huet's *Tractatus*.

6. The learned man was Augustin Calmet (1672–1757), Benedictine abbot of Senones and compiler of biblical commentaries. Mather's secondhand quotation from Huet is taken from an English translation of Calmet's celebrated *Dictionnaire historique*. See "Paradise," in *Great Dictionary*, vol. 2.

7. Mather pokes fun at the account in 3 Enoch 17:1–4 (OT pseudepigrapha), where Rabbi Ishmael identifies seven heavens and refers to the angelic Prince Sahaqi'el as the ruler of the fourth heaven, located in Zebul. See 2 Cor. 12:2–4, which speaks only of three heavens.

8. Huet, according to Calmet's excerpt, located Paradise near the confluence of the Tigris and Euphrates, called "*the river of the Arabs*" ("Paradise," in *Great Dictionary*). Whiston was in full agreement with this location, in *New Theory*, pt. II, p. 118.

9. Calmet, "Of the Situation of Paradise" (*Great Dictionary* 4:193–94); Strabo 11.2.17, 11.3.4.

10. Adrien Reland (1676–1718), Dutch professor of Oriental languages and church his-

tory at Utrecht. His speculations appeared in his geography of paradise, "De situ Paradisi terrestris." See also *MAM*, p. 55.

11. How much Mather relies on Samuel Lee's lost manuscript in "The First Paradise" is debatable; much more certain is the influence of Edward Wells, D.D. (1667–1727), rector of Cotesbach, Leicestershire, mathematician and geographer, whose *Historical Geography* supplied Mather with many passages. See 1:1–38; *MAM*, p. 148.

12. An imaginary alchemical substance believed to turn inferior metals into more precious metals, for example, silver into gold.

13. The subsequent text [ms. I, 5-I, 24], appearing also in "BA" (on Genesis 2), is in Mather's earlier hand and was evidently begun in 1712 (D 3:91).

14. The Greek historian and geographer Strabo (c. 64 B.C.–c. A.D. 21) refers to Orontes, a river near Antioch (Syria) variously as Typhon and Paradisus (6.2.9, 16.2.19). Claudius Ptolemaeus (Ptolemy), a Greek astronomer and geographer of Alexandria (fl. 121–51), remained the most reliable and comprehensive of the ancient geographers until modern times (See Ptolemy's *Geography* 5.14; hereafter *Ptolemy*). A Roman historian, biographer, and soldier, Gaius Plinius Secundus (c. 23–79) is best known for his encyclopedic *Natural History* (hereafter *Pliny*; see 5.18–19). The Roman historian Diodorus Siculus covers the history of the world from the beginning to Caesar's Gallic War, 54 B.C. (see 18.39.1).

15. The Adonis River (near Byblus) is associated with the legend of Adonis, who was killed on Mt. Libanus (Ovid, *Metamorphoses* 10; Strabo 16.2.18–19; *Ptolemy* 5.14).

16. Flavius Claudius Julian (332–63), Roman emperor and staunch opponent of Christianity.

17. Alabaster is the name derived from the Egyptian city Alabastra, famed for its quarries. Yet Mather refers to King David's quarries near Damascus (1 Chron. 29:2; *Pliny* 36.18). The river Chrysorrhoas is commonly identified as the river Pharphar, as in Strabo 16.2.16, 19, and *Ptolemy* 5.14.

18. King Hiram of Tyre, who supplied the building material for Solomon's temple after David's death (1 Kings 5:1–10, 7:1–8; 2 Chron. 2:11–14).

19. *Ptolemy* 5.19.

20. See Gen. 3:14, 18, 24; *Pliny* 12.63; Herodotus 3.108–11.

21. Sectarian followers of the Syrian ecclesiastic Nestorius, patriarch of Constantinople (d. c. 451), who held that the divine and human natures of Christ remained distinct. See *IC*.

22. Caspar, Melchior, and Baltharzar, the three Magi (Matthew 2).

23. Gog, also Gug, meaning "darkness" (Samaritan Pentateuch on Ezekiel 38, 39), is historically identified with Gyges, king of Lydia (Asia Minor). Yet most millennialists of the day identified it with the powerful Ottoman Empire, which played a significant role in Anglo-American eschatology. See Mede, *Paraleipomena*, p. 28; Mather's discussion "Where to find *Gog* and *Magog*" (below); *TLF*; *TDP*.

24. Mather quotes at second hand from *De Administrando Imperio* 50.96, by the Byzantine emperor Constantine VII Porphyrogenitus (905–59), whose work was excerpted by Guido Pancirolli (1523–99), Italian lawyer, antiquarian, translator, and author of *The History of Many Memorable Things*. Zenobia (fl. 266–72) was queen of Palmyra.

25. Mather customarily provides his own translation for Hebrew terms. "Before their face" is the literal translation; i.e., "in their presence."

26. Abraham's wife Sarah shared her lot with Keturah, one of Abraham's secondary wives, who bore him six sons, the progenitors of various northern Arabian tribes.

27. *Pliny* 6.32.158; *Ptolemy* 5.14. Ptolemy was nicknamed "the Nubian" because he was born in Nubia, a region in upper Egypt.

28. *Ptolemy* 5.14.

29. Medan was the third son of Keturah (*Ptolemy* 5.14).

30. *Ptolemy* 6.17. Mather refers to the Peutinger Tables (segmentum IX.4–5), a third- or fourth-century map consisting of twelve sections on a long, narrow strip, which survives in the copy made by the German scholar Konrad Peutinger (1465–1547).

31. Emisa, in *Ptolemy* 5.14, 16.

32. Shuah, the sixth son of Keturah, is believed to have been the ancestor of Bildad (Job 2:11). Procopius (b. Caesarea, d. 562) was a Byzantine historian, geographer, and statesman at the court of Justinian I. Mather refers to *Ptolemy* 5.14; Peutinger, segm. X.1.

33. *Ptolemy* 6.7; *Pliny* 6.32.156–59.

34. Made of copper, the brazen serpent of Moses (Num. 21:4–9; 1 Cor. 10:9) healed all faithful Israelites, whose lengthy peregrination is believed to have taken them to a camp-site at Punon (Num. 33:41–43). Jerome (c. 340–420), an important early church father, translated the Septuagint into Latin (Vulgate). His often-cited *De Situ et Nominibus Locorum Hebraicorum*, a geography of Hebrew places (*Patrologiae Latinae* [hereafter *PL*], vol. 23), lists the term Mather mentioned at *PL* 23.199. Gulielmus Tyrius, or William of Tyre (c. 1130–87), archbishop of Tyre (1175), wrote one of the most important medieval historiographies, *Historia rerum in partibus trans marinis gestarum* (begun 1169); the reference is to *PL* 201.209.

35. Aturia in Strabo 16.1.1, 3; Atera in *Ptolemy* 5.14.

36. *Ptolemy* 5.18. Marius Niger was a commentator on Ptolemy's geography. Mather re-fers to Niger's Commentary 5, in *Geographia Asiae*. The Hebrew particle is *El* ("lamed").

37. *Ptolemy* 5.14. The temple of Aphrodite at Aphaca was destroyed by Constantine.

38. *Ptolemy* 5.16. Arabia Petraea is the region including the Sinai Peninsula and nothern Saudi Arabia.

39. *Ptolemy* 5.16. The Greek terms, which translate, "Oboda" and "Place of the Naba-taeans," are those of the Byzantine grammarian and geographer Stephanus.

40. Alata in *Ptolemy* 5.18, in the Syrian desert.

41. Descendents of Abraham's son Ishmael by the patriarch's secondary wife Hagar (Gen. 16:15).

42. The Greek is "Hegra." Jerome's Latin ("Concerning Places") refers to *PL* 23.259.

43. The "Nabathean Regions" and "Nabathean Kingdoms" are mentioned in *Metamor-phoses* 1.61, by Publius Ovidius Naso (43 B.C.–c. A.D. 17), the Roman poet and dramatist. The *Pliny* reference is 5.21.87. See Hermes' winged ram and the Golden Fleece in Apol-lonius of Rhodes's *Argonautica* and Vergil's *Aeneid*.

44. "By inaccessible mountains" (*Pliny* 5.21.87).

45. King Malchus of Arabia Petraea was Caesar's ally during the Roman conquest of Egypt (c. 40 B.C.); Aretas was an Arab ruler of Damascus at the time of Paul's escape from that city; and the Saracens were Bedouin tribes along the Syrian frontier, whose name was later applied to the Moslem Empire before the Turkish conquests.

46. The Latin translates the Hebrew: "it was dark," "concealed," or "made obscure."

47. Meshech was not Kedar's brother but the son of Noah's son Japheth (Gen. 10:2; 1 Chron. 1:5; Ps. 120:5). Mather erroneously applies the name to Ishmael's fifth son, Mishma (Gen. 25:13–15; 1 Chron. 1:29–31). "Adra" is mentioned in *Ptolemy* 5.14, 16.

48. Marcus Junius Nipsus (second century), author of *Gromaticus* and surveyor of rivers and boundaries.

49. Ancient territory of Yemen, renowned for its fertile land and its prosperous people, hence "Arabia the Happy." "*Chisbam*" should be Mibsam, Ishmael's fourth son.

50. *Ptolemy* 5.18.

51. Stephanus's term is "Mesune"; the *Ptolemy* reference is 5.18.

52. Trachonitis is a volcanic region of the northeastern Transjordan area, in High Syria, covered with cinder cones (Luke 3:1). Stephanus's terms are "Surmaioi" and "Salamioi."

53. Mather's *"Noba"* (Nobah) is mentioned in Num. 32:39, 42, rather than in the Chronicles.

54. "In accordance with its eminence."

55. *Ptolemy* 6.7 calls them Ascitae, located near Syagrum, near the sea.

56. The country called Ausitis in the Septuagint is called Gaesa in *Ptolemy* 6.7, on Arabia Felix (Job 1:1).

57. These terms, signifying "fire," are associated with Zoroaster (Zarathustra), a Persian prophet (seventh–sixth century B.C.) whose adoration of the supreme god Ahura Mazda is connected with the worship of fire, the sun, and the stars.

58. Ur (southern Iraq) was the birthplace of Abraham (Gen. 11:28).

59. Laban's teraphim, or family gods, were stolen by Rachel (Gen. 31:30–35).

60. Jerome's descriptive geography (*PL* 23.903) relies on the famous *Ecclesiastical History* of Eusebius Pamphili (c. 260–341), bishop of Caesarea. Mather refers in the latter to 1.6.

61. Peutinger, segm. IX.5. The Roman temple is "To Diana," protectress of women (*Ptolemy* 5.1). Faunus (Mather's *"Fanum"*), protector of agriculture, is associated with the Arcadian Pan. One of Faunus's temples stood near Mt. Horeb.

62. Peutinger, segm. X.1–2.

63. *Ptolemy* 5.14.

64. Probably the city Bethauna, in *Ptolemy* 5.17.

65. The city is Apphadana in *Ptolemy* 5.17. Marcus Licinius Crassus Dives (c. 112–53 B.C.), Roman senator and general in the Parthian campaign, was killed near Carrhae. St. Stephen was the first Christian martyr (Acts 7:57–60). Mather refers to *Ptolemy* 5.18; Peutinger, segm. X.5-XI.1.

66. There is no twenty-fourth chapter in Judges. The most likely Scripture is Josh. 24: 8, 11.

67. Or Negeb, a desert area south of the mountains of Judah.

68. Jacob Golius (Gohl) (1596–1667), Dutch Calvinist, professor of mathematics and translator of Arabic manuscripts. Mather evidently refers to Golius's *Lexicon Arabico-Latinum*.

69. *Ptolemy* 5.17.

70. "Among all things."

71. Heb.: "Eden"; Lat.: "pleasure."

72. "Hedone"; i.e., "pleasure."

73. A mountain chain of Media, formerly called Orontes.

74. The golden fleece of Hermes's winged ram, which took Phrixus to Colchis (*Ptolemy* 5.9). Here the fleece was guarded by a sleepless dragon.

75. The burning pits of bitumen near Ecbatana—which the Macedonian conqueror Alexander the Great (356–323 B.C.) saw during his conquest of Syria and Medo-Persia (Herodotus 1.178–83).

76. Alexander's story is told in Plutarch's *Lives*, the famous character juxtapositions of sixty-six rulers by the Greek Plutarch (c. 45–120), a voluminous writer and minor philosopher. The Greek passage, from *Ptolemy* 6.2, translates, "Chasm of fire among the Ecbatanae." The *Pliny* reference is 6.17.43. And the Latin passage from Tibullus Albius (c. 48–19 B.C.), a Roman elegiac poet, translates, "Or the strange wave burns in the fields of

Aracta" (*Panegyricus Messallae* 3.7.142). Mather's version may be an adaptation of "aret, Araccaeis aut unda Oroatia campis" ("or the waters of Oroatis in the plains of Aracca" or of "Aret Arecteis haud una per ostia campis" (3.7.142).

77. Jerome, *Commentary on Genesis* IV.16 (*PL* 28.201); Ptolemy 6.2. Mather's Olearius is Adam Oelschlaeger (1603–71), a German philologist whose *Newe Orientalische Reise* appeared in an English translation as *The Voyages & Travels of the Ambassadors*.

78. Mather's reference to Pomponius Mela (fl. 40)—first Roman geographer to write a formal treatise on geography—is to *De Chorographia* 1.110, 111, and that to the Roman geographer Gaius Julius Solinus (fl. 200) is to *Collectanea Rerum Memorabilium* 15.17, a work largely gleaned from Pliny and Mela.

79. Mather refers to a hopelessly corrupted work based on first-century maps by Julius Aethicus (fl. fifth century); the reference is to *Cosmographia* 84.

80. Strabo 15.3.4–5, 16.1.1. Rabbi Benjamin (Ben Jonah) of Tudela (fl. 1150–85), the famous traveler and geographer of medieval Spain, was best known for *Itinerarium*.

81. A commentator on Ptolemy's work.

82. The location of Solomon's famed gold mines (1 Kings 10:11; 2 Chron. 8:18) is disputed. See Menasseh ben Israel's *Hope of Israel*, sec. 38, pp. 43–44; "Ophir," in *Calmet's Great Dictionary*, vol. 2; Wells (on whose text Mather relies heavily throughout) 1:5–6.

83. The Greek and Latin quotations from *Periplus of the Euxine Sea*, a work on circumnavigation by the Greek historian Flavius Arrianus (second century), respectively translate, "Country of Pasini," "Region of Pasini," and "Wall of Pasini."

84. The modern Bahrain island in the Persian Gulf.

85. "Huaila" (Hyaela) in *Ptolemy* 6.7.

86. Strabo 16.4.19.

87. Indian Ocean.

88. Mather refers to the Greek historian Herodotus (c. 485–428 B.C.) (1.202); to Tibullus (3.7.141); to the Roman historian Ammianus Marcellinus (c. 330–90) (23.6.40) and to the *History Against the Pagans* 2.6, by Paulus Orosius (fl. 414–20), a Spanish historian, presbyter, and pupil of Augustine. The quotation is from Tibullus: "The rushing Gyndes which maddened Cyrus" (*Panegyricus Messallae* 3.7.141).

89. Cyrus the Great (c. 559–529 B.C.), founder of the Persian Empire and conqueror of the Nabonidean Babylon (539 B.C.). Mather refers to Orosius 2.6.

90. The Greek epic poet, author of the *Odyssey* and *Iliad* (eleventh–seventh centuries B.C.).

91. Zerah was a Cushite general, defeated by King Asa (2 Chron. 14:1, 9–15). Heb. and Lat.: "going round" and "washing," "licking at."

92. The "Royal River" (*Ptolemy* 5.17) is also called Palla Cottas Canalis, a canal (not a river), which Ammianus Marcellinus attributes to Nebuchadnezzar. The yeshiva near Nehardea, which Bochart identifies as "*Naardensis Academiae Doctores ad Euphratem*" (*Opera Omnia*, pt. II, bk. 6, ch. 5, p. 818), was founded in the third century A.D.

93. "He defiled Assyrian Carrae with Latin blood" (*Pharsalia* 1.105), a comment by the Roman poet-historian Marcus Annaeus Lucanus (39–65).

94. The son of Cush (1 Chron. 1:10), Nimrod is believed to have been the founder of the cities of Babylon and Nineveh (Gen. 10:10, 11:3–4).

95. *Collectanea Rerum Memorabilium* 30.3.

96. Pliny 5.20.83–85. Babylon's doom is foretold in Jer. 51:37. The modern Felujah (Felugea), an ancient castle about fifty miles north of Babylon, is situated near the river canal Flumen Regium.

97. A mainstay in eschatological hermeneutics of the day, Daniel's Fourth Monarchy is commonly identified as the Roman Empire and the Catholic church (Mather's "Old & New *Babylon*"). For detail see Dan. 2:31–45; "BA"; "The Third Paradise" (below); *SCM*.

98. "Just like the dog near the Nile."

99. "It has divided."

100. Raleigh, or Ralegh (c. 1552–1618), Elizabethan soldier, mariner, and historian. His account of paradise, in *History of the World* (bk. 1, chs. 3–4), draws on "De paradiso commentarius," in *Epistola populi Nestoriani*, a collection of travelogues by the Belgian orientalist Andreas Masius (1514–73).

101. *Purchas His Pilgrimage*, a valuable collection of travel accounts, was compiled by Samuel Purchas, D.D. (1577–1628), a learned English divine and rector of St. Martin's, Ludgate.

102. Antonio Ferrari Galateo (1444–1516), Italian naturalist, antiquarian, geographer, and author of *De situ elementorum*; Jacques Jansonnius (1547–1625), Dutch professor of theology at Louvain; Jean-Baptiste Tavernier (1605–89), French traveler best known for his *Voyages en Turquie*.

103. "Enclosed place."

104. André Thevet (1502–90), French traveler and cosmographer; the citation is to his *Cosmographie de Levant*, ch. 39, p. 147.

105. Celebrated for its Sylvan beauty, Tempe is a valley gorge near Mt. Olympus in northeastern Thessaly. The Fortunate Islands (Canary Islands), like the Gardens of the Hesperides, were associated with the winterless abodes of the happy dead. The Hesperides (Bernicide) is a mountainous region on a northern African promontory near Benghazi (Libya), whose fabled terraces are placed in Cyrenaica. The mythical Atlantis in Plato's *Timaeus* (25) and *Critias* (109, 113), works by the famous Greek philosopher of Athens (c. 427–347 B.C.), is an island located in the Atlantic beyond the Pillars of Hercules (Straits of Gibraltar). The Greek poet-historian Hesiod (fifth or fourth century B.C.) locates the Elysian Fields and Isles of the Blessed "at the end of the world," where fortunate heroes are translated into life eternal (*Work and Day*). The paradisial orchards of King Alcinous, celebrated grandson of Poseidon and happy ruler of the Phaeacians on Scheria (*Odyssey* 7), need no elucidating.

106. In their prelapsarian condition, Adam and Eve are the OT types of the Second or Last Adam, Christ and his Bride (the church) (Rom 5:14; 1 Cor. 15:45). As the true savior, he is the Homeric counterpart to the false Orpheus, who failed to recover Eurydice from Hades, even though he was able to charm the rulers of the Underworld (Ovid, *Metamorphoses* 10.1–109).

107. The quotation from the Roman elegiac poet Sextus Propertius (b. c. 54–48 B.C.) translates, "Great is the reward, O men [of Rome], the most distant land prepares Triumphs, / The Tigris and Euphrates will flow under your sway" (3.3.3–4).

108. Here ends Mather's excerpt and summary of Samuel Lee's lost manuscript.

109. As was the fashion of the day, Mather's subsequent account is largely cribbed from Wells 1:1–49; Wells relied on Bochart's *Geographia Sacra*, in *Opera Omnia*, bk. 2, ch. 28; and on Huet's *Tractatus*. See Tuttle, "Libraries," p. 354. The passage, "Yett . . . Wells," was inserted in Mather's later hand.

110. Strabo 15.3.5. Jesus Ben Sirach's *Liber Ecclesiasticus* (Wisdom of Sirach) is a Greek translation of a Hebrew apocrypha. For textual similarities to Mather, see Wells 1:13–15.

111. Rabbi Benjamin of Navarre, in Wells 1:15.

112. Niger's Commentary 5 (Wells 1:15 n).

113. Also Shalmaneser, Assyrian king during the times of Hoshea (c. 740 B.C.), last king of the northern kingdom of Israel.

114. *Pliny* 6.27; *Ptolemy* 6.3 (Tabula 5 Asiae); Arrian, *Indica* 40.1–6 and *Anabasis* 7.

115. In *Perseus et Choephori* 421, by the Athenean poet and playwright (c. 525–456 B.C.).

116. The Jewish aristocrat and historian Flavius Josephus (b. 37/38) was best known for his *Jewish Wars* and *Antiquities of the Jews*. The Chaldean Paraphrasts, also called Targum (i.e., interpretation), is an Aramaic paraphrase of the Old Testament compiled in Babylon and Palestine when Hebrew ceased to be the standard language.

117. "Orientals": the Arabic language groups in the Middle East; *Pliny* 6.27.

118. Moses wrote in Arabia Petraea.

119. For similarities to this paragraph, see Wells 1:17–19.

120. *Loetum facere*: "to make fertile." Mather's quotation from the Roman poet Publius Vergilius Maro (70–19 B.C.) translates, "What makes the crops fertile" (*Georgics* 1.1).

121. For Mather's borrowings, see Wells 1:19–21.

122. According to Josephus (*Antiquities* 14.3), Aristobulus bribed the Roman general Gnaeus Pompeius Magnus (106–48 B.C.) and seized the crown and office of high priest from Hyrcanus (c. 68 B.C.). Aristobulus lost in the ensuing fraternal war when Pompey favored the cause of Hyrcanus, took Jerusalem (63 B.C.), and consecrated the spoils to Jupiter in the Capitol of Rome. The Greek words translate, "delight" and "delightful thing." For the rites of Adonis, see Ovid, *Metamorphoses* 10.519–30. Pluto (giver of wealth), the ruler of the Underworld, presided over both good and evil. In this sense, the Meadows of Pluto and the Gardens of the Hesperides are linked with the resting place of the dead in the Fortunate Islands and the Elysian Fields. For Mather's borrowings, see Wells 1:24–25.

123. Mather refers to *Annotationes* 1:4–5 of the great Dutch theologian, philologist, jurist, and statesman Hugo Grotius (1583–1645), whose philological and historical-contextual approach to the Scriptures greatly shaped modern biblical hermeneutics. For Mather's textual similarities, see Wells 1:27–28.

124. As is evident in the ms. from the change in handwriting, here ends the part of Mather's "First Paradise" that he wrote in 1712 and laid aside until shortly before his death (D 3:91; D 2:811). Ms. I, 1–4 and 25–28 constitute his later emendations. See also Mather's letters to Thomas Prince, in *Selected Letters of Cotton Mather*, pp. 410, 415.

125. In the subsequent cancellation (ms. I, 24) (see appendix A), Mather identifies the collector as Hans Heinrich Heidegger (1633–98), a Swiss Protestant theologian, professor of Hebrew and philosophy at Heidelberg and Zurich, who discusses the location of paradise and the descendants of Adam and Eve in vol. 1, ch. 4, of *Historia sacra patriarcharum*.

126. Joseph Pitton de Tournefort (1656–1708), French botanist, traveler, and physician. Mather quotes Tournefort's *Voyage du Levant*.

127. Huet's *Tractatus*.

128. Tournefort refers to the *Universal History* by the Greek historiographer Polybius (c. 205-c. 125 B.C.); to Appianus of Alexandria (early second century), a Roman historian, whose *De Bellis Civilibus* forms books 13–21 of his *Roman History*; and to the Greek historian Zosimus (under Theodosis II), who staunchly upheld the ancient gods (in *The Decline of Rome*) and blamed Christianity for the demise of Rome.

129. Nebuchadnezzar's many building activities included numerous canals connecting the Mesopotamian rivers. The Roman emperor Marcus Ulpius Traianus (98–117) invaded Armenia, Cappadocia, and Mesopotamia (113–15). Roman emperor Lucius Septimus Severus (193–211) was renowned for his successful campaigns in Egypt, Syria, and Mesopotamia.

130. For example, Thomas Burnet's *Sacred Theory* dismissed any efforts to look for evidence of Eden because it hypothesized that the antediluvian earth collapsing upon internal caverns erased any trace of the former garden (bk. I, chs. x-xi; see also bk. II, ch. i).

131. The modern city Tiflis or Tbilisi, capital of the Republic of Georgia, south of the Caucasus.

132. About 28 miles/45 km.

133. Heidegger's "Garden of the First Man" is from his *Historia*, vol. 1, ch. 4.

134. To Brochard (also Burcardus), a Westphalian Dominican friar (fl. 1232) at Avignon, is attributed *Directorium ad Passagium Faciendum ad Terram Sanctam*. The French aristocrat Jacques de Villamont (fl. 1560) is best known for his *Voyages*. Both accounts support the theory of Mather's "Helvetian," Heidegger, who also found an ally in Thomas Burnet, *Sacred Theory*, pp. 94, 98–101, 285.

135. Epiphanius (315–403), bishop of Salamos and opponent of Origen. His *Treatise on Weights and Measures* includes a geographical description of the area.

136. Jacques Davy Du Perron (1556–1618), eminently learned Catholic prelate, cardinal, and later archbishop of Sens, was criticized by Joseph Justus Scaliger (1540–1609), the famous Dutch Lutheran Renaissance historian, philologist, and chronologer. The celebrated French Jesuit and chronologer Dionysius Petavius (Denis Petau) (1583–1652), often called "Prince of the Chronologers," came to Scaliger's aid.

137. Mather pokes fun at *The Testimony of the Soul*, ch. 19, by Quintus Septimus Florens Tertullianus (c. 160-c. 225), one of the most important church fathers. Ambrose (c. 339–97), orator and bishop of Milan, asserted that the sun, frequently clouded in watery vapor, might eventually cool off (*Hexaemeron* 2.3, pts. 13–14). Justin Martyr (c. 100–165), an early Christian apologist, is best known for his *Dialogue with Trypho*. Lucius Caelius Lactantius Firmianus (c. 240-c. 320), the "Christian Cicero" of Bithynia, Asia Minor, objected that the circular representation of the earth would have people standing on their heads (*Divine Institutes* 3.24; see also Hippolytus's *Refutation of all Heresies* 1.5, 6). And Augustine (Aurelius Augustine) (354–430), bishop of Hippo, like Lactantius laughed at the idea of Antipodes with people standing on their heads (*City of God* 16.9). Mather also mocked these "unphilosophical" Fathers in *MCA* 1.1.1–2 and "General Introduction," par. 5. Increase Mather joined the merriment in *Future Conversion*, p. 32, and Sewall, in *Phaenomena*, pp. 34, 42.

138. "You have done admirably; I am much more uncertain than before."

139. "Who such things from the bottom—" (Terence, *Phormio* 459).

The Second Paradise

1. Fifth century B.C. A synopsis of "The Second Paradise" appears in *C*.

2. Also *Shekinah*, Heb.: "that which dwells" or "resides," "the dwelling" (Exod. 13:21).

3. The fate of the just and unjust after death has engaged man for millennia. According to Henaeth 60:8, 61:4, 12; Jub. 4:23, the elect after death—but before Resurrection—go to paradise, located in the far east, north, or west. Other texts, however, placed paradise in heaven, or the Third Heaven, for that is where God took paradise after Adam's fall (Henslav 8:1). Luke (16:23, 23:43) identifies paradise as a temporary resting place where the just remain in Abraham's bosom (see also Test. Abraham 20). The early Christians, however, interpreted this temporary state to mean "being with Christ" (Phil. 1:23; Acts 7:59).

4. Marcus Tullius Cicero (106–43 B.C.), Roman orator, statesman, and man of letters, found the term *Paradises* in *Oecomenicus* 4.20, by Xenophon, an Athenean historian and

general (c. 434-c. 357 B.C.), and rendered it, "A field fenced in and diligently planted" (*De Senectute* 17.59).

5. Paradise is discussed by Julius Pollux (second century), Greek rhetorician, sophist, and grammarian, in *Onomasticon* 1.228, 7.140, 9.8, 13; and by Philo Judaeus of Alexandria (c. 20 B.C.–A.D. 40), a Jewish philosopher and commentator on the Pentateuch, in *Genesin* 1.6–15, 56, in *De Fuga* 62–63, in *Legum Allegoriarum* I.43–63, and in *Opificio Mundi* 153–54.

6. The Roman grammarian and historian Aulus Gellius (c. 117–80) uses *Vivarium* to signify "a place where living animals are kept" (*Attic Nights* 2.20.1).

7. See Herodotus 3.108–11.

8. See my Introduction (ch. 1); Hobbes, pt. III, chs. 34, 38, pt. IV, chs. 44–46; Burnet, *Departed Souls*, chs. 3–4; More, *Immortality*, bk. 1. chs. 3, 9.

9. John Calvin (1509–64), French reformer and theologian of Geneva, was one of the most important Protestant theologians to influence the development of Puritanism. His *Psychopannychia, qua refellitur quorundam imperitorum error* (1542), written against the Anabaptists (1534), appeared in an English translation under the title *An Excellent Treatise of the Immortality of the Soule* (1581). My citation references to Calvin's *Psychopannychism* are based on the modern edition, in *Tracts and Treatises* 3:413–90. Mather quotes from *Immortality of the Soul*, by Hieronymous Zanchius (Girolamo Zanchi) (1516–90), Italian professor of theology at Strasbourg and Heidelberg: "It [Calvin's *Psychopannychia*] is most worthy of being read" (vol. 3, ch. 3); see Tuttle, "Libraries," p. 355. The state of the soul was debated by the Greek theologian and early church father Origen (c. 185–254) (*De Principiis* 2.3.1–4, 3.4.1–5); by Lactantius (*Against Heresies* 2.33); by Moïse Amyraut (1596–1664), French professor of theology at Saumur, in *The evidence of things not seen*; by the English Presbyterian and friend of the Mathers, Richard Baxter (1615–91), in *Immortality*; by Isaac Bates (fl. 1700), in *Not Death but Immortality* (see Tuttle, "Libraries," p. 316); and by the English nonconformist Presbyterian William Bates, D.D. (1625–99), in *Considerations*. See *MAM*, pp. 68, 100.

10. The Epicureans, disciples of the Greek philosopher Epicurus (324–270 B.C.), whose *On Nature* denied the immortality of the soul and thus rendered the concepts of reward and punishment after death null and void, were attacked in Jesus Ben Sirach, Liber Ecclesiasticus (41:1–4). The Roman poet-philosopher Carus T. Lucretius (c. 95–c. 51 B.C.) argued that the *anima* and *animus* (soul or living spirit) are the same as the body and thus have no independent existence, dying with the death of the body. The quotation from Lucretius reads, "It vanishes into thin Air" (3.195–258); see Plato's *Phaedo* 77–78.

11. *Garloup*: gallop. It is unclear which pope Mather had in mind, but this ignominious example incensed Mather sufficiently to resurrect this illustration from his *MP*, pt. III, p. 16.

12. The epitaph of the learned Italian scholar and physician Caesar Cremonius (1550–1631) translates, "All Cremonius lies here."

13. Unidentified.

14. Fig.: "spiritual wilderness."

15. Cebes of Thebes, the Greek philosopher, disciple of Socrates, and author of *Pinax*, allegorizes the soul and its condition before its union with the body, asserting that happiness lies in the development of the mind and the practice of virtue. His confession translates, "A disbelief to the majority." Cicero joins him with, "Crowds of those speaking against it" (*Tusculan Disputationes* 1.77). And Zanchius leaves room for Cicero's "In every thing the unanimity of all peoples must be considered a law of nature" (*Tusculan Disputationes* 1.30).

16. To corroborate the existence of the immortal soul and its lively continuation after the death of the body, many respected theologians and scientists of the day compiled their own collections of ghost stories. See More's appendix to *Treatise Against Atheisme* and his *Immortality*, bk. 1, ch. 13, bk. 2, ch. 16, which sought to invalidate Hobbes's materialist position (pt. III, ch. 34, pp. 286–87). Mather would have definitely disliked Spinoza's ratiocinations on ghosts had he known of the Dutch philosopher's correspondence with Hugo Boxel (1674), in Spinoza, *Correspondence* (*Works* 2:375–88).

17. Mather refers to the English statesman and playwright George Villiers (1628–87), second duke of Buckingham. Mather owned *Observationes Medicae* (Tuttle, "Libraries," p. 350), a medical handbook by Major Thomas Sydenham (1624–87), an English soldier and physician under Oliver Cromwell (see also *AB*). The nonconformist chaplain and surgeon John Webster (1610–82) authored *The Displaying of Supposed Witchcraft* (see Tuttle, "Libraries," p. 310). William Smythies (d. 1692), curate of St. Gile's Cripplegate, London, told the story Mather mentions here in his *True Account*. Mather's references to Nailor and Shaw are based on similar but undetermined accounts.

18. For similar collections of ghost stories and attestations, see *MP*; *WIW*; *MCA* 6.7.66–83; "CAm"; *D* 2:383. Increase Mather gives his in *Illustrious Providences*, chs. 5–7, 9. The popular *Frayeurs de la Mort*, by Charles Drelincourt (1595–1669), minister of the Reformed Church in Paris, was indeed reprinted many times over; Daniel Defoe added to the fourth edition (1706) his "Apparition of Mrs. Veal." See also *D* 2:74.

19. Mather retells the story of Joseph Beacon, apparently a transient resident of Boston, in his *WIW*, pp. 34, 136–39; and in *MCA* 6.7.77–78; and relates his own nightmarish experience in *D* 1:129–30. Through this and subsequent case studies, he counters Hobbes's rationalist analysis of dreams and apparitions, by emphasizing their verifiable impact on the visible world (*Leviathan*, pt. I, ch. 2, pp. 25–27; ch. 12, pp. 87–89; More, *Immortality*, bk. 1, chs. 9–10, 13; bk. 2, ch. 16).

20. A prostitute, mistress, or sweetheart.

21. The identity of Mehetabel Warner (c. 1676–96), a Boston woman who died in 1696, cannot be established with certainty. Perhaps this was Mehitabel (b. 21 Nov. 1673), daughter of Robert and Elizabeth Warner, listed in the *New England Historical and Genealogical Register* (hereafter *NEHGR*) 14 (1860): 135. Mary Johnson of Haverhill is unidentified. For similar ghost stories, see More, *Immortality*, bk. 2, ch. 16, pp. 293–96; I. Mather, *Illustrious Providences*, pp. 239–41; and Benjamin Franklin's Osborne, who "never fulfill'd his Promise" (p. 92).

22. Unidentified.

23. Potamiaina (d. c. 202/3), Christian martyr of Alexandria (Eusebius, *Ecclesiastical History* 6.5), reappeared three days after her death and persuaded her companion Basileides to follow her into martyrdom.

24. For Mather's possible reliance on Henry More and on Increase Mather, see my Introduction, ch. 3. See also *D* 1:129–30 and K. Thomas, ch. 19.

25. "Since the nature of the soul is simple, nor does it have in itself anything mixed with it that is unequal to it and dissimilar" (Cicero, *De Senectute* 21.78).

26. The dying words of Socrates (c. 470–399 B.C.), Athenian philosopher, were recorded in Plato's *Phaedo* 77–78. Tertullian's remark translates, "Not concerning trust of a known truth" (*On the Soul* 58). The dying Caesar comforted himself with the thought, "Beyond there is room for neither anxiety nor joy." The two quotations from Cicero translate, "Explain it, if it is possible," and "Some god will have seen" (*De Senectute* 21, 22). Plutarch's passage translates, "The legendary hope." Mather refers to the Dutch philologist and professor of history, Justus Lipsius (Joest Lips) (1547–1606), author of *De constantia*. The

Stoics were the disciples of the Athenian Zeno of Citium (c. 300 B.C.), whose philosophical system taught that man's soul is partly divine but partly perishable. Lucius Annaeus Seneca (the Younger) (c. 4 B.C.–A.D. 65) was the most important Roman Stoic philosopher next to Cicero. The quotation from Seneca ("Perhaps, if only the opinion of the wise men be true") and his disquisition on the immortality of the soul appear in *Epistulae Morales* 71.16, 102.21–30.

27. Apollinarius (the Younger) (c. 310–90), bishop of Laodicea, acknowledged the deity of Christ but denied that he had a human spirit even though he had a human body and soul. That is, while Christ possessed complete Godhead, he lacked complete manhood. Apollinarius's Christology was condemned by the Council of Alexandria (362) and by the Synod of Rome (374–80).

28. St. Stephen, the first Christian martyr (Acts 7:57–60).

29. Aristotle (384–322 B.C.), Greek philosopher and student of Plato, discusses this issue in *Nichomachean Ethics* 1.7–12 and in *On the Soul* 3.9–12. A close friend of Cicero, Pomponius Atticus (132–9 B.C.) was a chronicler of Roman history. Excommunicated in 231, the Alexandrian church father Origen (c. 185–254) debates this issue in his *De Resurrectione*, which survives in Jerome's *De Principiis* (4.1.36–37). Mather's "Oregins" is probably the third-century Neoplatonist author of *De Daemonibus*, often mistaken for his namesake, the church father (*Paulys Real-Encyclopaedie der Classischen Altertumswissenschaft*; hereafter *Pauly*). The apostle mentioned is Paul.

30. "Whatever for sufficiency is added, it will be attributed to superfluity."

31. "The rest will belong to death."

32. Mather reprints Richard Baxter's letter to Increase Mather (3 August 1691) in *MCA* 3.3.210–11. On his deathbed, Baxter was drawing comfort from reading Cotton Mather's biography of John Eliot, *TRR*, reprinted in *MCA* 3.3.170–210. Eliot (1604–90), Puritan apostle to the Narragansett Indians, translated the Bible into Algonquian and founded communities of Praying Indians.

33. Mather's epithet *"Soul-killing Swine"* applies to such Epicureans as Thomas Hobbes, to whom the soul was nothing more than a vital moving force that vanished at the death of the body. The quotation from Phocylides (b. c. 560 B.C.), a gnomic poet of Miletus, translates literally, "The soul, immortal and ageless, lives always" (Pseudo-Phocylides 115).

34. Mather evidently cites from memory the controversial *Discourse* by the clergyman Charles Leslie (1650–1722), who insisted that only those baptized by Episcopally ordained ministers were truly saved.

35. Justin Martyr (c. 100–165), an early Christian apologist killed during the anti-Christian uprisings in Rome under Marcus Aurelius. The specific works in question are *Dialogue with Trypho* (5 and 105) and *First Apology* (18).

36. For similar insights see "Of Man," in *CP*, pp. 221–304; Silverman, *Life and Times*, p. 252.

37. Mather discusses this physico-theological theory again and again, in "An Appendix Containing Some General Stores" ("BA"), in *CH*, and in his medical handbook *AB*, pp. 28–38. Except for minor substantive changes, "Capsula V. *Nishmath-Chajim*," in *AB*, became the basis for this section of "The Second Paradise." For helpful elucidations, see Beall and Shryock; Middlekauff, pp. 318–19; Erwin, ch. 5.

38. This tripartite distinction is based on Socrates's division into (a) intelligible Spirit, which is immortal, (b) Soul, which is mortal, (c) Body, which is mortal (Plato's *Phaedo*; Origen's *De Principiis* 3.4.2).

39. Johannes Baptista van Helmont (1577–1644), Flemish physician and naturalist. His

medical handbook *Ortus Medicinae* was published by his son Franciscus Mercurius van Helmont.

40. The quotation is from *Concerning the Origin of Things*, by Franciscus Oswaldus Grembs of Salzburg (fl. seventeenth century): "Some middle between the soul and the body and just as a shining and bright air."

41. An ether spirit belonging to the souls that have departed to the stars, the astral spirit was thought to be the carrier of life in the human body. This concept dates back to Neoplatonic, Neo-pythagorean, and Stoic philosophies, in which the early Aristotelean concept that stars and souls consist of the same quintessence—ether—is combined with the Platonic concept of the world soul (*anima mundi*). According to Porphyrios and Proclos, the bodies of demons and angels consist of ether, which also serves the souls as a vehicle, or body, mediating between the soul and the human body. Origen derives from this concept the quality of a revived human body. Both the Aristotelean concept of the astral spirit and the Neoplatonic concept of ether (*corpus spirituale*) enjoyed currency throughout the Middle Ages and Renaissance. Thus Paracelsus classifies all living things into (a) elementary, bodily, *visible* matter and (b) celestial, astral, *invisible* matter (*spiritus*). The latter was believed to be the essence of all matter and to be separable from the body by means of alchemical experiments. Even the disciples of the Greek physician Claudius Galenus (c. 129–99), the most celebrated authority until the sixteenth century, espoused a similar theory (see Galen 1.12; see also Aristotle, *On the Soul* 1.5). The French physician and naturalist Jean Fernel (c. 1497–1558) authored *Concerning the Hidden Causes of Things* (see 2.16), widely used until the eighteenth century (see I. Mather, *Illustrious Providences*, p. 170). The Greek text "To Enormon" (Galen 7.597) refers to Galen's idol, Hippocrates (c. 460-c. 357 B.C.), a Greek physician and the father of medicine.

42. Jan van Heurne (Johannes Heurnius) (1543–1601), a Dutch physician whose major work is *Institutiones Medicinae*. See I. Mather, *Illustrious Providences*, p. 173.

43. "Spirit to serve as salt" (Cicero, *De Finibus* 5.38).

44. "Craftsman and ruler of generation." See Silverman, *Life and Times*, p. 252.

45. I.e., Palaiphatos, mentioned in *Suidas*, a c. tenth-century compendium of abstracts from the classics. Though used as a pseudonym, Palaiphatos is believed to have been the fictitious name of a fourth-century Athenian comedian to whom all sorts of fictitious works were attributed (*Pauly*, pp. 2449–2555). Hence Mather's tongue-in-cheek reference.

46. Traducianism argues that the human soul, along with Original Sin, is passed on from parents to offspring during procreation. Condemned by Pope Anastasius II (498), Traducianism was upheld by Gregory of Nyssa, Tertullian (*On the Soul* 26–27), and Augustine, for whom it signified *spiritual* generation. The Latin passage translates, "Of light from light."

47. Borrowed from the god of the Underworld (*Dii Manes*), the term *Manes* is applied to souls separated from their bodies. It is in this context that Mather refers to Homer (*Odyssey* 10.563–80, 11.30–164), Plato (*Republic* 10.13–14), and Justin Martyr (*First Apology* 18–21 and, for his reaction to Plato and Aristotle, *Exhortation to the Greeks* 6).

48. The first two Greek terms signify "understanding," or "reason," and the last two terms suggest "soul." And Plutarch delivers his doctrine in *Sentiments Concerning Nature* 4.2–7, 23.

49. The Talmud is a compilation of the Jewish Mishnah (oral teachings) and of the Gemara (discussion of the Mishnah), existing in two versions: the Babylonian and Jerusalem Talmuds (c. fifth century). Nimensis (Nemesis) was a female deity widely revered

in Greece, Asia Minor, and Egypt, whose image was often imprinted on coins. The Greek passage, "Distinction according to shapes," alludes to the recognizable shapes of departed heroes, in Homer's *Iliad* 23 and *Odyssey* 11.

50. Mather refers to *Against Heresies* 5.6.1, by Irenaeus, bishop of Lyons (c. 130–200). The first Latin passage, "To preserve the nature of bodies," is from Irenaeus 2.34.1; Tertullian's "Image of the soul and its corporeal lines" is from his *Against Marcion* 2.9 (see also *On the Soul* 7 and 9). The vision of Thespis (Thespesius), a Greek tragedian of the sixth century B.C., is indeed an unpleasant one, since the souls of his heroes return with the ulcers of their passions (*AB*, p. 32).

51. See also Mather's unpublished letters to the Royal Society on how birds make nests and bees, honey: "The Nidification of our pigeons," in "CAm" (first series, 1712) and "*Meliossologia;* with a new Method of Bee-hunting," in "CAm" (1712–22 series).

52. See *CP*, p. 256.

53. The Latin phrases translate, "Motive Breath" and "Weights to be lifted up." Both appear to come from *De Motu Animalium*, by Giovanni Borelli (1608–79), an Italian physician and biologist who developed a mechanical interpretation of the process of life (iatrophysics).

54. For Mather's disquisition on the stomach, see *CP*, pp. 266–68. The Latin signifies, "Ask, seek."

55. Herophilus (c. fourth–third century B.C.) was one of the most notable physicians, anatomists, and physiologists of antiquity (Tertullian, *On the Soul* 10.4, 25.5). Otto Tachenius (fl. 1650s) was a German physician and chemist whose iatrochemical discoveries were published in *Hippokrates chimicus.*

56. Anodynes administered in a chalybeate liquid are pain-relieving drugs that have an iron taste. Georges Baglivi (1669–1707) was for Italy what Sydenham was for England. As a physician of the soul and body, Mather was thoroughly at home in the art of curing by consolation, for his third wife, Lydia Lee George, was given to bouts of insanity. See *D* 2:583–84, 723, 735, 742, 749–50, 755; *AB*, chs. 24–25; *CTM; BV.*

57. For Mather's insights on possession, see *MP; WIW;* "Thaumatographia Pneumatica," in *MCA* 6.7.66–83. Mather sneers at the Jewish sect of the Sadducees (formed c. 200 B.C.), who, like the Epicureans, denied the immortality of the soul and the existence of spirits. For similar reasons, Balthasar Becker (also Bekker) (1634–98), a Dutch Cartesian minister of Amsterdam, was removed from office (1692) when his *De betoverde weereld* gave a rationalist explanation of the "enchanted world," insisting that neither devil nor demon can possess man or incite him to evil.

58. Mather's reference to "Mr. *Nullibist*" appears to be a nickname for those—like Thomas Hobbes—who deny the immortality of the soul. Both Enoch (Heb. 11:5, 13) and Elias (Elijah) the prophet were translated into heaven without first incurring death (2 Kings 2:1–18).

59. The Beatific Vision as the final reward of just souls admitted to behold God face to face was an issue hotly debated throughout the ages. See Burnet's *Departed Souls*, ch. 3, esp. pp. 53–79.

60. The sermons on this issue of George Bull, D.D. (1634–1710), Episcopal bishop of St. David, appeared in his *Collected Works* 1:23–82, 168–92. The bishop of Lycia, Methodius Patarenes (d. c. 311), discussed the issue in *Banquet.*

61. The holy of holies, or *sanctum sanctorum* of the inner temple of Jerusalem, was separated from the *sanctum* by a curtain. Only the high priest was allowed to enter (Exod. 25:40; Deut. 10:14; Neh. 9:6; Matt. 27:51; Heb. 6:19, 10:20).

62. Probably Thomas Taylor, D.D. (1576–1633), Puritan divine and Hebrew lecturer at Christ College, Cambridge, a copy of whose *Works* was owned by the Mathers (Tuttle, "Libraries," p. 351).

63. The Manichaeans were a Gnostic sect founded by Mani (216–76), whose *Kephalaia*, a catechism, combined Gnostic elements with Hindu philosophy, according to which the elect after death are destined for deliverance from transmigration. The early church father Johannes Chrysostomus (c. 347–407), bishop of Constantinople, clarifies this issue in *Homily 73*.

64. "We are become content with these boundaries prescribed for us by divine influence; that the souls of the pious having endured the labor of warfare, yield into blessed rest where they await with fortunate joy the fruition of the promised Glory and that thus they hold all things in suspense until the Redeemer Christ should appear" (Calvin, *Psychopannychia*, pp. 435–36).

65. Ephraem Syrus (c. 306–73), a famous Mesopotamian hymnodist and Christian writer. His treatise *Of the Eternal Mansions* was a Latin translation of a Syriac work.

66. Mather refers to Justin Martyr's debate with Tryphon, the Greek grammarian of Augustan Rome (*Dialogue with Trypho* 5). Photius (c. 810–95) was a Byzantine scholar and patriarch of Constantinople; his *Bibliotheca* covers all sorts of secular and ecclesiastical knowledge.

67. The reference to Irenaeus is to 5.31.1–2. For Tertullian's Elysian pleasure ground, see *Apology* 47.12, *Against Marcion* 4.34, and *On the Resurrection of the Flesh*, ch. 17. (See also Burnet, *Departed Souls*, pp. 70–73.) Tertullian's lost treatise is mentioned in his *On the Soul* 55.

68. Caius (also Gaius) was the Roman presbyter and orthodox churchman (fl. third century) whose debate with the Montanists is mentioned in Eusebius's *Ecclesiastical History* 2.25. His Greek passage translates, "Into a shining place." Origen's sermon on Leviticus (*Homily 7*) debates the issue at hand. Theodoret (c. 393–466), bishop of Cyrrhus (Syria), authored his apologia *Graecorum Affectionum Curatio* in the Christological controversy with Nestorius and Cyril of Alexandria. Theophylact (eleventh century), archbishop of Achrida (1078), is best known for his commentaries on the Old and New Testaments. Chrysostom's discussion of Heb. 11:37–38 appears in *Homily 28.1–2*. And the closing Greek passage, probably from Chrysostom, translates, "To be held in honor together."

69. Mather refers to Ambrose's *Death as a Good* 11.48–49 and to Augustine's *City of God* 20.6–7. The works of John Frith (1503–33), a Marian martyr of Kent and author of *A Disputacion of Purgatory*, as well as those of William Tyndale (c. 1494–1536), the martyred reformer and translater of the Bible into English (1525), were reprinted by the famous martyrologist John Foxe, in *Works of W. Tyndall, John Frith*. Martin Luther (1483–1546), German reformer of Wittenberg who translated the Bible into German, actually rejected psychopannychism. See his *Lectures on Genesis* 25:7–10, pp. 312–13. See also Luther, *Works* 8:318, 15:147–50.

70. Convoked by Pope Eugene IV (1431–47) to safeguard the union with the Greeks, Armenians, and Jacobites, the council met at Florence from 1439 until 1442. See also Burnet, *Departed Souls*, p. 66.

71. Ludovicus Cappellus (Louis Cappel) (1585–1658) was a learned Huguenot professor of Hebrew at the Academy of Saumur (1626). Mather refers to his Latin work *State of the Souls*. The Latin passage translates, "A certain indescribable and glorious joy from that hope and most sure expectation."

72. "Hidden repositories of souls."

73. Thomas Cranmer (1489–1556), archbishop of Canterbury and Henry VIII's chief instrument of church reformation in England, was executed by Mary Tudor. Mather echoes Thomas Hobbes's refutation of purgatory in *Leviathan*, pt. IV, ch. 44. André Rivet, D.D. (1572–1651), French professor of theology at Leyden, delivered his refutation in *De Providentia Dei*; see Tuttle, "Libraries," pp. 346–47. See Vergil's *Aeneid* 6.331–1120.

74. Augustine's "Wherever it is lived well" appears in *Epistle* 57. For his discussion of purgatory, see *City of God* 20.24–25. See Burnet, *Departed Souls*, pp. 95–100.

75. The Greek passage from the Septuagint translates, "He who has wrought" (2 Cor. 5:5), which Mather applies to Bezaleel, the chief builder of the tabernacle of Moses (Exod. 31:1–5, 35:30–35). Mather's quotation from Tertullian translates, "Glory is plucked while they endure the Day of Judgment" (see *Apology* 48.2).

76. See Chrysostom's *Homily* 28.1–2, and *Homily on Saint Ignatius*, pts. 1 and 5.

77. The word from Rev. 14:13 translates, "Henceforth." Mather speaks of *two* resurrections: During the First Resurrection at the beginning of Christ's millennium, the elect who will reign with Christ in heaven will rise first (Rev. 20:4–6; 1 Thess. 4:16, 17). At the end of the millennium, the Second Resurrection, a general resurrection of the just and unjust alike, will occur at Judgment Day (Acts 24:15). The millennialist Thomas Goodwin, D.D. (1600–1680), president of Magdalen College, Oxford, addresses this issue in his *Exposition*, pt. II, ch. 7, sec. 9, pp. 195–205.

78. Titus Flavius Clemens (Clement of Alexandria) (fl. 193–216), Christian convert and prolific humanist writer. Mather evidently refers to *Stromata* 4.6–7.

79. An expository Midrash of Genesis, the Bereshit Rabba has been attributed to the amora Hoshaiah (fl. third century) of Palestine; it was used to instruct youths. The quotation from this work translates, "As long as the just live, they fight with their inborn concupiscence; when they are dead, then they rest."

80. The "Excellent Person" is Thomas Goodwin, and Mather quotes the running title of his *Discourse of the Blessed State*.

81. Mordecai is of course the uncle of Esther (2:5–7), and Bernard (1090–1153), abbot of Clairvaux, a biblical scholar of the Cistercian Order.

82. The voluminous works of Michael Psellus (c. 1019–78), first professor of philosophy at the newly founded university of Constantinople, were collected in *Bibliotheca Maxima Veterum Patrum*. Mather probably refers to *Iamblichvs*. The Book of Splendor (Midrash ha-Zohar), commonly called Zohar, investigates the mystical prophecies of the Torah and of other OT books. Modern critics attribute this work to Moses ben Leon (1250–1305), a Sephardic Jew. For Mather's passage, see "The Destiny of the Soul," in Gershom Scholem's edition, p. 92. Rabbi Phinehas B. Hama was a Palestinian amora of the fourth century. The identity of Rabbi Levi is still undetermined. Mather's *"Vestis Onychina"* translates, "A garment of Onyx-marble," certainly a *"Proper Indument"* or clothing for the just souls (see *D* 2:113). Tertullian's "A place of divine pleasantness" is mentioned in his *Apology* 45.13.

83. The good "Doctor" on whom Mather relies here is Thomas Goodwin, whose *Discourse of the Blessed State* is the work in question.

84. The Latin "Halls from far off" are the receptacles of souls that, says the unidentified Caraval, "Still wait in the halls of God." Mather preached on these celestial receptacles on at least three occasions (*D* 2:163, 285, 402). See Burnet, *Departed Souls*, pp. 95–105, 124–25.

85. The *Life* of the Scottish reformer George Wishart (c. 1513–46) appeared in Foxe's *Book of Martyrs* (1559).

86. Pious Shermerdine is probably Ralph Sherwine of Derbyshire, a Roman Catholic priest who was executed in London (1581) for allegiance to his faith; see Foxe, *Examination* 3:501–3.

87. William Ames, D.D. (1576–1633), leading English Puritan reformer, was an acclaimed theologian at Franeker (Tuttle, "Libraries," p. 314). Mather's Dr. Holland was probably Thomas Holland, D.D. (d. 1612), professor of divinity at Oxford and one of the translators of the KJV (1611); see also *PN*, p. 107.

88. Joachim Curaeus (1532–73) was a German physician and historian; his deathbed narrative appears in *Narratio Historica*. The Latin passage translates, "My breast now burns with the sight of life eternal, whose beginnings I truly feel in myself."

89. Fulvia-Olympia Morata (1526–55), a learned Italian humanist who died in Heidelberg, was married to Grunthler, a German physician of Heidelberg. Her biography and works appeared in *Mulieris Omnium Eruditissimae*. Melchior Adamus (d. 1622), German lexicographer, biographer of Martin Luther, and professor at Heidelberg, collected deathbed narratives in *Dignorum Laude Virorum*. And Gijsbert Voet (1589–1676), a Dutch Reformed theologian and staunch Calvinist, probably retold Morata's story in *Exercitiis Pietatis* (Tuttle, "Libraries," p. 353). Mather's translation, "I am full of Joy," is accurate.

90. Samuel Winter, D.D. (1603–66), provost of Trinity College, Dublin, was a student of Mather's maternal grandfather John Cotton (1585–1652), who was vicar of St. Botolph's, Boston, England, at the time. For information, Mather relied on Winter's *Life*, reprinted in Clarke's *Lives*, and in *Calamy's Account* (1713) (*D* 1:65; Tuttle, "Libraries," p. 354).

91. "The spirit went rejoicing and thus with hope relieved its losses."

92. Mather probably draws on Nathaniel Ranew's *Glory and Happiness, Discourses Concerning Death*, or *Preparation for Death*.

93. Curma of Tullium, near Augustine's seat of Hippo, was a member of the Senate. His death is related in Augustine's *Care for the Dead* 12. Mather derived such stories from Nathaniel Wanley (1634–80), vicar of Trinity, Coventry, and author of the popular *Wonders of the Little World* (*MCA* 2.12.54).

94. Battista Fregoso (1453–1504), an Italian theologian and author of *Baptistae Fulgosi*.

95. Thomas Wadsworth (1630–86), Puritan divine, friend of Richard Baxter, and author of *Immortality of the Soul*, tells the story of Cotton Mather's great-uncle Samuel Mather (1626–71), who is best known for his *Figures and Types of the Old Testament*. For a similar case see *PN*, p. 154.

96. Henry Atherton (c. 1649–95), a physician, commemorates his sister's death in *The Resurrection Proved*. Johannes Manlius (1497–1560) authored *Locorum Communium Collectanea*, a compilation of anecdotes of learned men. See also *D* 2:98–99, 101, 186.

97. Wilkins is difficult to identify. Both *NEHGR* and Pierce's edition of *The Records of the First Church in Salem* (hereafter *Records*) list numerous likely entries. Mather's deathbed narratives are all written like miniature Plutarchan biographies, in which a particular character trait parallels a particular Scripture woven into a person's deathbed experience. The Wilkins account illustrates the story of the lost sheep (Matt. 18:12–13; Luke 15:6). A longer version appears in *MCA* 6.4.3.21–22 and *C*, p. 157; see also *PN*, pp. 168–69; *D* 1:372–73.

98. *NEHGR* lists several persons by the name Thomas Parker. This deathbed account juxtaposes the joys of the convert who gains life eternal with the futility of the person who gains the whole world but loses his soul (Matt. 16:26; Mark 8:36). See *C*, pp. 157–58.

99. John Goodwin's story illustrates the fear of death overcome (Heb. 2:15). He was evidently the father of a posthumous daughter, Abiel, whose life of early piety Mather commemorates in *TFC*. See *MP*, pt. I, pp. 45–53; *C*, p. 158; *D* 1:137n, 596n, 2:694n.

100. This was probably Margaret Rix, who was received to full communion to the First Church of Salem in 1689 (Records, p. 170). She is evidently the same Margaret Rix who settled in Salem in 1652 with her husband, Thomas (NEHGR 8 [1854]: 49). Her story exemplifies endurance (Jas. 5:11; Matt. 10:22, 24:13; Mark 13:13) and was probably related by Mather's colleague, Rev. Nicholas Noyes (1647–1717). See also C, p. 161. Mather's "anhelations" is an archaic term for "panting" or "shortness of breath."

101. This is the deathbed narrative of Cotton Mather's own daughter, who died of consumption in 1716. Mather gives a detailed account of "Kathy's" deathbed struggle in his funeral sermon V. See also C, p. 160; D 2:371, 373–74, 388–89, 390–91.

102. This was Mather's youngest sister (1684–1710), who married Peter Oliver (March 1709/10) and died in childbed seven months later (D 2:38, 57, 59). Her account illustrates the theme of fear of death (Heb. 2:15). See also C, pp. 159–60.

103. This was probably Sarah Frothingham, who was admitted to full membership in the First Church of Charlestown on 23 Jan. 1703/4 (NEHGR 23 [1869]: 443). Her story illustrates Rev. 7:17. See C, p. 159.

104. There are two persons by the name Sarah Brown listed in Records (pp. 13, 47). This case (see C, p. 161) illustrates the popular theme of transformation from fear of death to confidence and joy (Ps. 126:5; Rev. 21:4), which also guided Mather's account of Katharine Holt Mather (PA, p. 86).

105. Apparently Lydia was the wife of John Baily (1644–97), minister of Watertown and later of the First Church of Boston. Her account exemplifies the theme "Death has no Terror" (1 Cor. 15:55) and appeared earlier in MCA 6.7.78–79. See D 1:244–45.

106. This unidentified justice of the peace probably died during the great smallpox epidemic of 1721–22. "Decumbiture" is an archaic term for taking to a sickbed.

107. Mather refers to the religious persecutions during the time of John Knox, in Scotland (sixteenth century), the persecutions during the Restoration, and the persecution of the French Huguenots after the Revocation of the Edict of Nantes (1685) by Louis XIV. Among the many sermons and tracts on that topic are his LTS and PB, the latter of which epitomizes Robert Woodrow's Sufferings of the Church of Scotland.

108. The "German Ephemerides," published by the Academia Naturae Curiosorum, was an annual publication of scientific discoveries appearing under the title Miscellanea curiosa sive ephemerides medico-physicarum Germanicarum. Mather, however, was not impressed by this publication. See CP, p. 227; MAM, p. 51.

109. The quotation from this unidentified work translates, "She, restored, did not give thanks for the services performed for her, but she poured fourth complaints, that the incomprehensible and unutterable calmness of the spirit had been snatched from her and the most pleasing pleasure and such felicity which mortals are unable to enjoy, unless they have been led to that state; that which comes by the name of Joy, offers only a very weak idea of that which she had enjoyed."

110. I.e., expressed little gratitude.

111. Johannes Ludovicus Hanneman (1640–1724), a German theologian and scientist, published a work on the Hesperidean Gardens, Nebo Chemicus. Philip Jacob Spener (1635–1705), "the Father of Pietism," was a German Lutheran reformer best remembered for his Pia Desideria. See D 2:490, 497, 499. Spener's Latin passages translate, "Perhaps we are without true philosophy," and "Perhaps."

112. "So may it happen to me."

113. In light of his earlier problems with the Boston haberdasher Robert Calef, whose More Wonders of the Invisible World had blamed Cotton Mather for the witchcraft hysteria (1692–93) and for endorsing Governor William Phips's inquiring after his fortune

from a witch (*More Wonders* 3:154–55), Mather was naturally concerned about protecting his reputation from any further charges. "There is a *Communion with the Departed Saints*," he protested, "which is indeed so far from its being *Unlawful* to be ask'd for and fought for, that our *Sanctity*, and a *Conversation in Heaven*, lies very much in the Study of it" (*C*, p. 39). Yet he was more circumspect in his intercourse with angels for fear they might turn out to be demons after all (*C*, pp. 92–93; *PN*, pp. 111–13, 119, 131, 133). For Increase Mather's views on this volatile issue, see *Illustrious Providences*, pp. 202–19, and *Angelographia*.

114. During the Second Resurrection, when all are awakened for the Last Judgment of the just and unjust, the latter will be condemned to eternal death (Second Death), from which there is no release (Rev. 20:10, 14, 15, 21:8; Matt. 25:41).

115. Seraphs are a higher order of angels (Isa. 6:1–7).

The Third Paradise

SECTION I

1. Quite different in style and content from the First Epistle of Peter (c. 65–150), the Second Epistle, like its probable source, the Epistle of Jude (c. 65) warns against false teachers who have crept into the early Christian assemblies.

2. Because Peter died during Emperor Nero's reign (54–68), Hugo Grotius denied that Peter could have authored the Second Epistle. The Apocalyptic doom pronounced on Jerusalem (2 Peter 3), Grotius insisted, must have been written after the Roman destruction of Jerusalem (70) by Simeon, bishop of Jerusalem, who lived until Trajan's times (*Annotationes* 2:390–94). Henry Hammond adopted Grotius's preterite method and allegorized Peter's doomsday prophecy as well, in *Paraphrase*, pp. 719–20, 728–29. Origen and Eusebius (*Ecclesiastical History* 3.25) questioned the authenticity of the Second Epistle, and it was canonized only with much hesitancy. See my Introduction, ch. 4.

3. Dr. Thomas Sherlock (1678–1761), bishop of London, whose "Authority of the Second Epistle of St. Peter" was appended to *Use and Intent of Prophecy*. This text and the subsequent *Discourses on the Use and Intent of Prophecy* are Sherlock's attack on Anthony Collins's *Grounds and Reasons*, a daring rejection of the NT literal abrogation of OT messianic prophecies. See my Introduction, ch. 1.

4. Much of Mather's discussion in section I of "The Third Paradise" is extracted from his manuscript annotations on "2. Peter chap. i" and "2. Peter chap. 3," in "BA."

5. The mystical "Whore of Babylon" (Rev. 17:4, 5).

6. Mather's irritated charge does not come as a surprise if we consider how much the allegorical and historical method threatened his literalist eschatology. See, e.g., John Lightfoot's adoption of Hammond's historical-preterite-allegorical method in *Works* 7:78–79, 112–27, 9:328, 354, 11:303–7; and the counterarguments in Burnet, *Departed Souls*, pp. 128–44, and *Sacred Theory*, pp. 295–96, 306–21, 334; and in Ray, pt. 3, pp. 300–321, 392–93.

7. An Egyptian bishop of Arsinoe (third century), Nepos authored the millenarian tract *Refutation of the Allegorists*, which promised a paradisial lubberland on earth during Christ's millennium. He was attacked by Bishop Dionysius of Alexandria (d. 265), and Eusebius relates the story in his *Ecclesiastical History* 7.24–25. Nepos's Greek passage reads, "Refutation of the Allegorizers." Johan Heinrich Hottinger (1620–67), a Swiss professor of Oriental languages at Zurich and Heidelberg, published on this issue *Analecta*

historico-theologica (Tuttle, "Libraries," pp. 307, 332). Hottinger's Latin passage translates, "They have done the greatest damage to Christianity, who without just and serious cause, have spurned literal expositions of Scripture."

8. Cestius Gallus marched against Jerusalem in 66 but withdrew his forces without taking the city, which was finally sacked by Titus in A.D. 70. Mather here targets Grotius, Hammond, Lightfoot, and their disciples, whose preterite-contextual-allegorist hermeneutics deprives 2 Peter 3 of its literalist futurist application.

9. Roman emperor Publius Aelius Hadrianus (Adrian) (117–23) built a shrine to Jupiter Capitolianus on the site of the destroyed temple in Jerusalem.

10. The ecclesiastical writer Salvian (c. 400–480) was a presbyter of the church of Marseilles. His Latin passage translates, "Apart from a certain very small number who flee evils, what else is there within the power of all other Christians than the dregs of vices" (*Ad Ecclesiam* 1.1). Mather's is a corrupted version of "penes omnis caeteros Christianus."

11. I.e., diminution.

12. Mark 13:31–37. Since humans cannot know the time of the Second Coming, they are exhorted to watch for their Master's return.

SECTION II

1. Ahmed El-Ghazali (Al-Ghazzali) (1059–1111), an Islamic theologian teaching at Baghdad, was one of the most important thinkers of Islam; his *Contradictions of the Philosophers* attempts to refute Greek metaphysics. "Keeping in Resenis" signifies "keeping in mind" or "in store."

2. Mather refers to the succession of kingdoms in Daniel's interpretation of the great image in Nebuchadnezzar's dream vision (Dan. 2:31–45).

SECTION III

1. An apocryphal narrative of Christ's infancy, known as the Book of James. It was translated into Latin by G. Postel (d. 1581) and appeared as *Protevangelion Jacobi*.

2. Spiritual Israel (the Christian church) becomes the surrogate of natural Israel, of which event Mather sees the OT type in Ezekiel's vision of the temple (Ezek. 40:5–42:20).

3. Unidentified. Mather tried to emulate the example of his Lutheran colleague (*D* 1:519).

4. Mather adopted this argument from Joseph Mede, who seems to have been the first to establish this connection (1629), in "Epistle XVII," in *Works*, pp. 767–68. According to Nicolaus Gulonius's sixth-century legend, Gregentius (d. 552), archbishop of Tephar (Arabia Felix), and Herbanus, a Jewish leader, debated whether Christ was indeed the long-expected Messiah. On the third day of the raging debate, Christ appeared miraculously in the clouds of heaven and "the Jews were all stricken blind, and received not their sight till they were all baptized" (Mede, *Works*, p. 768). In this manner, a vast multitude of Jews was converted in one day; but to ensure intermingling between Christians and Jews in an effort to erase their distinction, the Jewish converts, under pain of death, were forced to marry only Christians (see Radius). This popular legend appeared in Gulonius, *Sancti patris nostri Gregentii* and was of prime importance to Cotton Mather's eschatology. Yet for many years he vacillated about its veracity. Compare "PT," pp. 33–35; *TMT*, p. 104; *T*, III, secs. iii, vii, xi. His change of mind comes as no surprise, however, when we consider that Mather tried to corroborate his preterite-allegorical reading of Romans 11 with historical evidence from patristic legends.

5. Jerome's passage from the "Preface" to his *Commentary on Isaiah* translates, "That

he [Isaiah] is not to be called a prophet so much as an evangelist" (*PL* 28.772–73) and appears in Jerome's *Apology Against the Books of Rufinus* (*PL* 28).

6. Isaac ben Judah Abrabanel (Abravanel) (1437–1508) was a celebrated Portuguese rabbi, biblical exegete, millennialist, and treasurer to King Alfonso V of Portugal (hence Mather's subsequent reference to Philip's conversion of the *"Ethiopian Lord-Treasurer"* [Acts 8:27–39]). Mather relies on Abrabanel's messianic *Tower of Salvation*, a collection of commentaries on the minor and major prophets. Moses Alshekh (d. c. 1593) was a Greek rabbi and Cabbalist. And the Franciscan Nicholas de Lyre (Lyranus) (c. 1270–1349) was a French biblical commentator whose messianic tract *De Messia* was later attacked by Abrabanel in his commentary on Daniel, *Fountain of Salvation*.

7. Antonius Hulsius (Hulse) (1615–85), a Dutch Calvinist, published his correspondence with Jacob ben Joseph Abendana (1630–85), a biblical commentator and translator of the Mishnah. Hulsius's Latin passage translates, "Torment of Rabbis."

8. Grotius's *De Veritate* was one of the earliest missionary handbooks. In bk. 5, chs. 13–19, of this work, Grotius still insisted that Isaiah's prophecy of a virgin giving birth to a son (Isa. 7:14) was the OT type that was literally abrogated in Christ, the NT antitype (Matt. 1:22–23). Yet in his later work *Annotationes* (1:298–99), Grotius pointed at the incongruence of the two Scriptures and called for a strictly historical application of this prophecy to Isaiah's own time. Matthew's NT parallel was therefore not a literal fulfillment of this prophecy in Christ as the Messiah, he argued, but merely an inadmissable allegorization of its OT original. Mather's mixed admiration for Grotius becomes clear when he charges him with "Judaizing" the prophecies and blames him for such intellectual offspring as Anthony Collins, whose *Grounds and Reasons*, pt. I, ch. 8, pp. 39–50, was the most decisive Deist threat yet to the authority of the Bible. For Increase Mather's reaction to Grotius see *Future Conversion*, pp. 7–8.

9. Mather refers to Samuel White of Trinity College, Cambridge (fl. 1700), author of *A Commentary on the Prophet Isaiah*.

10. The English libertine John Wilmot, second earl of Rochester (1647–80), poet and courtier of Charles II. Infamous for his life-style during his early years, Rochester turned to religion when his health began to fail. His deathbed confession was published in Gilbert Burnet's *Passages*.

11. Mather's argument heavily relies on Whiston's *Accomplishment*; William Lowth's *Isaiah*, pp. vi–vii, 51–64; and Edward Chandler's *Defense of Christianity*, esp. chs. 3 and 6. Chandler's work, in turn, attacks Collins's *Grounds and Reasons*, pp. 39–50. Collins's work was a direct response to Whiston's *Essay Towards Restoring* and charged Whiston with trying to prove Christianity by introducing his own "Whistonian Bible" in an effort to represent OT prophecies of the Messiah as literally fulfilled in the New Testament. Mather intended to enter the debate with the publication of his "Triparadisus" in London.

12. The most decisive argument was waged over how to account for Matthew's allegorization of Isaiah (Matt. 1:22–23; Isa. 7:14). The debate reached its bursting point when Whiston, in his *Essay Towards Restoring*, blamed copyists of the *Masorah* (first century) for purposely introducing errors especially in those OT prophecies on which the early Christians depended for proof of their Messiah. See my Introduction, ch. 1; Reventlow, pp. 362–69; Force, *Whiston*, pp. 63–89.

13. John Green, curate of Thurnscoe. His *Letters* attacks Anthony Collins's anonymously published work by asserting a twofold interpretation of Isaiah's messianic prophecy (Isa. 7:14). Collins was only too glad to retort with his *Defense*.

14. This is the debate described above. William Lowth, D.D. (1660–1732), in his *Isaiah*, attacked Samuel White's *Commentary*. And as noted, Edward Chandler, D.D. (1668–

1750), bishop of Durham, lashed out against Anthony Collins's *Grounds and Reasons*, in *A Defence of Christianity*.

15. See Lowth, on Isaiah 35, in *Isaiah*.

16. This was Samuel Marochitanus (Marrochianus) (fl. late fifteenth century), a converso of Morocco, whose *Coming of the Messiah* was quoted in Mather's missionizing catechism for Jews, *FF*, p. 2.

17. Grotius, *Annotationes* 1:290–91.

18. David Kimchi (Kimhi) (c. 1160–1235) was a French rabbi, grammarian, and exegete; his works influenced Isaac Abrabanel's own exegesis. Mather probably drew for information on Kimchi's polyglot commentary on the minor prophets, *Hosee cum Thargum*. Abraham ben Meir Ibn Ezra (Aben Ezra) of Tudela (1092–1167) was a distinguished Jewish OT exegete, philosopher, poet, and physician of medieval Spain.

19. Herman Witsius (Wits) (1636–1708), eminent Dutch Calvinist and professor at Franeker, Utrecht, and Leyden. Mather's corrupted Latin text translates, "To observe the embarrassment of the blind and infidel Jews is necessary for those of us, for whom it is not religion to twist so plain a prophecy in a different direction." The Latin original in Wits reads, "Qua caeci caeteroquin Judaei observatione in ruborem eos ex nostris dari oportet, quibus tam insigne vaticinium aliovorsum torquere religio non est." This text is from "Dissertatio VIII. De Prophetia, Jesaiae XLII:1. Impleta in Jesu Matth. XII:16," sec. 4, in *Meletemata Leidensia*, p. 282; see also pp. 281–86.

20. Evidently Dr. Thomas Goodwin.

21. Mather slightly condenses this passage from Goodwin's *Christ Set Forth*, sec. 1, ch. 1, pp. 7–8.

22. Jerome's *Commentary on Isaiah* (50:10) (*PL* 24.582).

23. Geber was the father of one of Solomon's twelve deputies (1 Kings 4:7, 13, 19). Samson was the man who lost his hair to Delilah. His birth was announced to Samson's mother by an angel (Judg. 13:2–7). A similar angelic *nuncius* appeared to Mary, mother of Christ, and to the mother of John the Baptist (Luke 1:5–14, 26–38).

24. Judah Monis (d. 1760), who taught Hebrew at Harvard from 1722–1760 (*D* 2:741, 743). But see also Friedman, "Mather and the Jews" and "Early Jewish Residents." See also *D* 1:200, 300, 315, 2:62, 741n, and passim.

25. Mather refers to the translators of the KJV (1611) rather than those of the Septuagint (LXX) to which Mather refers below. The marginal reference to Lam. 4:20 mentioned here appears in the KJV next to Matt. 26:56.

26. Marrochianus's conversion was celebrated in his *Blessed Jew of Marocco*.

27. Mather employs Marrochianus's exegesis of Amos, Hosea, Micah, Nahum, Zephania, Habakkuk, and Zechariah (see Mather's commentary on these minor prophets in "BA").

28. John Beart, pastor of Bury, Suffolk, authored *A Vindication of the Eternal Law*. Mather follows Beart's exegesis below in rejecting Hos. 6:2 as the *"Third Redemption,"* the first two being Israel's redemption from Egyptian and Babylonian captivity.

29. Sebastian Münster (1488–1552) was a German Reformed theologian, Hebraist, and cosmographer; his most important works are *Biblia Hebraica* and *Cosmographia*. The quotation translates, "Christians understand this more truly, of the Third Day, on which Christ rose from the Dead."

30. Grotius's *Annotationes* 1:406 calls it Galgal.

31. Mather quotes the *Commentaria in Psalmos* of Joannes Baptista Folengius (Folengo) (1490–1559), an Italian Benedictine monk: "Christ is the fulfillment of the whole volume of the Psalms."

32. See Psalms 16; 56; 57; 60. Jacques Gousset (1635–1704), Huguenot pastor at Dort (1687), later professor of Greek and theology at Groningen.

33. This is Mather's peculiar mystical-allegorical-literal reconciliation of the historical method of Grotius, Hammond, Simon, and Collins with the literalist abrogation of OT prophetic types in the New Testament.

34. The "Gentleman" was Richard Simon (1638–1712), a French Catholic theologian, professor of philosophy, and biblical exegete, whose historical and textual criticism of the Bible in *L'Histoire critique du Vieux Testament* was highly controversial and gained him the censure of the church. For detail see my Introduction, ch. 1. The sentence passed on Simon was "A very criminal audacity." David Martin (1639–1721), Huguenot professor of theology and philosophy at Utrecht, published his French refutation of Simon's work in Utrecht (1717). It appeared in English in 1719. See Reventlow, pp. 335–41; Reedy, ch. 5.; Popkin, "Newton."

35. We can perhaps appreciate Mather's unusually passionate outburst if we remember what a phenomenal challenge this new historical and textual criticism of the Bible posed for the old-guard theologians whose faith in the promised Messiah was grounded in the bedrock of literalist typology. See my Introduction, ch. 1.

36. Until late in his life (c. 1720), Mather held fast to the premillennialist tenet of the literal restoration of the Jewish nation, whose return to Palestine was foretold by Paul (Romans 11). As Christopher Hill and others have shown, the literal fulfillment of this prophecy just before the Second Coming was doubted by few ("Till the Conversion"). Only those who viewed Romans 11 as an allegory of the Christian church would eventually dismiss its inherent typological correspondence with OT precedent (see my Introduction, chs. 2, 4). The sweeping implications of this issue for early American millennialists and their view of America's eschatological role I have discussed in my Introduction and in "*Israel Redivivus.*"

37. Heb.: "Not my people," the typological name of the second son of Gomer, by Hosea's wife (Hos. 1:8, 9). See Spinoza, *Tractatus*, ch. III, pp. 54–56. For Increase Mather's differing views on this issue, see *Mystery*, pp. 48–51, 69, 77, and his later work *Future Conversion*, p. 10.

38. Roman emperor Justinian (527–64) engaged in a massive construction of public buildings, which included Sancta Sophia at Constantinople, his grandest achievement and the temple to which Mather refers. Solomon's temple, the first temple in Jerusalem (c. 970–930 B.C.) was destroyed in c. 586 B.C. by the Babylonians. See also *ATC*, p. 24. The "*Little Stone*" is Christ's millennial kingdom foretold in Daniel's prophetic dream (2:45). See *SCM*.

39. Cotton Mather's catechism for the conversion of Jews, *FF*, is the epitome of his millennialist endeavor to speed up the Second Coming by bringing Israel into the Christian fold.

40. I.e., the Mosaic law.

41. "The prophet speaks in figures that are appropriate to his own period." John Calvin makes a similar point in his *Praelectiones in Ieremiam*, ch. 33:15, p. 67.

42. Son of the high priest of Israel, Onias IV (second century B.C.) faltered in his candidacy for his father's office. Onias went to Egypt and built a temple in Leontopolis (c. 145 B.C.). Josephus Flavius regarded Onias's temple as blasphemous, and the priests at Jerusalem did not recognize their rivals in Leontopolis. Vespasian closed the temple in 73 B.C. (Josephus, *Antiquities* 13.3 and *Wars* 7.10).

43. Son of Sargon II and king of Syria, Sennacherib carried on a campaign in Palestine that was successful until he threatened Hezekiah that he would besiege Jerusalem

(c. 732 B.C.) (2 Kings 18:17–35), at which time an angel struck down the invader (Isa. 37:9–37; 2 Chron. 32:21).

44. *Miscellanea Sacra*, by John Shute (1678–1734), first viscount Barrington, a lawyer, polemic, and Christian apologist.

45. Gr.: "The Saved" (Luke 13:23; Acts 2:47). Mather here leans on Lowth's *Isaiah*.

46. Pekah, king of Israel (c. 778–758 B.C.), formed an alliance with Rezins, king of Syria (c. 777–762 B.C.), to march against Judah (2 Kings 16:7–9). The prophet Isaiah doomed this alliance and predicted the failure of their mission (Isa. 7:6–7).

47. Jean D'Espagne (1591–1659) was a Huguenot theologian whose voluminous works were translated into English. Mather refers to D'Espagne's *Shibboleth*. The bishop of Rome is of course the pope as Antichrist in Protestant eschatology.

48. The religious center of the Ituraean tetrarchy, Heliopolis became a Roman colony (16 B.C.) and was renowned for its elaborate temples to Jupiter-Hadad, Bacchus, and other gods. Mather's reference to the Greek geographer Strabo is one of the many instances where Mather rejects Joseph Mede's eschatological view that Christ's millennial kingdom would be confined to the terrain of the Roman Empire ("Strabo's cloak") as the apostles knew it. Mather's irritation becomes intelligible when we remember that Mede's conjecture excluded the American hemisphere from the Christianography of the millennium. See Mede's *De Gogo & Magogo*, in *Works*, pp. 574–76; *MCA* 1.2.1–5; my article "*Israel Redivivus*," pp. 369–74 and app. 3, p. 395. William Jameson (fl. 1689–1720) was a blind Presbyterian controversialist who lectured at Glasgow (*D* 2:205; Tuttle, "Libraries," pp. 303, 307, 333; Silverman, *Selected Letters of Cotton Mather*, p. 179).

49. This was probably Abrabanel; the Latin translates, "This lock of the book is greater than the lock with which God closed our hearts."

50. The "Ingenious Man" was Lowth, in his *Isaiah*.

51. Probably John Templer, D.D. (d. 1693), an Episcopal sermonist and author of *Idea Theologiae Leviathanis*.

52. Cyrus the Great (c. 559–529 B.C.), founder of the Persian Empire and conqueror of Babylon. It was to him that Isaiah's prophecy—that the predicted fall of Babylon would usher in the release of the Jews from captivity—was applied.

53. St. Helena (c. 255–330), mother of Emperor Constantine (c. 274), established basilicas in Bethlehem and on the Mount of Olives, where according to tradition the cross of Christ was discovered. Artaxerxes I (Ahasuerus) (fl. 486–464 B.C.) was king of Persia; his Jewish consort, Esther (Mordecai's niece), used her influence to save her people from annihilation by Haman, Ahasuerus's grand vizier (Esth. 7:1–7).

54. For a defense of infant baptism, see New England's own Thomas Shepard (1605–49), *Church-Membership*.

55. See Mather's commentary on Zechariah in "BA." Mather's references to the typological parallels between Zechariah and the Gospels are as follows: (1) Christ's riding on a colt (Zech. 9:9; Matt. 21:5; John 12:15); (2) thirty pieces of silver (Zech. 11:12, 13; Matt. 26:15, 27:9); (3) scattering of the disciples (Zech. 13:7; Matt. 26:31; Mark 14:27); and (4) the piercing of Jesus (Zech. 12:10; John 19:34, 37).

56. The reference is to Daniel's interpretation of Nebuchadnezzar's visionary statue, whose various metals signified a succession of empires (Dan. 2:31–45).

57. Plutarch's *De defectu oraculorum* argues that the oracles became obsolete because decreasing numbers of people inquired after their fortunes. Whereas in ancient times three prophetesses served at Delphi, now only one was needed (*Moralia* 5.410–38).

58. See Mather's commentary on Zephaniah 3 in "BA."

59. Samuel Bochart's disquisition appears in *Opera Omnia*. Abrabanel's outcry trans-

lates, "Far be it from me that I should believe this." For Jerome's view on Joel, see *PL* 28.1083, and for that of Cyril of Alexandria, see *Patrologiae Graecae* (hereafter *PG*) 71.200, 225.

60. Mather's *PS* was a blank-verse translation of the Psalms, which he deemed "the most *Prophetical Book* in the World." See his "PROPOSAL for Printing by Subscription, PSALTERIUM AMERICANUM" (Boston, 1718); *D* 2:528, 540–41; Silverman, *Life and Times*, pp. 304–5. The "Learned Man" is evidently the famous Isaac Watts (1674–1748), author of *Psalms of David*, with whom Mather corresponded on the subject (*D* 2:142; Silverman, *Selected Letters of Cotton Mather*, pp. 311–12, 188–89).

61. Mather cites Rev. 17:1. For Jerome's Antichrist, see *Homily on Psalm 5*; and for Augustine, *City of God* 8.24 (Psalm 95).

62. Nicolaus Guertler, D.D. (1654–1711), Swiss theologian of Basel, professor of philosophy at Herborn (Germany) and Franeker (Holland). The actual title of his book is *Dissertationes de Jesu Christo in gloriam evecto* [*Disquisition on Christ raised in Glory*].

63. Abraham and Sarah were buried in the cave of Machpelah (Gen. 25:8–10).

64. Mather cites his own *PS*.

65. "To the leader in the generation" (Kimchi, *Commentariis in decem Psalmos*).

66. "Flood of Fire," or conflagration of the world at the Second Coming. Its OT type was Noah's flood (Ovid, *Metamorphoses* 1.254–61).

67. The "Sensible Interpreter" was William Lowth, on whom Mather relies throughout.

68. This is Mather's response to the disciples of Grotius and Hammond, who argued that the sacred oracles must be understood as historical literature whose prophetic purport has no literal fulfillment beyond the prophets' own times (see my Introduction, ch. 1).

69. Tophet (Isa. 30:33), a place of human sacrifice in the Valley of Hinnom, near Jerusalem, is used figuratively to signify "a place of burning," indicative of the destruction of Assyria predicted by Isaiah. Mather thus interprets the passage "*By the King*" to signify "by Satan," whose destruction in "*Everlasting Fire*" is here foretold. The "*Vicar* at *Rome*," who is to have a part in Satan's destruction, is, of course, the pope.

70. The expositor is John (Rev. 14:14–20, 19:11–16).

71. Actually, "In consummatione mundi," "the consumption [as by fire] of the world" (*PL* 24.331). Jerome is commenting here on Isa. 24:9.

72. An error for "*Holy Temple*" (KJV and Geneva).

73. The pope's headdress, the tiara, or triple crown, resembles a beehive, signifying the threefold power of the papacy.

74. In Hos. 2:21–23, *Jezreel* is used in its prophetic context of bringing back the remnant of Israel and Judah to the Promised Land (see Zech. 10:8–10). Jehu was the king of Israel (c. 843–816 B.C.) who opposed the worship of Baal but advocated the worship of calves at Dan and Bethel, for which practice he was reproached (2 Kings 10:29, 31). William Alleine, D.D. (1614–77), was nonconformist vicar of Bridgewater, Somerset, and private chaplain to Lord Digby of London. Mather evidently refers to Alleine's *Mystery of the Temple and City*.

75. See Grotius's *Annotationes* 1:409–10.

76. Sebastian Münster's Latin translates, "The expression of thanks concerning the glory of the righteous on the Day of Judgment."

77. For the debate on America's place in the Christianography of the millennium, see Mede, *Works*, pp. 574–76; Twisse, Epistle 42, in Mede (*Works*, pp. 798–99); Sewall, *Phaenomena*, pp. 27–64; C. Mather, *TA*, pp. 42–51; and Smolinski, "*Israel Redivivus*," pp. 369–82.

78. I.e., King David (Ps. 103:4, 5).

79. Joseph Mede (1586–1638), biblical scholar, astrologer, Egyptologist, was one of the most important millennialists of the early seventeenth century. The Mathers owned a copy of John Worthington's enlarged edition of Mede's *Works* (Tuttle, "Libraries," pp. 281, 309, 338).

80. Lowth, *Isaiah* (Isa. 45:18).

81. Ibid., p. 479. See also Isa. 60:21.

82. For these and subsequent passages from the Book of Psalms, Mather uses his own translation from *PS*.

83. Mather's lines are freely adapted from Homer's *Iliad* 20.54–71, 491–503.

84. Dionysius Cassius Longinus (213–73), Greek philosopher, visited Queen Zenobia of Palmyra on one of his travels to Emesa, Asia Minor. Longinus is mostly known for his *On the Sublime*, a literary treatise discussing the elements that constitute literary greatness in oratory and poetry.

85. The mischievous individual is probably Samuel White, who rejected the hyperbolic terms of the Psalms and insisted on a strictly historical approach to the prophecies. See also *D* 2:728. Mather's vehemence can be appreciated in light of Spinoza's anonymously published *Tractatus* (1670), where the Jewish philosopher voids such typological readings by attributing matters of style to the prophets' different temperaments and imaginative abilities (ch. II, pp. 29–32; ch. VI. pp. 94–95).

86. Sir Richard Blackmore (d. 1729), a physician and writer of verse and prose whose income had to be supplemented by teaching school. Blackmore's poetic works included a rhyming translation of the Psalms, *New Version of the Psalms of David*, and *Redemption*, for which he became the laughingstock of his contemporaries. Though Blackmore was later ridiculed by John Dennis and Alexander Pope (*Dunciad*), Cotton Mather liked Blackmore's poetry exceedingly and considered him "the equal of Homer & Vergil" (see Mather's annotations on Job 1:1–3 in "BA"; *D* 2:105, 141). So much for taste.

87. "*Teague*" is a derisive nickname for an illiterate Irishman. Scaliger's Latin response to the flattering Hibernian translates, "Sir, I do not understand Irish," and Mather's witticism, "Sir, I do not understand Irish Latin."

88. Psalms 147–50. From Heb.: *Alleluia*, signifying "Praise Ye Yah."

SECTION IV

1. This section is excerpted from Mather's "Article IX," appended to "The Four Gospels" in "BA." In turn, much of this section is cribbed from Dr. Humphrey Prideaux's *Old and New Testament*, vol. 2, bk. 9, pp. 397–406. The Sibylline oracles were a collection of exclamatory statements couched as prophetic riddles in hexameter verse, circulating in Athens during the fifth century B.C. Because of their strong messianic themes, they enjoyed widespread popularity. References are to J. J. Collins's edition.

2. Augustine's Latin passage translates, "If the Sibyls are held to have foretold true things, it avails [us] somewhat to prove the foolishness of the Pagans, but not to embrace their Authority" (*Sibyllinorum Verborum Interpretatio*) [*PL* 90.1181–86]; see also *City of God* 18.23]. Increase Mather's low opinion of the Sibyls is evident in *Future Conversion*, p. 23. Notwithstanding their cautious use, the Sibylline Oracles were hotly debated by William Whiston, who wrote *A Vindication of the Sibylline Oracles*, and by Edward Chandler, in *Defense of Christianity*, ch. 1, sec. 1, pp. 10–35.

3. Accounts of these ten Sibyls vary greatly, but all are said to have got their name from the first Sibyl, believed to be the daughter of Dardanus and Neso. The most famous of them all is the Cumaean Sibyl, who is supposed to have sold the oracles to Tarquinius.

4. Justin Martyr, *Exhortation to the Greeks* 37. Vergil describes the ecstatic nature of the Sibyls in *Aeneid* 6.77–102 and adapts the lines in his *Fourth Eclogue*, lines 1–61.

5. That is, in "A.C. 1539" ("Article IX," in "BA"). Onofria Panvinio (1529–68) was a learned Italian of Verona, an Augustinian monk, a historian, and a biographer. Among his most celebrated works is *De Sibyllis et Carminibus.*

6. Mather's account is based on the travel report of George Sandys and Lassel (Prideaux 2:398, n. 1).

7. Tarquinius Priscus (c. 616–579 B.C.), fifth king of Rome. The story of the sale of the Sibylline Oracles is told in Pliny, *Natural History;* in Lactantius, *Divine Institutes* 1.6 and *De Falsa Religione* 1.8; in Dionysius Halicarnas 4; and in Aulus Gellius 1.19.

8. The Capitol burned in 83 B.C. and was rebuilt in 76 B.C. The story is told in Appian, *De Bellis Civilibus* 1; in Tacitus, *Historia* 3.72; and in Lactantius, *De Falsa Religione* 1.6, *De Ira Dei* 22, and *De Falsa Sapientia* 1.17.

9. Octavius Caesar Augustus (63 B.C.–A.D. 14), first Roman emperor, was succeeded by the infamous Tiberius Julius Caesar Augustus (42 B.C.–A.D. 31). The story of the destruction of spurious versions of the oracles is told in Tacitus, *Annales* 6.12; in Suetonius 31; and in Dion Cassius 57.

10. See Plutarch's *De defectu oraculorum* (*Moralia* 5.410–38).

11. Flavius Honorius (384–423), Roman emperor of the West. In "BA," Mather identifies the year when the oracles were used for a final time as "A.C. 399." The *"Abominable Rites"* included human sacrifices (Prideaux 2:400, 402).

12. Publius Aelius Hadrianus, Roman emperor (117–38), chose as his successor Antonius Pius (Caesar Titus Aelius Hadrianus), who ruled Rome from 138 to 161. The reference to Adrian (Hadrian) appears in Sibylline Oracles 5.47, often quoted in Justin Martyr's *First Apology* 20 and *Exhortation to the Greeks* 16. Mather's entire paragraph closely follows Prideaux 2:400.

13. Isaak Casaubon (1559–1617), Swiss-French philologist and librarian to Henry IV of France and to James I of England. Among his many editions of the classics is Casaubon's edition of Panvinio's *De Sibyllis et Carminibus;* the Latin translates, "Those oracles, the more lucid they are, the more dubious they seem" (bk. 8).

14. Mather refers to bk. 3 of the oldest of the Jewish Sibylline Oracles, which identifies the Sibyl as one of Noah's daughters-in-law. This account closely resembles that of the Babylonian Sibyl Sambethe (Prideaux 2:401).

15. Sibylline Oracles 3.97–105; Justin Martyr, *Exhortation to the Greeks* 6, 37; Josephus, *Antiquities* 1.4–5.

16. Clement of Alexandria (150–215), Gnostic theologian, was born in Athens. Mather's references appear in Clement's *Protrepticus* 4.44, 54, 6.61, and *Stromateis* 5.1.5.1, 5.10.65.4.

17. Flavius Vopiscus (third century) was one of the six Scriptores Historia Augustae. Vopiscus's letter to Lucius Domitius Aurelianus (c. 215–75), subsequently emperor of Rome (270–75), appears in Vopiscus's biography *Aurelianus.* The Sibylline prophecies were written in Greek hexameter verse. To guarantee genuineness, they were often rendered in acrostics. For Cicero's views, see *De Divinatione* 2.54.110–11. The Greek quotation is from Augustine's *City of God* 18.23; it translates, "FISH" or "IKTHUS," and in Greek it represents the acrostic initials of "Jesus Christ the Son of God the Savior." See "Article IX," in "BA"; Prideaux 2:401–2.

18. This is, of course, Humphrey Prideaux, D.D. (1648–1724), dean of Norwich, on whose *Old and New Testament* Mather has been drawing all along.

19. Son of Beor (fifth century B.C.), Balaam lived in Pethor, upper Euphrates. Though not an Israelite, he acknowledged the God of Israel (Num. 22:5, 18).

20. In *Contra Celsum* 7. See Prideaux 2:406.

21. Chandler, pp. 10–35.

22. Hesychius of Alexandria (fifth century), lexicographer, whose lexicon is known from a Renaissance manuscript.

23. James Ussher (1581–1656) was archbishop of Armagh, a voluminous exegete, and author of *Annales Veteris et Novi Testamenti* (Tuttle, "Libraries," p. 310). Gerhard Johann Vossius (1577–1649) was a famous Dutch scholar, a professor of history at Amsterdam, and a friend of Laud and Ussher. His *Historia Pelagiana* was well received in England (Tuttle, "Libraries," p. 353). See also Augustine, *City of God* 18.23; Prideaux 2:402.

24. Caius Julius Caesar, the dictator (100–44 B.C.) was uncle and predecessor of Octavianus Caesar Augustus. Cicero offered his doubts in *De Divinatione* 2.54.110–11, and Vergil has the priestess address Aeneas with the words, "Anchises' son, true offspring of gods," in *Aeneid* 6.321. Emperor Octavius Augustus divorced his much older wife, Scribonia, on the day she gave birth to a Julia rather than a Julius (39 B.C.). And Vergil's prophecy of the great king appears in *Fourth Eclogue*, lines 4–17.

25. Herod the Great (c. 73–4 B.C.) was the son of Antipater, king of Judea, and builder of the last temple of Jerusalem. Herod's two sons were Herod Antipas (who executed John the Baptist) and Philippus Herodes, half-brother of Antipas. Asinius Pollio (76 B.C.–A.D. 4) was a distinguished poet, historian, and orator of the Augustan Age. Out of his love for literature, Pollio saved Vergil's property at Mantua from confiscation, and Vergil's *Fourth Eclogue* is dedicated to him. For close textual similarities to Mather's entire paragraph, see Prideaux 2:402; Chandler, p. 14.

26. Flavius Stilicho (fl. 395–408) was a Roman general under Emperor Flavius Honorius Augustus, upon whose decree Stilicho burned all remaining Sibylline Oracles and razed the temples to Apollo. See Augustine's *City of God* 18.53–54.

27. Mather's textual adaptation from his fuller discussion in "Article IX" ("BA") ends at this point.

28. Mather refers to the mystical temple in Ezekiel's vision (Ezek. 40:1–43:27), rather than the much-detested temple of Herod the Great. In Mather's mystical explication, the sizes of the outer and inner courts in Ezekiel's vision were in the same proportion as that of 365 days to 1,260 days/years, the period of Antichrist's reign (Rev. 11:3). For this typological reading, Mather drew on Joseph Mede's *Paraleipomena*, pp. 18–19, and *Works*, pp. 588–89.

29. Evidently from *Rutilii Itinerarium* 2: "Let it be of as much help as it can" (Prideaux 2:400).

30. Lactantius discusses the Sibylline Oracles at great length in his *Divine Institutes* 7.14–27, but Mather's Greek quotation, which translates, "Depriving all by a conflagration," is from Lactantius's *De Ira Dei* 23.5. Lactantius, of course, echoes the Sibylline passage, "Destroying the entire race of men at once by a great conflagration" (Sibylline Oracles 4.160–61). The Latin phrase, quoted from the *Chronicle* of the French monk Prosper Tiro (c. 390–463), translates, "The Earth will be destroyed and will perish." Mather translates the remainder of Prosper's epigrammatic couplet himself. The *Chronicle* was based on Jerome's translation of Eusebius's *Chronicles*; hence Mather's dismissal of Prosper's "*Second-hand* Things." Mather's colleague John Ray, fellow of the Royal Society, debated the same point in the third edition of his *Three Physico-Theological Discourses*, pp. 334–35.

31. "And at that time a mighty river of blazing fire / shall flow from heaven and consume every place" (Sibylline Oracles 2.196–97).

32. "There will be fire throughout the whole universe and this vast tomb has been prepared, / with sword and trumpet at sunrise" (Sibylline Oracles 4.173–74).

33. Samuel Mather, who followed his father into the ministry.

34. Samuel Mather's rhyming translation is loosely based on Sibylline Oracles 4.175–92.

SECTION V

1. This entire section echoes much of John Ray's *Discourses*, pp. 303–37, and of Thomas Burnet's *Sacred Theory*, pp. 246–64.

2. Josephus tells the story of the two pillars in *Antiquities* 1.2.3.

3. Evidently Mather means Raphael Mafejus (1452–1522), Italian geographer, historiographer, and biographer of various church fathers. The Scythians were a fierce, nomadic people who roamed throughout Asia, yet in the first century A.D., *Scythian* denoted "the worst of Barbarians" (see Col. 3:11).

4. Berossus (fl. c. 290 B.C.) was a historian and Babylonian priest of Belus. His *History of Babylon* covered Babylonia from the beginning to the death of Alexander the Great. The Roman philosopher Lucius Annaeus Seneca (c. 4 B.C.–A.D. 65) refers to Berossus in *Naturales Quaestiones* 3.20.8, 3.28.1–7, 3.29.1, 7.4.1, 7.28.1 (see also Ray, pp. 329–30). Mistakenly believed to be the name of an author, Suidas (Suda) is the title of a lexicon (c. tenth century) that abstracts works of many classical philosophers, historians, and biographers.

5. According to the *Life* of Zeno of Citium (c. 366–c. 264 B.C.) by Diogenes Laertius (bk. 7), Zeno's cosmos consisted of four elements—fire, air, water, and earth—all of which would again be absorbed by the primeval fire. Marcus Minucius Felix (fl. 200–240) was a distinguished Roman lawyer and author of a philosophical dialogue to which Mather refers (*Octavius* 34.1–4). The Latin passage, "The conflagration of the elements and the collapse of the world" (*Octavius* 34.3), is adapted from Lucretius 5 (see Ray, pp. 326–27).

6. Strabo 4.4.4–5. Jerome's commentary on Isa. 51:6 translates, "This is the opinion also of the philosophers of the world, that all things which we sell will perish by fire." Mather adapted his quotation from "Quae quidem et philosophorum mundi opinio est, omnia quae cernimus igni peritura" (*PL* 24.588).

7. Bishop Theophilus of Antioch (fl. 150–83) wrote his Christian apology *Ad Autolycum* in the form of a letter to a friend to whom he wished to teach the principles of the Christian faith. Mather's passage appears at 2.38. The bishop's namesake, Theophilus, patriarch of Alexandria, was a scrupulous opponent of Chrysostom and of the disciples of Origen. The quotation from the Alexandrian translates literally, "having drawn their doctrines from the fountain."

8. Cicero's *Somnium Scipionis* 6.20–21.

9. Justin Martyr's quotation of Sophocles translates, "The nurtured flame will burn up all things on the earth and above the earth" (*The Monarchy* 3).

10. Clement of Alexandria's quotation from Diphilus, the Athenian New Comedy poet (fl. 360-c. 290 B.C.), appears in *Stromateis* 5.14.121.1 and 5.14.133.3 (see also Ray, pp. 326–37).

11. Publius Ovidius Naso (43 B.C.–A.D. 17) was a prominent Roman poet. His singular compliment to Lucretius, which concludes, "When one day shall give the earth to destruction," appears in Ovid's *Amores* 1.15.23–24. Titus Lucretius Carus (c. 94–55 B.C.) was a Roman poet and philosopher whose only work was *De rerum natura*, which discusses

the materialist theory of Epicurus. The quotation from Lucretius translates, "All these a single day will blot out. The whole substance and structure of the world, upheld through many years, will crash. I am well aware how novel and strange in its impact on the mind is this impending demolition of heaven and earth" (5.95–98). For a close similarity to Mather's argument, see Ray, pp. 326–27. The "Infamous Pen" remains unidentified.

12. "It was in the fates that a time would come when sea and land, the unkindled palace of the sky and the beleaguered structure of the universe should be destroyed by fire" (*Metamorphoses* 1.256–58. See also Ray, pp. 333–34).

13. Marcus Anneaus Lucanus (A.D. 39–65) was a Roman poet, prolific writer, and nephew of the Roman philosopher Seneca. The quotation from Lucan translates, "A universal pyre is left over from the world" (*Bellum Civile* 7.814).

14. Lucan was forced to commit suicide by the Roman emperor Nero (54–68), who, according to legend, incinerated Rome (64) while reciting his poetry. Mather's translation is based on Lucan's *Bellum Civile* 7.815–22.

15. Unidentified.

SECTION VI

1. In this section, Mather tries to resolve the inherent paradox arising out of two contradictory prophecies. While Christ had warned his disciples that his return would be prognosticated by such stupendous prodigies of nature as wars, famines, pestilences, and earthquakes (Matthew 24; Mark 13; Luke 21), the Petrine prophecy augured that "the day of the Lord wil come as a thiefe in the night" (2 Pet. 3:10) and would catch the sleeping world off guard (D 2:737–38). Thomas Burnet, for one, did not resolve this issue in his *Sacred Theory* (bk. 3 chs. 11–12) by relying on the more spectacular elements of the conflagration story to carry his point. John Ray's *Discourses* (pp. 396–97) had done little better and had conceded to Grotius. And the great William Whiston skirted the issue entirely in his *New Theory* (pt. III, p. 287).

2. For Mather's physico-theological explication of this phenomenon (Dec. 1719), see VFH, "CAm," and D 2:596. "*Subitaneous*" signifies "sudden" or "unexpected." Mather here agrees with Thomas Burnet in rejecting the idea of a universal drought engendering the conflagration of the earth (*Sacred Theory*, pp. 264–70).

3. I.e., wailing or lamentations.

4. The destruction of the temple in A.D. 70 by Titus Flavius Vespasianus (39–81) during the sacking of Jerusalem (Matt. 24:29) was seen as a smaller type of things to come. For a similar argument, see Burnet's *Sacred Theory*, p. 296.

5. Ibid., bk. 3, ch. 7, p. 275.

6. The death during the eruption of Vesuvius (79) of Gaius Plinius Secundus (the Elder) (c. 23–79), Roman historian, biographer, and author of *Natural History*, is recorded by his nephew, Pliny the Younger (c. 61–112), in an epistle to Tacitus (*Epistle* 6.16). An earlier eruption of Vesuvius is described in Pliny the Elder's *Natural History* 2.106–7. For Mather's source, see Burnet, *Sacred Theory*, pp. 277–78.

7. The Latin passage in this quotation from Dion Cassius translates, "Many mighty men, exceeding human nature, of the kind described as Giants, partly on the mountain itself, partly in the surrounding territory, and in towns by day and by night, were seen to survey the earth and to traverse the air" (66.22–23). Mather interpolates the original into his manuscript text because it echoes the signs of the End described in Joel 2, Matthew 24, Mark 13, and Revelation 21. However, he borrows the English translation of Dion Cassius's narrative from Thomas Burnet's *Sacred Theory*, which he quotes verbatim with minor variations (p. 275). See also Ray, pp. 282–83.

8. "Such great fumes and heat burst forth from undepleted craters." Mather quotes Girolamo Borgia (1475–1550), Italian poet-historian, bishop of Massa Lubrense.

9. Pliny's *Epistle* 6.16, 20.

10. Pliny tells that his uncle and his slaves tied pillows on their heads to protect themselves from the falling cinders or "*Puntice-Stones.*"

11. From Lat. *indigitare*; i.e., to invoke (a deity); also obs. for "indication."

12. Perhaps Thomas Jackson, D.D. (1579–1640), president of Corpus Christi and dean of Peterborough.

13. "The form of which no other large tree than the Pine depicts" (*Epistle* 6.16).

14. "It does not please." Mather specifically targets William Whiston, who argued that a comet, which had caused the inundation by water in Noah's time, would also cause the flood of fire that would incinerate the earth at the Second Coming (*New Theory*, pt. II, pp. 182–224, 372–456, and app., pp. 459–78). But see Increase Mather's *Kometographia* and Mather Byles's "The Comet: A Poem."

15. Eugubinus Steuchus (Agostino Steuco) (c. 1497–1548), a learned Italian theologian, bishop of Cisamus, and author of the Latin text *On the Destruction of the World.* See also Burnet, *Sacred Theory*, pp. 241–42, 270, 321; Augustine, *City of God* 20.18.

16. Again Mather's disenchantment with Whiston's *New Theory* is apparent, for Whiston—like Burnet—had dared to limit the Mosaic creation account to the earth and its immediate atmosphere (pt. I, pp. 33–94).

17. St. Cyprian (c. 300), magician, astrologer of Antioch, and later bishop, beheaded by Diocletian at Nicomedia.

18. Mather pokes fun at the patristic legend according to which Emperor Domitian had the Apostle John cast into a "cauldron of boiling oil" from which the apostle miraculously emerged unscathed. Traditionally, John died at Ephesus in 100, during Trajan's reign.

19. Marcus Ulpius Traianus (53–117) wintered in Antioch, the capital of the Roman province of Syria, in 115, during the Parthian campaign. Trajan barely escaped with his life during the earthquake, which devastated the whole area (see Ray, p. 248).

20. See Rev. 6:16. Again, Mather relates this account in an effort to find evidence for the preterite fulfillment of the signs of the End (Matthew 24; Mark 13; Revelation 6).

21. Mather's source is Dion Cassius 68.24–25.

22. The "Learned Writer" is either Humphrey Prideaux or Thomas Burnet, on whose works Mather relies throughout.

23. Dion Cassius 68.25. Thomas Doolittle, in *Earthquakes Explain'd and Practically Improved* (p. 43), uses a similar, provocative description of what happened during the London earthquake of 1692. The similarities between the illustrations and the use of language suggest that Mather may have relied on Doolittle for graphic detail.

24. See Burnet, *Sacred Theory*, pp. 265–67, 283–88; Ray, pp. 381–88. Jerome's Latin translates, "The frenzy of the hungry broke out into abominable foods." And Lipsius's, "Concerning famine, we, or our age, assuredly see nothing of it, if we see Antiquity."

25. The reign of Titus Flavius Savinus Vespasianus, Roman emperor (79–81) was marked by repeated natural disasters, described in Ammianus Marcellinus 26.4 (see Ray, p. 14). The reign of the Eastern emperor Flavius Leo I (Leo the Great) (400–474) was attended by a series of catastrophes: A second earthquake that destroyed Antioch (458), the great fire of Constantinople (465), devastating floods (469), and another eruption of Mt. Vesuvius (472), with showers of ashes flying as far as Constantinople (to which Mather here refers), frightened the Romans in both parts of the divided empire (see also Ray, p. 283).

26. George Sandys (1578–1644), poet and author of the travel book *The Relation of a Journey.*

27. The quotation is from Mather's "*Cicero,*" the learned Athanasius Kircher (1602–80),

a German Jesuit, philologist, naturalist, geographer, and professor at the Collegium Romanum. Mather quotes from Kircher's *The Vulcano's*, which provides a detailed description of various volcanic eruptions.

28. Ps. 119:120. See *WA*.

29. A similar description appears in Burnet, *Sacred Theory*, p. 97; and Ray, p. 13.

30. Bernhard Varenius (Bernhard Varen) (c. 1621–51), German cosmographer and geographer. See Ray, p. 31.

31. The Banda Islands of East India; i.e., Indonesia, in the northeastern Banda Sea.

32. Sponsored by the Royal Society of London, the *Philosophical Transactions* appeared from 1665 onward. Mather himself published various scientific treatises in the *Transactions* and was elected a Fellow of the Royal Society in 1713 (Silverman, *Life and Times*, pp. 244–49 and passim).

33. I.e., the Gulf of Tatary, south of the Sea of Japan.

34. The fiery furnace of Nebuchadnezzar into which Shadrach, Meshach, and Abed-nego were cast (Dan. 3:1–30).

35. Plato's Atlantis. Faial, Pico, Terceira, and St. Michael (Sao Miguel) belong to the Portuguese Azores. See *D* 2:626; Mather's Letter to Mr. Chamberlain of the Royal Society, in "CAm" (1721–22 series); *WA*; Menasseh ben Israel, *Hope of Israel*, sec. 39, pp. 44–45.

36. Mather draws on Kircher's eyewitness account of 1638, recorded in his preface of *Mundus Subterraneous*.

37. Sixty fathoms are approximately 360 feet, and twenty leagues approximately 28 miles/45 km. For a similar account, see Ray, p. 22.

38. See *CP*, pp. 100–101; *CPI*, pp. 66–71; Ray, p. 22; Burnet, *Sacred Theory*, p. 273.

39. See Tacitus's description (*Annales* 13). Carbo is a dormant volcano in the northeast of the former Yugoslavia, in what was once a Roman province.

40. Mt. Hekla, an active volcano in southern Iceland (Burnet, *Sacred Theory*, p. 273).

41. Santorin (Thera, or Thira), the famous Greek Island in the Aegean Sea, is the eastern half of an exploded volcano, which erupted in c. 1500 B.C. and is believed to have destroyed the Minoan civilization on Crete.

42. Mt. Stromboli, 22 miles northeast of Liparia in a group of seven volcanic islands northeast of Sicily, is still active. Again Mather relies on Kircher's eyewitness account (see also Strabo 1.3.10).

43. The infamous Gaius Julius Caesar Germanicus (12–41), nicknamed Caligula ("Little Boots"), remembered mostly for his atrocities.

44. Heneage Finch, third earl of Winchelsea (d. 1689), the ambassador of Charles II to Constantinople. Winchelsea relates his eyewitness account in his public letter, *A True and Exact Relation*.

45. Nickname for Mt. Aetna (mentioned in the title of Finch's *Relation*).

46. Mather refers to the description of the 1669 eruption of Aetna by the Italian mathematician Giovanni Alfonso Borelli (1608–79), in *Historia*. See also Ray, pp, 19–21, 106, 287; Burnet, *Sacred Theory*, p. 274.

47. In Greek mythology, the rivers Acheron, Pyriphlegeton, and Cocytus flow into Hades. See Homer's *Odyssey* 10.513; Vergil's *Aeneid* 6.297; Plato's *Phaedo*.

48. Borrowed from Finch's *Relation*, this passage echoes a large number of doomsday prophecies (Isa. 30:33; Mal. 4:1–2; Job 37:1–5; Rev. 8:8).

49. Mather alludes to the destruction of Antioch (A.D. 115), as described by Dion Cassius (68.24–25), and to Burnet's theory that the crust of the earth rests on pillars above the caverns of the interior (*Sacred Theory*, bk. 1, chs. 5–6, 9–10). See also *CP*, pp. 101–2; Ray, pp. 21–22.

50. See I. Mather's *Illustrious Providences*, pp. 325–29.

51. See, for instance, Strabo 1.3.19–21, 4.1.6, 5.4.9.

52. Both Tyre and Sidon were important Mediterranean harbor towns and the frequent object of wrath of the OT prophets. For the earthquake during the Crucifixion, see Matt. 27:45, 51–54; Luke 23:44–45; Acts 16:25–38.

53. See also *CP*, p. 101; Burnet, *Sacred Theory*, p. 97; Ray, pp. 206–11.

54. "Fearful tremors were caused throughout the whole expanse of the Earth" (Ammianus Marcellinus 26.14).

55. Mather refers to New England's own Congregationalist pastor Peter Bulkeley (1583–1659) of Concord. The Latin, probably from Bulkeley's *Gospel-Covenant*, translates, "The axes of the earth totter, the structure of the earth is weakened, it trembles from the countenance of God enraged." See *MCA* 3.10.96–98 for Mather's biography; and Ray, pp. 291–94, for the earthquake in Sicily.

56. Both Catania and Syracuse are cities in southeastern Sicily.

57. Since approximately 1,500–2,000 people died during this disaster, it is not surprising that we find this story recorded in many places: *D* 1:142–43, 257n; *WIW*, pp. 77–78; Samuel Sewall's *Phaenomena*, pp. 38–39; Ray, pp. 251–60.

58. Mather may have received this eyewitness account from an unnamed Nonconformist minister (*D* 1:143, 550–51) or from Mather's friend and supporter Sir Charles Hobby (*D* 3:35). Sewall lists a number of eyewitnesses: William Harris, William Welsteed, Thomas Steel, and William Turner—all merchants (*Phaenomena*, p. 39).

59. "O hearts of men, harder than rocks."

60. The famous naval battle in which Roman emperor Octavian defeated Anthony at Actium, northeastern Greece (31 B.C.). Josephus tells the story in *Antiquities* 15.4–5 and *Wars* 1.19.1–4.

61. The OT story of Samson's death (Judg. 16:26–30).

62. I.e., roaring earthquakes, from Lat. *rugire*.

63. Mather identifies the two combatants as *"Caesar* and *Pompey"* but cancels this reference from his manuscript to give his allusion a wider application.

64. For the unnamed minister, see Mather's letter to his nephew John Cotton (*D* 1:142–43); for a parallel account, see Ray, pp. 252–55.

65. To lend his text a more ominous and universal quality, Mather changes the tense of the passage from past to future. See Jer. 4:20, 23–24.

66. The double destruction of Jerusalem and its temple by the Babylonian Nebuchadnezzar (c. 597 B.C.) and by Vespasian (A.D. 70) as signs of the future dissolution of the world during the Second Coming (see Burnet, *Sacred Theory*, p. 296).

67. Josephus, *Wars* 6.4–5.

68. Tacitus, *Historia* 5.13 and *Fragments of the Histories* 3; Josephus, *Wars* 6.9.3.

69. Mather paraphrases various doomsday prophecies from Isaiah, Jeremiah, and Zephania.

70. The quotation is from Henry More, D.D. (1614–87), student of Joseph Mede, Cambridge Platonist, and a favorite of Cotton Mather. Mather quotes the same passage in *WA*, p. 14, where he echoes More's discussion of the conflagration in *Immortality*, bk. 3, ch. 18, pp. 525–38. In his early eschatology, Mather had still believed in two conflagrations, a partial one at the beginning of the millennium and a global conflagration at the end ("PT," pp. 78–79). Apparently, he had changed his mind on this issue long before his father's death, but he did not reveal his insights until c. 1721 (*WA*, p. 12; *D* 2:740, 748). See also Mather Byles's poem "The Conflagration" (c. 1744).

SECTION VII

1. Mather rebukes his postmillennialist colleagues, including Daniel Whitby, who expected Christ's return at the end of the thousand-year period of rest, when the Christian church—free from religious contention and persecution—was to have attained its "Happy State" ("PT," pp. 57–59; Whitby, *True Millennium*).

2. Since the conflagration was intended to destroy Antichrist's empire, it appeared logical to most premillennialists that the *diluvium ignis* would begin in the heart of Italy (*CPI*, p. 69; *PSNE*, pp. 34–37; "PT," pp. 78–79; *D* 2:693–94, 740, 748). This old mainstay can also be found in Joseph Mede's *Paraleipomena*, p. 36; and in Burnet's *Sacred Theory*, pp. 289–91.

3. Mather refers to Satan's ousting from heaven (Rev. 12:7–12).

4. Mather sneers here at Grotius, Hobbes, Hammond, Lightfoot, Spinoza, and all those who tried to rationalize away the wonders of the invisible world (see "The Second Paradise").

5. Mather certainly knew what he was talking about (*MP*, pt. I, pp. 20–21, 26), for precisely such a case had happened in his own home—if the report of Robert Calef, Mather's old adversary, can be trusted; see Calef's letter (24 Nov. 1693), in *More Wonders* 2:57–58.

6. Vergil's Latin translates, "The sky lightens with quick-flowing flashes" (*Aeneid* 1.90).

7. The Saints of the First Resurrection. See Augustine, *City of God* 20.18, 22.19–21.

8. Exod. 33:20. The Hebrew term *Elohim*, i.e., God (pl.), signifies "majesty," "dignity," or "excellence."

9. Flavius Valerius Aurelius Constantinus (Constantine the Great) (ca. 274–337), the first Christian emperor of Rome, removed the seat of government from the ancient city of Rome to his new capital, Constantinople (Byzantium), in 330.

10. Mather refers to the selling of Joseph into Egyptian slavery (Gen. 37:23–24).

11. Mather describes the separation of the sheep from the goats (Matt. 25:31–46; Rev. 20:4–13) during the Second Resurrection at the end of the millennium. See secs. ix–x below.

12. "*De Regno Ecclesiae Glorioso*," which translates, "On the Glorious Kingdom of the Church," is probably the running title of a still unidentified work. The quotation from it translates, "Nothing is referred to here concerning the Resurrection of the Dead." Desiderius Erasmus (Erasmus of Rotterdam) (c. 1469–1536) was the great Dutch humanist and Augustinian monk (see Tuttle, "Libraries," pp. 307, 326). And Gregory of Nazianzus (329–89) was the Greek theologian, bishop of Constantinople, and Cappadocian father.

13. In an effort to solicit subscribers for the publication of his unpublished commentary "BA," Mather repeatedly quotes from his magnum opus; this excerpt comes from his annotations on Matthew 25 and Revelation 20. See "PT"; my Introduction, chs. 3–4.

14. Mather's signs preceding Christ's Second Coming (Matt. 24:3–51) include the persecution of the Huguenots of France. See *WWG; FW; ACF; SD; UGV; D* 1:199–200, 202, 205, 207–8, 261–63.

15. The "Infamous *Peace*" negotiated in the Treaty of Ryswick (1697) brought to a temporary halt the war between England, France, Spain, and Holland (see *D* 1:213, 214, 256, 397–99). For Mather's feelings on the Peace of Utrecht (1713), which concluded the War of the Spanish Succession (1701–13), see *D* 1:420, 2:171–74, 176. See Rice.

16. Elijah (Elias) was taken up into heaven in a whirlwind (2 Kings 2:1–13).

17. Palladius of Helenopolis (c. 365–425), early church historian and biographer, was primarily known for his *Lausiac History*, a collection of biographical anecdotes and miracles. Mather refers to the legendary debate between Archbishop Gregentius and the

Jewish leader Herbanus of Tephar (Arabia), during which dispute Christ was said to have appeared visibly in the clouds and brought about a large-scale conversion of many Jews. See also "PT," pp. 32–34; secs. iii above and xi below; Mede, *Works*, pp. 767–68; my Introduction, ch. 2, and Radius.

18. Before his miraculous conversion on the road to Damascus, Paul (i.e., Saul, "one of His Persecutors") hounded the early Christians.

19. Also *merkabah*: "chariot," or "heavenly throne" (Ezekiel 1, 10).

20. The *"Horrid Conspiracy"* in Mather's time was, of course, the spread of Deism, which rejected Christ's divinity, God's special providence, and the belief in the reward and punishment of good and evil.

21. Mather was in good company in calling down the fire of vengeance on an incredulous world. He could readily draw for support on Burnet's *Sacred Theory*, pp. 271–79, 289–92, 305; Ray's *Discourses*, pp. 381–93; and Whiston's *New Theory*, pt. II, pp. 285–87, 442–47.

22. Like most Protestant literalists among millenarians, Mather could not resist meting out a particular dose of punishment on Rome, the seat of Antichrist (see also Mede's *Paraleipomena*, p. 36; Burnet's *Sacred Theory*, p. 290).

23. The belief in lunar inhabitants was not entirely new in Mather's time; it had been popularized in Francis Godwin's *Man in the Moone*. William Whiston even thought it presumptuous for man to conceive of himself as the whole focus of God's creation and contended that there are millions of nobler intellectual beings out there in the solar system (*New Theory*, pt. I, pp. 71, 93).

SECTION VIII

1. Mather's quotation is from Homer's *Iliad* 6.180. Lycia is a celebrated mountain on the southern coast of Asia Minor, near Phrygia. The monstrous, fire-breathing creature called Chimaera is "lion before, serpent behind, and she-goat in the middle" (*Iliad* 6.181).

2. In Mather's cosmology, the progressive deterioration of nature toward a global conflagration was inevitable, given his causality. His colleague John Ray, however, though agreeing with Mather's literalist position, rejected the idea of nature's degeneration (Ray, pp. 269, 393–94).

3. The prophet was Jeremiah (44:22).

4. "The principal crime of the human race."

5. The Dalai Lama of Tibet, whom Mather also calls "Prester John" and "Pope of Barantola" (*ATC*, p. 37).

6. *"Mammetry,"* or *maumetry*, is an obsolete term for "idolatry," or "Muhammadanism." Islam prohibits the use of images of any sort; hence Mather's reference to iconoclasm. The most famous of Muhammad and Khadidja's daughters (sixth century), Fatima is revered throughout the Muslim world. For Mather's probable source, see Hugo Grotius's popular missionary handbook *De Veritate*, bk. 6.

7. For a description of *"Mystical Babylon,"* the symbolic woman called Babylon the Great, see Revelation 17. Puritans objected to the Roman Catholic doctrine of transubstantiation, the mystical transmutation of Christ's body in the host. To Mather, as well as other Protestants, this doctrine was tantamount to *"Artolatry,"* the worship of bread. See *Savoy Declaration*, ch. 30 ("Of the Lords Supper"), pp. 399–400; *MCA* 5.18–19.

8. From Lat. *excarnare*, signifying "to deprive or strip of flesh." Used as a noun, the term is also applied to the separation of the soul from the body at death (*Oxford English Dictionary*, hereafter *OED*). Mather has in mind the many tales of executions and mas-

sacres in John Foxe's *Book of Martyrs* and those in the Dutch equivalent by Thieleman J. van Braght, *The Bloody Theater or Martyr's Mirror* (1660).

9. Joannes Ludovicus De La Cerda (Juan Luis De La Cerda) (1560–1643) was a Spanish Jesuit and scribe, author of *Adversaria sacra*.

10. The title translates, *On the Small Number of Martyrs*. Neither the work nor its author has been identified.

11. "*Godless*," or "*blasphemous*."

12. Mather refers to the expansionist wars of the Austrian Holy Roman Emperor Leopold I of the House of Hapsburg (1640–1705), who persecuted Protestants in the Austro-Hungarian Empire; and of the French Sun King, Louis XIV of the House of Bourbon (1638–1715), during the War of the Spanish Succession (1701–13). To Mather, the bloody scourges of Austria and France easily matched those of antiquity, especially those of Roman emperor Gaius Aurelius Valerius Diocletianus (245–313), of Nero Claudius Caesar (37–68), and of Roman emperor Titus Flavius Domitianus (51–96).

13. Located in the northwestern part of the old City of London and famed for its ancient Bartholomew Fair, Smithfield served as a place of execution. See also *PN*, p. 107.

14. "It came to such a pass that among Christians, strivers after the Cross, it happened every day openly and publicly that the laws of heathen nations punished them harshly" (see Grotius, *Truth of the Christian Religion*, bk. 2, sec. 19, pp. 154–60).

15. Richard Kidder (1633–1703), bishop of Bath and Wells, Boyle lecturer, and controversial Latitudinarian. His relevant work is *A Demonstration of the Messias*.

16. Mather describes the same issue in *IC*.

17. "Let it only be well here."

18. The quotation from Bernard of Clairvaux (1091–1153) translates, "The very positions of ecclesiastical dignity also have passed into disgraceful pursuit of gain and the commerce of darkness: and it is not the salvation of souls but the opulence of riches that is sought in them." Bernard's lamentation for the corruptions of the church by Dives is given at length in his "Epistle XLII," chs. 2–3 (*PL* 182.463).

19. Mather preached against slavery early on, as is evident in his *NC* and *D* (1:176–77, 2:442), but he accepted from Governor Phips and from his own congregation the gift of a slave (*PN*, p. 59; *D* 1:203, 579). See also *D* 1:564–65; Silverman, *Life and Times*, pp. 263–65, 281, 369. One of the earliest abolitionist tracts in New England was written by Judge Samuel Sewall (*The Selling of Joseph*).

20. An ancient OT name for the Lord of Hosts, who accompanied the Israelites into battle.

21. Gaius Suetonius Tranquillus (c. 69-c. 125), Roman historian, authored *Vitae Duodecim Caesarum*, a biography of twelve Roman emperors. Mather refers to his description of Nero's sexual appetites (6.28–29).

22. Probably John Calvin. On the issue of adultery, see Calvin's *Institutes* 2.8.41–44; Mather's "Quo," vols. 47–48.

23. See Mather's comments on venereal diseases, "*Kibroth Hattaavah*," in *AB*, pp. 116–20.

24. For the colony's sentiments on "buggery," see William Bradford's *Of Plymouth Plantation*, ch. 32 (pp. 316–22) and app. 10 (pp. 404–13).

25. Mather refers to the British Isles.

26. What that challenge was I have been unable to determine. But for the Puritan views on the theater, see Lamont, *Politics*, ch. 2.

27. Through his third wife (Lydia Lee George), Mather incurred great financial obliga-

tions to the creditors of the George estate (D 2:630–31, 703, 707–8, 713, 739, 745). Wiser afterward, he published FD. See Silverman, Life and Times, pp. 312–15.

28. Mather may very well have himself in mind as the "Honest Writer," for his B makes the same point. The passage by the unidentified Roman translates, "The end of things is at hand."

29. The issue of the earth's combustibility was also discussed in Burnet's Sacred Theory, pp. 265–79; and in Ray's Discourses, pp. 381–415.

30. Jon. 4:11 tells of "sixscore thousand persons, that cannot discerne betweene their right hand and their left hand." Niniveh was destroyed by the Babylonian king Nebopolassar and the Median Cyaxares (c. 632 B.C.).

31. "Roan" is an archaic spelling for the French city Rouen. Mather reminds his audience of the Great Fire of London (2 Sept. 1666) as an example of what may lie ahead. For an eyewitness account, see The Diary of Samuel Pepys 2:282–91; The Diary of John Evelyn, pp. 209–16.

32. Lucian 23; Diodorus Siculus 2.7.2, 2.28.1–7; Herodotus 1.178, 185, 193. The quotation from Samuel Bochart translates, "Hence, I think that learned men wear themselves out in vain, in defining the location of Nineveh" (Geographia Sacra, bk. 4, ch. 20).

33. An affluent and powerful Achaean-Troezenian metropolis in the Gulf of Tarentum, Sybaris was destroyed by Croton (c. 510 B.C.), who diverted the river Crathis to wash away the rubble of the city. Both Strabo (6.1.13) and Diodorus (10.23, 12.9.1–10) speak of only 300,000 inhabitants. Perhaps Mather mistakenly thought of Tacitus's description of Thebes and its 700,000 inhabitants. Located in the eastern plain of Boeotia, Thebes was the most important city during the Boeotian Confederacy (fifth century B.C.) but was later destroyed by Alexander the Great.

34. Cassiopeia is the northern constellation between Andromeda and Cephus consisting of five bright stars. Mather probably refers to Tycho's supernova, which appeared in this constellation in 1572.

35. Vita Sanctae Genovefae describes how Geneviève (c. 422–512), patron saint of Paris, comforted the Parisians when the Huns invaded the city (451).

36. One of the oldest cities of ancient Greece, Corinth, located on the Peloponnesian isthmus, was destroyed by Roman consul L. Mummius (146 B.C.) in retaliation for the maltreatment of the Roman ambassadors by the Achaean League. Rebuilt in 44 B.C., it was visited by Paul in c. 50. It was completely destroyed by an earthquake in 521, and several times again by the Turks in the sixteenth and seventeenth centuries (Treaty of Carlowicz).

37. Mather refers to the sacking of Rome (A.D. 455) by the Vandal ruler Genseric (see sec. xii below).

38. For a more detailed discussion of the "Saracen Locusts" and the "Ottoman Horsemen" (the first two of the three final woe trumpets) in Mather's eschatology, see WWG, p. 41; TLF, pp. 31–44; WIW, pp. 90–91; TDP, p. 34; ATC, pp. 12–22; "PT," pp. 52–58; sec. xii below. Richard Knolles's Turkish History was of great interest to Mather.

39. The quotation from the celebrated Italian jurist Guido Panciroli's Rerum memorabilium translates, "Things utterly lost."

40. Mather himself was likely to bewail the loss of such treasures. When creditors of his third wife's estate claimed Mather's library as payment, he confided to his diary: "My very Library, the Darling of my little Enjoyments, is demanded from me." But he quickly detached himself from such vanities, adding, "'Tis inexpressible, how much this Condition pleases me, gladdens me" (D 2:708; see also D 2:745; PN, p. 42). His own library and that of his father together constituted probably the largest private holding of books

in the colonies; the Mather libraries were called "the Glory of New-England, if not of all America" (quoted in Silverman, *Life and Times*, pp. 262–63). How Mather acquired such treasures is recorded in his diary (*D* 1:214, 343, 368, 447, 532, 2:2). For the remains of these libraries, see Tuttle, "Libraries," pp. 269–356.

41. The holdings of this renowned library in Egypt were variously estimated at 700,000 volumes (Josephus, *Antiquities* 12.2) and 400,000 volumes (*Athenaeus* 1.3). Part of the library was destroyed during Julius Caesar's blockade of Alexandria and another part in the fourth century by Christian fanatics; the remainder fell prey to the flames (A.D. 640) when Khalif Omar sacked the city. It is evidently the latter whom Mather has in mind. See also Happel, "Die ptolemäische Bibliothek," pp. 173–74.

42. Located in the Mysian district of Teuthrania, Pergamus was endowed by Eumenes II (fl. 197–159 B.C.) with a vast library, inferior only to that of Alexandria (Strabo 13.623–24; *Athenaeus* 1.3). Its estimated 200,000 volumes were Anthony's gift to Cleopatra, who stored them in Alexandria. Thus the library of Pergamus vanished as well when the Alexandrian library was destroyed. Fire also destroyed the library of Constantinople, in 532, in a *diluvium ignis* that nearly incinerated the whole city.

43. Henricus Salmuth the Elder (fl. 1599) was a German jurist; his annotations were incorporated in the English translation of Guido Panciroli's *Rerum memorabilium*. In 1622, Maximilian I, duke of Bavaria, made a present of the Palatine Library of Heidelberg to Pope Gregory XV for his assistance during the Thirty Years War (1618–48). Happel described the loss of the rare treasures of Heidelberg in *Relationes Curiosae*, p. 170.

44. In an effort to settle his quarrel with Pope Clement VII, Holy Roman Emperor Charles V, king of Spain, sacked Rome in 1527 with his Spanish and German Lutheran troops. All the libraries discussed here incurred the same fate as the Tower of Sechem (Neapolis), in Palestine (near Nablus), which was destroyed during the Samaritan uprising by King Julianus (fifth century).

45. All the conflagrations Mather has mentioned typify the conflagration of Christ's Second Coming, of which his quotation asserts, "I have never seen a brighter fire."

46. Neither of the two martyrs has been identified, yet their lives can probably be found in Foxe's *Book of Martyrs*, from which Mather quotes: "O blessed Revelation; how well I am dealt with, who am burnt with you!"

47. Joannes Arndtius (Johann Arndt) (1555–1621), German Lutheran theologian and Pietist, best known for his *De vero christianisimo libri IV*. See *D* 2:337, 341, 348; and Tuttle, "Libraries," p. 315.

48. For similar mathematical exercises, see Burnet, whose calculations produced a figure of more than 10 billion antediluvians (*Sacred Theory*, p. 36), and Whiston, who arrived at nearly 550 billion people living before Noah's flood (*New Theory*, pt. III, p. 249).

49. For a further application of Burnet's theories of how the Flood occurred, see *Sacred Theory*, p. 101; Cotton Mather's letter to the Royal Society of London (8 June 1723), in "CAm" (first series). In 1705, Indians discovered the bones of a mammoth at Claverack (New York), which were taken as evidence of the antediluvian giants or nephilim, mentioned in Genesis (6:1–4). The account was published in the *Boston News-Letter* (30 July 1705), and Mather sent his scientific improvements on the subject to John Woodward of the Royal Society (1712), who published them in the *Philosophical Transactions of the Royal Society of London* 29 (1714): 62–63. See also Stanford.

50. The Tower of Babel (Gen. 11:4).

51. The extent of the conflagration was also limited to the earth and its atmosphere by Burnet (*Sacred Theory*, pp. 241–42, 270, 321), by Ray (pp. 403–15), by Whiston (*New Theory*, pp. 87–88), and before them by Augustine, *City of God* 20.18.

52. The quotation from Salonius, bishop of Genoa (d. c. 475), translates, "It will burn to as great an extent as the wickedness of men, and at the same rate as it is able [to burn] the defiled demons." This somewhat garbled quotation from Salonius's *In Ecclesiasten Expositio Mystica* reads in the original, "Tantum quippe ardebit coelum sursum et terra deorsum, quantum malitia hominum simul et daemonum coinquinari potuit" (*PL* 53.995), which translates, "It will certainly burn the heaven on high and the earth below to as great an extent as it is able [to burn] the wickedness of men and the defiled demons." That's enough, indeed!

SECTION IX

1. "In the force of fire [it] will go away" (Minucius Felix, *Octavius* 35).

2. Actually, Mather's quotation is not from Heb. 11:18 but from Heb. 11:9–10.

3. *"Peganius"* is the pseudonym of Christian Knorr von Rosenroth (1636–89), poet, Protestant theologian, and cabalist of Silesia. His Pietism was strongly influenced by Jacob Boehme. Mather apparently refers to Peganius's *Genuine Explication.* Modern critics have much to say about how American Puritans built their own "New Jerusalem" in New England as a shining beacon to the Old World. Yet scholars have rarely appreciated the term's disputed eschatological meaning among Mather's fellow exegetes, nor have they examined the startling implications suggested by the layers of different significations. For a helpful survey of early American millennialism, see Froom 3:98–115. See also my discussion in *"Israel Redivivus"* of Mather's New Jerusalem and its implication for the study of American Puritanism; my Introduction, ch. 4.

4. Tertullian's *Against Marcion* 3.24 describes the mirage of a walled city appearing in the air every morning for forty days. Tanaquillus Faber (Tannegui Lefèbvre the Elder) (1615–72) was a French biblical and classical philologist. He was joined on this issue by Walter Moyle (1672–1721), an English parliamentarian, botanist, and classical historian.

5. The passage from Tertullian, a native of northern Africa, translates, "We believe also in a kingdom guaranteed for us on earth, but in a different condition, namely after the Resurrection" (*Against Marcion* 3.24). See also Tertullian, *Spectacles* 30. The original is somewhat fuller and reads, "Confitemur in Terra nobis Regnum repromissum, sed ante coelum, sed alio statu, utpote post Resurrectionem (*PL* 2.355–56).

6. The running title of Mather's *C.*

7. "We speak of this city, the saints being admitted by Resurrection and renewed by an abundance of all spiritual goods without exception, in compensation of those which we disdained or lost in our age, provided for by God" (*Against Marcion* 3.24). The last Latin word in Mather's rendition, *"prospectum,"* is *"prospectam"* in the original (*PL* 2.356).

8. Mather is particularly displeased with the Anglican Henry Hammond and his allegorist disciples, to whom the prophetic terms of Rev. 21:1–4 signify no more than the condition of the millennial church on earth: "It signifies not the state of glorified Saints in heaven" but only "the pure Christian Church, joyning Christian practice with the profession thereof, & that in a flourishing condition, express'd by the *new heaven* and *new earth"* (*Paraphrase,* p. 837). See also Whitby's *True Millennium,* pp. 1–20.

9. "Entities of Reason."

10. The *"Seven-hilled City"* is Rome.

11. This is one of Mather's most-favored biblical phrases; it accrues central importance in *TA.* Unfortunately, modern critics have frequently misread his use of it to suggest that Mather saw Boston as the location for the literal New Jerusalem in America (see my Introduction, ch. 4, and *"Israel Redivivus"*).

12. For his description of the New Jerusalem, Mather relies ironically on ancient Babylon, its symbolic opposite. The description of Babylon occurs in Herodotus 1.178–80.

13. I.e., 990 yards, a little more than half a mile (c. 850 m).

14. Nebuchadnezzar's pride was punished with insanity for a period of seven years, during which he grazed like a bull (Dan. 4:30–33).

15. Joseph Justus Scaliger computed the weight of the Colossus of Rhodes, one of the Seven Wonders of the World. The statue, 32 m tall, guarded the entrance to the harbor but was destroyed during an earthquake in 224–223 B.C. It is not surprising that Scaliger was ridiculed for measuring the weight of a statue lost for more than 1,900 years. Mather's apology about measuring the size of the celestial Jerusalem is therefore well grounded. The German historian Eberhard Werner Happel related the same story and estimated the weight of the Colossus at 900,000 pounds of iron ore (*Relationes Curiosae*, pp. 87–90).

16. For the translation of the Saints to the celestial City, see Tertullian, *Against Marcion* 3.24; Mede's "Epistle XXII," in *Works*, pp. 775–76. Mather's *"Verticordious Grace"* is derived from *verticordia*, signifying "turner of hearts"; i.e., regenerative grace. The only example of its use cited in the *OED* is *MCA* 3.26.149.

17. There are several holy mountains: Mt. Sinai (Exod. 19:3, 20); Mt. Pisgah (Deut. 34:1–5); Mt. Horeb (1 Kings 19:8–12).

18. Mather may have himself in mind, for he often refers to Boston as an obscure village in the Scythian deserts of America.

19. "You will know when you become."

20. Echoing St. Thomas Aquinas's position, Mather describes the bliss of the Saints of the First Resurrection, who will experience the Beatific Vision at the beginning of the millennium. Mather's own mystical union and ecstatic visions are related in his diaries (*D* 1:239, 278, 422, 437–38, 471, 478–79, 483, 2:12, 545, 669, 696–97, 738–39) and in his autobiography (*PN*, pp. 112–13, 117–19, 133, 148, 162, 173). For a helpful introduction, see M. J. Redle's survey "Beatific Vision," in *Catholic Encyclopedia* 2:186–93.

21. The same passage appears with slight changes in *PN*, p. 298. This quotation echoes the account of Dr. Barnes's execution by burning (30 June 1526) related in *Lives, Sufferings, and Triumphant Deaths*, by Rev. John Foxe. See also *CP*, pp. 303–4, and *CCC*.

22. I.e., beginning.

23. Though asserting Christ's millennial kingdom on earth, Thomas Hobbes denied that the resurrected Saints would ascend to heaven (pt. III, ch. 38, pp. 335–37).

24. Heb.: "Jehovah is there."

25. An allusion to Plato's world of shadows, in "Allegory of the Cave" (*Republic* 7).

26. *"Zaphnath-Paaneah"* is Pharaoh's Coptic name for Joseph, who had revealed the mystery of Pharaoh's dream (Gen. 41:45).

27. "Things concerned with Life." Probably the running title of an unidentified work.

28. "The resurrection of the dead is the assured hope of Christians!" This is an adaptation of Tertullian's "Fiducia Christianorum, resurrectio mortuorum," in *De Resurrectione Carnis*, ch. 1 (*PL* 1.795).

29. "I shall rise again."

30. See Calvin's *Institutes* 3.25.3–8 and *Psychopannychia*, pp. 467–73.

31. Irenaeus 3.16.9, 5.7.1.

32. The *"Plastic Spirit"* is the same as Mather's *Nishmath-Chajim* (Garments of Light), or *"Luminous Air,"* occupying a middleground between the ethereal soul and the corporeal body." See "Second Paradise" above, sec. ii; Mather's medical handbook, *AB*, pp. 27–38; and the helpful discussion in Erwin, pp. 116–52.

33. The *shechinah* was visible on Moses's radiant face because he had been in the presence of Jehovah (Exod. 34:29–35; 2 Cor. 3:7, 13).

34. Timothy, who accompanied Paul on his journeys, frequently suffered from a stomach ailment (1 Tim. 5:23).

35. *De Cruciatibus Martyrum* (unidentified) translates, *On the Agonies of Martyrs*. The Roman soldier Tharacus (Tarachus) (c. 239–304) became a Christian martyr during the Diocletian and Maximilian persecutions. See Cyprian of Carthagena, in *Dissertatio Apologetica Pro SS. Perpetua* 6.6 (*PL* 3.148). The life of St. Blandina (d. 177), a virgin who was martyred with Bishop Pothinus in Lyons (France), is narrated in *Homilia De Sancta Blandina Lugdunensi* (*PL* 50.859).

36. Paul's epistles to the churches of Ephesus, Smyrna, Pergamus, Thyatira, Sardis, Philadelphia, and Laodicea. For the fate of these churches under the Ottoman yoke, see *ATC*.

37. Here Mather is evidently thinking of individuals like himself; he received much comfort from his anticipated reward in heaven (*D* 1:560, 2:41, 585, 641; *B*, p. xi; *PN*, pp. 14–15, 188, 197–229). See also Bernhard.

38. Esther's uncle Mordecai saved King Ahasuerus of Persia from assassination (Esth. 2:21–23, 6:6–11). Artaxerxes was king of Persia (c. 465–425 B.C.).

39. King David repented for the sin of numbering his people against the explicit command of God (2 Sam. 24:10). Peter wept bitterly for denying Christ three times (Matt. 26:75; Luke 22:62); and Paul (Saul), for having persecuted Christ (Acts 9:3–18).

40. After the death of John the Baptist, Moses and Elias (Elijah) appeared during Christ's transfiguration (Mark 9:1–8).

41. The "Minister" is Paul, in his Epistle to the Thessalonians.

42. In his Epistle to the Colossians (Asia Minor), Paul encourages Archippus to continue faithfully in his ministry (Col. 4:17; Philem. 2).

43. Literally, "O that happy Day."

44. Mather, who hoped to unite Lutherans and Calvinists through his Pietism (*D* 2:663), refers to the division during the debate of Marburg (1529) between the German reformer Martin Luther (1483–1546) and the Swiss reformer Huldreich (Ulrich) Zwingli (1484–1531) on the issue of transubstantiation. See I. Mather's "New Jerusalem," p. 402; "PT," pp. 10–11.

45. "*Minority*" (immaturity) is here used to suggest being under the Mosaic Law (works vs. faith alone); i.e, in the state of mortality (Gal. 3:23–26).

46. Mather makes explicit his distinction among essentially three classes of Saints: (1) The Raised Saints (First Resurrection), united with their etherealized bodies at the beginning of the millennium, will reign with Christ in the literal New Jerusalem in heaven and become the teachers of (2) the Changed Saints. Alive during the conflagration, the Changed Saints will be translated into their prelapsarian, immortal condition and returned to earth to increase and multiply for a thousand years. (3) The just and unjust dead, united with their restored bodies at the Last Judgment at the end of the millennium, will be raised to eternal life or death. Compare with Burnet's *Departed Souls*, pp. 89–106, and *Sacred Theory*, pp. 327–32.

47. See *PN*, pp. 119, 169–70; *D* 1:479, 2:190, 520–22, 577, 579, 590. The angelic function of the Raised Saints is also part of the eschatological thought of Joseph Mede (*Works*, pp. 773–75); Increase Mather ("New Jerusalem," pp. 383–84; *Angelographia; Future Conversion*, pp. 34–35); Richard Baxter (*Glorious Kingdom*, pp. 71–72). See also Whitby, *True Millennium*.

48. The term "*Nonage*" refers to the Jews under the OT Law of Moses before Christ's

abrogation. Here it is used to signify the mortal state ("*Vermicular State*") of the Raised Saints before their resurrection at the beginning of the millennium.

49. That Mather longed for such opportunites to do good while still on earth can be seen in *B*, pp. xi, xvi; *D*, 1:560; *PN*, pp. 188, 197–201, 204, 206, 208, 217–29.

50. "It is just and worthy of God to raise his servants to that place also where they are even afflicted in his name" (Tertullian, *Against Marcion* 3.24).

51. Mather's view is not unique, for several church fathers maintained the same thing. See, e.g., Augustine's *City of God* 22.17; Tertullian's *Prayer*, ch. 20. Though a product of his own time, Mather generally maintained an enlightened view of women and female education (*D* 2:153). For an excellent discussion of this topic, see Pattie Cowell's introduction to and edition of *ODZ*, esp. pp. v–xix.

52. Mather juxtaposes the benign regard for the unisex Saints in the City of God and the atrocious slaughter of women in Babylon to forestall starvation (c. 521 B.C.) (Herodotus 3.150). Mather promises his female readers a position of equality in the new world order. On Huldah, see 2 Kings 22:14; 2 Chron. 34:22.

53. Mather balances God's curse of Eve (Gen 3:16–17) against the achievements of Queen Zenobia of Palmyra (fl. 266–72), whose troops overran the Roman provinces of Syria, Egypt, and Asia Minor.

54. The Salic or Salique Law excluded women from accession to the French throne. On the position of women, see also Burnet's *Departed Souls*, p. 239; Augustine's *City of God* 22.17.

55. Evidently the work of that title by the German theologian Johann Friedrich Mayer (1650–1712).

56. The *Luz* or "Jew's bone" in Rabbinical tradition followed the eighteenth vertebra of the spine and was considered the source of Resurrection because of its indestructibility. See Burnet, *Departed Souls*, pp. 181–82.

57. As is well known, Mather's medical knowledge came from his early study of medicine when an unsettling stammer seemed to render him unsuitable for the ministry (Levin's *Cotton Mather*, pp. 2, 32–35). The *"Spina Dorsi"* is the backbone; *"Carina"* is "a genus of Heteropodous Molluscs, having a delicate shell of glassy translucency which protects the heart and liver" (*OED*). The *"Cerebrum"* is the anterior part of the brain, whereas the *"Cerebellum"* is "the little or hinder brain, situated behind and below the cerebrum, and above the *medulla oblongata*" (*OED*). The *Punctum saliens* (*"Salient Point"*) is an archaic term for "the heart as it first appears in an embryo; hence the first beginning of life or motion" (*OED*). The *"Medullary Matter"* is the spinal marrow, which was believed to provide the nutriments for the muscular and carneous parts of the body.

58. The *"Animal Oeconomy"* is Mather's archaic jargon for the household of the body system. *"Digestion"* here signifies "the process of maturing an ulcer" (*OED*), and *"Resolution"* suggests a "Relaxation or weakening of some part of the body" (*OED*).

59. Sarah, Abraham's wife, was buried in the Cave of Machpelah (Gen. 23:19). Jacques Saurin (1677–1730) was a celebrated French Protestant minister. Mather refers to Saurin's chapter "Abraham achète un sepulchre," in *Discours historiques* 1:325–44.

60. The *"Protoplast"* is of course Adam; i.e., "that which is first formed or created" (*OED*).

61. The Levite Heman, grandson of the Prophet Samuel, led his fourteen sons and three daughters in song through the temple (1 Chron. 6:33, 15:17–19; 2 Chron. 5:11, 12) and presided with Asaph and Jeduthun over the temple musicians during the reigns of David and Solomon (*Dictionary of the Bible* [hereafter *DOB*] 4:153–54).

62. The messengers were Magdalene and Mary, the mother of James (Matt. 28:1; Mark

16:1). *"Hephsibah"* and *"Beulah"* signify the happy condition of Jerusalem's restoration after the Babylonian captivity (Isa. 62:4).

63. The Hebrew term translates, "So," and was part of God's promise to Abraham (Gen. 15:5). Mather evidently relies on Moise Sefardi (Moses Sephardi) (b. 1062), a Spanish converso, physician, and polemicist who adopted the name Petrus Alfonsi when he became the court physician to England's King Henry I. Alfonsi's *Collection Against the Jews* is probably part of his apologia *Dialogi in quibus judaeorum opiniones confutantur.*

SECTION X

1. See Burnet, *Sacred Theory*, pp. 241–42, 270, 320–24, 331; Ray, pp. 301–20, 402–6; and Whiston, *New Theory*, pp. 87–88.

2. During Mather's time several theories coexisted on the meaning of the conflagration. Some believed it would be a complete annihilation of the earth; others, a complete liquifying and subsequent restoration, or the burning by fire of the earth's surface; still others believed it to be a metaphor for the cleansing of wickedness and for the regeneration of the heart of man (see Burnet, *Sacred Theory*, pp. 320–24, 331; Lactantius, *Divine Institutes* 7.23, 7.26; Irenaeus 5).

3. Robert Maton (1607-c. 1653) was an English millenarian divine with strong Fifth-Monarchist leanings. His tracts *Israels Redemption* and *Israels Redemption Redeemed* caused a minor controversy, for Maton actively engaged in gathering English Jews to lead them back to the Holy Land (see also Hill, "Till the Conversion," pp. 275, 284).

4. This was certainly the position of the New Englander Samuel Hutchinson (1618–67), whose *Declaration of a Future Glorious Estate*, pp. 27–30, asserted that the New Jerusalem would literally and corporeally descend over Judea, cleaving asunder the Mount of Olives in Jerusalem. It was also the claim of Increase Mather in *Mystery*, in "New Jerusalem," and in *Future Conversion*. Cotton Mather subscribed to this position as well until he adopted the preterite and allegorist position of Grotius, Hammond, and Lightfoot (see my Introduction and sec. xi below).

5. The bones of Jacob's son Joseph were carried back to Canaan during the Exodus (Gen. 50:22–26; Josh. 24:32; Heb. 11:32).

6. Arnobius the Younger (d. 451) was an African monk from whose *Commentarii in Psalmos* Mather quotes: "The world is to be reduced to nothing at the end of the age." See Ray, pp. 406–15; Burnet, *Sacred Theory*, pp. 319–32, 339.

7. Johann Gerhard (1582–1637) was a German Lutheran divine and professor of theology at Jena. His most important doctrinal work was *Loci theologici*, which included his discussion of the conflagration, *De Novissimis in Genere* (vol. 8, ch. 9–11) and *De consummatione seculi* (vol. 9, chs. 3–6). See also Tuttle, "Libraries," p. 329; *D* 2:768. For Martin Luther's position see his "Preface to the Second Epistle of St. Peter," p. 392. The Greek word translates, "substantial."

8. Irenaeus 5.36.1; Cyril of Jerusalem, *Catechesis* 15.3. Origen's position translates, "Purifying fire" (*Genesis Homilia VI, PG* 12.74–75). And Basil the Great of Caesarea (c. 329–79), the Cappadocian father, pleads for a "Restoration" and "Renewal" in *Commentarii in Isaiam Prophetam* 6 (*PG* 30.514).

9. Theophylact, archbishop of Achrida and Byzantine exegete (eleventh century), presents his view in *Expositio In Epist. II S. Petri Cap. III.* (*PG* 125.398–99). The sixth-century exegete Oecumenius discusses the issue in his commentary on *Epist. II S. Petri Cap. III.* 5–9 (*PG* 119.550). And Mather alludes to Epiphanius (c. 315–403), bishop of Salamis.

10. Proclus (d. c. 446), patriarch of Constantinople, says, "It will catch fire for [the purpose of] cleansing and renewal, the whole world [being] purged by fire after the descent

is made; but it will not achieve complete destruction and ruin." Jerome's commentary on Psalm 102 translates, "It is clear that heaven and earth do not perish, but are changed for the better." His gloss on 1 Cor. 7:31 translates, "The outward appearance, not the substance, passes away."

11. Augustine concurs with, "This world will pass away by a change of things, not by destruction of every kind" (*City of God* 20.16). Salonius, bishop of Genoa (d. c. 475), agrees, stating, "When cleansed by the fire of judgment, they will be improved, since they will be renewed, but will not be utterly destroyed" (*Ecclesiasten Expositio Mystica*; PL 53.995). Gennadius I (d. 471), patriarch of Constantinople, adds, "Let us not believe that the elements are to be obliterated by fire but [that they are to be] changed for the better" (*Dogma Ecclesiarum*, ch. 55).

12. Pope Gregory the Great (c. 540–604) embellishes the whole argument by saying, "Heaven and Earth pass away according to that image which they have now; but according to their essence they subsist unendingly." But the last word is given to the disciples of the Greek astronomer and mathematician Conon of Samos (third century B.C.), whose opinion is here summarized by St. Nicephorus (c. 758–829), patriarch of Constantinople: "In terms of form alone, but not in terms of matter."

13. Marcus Fridericus Wendelinus (1584–1652) was a German theologian and author of *Christianae Theologiae* (see Tuttle, "Libraries," p. 354). Henricus Valesius (Henri de Valois) (1603–76) was a French scholar of antiquity, lawyer, and royal historian to Louis XIV.

14. Mather alludes to Theodoret of Antioch (c. 393-c. 466), bishop of Cyrrhus, whose reference to the "NEW CREATURE" (Gal. 6:15) appears in *Interpretatio Epistolae ad Galatas* (PG 82.395–96). Theophylact's position appears in *Expositio in Epistolam ad Galatas* (PG 124.365). Philo Judaeus of Alexandria, Jewish exegete and philosopher (c. 20 B.C.–A.D. 50), developed an allegorical interpretation of the Old Testament. Mather may have in mind Philo's *De Opificio Mundi* 43–44 and *De Aeternitate Mundi* 69–50.

15. "Restoration" or "restitution."

16. Abraham Calovius (1612–86), orthodox Lutheran theologian, professor at Wittenberg, staunch opponent of the Socinians, and distinguished orientalist. Among his major works are *Systema locorum theologicorum* and *Biblia Illustrata*. Mather's quotation (probably from *Biblia*) translates, "Concerning the restitution to the former, or better, state."

17. As usual, Mather is incensed at the preterite and allegorical interpretations of Henry Hammond. Mather prefers to interpret this regeneration as a re-creation of the earth. Evidently he relies on Calovius's quotation from Justin Martyr's *Dialogue with Trypho* 113 for the Greek words, which translate, "Re-creation" and "Reconstruction."

18. "Larger and more flawless."

19. William Whiston developed a lengthy argument that the antediluvian world was much more fertile and healthy (*New Theory*, pt. III, pp. 246–84). Mather also alludes to God's cursing the soil with unfruitfulness (Lev. 26:20) and to his rainbow covenant with Noah (Gen. 9:8–17). Thomas Burnet maintained that the antediluvian world was entirely level, more fruitful than the present, and blessed with one uniform season (*Sacred Theory*, chs. 4–5, 9). But Dr. Thomas Sherlock (1678–1761), bishop of London, disputed Burnet's theory—as did virtually everybody—in *Use and Intent*. See Ray, pp. 8–60.

20. Gr.: "Inhabited." See also Burnet, *Sacred Theory*, pp. 327–32.

21. See Ray, pp. 411–15; Whitby, *True Millennium*, p. 6; Burnet, *Departed Souls*, p. 239.

22. "To enjoy God" and "to make use of his creatures." See also Mede, *Works*, pp. 811–12.

23. See Tertullian, *Against Marcion* 3.24; Mede, *Works*, pp. 775–76; I. Mather, *Future Conversion*, p. 30; Whitby, *True Millennium*, p. 5.

24. Cerinthius (fl. 100), a Gnostic, taught that Christ was merely human at birth but became divine through baptism, when a divine power descended on him, although this power left him at crucifixion. In objecting to the immoderate carnal banquets that Islam was believed to promise the just in a paradisial lubberland, Mather adopts the Augustinian position and pleads for moderation (*City of God* 20.7; see also Irenaeus, *Against Heresies* 5.35; Origen, *Contra Celsum* 2.112). Hedibia was the learned woman to whom Jerome addressed his Epistle 122, *De Poenitentia* (*PL* 22.1058).

25. Lactantius, *Divine Institutes* 7.24.

26. The Marcionites were the disciples of Marcion (d. 160), a Pontian heretic excommunicated in 144. Marcion rejected the Old Testament because it was essentially a codex of law (set up by the Demiurge) rather than a gospel of love like the New Testament. The OT God of law, Marcion taught, had nothing in common with the God of love, whom Christ revealed himself to be during his lifetime. Moreover, Marcion felt that only the Apostle Paul understood this dichotomy, while the other apostles and evangelists were oblivious to it. The other heresy of the Marcionites was that they, as Mather gives it in Greek, "preached celibacy" (Tertullian, *Against Marcion* 5.9–10).

27. Daniel Whitby traces the whole debate among the church fathers in *True Millennium*, p. 7. For Samuel Sewall's table discussion on this issue, see Davidson, pp. 22–23; see also Watters, chs. 1–3.

28. Tertullian mentions his lost work, *Hope of the Faithful*, in *Against Marcion* 3.24. See *PA*, p. 118. Although the anonymous work with Tertullian's title, *Spes Fidelium*, is not listed in Tuttle, "Libraries," it appears in Isaiah Thomas's "Catalogue of Dr. Cotton Mather's Library" (American Antiquarian Society).

29. Thomas Burnet, though also not distinguishing between the two classes of Saints (*Sacred Theory*, pp. 327–32), was quite impatient with expositors who wanted to restore the belly to the Raised Saints (*Departed Souls*, pp. 231–41). Saturninus (second century), a Syrian Gnostic and disciple of Simon Magus (the Samaritan sorcerer), was rebuked by the Apostle Peter (Acts 8:9–24) for teaching that man, a primitive species before a divine spark gave him reason, was made by a number of creator angels, who themselves had been brought forth by an unknown supreme father. This unknown being, according to Saturnius, sent Christ to destroy the God of the Jews (one of the creator angels) and to save those who had been endowed with the divine spark. Irenaeus castigated the Saturninians in *Against Heresies* 1.24.

30. In the Mosaic account, Jacob blessed his son Joseph and his offspring with the words, "Let them grow [as fish increase] into a multitude in the midst of the earth" (Gen. 48:16). Theodoricus Hackspan (1607–59), a German Lutheran exegete, philologist, and Orientalist, published several pertinent works on this issue, including *Observationes Arabico-Syriacae* and *Exercitatio de Cabbala Judaica*. Aristotle discusses the fertility of fish in *Generation of Animals* 3.1.751. Gaspar Schott (1608–66) was a German Jesuit, mathematician, and natural scientist. Mather's reference to Polytokie and his "Exemples" is unclear.

31. The Pentateuch relates the story of Jacob and 70 members of his family moving to Egypt. At their exodus from Egypt, their numbers are supposed to have reached 600,000 (Genesis 46; Exod. 1:5–7, 12:37).

32. Ludovicus Cappellus (Louis Cappel) (1585–1658), son of Jacques Cappel, was a French monk, professor of theology, biblical exegete, Hebraist, and grammarian. Augustinus Tor-

niellus (Agostino Ternielli) (1543–1622) was a learned Italian divine and author of *Annales Sacri et profani*, which explains many obscure references to OT chronology, geography, and topography.

33. Joannes Temporarius (b. c. 1535) authored the exegetical *Chronologicarvm demonstrationvm libri tres*, a chronological history of Christianity to 1580. The quotation translates, "Without any marvel of nature." Mather's defense of such hyperbolic multiplications comes as no surprise, for in the best Newtonian manner he endeavors to validate the accuracy of the Bible with the methods of the new sciences. See similar efforts in Burnet, *Sacred Theory*, p. 36; Whiston, *New Theory*, pt. III, p. 249.

34. Mather tries to come to terms with two distinct groups mentioned in Revelation 7: one consisting of 144,000, culled from the Twelve Tribes of Israel (Rev. 7:4–8) but surrogated in Mather's Spiritual Israel; and the other, a great multitude from all nations that no one could number (Rev. 7:9).

35. Celio Secondo Curione (1503–69), erudite Italian theologian, historian, and compiler. Mather refers to the popular work by Curio whose title translates, *On the Greatness of the Blessed Kingdom of God*.

36. Mather asserts a double Jerusalem here: The celestial New Jerusalem, a corporeal city where the Raised Saints obtain their Beatific Vision, is without a temple because God himself is there. Its earthly counterpart, the restored Judean capital, however, still maintains its temple. Yet Mather does not wish to press the point too much, as is evident from his dictum, "Let it be of as much value as it can."

37. That Mather's old boyhood teacher Ezekiel Cheever (1615–1708) continued to exert a tremendous influence on him, even in his mature years, can be seen in this revealing passage. See *CA*; Silverman, *Life and Times*, p. 14; Levin, *Cotton Mather*, pp. 13, 26.

38. "Satan's minions."

39. Busiris, Poseidon's son, is the mythological king of Egypt who sacrificed on the altar of Zeus every foreigner coming to the country. The reason for Mather's Plutarchan parallel to the French Louis XIV becomes evident when we remember the slaughter of the Huguenots after the Revocation of the Edict of Nantes (1685).

40. From Lat. *colaphus*, signifying "blow" or "buffet." Hence, "smitings."

41. Mather's barb comes as no surprise, when we bear in mind that the unidentified Venetian imbibed Origen's heretical notions on the destiny of the soul. In *De Resurrectione*, which survives in Jerome's *De Principiis* (4.1.36–37), Origen argued that souls, though equal at creation, could become angels or demons, because of their free will. Death, however, did not decide the final fate of the soul, for its ascent or descent went on uninterruptedly until the final *apocatastasis*, when all creatures—including the devil— would be saved.

42. Mather could not help but wonder about the sagacity of those of his fellow chiliasts who would date the millennium from the time of Luther, when the reformer published his 95 Theses (1517), or even from Constantine's time, when the Roman emperor was baptized on his deathbed (337). The latter conjecture was particularly objectionable, thought Mather, since Flavius Claudius Julianus ("Julian the Apostate") (332–63), the nephew of Constantine I, returned to the pagan gods of Rome and opposed the spread of Christianity even though he had been raised in the Christian church. If either of these two dates were correct, Mather snickered, then Christ's millennial reign of peace and tranquility would have long since eliminated the wars, persecution, and other bloodshed so rampant in Mather's own time. That efforts to date the millennium were no idle diversions can be gathered from a variety of sources. The Geneva Bible of 1602 inserted a chronological

table to that purpose in front of Revelation. See also Joseph Mede's *Paraleipomena*, p. 20; Thomas Goodwin's *Exposition*, pt. II, ch. 6 and ch. 7, sec. ix, pp. 157–58, 195–205; Burnet's *Sacred Theory*, p. 334; Mather's chronology in sec. xii below.

43. "The more difficult places" and "the insoluble points of sacred Scripture."

44. The reference is to Nathaniel Holmes, D.D. (1599–1678), Puritan exegete, Hebraist, and ardent millennialist. All Bible translations consulted render this Hebrew particle in Isa. 65:20 as "for" rather than "that." See Geneva Bible (1602); Douay; KJV; Revised Standard version; New English Bible; Jerusalem Bible.

45. The Chaldee version is the Targum of Jonathan bar Uzziel, also called the Babylonian Targum of the Prophets, a paraphrase of the OT prophets in Aramaic. The Greek version of the OT prophets, of course, is the Septuagint.

46. Mather's hieroglyphics could not be deciphered with certainty. Other possible readings of *"Aforcaeus"* are "Archaeus," "Ascraeus," "Asorceus," and the like. The Greek passage translates, "Child of a hundred years."

47. "Poison poured out into the church."

48. Probably Nicodemus, the Pharisee and Jewish ruler who believed in Christ but was afraid to acknowledge him publicly (John 3).

49. The five Danites were surveying their land inheritance in Canaan (Judg. 18:2, 7, 9, 10).

50. Josephus, *Wars* 4.8.3. Since William Whiston's translation of this work was not published until 1737, Mather evidently relied on Sir Roger L'Estrange's translation (1700), which was phased out when Whiston's appeared on the market.

51. Irenaeus (c. 125–203) was bishop of Lyons. His gloss and subsequent annotation on Isaiah appear in *Against Heresies* 5.34.2.

52. The hyperbolic passage is related at second hand from Papias (70–155) by Irenaeus. Papias was a martyred bishop of Hierapolis (Phrygia), whose works survive only in fragments (Irenaeus, *Against Heresies* 5.33). An emblematic representation of Papias's hyperbole appears in *Tabula Geographica, in qua Iisraelitarum* [sic] (c. 1590), by the Dutch theologian and geographer Petrus Plancius (1552–1622). The prophetic value of Papias's hyperbole was hotly debated among Mather's contemporaries. See I. Mather, *Future Conversion*, p. 22; Whitby, *True Millennium*, p. 4; Anthony Collins, *Grounds and Reasons*, pt. II, pp. 256–57.

53. Mather presents an imperfect quotation from Lactantius: "The Earth will open up its bounty, and will bring forth copious crops of its own accord. The crags of the mountains will ooze with honey; wines will run down through streams; and rivers will overflow with milk. Finally, the world itself will be glad, and the whole nature of the universe will rejoice, snatched away and freed from the dominion of evil, unrighteousness, and error" (*Divine Institutes* 7.24; for the Latin original, see *PL* 6.809).

54. The quotation is from Edward Chandler's discussion of Daniel's dream vision, in *A Defense of Christianity*. Always looking for non-Christian sources to corroborate the prophecies, Mather draws on Vergil's *Fourth Eclogue* (37 B.C.), in which the poet-seer prophesies the birth of a child attended by the coming of the Golden Age. Most critics identify the child in question as either the son of Consul Gaius Asinius Polio (c. 40 B.C.) or the anticipated son (who turned out to be a daughter) of Octavian and Scribonia. Because of its messianic overtones, Vergil's *Fourth Eclogue* was held in high esteem by Christian writers who viewed it as a pagan source announcing Christ's birth. See also Ovid's "The Four Ages," in *Metamorphoses* 1.88–162.

55. "The one who possesses it ought to be healthy."

56. The Apostle Luke is believed to have been a physician.

57. Louis XIV, on whom Mather bestows various unflattering epithets. See Mather's mock funeral sermon, *SD*. See also n. 59 below.

58. Cicero's tribute to the Roman triumvir Gnaeus Pompeius Magnus (106–48 B.C.) describes him as "a man of honor and high moral principle" (*Epistolae ad Atticum* 11.6).

59. Again, Mather's hatred for Louis XIV and his massacre of the Huguenots gets the better of him. Here he equates the French king with the gruesome Aztec god Vitziliputzli (Huitzilopochtli). The bloody rites of human sacrifice in the Mexican temple were well publicized in the English translation of Father José de Acosta's *Natural & Moral History* (2:327–31) and played a prominent part in Mede's exclusion of the American hemisphere from the geography of Christ's millennial kingdom (*Works*, pp. 574–76, and Mede's letter to Dr. William Twisse, "Epistle XLIII," in *Works*, pp. 799–801); see also *WIW*, pp. 201–2; "PT," pp. 68–69; *TA*, pp. 45–48; Sewall, *Phaenomena*, pp. 27–58. For a discussion of this issue, see my "*Israel Redivivus.*"

60. The famous naval battle of Actium (31 B.C.), during which Octavian (the later Roman emperor) defeated the superior forces of Anthony and Cleopatra, queen of Egypt. It is she that Mather has in mind, along with Helen of Troy in Homer's *Odyssey*.

61. The Roman biographer and historian Trebellius Pollio (fl. third century A.D.) authored *The Thirty Tyrants*, a biographical history that also mentions Gunnar and Oisten. Mather's Latin passage translates, "Because I did not find a worse one."

62. Also *Abrech*, from Heb. *avrekh*. Probably a title, but neither its etymology nor its precise meaning is known (see Gen. 41:43).

63. It is unclear who that voluminous writer was of whom it was pretended "they learn everything that can be known."

64. Mather's less-than-flattering epithet for Aristotle—"babbling"—comes as no surprise. The Greek philosopher had fallen on hard times in the colleges (Burnet, *Sacred Theory*, pp. 42–53). For Mather's recommendation for improving Harvard's curriculum, see *MAM*; and for his donations of Pietist books, see *D* 2:192, 194, 348, 380–81, 405–6, 723–24.

65. Founded in 1694 by Frederic I (1657–1713), first king of Prussia, the University of Halle in Saxony was renowned for its school of Protestant theology, at which Mather's long-time correspondent August Hermann Francke (1633–1727), a German Pietist, was teaching. See Kuno Francke; Benz, "Ecumenical Relations"; Lovelace; Hambrick-Stowe.

66. Henry More, D.D. (1614–87), student of Joseph Mede, learned theologian of Christ College, and Cambridge Platonist.

67. Andrew Willet, D.D. (1562–1621), rector of Childerley, Cambridgeshire, staunch opponent of Catholicism, biblical scholar, and contemporary of William Perkins at Christ College, Cambridge.

68. The "Old Conquerors" placed their trophies in the Capitolium in ancient Rome, consisting of three temples dedicated to Jupiter Optimus Maximus, Minerva, and Juno.

69. See Mede, *Paraleipomena*, pp. 23–34; Johnson, pp. 34–35; I. Mather, *Future Conversion*, p. 34.

70. Mather alludes to the "fired Granado" thrown into one of his bedrooms by a vengeful Bostonian (14 Nov. 1721). The outraged neighbor apparently tried to stop Mather from "spreading the smallpox" through inoculation during the epidemic then raging in Boston (*D* 2:657–58). See Winslow, pp. 32–58, 78–87.

71. Though evidently based on a historical individual, Gog and Magog in Ezekiel's prophecy (chs. 38–39) are generally identified with Satan and his minions in the Apocalypse (Rev. 20:7–12). Mather relies on Rabbi David De Pomis's *Zemah David* (see n. 74 below) and on Pierre Poiret's *L'Œconomie Divine*, whose argument Mather had rejected

earlier (1703) as a "Fancy rather [to be found] in a Poem of *Milton*, than in a Treatise of Divinity" ("PT," pp. 67–68; see also pp. 65–67). See also Mede, *Paraleipomena*, pp. 28–29.

72. Mather evidently consulted with Thomas Prince on the identity of Gog and Magog (*D* 2:792). For similar concerns, see Burnet's *Departed Souls*, pp. 195–96; Whitby, *True Millennium*, p. 6.

73. Pierre Coton (1564–1626), illustrious French Jesuit, spiritualist, and controversialist.

74. Also *Zemah David*, a trilingual dictionary (Hebrew, Latin, and Italian) compiled by David De Pomis (1525–93), an Italian rabbi, linguist, physician, and philosopher. The Messiah, son of Joseph, is prophesied to be slain by Armilus in a global war that will precede the redemption through the Messiah, son of David (*Encyclopaedia Judaica*; hereafter *EJ*).

75. Joseph Mede, the famous English millennialist, historian, philologist, and biblical scholar, argued that America might escape the conflagration because it was the hiding place of Gog and Magog ("De Gogo & Magogo in Apocalypsi Conjectura," in *Works*, pp. 574–76; see also pp. 796–802). Mather did not like this conjecture at all and militated against it wherever he had a chance: *WIW*, pp. 96–97, 201–2; *MCA* 1.1.7.4–5, 2.7.1–2; "PT," pp. 68–69; *TA*, pp. 45–48; *IC*, pp. 24–25. See also Sewall, *Phaenomena*, pp. 27–29, 52–55; Noyes, pp. 32–34.

76. Cyrus the Elder (559–529 B.C.), founder of the Medo-Persian Empire, was idealized by the Greek historian Xenophon (c. 430–354 B.C.) in his biography *Cyropaedia*. Mather quotes Cyrus's dying words to his two sons, "Learn from the things that have happened before" (*Cyropaedia* 8.7.24). For the same quotation, see *MCA*, "General Introduction," par. 3.

77. Mather refers to Joachim Lange (1670–1744), German Lutheran Pietist, exegete, Hebraist, grammarian, and professor of theology at Halle. Of Lange's many publications, Mather owned *Causa Dei* and *Medicina mentis*. See *MAM*, p. 35; *D* 2:337, 348, 405, 451; Tuttle, "Libraries," p. 335.

78. Israel's peregrination through the wilderness as seen in Ezekiel 20; in Amos 5, 6; and by Stephen in Acts 7:22–44.

79. Also Beelzebub, a name often applied to Satan as ruler over demons (Matt. 10:25, 12:24–29; Mark 3:22–27; Luke 11:15–19).

80. Pierre Poiret (1646–1719) was a French theologian and mystical Protestant writer. Although Mather had rejected Poiret's Miltonian fancy in his early eschatology ("PT," pp. 67–68), by this time he approved of Poiret's providence book, *L'Œconomie Divine*; his reference is to bk. 5. ch. 15. p. 469 (see I. Mather's *Future Conversion*, p. 35). Mather also relies on John Smith (fl. 1675–1711), Anglican divine, rector of St. Mary's, Colchester, who authored *Christian Religions Appeal*. See also *MAM*, p. 34.

81. Mather refers to Thomas Staynoe, B.D. (d. 1708), chaplain to Queen Mary (William III), who authored *Salvation by Jesus Christ alone*. Who Mather's learned annotator of Revelation is I never did discover.

82. Joseph Justus Scaliger's Latin passage translates, "It is one part of human wisdom to be willing, with resignation, not to know."

83. For various theories on this issue, see Augustine, *City of God* 20.7, 11; Mede, *Paraleipomena*, p. 28; Noyes, pp. 69–76.

84. Mather quotes from the seventh edition (folio) of John Foxe's martyrology *Acts and Monuments* (1632). Like Fox, he was no stranger to such flashes of insight and prophetic revelation, notwithstanding his caveat in the subsequent paragraphs (*D* 1:191, 195, 213, 377–78, 431–32, 446, 2:722). For the time calculation, see Rev. 11:2, 13:5 ("Forty-two months"), 12:14 ("Time, Times & half Time"), 11:3, 12:6 ("Twelve-hundred & Sixty

days"). See sec. xii below and my Introduction, ch. 4. Marcus Aurelius Valerius Maxentius, Roman emperor (306–12), was noted for his cruel persecutions of Christians, and
so was Publius Flavius Galerius Licinius, Roman emperor (307–24). Constantine I (the
Great), Roman emperor of the East, killed Maxentius in 312 and Licinius in 324.

85. Ezek. 4:6: "I have appointed thee each day for a year."

86. For the same argument, see Whitby, *True Millennium*, p. 22.

87. Satan and his minions, who have been damned for a period of 7,000 years: from
Adam's Fall (Gen. 3:1–7; Job, chs. 1–2) to Satan's binding in the abyss at the beginning of
the millennium (6,000 years). His release is to occur 1,000 years later, at the end of the
millennium (Rev. 20:1–7).

88. The great multitude (Rev. 20:8), whom Mather identifies as the offspring of the
Changed Saints from all nations and people living and multiplying on the New Earth.

89. See Staynoe's *Salvation*, which asserted that Satan when loosed at the end of the
millennium would succeed in deceiving the offspring of the Changed Saints. Like many
of his contemporaries, Mather distinguished between two resurrections: At the beginning of the millennium, the Saints of the First Resurrection (Rev. 20:4, 6) would become
the Raised Saints and rulers in the celestial New Jerusalem, from where they would govern the Changed Saints and their descendants on earth. At the end of the millennium,
all others (just and unjust) would be raised (Second Resurrection) to receive their reward
(Rev. 20:11–15).

90. A likely source for Mather's theories is More, *Immortality*, bk. 3, chs. 1, 4, 5, 11, 18.

SECTION XI

1. See Mather's treatment of the prophetic visions of Daniel (2:31–45, chs. 7 and 8,
9:24–27) in "BA"; Newton, pt. I, pp. 128–43.

2. Mather dates the beginning of Daniel's Seventy Weeks (9:24–27), a crucial link in
establishing his prophetic time scheme, from the twentieth year of Artaxerxes Macro-
cheir's reign (Neh. 2:1) (c. 455 or 445 B.C.); he then calculates the years of Christ's birth
and death and develops a time frame to predict his Second Coming. See also Mede,
"Discourse XXV," in *Works*, esp. pp. 103–6. See sect. xii below.

3. "I should not disapprove of the pious pursuit of those who wisely compare the meditations in prophetic and apostolic writings with the outcome itself, the best interpreter
of predictions, and infer that the final day is close at hand" (Johann Gerhard, "De extremo
judicio consummatione seculi, inferna, vita aeterna," in *Loci theologici*, vol. 9).

4. For my discussion of this issue, see my Introduction, ch. 2, and "*Israel Redivivus.*"
For Mather's earlier views see *TLF; FF; D* 1:298, 315; *ATC*, app.; *ACF;* "PT"; *TMT; M; FE.*

5. "It can be concluded in the negative; the Jews have not yet been converted; therefore,
the end of the world is not at hand." This passage is evidently quoted at second hand
from Gijsbert Voetius (Voet), *Disputatione* (see I. Mather's author's preface in *Mystery*,
sig. c-c4, p. 5).

6. The unnamed author is James Calvert (d. 1698). Mather's quotation translates, "Is
not an opinion and presumption, even though prevalent and eagerly received by the
whole world, nonetheless without doubt an empty one?" Calvert's allegorist position is
delineated in his *Naphtali.* See I. Mather's confutation in *Future Conversion*, p. 1.

7. The unidentified pen is evidently none less than that of Increase Mather, who admits, "The opinion of those who pass on the idea that the coming of the Lord will not
take place, except after an infinite number of years, pours exceeding stupor into the hearts
of men, and for this reason is not to be received automatically" (*Diatriba*).

8. For this typological parallel, see Thomas Goodwin's *Exposition*, pp. 195–97.

9. This is evidently the baptismal controversy with the Novationists (255–57). In an effort to preserve the unity of the church, Cyprian (fl. 249–58), bishop of Carthagena, rejected all baptismal or sacramental rites performed outside the church. Crescentius is probably the Christian writer (early fourth century) who disputed with Bishop Alexander of Alexandria the date of the celebration of Easter (*Pauly*).

10. In "PT" (p. 24), Mather had still rejected the historical and allegorical method of Sir John Lightfoot of Ely (1602–75), which asserted a preterite fulfillment of Paul's prophecy (Romans 11). Having since become a disciple of Grotius, Hammond, and Lightfoot, Mather could now quote him with good conscience. The passage is from sec. xii: "Concerning the Calling of the Jews," in Lightfoot's tract *Harmony*, p. 409. See I. Mather's *Future Conversion*, pp. 7–9.

11. The commonness of the name Rabbi Isaac prohibits any identification (see *EJ*). Mather's address to him translates, "I wish, my Lord, to be made certain through you, and by the witnesses of the Law and the Prophets and other Scriptures."

12. Reportedly, the various groups that returned to Jerusalem under Ezra consisted of the descendants of the original Twelve Tribes (hence Mather's "DODEKAPHYLON"), whose union as one nation had been foretold by Jeremiah (33:7) and in Ezekiel's vision of the "two sticks made one" (37:15–28).

13. Jeroboam, son of Nebat, an Ephraimite in Solomon's service, was established king over the Ten-Tribe Kingdom of Israel after Solomon's death (c. 997 B.C.). Jeroboam set up a temple of his own, with two golden calves and non-Aaronic priests at its center. Resenting this apostasy, many Israelites resettled in Judah (1 Kings 12:26–33; 2 Kings 23:15; 2 Chron. 11:13–17, 13:9). King Hezekiah of Judah (c. 727–698 B.C.), eager to undo his father's neglect of the temple, sent messengers to the northern Kingdom of Israel, inviting it to join in worship at Jerusalem. Yet only representatives of the tribes of Asher, Manasseh, and Zebulun honored Hezekiah's invitation (2 Chron. 30:1–20; Num. 9:1–13).

14. Grotius, *Annotationes* 1:170. Hoshea was the last king of Israel, during whose reign the Ten Tribes became tributaries to King Shalmaneser V of Assyria, who initiated their deportation (c. 722 B.C.).

15. Descendants of Jacob's son Simeon, the Simeonites belonged to the Ten Tribes of Israel and reportedly killed the marauding Amalekites during Hezekiah's reign (1 Chron. 4:42–43). This battle, however, took place long before the composition of Chronicles, which modern estimates place between 350 and 250 B.C. (*DOB* rev. ed.). King Josiah of Judah (c. 639–609 B.C.) cleansed his kingdom from apostate worship (2 Chron. 34:3–8).

16. Mather describes the Assyrian cities of the Shalmaneserian Deportation (2 Kings 17:6, 18:11; 1 Chron. 5:26). See Strabo 16.1; Herodotus 7.62; Wells, 2:94–95. To validate the historical account, Mather draws on the apocryphal Tobit (1:17–22), an account of the courageous Naphthalite, who defied Sennacherib's prohibition to bury the bodies of executed Israelites.

17. Mather refers to chs. 3–14 of the Second Book of Esdras in the Pseudepigrapha (i.e., 4 Esdras in the Vulgate), also called Apocalypse of Ezra, which is the source of the legendary Ten Lost Tribes of Israel (2 Esd. 13:39–48). Subject to great eschatological speculation throughout the seventeenth century, the Lost Tribes were thought to have removed into "a further countrey, where neuer mankind dwelt," called "Arsareth" (2 Esd. 13:41–45). However, they were expected to reunite with their Jewish brethren just before the Second Coming. See Fletcher and Lee, pp. 25–28, 50–56, 63–88.

18. Because of its millenarian significance, the *ubi sunt* of the Ten Lost Tribes of Israel was much debated, and many reports from the New World sought to deliver proof that they lived in hiding in the Peruvian mountains of Quito. In his *Chronographia*, bk. 1,

Gilbert Genebrard suggested South America as the faraway country "Arsareth." Yet Cotton Mather pokes fun at his colleague Thomas Thorowgood (c. 1595–1669), who gave new life to this speculation in *Iewes in America* and *Digitus dei*. See Huddleston, pp. 33–48, 128–38; my Introduction, ch. 2.

19. Rabbi Menasseh ben Israel (1604–57) of Amsterdam was the most prominent Hebraist of his age. See Roth; Katz, *Philo-Semitism*. Cotton Mather refers to Menasseh's *Esperanza de Israel*, which relates Antonio de Montezinos's eyewitness account (1644) of the Lost Tribes in Peru. Translated into English, Menasseh's work (esp. pp. 11–17, 26–31, 39–56) fueled the millennialist fervor of Thomas Thorowgood, John Dury, and New England's own John Eliot. See Mede, *Works*, pp. 74–77, 799–800; *MCA* 3.3.192–93; Sewall, *Phaenomena*, pp. 29–47; Noyes, pp. 68–99; Burnet, *Sacred Theory*, pp. 193–95; Whiston, *Literal Accomplishment*, p. 116, and *Sermons and Essays*, pp. 224–25, 233–34.

20. For the Babylonian Captivity of the Moabites, Ammonites, and Idumaeans and their subsequent release, along with the Jewish nation, see Josephus, *Antiquities* 10.9.7. John Lightfoot's discussion appears in "Addenda to 1 Cor. XIV," in *Works* 12:570–73. The same tradition is related in The Order of the World (Seder Olam Rabbah and Seder Olam Zuta).

21. Mather refers to the Babylonian Talmud and to Jonah, who calls himself a Hebrew (1:9). Elijah Levita (Bahur ben Asher ha-Levi Ashkenazi) (c. 1468–1549), a learned Hebraist, grammarian, philologist, and lexicographer, taught Hebrew in Italy. His *Tishbi* is a celebrated lexicon of talmudic and medieval Hebrew and Yiddish vocalizations, of foremost importance to the study of Hebrew grammar.

22. The Idumaeans were subjugated and naturalized by King John Hyrcanus (134–104 B.C.), high priest of Judea (Josephus, *Antiquities* 13.9.1; Isa. 11:13–14; Obad. 10, 17–21; Dion Cassius 37.16.5–17.4. The Greek translates, "Their institutions."

23. Josephus, *Antiquities* 11.1.1–3; Ezra 1:1–11.

24. A prophet of the House of Asher, Anna predicted the imminence of the Messiah (Luke 2:36–38). In Anna, Mather finds evidence for his argument that the Ten Tribes of Israel, to which the House of Asher belonged, were not lost but rather that a remnant of each had returned out of Babylon.

25. The Hasmonean Revolt against Antiochus IV Epiphanes (175–164 B.C.), as characterized in Josephus, *Antiquities* 14.16.1–4.

26. The Latin translates, "Not much farther." And the description of Iamnia can be found in Strabo 16.2.28.

27. Mather relies on Herman Wits and Gijsbert Voet.

28. Cornelius à Lapide (Cornelius van den Steen) (c. 1566–1637) was a Jesuit of Flanders, professor of theology, exegete, and compendious writer.

29. Mather integrates the philological insights of the new hermeneutics of his day. While chs. 1–8 of Zechariah are attributed to the prophet Zechariah, chs. 9–14 are believed to be of later origin. Differences in content, language, and form suggest an anonymous writer whose prophecies were attached to Zechariah and came to be called Deutero-Zechariah.

30. Franciscus Vatablus (François Waterbled, called Vatable) (d. 1547, Paris) was appointed professor of Hebrew at the College of Three Languages, Paris, by King François I of France. Thomas Gataker (1574–1654), learned member of the Westminster Assembly and Puritan divine, opposed the execution of Charles I. Among his works are *Opera Critica* (see Tuttle, "Libraries," p. 329). The *"Exiccation"* of the Euphrates was, of course, the drying up (exsiccation) of that river at the fall of Babylon (Herodotus 1.191; 2 Esd. 13:46–47).

31. Matthias Flacius Illyricus (Matija Vlačić Ilir) (1520–75), German Lutheran church

historian and professor of theology at Wittenberg and Jena, is remembered for his compilation of *Historia ecclesia Christi*, a Lutheran church polemic known as the *Magdeburg Centuries* (*MAM*, pp. 65, 66). Mather's reference to Theodoret (c. 393–466), bishop of Cyrrhus, is to his *Interpretatio Zachariae Prophetae* (*PG* 81.1642).

32. Jerusalem was sacked by General Titus (70), son of Roman emperor Titus Flavius Vespasianus (69–79). According to the historian Josephus, more than a million Jews were killed or taken captive and sold into slavery (*Wars* 6.9.3). The three factions mentioned by Mather were the Pharisees, Sadducees, and Scribes—all fulfilling their priestly offices in various capacities (Josephus, *Antiquities* 13.10.6).

33. Perhaps Beroean (Acts 17:10–15), one of the citizens of a Macedonian town who carefully compared Paul's preaching with their Scriptures.

34. Mather discusses Zechariah 12, which foretells the destruction of Jerusalem and the Coming of the Messiah. Hugo Grotius insists on a strictly historical reading of this prophecy (*Annotationes* 1:443–44). And *"Jackson"* is probably Thomas Jackson, D.D. (1579–1640), dean of Peterborough.

35. See Calvert; Calvin, *Novum Testamentum Commentarii*, 5:137, 166–84.

36. Lat.: "The mind of the law is law." In Mather's preterite and allegorical reading of Romans 11, the descendants of the Christianized Jews and all true believers among the Gentiles are now the Surrogate Israel. Giles Fletcher and Samuel Lee (Cotton Mather's father-in-law) specifically warned against such an allegorical reading in *Israel Redux*, pp. 100–106.

37. "Through Cyrus temporally, through Christ spiritually." Compare with I. Mather's *Mystery*, pp. 1–11. See also my discussion in *"Israel Redivivus,"* pp. 361–69.

38. Hebrew reference unclear.

39. Eusebius Pamphili reports that Domitian Caesar, who feared the coming of Christ, questioned the descendants of the Davidic family about Christ's kingdom (*Ecclesiastical History* 3.20). The passage is a paraphrase of Matt. 16:27; Acts 10:42; Rom. 2:6; 2 Tim. 4:1; Rev. 2:23, 11:15.

40. The quotation from Petrus (Van der Cun) Cunaeus (1586–1638), Dutch Hebraist, jurist, and antiquarian at Franeker, translates, "It belongs to mankind to have opinions on those matters, but to God to know them." Mather probably refers to Naphthali Ben Isaac Kutz (1645–1719), a Polish rabbi and famous Cabalist of Poznan. And Juan Bautista Villalpando (1552–1608) was the Spanish Jesuit who authored *Apparatus urbis ac templi Hierosolymitani*.

41. William Whiston (1667–1752), Anglican divine and ardent millennialist, succeeded Isaac Newton as Lucasian Professor of Mathematics at Cambridge (see Force, *Whiston*). Mather refers to *Accomplishment* and *Sermons and Essays*, pp. 220–34. See also Toland; Tuttle, "Libraries," p. 354; *D* 2:106, 205, 230; *MAM*, pp. 54, 69, 150. For an early examination of Whiston's influence on Mather see Tuttle's "William Whiston and Cotton Mather," *Publication of the Colonial Society of Massachusetts* 13 (1912): 197–204.

42. Theodoret opposed the Christology of Cyril of Alexandria because of its similarity to Apollinarianism. Apollinarius the Younger of Beirut (c. 310–90) held that while Christ's body and soul were human, his spirit was not, for it had been replaced by the divine Logos. Consequently, Christ lacked complete manhood even though he had perfect Godhead (see Theodoret's *Against Heresies* 4.8 and *De Incarnatione*). Mather refers to John Toland (1670–1722), an Irish Deist whose *Nazarenus* asserted (p. vi and chs. 16–17, pp. 62–69) that Christ had not at all abrogated the Mosaic pedagogy and that Christianized Jews and Gentiles alike were therefore bound to observe the Mosaic Law for all time. Accordingly, faith (Christ) and works (Mosaic Law) had to be observed together. Mather's

early millennialism essentially agreed with Toland's position on the eschatological role of the Jewish nation; however, with his new preterite-allegorical exegesis of Romans 11, Mather could now afford to sneer at his embattled colleague. See also Scult, pp. 40–42.

43. William Lowth, bishop of Winchester, dealt with this issue in his popular work *Larger and Lesser Prophets* and especially in *Ezekiel*. Mather's five following paragraphs on Ezekiel's visionary temple are excerpted from his own commentary on Ezekiel 40–48 in "BA." See Whitby's *True Millennium*, pp. 9–14.

44. I.e., Zerubbabel's temple, built c. 536–515 B.C., after the Babylonian Captivity had ended. It fell far short of the magnificent edifice described in Ezekiel's vision (chs. 40–48) and even of Solomon's temple (2 Sam. 7:1–6; 1 Kings 5:3–5 and chs. 6, 7, 8), which had endured until its desolation by Nebuchadnezzar (c. 597 B.C.).

45. In many respects, Mather speaks of five separate temples: Solomon's temple; Ezekiel's visionary temple; Zerubbabel's temple; Herod's temple; the mystical temple of Christ's Saints, typified by the three literal predecessors (1 Kings 8:27; Isa. 66:1; Acts 7:48, 17:24; Heb. 8:5; Eph. 2:19–22; 1 Pet. 2:1–9).

46. Ezekiel's vision describes the territorial allotments for each of the tribes. These territories, of equal width, are arranged from north to south with exact lines running east to west and a *"Princes Portion"* (oblation) lying to the east and west side of a square of 25,000 cubits, extending from the Jordan to the Mediterranean (Ezek. 48:1–22).

47. Constantin L'Empereur (Van Oppyck) (1591–1648), Dutch professor of Hebrew and theology at Leyden, edited and translated into Latin various Hebrew commentaries by Isaac Abrabanel and Moses Kimchi. Mather refers to L'Empereur's quotation from R. David Kimchi (c. 1160–1235), a French exegete and grammarian famous for the philological and grammatical study *Mikhol* (1532) and for his lexicon *Sefer ha-Shorashim* (before 1480). Mather enlists in his argument John Lightfoot's *Temple*, ch. 10, which argues that Zerubbabel's temple was modeled after that in Ezekiel's vision but matched neither its dimensions nor its splendor (p. 251; see also pp. 217, 248, and Lightfoot's *Works* 12:271). William Greenhill (1591–1671), nonconformist divine, member of the Westminster Assembly (1643), and benefactor of Harvard College, wrote a preface to Increase Mather's *Mystery*. Cotton Mather here refers to Greenhill's literalist compendium *Exposition of the Prophet Ezekiel* (see *MAM*, p. 83).

48. This secondhand quotation from Cornelius à Lapide's *Commentaria* translates, "All things which are written in Ezekiel about Jerusalem are without doubt to be understood of the heavenly City, the Jerusalem above." See Mather's Rabbi "Antipass" (*T*, p. 459).

49. William Alleine, D.D. (1614–77), nonconformist vicar of Bridgewater, Somerset, ousted by the Act of Uniformity. Mather refers to Alleine's *Mystery of the Temple and City*; he summarizes the main points of Alleine's allegorization of the temple in "Ezekiel, ch. 40," in "BA."

50. Here ends Mather's excerpt from "Ezekiel, ch. 48" ("BA").

51. I.e., Mather's Spiritual (Surrogate) Israel, rather than Natural Israel. For a careful review of the contemporary debate see Whitby, *True Millennium*, "Paraphrase on . . . Romans [ch. IX–X]," pp. 53–64, and "Appendix to [Romans] Chap. XI."

52. Cotton Mather specifies two prominent Continental literalists. Jacob Alting (1618–79), German Hebraist, was the son of the Calvinist theologian at Groeningen Johann Hendrik Alting (1583–1644). Jacob Alting's commentary on Romans 11 appears in his *Opera omnia theologica*, vol. 4. Franciscus Junius (François du Jon) (1545–1602) was a French Reformed theologian, son of Immanuel Tremellius (1510–80), a learned Protestant divine and converso of Ferrara, who taught Hebrew at Cambridge, Heidelberg, and Sedan. Father and son together translated *Biblia Sacra* into Latin from a Greek origi-

nal. For helpful secondary works on the restoration of the Jewish nation, see Hill, "Till the Conversion"; Toon, *Puritans*; Culver; Ehle; Ball; Katz; Popkin, *Millenarianism and Messianism*.

53. Mather refers to Jacobus Johannes Batelier (Batalerio) (1593–1672), author of *Dissertatio de Israelitarum conversione*, and to David Pareus (1548–1622), German Lutheran-Calvinist theologian at Heidelberg (1591), from whose *Opera theologica exegetica* (vol. 1) Mather quotes the passage, "I confess that it is with trepidation that I undertake to expound these points." See Tuttle, "Libraries," p. 341. Both Increase and Cotton Mather had rejected these allegorists, the latter in "PT," pp. 23–35, and the former in *Future Conversion*, pp. 1–2, and in *Mystery*.

54. This was the first missionary journey of Paul and Barnabas (c. 47–48). See Acts 13:1–14:18.

55. Mather here embraces the preterite-allegorical position of Grotius (*Annotationes* 2:270–73), of Hammond (*Paraphrase*, pp. 433–37), and of Lightfoot (*Works* 3:408–12, 6:393–94, 12:441–46), primarily because he needs to establish that the Christian church as Surrogate Israel has inherited God's promise to Israel.

56. "That God would be more estranged from Israel than from the Gentiles."

57. Mather's imagery is taken from Paul's illustration of God's adopting the Gentiles (Rom. 11:17–24). Theophrastus of Eresos (c. 370-c. 288 or 285 B.C.), pupil of Aristotle, describes and classifies plants in his *Enquiry into Plants* 2.2.5, 3.12.1–3.

58. I.e., pruning.

59. Mather paraphrases Paul's parable of the olive tree (Rom. 11:13–26).

60. Rabbi Eliezer Ben Hyrcanus (fl. first century), great Jewish scholar and Talmudist, supported the popular view that the Ten Tribes of Israel still lived beyond the Euphrates, from where they would return (see Josephus, *Antiquities* 11.6; 2 Esd. 13:39–45). For Mather's source, see *Antiquities* 12.2; Epistle of Aristeas. And Justin Martyr's Greek, which translates, "Every day," appears in *Dialogue with Trypho* 47 and *First Apology* 63.

61. For this holocaust, see Josephus, *Wars* 6.4–7.1.1. Mather's *"Bitter"* refers to the bitter herbs of Passover (Exod. 12:8).

62. The Christian historian and hagiographer Sulpicius Severus (c. 360–420) describes this issue in his *Chronicle* 2.45, and Justin Martyr does so in his *First Apology* 69–71. Johann Clemens Drusius (Jan van der Driesche) (1550–1616) was a Dutch theologian, Hebraist, and professor of Oriental languages at Oxford and Franeker. See Tuttle, "Libraries," p. 324; Whitby, "Appendix to [Romans] Chap. XI."

63. This is the patristic legend Mather discusses over and over again in an effort to validate his preterite fulfillment of Romans 11. The Greek passage translates, "More worthy" or "honorable." For a synopsis of the debate between Gregentius and Herbanus, see my n. 4 to sec. III above; Mede, *Works*, pp. 767–68; *TMT*, p. 104; William Thomas Radius's edition of *The Discussion of St. Gregentius*.

64. "Let Apella the Jew believe it."

65. Gr.: "Filling up" (Rom. 11:25, 26); Lat.: "The precious stone fills up the cavity of the ring." For Increase Mather's contrary view, see *Mystery*, pp. 1–11; and my discussion in *"Israel Redivivus,"* pp. 361–69.

66. This was John Seager (Seger) (d. 1656), author of the millennialist tract *A Discovery*. For the widespread millennial expectations among the Fifth Monarchists during Cromwell's Interregnum, see P. G. Rogers; Capp, *Fifth Monarchy Men*; Maclear.

67. Mather refers to the Fourth Monarchy (the Roman Empire), represented by the iron legs in Daniel's interpretation of Nebuchadnezzar's golden-headed image (2:31–33, 40–42).

68. Mather's translation is correct.

69. Cotton Mather could by this time embrace the allegorical views of Richard Baxter, the renowned English Presbyterian and friend of Increase Mather (*Selected Letters*, pp. 415–16). Baxter's *Glorious Kingdom* originated as an extended refutation of the ardent millennialism Thomas Beverley propounded in *Thousand Years Kingdom*. Although Increase wrote *Future Conversion*, his reply to and refutation of Baxter's *Glorious Kingdom*, as early as 1695, he did not publish it until long after Baxter's death (see esp. ch. 1). See also Michael G. Hall, pp. 274–79.

70. Contrast Jonathan Edwards's views in "Apocalypse," pp. 134–35.

71. This position was also tendered by Menasseh ben Israel in *Hope of Israel*, sec. 17, pp. 31–34; and by Fletcher and Lee in *Israel Redux*, pt. I, pp. 7–8, 44–63.

72. *PL* 23.903.

73. Voetius: "That no tribes of Israel, or their remnants, survive today outside the Jewish nation." Johannes van der Vorst (Vorstius) (1623–76), German Protestant theologian and philologist of classical and Oriental languages: "That today certain genuine remnants of those tribes are found on the earth is a most empty dream."

74. R. Benjamin of Tudela (fl. c. 1150–73) was the great Jewish traveler of medieval Spain whose *Itinerarium* describes the descendants of the Ten Lost Tribes of Israel as still inhabiting the Persian towns of Nishapur and Khaybar (see Adler, p. 53). A similar claim was made by R. Abraham ben-Mordecai Peritsol (also Peritzol or Farissol) (d. 1528), the learned French rabbi of Avignon, geographer, and exegete, whose cosmography, *Itinera Mundi* (chs. 18, 30), is relevant here. Cotton Mather liked these accounts as little as that of Antonio de Montezinos, which placed the Ten Lost Tribes in the Peruvian mountains of Quito. In the same vein, Mather discards the pseudepigraphic Epistle of Aristeas, according to which legend (third century B.C.) the Hebrew Scriptures were translated into Greek (the Septuagint) by 72 famous scholars from Jerusalem in 72 days. This legend appeared to Mather as incredible as the ancient talmudic story that relates how Josiah hid Moses's Ark of the Covenant (Jer. 27:15–22) and the temple utensils in a cave on Mt. Nebo to avoid their desecration during the Babylonian Captivity (Shekalim 6:1–2; Yoma 53b-54a, talmudic tractate; 2 Macc. 2:1–7).

75. See Mather's discussion of Pietist conversions in Malabar, eastern India, in *IC*, pp. 44 ff.; Lovelace, pp. 32–33. Mather unites the Christianized Indians of the East with John Eliot's praying Narraganset Indians of Massachusetts in the West (*MCA* 6.6.50–65). See Holstun, pp. 102–65. For Jacob's sons and the patriarch's wrestling with an angel, see Gen. 29:33–34, 32:22–28.

76. An allusion to the miraculous appearance of Christ in the legend of Gregentius and Herbanus and to Paul's sudden conversion as a type of what would happen to Israel. For Mather's source, see Mede (*Works*, pp. 761, 767–68, and *Paraleipomena*, pp. 24, 37–40). See "PT," pp. 33–34; my Introduction, ch. 2.

77. Chrysostom's Greek translates literally, "Will prevail until the end." Mather's translation from Origen, *Contra Celsum* 4.22 (*PG* 11.1056C), is quite literal.

78. Mather refers to Hieronymus Zanchius (Girolamo Zanchi) (1516–90), Italian-born Calvinist theologian and renowned professor of theology at Strassburg and Heidelberg. Mather may have in mind Zanchius's Latin commentary on Thessalonians (2 Thess. 1:8), in *Opera omnia theologica*, vol. 6.

79. Compare with Whitby's *True Millennium*, pp. 5, 9.

80. "Even we were of this opinion at one time."

81. "EXPECTANDA" was the running title of his sermon *TLF*. His quotation is from pp. 9–10 of this text. For Mather's earlier belief in the doctrine of the national conversion,

see *TDP*, p. 34; *FF*; *ATC*, pp. 38, 56, and app.; "PT," pp. 23–34; *B*, p. 168; *TMT*, pp. 10–27, 103–8; *ME*, pp. 39–40; *FE*; *IC*, pp. 18, 46–49. From c. 1721 onward, Mather no longer subscribed to this belief, as is evident in *WA*, pp. 12–16; *TB*, pp. 16 ff.; *TL*, pp. 28 ff.; and *D* 2:733.

82. Actually Mather was about 29 when his *TLF* appeared in 1691.

83. Mather used the Hebrew appellation, which translates, "My Lord, My Father," to protect the identity and reputation of Increase Mather, who had died about three years earlier. Cotton had good precedent for this filio-pietistic locution, for as he reports in his *MCA*, "R. David Kimchi did use to Quote R. Joseph Kimchi, under the Title of *Adoni Avi*" (7.30.103; see also *DL*, p. 193; *D* 2:313, 430; *Selected Letters*, p. 415). See also Bercovitch, "Cotton Mather," p. 103. Mather refers to his father's *Future Conversion* but quotes the title from memory. This work was preceded by Increase Mather's *Diatriba* and of course by *Mystery*. For a helpful discussion of Increase Mather's eschatology, see Middlekauff, ch. 10; Miller, *Colony to Province*, pp. 185–90, and *Errand*, pp. 217–39; Bercovitch, "Horologicals"; M. G. Hall, pp. 77–78, 274–79.

84. The passage is a synoptic paraphrase of "Article XIV. Sober Chiliasm," in *PA*, pp. 117–19.

85. Mather refers to 2 Peter 3 but quotes from Acts 3:18–21. He expressed his doubts as early as 1703 ("PT," pp. 78–80).

86. Mather quotes almost verbatim from his father's *Future Conversion*, p. 30. The passage from Lactantius translates, "Certain [nations] will be left behind to be exhibited in triumph by the righteous" (*Divine Institutes* 7.24.3). For a synoptic view of the early chiliasts, see Burnet, *Sacred Theory*, pp. 258–59, 346–49.

87. For Mather's likely source of this interpretation, see Mede, *Paraleipomena*, p. 36, and *Works*, pp. 773–76; Burnet, *Sacred Theory*, pp. 262, 289–91. Drue Cressener, D.D. (c. 1638–1718), vicar of Soham, Cambridgeshire, was the author of the millenarian tract *The Judgments of God*.

88. The author of *Good Things to Come* is identified only as "P.G.B." This publication reshaped Mather's eschatological views (see my Introduction, chs. 2–3; *WA*, pp. 12–16). Mede had not yet harmonized the Rapture with his own eschatological system (see "Epistle XXI" and "Epistle XXII," in *Works*, pp. 773–76).

89. Mather pokes fun at Juan Caramuel de Lobkowitz (1606–82), Spanish Cistercian, bishop successively of Campagna, Satriano, and Vigevano. In his controversial *Theologia Moralis*, Caramuel argued that the nature of the Decalogue was not fixed but mutable and that God could change it at will; hence Mather's Latin charge of "the change of precepts."

90. This line of argument was tantamount to the postmillennialist position of Daniel Whitby and of Jonathan Edwards.

91. Mather excoriates the allegorists Grotius, Hammond, and Lightfoot, whose historicizing of the Petrine conflagration (2 Peter 3) quenched its fire and confined it to the historical destruction of Jerusalem (A.D. 70). See also *D* 2:740, 748.

92. This passage, probably from Mede's *Clavis Apocalyptica*, translates, "After I had finally tried everything else in vain, I yielded to the paradox, affected by the clarity of the thing itself."

93. The first Latin passage translates, "I have frequently and exceedingly marveled with myself." Rabbi Samuel Mar (Samuel Yarhina'ah) (second-third century) was an astrologer, physician, Talmudist, and jurist. In the talmudic tractates Barakhot (34b) and Sanhedrin (99a), R. Samuel argues that the messianic condition of Israel will differ from its second-century state only in that Israel will then be liberated from the yoke of alien rulership (*EJ* 3:1356). Mather's quotation translates literally, "The kingdoms are to be subjugated."

94. The temporary punishment of Miriam, sister of Moses, with leprosy (Num. 21:1–15) is the OT type of the church's restoration. Likewise, Persian Queen Vashti, wife of Ahasuerus (Xerxes I), fell into disfavor (c. 480 B.C.) when she slighted her regal husband (Esth. 1:1–22). *Sic transit gloria mundi.*

95. Thomas Fuller (1608–61), prebendary of Sarum and prolific writer of many acclaimed histories. His *History of the Holy Warre* went through many editions (Tuttle, "Libraries," p. 328).

96. The temple utensils, including the menorah of Solomon's temple, were first carried into Babylonian exile after the fall of Jerusalem (c. 597 B.C.). Upon the Israelites' return, the utensils were placed in Zerubbabel's temple; they were again carried off by Antiochus IV Epiphanus (175–164 B.C.), replaced a little later by Judas Macchabee (1 Macc. 4:49), and replenished again by Herod the Great (Josephus, *Antiquities* 3.6.1, 15.11.1; *Wars* 1.21.1). Again taken by Vespasian's general Titus at the sacking of Jerusalem, they were carried to Rome in triumph, where they remained until the fifth century (Josephus, *Wars* 7.5.5). Roughly 400 years later, according to the sixth-century Byzantine historian Procopius, the dreaded Vandal Genseric (d. 477) sacked Rome (June 455) and removed the utensils to Carthagena, his north-African capital (*Wars of the Vandals* 1.4.5). Procopius reports that Belisarius, general of Justinian I, retrieved the treasures of the Jews at the fall of Carthagena (533) and transported them to Constantinople. Mather obviously relies for information on Procopius, who relates that Justinian hastily returned the vessels to Jerusalem after he had been warned that they had brought nothing but disaster to both Rome and Carthagena. After repeated invasions of Jerusalem by the Persians and Arabs (seventh century), the golden vessels disappeared forever. While modern historians give little credit to Procopius's version, late medieval accounts report that the menorah had been seen in the palace library of Emperor Julian during the seventh century, and Emperor Constantine Porphyrogenitus (905–59) mentions that such a lampstand was in use during religious celebrations. In either case, the vessels would have been lost when Constantinople was destroyed during the Fourth Crusade (1204). Today, a depiction of the menorah can still be seen in Rome on the Arch of Titus, which commemorates his victory.

97. Roman emperor Julian the Apostate (332–63) renounced the church and became a vigorous opponent of Christianity.

98. This is Mather's wry effort to unnerve his placid readers asleep in their expectation of future signs prognosticating the Second Coming.

SECTION XII

1. The reference is to the prophetic succession of empires—Babylon, Medo-Persia, Greece, and Rome—in Nebuchadnezzar's dream (Dan. 2:31–45). See also Mather's commentary on Daniel 2 in "BA."

2. Xerxes I, king of Persia (486–465 B.C.) despoiled Babylon's temples to replenish his own war coffers. Diodorus Siculus reports that the treasures of the temple of Belus amounted to 6,000 talents (*Universal History* 2.9.5, 8). Mather refers also to the chronological *Physical History* by Julius Pollux, a ninth-century Byzantine ecclesiastical writer.

3. Mather praises William Burnet (1688–1729), colonial governor of New York, whose sole claim to fame is *An Essay on Scripture-Prophecy.* See *D* 2:804–6; Tuttle, "Libraries," p. 302. The Latin, which translates, "On the Four Greatest Empires," alludes to Burnet's main argument, esp. pp. 40–63.

4. The Fourth Empire (Rome and the kingdom of Antichrist), represented by the statue's feet of iron mixed with clay, is struck down by a mystical stone cut from the mountain (Christ's millennial kingdom). See Mather's eschatological sermon *SCM.*

5. In his commentary on Daniel 2 ("BA"), Mather provides his political identification of the statue's ten toes as the ten European monarchies dominated by the Papal See during the pontificates of Gregory VII to Leo X: "The *Feet*, which constitute the *Papal Empire*, are Terminated in *Ten Toes*. And thus, there are *Ten Kingdomes*, to bee found in it. The Time from *Gregory* VII to *Leo* X a Space of 430 years, was the most Remarkable, for the Arbitrary Domination of the *Popes*, over the *Kingdomes* of *Europe*; and you find the Number of them to bee *Ten*, all along this doleful Time. i. The Emperour of *Germany*. 2. The King of *France*. 3. The King of *England*. 4. The King of *Poland*, & *Suedeland*. 5. The King of *Hungary*. 6. The King of *Denmark*. 7. The King of *Scotland*. 8. The King of *Spain*, and *Sicily*. 9. The King of *Portugal*. 10. The King of *Navar*. Kings, as, unaequal in Power, as *Toes* are in Bigness." Compare with I. Mather's variant reading in *Strange Doctrine*, app.

6. "And likewise there are four monarchies." For Mather's source of synchronizing these prophecies, see Mede, "Discourse XXV" and "Some Remaines," in *Works*, pp. 103–5, 582–85.

7. Arthur Ashley Sykes, D.D. (1684–1756), was a Latitudinarian, a controversialist, and a voluminous writer. His *Difference* is an exegesis of Daniel. (See commentary on Matthew 3, in "BA.")

8. This is the doubting Thomas mentioned in John 20:24–29.

9. "Parousia"; i.e., Christ's presence at the Second Coming.

10. Stephen's vision at the moment of his martyrdom (Acts 7:55–56) and John's vision expressed in Revelation.

11. For his sermons and tracts predicting the year 1697 as the *annus mirabilis*, see *TLF*; *PMDJ*; *MC*; *WIW*; *TDP*. For his generic reference to Christ's imminence, see *DL*; *FF*; *ATC*. For works announcing the year 1716, see "*PT*"; *B*; *TMT*; *SCM*; *M*; my Introduction, ch. 4, notes 11–12; and for those claiming 1736, see, in addition to the present study, *C*; *TB*; *TL*; *BO*; "*BA*."

12. See I. Mather's *Mystery*, pp. 130–31.

13. See I. Mather's *Strange Doctrine*, pp. 92 ff. See also Rev. 11:2, 3, 13:1–5.

14. The sack of Rome (455) was a fulcrum for most millennialists who followed Mede's calculation tables.

15. Mather refers to *République des Lettres* by Pierre Bayle (1647–1716), Huguenot philosopher and professor of history at Rotterdam. Jean Pierre Nicéron (1685–1738) has provided extremely helpful biographies of the philosophic society's members, in *Memoirs*.

16. "All expectation seems to be of no more than two hundred years" (Lactantius, *Divine Institutes* 7.25, *PL* 6.812). Mather's argument closely follows Ray, p. 398.

17. Hesychius (fl. 418), bishop of Salona (Dalmatia), with whom Augustine corresponded on the issue of the end of the world (Augustine, *Epistle 198*, *PL* 33.899–925; see also *City of God* 20.5).

18. The Latin of Pope Gregory the Great translates, "That his own generation was not a long way from the end of the world" (see *Epistle 29*, *PL* 77.875). His successor and precursor is, of course, the Protestant Antichrist identified with the Papal See.

19. Johannes Trithemus (Tritheim) (1462–1516) was a German reformer, Benedictine scholar, and abbot of Sponheim. Bernard (1090–1153) was a Cistercian monk, abbot and founder of the Abbey of Clairvaux; Mather refers to his *Epistle 56* (*PL* 182.60). And St. Norbert of Xanten (c. 1080–1134) was the mendicant monk and rabid millenarian of Prussia. For detail see Cohn, pp. 47–50.

20. Johannes Thurmayr Aventinus (1477–1534), German humanist, historiographer, and friend of Melanchthon, was best known for his history of Bavaria, *Annales ducum*

Boiariae. Arnold of Villanova (c. 1240–1311), Spanish physician and lay theologian, authored *Tractatus de tempore adventus Antichristi.*

21. Philipp Camerarius (1537–1624), councillor of the Free State of Nuremberg. The quotation, probably from his *Operae Horarum Subcisivarum,* translates, "They will see him whom they pierced." See Tuttle, "Libraries," p. 320. Abraham Bucholtzer (1529–84) was a German ecclesiastical writer and chronologer. The Latin passage, probably from the apocalyptical work *Index Chronologicus,* translates, "Jesus of Nazareth, King of the Jews."

22. The chronogram translates, "The Coming of the Lord." Its numerical value or date cannot be determined, since none of its letters are distinguished in size. The second Latin passage translates, "The days shall be shortened"; its mystical (cabalistic) significance Mather rejects with the help of St. Remaclus (d. c. 675), abbot of Solignac and Cugnon, Luxembourg.

23. The *Familiarium Colloquiorum Libellus* of Johannes Posselius (1528–91), German classical scholar and philologist, was owned by the Mathers (Tuttle, "Libraries," p. 343). The Gregorian calendar replaced the less accurate Julian Calendar (45 B.C.) on 4 Oct. 1582, adding ten days to rectify the equinoctical deviation. In that year, Pope Gregory XIII instituted the Gregorian Easter cycle, which replaced the less accurate sixth-century Dionysian cycle. Thus, Posselius's doomsday prediction was for c. 1622. Among the expositors who looked for the End in 1656 were John Tillinghast, in *Knowledge of the Times,* pp. 303–8; and George Joye, in *Coniectures,* sig. B i–iii. And the gentleman who earned himself the nickname of "*Doomsday*" was either Thomas Goodwin, whose *Exposition,* pp. 157–58, 195–205, gave great significance to these dates, or Thomas Beverley, who published numerous tracts proclaiming 1697 as the end of the world.

24. I.e., "Six hundred threescore and six" (Rev. 13:18). Its eschatological significance is discussed in Stein, "Cotton Mather and Jonathan Edwards."

25. Lat.: "Woe, popes, are the general exclamations." John Napier (Neper) (1550–1617), baron of Merchiston, was the inventor of logarithms (Tuttle, "Libraries," p. 339).

26. Lat.: "The eighty-eighth miraculous year." Hieronymous Cardanus (Girolamo Cardano) (1501–76) was a learned Italian mathematician, philosopher, and physician of Milano (Tuttle, "Libraries," p. 320). Thomas Beverley (fl. 1670–1701), nonconformist clergyman of Cutler's Hall, London, was an avid premillennialist and zealous proponent of 1697 as the end of the world. For Mather's own hope for this period see *PN,* pp. 128–29, 138–39, 148–53; *D* 1:199–200, 207–8, 212–14, 222–26.

27. Giovanni Pico della Mirandola (1463–94), Italian humanist and philosopher, was one of the first Renaissance Christians to study the Cabala. Mirandola's Latin translates, "We can discover by the most secret way of the Cabala that the end of the age will be about 514 years and 25 days from now."

28. Mather refers to the apocryphal work Apocalypse of Elijah, also known as Apocalypse of Elias the Prophet. Similar eschatological views were popular during the talmudic period. According to the talmudic tractates Avodah Zarah 9a and Sanhedrin 97a-b, the existence of the world is restricted to 6,000 years (*EJ* 11:88). See Burnet, *Sacred Theory,* pp. 258–61; Ray, pp. 399–400.

29. Whoever the author—Anton, Erhart, Johann, Samuel-Fryderyk, or Wolfgang Adam Lauterbach—the Latin distich translates more literally, "The world will endure for only 6,000 years; / after that it will all collapse, overcome by the fire that has been sent."

30. Mather refers to Quirinus Reuterus (1558–1613), a German Reformed theologian and teacher at Heidelberg, who ascribed this talmudic tradition to a pre-Christian rabbi rather than to Elias the Tishbite. For Mather's own source, see Ray, p. 400.

31. "In the sixth generation" (Plato, *Philebus* 66.8).

32. Justin Martyr, in *First Apology* 20, *Second Apology* 7, *Dialogue with Trypho* 80–81; Hippolytus (c. 170–236), in *Refutation of all Heresies*, ch. 21, p. 247, and *Treatise on Christ and Antichrist*, chs. 43–47, pp. 212–14; Irenaeus, in *Against Heresies* 5.28.2–3, 5.30.1–3; Cyprian, in *Exhortation to Martyrdom* 11; Lactantius, in *Divine Institutes* 7.14; Jerome, in *Commentary on Isaiah* 5.20.210 (*PL* 24.193) and *Commentary on Galatians* 2.4.474 (*PL* 26.418); and Augustine, in *City of God* 20.7, 9, 13.

33. "Every expectation."

34. In biblical numerology, the number seven signifies completeness. For Enoch's genealogy see Gen. 5:1–21; the Apocrypha 2 Enoch 67.

35. Christ's transfiguration was witnessed by Peter, John, and James (Matt. 16:28, 17:1–8). And Christ's miracle at the wedding in Canaan (John 2:1–9) typifies the 6,000 years of man. The Apocalypse of Elias counted the six millennia of man from the creation to A.D. 2,000. Hence Mather's argument in the next paragraph that according to this scheme Christ's millennium could be expected in 270 years from 1730; however, this scheme contradicted the chronology of the Samaritan Pentateuch (published in an edition by John Lightfoot), which Mather considered more accurate.

36. This date provides evidence that Mather was still working on his manuscript in 1727. Compare *D* 3:91 with *D* 2:811.

37. Both Ambrose and Basil wrote works entitled *Hexaemeron*, which discuss the six creative days of Genesis.

38. Pierre Jurieu (1637–1713), French Calvinist and millenarian, whose *Accomplishment of the Scripture Prophecies* predicted that the triumph of the Protestant church would occur in 1689. See also *TLF*, pp. 47–49.

39. The reputation of Henry Ainsworth (1571–1622/23), leader of the Elizabethan Separatist group settling in Amsterdam, was tarnished when his opponents accused him of Brownism. The quotation is evidently taken from his *Annotations*. See also Tuttle, "Libraries," p. 313; Edwards, *History*, pp. 306 ff.

40. See "PT," p. 89; Ray, pp. 320–25.

41. The reference is to Augustine of Hippo Regius, northern Africa. On the behest of Erasmus, Augustine's *De Civitate Dei* was first printed in 1522 by the Spanish humanist, philosopher, and reformer Juan Luis Vives (1492–1540), who added his own commentary to this edition.

42. Mather quotes from the commentary of Vives: "Let us keep watch and pray that the Lord will come more quickly"; "Let us keep watch and pray that the Lord will indeed come late, but our life is short"; "Let us keep watch and pray, because we do not know when the Lord is going to come." And Mather joins Augustine with "We do not know when." Augustine's discouragement of such calculations is perhaps best expressed in his epistles to Hesychius, bishop of Salona (*Epistle 197* and *Epistle 199*), and in his treatise *On the End of the World* (*PL* 33.899–925).

43. Hieronymous Zanchius's Latin passages translate: "In what year and what century the Lord is going to return, we do not know, and can in no way know"; "We must each continuously reflect that it may possibly turn out that the Lord comes more quickly than the world thinks"; "We must keep watch and pray unceasingly, and keep hold of lamps furnished with the oil of faith and good works, just as if he were to come tomorrow."

44. Even though most of the Koran (c. 616–50) relied for transmission on oral tradition committed to memory, some revelations were written on anything available at the moment. Mather's sneer seems unfounded in light of Muhammad's warning to skeptics who think that Judgment Day is still 50,000 years off ("The Ladders," in *The Koran*, p. 57).

45. Mather warns all those who like Samson have relinquished their watchfulness (Judg.

16:4–21). In this hedged manner, Mather can indeed predict the year 1736 as the next *annus mirabilis* without sounding like a rabid millenarian (*D* 2:733).

46. The number from the chronogram of the Greek word *Lateinos* ("Latin") is the dreaded 666 of Rev. 13:18 (Irenaeus, *Against Heresies* 5.30.3). The endeavor of Hugo Grotius and Henry Hammond to provide a strictly historical-contextual interpretation of the prophecy led to different results from those desired by most Protestants, who eagerly sought to establish the pope as Antichrist. Grotius opts for the Roman people as Antichrist (*Annotationes* 1:389), and Hammond, explicitly discouraging such numerological fooleries, so identifies Emperor Domitian (*Paraphrase*, pp. 813, 814). See Tuttle, "Libraries," p. 330. For Mather and his fellow millennialists, a "blinded condition" worse than Sodom's was endemic among those with Roman Catholic leanings.

47. This "Sylvester of the Sacred Rock" is probably Gerbertus (c. 945–1003), later Pope Sylvester II (999–1003), who was known for his ardent defense of the papacy. The Latin passage translates, "Our Lord God the Pope."

48. Jacques Davy Du Perron (1556–1618) was an eminently learned French Roman Catholic prelate, cardinal, and later archbishop of Sens. Mather refers to Perron's 1611 thesis, which asserted the infallibility of the pope and the power of his council. Gabriel Vasquez (1551–1604) was a Spanish Jesuit and professor at Alcala; and Diogo Payva d'Andrada (the Elder) (1528–75), a Portuguese Jesuit theologian and treasurer to King John.

49. Robert Bellarmine (1542–1621), Jesuit theologian and controversialist, engaged James I of England in a disputation about Protestantism, in *Disputationes de Controversiis Christianae Fidei*. Mather's quotation translates, "The power of making what is not a sin from a sin, and a sin from what is not a sin."

50. Pierre du Moulin (1568–1658) was a Reformed Huguenot theologian, controversialist professor of philosophy and Greek at Leyden, and author of the work to which Mather refers. See also Tuttle, "Libraries," p. 325. Walter Garret (fl. 1700) was an English millennialist who published several eschatological treatises. "*A Discourse concerning Antichrist*" is probably the running title of an unidentified work. Mather's Latin translates, "As big as all."

51. Caesar Baronius Soranus (1538–1607) was an Italian cardinal, church historian, and Vatican librarian; his *Annales ecclesiastici* was begun as a refutation of the Lutheran Church chronology known as the *Magdeburg Centuries* (*MAM*, p. 68). Bellarmine's work in question is his edition of Baronius's *De Antichristo*.

52. Mather refers to Matthias Flacius Illyricus, the leading force behind the polemical *Magdeburg Centuries*. The Greek preposition signifies "on behalf of," "by," "upon," "about." Martin Luther translated the New Testament into the German vernacular in 1522. The objectionable passage appears in 2 Thess. 2:1 (see also "BA").

53. Augustine, *City of God* 20.19; Jerome, *Dialogus Contra Luciferianos* (*PL* 23.190).

54. Mather objects to all those who would impose an allegorical meaning on the Second Coming. To Mather, this endeavor is tantamount to the "enthusiasm" of the Quakers and their inner experience of Christ. See *MCA* 2.4.11–12, 7.1–4, and app., article xxix; Worrall, pp. 43–59. Mather's reference to the bishop of Ossory, a Catholic diocese in southeastern Ireland and See of Kilkenny, has not yet been traced.

55. This synchronization of the Four Empires (Dan. 2:32–45) with the Four Beasts (Dan. 7:1–28 and Revelation 13) is essentially the work of Joseph Mede (esp. *Works*, pp. 104–5). See Mather's commentary on these chapters in "BA"; Augustine's *City of God* 20.23.

56. Rabbi Solomon is unidentified.

57. Jerome's passage translates, "Let us say, therefore . . . what all the ecclesiastical writers have handed down." See Jerome's commentary on Daniel 7 (*PL* 25.551).

58. Juan de Maldonado (1534–83) was a Spanish Jesuit theologian; his *Commentarii in Prophetas quatuor* is probably the work in question (see Tuttle, "Libraries," p. 337). Tomas Malvenda (1566–1628) was a Spanish Dominican historian and exegete; his *De Antichristo libri XI* is pertinent to Mather's discussion.

59. Ps. 14:1. Paul's paraphrase appears in Rom. 3:10.

60. Mather refers to the invasions by the Visigoths, an eastern Germanic tribe. Under Fritigern, the Visigoths marched on Constantinople and defeated Emperor Valens (378). Alaric (c. 370–410) was the first Visigoth king to invade Italy (401) and to sack Rome (410). In 455, Rome was pillaged again by the Vandal Genseric (429–77). Mather identifies the ten provinces as "i. *Spain.* 2. *Gaul.* 3. *Germany.* 4. *Britain.* 5. *Pannomia, & Moesia.* 6. *Greece.* 7. *Asia,* ye Less. 8. *Syria.* 9. *Egypt.* 10. *Africa.* The Islands of the Mediterranean wee need not Number; for they were but Appendages to the Continent. *Italy,* which was ye *Head,* that bore all ye *Horns,* is therefore not reckoned One of them" ("Daniel, ch. 7," in "BA").

61. The Midrash Tehillim (Aggadat Tehillim) is a collection of Psalms and Rabbinical homilies, with an exegesis of the Psalms, of uncertain date. Mather establishes a typological link between the Roman provinces mentioned above and the ten sons of Haman, prime minister of Ahasuerus (Xerxes I) of Persia, whose persecution of the Israelites was thwarted by Esther (Esth. 9:10, 12).

62. Evidently Mather has in mind the deposition of the Stuart monarch James II (1685–88), who fled into French exile during the Glorious Revolution (1688). The new *"Crown'd Head"* replacing him was the stadtholder of Holland, William of Orange. See *TLF; PMDJ; WWG; TDP.*

63. Mather refers to the defeat of the Spanish Armada (1588); the Gunpowder Plot (1605); and the War of the Spanish Succession (1701–13), which erupted when Louis XIV attempted to secure for his grandson the vacant throne of Spain. See *WWG; TLF; SD; UGV; D* 1:397–99, 420, 2:171–74, 176.

64. A legislative commission of ten Romans under the presidency of Appius Claudius temporarily supplanted the Roman magistracy (451–449 B.C.) and incorporated important elements of Greek law into the Twelve Tables of the Roman law.

65. Pope Marcellus I, bishop of Rome (308–9), reorganized the church of Rome during the Diocletian persecution. When Heraclius challenged Marcellus's authority, a great disorder arose, and Emperor Maxentius (306–12) tried to restore public peace by exiling Marcellus from Rome. According to a fifth-century legend, to which Mather alludes here, Maxentius turned Marcellus's main church into a stable, where the pontiff died from the exertions of working as a stable boy (*Passio Marcelli; Liber pontificalis*).

66. Carlo Sigonio (c. 1520 or 1524-84) was an Italian historian and professor of classical languages; his *Regne Italiae* and *Occidentali Imperio* furnished Mather with information on the invading Germanic tribes—Heruli, Lombards, and Ostrogoths—who established kingdoms in northern Italy. For more detail, see Hugo Grotius, *Historia Gothorum.*

67. Porphyry (c. 232-c. 303) was a Greek Neoplatonist philosopher, student of Plotinus at Rome, and staunch opponent of early Christianity. His *Against the Christians* attacks various points of OT and NT chronology, most notably the date of Daniel. Modern critics assign the writing of Daniel to 168–165 B.C.

68. Johann Heinrich Bisterfeld (d. 1655), German professor of theology at Weissenburg.

69. Again Mather takes issue with Hugo Grotius's historical-contextual interpretation of the prophecies. See Grotius's commentary on Dan. 7:12, "*Quasi filius hominis,* Populus Romanus," in *Annotationes* 1:389. The reference to Matt. 26:64 appears in *Annotationes* 2:106.

70. Rev. 11:3 (1260 days : 360 = 3.5; i.e., Time, Times, and Half a Time). See Mede, *Works*, pp. 105 ("Discourse XXV"), 588–91, 597–99 ("Remaines").

71. The "godly Presbyter of *Marseille*" is Salvian (c. 400–480), whose lamentation translates, "That it was not their own work that they were doing, for they were being led and spurred on by divine command" (*De Gubernatione Dei* 7.12). Mather here relies on Jornandes (Jordanes) (fl. 550), an important historian and bishop of Ravenna, who authored *De summa temporum vel origine actibusque gentis Romanorum* and a history of the Goths, *De origine actibusque Getarum gentis*.

72. "The Scourge of God," the rightful byname of Attila the Hun (434–53). Perhaps the greatest adversary of the Roman Empire in the fifth century, Attila ravaged the Eastern Empire (440) and then invaded Gaul (451) and finally Italy (452).

73. After the sack of Rome in June 455, the Vandal Genseric appointed the Roman emperors for the next 21 years. The Greek phrase translates, as Mather notes, "The tenth."

74. Samuel Lee (1625–91) was Mather's father-in-law. Among Lee's millennialist tracts is the one Mather mentions, whose title translates as *On the Destruction of Antichrist*.

75. Flavius Honorius (384–423) was the Roman emperor of the West during whose reign (393–423) the imperial government was moved to Ravenna (402). The move left the city of Rome to Pope Innocent I (402–17), whose influence on Honorius enabled the pontiff to increase his papal and civil power in both the Eastern and the Western empires.

76. Pope Leo I (Leo the Great) (440–61) extended his papal command to Gaul, Spain, Africa, and all the western Provinces, whereupon he pressed Emperor Valentinian III to grant jurisdiction over these areas to the Roman See (*Novel. Valent. 17*: 8 July 445). *De Apostolis* (*On the Apostles*) is one of Leo's 96 still-extant sermons. In traditional Protestant fashion, Mather equates the mystical Babylon the Great (Rev. 17:5) with the New Babylon, the Roman Catholic church.

77. In an effort to stop doctrinal and political quarrels arising from the Council of Ephesus (431), the newly risen emperor of the East, Marcian (396–459), convoked the Council of Chalcedon (451) in Asia Minor—a convocation that Marcian's predecessor, Emperor Theodosius II, had set in motion against the wishes of Pope Leo I and Western emperor Valentinian III. Marcian presided over an assembly of only 350–60 Eastern bishops, Leo's Western party being represented by only three legates and two bishops from Africa (a later tradition sets the attendance at 600–630). The *Definition of Chalcedon* (451) confirmed the papal primacy of the See of Rome (Mather's "*Caput Ecclesiarum*"; i.e., head of the church). Hence his reference to Pope Leo I as the fierce OT Philistine Goliath (1 Sam. 17:23).

78. Flacius Placidus Valentinianus III (419–55) became Roman emperor of the West at the age of six (425) and ruled Rome until his assassination. General Flavius Aetius completely dominated his government and proved to be invaluable during Attila's invasion of Gaul. But Valentinian III, doubting his general's loyalty when Attila returned in 451, killed Aetius with his own hands (454), for which deed Valentinian was assassinated by loyal cohorts of the general.

79. Petronius Maximus (396–455), Roman emperor of the West for ten weeks, succeeded Valentinian III (455). His regal power was short-lived: When Genseric's Vandal troops took the city of Rome, an enraged mob of Romans tore the fleeing Maximus to pieces.

80. Such an army of Protestant writers on Antichrist has been gathered in *Cyclopaedia*, edited by M'Clintock and Strong, 1:256–61.

81. See my Introduction, ch. 4. For Mather's earlier exegesis, see *TLF*, pp. 27–31, 38–42; *WIW*, pp. 83–90. For similarities see Fletcher and Lee, *Israel Redux*, pp. 114–25.

82. On Charlemagne and his successor, see my Introduction, ch. 4., n. 32. Mather's "*Débonnaireté*" signifies "compliance" or "piety."

83. Following Mede's example (in *Works*, pp. 586–89, and *Paraleipomena*, pp. 18–23), Mather synchronizes John's vision of the temple's inner and outer court (Rev. 11:1–2) with Ezekiel's vision of the temple (Ezekiel 40). According to Mede's scheme, John's Revelation was given in A.D. 94. See also Thomas M. Davis, pp. 11–45.

84. See *D* 2:763, 804, 805–6. Constantine the Great became Roman emperor in 306 and was actually baptized on his deathbed in 336/37, although, according to a fifth-century legend, he was baptized by Pope Sylvester I (314–35) in the year 324. Thus Mather's calculation required some juggling and readjusting. (See my Introduction, ch. 4, for detail.) Mather's calculation seems rather inept at first glance, for Emperor Theodosius I (379–95) divided the empire between his two sons in 395 rather than 456.

85. To avoid exhausting his readers, Mather refers them for further detail to Walter Cross (d. c. 1701), pastor of Moorfield, London, author of *The Taghmical Art*.

86. King of Salem and the first priest mentioned in the Old Testament (Gen. 14:18, 22), Melchizedek is called "King of Peace" (Heb. 7:1–3) and thus taken for a type of Christ.

87. Nicholas of Cusa (1401–64) was a German mathematician, a cardinal, a bishop of Brixen, Italy, and the author of *Prohemium*. The Latin translates, "But after that time there will be the ascent of the church, with Christ her betrothed arriving at the Judgment." Mather equates Cusanus with Caiaphas (c. 18–36/37), Sadducee and high priest of Jerusalem during the ministry of Christ, because during Christ's trial Caiaphas predicted that Jesus would die for Israel (John 11:49–53).

88. William Whiston, whose anti-Trinitarian Arianism led to his expulsion from Trinity College, Cambridge (1710), was one of the foremost physico-theologians, scientists, and millennialists of his day. Mather refers to Whiston's millenarian *Revelation of St. John* as well as *The Accomplishment of Scripture Prophecies*, both of which he much admired. Mather was deeply shaken by Whiston's captivating anti-Trinitarian research (*D* 2:106–7, 109, 186, 205, 225, 230, 817), yet must have forgiven him when Whiston published his *Literal Accomplishment* and his *Supplement to the Literal Accomplishment*, both attacking Anthony Collins's dismissal of Christianity as Judaism allegorized (*Grounds and Reasons*). Governor William Burnet's *Scripture-Prophecy*, which Mather welcomed enthusiastically, is essentially an exegesis of Daniel and Revelation in the best tradition of the day (*D* 2:805–6; Tuttle, "Libraries," p. 302). Both William Burnet and William Whiston were greatly influenced by Sir Isaac Newton (1642–1727), the greatest physicist of his day. An ardent millennialist, Newton had the acumen to keep private his research on biblical prophecies. Except for his posthumously published *Observations*, virtually all of his voluminous tracts on eschatological matters remain unpublished. See Force, *Whiston*; Popkin, "Newton"; Manuel, pp. 361–80.

89. Newton develops this argument at length (pt. II, ch. 3, pp. 276–307).

90. Romulus Augustus, last of the Roman emperors of the West (475–76), was deposed by Odoacer the Hun in 476. Ironically, Romulus Augustulus (little Augustus) bore the names of two illustrious ancestors: Romulus, the first king of Rome; and Augustus, first Roman emperor. In reminding his readers that the chronology of the Samaritan Pentateuch was more accurate than that of the Septuagint and pointed toward 1736—the date one arrives at if Antichrist's 1,260-year reign is dated from 476, rather than 456—Mather follows good precedent. See Mede; Fletcher and Lee, pp. 114–25; I. Mather, *Future Conversion*, p. 26, and *Strange Doctrine*, p. 109 (app.); William Burnet, pp. 103–9, 146–67.

91. The Ottoman Empire faced its most powerful opposition in 1683, when Jan Sobieski, king of Poland (1674–96), and Prince Eugene of Savoy (1663–1736), with the Holy

League of Hapsburg, Venice, and Russia, defeated the Turks who were besieging Vienna for a second time. Between 1683 and 1699, the Ottoman Empire fought disastrous wars against the Holy League, culminating in the Treaty of Carlowicz (1699). See *TLF*, pp. 31–42; *WIW*, pp. 51–52, 90–92; *TDP*, pp. 34–36; *ATC*, pp. 13–43; "PT," pp. 52–57; *DL*; *D* 1:207, 212–13, 214, 243.

92. Benjamin Marshall (b. 1682), rector of Naunton, wrote several hermeneutical works on Daniel. Mather particularly approved of Marshall's *Chronological Treatise upon the Seventy Weeks* and *Chronological Tables*. For further detail, see Mather's commentary on Daniel in "BA"; Mede, *Works*, p. 105; Goodwin, *Works* 3:195–205; Newton, pp. 129–44.

93. Mather's interpretation of Daniel's Seventy Weeks (9:24–27) runs as follows: The Messiah was to be crucified 69 prophetical weeks or 483 years (69 × 7) after King Artaxerxes Longimanus, in the twentieth year of his reign (Neh. 2:1, 4–8), issued his decree for the rebuilding of the temple in Jerusalem. The time allotted for the reconstruction of the city and its temple was 7 prophetical weeks (49 years); thus 62 prophetical weeks (434 years) after the completion of the temple, Christ's Crucifixion was to be expected at the Passover, at the end of the sixty-ninth prophetical week from Artaxerxes's original decree. The remaining seventieth week, however, was not to be calculated according to the rule of "a day for a year" that Mather has applied so far. For here "has been the Rock," Mather triumphs later in the paragraph, "which all the Expositors of this Illustrious Prophecy have splitt upon."

94. Before explaining the vision of the Seventy Weeks, the angel Gabriel hails Daniel with the words, "Greatly beloved" (Dan. 9:23); later the angel uses a similar appellation for Mary, mother of Christ (Luke 1:28).

95. In *Tetrabiblos*, the Greek astronomer, mathematician, and geographer Claudius Ptolomaeus (second century A.D.) argued that human behavior could be determined by the position of the celestial bodies. This astrological fatalism determined not only man's moral character and talent but also his destiny. As Seneca put it: "Our fates lead us, and the hour of birth has determined how much time remains for each" (*De providentia* 5.7).

96. Mather refers to the Roman general Cornelius Domitius Corbulo (d. A.D. 66), who was forced to conclude a treaty with Vologeses and his Parthian brother Tiridates when Corbulo's troops under Cestius Gallus (d. 67) suffered defeat during the Parthian campaign (63). When Tiridates invaded Armenia again, Corbulo finally forced the Parthian to surrender (64). The quotation from Tacitus translates, "Not otherwise than a fixed peace" (*Annales* 15.26–28).

97. Roman emperor Titus Flavius Vespasianus (69–79) took over the military rule of Judea (67) when Cestius Gallus, governor of Syria, died during the Parthian campaign against Vologeses and Tiridates. In 66, the year before his death, Cestius Gallus had marched on Judea in an effort to quell the Jewish revolt against Rome. He besieged Jerusalem, thrust his forces all the way up to the outer temple walls, but inexplicably withdrew without carrying out the destruction of the city. Yet three and a half years later, General Titus (the later Roman emperor Vespasian [69–79] and son and namesake of the Roman emperor at that time) returned with his troops during the Passover celebrations, besieged Jerusalem again, entered the city (70), and set the temple on fire a few days later. See Josephus, *Wars* 7.1.1; Eusebius, *Ecclesiastical History* 3.5.

98. According to Dan. 12:11, 12, an additional 30 and 45 prophetic days/years are allowed to elapse after the destruction of the temple and before the Second Coming of Christ. Antichrist's reign may therefore be extended from 1,260 years to 1,290 years or even 1,335 years. Mather's scheme, derived from Benjamin Marshall and William Burnet, postpones the *annus mirabilis* for a total of 75 years (see "Daniel, ch. 12," in "BA").

99. "The Age of the Holy Spirit."

100. Friedrich Balduin, D.D. (1575–1627) was a professor of theology at Wittenberg and an avid millenarian. Johann Heinrich Bullinger (1504–75), a Swiss reformer of Zurich, chastises those misguided millennialists who believe "that in the space of such a short time they have enough resources." See also Cohn.

101. Michael Stifel (1487–1567) was a Lutheran divine of Saxony, a mathematician, and an apologist. Among his numerological interpretations of Daniel and Revelation is *Ein sehr wunderbarlich Wortrechnung* and among his pronouncements of doom, *Vom End der Welt*. Mather's source is "Bucholtzer" (*T*, p. 465).

102. John Mason (c. 1646–94), rector of Water-Stratford (1674), was given to melancholy after his wife's death (1687). Notorious for his eschatological speculations about the End, Mason published his popular *Midnight Cry* and set up a community on "Holy Ground" near his vicarage, where his followers awaited Christ's return. Meetings were held there even 16 years after Mason's death in 1694 (*Dictionary of National Biography*).

103. "And indeed it must happen in this way."

104. Mather refers to Hieronymous Zanchius's *De fine Seculi* (*On the end of the Age*). The Latin passages translate, respectively, "Not far away" and "Before long."

105. Andreas Meusel (Musculus) (1514–81) was a German Lutheran theologian, millennialist, and opponent of Calvinism. The odd running title translates, "Whether that boy, who is going to overcome the Final Day, will put on just shoes?"

106. Cunmannus Flinsbachius (fl. 1550–70) was a Swiss theologian and author of the Latin *Conjectures of the End Times*.

107. Perhaps a reference to Martin Luther's diatribe *Against Latomus*, p. 139.

108. Even after the Salem Witchcraft debacle (1691–93), Mather held fast to his *WIW*. For his Pietist ecumenism grounded in millenarian speculations, see Lovelace, pp. 32–72.

109. Thomas Venner (d. 1661), one of the earliest settlers of the Bay Colony and a cooper by trade, returned to England during the Interregnum and plotted to bring about Christ's Fifth Monarchy by overthrowing the government (1657). Venner and a number of his followers were executed in front of his meetinghouse in early January 1661 (*DNB*). See Maclear; Banks; Hill, *World Turned Upside Down*, pp. 107–50, and *Collected Essays*, vol. 2, pt. III.

110. "Watchman."

APPENDIX A:
MANUSCRIPT CANCELLATIONS
AND INTERPOLATIONS

Several considerations led me to believe that recording Mather's excisions and interpolations in an appendix would help establish the final version of "Triparadisus" as he intended it for the press. His innumerable alterations would have seriously affected the clarity of the text had they been recorded in it. Moreover, readers who are more concerned with Mather's millennialism and hermeneutics than with matters textual and editorial are thus furnished with a readable edition. Those interested in the composition and editorial process can collate the final product with the entries in this appendix and the one that follows.

The following list is a complete and faithful record of Mather's corrections as they occur in the manuscript. They include a large variety of changes, ranging from corrections of misspelled words, upper- or lowercasing of word-initial letters, and repunctuations to cancellations of individual letters, words, phrases, clauses, paragraphs, or entire pages of manuscript text. Generally, Mather used single, double, triple, or quadruple carets to indicate the exact placing of his interlineations and marginal insertions. However, Mather's carets have been recorded here only when he canceled a caret or careted passage. It appeared unnecessary to record how many carets he used in each case, for they were only to remind him of the sequence in which these interlineations or marginal insertions were to be added. Similarly, to record the innumerable smudges caused by ink spots or foxing seemed unwarranted. Such additional recording would have inflated the bulk of this appendix to an unmanageable size. Consequently, smudges have been recorded only if they completely obscure legibility.

I have used the following descriptors:

[.]   to indicate an illegible canceled letter, the number of bracketed ellipsis marks corresponding with the number of letters—if that could be determined.

[.]   to indicate an illegible underscored and canceled letter, the number of underscored ellipsis marks corresponding with the number of letters—if that could be determined.

[*]   to indicate an illegible canceled word, the number of bracketed asterisks indicating the number of canceled words.

[*]   to indicate an illegible underscored and canceled word, the number of underscored asterisks indicating the number of canceled underscored words.

)(to indicate *marginal* interpolations.

( )   to indicate *interlinear* insertions.

| | to indicate interpolations *within* marginal or interlinear insertions, thus,)| |(and ⟨| |⟩.

\ \   to indicate a canceled passage, thus, \Curious\.

*   to indicate a correction written over, i.e., in the same place as, the earlier passage. Thus, he * im indicates that *he* replaces *im* in the manuscript.

\#   to indicate "followed by." Thus, of| # \this\ indicates that the word *of* in the final text is followed in the manuscript by a canceled *this.*

@   to indicate "preceded by."

(?)   to indicate a doubtful reading, thus, *st*(?).

Numerals refer to page and line numbers in the present edition. The words followed by closing brackets occur in the final text and function here as locators.

91.8. of| # \the OLD WORLD, OUR PROTOPLASTS\; \(our *Protoplasts,* fir *Eden.*)\. 9. ⟨Instructive⟩| \Curious\. 16. NEW] # \HEAV\. 21. *Already*] # \fulfill'd\. 21. *All*| 'A' * 'a'. 25. The] 'he' * 'is'. 28. THIS] @ \this\. 29. ⟨here⟩].

93.4. PARADISE] @ \Para\. 12. O] # \our\. 13. *Truth*;] # \o\. 19. \The P\ centered between lines 19 and 20. 29. ⟨of⟩|. 30. But,] # \Alass,\. 35. stood.] '.' * ','. 37. as] # \w\. 39. for] # \us\. 44. *Delectable*| # \Se\. 45. ⟨of⟩|.

94.1. ⟨caus'd and left⟩| \made\. 2. *World*] 'ld' * 'st'(?). 3. ⟨written an⟩| \given us the\. 5. ⟨Ancient⟩|. 6. ⟨much⟩|. 6–8.)as . . . that⟨|. 8. Steering] @ \And\. 11. Great] @ \Many\. 14.)of their . . . or,⟨|. 17. their] # \Treatises.\. 17.)most Elaborate Composures.⟨|. 17. Elaborate| 'E' * 'C'. 23. ⟨did⟩|. 23. proceed] \ed\ of earlier 'proceeded'. 24.)nor . . . *That*;⟨|. 24. upon] 'u' * 'e'(?). 25. ⟨taste⟩| \decay\ (?). 26. any] # \where *Together* to\. 27. But] @ \He\. 32. Occasion.] Mather begins a new paragraph and cancels three lines of several false starts: \Tis from that Work, that ⟨I fetch⟩ what I *Extracted* and *Contracted* from the *Rich Oar* then before me, shall be now, in a few exhibited.\. 34. ⟨on⟩| \at\. 35. *Man*| @ \Person\. 36. ⟨discouraging⟩|.

95.1. Equator:] ':' @ uncanceled '.' 2. *Nile*| # \derived.\. 7. ⟨very learned⟩| \learned Author of *Polymathean*\. 7.)[HUET Bishop of Avranches](. 9. ⟨near⟩]. 12. Successive| ⟨ive⟩. 13. but] @ \for\. 14. *Contracted*| @ *Extracted* and\. 15. ⟨the . . . that⟩| \the\. 15. upon;| ';' * ':'. 15–16. ⟨give . . . wherein⟩| \it is thus that\. 16. calcined] 'e' * '''. 16.)improv'd & strengthened⟨|. 20. *Experiments*;] ';' * ','. 23. Ms. I, 5, and first half of ms. I, 6, are canceled:

\The First ESSAY.

on,

THE PARADISE OF THE OLD WORLD

Among the Stars that Visited and Enlightened the Western Haemisphere, one of an uncomôn Lustre, was the very Learned Mr. SAMUEL LEE, who spent some of his Latter Dayes in *America.* This Eminent Person deserved well of the World, and very much obliged the Church of God, by *Writing of Excellent Things,* whereof many have been published. They were *all* Valuable, *Quiquid tam doctis manus candidit.* But his Noble Treatise, *Of* SOLOMONS *Temple,* which he Entituled, *Orbis Miraculum,* are a First rate among them. The *Treatise* worthy of the *Title,* which it putts upon the *Temple,* and the Author doing the part of an *Araunah* for it. He had also praepared several other Composures for the publick, which have dy'd in *Abortive Manuscript,* without Hope of a Resurrection. Among these, one was a Discourse, *of a Three-fold Paradise,* in which he never proceeded, that I could Learn, any farther than the *Terrestial;* but is called away to enjoy the *Coelestial,* before he had gone so far as to write upon it. This Manuscript also gone, I doubt, beyond the hope of any *Eben-Tognin* to recover it; But it happened, that in the few Hours, while it staid in my Hands, I carefully Abridged it, and Siezed upon all that appeared unto me Material and Serviceable, for the Design of Enriching our BIBLIA

AMERICANA, with a very Entertaining Illustration upon the Scituation of the *Paradise* to be treated on.

[ms. I, 6] I waved what *Bochart* and *Huet*, (them whom the Two Communions have scarce ever afforded greater Literators,) had written on that Subject, and praeferr'd what my most honour'd Friend had perform'd upon it; of whose Name I was also willing to have our Collection Enjoy the Honour, on this Occasion. Some that have been desirous to have as much as tis possible of that Learned Mans composure come into the publick, and there withal to have the *Desiderata* supplied, with some communications on the Arguments which he had not prosecuted, have proposed that what is *now* to be done (rather than *just nothing*) should come into the hands of those, whose *Heart-strings* are tuned for it.

What had been *Extracted* and *Contracted* from the *Rich Oar*, which I had with me, now runs in such Terms as these.\

95.25. ⟨we⟩] * 'f'. 29. Amos. I. 5.] 'I' * 'I'. 33. Delicacies] 'D' * 'd'. 34. XLIII.] * '43'. 40. ⟨XXVIII⟩] \28\. 42. Amos I. 5.] 'I' * 'i'. 43. ⟨Captives⟩].

96.3. ⟨XXXVII.⟩] \37.\. 9–10. Ingenious] 'o' * 'u'. 14. Gen. II.] 'II' * '2'. 20. Countr⟨e⟩y] @ \Coun\. 24. mentioned] 'ed' * 's'. 27. XXIV.] * '24'. 34. XXV.] * '25'. 38. Gen. XVI.] 'G' * 'g'; 'XVI' * '16'. 38. *Dwell*] 'D' * 'd'. 42. XXV] * '25'. 43. seems] @ \seems\. 46. ⟨XXXVII.⟩] \37.\. 46. ⟨VIII.⟩] \8\.

97.3 went] # \no\. 6. ⟨XXV.⟩] \25\. 7. ⟨XXV.⟩] \25\. 8. *Quennessari*] first 'e' * 'a'(?). 9. *Haleb*] 'l' * 'b'. 14. migrations] \ti\. 16. *Peutinger*] 'u' * 'n'. 22. *Gadara*] first 'a' * 'u'. 24. *Palmyra*] ⟨my⟩ \miy\. 25. *Sabaeans*] 'ae' * 'e'. 28. brother] 'b' * 'B'. 29. *Punon*] 'o' * 'a'. 29. XXI] * '21'. 30. Place] 'P' * 'p'. 33. ⟨XXXVI.⟩] \36.\. 39. *Palmyra*] 'm' * 'mi'. 41. ⟨XLVII.⟩] \47.\. 44. ⟨LX.⟩] \60.\.

98.7. ⟨the⟩ *Rhaabeni*]. 9. ⟨is⟩] \I have\ 9. Illustrated] # \unto you\. 10. remained] 'r' * 'R'. 18. XXV] * '25'. 26. *Fat*] @ \fat\. 26. ⟨LX.⟩] \60.\. 27. Sled⟨s⟩] \ges\. 30–31. II Cor. XI.32.] 'II' * '2'; 'XI' * '11'. 32. ⟨XXXVI.⟩] \36.\. 36. ⟨CXX.⟩] * \120.\. 39. ⟨XLIX⟩] \49\. 40. *Adubeni*] 'i' * 'e'. 43. *Stephanus*] 'an' * 'en'. 45. ⟨CXX.⟩] \120.\.

99.2. ⟨XLIX.⟩] \49.\. 4. *Thema*;] ';' * '.' 6. III.] * '3.'. 9. ⟨LXVIII.⟩] \68.\. 11. XV] * '15'. 14. *Hagar*] 'r' * 'i'. 24. ⟨has been⟩] \I have\. 24. ⟨XXIX.⟩] \29.\. 37. X.] * '10.'. 39. is] * 'in'. 39. ⟨judged⟩] \indeed\. 42. inproper] 'np' * 'm'. 43. his] 'i' * 'e'.

100.2. *Peutinger*] 'u' * 'n'. 7. *Peutinger*] 'u' * 'n'. 7. Tables] underscoring canceled. 7. and the] 'e' * 'is'. 8. *Agrei*] @ \Agraei\. 10. *Peutinger*] 'u' * 'n'. 12. XIV] * '14'. 18. Scriptures] @ \Script\. 19. *Kedemah*] 'K' * 'k'. 22. Ar⟨a⟩menia]. 26. *Crassus*] 'ra' * 'a'. 27. ⟨XLVII.⟩] \47.\. 28. *Peutinger*] 'u' * 'n'. 33. VI.] * '6'. 33. ⟨VIII.⟩] \8.\. 33. ⟨XXIV.⟩] \24.\. 34. XI.] * '11'. 37. ⟨XIII.⟩] \13.\. 44. X] * '10.'.

101.3. ⟨XXXIII.⟩] \33.\. 8. Entertainment] first 'nt' * 'te'. 10. omnia] 'o' * 'm'. 12. call] @ \called\. 13. been] @ \being\. 23. *Genesis*] 'i' * 'l'. 26. *Phasis*] @ \Phasis\. 28. Travel] 'l' * 'll'. 29. ⟨III.⟩] \3.\. 29. Flaming] @ \Fla\. 30. and] # \t\. 37. ⟨VI.⟩] \6.\. 42. X.] * '10.'.

103.1. IV.] * '4.'. 7. Amos. I.] 'I' * 'I'. 30. *Pison*] long-tailed 's' * 's'. 32. *Pliny*] 'i' * 'y'. 34. II.] * 'i'. 38. ⟨XXV.⟩] \25.\. 38. I. Sam. ⟨XV.⟩ 7.] 'I' * 'i' ⟨XV.⟩ \15.\. 38. *Hailah*] 'h' * 't'. 39. *Magirus*] # \.\.

104.8. Gulf] 'f' * 'p'. 9. *Bedolach*] 'a' * 'e'. 19. Sardonyx] 'y' * 'i'. 20. ⟨or⟩]. 20. Exudations] 'x' * 'u'. 22. *Chaulan*] 'h' * 'a'; 'n' * 'h'. 29. II] * 'ii'. 33. *Dementia*] 'en' * 'u'. 37. II] * '2'. 40. II Chron. ⟨XIV.⟩ 9.] 'II' * '2'; ⟨XIV.⟩ \14.\.

105.7. III.] * 'iii'. 9. *Dart*] 'D' * 'd'. 20. ⟨X.⟩] \10.\. 21. *Nimrod*;] ';' * '.'. 29. Chaldaean] underscoring canceled. 43. Easy] 'E' * 'e'. 43. Tedious] 'T' * 't'. 44. proofs] 's' * 'e'.

106.6. *Mosul*,] # \in Lat. 36. gr. 50. min.\. 13. II] * '2'. 16. II] * '2'. 19. ⟨XXII.⟩] \22.\.

27. IV] ˟ '4'. 28. and *Eve*] 'and' ˟ '&'. 39. ⟨on the⟩] \on some Communications in\. 39–40. ⟨I . . . of.⟩] \from a learned Friend, Mr. *Samuel Lee.*\. 40–42.)Yett . . . *Wells*,⟨]. 41. *Huet*;] # \an\. 41. them;] # \In\. 42. who] @ \I will now add, That there is one Dr. *Wells*\. 44. offer] # \you\.

107.7. *Petraea*] first 'e' ˟ 'ae'. 9. Name] 'N' ˟ 'n'. 23. *Benjamin*] 'in' ˟ 'en'. 24. *Elam*] 'm' ˟ 'n'. 29. beleeve] third 'e' ˟ 'i'. 45. *Diklat*] 'k' ˟ 'g'.

108.15. *Pleasantness*] @ \Pleas\. 15. washed] # \,\. 33. *Adon*] 'A' ˟ 'E'. 34. Gardens] @ \Gar\. 43. incline] first 'i' ˟ 'e'.

109.3. yeeld] first 'e' ˟ 'i'. 4. ⟨Thus our Collector⟩] added in Mather's later hand when he canceled the remaining eight lines of ms. I, 23 and all of ms. I, 24:

Heidegger is of Opinion, That the true Seat of *Paradise*, was in that part of the *Holy Land*, which was called, *Genesar*; and which comprehends, the Sea of *Galilee*, the illustrious Field and Vale of *Jericho*, and the Countrey which the *Dead Sea* has now buried under water.

The *River of Paradise*, he takes to be the *River of Jordan*. The Four famous Rivers of *Pison*, and *Gihon*, and *Hiddekel*, and *Euphrates*, he takes to hold such a Subterraneous Communication with *Jordan*, which we know, has no outlett above [ms. I, 24] Ground, that *Jordan* may be justly esteemed the Source of them all. He thinks, an Inspection of the Maps, would invite one to such Apprehensions. Both *Brocardus* and, *Villamontius*, do mutter something of such a matter. Yea, the very Name of *Jordan*, seems originally to have been / נהו צרן / The River of Eden.

Moreover, the Name of *Genesar* is as much as to say / נשׂו / *Hortus princeps*, or *Hortus principis*; to wit, The *Garden* of Adam. It is Remarkable, That in *Ecclesiasticus*; ch. ⟨XXIV.⟩ v. 35, 36. Those *Five* are joined, as the Five Rivers of Divine Wisdome; *Pison, Tigris, Euphrates, Jordan* and *Gihon*.

The Word used for, the *watering* of *Paradise* by its *River*, is the same that we find used for this very Countrey; Gen. XIII.10.— *The Plain of Jordan was well-watered every where.* Compare, Josh. III.15. It is probable, That Paradise was not far from the Place, where *Adam* was created. And it is probable that *Adam* was created in the Field of *Damascus*; which was not far from hence. We may gather from *Josephus*, that this was a very ancient Tradition among the People of God. And *Adrichomus* magnifies the *Red Earth* of that place, *Ager Damascenus habet Terram Rubram, et mire tractabilem, quam Saraceni deferunt in AEgyptum, Indiam, AEthiopiam, care vendentes.*

Accordingly, *Basil* mentions an Ancient Tradition ως πρωτη η Ιουδαια ανϑρωπον εχειν οικητορα˙ That the Land of *Judaea*, was the first Land, that ever had a man for its Inhabitant. Yea, there is a well-known Tradition, That *Adam* was buried in Mount Calvary.

The Admirable Fertility and Amaenity of this Region agrees well enough, to our Assignation of it, for the Seat of *Paradise*. If you consult such Witnesses as *Hegerippus* and *Brocardus*, they will tell you enough, to make you fall in Love with the Countrey. We will not insist on the plentiful Growth of that Fruit there, which is to this Day commonly called, *The Apple of Paradise*. It is Expressly said of this place; Gen. XIII.10. *It was well watered ꝸ as the Garden of the Lord.* The / כ / which we render, *As*, may not be αιτιαϯικον to make a Comparison, but, συγκριτον. to mention the *Cause*, why it was *well-watered*;— namely, *As being the Garden of the Lord.* Thus our *Heidegger*.\

109.6. ❡3.] '3' ˟ '4'. 15. Euphrates] @ \Ep\. 18. notwithstand⟨ing⟩]. 31. assign] @ \find\. 110.2. *Iberia*] @ \Armenia and\. 8. *Terrestrial*] @ \Ga\. 9. ⟨Ancient⟩]. 10. to] 't' ˟ 'f'. 14. he] @ \he\; 'h' ˟ 'w'. 16. The Four] 'he' ˟ 'his'. 21.)HIM⟨]. 21. Usual] @ \him\. 22. rare] @ \r\. 22. endeavours] @ \prosecutes\. 23. ⟨of⟩]. 25. accurate] @ false start. 25–

26. *Astronomy*,]] Mather's ']' ˟ ')'. 26. Rivers] @ \Four\. 29. which] # \[˟]\. 29. ⟨one⟩] @ \me\. 33.)which . . . for.⟨. 34. ⟨unphilosophical⟩]. 34. *Ambrose's* # \of\. 35. Scorn] # \full occasion\. 36. hear] # \that\. 41–42.)Points . . . of.⟨]. 41. Points] 't' ˟ 's'. 44. A] # \The\.

112.9–10.)the amiable . . . *Earth*,⟨]. 9–10. the amiable] @ \a and the admirable, Spott of Earth\. 11. Parents] # \had their Seat\. 12. ⟨so . . . *Thorns*,⟩] \such,\. 15. Stedy] @ \Con\. 15. a] @ \an\. 15. *World*;] # canceled double caret. 16. Dawn] @ \Time when\. 16. would] # \shine down from thence\. 18–21.)From . . . *Israel*.⟨]. 20. is to] # \[˟] From the [˟] times\. 21. Days,] # \d *desired an Heav-*\. 22. *Countrey*;] ';' replaces ',' # canceled caret. 25. ⟨paenitent⟩] \poor\. 26–27. ⟨of God⟩]. 27. visibly] @ \ap\. 30. *Expiration*] 'tio' ˟ 'on'. 31. ⟨the Wise among them⟩] \they\. 35. *enter*] 't' ˟ 'd' 37. Souls,] @ \Departed\; # \[˟ ˟]\. 40. *Beauty*;] ';' replaces ','. 41. I *made*] @ \eno\ {?}.

113.1. alone] @ \will alone\. 5. *Separate*] @ \Souls of\. 7. ⟨Beloved⟩]. 7.)[and . . . *Birds*,]⟨]. 18. Good] @ \Honest\. 21. *Rational*] @ \Soul\. 22. one] 'o' ˟ 'w'. 22. been] # \d\. 22. Sufficiently] # \conf\. 22–23. Disturbed] 'D' ˟ 'd'. 23–24.)[in . . . *legatur*,]⟨]. 23. Book,] # \de Ps\. 35. was] # \his\. 38. having] # \the\. 40. *Immortality*;] # second ';'. 40. *Probabilities*] 'ti' ˟ 'es'. 41. *thou*] # \hast been\. 44. once] # \a\.

114.1 ⟨after . . . Ages,⟩]. 1. *Fable*:] ':' @ ',.'. 2. its] ˟ 'in'. 4. *changed*;] ';' @ ',.'. 7. &] # \I\. 8. ⟨Now⟩]. 9. *Vice*] @ \[˟]\. 10. It is] # \used in\. 11. *Nothing*] 'N' ˟ 'n'. 19. it.] '.' ˟ ';' # \asserts it\. 19–29.)*Cebes* . . . *Nature*?⟨]. 19. *Cebes*] # \[. .]\. 20. Many.] # \the most of mens\. 21. &] @ \in\. 21. it.] '.' ˟ ';'. 23. *suspected*] second 's' ˟ long-tailed 's'. 26. all] # \all\. 30. What] # \shall be\. 31. them⟨selves⟩]. 32. an] @ \the E\. 33. detected.] '.' ˟ ',.'. 34. such] @ \those App\. 34. unquaestionable] # *Matter of Fact*,\. 34. the] ˟ \any\. 36. ⟨can⟩]. 36. make] \s\ of 'makes'. 37. compell] 'c' ˟ 't'. 37. Beleef] @ \Credo\. 41. ⟨and Unreproachable⟩]. 42. ⟨it as⟩]. 43. *Memorable*] plural \s\. 44. good] @ \conside\.

115.1. to?] \un\ of 'unto'. 7–8. ⟨or Three⟩]. 8. that] # \the thing may be esta\. 8. ⟨or Three⟩]. 9–13.)them . . . unto.⟨]. 16. whether] 'h' ˟ 'e'; # \w\. 17. Latter,] # \of them\. 19–20. ⟨[which . . . wore]⟩]. 22. sayd] 'd' ˟ 's'. 23. *Joseph*] @ \Sa\. 31. you] 'y' ˟ 'h'. 32. heard;] ';' @ ',.'. 42. in] \to\ of 'into'. 42. the] # \Fire\. 43. wounded] @ \wounded\.

116.2. but] ˟ 'his'. 2. the Friends] 'he' ˟ '[. .]'. 2. Deceased] 'c' ˟ 's'. 3. and] @ \and prose\. 12. should] # \happen\. 13. ⟨Real⟩]. 15. Fear] 'F' ˟ 'f'. 21. concluded] @ \[˟ ˟]\. 21. ⟨this⟩ # \⟨was Audible⟩\ ˟ \this\. 21. but] @ \but\. 27. Experiment] # \,\. 28. Noise] 'is' ˟ '[. .]'. 32. Woman,] # second ',.'. 32. Next] @ \next\. 33. Night] # \th\.

117.4. Confirmation] 'io' ˟ 'm' (?). 5. on] # \my\. 7. Watts] 'tt' ˟ 'ts'. 13. *Piety* @ \Pie\. 14. not] @ \much\. 15. his] # \at receiving th\. 15. as] # \if [˟]\. 18. unto] @ \Eno\. 20. Magistrate] @ \Court\. 26. of them,] # second ',.'. 27. that] # \at the very Time, they were\. 30. Appeared] @ \profess'd themselves to be.\. 32. ⟨so⟩]. 35. On] 'O' ˟ 'I'. 36. so.] # \A Good [. . .]\. 38. *Ly*] @ \Ly\. 38. to be] # \and\. 40. still] @ \yett they\. 44. ⟨it is⟩]. 44. nor.] @ \It is\. 44. of] # \Pri\.

118.4. unto] # [˟]. 4. Faculty] 'l' ˟ 't'; # \,\. 11. ⟨wittingly and willingly⟩]. 15. Body.] '.' ˟ ',.'. 22. setts] # \all the\. 23. and] @ \But if\. 24. cease] @ \be a means\. 31. *confidently*,] # ';'. 31–32.)nor . . . |Man| . . . so.⟨]. 33. *veritatis*.] # false starts \For our *Aristotle* has a Saying, Tis' abs Both *Socrates* and *Cebes* confess, [˟ ˟ ˟]\. 38. us,] ',' @ \[.]\. 39. which] @ \[˟ ˟ ˟]\. 39. *Quaestion*.] # *Lipsius* owns, it was a Controverted\. 39. about,] # \the\. 41. ⟨or⟩] \and\. 45. very] @ \[. . .]\. 45. *Confidently*] 'nt' ˟ 'm'.

119.1. us.] # \We are\. 1. have] # \well\. 2. are] @ \We\. 3. has] @ \as\. 6. Himself] @ \hi\. 8. that instructs] @ \he t\. 20. SAVIOUR.] '.' ˟ ',.'. 20. intended] 't' ˟ 'd'. 24. Passage,—] # \Not able to kill\. 25. T'wil] @ \I\. 26. Determination] @ \& Victori\. 31. His Army] 'H' ˟ 'h'. 31. at His] 'H' ˟ 'h'. 32. HIM] @ \Him\. 32. before] # \don\. 36. *GOOD*]

@ *Good* o\. 36. have] # \[. .]\. 38. ⟨*Hope*⟩] *Faith*\. 45. full] # \Testimony receives\.
    120.1. when] @ \plainly\. 2. which] # \the\. 3. was] @ \wa\. 4. says] 'y' ˟ 'id'. 6. That]
@ \f\ (?). 7. that] # \may not be utter\. 7. According] 'A' ˟ 'a'. 8. has an] # *Eye* to see\.
13. held] @ \denied\. 18–19.)However . . . rest.⟨]. 23. have] # \been laid in\. 24. at] # \t\.
25. *Be*] '*B*' ˟ '*b*'. 25. *far*] @ \State\. 26. & ⟨one⟩]. 27. ⟨the . . . or⟩].
    121.1–3.)It . . . |says| . . . *Dy*.⟨]. 14. ⟨did⟩]. 15–16.)written . . . died,⟨]. 16. have] @ \still\.
18. *Inference*!] # \from This\. 20. of] # \of\. 22. And] 'A' ˟ 'a'. 27. certain] # \more\.
30. ⟨we⟩]. 31. and] 'a' ˟ '&'. 34. *Soul*] # \, which\. 34. *Immortal*,] # \[˟˟˟˟˟]\. 35. *Nor*] @
Never grows old, but lives perpetually.\. 36. One] @ \I suppose when\. 38. Word] # \,\.
41. of] 'f' ˟ 'n'. 42. ⟨What . . . *Folly*!⟩]. 43. him] 'm' ˟ 's'; # \cause\. 44. ⟨And⟩]. 44. any] 'a' ˟
'A'.
    122.1–3.)(notwithstanding . . . *Dialogue*,)⟨]. 6. But] # \now, any more would be indeed
Superfluous.\. 6. But] # \ˆ)what has been said has now been so *Sufficient*, that⟨\]. 11.
GOD,] # \who is every where continually at wo\. 11.)& who⟨]. 16. produce] # \Eff\. 18.
beyond] # \the\. 18. *Principles*,] # second ','. 22. *Life*] 'f' ˟ 'v'. 25. them;] ˟ ','. 25. And] 'A'
˟ 'a'. 31. *Things*;] ';' ˟ ','. 41. *Aura*] 'ur' ˟ 'ra'.
    123.7. So,] # \that\. 8. *Soul*,] ',' ˟ ';'. 12. *Air; and*] # \is\. 23. Feels;] ';' ˟ ','. 31. will] #
\help unto\. 35. *Infants*] 't' ˟ 's'. 45. It] # \is at\. 45. it is] # \th\.
    124.2. all the] \ir\ of earlier 'their'. 4. ⟨They speak of⟩] *Homer* insists\. 9–21.)In . . .
Two.⟨]. 11. *Man*] '*M*' ˟ '*m*'. 22. *Man*] \[which the *Talmuds* make an *History* of a Man,
whose Name they say, was *Nimensis*] He\. 25. Ancients] @ \⟨Chri⟩\. 25. *Parable*;] # \and
their Op\. 37. by the] 'e' ˟ 'is'. 40. *Mellification*] '*M*' ˟ '*m*'. 40.)the . . . *Bevers*,⟨]. 40.
Architecture] @ \House building\.
    125.1–9. It . . . it.⟨]. 8. *Regards* @ \Facult\. 14. *Abiding*] '*id*' ˟ '*fi*'(?). 15. an] @ \an\. 29.
A] # \The\. 31. *Philosophers*,] # \an Physicians,\. 33. ⟨in⟩]. 33. *Tastable*] @ *Tasteable*\.
38. It is] # \mor\. 38. *Nishmath*] final '*h*' ˟ '*th*'. 42. discovered,] # second ','. 42. *Enforcing*]
'*r*' ˟ '*c*'. 43. *Microcosmic*] first '*c*' ˟ '*r*'.
    126.1. to] # \B\. 4–6.)and . . . |can| . . . potent:⟨]. 5. *Spirits*,] # \in\. 6. wherein] # \Ad\.
6. potent:] # \)Th⟨\. 8. *Passions*] # \in the Mi\. 9. ⟨in⟩] \with\. 10.)&⟨]. 14. their] # \s\.
16. Men a] # \marvell\. 17. when] '*he*' ˟ '*en*'(?). 19. Difficulties,] # \b\. 24. confined,] #
second ','. 29. To] @ \I\. 34. ⟨*Man* . . . A⟩]. 34. up] '*p*' ˟ '*b*'. 34. *Place*] @ \a\. 37. thing] # \by
no means\. 39. *Body*.] # \Mr. *Nullibist*, Man gives up the Ghost,\. 40. *Nullibist*] second
'*i*' ˟ '*s*'(?).
    126.42–127.2.)*Place* . . . of.⟨]. 126.42. lead] @ \point\.
    127.1. PARADISE] final '*E*' ˟ '*e*'. 3. Now,] @ \Sect. III. But a PARADISE for the *Im-
mortal Soul*, is what we are now seeking for.\. 4. PARADISE] @ \Para\. 4. *Departed*] @
\T\. 10. unto.] # \The Ancients we do\. 11. it was] # \gene\. 12. Sufferings] # \for the
Kingdome\. 12. ⟨*Faith and*⟩]. 17. of] # \an\. 17. *Comforts*,] # \and sett before him\. 22.
Small Type] @ \Little Type\. 22. which is] # \called\. 23. ⟨and . . . *Nehemiah*⟩]. 24–25.
⟨of . . . GOD.⟩] \of that *Heavenly World*.\. 25. Habitation] # \GOD\. 27. Accounts,] #
\while an\. 29–30.)too . . . it!⟨]. 31. What] @ \The Intercourse\. 31. may] @ \carries\.
37. thee,] # second ','. 38–39.)I . . . think,⟨]. 38. *Thou*] @ \w\. 40. ⟨thou⟩] \you\. 41. it,] #
second ','.
    128.3. thither] '*ith*' ˟ '*ere*'. 5. SAVIOUR] 'A' ˟ 'a'. 9. Accordingly] @ \It is well\. 15.
not] # \an\. 18–27.)When . . . also.⟨]. 19. *FATHERs*] divides '*FAT-HERs*'; then \T\ and
corrects to '*FA-THERs*'. 21. Rejecting] @ \With\. 22. which] '*hich*' ˟ '*ho*' of earlier '*who*'.
22. determine] @ \did,\. 24. suppose] final '*e*' ˟ '*t*'. 28. tho'] # \it may be\. 29. *short*] @

\on more accounts than one\. 30. shall] # \shall fetch them ⟨out⟩ from thence to receive\.
34. is] # \yett\. 44. which ⟨the⟩]. 45. be] 'e' * 's'. 45. dis⟨pensed unto us.⟩].

129.1. *Deep*] @ \the\. 2. *Appearing*] 'A' * 'a'. 8. We will] @ \I will\. 11. II. 34.] '3' * '[.]'.
12. in ⟨that⟩]. 13. which] @ \from\. 13. ⟨was not what⟩]. 15. to the] # \the\. 15. fetch] #
\⟨our⟩\. 19–20.)says . . . *Just.*⟨]. 27. is to be] # \at our reve\. 28. And] @ \Unt\. 37. Are]
\, Do\. 38–41.)The . . . *Everlasting.*⟨]. 38. SAVIOUR] 'A' * 'a'. 39. also] # \In\. 40. will]
@ \is to\. 41. *Dead,*] ',' * 'g'.

130.3. for] @ \fo\. 4. fully] # \granted and\. 6–7. ⟨Shall . . . |[Psal. CXIX. 100]| . . . *An-
cients?*⟩]. 8. *Ancients.*] '.' * ';'. 8–15.)Tis . . . |Ly| . . . |in *Heaven*| . . . for.⟨]. 10. Language.] '.' *
','. 14. their] # \Pe\. 18. *Justin,*] # second ','. 22. says] 'y' * 'is'. 24. took] # \P\. 25. *Hades;*]
';' @ '.'. 26–27. ⟨|perhaps . . . repast|⟩]. 29–30.)Nor . . . Impatience:⟨]. 33. *Habitation*] 'H'
* 'P'. 34. suppose,] # \ar\. 35. think,] # \upo\. 40–41.)*Theophylact* . . . Same.⟨]. 43. *We*]
# \[. .]\. 45. thrown] @ \added\.

131.1. ⟨in this Matter;⟩] @ \⟨upon⟩\. 7–13.)too . . . |of| . . . *Blessedness.*⟨]. 10. and] # \left
not the g\. 12. with] # \the rest of the Reformers, wo who\. 14. The ⟨Ancient⟩] first 'e' *
'is'. 16. ⟨indeed⟩]. 19. *latter* # \d\. 19–20. ⟨On . . . Hand,⟩]. 19. On] 'O' * 'i'. 22. it] @ \it\.
30. &] # ⟨by⟩ \not [*] the Top of\. 31. State] underlining canceled. 34. *Popish*] # \Purgat\.
34. allows] # \the Happiness\. 35. ⟨their⟩]. 38. *expectatione*] 'x' * long-tailed 's'. 42. ⟨he⟩].

132.6. very] # false start. 10. for ⟨the⟩]. 18. Not] @ \The Sixth Æ\. 21–23.)According . . .
it.⟨]. 23. a] @ \the\. 25. ⟨in⟩]. 26. *Flames,*] # \must give,\. 26. must] # \, give now\. 29.
unspeakably] 'y' * 'e'. 29. our] @ \Present St\. 30. through a] \n\ of earlier 'an'. 30. ⟨forlorn
& wretched⟩] *Howling*\. 30. *Wilderness.*] '.' * ',' # \or Land of *Droughts & Pitts & Fl
Fiery flying Serpents.*\. 30–35.)They . . . Resurrection.⟨] @ \⟨Even⟩\. 31. this] @ \the\. 31.
express] \themselves upon it. The Plea.\. 32. it,] # second ','. 33. *Resurrection,*] # second
','. 36. Faithful] # \be be\. 42. Catechism] 's' * 'm'. 42. The] @ \They\.

133.5. where] 're' * 'n'. 6. with] @ \And\. 18. it.] # \The\. 25. *Rejoicing*] 'ci' * 'n'. 27.
Chrysostom,] # \who\. 29. ⟨does⟩]. 29. place] \s\ plural. 30. and ascribe] # \th\. 31. no]
@ \indeed\. 37. *Antichrist*] # \,\. 40. as] # \foretelling\. 41. ⟨be⟩ *Now*] 'N' * 'n'; # \be\.
43. *hundred*] 're' * 'er'. 45. most] 'm' * 'g'.

134.4. ⟨therewith⟩]. 8. *Consolations*] pl. 's' added. 10–16.)That . . . *Mansions!*⟨]. 12.
others] # \Ancient\. 14. *Chambers,*] # second ','. 20. [Psal.] @ \[[. . .]\. 22. *Enemies,*] #
\and *Escaped* from\. 23. from] # \the T\. 26.)Even . . . *quiescunt.*⟨]. 30. ⟨on⟩] \on\. 40.
this] # \wh\. 40. Worlds!] '!' * '.'. 45. ⟨be⟩].

135.3. *Mordecai*] 'M' * 'm'. 4. and] @ \Thou\. 5–8.)And . . . |*Joyful*| . . . Blessedness.⟨].
8. of] # \their\. 12. then] 'en' * 'ere'. 19. ⟨Stephen⟩] \the Martyr\. 20. ⟨of the Master,⟩]
'ster' * 'ker'. 24. implies] @ \em\. 24. appointed] @ \allow'\. 24–25.)Certainly . . .
Worshippers.⟨]. 30. *Scriptures,*] # second ','. 31. ⟨with⟩. 32–33. *Chaldaic*] # \O\. 33. He
says;] # second ';'. 37. *Glory,*] # second ','. 39. *Bodies*] @ *Just*\. 43. ⟨come⟩] \mani\. 44.
Light,] # second ','.

136.1–2. ⟨in . . . Testament⟩]. 2. of] 'o' * 'O'. 3. the *Stars*] @ \[*] ever\. 7. *Vestis*] 'Ve'
* 'W'. 6. them;] ';' @ ','. 12.)and⟨]. 16–17.)or . . . *Second.*⟨]. 17. *First*] 'F' * 'f'. 26. were]
@ \where\. 28. It] @ \Th\. 30. brought] # \with a\. 30. ⟨Excellent⟩]. 34. admitted] @
\raised\. 39. that] \b\. 39. ⟨after⟩] \at\. 40. agree with] # \Him\. 42. seems,] # \that
the\. 44. for] \t\ of 'fort'.

137.2. *Frequent,*] # second ','. 2. ⟨Visitations⟩] *Visits*,\. 2. where] @ \of [*]\. 2. Souls]
@ *Separate*\. 3. *Paradise*] @ \A a\. 3. ⟨grants⟩] \on those Occasions makes\. 5. by] 'y'
* 'e'. 5. Raised] @ \a\. 6. withal;] ';' @ ','. 7. But] 'B' * 'b'. 8. to] # \such\. 16. *Angels*] #

\,\. 19. *Israel*ͺ] ';' @ '.'. 22–25.)*Bull . . . Appearance*.⟨]. 29. Variety] @ \Differen\. 34–35. *Successive*] '*ive*' * '*es*'. 37. is] @ \is\. 37. ⟨Disproportion⟩] *Distance*\. 41. ⟨we⟩]. 41. far] # \elevat\.

138.4 *Coelestial*] '*C*' * '*T*'. 6. :] * 'ͺ'. 6. Perswasion,] # *Blessed is the Man*\. 10. However] @ \Wh\. 11. have] # \gone away [*,]\. 17. *Shermerdine*] first '*r*' * '*d*'(?]. 26. Faithful] @ \Sa\. 28. ⟨the⟩]. 32. *Visionaries*.] '.' * 'ͺ'. 32. ⟨They . . . *Discretion*.⟩] \and must b\. 42. *Terrors*ͺ] * 'ͺ'. 44. *CHRIST!*] '*!*' * '.'.; # \Lord, when wilt tho\.

139.1. *When!*] '*!*' * 'ͺ'; # \When\. 1. Soul] # *out of the*\. 1. away] '*aw*' * '*w*'. 4. And,] # \where if I pl\. 11. *sentio*] # \in\. 13–23.)That . . . *more*.⟨]. 13. celebrated,] # \not\. 13. by] # \only\. 14. so] # \and\. 17. in] * '*m*'. 33. which] @ \wh\. 34. ⟨*sic*⟩]. 36. Person] # \on\. 38. apprehend] @ \think\.

140.2. *Terribleness*] @ \t\. 7. Stories] @ \swell\. 8. ⟨or⟩] \&\. 8–12.)ǀMore Particularlyǀ . . . ǀbe nowǀ . . . them.⟨]. 8.)ǀMore Particularlyǀ] \A *Wanly* ma among others, may be consulted on this Occasion.\. 10. it:] # \I\. 13. of] # \naming (?)\. 14. ⟨from . . . *Age*,⟩]. 16. ⟨in⟩] \at\. 18. *World*] @ *Place*\. 21. ⟨from another *Place*,⟩]. 23–24.)with . . . him.⟨]. 25. ⟨him⟩]. 32. would] @ \had gr\. 33. lett] # \them know\. 33. his] '*is*' * '*m*'. 35. to] # \[. .]\. 36–37. ⟨as . . . him,⟩]. 40. The] @ \What has been p\. 41. his,] # \who after\. 42. lain] '*n*' * '*i*'. 42. Life,] # \upon her,\. 44. *Extasy*ͺ] 'ͺ' * '.'. 45. *Borellus*] '*o*' * '*er*'.

141.1. shall] # \o\. 1. ⟨only⟩] \b\. 1. few] # \of\. 2. *Paradise*,] # second 'ͺ'. 2. ⟨with⟩]. 2. which] # \have been\. 3. and] # \of\. 3. ⟨upon . . . them⟩]. 6. who] # \had\. 7. died,] # second 'ͺ'. 10. ⟨Weeks⟩] \Years\. 12. *Grace!*] '*!*' * 'ͺ'. 15. Hours] # \[.]\. 16. revived] '*i*' * '*e*'. 28. Seven] @ \But\. 40. and] # \(if)\. 41. were] # \⟨[.]⟩\. 43. ⟨No⟩] \Who\.

142.2. after] # \, he dep\. 23. *Rix*] @ \Rx\. 25. ⟨by⟩]. 26. Intimate] # \Friend, who\. 26. &] # \F\. 29. for her] '*her*' * '&'. 34.)as⟨]. 36. kept] # \full of\. 36. Heavenly] '*H*' * '*h*'. 37. to] # \the\.

143.12–13. *to me*] '*to*' * '*m*'. 15. ⟨her⟩] \the\. 24. Among] '*A*' * '*a*'. 29. after ⟨a⟩]\her\. 30. now] @ \arri\.

144.3. *Admonitions*,] # \who\. 22. ⟨always⟩]. 23. very *Tearful*] '*v*' * '*T*'. 23. well as] # \Fear\. 25. alone] @ \a\. 28. *Eyes*ͺ] # *After this Hour, thou shalt ne*\. 28. She] '*Sh*' * '*T*'. 32. *Voice*] @ \the\. 41–45.)She . . . Lord.⟨]. 42. promise] '*p*' * '*b*'.

145.3. *SAVIOUR*] '*R*'* '*r*'. 7. him] '*h*' * '*H*'. 10. Head.] # \Lett all take\. 13. Her] '*He*' * '*Th*'. 21. asserted] # \it\. 24. X.] \⟨X.⟩\ 26. Persons] # \an (?)\. 31. hearing ⟨of⟩]. 33. examined,] # \whether\.

146.10. ⟨in⟩] \by\. 14. One] '*e*' * '[. .]'. 15. ⟨of all⟩] \the\. 20. Insensible] @ \sense\. 24. ⟨French⟩]. 25. *Medicus*] # *Gallicus*\. 30. ⟨how⟩]. 30–38.)For . . . ǀSheǀ . . . in.⟨]. 30. of] # \the English\. 31. y^m] '*y*' * '*it*'. 32. Recovered,] # \she\. 32. conn'd] second '*n*' * '*d*'. 33. Complaints,] '*s*' * 'ͺ'. 37. mean] # *Idea*\.

147.3.)no . . . so.⟨]. 4. *Narratives*] @ \Histor\. 4. and] '*a*' * '*e*'. 4. that] '*at*' * '*e*'. 4. ⟨of⟩] \Time of\. 8. Consolations] '*olat*' * '*idera*'. 20. there] '*t*' * '*f*'. 20. from] # \its being\. 27. in] '*i*' * '*o*'. 27. Earth,] # \are *Laid on the Earth*,\. 29–30. And they] '*nd*' * \[. .]\; '*t*' * '*T*'. 30–32.)To . . . Souls.⟨]. 32. ⟨like *Fools*,⟩]. 35. ⟨in *Paradise*.⟩] \above\. 35. Doubtless,] # \They had rather Dy or\. 37–38.)Lett the ǀGloriesǀ . . . *Paradise*.⟨]. 37. ǀGloriesǀ] \vanities\. 39. How] # \do\. 39. ⟨Pomp⟩] \Glory\. 43. *Stone*] # \bring up\. 43. Altar] @ \Coelestial\. 43. ⟨in *Paradise*⟩].

148.1. When] @ \In this w\. 3. ⟨may⟩] \should\. 4. *Worship* of] # \GOD,\. 5. Him!] '*!*' * \ͺ\. 5. In] @ \If we become\. 6. Manner,] 'ͺ' * 'ͺ'. 6. ⟨*Paradise*⟩] *Heaven*\. 8. against] @ \of\. 10. worship] # *GOD*,\. 14. ⟨the⟩]. 14. *Soul*] pl. \s\. 15. &] # \Lett\. 16. *Inheritance*] # \re\. 17. Cry,] * second 'ͺ'. 18. Are] @ \It ma\. 19. They] @ \Ma\. 22. and may] #

\continually\. 24. *Evident*] @ \Tok\. 25. may] # \fetch\. 31. ⟨here.⟩] 36. espouse] 'u' * 's'.
36. *Holiness,*] # second ',' 36. but ⟨a⟩]. 36. As a] @ \and the *Little Flock*\. 37. *two of*] #
\kind\. 40. They] 'e' * 'y'. 43. ⟩weigh⟨]. 43. Foolish] @ \Fool\. 44. People] # \[*]\. 44. of
⟨a⟩]. 44. The] @ \Finally,\.

   149.5. Look] @ \but\. 6. The⟨ir⟩]. 16. not] 'n' * 'c'. 16. them] 'em' * 'eir'. 17. Hear] 'H'
* 'h'. 20. Thus,] @ \Le\. 23. there.] '. * ':'. 30. *their*] 'ir' * 'n'. 34. him,] 'm,' * 'ms'. 34–
39. ⟩Reader, . . . *away.*⟨]. 38. Way be] # \dislodged fr\. 38. and] # \the *Nest*\. 39. ⟨any of
the⟩] \the\. 40. Schools] # \up [?]\. 40. ⟨where . . . to,⟩] \among the Children of Men,\.
43.] Quaestion] 'ae' * 'a'.

   150.3. *Nation,*] # *may e*\. 6. to] # \to\. 6. ⟨most⟩]. 7. Matter] @ \a P\. 7. ⟨with him,⟩].
12. *Work,*] # \of GOD\. 13. upon] @ \begun\. 18. what] @ \that\. 20. Glory,] ';' * ','. 32.
united,] # second ','. 33. Justified] 'J' * 'i'; 'f' * 'i'. 43. heartily] @ \heartily\. 43. Methods,]
',' * ','. 43. tho'] 't' * 'f'.

   151.3. ⟩*in*⟨].

   153.1. \May 28\ in upper left-hand corner; '8' * 'o'. 6. An] @ \ii\. 10. ⟨the . . . Ruines⟩]
\little but the Reverse\. 10. have] # \b\. 10. considered] # \as with\. 11–13. ⟩in . . . him.⟨].
14. And] # \with a Reflection\. 14. the *Sorrow*] 'yᵉ' * 'a' 15. obliged] @ \u\. 16. ⟨*Heavenly*⟩].
17. ⟨by the *Second Adam*⟩]. 17. *Spirits,*] @ *Better Part,*\ # \at the End of our Life\. 18.
done] # \at\. 19. But] @ \Sh Sh\. 20. and] # \⟨even ear⟩\. 20. ⟨even⟩]. 21. exceed] # \that\.
21. exhibited] # \Four Thousand\. 24–31. ⟩It . . . |He| . . . exemplified.⟨]. 26. ⟩|He|⟨] \Even\.
29. *remaineth*] 't' * 'd'. 29. Thus] @ \A\. 33. But,] # ','. 33. ⟨amazing⟩] \Tremendous\. 34.
have] @ \be\. 35. and] # \Increa\. 35. ⟨it,⟩] \it\. 37. *Purify*] 'y' * 'ie'. 40. ⟨the⟩] \an\. 40.
Earth,] # \where the Children of M\. 43. ⟩black &⟨]. 43. Wickedness] 'd' * 'n'. 43. for] #
\it,\. 43. ⟨and⟩ ⟨has⟩]. 44. been] 'en' * 'ing'. 44. ⟨so fulfill'd⟩] \accomplished\. 44. ⟩that⟨] \of
that we know\.

   154.1. treat] # \mak\. 2. *Earth, Earth, Earth*] third '*E*' * '*H*'. 2. Word] 'd' * 'l'. 3. Yea,]
\And,\. 3. *World*] '*l*' * '*d*'. 4. Matter] # \was never addre\.

   155.1. I. The] '*I*' @ \i\. 1. Earth] 'th' * 'h'. 7. ⟨of⟩]. 8. on] @ \up\ of 'upon'. 9. *Style*] @ \s\.
9–20. ⟩the . . . to!⟨]. 15. Reason],] # \why\. 21. ⟨⟨one . . . *Three*⟩⟩] @ \[***]\. 21. ⟨*First*⟩] @
\⟨Bel⟩\. 22. Instruction] @ \a\. 23. ⟨instructed⟩] \favour'd\. 25. SPIRIT,] '*PIRIT*' * 'pirit'.
26. *By*] @ *The World, being overfl that then was, being overf being overflowed with
Water* perished. But the\. 29. FIRE] '*I*' * '*i*'. 30. Day] '*D*' * '*d*'. 34–35. ⟨by . . . World⟩]. 35.
⟨*By*⟩]. 35. One] '*O*' * '*B*'. 37–39. ⟩But, |Many| . . . |Or,| . . . with.⟨]. 37. ⟩|Many|⟨] \[*] People\;
'*M*' * '*m*'. 39. of] # \th\. 39. a] # \Prophecy is\.41. only] # \of a certain\. 41. ⟨unknown⟩
Event,] # \to\. 43. *Conflagration*] # \is an Allegory\. 44. ⟨what . . . an⟩] \was it a meer
Allegorical\. 44. *Inundation,*] # \in the\.

   156.1. for] @ \of whic\. 4–5. ⟨the . . . whose⟩] \People\. 5–6. ⟩impious . . . *imprisoned,*⟨].
6. ⟨such⟩] \such\. 8. other] # \it\. 10. ⟨as . . . *Iniquities*⟩]. 10. which] # \many People in\.
10. be] # \[. . . .]\. 11–12. ⟩the . . . *Judgment,*⟨]. 13. ⟨*Deceive not yourselves,*⟩]. 14. There]
@ \Y\. 17. *Summer,*] # \Yea\. 17. pour] # \these\. 18. *Wretched*] '*W*' * '*T*'. 20. Times;] #
\are fond of\. 20. Fire,] # \⟨[. .]⟩\. 21. ⟨devoted⟩] \dam'd\. 23. a] # \notable\. 24. may] #
\may\. 25. is] @ \are\. 25. Shall # \th\. 26. when] '*n*' * '*re*'; # \in\ of earlier *wherein*. 28.
in] @ \wherei\. 29. Son] @ \gl\. 29. GOD,] # \will make His\. 31. ⟨hideous⟩]. 32. shall]
\break forth from the break\. 33. *Figures*] # \under\. 33. hoped,] # \the [*]\. 33. were]
\a\]. 33. ⟨under which⟩] \to the [**] of\. 34. *Rocks*] @ \M\. 35. Him] @ \the Livi\. 35.
We] # \The The\. 35. have] # ⟨[*]⟩. 37. *Allegorical*] '*A*' * '*h*'. 38. *Nepos*] @ \Ne\. 43. But]
\the Event\. 43. if] # \nothing\.

   157.2. [ms. III, 4] opens with centered \III. The PETRINE Prophecy, of the CONFLA-

GRATION, rescued from a wrong Interpretation.\. 2. *away*,] # second ','. 3. foretold by] # \our Apostle, from\. 10. could] 'ou' * 'an' of earlier 'can'. 18.)what?⟨|. 20. Our] @ \Indeed,\. 22. But] # \w\. 28–38.)This . . . World; It |is| . . . And⟨|. 28.)This] @ \It is\. 29. against] # \the [. .] [. .] [. .]\. 30. a] # \Vast *Change* upon\. 31. for] @ \be-c\. 33. what] # \[. .]\. 35. It ⟨is⟩]. 35. Spectacle] # \which is com\. 35. Them] 'm' * 'y'. 36. occur'd] @ \in an\. 37. *Jerusalem*,] # \I could alm\. 38. that] # \here ha\. 38. Censures] @ \Apostolical\; # \may b\. 42. ⟨his⟩] \his\.

158.2. ⟨Was⟩] \And\. 8. horrible] # \[*]\. 12. *Righteousness*:] ':' * ';' (?]. 13. ⟨not⟩] 13. COME] 'M' * 'm'. 18–19. *Peculiar*] @ *Influence*\. 22. ⟨of⟩]. 26. But] @ \M\. 28. This] @ \The Pri\. 29. *All*] 'A' * 'a'. 30. Destruction] @ \Destr\. 30. *Jerusalem*,] # second ','.

159.2. II.] second numeral 'I' * 'V'. 7. Compassion] 'C' * 'a'. 7. on] # \His People\. 8. *Death*,] # \and w\. 9. ⟨of⟩ us]. 9. *Truth*] pl. \s\; # \and ar\. 10.)are⟨|. 10. us.] '.' * ';'. 10. ⟨'Tis a Book⟩] \and\. 10. ⟨particularly⟩] @ \⟨in⟩\. 11. ⟨the *Peculiar*⟩]. 13. *Events*] # \wch\. 14. There] @ \I\. 16. *wrote*] 'wrot' * 'mad'. 17. them.] # \The Mysteries Reveled in this Book\. 18. Reveled] 'R' * 'r'. 19. ⟨and . . . GOD⟩]. 19. that] # \men GOD must be the Author & Fountain of the nothing but the Light of GOD [w] the\. 21. Assertions] 'A' * 'a'. 22. from] # \GOD,\. 23. ⟨directed⟩] \prescribed\. 23. the] # \I T\. 24. *Holy*,] # \that we must be\. 24. as] # \,\ 24. to] # \leave\. 25. should] # \communi\. 25–27.)The . . . GOD.⟨|. 29. ⟨with⟩] \such\. 29. the] @ \as as [.] [. .]\. 30. ⟨attaining⟩] \coming\. 31. It] @ \Th\. 33. ⟨it⟩]. 33. this] @ \[*]\. 34. Matchless] # \& & Holy\. 34. All] @ \so then, if\. 38. If] @ \None Such a Thing\. 38. hath] 'th' * 've'; # \the\. 39. by] # \Fire, an\. 40. ⟨thereupon⟩]. 41. no] # *Sin*,\. 159.43–160.2.)besides . . . |that would| . . . *together*:⟨|. 159.43. upon] # \the\. 159.44.)|that would|⟨| \to\. 159.44. Tremendous] @ \Con\.

160.2. No] 'N' * 'n'; # \this [*]\. 3. ⟨every where⟩]. 3. ly] # \scatt\. 4. of] # \the Storm\. 4. ⟨like⟩]. 5. *Fire*,] # second ','. 5. We] @ \ˆ ˆ\. 5. will] # \From the *Old Testament*\. 5. That] @ \a\. 6. ⟨brought⟩]. 6–8.)keeping . . . Purpose,⟨|. 7.)Resenis⟨| \of passages\; # \)a Vast Army, & ren\. 7. GOD,] # \of\. 7. at] @ \a\. 8. Sacred] @ \Sacred\. 11. foretold,] @ \ex\. 11. ⟨Dan. VII. 9, 10, 11.⟩]. 12. *Fiery*] 'er' * 're'. 15. *away*,] # \wa\. 15–17.)It . . . *Cup*.⟨|. 15. *Time*.] # \It is foretold; *Isa*, LXVI. 15, 16. *Behold, The Lord will come with Fire, & with his Chariots like a Whirlwind, to render his Anger with Fury, and his Rebuke with Flames of Fire. For by Fire and by his Sword, will the Lord plead with all Flesh; and the Slain of the Lord shall be many.*\. 17–18. It is . . . A] Accidentally canceled, but not obliterated; these lines are a continuation of the preceding obliteration of Isa. 56:15–16. 21. That] @ \P\. 21. such] @ \these\. 21. into] # *Smoke*\. 23. *Testament*,] # \which can have\. 24–29.)If . . . Eye;⟨|. 24. the Apostle] @ \if\. 25. *John*,] # \may be\. 25. in] @ \with\. 27. It] @ \There can be no\. 28. with] # \an Eye\. 29. [2. Thess.] @ \Here it is foretold,\. 29. *Heaven*,] # \in flaming Fire,\. 35. ⟨since . . . there⟩]. 35. *Fact*] # \more\. 37. Now,] # \the\. 38. Great] @ \Glorio\. 42. us.] # *Now*\. 42.)Yea,⟨|. 42. has] # \[*] made\. 45. The] 'T' * 't'. 45. *thrown*] @ \st\.

161.4–12.)Yea, . . . *Just*.⟨|. 4.)Yea⟨| @ \)And,⟨\ # \How\. 4. was the] # \Wit\. 7. [Joh. V. 27, 28] '7' * '8'; second '2' * closing bracket ']'. 12. After] 'A' * 'a'; @ \And, [Luk. XXI. Now,\. 15. ⟨in⟩]. 16. with] # \the\. 16. ⟨a⟩]. 17. After] # \this Gos\.

162.2. III.] second numeral 'I' * 'V'. 9. yett] # \there are so\. 9. *Decla⟨ra⟩tions*] # \of\. 9. ⟨in⟩] \in\. 11. ⟨Scrutiny and⟩ ⟨diligently⟩]. 12. *of the*] 't' * 'C'. 12. concerning] # \what the\. 18. of the] # \Sacred\. 18. ⟨Divine⟩]. 19. And] # \ena- [. . .]\. 21. *Strangers*] # \& Sojourners\. 25. Embassadors] # \from ⟨of⟩ Heaven to the\. 28. And] 'A' * 'a'. 29. them the] # \Great\. 29. *Grand*] 'G' * 'g'. 29. which] # \concerned the Kingd\. 29. to] # \be\. 29.)in⟨| # \unto\. 31. none] 'ne' * 'm'. 32.)that⟨| # \which\. 33. ⟨at once to⟩]. 33. ⟨*Sublime*⟩]

\Vast\. 34. ⟨Aims⟩] \Views &\. 35. This] # \G\. 37. shall] @ \are\; # \anon see\. 37. to]
\see\. 37. ⟨behold⟩]. 40. In] @ \There\. 41. ⟩THREE⟨] # \Three\. 42. View;] ';' @ ','. 42.
tho'] # \there were\. 44. THREE] 'HRE' * 'Grea'.
   163.3–4. fixed upon] @ \se\; # \and wherein Things\. 9. GRAND] @ \Grand E\. 9.
GOD,] # \being\. 12. descended] 'sc' * 'cd'. 18. ⟨the⟩] \th\. 20. Light] @ \V\. 21. few] 'f'
* 'a'. 22. ⟩that is Master⟨]. 22. ⟨Penetration⟩] \Sagacity\. 23. into] @ \in\. 26. Prophet,] #
\namely\. 29. [I.]] # \VI.\. 30. GRAND] 'G' * 'g'. 34. ⟨occurr'd⟩] \was\; \⟨ha⟩\. 34. was] #
\The W\. 35–36. ⟩the . . . Incarnate;⟨ 36. promised] # \& expected\. 37. ⟨in⟩]. 37. the] @
\of\.
   164.2. the] @ \T the Reformed B\. 3. inexpressible] # \Satisfaction\. 4. ⟨Consolation.⟩].
5. ⟨in which⟩] \wherein\. 6. and there] @ \and the\; # \are\. 6. something] # \that when
much [*]\. 8. ⟩Writers⟨] # \Divines\. 10. ⟩Reason⟨] # \Occasion\. 10. insult] # \,\. 11. is]
@ \are\. 12. ⟨Tho'⟩] \However,\. 14. Interpreter] @ \Expression\. 15. See ⟨and⟩] \To it\.
16. ⟨in other Points⟩]. 16. ⟨Good Men⟩] \Gentlemen\. 17. ⟨on . . . hand⟩]. 18–19. ⟩what . . .
more,⟨]. 18. does] # \Austin\. 19. particularly] @ \[*]\. 21. ⟨in that Passage⟩]. 22. before]
'b' * 'th'. 22. ⟨in⟩]. 23. apprehend] # \our Saviour intend\. 23. which] 'ich' * 'at'. 25. The.]
new paragraph @ \In what we may call, The Gospel of Is\. 27–28. ⟩We . . . evangelista.⟨].
29. that] # \it b the Gospel\. 31. Our] @ \The\. 32. it] * 'is'. 34–35. ⟨Obstinate . . . Jews⟩].
35. their] 'eir' * 'ere'. 37. and] # \[. .]\. 39. Isaiah] # \has\ * \had\. 43. this] \I\. 44.
this] 'is' * \at\. 45. if] # \a\. 45. Philip] # \the Evangelist\.
   165.2. ⟨even⟩]. 7. Virgin] first 'i' * 'a'. 12. mean] # \b\. 13. Now] @ \But no\. 15. Whereas]
\But suppose the Typical Explication\. 16. The] 'h' * 'o'. 18. Dark] @ \Time\. 22. House
⟨of⟩]. 26. ⟨for⟩] \as\. 29. Ahaz] # \ref\. 32. GOD,] # second ','. 32. ⟨upon⟩] \upon\. 33.
⟨unto⟩] \to\. 34. The] @ \a God had now no\. 34. Ahaz] @ \our\. 35. after] # \he had\.
35. putt] 'tt' * 'n' (?). 35. one] 'n' * 'ur'. 37. Exclusion] 'c' * 't'. 40. Ahaz] # \should utterly
fail,\. 43. who] @ \shou\. 43. IMMANUEL] 'E' * 'e'. 44. from a] \n\ of earlier 'an'. 44.
⟨Pure⟩] \unspotted\.
   166.4. be] 'e' * 'd'. 5. little.] '.' * ','. 5. ⟩Ivery] . . . Victorious⟨]. 5. taken] 'k' * 'f'. 9. have] @
\be\. 11. Literal] @ \sub\. 14. gives] @ \makes\. 14. ⟨till now,⟩]. 15. Imposter] @ \Tr\. 16.
Introduction,] # second ','. 19. remarks] @ \obs\. 23. Praedictions] # \was to\. 32. ⟨very⟩].
33. performed] # \above seven hundred Years afterwards.\. 34. after] @ \after\. 34. Years]
\h\. 35. since] # \the\. 35. fulfill'd,] # \be no longer\. 39. them,] # \comes\. 39. is] 's' *
'n'. 40. ⟨All . . . Grass⟩]. 40. ⟨a Promise,⟩] \That,\. 41. Empire] # \of the mighty Babylon\.
43. stand] @ \resist the\. 43. ⟩Men &⟨]. 44. ⟨and frail⟩]. 44. ⟨Return⟩] \Restoration\.
   167.2. Harbinger] @ \Fore\ (?). 3. Read] 'R' * 'r'. 10. Lord,] # second ','. 11. unto] @
\upon\. 12. ⟨repairing⟩] \returning\. 12. when] @ \m\. 13. again] # \to\. 14. A] * 'a'. 15.
Lowthe] @ \W\. 15. Learned] @ \[. . . .]\. 17. SAVIOUR] 'R' * long-tailed 's'. 17. The]
@ \In the y\. 18. ⟩Joy⟨] # \Joy\. 19. Instructed] @ \cultivated\. 20. ⟨the⟩]. 23. People]
@ \most\; # \to\. 25–26. because] # \for many the th\. 28. and] @ \th\. 31. alone] @
\alone\. 33. Jews] # \(as the Doctor observes)\. 34–35. ⟨reckoned that⟩] \from\. 35. carried]
@ \a\. 36. Diseases] 'D' * 'd'. 36. are] @ \have a\. 39. SAVIOURs] # \visible A\. 40.
understood] @ \under\. 44. themselves,] @ ';'.
   168.3. them,] # ','. 7. foretold] @ \'\. 7. Magicians] @ \'\. 8. Christs,] # second ','. 10.
Essays] @ \two larger\. 10. There] @ \That\. 12. Watching,] @ \wch\. 12. appearing] @
\to\; # \in them\. 12. therein] * 'them'. 15. ⟩In⟨]. 15. what] 'at' * 'en'. 15. [Isa. XXII. 20–
24.]] 'o' * 'i'. 16. SAVIOUR] @ \Saviou\. 17. referr'd] @ \intended f\. 17–18. ⟩hearken . . .
us,⟨]. 18. That] @ \be willing,\. 19. means] @ \should\. 20–21. Sennacherib?] '?' * ':'. 22.
⟨indeed⟩]. 23. ⟨him⟩] \us\. 25. ⟨a⟩]. 26. One] # \that com\. 33. what] @ \that\. 35. Jew,] #

',′. 41. which] @ \th\. 42. discern] # \ˆthe *Messiah* there,\. 42. ⟨a⟩]. 42. *Kimchi*] # \does\.
169.9. Him] @ \t\. 12. meant,] # \by the Serv a in\. 13. *Light.*] # second '.′. 22. most] @
\Proph\. 23. This] @ \In him\. 26. read] @ \sai\. 26. *The*] @ \A New\. 27. *Mighty Man*]
@ *Man*\. 28. ⟨their⟩] \the,\. 30.)However,⟨]. 31. *Jew*] @ \Learned\. 35. *Lord*] @ \L\. 37.
Him] # \a\. 39. it] # \a\. 40. Text,] # \i\. 42. Meditating] @ \feeding\.
   170.2. and] @ \In\. 4. His] @ \his\. 6. ⟨my⟩]. 8. who] @ \of whom\. 12. give] @ \call\.
12. what] # \[*]\. 14. That] @ \On\. 14. Pious] @ \Hon\. 14. glosses] @ \reads, He\. 14.
HE] * '*he*′. 15. *smitten*] # \h\. 17. the Clause] first 'e′ * 'at′. 21. *surrexit*] first 'r′ * division
mark '-′. 22. may] 'y′ * '/′. 22. *Amends*] '*A*′ * '*a*′. 24. Word] 'd′ * 'l′. 26. *All*] @ \Here is
the\. 29. For] 'or′ * 'ed′ (?). 32. how] @ \I\. 38. Bonds] '*B*′ * '*b*′. 39. His] @ \the\. 42. *Their*]
'*i*′ * \n\ (?). 44. *The*] @ \y\. 44. mean] @ \to say\. 45. And] # \of\. 45. who,] # \m,\. 45.
⟨He⟩] \of Him,\.
   171.1. is,] # \it possible to understand,\. 1. *Branch*] '*B*′ * '*b*′. 2. whom] # \the [*,]\. 3.
)Who . . . him?⟨]. 3. but] @ \ca\. 4. And] # \the People tell of\. 4. foretells] 't′ * 'l′. 5. was]
\eminently\. 9. ⟨of which⟩] \whereof\; # \the our\. 9. *Folengius*] '*u*′ * '*y*′. 10. *est.*]
\W\. 10. Christian,] # \Disc\. 11. this] @ \y\. 11. Will] @ \Skill &\. 11. and] \a\ * \t\. 12.
dost] @ \comest\. 14. ⟨as⟩]. 16.)We have⟨]. 23. ⟨a Sovereign⟩]. 24. by] @ \than\. 26. was] #
\per\. 26. ⟨& giving⟩]. 28–32.)Passing . . . That⟨]. 32. ⟨tho′⟩] @ \But\. 32. *David,*] # \in\.
33. yett] # \S\. 34. are] @ \are\. 36. ⟨and . . . are⟩]. 36. not] @ \is\. 37. our] @ \and\. 37.
⟨also⟩]. 37. proved] 'd′ * 's′. 37. Psalm] # \[*] was not fulfilled in *David*\. 39. ⟨Figurative⟩,]
Mystical\. 40. severely] @ \in\. 42. *Martyn*] 'y′ * '*i*′. 43. *Criminal*] # \Undertaking\.
   172.2. the] # \se\. 2. engage] @ \combate encounter,\. 24. *in*] '*i*′ * '*H*′. 25. ⟨exploded⟩]
\defied & rejected\. 26–28.)in . . . *Aliens*,⟨]. 28. see] @ \d\. 29. most] # \coelesti Illustri-
ous & Coel singul pr\. 30. Invaluable] @ \Inva\. 35. ⟨in⟩] \[*]\. 37. sure,] # ',′. 37–38.)as . . .
Him,⟨]. 42. [2.]] # \VII.\. 43. GENTILES] @ *Gentiles*\. 45. this] 'is′ * 'e′. 45. ⟨First⟩]. 45.
unto it,] # \it *Pleased* the *Heavenly Father*, who is\. 46. ⟨&⟩].
   173.2. *Part*] # \of them w\. 4. until] # \Shiloh\. 5. came,] ',′ * ';′. 5. of ⟨the⟩]. 6. as] #
\[. . .]\. 9. and] # \upon the Accomplishment of this\. 9. ⟨in⟩] \upon\. 11. was] # \horri
with\. 12. *Gabriel*] '*G*′ * '*g*′. 12. ⟨are . . . read,⟩]. 15. *Prince,*] # \our\. 16. *GOD.*] # \An\.
17. *Daniel*] @ \Daniel\. 18.)which . . . *Israel.*⟨]. 18. GOD] # \unto A\. 19. *Countrey*] #
\[which can\. 20. ⟨to⟩] @ \⟨here⟩\; \to take place of\. 20. ⟨here,⟩] \in the united\; \⟨has⟩\
interlined above \united\. 21. is ⟨of⟩ # \⟨a⟩\. 21. *Name*] @ \Gr a\. 22. and] @ \to plead\.
25. Servant] @ \Lover of CHRIST &\. 28. Dead,] # second ',′. 29. into] # \to\. 30. *in-
wardly*;] ';′ @ ',′. 33. truly] @ \a\. 34. *Ethiopian,*] # \who fear\. 35. any] '*a*′ # '*E*′. 36.)as . . .
any⟨]. 36. one] @ \as\. 37. *Issue*] @ *Iss of*\. 39. them:] ':′ # '.′. 41. The] 'e′ # 'at′. 42. for]
@ \for\. 42. ⟨the⟩ *Israelitizing*] \the\. 42. *Gentiles,*] # \ever falls\. 42.)ever⟨] # \into an
Astonish\. 43. *Mystery*!] '!′ * ':′; # \falls into,\. 43. Raptures] @ \pious\. 44. it!] '!′ * ';′.
44. Almost] '*A*′ * '*a*′. 44. ⟨& faints⟩]. 46. be] # \built on\.
   174.1–3.)yea . . . *Solomon,*⟨]. 2. than] # \that buil a\. 7. what] @ \up\. 8. *Faith*] @
\P\. 9. lost] @ \found among the *Gentiles* , while\. 10. obeyed] second 'e′ * apostrophe of
earlier 'obey′d′. 10. them] @ \the Jews\. 13. ⟨& . . . *Land*⟩] \among the People of GOD,\. 15.
⟨there⟩]. 17.)Triumphing . . . *Death,*⟨]. 19–20. *Righteousness*!] '!′ * ';′. 21. ⟨more Manly⟩].
23. ⟨a marvellous,⟩]. 23. amazing] # *Revolution!* Dispensation.\. 24. ⟨*Revolution.*⟩]. 24.
well] 'w′ * 'b′. 25. lett] @ \in\. 26. ⟨this⟩]. 28. Tis] # \true the People often\. 28. as.] @
\Judicious\. 28. ⟨sharp-sighted⟩]. 31. ⟨Seeking of⟩] \Serving\. 34. this,] # \wh\. 34. *Altar*
\for\. 37. *Jews*] # \vehem\. 38. asserted] @ \the argue\. 38. lawfully] @ \legally be\.
39. It @ \So that\. 40. Completion] @ \Ac Ac\.
   174.40–175.4.)for . . .]up] . . . Gospel.⟨]. 174.41. Service] @ \W\. 175.2. *Egypt*] @ \It

is to\. 3. GOD,] # second ',/'. 3. of] @ \them\. 8–9.)which . . . illustrated.⟨|. 11. *Idolatry*]
\of the Gentiles\. 12. ⟨*Civic*⟩] # \⟨[. .]⟩\. 14. Given of the] # \Law\. 14–15.)*Levitic*
Institutions.⟨|. 15. These] 's' ˙ 'y'. 17. *Things*] @ \Idol\. 22. *Leviticus*:] ':' # ',/'. 24. *Prose-*
lytes] # \be embrace\. 25. Church] @ \Christian Jews\. 28. Christianized] 'C' ˙ 'P'. 29.
⟨*Burthen*⟩]. 30. Claim] @ \Expectation\. 38. *Messiah*] 'M' ˙ 'm'. 39. but] # \also\.

176.3. to] \un\ of 'unto'. 3–4.)wherein . . . them.⟨|. 4. Pretence] 'en' # 'm'. 6. the] #
\the\. 6. *Isaiah*] # \a\. 8. ⟨His . . . about.)]. 8. In] @ \By The\. 9. IV. 2, 3.] '.' ˙ ',' 9. and]
@ \XXXX\. 10. saw] # \,\. 12. rest] @ \rest R\. 14. ⟨also)]. 25. with] @ \to\. 26. *Judah*;]
# \it refers to the\. 26–27. *Gospel*?] '?' ˙ ',/'. 31. where] 'ere' ˙ 'ich'. 37. unto a] 'a' ˙ 'the'.
38. ⟨called,)]. 41. Nations] @ \Gent\. 42. *Piety*] @ \Piety exp\. 45. ⟨an Intimation⟩] \a
Prophecy\.

177.5.)Stark⟨|. 8. ⟨*Mountain*)]. 10. Upon] # \the Sealed\. 11. some] @ \man\. 12. ibid.]
@ \v.\. 14. *Romans*,] # second ',/'. 14. them!] '!' ˙ ':' 16–20.)Tis . . . withal.⟨|. 17. Man,] #
\Th\. 19. be] @ \enjoy\. 21. Glories] # \of,\. 24. Isa.] @ \whe\. 25. foretell] @ \tell\. 27.
Assyrian] 'A' ˙ 'T'. 27. now] # \says.\. 36. *and*] # \of Ethiopia\. 38. Conquests,] # ',/'. 39.
understood] @ \meani\. 40.)to be⟨|.

178.1. *Chaldaean*] 'h' ˙ 'a'. 10. Apostle,] # \un\. 11. ⟨had been)] \was\. 13. more] # \,\.
13. of] @ \in\. 20. Excellent] # \Magn\. 24. of] @ \aforetime.\. 25–26.)|We| . . . But,⟨|.
25. prophesies] # \of a\. 27. It is] @ \That\. 28. *Zechariah*,] ',/' ˙ ';'. 30–31. ⟨And . . .
removed.)]. 32. Zech.] 'Zec' ˙ 'Jer'. 38. Ministry.] # \ˆ ˆ)From the Prophecies of *Ezekiel*
we will in this Place mark no Deliberations; But we will observe, That the Prophets of a
Restored Israel there have this their *Key*, in what is foretold, [Ezek. XXXVII.12.] *Behold;*
O my People; I will open your Graves, & cause you to come up out of your Graves.
A Thing to be literally accomplished. Its being at the Time, when the Holy One says,
My Tabernacle shall be with them; yea, I will be their God, & they shall be my People;
the [\Bles\] Apostle *John* assures us, the *Resurrection* there foretold, is to be *A Thing to*
be literally accomplished.\. 45. *Mercy* to] @ \the\.

179.2. *Habakkuk*] second 'a' ˙ 'b'; first 'k' ˙ 'a'. 5. ⟨Work,)] \Thing\. 9. ⟨vanished)]
\extinguished\. 13. even] @ \a\. 16. his] 'h' ˙ 'H'. 21. as] @ \an\. 24. But] @ \And\. 26.
⟨our)] \the\. 29. ⟨which)]. 33. Hereupon,] # \the L\. 42. ⟨Prophecy of the)] \passage\. 42.
Locusts] # \in the *Prophecies* of\. 43. whether] # \the the they\. 43. *Literally*] @ \His-*
torically and\; # \acco and Historic\. 45. *Monarchies*] @ \famous\. 45. Monarchies] 'i' ˙
'e'.

180.2.)from⟨|. 2. which] @ \by\. 2. have] # \been tormented so\. 4. And] 'A' ˙ 'a'. 7.
lamented] @ \d\; # \in the\. 7. ⟨a)]. 9. ⟨who fancies)]. 12. that] # \is is\. 12. horrid] @ \a\.
14. Wretches] @ \[. .]\. 14. will] @ \[.]\. 14. calculated] second 'a' ˙ 'e'. 16–20.)*Jerom* . . .
them.⟨|. 19. That] # \the *Church*, as State of the Church ap\. 22. *look*] @ \tell the\. 28–
29. ⟨In . . . Verses,)]. 31. Next] @ \I\. 33. Hereupon] @ \Thirdly,\. 35. SAVIOUR] 'SA-' #
\viour\. 39. [3.]] # \VIII.\. 39. *Golden*] @ \Key\. 39. EVENT;] # \Th\. 44. The] @ \T\.

181.3. ⟨there shall be)\. 5.)continually⟨|. 5–6. descending] # \from time to t\. 16. *Wise,*]
',/'. 19. Godly] @ \Holy\. 21.)That . . . the⟨|. 21. *Land*] @ \⟨That he would give him)\
\the\. 21. *Possession,*] # \did he think, that there was no more in\. 23. A] ˙ 'a'. 24. was]
\[˙]\. 24. days;] ';' ˙ '!' # \ˆ)and what was *he* the Better for his Posterity having it, {and
but for *a while* neither, & generally in much Miseries & Confus⟨\. 27. *foot,*] # \of Land,\.
28. World!] # \Are\. 28. Intimations,] # second ',/'. 29. him] # \,\. 29. would] @ \no\. 31.
Dead?] # \What was he the Better for it\. 31. *Favourite*] 'F' ˙ 'f'. 33. have] @ \fo\. 35.
as] # \proclamed\. 35. ⟨often . . . Proclamation)]. 37. *polluted.*] '.' ˙ ',/'. 37. this] @ \the\.
38. plain] # \, & f\. 39. so;] # \ˆ Now, if the Glorious GOD,\. 40. ⟨if)] @ \⟨if)\. 42. ⟨But)]

\Now\; 'B' * 'b'. 42. *unto*] @ \To\. 43. Wherefore,] # \in the Day\. 43. when] # \GOD\. 43. *Blessed*] # \adm\. 44. from] # \amon\. 44. and] # \brou\. 44. which] # \will\.

182.1. ⟨Delivered)⟩ \restored into from all the\. 1. and be] 'b' * 'e'. 1. from] 'ro' * 'or'. 3. *Offspring*] # \and\. 7. *That*] # \a\. 7. *CHRIST*;] ';' @ ','. 10. ⟩THIS . . . *Covenant*.⟨] @ \This\. 12. Blessed] @ \admira\. 13. Wisdome] # \)brings⟨ fetches be\. 13. ⟨He brings)⟩. 14. promised] @ \said\. 18. must] 'u' * 'a'. 20. *Dead*] @ \GO\. 25. will] # \be\. 28. or] # \beyond th\. 29. have] @ \cont\. 29. ⟨*Death* and)⟩. 29. *Sin*,] # \and *Death*\. 30. these] # \GOO\. 31. *Patriarchs*.] @ \ancient\; '.' * ':'. 34. *NOW*] @ \they\. 36. which] # \without us,\. 36. *us*,] # second ','. 37. must] @ \in\. 37. into] @ \by\. 40. ⟨People)⟩ \Persons\. 40–41. ⟩and . . . *Heaven*.⟨] 43. us.] # \The P Our\. 43. ⟨The)⟩.

182.45–183.1. ⟩or . . . do.⟨]. 183.3. Thoughtful] 't' * 'f'. 4. what] # \we render, Psal. CV.8.\. 7. ⟨we)⟩ \you\. 8. Law,] # ','. 9. *Sabbatism*] @ \Gr\. 10. point] # \at\. 12. *Thousand*,] # \[\. 15. may] # \no\. 17. ⟨*Second*)⟩. 18. below,] # \enjo\. 18. in] # \a\. 20. Him:] ':' @ ','. 20. ⟨what . . . in)⟩. 20. GOD,] # \will no\. 21. ⟨the *Promise*,)⟩ \a, before that Revolution,\. 23. ⟨and)⟩ @ \⟨yett)\. 23. *Unreasonable*;] # \yea, *Irreligious*\. 25. is] # \,\. 30. another] @ \another\. 31. which] # \Antiqui\. 31. *We*] # \do very little trem\. 33. But] @ \Lett\. 33. what] # \I\. 34. FIRE] @ *Fire*,\ 35. fill] # \the\. 35. ⟨horrid and)⟩. 35. and] # \be\. 37.)of⟨]. 37. the] @ \succeeded with\. 38. still] # \,\. 39. us;] # \who would\. 41. ⟨the Phrase)⟩ \is\. 43. uses] # \it\. 45. 18.] '8' * '5'.

184.11. *Mouth*,] ',' @ ','. 12. ⟨our)⟩. 15. on] # \his and Satans\. 27. But] # \I insist upon the\. 27. Way] @ \Apostolical\; # \of appl\. 28. apprehend] @ \look on the P\. 32–37.)why . . . Admonitions.⟨]. 36. the most] @ \a\. 38. Of] # \That\.

185.3. *another*] # \the\. 9. shall] # \then\. 10. that] # \was not is not\. 22. *praepared*,] # ','. 24. ⟨an) ⟨for it)⟩. 26. whom] # \the\. 27. His] # *Vicar*\. 32. *Fire!*] '!' @ '.'. 39. ⟨the . . . of)⟩ *Idumae*\. 39. *Edom*] # \ae\. 39. made] 'm' * 's'. 43.] ⟨and Poetically)⟩. 44. they] # \us\. 45. But] # \an at\. 45. ⟨an)⟩.

186.1. has] # \deter\. 1. *Apocalypse*] # \[. .]\. 2–20. ⟩And . . . demonstrated.⟨]. 7. |shalt do|] \didst\. 8. |when|]. 8. |hast|]. 8. *come*] \st\ of '*comest*'. 8. |shall flow|] *flowed*\. 11. |unknown|]. 11. |here|]. 12. *for*] # \them that\. 12. |of GOD|]. 13. refers] @ \refer wh\. 15. *Rebuke*] pl. \s\. 15. of] # *Fir*\. 20. Compare] @ \[\. 22. the Grand] 'e' * 'i'. 26–28. ⟨So . . . *Saeculi*.)⟩]. 30. of] @ \Th\. 33. blazes] 'z' * 's'. 35.] the end of MS. III, v28 is marked by a wavy line to separate long marginal insertion from the last line of the text. 40. visible,] # \on the\.

187.4. *Fire*,] # second ','. 17–18.)All . . . *Jealousy*.⟨]. 19. conclude,] # \wi the\. 23. ⟨for)⟩. 24. *forth*,] # \in its Operations\. 24. *Eyes*,] # \with\. 24. that] @ \a\. 26. borrows] @ \is\. 39. honest] @ \most worthy\.

188.5. ⟨Recovery)⟩ \Reduction\. 6. RETURN] 'E' * 'e'. 7. Prayer] @ \Song of\. 10. Sense] long-tailed 's' * 's'. 16. ⟨coming to)⟩. 19. read] # \in the Prophecies of *Jeremiah*;\. 19. ⟨in . . . *Jeremiah*,)⟩. 24.)As⟨]. 24. his] 'h' * 'H'. 24. quoted,] # \is; They\. 31–39.)In . . . *accomplished!*⟨]. 33. come] # \ou\. 39. *accomplished!*⟨] Subsequent, canceled passage lacks a positioning caret: \)And, Isai. who |one may| who answer'd read, the *General Conflagration*, by the Light of that Prophecy; [Zeph. III. 8.] *All the Earth shall be devoured, with the Fire of my Jealousy*.⟨\. 43. brief,] @ \Not\; # \No\. 43. Sharp,] # \No\. 43. *Gratiarum*] '*Gratia-*' *piorum*\. 44. Paul] # \to bear him ou\.

189.2. World,] # \the\. 2. This] @ \Fro\ 3. *handle*] @ \proceed in\. 6. Prophecies] @ \Promis\. 6. be] 'b' * 'B'. 11. Some] @ \a few be lef\. 15. ⟨all)⟩. 15. behold] @ \be\. 15. Lord,] # \appear\. 20. cry] # \ou\. 21. FIRES] @ *Fires*,\. 22–23. ⟨Now . . . you.)⟩]. 23. were] @ \wh\. 23. ⟨in . . . Style)⟩ \in the Prophetic\. 28. Number!] '!' @ ','. 30. and] # \be

[. .]\. 30. ⟨may . . . be⟩]. 32. wonderful] @ \mirac\. 32. Revolution] 'v' * s'. 33. up] 'u' * 'f'.
33.)yea,⟨]. 33. no] @ \&\. 35. Lord] # \sh\. 35. and] # \before His Ancient People glor\.
36. Heavenly] @ \Mo Coel\. 38. accomplished] 'lish' * 'ani'. 39. enlightens] @ \ligh\. 41.
Daniel,] # \i\.

190.4–5.)One . . . |Writing . . . Prophecy| . . . that⟨]. 5. the] # \e\. 5. has] 'a' * 'u'. 5. that]
@ \such\. 6. from] @ \of y\. 7. the] 'e' * 's'. 8. applying,] # \what\. 9. has] # \one\. 13.
It] @ \S\. 16–20.)It . . . Servants.⟨]. 18. forever;] ';' @ '.' 21. Isa. LIV.] 'I' * 'V'. 22. John]
\finds them\. 22. ⟨makes⟩]. 23. Tis] @ \There\. 24. ⟨which . . . Restitution.⟩]. 26. read,]
\of,\. 28. of] # \[.]\. 28. Earth,] # \which he\. 31. World,] # \an\. 36. Earth,] # \are\.
37. Conflagration] plural \s\. 38. how] @ \was\. 38–39. frequently,] # \how notably,\. 39.
pointed] @ \display\.

190.40–191.3.)Among . . . of.⟨]. 190.40. the Last] first 't' * 'T'. 191.4. What,] # \we\.
4. are] # \to seek in the\ 5. memorable] @ \G\. 6. always] # \mea\. 7. ⟨all⟩]. 8. ⟨all⟩]. 9.
⟨are to⟩]. 9. and] # \are also\. 10. ⟨to be⟩]. 10. Obtaining] 'g' * 'i'. 10. Mercy,] # second ','.
10. and] # \see GOD\. 11. these] @ \a\. 12–13. in the World] 'e' * 'is'; # \, where the
Servants of GOD are to Ble\. 14. see] # \The Wicked shall perish, and the Enemies of
the Lord shall be as the Fatt of Lambs, they shall consume in Smoke, they shall consume
away.\. 15–18.)Ill . . . SMOKE.⟨ 20. when] # \the Evil-doers shall be cut off, then they
that wait on the Lord shall inherit the Earth. The Righteous then shall inherit the Earth,
& shall dwell therein forever.\. 20–21. when] #)|All| . . . thence.⟨]. |All|] 'A' * 'T'. 26.
come,] 'e' * 'f'. 26. Sinners] @ \when\. 26. will] * 'shall'. 27. ⟨from Earth⟩ consumed,] #
\out of the Earth, & the Wicked shall\. 27. ⟨and the Impious⟩]. 28. Lord,] # \⟨He does⟩
Looks on the Earth & it trembles; He touches the Hills and they Smoke.\. 28–29.)He . . .
smoke.⟨]. 30. that,] # \H\. 30. Bible.] '.' * ','; # \A HALLELUIAH The Grand Occasions
for\. 30. HALLELUIAHs] # \are introduced, by this Dispensation\. 31. this] # \Disa\. 31.
World] # \⟨here foretold⟩ shall introduce it,\. 32. on:] # \Lord, Thou shalt Send forth thy
Spirit, and the things are Created over again; and thou Renewest the Face of the Earth;
& So, The Glory of the Lord shall endure forever; the Lord shall p Th\. 32. They] # \||\.
33. anew:] # \||\. 33. Earth] # \||\. 33. give.] # \||\. 34. GOD,] # \||\. 34. forever;] # \||\.
35. GOD] # \||\. 36. with] # \such\ 40. FIRE] # \that shall flame from thence shall with
a\. 42. Wonderful] # \Le ma\. 44. to] @ \of\. 44. Transcription] divides 'Trans- scription'
then cancels first 's'. 45. keeping] # \exactly to the\. 45. strictly] second 't' * 'k'.

192.2. were] @ \were\. 5. display'd] @ \, unde\. 6. Spreading] @ \Eagl the\. 12. Voice;]
','. 14. and] 'n' * 'd'. 14. fetch] # \an Inst\. 16. thy] # \Je [Jewe\. 16. Christians,] # ^
\Ta\. 17. ⟨Do You⟩]. 18–35.)A . . . Irlandica.⟨]. 24. |such|]. 22. convuls'd,] # second ','. 25.
an] \d\ of 'and'. 27. used] @ \use\. 28. too] # \a Da\. 28. The] @ \Yett\. 45. it?] '?' @ ','.

193.1. ⟨O⟩ Lett the many] \and\. 2. dense] @ \des\. 5. Melting] @ \Melting\. 6. Face\
'F' * 'f'. 9. a] \n\ of 'an'. 9. ⟨Line⟩] \Hint\. 9. ⟨no more than⟩]. 10. ⟨writing . . . Hebrews⟩]. 17.
Thou] # \shalt be chang'd\. 19. ⟨the present⟩]. 21.)us⟨]. 22. established.] # \Such Things
have we learnt from the Scripture ⟨of⟩ Truth. [\O\] Christians, employ you\. 23. Tho'] @
\And y\. 23. the] # \a\. 24. Song] # \formed in\. 25. but] 'b' * '&'.

194.2. IV.] # \IX\. 7. ⟨in⟩] \from\. 9–15.)But . . . them.⟨]. 9. speak] @ \speak l\. 10.
will] @ \do i\. 14. show] @ \tell\. 14. Nations] * 'Pagans'; # \in\. 14. FIRE] @ \F\. 16.
pay\ @ \l\. 16. possessed] @ \wearing the Name of Sibyls, so w\. 21. ⟨Cell⟩] \Pair\. 21.
⟨Enthusiasms⟩] \Oracles\. 26. by] @ \of\. 27. were] # \lodged\. 27. ⟨then putt up⟩]. 28.
Capitol] @ \Sepu\. 30. ⟨they⟩] \we\. 38. ⟨now⟩]. 40. ⟨Christian⟩]. 41. period] @ \year y g
y\. 42–45.)this . . . Original.⟨]. 44. discover] # \a\.

195.1.. Eight] 'E' * 'e'. 3. And] 'A' * 'a'. 4. Because] 'B' * 'b'. 4–6.)Tis . . . suspectiora.⟨].

6. *sunt,*] # ','. 6. ⟨them⟩] \it\. 8. *Sibyl*] @ \Sib\. 11. could] @ \app\. 13. affirm] @ \aff\. 13. *Paul*] 'u' ˇ 'l'. 14–16.)|And yett;| . . . them.⟨]. 17. *Acrosticks*] 'k' ˇ 's'. 19. were ⟨of⟩]. 21. After] @ \Th The Determin\. 21. [ms. III, 36] '6' ˇ '4'. 27. might] # \wor\. 29. yea] 'y' ˇ '&'. 30. *Heathen*] 'H' ˇ 'h'. 32. *Christianity*] 's' ˇ 't'. 33. ⟨it⟩]. 33. make] @ \Christianity, see frequently\. 33. ⟨that . . . they⟩] \as to\. 36. ⟨of a Piece;⟩] \alike;\. 36. the noble] @ \ˆChristianity\. 37. ⟨from⟩] \by\. 37. Authority] @ \whole\. 37. *Whole*] # \,\.

196.2. *Signifies*] third 'i' ˇ 'e'; 'e' ˇ 's'. 4. *Sibyl*] 'i' ˇ 'y'; # \was\. 6. ⟨whereas⟩]. 7. the Greek] 't' ˇ 'T'. 8. therefore] second 'e' ˇ 'f'. 13. hands;] ';' @ ','. 15. make] @ \b\. 20. in] 'i' ˇ 'y'. 20. ⟨the *Sixth Æneid,*⟩]. 24. Hopes] @ \Hopes\. 26. In] 'I' ˇ 'i'. 27. *Sibylline*] # \Verses, h\. 32. Days] @ \Age turne\. 32. Even] # \the\. 32. yea,] 'ea' ˇ 'es y'. 38. that] # \P\. 38. whom] 'o' ˇ 'n'. 38. However] @ \Bu\. 43. ⟨rife⟩] \yett\. 45. And] 'A' ˇ 'a'.

197.1. ⟨intimated and countenanced⟩] \favoured\. 2. run] # \Since the ⟨First⟩ Appearing of *Christianity;*\. 2–3.)Out . . . SAVIOUR;⟨]. 2. Out,] # [. . .]\. 2. CCCXCVIII] 'VIII' ˇ 'LXI'. 3. *Pagans*] # \much\. 4. *Revolution*] # \try\. 6. ⟨even⟩]. 10. Alass,] second 's' ˇ ','. 11.)made⟨]. 11. fearful] \ly\. 12. Lett] @ \The\. 13. M.CC.LX.] first 'C' ˇ 'D'. 13. and] # \[.]\. 17. Truth] @ \in\. 19. on] # \the *Sibylline*\. 21. which] # \Honorius\. 22–24.)least . . . World.⟨]. 23. was] 'w' ˇ 'a'. 25. them;] # \where they d\. 26. *Mankind,*] # second ','. 28. us] # \of Tel\. 34. These] @ \An po th\; 's' ˇ 'r'. 34. ⟨Two⟩] \Two\. 34. Purpose,] # second ','. 36. [ms. III, 38] '38' ˇ '46'.

198.1. Perhaps] @ \That\. 1. if] @ \w\. 2.)instead of a *Transcription*⟨]. 2. *Translation,*] # second ','; @ \as if you\. 2. ⟨my⟩] \Pen of the great [ˇˇ] of my A a [.]\. 3. of] # \write\. 3. Writing,] # \says\. 7. Silver] @ \⟨Silver⟩\ \gaudy Wings\. 12. ⟨comes⟩] \roams\. 14.)The Race of Men⟨] # \Mankind ⟨do⟩\. 14. unto] # \the\. 18. When] @ \When the Great GOD, [\the\] the Fire who kindled, sees, The World so gone, Hee'l bid the Flames to cease.\. 20. ⟨then will⟩] @ \⟨putt⟩\. 20. will] \do gracious\. 22. shall] # \y\. 23. *Judgment*] # \look'd of\. 24. Most] @ \Glorious GOD\. 24. ⟨His Truth shall⟩] \shall Righteous\. 25. Love.] # \[.]\. 30. ⟨live⟩]. 34. They'l] 'Th' ˇ 'C'. 34. see,] # \, B\.

199.2. V.] # \X\. 6. *Them*] @ \what\. 7.)even . . . Immemorial,⟨]. 7. Time] 'T' ˇ 't'. 7. the] # \Trad\. 9. *Josephus*] @ \The Story told by\. 10. ⟨Double⟩]. 11. World,] # \by Fire, which he received\. 13. But] @ \An\. 14. who] # \s\. 14. *Readers,*] # second ','. 14. with] # \inser\. 15. in] @ \b\. 16. argue] # \The\. 18. Among] @ \So\. 18. The] \se\. 18. ⟨Philosophers⟩]. 19. self-conceited] 's' ˇ 'w'. 20. *East,*] # \Indies to this Day continue so\. 21. *East;*] # second ';'. 24. It] @ \The\. 26. ⟨from *Them*⟩]. 26. *Conflagration.*] '.' ˇ ','; # \who indeed render it\. 29. *Greece;*] ';' # '.'. 29–32.)*Minutius* . . . But⟨]. 29. *Epicureans*] @ \p\. 31. of] # \them\. 31. that] # \it was\. 36–43.)So . . . *Fountain.*⟨]. 38. |of|] # \of Antio\. 38. *Antioch*] \ensis,\. 39. *Autolycus*] 'us' ˇ 'as'. 39. observes:] *Quod Conflagrationeu mundi nolentes volentes consertinet cum prophetis philosophis quamus Temporis espectu.*\.

200.1. Vain] @ \me\. 1. there] # \is no room it\. 3. away]. # \,\. 4–5. concerning] @ \of\. 5. Day] @ \consu\; # \make\. 11. ⟨all⟩]. 11. ⟨Devouring⟩] \destroying\. 12. *Diphilus;*] # \of the very\. 13. few] @ \press\. 15. would] # \m co\. 28. the] 'he' ˇ '&'. 29. fatal] @ \f\. 33. [ms. III, 40] '0' ˇ '8'. 33. ⟨His Admirer⟩]. 33. stand] # \a\. 36. *reminiscitur*] 'c' ˇ 't'.

201.2–4.)as . . . upon.⟨]⟨]. 5. *superest*] @ \m\. 6. \But here's enough\. 7–14.)Speaking . . . enough.⟨]. 15. A] ˇ 'a'. 23. the] 't' ˇ 'e'. 26.)and . . . *Noah,*⟨]. 26. Sons] 'n' ˇ 's'. 27. Men,] # \even among the First Sons of *Noah,*\. 28. Matter] # \,\. 29. when] @ \lett it be\. 33–34.)[see . . .]⟨]. 34. the] # \Confla General\. 35.)we see,⟨].

202.2. VI.] 'V' ˇ 'X'. 2. SIGNS] @ \Si\. 5. ⟨first⟩]. 7. REDEEMER] first 'E' ˇ 'e'; @ \Rede\. 8. *Signs*] # \as\. 10. Hereupon] @ \But, I\. 13. That] @ \ˆ)and⟨\. 14. they] # \were Eating &)

Drink\. 14. carried] 'c' * 's'. 16. ⟨very⟩]. 16. Noah] # \the\. 17. That] @ \And,\. 21. without|
\any Dream\. 21. any] # \Eve\. 21. near,] # \ There\. 23–25. ⟩The . . . Midnight.⟨]. 25. ⟨&
awakening⟩]. 25. Approach,] # \be\. 26. Conjectures] 'Con-' # \I have conjec\. 26. ⟨some,⟩|
\a Learned Man,\. 27. Inflammability,] # \still\. 29. are] # \altogether unsurpassed\. 30.
In] @ \Is th In the multitude of my thoughts within me, I have been ready to propose
whether\. 30. I] @ \I a\. 31. some] @ \y\. 32. ⟨really⟩]. 32–33. ⟩not . . . it;⟨]. 35. and] #
\But\. 37. ⟨Disquisition⟩] \Contemplation\. 38. ⟨our Lord has⟩]. 38. given] @ \are\; # \for
the\. 38. ⟨of His⟩]. 39. should] # \be\. 39. JUST] @ \Just Before\. 40. ⟩or |be| . . . it:⟨]. 40.
But] # \Such as may\. 41. may] @ \m\. 41. a] \re\. 42. done: @ \[*]\.

202.42–203.1. ⟩or, . . . for.⟨]. 2. Signs] # \given L\. 2–3. ⟨came to pass.⟩] \were accom-
plished.\. 3. ⟨be⟩]. 4. and] # \an\. 5. had] # \express'd\. 10. Come,] # \to the wor\. 12.
⟨the⟩ Earth]. 18. ⟩Immediately . . . Days,⟨]. 18. Immediately] 'ia' * 'te'. 26. Now,] # \if\. 26.
⟨hereupon⟩]. 27. Remarks;] 'r' * 'k'; # \The First Remark is\. 30. foretold] # \in Luke\.
31. that] # \He was\. 31. has] # \had\. 31. actually] 'a' * 'b'. 32. His] # \Come\. 32. Fire,]
\as\. 34. ⟨in⟩]. 35. alarmed] 'med' * 'umed'. 35. such] @ \those Pro\. 36. Signs] # \are\.
38. are] # \m\. 38. Past,] # \be\. 45. there] @ \are\.

204.1. Signs] @ \XII.\. 1. ⟨from⟩] \out\. 3. Lett] @ \Lett i\. 3. That] # \Immediately
after\. 4. ⟨Ascended⟩]. 5. Tribulation] # \which were in t\. 11–13. ⟩Without . . . History:]⟨].
11. who] # \paid\. 15. View,] # \the Com\. 16. and the] @ \to\. 18. about] @ \[*]\. 19.
⟨[Lib. 66.]⟩]. 20–22. ⟩Yea . . . videbantur.⟨]. 22. obire,] # \atqe in oppidis interdiu noctuque
in terram obire,\. 25. ⟨either sunk in or⟩] \be\. 25. down.] '.' * ','; # \or were sunk in\. 25.
At the] # \the\. 29. And] 'A' * 'a' 31. Womb] @ \Mouth\. 32. AIR] @ \Air\. 33. DAY] 'A'
* 'a'. 34. fright⟨ed⟩]. 40. Land] # \[*]\. 43. so] # \,\.

205.2. Africa,] 'ca' * 'a,'. 2. and] # \into\. 4. Sun.] '.' * ','. 9. ⟨with which⟩] \that all\.
10. from] # \it\. 10. ⟨as far as⟩]. 10. Africa] @ \Asia and\. 10–11. ⟩Tantus . . . —⟨]. 11.
Borgius] # \upon\. 12. ⟨Large⟩]. 12. it;] # \If they did make any, they are lost. But\. 13–14.
⟩thought . . . &⟨]. 14. Redemption] 'm' * 'i'. 14. REDEEMER] final 'E' * 'R'. 14–17. ⟩and . . .
Sodom!⟨]. 14. and, the] # \Giants\. 15. |more . . . Figures|]. 15. |in|]. 18. that] # \the\. 19. ⟨so
fully⟩]. 19. who] # \never had readd our New Testament\. 20. ⟨rendred⟩]. 21. Admirable]
@ \a Serviceable\. 22. ⟨confirm⟩]. 23. ⟨an . . . Matter;⟩]. 24. ⟩that had| . . . it,⟨]. 24. enquired]
'ed' * 'ing'. 25. &] * 'et'. 25. Vesuvius,] # \m\. 26. has] @ \do\. 27. Cinders] @ \Ash\.
28. Swelling] @ \horrid Consternation\. 30. their] @ \the\. 32. ⟨anxious⟩] \fearful\. 32.
Relatives] # \losing after one another\. 33. in] # \the Pitchy Darkness, wher\. 33. which]
@ \wherein\. 34. Devastations] @ \Deva\. 35. Picture] @ \Confl\. 38. Event] @ \W Wa\.
44. those] @ \fo\.

206.1. Tis a] @ \Now,\. 3. what] @ \the\. 9. ⟨Interpretation⟩] \Explanation;\. 11.
Comets] # \in their Elliptic Motions,\. 12. ⟨I find⟩] \It is\. 15. will] # \m\. 15–16. ⟩may . . .
and⟨]. 16. be] # \[. .]\. 17–18. ⟩and . . . Lightening.⟨]. 18. will] @ \is\. 18. Great Thing,]
'G' * 'g'; # \done,\. 20. But] @ \At the same time, the Powers of He\. 22. Tis] @ \[.]\.
22. Day] # \m\. 22. ⟨in⟩]. 23. Verse] # \]\. 24. the] @ \Capa\. 27. it] @ \they\. 27. be] #
\justly s\. 29. Vesuvian] @ \Er\. 30. Tis] @ \And, when our SAVIOUR added, [Mar. XIII.
15, 16.]\. 30. Rome] @ \^\. 30. ⟩the . . . terrified,⟨]. 31. overwhelmed:] # \^\. 32. when] #
\Titus\. 33. Considerable] @ \Grea\. 34. ⟨consumed⟩] \burnt\. 34–35. ⟩some . . . others,⟨].
35–36. ⟨which . . . Fire⟩]. 36. many] @ \wherein ^\. 43. Ten] @ \t\.

207.4. ⟨2⟩] # \XIII.\. 6. ⟩Wells,⟨]. 7. Great] @ \Gre\. 8. within] @ \as th\. 8. ⟨before⟩]
\while\; @ \⟨and⟩\. 9. John] # \was yett living,\. 9. Grave,] # \the\. 10. Circumstances] #
\th\. 10. ⟨obliged⟩] \obliged\. 11. ⟨Cognisance⟩] \Notice\. 12. and at] # \at\. 13. Representative.] # second '.'. 14. Amazing] @ \Ho\. 15. Sea] # \wrought, & swell'd\. 16. heav'd;] #
\and Buildings of all Sorts the\. 17. ⟩The . . . People;⟨]. 17. so,] 's' * ';'; # \that\. 18. ⟨The⟩].

18. People] @ \they\. 18. see] # \nor hear\. 19. hid] @ \hid\. 20. famished,] # \that\. 21. frighting] @ \terri\. 28–29.)What . . . *Rebound.*⟨]. 29. *Antiochians,*] # \[as\. 31. the] @ \[. .]\. 39. from] @ \[*]. 40. *Embassadors*] '*E*' * '*S*'. 41. celebrated] @ \me\. 43. did] @ \red\. 44. Judge] @ \M\. 44. World] @ \Whole\.

208.4. But] @ \Listen to\. 4. ⟨as⟩]. 5. ⟨know . . . of)] \are acquainted with\. 6. *Places,*] # \Bu\. 10. *Drought*] '*o*' * '*r*'. 10. and] @ \ˆ)especially tha⟨\. 12. *World*] # \knew not what were at\. 12. an] '*a*' * '*h*'. 14. Yea] @ \In\. 17. Now,] # \tho'\. 17. the *Signs,*] \m\ of earlier '*them*'. 19. *Ungodly*] @ \Gr\. 20. ⟨Abundant,⟩] \sufficient\. 20. that] @ \& w\. 21. or] # \we\. 21. ⟨the Sleeping World⟩]. 23. ⟨hereupon to)]. 23. labour] @ \to say upon them; That for ought\. 25. *Night*] '*N*' * '*n*'. 28. (3)] # \XIV.\. 30. But] # \that the Incessant War\. 32. &] # \in warning\. 32. to] # \that\. 32. overtake] '*take*' * '*whelm*'. 36. wherein] '*i*' * ',*'*. 37. ⟨as . . . it)]. 41–42.)What . . . *Perusal.*⟨]. 41. amazing] @ \dreadful Mountain\. 45. visiting] '*ing*' * '*ed the*'.

209.1. ⟨horrible)]. 4. methoughte] @ \he th\. 12. *that*] # *Last Day, where in*\. 15–18.)The . . . *Judgments.*⟨]. 16. diffused] # \thro'\. 18. me] # \again\. 18. *repeat*] # \what I have heretofore given in a Little Essay in *The World Alarm'd*\. 19. Commotions] @ \horrid\. 19. Convulsions] @ \hideous\. 26–27.)in . . . *Volcano's*)⟨]. 28. Mountains] '*t*' * '*i*'. 30. in] @ \are\. 31–32.)where . . . 'em:⟨]. 32. And] '*A*' * '*a*'. 33–35.)The . . . it.⟨]. 35. without] # \some such In it, outcry as that Lord, I may\. 35. ⟨At)] \W\. 36. the] '*t*' * '*T*'. 36. Outbreakings] @ \[*] terrible\. 38. *Fiery*] @ \horrificent Erruptions\. 38. that] \on the Plain of\. 41–42. the Matchless] '*ye*' * '*g*'. 44. ⟨In . . . 1638.)]. 44. 1638] '*3*' * '*4*'. 44. after] # \e\. 45. from] @ \of\.

210.4. added] # \mu\. 8. anon] # \to\. 8. Miles] '*M*' * '*m*. 10. ⟨praevious)]. 12. ⟨both)]. 15. ⟨incomputable and)]. 16. *Volcano's* first '*o*' * '*a*'. 24. ⟨Monserat)] *Antiqua,* which is *Without Water,* is not always *Without Fire*; but\. 25. every] @ \are\. 29–32.)Even . . . *Water.*⟨]. 31. Dust] @ \Stones, &\. 33–36.)formed . . . *Santorin.*⟨]. 35. another] @ \there was\. 36. *Italy, Italy,*] final '*y*' * '*n*'; final ',' * \y\. 38. Conservatory] '*C*' * '*t*'. 38. we] * '*is*'. 39. And,] @ \and\; # \have\. 40. shall] # \not\. 41. *Vulcanello's* '*u*' * '*a*'. 42. Vicinage] @ \New\. 42. we] # \in\. 44. *Ancient*] pl. \s\.

211.1. flaming:] # '.'. 1–2.)and . . . *Day.*⟨]. 1. *Everlasting*] '*r*' * '*l*'. 2. more] @ \to\. 3. No] @ \Th\. 3. ⟨a)]. 4. them.] # \They have caused whole Nations to tremble. We shall\. 4. wide] @ *Crater*\. 5. Whole] * '*all*'. 5. that] '*t*' * '*w*'(?). 5. One] # *Paroxysm* of *Paroxysm*\. 6. ⟨so lately as)]. 7. *Winchelsea*] poss. case \'s\; # \Account, has relates.\. 7. Ey-Witness.] '.' * ','. 8. ⟨with)]. 9. also] @ \only gi\. 10. Prodigy] @ *Phaenomena*\. 11. of] # \so unusually\. 11. and] # \so\. 12. ensued] # \an\. 14. Tumbling] @ \falling Houses\. 14. yett] # \the\. 15. ⟨Reeling and Staggering)\. 17. their] '*i*' * '*y*'. 19. ⟨at once,)]. 21. were] @ \was accom\. 21. with] # \the a\. 22. that] # \outdid the\. 23.)Great⟨]. 23. Stones] @ \Huge\. 26–30.)Yea, . . . *Waters.*⟨]. 27. Furious] @ \Ra- ging\. 29. Mighty] '*h*' * '*t*'. 30. was,] # \A a b\. 31. River] @ \Torrent of\. 32. *Fiery*] '*F*' * '*f*'. 32. all] '*a*' * '*y*'. 33. ⟨which was mostly)]. 34. where] # \it\. 34. Torrent] plural \s\. 36. along,] # \in its Way\. 36. in] '*n*' * '*ts*'. 38. floating] '*n*' * '*i*'. 39. River] @ \Stones of\. 40. Furnace] @ \great\. 40. *Iron*] @ *Burn*\. 40–41.)Thus . . . *troubled.*⟨]. 41. Acute] # \and Accurate\. 42. *Pisa,*] # \surveyin\. 42. ⟨an accurate)] \a\. 42. Survey,] # \of it pen thereof\. 43. amount] @ \be\. 45. Cubical] # \,\.

212.3. Almost] @ \Truly,\. 3. ⟨One says upon it,)]. 5–7. ⟨At . . . them.⟨]. 7. |with|]. 7. ⟨The)] \My\. 7. *Winchelsea*] # \said, No Pen can express how terri- ble\. 9. *express*] @ \dis\. 9. *terrible*] # \t\. 13. *Wickedness.*] # \ˋ\. 13. *Mountains*] '*un*' * '*na*'. 13. Lo] @ \G\. 16. wilt] '*w*' * '*a*'. 19. *Such*] @ \Wh\. 19. ⟨things)]. 20. in] # \(the)\. 20. the] @ *Ruines* [.]\. 22. GOD,] # \unto\. 24. *Antioch*] # \felt\. 25. In] @ \Once\. 27. make] @ \m\. 27.

cause] @ \make ma\. 30. hollow] @ \Recesses of the\. 33. *Particular*] @ \All\. 33. make]
\a\. 34–36. ⟩*England* . . . *Hell-kettles.*⟨]. 36. ⟨has had⟩]. 36. *Italy.*] '.' * ';'; # \where,
how\. 37. which] # \who\. 37. has] # \covered man\. 37. ⟨the⟩ Land]. 39. ⟨Ships . . . and⟩].
40. yea,] * 'and'. 40. Cities] # \have been\. 40–41. ⟩*Thirty* . . . *Hell-kettles.*⟨]. 41. What] #
\were\. 42. ⟨there⟩]. 42. have] @ \have no\; # \⟨tis, true, tho' *Some,* yett not *Much*⟩\ \a
Slender\. 42–43. ⟩tis . . . *Much,*⟨]. 43. Account!] # \We have some Acc a large Account of
a\. 43. ⟨in⟩]. 43. ⟨and others⟩]. 44. ⟨in Writings⟩]. 45. find] @ \have\; # \[.]\.

212.45–213.2. ⟩*Austin* . . . Ruines.⟨]. 2. In] @ \And\. 4. attended] @ \follow\. 5. splitt] @
\tore\. 5. ⟨on⟩]. 5. Judicious] # \Protestants,\. 7. all] @ \as\. 8. Whether] @ \But since\. 9.
France] @ \u\. 10. *Separation,*] # \as whole\. 11. ⟨judged⟩] \thought\. 15. This] @ \the\.
15. it] # \more\. 16. Sins] # \a\. 17. may] # \⟨be⟩\. 20. some,] # \⟨to⟩\. 20. of] @ \which a
Great Part of the World\. 22. 365.] '3' * '5'. 25. *with*] \out\. 26. such;] ';' # '.'. 26. which] #
\many Cities were su\. 27. when] # \that\. 27–28. ⟩as . . . Writing.⟨]. 30. But] # \History\.
30. pass] # \[. .]\. 34. together.] '.' * ','; # \as an Intro a *Alarum* the\. 35. began] @
\shook\. 36. People,] # \into some Consultations\. 39. ⟨*made in the Earth,*⟩]. 39. by] @
\produced\. 40. *Cantania*] 'i' * 'e'. 40. ⟨was . . . situated,⟩]. 40. University,] # \in it,\. 43.
Canons] 'ns' * 'n'. 43. ⟨New⟩]. 44. advanced] @ \appeare\.

214.2. Storm] @ \Earth\. 3. in] @ \above Seven thousand\. 5. of,] # \Nic\. 7. one] #
\left\. 7. ⟨had happened.⟩] \became of the rest.\. 7–8. ⟩Nothing . . . populous.⟨]. 8. O] @ \In
some of the Cities that were not utterly destroy'd,\. 11. They,] 'y' * 'ir'. 12. In] @ \One\.
14. The] @ \He wonderful Thunders\. 14. Heavens] # \were\. 14. ⟨one Flash whereof⟩]
\that\. 17. ⟨in⟩] \with\. 18. Calculation] @ \Comprehe\. 19. *doing*] pl. \s\. 20. that] #
\Is\. 21. That] 'a' * 'e'. 21. of] # \our\. 21. ⟩West⟨]. 22–23. ⟩after . . . Eleven,⟨]. 22. *calm*]
@ \[. .]\. 22. clear] 'c' * 'f'. 24. *Mills*] 'M' * 'S'. 25. threw] 'ew' * 'esh'. 25. *Mountains*]
\tan\ after '*Mount*-'. 25. The] 'e' * 'a'. 27. Places] @ \multitude\. 29. ⟨thrown⟩] \spewd\.
30. ⟨were⟩] \were\. 31. ⟨an⟩] \a total\. 34. ⟨rumbling⟩] \thundring\. 35. Thunderclaps] @
\of\. 35. ⟨mighty . . . hott⟩] \[*] such\. 35. there,] # \as we\. 36. in,] # \upon them\. 38.
add] @ \m\. 38. ⟨we⟩]. 38. *Ambrose's*] 'o' * 'e'. 39–44. ⟩*Truly* . . . *Judah.*⟨]. 41. what] # \an
Earth\. 41. Rebellions] # \against the Al\.

215.2. and] # \the De\. 3. there] @ \⟩*Judaea* was horribly shake\. 3. *Judaea* was] #
\horribly *Shaken,* and near\. 6. fell,] # \upon\. 7. waiting] # \upon P\. 13. Verily] @
\With\. 13. ⟨Voice⟩]. 14. ⟨we have⟩]. 14. Lord] # \[.]\. 14. us;] # \The Th\. 18. *from*] @
\in\. 19. Sinners] @ \greater\. 20. *in the*] \ir\ of earlier 'their'. 20. *Ways*] @ \Wicked\,
above which \⟨few⟩\. 20. ⟨of their *Folly*⟩]. 20. Nay,] # \[*and it will
not Repent!*]\. 22. in] # \those Earthquakes\. 22. wherein] @ \which\. 23. extensive] *
'terrific'. 24. *Harvest*] @ \H\. 26. But] @ \W\. 26. ⟨in⟩] \at\. 26. ⟨Hours⟩] \Time\. 26. ⟨of
a⟩] \of the\. 27. Men] # *Caesare* and *Pompey*\. 27. ⟩who . . . World;⟨]. 28. engaged the]
\m\ of earlier 'them'. 29. thus,] @ \As little Notice will\. 29. will] 'i' * 'o'. 29. be] # \so\.
30. that] # \w\. 30. GOD] @ \the\. 32. may] @ \won\. 32. what] # \the B\. 32. ⟩a⟨]. 32.
Bishop] @ \Sicilian\. 32. ⟨of Sicily⟩]. 33. wherewith] @ \when the\. 36–38. ⟩*Whole* . . .
them.⟨]. 41. Owners;] ';' @ ','. 42. carry] @ \[.]\.

216.1. this] @ \the\. 1. continual] @ \wh\. 6. ⟨Peece⟩] \Peec\. 6. ⟨is our⟩] \we\. 8. ⟨4⟩] #
\XV.\; @ \An\. 11. a] @ \the Destruction\. 12. Men] @ \we\. 13. They] @ \Behold the\.
19. ⟩even⟨]. 20. *World;*] # \and all\. 21. would] @ \they w\. 23. ⟨more particularly⟩]. 24.
up⟨on⟩]. 26. Representation] @ \Map\. 27–28. ⟩*Behold* . . . *Vengeance.*⟨]. 28. The] * 'Yᵉ'
@ \As\. 32. the] 'e' * 'is'. 34. In] @ \the\. 34. *former,*] # second ','. 35. ⟨entirely⟩]. 35–36.
⟨that . . . on;⟩]. 38. not] # \stay\. 39. so much] @ \in denying\; # \as\. 42. *FATHER*] 'A'
* 'a'. 42. ⟨Judgment⟩] *Vengeance*\. 43. that] # \has\. 43. He] 'H' * 'a'. 43. offended] 'o' *
'e'. 44. *Judaeical*] @ \De- struc\.

217.1. first,] # \there\. 1. ⟨Fire⟩] \Flames were\. 1. The] # \[***]\. 2. Children] \27
26\ in upper left-hand corner of ms. 2. Towns] @ \⟨#⟩\. 3. And] # \of the th\. 6. Lord]
@ \Gl\. 6.)a . . . Prophet,⟨]. 6. warning] @ \with an E\. 10. Superi⟨our⟩] '⟨our⟩' \er\ of
earlier 'Superier'. 13. Number] @ \Number of\. 15. the] 't' * 'T'. 15. Parts,] # \at & for the
Celebration of the Passe\. 16. Enemy] 'y' * 'ie'. 17–18.)[which . . . not,]⟨]. 19. Josephus] #
\Eleven\. 22. But] @ \What\; # \what w Land ⟨[*]⟩\. 24. also] # \wa\. 26.)Superb &⟨].
27. ⟨Desperate⟩]. 29. Noises] @ \Nois\. 29. Clamours,] # \& the universal Confusion of\.
31. ⟨he has⟩]. 34. with] @ \was now on Fire\. 35. And] # \Go the Glorious\. 35.)Our⟨]. 37.
unto] # \all\. 37. rest] # \Nations\. 41. What] @ \It It is\. 42. but] # \thereof\.

218.2. ⟨in the Day⟩]. 2. Wrath;] # \Yea, His Wrath\. 3. perish] # \for\. 3. for] @ \by\;
'o' * 'a'. 8. described] @ \t\. 10. we] @ \I\. 10. Lines] @ \Words\. 14. heated] @ \bur\. 20.
swallowed] @ \carried down\. 21. fiery] 'ie' * 'ei'. 26.)permitt . . . it;⟨]. 26. As] 'A' * 'a'.
28. ⟨than⟩] \tha\. 29. say] # \,\. 29. Ariel,] # \wh\.

219.2. VII.] # \XVI\. 4. will] # \have no be s\. 4. no] # \A\. 4. All] 'A'.* \a\. 5–7.)IThey
will| . . . Amusements.⟨]. 5. be] @ \but\; # \Asleep\. 8. Mighty] 'ght' * 'ht'. 9–10. Un-
known Hand] @ \Ha\; # \b\. 10. write] # \a\. 11–15.)Old . . . into.—⟨]. 12. as] # \a Despe-
rately Wick\. 13. and] # \after y [*]\. 14. unmindful] italics canceled. 15. All] # \People\.
16. Men] @ \Worldly People will be as violently\. 16. violently] @ \strongly\. 18. be] @
\[.]\; # \enga\. 19. ⟨Voluptuous and their⟩ ⟨their⟩]. 19. ⟨Purposes,⟩] \Intentions;\. 19. if]
@ \those\. 20. to] # \give\. 20. And,] @ \In Resigna [**]\; # \chiefly,\. 23. wherein] #
\they shall be punished,\. 23–27.)and . . . Drunkenness!⟨]. 23. as] # \Blind\. 24. |will they
be|. 25. down] @ \show\. 25. Hell] @ \F\. 26. How] @ \Sur\. 28. ⟨a⟩]. 28. Servants,] ',' *
';'; # \and and with\. 28. and] # \a\. 29. ⟨Roman⟩]. 30. Edicts] @ \and an\. 31. Slaughter;]
';' @ ','. 31. and] # \nothing but,\; # \Eter\. 32. putt] 'p' * '[.]'. 32. They] @ \The most\.
33. Slumbring:] ':' @ '.'. 35. Happy] @ \a long prospe\. 35. arrive] @ \be\. 35. by] @ \up\.
38. ⟨perhaps first most⟩] \the especially,\.

219.38–220.1.)where . . . withal.⟨]. 219.40. ISon of Perdition|] \Man of Sin\. 219.44.
Angels of] # \Heaven\. 220.1. ⟨soon⟩]. 2. ⟨and Flashes,⟩]. 6. ⟨astonish . . . Coming!⟩]. 6.
World] @ \Earth\. 6–8.)Heaven . . . in.⟨]. 6.)Heaven] @ \The\. 7. ISome|] \&\. 7. |with|].
8. in.] # \withal.\. 10. Daemons] 'n' * 's'. 11. ⟨that⟩] \which\. 11. above] @ \a\. 12. talk] 'l'
* \k\. 13. ⟨Praesumpteous⟩]. 14. of] 'o' * \&\; # \the those Dunces the Schoolmen, ⟨even⟩
Subtilize them into Impassibility;\. 15. ⟨Metaphysical⟩] \Learning &\. 16. ⟨them⟩]. 16. ⟨a
Sort of⟩]. 19. ⟨as⟩]. 20. To] @ \I will [*]\. 21. ⟨in⟩ them] \by\. 23. and] @ \⊕\. 32. whither]
\,\. 34.)& Revenge⟨]. 37. Serpent.] '.' * ',';⟩ # \and s\. 38. Heavens,] # \and the most H\.

220.39–221.4.)We . . . it?⟨]. 220.41. describe] # \the [.]\. 220.42. of GOD.] @ \`\; #
\The Executioners\. 221.5. than] @ \of the\. 7. as] # \accom s\. 13. Rise] 'R' * 'r. 15.
And] 'A' * 'a'. 16. in] # \it. But\. 16–22.)The . . . comprehend!⟨]. 17. when] @ \& be\.
22. also,] # \will be the Time, of when\. 23. GREAT] 'T' * 'a'. 24–25 ⟨transcending . . .
Law,⟩]. 26. And] # \we are express\. 29. forth.] # \The Spirits of them that have been
the Faithful of the Blessed JESUS\. 29. He that] @ \He that\; # \cried with a loud\. 31.
Lazarus,] # \Come forth!\. 33. FORTH] 'T' * 'E'. 38. Our] @ \Our\. 38. SAVIOUR] @
\REDEEMER,\. 39. CHRIST,] # \exerting the Power of a GOD,\. 40.)as . . . Magnetism⟨].
40. find] @ \fe\; # \what\. 41. serve] @ \serv\. 44. to] * 'is'; # \,\.

222.2. ⟨of old⟩] \of old\. 2. fly] 'f' * 'F'. 4. High] @ \Prai\. 4. and] # \astonished\. 4.
⟨amazed⟩] \as Persons in a Drea\. 5–8.)when . . . them;⟨]. 6. transported] 'trans-' * \ˆ
and coming again with Joy, bringing the She\. 7. thus] # \Topston\. 8. Squadron of] @
\Regiments\; # \Angels,\. 9. help] 'l' * 'p'. 9. which] @ \of\. 10. these] # \Raised Ones
become\. 11. ⟨out of⟩] \from\. 12. doubtless] # \[*]\. 12. [what] '[' * '(. 15. now] # \to con-

clude, That upon these\. 15. these] first 'e' * \is\. 16.)awful . . . *Seraphim*!⟨|. 18. *waiting*]
@ \now standing most obediently standing\. 19. will] 'w' * 'b'. 22. *Behold*] @ *Every*\. 25.
⟨from)] \from\. 25. a Long &] @ \Long\; 'L' * 'C'; '&' * 'a'. 26. *on*] 'o' * 'w'. 27. *Midnight*]
@ \Might\. 31. with] 'w' * '&'. 32. ⟨their) *Idols*]. 32. ⟨To)] \That\. 32. describe] \ing\; @
\For the\. 32–33.)the . . . at⟨|. 33. that] @ \of\. 34–39.)What . . . *Empire*.⟨|. 41. *Blood*,] ','
* ';'. 42. ⟨wherewith)] \)with which⟨ that\. 44–45. ⟨not . . . do.)].

223.2. ⟨will)]. 3. *say*] 'y' * 'id'. 5. What] # \shak\. 6. ⟨what . . . Looks,)]. 6. be,] # \[.]\. 7.
⟨Eternal GOD)] *Glory*,\. 8–10.)What . . . *Days*!⟨|. 8. upon] # \an ungodly an\. 10. what]
@ \⟨what)\. 11–12. Miserable People] 'P' * 'L'; @ \Peopl\. 12. with] @ \b\. 13. The] @
\Ever\. 17. Lend thy] 'y' * 'i'. 17. Use] @ \Make\. 17. the] 'e' * 'y'. 18. to] @ \with in\. 18.
limn] @ \pri\. 18. out] @ \the\. 18. *Terrible*] @ \amazing Terrors of the\. 22. *surpass*]
'r' * '[.]'; second 's' * long-tailed 's'. 26. *know*] @ \kno\. 27. are] @ \m\. 28. ⟨the)]. 28.
revealed] 'ed' * 'ing'. 31. deeply] @ \lively\. 31. and] # \a conspicuous Care to\. 33. have]
@ \express\. 35. *Devotions*] @ \The\; # \to\. 35. ⟨towards)]. 38–41.)A . . . Pitty.⟨|. 41.
whom] # \they\. 45. *Mark*] 'a' * 'A'.

224.1. these] 't' * 'T'. 1. genuine] # \Sons of\. 3. Mountain] @ \Arabian\. 7. Best] #
\Saint upon Earth,\. 7. *Saints*,] # \now on the Earth\. 8. they] @ \is\. 8. devoured,] #
\have cause exceed\. 10. have] @ \[. .]\. 10–12.)Will . . . *Tempest*!⟨|. 10. Will] # \th\.
12. These] first 'e' * 'i'. 12. ⟨now)] \also\. 14. when] @ \He\. 15. and will] # \preven\. 20.
⟨To understand)] \The To interpret,\. 20.)*The*⟨| # \what were and of, All\. 21. referred]
@ \meant\. 22. upon] @ \upon [.] that is to take\. 24.)about⟨|. 24. *Day*] 'D' * 'd'. 25.
Especially] 'E' * 'e'. 25. Supposing] @ \a\. 25. *Righteous*] 'g' * \s\. 26. ⟨then)]. 27. among]
@ \a in the\. 28–29.)A . . . Resurrectione.⟨|. 33. Ungodly] @ \Wick-\. 33. ⟨the Decreed)].
34. lying] @ \being\. 39. the Lord] 'y^e' * 'o'.

225.4–5. under the] 't' * 'g'. 15. is] @ \y\. 16. Works] @ \F\. 16. ⟨with)] \and\. 18–22.
)and . . . *Cup*.⟨|. 22. ⟨However . . . be)] \Tho' tis\. 23. most] @ \and\. 26–29.)[Matth. . . .
us;⟨|. 34. Determining] @ \the Redemp\. 34. now] @ \find\; # *find Mercy*\. 35. what]
@ \[. .]\. 39. *Babylon*. '.' * ','; # \And other Countreys besides France, & Palatin\. 39–
40. ⟨Hungarians, & with)]. 42. ⟨Charitable)]. 43. SAVIOUR] # \,\. 44. them] @ \them,
while\. 44–45.)and . . . own.⟨|.

226.1. *Hands*] # \will\. 1. ⟨it)]. 3–6.)They . . . before.⟨|. 5. nothing.] # *Peace* will be
once\. 5. concluded] second 'c' * 'd'. 9–11.)Indeed . . . Saved.⟨|. 9.)Indeed] @ \The Diff\.
12. ⟨who) knows] \that\. 13. How] # \,\. 13–15.)It . . . do?⟨|. 15. satisfy] @ \certain\. 15–
16. ⟨if . . . than)] \to find and\. 16. *deliver*] second 'e' * 'r'. 18. *Supernatural*] @ \Mercy\.
19. ⟨Recorded)] \mentioned\. 24. *Sinjed*] 'j' * 'g'. 25. had] @ \had\. 26.)any time⟨|. 27.
upon] @ \in\. 28. ⟨any where)]. 30. Cause] # \to say\. 30. ⟨to)]. 31. when] # \So\. 31. *Lot*]
't' * 'tt'. 33. ⟨inexorably)]. 33. *Anger*,] # *& repented not*,\. 35. thus,] # \the *Angels*\. 35.
the] 't' * 'g'. 35. In] @ \Pl\. 39. And,] # \[i. Cor.\. 43. survive] @ \escape\. 43. Destroy] @
\Consum\. 44. into] @ \when\. 44. where] 'r' * 'n'.

226.45–227.2.)having . . . them,⟨|. 226.45. having] @ \[.]\. 227.1. now] @ \are\; #
\attend them\. 2. should] @ \with the Seeds of *Sin* & of *Death* in them,\. 2. admitted] @
\taken\; # \where not Defiling\. 3. They] 'e' * '''. 4–6.)In . . . them.⟨|. 4. this] @ \all\. 6.
render this] 'i' * 'e'. 9. him,] ',' * ';'. 12. before] @ \m\. 13. and] # \then he was *Deathless*
th\. 14. upon] @ \when he\. 16–18.)*will* . . . for,⟨|. 19. Our] @ \ˆ ˆ\. 19. thus] # \ˆ None
to stand\. 19. and] # \fo\. 20. for,] \ˆ\. 20. the] 't' * 'T\; @ \ˆ The World is n\. 20. it;] #
\ˆ\. 21. for] # \is\. 21. *Mercy*] # \[. .]\. 22. ⟨its Portion)] \dispensed unto it.\. 22. now] @
\calls for\. 23–26.)Nothing . . . *together*!⟨|. 23. It] @ \the *End* whereof must\. 24. unto] #
\w\. 24. of] @ \them and of them what\. 29. of] # \it\. 32. Fainting,] @ \Choak\; # \for

the\. 35. them.] # \They *smite upon their Breasts,*\. 35. *Breasts*] @ \Breats\. 36. *moved*]
\,\. 36. *Aspine-Leaf.*] '.' * ','; # \in an\. 39. *Him⟨self⟩*]. 41. ⟩*is come,*⟨]. 41. *the End*] @
\[*]\. 43. ⟨it⟩]. 43. the] # \[*] about\. 45. and] @ \^\; # \contin\.
   228.1. *The Time*] @ \& Thou who d\. 3. *my Eye*] @ *you shall*\. 4. *Pitty;*] ';' @ ','.
4. Ones] 'O' * 'A'. 4. *know*] @ \now\. 5. *you.*] 'o' * 'e'. 5–15. ⟩But . . . for.—⟨]. 15. *our*] *
the\. 17. now] @ \appears\. 18. which had] # \said\. 19. the] @ \[.]\. 20. covered] @
\enveloped Him,\. 24. under] @ \for\. 24. ⟨inconceivably⟩]. 25. ⟨the⟩]. 26. ⟨glittering⟩] \G\.
31. shall] # \See not only\. 31. ⟨wonderful⟩] \fulge\. 31. *Face* of] # \an\. 31. the Great] @
High-Priest of\. 32. now] # \[*]\. 34. most] @ \[.]\. 37. ⟨all⟩ *together*] ⟨all⟩ \al\ of earlier
'*altogether*'. 38. of . . . not] italics canceled. 40. *himself*] 'h' * 'H'. 41. what] # \makes\.
42. ⟨nefandous⟩]. 43. every] @ \^ had\. 45. *say*] @ \call\.
   229.1. impiously] @ \im\. 3. ⟩What . . . MAJESTY.⟨]. 4. Upon] @ \And he sees a multi-
tude of those who durst not go so far, but yett make themselves Accessories to the *Plott,*
by maintaining, That the Faith of His *Godhead* is not essential; People may be Good
Christians without the *Faith* of His *Godhead.*\. 5. Provoking] 'ing' * 'ed'; @ \Sigh\. 6.
⟨the⟩ *Ministers*] \the\. 8. *Eyes* will] # \no\. 9. *Terrible.*] # \Their *Opened Eyes*\. 10. And,]
'A' * 'a'. 11. *Horses*] @ \Cha\. 12. Comfort] @ \Defence\. 12–14. ⟩before] . . . These⟨]. 12.
whom] # \is Greater than any Emper Conqueror or Emperour\. 14. Throne] @ \P\. 15.
These] # \S *Burners* full\. 15. *Seraphim,*] # \and *Angels* that now will have *Power over*
the Fire,\. 16. ⟨in⟩]. 18. were] @ \lay\; # \fallen under his\. 19. humbly] @ \propose\. 19.
SON] @ \Son\. 20. GOD] # '''' * ';'. 20. ⟨about . . . them;⟩]. 22. WORD] @ \Word is wai\.
24. seeing] @ \cried with a Lo\. 25. And] @ \Thus, our Almighty\. 27. *Tread*] @ \[.]\.
27. will] # \utter\. 28. ⟨at⟩]. 29. A Voice] @ \Yea, the Le\; # \⟨of this Importance⟩\. 32.
they] # \have\. 32. *deserve*] final 'e' * d. 33. given.] # \Inconceivable Showres\. 34–36.
⟩With . . . it!⟨]. 34. *thunder*] # \upon *His Adversaries,*\. 35. Ten] # \[.]\. 38. *Enemies.*] '.'
* ':'. 41. Veins] @ \W\. 41. ⟨where⟩]. 42. Ten] @ \^\. 43. Flames,] @ \Smoke, and\; # \&
Cinders,\. 44. Thousands] @ \Ten\. 45. ⟨Massy⟩] \Vast\.
   230.1. mighty] @ \which\. 2. upon] @ \and much\. 5. *Her*] 'H' * 'h'. 5. carry] @ \exceed
all\. 5. and] # \^ ^\. 6. stood,] # \there\. 6. into] # \a Lake\. 7. *Brimstone*] 'i' * 's'. 7.
furlongs] 'r' * 'l'. 9. *Desolation.*] pl. \s\. 9. One] @ \sho\. 10–19. ⟩O . . . know;⟨]. 14.
Inhabitants] 'ab' * '[. .]'. 16. dire,] # \&\. 17. there |be|\. 21. *Transported*] @ \Esc\. 21.
will] @ \will y\. 29. *Portion*] \⟨[*]⟩\. 29. *We are*] @ \But\. 30. on, ⟨O⟩] *the*\. 30. & ⟨O⟩]
\Thou\.
   231.1. VIII.] @ \X\; final 'I' * 'i'. 2. How] 'H' * 'h'. 4. But,] # '[.]'. 6. ⟨Stately⟩] \Wealthy\.
6. *Cities*] 'C' * 'S'. 7. admirable] @ \and\. 7. Industry] @ \Skill and\. 10. be] @ \can\.
12–19. ⟩The . . . *Poets.*⟨]. 16. now] @ \kn\. 23. Peremptorily] @ \Exp\. 24. There] @ \A
Word,\. 27. be] @ \be\. 30. Disowns] @ \She\. 30. our] @ \Him the\. 30. Creator] 'C'
* '[.]'. 32. Reproach] @ \De\. 35. it heaps] 'it' * '[. .]'; 'h' * 'b'. 37. enough;]';' * ':'. 38.
know] @ \k\. 38. procured] # \a Desolation\. 39. there] # \are *Men* at one time Ali\. 40.
Alive . . . Earth] italics canceled. 40. That] @ \For\. 40. *Angels,*] @ \Apostate\. 42. Now,]
@ \Ca\; # \the Judg at the\. 43. Thousands] @ \Innumerable\. 44. should] # \under\.
   232.2. infinitely] @ \inf the\. 3. thought] @ \thot\. 3. Judge] @ \That\; # \, by th\.
7–15. ⟩The . . . People!⟨]. 8. |at|]. 14. The] 'T' * 't'. 15. Here] @ \Veri the Wrath\. 16. Im-
portance] @ \accurate,\. 18. ⟨a⟩]. 20. Reported] 'por' * 'ort'. 20. *Earth*] @ \Land\. 22. But,]
\wch\. 22. What] @ \horrid, &\. 24. ⟨be⟩]. 26. ⟨but⟩]. 27. *Ungodliness*] @ \Unkindness
of the Doings of a Worl\. 28. ⟩be⟨]. 34. Degenerate] @ \Mankind,\; 'D' * ','. 37. ⟨O Ye
Heavens,⟩]. 39. Unsanctified] 'c' * 'f'. 39. ⟨continually⟩] \perpetually\. 42. but] # \prop\.
42–45. ⟩means . . . them.⟨].

233.1. We] @ \But,\; 'W' * 'H'. 2. ⟨most⟩]. 3. ⟨nothing but⟩]. 9. *Devils*] @ \Dev the\. 9.
⟨Among the rest,⟩] @ \⟩Among the rest,⟨\. 9. which] 'ic' * 'at'. 11–13. ⟩And . . . them!⟨]. 12.
hold] 'ld' * 'v'. 13. ⟩so⟨]. 13. *Iconoclastic*] @ \their\. 13. has] @ \has there\. 14–15. ⟩and . . .
Mammetry;⟨]. 16. *Imposters*] # \to by whom they\. 17–19. ⟩and . . . so.⟨]. 18. Intercede] @
\to\. 20. day] # \on the Earth are o\. 21. ⟨*Gentilism.*⟩] *Paganism.*\. 23. Nonsensical] @
\Nonsensi\. 32. express] \ion\; @ \make\. 32. *Thou*] @ \Righteousness\. 35. *Iniquity,*]
second ','. 35. ⟨the⟩ *Blood*] \[b..]\.
233.36–234.1. ⟩The . . . up.⟨]. 233.40. |*Abetting*|] \in justifying\. 233.40. these] @ \|warn-
ing|\. 234.4. People] @ \Innocent\. 5. ⟩whose *Memorials*, go up,⟨]. 7–10. ⟩An . . . *Souls.*⟨]. 7.
Approach] # \^\. 9. them] 'm' * 'e'. 9. rowsed] @ \[.]\. 11. Worrying] @ \the\. 12. *Folio's*]
's' * 'y' # \s\. 13. ⟨they⟩]. 13. ⟨Barbarities⟩] 'Ba' * 'Id' \Cruelties\. 14. *Scarlett*] @ \Ten-
horned\. 15–25. ⟩An . . . Indeed,⟨]. 15. |cruel|] \hideous\. 15. occurring] @ \done\. 15. but]
@ \One\. 16. a] @ \an\. 16. *four*] @ \tw\. 19. I] @ \Indeed\. 21. Hott] @ \Long\. 24. And]
* 'But'. 24. *Drunk*] @ \Drunk\. 25. When] @ \After\; @ \^ ⟨Before thus⟩\. 28. Regions,]
@ \Territory\. 29. had] 'h' * 'a'. 30. And] * 'But'. 31. Bruitish] @ \Wicked Inju Sh\. 34–35.
⟨Actions . . . What⟩]. 35. Butcheries] @ \B Cruelties and\. 38. *Dioclesian*] 'sia' * '[. . .]'.
235.2. *Lives,*] # \^ before the Course of Nature should bring in Tes\. 4. *Sacrificed*] @
\Sac\. 5. *Antichrist*] @ \Babylone\. 7. ⟨a⟩] \a\. 7. *Persecution;*] ';' * '?'. 11. see] # \wh\.
12. into,] # \we shall f\. 14. *trespassing*] 'n' * 'g'; # \g\. 15–29. ⟩What? . . . GOD!⟨]. 15.
Alas] 'A' * 'a'. 16. *Christians*] @ \[.]\. 19. A] * 'a'. 24. Yea,] 'Y' * 'T'. 27. throw] # \in\.
28. of] # \[.]\. 29. What] @ \It is m\. 23. and] @ \that if any\. 35. oblige] @ \det\. 36–40.
⟩Men . . . it.⟨]. 37. of] @ \^\. 39. become] @ \a\. 40. Impossible] # \for\. 40. doing] @ \the
managin\. 41. Good] @ \Wel\. 42. basely] @ \pro\. 43. Wretches] @ \Men\. 44. fleece] @
\[.]\. 45. ⟨wrong⟩] # \Wron Unjust\. 45. are] @ \in ⟨and⟩ what\. 45. found] # \in\.
236.2. And] @ \and\. 2. ⟨not⟩]. 3–9. ⟩The . . . *Lord*!⟨]. 4. which] # \th\. 5. is] @
\will\. 6. Neglected,] # \and\. 9. Continually] 'C' * 'S'. 10. that] # \[*] manage the
Rit\. 10. ⟨Superstitious & Unprofitable⟩]. 12. are] @ \are [. . .]\. 13. where⟨in⟩] \of\. 13.
Guides] @ \Instructors\. 18–19. ⟩The . . . by.⟨]. 19. Concern] 'nc' * 'ce'; @ \Int\. 20–24.
⟩and . . . Hence⟨]. 24. contempt] @ \c n\. 25. *Little*] @ \Church Honest\. 25. Saecular] @
\Grandeur\. 26. ⟨Miscreants⟩] \Fellows\; # \Wor\. 29. ⟨*Turn yett again!*⟩] \Yett more;\.
29. *abound*] # \among\. 31. but] @ \and v\. 33–38. ⟩indeed . . . *Abominations.*⟨]. 34.
Heaven,] # \[*]\. 35. Heaven.] # \I\. 35. and] @ \th\. 37. *Door*] # \Add To these things it
may be added;\. 41. and] @ \almo\. 44. gives] @ \who\.
237.2. Whole] @ \Yea,\. 5. even] @ \name\. 6. ⟨in⟩] \of\. 7. if,] 'f' * 's'. 8. known]
@ \which was\. 13. *Crime*] @ \Fire\. 14. *Sodom* &] # \her Daugh Daughters,\. 15–16.
⟩even . . . *Mahometans,*⟨]. 16. quickly] 'k' * 'c'. 17. more] # \Desol\. 18. ⟨were to⟩ ⟨now⟩]. 19.
that] @ \wh\. 20. grassant] @ \us\. 21–25. ⟩The . . . upon!⟨]. 22. of.] '.' * ','. 24. Vengeance]
\e\ between 'n' and 'g'. 26. *Just*] 'J' * 'T'. 28. ⟨in the *Nation,*⟩] \here\. 28. Challenge] final
'e' * 's'. 28. made] 'm' * 's'. 29. ⟨loud⟩] \loudly do they invoke Heaven to p\. 31. committed]
@ \⟨annually⟩\. 31–32. ⟨on . . . there,⟩]. 32. there] first 'e' * 'u'. 33. ⟩Besides . . . *Pardon.*⟨]. 35.
ripe] @ \ri\. 36–38. ⟩An . . . *rerum.*⟨]. 37. such] # \such\. 39. yett] 'tt' * 't'. 39. *Indictment*]
'm' * '[.]'. 42–43. ⟩What . . . it!⟨]. 45. a] * 't'.
238.7. ⟩World,⟨]. 13. ⟨& arraigned Him⟩]. 13–15. ⟩They . . . Him;⟨]. 16. *Buffeted*] 'u' *
'e'; @ \b\. 16. They] # *Nail'd* Him to a Cross\. 17. this] @ \these\. 18. ⟨in Bitter⟩]. 18.
Torments,] # \Sug mids\. 19. ⟨dash'd⟩] *mixed*\. 19–20. augment] @ \incre\. 20. and] @
\The w\. 22–24. ⟩A . . . upon!⟨]. 23. of] @ \of\. 23. How] @ \how\. 25–26. ⟨that *Precious
Blood*⟩]. 26. into] @ \it\. 26. No,] @ \No,\. 26. was] # \[. .]\. 27. ⟩We . . . *Ground.*⟨]. 28.
Tho'] @ \N No, No, Alaz, the Cryin\; # \I\. 29. who] # \with a Repenting Faith, do plead

it\. 29. what] 'w' ˟ 't'; @ \the Sin\. 34. Forlorn] @ \Wicked\. 34. ⟨Polluted⟩] \Perpetual\. 35. The] @ \In the\. 35. Resentments] # \an\. 35. ⟨to⟩] \for\. 36. ⟨hereupon⟩] \upon it\. 37. *THAT*] @ \th\. 37–44. ⟩The . . . murdered!⟨]. 38. *slain*.] # \ˆˆ Every Day to be wondred at! an\. 45. ⟨*Detestable*⟩] # \⟨*World Exe*⟩ *Detestable World Vile*\. 45. *Earth*] \⟨*Execrable*⟩\.

239.1. *Coals*] # \of I\. 2. is] # \⟨{to b}⟩\. 2. ⟨every . . . at!⟩]. 3. more] # \Finally\. 4. Load] @ \M\. 4. which] 'ic' ˟ 'er'. 5. Generation] final 'n' ˟ 'ns'. 7. *Earth,*] # second ','. 11. *This Generation*] @ \The\; # \has\. 12. *Approved*] 'A' ˟ 'a'. 13. *Darkness*.] '.' ˟ ','. 13–18. ⟩It . . . *Decision*!⟨]. 14. *grown*] @ \grow\. 19. ⟨*Amorites* and the⟩]. 19. *full*,] # second ','. 20. *Measure*] 'M' ˟ 'S'. 22. *Guilt*] 'l' ˟ 't'. 24. *Con*)f⟨*lagration*] 'l' ˟ 'f'. 25. *Guilty*] @ \Gu\. 27. now] @ \may\. 28. *bear*] \for\ of original *'forbear'*. 29. committed] 'e' ˟ apostrophe. 30. ⟨Certainly⟩]. 31. *Guilt* @ \enou\. 31. burning] @ \Ind\. 36. but] # \such Materials, as\. 37. *Asbestine*] 'in' ˟ 'um'. 37. ⟨Clothe⟩] \Materials\. 37. ⟨Sheets,⟩] *Clothe*\. 40. used] @ \us\. 40. *it be*] 't' ˟ 's'. 42. Occasion] 'i' ˟ 'o'.

239.43–240.8. ⟩I . . . say,⟨]. 239.43. *Few*] 'F' ˟ '64'. 239.43. *All*] 'A' ˟ 'a'. 239.44. passing] \⟨Lyi⟩\. 240.4. Accounts] # \;\ 6. that,] # second ','. 8. But] @ \Again,\. 10. *Seats*] @ \Stately *Palaces*,\. 12. ⟨vast⟩]. 13. ⟨together⟩]. 13. *Cities*] # \,\. 13. yett] 'tt' ˟ 't'. 15. ⟨overthrown . . . not*.*⟩]. 17. spend] @ \execute\. 22–23. ⟩which . . . Inhabitants,⟨]. 22. exceeds] @ \ˆ yett\. 24. *September*] 'p' ˟ 'te'. 24. But] 'B' ˟ 'A'. 26. There] @ \There\. 26. could] @ \any\. 27. Desultory] 'u' ˟ 'a'. 27. ⟨very⟩] \the\. 28. *Herodotus*] @ \Even\. 33. definiendo] 'o' ˟ 'e'. 34. Prophecy!] '!' @ ';' 39. *Tacitus*] 'u' ˟ 'a'. 40. ⟨Wicked⟩] *Mighty*\. 42. thought] # *Incredible*\. 43. *Wicked*] @ \Ci\. 44. when] # \the Lord\. 45. *Slain*] @ \m Sword of t\.

240.45–241.1. ⟩Thy . . . *Vanity*!⟨]. 2. *Ambassadors*] 'A' ˟ 'E'. 4. that] @ \th\. 4. hoped] @ \would\. 5. would] @ \th\. 5. ⟨too,⟩]. 9. And,] @ \What\. 10. should] @ \be\. 10–11. reduced] @ \brought t\. 11. *Ruines*?] # \W\. 11. which] @ \whom\. 12. ⟩upon . . . GOD,⟨]. 13. ⟨comprehend⟩] \conceive the where\. 15. ⟨called in⟩] \the Sar\. 16. made] # \a Prodigious\. 18. buried] # \un in\. 19. *All*] 'A' ˟ 'a'; @ \the\. 19. have] @ \[.]\. 20. And,] # ','. 21. the *Trumpetts,*] @ \the *Trumpetts,*\; # \which is to\. 22. upon] # \an Incurable World\. 23. no less] @ \to\. 24. *Him*] 'H' ˟ 'h'. 27–34. ⟩In . . . *Ages*?⟨]. 32. |Arts|] @ \⟨Arts [˟]⟩\ *Sciences*\. 32. the] 'he' ˟ \[. .]\. 34. *Ages*?] @ *Days*?\. 36. Their] 'ir' added to original 'The'; # \ˆ ⟨M⟩\. 37. But,] # \in these *Libraries*, how many Thousands of Books,\. 38. *Library*] @ \Alexandrian\. 39. kindled] @ \en\. 40. the *World,*] @ *Mankind*\. 41. become] 'm' ˟ 'i'. 43. Scholar] @ \cannot\. 43. ⟨⟨with *Salmuth*⟩⟩]. 44–45. ⟨which . . . *Vaticans,*⟩]. 45. *Vatican*:] @ \ˆ\.

242.1. German] @ \Ge Spaniads\. 3. ⟨a⟩] \the\. 3. *Fire*] # \now ready to break forth upon it,\. 4. should be] @ \be an\. 6. that] # \it\. 6. if] # \m\. 7. ⟨but . . . *Ignem;*⟩]. 8. a] @ \a\. 9. them;] # \and are\. 9. consist⟨ing very much⟩]. 11. them;] ';' ˟ ':'. 11–25. ⟩Indeed . . . *Read.*⟨]. 12. one] # \[.] [.]\. 17. it;] # \ˆ ⟩but have that Complement made upon it, *Nunquam vidi clariorem Ignem*!⟨]. 22–23. the Words] 'e' ˟ 'is'; # \shall\. 26. once] # \u\. 27. of] 'o' ˟ 'a'. 28. *Populous.*] # \Let us make\. 28. *Antediluvian*] 't' ˟ 'd'. 30. *Centuries,*] 'i' ˟ 'e'. 37. ⟨twice⟩]. 38. as are] @ \again\; # \now\. 42. by] @ \of\. 42. *Ark,*] # \w\. 44. we have] @ \ˆ ⟨and⟩\; # \also\. 44. *Antediluvian*] 't' ˟ 'd'. 45. show] @ \)also⟨\.

242.45–243.1. Unquaestionable] @ \Undoubted,\. 243.1. Remembrances] first 'm' ˟ 'e'. 2–6. ⟩The . . . *Illustrious.*⟨]. 2. astonishing] # \Peece of Archi Edifice of\. 5. make] @ \[˟˟]\. 6. *Populous*] @ \replenish peopled\. 6. *Illustrious*] @ \T\. 12. From] @ \Who\. 13. *Mightily*] @ \spe mighty\. 17. *Conflagration*] # \written\. 19–20. inconceivably] @ \Inconceiv\. 21. old] # \sett unto it; the Ear\.

244.2. *IX.*] # *XVIII.*\. 5. ⟨*Intention*⟩] \Import\. 5. *Clause,*] # \The\. 6–8. ⟩or, if . . .

abiturum,⟨|. 6. Defer] 'D' ⁕ 'd'; @ \forbear\. 10. The] @ \The first\. 10. ⟨is to⟩] \will\.
11. having] @ \being so far exting]. 12. ⟨there will⟩]. 12. now] # \will\. 14. *remembred*]
first 'r' ⁕ 'R'. 15. have] # \the\. 16. ⟨the *Fire* of GOD⟩]. 16. is] @ \it\. 18. ⟨a little⟩]. 18.
before] second 'e' ⁕ 't' 19. HEAVENS] first 'E' ⁕ 'A'. 21. Oracles] 'c' ⁕ 'a'. 21. informed] @
\told\. 22. *CITY*] @ *City*\. 23.)having . . . *Foundations,*⟨|. 24. consisting] @ \compa\.
24. *Pure Gold*] @ \what\. 29. each] @ \ea\. 31–35.)not . . . *ever.*⟨|. 32. No;] @ \It will\.
36. whereof] \⟨a⟩\. 36. an⟨other⟩]. 36. with] @ \[Heb. XI. 1\. 39. Patriarchs,] 'i' ⁕ 'e'. 42. It]
@ \[.]\. 42–43. *Creatures*] @ \'\. 43. live] @ \'\. 43. so,] @ \'\; # \they b\. 45. *Place*] @
\'\. 45. where] @ \'\. 45. Noblest] 'N' ⁕ 'n'; @ \'\.

    245.1. *Heavens*] '-vens' @ \'\. 2. the best] @ \'\. 3. *Bodies;*] # \The Myria\. 4. ⟨Him-
self,⟩]. 5. But] # \i\. 7–16.)I . . . then,⟨|. 8. But] ⁕ 'And'. 13. it,] # \ˆ I object nothing to
That! But then,\. 13. fond] @ \so lothe may will\. 16. But] 'B' ⁕ 'b'. 16. which] 'ich' ⁕ 'ose';
@ \which will\; # \is\. 17. ⟨be⟩]. 17. where] @ \where\. 18. ⟨than . . . is,⟩]. 18. the] \m\
of earlier 'them'. 18. ⟨Nations.⟩. 20. Now,] # \the\. 21. LORD] @ \Lord\. 23. What] @
\What\. 25. to] # \go gov Reign\. 25. ⟨Reign over⟩ \govern\. 25–28.)This . . . here.⟨| 27.
Rose] @ \[..]\. 30. ⟨End⟩] \Conclusion\. 31–37.)While . . . them.⟨|. 31. quaestion] @ \susp\.
38. ⟨venerable *African,*⟩]. 38. ⟨venerable⟩] # \⟨godly⟩\. 41. *Holy City*] @ \City [. . .]\. 41.
The] @ \They\. 42. ⟨Our⟩] \The\. 42. *Mother*] # \of us all,\. 45. adds] # \an A..\.

    246.1. granted] \⟨only but⟩\. 1. ⟨not⟩]. 1. ⟨only . . . Army.⟩]. 2. He] @ \also.\. 3. beheld]
second 'e' ⁕ 'o'. 3. Astonishment] @ \Admiration\. 4. says] @ \[.]\. 7. *Hanc*] # \dicimus\.
9–10.)Now tho' I⟨|. 10. the] # \strange\. 10. Yett] ⁕ 'But'. 12. the] 't' ⁕ 'h'. 13. *Christian*]
@ \Reade\. 13. taking] 'g' ⁕ 's'; @ \considering\. 16. *Notion*] \And now\ between 'No-
' and '-tion'. 16. *Groundless*] 'G' ⁕ 'g'. 18–33.)A . . . them.⟨|. 22. *Chimaerical*] first 'i' ⁕
'e'; @ \a\. 22. indeed] \in\ of earlier 'in-' 'deed'. 25. it,] # \in it\. 27. entreat] # \That a
Temple\. 28. meer] @ \p\. 40. ⟨That's enough!⟩]. 43. ⟨mostly⟩].

    247.2. Besides] @ \By the Streets thus crossing each other\. 5. Four] 'F' ⁕ 'f'. 10. ⟨there⟩]
\they\. 12. *Nebuchadnezzar*] second 'e' ⁕ 'z'. 13. the] \m\ of earlier 'them'. 13. ⟨People . . .
triumphed⟩. 14. who] # \as L\. 15. as] @ \an\. 15–16.)It . . . *Nations.*⟨|. 17. ⟨It . . . finished;⟩].
19. *New*] @ \Celes\. 24. having] @ \of T\. 24. *Things hoped*] @ \a\. 30. and ⟨an *Hun-
dred Times*⟩]. 31–32. Addition] 'A' ⁕ 'a'. 32–43.)I . . . *Room.*⟨|. 33. detected] # \in of\.
38. calculate] @ \try to\. 40. |*City*|] ⟨i⟩ \e\. 45. subdue] @ *Conquer* the\. 45. Minds] #
\and\.

    248.2. be] @ \be\. 2. ⟨His⟩] *the Holy*\. 3. *Holy*] @ \Bel\. 4. ⟨which⟩]. 4. does] @ \does\.
6. ⟨them⟩]. 7. *for*] 'f' ⁕ 'u'. 9. assembled] # \now\. 12. HOLY] @ \Hol\. 15. *Kindness*] 'K'
⁕ 'c'. 16. This] @ \This\. 17. CITY,] # \in\. 17–23.)will . . . *away.*⟨|. 26. shall] # \then\.
29. brought] @ \has\. 31. *which*] 'hi' ⁕ 'ha'. 34. exceeds] first 'e' ⁕ 's'. 35. *saw*] @ \to\.
36. Indeed] @ \The most Ef\. 38. ⟨what . . . is⟩]. 38. *Way*] # \which we know\. 39. But] @
\The View is a little d\. 39. ⟨aforehand⟩].

    248.44–249.3.)These . . . *here!*⟨|. 249.2. |but|]. 3. must] # \have\. 6. ⟨into⟩]. 6. which] #
\He\. 6. ⟨Eternal⟩]. 6. People.] # \As there is\. 7. THREE] @ \Thr\. 8. Incomprehensible]
'comprehensible' ⁕ 'conceivable'. 8. But] @ \⟨are unto them⟩\. 8–9. ⟨and Unfathomable⟩].
9. ⟨some from among⟩] \a Number of\. 10. those] # \Deli\. 11. This] 'T' ⁕ 't'; @ \We
have\. 15. becoming] 'i' ⁕ 'e'. 16. they] \B\ appears below 'y'. 19. *GOD;*] # '.'. 21. in] #
Thoughts of min and\. 22. ⟨Closing⟩] # \⟨in⟩\ \Centering in\. 22. ⟨with⟩] @ \Casting\.
23–28.)We . . . there.⟨|. 26. End of] # \the a\. 28. *Heavens,*] # \we shall\. 33. *enquiring*]
@ \Travelling to it with a Face thitherward,\. 34. such] @ \th\. 39. arising] @ \th\.

    250.7. *Inchoation*] 'ch' ⁕ 'di'. 8. aspiring,] # \to\. 10–16.)None . . . *GOD.*⟨|. 14. have]
@ \are\. 18. every] # \One\. 19. no] # \for\. 19. ⟨inaestimable⟩]. 20. ⟨is⟩] @ \⟨was⟩\ \is\.

21. Old] 'O' * 'V'. 23. Book] @ \Sai\. 26. ⟨ever⟩ be]. 26. spoken] # \. There will [.]\. 27. ⟨Mind;⟩] \Mind;\; @ \⟨[*]⟩\. 27. not] 't' * 'nor &'; @ \And\. 27. ⟨any⟩ but]. 27. ⟨ever⟩]. 28. ⟨there.⟩] \in any Mind:\; 'er' * 'is'. 28. All] @ \Every O\. 29. Soul;] # \and m\. 29–30. ⟨and Virtues⟩]. 30. and] # \Bles-\. 30. ⟨Bles⟩sings]. 32. an] @ \some\. 33. Use] # \in\. 34. to one another,] italics canceled. 35. Obedience] @ \Conformity &\. 36. City.] '.' * ','. 39–40. ⟨Who . . . Death!⟩]. 40. now] @ \here\. 41. ⟨Verminous⟩]. 42. ⟨Mischiefs⟩] \Things\. 43. ⟨into⟩]. 43. ⟨have now⟩] @ \are\. 43. will] @ \into,\. 44. no] @ \b\.

251.5. ⟨an⟩]. 5. a] @ \R\. 6. Having] @ \A\. 9. ⟨made⟩]. 9. His] 'H' * 'h'. 10. them:] ':' * '!'; # \A Pe there will A P Enlivened by the Spirit of Life, in their Glorious KING, every will\. 11. Soul,] # \in that\. 12. Enlivened,] # \by\. 13. began] # \upon the Elect Vess\. 15–16. ⟩Even . . . Earth,⟨]. 15. ⟩Even⟨] 'E' * 'e'. 16. those] @ \th\. 18. ⟨proper Means⟩]. 20. ⟨in all things⟩]. 21. desired] @ \Conformi\. 22. that] # \in\. 22. on] 'o' * 'i'. 24. With] # \with a S\. 24. Satisf⟨action of⟩] 'action' * \ied\. 25–36. ⟩A . . . be.⟨]. 27. while] @ \[*]\. 29. assiduously] @ \ear-\. 31. |their|] \his\. 32. |will|] \do it\. 37. KING] @ \King\. 38. What] @ \[.]\. 45. to] @ \f\.

252.3. will] @ \is\. 4. ⟨They⟩] \We\. 4. have] @ \see\. 11. Voice,] @ \a\. 11. Big] @ \gre\. 12. ⟨Almighty⟩] \Omnipotent\. 14–15. ⟩The . . . there.⟨]. 14. JEHOVAH] 'O' * 'A'. 18. from] @ \w\. 18. Righteousness:] # \⟨and fill'd with⟩\. 18–19. ⟩and |Bless'd and| . . . for.⟨]. 20. ⟨will be⟩] \are\. 20. ⟨into . . . it,⟩]. 21. All] 'A' * 'T'. 22. ⟨has been⟩] \is\. 24. be] @ \now\; # \enriched b\. 25. ⟩In . . . them!⟨]. 27. Tis] @ \A\. 30. shine.] # \A Thoug ex Accurate Knowledge will\. 30. ⟨Precious⟩] \Immense\. 31. withal!] # \The Knowled\. 32. O] @ \A\. 34. Spirits] @ \bright Penetrati Bright Intelli\. 38. Various] @ \Wrong Apprehen\. 38. many] @ \thin\. 40. there.] # \The Saints will have no Jars\.

253.5. Those] @ \In the\. 6. ⟨us⟩] \us when,\. 6. ⟨they who⟩] \we\. 7. shall] @ \There, Then, they]. 7. GOD,] # second ','. 9. Bible,] # second ','. 14. Among] 'A' * 'a'; @ \I have somewhere [.] seen such a Passage as this;\. 14. were] @ \had y\. 36. most] @ \glo\. 36–42. ⟩But . . . GOD:⟨]. 40. very] @ \con\.

254.2. From] @ \We look\. 2. for] # \our\. 3. Bodies,] 'ie' * 'y'. 5. A] @ \I\. 8. Expectation] @ \Expectation, which\. 9. who] 'o' * 'i'. 9. Old] @ \feeble Bod\. 9. ⟨and⟩] \foul,\. 10. Creed;] # \Resurrectio\. 11. who] # \only\. 13. ⟨in⟩]. 13. expired.] # \withal.\. 14. inspired] 'p' * 's'. 17. fast] @ \fa\. 21–32. ⟩When . . . awake.⟨]. 25. Dead.] '.' * ','. 25. Their] @ \^ ^\. 29. Knew,] # \The Living\. 30. Redeemer:] ':' * ';'. 32. Such] 'S' * 'R'; @ \this\. 32. has ⟨over⟩] \once\. 33. and ⟨over⟩]. 33. could] @ \qu\. 34. Power,] @ \Scripture an and\ # \of GOD\. 35. former assures] # \th\. 36. ⟨confirmed⟩] @ \⟨co⟩\ \confirmed\. 36. ⟨in⟩] \in\. 36. the] 'e' * 'is'. 36. it,] # \by His own Rising from the Dead,\. 40. that] # \gave His own\. 41. Risen] # \,\. 43. He who] # \who\.

254.45–255.1. ⟩as . . . Sacraments;⟨]. 255.1. SAVIOUR] 'R' * 'r'. 1. instituted] 'st' * [..]. 3. will] # \bring us\. 3. day] # \cause our Bodies to [*]\. 3. wherein] @ \[.]\. 4. shall] # \sitt with Him in Heavenly Places, and\. 5. ⟨is⟩] \has been\. 5–6. Possession] 'P' * 'p'. 7. We] 'W' * '[' . 14. ⟨Faith,⟩] \Consolation\. 18–20. ⟩and . . . Potter,⟨]. 19. Work,] # \which it\. 20. withal:] 'th' * 'al'; ':' * '.'. 24. perhaps] 'p' * 'h'. 27. Immortal] @ \They will have\. 31. that] 'at' * 'ey'. 33. under] @ \with it\. 34. We] @ \Of these\. 34. informed,] # second ','. 34. shall] @ \s\. 42. that] 'at' * 'eir'. 45. ⟨now⟩]. 45. this] @ \now\.

256.9. ⟨An⟩] \The\. 12–13. ⟩Our . . . Eagles.⟨]. 13. ⟨Behold, The Bodies⟩]. 13. which] 'ic' * 'en'; @ \Behold the Faithful That is ⟨Here⟩\. 16. with the] 't' of 'the' * 'a'. 17. ⟩as⟨]. 18–24. ⟩All . . . done.⟨]. 19. bearing] @ \for a T\; # \a\. 20. been] 'n' * 'b'. 22–23. |Even ⟨a⟩ . . . and ⟨a⟩ . . . Sufferings.|]. 23. |Thus|] \So\. 26. ⟨Everlasting . . . Overwhelming⟩]. 32. Here] @ \The [..]\. 33. [ms. III, ix, ⟨81⟩] \81\. 35. Promise] @ \Word\. 36. pass] # \in the into unrecompe\. 38. Compleat] @ \T\. 38. ⟨Promise⟩] \Word\. 39–44.)All . . . for!⟨]. 41. *Raised*] # \Sai\. 42. thy] 'y' * 'e'.

257.1–2.)when . . . *City*,⟨]. 1. *Behold*] @ \Lo\. 3. abundantly] @ \abound\; # \satisfy\. 3. ⟨assure⟩]. 6–13.)*Mouth* . . . for.⟨]. 11. GOD] @ \God\. 12. Yea,] # second ','. 16. and] # \an\. 16. ⟨an Equal⟩]. 21. Imagine] 'I' * 'i'. 22. *Title*] # \of\. 23. to ⟨the⟩] \Eternal\. 25. When] @ \By no means!\. 28. *Heaven*] # \too\. 29. SPIRIT] # \had\. 30. ⟨by . . . them⟩]. 32. they] # \should\. 34. had] # \their\. 35. from] # \from\. 35. the] \ir\ of earlier 'their'; @ \He h\. 36. His] 'is' * 'a'. 37–39.)*Invisible* . . . *Blessed*.⟨]. 38. |shown and|]. 39. Part] @ \Pa\. 44. ⟨entred⟩]. 44. and] # \:\. 45. Humble] @ \Hun\.

258.1. ⟨written⟩] @ \⟨&⟩\. 2–7.)In . . . *GOD*.⟨]. 4. Golden] @ \Lac\. 7. from] @ \who *knows* their war\. 12. ⟨Acknowledgments of⟩] *Devotions* to\. 13. *Ben*⟨*efactions*⟩] \ignities\. 13–15.)How . . . them!⟨]. 16. for] # \the undefiled Inheri\. 20–21.)With . . . *Talents*:⟨]. 21. Various] 'V' * 'v'. 23. With] @ \Finally;\. 24. ⟨and . . . *Patience*⟩]. 31–32.)Their . . . *Crowned*.⟨]. 32. ⟨it⟩]. 32. shall] @ \they\. 33. ⟨it⟩] @ \ˆ⟨it⟩\. 34. be] # \found that their\. 35. and] # \th\. 35–42.)It . . . *Distinctions*.⟨]. 37. there] @ \in\. 42. before] # \a Glorious\. 44. SPIRIT;] @ \the Works of His Holy\.

259.3. Beleever] @ \B\. 3. In] @ \Our Bible A\. 4. given] 'ven' * '[. . .]'. 8–18.)concerning . . . Him.⟨]. 12. *Thoughts*] @ \Th\. 15. unto] # *David*,\. 20. of] # \the *Kingdome*,\. 20. ⟨great⟩]. 21. Favour,] # \and\. 21. City,] # \of the Empire,\. 26. before] # \the Least & His *Holy Ones*,\. 26. than] # \an *Ahashuerus*,\. 28. ⟨Humble⟩]. 28. be] @ \a\. 30. *made*] @ \made\. 31. Endeavour] @ \Hono\. 33. Great] # \and as Good\. 33. few] # \, have in this\. 35. which] @ \as\. 36. printed] @ \wri\. 36. ⟨the⟩] \that He such\. 39. Obscurity] # \,\. 41. passed] 'p' * 'b'. 42–43.)It . . . *Invisible*;⟨]. 44. *Theatre*] 'ea'* 're'.

260.1. *Alms*] 'A' * 'a'. 1. ⟨went⟩] \are Gen\. 2. be] @ \be\. 3. them.] # \It una- ˆˆ)voidably f⟨\. 4. what] @ \the\. 6. *Self-Annihilation*] 'a' * 'i'. 6. that] @ \that\. 7. LORD] 'O' * 'or'. 10. ⟨of the Earth⟩]. 12. the *Worm*,] \e\ of earlier 'thee'. 12. defrauding] @ \and Gr\. 12. His] # \Prai\. 12. ⟨Praises⟩,] \Acknowledgments\. 13. an] 'a' * 'd'. 20–21.)and . . . *Bitterly*,⟨] @ \ˆ\. 22. also] # \als\. 24–26.)Yea . . . them.⟨]. 25. Themselves] @ \to\. 26. GOD] @ \GOD is glorifie Th\. 26. *Praise*] # \;\. 31. *Ancients*] @ \Elde\. 35. ⟨*Conversations* and⟩]. 41. But] # \how\. 41. ⟨any . . . we⟩] \those whom we do not\. 42. whose] @ \who had\. 45. It] @ \Set thems\.

261.4–5.)|But| . . . Contemplation!⟨]. 4. |But|] \And\. 6–7.)that . . . do,⟨]. 6. *Sojourn*] 'r' * 'n'. 7. with] # \a An Anp\. 12. embrace] # \as\. 12. another] # \in\. 14. another,] # second ','. 17. ⟨and . . . *Prayers*⟩]. 19. *Distresses*!] '!' * ','. 19. In] @ \and in answering\. 20. will] 'ill' * 'ould'. 23. They] @ \Those w\. 28. ⟨at and by⟩]. 28. *Just*] @ \Sai\. 29. Praesumption] @ \Intim\. 30.)in⟨]. 31. should] # \be more\. 34. Then] # \ˆ⟨a⟩\. 36. that] # \thus\. 36. ⟨so⟩]. 42. From] @ \And\. 44.)did⟨]. 45. gain,] # \and\.

262.3. *GOD*.] '.' * '!' 4–5.)*Employments* . . . *GOD*!⟨]. 5. Expectations?] # \ˆ\. 7. *unto* @ \⊙ so\. 16. People] # \that rise\. 17. it] * 'H'. 18–20.)They are |the| . . . SAVIOUR.⟨]. 19. |own|]. 19. *Dead*,] # \that\. 24. *Lead*] @ \them\. 24. *Help*] @ \them\. 26. Students] @ \a Gent\. 28. Church] @ \Men\. 29. Ministr⟨ation⟩] \y\ of earlier 'Ministry'. 29. *Angels*] @ \Holy\. 30. ⟨to⟩]. 31. ⟨the⟩]. 31. receive] @ \be\. 31. the] \ir\ of earlier 'their'. 31. Ministr⟨ation⟩] \y\ of earlier 'Ministry'. 32. *Ended*,] # \or the Objects of it will\. 36. ⟨a Sort of⟩] \the a\. 37. Ministration] @ \Ange\. 37. Mind] @ \Ple\. 39. ⟨on *Sinai*⟩]. 42. having] @ \with\. 43. As] @ \A\. 44. Yea,] # \it\.

263.3. for] @ \to\. 3. Management] @ \Government\. 3. ⟨Grand⟩]. 3–4.)and . . . *GOD*.⟨]. 4. There] @ \Thus the Heavens w\. 6. transported] @ \carried\. 6. into] @ \it\; # \the\. 8. may] # \fly down, to do their\. 9. Transportation.] # \ˆˆ)While these⟨\. 9. then] 'n' * 'm'. 10. that] # \always\. 13. of &] # \converse with\. 13. the⟨ir⟩]. 14. ⟨Illustrious and Superiour⟩] \Glorified\. 14. Brethren] 'B' * 'b'. 14. bear] # \a Fellowshi\. 15. them.] '.' * ','. 15. If] @ \as\. 16. ⟨in . . . Ezekiel⟩]. 18. People] # \[.]\. 20. in] # \their more Vermicular State, or,\. 20. ⟨most Religiously and⟩]. 21. Thankful,] @ \and con perpetually\. 21. Angels,] # \to whom there was committed\. 22. Church,] # \in the World,\. 22. ⟨for very many⟩] \in the Machin of Peace to regulate the\. 27. Dispatch] # \they made\. 29. Lord.] '.' * ';'. 31–40.)While . . . do.⟨]. 32. yett] * 'the'. 34. |Advantages|] \Opportunities\. 35. Those] 'o' * 'i'. 36. of Good;] # \Thy Opportunity to Do Good,\. 38. be] # \Unaccounta-\. 38.)|Inconceiva-|bly⟨]. 39. unto] @ \unto\. 40. what] # \the d\. 42. might] 'i' * 'a'. 42. ⟨if⟩]. 42. their] 'i' * 'y'. 42. unhappily] 'i' * 'y'. 44. Laws] # \full\. 45. Places,] # \as\.

264.1. and ⟨would⟩]. 3. Be] # \[.]\. 4. At] @ \At\. 4. Honourable] # \Places bestow'd upon you\. 7. shall they] 'y' * 'S'. 11. Earth,] # \be Recon have\. 13. It] @ \When\. 18. ⟨a⟩]. 24. a] @ \the\. 24–26.)has . . . ipsius⟨]. 25. illic] second 'i' * 'o'. 28. City;] # '.'. 29. ⟨they had⟩]. 29. the] # \St\. 30–31.)There . . . Jerusalem!⟨]. 32. not] # \not in\. 31. exemplary] @ \full\. 40. But,] # \what\.

264.43–265.1.)It . . . City.⟨]. 264.44. Reality] @ \Origi\. 264.45. of;] # \ˆMost certainly,\. 265.4–5. ⟨Difference,⟩] \Distinction\. 5–6.)Lett . . . Father?⟨]. 9–10. ⟨[particularly . . . Biblica,]⟩]. 12. One] 'O' * 'B'. 12. ⟨whole⟩ ⟨Humane⟩] \Animal\. 15. Cerebrum] 'br' * 'ot'. 19. ⟨that⟩]. 22. First Father] 'a' * 'i'. 28. by] @ \quickly\; # \the\. 32. Flesh] 'F' * 'b'. 38. ⟨fashion⟩] \form\. 41. They] # \shall In- herit\.

265.41–266.6.)When . . . for!⟨]. 7. ⟨may think they⟩]. 9. might] # \more Significant that\. 9. But,] # \[.]\. 13. Men,] # \shall\. 13.)shall⟨]. 13. them,] # \come unto an End. Shall\. 14. ⟨uncouth⟩]. 15. ⟨some Countreys⟩]. 15. here.] @ \many Nations\. 15. your] # \Glorious GOD Lord,\. 15. ⟨most . . . make⟩]. 16. GOD,] # \in\. 16–17. among . . . there.⟨]. 16. among] @ \th\. 16. |attend upon|] \praise\. 17. Yea,] @ \His Holy City, of old here\. 17. Apostolical] @ \Church State of the Gospel,\. 18. take] @ \teach\. 18. ⟨any . . . Teaching⟩]. 18. any] @ \⟨do⟩\. 18–19. Christian] @ \present Order of the Church,\. 19. yett] # \the Days will He is\. 19. you] # \to be\. 19–20. ⟨to . . . Part⟩]. 19. ⟨to do⟩] # \⟨something⟩\. 20. below] 'b' * 'B'. 21. of ⟨the⟩]. 23. Separate] @ \Sp\; # \Sh\. 28. ⟨at Length⟩] \lately\. 29. Several] @ \the\. 32. The] @ \No\. 33. Marriage] @ \esp\. 33. GOD.] # \There is no Salique Law of any Force in the Holy\. 33. that] 'a' * 'e'. 34. carry the] @ \publish\; 't' * 'a'. 34. REDEEMER] # ˆ * '?'. 34–35. ⟨unto His Disciples?⟩].'36. which] @ \when\. 37. will] @ \it\. 37. it?—] # canceled lines that start a new paragraph:

\Thus ⟨we⟩ have taken a Short View of the Blissful Seats, where we shall be Forever with the Lord.

It will not impair our Portion there, if we step down for a while, to the New Earth, which will be Part of the [\the\] Heavenly Countrey, to be look'd for.\. 37. In] @ \Touching\. 39. Period;] ';' @ ','. 41. informed] @ \assured me\. 43. toward] \s\. 44. Judaeos] 'o' * 's'. 45. We] # \have been\.

267.3. has] # \been\. 4. Stones] @ \f\. 6. Him;] 'H' * 'h'. 8. ⟨Posterity⟩] \Offspring\. 8. in] # \the Prosperity\. 14. Earth,] # '.'

268.2. X.] # \XIX.\. 2. EARTH] # \described.\. 4. Our] @ \We\. 6. ⟨An Earth,⟩] \Thy GOD as\. 6. ⟨no longer⟩]. 7. ⟨no longer⟩]. 7. that] # \av\. 8. a Quiet] 'a' * 'at'. 13. will] # \continue\. 13. ⟨persist . . . proceed⟩]. 13. ⟨persist⟩ \consume\. 14. But] # \it will\. 16–25.)In . . . Thousand.⟨]. 21 we shall] 'e' * 'i'. 21. Years] @ \Days wherein\. 26. ⟨much⟩] \far\. 27. ⟨the . . . GOD⟩] \its terrible Execution\. 30. Fire] # \now\. 31. ⟨Innocent⟩]. 31. ancient] @ \famous Law\. 34. that] @ \there\. 36. ⟨Ungodly⟩] \Wicked\. 37. of] * 'in'. 40. unto] # \the Pa- triarch\. 42–43.)will . . . on.⟨]. 45. ⟨out⟩].

269.2. when] # \they\. 2. should be] # \Raised unto\. 3. ⟨Restored unto⟩]. 5. over That]

'T' * 't'. 12. promised] # \fo\. 12. Day] 'D' * 'd'. 13. Indeed,] # \Ther\. 14. as] @ \sh\.
17. be] 'b' * 'to'. 18–19.)without . . . Caverns,⟨]. 21. express] \ly\ of earlier 'expressly';
\declare\. 21–22.)the . . . Terms;⟨]. 24. Earth is] 'is' @ \shall\; # \passed away, &
there\. 24–26.)And . . . AWAY;⟨]. 26–28.)That . . . BE.⟨]. 28. One] 'O' * 'W'. 29. Deed] @
\Promise of of Engagem\. 29. ⟨for)] \of\. 29. Land,] # second ','. 30. Investing] # \Abr\.
31. ⟨then)] \then\. 32. Countrey] # \his Canaan here\. 33–34.)whether . . . unto!⟨]. 33.
lor . . . the]. 33. may] @ \may ever b\. 35. Indeed,] # \a whole No Gerhard, constantly\.
35. empannel] @ \brin\; # \about\. 37. for] # \a Mind\. 38. But,] # \Lett\. 38. with] @
\mastering\; # \the Voice of\. 39. having] 'h' * 'S'. 39. strongly] @ \to\. 40–42.)and . . .
yett⟨]. 41. World,] # \at the err\. 42. there] # \is en\. 43. VOICE] 'ICE' * 'IECE'. 43. ⟨more
generally)]. 44. World] @ \une d Earth\. 44–45. ⟨I . . . many.)].

270.1. Cyril] 'y' * 'u'. 3–9.)To . . . for.⟨]. 4. Basil] @ \^\; # \supposes\. 4. Theophylact,] @ \And\; # \di\. 7. will] # \not it\. 11. it,] # \Perditis non Interitum sanat,\. 13.
And] 'A' * 'a'; # \brin\. 13. The] 'he' * 'is'. 15. Interitu] # \[*]\. 15. And] @ \Who\. 21–
22. Company,] # second ','. 22. go] 'g' * long-tailed 's'. 22. Opinion] @ \Heresy of the\.
26. Evaporation] @ \Substantial\. 27. But] @ \Nevertheless\. 27. ⟨yett)]. 30–36.)I . . .
GOD.⟨]. 30. among] 'a' * 'A'. 31. such] # \a\. 35. |will]]. 36. says, Behold] 'B' * ']'.

270.42–271.5.)NEW . . . Condition.⟨]. 270.44. Theophylact,] # \as\. 270.45. it] @
\we\. 271.1. What] 'Wh' * 'to s'. 4. interpreting] @ \the\. 6. ⟨The Thing whereof)] @
\Nevertheless\. 11. PARADISE] @ \Para- dise the\. 12. before] # \the b\. 14. Prophets]
\since the World began\. 15–26.)Calovius . . . Briefly,⟨]. 22. one] # \says of\. 24. Cre-
ation] # \done ov\. 26. CREATED] @ \made\. 28. Recovered] @ \rather better co\.
28. into] 'o' * 'a'. 29. before,] # \By one\. 31. Heavenly] first 'e' * 'a'. 31. ⟨in)]. 31–33.
⟨GOD . . . wonderfully.)] \will have the Aspect and the Savour of, A Field which the Lord
has [\Blesse\] BLESSED.\. 37. awfully] @ \a\. 38. and] # \some\. 39. as] # \N\. 40. Toil
of] # \Mankind,\. 42. that] # \the\. 43. from] 'f' * 'b'. 43. ⟨our)]. 44. fulfilling] # \H\. 45.
had] 'd' * 's'. 45. ⟨for us)].

272.7. And] @ \THEN\. 8. is] # \shall\. 9. THEY] @ \They\. 9. will] @ \sh\. 15. cre-
ated] @ \made it not in Vain,\. 16. ⟨Word)]. 17. We] @ \[.]\; # \But inherit it\. 17. Earth,]
second ','. 18. called] 'c' * 'b'. 19. Most] @ \It will\. 20. The] @ \We are ass\. 22. ⟨In . . .
it,)] \We are assured,\. 23. ⟨we have)]. 25. ⟨They . . . And,)]. 25. of] @ \For,\. 27. that] # \are
the Children of GOD, by being\. 29. in] \t\. 30. Earth] 'E' * 'e'; @ \Heavens\. 31. Suitable]
@ \I\. 34. and] # \f\. 35. Hence] # \the Inhabitants of\. 39–40.)Or, . . . Parables!—⟨]. 39.
hastily] @ \as\. 40. an,] ',' * [.]. 42. Lovely] \Happy\. 42. shall] # \escape the Terror\. 44.
Coming,] # \in His Him\.

273.3. Ministry,] # \[.]\. 5. and ⟨from)]. 5. will] # \the\. 6. Field] @ \Earth,\. 6. on] 'o' *
'i'. 7. Rebelled] @ \fell from th\. 9. which] # \made\. 10. Judge;] ';' * ':'. 12–13.)They . . .
Above:⟨]. 12. Heavenly] @ \Mate\. 12. |Tempers|] \Disposi- tions in a Sa He Symphon\.
14. ⟨Devotion:)] \Piety:\. 18. They] 'ey' * 'er'. 18. Virtuous,] @ \Holy,\. 18. ⟨and)]. 19–20.
)They . . . Creaturis,⟨]. 22. ⟨while)] \tho'\. 23. Rate] 'R' * 'h'. 24. KING] 'K' * 'R'. 26. it,]
',' # ','. 28. These] @ \It is\. 30. Both] @ \Together\. 31. in ⟨the)]. 32. ⟨all . . . of)]. 32. ⟨of)].
36. expound] @ \to\. 37. apply] @ \apply th\. 37. differeth] @ \⟨will)\; # \differeth\.

274.4. we] @ \^\; # \m\. 5. Jerom] 'o' * 'st'. 5. ⟨and Push)]. 6. ⟨It . . . Mahometan!)]. 6.
rail] # \perhaps [a..]\. 7. ⟨as . . . it,)]. 7. with] 'w' * 'a'. 9–16. ⟨Or . . . Hearing.⟨]. 18. what] #
\can\. 19. render] # \them\. 19. ⟨it)]. 20. ⟨are)]. 21. must] 'm' * 'T'. 22. World] # \recovered
out of the Fire\. 23. Things] @ \Ob\. 26. ⟨our Protoplast)] \had\. 28. his] 'h' * 'H'. 28. in]
\His\. 28. the Tendencies] @ \[.]\. 29–41.)Vile . . . Earth.⟨]. 42. lost,] # \we have lately
had some Amends made us\. 45. Raised Saints] @ \Ra\.

275.2. propose] second 'p' * long-tailed 's'. 5. there:] ':' * ';'. 19–21.)But . . . them.⟨]. 21.

|up|on]. 26. *GOD*;] # \and my Tabernacle shal\. 27. *THEY*| '*HEY*' ˅ '*hey*'. 28. Thus] @ \I Yea, w\. 28. Word] @ \Wor\l\d\. 29. which] @ \Now,\. 33. *away*] @ \w\. 37. almost] @ \as i\. 39. this] '*is*' ˅ '*e*'. 41. ⟨*Fish-like*⟩]. 43. ⟨of⟩ which]. 44. Collection:] ':' ˅ '!'. 45. that] @ \h\.

276.5. ⟨even⟩]. 7. Demonstrates] @ \, even with\. 8. Allowances,] # \And\. 11. Armed] '*A*' ˅ '*a*'. 12–13.)But . . . say,⟨]. 13–14.)the . . . and⟨]. 14. from] # \the *Flames* of\. 17–19.)It . . . *numbered*.⟨]. 18. And,] # \ˆˆ It is expressly said,\. 21–23.)We . . . No.⟨]. 22. his] # \P\. 23. come] @ \[. .]\. 24. which] @ \whom\. 29. *them*] # \they appe\. 31. Representation] '*a*' ˅ '*i*'. 32. told] # \what I Read There, I will\. 32. ⟨I apply⟩] \and expound\. 34. find] # \a Pro\. 34. *One*] @ \a\. 35. the Mark] '*e*' ˅ '*is*'. 39. *Israel*,] # \we shall do but as it\. 42. *Conflagration*] first '*a*' ˅ '*g*'. 42–43.)They . . . so.⟨]. 42. They] @ \⟨it⟩\. 45. *Multitude*] @ \[.]\.

277.2. ⟨is⟩]. 10. ⟨the *Blessedness* of⟩]. 10. *Come*!] # \me\. 11. *Holy*] @ \People of\. 12. Engagement] '*t*' ˅ '*ts*'. 15.)and⟨]. 18. *Earth*,] # \had at least ultim\. 19. refer] second '*r*' ˅ '*rs*'; @ \re\. 22. and] # \[˅]\. 22. sends] @ \sends when\. 24. entirely] @ \Delivered\. 26. it,] # second ','. 31. to] ˅ '*no*'. 33–34.)Certainly, . . . him!⟨]. 34. GOD] # \with whom He *walked*, was Tr\. 38. What] @ \This\. 39. ⟨of⟩]. 40. *Fiction*] @ *Romish*\. 41. Holy] # \,\. 43. say] # \to\. 44.)of . . . to⟨].

278.1. the] '*t*' ˅ '*T*'. 2. *Lord*,] # \the *In*\. 7. *think*] # \of the New\. 8. whom] '*w*' ˅ '*t*'. 9–10. upon me;] # \','\. 16. *that*] '*ha*' ˅ '*y*'. 17. ⟨them⟩]. 20. their] '*i*' ˅ '*y*'. 22–24.)The . . . *Iniquities*.⟨]. 24. can] # \it be said\. 27. pray,] # second ','. 27. ⟨*come*⟩]. 28. And] '*A*' ˅ '*a*'. 34–35.)If . . . there!⟨]. 38. *Strong*] @ \Stron\. 39. that] '*a*' ˅ '*is*'. 40.)The . . . them,⟨]. 40. tempting] @ \[. | vexing\. 40. the] '*t*' ˅ '*T*'. 41. the] @ \[.]\.

279.2. ⟨After . . . so⟩]. 4. their] '*he*' ˅ '*at*'. 8. Scandalous] '*o*' ˅ '*u*'. 10. ⟨sunk and⟩]. 12–13.)and . . . Land,⟨]. 12. no] '*n*' ˅ '*m*'. 18. or, the] '*t*' ˅ '*T*'. 18. SATAN] @ \Satan\. 24. *Power*] # \,\. 26. *this World*;] # *e*⟩\. 26.)a⟨]. 26. *World*,] @ \of the\. 27. very] @ \And we can\. 28. ⟨by the . . . GOD,⟩]. 31. hideous] @ \horrible Thi\. 32. implied] # \,\. 32. *Satan*,] # \is\. 32. *Head*] @ *Grand Seigneur* of the Devi Head ⟨and⟩ of the *Devils*\. 34. ⟨what *Iniquities*, and⟩]. 35. World] '*W*' ˅ '[.]'. 36–37.)from the |Egyptian| . . . Tyrants⟨]. 37. *Busiris*] # \of E\. 40–41. [ms. III, x, 18v] '*8*' ˅ '*6*'. 43. but] @ \especially\. 44. *Energy*] @ \Influences\. 44. ⟨when⟩].

280.2. Hands,] # \in his and obtain a\. 3. them.] # \Such *Idaea's* of the Matter, the Gospel of our GOD has given us.\. 5. ⟨*Dark*⟩]. 8. bitter] @ \[˅]\. 11. Masses] final '*s*' ˅ long-tailed '*s*'. 12. expected,] # \was had\. 14. One] '*O*' ˅ '[.]'. 15. maintain] @ \m\. 15. ⟨Promised⟩]. 16. Some,] # \in Lu\. 16. *Luthers* Time;] '*T*' ˅ '*t*'. 17.)[In . . . *Julian*!]⟨]. 19. from] # \any P\. 19. *Pandaemonium*] '*P*' ˅ '*D*'. 21. unaccountably] '*ta*' ˅ '*ab*'. 23. NEW] @ \New\. 24. THEN] @ \The\. 26. How] @ \Then\. 26. down] # \, whic\. 32. *New*] # \-\. 33–36.)This . . . Day.⟨]. 34. |with|]. 34. their] @ \the\; # \-\. 35. *they*] @ \they\. 39. *Earth*] # \associated with them,\. 43. *Bind*] '*B*' ˅ '*b*'; # \)which⟨\. 43–44.)those . . . World,⟨]. 43. are] # \now\. 44. *in*] @ *these Kings* ˆ of This World,\.

281.1–3.)in . . . them.⟨]. 4. There] @ \But\. 4. Another] '*A*' ˅ '*a*'. 5. DEATH] @ \Deat\. 8–11.)And . . . Miseries.⟨]. 12. as] @ \H\. 13. which] # \consumed all the\. 16. *Written*] # \for\. 18. has] # \plainly in\. 19. minding,] # \many tim\. 19. gloss] # \which\. 22. Here] @ \At Coming of the Lord, there will\. 23. at] @ \found\. 28. The] '*e*' ˅ '*at*'. 28. not] @ \never\. 30. said,] # \I will Ransome them from the Grave, I will\. 31. *These*] '*T*'˅ '*t*'. 34–41.)When . . . them!⟨]. 38. *them*:] # \','. 39. |to|]. 42. ⟨is⟩]. 43. *Deathless*] @ \S\. 44. Striving] @ \Wi\. 44. read] # \, [Isai. LXV\.

282.3. being] @ \[˅]\. 5. ⟨*Statute*⟩] \Law\. 6. *City*:] # \In time, [˅˅] such a day as This

was not now to be chosen, [*] For a I was in much Distress as\. 8. from] # \Hos\. 9. may]
@ \should\. 17. himself] # \a *Vio- lent Death,*\. 19. against.] # second '.'. 19. Thus] 'T' #
't'. 21. *Tree,*] @ \was\. 22. it.] # second '.'. 24. an,] 'n' * ','. 28. without] # \[.]\. 28. and
⟨without⟩]. 33. Time,] # ','. 36–38.)And . . . *GOD.*⟨|. 37. having] # \a\. 37. |every where|].
38. ⟨the⟩ Influences]. 43. ⟨very⟩].

283.2–9.)It . . . *Place.*⟨|. 11. SACRED] @ \Sa\. 13. *Ground*] 'n' * 'd'. 16. And] 'n' * 'T'. 17.
Extraordinary] 'ar' * 'y'. 18. Things] @ \w\. 21–22.)This . . . *Mysteries.*⟨|. 22. our] * \^\.
22. ⟨of the)]. 22–23. Instances.] # \of it.\. 28. Waters] # \,\. 32. ⟨indeed)]. 36–39.)As . . .
it:⟨|. 44. The] @ \By\. 45. *Death:*] ':' @ ','.

284.6. more] @ \Im\. 7. concerning] @ \of the\. 7. ⟨Every)] \the\. 7. ⟨*Vine*)] \Vines\. 7.
having] # \each of them\. 7. in] @ \and\. 8. ⟨Every)] \one\. 8. on] 'o' * 'i'; @ \and\. 10.
⟨Ten)] \Twelve\. 10. Wine] @ \muc\. 11–13.)[Two . . . *Talmudism*!]⟨|. 13. ⟨more *Sober*)]. 18.
more] @ \m\. 18. Expositor] @ \,\. 18. Prophecies.] '.' * ','; # \of m\. 19. when] @ \wh\.
19. Read] # \,\. 22. Revolution] # \[\. 23. World] # \,\. 35. Commodities,] # second ','.
37. *Ivy.*"] # \I do\. 39. Prophecies] # \, the\. 41. NOW] @ \To\.

285.2.)For . . . *oportet.*⟨|. 8. Tree] # \of Life\. 8. Health] 'th' * 'hy'. 11. will] # \be\.
12–13.)and . . . *Imagination*!⟨|. 15. Kingdom] @ \KINGDOM\. 16. Happy] @ \^\. 17.
Unhappy] 'h' * 'p'. 19. *Intemperance*] @ \or\. 27. what] @ \ho\. 29. of their] @ \of\.
30. another] # \Vi\. 30. how] @ \what\. 31. ⟨and Idle Capricio's)]. 31. Idle] @ \⟨ho⟩\. 31.
Cyclopean] @ \M\. 40. placed] @ \sett over\. 40. Capacities] @ \Dignities\. 40. do] 'd' *
'D'. 41. Providence] @ \the\. 42–44.)or, . . . them?⟨|. 45. ⟨merciful)]. 45. and the] \ir\.

286.1. wherewith] @ \with\. 1. *Good*] @ \Laws,\. 8. GOD] # \here\. 12. Greater] @
\Smaller\. 16. *Shepherds*] @ \Office\. 20. ⟨who . . . and)]. 20. will] @ \may\. 21. Under]
@ \Com\. 23. ⟨will)]. 23. them] \selves an\. 24. astonishing] @ \astoni\. 29. have] # \a\.
29. allow'd] @ \assur assurin\. 29. than] # \he th\. 29. was to] # \him\. 29–30. ⟨that . . .
Writer)]. 30. whom] # \they\. 33–38.)The . . . *University.*⟨|. 34. |our|]. 37. Part of] # \our\.
37. |the World,|]. 38. *Earth*] # \without Sin, ⟨and *Death*⟩ as\. 39. ⟨So . . . *Sinless*)].

287.3–10.)And . . . *goeth.*⟨|. 4. |are|]. 4. yett] # \we make a\. 12. who,] # \deserve
that their\. 16. ⟨with)] \from\. 18. than] @ \do\. 20. *Glory*] @ \H\. 24. ⟨will do so,)]. 28.
LORD!] # \Who can comprehend the Cause.\. 30. ⟨that)]. 30. *very*] # \⟨f⟩ off Twenty\.
31. ⟨Hundred)]. 31. now] @ \is\; # \very\. 33. Who] @ \But\. 34.)Glad⟨|. 34. *Shouts*] @
Joyful\; # \of\. 34. made] @ \heard\. 37. ⟨Reviving and Comforting)]. 38. will] # \this
Almighty King scatter amon\. 38. ⟨a). 42. ⟨for a while)]. 42. them,] # ','. 42. still] # \may\.

288.1. LORD] 'ORD' * 'ord'. 2. up] \on\ of earlier 'upon'. 7. ⟨Paul)]. 15. ⟨who)] \that\.
18. says,] @ long-tailed \s\. 18. ⟨Our . . . Paul,)]. 18. *Epistles*] \Epi\. 20. of] @ \to\. 21.
what] @ \th\. 23. who] @ \wou\. 24. *Heathens*] @ \Gent.\. 25. that] first 't' * 'T'. 26.
⟨tho' . . . one,)] \of Inter\. 26.)of⟨|. 28. ⟨first)]. 30. far] # \into [. .]\. 33. ⟨You)]. 33. there] @
\I\. 34. Elaborate] @ \Comm\. 34. Again] 'A' * 'a'. 35. not] @ \^\. 35. ⟨here)]. 35. Evident]
@ \P\. 36. have] @ \be\. 37. and] # \by A\. 37. by] 'b' * 'a'. 38. until] # \This Tim\. 39.
Subject] \ed\ of earlier '*Subjected*'. 40. ⟨to)]. 40. first] # \[. .]\. 43. them;] # \they b\.

289.1–2.)Alas, . . . *Cursed*!⟨|. 2. the] \ir\. 2–3. ⟨which . . . and their)]. 3. *Constitution*]
@ \and\. 3. from] # \these Pros\. 4. this] 'is' * 'es'. 4. for] # \an Amendme\. 7. *Feet,*] #
\^ ^\. 8. intended] 't' * 'd'; @ \dep\. 8–11.)and . . . them;⟨|. 8. for,] ',' * ';'. 13. Behold] @
\And\. 16. Unto] @ \An\. 16. ⟨offer)] \tender\. 17. the Express] @ \the\. 17. Chapter] @
\Cha\. 17. it,] # \a,\. 20. Q.] \⟨[.])\. 20. ⟨Will)] \Shall\. 21. Isa. LXV.] 'L' * 'X'. 26. *like
the*] # *ese*;\. 28. appear] @ \app\. 29. ⟨Old)]. 34. much] 'm' * 's'. 35. *Time*] pl. \s\. 38–
40.)The . . . they;⟨|. 38. *Nations*] # \that\. 41. ⟨True)] \Right\. 42. Chiliasm,] # \are\. 42.
passing] 'i' * '[.]'. 44. *Answer*] 'A' * 'a'. 44. that] 'at' * 'en'. 44. think] @ \the\.

290.1–5.)How Impertinent. . . *Magog*?⟨|. 6. Now,] # \as our SAVIOU\. 10. Ask] 'A' *

'a'. 13. I will ⟨tell⟩|. 15. *TEETH*| @ *Teet*\. 15–19. ⟩To . . . |try to| . . . Magog.⟨|. 15. To|
@ \Or,\. 20. Enough| # \to Ask a Quaestion\. 20. *Five*| # *Years*\. 22–23. *Abraham,*| #
\at least\. 29. *will*| # *the*\. 30. Here| # \he\. 32. one| @ \I be allowed\. 34. *Heavens*|
\apl\. 35. most] @ \m\. 36–37. Unaccountable] @ \Att\. 45. present,] # second *','*. 45.
⟨been⟩|. 46. Quaestionable| *'Q'* * *'q'*.

291.3–15. ⟩One thing |which does| . . . *John*:⟨|. 3. |which does|| \that\. 4. about *Gog*]
\ˆˆˆ\. 4. is,] @ \[.]\. 6. Action| @ \ac\. 10. who] @ \[. .]\. 13. will| # \ad be\. 17.
Accounts,] # \we will not give that of Monsr. Poiret in his\. 17. One] @ *L'Oeconomie
Divine,* That\. 21. humbly| @ \mak\. 23. ⟨own⟩]. 24. ⟩I . . . upon⟨|. 29. Literal] @ \Literal\;
Serpent\. 30. ⟨Did he not⟩|. 30. make| # \an Assault upon our\. 30. ⟨Effectual⟩|. 32.
Increasing] *'ing'* * *'e of'*. 32. ⟨we⟩ have|. 32. that| # \in that\. 35–37. ⟩Tis . . . *come?*⟨|. 35.
not] @ \of\. 38. ⟨such as⟩|. 38–39. ⟩and . . . them,⟨|. 39. seem] # \strange\. 40. strange| \,\.
43. ⟨in . . . *Calf*,⟩|. 44. at] @ \wch\. 45. Terrors,] @ \[. . .]\.

292.2. them,] # \def\. 4. ⟨above . . . for⟩| \an Infinite Quantity of\. 5. is an] @ \are\.
8–11. ⟩were . . . them?⟨|. 10. and] @ \did\. 12. ⟨I offer This.⟩|. 13–14. ⟨or the *Wicked,*⟩|. 14.
The] @ \This Enquiry\. 16. by| * *'in'*. 16–17. ⟩in . . . *alone,*⟨|. 17. ⟨it⟩|. 18. well| @ \is\;
\worth\. 19. ⟨notably⟩|. 19. Notion,| # second *','*. 20. being] # \[Ezek. XXXII. 27.]\. 23.
these] @ \do\. 23. ⟨unto him,⟩|. 24–26. ⟩And . . . it.⟨|. 26. forbear] # \for-\. 27. ⟨of⟩|. 28.
for this] *'f'* * *'F'*. 29. Nor] @ \It was\. 30–31. ⟩Want . . . *velle.*⟨|. 32. Things] # \to be\. 38.
Silence,] # \upon\. 43. GOD,] # \M Joh\. 45. as] # \[.]\.

293.4. *Sabbaths*.| # \All he\. 10. ⟨altho'⟩| \however\. 10. *Pagan*| *'g'* * *'p'*. 11. ⟨is⟩| \wa\.
12. Time| # \,\. 12. Days] @ *Years*\. 15. as] @ \of\. 16. *Lords-day,*] # \as\. 18. with which|
@ \whi\; # \⟨Sco⟩\. 18. ⟨or⟩|. 18. the *Sleepers*] @ \and\. 19. away| # \the\. 22. *You*| *'y'*
* *'th'*. 23. *shall*] second *'l'* * *'t'*. 23. *You are*| *'y'* * *'th'*; *'re'* * *'rt'*. 27. ⟨something that⟩|
\what\. 29. then] *'n'* * *'re'*. 31. and| *'a'* * *'&'*. 33. a] * *'t'*. 34. from] # \y\. 34. suffering| #
\Impress\. 36. Thirdly] *'Th'* * *'Se'*. 36. *Damned*| *'D'* * *'d'*. 40. Fourthly] @ \The\.

294.2. Game] # \,\. 4. be| # \onl\. 6. Accept| *'A'* * *'a'*. 7. is| *'i'* * *'a'*. 8. be| # \destroy'd
by Fire\. 8. a] @ \an\. 9–10. *Resurrection*] @ \Third\. 11. Not] @ \none\. 14. to| # \these
it;\. 14. *The*] *'T'* * *'t'*; @ \App\. 19. Yea,| # \we\. 20–22. ⟩will . . . so.⟨|. 21. render| second
'e' * *'r'*. 25. *Ghosts*] @ \wicked\. 27. *Dy*| *'y'* * *'ie'*. 30. GOD?] *'?'* * *'!'*. 31. Yea,| *'a'* * *'[.]'*. 31.
when] @ \ˆ⟨Sometimes⟩\. 31. molested] # \among us,\. 32. ⟨some⟩| \the\. 43. enjoy'd,] #
\either\. 43. or] @ \and th\.

295.2. XI.| # \XX.\. 8. *Glory,*] # \enq\. 9. from] *'f'* * *'t'*. 11. *Promised*] @ \King\. 12.
Power.] # \Now, Som The\. 13. of GOD] *'o'* * *'g'*. 13. JESUS,] # \to be\. 14. so| @ \as Com\.
16. Commission| @ \Direction and\. 16. ⟨the⟩|. 17. *Daniel,*] @ \Dan\. 18. *Beloved*] first
'e' * *'l'*. 19–20. Prophecies:| *':'* * *';'*. 20. ⟩and . . . so.⟨|. 20. told| # \the\. 21. ⟨according . . .
Prophecies,⟩|. 22. Followers] # \of it, & wi\. 23. to| # \[. .] b\. 24. *Periods*| # \[. .]\. 24.
those] # \Prophecies\. 25. ⟨&⟩ three|. 25. *thirty*| *'th'* * *'fi'*. 25. But,| # \if\. 26. for] @ \at\.
27. for] @ \of\; # \the\. 29. TIME?] *'?'* @ *','*. 29. the] @ \our\. 29. enabling| @ \to\. 31. He|
@ \His FATHER gave\. 33. Whereupon,| @ \A\. 33. ⟨Apostle⟩|. 33. in] @ \with the\. 34.
have] @ \Reign [. .]\. 35. ⟨Apostle⟩|. 38. Nevertheless| @ \New\. 38. that] @ \that\. 39–
43. ⟩and . . . *colliquit:*⟨|. 39–40. Allowance] @ \Advance of\. 42–43. *in PROPINQUO*|
'IN' * *'in'*. 44. Times| # \e⟩\. 44. ⟨or the⟩|.

296.1. away,] # \the wh\. 2. Matter,| # \that must\. 2. ⟨to⟩ @ \⟨who⟩\. 2. Accom-
plished.] # \Th\. 2. binds| @ \brings and keeps\. 3. ⟨on⟩|. 10–12. ⟩the . . . *Finis.*⟨|. 16.
Abetters] @ \Abetters\. 17. as great| @ \the gre\. 18. Men.] # \ˆ\. 19. an| *'n'* * *'s'*; #
\groundless & carnal\. 20. ⟨really⟩| \altogether\. 20. ⟨very . . . to⟩| \well consistent with\;
⟨to⟩ # \⟨the⟩\. 20. ⟨whole⟩|. 21–23. ⟩Or . . . *vana?*⟨|. 25. ⟨because . . . to⟩| \thinking for\.

25. of] # \His those\. 25. ⟨His⟩]. 25. ⟨Glorious⟩] \Holy\. 26–27.)How . . . out!⟨]. 32. ⟨a Wonderful⟩] \Vast\. 33. ⟨throughout . . . World,⟩]. 34. *Sleep,*] # \at the Coming of the\. 35.)&⟨]. 35. Impiety] @ \)of⟨ thro of ⟨to)\. 35. ⟨that was⟩] \in the old wherein the Flood over- took so and the an\. 35. ⟨Day⟩] \Co- ming\. 37. feel] @ \fee\. 38. ⟨to)]. 39. whether] # \[.]\. 39. ⟨ourselves,⟩]. 40. from] # \a\. 40. Apprehension,] @ \our\; # \of\. 42. ⟨unto)]. 42. Fathers?] # \I freely avow'd that I lived in that Opinion for Seven times Seven Years together, and wrote as well as I could, more than once, for\. 44. Disputing] 'D' * 'd'. 45. *Demonstrations*] @ \Argume\.

297.1. ⟨while they⟩] \may\. 1. *Modesty,*] # \much sooner than m\. 1–3.)I . . . *Cyprian.*⟨]. 3. *Lightfoot,*] @ \Mod\. 5. Christians,] # \that\. 6. Alloy] 'y' * 'w'. 7. *Charitable*] # \˘⟨a) *Opinion of so many and so godly Chris-*\. 7. *Opinion* # \th from Ad [* * *]\. 8.)about . . . *World,*⟨]. 8. see] @ \know\. 11. address] @ \d\. 14.)I.⟨]. 14. now] # \inte\. 16. Already;] 'A' * 'a'. 18. ⟨Conflagration.⟩] \Coming of the LORD.\. 18. *Key*] 'K' * 'k'. 20. all] @ \any\. 22. as] # \[. . .]\. 23. what] @ \the *Clouds*\. 28. been] # \(before)\. 30. *Israel.*] '.' * ',.'. 30–31. DODEKAPHYLON] 'A' * 'E'. 31–38.)The . . . *Autumn.*⟨]. 34. whom] # \And an\. 38. Besides] @ \Befo\. 38. after] # \Jerob\.

298.1. *Anarchy*] @ \Confusion and\. 2–3.)*Salmanasserian*⟨] \De\. 3. away;] ';' * ':'. 9. ⟨Great⟩]. 11. to] @ \to\. 12. better] @ \were better *Judaeans,*\. 13. *Israelites,*] first 'e' * 'b'. 15. between] @ \w\. 17.)was⟨]. 17. not] @ \did\. 17. profitable] 'f' * 'v'. 20. *Ezekiel*] 'z' * 'e'. 20. and,] # \no doubt\. 21. doubt,] @ \d\. 21. them;] ';' * ':'. 23. Travel,] # \⟨of a Year and half)\. 23–24.)and . . . *Ramble,*⟨]. 24. ⟨far distant⟩]. 24. ⟨Indeed⟩] \tho'\. 26–28.)albeit . . . *that*⟨]. 27. can't] @ \will n\. 28. Blood,] # \[.]\. 28. ⟨passing from *Scythia*⟩]. 28. found] # \in the Veins\. 33. *Ten*] @ \Two\. 38. And] 'A' * 'a'. 41. all] @ \any\. 41.)the⟨ *Particular*]. 44. Tis] 'T' * 't'.

299.1. accordingly,] # \we find,\. 2. possessed] 'esse' * 'poss'd'. 3–4. *Dedication*] 'c' * 'd'. 5. *Israel;*] # \is a Decisive Passage\. 6. *Quota*] @ \N\. 8. Empire] @ \D\. 10. that] # \was to\. 12. become] \what\. 13. the] 't' * 'T'. 14. *Jew;*] ';' @ ','. 14. so] @ \E\. 15. Yea,] # \the\. 16. procures] @ \in\. 16. *Jews,*] # \[**]\. 17. *Jews,*] # \were so\. 19. ⟨from)] \to\. 20. *Jerusalem*] @ \y\. 20. Feast] 'F' * 'f'. 21. testified] final 'd' * 's'. 23. Epistles.] # \Unto\. 24. sent] 't' * 'd'. 26. to] @ \that\. 30. ⟨*Edomites* . . . *Amonites*⟩] *Idumaeans*\. 31–32.)and . . . *Prophecies;*⟨]. 32. unto] 't' * 'o'. 35. so.] '.' * ':'. 35. *Jeremiah*] @ \The Peopl\. 38. now] # \so\. 40. knew] @ \sho\. 40. *Asher,*] # \many of them knew\. 42. ⟨uninterrupted⟩] \exact\. 44. as] * 'tis'.

300.4. *Twelve*] @ \A\. 7. *Italy*] 'y' * 'ia'. 7. scarce] @ \had\. 8. And ⟨at)] 'nd' * 'fter'. 15. here,] ',' * ';'. 19. These] \th\. 24. their Devotions] 'r' * 'd'; 'D' * 'd'; 'n' * 'it'. 26. ⟨Repentance⟩] \Recovery\. 27. their] # \con\. 27. and their] # \memorable Recovery\. 29. Fulfilment] @ \Prophecy\. 30. *Ephraim.*] '.' * ','. 30. And,] 'A' * '['. 33. referr'd] @ \s\. 34. *their*] @ \the\. 36. From] @ \That\. 38. Cause] @ \Occa\. 39. Appetites,] 'es' * 'it'. 40. *Full*] @ \Full\. 40. ⟨of the)]. 42. Prophecies,] ',' * ';'; # \[Isa. XI.13.\. 43. *Envy Judah,*] # ','. 45. should] @ \la\.

301.10–11. Congruous] # \Conclusion to the Old Test\. 11. ⟨and all along⟩]. 12. *Gate,*] # ⟨'⟩ * '&'. 12–13.)and . . . and⟨]. 12. *Wings*] # \therein\. 16. ⟨of)]. 18. some] \thing\ of earlier 'something'. 18. Book,] # \which\. 19. ⟨that)]. 19. *Zechariah,*] # \it is evident that the Six Last Chapters of that Book,\. 27. *Calvin*] 'C' * 'c'. 30. ⟨any of these⟩] \led them [*] them\. 31. *this.*] 'is.' * 'ese'. 32. brought] @ \of\. 33. *Their*] 'T' * 't'. 34. of] @ \an Opposi\. 35–39.)Then . . . us!⟨]. 37. |their|] \Pec-\. 40. Chap. XII. 12.] '2' * 'o'. 41. *Mourning*] @ \[.]\. 42. the Beleeving] 'h' * '[.]'. 43. to the *Heart*] @ \As for the Circumstances of the Battel, in the *Last* Chapter of these Prophecies, I refer you, first unto a *Grotius*, or, if he will not satisfy, then unto a *Jackson*, to declare, how literally all has been accomplished—\. 44. *Shimei*] first '*i*' * '*e*'.

302.3. mention'd] @ \which\. 4. Signal] @ \Remark\. 9. *Siege*] @ *Battel*, in the Last Chapte\. 11–17.)we . . . SAVIOUR.⟨]. 12. in abandoned Circumstances] underscoring canceled. 12–13. (|far . . . than|]. 16. finds] @ \does\. 16. *Cyrus,*] @ \his\. 18. ⟨still . . . some⟩] \any\. 19. *Israel,*] # \have not been\. 20–21.)*Mens* . . . and⟨]. 22. *Circumcision.*] # \And tho'\. 22. is] @ \is i\. 23. ⟨they were⟩] \it was\. 24. *Heirs*] @ \Subjects\. 25. ⟨them⟩].

302.28–303.2.)They . . . not.⟨] marginal interlineation replaces canceled passage: \It is evident, That the Title of, *The Holy People*, in the Prophecies of *Daniel* putt upon the *Surrogate Israel*. Since the Fulfilling of that, which is also found in His Prophecies, [Ch. IX. 26.] That the *Jews*, after the *Cutting off of the Messiah*, should be, *No more His People*; but *Messiah* was to be the *Prince* of a *Future People*. And whereas we read, [Hos. III. 4.] That *Israel* should *abide many Days*, in [\d\] abandoned Circumstances, but *Afterward they should Return & Seek the Lord their GOD, and fear the Lord & His Good One in the Latter Days*;\. 302.34. *Unbeleef*] '*U*' * '*u*'. 302.35. *without*] @ \[. .]\. 302.41. *With*] @ \And we can\.

303.3. Roll] @ \there is a\. 6. *All*] @ \all\. 7. us!] '*u*' * '!'. 8. *Davidic*] @ \Family\. 8. have] @ \ad\. 10. *not a*] # \Worldly an Earthly\. 13. *Works.*] # \Tes\. 17. ⟨Best⟩]. 17. *Unfold*] '*U*' * '*u*'. 18. To] @ \To\. 20. reserved] @ \laid up for\. 21. in] # \it\. 24. with] @ \and have\. 27. ⟨to⟩]. 29. ⟨one of⟩]. 31–33.)I . . . *scire,*⟨]. 33. ⟨Some . . . Pain⟩] \It afflicts one\. 33. see a] # \[.]\. 34. ⟨*wrestling*⟩] \attempting\. 35. Land] # \of this Vision\. 35. ⟨whereof . . . here,⟩]. 37. described;] # \ˆ\. 37–38.)And . . . *Vain.*⟨] @ \ˆ)We will not so spend our Time at the *Labour in Vain.*⟨\. 38. at the] cancels underscoring. 38. |as|]. 43. can] @ \will\; # \any Theo\.

303.44–304.1.)and . . . upon?⟨]. 304.1. laugh] \t\ of earlier '*laught*'. 2. ⟨nor . . . *Toland.*⟩]. 2. do?—] # eight canceled ms. lines beginning a new paragraph. This cancellation is part of a larger excision recorded below. Beginning with [* *] below, Mather copied the canceled text—excepting minor changes—and inserted it in 305.33: \Sometimes I have begun to consider, whether the Intention of this *Vision*, might be to give a Direction unto the [\Returning Israelites\] *Redeemed Israelites*, how to proceed in the [\⟨Resettlement⟩\] Management of their Affairs; ⟨according to⟩ which, if they had gone [\with\] on to do, all they could, with a *Strong Faith*, and an unwea- ried & inflexible Resolution, to do as well as they could, [* *] the Almighty GOD who told them, *The*\.

At this point, Mather inserts four new pages, ms. III, xi, ⟨1r⟩-ms. III, xi, ⟨2r⟩, and cancels ms. III, xi, 114, and eleven and a half lines of ms. III, xi, 20v. These subsequently canceled lines are a continuation of the cancellation recorded above:

\[ms. III, xi, 114]\ '*Silver is mine* [\,\] *& the Gold is mine*, would have carried them along; They would anon have had a Territory Six hundred & Eighty two Miles [\in Len\] (or, [\tak\] adding the *Princes Portion*, Seven hundred & Eight Miles) in *Length*, and at [\Last\] least One hundred & Sixty Miles in *Breadth*, besides future Enlargements; A *City* Fourty two Miles in Compass; with a *Temple*, the Ground-Plott whereof would have contained in Compass, four Miles & above a Quarter. But [\P\] an *Evil Heart of Unbeleef*, discouraged by *Poverty*, made them lay aside their [\[*]\] Prospect & Prosecution of such Dimensions. And—But I soon laid aside the *Conjecture*: T' *will not do!*

—I must again retire to *Yolam Havah*. If it be true, what is asserted by [*Josephu*\] *David Kimchi*, as *L'Empereur* quotes him, That the *Returned Israelites* had the Temple of *Ezekiel* in their View, when they erected their *Temple*, [# second \,\] but as [\[.]\] *Cunaeus* notes, no further than they were capable of Conforming to that Model; and as

Lightfoot adds, they could not come up to the Bulk & Cost of *That*; yett we must consent, unto our *Greenhill*, and others, that there was much of the *Mystical*, and the *Typical*, in the Visions. More particularly, There is a Weight in [\that of *Antipass*;\] ⟨what falls from one of the *Romish* Rabbis;⟩ *Omnia quae in* Ezekiele *de* Jerusalem *scribuntur, de Sancta civitate, superna Jerusalem absqe dubit sunt intelligenda.* Yea, Tis a Saying of the *Jewish* Rabbi's themselves; *The City described in the Last Chapters of* Ezekiel, *are to be interpreted concerning the Jerusalem that is Above.* For this Cause, I [\must take\] ⟨look on⟩ the Essay of that Gracious Man, *William Allein* of *Bristol*, [\to\] ⟨as⟩ the best, & the nearest unto the Truth of any that I have ever yett mett withal. [\When the\] In short, when the *New Heavens* and the *New Earth* arrive, these *Nine Chapters* will be better *understood*, than they are like to be before: And I verily beeleeve, they will never be any further *fulfilled* than they have been, [\[..]\] until *Then*. That which would [\perswade\] a little Incline one the rather to take up with such Sentiments, is, That when *Moses*, and afterwards when *David*, and [ms. III, xi, 20v] afterwards when *Isaiah*, were by the *Hand of GOD* upon them, transported into the [\Heavenly World,\] *Coelestial World*, they all had exhibited unto them, a Temple, after the *Pattern* whereof the [\Tabernacle\] *Tabernacle* of *Moses*, & so the *Temple* of *Solomon*, were formed: And these *Holy Places*, as our Apostle tells us, were but [\little\] ⟨small⟩ *Figures of the TRUE*, even of *Heaven itself.* But that which ⟨yett⟩ more confirms the Sentiment, is, That our *Ezekiels* Vision, is ushered in, with, *The Resurrection of the Dead*, and the *State*, wherein, *The Tabernacle of GOD shall be with Men, and He will be their GOD.*\.

Here ends Mather's excised passage. Subsequent emendations resume with ms. III, xi, [1r].

304.3. ⟨like⟩] \as\. 3. utterly] @ \utterly\. 5. Inquisitive] @ \successful\. 7. them,] @ \those\. 9. This] 'i' * 'e'; # \S\. 9–10.)First, . . . Visions.⟨]. 15. *Eyes:*] @ ','. 20. for the] 'h' * '[.]'. 29.)with⟨]. 38–41.)The . . . short,⟨]. 39. that] # \gave a model\. 42. ⟨the People;⟩] \them;\.

305.1. more] # \me\. 2. *Prophecy,*] # second ','. 14. among] @ \unto them\. 18. yea] 'y' * '&'. 24. *Holy*] @ \Faithful\. 24.)does⟨]. 24. *Promised*] @ \La\. 27. know,] # \we know\. 27. how] # \P\. 27. their] 'eir' * 'ere'. 29. ⟨be⟩ traps]. 30. *Scourges*] # \of\. 31. had] 'h' * 'st'. 33. them,] # \⟨#⟩\ and \)# 5 A.⟨.\. 34. would] @ \w\. 34. ⟨Countrey⟩] \Territory\. 41. retire] @ \return ag\. 41. true] @ \so\.

306.6. Ezekiel,] # \[.]\. 13. transported] @ \them\. 14. after] # \which\. 17. Heavenly] @ \State\. 18–24.)an . . . more.⟨]. 19. *Zerobabel*] first 'b' * 'a'. 21. ⟨The⟩]. 23. may] @ \dismiss\. 24–25. ms. III, xi, 114 *canceled*; see commentary at 304.2. 26–37.)One . . . accomplished.⟨]. 27. yett] @ \to\. 27. *Jews,*] # \it has\. 40. World] 'W' * 'ea'. 43. ⟨Our⟩] \The\. 45. *be*] @ \is\.

307.1. *Olive-tree;*] # \and\. 2. there] 'r' * 'e'. 4.)& . . . *Junius,*⟨]. 5. thought] @ \p\. 5. that] 't' * '[.]'. 7. Lett] # \h\. 9. ⟨upon . . . all⟩]. 10–13.)as . . . *Romans.*⟨]. 12. But] @ \Bu\. 15.)by . . . *Apostles,*⟨]. 18. receive] \d\ of earlier 'received'. 20. unto] @ \b\. 20–21. *Two New*] 'N' * 'A'; @ \two\. 22. Purpose.] '.' * ','. 22. The] @ \wh\. 22. ⟨for the Present⟩]. 22.)had⟨]. 23. now] @ \were\. 23. ⟨been⟩]. 23.)the . . . them;⟨]. 24. upon] 'u' * 'a'. 26. Behold] # \,\. 27. occur] @ \o\. 28. till] # \the pa best part of\. 28. ⟨perhaps⟩]. 28. ⟨be sure,⟩]. 31. *Rejected of GOD,*] # \that\. 33. entirely] @ \forever sh\. 36. *Arrogancy*] 'y' * 'e'. 36. *Fall*] 'F' * 'f'. 41. and,] # \beware,\. 45. directs] @ \& accordingly\.

308.1–5.)|Every body| |knows| . . . *Unnatural.*⟨]. 1. |Everybody|] \˜ does\. 1. the *Oleaster*] @ \˜ Be sure\. 5. would] @ \was\. 7. ⟨by the *Faith*,⟩]. 9. ⟨*Theophrastus*,⟩] \that Author,\. 9. but] 'b' * '[.]'. 11. ⟨*Inoculation*⟩] \Grafting\. 13. ⟨not very well⟩] \little\. 13. *Semination*]

@ \Seed\. 14. Grafted] 'G' * 'g'. 16. Stock,] # \be\. 16. to their] 'to' * '˜' * 'to'; \⟨to be grafted⟩\. 16. and] # \upon\. 18. Excellent] @ \be\. 19. And] @ \But [. .]\. 23. Numbers] # \It came to pass accordingly!\. 32. ⟨We find⟩]. 32. making] 'i' * 'e'; # \him Back\. 32. turned] @ \turn\. 36. assign'd] @ \brought\. 37. what] # \h\. 40–41.)[without . . . Bitter]⟨]. 43–44.)as . . . him,⟨]. 44. Jerusalem,] @ \Jerus\.

309.2. yett] @ \Great\. 3. SAVIOUR.] '.' @ ','. 4. Constantine,] # \when\. 4. possible] @ \[.]\. 5–7.)the . . . Gentiles:⟨]. 9. Appearing] 'ring' * 'rance'; @ \Arri\. 10. ⟨above . . . Earth.⟩]. 11. did] @ \were\. 12–13. ⟨their . . . in⟩]. 13. Long] 'L' * 'S'. 14. ⟨in Marriages⟩]. 21. People,] # \for Jews\. 24. Nations,] # \of the World\. 28. does] @ \is to\. 30–32.)and . . . Israel;⟨]. 36.)Even . . . Annuli.⟨]. 38. The] @ \F\. 40. ⟨that⟩]. 40. Body] # \may be Supplied\.

309.43–310.1.)There . . . |we| . . . But—⟨]. 309.44. |we|] \˜\. 310.10. bestow'd] @ \in\. 11. made] @ \that\. 12. Maintainers] 'r' * 's'. 15. Times,] # second ','. 16. ⟨are⟩] \is\. 18. otherwise] @ \any\. 20. Root] @ \Rush\. 20. we] @ \I\. 25. Idolatries,] # \there\. 25. ⟨with a MOREOVER,⟩]. 27. ⟨it⟩]. 31. Relaps'd] 'R' * 'r'. 31. ⟨Them;⟩]. 31. And] @ \T\. 33. which] # \th\. 33. brought on,] # second ','. 40. What?] # \Whe\. 41. LORD] @ \m\. 45. No,] \w,\ of earlier 'Now'.

311.1–2.)and . . . nigh.⟨]. 2. But] @ \Lo, This is our GOD, we have waited for Him, we will be glad & rejoice in His Salvation.]. 2. But] 'B' * 'F'. 3. Unbeleef,] # \[*] and will [. .]\. 4. them,] # \an wh\. 4. ⟨must⟩]. 6. National] @ \Conversion\. 9. can] 'c' * \[.]\; @ \shall\. 11. justly] 'st' * 'ly'. 16. Sunk] @ \demolishe\. 16–21.)If . . . it?⟨]. 19. Jew.] # \To except you\. 24. All] 'A' * 'a'. 30. ⟨more particular⟩]. 31. even] @ \th\. 31. Twelve] \s\. 34. Coalition] @ \Col\. 35. ⟨now⟩]. 35–38.)In . . . Yea,⟨]. 38. Some Learned] 'S' * 's'; @ \And particularly\. 39. They.] @ \the Ten Tribes\. 40. their] 'i' * 'r'. 40–42.)It . . . But⟨]. 41. existing] @ \cap\. 42. ⟨even⟩]. 42–43. answering] @ \an\. 43. repeat] @ \resen\. 43. ⟨a⟩] \our Wi\. 45. ⟨a⟩] \our\. 45. reperiri] # \,\.

312.3. Away] @ \They ar\. 5. Gentlemen] @ \[*]\. 12. become] @ \[*]\. 13–14.)while . . . Dogs.⟨]. 16. Gentile] @ \Place\. 16. Most] @ \[. .]\. 17. that] first 't' * 'c'; @ \k\. 18–19.)The . . . it!⟨]. 20. now] # \th\. 21. Abraham.] '.' * ','; # \and there is of that Promise\. 21. Abdicated] # \and an Abominable\. 22. ⟨of old⟩]. 23. He be] @ \be\. 28.)and . . . Him,⟨]. 29. This] @ \And\. 29. and] 'n' * 'l'. 30. ⟨more⟩]. 34. themselves!] # \But Shiloh is come, and now\. 36. learn,] # \That one true Beleever on His\. 38. come;] @ \come\. 39. Holy One] @ \Go\. 40. Ethiopians .] '.' * ','. 42. Massachusetts⟨ians⟩]. 42. shall] # \Fear of GOD and work Righteousness, & is k\. 42. thro'] # \be\. 43. ⟨be⟩] \as\.

313.3. GOD] # \,\. 3. a] # \Particularly\. 3. ⟨Distinguishing Regard⟩]. 4. ⟨the Flesh, of⟩]. 11. ⟨I . . . say,⟩]. 22–26.)But . . . Phoenix?⟨]. 24. All] @ \[. . .]\. 29–30.)For . . . Glory.⟨]. 31. ⟨it⟩]. 33. continue] # \continue\. 34. OTI] # \[. . .]\. 313.35–314.3.)Once . . . Objection.⟨]. 313.37. Faith] # \,\. 40. such] # \lg\. 40. a] # \[.] Unbeleef as That, and the\. 42. can such] @ \will\. 44. on the] \ir\ of earlier 'their'. 44. |oppressling|].

314.2. |Work|] \Christs\. 2. |do|]. 4. ⟨against⟩] \[*] of\. 4. ⟨Arguing,⟩] \Awaking,\. 6. which] # \comes like\. 9. There] @ \And\. 14. ⟨whereof⟩] \of which\. 18. was] # \promised unto\. 21. as] # \were once\. 25. ⟨Or . . . briefly,⟩]. 28. and] # \experience himself\. 32. Etiam . . . aliquando.—⟨]. 32. ⟨myself⟩]. 35. Davidical] @ \V\. 36. Kingdom] # \e\ of earlier 'Kingdome'. 39. forever.] # '.'. 43. I] # \mistook the True Israel\. 43. was] 'w' * 'I'. 44. ⟨very⟩]. 44. ⟨[between . . . Thirty.]⟩].

315.1. ⟨I Recant; I Revoke|⟩]. 1–4.)Then |indeed,| . . . But.⟨]. 2. the Promised Kingdom,] @ \the\; # \was to be\. 3. Earth,] # ','. 4. and] @ \and\. 4. Years] \,\. 4. together,] @ \[*]\. 4. felt] @ \was I\. 4. Myself] 'M' * 'm'. 6. ⟨as . . . puzzled⟩]. 7. And] # \d\. 11. Second] 'e' * '[.]'. 14. the Parentator] @ \m\ of earlier 'my'. 14. died] @ \did\. 17. His] @ \His k\. 18.

until] '*i*' * '*u*'. 20. I insisted] @ \ıWhenı\; # \once\. 20.)I . . . that⟨]. 20. see,] @ \say\. 22. *Conflagration*] '*r*' * '*a*'. 24. ⟨Return and⟩]. 26. out] @ \and then\. 29–30.)which . . . upon.⟨]. 31. and] # \then might\. 31. Method] @ \Proof would certainly\. 34–35. ⟨and . . . *Writer.*)]. 36. ⟨after all⟩] \I could not;\; @ \⟨anon⟩\. 36.)ıI find,ı . . . *Unscriptural.*⟨]. 36. ıI findı] '*n*' * '*y*'; \`\. 37. ⟨do not, I⟩]. 36. It] @ \a\. 37. ⟨any⟩] \a *Fire*\. 38. Lord;] ';' * ':'. 38. I] @ \a\. 40. *Conflagration*] @ *Fire*\. 43. and] # \I\. 43. *understand*,] # \I was particularly by\.

316.1. explained] '*d*' * '*s*'; # \;\. 2. ⟨of the *Translated*⟩]. 3. and] @ \And\. 5–7.)and . . . unto.⟨]. 9. ⟨yett⟩]. 9. hope,] # \I sho\. 9. he] @ \I should\. 13. *the Lord*] '*t*' * '*c*'. 13. to] # \intend the Same\. 13. Same.] # \Transaction.\. 14. Now,] # \no bo\. 16. *Earth:*] ':' * ';'. 17. And] # \onl of the may but, had\. 18. Strain] '*tr*' * '[. .]'. 20. But] @ \Now,\. 21. ⟨can⟩] \shall\. 23. Or] # \if the *Converting* of them at the Instant could Qualify any [. . .]\. 23. Conviction] # \Co\. 24. for] # \what the\. 24. Rapture] # \to be then\. 24. Converting] '*t*' * long-tailed '*s*'. 26–31.)the . . . Travels!—⟨]. 26. the] @ \ıforı\. 29. what?—] # *Forward & Sudden Declarations.*\. 33. *Stubble*] @ \Sal\. 34. *Day which*] a whole series of what appears to be S's or doodles of diminishing size occurs in the left-hand margin. 35. That] # \so many\. 36. by] # \almost *all* the Servants of GOD in the W\. 37. for,] # \the\. 40. *succubus!*] # canceled paragraph (5 1\2 lines): \But then, *Franzius* has taught me what Sort of Conclusion to break off withal; *Hanc meam ut privatem Declarationem lector benevolus mihi soli ascribat et indulgeat; eam probe examine, et de eadem quantum ipsi debet tribut ferum liber rerum preferat Iudicium.*—\. 41–42.)[and . . . *fui!*]⟨]. 42. *Christians*] @ \Wise\. 44. *Samuel:*] # \All the Diff\.

317.1. Days,] # *the* Kingdoms will be\. 2. *under.*] # \The Dom\. 9–10. *Restoration*] @ \Destruc\. 13. *Death.*] # second '.'. 17. from] @ \out of\. 24. ⟨out⟩]. 25. Renounce] @ \either forfeit his Li\. 26. I am] @ \We may before we are aw\. 28. propose] # \any thing like an T\. 29. *Nation*] @ \Jewish\. 31. *Golden*] @ \V\; four separate doodles in form of interconnected S's occur in the margin. 38. thither,] # \&\. 38. ⟨that . . . be⟩]. 38. laid] # \them\. 39–40.)(if . . . were)⟨]. 42. more.] # \` I\. 43–44.)All . . . surviving.⟨]. 43. *Vespasians*] @ \the\. 44. surely,] @ \I\.

318.5. of the] a canceled vertical inscription reading \for Dr Mather\ (c. 6 cm]—in a different hand—is written across the ms. page. 9. consumes] '*c*' * '*s*'. 9. Materials] '*ria*' * '[. .]'.

319.2. XII.] # \XXI.\. 2. *WHEN*] '*H*' * '*S*'. 8. ⟨unto⟩] \to\. 12. of] # \the Exhibition which he had given\. 16. Thirty] '*t*' * '[.]'. 18. And] @ \Th\. 29. justly] @ \[.]\. 35. Vision.] '.' * ';'; # \and We will n\. 36. Present] @ \Purpose\. 37. ⟨Extinction⟩] \Expiration\. 39.)[Compare . . . 44.]⟨]. 41. ⟨a Quality⟩] \to w\. 42. which] # \is, what\. 42. ⟨[Col. II. 11.])].

320.1. Original,] # second ','. 3. look] @ \look f\. 4. *Stone*,] ',' * ','. 5. *Strong*] '*S*' * '*R*'. 7. partake] @ \for\. 8. This] @ \Thes Sub These\. 8. are] @ \for\. 18. Compare,] @ \[\. 20. Jewish] @ \[.]\. 22. not] @ \th\. 22. *comes*] # \m\. 24. perish] @ \to\. 25. whereupon] @ \wher\. 27. became] @ \beheld an\. 30. their] @ \expired\. 35. *hand*;] # '.'. 37. understood] # \[.]\. 38. by] # \Mr. Sykes\. 39. ⟨as⟩]. 44. *Same Kingdom.*] '.' * '*e*' of '*Kingdome*'.

321.1.)and . . . *Parables*;⟨]. 6. *Greater*] '*G*' * '*g*'. 10. *Testament*,] # ','. 13. Commencement] @ \Beginning of th\. 15. *Power.*] # \This is the *Kingdom* that\. 17. capable] @ \serviceable in this\. 22. yett] @ \Eat\. 24. And our LORD] # \own'd\. 24. ⟨Confessed⟩]. 30. ⟨in⟩]. 31. Commands] # \contrary\. 34. Placing] @ \in payi\. 35. ⟨our⟩]. 35. ⟨a⟩].

322.1. the] @ *Daniels* Prop\. 1. *over all*] @ \of\. 11. respect] @ \regard\. 12. describes] # \Him,\. 15. The] @ \In\. 16. *Eighth*] '*th*' * ', V'; # \Ve\. 16. ⟨in⟩] \of\. 21. *Works.*] '*Wo*' * '[. .]' 22. this] '*t*' * '*h*'. 23. see] @ \see\. 24–26.)*Stephen* . . . so!⟨]. 28. ⟨have⟩]. 29. All] #

\XXI. *When* the Grand REVOLUTION is\. 30. The] @ \to be look'd for.\. 31–35.)that . . .
things?⟨]. 32. |be|]. 37. KING] @ \Glorious\. 42. *Now*] *'N'* * *'n'*.
   323.2. Lett] @ \Lett\. 2. disturbed] # \,\. 3. ⟨in⟩]. 6. kept] @ \concel'd\. 8. generally] #
\understood it,\. 8. Prayed] # \ad\. 10. of;] # '.'. 13. that] * 'had'. 16. *Age,*] @ *Age*\. 16.
⟨it⟩]. 19. ⟨Ask⟩] \enquire\. 21. He] @ \h\. 25. to] * 'H'. 25. for His] 'H' * 'h'. 26. *Apostasy*]
\[. .] should give [*]\. 26. ⟨give⟩]. 27. erect] @ \have his Reign\. 29. would] \[. .]\.
30. ⟨Broken⟩]. 31. perish] # \at the\. 31. in] @ \burn\. 32.)after⟨]. 32. ⟨were⟩]. 32. expired.]
\I\. 33. been] second 'e' * 'n'. 37. Great] @ \M\. 39. They] 'T' * 't'. 39. That] 'T' * 't'
40. *Daniel,*] # \to be sett up in the Days V\. 41. *on't!*] # \And\. 42. since] @ \from\. 43.
That] # \the Period fix\. 44. *Daniel,*] # \for\. 44. Birth] @ \coming\. 45. *on't!*] # \Yea,
our Lord\. 45. Observers] # \,\.
   324.1. *Time,*] # \and se\. 7. him,] @ \Hi\; # \this e\. 9. *befriend,*] # \wise Chris, the
Christians\. 13–21.)a . . . Chronologer.⟨]. 17. Holy] @ \Spir\. 21. as] # \nota\. 22. true,]
\there\. 23. precarious] 'a' * 'er'. 23. ⟨seduced⟩] \betrayed\. 23. ⟨vain⟩] \such\. 24. and
⟨the⟩]. 25. *World*] 'l' * 'd'. 25. their] @ \themselv\. 31. CCCLXV] 'L' * 'X'. 32. Appearing]
@ \Pre\. 32. suspected] @ \bes\. 34. Years] # \^)seasonable⟨\. 34. would] 'w' * '[.]'. 36.
Age,] # two commas \con\. 37. ⟨A⟩] \Thy\. 37. ⟨of thine,⟩]. 38. M.CC.LX.] 'M.' # \X\. 43.
then] # \at the Door,\. 44. about] # \the Year io\. 45. World] # \be\. 45–46. presently]
@ \[*]\. 46. *nova*] # \relates that)about⟨ A.C. 106. *Constantem fuisse famam, imminaes
excidit futura tenorum orbi.—* Sett ⟨assign'd⟩ the Year, 1335.\.
   325.1. *Antichrist,*] # second ','. 1–3.)all . . . nor⟨]. 3. furiously] @ \roaring\. 5. what]
@ \the L\. 5.)That⟨]. 5. a very] @ \of\. 5. Man,] # second ','. 6. Mathemat⟨ician,⟩]
\ian,\ of earlier 'Mathematian'. 7. sett] # \th\. 7. *Bucholtzer*] @ \An\. 8. Discoveries]
@ \Vaticinations\. 9. discovered] @ \foun\; # \Strange [. . .]\. 9. ⟨a . . . of⟩]. 10. *abbre-
viabuntur.*] # second ','. 11. *Remaclus,*] # second ','. 13. Forty] @ \F\. 13. Remarkable]
\mak\ between 'Re-' and 'markable'. 13. *Passeover*] # \ever now & then, bring on some
great Ev\. 19. Terrors] @ \Expectations [.]\. 20. Nickname] @ \Nic\. 21. given] @ \a\.
22. Tip-toe] @ \m\. 23. ⟨among the Grammatical⟩]. 23. *Theses*] 'es' * 'is'; @ \Punning\.
23. ⟨for⟩] \of\. 23. Year,] # \VAE PAPAE sunt communes\. 25. ⟨besides *Napiers,*⟩]. 26.
1700.] # \what was *Cusanus's* Year.\. 27. *Cardan*] @ \But\. 28. keeps] # \[*]\. 28. these]
\have seen\. 28. had] # \be\. 29. ⟨same⟩]. 29. with] @ \hon\. 29. *Beverly*] 'y' * 'e'; # \'s
Ninety Sev\. 29. ⟨in⟩] # \with\. 30–33.)famous . . . Portion.⟨]. 37. ⟨its⟩] \the\. 39. in lower
left-hand margin of ms. XII, 124, the following numbers occur as follows:

                                 437
                                 147
                                  59
                                 ———
                                 815.

   44. ⟨Tis true⟩] \)Albeit⟨ the\; @ 'll'. 44. is] * 'was'. 45. *Jew*] @ \Gentleman\; # \th\. 45.
living] # \Two\. 46. Birth] @ \Imm\. 46. SAVIOUR;] ';' * ''''.
   325.46–326.4.)Yett . . . *Plato!*⟨]. 326.2. Age.] # \^ as well as f (which is a little strange The
Ancient Pagans, who had a [*] I ^ [Tho'\. 2. |also|]. 4. *Plato!*] # ']'. 4. ⟨Be sure,⟩] \Yett\. 5.
it:] # \^ *Irenaeus* and\. 5. ⟨and *Hyppolytus*⟩]. 5. ⟨and *Cyprian*⟩]. 6. ⟨and *Austin,*⟩] \himself
seems to\. 6–7. ⟨and . . . it.⟩]. 6. least] # \by\. 7. And,] # \according to\. 9. into] # \their
Notio\. 10–13.)I . . . Ages.⟨]. 11. declaring] @ \de\. 11. will] @ \is\. 12. for] 'o' * 'a'. 12.
|*Valuable*|] \)*Considerable,*⟨]. 12. made] @ \be\. 15. *Genesis,*] 'G' * 'g'. 17. Few] @ \Scarce
any of them\. 17. of *That*] # \,\. 20. which] 'w' * 'to'. 23. ⟨had⟩] \brought\. 24. which] @
\[*]\. 25. ⟨He . . . *Sabbatism.*⟩]. 27. much ⟨of⟩]. 27. Labour.] # \to them. Every *Seventh* of

Week\. 29. *Restitution*] @ \Redi\. 30. *of Man*] # \coming\. 31–37.)It . . . it.⟨]. 32. no] *
'[. .]'. 37. *Seven times*] # \Accordi\. 39. at,] # second ','. 41. ⟨are⟩]. 42. the Vulgar,] @ \w\;
'V' * 'v'; # \[.]\. 42. 1727.] # ','. 42. 1730.] # ','. 43. since] @ \wh\. 43. our CERTAINTY,]
@ \the unc\. 44. KNOWING] @ \N Know\. 44. MAY BE,] # second ','. 45. Behold] 'B' *
'b'. 46. to spoil] @ \give a S\. 46. *come.*] '.' * ','.

327.1. *Foundation*] @ \Sure\. 1. Six Eminently] @ *Seven Periods*\; # \disti\. 2.
Conspic⟨u⟩ously]. 4. be] @ \de\. 7. ⟨a⟩]. 8. deserves] # \a Cultiva\. 9. T'wil] @ \ˆˆ\. 9–24
)*his* . . . 17.]⟨]. 10. transcribe] # \the Words of an Author\. 11. quote] # \a Wri\. 12. Ex-
pression] pl. \s\ 13. Gen. I. 21.]] ']' * ⟨with⟩. 15. Flood] 'l' * 'o'. 20. unto] @ \u\. 21. Ghost]
'G' * 'S'. 26. *Ours,*] # \[which\. 26. ⟨not⟩] \be may asser\. 27. Heaven-born] @ \Glorious
Re\. 27–28. ⟨(from . . . Evidence)⟩]. 30. in] # \the Year 1736. j\. 32. what] @ \be\. 32. ⟨be⟩].
35. ⟨Glory of⟩] \Bishop of\. 36. writes] # \in his Notes\. 38. upon.] '.' * ','. 43. *Quandò*] #
Dom\. 44. *Zanchy,*] # \of whom it\. 45. [⟨perhaps⟩]. 46. complied] @ \anon yett\.

328.4. *sit.*] @ \a\. 4–10.)Indeed| . . . us.⟨]. 5. were] 'e' * 'h'. 6. Imposter] @ \[. . .]\. 8.
FIRE,] # \&\. 9. any] @ \all the\. 11. ⟨move,⟩] \Argue for,\. 11. without] @ \We NOW\. 13.
that] * 'what'. 14. or] @ \hin th\. 18. Sentiments] @ \The\. 21. ⟨to⟩]. 21. is,] # second ','.
22. LORD,] @ \Lo\. 22. so] # *Conflagration* which is to\. 24. *Romish*] 'i' * 'o'. 24. which]
\is as far as the Divine Oracles have taught us is m\. 25. NOW] @ \now\. 29. made]
\,\. 31. There are] @ \It is [*]\; # \are\. 33. make] @ \[*]\. 34. great] @ \as\. 35. which]
@ \[. . .]\; # \the Day of\. 35. come to] @ \Jud\. 36–39.)Even . . . LATEINOS.⟨]. 39. All
⟨the⟩]. 40. Ill-designing] first 'g' * 'n'. 42. for] @ \from\; # \m\. 45. ⟨*Pope*⟩] \which\.

329.4. Earth, but] # \[. . .]\. 8. Impiety,] # second ','. 9–11.)Where . . . But—⟨]. 9.
is] \⟨h⟩\. 13. ⟨a⟩] \Tho\. 13. Thousand] # \more\. 15. *Rome.*] '.' * '!'. 16–22.)whose . . .
Antichrist.⟨]. 20. *Bishop,*] # \and unaware pro\. 20. as] # \ˇ Probable Ratiocinations.\.
21. sitting] @ \[*]\. 23. All] @ \We\. 27. *Thessalonician*] 'c' * 'a'; @ \Ga\. 27. been] #
Shaken\. 31. might] @ \led them i\. 32. ⟨that . . . say,⟩] \or the Pretence of Some to\. 32–
33. ⟨the . . . them;⟩]. 33. Rational] @ \Ration\. 34. ⟨Probable Ratiocination;⟩]. 34. ⟨Former⟩]
Genuine\. 34. Epistle] 'e' * 'es'. 40. Praeposition,] 's' * '[.]'. 43. he] @ \H\. 44. Godly] 'G'
* 'T'. 45. ⟨or,⟩].

330.1. NEXT] @ \Next Thing\. 1. FIRST] @ \first\. 3. it,] # \as\. 6. ⟨only⟩]. 7. which] @
\very\. 8. ⟨quite⟩]. 10. so!] '!' @ ','. 13. gives] @ \leaves us no\. 14–21.)One . . . |mean| . . .
Impertinencies!⟨]. 18. |mean|] \mean [*]\. 23–25.)which . . . *Antichrist*;⟨]. 25. That in] 'T' *
't'. 26. *People:*] ':' @ '.'. 26. Upon] 'U' * '[.]'. 28. *Clouds*] l-shaped doodles in lower left-
hand corner. 30. misled] @ \been\. 33. ⟨first⟩] \first\. 34. *Gospel,*] # \(\. 34. *Reformation,*]
\)\. 35. ⟨our Lords⟩] \His\. 36. Return] @ \Appearing;\. 36. there] @ \then\. 37. *He*] @
\with\. 39. is a] * 'a'. 40. for the] \i\ between 'th' and 'e'. 40. we] # \shou\. 43. *Heighth!*]
'!' @ ','.

331.3. ⟨then⟩]. 7. *Four*] @ *Kingdoms*\. 9. Shape of] @ \Metals\. 9. But] @ \N\. 16.
Nameless] 'N' * 'n'. 26. Nine] 'N' * 'n'. 27. bring] @ \be should attest,\. 28. *Beast*] 'a' *
's'. 28. them] 'em' * 'ei'.

332.9. Division] @ \Divi\. 10. *Ten*] \Roman\. 11. preserved] # \[. .]\. 13. Place.] @
\Place\. 13–16.)Behold . . . *Europe!*⟨]. 13. very] @ *Day yett*\. 14. disappearing] @ \wi\.
14. |a Distinct|] @ \the\. 15. remarkable] 'e' * 'y'. 16. How] 'H' * 'h'. 16. Attempts] \⟨use⟩\.
17. ⟨Nine⟩] \last\. 17. in] # \,\. 17. *Universal*] 'U' * 'M'. 18. Abortive.] '.' * ','. 20–29.
)Among . . . it.⟨]. 25. the] \se\ of earlier 'these'. 34. the Bishop] 't' * 'h'. 36. ⟨*Grand*⟩]. 40. is
not] @ \Observation\; # \a Thing\. 42. ⟨a⟩] \the\. 43. first on the Kingdom] \e\ of earlier
'Kingdome'.

333.1. ⟨most notably⟩]. 1. expound] # \the Pro\. 3. and ⟨his⟩] \him\. 8. That] # \the\.

11. *Thrones* be] 'r' * 'o'; # \pitched dow\. 13. *Throne*:] # \w\. 15. be] # \like\. 16. ⟨ᴇ⟩].
17. *Him*.] '.' * ','. 17. *Beast*] @ *Body of the*\. 19. [A Title] \which had much\ between '['
and 'A'. 20. ⟨the Same with⟩]. 20. *Son*] @ \Sam\. 27. ⟨*Empire*⟩] *Monarchy*\. 32. Judge,] #
\and y\. 33. *ministring*] third 'i' * 'y'. 34. on this] @ \some\; # \Occa\. 40. ⟨for⟩] \in\.
45. what] # \our\.

334.1–8. ⟩That . . . There⟨]. 3. how] @ \th\. 8. can] @ \And none, what\. 8. ⟨nothing⟩]. 9.
than] 'n' * 't'. 9. that] # \Sec Comin\. 11. Term] # \allowed for the\. 13. TIME] 'I' * 'i'. 15–
17. ⟩whereof . . . Typical.⟨]. 17. that] # \⟨according to the Rule first given to the Prophet
Ezekiel,⟩ [.]\. 18. have] 've' * 'ppe'. 21. ⟨ANTICHRIST⟩] \Antichrist,\. 21. *determined*]
@ \d\. 22. *is with*] @ \Him;\. 24. Certainty] @ \any\. 25. when] # \they are e\. 26.
Words;] ';' * '!'. 30. ⟨rising⟩] \appearing\. 30. broken] @ \Ro-\. 33. *Roman*] 'm' * 'an'. 33.
⟨Devastations⟩] \Desolations—\. 34–35. themselves] # \were sensible, that they are\. 37.
Marseilles] 'a' * 'e'. 37–38. *Jornandes*] @ \And\. 38. have] @ \be putt\. 39. Expeditions.]
','. 41. ⟨Heart and Strength⟩] \Heart & Strength\. 41. and] # \Strength\.

335.1. conquered;] # ','. 5. And] # \there\. 7. TENTH] 'E' * 'e'. 7. ⟨& Last⟩]. 7. which] #
\for\. 7. for] \⟨m⟩\. 9. *Ten*] @ \then\. 10. whom,] # \none\. 11. Now] 'N' * 'T'. 13. to the] #
Bishop Emper Bi\. 16. *reveled*.] # \Not only the *Pagan*, but also the *Christian*, Power\.
18. ⟨now⟩]. 19. ⟨*Roman*⟩]. 19. *Empire*] # \declined, Insom\. 21–22. ⟩[And |methinks| . . .
Empire!]⟨]. 21–22. Commencement] @ \Be\. 26. Bishops] 'i' * 'e'. 27. Bishop] @ \Rom\.
32. *Roman*] 'm' * 'a'. 36–37. ⟨who . . . there⟩] \Genseric\. 37. killed] # *Maximus,*\. 38.
Rome:] # \⟨and left it, A.C. 455.⟩\. 38–39. ⟩and . . . 455.⟨]. 41. *Time,*] # \the Protestant,\.
42. as well] 'a' * '[.]'. 42. ANTICHRIST,] 'N' * 'n'. 45. TIME] @ \Time,\.

336.3. him] # \in\. 6. ⟩A.C. 815.⟨]. 6. Period;] # \reached [.]\. 11. who] # \b\. 12. Per-
fidiously] @ \Cruelly\. 12. and] # \Inh\. 16. *Halves*] # \as they have\. 28. *time*;] # '.'. 34.
[Rev.] @ \There is fir\. 37. Still 'S' * 'T'. 40. Years.] '.' * ','.

337.4. Time] 'T' * 't'. 5. This] @ \Tim\. 9. M.DCC.XVI.] second period # \.\. 10. Mar-
vellous] 'M' * 'C'; # \Coinci\. 10. of] @ \these,\. 11. invite] @ \perswade\. 12. *Twelve*] #
\[.]\. 12. wherein] @ \to be\. 16. acute] @ \ing Cro\. 16. *Art,*] # second ','. 18. Faithful]
'i' * 't'. 21. ⟨glorious⟩] \Blessed\. 27. *Year*] @ *Day* for a\. 28. World,] # second ','. 29.
CCCLXV] @ \365\. 30. he] # \not only\. 36. Date] # \of the\. 38. Quickly] @ \shortly
loo\. 39. be] @ \as\. 42. ⟨any more⟩] \them,\. 44. ago;] # '.'. 45. done] # \by &\.

338.1. SAVIOUR,] # \from\. 1. ⟨and to⟩]. 2. and] # \you m\. 4. may] @ \will see\. 5.
CHURCH,] 'U' * 'R'. 6. ⟨down⟩]. 6. with] @ \and\. 6. him] 'h' * 'H'. 7. Year] @ \of\. 8. *Post*]
autem\. 9. ⟨*autem*⟩]. 10. write] @ \speak\. 11. *Works,*] # ','. 13. ALL] first 'L' * 'l'. 15.
Fulfill'd] apostrophe * 'e'. 19. ⟨is,⟩]. 20. ⟨an Acute⟩] \the\. 20. Whiston] @ *Joseph*\. 20. un-
happy] @ \unha\. 21. lose] # \t\. 22. valuable] # \a\. 22. Studies.] '.' * ','. 22. *Prophecies,*]
'ci' * 'n'. 27. *Strokes*;] # ','. 28. ⟨in them,⟩]. 29. without] final 't' * '[.]'. 31–35. ⟩*Foretold* . . .
Heavens!⟨]. 32. Instances,] # second ','. 33. *All*] 'A' * 'a'. 36. which] # \Interpreters\. 36.
Arbitrary] @ \Arb\. 41–44. ⟩One . . . Trumpetts.⟨]. 41. One] @ \Th\. 41. that] # \a little\.
43. finds] @ \is\. 45. As] 'A' * 'a'; @ \And\.

339.6. *Creation*.] '.' * ';'. 6. are] 're' * 'n'. 7. Seven] @ \while Serving\. 7. Ten] 'T' *
't'. 8. according] @ \was [. .]\. 9. M.CC.LX.] @ \M.D.CC\. 10. now] # \gene\. 10–11.
⟨must Reply,⟩] \must still say,\. 14. allow] @ \reckon it\. 16. when] # \the Emperour
Augustu\. 16. ⟨Last⟩]. 16. *Au⟨gu⟩stulus*] \gu\. 18. until] @ \an\. 19. to,] # \the Y\. 21. I] @
\Secondly;\. 21. is] 'i' * 'u'. 23. not] # \a Promise\. 24. which] # \the\. 24. of] 'o' * 'p'. 24–
26. ⟩What . . . supposed.⟨]. 25–26. Sometimes] @ \be\. 26. ⟨a . . . than⟩]. 28. upon] @ \on
the Ot\. 28. 1697.] # \and so the Yett the Angel of the And\. 29. ⟩|⟨]. 29. SEVENTY] @ \
Sevent\. 30. wondrous] @ \wonderful\. 31. A] * 'T'. 38. ⟨then⟩]. 41. *Prophet*] # \⟨upon⟩\

\that he\. 41. upon] @ \up di\. 42.)Dispatch⟨]. 42. of *Sixty*] @ \running through\. 43. *Thirty*] @ *Fourty f*\. 44. ⟨*Hundred*⟩]. 45. aforesaid] 'i' * 'd'.

340.3. from] # \the\. 4. There] @ \B\. 13–15.)And . . . Secret.⟨]. 15. But] @ \Afterw\. 16. ⟨miserable⟩]. 16. had] # \gotten a\. 18. ⟨*Little*⟩] *Short*\. 19. *Anon*] 'A' * 'S'. 20. ⟨of⟩]. 20. *Desolation*] 'n' * 'ns'. 21. *Inundation*] @ \Desola\. 25. was,] # \h\. 25. ordered] \,\. 28. in⟨to⟩]. 31. it;] ';' @ ','. 36. in] @ \in\. 42–43.)with . . . Devotions,⟨]. 44. *Holy*] @ *Temple,*\.

341.1. what] @ \qu\. 5. Years;] # '.'. 5. And] 'A' * 'a'. 5. running] # \of\. 6. ⟨M.⟩CCC.XXXV.]. 6. ⟨*looks for*⟩] *waits*\. 6. comes] # \[. . .]\. 20. the *Hour*] 'e' * 'is'. 21. all] @ \the\. 22. informed] @ \told\. 24. carried] @ \by some\. 32. Yea,] # *Bucholtzer*\. 32. ⟨others⟩] \⟨Author⟩\. 32. tell] \s\ of earlier 'tells'. 33. boast] @ \present\. 36. ⟨& . . . Husbandry,⟩]. 37. lately,] # \In\. 38. ⟨brought⟩] \cast\. 40. *August*] # \that\. 40. And] # \in\. 40. ⟨One . . . *Mason*,⟩]. 41. our] @ \the\.

342.1. the] 't' * long-tailed 's'. 2. ⟨General⟩]. 3. ⟨& hearten⟩]. 3–4.)with . . . *Laughter.*⟨]. 4. Matter] 'r' * 'f'. 4. *Inextinguishable*] 'I' * 'i'. 4. *Et*] @ \within\. 5. that PIETY] second 't' * '[.]'. 7. ⟨yett⟩]. 8. *Dy*] 'y' * 'ie'. 9. leave] first 'e' * 'a'. 11. if] @ \not knowi\. 17. now] @ \CANN\. 17. OFF,] ',' * ';'. 19. WHAT] 'T' * 'F'. 20. earnest] @ \the\. 21. and] # \,\. 29. what] @ \we\. 29. ⟨been⟩]. 30. ⟨last⟩]. 34. is] @ \was\. 37. then] @ \would was\; # \within *Two Years Hundred Years*\. 38. ⟨a Grant of⟩]. 38. *Signs*] # \granted,\. 40. ⟨short-winded⟩] \praecipitous\. 40. Way] # \of which prevails,\. 40. upon] @ \on\.

343.1. ⟨makes⟩] \passes\. 5–13.)It . . . Briefly,⟨]. 5. indeed] @ \i\. 5. forbear] # \all\. 5. *Steps,*] # \[And when\. 6. |any|]. 6. Promise] @ \Prospect\. 7. |seeing|]. 9. as] # \such Thi\. 10. Company,] # \so were\. 11. Frenzy] 'F' * 'f'. 11. |Now|]. 11. some] @ \the\. 15. Lett the] @ \But,\; # \B\. 16. as] 's' * '[.]'. 18. due] @ \all\. 18. ⟨CHRIST is NOW⟩] *the Lord is*\. 18. hand;] # \and\. 20. upon] # \ ten canceled ms. lines: \And this is, *The Conclusion of the Matter. Seeing all these things shall be dissolved,* and it will *not be long,* but we know *not how soon,* before the *Dissolution* come, Lett the *Confidence* of Every Man advise him, *What Manner of Persons ought we to be, in all Holy Conversation & Godliness*!

I have nothing to add, but; an Instance of PIETY, with which I find myself supplied, for *The Conclusion of the Matter.*\.

343.25. sensibly] @ \ad\. 25. annexing] @ \the\. 28. Him] @ \hi\. 29. who] @ \wh\. 29–37.)into . . . *Christians.*⟨]. 31. make] @ \bring this Report\. 32. being] # \Rewar fully depen\. 33. at the] \ir\ of earlier 'their'. 33. *Resurrection*] # *from*\. 42. influenced] @ \agreea\. 43. say:] ':' @ ','. 43. QUICKLY] @ \Quick\.

344.2. His] @ \th\. 3. he] @ \h\. 4. is] 's' * 'f'. 8. ⟨an⟩] \some\. 8. of] 'o' * 'u'; # \T\. 17. THE] 'H' * 'h'. 20. very Near] 'N' * 'n'. 21. a] # \A tremendous\. 22. but] # \he ⟨our GOD⟩ in a *Restitution of all Things* who is a\. 23. He] @ \He\. 28. ⟨His⟩] \the\. 29. and] @ \be be\. 29–33.)Since . . . *Kingdom.*⟨]. 30. *Man*] 'M' * 'm'. 33. *Mind*] 'M' * 'Br'. 34. ⟨now⟩]. 44. ⟨Wishes⟩] \Desires\.

345.1. I] # \may\. 1. the] \r\. 3. I] # \my\. 3. Desire,] first 'e' * 'E'; # \is\. 3. when] # \GOD my\. 10. that] 'hat' * 'tis'. 10. the] # *Suffering of my S*\. 11. thy] 'y' * 'e'. 12. most] @ \[. .]\. 14. out;] ';' * ':'. 15–16. ⟨make me⟩]. 18. *Tares*] # \ˆ ˆ)[*Lord, Gather not my Soul with Sinners!*]⟨\. 19–19. ⟨I . . . be⟩]. 20. ⟨*Lord . . . Sinners!*⟩]. 20–27.)*My . . . me!*⟨]. 20. *Groans*] @ \Man\. 23. Herein] @ \Tho\. 24. now] 'n' * 'o'. 28. CHRIST] # \,\. 28. ⟨|who . . . Life,|⟩]. 29. my] @ \I now\. 30. unto] # \Him\. 31. me;] ';' @ ','. 31–32.)sensible . . . me,⟨]. 34. *Vital*] # *Hold*\. 37.)As . . . *One,*⟨]. 40. ⟨very⟩]. 41–42.)Willing . . . *Him.*⟨]. 44. ⟨a⟩].

346.1. submitt] @ \be be\. 2. *Friendless*] @ \Val\. 4. promote] @ \serve\. 4. ⟨for⟩] \in\.

4–5.)His . . . Articles!⟨|. 5. *Remembrance*| # \I may\. 5. may] # \afforded\. 6. ⟨it⟩|. 8. ⟨most⟩|. 9. to] @ \which\. 11. give] 'i' * 'a'. 12–13. ⟨And . . . ta{ke}⟩] \ˆBy such {who} *walk with GOD*, would I be distinguished\. 13–14.)to . . . *Evil.*⟨| # \⟨ˆI would spend my Time⟩\. 15. a] * 'f'. 15–16. ⟨as . . . *torn*|⟩]. 16. ⟨on the Wing⟩] \hastening\. 18. ⟨are the⟩] \my\. 18. *Talents*] # \are, ⟨[m... *torn*|⟩\. 18. ⟨wherewith . . . endew'd⟩]. 18.)me, &⟨|. 19.)them⟨|. 19–20. ⟨as . . . *Good,*⟩] \with a *Faithful*\. 20. *Steward*] *ship*\ of earlier '*Stewardship*'. 20. ⟨*Favours* . . . me.⟩]. 21. by] 'y' * 'e'; # \distinguished from a vain, mis{erable,} ungodly World, by sin\. 22. ⟨shun⟩] \World\. 22. of] # \an ungodly World [*] an ungodly World,\. 24–32.){I} . . . *me!*⟨|. 26. *Controversies*] # \[..]\. 28. He] @ \at\. 29. *Nations*] # \ˆunder the Oppressions of Antichrist;\. 33. And] @ \I Desire, That I'm\. 33. ⟨Great⟩]. 34. maintain] @ \exercise myself in\. 36–42.)I . . . of.⟨|. 37. |Chosen|] \Children\. 38. SAVIOUR,] # second ','. 38. |much|]. 43. That] # \I may be\. 45. ⟨under . . . *Antichrist,*⟩].

347.3. their] 'ir' * 'm'. 4. ⟨And⟩]. 4. *them*!] '!' * ';'. 5. ⟨Now⟩]. 9. be] # \order\. 9. ⟨I⟩]. 10. *Purchase*] @ \be as that I\. 11. thing] # \B\. 14. *Cold*] 'C' * 'G'.

APPENDIX B: EDITORIAL
EMENDATIONS

The following list is a complete record of editorial emendations as they appear in the present edition. These emendations include corrections of misspelled words; deletions of erroneous punctuation marks, letters, and word repetitions; insertions of punctuation marks, missing letters, and words; adjustments of indentations; corrections of erroneous biblical chapter and verse citations; regularizations of spelling and hyphenation. In the subsequent list, the word *regularize* is used when Mather deviates from his own norm. For instance, Mather's compounds *"Nishmath-Chajim"* and *"High-Priest"* are generally hyphenated, and wherever he forgets to do so, I have supplied the hyphen.

See appendix A for editorial symbols used.

97.22. *Peutinger*] regularized from 'Pentinger'. 101.5. *Peutinger*] 'Pentinger'. 103.20. (i, e, . . .)] opening parenthesis replaces '['. 106.27. *Terrestrial*] 'Terrestial'. 107.10. considered. Most] 'considered, most'. 115.25. *debauched*] 'ed' added. 117.45. no *Separable Parts*] 't' of 'not' dropped. 118.31. *confidently,*] ',' replaces ';'. 119.15. [Matth. XVI. 26.]] 'XV'. 122.21. Abbreviation] 'Abbrevation'. 123.34. *Nishmath-Chajim*] hyphen added to regularize spelling. 123.35. Imagination] plural 's' dropped. 125.28. *Nishmath-Chajim*] hyphen added. 126.8. *Passions of the Mind*] 'the' added. 126.25. they] 'thay'. 128.8. *High-Priest,*] hyphen added. 128.36–37. [ms. II, 28] misnumbered '29'. 131.1. themselves] ':' deleted. 135.4. *putt off*] second 'f' added. 137.22. *Bull*] # '//'. 138.32. They] 'Thyy'. 146.26. *ereptu*] 'erepta'. 146.37. of what] second 'of' deleted. 149.37. obtain] 'obain'. 155.1. I. The Present] @ 1½ inch wavy line to signal beginning of a new page. 155.10. (and] # '//' to separate insertion from main manuscript text. 155.25–26. 2 Pet. III. 5, 6, 7, 10, 11.] verse '5' emended from '1'. 156.4–5. the *Disobedient* People in whose] 'the *Disobedients* \People\ in whose'. 156.8. Twelve letters or doodles appear in the right-hand margin of [ms. III, v2]. 156.27. wherein] 'whenin first'. 160.24. the Apostle] second 'the' dropped. 163.29. *Prophecy*] 'Prophey'. 167.7–8. *High-Way*] hyphen added to regularize his spelling. 168.6. It was] opening single quotation mark erroneously left uncanceled. 168.12. the Great REDEEMER] 'the' added. 168.18. [Isa. XXVIII. 16.]] 'XVII'. 168.42. does discern] 'dos'. 169.23. Predecessor] 'Predcessor'. 170.26. SAVIOUR] 'SAVIouR'. 171.17. Zion.] '.' replaces ','. 171.25. the [ms. III, v16] Promised] second erroneous 'the' preceding 'Promised' deleted. 171.31. Observation] 'Obse- vation' 176.16. [Isa. VIII. 14.] '16'. 180.10. dispersed] 'dispressed'. 180.36–37. when we shall have no Enemies to conflict withal.] 'when we shall no Enemies to conflicted withal.' 190.32. [Isa. LX. 21.]] '20'. 190.40. *the Last*] # '||' to separate marginal insertion from main text. 191.13. have no] @ second 'have'; here deleted. 191.15–24. Mather uses two slashes '//' to indicate line breaks after the following words: *'Foes'; 'GOD'; 'Lambs;' 'SMOKE.'; 'Ones'; 'Earth:'; 'Him'; 'thence.'* 192.15. from the First] 'fro' expanded. 198.35. Bless.] terminal punctuation mark added. 199.6. Tradition] restored from Mather's erroneous cancellation. 200.36. *adfore*] 'affore'. 205.14. REDEEMER] 'REDEMER'. 207.8. after this, and ⟨and before⟩] second '⟨and⟩' dropped. 207.11. unto some] second 'Some' dropped.

210.13–14. there had been Fifty Canon] 'had' added. 215.6. Eighteen] 'Eigtheen'. 223.44.
[ms. III, 59] '(125' in upper right-hand corner of ms. page deleted. 225.26. [Matth. XXIV. 31.]
'XXV'. 226.36. [1. Thess. IV. 16, 17.] 'IV. 17'. 228.31. the Great] 'of the Great'. 233.40. too]
second ⟨too⟩ deleted. 235.29. *unto thee, my GOD!*] one-inch horizontal brace below passage deleted. 235.40. Purpose in it.] two parallels 'II' deleted. 236.2. *Wicked!*] two parallels
'II' deleted. 236.28. *it so!*] two parallels 'II' deleted. 236.29–30. [ms. III, v67] '33.' appears
in upper left-hand margin. 237.18. single out] 'out' added. 237.24. Vengeance] 'Vengance'.
240.21. Inhabitants;] 'In- bitants'. 241.42. destroy'd a *Library*] second indefinite article
'a' dropped. 242.1. Souldiers;] 'Soulders'. 242.44. *Antediluvian*] '*Antedilvian*'. 244.29. *Fifteen*] underscoring regularized. 247.13. triumphed] second interlined ';' deleted. 248.17.
STRONG] 'SRRONG'. 252.20. over the *City*] 'the' added. 256.17. as] two parallels 'II'
deleted. 257.33. Matter] 'Ma- ter'. 260.36. *know one another?*] '*know one other*'. 263.20.
yett in their] second 'in' dropped. 265.42. [Gen. XXIII.4.] '8'. 266.45. the same] 'the san'.
268.45. came out,] ',' after '*came*' dropped. 269.34. *Israel*] '*Irael*'. 271.3. upon it. [ms. III,
x, 6v] I say] second 'I say' deleted after 'it.' 271.6. [Act. III. 21.] 'II'. 276.18. [Hos. I. 10.]
'11'. 278.18. in the World,] second 'in' dropped. 282.8. *Holmes*] '*Homes*'. 285.20–21. one
of [ms. III, x, 26v] the Greatest] missing definite article 'the' added. 287.30. *Behold &
Possess*] underscoring for 'Possess' added to regularize. 287.31. *Salvation*] '*tion*' added
to earlier '*Salva-*' 292.16. *Staynoe*] '*Stanyoe*'. 292.27. *Staynoes*] '*Stanyoes*'. 295.10–11.
should enjoy] second '*should*' dropped. 294.18. (we may call him,)] second 'may' deleted.
296.6. descended from the] second 'from' deleted. 297.9. *Difficulties, which it is encumbred with.*] 'which' replaces erroneous 'with'. 298.2–3. *Salmanasserian*] @ two parallels
'II' to separate interlinear insertion from marginal insertion. 300.15. [Jer. XXXI.6.]] 'XXX'.
303.6. *ALL come to pass.*] '*to*' added. 303.28. *Read this, I pray thee,*] ',' after '*pray*' deleted.
304.32. rolled along,] ',' after 'rolled' deleted. 313.31. *Beleeve it,*] ',' deleted after '*Beleeve*'
and placed after '*it*'. 321.11. [Mar. IX.1.]] corrected from original 'XI'. 325.44. Tis true] @
two parallels 'II' to separate text from marginal insertion. 326.46. here, to spoil] second 'to'
deleted. 327.45. [perhaps *Too far!*]] brackets around interlined ⟨perhaps⟩ dropped. 328.26.
[2. Thess. II. 8.] 'I'. 334.9. that the *Second Coming*] second 'the' deleted. 334.17. fully
understood, that these] second 'that' deleted. 334.37. the godly Presbyter] second 'the'
deleted. 335.25. Emperour] regularized from 'Emperor'. 335.28. *Goliath*] '*Goliah*'. 337.14.
Exinanitions] '*Exina-* sions'. 338.1. His Life ⟨and to⟩ the Day] second 'to' deleted. 338.36.
Arbitrary Interpreters,] ',' after '*Arbitrary*' deleted. 340.38. began.] '*begin*'. 343.25. sensibly
advantageous] 'advantages'. 344.28. on ⟨His⟩ Wicked Enemies,] ',' after 'Wicked' deleted.
344.30. *in which He will Judge the World, by that*] ';' after '*Judge*' deleted. 344.40. *Living
GOD.*] '*Livin*'. 345.11. *work in me what shall*] second '*what*' deleted.

APPENDIX C:
BIBLICAL CITATIONS
AND ALLUSIONS

The following list includes only those references that Cotton Mather does not specifically identify in his manuscript. Page and line numbers are given in front of the biblical
citation references.

93.18	1 Cor. 15:45	93.29	Isa. 51:3	93.31	Gen. 3
93.38	John 14:2–3	93.42	2 Kings 25	93.42	Neh. 1
94.1	Gen. 7, 8	94.2	2 Pet. 3:6	94.3	Gen. 2:10–14
94.38	Rev. 8:13	94.40	2 Pet. 2:4	95.14	Matt. 25:14–30
95.14	Luke 19:12–27	95.36	2 Kings 5:12	95.40	1 Kings 5:1–10
95.43	2 Kings 16:7–9	96.7	Gen. 3:14, 18	96.26	Matt. 2
96.28	Ezek. 38, 39	97.20	Job 2:11	97.23	Gen. 25:1–3
97.23	1 Chron. 1:32	97.26	Job 1:14–15	97.30	Gen. 21:4–9
97.30	Num. 33:41–43	97.38	Gen. 25:1–3	97.43	Gen. 14:5
97.43	Deut. 2:10–11	98.1	Gen. 25:2–4	98.1	1 Chron. 1:3
98.1	1 Chron. 1:33	98.15	Gen. 16:15	98.16	Gen. 12:10, 16
98.24	Gen. 25:13–16	99.6	Luke 3:1	99.11	Num. 31:39, 42
99.29	Job 1:1	99.34	Gen. 11:28	99.38	Gen. 31:30–35
99.42	John 14:2	99.44	Gen. 36:34	99.44	Jer. 49:7, 20
100.4	1 Kings 19:8	100.4	Exod. 33:6	100.5	1 Chron. 1:32
100.13	Job 2:11	100.19	Num. 22:5, 18	100.23	Gen. 27:41–46
100.23	Gen. 28:1–2	100.30	1 Kings 9:17–19	100.30	2 Chron. 8:1, 4
100.33	Judg. 6:3	100.33	Judg. 8:10	100.35	Gen. 8:4
100.41	Gen. 11:2	100.45	Gen. 10:1	101.30	Gen. 3:24
103.13	Gen. 4:16, 17	103.43	1 Kings 10:11	103.43	2 Chron. 8:18
104.19	1 Chron. 29:2	104.35	2 Kings 25:22–26	104.35	2 Chron. 36:20
104.35	Isa. 44, 45	104.35	Jer. 50, 51	104.39	2 Chron. 14:1–9
104.41	Exod. 2:21	105.19	1 Chron. 1:10	105.34	Jer. 51:37
105.37	Dan. 2:31–45	105.45	Gen. 8:4	106.9	Nah. 1:1
106.9	Nah. 2:8–3:19	106.9	Zeph. 2:13–15	106.9	Jer. 46:2
106.18	Job 2:11	106.28	Rom. 5:14	106.28	1 Cor. 15:45
108.7	Gen. 2:14	108.40	Gen. 4:11–16	112.8	Amos 3:2
112.13	Exod. 3:8, 17	112.13	Exod. 13:5	112.26	Ps. 49:15
112.26	Deut. 12:11	112.26	Deut. 14:23	112.29	Luke 23:43
112.29	Luke 16:23	112.29	Phil. 1:23	112.29	Acts 7:59
113.31	Gen. 19:30–38	113.31	1 Sam. 11:1–11	113.31	Jer. 9:25
113.43	Prov. 20:27	114.4	Ps. 102:26–27	119.3	Titus 1:2
119.3	Heb. 6:18	119.19	Mark 8:37	119.24	Matt. 10:28

120.2	Acts 18:9	120.2	Acts 9:1–9	120.38	1 Cor. 13:8–13
120.38	1 Cor. 15:45	120.38	1 Pet. 3:18	120.38	John 6:63
120.38	1 Tim. 6:15	120.38	Rom. 8:38–39	121.9	Job 1:2
121.9	Ps. 49:17	122.23	Matt. 10:26, 28	122.6	1 Thess. 5:23
122.6	1 Cor. 15:42–49	122.30	Heb. 4:12	124.22	Luke 16:19–31
124.30	1 Cor. 15:49	126.40	Heb. 11:5, 13	126.40	2 Kings 2:1–18
127.6	Exod. 34:28–35	127.6	2 Cor. 12:2–4	127.8	2 Cor. 12:2
127.20	Matt. 27:51	127.20	Heb. 6:19	127.20	Heb. 10:20
127.23	Neh. 9:6	127.23	1 Pet. 2:5	127.31	Luke 23:33, 43
128.8	Heb. 10:12	128.12	Luke 23:43	128.18	John 14:2
128.35	Rom. 6:23	128.35	James 1:15	129.37	Matt. 25:14–31
130.41	Heb. 11:37–38	131.43	Num. 20:17	132.12	Rev. 1:5
132.12	Rev. 7:14	133.4	2 Cor. 5:5	133.12	Lev. 19:13
133.23	Ps. 126:5–6	133.23	1 Cor. 15:42	133.41	Rev. 20:4–6
133.41	1 Thess. 4:16	133.41	Acts 24:15	134.9	Ps. 63:5
135.3	Ps. 30:11	136.2	Dan. 12:3	136.3	Matt. 13:43
136.31	Phil. 3:8	137.31	2 Cor. 3:10	137.36	2 Cor. 3:18
137.36	1 Tim. 6:16	147.27	Lev. 20:6, 27	147.35	Rev. 20:10–15
147.35	Rev. 21:8	147.35	Matt. 25:41	147.42	Isa. 6:1–7
147.43	Rom. 12:11	148.5	Neh. 9:6	148.16	1 Pet. 1:4–5
148.19	Exod. 16	148.19	1 Cor. 10:3	148.27	Isa. 41:31
148.40	Rev. 7:9	149.10	Jer. 17:9	150.19	2 Sam. 23:5
150.20	1 Pet. 1:8	150.23	Ps. 1:8	150.23	Ps. 119:6
150.44	Heb. 12:11	151.1	Dan. 12:13	153.15	Gen. 3:17, 18
153.12	Gen. 4:12	153.19	1 Chron. 16:31	153.20	Acts 3:21
153.23	Isa. 65:17	153.26	Jer. 18:4	153.27	2 Cor. 3:10–11
153.29	Isa. 42:9	153.29	Rev. 21:5	153.38	Ps. 87:3
154.2	Jer. 22:29	154.3	Ps. 49:1	155.34	Rev. 17:4–5
155.44	2 Pet. 3:6	157.42	2 Pet. 3	157.43	Rev. 20; 21; 22
158.20	Mark 13:31–37	158.25	2 Pet. 3:7	159.7	Ps. 107:10
159.32	Isa. 40:15	159.42	Rev. 19:9	160.8	Deut. 17:6
160.11	Dan. 2:31–45	160.25	Rev. 20:10, 14–15	160.37	1 Pet. 1:3
160.39	Acts 17:31	162.20	1 Chron. 29:15	163.6	Josh. 21:45
163.34	1 Tim. 3:16	163.41	Luke 24:27	164.3	Matt. 13:46
164.29	John 12:41	164.34	Acts 8:27–39	165.19	Isa. 7:1, 3
165.19	Isa. 8:18	165.19	Isa. 10:21	165.23	Isa. 7:5–6
165.31	Matt. 4:7	165.31	Isa. 7:2–12	165.32	2 Kings 16:3–4
165.32	2 Chron. 28:3–4	166.11	Matt. 1:23	166.11	Isa. 7:14
166.26	Rom 4:20	166.30	Isa. 7:15–16	166.39	Isa. 40:3, 6
166.39	Matt. 3:3	166.39	Mark 1:3	167.3	Isa. 35:1
167.21	Isa. 35:2	167.25	Isa. 35:7	167.28	Isa. 35:9
168.2	Matt. 11:3, 5	168.12	Ps. 130:6	168.23	1 Pet. 2:6, 7
168.31	Isa. 41:25	168.33	Isa. 41:27	169.9	Isa. 50:5, 6
169.13	Isa. 50:10	169.27	1 Kings 4:7, 13	169.27	Judg. 13:2–7
169.27	Luke 1:5–14	169.27	Luke 1:26–38	169.38	Matt. 26:56
169.39	Lam. 4:20	169.39	Acts 2:23	170.8	Hab. 3:4
170.11	Zech. 13:7	170.14	Hos. 6:2	170.44	Hag. 2:7
171.3	Mal. 3:1, 14	171.3	Mal. 4:2	171.13	Ps. 16; 56; 57

171.13	Ps. 60	172.14	Matt. 28:1–20	172.43	Exod. 19:5
174.43	Ps. 135:4	174.43	Deut. 7:6	173.4	Gen. 49:10
173.4	Ezek. 21:26–27	173.4	Luke 1:32–33	173.21	1 Chron. 1:9
173.27	Gen. 22:18	173.29	1 Pet. 2:4	173.30	Rom. 2:28–29
173.33	Phil. 3:3	173.39	Hos. 1:8–9	173.45	Rom. 11:43
174.6	Dan. 2:45	174.45	2 Kings 18:17–35	174.45	Isa. 37:9–20
174.45	Isa. 37:33–37	174.45	2 Chron. 32:31	175.4	Eph. 3:6
175.16	Exod. 12:48–49	175.45	Lev. 19:33–34	175.45	Lev. 24:22
175.45	Gal. 5:3	176.13	Luke 13:23	176.13	Acts 2:47
176.18	2 Kings 16:7–9	176.18	Isa. 7:6–7	177.41	Rev. 21:2, 9–27
178.10	Gal. 4:27	178.10	Rom. 10:15	178.31	Zech. 9:9
178.31	Matt. 21:5	178.31	John 12:15	178.31	Zech. 11:12–13
178.31	Matt. 26:15	178.31	Matt. 27:9	178.31	Zech. 13:7
178.31	Matt. 26:31	178.31	Mark 14:27	178.31	Zech. 12:10
178.31	John 19:34, 37	179.10	Dan. 2:31–45	179.19	Amos 2:8
179.35	Zeph. 3:8	179.42	Joel 1:4; 2:25	179.42	Rev. 9:3, 7
180.18	Rev. 17:1	180.22	Gen. 15:5	180.30	Acts 9:31
180.43	Titus 2:13	181.7	Isa. 65:21, 23	181.16	Prov. 1:6
181.21	Gen. 17:8	181.27	Gen. 25:8–10	181.36	Mic. 2:10
182.10	Matt. 22:31–32	182.34	Heb. 11:13–16	182.40	Matt. 6:10
182.44	1 Chron. 4:10	183.4	Ps. 105:8	183.12	Job 8:8
183.12	Deut. 4:32	183.27	Jer. 33:14	183.36	Deut. 33:23
184.3	1 Thess. 4:17	184.14	2 Thess. 1:8	184.17	Matt. 24:30–31
185.21	2 Kings 23:10	185.21	Isa. 30:33	185.39	Isa. 34:9–15
185.39	Jer. 49:7–22	185.44	Rev. 14:14–20	185.44	Rev. 19:11–16
186.9	Isa. 64:3	186.17	Isa. 66:14	187.13	Zeph. 1:16, 18
187.32	2 Kings 10:29	187.41	Hos. 2:21–23	187.41	Zech. 10:8–10
188.14	Hos. 14:7	188.37	Ezek. 37:27	188.45	1 Cor. 15:54
189.1	Rev. 7:17	189.1	Rev. 21:4	189.6	Isa. 24:1–23
189.37	Heb. 12:22	189.39	Isa. 60:19	189.41	Dan. 2:35
189.43	2 Thess. 1:7	190.5	Ps. 103:4–5	190.13	Isa. 45:18
190.21	Isa. 54:11–12	190.23	Rev. 21	190.26	Job 28:6
190.34	Matt. 5:5	190.35	2 Pet. 3:13	190.45	Rev. 8–11
191.6	Matt. 5–7	191.25	Ps. 37:20, 22	191.29	Ps. 144:5
191.35	Ps. 104:30–31	191.41	Ps. 21:8–9	192.36	Ps. 147–150
193.22	Ps. 102:16	193.22	Ps. 102:25–28	193.31	Deut. 32:22, 43
195.30	Acts 16:16–19	197.13	Ezek. 40–43:27	197.13	Rev. 11:3
199.9	Gen. 4:17	199.9	Gen. 4:26	199.9	Gen. 5:3–8
199.9	1 Chron. 1:1–4	199.21	Col. 3:11	202.6	Matt. 24:3–5
202.19	Matt. 24:38	202.19	Thess. 5:3	203.29	Matt. 24:29
204.4	Acts 2:1–7.	204.4	Acts 2:17	205.41	Joel 2:28, 30
205.42	Mark 14:9	205.42	Matt. 24:24	206.18	Luke 10:18
206.18	John 12:31	207.20	Rev. 6:16	207.28	Matt. 24:17–18
207.28	Mark 13:15	208.4	Matt. 24:7	208.19	2 Pet. 3:7
208.30	2 Pet. 3:9	209.17	Ps. 119:120	209.39	Dan. 3:1–30
211.30	Rev. 14:2	211.30	Rev. 19:6	211.31	Rev. 19:20
211.31	Rev. 20:10, 14	211.41	Ps. 46:1–3	212.8	Isa. 30:33
212.13	Rev. 8:8	212.13	Job 37:1–5	212.13	Mal. 4:1–2

213.4	Matt. 27:45, 51	213.18	Amos 9:3	213.32	Ps. 46:8
214.9	Ps. 9:6	214.17	Ps. 73:19	214.44	Zech. 14:5
215.2	Hag. 2:6–7	215.6	John 5:2	215.10	Luke 13:4–5
215.12	Judg. 16:26–30	215.24	Jer. 4:20, 24	216.25	Isa. 1:4
216.40	John 5:22	217.2	Isa. 33:20	217.5	Isa. 64:11
217.14	Rom. 11:9	217.21	Rev. 16:14	217.25	Isa. 9:5
217.36	Deut. 4:24	217.36	Heb. 12:29	217.45	Lam. 1:12–13
219.5	2 Pet. 3:4	219.10	Dan. 5:1–31	219.15	Luke 12:19
219.21	2 Pet. 2:10	219.27	Luke 21:34	219.38	Rev. 17:4–5
219.40	2 Thess. 2:8	219.42	Matt. 24:27–28	220.5	Luke 21:26–27
220.5	2 Pet. 3:12	220.10	Rev. 12:7–12	220.12	Eph. 6:12
221.4	Joel 2:3, 5, 6	221.4	Joel 2:10, 11	221.15	2 Pet. 3:10
221.19	Job 37:3	221.23	Zech. 9:14	221.25	Exod. 19:16
221.25	Exod. 19:19	221.28	John 5:25	221.28	John 5:28
221.31	John 11:43–44	221.36	Isa. 26:19–21	221.39	1 Cor. 15:52–54
221.42	Phil. 3:21	222.12	1 Sam. 2:8	222.16	Exod. 33:20
222.18	Dan. 7:9, 10	222.23	Rev. 1:7	223.5	Rev. 6:12, 14–17
223.5	Isa. 34:4	223.9	Jas. 5:3	223.16	Jer. 30:5–7
223.18	Joel 2:31	223.23	Matt. 24:21	223.26	Eph. 2:2
223.28	Rom. 1:18	223.32	Eph. 4:30	223.38	1 Pet. 1:4–5
223.41	Gen. 37:23–24	223.45	Ezek. 9:5–6	224.9	Exod. 19:16, 18
224.9	Heb. 12:18–21	224.11	Ps. 55:6–7	224.18	Isa. 25:9
224.19	Matt. 25:31–46	224.21	Matt. 24:30	224.41	Matt. 25:1–30
225.8	1 Thess. 4:17	225.10	Matt. 13:40–43	225.10	2 Pet. 3:7
225.13	Acts 24:15	225.13	Rev. 20:4–6, 12	225.13	Rev. 20:12–14
225.36	Matt. 24:3–51	226.17	2 Pet. 2:9	226.21	Rev. 10:7
226.22	Dan. 3:27	226.31	Zech. 3:2	226.31	Gen. 19:16
227.3	1 Cor. 15:50	227.9	2 Kings 2:11	227.18	Luke 17:34, 36
227.33	Dan. 5:6	227.36	Isa. 7:2	227.40	Isa. 1:24
227.41	Ezek. 1:24	227.43	2 Cor. 6:15	227.44	Isa. 33:12
228.5	Ezek. 7:2–4, 9	228.18	Isa. 53:3	228.22	Acts 26:13
228.29	Rev. 1:14–17	228.33	Isa. 63:1, 3, 6	229.5	Jer. 5:9, 29
229.5	Jer. 9:9	229.7	Ps. 103:21	229.9	Judg. 13:6
229.19	2 Kings 6:21	229.21	Hab. 1:13	229.26	Rev. 14:18–19
229.26	Joel 3:13	229.32	Luke 19:27	229.35	1 Sam. 2:10
229.40	Isa. 30:30	230.4	Rev. 17:2; 14:8	230.4	Josh. 6:17
230.7	Rev. 21:8	230.7	Rev. 14:20	230.12	Ps. 76:6–7
230.16	Lam. 4:11	230.23	Rev. 16:5, 7	231.10	Ps. 17:14
231.10	Rev. 18:9–19	231.24	2 Pet. 3:10–11	231.32	Prov. 26:10
231.41	Jude 6	231.41	2 Pet. 2:4	232.11	Ps. 22:14
232.20	1 John 5:19	232.24	Jer. 44:22	232.30	Jer. 5:30
232.36	Isa. 17:6	232.40	Jer. 2:12	232.45	Isa. 27:11
233.25	Deut. 12:2–3	233.28	Deut. 13:16	233.34	Rev. 16:5–6
233.34	Isa. 26:21	234.7	Rev. 6:9, 10	234.14	Rev. 17:6
235.6	Dan. 7:11	235.28	Ezra 9:10	236.2	Eccles. 3:16–17
236.4	Ps. 50:3	236.17	Isa. 56:10–12	236.36	Jas. 5:4, 8, 9
236.37	Ezek. 8:6, 13–15	236.42	Mal. 4:1	237.43	Rev. 17, 18
238.4	Rev. 18:8–10	238.23	Heb. 6:6	238.27	Luke 22:44

238.28	Ezek. 24:6–9	238.33	Heb. 10:29, 40	238.33	Heb. 6:6
238.37	Hos. 8:13; 9:9	239.2	Ps. 120:3–4	239.8	Matt. 23:32, 36
239.9	Jude 11	239.18	Joel 3:13–14	239.19	Amos 2:9
239.23	Jer. 44:22	239.40	Acts 26:8	240.15	Deut. 29:23
240.20	Jon. 4:11	240.45	Isa. 66:16	241.26	Zeph. 3:7–8
242.25	Isa. 34:9, 16	242.39	2 Pet. 3:6	243.2	Gen. 11:4
243.12	Rev. 7:4–8	244.5	Rev. 21:1	244.32	Col. 1:12
244.35	Dan. 12:3	244.38	Heb. 11:13, 9–10	245.28	Matt. 27:52–53
246.25	Eccles. 10:10	246.33	Heb. 10:34	247.18	Ps. 119:37
247.18	Lam. 2:15	247.18	Ps. 48:1–3	247.24	Heb. 11:1
247.27	Dan. 4:30–33	247.30	Isa. 14:6	247.40	John 14:2
247.42	Luke 16:9	248.2	Rom. 9:11	248.2	Col. 1:13
248.7	Luke 1:17	248.8	Ezek. 1:1	248.16	Ps. 31:19, 21
248.18	Isa. 26:2	248.23	Rev. 21:3–4	248.27	Exod. 19:3, 20
249.3	Luke 9:33	249.19	Eph. 1:23; 3:19	249.23	Ps. 16:11
249.30	Eph. 3:20	249.32	2 Sam. 23:5	250.12	Rev. 20:6
250.16	John 3:9–10	250.18	Ps. 24:3–4	250.20	1 Pet. 1:4
250.23	Isa. 1:26	250.39	Rom. 12:9; 7:24	251.7	Heb. 3:12
251.23	Isa. 53:11	251.25	Isa. 8:18	251.31	Ps. 86:2–7
251.34	2 Cor. 3:18	251.35	Eph. 5:1	251.38	Ps. 103:19
251.40	1 Pet. 2:9	251.42	Judg. 8:18	252.5	Col. 2:9
252.7	Neh. 9:5	252.10	Rev. 1:16	252.17	Mal. 4:2
252.23	1 Pet. 1:8	252.23	Eph. 3:19	252.29	Cant. 2:17; 4:6
252.33	1 Cor. 13:12	253.4	John 3:7	253.6	Ps. 73:16
253.7	2 Pet. 3:16	253.10	Gen. 41:45	253.12	Eccles. 11:7
253.39	Ps. 72:6, 16	254.19	Job 14:14	254.30	Ps. 49:15
254.32	Dan. 12:2	254.37	Luke 7:11–15	254.37	Luke 8:49–56
254.37	John 11:38–44	254.37	Mark 16:9	254.43	2 Cor. 4:14
255.16	Rom. 5:5	255.18	Hos. 13:14	255.19	Jer. 18:4
255.24	1 Cor. 15:36–44	255.28	Rev. 21:4	255.34	Dan. 12:3
255.37	Exod. 34:29–35	255.39	Matt. 13:43	255.41	Ps. 105:37
255.43	1 Tim. 5:23	256.2	Josh. 14:10–11	256.11	Isa. 40:31
256.16	Ps. 68:13	256.17	Ps. 139:9	256.28	Rev. 1:5
256.37	Luke 14:14	256.38	Eph. 6:8	256.45	2 Tim. 4:8
257.1	Rev. 22:12	257.4	Ps. 58:11	257.5	Ps. 103:4
257.36	Rom. 5:2	257.43	Phil. 4:3	258.6	1 Pet. 4:19
258.8	Rev. 2:2	258.11	Gal. 2:20	258.17	1 Tim. 6:18–19
259.4	1 Tim. 5:21	259.9	Heb. 4:12	259.13	2 Pet. 1:11
259.17	Eph. 6:6	259.20	Esther 2:21–23	259.20	Esther 6:6–11
259.32	Esther 6:11	259.32	Esther 10:1–3	259.39	Num. 1:16; 16:2
260.1	Acts 10:4	260.21	2 Sam. 24:10	260.21	Matt. 26:75
260.29	Isa. 43:25	260.37	Mark 9:1–8	261.4	Col. 4:17
261.23	Heb. 12:23	261.28	Luke 20:35–36	261.36	Rev. 5:8–12
261.37	Heb. 1:14	261.39	Gal. 3:23–26	261.44	1 Thess. 2:7
262.2	Isa. 58:2	262.3	Ps. 46:4	262.5	Heb. 4:9
262.8	Rev. 2:27	262.15	Exod. 20:7	262.20	Heb. 6:12
262.20	Rev. 2:26	262.42	Rev. 14:6	263.1	Matt. 19:28
263.11	Rev. 22:4	263.17	Ezek. 42:14	263.17	Ezek. 44:19

263.44	Prov. 20:6	264.3	Jas. 5:8	264.8	Exod. 3:8, 17
264.30	2 Kings 22:14	264.35	1 Pet. 3:3–5	264.36	Num. 26:59
264.36	Exod. 15:20–21	264.38	Gen. 3:16–17	265.29	Gen. 2:18–23
265.33	Eph. 3:4	265.33	Col. 4:3	265.35	Luke 20:36
265.37	Eph. 5:30	265.39	Ezek. 1:28	265.39	Rom. 6:5
265.41	Isa. 60:21	265.42	Gen. 23:19	266.5	Heb. 12:23
266.18	1 Tim. 2:12	266.25	1 Chron. 6:33	266.25	1 Chron. 15:17
266.29	1 Chron. 15:21	266.33	Matt. 28:1	266.37	Isa. 62:4
266.40	Gen. 15:5	267.4	1 Pet. 2:5	267.4	Luke 14:21, 23
267.10	Luke 24:5	268.4	Isa. 49:13	268.5	Ps. 104:30
268.5	Ps. 119:64	268.7	Num. 13:32	268.12	Hab. 1:13
268.18	Rev. 20:2–7	268.21	Ps. 90:4, 15	268.21	2 Pet. 3:8
268.31	Exod. 3:2	268.41	Gen. 13:15	268.45	Heb. 11:14–16
269.10	Matt. 2:12	269.15	Ezek. 36:35	269.18	Gen. 50:22–26
269.18	Josh. 24:32	269.23	2 Pet. 3:10–11	269.24	Rev. 21:1
269.24	Luke 21:33	269.26	Isa. 65:17	269.28	Ps. 37:9–10
270.14	1 Cor. 7:31	270.36	Rev. 21:5	270.37	Isa. 65:17
270.41	2 Cor. 5:17	271.14	Luke 1:70	271.29	Rom. 5:12
271.33	Ps. 67:4–6	271.37	Lev. 26:20	271.38	Gen. 9:8–17
271.40	Gen. 5:29	271.45	1 Tim. 4:8	271.45	2 Tim. 1:1
272.7	Isa. 51:3	272.8	Ezek. 36:35	272.21	Mal. 4:1
272.22	Rev. 11:18	272.24	Ps. 104:35	272.27	Ezek. 28:26
272.30	Matt. 22:30	272.30	Mark 12:35	272.40	Ezek. 20:49
272.43	Ps. 73:19	272.44	1 Thess. 4:17	273.12	Isa. 65:22
273.16	1 Pet. 1:15	273.28	1 Thess. 4:17	273.28	1 Cor. 15:51–54
273.28	Rev. 20:4–15	273.33	Rev. 7:17	273.33	Isa. 25:8
273.33	Ps. 94:13	273.35	Ps. 147:4	273.37	1 Cor. 15:41
274.2	Luke 20:36	274.4	Ezek. 28:26	274.4	Isa. 65:22
274.16	Job. 11:12	274.18	2 Pet. 3:13–14	274.38	John 21:1–14
274.38	Luke 24:30–31	274.39	Gen. 18:1–8	275.1	Luke 20:27–38
275.20	Acts 8:9–24	275.24	Ezek. 36:38	275.28	Ezek. 37:23–25
275.33	Rev. 21:3–4	275.35	Ezek. 36:8–10	275.41	Gen. 48:16
276.1	Exod. 1:5–7	276.1	Exod. 12:37	276.11	Gen. 46:27
276.11	Exod. 48:1	276.14	Rev. 7:4–9	276.23	Ps. 27:13
276.30	Ps. 33:5	276.30	Zech. 9:10	276.30	Num. 23:9–10
276.34	Rev. 7:4	276.43	Rev. 14:3	277.9	Rev. 7:9, 16–17
277.15	Rev. 7:15	277.17	Rev. 21:22	277.22	Rev. 14:13
277.26	Luke 1:74–75	277.29	Isa. 43:2	277.34	Gen. 5:24
277.34	Heb. 11:5	277.34	Heb. 11:13	277.37	Mal. 3:2–3
277.45	Zech. 3:2–4	278.13	2 Pet. 3:7	278.15	Ezek. 30:24
278.16	Rom. 7:24	278.22	Ps. 38:5–7	278.24	Ps. 130:8
278.25	Rev. 22:3	278.27	Matt. 6:10	278.31	1 John 3:8
278.36	Rev. 20:1–3	278.39	Luke 11:22	278.43	2 Pet. 1:21
279.3	Deut. 12:8–9	279.11	Ps. 78:37	279.16	2 Chron. 30:19
279.21	Job 1:7	279.21	Job 2:2	279.22	1 John 5:19
279.25	Heb. 2:14	279.30	Eph. 2:2; 6:12	279.33	John 12:21
279.33	John 14:30	279.39	Prov. 30:19	279.42	Acts 26:18
280.29	Isa. 14:7, 12–15	280.36	Eph. 6:11, 13	280.43	Isa. 14:2

280.45	Ps. 149:809	280.45	1 Cor. 6:3	281.3	Jude 6
281.12	Judg. 13:23	281.16	Isa. 4:3	281.28	1 Cor. 15:51
281.29	Heb. 2:15	281.30	Hos. 13:14	281.34	Job 33:24–28
281.35	Ps. 91:4	281.40	Ps. 91:7–8, 11–12	282.4	Gen. 5:3–21
282.9	Isa. 65:20	282.21	Isa. 65:22	282.37	Acts 14:22
282.43	Judg. 18:9–10	282.44	Rev. 22:3	283.3	Gen. 27:27–28
283.14	2 Kings 2:19–20	283.37	Deut. 15:9	283.41	Isa. 30:25
285.8	Ps. 67:2	285.37	1 Sam. 17:46	285.37	Dan. 7:3–8
285.37	Dan. 2:31–45	286.2	Luke 19:14	286.3	Ps. 109:6
286.8	Luke 20:36	286.11	Isa. 60:17–18, 21	286.21	Gen. 41:43
286.23	Rev. 1:5	286.28	Luke 7:28	287.7	Matt. 17:1–8
287.20	Rev. 21:26	287.28	Acts 3:19	287.32	Isa. 56:1
287.33	Isa. 33:17	287.43	1 Thess. 4:17	288.19	2 Pet. 3:15–16
288.32	Matt. 18:3	289.6	Heb. 2:7–8	289.12	Ps. 8:1, 9
289.14	Acts 3:21	289.38	Ezek. 38, 39	289.38	Rev. 20:7–12
290.8	Matt. 21:24	290.16	Rev. 2:26	290.32	Gen. 15:12
290.38	Ps. 59:14	291.5	Rev. 20:8	291.12	Ezek. 38:2, 17
291.37	Rev. 20:2, 7	291.40	1 Kings 22:22	291.43	Exod. 32
291.44	Job 26:11	291.46	Ezek. 20	291.46	Amos 5, 6
291.46	Acts 7:22–44	292.3	Exod. 13:21	292.4	Exod. 16:12–15
292.10	Matt. 10:25	293.2	Rev. 11:2–3; 13:5	293.2	Rev. 12:6, 14
293.14	Ezek. 4:6	293.25	Rev. 20:5	293.36	Gen. 3:1–7
293.36	Rev. 20:1–15	293.40	Rev. 20:8	294.45	Job 1:6–7
294.45	Rev. 12:7–12	295.5	Matt. 24:3	295.11	Acts 1:7; 3:21
295.17	Dan. 2:31–45	295.17	Dan. 7, 8	295.17	Dan. 9:24–27
295.18	Dan. 10:11	295.18	John 21:7	295.25	Dan. 12:12
295.29	Acts 1:6–7	295.31	Rev. 5:1–9	295.32	Rev. 6:1; 22:6
295.33	2 Thess. 2:3	295.35	Rev. 13:20	295.37	Job 15:20
295.44	Acts 1:7	296.4	2 Pet. 3:10	296.26	Rom. 11:33
296.35	1 Pet. 3:20	296.37	Mark 13:32–37	296.37	Matt. 25:1–14
296.40	Zeph. 1:7	296.40	2 Thess. 2:2	297.39	1 Kings 12:26–33
297.39	2 Kings 23:15	297.42	2 Chron. 30:1–20	297.44	2 Chron. 31:1
298.4	Isa. 17:6	298.5	Amos 3:12	298.8	2 Chron. 34:3–8
298.14	2 Kings 17:6	298.14	2 Kings 18:11	298.14	1 Chron. 5:26
298.35	Jer. 25:12	298.35	Jer. 25:21	298.35	Jer. 27:1–8
298.35	Jer. 48:47	298.35	Jer. 49:1–7	298.43	Neh. 7:6
299.4	Ezra 6:16–17	299.11	Gen. 49:10	299.13	Jonah 1:9
299.16	Isa. 11:13–14	299.16	Obad. 10, 17–21	299.20	Luke 24:47
299.20	Acts 3:36; 26:7	299.22	James 1:1	299.25	Ezra 1:1
299.25	Ezra 7:1, 6, 13	299.40	Luke 2:36–38	300.23	Matt. 10:6
300.34	Ezek. 16:55, 61	300.37	Ezek. 36:25–26	300.41	Jer. 33:14
301.12	Acts 2:1–10	301.13	Matt. 23:37	301.13	Luke 13:34
301.26	Zech. 10:6, 11	301.28	Isa. 44:27; 45:1	301.34	John 19:15
301.44	Zech. 12:12–14	302.1	Luke 3:23–38	302.3	Matt. 1:1–16
302.4	2 Sam. 11:2–27	302.4	2 Sam. 12:13–16	302.4	2 Sam. 24:10–17
302.8	Gen. 24:7	302.9	Zech. 12	302.15	Hos. 3:5
302.24	Phil. 3:3	302.24	Heb. 6:17	302.24	Gal. 3:29
303.2	Josh. 21:45	303.2	Ps. 89:33	303.6	Josh. 21:45

SELECTED BIBLIOGRAPHY

PRIMARY WORKS

Abrabanel, Isaac ben Judah (Abravanel). *Commentarii in Esaiae Prophetam 30*. Leyden, 1631.

———. *Ma'yenei ha-Yeshu'ah*. [*Fountain of Salvation*]. Ferrara, 1551.

———. *Migdal Yeshu'ot*. [*Tower of Salvation*]. Ferrara, 1528.

Acosta, José de. *The Natural & Moral History of the Indies* (1590). 2 vols. Edited by Clements R. Markham. 1880. First English Edition 1604. Reprint. New York: Burt Franklin, 1970.

Adamus, Melchior. *Dignorum Laude Virorum, Quos Musa Vetat Mori, Immortalitas*. Third Edition. Frankfurt, 1705.

Aeschylus. *Perseus et Choephori*. [Loeb].

Aethicus, Julius. *Cosmographia*. Edited by Heinrich Wuttke. Leipzig: Dyk'sche Buchhandlung, 1853.

Ainsworth, Henry. *Annotations upon the Five Bookes of Moses, the Booke of Psalmes, and the Song of Songs*. London, 1627.

Alfonsi, Petrus (Moise Sefardi, Moses Sephardi). *Dialogi in quibus Iudaeorum opiniones confutantur*. Coloniae, 1677.

Alleine, William. *The Mystery of the Temple and City, described in the nine last Chapters of Ezekiel, unfolded*. London, 1679.

Alsted, Johann Heinrich. *Diatribe de mille annis Apocalypticis*. Herborn, 1627. Translated by William Burton as *The Beloved City*. London, 1643.

Alting, Jacob. *Opera omnia theologica, analytica, exegetica*. 5 vols. Amsterdam, 1687.

Ambrose, St. *Death as a Good*. In Deferrari, *Fathers*. 65:69–113.

———. *Hexaemeron*. In Deferrari, *Fathers*. 42:3–283.

Ammianus Marcellinus. *History*. [Loeb].

Amyraut, Moïse. *Discours de l'Estat des fidèles après la mort*. Saumur, 1646. Translated as *The evidence of things not seen; or, Diverse scriptural, and philosophical discourses; concerning the state of good and holy men after death*. London, 1700.

Apollonius of Rhodes. *Argonautica*. [Loeb].

Appianus. *De Bellis Civilibus*. [Loeb].

———. *Roman History*. [Loeb].

Aristeas. *Epistle of Aristeas*. In *The Old Testament Pseudepigrapha*. 2 vols. Edited by James H. Charlesworth. New York: Doubleday, 1985. 2:7–34.

Aristotle. *Generation of Animals*. [Loeb].

———. *Nichomachean Ethics*. [Loeb].

———. *On the Soul*. [Loeb].

Arndt, Johann (Joannes Arndtius). *De vero christianisimo libri IV*. Lunaeburgae, 1606–10.

Arnobius the Younger. *Commentarii in Psalmos*. [*PL* 53].

Arrianus, Flavius. *Anabasis*. [Loeb].

———. *Indica*. [Loeb].

———. *Periplus of the Euxine Sea*. C. 132. [Loeb].

Athenaeus. *Deipnosophistai*. C. 200 [Loeb].

Atherton, Henry. *The Resurrection Proved; or, The life to come demonstrated. Being a strange but true relation of what hapned to Mris Anna Atherton*. London, 1680.

Augustine, St. *Care for the Dead*. In Deferrari, *Fathers*. 27:351–84.

———. *De Civitate Dei* (413–26). Translated by Marcus Dods as *The City of God*. New York: Modern Library, 1950.

———. *Epistle 57*. In Deferrari, *Fathers*. 12:295–6.

———. *Epistle 197*. [*PL* 33].

———. *Epistle 198*. [*PL* 33].

———. *Epistle 199*. [*PL* 33].

———. *Epistle to Hesychius* (197–99). [*PL* 33].

———. *On the End of the World*. [*PL* 33].

———. *Sibyllinorum Verborum Interpretatio*. [*PL* 90].

Aventinus, Johannes Thurmayr. *Annales ducum Boiariae*. Lipsiae, 1522.

Baglivi, Georges. *Opera Omnia Medica Practica et Anatomica*. Lyon, 1704.

Balduin, Friedrich. *Adventus Christi typicus*. Wittenberg, 1621.

———. *De Antichristo disputatio*. Wittenberg, 1606.

———. *Diatribe theologica de Antichristo*. Wittenberg, 1615.

Barnabas, St. *Catholic Epistle*. In Roberts, *Ante-Nicene*. 1:133–49.

Baronius Soranus, Caesar. *Annales ecclesiastici*. 12 vols. Rome, 1598–1607.

———. *De Antichristo, quod nihil commune habeat cum Roman Pontifice*. In St. Robert Bellarmine, *Opera Omnia*. 1:709–800.

Basil the Great of Caesarea, St. *Commentarii in Isaiam Prophetam*. [*PG* 30].

———. *Hexaemeron*. In Deferrari, *Fathers*. 46:3–150.

Batalerio, Jacobus Johannes (Batelier). *Dissertatio de Israelitarum conversione à Divo Paulo ad Romanos undecimo capite praedicta*. Hagae, 1669.

Bates, Isaac. *Not Death but Immortality, the desir'd Relief of the Burthen'd Christian*. London, 1708.

Bates, William. *Considerations of the existence of God, and of the immortality of the soul*. London, 1676.

Baxter, Richard. *The Certainty of the World of Spirits*. London, 1691.

———. *The Glorious Kingdom of Christ, described and clearly vindicated, against the bold asserters of a future calling and reign of the Jews ... Answering Mr. Tho. Beverley*. London, 1691.

———. *Of the immortality of man's soul, and the nature of it and other spirits*. London, 1682.

Bayle, Pierre. *Nouvelles de la République des Lettres*. Amsterdam, 1718.

Beart, John. *A Vindication of the Eternal Law, and Everlasting Gospel*. London, 1707.

Becker, Balthasar (Bekker). *De betoverde weereld, zynde een grondig ondersoek van't gemeen gevoelen aangaande de geesten* [*The Enchanted World*]. Amsterdam, 1691–93.

Bellarmine, St. Robert. Editor. *De Antichristo, quod nihil commune habeat cum Roman pontifice*. By Caesar Baronius Soranus. In *Bellarmine, Opera Omnia*. 1:709–800.

———. *Disputationes de Controversiis Christianae Fidei adversus hujus temporis Haereticos*. Ingoldstadt, 1586–93.

———. *Opera Omnia*. 7 vols. Colonia Agripinensis, 1620.

Benjamin of Tudela (R. Ben Jonah). *Sefer ha-Massa'ot*. Constantinople, 1543. [*Itinerarium*. Ferrara, 1556].

Bernard, St. *Epistle 56*. [*PL* 182].

Beverley, Thomas. *A Scripture-line of Time.* London, 1684.

———. *The Thousand Years Kingdom of Christ, in its full Scripture-State: answering Mr. Baxter's new treatise, in opposition to it.* London, 1691.

Bisterfeld, Johan Heinrich. *Scripturae Sacrae divina eminentia et efficientia.* Lugduni Batavorum, 1654.

Blackmore, Sir Richard. *A new version of the Psalms of David.* London, 1721.

———. *Redemption: a divine poem, in VI Books.* London, 1722.

Bochart, Samuel. *Dissertatio de paradiso terrestri.* In Bochart, *Opera Omnia.*

———. *Geographia Sacra.* Cadomi, 1646.

———. *Samuelis Bocharti, Opera Omnia. Hoc Est Phaleg, Chanaan, et Hierozoicon.* Fourth Edition. Lugduni Batavorum, 1712.

Borelli, Giovanni Alfonsi. *De motu animalium.* 2 vols. Romae, 1680–81.

———. *Historia, et meteorologia incendii AEtnaei anni 1669.* 1670.

Borgius, Hieronymus (Girolamo Borgia). *Carmina lyrica et heroica.* Venice, 1666.

———. *Historiae de bellis Italia.* Romae, 1544.

Bradford, William. *Of Plymouth Plantation.* Edited by Samuel Eliot Morison. New York: Alfred A. Knopf, 1984.

Braght, Thieleman J. van. *The Bloody Theater or Martyr's Mirror* (1660). Lancaster, 1837.

Brightman, Thomas. *A Revelation of the Apocalyps.* Amsterdam, 1611.

Brochard (Burcardus de Monte Sion). *Directorium ad passagium faciendum ad terram sanctam.* 1345.

Bucholtzer, Abraham. *Index chronologicus: monstrans annorum seriem a mundo conditio ad annum nati Christi 1580.* Gorlicii, 1580.

Bünting, Heinrich. *Itinerarium sacrae scripturae.* Helmstedt, 1581.

Bulkeley, Peter. *The Gospel-Covenant; or, The Covenant of Grace Opened.* London, 1646. Second Edition. London, 1651.

Bull, George. *Collected Works.* 7 vols. Edited by Rev. Edward Burton. London: Clarendon Press, 1827.

Burnet, Gilbert. *Some Passages of the Life and Death of Rochester.* London, 1680.

Burnet, Thomas. *Archaeologia philosophicae.* London, 1692.

———. *The Sacred Theory of the Earth.* London, 1684. Edited by Basil Willey from the 1691 edition. Carbondale: Southern Illinois University Press, 1965.

———. *A Treatise Concerning the State of Departed Souls Before, and At, and After the Resurrection* (1681). Second Edition. London, 1730.

Burnet, William. *An Essay on Scripture-Prophecy, wherein it is endeavoured to explain the three periods contain'd in the XIIth chapter of the prophet Daniel. With some arguments to make it probable, that the first of the periods did expire in the year 1715.* New York, 1724.

Byles, Mather. "The Comet: A Poem." Boston, 1744.

———. "The Conflagration." In *Works.* Compiled by Benjamin Franklin V. Delmar, NY: Scholars' Facsimiles & Reprints, 1978.

Calef, Robert. *More Wonders of the Invisible World.* London, 1700. In *The Witchcraft Delusion in New England.* 3 vols. Edited by Samuel G. Drake. 1866. Reprint. New York: Burt Franklin, 1970. Vol. 3.

Calmet, Augustin. *Calmet's Great Dictionary of the Holy Bible.* 5 vols. Charlestown, MA: Samuel Etheridge, 1812.

———. *Dictionnaire historique, critique, chronologique, géographique, et littéral de la Bible* (1718). 4 vols. Paris, 1730.

Calovius, Abraham. *Biblia Illustrata.* 4 vols. Dresden, 1719.

———. *Systema locorum theologicorum.* 12 vols. Witebergae, 1655–77.

Calvert, James. *Naphtali; seu, Colluctationes theologicae cum tribus ingentibus dubiis, viz. De reditu decem tribum. De Conversione Judaeorum.* London, 1672.

Calvin, John. *Institutes of the Christian Religion.* Library of Christian Classics. Vols. 20–21. Edited by John T. McNeill. Philadelphia: Westminster Press, 1960.

———. *Ioannis Calvini in Novum Testamentum Commentarii.* 5 vols. Edited by A. Tholuck. Berolini: Gustavum Eichler, 1834.

———. *Praelectiones in Ieremiam.* In *Ioannis Calvini Opera Quae Supersunt Omnia.* 67 vols. Brunsvigae: Schwetschke, 1863–1900. Vol. 39.

———. *Psychopannychia, qua refellitur quorundam imperitorum error.* Geneva, 1542.

———. *Psychopannychia; or, A Refutation of the Error that the Soul Sleeps in the Interval Between Death and the Judgment* (1542). First translated into English as *An Excellent Treatise of the Immortality of the Soul.* London, 1581. In *Tracts and Treatises in Defense of the Reformed Faith.* 5 vols. Translated by Henry Beveridge. Grand Rapids: Wm. B. Eerdmans Publishing Co., 1958. 3:413–90.

Camerarius, Philipp. *Operae horarum subcisivarum.* Frankfurt, 1644–50.

Cappellus, Ludovicus (Louis Cappel). [*Concerning the State of the Souls after Death*]. In *Commentarii et notae in Vetus Testamentum.* Amsterdam, 1689. Pp. 243–62.

Caramuel de Lobkowitz, Juan. *Theologia moralis.* Louvain, 1643.

Cardanus, Hieronymus (Girolamo Cardano). *De utilitate ex adversis capienda libri IV.* Franeker, 1648.

Casaubon, Isaac. Editor. Onofria Panvinio, *De Sibyllis et Carminibus.* Heidelberg, 1588.

Chandler, Edward. *A Defense of Christianity From the Prophecies of the Old Testament Wherein are Considered All the Objections against this Kind of Proof, Advanced in a Late Discourse of the Grounds and Reasons of the Christian Religion.* London, 1725.

Chrysostomus, Johannes. *Homily on Saint Ignatius.* In Schaff, *Nicene.* 9:137–40.

———. *Homily 28.* In Deferrari, *Fathers.* 33:267–77.

———. *Homily 73.* In Deferrari, *Fathers.* 41:281–91.

Cicero. *De Divinatione.* [Loeb].

———. *De Finibus.* [Loeb].

———. *De Senectute.* [Loeb].

———. *Epistolae ad Atticum.* [Loeb].

———. *Somnium Scipionis.* [Loeb].

———. *Tusculan Disputationes.* [Loeb].

Clarke, Samuel. *Lives of Eminent Persons.* London, 1683.

Clement of Alexandria, St. *Protrepticus.*

———. *Stromateis.* In Roberts, *Ante-Nicene.* 2:299–567.

Collins, Anthony. *A Defense of the Argument for the Truth of Christianity from miracles, and the gospel application of several passages in the Old Testament.* London, 1728.

———. *A Discourse of the Grounds and Reasons of the Christian Religion.* London, 1724.

Collins, J. J. Editor. The Sibylline Oracles. In *The Old Testament Pseudepigrapha.* 2 vols. Edited by James H. Charlesworth. Garden City, NY: Doubleday, 1983. 1:317–472.

Constantine VII. Porphyrogenitus. *De Administrando Imperio.* Budapest: Pazmany Peter Tudomanyegyelemi, 1949–62.

Cotton, John. *A Brief Exposition With Practical Observations Upon the Whole Book of Canticles.* Second Edition. London, 1655.

Cressener, Drue. *The Judgments of God upon the Roman-Catholick Church . . . unto its last end.* London, 1689.

Cross, Walter. *The Taghmical Art; or, The art of expounding scripture by the points.* London, 1698.

Cunaeus, Petrus (Van der Cun). *De Republica Hebraeorum.* Leiden, 1617.

Curaeus, Joachim. *Narratio Historica de Vita et Morte Ioach. Curei.* Witebergae, 1601.

Curione, Celio Secondo. *De amplitudine beati regni Dei, dialogi sive libri duo.* [*On the Greatness of the Blessed Kingdom of God*]. Goudae, 1614.

Cyprian, St. *Exhortation to Martyrdom.* In Deferrari, *Fathers.* 36:311–44.

Cyprian of Carthagena, St. *Dissertatio Apologetica Pro SS. Perpetua.* [*PL* 3].

Cyril of Alexandria, St. *Joel.* [*PG* 71].

Cyril of Jerusalem, St. *Catecheses.* In Deferrari, *Fathers.* 61:89–249; 64:3–140.

D'Asigny, Marius. Translator. *A Christian's Defence against the Fear of Death.* London, 1675.

D'Espagne, Jean. *Shibboleth; or, The Reformation of several Places in the Translation of the French and of the English Bible* (1633). London, 1655.

Deferrari, Ray Joseph, and Ludwig Schopp. Editors. *The Fathers of the Church.* 89 vols. New York: Fathers of the Church, Inc., 1948–82.

De La Cerda, Joannes Ludovicus (Juan Luis De La Cerda). *Adversaria sacra, quibus fax praefertur ad intelligentiam multorum scriptorum sacrorum.* Leon, 1626.

De Pomis, R. David. *Zemah David.* Venice, 1587.

Diodorus Siculus. *Universal History.* [Loeb].

Dion Cassius. *Roman History.* [Loeb].

Dionysius Halicarnas. *Roman Antiquities.* [Loeb].

Doolittle, Thomas. *Earthquakes Explain'd and Practically Improved.* Boston, Reprinted by Benjamin Harris, 1693.

Drelincourt, Charles. *Les Consolations de l'âme fidèle, contre les frayeurs de la mort.* Geneva, 1669. Transl. by Marius D'Asigny.

Drusius, Johann Clemens (Jan van der Driesche). *Critici Sacri.* Antverp, 1616.

Dury, John. *An Epistolicall Discourse of Mr. John Dury to Mr. Thorowgood. Concerning his conjecture that the Americans are descended from the Israelites.* London, 1650.

Edwards, Jonathan. *A History of the Work of Redemption* (1774). In *The Works of President Edwards.* 4 vols. New York: Robert Carter & Brothers, 1864. 1:295–516.

———. "Notes on the Apocalypse." In *The Works of Jonathan Edwards.* Edited by Stephen J. Stein. 8 vols. New Haven: Yale University Press, 1977. 5:95–305.

———. *Sinners in the Hands of an Angry God.* In *Works* (1864). 4:313–21.

———. *Thoughts on the Revival of Religion in New England* (1740). In *Works* (1864). 3:274–425.

El-Ghazali, Ahmed (Al-Ghazzali). [*Contradictions of the Philosophers*].

Ephraem, St. Syrus. *Of the Eternal Mansions.* C. fourth century.

Epicurus. *De rerum natura.* [*On Nature*]. In *Opere.* Torino: G. Einaudi, 1973.

Epiphanius, St. [*Treatise on Weights and Measures*]. In Dionysius Petavius, *Opera Omnia.* 2 vols. Cologonia Agripinensis, 1682. Vol. 2.

Eusebius Pamphili. *Chronicles.* [*PL* 8].

———. *Ecclesiastical History.* In Deferrari, *Fathers.* Vols. 19 and 29.

Evelyn, John. *The Diary of John Evelyn.* Edited by John Bowle. New York: Oxford University Press, 1985.

Fernel, Jean. [*Concerning the Hidden Causes of Things*]. In *Universa Medicina.* Lutetiae Parisiorum, 1554.

Finch, Heneage (Third Earl of Winchelsea). *A True and Exact Relation of the late prodigious earthquake & eruption of Mount Ætna, or Monte Gibello.* London, 1669.

Flacius Illyricus, Matthias (Matija Vlačić Ilir). Compiler. *Historia ecclesia Christi* [*Magdeburg Centuries*]. Basel, 1559–74.

Fletcher, Giles, and Samuel Lee. *Israel Redux; or, The Restauration of Israel exhibited in two short treatises.* London, 1677.

Flinsbachius, Cunmannus. [*Conjectures of the End Times*]. In *Genealogiae Christi et omnium populorum tabulae.* Basileae, 1567.

Folengius, Joannes Baptista (Folengo). *Commentaria in Psalmos.* Bâle, 1557.

Foxe, John. *The Actes and monuments of these latter and perilous dayes.* [*Book of Martyrs*]. London, 1559.

———. *Acts and Monvments of Matters Most speciall: The seventh time newly imprinted.* 3 vols. London, 1632.

———. *An Examination of Fox's Calendars of Protestant Saints, Martyrs, & Catholic Missionary Priests.* 3 vols. London, 1826.

———. Editor. *The Whole Works of W. Tyndall, John Frith, and Doct. Barnes.* London, 1573.

Foxe, John. *A History of the Lives, Sufferings, and Triumphant Deaths.* New York, 1855.

Franklin, Benjamin. *The Autobiography of Benjamin Franklin.* Edited by Leonard W. Labaree. New Haven: Yale University Press, 1964.

Fregoso, Battista. *Baptistae Fulgosi de dictis factisqe memorabilibus collectanea.* Mediolani, 1496.

Frith, John. *A Disputacion of Purgatorye.* In John Foxe, editor. *The Whole Works of W. Tyndall, John Frith, and Doct. Barnes.* London, 1573.

Fuller, Thomas. *The History of the Holy Warre.* London, 1639.

Galateo, Antonio Ferrari. *De situ elementorum, De situ terrarum, De mari et aquis et fluviorum origine.* 8 vols. Bâle, 1558.

Galenus, Claudius. *On the Natural Faculties.* [Loeb].

Garret, Walter. [*A Discourse Concerning Antichrist*]. In *Decium Caput Apocalyseos.* London, 1698.

Gataker, Thomas. *Opera Critica.* Trajecti, 1698.

Gellius, Aulus. *Attic Nights.* [Loeb].

Genebrard, Gilbert. *Chronographia in duos Libros Distincta.* Paris, 1567.

Gennadius of Constantinople. *Dogma Ecclesiarum.* [*PL* 58].

Gerhard, Johann. *De consummatione seculi.* In *Loci theologici.* Vol. 9.

———. *De extremo judicio consummatione seculi, inferna, vita aeterna.* In *Loci theologici.* Vol. 9.

———. *De Novissimis in Genere.* In *Loci theologici.* Vol. 8.

———. *Loci theologici cum pro adstruenda veritate* (1610–22). 9 vols. Berlin, 1863–70.

———. *Meditatione Sacrae.* 1606.

Godwin, Francis. *The Man in the Moone.* London, 1638.

Golius, Jacob. *Lexicon Arabico-Latinum, Contextum ex probationibus orientis Lexicographis.* Leyden, 1653.

Good Things to Come; or, A setting forth of some of the great things that will contemporize and take place when our Lord Christ shall come again, mentioned in the Holy Scripture . . . By P.G.B. London, 1675.

Goodwin, Thomas. *Christ Set Forth in His Death.* London, 1651. In Goodwin, *Works.* 4:1–91.

———. *A Discourse of the Blessed State of Glory which the Saints Possess After Death.* In *Works.* 7:339–471.

———. *An Exposition of the Revelation.* In *Works.* 3:1–225.

————. *The Works of Thomas Goodwin*. 12 vols. Edited by John C. Miller. Edinburgh: James Nichol, 1860–66.

Gousset, Jacques. *Commentarii linguae ebraicae*. Amstelaedami, 1702.

Green, John. *Letters to the author of the Discourse of the Grounds and Reasons of the Christian Religion*. London, 1726.

Greenhill, William. *Exposition of the Prophet Ezekiel*. 5 vols. 1645–62.

Gregory the Great. St. *Epistle 29*. [*PL* 77].

Grembs, Franciscus Oswaldus. [*Concerning the Origin of Things*]. In *Arbor integra et ruinosa hominis. Id est: Tractatus medicus theoretico practus*. Frankfurt, 1657.

Grotius, Hugo. *Annotationes in Vetus et Novum Testamentum Juxta Editionem Amstelaedamensem, MDCLXXIX* (1642). 2 vols. London, 1727.

————. *De Origine Gentium Americanarum*. Paris, 1642.

————. *De Veritate Religionis Christianae*. Paris, 1627. Translated as *Of the Truth of the Christian Religion in Six Books*. Eighth English Edition. London, 1779.

————. *Historia Gothorum, Vandalorum, & Langobardorum*. Amsterdam, 1655.

Guertler, Nicholas. *Dissertationes de Jesu Christo in gloriam evecto*. Franeker, 1740.

Gulonius, Nicolaus. *The Discussion of St. Gregentius, archbishop of Taphar with the Jew Herban*. Translated and edited by William Thomas Radius. Ann Arbor: University of Michigan Press, 1939.

————. *Sancti patris nostri Gregentii, archiepiscopi Tephrensis, Disputatio cum Herbano Iudaeo*. Lvtetiae [Paris], 1586.

Hackspan, Theodoricus. *Exercitatio de Cabbala Judaica*. Altdorphi, 1660.

————. *Observationes Arabico-Syriacae in quaedam Loca Veteris et Novi Testamentum*. Altdorphi, 1639.

Hammond, Henry. *A Paraphrase and Annotations Upon all the Books of The New Testament* (1653). In *Works*. 3:3–841.

————. *A Second Defence of the Learned Hugo Grotius* (1655). In *Works*. 2:77–82.

————. *The Works of the Rev. and Learned Henry Hammond*. 4 vols. Seventh Edition Corrected and Enlarged. London, 1702.

Hanneman, Johannes Ludovicus. *Nebo Chemicus, au viatorium ostendens viam in Palestinam auriferam*. Kiloni, 1714.

Happel, Eberhard Werner. *Relationes Curiosae* (1684). In *Größte Denkwürdigkeiten der Welt oder Sogenannte Relationes Curiosae*. Edited by Uwe Hübner and Jürgen Westphal. Berlin: Rütten & Loening, 1990.

Heidegger, Hans Heinrich. *Historia sacra patriarcharum, exercitationes selectae*. 2 vols. Amsterdam, 1667–81.

Helmont, Johannes Baptista van. *Ortus Medicinae*. Amsterdam, 1648.

Herbert, George. "The Church Militant" (1633). In *The English Poems of George Herbert*. Edited by C. A. Patrides. 1974. London: J. M. Dent, 1984. Pp. 193–200.

Herodotus. *The History*. Translated by David Grene. Chicago: University of Chicago Press, 1987.

Hesiod. *Work and Day*. [Loeb].

Heurne, Jan van (Johannes Heurnius). *Institutiones Medicinae*. 4 vols. Lugduni Batavorum, 1592.

Hippolytus Martyr, St. "Appendix to the Works of Hippolytus." In Roberts, *Ante-Nicene*. 5:247.

————. *Refutation of all Heresies*. In Roberts, *Ante-Nicene*. 5:9–162.

————. *Treatise on Christ and Antichrist*. In Roberts, *Ante-Nicene*. 5:212–14.

Hobbes, Thomas. *Leviathan; or, The Matter, Forme and Power of a Commonwealth*

Ecclesiasticall and Civil (1651). Edited by Michael Oakeshott. New York: Collier Books, 1962.

Holmes, Nathaniel. *Exercitations on the Chiliasme, the Burning of the World.* London, 1664.

———. *Miscellania; Consisting of three treatises.* London, 1666.

———. *The Resurrection revealed, & raised above doubts.* London, 1661.

Homer. *Iliad.* [Loeb].

———. *Odyssey.* [Loeb].

Homilia De Sancta Blandina Lugdunensi. [PL 50].

Horn, Georg (Hornius). *De origine Gentium Americanarum* [*De Originibus Americanis*]. The Hague, 1652.

Hottinger, Johan Heinrich. *Analecta historico-theologica* (1625). Tiguri, 1652.

Huet, Pierre Daniel. *Tractatus de situ Paradisi terrestris, adjecit ejusdem commentarius de navigationibvs Salomonis.* Amsterdam, 1698.

Huit, Ephraim. *The Prophecies of Daniel Explained.* London, 1643.

Hutchinson, Samuel. *A Declaration of a Future Glorious Estate of a Church to be Here upon Earth.* London, 1667.

Irenaeus, St. *Against Heresies.* In Roberts, *Ante-Nicene.* 1:309–567.

Jackson, Thomas. *Works.* 3 vols. London, 1673.

Jerome, St. *The Apology Against the Books of Rufinus.* [PL 28].

———. *Commentary on Daniel.* [PL 25].

———. *Commentary on Genesis IV.16.* [PL 28].

———. *Commentary on the Epistle to the Galatians.* [PL 26].

———. *Commentary on the Prophet Isaiah.* [PL 24].

———. *De Poenitentia.* [PL 22].

———. *De Principiis.* In Roberts, *Ante-Nicene.* 4:71–123.

———. *De Situ et Nominibus Locorum Hebraicorum.* [*Books of Hebrew Names and Places*]. [PL 23].

———. *Dialogus Contra Luciferianos.* [PL 23].

———. *Homily on Psalm 5.* In Deferrari, *Fathers.* 48:15–24.

Johnson, Edward. *Wonder-Working Providence of Sions Saviour in New England* (1654). In *Johnson's Wonder-Working Providence.* Original Narratives of Early American History. Edited by J. Franklin Jameson. New York: Charles Scribner's Sons, 1910.

Jornandes of Ravenna (Jordanes). *De origine actibusque Getarum gentis.* Sixth century.

———. *De summa temporum vel origine actibusque gentis Romanorum.* Sixth century.

Josephus, Flavius. *Jewish Wars* (c. 75) and *Antiquities of the Jews* (c. 93). In *The Complete Works of Josephus.* Translated by William Whiston. Grand Rapids: Kregel Publications, 1960.

Joye, George. *The coniectures of the ende of the worlde.* Antverp, 1548.

Jurieu, Pierre. *The Accomplishment of the Scripture Prophecies; or, The approaching deliverance of the Church.* Amsterdam, 1686. London, 1687.

———. *The Balance of the Sanctuary.* London, 1686.

Justin Martyr, St. *Dialogue with Trypho.* In Deferrari, *Fathers.* 6:147–366.

———. *Exhortation to the Greeks.* In Deferrari, *Fathers.* 6:373–436.

———. *First Apology.* In Deferrari, *Fathers.* 6:33–111.

———. *The Monarchy, or the Rule of God.* In Deferrari, *Fathers.* 6:443–55.

———. *Second Apology.* In Deferrari, *Fathers.* 6:119–35.

Kidder, Richard. *A Demonstration of the Messias, in which the truth of the Christian Religion is proved especially against the Jews.* London, 1684–1700.

Kimchi, David (Kimhi). *Commentariis in decem Psalmos priores Heb. & Lat.* In Adrian Reland, *Analecta Rabbinica.*

———. *Hosee cum Thargum . . . & commentariis . . . R. Abraham Aben Ezra . . . & David Kimchi.* Parisiis, 1556.

———. *Mikhol.* 1532.

———. *Sefer ha-Shorashin.* C. 1480.

Kircher, Athanasius. *Mundus subterraneous, in XII libros digestus.* Amsterdam, 1665. Translated as *The Vulcano's; or, Burning and Fire-Vomiting Mountains, famous in the World.* London, 1669.

Knolles, Richard. *The Turkish History From the Original of that Nation to the Growth of the Ottoman Empire.* 2 vols. London, 1687.

The Koran. Translated by N. J. Dawood. Harmondsworth: Penguin Books, 1974.

Lactantius. *De Falsa Religione.* In Deferrari, *Fathers.* 49:15–93.

———. *De Falsa Sapientia.* In Deferrari, *Fathers.* 49:164–244.

———. *De Ira Dei.* In Deferrari, *Fathers.* 54:59–116.

———. *Divine Institutes.* [PL 6]. In Deferrari, *Fathers.* 49:3–541.

Laertius, Diogenes. *Life of Zeno.* [Loeb].

Lange, Joachim. *Causa Dei et religionis Judaeis revelatae.* Halle, 1726.

———. *Medicina mentis.* Berlin, 1708.

La Peyrère, Isaac de. *Prae-adamitae* (1655). Translated as *Men Before Adam.* London, 1656.

Lapide, Cornelius à (Cornelius van den Steen). *Commentaria in Vetus et Novum Testamentum.* Antverp, 1616–79.

Lee, Samuel. *De Excidio Antichristi.* London, 1659.

———. *The Great Day of Judgment.* Boston, 1692.

———. *Orbis Miraculum, or the Temple of Solomon.* London, 1659.

L'Empereur, Constantin (Van Oppick). *Clavis Talmudica.* 1634–1714.

Leslie, Charles. *A Discourse shewing who they are that are now qualifi'd to administer Baptism and the Lord's Supper. Wherein the Cause of Episcopacy is briefly treated.* London, 1698.

Levita, Elijah (Bahur ben Asher ha-Levi Ashkenazi). *Tishbi.* 1541.

Lightfoot, John. *The Harmony, Chronicle, and Order of the New Testament.* London, 1655. In Lightfoot, *Works.* 3:1–471.

———. *Hebrew and Talmudical Exercitations upon the Romans.* In *Works.* 12:1–593.

———. Editor. *The Samaritan Pentateuch.* In Brian Walton, *Biblia Sacra Polyglotta.* London, 1657.

———. *The Temple, especially as it stood in the Days of Our Saviour.* London, 1650. In *Works.* 9:207–481.

———. *The Whole Works of the Rev. John Lightfoot, D.D.* Edited by John Rogers Pitman. 13 vols. London, 1822–25.

Lipsius, Justus (Joest Lips). *De constantia. Manuductio ad Stoicam philosophiam.* Antverp, 1605.

Longinus. *On the Sublime.* [Loeb].

Lowth, William. *A Commentary on the Larger and Lesser Prophets.* London, 1714–25.

———. *A Commentary on the Prophet Isaiah.* London, 1714.

———. *A Commentary upon the Prophet Ezekiel.* London, 1723.

Lucanus, Marcus Annaeus. *Bellum Civile.* [Loeb].

———. *Pharsalia.* [Loeb].

Lucian. *Charon, or the Inspectors.* [Loeb].

Lucretius. *De rerum natura.* [*On the Nature of the Universe*]. [Loeb].

Luther, Martin. *Against Latomus* (1521). In *Luther's Works.* 32:133–260.

———. *Lectures on Genesis* 25:7–10. In *Luther's Works.* 4:300–409.

———. *Luther's Works.* 55 vols. Edited by Jaroslav Pelikan. St. Louis: Concordia Publishing House, 1964.

———. "Preface to the Second Epistle of St. Peter." In *Luther's Works.* 35:390–92.

Lyranus. (Nicholas de Lyre). *De Messia . . . ad Judaei argumenta, De diversis contra Judaeos.* C. 1300.

Maldonado, Juan de. *Commentarii in Prophetas quatuor, Jeremiam, Baruch, Ezechielem, & Danielem.* Lyons, 1606.

Malvenda, Tomas. *De Antichristo libri XI.* Rome, 1604.

Manlius, Johannes. *Locorum communium collectanea.* Budissinae, 1565.

Marcellinus, Ammianus. *Ammianus Marcellinus.* [Loeb].

Marochitanus, Samuel (Marrochianus). *The Blessed Jew of Marocco; or, A Blackmoor made White, Being a demonstration of the true Messias of the Law and Prophets.* York, 1648.

———. [*The Coming of the Messiah*]. Amsterdam, 1648. In *Bibliotheca Maxima Veterum Patrum et antiquorum Scriptorum ecclesiasticorum.* 27 vols. Lyons, 1677. Vol. 18.

Marshall, Benjamin. *Chronological Tables. In which are contain'd not only all the chief things of sacred history from the creation of the world 'till Christ's time, but also all other the most remarkable things of those times that are recorded in any of the antient writers now extant.* Oxford, 1712–13.

———. *A Chronological Treatise upon the Seventy Weeks of Daniel.* London, 1725.

Martin, David. *A Critical Dissertation . . . against the objections of Mr. Simon and the Modern Arians* (1717). London, 1719.

Masius, Andreas. *Epistola populi Nestoriani, quam anno MDLII ex Mozal.* Antverp, 1573.

Mason, John. *The Midnight Cry. Sermon on the Parable of the Ten Virgins.* London, 1691.

Mather, Cotton. *An Advice, to the Churches of the Faithful.* Boston, 1702.

———. *American Tears Upon the Ruines of the Greek Churches.* Boston, 1701.

———. *The Angel of Bethesda.* Edited by Gorden W. Jones. Barre, MA: American Antiquarian Society and Barre Publishers, 1972.

———. *The Armour of Christianity.* Boston, 1704.

———. *Balsamum Vulnerarium.* Boston, 1692.

———. *Batteries upon the Kingdom of the Devil.* London, 1695.

———. "Biblia Americana." MS. 6 folio vols. Massachusetts Historical Society.

———. *Boanerges.* Boston, 1727.

———. *Bonifacius: Essay Upon the Good.* Boston, 1710.

———. *Bonifacius.* Edited by David Levin. Cambridge: Harvard University Press, 1966.

———. *Brontologia Sacra.* London, 1695.

———. *The Case of a Troubled Mind.* Boston, 1717.

———. *A Christian Conversing with the Great Mystery of Christianity.* Boston, 1709.

———. *The Christian Philosopher.* London, 1720/21.

———. *Christianus per Ignem.* Boston, 1702.

———. *Coelestinus.* Boston, 1723.

———. *Coheleth.* Boston, 1720.

———. *The Comfortable Chambers.* Boston, 1728.

———. *A Companion for Communicants.* Boston, 1690.

———. *Corderius Americanus.* Boston, 1708.

———. "Curiosa Americana." MS. American Antiquarian Society.

———. *The Day, & the Work of the Day.* Boston, 1693.

———. *Decennium Luctuosum.* Boston, 1699.

———. *The Diary of Cotton Mather.* Edited by Worthington C. Ford. Collections of the Massachusetts Historical Society. 7th series. Vols. 7–8. Boston, 1911–12.

———. *The Diary of Cotton Mather . . . for the Year 1712.* Edited by William R. Manierre II. Charlottesville: University Press of Virginia, 1964.

———. *Fair Dealing between Debtor and Creditor.* Boston, 1715/16.

———. *Fair Weather.* Boston, 1692.

———. *Faith Encouraged.* Boston, 1718.

———. *The Faith of the Fathers.* Boston, 1699.

———. *Frontiers Well-Defended.* Boston, 1707.

———. *A Glorious Espousal.* Boston, 1719.

———. *The Glorious Throne.* Boston, 1714.

———. *The Heavenly Conversation.* Boston, 1710.

———. *An Heavenly Life.* Boston, 1719.

———. *India Christiana.* Boston, 1721.

———. *A Letter Concerning the Terrible Sufferings of our Protestant Brethren.* Boston, 1701.

———. *Magnalia Christi Americana.* London, 1702. Facsimile reprint. New York: Arno Press, 1972.

———. *Malachi.* Boston, 1717.

———. *Manuductio Ad Ministerium.* Boston, 1726.

———. *Memorable Providences.* Boston, 1689.

———. *Menachem.* Boston, 1716.

———. *A Midnight Cry.* Boston, 1692.

———. *The Negro Christianized.* Boston, 1706.

———. *Observanda.* Boston, 1695.

———. *Ornaments for the Daughters of Zion.* Cambridge, 1691. Facsimile reprint of the Third Edition (1741). Edited by Pattie Cowell. Delmar, NY: Scholar's Facsimiles & Reprints, 1978.

———. *The Palm-bearers.* Boston, 1725.

———. *Parentator* (1724). In *Two Mather Biographies.* Edited by William J. Scheick. Bethlehem, PA: Lehigh University Press, 1989.

———. *Paterna: The Autobiography of Cotton Mather.* Edited by Ronald A. Bosco. Delmar, NY: Scholar's Facsimiles & Reprints, 1976.

———. *Perswasion from the Terror of the Lord.* Boston, 1711.

———. *Preparatory Meditations upon the Day of Judgment,* prefixed to Lee, *Great Day.*

———. *The Present State of New England.* Boston, 1690.

———. "Problema Theologicum." MS. American Antiquarian Society. 1703.

———. *Psalterium Americanum.* Boston, 1718.

———. "Quotidiana." MS. American Antiquarian Society.

———. *Ratio Disciplinae Fratrum.* Boston, 1726.

———. *The Salvation of the Soul Considered.* Boston, 1720.

———. *Selected Letters of Cotton Mather.* Edited by Kenneth Silverman. Baton Rouge: Louisiana State University Press, 1971.

———. *Shaking Dispensations.* Boston, 1715.

———. *A Short History of New-England.* Boston, 1694.

———. *Some Seasonable Enquiries Offered.* Boston, 1723.

———. *A Speech made unto His Excellency, Samuel Shute.* Boston, 1720.

———. *The Stone Cut out of the Mountain.* Boston, 1716.

——. *Suspiria Vinctorum*. Boston, 1726.

——. *Tela Praevisa*. Boston, 1724.

——. *Terra Beata*. Boston, 1726.

——. *Terribilia Dei*. Boston, 1697.

——. *The Terror of the Lord*. Boston, 1727.

——. *Theopolis Americana*. Boston, 1710.

——. *Things for a Distressed People to think upon*. Boston, 1696.

——. *Things to be Look'd for. Discourses on the Glorious Characters, with Conjectures on the Speedy Approaches of that State, which is reserved for the Church of God in the Latter Days*. Cambridge, 1691.

——. *Things to be More Thought upon*. Boston, 1713.

——. *Thoughts for the Day of Rain*. Boston, 1712.

——. *Tokens for the Children of New-England*. Third Edition. Boston, 1728.

——. "Triparadisus: A Discourse Concerning the Threefold Paradise" (1712, 1726/27). MS. American Antiquarian Society. All references are to the present edition of this text.

——. *The Triumphs of the Reformed Religion in America*. Boston, 1691.

——. *Une Grande Voix Du Ciel A La France*. Boston, 1725.

——. *Unum Necessarium*. Boston, 1693.

——. *Utilia*. Boston, 1716.

——. *Victorina*. Boston, 1717.

——. *A Voice from Heaven*. Boston, 1719.

——. *The Voice of God in a Tempest*. Boston, 1723.

——. *What Should be most of all Tho't upon*. Boston, 1713.

——. *Winter-Meditations*. Boston, 1693.

——. *The Wonderful Works of God Commemorated*. Boston, 1690.

——. *The Wonders of the Invisible World*. Boston, 1693. In *The Witchcraft Delusion in New England*. 3 vols. Edited by Samuel G. Drake. 3 vols. 1866. Reprint. New York: Burt Franklin, 1970. Vol. 1.

——. *The World Alarm'd*. Boston, 1721.

Mather, Increase. *Angelographia*. Boston, 1696.

——. *A Call from Heaven*. Boston, 1685.

——. *Diatriba de Signo Filii Hominis, et de Secundo Messiae Adventu*. Amsterdam, 1682.

——. "A Discourse Concerning the glorious state of the church on earth under the New Jerusalem" (c. 1692–95). Edited by Mason I. Lowance and David Watters. In "Increase Mather's 'New Jerusalem': Millennialism in Late Seventeenth-Century New England." *Publications of the American Antiquarian Society* 87 (1977): 343–408.

——. *A Disquisition Concerning the State of the Souls of Men After the Death of the Body*. Boston, 1707.

——. *A Dissertation, Wherein the Strange Doctrine*. Boston, 1708.

——. *A Dissertation Concerning the Future Conversion of the Jewish Nation*. London, 1709.

——. *An Essay For the Recording of Illustrious Providences*. Boston, 1684.

——. *Meditations on the Glory of the Heavenly World*. Boston, 1711.

——. *The Mystery of Israel's Salvation*. London, 1669.

——. *Kometographia*. Boston, 1683.

Mather, Samuel [great uncle]. *The Figures and Types of the Old Testament*. Dublin, 1683.

Mather, Samuel [son]. *The Life of the Very Reverend and Learned Cotton Mather.* Boston, 1729.

Maton, Robert. *Israels Redemption; or, The propheticall history of our Saviours kingdome on earth.* London, 1642.

———. *Israels Redemption Redeemed; or, The Jewes generall and miraculous conversion.* London, 1646.

Mayer, Johann Friedrich. *Bibliotheca Biblica: complectens Qui perpetuos in Scripturam S. Commentarios scripserunt ex Reformatorum ordine.* Gryphiswaldiae, 1690.

Mede, Joseph. *Clavis Apocalyptica.* London, 1627.

———. *Paraleipomena. Remaines On some Passages in the Revelation.* London, 1640.

———. *The Works of the Pious and Profoundly Learned Joseph Mede.* Edited by John Worthington. Fourth Edition. London, 1677.

Menasseh ben Israel, *Esperanza de Israel.* Amsterdam, 1648. Translated as *Spes Israelis.* Amsterdam, 1650. Translated as *The Hope of Israel* (1650). Second Edition. London, 1652.

Methodius Patarenes. *The Banquet of the Ten Virgins; or, Concerning Chastity.* In Roberts, *Ante-Nicene.* 6:309–55.

Minucius Felix, Marcus. *Octavius.* In Deferrari, *Fathers.* 10:321–402.

Miscellanea curiosa sive Ephemeridum medico-physicarum Germanicarum; decuriae. Norimbergae, 1670–1706.

Montezinos (Montezinus), Antonio de. *Relacion de Aharon Levi, alias Antonio de Montezinos* (1644). In Menasseh ben Israel, *Hope of Israel.* Pp. 11–17.

Morata, Fulvia Olympia. *Olympia F. Moratae, Mulieris Omnium Eruditissimae, Latina et Graeca.* Basileae, 1558.

More, Henry. *Apocalypsis Apocalypseos; or, The Revelation of St. John the Divine revealed.* London, 1680.

———. *The Immortality of the Soul.* London, 1659.

———. *A Plain and Continued Exposition of the Several Prophecies or Divine Visions of the Prophet Daniel.* London, 1681.

———. *Treatise Against Atheisme.* London, 1653.

Moses ben Leon. *Zohar.* In *Zohar: The Book of Enlightenment.* Edited by Gershom Scholem. Translated by Daniel Chanan Matt. New York: Paulist Press, 1983.

Moulin, Pierre du. *Vates, seu de praecognitione futurorum et bonis malisque Prophetis.* Leyden, 1640.

Münster, Sebastian. *Biblia Hebraica.* Basileae, 1534–35.

———. *Cosmographia.* Basileae, 1544.

Napier, John (Neper). *A plain discovery of the whole Revelation of St. John.* Edinburgh, 1645.

Nepos. *Refutation of the Allegorists.* Third century.

Newton, Sir Isaac. *Observations upon the Prophecies of Daniel, and the Apocalypse of St. John.* London, 1733.

Nicéron, Jean Pierre. *Mémoires pour servir à l'Histoire des hommes illustres dans la république des lettres.* 44 vols. Paris, 1729–45.

Nicholas of Cusa. *Prohemium.* Paris, 1514.

Niger, Marius. *Geographia Asiae.*

Noyes, Nicholas. *New-Englands Duty and Interest.* Boston, 1698.

Oakes, Urian. *New-England Pleaded with.* Cambridge, 1673.

Oecumenius. *Epist. II S. Petri Cap. III. 5–9.* [PG 119].

Olearius, Adam (Oelschlaeger). *Newe Orientalische Reise* (1647). Translated as *The Voyages & Travels of the Ambassadors sent by Frederick duke of Holstein, to the great Duke of Muscovy, and the King of Persia*. London, 1662.

Origen. *Contra Celsum*. [*PG* 11].

———. *De Principiis*. In Roberts, *Ante-Nicene*. 4:71–123.

———. *De Resurrectione*. [*PG* 13].

———. *Genesis Homilia VI*. [*PG* 12].

———. *Homily 7*. In Deferrari, *Fathers*. 71:127–35.

Orosius, Paulus. *History Against the Pagans*. In Deferrari, *Fathers*. 50:1–366.

Ovid. *Amores*. [Loeb].

———. *Metamorphoses*. [Loeb].

Palladius of Helenopolis. *Lausiac History*. C. 419–20.

Panciroli, Guido. *Rerum memorabilium*. Venice, 1599. Translated as *The History of Many Memorable Things lost . . . with a Commentary . . . from Salmuth's annotations*. London, 1715.

Panvinio, Onofria. *De Sibyllis et Carminibus Sibyllinus*. Venice, 1558.

Pareus, David. *Opera theologica exegetica*. 3 vols. Frankfurt, 1647.

Parkman, Ebenezer. *The Diary of Ebenezer Parkman, 1703–1782*. Edited by Francis G. Walett. Worcester: American Antiquarian Society, 1974.

Peganius, A. B. (Christian Knorr von Rosenroth). *A Genuine Explication of the Visions of the Book of Revelation*. London, 1670.

Pepys, Samuel. *The Diary of Samuel Pepys*. 2 vols. Edited by Henry B. Wheatley. New York: Random House, n.d.

Peritsol, R. Abraham ben Mordecai (Peritzol, Farissol). *Itinera Mundi* (1524). Venice, 1587.

Perron, Jacques Davy Du. *Opera Omnia*. 3 vols. Paris, 1620. 2 vols. Cologne, 1682.

Peutinger, Konrad. *Die Peutingersche Tafel*. Edited by Konrad Miller. Stuttgart: F. A. Brockhaus, 1962.

Philo Judaeus. *De Aeternitale Mundi*. [Loeb].

———. *De Fuga et Inventione*. [Loeb].

———. *De Opificio Mundi*. [Loeb].

———. *Legum Allegoriarum*. [Loeb].

———. *Questiones et Solutiones in Genesin*. [Loeb].

Photius of Byzantium. *Bibliotheca*. C. 858. [*PG* 103–4].

Pierce, Richard D. Editor. *The Records of the First Church in Salem, 1629–1736*. Salem: Essex Institute, 1974.

Plato. *Critias*. [Loeb].

———. *Phaedo*. [Loeb].

———. *Philebus*. [Loeb].

———. *Republic*. [Loeb].

———. *Timaeus*. [Loeb].

———. *Work and Day*. [Loeb].

Pliny (the Elder). *Natural History*. [Loeb].

——— (the Younger). *Epistulae curatius scriptae*. [Loeb].

Plutarch. *De defectu oraculorum*. In *Moralia V* [Loeb].

———. *Lives of the Noble Grecians and Romans*. [Loeb].

———. *Moralia*. [Loeb].

———. *Sentiments Concerning Nature*. [Loeb].

Poiret, Pierre. *L'Œconomie Divine, ou système universel et démonstré des ouvres et des desseins de Dieu envers les hommes.* Amsterdam, 1687. Translated as *The Divine Œconomy.* 6 vols. London, 1713.

Pollux, Julius. *Onomasticon.* [Loeb].

——. *Physical History.* [Loeb].

Polybius. *Universal History.* [Loeb].

Pomponius Mela. *De Chorographia.* [Loeb].

Porphyry. *Against the Christians.* C. 268.

Posselius, Johannes. *Familiarium colloquiorum libellus Graece & Latine, auctus & recognitus.* London, 1681.

Postel, G. Editor and translator. *Protevangelion Jacobi, fratris domini, de natalibus Jesu Christi, et virginis Mariae.* Basileae, 1552.

Prideaux, Humphrey. *The Old and New Testament Connected in the History of the Jews, and Neighbouring Nations* [1716–18]. 2 vols. Fifteenth American Edition. New York: Harper & Brothers, 1871.

Procopius. *Wars of the Vandals.* [Loeb].

Propertius, Sextus. *Proportius.* [Loeb].

Prosper Tiro. *Chronicle.* C. 378.

Psellus, Michael. *Iamblichvs de mysteriis AEgyptiorum, Chaldaeorum, Assyriorum.* Venice 1516. In *Bibliotheca Maxima Veterum Patrum et antiquorum scriptorum ecclesiasticorum.* 27 vols. Lugduni Batavorum, 1677.

(Pseudo-) Phocylides. *The Sentences of Phocylides.*

Purchas, Samuel. *Purchas His Pilgrimage.* London, 1613.

Ptolomaeus, Claudius. *The Geography of Claudius Ptolemy.* Translated and edited by Edward Luther Stevenson. New York: Public Library, 1932.

——. *Tetrabiblos.* C. 150.

Raleigh, Sir Walter. *History of the World.* London, 1614.

Ranew, Nathaniel. *The Glory and Happiness of the Saints,* London, 1692.

——. *Practical Discourses Concerning Death.* London, 1692.

——. *Preparation for Death.* London, 1692.

Ray, John. *Three Physico-Theological Discourses.* Third Edition. London, 1713.

Reland, Adrien (Reeland, Adrian). *Analecta Rabbinica.* Second Edition. Trajecti, 1723.

——. "De situ Paradisi terrestris." In *Dissertationes miscellanearum pars tres.* 3 vols. Trajecti, 1706–8. Vol. 1.

Rivet, André (Verdaeus). *De Providentia Dei . . . De Purgatorio et Indulgentiis.* Lugduni Batavorum, 1625.

Roberts, Alexander, and James Donaldson. Editors. *The Ante-Nicene Fathers.* 10 vols. New York: Charles Scribner's Sons, 1903–26.

Salonius of Genoa. *In Ecclesiasten Expositio Mystica.* [*PL* 53].

Salvian of Marseilles. *Ad Ecclesiam.* In Deferrari, *Fathers.* 3:265–372.

——. *De Gubernatione Dei.* In Deferrari, *Fathers.* 3:21–232.

Sandys, George. *The Relation of a Journey begun an. Dom. 1610, in Four Books.* London, 1615.

Saurin, Jacques. *Discours historiques, critiques, théologiques, et moraux; sur les événemens les plus memorables du Vieux et du Nouveau Testament.* 11 vols. Amsterdam, 1720. Translated as *Dissertations, historical, critical, theological and moral, on the most memorable events of the Old and New Testaments.* London, 1723.

Savoy Declaration of Faith [1658, 1680]. In Williston Walker, *The Creeds and Platforms of Congregationalism.* 1893. Reprint. Philadelphia: Pilgrim Press, 1960. Pp. 340–408.

Schaff, Philip. Editor. *Nicene and Post-Nicene Fathers*. 14 vols. First Series. New York: Charles Scribner's Sons, 1886–89.

Schaff, Philip, and Henry Wace. Editors. *Nicene and Post-Nicene Fathers*. 14 vols. Second Series. New York: Charles Scribner's Sons, 1900–1904.

Seager, John (Seger). *A Discovery of the World to Come*. London, 1650.

Seneca, Lucius Annaeus. *Bellum Civile*. [Loeb].

———. *De providentia*. [Loeb].

———. *Epistulae Morales*. [Loeb].

———. *Naturales Quaestiones*. [Loeb].

Sewall, Samuel. *The Diary of Samuel Sewall, 1674–1729*. 2 vols. Edited by M. Halsey Thomas. New York: Farrar, Straus & Giroux, 1973.

———. *The Letter-Book of Samuel Sewall, 1674–1729*. In *Collections of the Massachusetts Historical Society*. Sixth series. Vols. 1–2. Boston, 1886–88.

———. *Phaenomena quaedam Apocalyptica* (1697). Second Edition. Boston, 1727.

———. *The Selling of Joseph*. Boston, 1700.

Shepard, Thomas. *The Church-Membership of Children, and Their Right to Baptisme*. Cambridge, 1663.

Sherlock, Thomas. *Discourses on the Use and Intent of Prophecy*. London, 1726.

———. *The Use and Intent of Prophecy, in Several Ages of the World*. London, 1725.

Sherwin, William. *The Doctrine of Christ's Glorious Kingdom*. London, 1672.

———. *The Saints Rising at the first blessed Resurrection*. London, 1674.

———. *The Times of Restitution of all things*. London, 1675.

Shute, John. *Miscellanea Sacra; or, A New Method of considering so much of the History of the Apostles, as is contained in Scripture*. 8 vols. London, 1725.

Sigonio, Carlo. *Historiarum de Occidentali Imperio libri XX*. Bononiensis, 1578.

———. *Historiarum de regne Italiae Libri XV*. Venetiis, 1574.

Simon, Richard. *L'Histoire critique du Vieux Testament*. Paris, 1678. Translated by Henry Dickinson as *A Critical History of the Old Testament*. London, 1682.

Sirach, Jesus Ben. Liber Ecclesiasticus. [Wisdom of Sirach, The Wisdom of Jesus, Son of Sirach]. Hebrew: 196 B.C.; Greek translation: 132 B.C.

Smith, John. *Christian Religions Appeal from the Groundless Prejudices of the Sceptick to the Bar of Common Reason*. London, 1675.

Smythies, William (Smithies, Smithyes). *A true Account of the Robbery and Murder of J.[ohn] Stockden, Victualler in Grub-Street, and of the Discovery of the Murderers, by the several Dreams of Elizabeth, the Wife of T. Greenwood*. London, 1698.

Solinus, Gaius Julius. *Collectanea Rerum Memorabilium*. Edited by Thomas Mommsen. 1895. Reprint. N. P. Weidmann, 1979.

Spener, Jacob. *Pia Desideria*. Frankfurt, 1675.

Spes Fidelium; or, The Believers Hope. Being an Epistolary Dissertation, wherein the Doctrine of the Millennium . . . is asserted. London, 1714.

Spinoza, Benedict (Baruch) de. *The Chief Works of Benedict de Spinoza*. 2 vols. Translated by R. H. M. Elwes. 2 vols. 1883. Reprint. New York: Dover, 1951–55.

———. *Tractatus Theologico-Politicus* (1670). In *Works* 1:1–278.

———. *Correspondence*. In *Works* 2:275–420.

Staynoe, Thomas. *Salvation by Jesus Christ alone*. London, 1700.

Stephanus. *Geographical Dictionary*. C. 500.

Steuchus, Eugubinus (Agostino Steuco). [*On the Destruction of the World*]. In *Opera Omnia*. 3 vols. Venetiis, 1591.

Stifel, Michael. *Ein sehr wunderbarlich Wortrechnung, sampt einer merklichen erklerung etlicher Zalen Danielis and der Offenbarung Sanct Johannis*. Nuremberg, 1553.

——. *Vom End der Welt and Zukunft des Endtchrists*.

Strabo. *Geography*. [Loeb].

Suetonius, Gaius Tranquillus. *Vitae Duodecim Caesarum* [*The Lives of the Caesars*]. [Loeb].

Sulpicius Severus. *Chronicle*. In Schaff and Wace, *Nicene*. 11:71–122.

Sydenham, Thomas. *Compleat Method of Curing almost all Diseases*. London, 1695.

——. *Observationes Medicae*. London, 1676.

Sykes, Arthur Ashley. *The Difference between the Kingdom of Christ and the Kingdom of this World*. London, 1717.

Tachenius, Otto. *Hippokrates chimicus*. 1660.

Tacitus. *Annales*. [Loeb].

——. *Fragments of the Histories*. [Loeb].

——. *Historia*. [Loeb].

Tavernier, Jean-Baptiste. *Voyages en Turquie, en Perse et aux Indes*. Paris, 1679.

Taylor, Thomas. *The Works of . . . Thomas Taylor*. London, 1659.

Templer, John. *Idea Theologiae Leviathanis*. London, 1673.

Temporarius, Joannes. *Chronologicarvm demonstrationvm libri tres*. Frankofvrti, 1596.

Terence. *Phormio*. [Loeb].

Tertullian. *Adversus Marcionem Libri V*. [*PL* 2]. Translated as *The Five Books Against Marcion*. In Roberts, *Ante-Nicene*. 3:269–475.

——. *Apology*. In Roberts, *Ante-Nicene*. 3:17–60.

——. *De Resurrectione Carnis*. [*PL* 1]. In Roberts, *Ante-Nicene*. 3:545–95.

——. *On the Soul*. In Roberts, *Ante-Nicene*. 3:181–235.

——. *Prayer*. In Roberts, *Ante-Nicene*. 3:61–78.

——. *Spectacles*. In Roberts, *Ante-Nicene*. 3:79–91.

——. *The Testimony of the Soul*. In Roberts, *Ante-Nicene*. 3:175–80.

Theodoret of Antioch. *Against Heresies*. C. 451.

——. *De Incarnatione*. [*PG* 84].

——. *Graecorum Affectionum Curatio*. [*PG* 84].

Theodoret of Cyr. *Interpretatio Epistolae ad Galatas*. [*PG* 82].

——. *Interpretatio Zachariae Prophetae*. [*PG* 81].

Theophilus of Antioch. *Ad Autolycum*. C. 180. In Roberts, *Ante-Nicene*. 2:85–121.

Theophrastus of Eresos. *Enquiry into Plants*. [Loeb].

Theophylact. *Expositio in Epistolam ad Galatas*. [*PG* 124].

——. *Expositio In Epistolam II S. Petri Cap. III*. [*PG* 125].

Thevet, André. *Cosmographie de Levant*. Lyon, 1556.

Thorowgood, Thomas. *Digitus dei: new discoveryes; with such arguments to prove that the Jews (a Nation) or people lost in the world for the space of near 200* [sic] *years, inhabite now in America*. London, 1652.

——. *Iewes in America; or, Probabilities that the Americans are of that race*. London, 1650.

Tibullus Albius. *Panegyricus Messallae*. [Loeb].

Tillinghast, John. *Knowledge of the Times; or, The Resolution of the question, how long it shall be unto the end of the wonders*. London, 1654.

Toland, John. *Nazarenus; or, Jewish, Gentile, and Mahometan Christianity*. London, 1718.

Tournefort, Joseph Pitton de. *Relation d'un Voyage du Levant*. Paris, 1717.

Torniellus, Augustinus (Agostino Ternielli). *Annales Sacri et profani . . . a Mundi creatione*. Frankfurt, 1647.

——. *Annales Sacri et profani ab orbe condito*. Frankfurt, 1611–13.

Trebellius Pollio. *The Thirty Tyrants*. [Loeb].

Tremellius, Immanuel, and Franciscus Junius. Translators. *Biblia Sacra, sive Testamentum Vetus ab Im. Tremellio & Fr. Iunio ex Hebraeo Latine redditum*. London, 1661.

Trithemus Johannes. *De Scriptoribus Ecclesiasticis*. 1492. Extracted in *Joannis Trithemii opera historica*. Frankfurt, 1601.

Twisse, William. "Epistles." In Joseph Mede, *Works*. Pp. 764–68, 798–99.

Ussher, James. *Annales Veteris et Novi Testamenti*. London, 1650. Translated into English. 1658.

Valesius, Henricus. *Ecclesiasticae historiae libri quinque cum interpretatione Latina et annotationibus Henrici Valesii*. Oxford, 1654.

Varenius, Bernhardus (Bernhard Varen). *Cosmographia and Geographia*. London, 1683.

——. *Geographia Generalis*. Translated by Isaac Newton. London, 1650.

Vázquez de Espinosa, Antonio. *Description of the Indies* (c. 1620). Translated by Charles Upson Clark. Smithsonian Miscellaneous Collections. Vol. 102. 1942. Reprint. Washington, DC: Smithsonian Institution Press, 1968.

Vatablus, Franciscus (François Waterbled). *Annotationes in Vetus et Novum Testamentum, Critici Sacri*. Salmant, 1584.

Vergil. *Aeneid*. [Loeb].

——. *Fourth Eclogue*. [Loeb].

——. *Georgics*. [Loeb].

Villalpando, Juan Bautista. *Apparatus urbis ac templi Hierosolymitani* (1604). In Jeronimo de Prado, *In Ezechielem explanationes et apparatus urbis, ac templi Hieroesolymitani*. Rome, 1596–1604.

Villamont, Jacques de. *Les Voyages dv Sr. de Villamont*. Arras, 1598.

Villanova, Arnold of. *Tractatus de tempore adventus Antichristi et fine mundi*. C. 1300.

Vita Sanctae Genovefae. C. 520. Edited by K. Kuenstle. Stuttgart, 1910.

Voet, Gijsbert (Voetius). *Disputatione de generati conversione Judaeorum*. Amstelaedami, 1665.

——. *Exercitiis Pietatis*. Amstelaedami, 1679.

Vopiscus, Flavius. *Aurelianus*. [Loeb].

Vossius, Gerhard Johann. *Historia Pelagiana*. Amstelaedami, 1631.

Wadsworth, Thomas. *The Immortality of the Soul*. London, 1671.

Walton, Isaac. Editor. *Biblia Sacra Polyglotta*. London, 1657.

Wanley, Nathaniel. *The Wonders of the Little World*. 6 vols. London, 1676.

Watts, Isaac. *Psalms of David Imitated in the Language of the New Testament*. London, 1719.

Webster, John. *The Displaying of Supposed Witchcraft; wherein is affirmed that there are many sorts of deceivers and imposters, and divers persons under a passive delusion of melancholy and fancy; but that there is a corporeal league between the devil and the witch, &c., is utterly disproved*. London, 1677.

Wells, Edward. *An Historical Geography of the Old Testament* (1711–12). In *An Historical Geography of the Old and New Testament*. 2 vols. Oxford: Clarendon Press, 1819. Vol. 1.

Wendelinus, Marcus Fridericus. *Christianae Theologiae*. Amsterdam, 1653.

Whiston, William. *The Accomplishment of Scripture Prophecies. Being Eight Sermons Preached at the Cathedral Church of St. Paul in the year MDCCVII*. London, 1708.

———. *An Essay on the Revelation of St. John, So far as concerns the Past and Present Times*. London, 1706.

———. *An Essay Towards Restoring the True Text of the Old Testament, and for Vindicating the Citations thence made in the New Testament*. London, 1722.

———. *The Literal Accomplishment of Scripture Prophecies*. London, 1724.

———. *A New Theory of the Earth* (1696). Fifth Edition. London, 1737.

———. *Sermons and Essays Upon Several Subjects*. London, 1709.

———. *A Supplement to the Literal Accomplishment of Scripture Prophecies*. London, 1725.

———. *A Vindication of the Sibylline Oracles*. London, 1715.

Whitby, Daniel. "A Paraphrase on . . . Romans [ch. IX–XI]," and "An Appendix to [Romans] Chap. XI. Containing A Discourse of the calling of the Jews to the Christian Faith." In *A Paraphrase and Commentary on the New Testament*. 2 vols. Edinburgh, 1761. 1:53–73, 95–107.

———. *A Treatise of the True Millennium* (1703). In *A Paraphrase*. 2:1–24.

White, Samuel. *A Commentary on the Prophet Isaiah, wherein the literal sense of his prophecy's is briefly explain'd*. London, 1709.

Wigglesworth, Michael. *The Day of Doom* (1662). In *Seventeenth-Century American Poetry*. Edited by Harrison T. Meserole. 1968. Reprint. New York: Norton, 1972. Pp. 55–113.

Willard, Samuel. *The Fountain Opened; or, The Admirable Blessings plentifully to be Dispensed at the National Conversion of the Jews* (1700). Third Edition. Appended to Samuel Sewall, *Phaenomena quaedam Apocalyptica*. Pp. 1–16 (Second Pagination). Boston, 1727.

William of Tyre. *Historia rerum in partibus trans marinis gestarum*. [PL 201].

Williams, Roger. *A Key into the Language of America*. London, 1643.

Winter, Samuel. *The Life of Samuel Winter, D.D.* (1671). In *Clarke's Lives of Eminent Persons*. London, 1683.

Winthrop, John. *A Model of Christian Charity* (1630). In *Puritan Political Ideas*. Edited by Edmund S. Morgan. New York: Bobbs-Merrill Co., 1965. Pp. 75–93.

Witsius, Herman (Wits). *Meletemata Leidensia*. Basileae, 1739.

Woodrow, Robert. *The History of the Sufferings of the Church of Scotland, from the Restauration to the Revolution*. Edinburg, 1721–22.

Xenophon. *Cyropaedia*. [Loeb].

———. *Oecomenicus*. [Loeb].

Zanchius, Hieronymous (Girolamo Zanchi, Zanchy). *De fine Seculi in 1 John 2.18*. In Zanchius, *Opera*. 7:78–92.

———. *[Immortality of the Soul]*. In *Opera*. Vol. 3.

———. *Opera omnia theologica*. 8 vols. Heidelberg, 1619.

Zosimus. *The Decline of Rome*. San Antonio: Trinity University Press, 1967.

SECONDARY WORKS

Adler, Elkan Nathan. *Jewish Travellers in the Middle Ages*. New York: Dover, 1987.

Ball, B. W. *A Great Expectation: Eschatological Thought in English Protestantism to 1660*. Leiden: E. J. Brill, 1975.

Banks, Charles E. "Thomas Venner: The Boston Wine-Cooper and Fifth Monarchy Man." *New England Historical and Genealogical Register* 47 (1893): 437–44.

Baritz, Loren. *City on a Hill: A History of Ideas and Myths in America.* New York: John Wiley & Sons, 1964.

Beall, Otho T., and Richard Shryock. "Cotton Mather: First Significant Figure in American Medicine." *Publications of the American Antiquarian Society* 63 (1954): 35–274.

Benz, Ernst. "Ecumenical Relations Between Boston Puritanism and German Pietism: Cotton Mather and August Hermann Francke." *Harvard Theological Review* 54, no. 3 (1961): 159–93.

———. "Pietist and Puritan Sources of Early Protestant World Missions." *Church History* 20, no. 2 (1951): 28–55.

Bercovitch, Sacvan. *The American Jeremiad.* Madison: University of Wisconsin Press, 1978.

———. "Cotton Mather." In *Major Writers of Early American Literature.* Edited by Everett Emerson. Madison: University of Wisconsin Press, 1972. Pp. 93–149.

———. "Horologicals to Chronometricals: The Rhetoric of the Jeremiad." In *Literary Monographs.* Vol. 3. Edited by Eric Rothstein. Madison: University of Wisconsin Press, 1970. Pp. 1–125.

———. *The Puritan Origins of the American Self.* New Haven: Yale University Press, 1975.

Berens, John F. *Providence and Patriotism in Early America, 1640–1815.* Charlottesville: University Press of Virginia, 1978.

Bernhard, Virginia. "Cotton Mather and the Doing of Good: A Puritan Gospel of Wealth." *New England Quarterly* 49 (1976): 225–41.

Boas, Ralph and Louise. *Cotton Mather: Keeper of the Puritan Conscience.* New York: Harper & Brothers, 1928.

Boyer, Paul, and Stephen Nissenbaum. *Salem Possessed: The Social Origins of Witchcraft.* Cambridge: Harvard University Press, 1974.

Bozeman, Theodore D. "The Puritans' 'Errand into the Wilderness,' Reconsidered." *New England Quarterly* 59 (1986): 231–51.

———. *To Live Ancient Lives: The Primitivist Dimension in Puritanism.* Chapel Hill: University of North Carolina Press, 1988.

Breitwieser, Mitchell R. *Cotton Mather and Benjamin Franklin.* Cambridge: Cambridge University Press, 1984.

Brumm, Ursula. *American Thought and Religious Typology.* Translated by John Hoaglund. 1963. Reprint. New Brunswick: Rutgers University Press, 1970.

Canup, John. *Out of the Wilderness: The Emergence of an American Identity in Colonial New England.* Middletown: Wesleyan University Press, 1990.

Capp, Bernard S. *The Fifth Monarchy Men: A Study in Seventeenth-Century English Millenarianism.* Totowa, NJ: Rowman & Littlefield, 1972.

———. "The Political Dimension of Apocalyptic Thought." In *The Apocalypse in English Renaissance Thought and Literature.* Edited by C. A. Patrides and J. Wittreich. Pp. 94–124.

Clendinnen, Inga. *Aztecs.* Cambridge: Cambridge University Press, 1991.

Clouse, Robert G. "Johann Heinrich Alsted and English Millennialism." *Harvard Theological Review* 62 (1969): 189–207.

———. "The Rebirth of Millenarianism." In Toon, *Puritans.* Pp. 56–65.

Cohn, Norman. *The Pursuit of the Millennium.* Revised Edition. New York: Oxford University Press, 1970.

Culver, Douglas Joel. "National Restoration of the Jewish People to Palestine in British Nonconformity, 1585–1640." Ph.D. diss., New York University, 1970.

Davidson, James W. *The Logic of Millennial Thought.* New Haven: Yale University Press, 1977.

Davis, Delmer Ivan. "Critical Editions of Samuel Sewall's *Phaenomena quaedam Apocalyptica* and *Proposals Touching the Accomplishment of Prophecies Humbly Offered.*" Ph.D. diss., University of Colorado, 1968.

Davis, Thomas M. "The Tradition of Puritan Typology." In *Typology and Early American Literature.* Edited by Sacvan Bercovitch. Amherst: University of Massachusetts Press, 1972. Pp. 11–45.

De Jong. J. A. *As the Waters Cover the Sea.* Kampen: J. H. Kok N.V., 1970.

Delbanco, Andrew. *The Puritan Ordeal.* Cambridge: Harvard University Press, 1989.

Demos, John Putnam. *Entertaining Satan: Witchcraft and the Culture of Early New England.* New York: Oxford University Press, 1982.

De Sola Poole, D. "Hebrew Learning Among the Puritans of New England Prior to 1700." *Publications of the American Jewish Historical Society* 20 (1911): 31–83.

Drake, Samuel G. Editor. *The Witchcraft Delusion in New England.* 3 vols. 1866. Reprint. New York: Burt Franklin, 1970.

Ehle, Carl Frederick, Jr. "Prolegomena to Christian Zionism in America: The Views of Increase Mather and William E. Blackstone Concerning the Doctrine of the Restoration of Israel." Ph.D. diss., New York University, 1977.

Elliott, Emory. *Power and the Pulpit in Puritan New England.* Princeton: Princeton University Press, 1975.

Erwin, John S. *The Millennialism of Cotton Mather: An Historical and Theological Analysis.* Studies in American Religion. Vol. 45. Lewiston, NY: Edwin Mellen Press, 1990.

Force, James E. "The Newtonians and Deism." In *Essays on the Context, Nature, and Influence of Isaac Newton's Theology.* Edited by James E. Force and Richard H. Popkin. Dordrecht: Kluwer Academic Publishers, 1990. Pp. 43–73.

———. *William Whiston: Honest Newtonian.* Cambridge: Cambridge University Press, 1985.

Francke, Kuno. "The Beginning of Cotton Mather's Correspondence with August Hermann Francke." *Philological Quarterly* 5 (1926): 193–95.

Franklin, Phyllis. *Show Thyself a Man.* The Hague: Mouton, 1969.

Friedman, Lee M. "Cotton Mather and the Jews." *Publications of the American Jewish Historical Society* 26 (1918): 201–10.

———. "Early Jewish Residents in Massachusetts." *Publications of the American Jewish Historical Society* 23 (1915): 79–90.

Froom, Le Roy. *The Prophetic Faith of Our Fathers: The Historical Development of Prophetic Interpretation.* 4 vols. Washington, DC: Review & Herald Publishing Association, 1946–54.

Gay, Peter, *A Loss of Mastery.* Berkeley: University of California Press, 1966.

Gilsdorf, Joy B. "The Puritan Apocalypse: New England Eschatology in the Seventeenth Century." Ph.D. diss, Yale University, 1964.

Graubard, Mark. *Witchcraft and the Nature of Man.* Lanham, MD: University Press of America, 1984.

Gura, Philip. *A Glimpse of Sion's Glory.* Middletown: Wesleyan University Press, 1984.

Hall, David D. Editor. *Witch-Hunting in Seventeenth-Century New England: A Documentary History, 1638–1692.* Boston: Northeastern University Press, 1991.

Hall, Michael G. *The Last American Puritan: The Life of Increase Mather.* Middletown: Wesleyan University Press, 1988.

Hambrick-Stowe, Charles E. *The Practice of Piety: Puritan Devotional Disciplines in Seventeenth-Century New England.* Chapel Hill: University of North Carolina Press, 1982.

Hansen, Chadwick. *Witchcraft at Salem.* 1969. Reprint. New York: New American Library, 1970.

Hatch, Nathan O. *The Sacred Cause of Liberty: Republican Thought and the Millennium in Revolutionary New England.* New Haven: Yale University Press, 1977.

Heimert, Alan. *Religion and the American Mind.* Cambridge: Harvard University Press, 1966.

Hill, Christopher. *The Collected Essays of Christopher Hill.* 2 vols. Amherst: University of Massachusetts Press, 1986.

———. "Religion and Politics in Seventeenth-Century England." In *Collected Essays.* 2:175–201.

———. "Till the Conversion of the Jews." In *Collected Essays.* 2:269–300. Reprinted in *Millenarianism and Messianism in English Literature and Thought, 1650–1800.* Edited by Richard H. Popkin. Leiden: E. J. Brill, 1988. Pp. 12–36.

———. *The World Turned Upside Down.* 1972. Reprint. Harmondsworth: Penguin Books, 1975.

Holmes, Thomas J. *Cotton Mather: A Bibliography of His Works.* 3 vols. Cambridge: Harvard University Press, 1940.

Holstun, James. *A Rational Millennium: Puritan Utopias of Seventeenth-Century England and America.* New York: Oxford University Press, 1987.

Huddleston, Lee Eldridge. *Origins of the American Indians.* Austin: University of Texas Press, 1967.

Huhner, Leon. "The Jews of New England (Other than Rhode Island) Prior to 1800." *Publications of the American Jewish Historical Society* 11 (1903): 75–99.

Hutchison, William R. *Errand to the World: American Protestant Thought and Foreign Missions.* Chicago: University of Chicago Press, 1987.

Isani, Mukhtar Ali, ed. "The Pouring of the Sixth Vial: A Letter in a Taylor-Sewall Debate." *Massachusetts Historical Society Proceedings* 83 (1971): 123–29.

Karlson, Carol F. *The Devil in the Shape of a Woman.* 1987. Reprint. New York: Vintage Books, 1989.

Katz, David S. "English Redemption and Jewish Readiness in 1656." *Journal of Jewish Studies* 34 (1983): 73–76.

———. *Philo-Semitism and the Readmission of the Jews to England, 1603–1655.* Oxford: Clarendon Press, 1982.

Kittredge, George L. *Witchcraft in Old and New England.* 1929. Reprint. New York: Russell & Russell, 1956.

Korshin, Paul J. *Typologies in England, 1650–1820.* Princeton: Princeton University Press, 1982.

Lamont, William M. *Richard Baxter and the Millennium.* Totowa, NJ: Rowman & Littlefield, 1979.

Lamont, William M., and Sibyl Oldfield. Editors. *Politics, Religion and Literature in the Seventeenth Century.* Totowa, NJ: Rowman & Littlefield, 1975.

LaPlanche, François. *L'Écriture, le sacré et l'histoire: Erudits et politiques protestants devant la Bible en France au XVIIe siècle.* Amsterdam: APA-Holland University Press, 1986.

Levin, David. *Cotton Mather: The Young Life of the Lord's Remembrancer, 1663–1703*. Cambridge: Harvard University Press, 1978.

——. Introduction. In Cotton Mather, *Bonifacius*. Edited by David Levin. Cambridge: Harvard University Press, 1966.

——. "Trying to Make a Monster Human." In *Forms of Uncertainty: Essays in Historical Criticism*. Charlottesville and London: University Press of Virginia, 1992. Pp. 157–76.

——. "When Did Cotton Mather See the Angel?" *Early American Literature* 15 (1980): 271–75.

Levy, Babette M. *Cotton Mather*. Boston: Twayne Publishers, 1979.

Lovejoy, David S. *The Glorious Revolution in America*. 1972. Reprint. Middletown: Wesleyan University Press, 1987.

Lovelace, Richard F. *The American Pietism of Cotton Mather*. Washington DC: Christian University Press, 1979.

Lowance, Mason I., Jr. *The Language of Canaan*. Cambridge: Harvard University Press, 1980.

——. "Typology and Millennial Eschatology in Early New England." In *Literary Uses of Typology*. Edited by Earl Minor. Princeton: Princeton University Press, 1977. Pp. 228–73.

Lowance, Mason I., Jr., and David Watters. "Increase Mather's 'New Jerusalem': Millennialism in Late Seventeenth-Century New England." *Publications of the American Antiquarian Society* 87 (1977): 343–408.

Lowrie, Ernest Benson. *The Shape of the Puritan Mind: The Thought of Samuel Willard*. New Haven: Yale University Press, 1974.

Maclear, James F. "New England and the Fifth Monarchy: The Quest for the Millennium in Early American Puritanism." *New England Quarterly* 32 (1975): 223–60.

Manuel, Frank E. *A Portrait of Isaac Newton*. 1968. Reprint. Washington, DC: New Republic Books, 1979.

Marvin, Abijah P. *The Life and Times of Cotton Mather*. Boston: Congregational Sunday-School & Publishing Society, 1892.

M'Clintock, John Rev. Editor. *Cyclopaedia of Biblical, Theological, and Ecclesiastical Literature*. 12 vols. Grand Rapids: Baker Book House, 1968.

Meserole, Harrison T. Editor. *Seventeenth-Century American Poetry*. 1968. Reprint. New York: W. W. Norton, 1972.

Middlekauff, Robert. *The Mathers: Three Generations of Puritan Intellectuals, 1596–1728*. New York: Oxford University Press, 1971.

Miller, Perry. *Errand into the Wilderness*. 1956. Reprint. New York: Harper & Row, 1964.

——. *Jonathan Edwards*. 1949. Reprint. Westport, CT: Greenwood Press, 1973.

——. *The New England Mind: From Colony to Province*. 1953. Reprint. Cambridge: Harvard University Press, 1983.

——. *The New England Mind: The Seventeenth Century*. 1939. Reprint. Cambridge: Harvard University Press, 1982.

Morgan, Edmund S. Editor. *Puritan Political Ideas*. New York: Bobbs-Merrill Co., 1965.

Murdock, Kenneth B. *Increase Mather: The Foremost American Puritan*. Cambridge: Harvard University Press, 1925.

Niebuhr, H. Richard. *The Kingdom of God in America*. 1937. Reprint. Middletown: Wesleyan University Press, 1988.

O'Higgins, James, S.J. *Anthony Collins: The Man and His Works*. The Hague: Martinus Nijhoff, 1970.

Owen, Denise E. "Satan's Fierce Darts: Explorations in the Experience and Concept of the Demonic in Seventeenth-Century New England." Ph.D. diss., Princeton University, 1974.

Parrington, Vernon L. *Main Currents in American Thought.* 3 vols. New York: Harcourt Brace, 1927.

Patrides, C. A., and Joseph Wittreich. Editors. *The Apocalypse in English Renaissance Thought and Literature.* Ithaca: Cornell University Press, 1984.

Paulys Real-Encyclopaedie der Classischen Altertumswissenschaft. 49 vols. Stuttgart: Metzlersche Verlagsbuchhandlung, 1894–1967.

Plomer, H. R. *Dictionary of Printers and Booksellers.* London: Bibliographic Society, 1977.

Pope, Alan. "New England Versus the New England Mind: The Myth of Declension." *Journal of Social History* 3, no. 2 (1969–70): 95–108.

Popkin, Richard H. Editor. *Millenarianism and Messianism in English Literature and Thought, 1650–1800.* Leiden: E. J. Brill, 1988.

———. "Newton as a Bible Scholar." In *Essays on the Context, Nature, and Influence of Isaac Newton's Theology.* Edited by James E. Force and Richard H. Popkin. Dordrecht: Kluwer Academic Publishers, 1990. Pp. 103–18.

Quistorp, Heinrich. *Calvin's Doctrine of the Last Things.* Translated by Harold Knight. London, 1955.

Radius, William Thomas. Editor. *The Discussion of St. Gregentius, archbishop of Taphar, with the Jew Herban.* Ann Arbor: University of Michigan Press, 1939.

Reedy, Gerard, S.J. *The Bible and Reason: Anglicans and Scripture in Late Seventeenth-Century England.* Philadelphia: University of Pennsylvania Press, 1985.

Reventlow, Henning Graf. *The Authority of the Bible and the Rise of the Modern World.* Translated by John Bowden. 1980. Reprint. Philadelphia: Fortress Press, 1985.

Rice, Howard. "Cotton Mather Speaks to France: American Propaganda in the Age of Louis XIV." *New England Quarterly* 16 (1943): 193–233.

Rogers, Jack B., and Donald K. McKim. *The Authority and Interpretation of the Bible: An Historical Approach.* New York: Harper & Row, 1979.

Rogers, P. G. *The Fifth Monarchy Men.* London: Oxford University Press, 1966.

Roth, Cecil. *A Life of Menasseh Ben Israel.* Philadelphia: Jewish Publication Society, 1945.

Rumsey, Peter Lockwood. *Acts of God and the People, 1620–1730.* Studies in Religion, No. 2. Ann Arbor, Michigan: UMI Research Press, 1986.

Sanders, Ronald. *Lost Tribes and Promised Lands: The Origins of American Racism.* Boston: Little, Brown, 1978.

Sanford, Charles L. *The Quest for Paradise: Europe and the American Moral Imagination.* Urbana: University of Illinois Press, 1961.

Scheick, William J. Editor. *Two Mather Biographies.* Bethlehem, PA: Lehigh University Press, 1989.

Scholem, Gershom. *Kabbalah.* 1974. Reprint. New York: New American Library, 1978.

Scult, Mel. *Millennial Expectations and Jewish Liberties.* Leiden: E. J. Brill, 1978.

Silverman, Kenneth. *The Life and Times of Cotton Mather.* New York: Harper & Row, 1984.

———. Editor. *Selected Letters of Cotton Mather.* Baton Rouge: Louisiana State University Press, 1971.

Smith, David E. "Millenarian Scholarship in America." *American Quarterly* 17 (1965): 535–49.

Smolinski, Reiner. "An Authoritative Edition of Cotton Mather's Unpublished Manuscript 'Triparadisus.'" 2 vols. Ph.D. diss., Pennsylvania State University, 1987.

———. "*Israel Redivivus*: The Eschatological Limits of Puritan Typology in New England." *New England Quarterly* 63, no. 3 (1990): 357–95.

Stanford, Donald E. "The Giant Bones of Claverack, New York, 1705." *New York History* 40 (1959): 47–61.

Starkey, Marion L. *The Devil in Massachusetts*. New York: Alfred A. Knopf, 1950.

Stein, Stephen J. "Cotton Mather and Jonathan Edwards on the Number of the Beast: Eighteenth-Century Speculation about the Antichrist." *Publications of the American Antiquarian Society* 84 (1974): 293–315.

———. "Transatlantic Extensions: Apocalyptic in Early New England." In *Apocalypse*. Edited by C. A. Patrides and Joseph Wittreich. Pp. 266–98.

Stout, Harry S. *The New England Soul*. New York: Oxford University Press, 1986.

Strong, James, and Rev. John M'Clintock. *Cyclopaedia of Biblical, Theological, and Ecclesiastical Literature*. 12 vols. Grand Rapids: Baker Books House, 1968.

Sutton, Walter. "Apocalyptic History and the American Epic: Cotton Mather and Joel Barlow." In *Toward a New American Literary History*. Durham: Duke University Press, 1979. Pp. 69–83.

Tanselle, G. Thomas. "The Editing of Historical Documents." *Studies in Bibliography* 31 (1978): 1–56.

Thomas, Isaiah. "Catalogue of Dr. Cotton Mather's Library." American Antiquarian Society.

Thomas, Keith. *Religion and the Decline of Magic*. New York: Charles Scribner's Sons, 1971.

Tichi, Cecelia. *New World, New Earth*. New Haven: Yale University Press, 1979.

———. "The Puritan Historians and Their New Jerusalem." *Early American Literature* 6 (1971): 143–55.

Toon, Peter. Editor. *Puritans, the Millennium and the Future of Israel: Puritan Eschatology 1600 to 1660*. Cambridge: James Clarke & Co., 1970.

———. "The Question of Jewish Immigration." In Toon, *Puritans*. Pp. 115–25.

Trefz, Edward K. "Satan as the Prince of Evil: The Preaching of New England Puritans." *Boston Public Library Quarterly* 7 (1955): 3–22; 8 (1956): 1–84.

Tuttle, Julius H. "The Libraries of the Mathers." *Publications of the American Antiquarian Society* 20 (1910): 269–356.

———. "William Whiston and Cotton Mather." *Publications of the Colonial Society of Massachusetts* 23 (1912): 197–204.

Tuveson, Ernest Lee. *Millennium and Utopia*. Berkeley: University of California Press, 1949.

———. *Redeemer Nation: The Idea of America's Millennial Role*. Chicago: University of Chicago Press, 1968.

Van Cromphout, Gustaaf, "Cotton Mather: The Puritan Historian as Renaissance Humanist." *American Literature* 49 (1977): 327–37.

———. "Cotton Mather as Plutarchan Biographer." *American Literature* 46 (1975): 465–81.

Vartanian, Pershing. "Cotton Mather and the Puritan Transition in the Enlightenment." *Early American Literature* 7 (1972): 213–24.

Vaughn, Alden T. *New England Frontier*. Boston: Little, Brown, 1965.

Walker, Williston. *The Creeds and Platforms of Congregationalism*. 1893. Reprint. Philadelphia: Pilgrim Press, 1960.

Watters, David H. *"With Bodilie Eyes": Eschatological Themes in Puritan Literature and Gravestone Art*. Ann Arbor: UMI Research Press, 1981.

Weisman, Richard. *Witchcraft, Magic, and Religion in Seventeenth-Century Massachusetts.* Amherst: University of Massachusetts Press, 1984.

Wendell, Barrett. *Cotton Mather.* 1891. Reprint. New York: Chelsea House, 1980.

Winslow, Ola E. *A Destroying Angel: The Conquest of Smallpox in Colonial Boston.* Boston: Houghton Mifflin, 1974.

Woody, Kennerly M. "Bibliographical Notes to Cotton Mather's *Manuductio Ad Ministerium.*" *Early American Literature* 6, no. 1 (1971): 1–98.

———. "Cotton Mather's *Manuductio Ad Ministerium:* The 'More Quiet and Hopeful Way.'" *Early American Literature* 4, no. 2 (1969): 3–48.

Worrall, Arthur J. *Quakers in the Colonial Northeast.* Hanover: University Press of New England, 1980.

INDEX